WHERE WE ARE NOW

The framework above introduces each chapter and makes the following point: That to formulate and apply HR practices such as testing and training you should understand the strategic and legal context in which you are managing.

THIRTEENTH EDITION

HUMAN RESOURCE MANAGEMENT

GARY DESSLER

FLORIDA INTERNATIONAL UNIVERSITY

PEARSON

Boston   Columbus   Indianapolis   New York   San Francisco   Upper Saddle River
Amsterdam   Cape Town   Dubai   London   Madrid   Milan   Munich   Paris   Montreal   Toronto
Delhi   Mexico City   Sao Paulo   Sydney   Hong Kong   Seoul   Singapore   Taipei   Tokyo

Editorial Director: Sally Yagan
Acquisitions Editor: Brian Mickelson
Editorial Project Manager: Sarah Holle
Director of Marketing: Maggie Moylan
Senior Marketing Manager: Nikki Ayana Jones
Marketing Assistant: Ian Gold
Senior Managing Editor: Judy Leale
Production Project Manager: Kelly Warsak
Senior Operations Supervisor: Arnold Vila
Operations Specialist: Cathleen Petersen
Creative Director: Blair Brown
Senior Art Director: Kenny Beck
Text Designer: LCI Design
Cover Designer: LCI Design
Cover Art: LCI Design
Manager, Rights and Permissions: Estelle Simpson
Media Project Manager: Lisa Rinaldi
Senior Media Project Manager: Denise Vaughn
Full-Service Project Management: Jennifer Welsch/Bookmasters
Composition: Integra Software Services Pvt. Ltd.
Printer/Binder: Quebecor World Book Services
Cover Printer: Lehigh-Phoenix Color
Text Font: 11/12 Minion

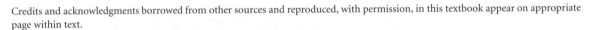

Credits and acknowledgments borrowed from other sources and reproduced, with permission, in this textbook appear on appropriate page within text.

Many of the designations by manufacturers and seller to distinguish their products are claimed as trademarks. Where those designations appear in this book, and the publisher was aware of a trademark claim, the designations have been printed in initial caps or all caps.

Library of Congress Cataloging-in-Publication Data
Dessler, Gary
   Human resource management/Gary Dessler.—13th ed.
     p. cm.
   Includes bibliographical references and index.
   ISBN-13: 978-0-13-266821-7 (hardcover: alk. paper)
   ISBN-10: 0-13-266821-1 (hardcover: alk. paper)
    1. Personnel management. I. Title.
   HF5549.D4379 2012
   658.3—dc23

                    2011037044

10 9 8 7 6 5 4 3 2 1

ISBN 10: 0-13-266821-1
ISBN 13: 978-0-13-266821-7

DEDICATED TO SAMANTHA AND TAYLOR

BRIEF CONTENTS

CONTENTS

PART TWO   RECRUITMENT, PLACEMENT, AND TALENT MANAGEMENT   102

4   Job Analysis and the Talent Management Process   102

6 Employee Testing and Selection   174

PART FIVE   EMPLOYEE RELATIONS   458

14   Ethics and Employee Rights and Discipline   458

16 Employee Safety and Health 530

17 Managing Global Human Resources 576

18 Managing Human Resources in Small and Entrepreneurial Firms 604

APPENDICES

Human Resource Management, 13th edition provides students in human resource management courses and practicing managers with a comprehensive review of essential personnel management concepts and techniques in a highly readable and understandable form. As this new edition goes to press, I feel even more strongly than I did when I wrote the first that all managers—not just HR managers—need a strong foundation in HR/personnel management concepts and techniques to effectively do their jobs. Particularly in these difficult economic times, where students want to be able to apply at work what they learn in class, this edition continues to particularly focus on practical applications that all managers can use in carrying out their HR-related responsibilities. If you adopted the previous edition, you will find transitioning to the 13th edition easy, as the chapter outline (as well as the outline for each chapter) is more or less the same.

I had two goals in writing the 13th edition. In brief, I wanted it to provide a "high-level" book's complete coverage with a "lower-level" book's readability, user-friendliness and (relative) brevity. To that end, I've made six major changes to this edition.

1. **Dozens of new topics.** These include new, expanded treatments of reliability, validity, generalizability, utility, person-job fit, person-organization fit, and bias in Chapter 6 (Employee Selection), as well as the standard deviation rule in equal employment compliance, retaliation, job satisfaction and withdrawal, managing voluntary turnover, management's willingness to take a strike, cross training, the Myers-Briggs type indicator, workflow analysis, job design in job analysis, task analysis and task statements, the psychological contract, job hazard analysis, safety awareness programs, operations reviews, competencies of HR professionals, managing voluntary turnover, employee engagement, the process of job withdrawal, cumulative trauma disorders, a thoroughly revised and expanded description of the ADDIE training process in Chapter 8, and new material on employee rights in Chapter 14 (Ethics and Employee Rights and Discipline). This edition also contains many dozens of new recent citations.

2. **A new boxed feature, *The Strategic Context*, paired with new strategic human resource management opening scenarios.** These boxes illustrate the strategic context of each chapter's material—for instance, how L.L.Bean's employee selection standards help to produce the employee competencies and behaviors that in turn support L.L.Bean's customer service strategy. The new chapter opening model says this: that (1) the company's human resource policies and practices should (2) produce the employee competencies and behaviors that (3) the company needs to implement its strategic plan.

3. **New *HR as a Profit Center* boxed features.** I've added a new focus throughout the book on the value proposition and on HR strategy, metrics, and analysis. The new HR as a Profit Center features give readers actual examples of human resource management practices they can apply on their jobs to cut costs, boost revenues, and improve performance.

4. **A completely revised Chapter 10 on Employee Retention, Engagement, and Careers,** and a completely rewritten and practical discussion in Chapter 11 of how to actually develop a market competitive salary structure.

5. **Eighteen new videos** all reviewed by me and with discussion questions and a synopsis for each video included at the end of each part of the textbook. We have a total of 28 videos on the DVD.

6. **All in a slimmer package.** This 13th edition is about 10% (73 pages) shorter than the 12th edition, which I accomplished mostly by pruning material.

NEW FEATURES

As noted previously, I've added two important boxed features.

Strategic HR opening scenarios paired with a new boxed feature, *The Strategic Context.* What HR practices and policies do we need to produce the employee competencies and behaviors required to achieve our strategic goals? The new *The Strategic Context* features (linked to the opening scenarios) show how companies make human resource management decisions within the context of their strategic initiatives. Examples include how Whirlpool uses candidate interviewing to build its customer base (Chapter 7), and how Google fosters the employee interaction its strategy depends on with a "crowd sourcing" selection process (Chapter 6).

New *HR as a Profit Center* **boxed feature.** Today's students want to apply what they learn in class to their jobs, and today's employers expect human resource management to add measurable value to the company. Our new *HR as a Profit Center* features show actual examples of how human resource management practices do this. Examples include how the Atlantic American insurance company conducted a workflow analysis to identify inefficiencies in how it processes its insurance claims (Chapter 4), and how KeyBank produced a $1.7 million cost savings in teller turnover in one year, simply by making better hiring decisions to reduce training costs (Chapter 6).

In addition, I've retained these important 12th edition features.

Evidence-Based Human Resource Management illustrates why and how managers base human resource decisions on measurable, data-based evidence.

Improving Productivity Through HRIS demonstrates how managers use technology to improve the productivity of HR.

Managing the New Workforce illustrates the skills managers need to manage today's diverse employees.

Previous editions of this textbook were the first to provide specific, actionable explanations and illustrations showing how to use devices such as the HR Scorecard process (explained fully in Chapter 3) to measure HR's effectiveness in achieving the company's strategic aims. In this 13th edition, a continuing "Hotel Paris" case at the end of each chapter gives readers practice in applying strategic human resource management in action. Coverage of the core concepts of strategic HR appears in Chapter 3.

Video Cases

To provide professors, students, and practicing managers with a richer and more flexible textbook, I have incorporated 18 new video cases at the end of the book's five parts. The *in-book video cases* provide a basis for in-class discussion of the videos available to adopters; I reviewed the videos and wrote the questions.

Comprehensive Cases

To continue with the theme of a richer, more flexible textbook, professors, students, and practicing managers will find I've again included five comprehensive cases in an appendix at the end of the book. I personally wrote the five *comprehensive cases* to provide students and faculty with an opportunity to discuss and apply the book's concepts and techniques by addressing more comprehensive and realistic case-based issues.

SHRM HRCI Review Questions

The profession of HR management is becoming increasingly demanding. Responding to these new demands, thousands of HR managers have passed the various certification exams offered by the Human Resource Certification Institute (HRCI), thus earning the designations Professional in HR (PHR), Senior Professional in HR (SPHR), and Global Professional in HR (GPHR) (as well as a special exam for California HR professionals).

This edition again contains, in each chapter, an *HRCI-related exercise* students can use to apply their knowledge of that chapter's material within the HRCI exam context, as well as a comprehensive listing of the topics that these exams address, in a HRCI guidelines appendix.

SUPPLEMENTS

Instructor Supplements

Instructors can access downloadable supplemental resources by signing into the Instructor Resource Center at www.pearsonhighered.com/educator.

It gets better. Once you register, you will not have additional forms to fill out or multiple user names and passwords to remember to access new titles and/or editions. As a registered faculty member, you can log in directly to download resource files and receive immediate access and instructions for installing Course Management content to your campus server.

Need help? Our dedicated Technical Support team is ready to assist instructors with questions about the media supplements that accompany this text. Visit http://247pearsoned.custhelp.com/ for answers to frequently asked questions and toll-free user support phone numbers. The following supplements are available to adopting instructors.

INSTRUCTOR'S MANUAL This comprehensive supplement provides extensive instructional support. The instructor's manual includes a course planning guide and chapter guides for each chapter in the text. The chapter guides include a chapter outline, lecture notes, answers to discussion questions, definitions to key terms, and references to the figures, tables, cases. The instructor's manual also includes a video guide.

TEST ITEM FILE The test item file contains approximately 110 questions per chapter including multiple-choice, true/false, and short-answer/essay-type questions. Answers are provided for all questions along with difficulty ratings. In addition, the Test Item File includes questions that are tagged to Learning Objectives and to AACSB Learning Standards to help measure whether students are grasping the course content that aligns with AACSB guidelines.

TESTGEN SOFTWARE Pearson Education's test-generating software is available from www.pearsonhighered.com/irc. The software is PC/MAC compatible and preloaded with all of the Test Item File questions. You can manually or randomly view test questions and drag and drop to create a test. You can add or modify test-bank questions as needed. All of our TestGens are converted for use in Blackboard and WebCT and are available for download from www.pearsonhighered.com/irc.

BLACKBOARD/WEBCT BlackBoard and WebCT Course Cartridges are available for download from www.pearsonhighered.com/irc. These standard course cartridges contain the Instructor's Manual, TestGen, Instructor PowerPoints, and when available, Student Powerpoints and Student Data Files.

INSTRUCTOR POWERPOINT PRESENTATION This presentation includes basic outlines and key points from each chapter. It includes figures from the text but no forms of rich media, which makes the file size manageable and easier to share online or via email.

VIDEOS ON DVD Adopters can access the 18 videos referenced in the part-ending cases, as well as 10 additional videos, on the 2013 Human Resource Management Video Library DVD. These videos have been produced to depict real-world HRM issues and give students a taste of the multi-faceted nature of HRM in real companies.

Student Supplements

MYMANAGEMENTLAB MyManagementLab (www.mymanagementlab.com) is an easy-to-use online tool that personalizes course content and provides robust assessment and reporting to measure student and class performance. All the resources you need for course success are in one place—flexible and easily adapted for your course experience.

COURSESMART ETEXTBOOKS ONLINE CourseSmart eTextbooks were developed for students looking to save on required or recommended textbooks. Students simply select their eText by title or author and purchase immediate access to the content for the duration of the course using any major credit card. With a CourseSmart eText, students can search for specific keywords or page numbers, take notes online, print out reading assignments that incorporate lecture notes, and bookmark important passages for later review. For more information or to purchase a CourseSmart eTextbook, visit www.coursesmart.com.

ACKNOWLEDGMENTS

Everyone involved in creating this book is very proud of what we've achieved. *Human Resource Management* is one of the top-selling books in this market, and, as you read this, students and managers around the world are using versions translated into a number of languages, including Thai, French, Spanish, Indonesian, Russian, and both traditional and simplified Chinese.

Although I am, of course, solely responsible for the content in *Human Resource Management*, I want to thank several people for their assistance. This includes, first, the faculty who reviewed this and the 12th edition:

Kyle Stone, *Fort Hayes State University*
George Wynn, *University of Tampa*
Edward Ward, *Saint Cloud State University*
Daniel Grundmann, *Indiana University*
Clare Francis, *University of North Dakota*
John Durboraw, *Columbia College*
Mary Kern, *Baruch College*
Lucy Ford, *St. Joseph's University*
Tom Zagenczyk, *Clemson University*
Leonard Bierman, *Texas A&M University*

I would also like to thank the supplements authors for the 13th edition for their hard work on updating and improving the supplements. They include George Wynn, University of Tampa; Emily Yelverton, and Alyssa Lambert, Indiana University Southeast. I appreciate comments, and you can reach me most easily at the address I use for this book, gsdessler@gmail.com.

At Pearson/Prentice Hall, I am again grateful for the support and dedicated assistance of a great publishing team. Sally Yagan, Editorial Director; Brian Mickelson, Acquisitions Editor; Judy Leale, Senior Managing Editor; Kelly Warsak, Production Project Manager; and Ashley Santora, Director of Editorial Services, along with Jen Welsch at BookMasters, worked hard to make this a book that we're all very proud of. Thanks to Nikki Ayana Jones, Senior Marketing Manager, and the Pearson sales staff, without whose efforts this book would no doubt languish on the shelf. I want to thank all the people at Pearson International for their efforts and effectiveness in managing the internationalization of this book.

At home, I want to acknowledge and thank my wife, Claudia, for her support during the many hours I spent working on this edition; my son, Derek, certainly still the best people manager I know and a source of enormous pride; as well as Lisa, Samantha, and Taylor, who are always in my thoughts. My parents were always a great source of support and encouragement and would have been very proud to see this book.

Gary Dessler

1

Introduction to Human Resource Management

Source: Paul Beaty/AP Images.

LEARNING OBJECTIVES

1. Explain what human resource management is and how it relates to the management process.

2. Show with examples why human resource management is important to all managers.

3. Illustrate the human resources responsibilities of line and staff (HR) managers.

4. Briefly discuss and illustrate each of the important trends influencing human resource management.

5. List and briefly describe important traits of today's human resource managers.

6. Define and give an example of evidence-based human resource management.

7. Outline the plan of this book.

Most L.L.Bean customers find its customer service staff to be knowledgeable, helpful, and understanding. Its managers know that courteous, expert workers are the key to such customer service, and that it takes the right human resource practices to attract and cultivate such employees. The company knows what it's looking for. Its Web site says candidates should be Friendly, Dependable, Helpful & Authentic; Trustworthy & Honest; Experienced & Innovative; Outdoor Oriented & Environmentally Aware; and want to have Fun.[1] The company uses an array of human resource practices, including competitive pay, cash performance bonuses, multiple medical and insurance plans, and "outdoor experience days" to attract and cultivate such employee behaviors.[2] The success of L.L.Bean's customer service strategy depends on its human resource management practices.

Access a host of interactive learning aids at **www.mymanagementlab.com** to help strengthen your understanding of the chapter concepts.

WHERE ARE WE NOW . . .

The purpose of this chapter is to explain what human resource management is, and why it's important to all managers. We'll see that human resource management activities such as hiring, training, appraising, compensating, and developing employees are part of every manager's job. And we'll see that human resource management is also a separate function, usually with its own human resource or "HR" manager. The main topics we'll cover include the meaning of human resource management; why human resource management is important to all managers, global and competitive trends, human resource management trends, and the plan of this book. The framework above (which introduces each chapter) makes this point: That the firm's HR polices and practices should produce the employee skills and behaviors the company needs to achieve its strategic aims.

1 Explain what human resource management is and how it relates to the management process.

WHAT IS HUMAN RESOURCE MANAGEMENT AND WHY IS IT IMPORTANT?

What Is Human Resource Management?

L.L.Bean is an *organization*. An **organization** consists of people with formally assigned roles who work together to achieve the organization's goals. A **manager** is the person responsible for accomplishing the organization's goals, who does so by managing the efforts of the organization's people.

Most experts agree that *managing* involves five functions: planning, organizing, staffing, leading, and controlling. In total, these functions represent the **management process**. Some of the specific activities involved in each function include:

- **Planning.** Establishing goals and standards; developing rules and procedures; developing plans and forecasting.
- **Organizing.** Giving each subordinate a specific task; establishing departments; delegating authority to subordinates; establishing channels of authority and communication; coordinating subordinates' work.
- **Staffing.** Determining what type of people you should hire; recruiting prospective employees; selecting employees; training and developing employees; setting performance standards; evaluating performance; counseling employees; compensating employees.
- **Leading.** Getting others to get the job done; maintaining morale; motivating subordinates.
- **Controlling.** Setting standards such as sales quotas, quality standards, or production levels; checking to see how actual performance compares with these standards; taking corrective action, as needed.

In this book, we are going to focus on one of these functions—the staffing, personnel management, or *human resource management (HRM) function*. **Human resource management** is the process of acquiring, training, appraising, and compensating employees, and of attending to their labor relations, health and safety, and fairness concerns. The topics we'll discuss should therefore provide you with the concepts and techniques you need to perform the "people" or personnel aspects of your management job. These include:

- *Conducting job analyses* (determining the nature of each employee's job)
- *Planning labor needs* and *recruiting* job candidates
- *Selecting* job candidates
- *Orienting and training* new employees
- *Managing wages and salaries* (compensating employees)
- *Providing incentives and benefits*
- *Appraising performance*
- *Communicating* (interviewing, counseling, disciplining)
- *Training and developing* managers
- *Building employee commitment*

And what a manager should know about:

- Equal opportunity and affirmative action
- Employee health and safety
- Handling grievances and labor relations

2 Show with examples why human resource management is important to all managers.

Why Is Human Resource Management Important to All Managers?

These concepts and techniques important to all managers for several reasons.

AVOID PERSONNEL MISTAKES First, having a command of this knowledge will help you avoid the sorts of personnel mistakes you *don't* want to make while managing. For example, no manager wants to:

- Hire the wrong person for the job
- Experience high turnover
- Have your people not doing their best
- Waste time with useless interviews
- Have your company taken to court because of your discriminatory actions
- Have your company cited under federal occupational safety laws for unsafe practices
- Have some employees think their salaries are unfair relative to others in the organization
- Allow a lack of training to undermine your department's effectiveness
- Commit any unfair labor practices

Carefully studying this book will help you avoid mistakes like these.

IMPROVE PROFITS AND PERFORMANCE Similarly, effective human resource management can help ensure that you get results—through people. Remember that you can do everything else right as a manager—lay brilliant plans, draw clear organization charts, set up world-class assembly lines, and use sophisticated accounting controls—but still fail, by hiring the wrong people or by not motivating subordinates. On the other hand, many managers—presidents, generals, governors, supervisors—have been successful even with inadequate plans, organizations, or controls. They were successful because they had the knack of hiring the right people for the right jobs and motivating, appraising, and developing them. Remember as you read this book that *getting results* is the bottom line of managing, and that, as a manager, you will have to get those results through people. As one company president summed up:

> For many years, it has been said that capital is the bottleneck for a developing industry. I don't think this any longer holds true. I think it's the work force and the company's inability to recruit and maintain a good work force that does constitute the bottleneck for production. I don't know of any major project backed by good ideas, vigor, and enthusiasm that has been stopped by a shortage of cash. I do know of industries whose growth has been partly stopped or hampered because they can't maintain an efficient and enthusiastic labor force, and I think this will hold true even more in the future.[3]

Indeed, we'll see that because of global competition, technological advances, and the changing nature of work, that president's statement has never been truer than it is today.

organization
People with formally assigned roles who work together to achieve the organization's goals.

manager
The person responsible for accomplishing the organization's goals, and who does so by managing (planning, organizing, staffing, leading, and controlling) the efforts of the organization's people.

management process
The five basic functions of planning, organizing, staffing, leading, and controlling.

human resource management (HRM)
The process of acquiring, training, appraising, and compensating employees, and of attending to their labor relations, health and safety, and fairness concerns.

YOU TOO MAY SPEND SOME TIME AS AN HR MANAGER   Here is a third reason to be familiar with this book's contents. You may well make a planned (or unplanned) stopover as a human resource manager. For example, Pearson Corporation (which publishes this book) recently promoted the head of one of its publishing divisions to chief human resource executive at its corporate headquarters. After General Motors emerged from bankruptcy a few years ago, it replaced its human resource director with Mary Barra, GM's vice president for global manufacturing engineering, an executive with no human resource management experience.[4] One survey found that about one-fourth of large U.S. businesses appointed managers with no human resource management experience as their top human resource executives. Reasons given include the fact that these people may give the firms' HR efforts a more strategic emphasis, and the possibility that they're sometimes better equipped to integrate the firm's human resource efforts with the rest of the business.[5]

However, most top human resource executives do have prior human resource experience. About 80% of those in one survey worked their way up within HR.[6] About 17% of these HR executives had earned the Human Resource Certification Institute's Senior Professional in Human Resources (SPHR) designation, and 13% were certified Professionals in Human Resources (PHR). The Society for Human Resource Management (SHRM) offers a brochure describing alternative career paths within human resource management. Find it at www.shrm.org/Communities/StudentPrograms/Documents/07-0971%20Careers%20HR%20Book_final.pdf.

HR FOR ENTREPRENEURS   Finally, another reason to study this book is that you might end up as your own human resource manager. More than half the people working in the United States—about 68 million out of 118 million—work for small firms. Small businesses as a group also account for most of the 600,000 or so new businesses created every year. Statistically speaking, therefore, most people graduating from college in the next few years either will work for small businesses or will create new small businesses of their own. Especially if you are managing your own small firm with no human resource manager, you'll have to understand the nuts and bolts of human resource management.[7] We'll specifically address HR for entrepreneurs in Chapter 18.

Line and Staff Aspects of Human Resource Management

> **3** Illustrate the human resources responsibilities of line and staff (HR) managers.

All managers are, in a sense, human resource managers, because they all get involved in recruiting, interviewing, selecting, and training their employees. Yet most firms also have human resource departments with their own top managers. How do the duties of this human resource manager and department relate to the human resource duties of sales and production and other managers? Answering this requires a short definition of line versus staff authority.

Authority is the right to make decisions, to direct the work of others, and to give orders. Managers usually distinguish between line authority and staff authority.

In organizations, having what managers call **line authority** traditionally gives managers the right to *issue orders* to other managers or employees. Line authority therefore creates a superior (order giver)–subordinate (order receiver) relationship. When the vice president of sales tells her sales director to "get the sales presentation ready by Tuesday," she is exercising her line authority. **Staff authority** gives a manager the right to *advise* other managers or employees. It creates an advisory relationship. When the human resource manager suggests that the plant manager use a particular selection test, he or she is exercising staff authority.

On the organization chart, managers with line authority are **line managers**. Those with staff (advisory) authority are **staff managers**. In popular usage, people tend to associate line managers with managing departments (like sales or production) that are crucial for the company's survival. Staff managers generally run departments that are advisory or supportive, like purchasing, and human resource management. Human resource managers are usually staff managers. They assist and advise line managers in areas like recruiting, hiring, and compensation.

Line authority gives the manager the right to issue orders.

Line Managers' Human Resource Duties

However, line managers still have many human resource duties. This is because the direct handling of people has always been part of every line manager's duties, from president down to first-line supervisors. For example, one major company outlines its line supervisors' responsibilities for effective human resource management under these general headings:

1. Placing the right person in the right job
2. Starting new employees in the organization (orientation)
3. Training employees for jobs that are new to them
4. Improving the job performance of each person
5. Gaining cooperation and developing smooth working relationships
6. Interpreting the company's policies and procedures
7. Controlling labor costs
8. Developing the abilities of each person
9. Creating and maintaining department morale
10. Protecting employees' health and physical condition

In small organizations, line managers may carry out all these personnel tasks unassisted. But as the organization grows, they need the assistance, specialized knowledge, and advice of a separate human resource staff. The human resource department provides this specialized assistance.

Human Resource Manager's Duties

In providing this specialized assistance, the *human resource manager* carries out three distinct functions:

1. **A line function.** The human resource manager directs the activities of the people in his or her own department, and perhaps in related areas (like the plant cafeteria).
2. **A coordinative function.** The human resource manager also coordinates personnel activities, a duty often referred to as **functional authority** (or functional control). Here he or she ensures that line managers are implementing the firm's human resource policies and practices (for example, adhering to its sexual harassment policies).
3. **Staff (assist and advise) functions.** Assisting and advising line managers is the heart of the human resource manager's job. He or she *advises* the CEO so the CEO can better understand the personnel aspects of the company's strategic options. HR *assists* in hiring, training, evaluating, rewarding, counseling, promoting, and firing employees. It administers the various benefit programs (health and accident insurance, retirement, vacation, and so on). It helps line managers comply with equal employment and occupational safety laws, and plays an important role in handling grievances and labor relations. It carries out an

---

authority
The right to make decisions, direct others' work, and give orders.

line authority
The authority exerted by an HR manager by directing the activities of the people in his or her own department and in service areas (like the plant cafeteria).

staff authority
Staff authority gives the manager the right (authority) to advise other managers or employees.

line manager
A manager who is authorized to direct the work of subordinates and is responsible for accomplishing the organization's tasks.

staff manager
A manager who assists and advises line managers.

functional authority
The authority exerted by an HR manager as coordinator of personnel activities.

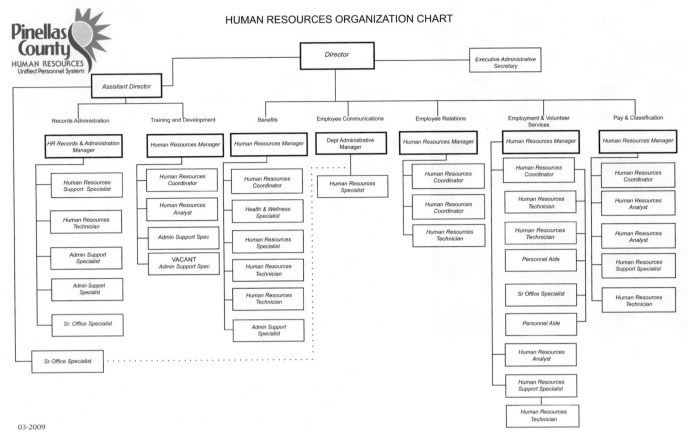

FIGURE 1-1 Human Resources Organization Chart

Source: www.co.pinellas.fl.us/persnl/pdf/orgchart.pdf, accessed April 1, 2009. Used with permission of Pinellas County Govt.

innovator role, by providing up-to-date information on current trends and new methods for better utilizing the company's employees (or "human resources"). It plays an *employee advocacy* role, by representing the interests of employees within the framework of its primary obligation to senior management. Although human resource managers generally can't wield line authority (outside their departments), they are likely to exert *implied authority*. This is because line managers know the human resource manager has top management's ear in areas like testing and affirmative action.

The size of the human resource department reflects the size of the employer. For a very large employer, an organization chart like the one in Figure 1-1 would be typical, containing a full complement of specialists for each HR function.

Examples of human resource management specialties include:[8]

- **Recruiters.** Search for qualified job applicants.
- **Equal employment opportunity (EEO) coordinators.** Investigate and resolve EEO grievances; examine organizational practices for potential violations; and compile and submit EEO reports.
- **Job analysts.** Collect and examine information about jobs to prepare job descriptions.
- **Compensation managers.** Develop compensation plans and handle the employee benefits program.
- **Training specialists.** Plan, organize, and direct training activities.
- **Labor relations specialists.** Advise management on all aspects of union–management relations.

FIGURE 1-2 HR Organization Chart (Small Company)

At the other extreme, the human resource team for a small manufacturer may contain just five or six (or fewer) staff, and have an organization similar to that in Figure 1-2. There is *generally* about one human resource employee per 100 company employees.

New Approaches to Organizing HR

Employers are also offering human resource services in new ways. For example, some organize their HR services around four groups: transactional, corporate, embedded, and centers of expertise.[9]

- The *transactional HR* group uses centralized call centers and outsourcing arrangements (such as with benefits advisors) to provide support for day-to-day transactional activities (such as changing benefits plans and employee assistance and counseling). In one survey, about 75% of respondents said their firms were providing transactional, administrative human resource services through such arrangements.[10]

- The *corporate HR* group focuses on assisting top management in "top level" big picture issues such as developing and explaining the personnel aspects of the company's long-term strategic plan.

- The *embedded HR* unit assigns HR generalists (also known as "relationship managers" or "HR business partners") directly to departments like sales and production. They provide the localized human resource management assistance the departments need.

- The *centers of expertise* are like specialized HR consulting firms within the company—for instance, they provide specialized assistance in areas such as organizational change.

IBM EXAMPLE Randall MacDonald, IBM's senior vice president of human resources, noted that the traditional human resource organization often isolates HR functions into "silos" such as recruitment, training, and employee relations. He says this silo approach often means there's no one team of human resource specialists focusing on the needs of specific groups of employees.

MacDonald therefore reorganized IBM's human resource function. He segmented IBM's 330,000 employees into three sets of "customers": executive and technical employees, managers, and rank and file. Separate human resource management teams (consisting of recruitment, training, and compensation specialists, for instance) now focus on serving the needs of each employee segment. These specialized teams help ensure that the employees in each segment get precisely the talent, learning, and compensation they require to support IBM's needs.[11]

Cooperative Line and Staff HR Management: An Example

Because line managers and human resource managers both have human resource management duties, it is reasonable to ask, "Exactly which HR duties are carried out by line managers and which by staff managers?" No one division of responsibilities would apply to all organizations, but we can generalize.

FIGURE 1-3 Employment and Recruiting—Who Handles It? (Percentage of All Employers)

Source: HR Magazine, Copyright 2002 by Society for Human Resource Management (SHRM).

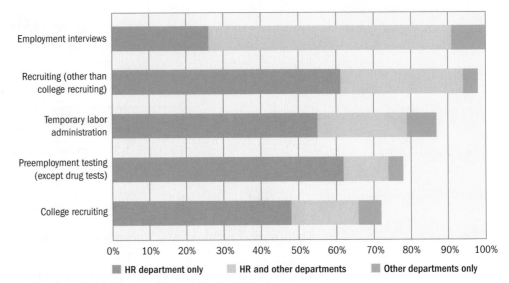

Note: Length of bars represents prevalence of activity among all surveyed employers.

The most important generalization is that the line–staff relationship should be cooperative.[12] For example, in recruiting and hiring, the line manager describes the qualifications employees need to fill specific positions. Then the human resource team takes over. They develop sources of qualified applicants, and conduct initial screening interviews. They administer the appropriate tests. Then they refer the best applicants to the line manager, who interviews and selects the ones he or she wants. In training, the line manager again describes what he or she expects the employee to be able to do. Then the human resource team devises a training program, which the line manager then (usually) administers.

Some activities are usually HR's alone. For example, 60% of firms assign to human resources the exclusive responsibility for preemployment testing, 75% assign it college recruiting, and 80% assign it insurance benefits administration. But employers split most activities, such as employment interviews, performance appraisal, skills training, job descriptions, and disciplinary procedures, between HR and line managers.[13]

Figure 1-3 illustrates the typical HR–line management partnership. For example, HR alone typically handles interviewing in about 25% of firms. But in about 60% of firms, HR and the other hiring departments are both involved in interviewing.

In summary, human resource management is part of every manager's job. Whether you're a first-line supervisor, middle manager, or president—or whether you're a production manager or county manager (or HR manager)—*getting results through people* is the name of the game. And to do this, you will need a good working knowledge of the human resource management concepts and techniques in this book.

THE TRENDS SHAPING HUMAN RESOURCE MANAGEMENT

4 Briefly discuss and illustrate each of the important trends influencing human resource management.

What human resource managers do and how they do it is changing. Some of the reasons for these changes are obvious. One is technology. For example, employers now use their intranets to let employees change their own benefits plans, something they obviously couldn't do years ago. Other trends shaping human resource management include globalization, deregulation, changes in demographics and the nature of work, and economic challenges (summarized in Figure 1-4). Let's look at these trends next.[14]

FIGURE 1-4 Trends Shaping
Human Resource Management

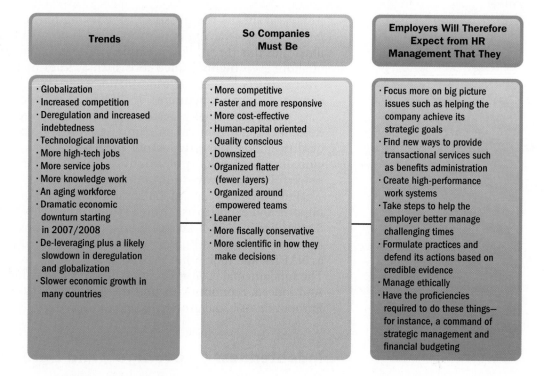

Trends	So Companies Must Be	Employers Will Therefore Expect from HR Management That They
· Globalization · Increased competition · Deregulation and increased indebtedness · Technological innovation · More high-tech jobs · More service jobs · More knowledge work · An aging workforce · Dramatic economic downturn starting in 2007/2008 · De-leveraging plus a likely slowdown in deregulation and globalization · Slower economic growth in many countries	· More competitive · Faster and more responsive · More cost-effective · Human-capital oriented · Quality conscious · Downsized · Organized flatter (fewer layers) · Organized around empowered teams · Leaner · More fiscally conservative · More scientific in how they make decisions	· Focus more on big picture issues such as helping the company achieve its strategic goals · Find new ways to provide transactional services such as benefits administration · Create high-performance work systems · Take steps to help the employer better manage challenging times · Formulate practices and defend its actions based on credible evidence · Manage ethically · Have the proficiencies required to do these things— for instance, a command of strategic management and financial budgeting

Globalization and Competition Trends

Globalization refers to the tendency of firms to extend their sales, ownership, and/or manufacturing to new markets abroad. Examples surround us. Toyota produces the Camry in Kentucky, while Dell produces PCs in China. Free trade areas—agreements that reduce tariffs and barriers among trading partners—further encourage international trade. NAFTA (the North American Free Trade Agreement) and the EU (European Union) are examples.

Companies expand abroad for several reasons. *Sales expansion* is one. Walmart is opening stores in South America. Dell, knowing that China will soon be the world's biggest market for PCs, is aggressively selling there.

Firms go abroad for other reasons. Some manufacturers seek *new foreign products* and services to sell, and to *cut labor costs*. Thus, some apparel manufacturers design and cut fabrics in Miami, and then assemble the actual products in Central America, where labor costs are relatively low. Sometimes, it's the prospect of *forming partnerships* that drives firms to do business abroad. When IBM sold its PC division to the Chinese firm Lenovo, it did so partly to cement firmer ties with the booming China market.

For businesspeople, globalization means more competition, and more competition means more pressure to be "world-class"—to lower costs, to make employees more productive, and to do things better and less expensively. As one expert puts it, "The bottom line is that the growing integration of the world economy into a single, huge marketplace is increasing the intensity of competition in a wide range of manufacturing and service industries."[15] Both workers and companies have to work harder and smarter than they did without globalization.[16]

Globalization therefore brings both benefits and threats. For *consumers* it means lower prices and higher quality on products from computers to cars, but for

globalization
The tendency of firms to extend their sales, ownership, and/or manufacturing to new markets abroad.

workers it means the prospect of working harder, and perhaps less secure jobs. *Job offshoring*—having employees abroad do jobs that Americans formerly did—illustrates this threat. For example, in the next few years, many employers plan to offshore even highly skilled jobs such as sales managers, general managers—and HR managers.[17] (On the other hand, what *USA Today* calls "A small but growing band of U.S. manufacturers—including giants such as General Electric, NCR, and Caterpillar" are actually "reshoring" jobs—bringing them back to the United States. Reasons range from rising shipping and labor costs abroad to occasional poor quality goods and intellectual property theft abroad.)[18] For *business owners*, globalization means (potentially) millions of new consumers, but also new and powerful global competitors at home.

For 50 or so years, globalization boomed. For example, the total sum of U.S. imports and exports rose from $47 billion in 1960, to $562 billion in 1980, to about $4.1 *trillion* in 2010.[19] Economic and political philosophies drove this boom. Governments dropped cross-border taxes or tariffs, formed economic "free trade areas" such as NAFTA, and took other steps to encourage the free flow of trade among countries. The fundamental economic rationale was that by doing so, all countries would gain. And indeed, economies around the world, not just in the United States but also in Europe and Asia, did grow rapidly.

Indebtedness ("Leverage") and Deregulation

Other trends contributed to this economic growth. Deregulation was one. In many countries, governments stripped away regulations. In the United States and Europe, for instance, the rules that prevented commercial banks from expanding into stock brokering were relaxed. Giant, multinational "financial supermarkets" such as Citibank quickly emerged. As economies boomed, more businesses and consumers went deeply into debt. Homebuyers bought homes, often with little money down. Banks freely lent money to developers to build more homes. For almost 20 years, U.S. consumers actually spent more than they earned. On a grander scale, the United States itself increasingly became a debtor nation. Its balance of payments (exports minus imports) went from a healthy positive $3.5 billion in 1960, to a not-so-healthy *minus* $19.4 billion in 1980 (imports exceeded exports), to a huge $497 billion deficit in 2010.[20] The only way the country could keep buying more from abroad than it sold was by borrowing money. So, much of the boom was built on debt. By 2011, Standard & Poor's said it would lower the ratings of U.S. sovereign (treasury) bonds, fearing Washington policymakers could not get a handle on the huge indebtedness. Rating agencies had already lowered their ratings on the bonds of countries such as Japan and Greece.

Source: Digital Vision/Thinkstock.

Many blue-collar workers no longer do hard physical labor with dangerous machinery like this. Instead, as explained in the text, Chad Toulouse spends most of his time as a team leader keying commands into computerized machines.

Technological Trends

Everyone knows that technology changed almost everything we do. We use smartphones and iPads to communicate with the office, and to plan trips, manage money, and look for local eateries. We also increasingly use technology for many human resource management–type applications, such as looking for jobs.

Facebookrecruiting is one example.[21] According to Facebook's *Facebookrecruiting* site, employers start the process by installing the "Careers Tab" on their Facebook page. Once installed, "companies have a seamless way to recruit and promote job listings from directly within Facebook."[22] Then, after creating a job listing, the employer can advertise its job link using Facebook Advertisements.

Trends in the Nature of Work

Technology has also had a huge impact on how people work, and therefore on the skills and training today's workers need.

HIGH-TECH JOBS For example, skilled machinist Chad Toulouse illustrates the modern blue-collar worker. After an 18-week training course, this former college student works as a team leader in a plant where about 40% of the machines are automated. In older plants, machinists would manually control machines that cut chunks of metal into things like engine parts. Today, Chad and his team spend much of their time keying commands into computerized machines that create precision parts for products, including water pumps.[23] As the U.S. government's *Occupational Outlook Quarterly* put it, "knowledge-intensive high-tech manufacturing in such industries as aerospace, computers, telecommunications, home electronics, pharmaceuticals, and medical instruments" is replacing factory jobs in steel, auto, rubber, and textiles.[24]

SERVICE JOBS Technology is not the only trend driving the change from "brawn to brains." Today over two-thirds of the U.S. workforce is producing and delivering services, not products. Between 2004 and 2014, almost all of the 19 million new jobs added in the United States will be in services, not in goods-producing industries.[25]

Several things account for this.[26] With global competition, more manufacturing jobs have shifted to low-wage countries. For example, Levi Strauss, one of the last major clothing manufacturers in the United States, closed the last of its American plants a few years ago.

Furthermore, higher productivity enables manufacturers to produce more with fewer workers. Just-in-time manufacturing techniques link daily manufacturing schedules more precisely to customer demand, squeezing waste out of the system and reducing inventory needs. As manufacturers integrate Internet-based customer ordering with just-in-time manufacturing, scheduling becomes more precise. For example, when a customer orders a Dell computer, the same Internet message that informs Dell's assembly line to produce the order also signals the screen and keyboard manufacturers to prepare for UPS to pick up their parts. The net effect is that manufacturers have been squeezing slack and inefficiencies out of production, enabling companies to produce more products with fewer employees. So, in America and much of Europe, manufacturing jobs are down, and service jobs up.

KNOWLEDGE WORK AND HUMAN CAPITAL In general, the best jobs that remain require more education and more skills. For example, we saw that automation and just-in-time manufacturing mean that even manufacturing jobs require more reading, math, and communication skills.[27]

For employers this means relying more on knowledge workers like Chad Toulouse, and therefore on *human capital*.[28] **Human capital** refers to the knowledge, education, training, skills, and expertise of a firm's workers.[29] Today, as management guru Peter Drucker predicted years ago, "the center of gravity in employment is moving fast from manual and clerical workers to knowledge workers."[30] Human resource managers now list "critical thinking/problem-solving" and "information technology application" as the two skills most likely to increase in importance over the next few years.[31] The accompanying HR as a Profit Center feature illustrates how human resource management methods can boost profitability by building and capitalizing on such employee skills.

human capital
The knowledge, education, training, skills, and expertise of a firm's workers.

HR AS A PROFIT CENTER

Boosting Customer Service

A bank installed special software that made it easier for its customer service representatives to handle customers' inquiries. However, the bank did not otherwise change the service reps' jobs in any way. Here, the new software system did help the service reps handle more calls. But otherwise, this bank saw no big performance gains.[32]

A second bank installed the same software. But, seeking to capitalize on how the new software freed up customer reps' time, this bank also had its human resource team upgrade the customer service representatives' jobs. This bank taught them how to sell more of the bank's services, gave them more authority to make decisions, and raised their wages. Here, the new computer system dramatically improved product sales and profitability, thanks to the newly trained and empowered customer service reps. Today's employers want and need human resource practices like these that improve employee performance and company profitability.[33]

Workforce and Demographic Trends

All of this is occurring along with big changes in workforce and demographic trends.

DEMOGRAPHIC TRENDS   Most importantly, the U.S. workforce is becoming older and more multiethnic.[34] Table 1-1 provides a bird's-eye view. For example, between 1998 and 2018, the percent of the workforce that it classifies as "white, non-Hispanic" will drop from 83.8% to 79.4%. At the same time, the percent of the workforce that is black will rise from 11.6% to 12.1%, those classified Asian will rise from 4.6% to 5.6%, and those of Hispanic origin will rise from 10.4% to 17.6%. The percentages of younger workers will fall, while those over 55 of age will leap from 12.4% of the workforce in 1998 to 23.9% in 2018.[35]

At the same time, demographic trends are making finding and hiring employees more challenging. In the United States, labor force growth is not expected to keep pace with job growth, with an estimated shortfall of about 14 million college-educated workers by 2020.[36] One study of 35 large global companies' senior human resource officers said "talent management"—in particular, the acquisition, development, and retention of talent to fill the companies employment needs—ranked as their top concern.[37]

"GENERATION Y"   Also called "Millennials," Gen Y employees are roughly those born 1977–2002. They take the place of the labor force's previous new entrants,

TABLE 1-1 Demographic Groups as a Percent of the Workforce, 1998–2018

Age, Race, Ethnicity	1998	2008	2018
Age: 16–24	15.9%	14.3	12.7
25–54	71.7	67.7	63.5
55+	12.4	18.1	23.9
White, non-Hispanic	83.8	81.4	79.4
Black	11.6	11.5	12.1
Asian	4.6	4.7	5.6
Hispanic origin	10.4	14.3	17.6

Source: Adapted from www.bls.gov/news.release/ecopro.t01.htm, accessed May 10, 2010.

Generation X, those born roughly 1965–1976 (and who themselves were the children of, and followed into the labor force, the Baby Boomers, born just after the Second World War, roughly 1944–1960).

Although every generation obviously has its own labor force entrants, Gen Y employees are different. For one thing, says one expert, they have "been pampered, nurtured, and programmed with a slew of activities since they were toddlers, meaning they are both high-performance and high-maintenance."[38] As a result:

1. They want fair and direct supervisors who are highly engaged in their professional development.
2. They seek out creative challenges and view colleagues as vast resources from whom to gain knowledge.
3. They want to make an important impact on Day 1.
4. They want small goals with tight deadlines so they can build up ownership of tasks.
5. They aim to work faster and better than other workers.[39]

Fortune Magazine says that today's "Generation Y" employees will bring challenges and strengths. It says they may be "the most high-maintenance workforce in the history of the world." Referring to them as "the most praised generation," the *Wall Street Journal* explains how Lands' End and Bank of America are teaching their supervisors to complement these new employees with prize packages and public appreciation.[40] But, as the first generation raised on cell phones and e-mail, their capacity for using information technology will also make them the most high-performing.

RETIREES Many human resource professionals call "the aging workforce" the biggest demographic trend affecting employers. The basic problem is that there aren't enough younger workers to replace the projected number of baby boom era older-worker retirees.[41]

Employers are dealing with this challenge in various ways. One survey found that 41% of surveyed employers are bringing retirees back into the workforce, 34% are conducting studies to determine projected retirement rates in the organization, and 31% are offering employment options designed to attract and retain semi-retired workers.[42]

NONTRADITIONAL WORKERS At the same time, there has been a shift to nontraditional workers. Nontraditional workers include those who hold multiple jobs, or who are "contingent" or part-time workers, or who are working in alternative work arrangements (such as a mother–daughter team sharing one clerical job). Today, almost 10% of American workers—13 million people—fit this nontraditional workforce category. Of these, about 8 million are independent contractors who work on specific projects and move on once they complete the projects.

Technological trends facilitate such alternative work arrangements. For example, professional online Web sites such as LinkedIn (www.linkedin.com) enable free agent professionals to promote their services. Thanks to technology, people working from remote locations at least once per month rose about 39% from 2006 to 2008 to just over 17 million people. Seeking the collaboration that's often missing when one works alone, "co-working sites" are springing up. These offer freelance workers and consultants office space and access to office equipment (and of course an opportunity to interact with other independent workers) for fees of perhaps $200 or $300 per month.[43]

WORKERS FROM ABROAD With retirements triggering projected workforce shortfalls, many employers are hiring foreign workers for U.S. jobs. The country's H-1B visa program allows U.S. employers to recruit skilled foreign professionals to work in the United States when they can't find qualified U.S. workers. U.S.

FIGURE 1-5 Gross National Product (GNP)

Source: U.S. Department of Commerce: Bureau of Economic Analysis, http://research.stlouisfed.org /fred2/fredgraph?chart_type=line&s[1] [id]=GNP&s[1][transformation]=ch1, accessed April 18, 2009.

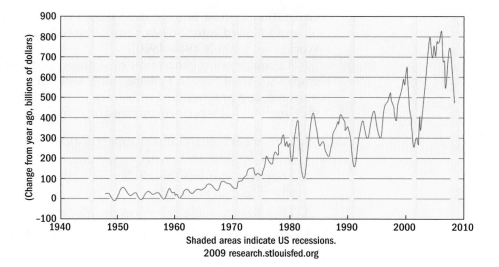

employers bring in about 181,000 foreign workers per year under these programs. Particularly with high unemployment, such programs face opposition. For example, one study concluded that many workers brought in under the programs filled jobs that didn't actually demand highly specialized skills, many paying less than $15 an hour.[44]

Economic Challenges and Trends

All these trends are occurring in a context of economic upheaval. As shown in Figure 1-5, gross national product (GNP)—a measure of U.S. total output— boomed between 2001 and 2008. During this period, home prices leaped as much as 20% per year. (See Figure 1-6.) Unemployment remained at about 4.7%.[45] Then, around 2007–2008, all these measures seemingly fell off a cliff. GNP fell. Home prices dropped by 20% or more (depending on city). Unemployment nationwide rose to more than 9.1%.

Why did all this happen? That is a complicated question, but for one thing, all those years of accumulating excessive debt seems to have run their course. Banks and other financial institutions (such as hedge funds) found themselves with trillions of dollars of worthless loans on their books. Governments stepped in to try to prevent their collapse. Lending dried up. Many businesses and consumers simply stopped buying. The economy tanked.

Economic trends will undoubtedly turn positive again, perhaps even as you read these pages. However, they have certainly grabbed employers' attention. After what the world went through starting in 2007–2008, it's doubtful that the deregulation, leveraging, and globalization that drove economic growth for the previous 50 years

FIGURE 1-6 Case-Shiller Home Price Indexes

Source: S&P, Fiserv, and MacroMarkets, LLC, http://www. clevelandfed.org/research/trends/ 2009/0309/04ecoact.cfm, accessed April 18, 2009.

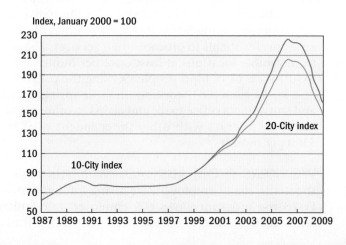

will continue unabated. That may mean slower growth for many countries, perhaps for years. This means challenging times ahead for employers. The challenging times mean that for the foreseeable future—and even well after things turn positive—employers will have to be more frugal and creative in managing their human resources than perhaps they've been in the past.

THE NEW HUMAN RESOURCE MANAGERS

Trends like these mean changes in human resource management practices, and in what employers expect from their human resource managers. We'll look at some specifics.

Human Resource Management Yesterday and Today

For much of the twentieth century, personnel/HR managers focused on "day-to-day" transactional types of activities. For example in the earliest firms, they first took over hiring and firing from supervisors, ran the payroll department, and administered benefits plans. As expertise in areas like testing began to appear, the personnel department began to play an expanded role in employee selection and training.[46] The emergence of union legislation in the 1930s added, "Helping the employer deal with unions" to its list of duties. Then, as Congress passed new equal employment legislation in the 1960s and 1970s, employers began leaning on their human resource managers' expertise for avoiding and managing discrimination claims.[47]

Today, we've seen that trends like globalization, indebtedness, and technology confront employers with new challenges, such as squeezing more profits from operations. Employers expect their human resource managers to have what it takes to address these challenges. We can list 10 characteristics of today's human resource professionals.

They Focus More on Strategic, Big Picture Issues

| 5 | List and briefly describe important traits of today's human resource managers. |

Today's human resource managers are more involved in longer term, strategic "big picture" issues. We'll see in Chapter 3 (Strategy) that *strategic human resource management* means formulating and executing human resource policies and practices that produce the employee competencies and behaviors the company needs to achieve its strategic aims. We illustrate this throughout this book with The Strategic Context features such as the accompanying one.

THE STRATEGIC CONTEXT

Building L.L.Bean

Strategic human resource management means formulating and executing human resource policies and practices that produce the employee competencies and behaviors the company needs to achieve its strategic aims.

L.L.Bean illustrates how companies do this. The heart of L.L.Bean's strategy has always been offering great outdoor equipment with outstanding service and expert advice. As its company history said, "L.L.Bean, Inc., quickly established itself as a trusted source for reliable outdoor equipment and expert advice. The small company grew. Customers spread the word of L.L.Bean's quality and service."[48]

To provide such service, L.L.Bean needs employees with special, outdoors-skills performing in a special way. As its Web site says, "L.L.Bean attracts a special sort of person. Like our customers, we are passionate about the L.L.Bean brand and our love for the outdoors. You already know the outstanding service L.L.Bean customers receive. Now imagine how we treat our employees."[49]

L.L.Bean's HR policies and practices attract and develop just such employees. For one thing, the company knows just who to recruit for. It wants sociable, friendly, experienced, outdoors-oriented applicants and employees.[50] To attract and

(Continued)

cultivate these sorts of employee competencies and behaviors, the company uses multiple interviews to screen out applicants who might not fit in. And L.L.Bean offers an outdoors-oriented work environment and competitive pay and benefits.

To help encourage great employee service, L.L.Bean also provides a supportive environment. For example, when its Web sales recently for the first time exceeded phone sales, L.L.Bean closed four local call centers, but arranged for the 220 employees to work from their homes. And instead of sending jobs abroad, the company keeps its jobs close to the town where Leon Leonwood Bean started his company almost 100 years ago.[51] L.L.Bean's managers built the firm's strategy and success around courteous, expert service. They know that having the right employees is the key to its success, and that it takes the right blend of human resource practices to attract and nurture such employees.

As at L.L.Bean in the Strategic Context feature, today's employers want their HR managers to put in place practices that will help the company achieve its strategic aims. Employers want them to be the firms' internal consultants, by identifying and institutionalizing changes that help employees better contribute to the company's success, and by helping top management formulate and execute its long-term plans.[52] HR managers no longer just do everyday transactional things like signing on new employees or changing their benefits plans.

They Use New Ways to Provide Transactional Services

But then, how do employers perform these day-to-day transactional tasks?[53] The answer is that today's human resource managers must be skilled at offering these transactional HR services in innovative ways. For example, they *outsource* more benefits administration and safety training to outside vendors.[54] They use technology, for instance, *company portals* that allow employees to self-administer benefits plans, *Facebookrecruiting* to recruit job applicants, *online testing* to prescreen job applicants, and *centralized call centers* to answer HR-related inquiries from supervisors. Table 1-2 lists some other examples of how employers use technology to support human resource management activities.[55]

As another example, more employers are installing their own internal social networking sites. For example, after the real estate bubble burst several years ago, many realtors from Long Realty in Tucson, Arizona, wanted a place where they could discuss the current market and how to deal with it. Long Realty therefore set up Long Connects. This internal social networking site lets its employees share experiences, suggestions, and advice without exposing their comments to the wider world (as would posting them on Facebook). IBM calls its internal social network site w3. IBM's employees around the world use w3 to "create personal profiles similar to those on

TABLE 1-2 Some Technology Applications to Support Human Resource Activities	
Technology	**How Used by HR**
Streaming desktop video	Used to facilitate distance learning and training or to provide corporate information to employees quickly and inexpensively
Internet- and network-monitoring software	Used to track employees' Internet and e-mail activities or to monitor their performance
Data warehouses and computerized analytical programs	Help HR managers monitor their HR systems. For example, they make it easier to assess things like cost per hire, and to compare current employees' skills with the firm's projected strategic needs

LinkedIn, bookmark web sites and news stories of interest, comment on company blogs, contribute to wikis, share files, and gain knowledge from white papers, videos, and podcasts."[56]

They Take an Integrated, "Talent Management" Approach to Managing Human Resources

Next, with employers competing for talent, no one wants to lose any high-potential employees, or to fail to attract or fully utilize top-caliber ones.[57] One survey of human resource executives found that "talent management" issues were among the most pressing ones they faced.[58] Human resource managers are therefore emphasizing talent management.

WHAT IS TALENT MANAGEMENT? **Talent management** is the *goal-oriented* and *integrated* process of *planning, recruiting, developing, managing, and compensating* employees.[59] It involves instituting a coordinated process for identifying, recruiting, hiring, and developing high-potential employees.

What does this mean in practice? For one thing, talent management means being more focused in how you manage your company's talent. For example, IBM segmented its employees into three groups. Now it can fine-tune the way it serves the employees in each segment. As another example, many employers are segmenting out their most "mission-critical" employees, and managing their development and rewards separately from the firms' other employees. We'll look more closely at talent management techniques starting in Chapter 4.

They Manage Ethics

We'll see in Chapter 14 (Ethics) that 6 of the 10 most serious workplace ethical issues—workplace safety, security of employee records, employee theft, affirmative action, comparable work, and employee privacy rights—were human resource management related.[60] *Ethics* means the standards someone uses to decide what his or her conduct should be. For example, prosecutors filed criminal charges against several Iowa meatpacking plant human resource managers who allegedly violated employment law by hiring children younger than 16.[61] Every human resource manager (and line manager) needs to understand the ethical implications of his or her employee-related decisions.

They Manage Employee Engagement

In today's challenging environment, no employer can afford to have its employees physically present but "checked out" mentally. The Institute for Corporate Productivity defines engaged employees "as those who are mentally and emotionally invested in their work and in contributing to an employer's success." Unfortunately, studies suggest that less than one-third of the U.S. workforce is engaged.[62] One Gallup study estimated that $350 billion is lost annually in the United States alone on damage done by disengaged workers.[63] Today's human resource managers need the skills to foster and manage employee engagement.

They Measure HR Performance and Results

In today's performance-based environment, employers expect their human resource managers to take action based on measurable performance-based criteria. For example, IBM's Randall MacDonald needed $100 million from IBM to reorganize its HR

talent management
The goal-oriented and integrated process of planning, recruiting, developing, managing, and compensating employees.

operations. He told top management, "I'm going to deliver talent to you that's skilled and on time and ready to be deployed. I will be able to measure the skills, tell you what skills we have, what [skills] we don't have [and] then show you how to fill the gaps or enhance our training."[64]

SAMPLE METRICS   To make claims like these, human resource managers need performance measures (or "metrics"). For example, median HR expenses as a proportion of companies' total operating costs average just under 1%. There tends to be between 0.9 and 1.0 human resource staff persons per 100 employees.[65] To see how they're doing compared to others, employers obtain customized benchmark comparisons from services such as the Society for Human Resource Management's Human Capital Benchmarking Service.[66] We'll look at improving performance through human resource management more closely in Chapter 3.

They Use Evidence-Based Human Resource Management

6 Define and give an example of evidence-based human resource management.

Basing decisions on the evidence, as practiced by IBM's Randall MacDonald ("I will tell you what skills we have . . .") is the heart of *evidence-based human resource management.* This is the use of data, facts, analytics, scientific rigor, critical evaluation, and critically evaluated research/case studies to support human resource management proposals, decisions, practices, and conclusions.[67] Put simply, evidence-based human resource management is the deliberate use of the best-available evidence in making decisions about the human resource management practices you are focusing on.[68] The evidence may come from *actual measurements* you make (such as, how did the trainees like this program?). It may come from *existing data* (such as, what happened to company profits after we installed this training program?). Or, it may come from published critically evaluated *research studies* (such as, what does the research literature conclude about the best way to ensure that trainees remember what they learn?).

They Add Value

This focus on performance, measurement, and evidence reflects another characteristic of today's human resource managers. From top management's point of view, it's not sufficient that HR management just oversee activities such as recruiting and benefits. It must *add value*, particularly by boosting profitability and performance in measurable ways. Professors Dave Ulrich and Wayne Brockbank explain this in terms of what they call "The HR Value Proposition."[69] They say the human resource manager's programs (such as screening tests and training tools) are just a means to an end. His or her ultimate aim must be to add value. "Adding value" means helping the firm and its employees gain in a measurable way from the human resource manager's actions.

We'll see in this book how human resource practices improve organizational profitability and performance. For example, studies of personnel testing's effectiveness conclude that screening applicants with personnel tests can produce employees who perform better.[70] Similarly, well-trained employees perform better than untrained ones, and safe workplaces produce fewer lost-time accidents and accident costs than do unsafe ones.

Putting in place a *high-performance work system* is one way to add value. Such a system is a set of human resource management practices that together produce superior employee performance. One study looked at 17 manufacturing plants, some of which adopted high-performance work system practices. For example, the high-performance plants paid more (median wages of $16 per hour compared with $13 per hour for all plants), trained more (83% offered more than 20 hours of training per year, compared with 32% for all plants), and used more sophisticated recruitment and hiring practices (tests and validated interviews, for instance). These plants also had the best overall profits, operating costs, and turnover.[71] We'll discuss high-performance work systems in Chapter 3.

They Have New Competencies[72]

Adding value, strategizing, and using technology all require that human resource managers have new competencies. They still need proficiencies in human resource management functional areas such as selection, training, and compensation. But they also require broader *business competencies.*

For example, human resource managers must "speak the CFO's language" by proposing and explaining human resource plans in measurable terms (such as return on investment), and be able to measure HR's impact.[73] To assist top management in formulating strategies, the human resource manager must understand strategic planning, marketing, production, and finance.[74] With companies grappling to adjust to competition, the human resource manager must be skilled at formulating and implementing large-scale organizational changes, designing organizational structures and work processes, and at understanding what it takes for the company to compete in and succeed in the marketplace.[75]

THE HUMAN RESOURCE MANAGER'S COMPETENCIES The accompanying Figure 1-7 provides one view of the competencies today's HR managers need.[76] Professor Dave Ulrich and his colleagues say that today's human resource managers need the knowledge, skills, and competencies to be:

- **Talent Managers/Organization Designers,** with a mastery of traditional human resource management tasks such as acquiring, training, and compensating employees.

- **Culture and Change Stewards,** able to create human resource practices that support the firm's cultural values.

- **Strategy Architects,** with the skills to help establish the company's overall strategic plan, and to put in place the human resource practices required to support accomplishing that plan.

- **Operational Executors,** able to anticipate, draft, and implement the human resource practices (for instance in testing and appraising) the company needs to implement its strategy.

- **Business Allies,** competent to apply business knowledge (for instance in finance, sales, and production) that enable them to help functional and general managers to achieve their departmental goals.

- **Credible Activists,** with the leadership and other competencies that make them "both credible (respected, admired, listened to) and active (offers a point of view, takes a position, challenges assumptions.)"[77]

FIGURE 1-7 The Human Resource Manager's Competencies

Source: Used with permission of The RBL Group, www.rbl.net, accessed April 4, 2011.

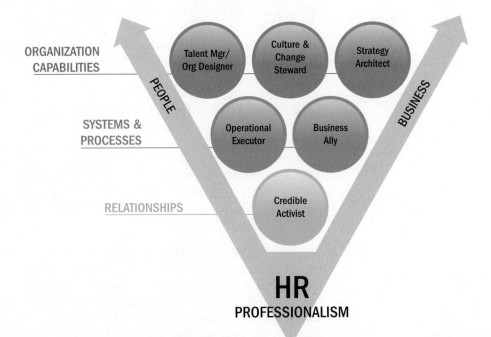

HR Certification

As the human resource manager's job becomes more demanding, human resource managers are becoming more professional. More than 115,000 HR professionals have already passed one or more of the Society for Human Resource Management's (SHRM) HR professional certification exams. SHRM's Human Resource Certification Institute offers these exams. Exams test the professional's knowledge of all aspects of human resource management, including ethics, management practices, staffing, development, compensation, labor relations, and health and safety. Those who successfully complete all requirements earn the SPHR (Senior Professional in HR), GPHR (Global Professional in HR), or PHR (Professional in HR) certificate. You will find certification-related exercises in the end-of-chapter exercises throughout this book. The test specifications for the HRCI exams, as well as new SHRM-related learning guidelines and exercises for human resource management courses, are in the SHRM appendix at the end of this book. Managers can take an online HRCI assessment exam at www.HRCI.org (or by calling 866-898-HRCI). SHRM provides an assurance of learning assessment preparation guide book for students.[78]

Finally, with all the changes taking place, the employment prospects for human resource managers look good. The U.S. Department of Labor projects that employment for human resource, training, and labor relations professionals will experience much faster than average growth in the next few years.[79] Top-ranked human resource managers earn multimillion dollar total take-home pay.[80]

7   Outline the plan of this book.

THE PLAN OF THIS BOOK
The Basic Themes and Features

In this book, we'll use several themes and features to highlight particularly important issues, and to provide continuity from chapter to chapter.

PRACTICAL TOOLS FOR EVERY MANAGER   First, human resource management is the *responsibility of every manager*—not just those in human resources. Throughout every page in this book, you'll therefore find an emphasis on practical material that you as a manager will need to perform your day-to-day management responsibilities, even if you never spend one day as an HR manager.

HR AS A PROFIT CENTER   Second, we've seen that employers need human resource management practices that add value. To illustrate this throughout the book, each chapter contains illustrative "HR as a Profit Center" features. These show actual examples of how human resource management practices add measurable value.

THE STRATEGIC CONTEXT   Third, we've seen that at companies such as L.L.Bean, *strategic human resource management* means formulating and executing human resource policies and practices that produce the employee competencies and behaviors the company needs to achieve its strategic aims. We'll use boxed "The Strategic Context" features in most chapters to help illustrate the strategic context of each chapter's material—for instance, how L.L.Bean's employee selection standards help support the firm's strong customer service philosophy, and thus its strategy.

EVIDENCE-BASED HR   Fourth, the intensely competitive nature of business today means human resource managers must defend their plans and contributions in measurable terms. Chapter 3 (Strategy) explains how managers do this. We also use (1) "Evidence-Based HR" features in most chapters to present examples of how managers manage based on facts and evidence, and (2) brief "Research Insights" to illustrate the evidence that supports what HR managers do.

CHAPTER CONTENTS OVERVIEW

Following is a brief overview of the chapters and their content.

Part 1: Introduction

Chapter 1: Introduction to Human Resource Management. The manager's human resource management jobs; crucial global and competitive trends; how managers use technology and modern HR measurement systems to create high-performance work systems.

Chapter 2: Equal Opportunity and the Law. What you should know about equal opportunity laws and how they affect activities such as interviewing, selecting employees, and evaluating performance.

Chapter 3: Human Resource Management Strategy and Analysis. What is strategic planning; strategic human resource management; building high-performance HR practices; tools for evidence-based HR.

Part 2: Recruitment, Placement, and Talent Management

Chapter 4: Job Analysis and the Talent Management Process. How to analyze a job; how to determine the human resource requirements of the job, as well as its specific duties, and what is talent management.

Chapter 5: Personnel Planning and Recruiting. Human resource planning; determining what sorts of people need to be hired; recruiting them.

Chapter 6: Employee Testing and Selection. Techniques you can use to ensure that you're hiring the right people.

Chapter 7: Interviewing Candidates. How you can interview candidates effectively.

Part 3: Training and Development

Chapter 8: Training and Developing Employees. Providing the training and development to ensure that your employees have the knowledge and skills needed to accomplish their tasks.

Chapter 9: Performance Management and Appraisal. Techniques you can use for appraising employee performance.

Chapter 10: Employee Retention, Engagement, and Careers. Coaching employees; managing careers; techniques such as career planning and promotion from within; talent management methods.

Part 4: Compensation

Chapter 11: Establishing Strategic Pay Plans. How to develop equitable pay plans for your employees.

Chapter 12: Pay for Performance and Financial Incentives. Pay-for-performance plans such as financial incentives, merit pay, and incentives that help tie performance to pay.

Chapter 13: Benefits and Services. Providing benefits that make it clear the firm views its employees as long-term investments and is concerned with their welfare.

Part 5: Employee Relations

Chapter 14: Ethics and Employee Rights and Discipline. How you can ensure ethical and fair treatment through grievance and discipline processes.

Chapter 15: Labor Relations and Collective Bargaining. How to deal with unions, including the union organizing campaign, negotiating and agreeing upon a collective bargaining agreement between unions and management, and managing the agreement via the grievance process.

Chapter 16: Employee Safety and Health. How you can make the workplace safe, including the causes of accidents, and laws governing your responsibilities for employee safety and health.

Chapter 17: Managing Global Human Resources. Special topics in managing the HR side of multinational operations.

Chapter 18: Managing Human Resources in Entrepreneurial Firms. Special topics you can use in managing human resources in smaller firms, including using Internet and government tools to support the HR effort, leveraging small size, using professional employer organizations, and managing HR systems, procedures, and paperwork.

The Topics Are Interrelated

In practice, don't think of each of this book's 18 chapters and topics as being unrelated to the others. Each topic interacts with and affects the others, and all should align with the employer's strategic plan. For example, hiring people who don't have the potential to learn the job will doom their performance regardless of how much training they get.

Figure 1-8 summarizes this idea. For example, how you test and interview job candidates (Chapters 6 and 7) and train and appraise job incumbents (Chapters 8 and 9) depends on the job's specific duties and responsibilities (Chapter 4). How good a job you do selecting (Chapter 6) and training (Chapter 8) employees will affect how safely they do their jobs (Chapter 16). An employee's performance and thus his or her appraisal (Chapter 9) depends not just on the person's motivation, but also on how well you identified the job's duties (Chapter 4), and screened and trained the employee (Chapters 6 and 7). Furthermore, we saw that how you recruit, select, train, appraise, and compensate employees should make sense in terms of producing the employee behaviors required to support the company's strategic plan.

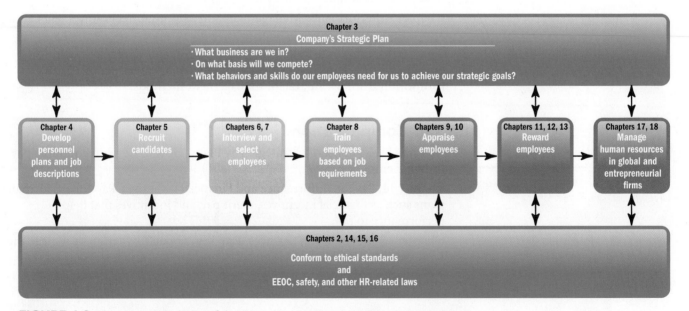

FIGURE 1-8 The interrelatedness of the Basic Human Resource Management Process

REVIEW

MyManagementLab Now that you have finished this chapter, go back to **www.mymanagementlab.com** to continue practicing and applying the concepts you've learned.

CHAPTER SECTION SUMMARIES

1. All managers should **understand the importance of human resource management**. Doing so helps managers avoid problems like hiring the wrong person for the job. And more important, it can help ensure that managers get results through people. Line managers' human resource duties include placing the right person on the job, and orienting and training new employees. The human resource manager's duties include supervising his or her own employees, coordinating the company's overall personnel policies, and assisting and advising line managers in the areas of human resource management.

2. **A changing environment today** is influencing what human resource managers do and how they do it. Globalization means more competition, and more competition means more pressure to lower costs and to make employees more productive and quality conscious. Technology is requiring more employees to be technologically well informed and pressuring employers to improve their human resource processes by applying new technological tools. There is more emphasis on "knowledge work" and therefore on building "human capital," the knowledge, education, training, skills, and expertise of a firm's employees. Workforce and demographic changes mean that the workforce is becoming older and more diverse.

3. Changes like these are manifesting themselves in **important trends in human resource management**.
   • Traditionally, personnel/HR managers focused on transactional issues such as hiring and firing employees and running the payroll department.

• Today, with employers competing in a challenging new environment, employers expect and demand more from their HR managers.

• For example, they expect their human resource management teams to focus more on big picture issues including instituting human resource policies and practices that support the companies' strategic objectives; to find new, more efficient ways to provide transactional services; and to have new proficiencies, for instance, in terms of strategizing and commanding a broader array of business knowledge.

• As part of this, employers expect their human resource managers to be able to create high-performance work systems that produce superior employee performance.

• To do so, HR managers should be able to apply evidence-based human resource management, which means the use of data, facts, analytics, scientific rigor, critical evaluation, and critically evaluated research/case studies to support human resource management proposals, decisions, practices, and conclusions.

4. In understanding the overall plan of this book, keep several important themes in mind: that human resource management is the responsibility of every manager, that the workforce is increasingly diverse, that employers and their human resource managers face the need to manage in challenging economic times, and that human resource managers must be able to defend their plans and contributions in measurable terms—to use evidence-based management—to show they've added value.

DISCUSSION QUESTIONS

1. Explain what HR management is and how it relates to the management process.
2. Give examples of how HR management concepts and techniques can be of use to all managers.
3. Illustrate the HR management responsibilities of line and staff managers.
4. Why is it important for companies today to make their human resources into a competitive advantage? Explain

how HR can contribute to doing this. What are some examples of employers who do this?

5. Think of some companies that you are familiar with or that you've read about where you think the human resource managers have been successful in "adding value". What do the HR managers do to lead you to your conclusion?

INDIVIDUAL AND GROUP ACTIVITIES

1. Working individually or in groups, develop outlines showing how trends like workforce diversity, technological innovation, globalization, and changes in the nature of work have affected the college or university you are attending now. Present in class.

2. Working individually or in groups, contact the HR manager of a local bank. Ask the HR manager how he or she is working as a strategic partner to manage human resources, given the bank's strategic goals and objectives. Back in class, discuss the responses of the different HR managers.

3. Working individually or in groups, interview an HR manager. Based on that interview, write a short presentation regarding HR's role today in building competitive organizations.

4. Working individually or in groups, bring several business publications such as *Bloomberg BusinessWeek* and the *Wall Street Journal* to class, or access them in class via the Web. Based on their contents, compile a list titled "What HR Managers and Departments Do Today."

5. Based on your personal experiences, list 10 examples showing how you used (or could have used) human resource management techniques at work or school.

6. Laurie Siegel, senior vice president of human resources for Tyco International, took over her job just after numerous charges forced the company's previous board of directors and top executives to leave the firm. Hired by new CEO Edward Breen, Siegel had to tackle numerous difficult problems starting the moment she assumed office. For example, she had to help hire a new management team. She had to do something about what the outside world viewed as a culture of questionable ethics at her company. And she had to do something about the company's top management compensation plan, which many felt contributed to the allegations by some that some former company officers had used the company as a sort of private ATM.

   Siegel came to Tyco after a very impressive career. For example, she had been head of executive compensation at Allied Signal, and was a graduate of the Harvard Business School. But, as strong as her background was, she obviously had her work cut out for her when she took the senior vice president of HR position at Tyco.

   Working individually or in groups, conduct an Internet search and library research to answer the following questions: What human resource management–related steps did Siegel take to help get Tyco back on the right track? Do you think she took the appropriate steps? Why or why not? What, if anything, do you suggest she do now?

7. The HRCI "Test Specifications" appendix at the end of this book (pages 633–640) lists the knowledge someone studying for the HRCI certification exam needs to have in each area of human resource management (such as in Strategic Management, Workforce Planning, and Human Resource Development). In groups of four to five students, do four things: (1) review that appendix now; (2) identify the material in this chapter that relates to the required knowledge the appendix lists; (3) write four multiple-choice exam questions on this material that you believe would be suitable for inclusion in the HRCI exam; and (4) if time permits, have someone from your team post your team's questions in front of the class, so the students in other teams can take each others' exam questions.

EXPERIENTIAL EXERCISE

Helping "The Donald"

Purpose: The purpose of this exercise is to provide practice in identifying and applying the basic concepts of human resource management by illustrating how managers use these techniques in their day-to-day jobs.

Required Understanding: Be thoroughly familiar with the material in this chapter, and with at least several episodes of *The Apprentice* or *The Celebrity Apprentice*, the TV shows in which developer Donald Trump starred.

How to Set Up the Exercise/Instructions:

1. Divide the class into teams of three to four students.
2. Read this: As you may know by watching "the Donald" as he organizes his business teams for *The Apprentice* and *The Celebrity Apprentice*, human resource management plays an important role in what Donald Trump and the participants on his separate teams need to do to be successful. For example, Donald Trump needs to be able to appraise each of the participants. And, for their part, the leaders of each of his teams need to be able to staff his or her team with the right participants, and then provide the sorts of training, incentives, and evaluations that help their companies succeed and that therefore make the participants themselves (and especially the team leaders) look like "winners" to Mr. Trump.
3. Watch several of these shows (or reruns of the shows), and then meet with your team and answer the following questions:
   a. What specific HR functions (recruiting, interviewing, and so on) can you identify Donald Trump using on this show? Make sure to give specific examples based on the show.
   b. What specific HR functions (recruiting, selecting, training, etc.) can you identify one or more of the team leaders using to help manage their teams on the show? Again, please give specific answers.
   c. Provide a specific example of how HR functions (such as recruiting, selection, interviewing, compensating, appraising, and so on) contributed to one of the participants coming across as particularly successful to Mr. Trump. Can you provide examples of how one or more of these functions contributed to a participant being told by Mr. Trump, "You're fired"?
   d. Present your team's conclusions to the class.

APPLICATION CASE

JACK NELSON'S PROBLEM

As a new member of the board of directors for a local bank, Jack Nelson was being introduced to all the employees in the home office. When he was introduced to Ruth Johnson, he was curious about her work and asked her what the machine she was using did. Johnson replied that she really did not know what the machine was called or what it did. She explained that she had only been working there for 2 months. However, she did know precisely how to operate the machine. According to her supervisor, she was an excellent employee.

At one of the branch offices, the supervisor in charge spoke to Nelson confidentially, telling him that "something was wrong," but she didn't know what. For one thing, she explained, employee turnover was too high, and no sooner had one employee been put on the job than another one resigned. With customers to see and loans to be made, she continued, she had little time to work with the new employees as they came and went.

All branch supervisors hired their own employees without communication with the home office or other branches. When an opening developed, the supervisor tried to find a suitable employee to replace the worker who had quit.

After touring the 22 branches and finding similar problems in many of them, Nelson wondered what the home office should do or what action he should take. The banking firm generally was regarded as being a well-run institution that had grown from 27 to 191 employees during the past 8 years. The more he thought about the matter, the more puzzled Nelson became. He couldn't quite put his finger on the problem, and he didn't know whether to report his findings to the president.

Questions

1. What do you think is causing some of the problems in the bank's home office and branches?
2. Do you think setting up an HR unit in the main office would help?
3. What specific functions should an HR unit carry out? What HR functions would then be carried out by supervisors and other line managers? What role should the Internet play in the new HR organization?

Source: From Claude S. George, *Supervision in Action*, 4th ed., 1985. Adapted by permission of Prentice Hall, Inc., Upper Saddle River, NJ.

CONTINUING CASE

CARTER CLEANING COMPANY

Introduction

A main theme of this book is that human resource management activities like recruiting, selecting, training, and rewarding employees is not just the job of a central HR group but rather a job in which every manager must engage. Perhaps nowhere is this more apparent than in the typical small service business. Here the owner/manager usually has no HR staff to rely on. However, the success of his or her enterprise (not to mention his or her family's peace of mind) often depends largely on the effectiveness through which workers are recruited, hired, trained, evaluated, and rewarded. Therefore, to help illustrate and emphasize the front-line manager's HR role, throughout this book we will use a continuing case based on an actual small business in the southeastern United States. Each chapter's segment of the case will illustrate how the case's main player—owner/manager Jennifer Carter—confronts and solves personnel problems each day at work by applying the concepts and techniques of that particular chapter. Here is background information that you will need to answer questions that arise in subsequent chapters. (We also present a second, unrelated "application case" case incident in each chapter.)

Carter Cleaning Centers

Jennifer Carter graduated from State University in June 2005, and, after considering several job offers, decided to do what she always planned to do—go into business with her father, Jack Carter.

Jack Carter opened his first laundromat in 1995 and his second in 1998. The main attraction of these coin laundry businesses for him was that they were capital- rather than labor-intensive. Thus, once the investment in machinery was made, the stores could be run with just one unskilled attendant and none of the labor problems one normally expects from being in the retail service business.

The attractiveness of operating with virtually no skilled labor notwithstanding, Jack had decided by 1999 to expand the services in each of his stores to include the dry cleaning and pressing of clothes. He embarked, in other words, on a strategy of "related diversification" by adding new services that were related to and consistent with his existing coin laundry activities. He added these for several reasons. He wanted to better utilize the unused space in the rather large stores he currently had under lease. Furthermore, he was, as he put it, "tired of sending out the dry cleaning and pressing work that came in from our coin laundry clients to a dry cleaner 5 miles away, who then took most of what should have been our profits." To reflect the new, expanded line of services, he renamed each of his two stores Carter Cleaning Centers and was sufficiently satisfied with their performance to open four more of the same type of stores over the next 5 years. Each store had its own on-site manager and, on average, about seven employees and annual revenues of about $500,000. It was this six-store chain that Jennifer joined after graduating.

Her understanding with her father was that she would serve as a troubleshooter/consultant to the elder Carter with the aim of both learning the business and bringing to it modern management concepts and techniques for solving the business's problems and facilitating its growth.

Questions

1. Make a list of five specific HR problems you think Carter Cleaning will have to grapple with.
2. What would you do first if you were Jennifer?

KEY TERMS

organization, *4*

manager, *4*

management process, *4*

human resource management (HRM), *4*

authority, *6*

line authority, *6*

staff authority, *6*

line manager, *6*

staff manager, *6*

functional authority, *7*

globalization, *11*

human capital, *13*

talent management, *19*

ENDNOTES

1. http://llbeancareers.com/culture.htm, accessed February 28, 2010.
2. http://llbeancareers.com/culture.htm, accessed February 28, 2010.
3. Quoted in Fred K. Foulkes, "The Expanding Role of the Personnel Function," *Harvard Business Review*, March–April 1975, pp. 71–84. See also http://www.bls.gov/oco/ocos021.htm, accessed October 3, 2011.
4. Jeremy Smerd, "Outsider Thinking for GM HR," *Workforce Management*, August 17, 2009, pp. 1–3.
5. Steve Bates, "No Experience Necessary? Many Companies Are Putting Non-HR Executives in Charge of HR with Mixed Results," *HR Magazine* 46, no. 11 (November 2001), pp. 34–41. See also Fay Hansen, "Top of the Class," *Workforce Management*, June 23, 2008, pp. 1, 25–30.
6. "A Profile of Human Resource Executives," *BNA Bulletin to Management*, June 21, 2001, p. S5.
7. This data comes from "Small Business: A Report of the President" (1998), www.SBA.gov/ADV/stats, accessed March 9, 2006. See also "Statistics of U.S. Businesses and Non-Employer Status," www.SBA.gov/ADV oh/research/data.html, accessed March 9, 2006.
8. Some employers, like Google, are adding "chief sustainability officers" within human resource management who are responsible for fostering the company's environmental sustainability efforts. Nancy Woodward, "New Breed of Human Resource Leader," *HR Magazine*, June 2008, pp. 53–57.
9. See Dave Ulrich, "The New HR Organization," *Workforce Management*, December 10, 2007, pp. 40–44; and Dave Ulrich, "The 21st-Century HR Organization," *Human Resource Management* 47, no. 4 (Winter 2008), pp. 829–850.
10. Robert Grossman, "Saving Shared Services," *HR Magazine*, September 2010, pp. 26–31.
11. Robert Grossman, "IBM's HR Takes a Risk," *HR Management*, April 2007, pp. 54–59.
12. In fact, one study found that delegating somewhat more of the HR activities to line managers "had a positive effect on HR managers' perceptions of their units' reputation among line managers." Carol Kulik and Elissa Perry, "When Less Is More: The Effect of Devolution on HR as a Strategic Role and Construed Image," *Human Resource Management* 47, no. 3 (Fall 2008), pp. 541–558.
13. "Human Resource Activities, Budgets, and Staffs, 1999–2000," *BNA Bulletin to Management*, June 20, 2000.
14. For discussions of some other important trends, see, for example, Society for Human Resource Management, "Workplace Trends: An Overview of the Findings of the Latest SHRM Workplace Forecast," *Workplace Visions*, no. 3 (2008), pp. 1–8; and Ed Frauenheim, "Future View," *Workforce Management*, December 15, 2008, pp. 18–23.
15. Ibid., p. 9. See also Society for Human Resource Management, "The Impact of Globalization on HR," *Workplace Visions*, no. 5 (2000), pp. 1–8.
16. See, for example, Society for Human Resource Management, "Promoting Productivity," *Workplace Visions*, no. 1 (2006), pp. 1–8.
17. Roger J. Moncarz, Michael G. Wolf, and Benjamin Wright, "Service-Providing Occupations, Offshoring, and the Labor Market," *Monthly Labor Review*, December 2008, pp. 71–86.
18. www.usatoday.com/money/economy/2010-08-06-manufacturing04_CV_N.htm, accessed May 8, 2011.
19. www.census.gov/foreign-trade/statistics/historical/gands.pdf, accessed May 8, 2011.
20. Ibid.
21. http://facebookrecruiting.net/, accessed May 8, 2011.
22. Ibid.
23. Timothy Appel, "Better Off a Blue-Collar," *The Wall Street Journal*, July 1, 2003, p. B-1.
24. Roger Moncarz and Azure Reaser, "The 2000–10 Job Outlook in Brief," *Occupational Outlook Quarterly*, Spring 2002, pp. 9–44.
25. See "Charting the Projections: 2004–2014," *Occupational Outlook Quarterly*, Winter 2005–2006.
26. Ibid.
27. See, for example, "Engine of Change," *Workforce Management*, July 17, 2006, pp. 20–30.
28. Moncarz and Reaser, "The 2000–10 Job Outlook in Brief."
29. Richard Crawford, *In the Era of Human Capital* (New York: Harper Business, 1991), p. 26.
30. Peter Drucker, "The Coming of the New Organization," *Harvard Business Review*, January–February 1998, p. 45. See also James Guthrie et al., "Correlates and Consequences of High Involvement Work Practices: The Role of Competitive Strategy," *International Journal of Human Resource Management*, February 2002, pp. 183–197.
31. Society for Human Resource Management, "Workforce Readiness and the New Essential Skills," *Workplace Visions*, no. 2 (2008), p. 5.
32. "Human Resources Wharton," www.knowledge.wharton.upe.edu, accessed January 8, 2006.
33. See, for example, Anthea Zacharatos et al., "High-Performance Work Systems and Occupational Safety," *Journal of Applied Psychology* 90, no. 1 (2005), pp. 77–93.
34. "Charting the Projections: 2004–2014," *Occupational Outlook Quarterly*, Winter 2005–2006, pp. 48–50; and www.bls.gov/emp/emplabor01.pdf, accessed October 20, 2008.
35. "Percent Growth in Labor Force by Race, Projected 2008–18," *Occupational Outlook Quarterly*, Winter 2009–2010, p. 35; "Percent Growth in Labor Force by Ethnic Origin, Projected 2008–2018," *Occupational Outlook Quarterly*, Winter 2009–2010, p. 36.
36. Tony Carneval, "The Coming Labor and Skills Shortage," *Training & Development*, January 2005, p. 39.
37. "Talent Management Leads in Top HR Concerns," *Compensation & Benefits Review*, May/June 2007, p. 12.
38. Bruce Tulgan, quoted in Stephanie Armour, "Generation Y: They've Arrived at Work with a New Attitude," *USA Today*, www.usatoday.com/money/workplace/2005-11-06-gen-y_x.htm, accessed May 10, 2010.

39. Stephanie Armour, "Generation Y: They've Arrived at Work with a New Attitude," *USA Today*, www.usatoday.com/money/workplace/2005-11-06-gen-y_x.htm, accessed May 10, 2010.

40. Nadira Hira, "You Raised Them, Now Manage Them," *Fortune*, May 28, 2007, pp. 38–46; Katheryn Tyler, "The Tethered Generation," *HR Magazine*, May 2007, pp. 41–46; Jeffrey Zaslow, "The Most Praised Generation Goes to Work," *The Wall Street Journal*, April 20, 2007, pp. W-1, W-7.

41. "Talent Management Leads in Top HR Concerns," *Compensation & Benefits Review*, May/June 2007, p. 12.

42. Society for Human Resource Management, Jennifer Schramm, "Exploring the Future of Work," *Workplace Visions*, no. 2 (2005), p. 6; Rainer Strack, Jens Baier, and Anders Fahlander, "Managing Demographic Risk," *Harvard Business Review*, February 2008, pp. 119–128.

43. Adrienne Fox, "At Work in 2020," *HR Magazine*, January 2010, pp. 18–23.

44. Rita Zeidner, "Does the United States Need Foreign Workers?" *HR Magazine*, June 2009, pp. 42–44.

45. www.bls.gov/opub/ted/2006/may/wk2/art01.htm, accessed April 18, 2009.

46. "Immigrants in the Workplace," *BNA Bulletin to Management Datagraph*, March 15, 1996, pp. 260–261. See also Tanuja Agarwala, "Human Resource Management: The Emerging Trends," *Indian Journal of Industrial Relations*, January 2002, pp. 315–331.

47. "Human Capital Critical to Success," *Management Review*, November 1998, p. 9. See also "HR 2018: Top Predictions," *Workforce Management* 87, no. 20 (December 15, 2008), pp. 20–21.

48. www.llbean.com/customerService/aboutLLBean/images/110408_About-LLB.pdf, accessed June 1, 2011.

49. www.llbean.com/, accessed June 1, 2011.

50. http://llbeancareers.com/culture.htm, accessed February 28, 2010.

51. Michael Arndt, "L.L.Bean Follows Its Shoppers to the Web," *Business Week*, March 1, 2010.

52. A survey found that HR managers referred to "strategic/critical thinking skills" as the top "most important factor in attaining next HR job." See "Career Development for HR Professionals," *Society for Human Resource Management Research Quarterly*, second quarter 2008, p. 3.

53. John Boudreau and Peter Ramstad, *Beyond HR: The New Science of Human Capital* (Boston: Harvard Business School Publishing Corporation, 2007), p. 9.

54. For example, see Sandra Fisher et al., "Human Resource Issues in Outsourcing: Integrating Research and Practice," *Human Resource Management* 47, no. 3 (Fall 2008), pp. 501–523; and "Sizing Up the HR Outsourcing Market," *HR Magazine*, November 2008, p. 78.

55. Studies suggest that IT usage does support human resource managers' strategic planning. See Victor Haines III and Genevieve LaFleur, "Information Technology Usage and Human Resource Roles and Effectiveness," *Human Resource Management* 47, no. 3 (Fall 2008), pp. 525–540. See also R. Zeidner, "The Tech Effect on Human Resources," *HRMagazine* (2009 HR Trendbook supp), pp. 49–50, 52.

56. Susan Ladika, "Socially Evolved," *Workforce Management*, September 2010, pp. 18–22

57. Paul Loftus, "Tackle Talent Management to Achieve High Performance," *Plant Engineering* 61, no. 6 (June 15, 2007), p. 29.

58. "Survey: Talent Management a Top Concern," *CIO Insight*, January 2, 2007.

59. www.talentmanagement101.com, accessed December 10, 2007.

60. Kevin Wooten, "Ethical Dilemmas in Human Resource Management," *Human Resource Management Review* 11 (2001), p. 161. See also Ann Pomeroy, "The Ethics Squeeze," *HR Magazine* 51, no. 3 (March 2006), pp. 48–55.

61. "Meatpacking Case Highlights HR's Liability," *Workforce Management*, September 20, 2008, p. 6.

62. Dean Smith, "Engagement Matters," *T+D* 63, no. 10, October 2009, p. 14.

63. Quoted in Smith, "Engagement Matters."

64. Robert Grossman, "IBM's HR Takes a Risk," *HR Management*, April 2007, pp. 54–59. See also Robert Grossman, "Close the Gap Between Research and Practice," *HR Magazine*, November 2009, pp. 31–37.

65. Chris Brewster, et al., "What Determines the Size of the HR Function? A Cross National Analysis," *Human Resource Management* 45, no. 1 (Spring 2006), pp. 3–21.

66. Contact the Society for Human Resource Management, 703.535.6366.

67. See, for example, www.personneltoday.com/blogs/hcglobal-human-capital-management/2009/02/theres-no-such-thing-as-eviden.html, accessed April 18, 2009.

68. The evidence-based movement began in medicine. In 1996, in an editorial published by the *British Medical Journal*, David Sackett, MD, defined "evidence based medicine" as "use of the best-available evidence in making decisions about patient care" and urged his colleagues to adopt its tenets. "Evidence-Based Training™: Turning Research Into Results for Pharmaceutical Sales Training," An AXIOM White Paper © 2006 AXIOM Professional Health Learning LLC. All rights reserved.

69. Susan Wells, "From HR to the Top," *HR Magazine*, June 2003, p. 49.

70. Mitchell Rothstein and Richard Goffin, "The Use of Personality Measures in Personnel Selection: What Does Current Research Support?" *Human Resource Management Review* 16 (2006), pp. 155–180; Helen Shipton et al., "HRM as a Predictor of Innovation," *Human Resource Management Journal* 16, no. 1 (2006), pp. 3–27; Luc Sels et al., "Unraveling the HRM–Performance Link: Value Creating and Cost-Increasing Effects of Small-Business HRM," *Journal of Management Studies* 43, no. 2 (March 2006), pp. 319–342; and Jaap Paauwe and Paul Boselie, "HRM and Performance: What's Next?" *Human Resource Management Journal* 15, no. 4 (2005), pp. 68–82.

71. "Super Human Resources Practices Result in Better Overall Performance, Report Says," *BNA Bulletin to Management*, August 26, 2004, pp. 273–274. See also Wendy Boswell, "Aligning Employees with the Organization's Strategic Objectives: Out of Line of Sight, Out of Mind," *International Journal of Human Resource Management* 17, no. 9 (September 2006), pp. 1014–1041. A recent study found that some employers, which the researchers called *cost minimizers*, intentionally took a lower cost approach to human resource practices, with mixed results. See Soo Min Toh et al., "Human Resource Configurations: Investigating Fit with the Organizational Context," *Journal of Applied Psychology* 93, no. 4 (2008), pp. 864–882.

72. Except as noted, most of this section is based on Richard Vosburgh, "The Evolution of HR: Developing HR as an Internal Consulting Organization," *Human Resource Planning* 30, no. 3 (September 2007), pp. 11–24.

73. Dave Ulrich and Wayne Brockbank, *The HR Value Proposition* (Boston: Harvard Business School Publishing, 2005).

74. See, for example, "Employers Seek HR Executives with Global Experience, SOX Knowledge, Business Sense," *BNA Bulletin to Management*, September 19, 2006, pp. 297–298; and Robert Rodriguez, "HR's New Breed," *HR Magazine*, January 2006, pp. 67–71.

75. Ibid.

76. www.elearning.shrm.org/newhrcompetency.aspx, accessed April 4, 2011.

77. Ibid.

78. SHRM no longer makes it possible for college graduates without HR experience to sit for one of the chairman certification exams. However, it does provide a SHRM Assurance of Learning Assessment Preparation Guidebook. This helps students study for a SHRM exam that aims to verify that the student has acquired the knowledge required to enter the human resource management profession at the entry level. See www.SHRM.org/assuranceoflearning/index.html, accessed April 4, 2011.

79. "Efforts to recruit and retain employees, the growing importance of employee training, and new legal standards are expected to increase employment of these workers." "The 2008–2018 Job Outlook in Brief," *Occupational Outlook Quarterly* 54, no. 1 (Spring 2010), p. 9.

80. For example, in 2009, the head of human resources and labor relations at Delta Air Lines earned about $5 million in total compensation, and the senior vice president for human resources at eBay earned over $4 million. Jessica Marquez, "As the Economy Goes," *Workforce Management*, August 17, 2009, pp. 27–33.

2

Equal Opportunity and the Law

LEARNING OBJECTIVES

1. Explain the importance of and list the basic features of Title VII of the 1964 Civil Rights Act and at least five other equal employment laws.

2. Explain how to avoid and deal with accusations of sexual harassment at work.

3. Define *adverse impact* and explain how it is proved.

4. Explain and illustrate two defenses you can use in the event of discriminatory practice allegations.

5. Cite specific discriminatory personnel management practices in recruitment, selection, promotion, transfer, layoffs, and benefits.

6. List the steps in the EEOC enforcement process.

7. Discuss why diversity management is important and how to institutionalize a diversity management program.

A federal district court in New York recently approved a $175 million settlement by Novartis Pharmaceuticals Corp. to pay a class of about 6,000 female current and former sales representatives to settle their sex discrimination class action suit.[1] As you'll see at http://eeoc.gov/eeoc/newsroom/index.cfm, hardly a day goes by without equal opportunity–related lawsuits at work.

Access a host of interactive learning aids at **www.mymanagementlab.com** to help strengthen your understanding of the chapter concepts.

WHERE ARE WE NOW . . .

Every HR action you take as a manager, from interviewing applicants to training, appraising, and rewarding them, has equal employment implications. Therefore, the purpose of this chapter is to provide you with the knowledge to deal effectively with equal employment questions on the job. The main topics we cover are equal opportunity laws enacted from 1964 to 1991, the laws from 1991 to the present, defenses against discrimination allegations, illustrative discriminatory employment practices, the EEOC enforcement process, and diversity management.

1 Explain the importance of and list the basic features of Title VII of the 1964 Civil Rights Act and at least five other equal employment laws.

EQUAL EMPLOYMENT OPPORTUNITY 1964–1991

American race relations were not always as tolerant as President Barak Obama's election might suggest. It took centuries of legislative action, court decisions, and evolving public policy to arrive at this point.

Legislation barring discrimination against minorities in the United States is therefore nothing new. The Fifth Amendment to the U.S. Constitution (ratified in 1791) states that "no person shall be deprived of life, liberty, or property, without due process of the law." The Thirteenth Amendment (1865) outlawed slavery, and courts have held that it bars racial discrimination. The Civil Rights Act of 1866 gives all persons the same right to make and enforce contracts and to benefit from U.S. laws.[2] Other laws and various court decisions similarly made discrimination against minorities illegal by the early 1900s, at least in theory.[3]

But as a practical matter, Congress and presidents avoided dramatic action on implementing equal employment until the early 1960s. At that point, civil unrest among minorities and women and changing traditions prompted them to act. Congress passed a multitude of new civil rights laws.

Title VII of the 1964 Civil Rights Act

Title VII of the 1964 Civil Rights Act was one of the first of these 1960s-era laws. As amended by the 1972 Equal Employment Opportunity Act, Title VII states that an employer cannot discriminate based on race, color, religion, sex, or national origin. Specifically, it states that it shall be an unlawful employment practice for an employer:

1. To fail or refuse to hire or to discharge an individual or otherwise to discriminate against any individual with respect to his/her compensation, terms, conditions, or privileges of employment, because of such individual's race, color, religion, sex, or national origin.

2. To limit, segregate, or classify his/her employees or applicants for employment in any way that would deprive or tend to deprive any individual of employment opportunities or otherwise adversely affect his/her status as an employee, because of such individual's race, color, religion, sex, or national origin.

WHO DOES TITLE VII COVER? Title VII covers just about everyone. It bars discrimination on the part of most employers, including all public or private employers of 15 or more persons. It also covers all private and public educational institutions, the federal government, and state and local governments. It bars public and private employment agencies from failing or refusing to refer for employment any individual because of race, color, religion, sex, or national origin. And it bars labor unions with 15 or more members from excluding, expelling, or classifying their membership based on race, color, religion, sex, or national origin.

THE EEOC Title VII established the **Equal Employment Opportunity Commission (EEOC)** to administer and enforce the Civil Rights law at work. The commission itself consists of five members appointed by the president with the advice and consent of the Senate. Each member serves a 5-year term. In popular usage, the EEOC also includes the thousands of staff the EEOC has around the United States. They receive and investigate job discrimination complaints from aggrieved individuals. When the EEOC finds reasonable cause that the charges are justified, it attempts (through conciliation) to reach an agreement. If this fails, it can go to court. The EEOC may file discrimination charges on behalf of aggrieved individuals, or the individuals may file on behalf of themselves.[4] We'll discuss the EEOC procedure later in this chapter.

Executive Orders

Various U.S. presidents signed executive orders expanding equal employment in federal agencies. For example, the Johnson administration (1963–1969) issued Executive Orders 11246 and 11375. These didn't just ban discrimination. They also required that government contractors with contracts of over $50,000 and 50 or more employees take **affirmative action** to ensure employment opportunities for those who may have suffered past discrimination. These orders also established the **Office of Federal Contract Compliance Programs (OFCCP)**.[5] It implements the orders and ensures compliance. President Obama's administration recently directed more funds and staffing to the OFCCP.[6]

Equal Pay Act of 1963

Under the **Equal Pay Act of 1963** (amended in 1972), it is unlawful to discriminate in pay on the basis of sex when jobs involve equal work; require equivalent skills, effort, and responsibility; and are performed under similar working conditions. Pay differences derived from seniority systems, merit systems, and systems that measure earnings by production quantity or quality or from any factor other than sex do not violate the act.

Age Discrimination in Employment Act of 1967

The **Age Discrimination in Employment Act of 1967 (ADEA)** made it unlawful to discriminate against employees or applicants who are between 40 and 65 years of age. Subsequent amendments eliminated the age cap, effectively ending most mandatory retirement at age 65. Most states and local agencies, when acting in the role of employer, must also adhere to provisions of the act that protect workers from age discrimination.

You can't get around the ADEA by replacing employees over 40 years of age with those who are also over 40. In *O'Connor v. Consolidated Coin Caterers Corp.*, the U.S. Supreme Court held that an employee who is over 40 years of age might sue for discrimination if a "significantly younger" employee replaces him or her, even if the replacement is also over 40. The Court didn't specify what "significantly younger" meant, but O'Connor had been replaced by someone 16 years younger.[7]

Younger managers especially may have to guard against ageist prejudices. For example, a 54-year-old former manager recently alleged that Google fired him because he wasn't a "cultural fit," according to his own manager. This and other allegedly ageist statements by Google executives prompted the California Court of Appeals to let the manager's case proceed.[8]

The ADEA is attractive to plaintiffs' lawyers. It allows jury trials and double damages to those proving "willful" discrimination.[9]

Vocational Rehabilitation Act of 1973

The **Vocational Rehabilitation Act of 1973** requires employers with federal contracts of more than $2,500 to take affirmative action in employing handicapped persons. It does not require hiring unqualified people. It does require an employer to take steps to accommodate a handicapped worker unless doing so imposes an undue hardship on the employer.

Title VII of the 1964 Civil Rights Act
The section of the act that says an employer cannot discriminate on the basis of race, color, religion, sex, or national origin with respect to employment.

Equal Employment Opportunity Commission (EEOC)
The commission, created by Title VII, is empowered to investigate job discrimination complaints and sue on behalf of complainants.

affirmative action
Steps that are taken for the purpose of eliminating the present effects of past discrimination.

Office of Federal Contract Compliance Programs (OFCCP)
This office is responsible for implementing the executive orders and ensuring compliance of federal contractors.

Equal Pay Act of 1963
The act requiring equal pay for equal work, regardless of sex.

Age Discrimination in Employment Act of 1967 (ADEA)
The act prohibiting arbitrary age discrimination and specifically protecting individuals over 40 years old.

Vocational Rehabilitation Act of 1973
The act requiring certain federal contractors to take affirmative action for disabled persons.

Pregnancy Discrimination Act of 1978

The **Pregnancy Discrimination Act** of 1978 prohibits using pregnancy, childbirth, or related medical conditions to discriminate in hiring, promotion, suspension, or discharge, or in any term or condition of employment. Furthermore, under the act, if an employer offers its employees disability coverage, then it must treat pregnancy and childbirth like any other disability, and include it in the plan as a covered condition.[10]

More women are suing under this act. Pregnancy discrimination claims to the EEOC rose about 50% from 2000 to 2010, to 6,119 charges in fiscal year 2010.[11] (Progressive human resources notwithstanding, one firm, an auto dealership, fired an employee after she said she was pregnant. The reason? Allegedly, "In case I ended up throwing up or cramping in one of their vehicles. They said pregnant women do that sometimes, and I could cause an accident, which might mean a lawsuit against them.")[12] Managers therefore shouldn't jump to conclusions. They should base "any [such] decision on whether an employee can do the job on medical documentation, not on a manager's interpretation."[13]

Federal Agency Guidelines

The federal agencies charged with ensuring compliance with these laws and executive orders issue their own implementing guidelines. These spell out recommended procedures for complying with the law.[14]

The EEOC, Civil Service Commission, Department of Labor, and Department of Justice together issued **uniform guidelines**. These set forth "highly recommended" procedures regarding things like employee selection, record keeping, and preemployment inquiries. As an example, they specify that employers must *validate* any employment selection devices (like tests) that screen out disproportionate numbers of women or minorities. And they explain how to validate a selection device. (We explain this procedure in Chapter 6.) The EEOC and other agencies also periodically issue updated guidelines clarifying and revising their positions on matters such as sexual harassment. (The OFCCP has its own guidelines.) The American Psychological Association has its own (non–legally binding) Standards for Educational and Psychological Testing.

Early Court Decisions Regarding Equal Employment Opportunity

Several court decisions between 1964 and 1991 helped clarify courts' interpretations of EEO laws such as Title VII.

GRIGGS V. DUKE POWER COMPANY *Griggs* was a landmark case, because the Supreme Court used it to define unfair discrimination. Lawyers sued the Duke Power Company on behalf of Wilie Griggs, an applicant for a job as a coal handler. The company required its coal handlers to be high school graduates. Griggs claimed this requirement was illegally discriminatory. He said it wasn't related to success on the job, and it resulted in more blacks than whites being rejected for these jobs. Griggs won the case. The Court's decision was unanimous. In his written opinion, Chief Justice Burger laid out three crucial guidelines affecting equal employment legislation.

- First, the Court ruled that the *discrimination does not have to be overt to be illegal*. In other words, the plaintiff does not have to show that the employer intentionally discriminated against the employee or applicant. Instead, the plaintiff just has to show that discrimination took place.

- Second, the Court held that an employment practice (in this case, requiring the high school degree) *must be job related* if it has an unequal impact on members of a **protected class**. (For example, if arithmetic is not required to perform the job, don't test for arithmetic.)

- Third, Chief Justice Burger's opinion placed the *burden of proof on the employer* to show that the hiring practice is job related. Thus, the employer must show that the employment practice (in this case, requiring a high school degree) is necessary for satisfactory job performance if the practice discriminates against members of a protected class. In the words of Justice Burger,

> The act proscribes not only overt discrimination, but also practices that are fair in form, but discriminatory in operation. The touchstone is business necessity. If an employment practice which operates to exclude Negroes cannot be shown to be related to job performance, the practice is prohibited.[15]

For employers, *Griggs* established these five principles:

1. A test or other selection practice must be job related, and the burden of proof is on the employer.
2. An employer's intent not to discriminate is irrelevant.[16]
3. If a practice is "fair in form but discriminatory in operation," the courts will not uphold it.
4. *Business necessity* is the defense for any existing program that has adverse impact. The court did not define business necessity.
5. Title VII does not forbid testing. However, the test must be job related (valid), in that performance on the test must relate to performance on the job.

ALBEMARLE PAPER COMPANY V. MOODY   In the *Albemarle* case, the Court provided more details on how employers could prove that tests or other screening tools relate to job performance.[17] For example, the Court said that if an employer wants to test candidates for a job, then the employer should first clearly document and understand the job's duties and responsibilities. Furthermore, the job's performance standards should be clear and unambiguous. That way, the employer can identify which employees are performing better than others. The Court's ruling also established the EEOC (now Federal) Guidelines on validation as the procedures for validating employment practices.

EQUAL EMPLOYMENT OPPORTUNITY 1990–91–PRESENT
The Civil Rights Act of 1991

Several subsequent Supreme Court rulings in the 1980s had the effect of limiting the protection of women and minority groups under equal employment laws. For example, they raised the plaintiff's burden of proving that the employer's acts were in fact discriminatory. This soon prompted Congress to pass a new Civil Rights Act. President George H. W. Bush signed the **Civil Rights Act of 1991 (CRA 1991)** into law in November 1991. The effect of CRA 1991 was to roll back equal employment law to where it stood before the 1980s decisions. In some respects, it even placed more responsibility on employers.

Pregnancy Discrimination Act
An amendment to Title VII of the Civil Rights Act that prohibits sex discrimination based on "pregnancy, childbirth, or related medical conditions."

uniform guidelines
Guidelines issued by federal agencies charged with ensuring compliance with equal employment federal legislation explaining recommended employer procedures in detail.

protected class
Persons such as minorities and women protected by equal opportunity laws, including Title VII.

Civil Rights Act of 1991 (CRA 1991)
The act that places the burden of proof back on employers and permits compensatory and punitive damages.

BURDEN OF PROOF First, CRA 1991 addressed the issue of *burden of proof*. Burden of proof—what the plaintiff must show to establish possible illegal discrimination, and what the employer must show to defend its actions—plays a central role in equal employment cases.[18] Today, in brief, once an aggrieved applicant or employee demonstrates that an employment practice (such as "must lift 100 pounds") has an adverse impact on a particular group, then the burden of proof shifts to the employer, who must show that the challenged practice is job related.[19] For example, the employer has to show that lifting 100 pounds is actually required for performing the job in question, and that the business could not run efficiently without the requirement—that it is a business necessity.[20]

MONEY DAMAGES Before CRA 1991, victims of *intentional* discrimination (which lawyers call *disparate treatment*) who had not suffered financial loss and who sued under Title VII could not then sue for compensatory or punitive damages. All they could expect was to have their jobs reinstated (or to get a particular job). They were also eligible for back pay, attorneys' fees, and court costs.

CRA 1991 makes it easier to sue for *money damages* in such cases. It provides that an employee who is claiming intentional discrimination can ask for (1) compensatory damages and (2) punitive damages, if he or she can show the employer engaged in discrimination "with malice or reckless indifference to the federally protected rights of an aggrieved individual."[21]

MIXED MOTIVES Finally, CRA 1991 states:

> An unlawful employment practice is established when the complaining party demonstrates that race, color, religion, sex, or national origin was a motivating factor for any employment practice, even though other factors also motivated the practice.[22]

The last phrase is pivotal. Some employers in so-called **"mixed motive" cases** had taken the position that even though their actions were discriminatory, other factors like the employee's dubious behavior made the job action acceptable. Under CRA 1991, an employer cannot avoid liability by proving it would have taken the same action—such as terminating someone—even without the discriminatory motive.[23] *If there is any such motive, the practice may be unlawful.*[24]

The Americans with Disabilities Act

The **Americans with Disabilities Act (ADA)** of 1990 prohibits employment discrimination against qualified disabled individuals.[25] It prohibits employers with 15 or more workers from discriminating against qualified individuals with disabilities, with regard to applications, hiring, discharge, compensation, advancement, training, or other terms, conditions, or privileges of employment.[26] It also says employers must make "reasonable accommodations" for physical or mental limitations unless doing so imposes an "undue hardship" on the business.

The ADA does not list specific disabilities. Instead, EEOC guidelines say someone is disabled when he or she has a physical or mental impairment that "substantially limits" one or more major life activity. Impairments include any physiological disorder or condition, cosmetic disfigurement, or anatomical loss affecting one or more of several body systems, or any mental or psychological disorder.[27] The act specifies conditions that it does not regard as disabilities, including homosexuality, bisexuality, voyeurism, compulsive gambling, pyromania, and certain disorders resulting from the current illegal use of drugs.[28] The EEOC's position is that the ADA prohibits discriminating against people with HIV/AIDS (and numerous state laws also shield such people).

MENTAL IMPAIRMENTS AND THE ADA Mental disabilities account for the greatest number of ADA claims.[29] Under EEOC ADA guidelines, "mental impairment" includes "any mental or psychological disorder, such as . . . emotional or mental illness." Examples include major depression, anxiety disorders, and personality disorders. The ADA also protects employees with intellectual disabilities, including those with IQs below 70–75.[30] The guidelines say employers should be alert to the possibility that traits normally regarded as undesirable (such as chronic lateness, hostility, or poor judgment) may reflect mental impairments. Reasonable accommodation, says the EEOC, might then include providing room dividers, partitions, or other barriers between work spaces.

QUALIFIED INDIVIDUAL   Just being disabled doesn't qualify someone for a job, of course. Instead, the act prohibits discrimination against **qualified individuals**—those who, with (or without) a reasonable accommodation, can carry out the *essential functions* of the job. The individual must have the requisite skills, educational background, and experience to do the job. A job function is essential when, for instance, it is the reason the position exists, or it is so highly specialized that the employer hires the person for his or her expertise or ability to perform that particular function. For example, when an Iowa County highway worker had an on-the-job seizure, his driver's license was suspended and the state fired him. The court ruled that he had no ADA claim because he couldn't perform the essential functions of the job.[31]

REASONABLE ACCOMMODATION   If the individual can't perform the job as currently structured, the employer must make a "reasonable accommodation" unless doing so would present an "undue hardship." Reasonable accommodation might include redesigning the job, modifying work schedules, or modifying or acquiring equipment or other devices (such as adding curb ramps and widening door openings).[32] For example, the National Federation of the Blind estimates that about 70% of working age blind adults are unemployed or underemployed, although they have the requisite education. Yet existing technologies would enable most of these people to work successfully in numerous job functions. One such technology is a screen-reading program called Jaws, which converts text from a computer screen into Braille while speaking it.[33]

Attorneys, employers, and the courts continue to work through what "reasonable accommodation" means.[34] In one classic case, an employee with a bad back who worked as a door greeter in a Walmart asked if she could sit on a stool while on duty. The store said no. She sued. The federal district court agreed with Walmart that door greeters must act in an "aggressively hospitable manner," which can't be done sitting on a stool.[35] Standing was an essential job function. You can use technology and common sense to make reasonable accommodation. Figure 2-1 summarizes several examples.

TRADITIONAL EMPLOYER DEFENSES   Employers traditionally prevailed in almost all—96%—federal circuit court ADA decisions.[36] A U.S. Supreme Court decision typifies what plaintiffs faced. An assembly worker sued Toyota, arguing that carpal tunnel syndrome prevented her from doing her job.[37] The U.S. Supreme

FIGURE 2-1 Examples of How to Provide Reasonable Accommodation

- Employees with *mobility or vision impairments* may benefit from voice recognition software.
- Word prediction software suggests words based on context with just one or two letters typed.
- Real-time translation captioning enables employees to participate in meetings.
- Vibrating text pagers notify employees when messages arrive.
- Arizona created a disability friendly Web site to help link prospective employees and others to various agencies.

"mixed motive" case
A discrimination allegation case in which the employer argues that the employment action taken was motivated not by discrimination, but by some nondiscriminatory reason such as ineffective performance.

Americans with Disabilities Act (ADA)
The act requiring employers to make reasonable accommodations for disabled employees; it prohibits discrimination against disabled persons.

qualified individuals
Under ADA, those who can carry out the essential functions of the job.

Technology enables employers to accommodate disabled employees.

Source: Robin Sachs/PhotoEdit Inc.

Court ruled that the ADA covers carpal tunnel syndrome only if her impairments affect not just her job performance, but also her daily living activities. The employee admitted that she could perform personal chores such as washing her face and fixing breakfast. The Court said the disability must be central to the employee's daily living (not just job).[38]

THE "NEW" ADA   The era in which employers prevail in most ADA claims probably ended January 1, 2009. On that day, the ADA Amendments Act of 2008 (ADAAA) became effective. The EEOC had been interpreting the ADA's "substantially limits" phrase very narrowly. The new ADAAA's basic effect will be to make it much easier for employees to show that their disabilities are limiting. For example, the new act makes it easier for an employee to show that his or her disability is influencing one of the employee's "major life activities." It does this by adding examples like reading, concentrating, thinking, sleeping, and communicating to the list of ADA major life activities. As another example, under the new act, an employee will be considered disabled even if he or she has been able to control his or her impairments through medical or "learned behavioral" modifications. The bottom line is that employers will henceforth have to redouble their efforts to make sure they're complying with the ADA and providing reasonable accommodations.[39]

Many employers simply take a progressive approach. Research shows that common employer concerns about people with disabilities (for instance, that they can't perform physically demanding tasks, are less productive, and have more accidents) are generally baseless.[40] So, for example, Walgreens has a goal of filling at least one-third of the jobs at its two large distribution centers with people with disabilities.[41]

Figure 2-2 summarizes some important ADA guidelines for managers and employers.

FIGURE 2-2 ADA Guidelines for Managers and Employers

- *Do not* deny a job to a disabled individual if the person is qualified and able to perform the essential job functions.
- *Make* a reasonable accommodation unless doing so would result in undue hardship.
- *Know* what you can ask applicants. In general, you may *not* make preemployment inquiries about a person's disability before making an offer. However, you *may* ask questions about the person's ability to perform essential job functions.
- *Itemize* essential job functions on the job descriptions. In virtually any ADA legal action, a central question will be, what are the essential functions of the job?
- *Do not* allow misconduct or erratic performance (including absences and tardiness), even if that behavior is linked to the disability.

Genetic Information Nondiscrimination Act of 2008 (GINA)

The Genetic Information Nondiscrimination Act (GINA) prohibits discrimination by health insurers and employers based on people's genetic information. Specifically, it prohibits the use of genetic information in employment, prohibits the intentional acquisition of genetic information about applicants and employees, and imposes strict confidentiality requirements.[42]

State and Local Equal Employment Opportunity Laws

In addition to federal laws, all states and many local governments prohibit employment discrimination. The effect of the state or local laws is usually to cover employers who federal laws might otherwise miss. Many cover employers (like those with less than 15 employees) not covered by federal legislation.[43] In Arizona, for instance, plaintiffs can bring sexual harassment claims against employers with as few as one employee. Some extend the protection of age discrimination laws to young people, barring discrimination against not only those over 40, but also those under 17. (Here, for instance, it would be illegal to advertise for "mature" applicants, because that might discourage some teenagers from applying.)

State and local equal employment opportunity agencies (often called "Human Resources Commissions" or "Fair Employment Commissions") also play a role in equal employment compliance. When the EEOC receives a discrimination charge, it usually defers it for a limited time to the state and local agencies that have comparable jurisdiction. If that doesn't achieve satisfactory remedies, the charges go back to the EEOC for resolution.

Table 2-1 summarizes selected equal employment opportunity laws, actions, executive orders, and agency guidelines.

ENFORCING EQUAL EMPLOYMENT LAWS WITH INTERNATIONAL EMPLOYEES Most employers' workforces are increasingly international, and this complicates applying equal employment laws. Guidelines for applying EEO laws in an international context follow.[44]

- U.S. EEO laws *do* apply inside the United States when the employer is a U.S. entity and the employee is *not* a U.S. citizen but *is* legally authorized to work in the United States. In some cases, U.S. laws may apply to workers who are *not* authorized to work in the United States.[45]

- U.S. EEO laws *do* apply to jobs located inside the United States when the employer is a foreign entity *not* exempted by a treaty and the employee is authorized to work in the United States.

- U.S. EEO laws *do not* apply to jobs located outside the United States when the employer is a foreign entity, even if the employee is a U.S. citizen.

- U.S. EEO laws *do not* apply to foreign citizens in jobs located outside the United States, even if the employer is a U.S. entity.

- U.S. EEO laws *do* apply to jobs located outside the United States when the employer is a U.S. entity and the employee is a U.S. citizen, if compliance with U.S. laws would *not* violate foreign laws.

Sexual Harassment

Under Title VII, **sexual harassment** generally refers to harassment on the basis of sex when such conduct has the purpose or effect of substantially interfering with a person's

sexual harassment
Harassment on the basis of sex that has the purpose or effect of substantially interfering with a person's work performance or creating an intimidating, hostile, or offensive work environment.

TABLE 2-1 Summary of Important Equal Employment Opportunity Actions

Action	What It Does
Title VII of 1964 Civil Rights Act, as amended	Bars discrimination because of race, color, religion, sex, or national origin; instituted EEOC.
Executive orders	Prohibit employment discrimination by employers with federal contracts of more than $10,000 (and their subcontractors); establish office of federal compliance; require affirmative action programs.
Federal agency guidelines	Indicate guidelines covering discrimination based on sex, national origin, and religion, as well as employee selection procedures; for example, require validation of tests.
Supreme Court decisions: *Griggs v. Duke Power Co., Albemarle v. Moody*	Rule that job requirements must be related to job success; that discrimination need not be overt to be proved; that the burden of proof is on the employer to prove the qualification is valid.
Equal Pay Act of 1963	Requires equal pay for men and women for performing similar work.
Age Discrimination in Employment Act of 1967	Prohibits discriminating against a person age 40 or over in any area of employment because of age.
State and local laws	Often cover organizations too small to be covered by federal laws.
Vocational Rehabilitation Act of 1973	Requires affirmative action to employ and promote qualified handicapped persons and prohibits discrimination against handicapped persons.
Pregnancy Discrimination Act of 1978	Prohibits discrimination in employment against pregnant women, or related conditions.
Vietnam Era Veterans' Readjustment Assistance Act of 1974	Requires affirmative action in employment for veterans of the Vietnam war era.
Ward Cove v. Atonio	Made it more difficult to prove a case of unlawful discrimination against an employer.
Americans with Disabilities Act of 1990	Strengthens the need for most employers to make reasonable accommodations for disabled employees at work; prohibits discrimination.
Civil Rights Act of 1991	Reverses various U.S. Supreme Court decisions; places burden of proof back on employer and permits compensatory and punitive money damages for discrimination.
ADA Amendments Act of 2008	Makes it easier for employee to show that his or her disability "substantially limits" a major life function.
Genetic Information Nondiscrimination Act	Signed into law in May 2008, prohibits discriminating against employees and applicants based on their genetic information.

Source: The actual laws (and others) can be accessed via a search at www.usa.gov/Topics/Reference_Shelf.shtml#Laws, accessed August 24, 2007.

work performance or creating an intimidating, hostile, or offensive work environment. Sexual harassment violates Title VII. In one recent year, the EEOC received 11,717 sexual harassment charges, about 15% of which were filed by men.[46]

EEOC guidelines emphasize that employers have an affirmative duty to maintain workplaces free of sexual harassment and intimidation. As we noted earlier, CRA 1991 permits victims of intentional discrimination, including sexual harassment, to have jury trials and to collect compensatory damages for pain and suffering and punitive damages, in cases where the employer acted with "malice or reckless indifference" to the person's rights.[47]

The U.S. Supreme Court held (in *Oncale v. Sundowner Offshore Services Inc.*) that same-sex sexual harassment is also actionable under Title VII.[48]

Minority women are most at risk. One study found "women experienced more sexual harassment than men, minorities experienced more ethnic harassment than whites, and minority women experience more harassment overall than majority men, minority men, and majority women."[49]

The **Federal Violence Against Women Act of 1994** provides another path women can use to seek relief for violent sexual harassment. It provides that a person "who commits a crime of violence motivated by gender and thus deprives another" of her rights shall be liable to the party injured.

WHAT IS SEXUAL HARASSMENT? EEOC guidelines define sexual harassment as unwelcome sexual advances, requests for sexual favors, and other verbal or physical conduct of a sexual nature that takes place under any of the following conditions:

1. Submission to such conduct is made either explicitly or implicitly a term or condition of an individual's employment.

2. Submission to or rejection of such conduct by an individual is used as the basis for employment decisions affecting such individual.

3. Such conduct has the purpose or effect of unreasonably interfering with an individual's work performance or creating an intimidating, hostile, or offensive work environment.

PROVING SEXUAL HARASSMENT There are three main ways someone can prove sexual harassment.

1. *Quid Pro Quo.* The most direct is to prove that rejecting a supervisor's advances adversely affected what the EEOC calls a "tangible employment action" such as hiring, firing, promotion, demotion, and/or work assignment. In one case, the employee showed that continued job success and advancement were dependent on her agreeing to the sexual demands of her supervisors.

2. **Hostile Environment Created by Supervisors.** One need not show that the harassment had tangible consequences such as demotion. For example, in one case the court found that a male supervisor's sexual harassment had substantially affected a female employee's emotional and psychological ability to the point that she felt she had to quit her job. Therefore, even though the supervisor made no direct threats or promises in exchange for sexual advances, his advances interfered with the woman's performance and created an offensive work environment. That was sufficient to prove sexual harassment. Courts generally do not interpret as sexual harassment sexual relationships that arise during the course of employment but that do not have a substantial effect on that employment.[50] The U.S. Supreme Court also held that sexual harassment law doesn't cover ordinary "intersexual flirtation." In his ruling, Justice Antonin Scalia said courts must carefully distinguish between "simple teasing" and truly abusive behavior.[51]

3. **Hostile Environment Created by Coworkers or Nonemployees.** The questionable behavior doesn't have to come from the person's supervisor. For example, one court held that a mandatory sexually provocative uniform led to lewd comments by customers. When the employee said she would no longer wear the uniform, they fired her. The employer couldn't show there was a job-related necessity for requiring the uniform, and only female employees had to wear it. The court thus ruled that the employer, in effect, was responsible for the sexually harassing behavior. Such abhorrent client behavior is more likely when the clients are in positions of power, and when they think no one will penalize them.[52] EEOC guidelines also state that an employer is liable for the sexually harassing acts of its nonsupervisor employees if the employer knew or should have known of the harassing conduct.

WHEN IS THE ENVIRONMENT "HOSTILE"? Hostile environment sexual harassment generally means that the intimidation, insults, and ridicule were sufficiently severe to alter the working conditions. Here courts look at several things.

2 Explain how to avoid and deal with accusations of sexual harassment at work.

Federal Violence Against Women Act of 1994
The act that provides that a person who commits a crime of violence motivated by gender shall be liable to the party injured.

These include whether the discriminatory conduct is *frequent or severe*; whether it is *physically threatening* or humiliating, or a mere offensive utterance; and whether it unreasonably *interferes* with an employee's work performance.[53] Courts also consider whether the employee subjectively *perceives* the work environment as being abusive. For example, did he or she welcome the conduct or immediately show that it was unwelcome?[54]

SUPREME COURT DECISIONS   The U.S. Supreme Court used a case called *Meritor Savings Bank, FSB v. Vinson* to endorse broadly the EEOC's guidelines on sexual harassment. Two other Supreme Court decisions further clarified sexual harassment law.

In the first, *Burlington Industries v. Ellerth*, the employee accused her supervisor of *quid pro quo* harassment. She said her boss propositioned and threatened her with demotion if she did not respond. He did not carry out the threats, and she was promoted. In the second case, *Faragher v. City of Boca Raton*, the employee accused the employer of condoning a hostile work environment. She said she quit her lifeguard job after repeated taunts from other lifeguards. The Court ruled in favor of the employees in both cases.

IMPLICATIONS   The Court's written decisions have two implications for employers and managers. First, in *quid pro quo* cases it is *not* necessary for the employee to suffer a tangible job action (such as a demotion) to win the case.

Second, the Court laid out an important defense against harassment suits. It said the employer must show that it took "reasonable care" to prevent and promptly correct any sexually harassing behavior *and* that the employee unreasonably failed to take advantage of the employer's policy. The implication is that an employer can defend itself against sexual harassment liability by showing two things:

- First, it must show "that the employer exercised reasonable care to prevent and correct promptly any sexually harassing behavior."[55]
- Second, it must demonstrate that the plaintiff "unreasonably failed to take advantage of any preventive or corrective opportunities provided by the employer." The employee's failure to use formal reporting systems would satisfy the second component.

Prudent employers promptly took steps to show they did take reasonable care.[56] Steps to take include:[57]

- Take all complaints about harassment seriously.
- Issue a strong policy statement condemning such behavior. It should describe the prohibited conduct, assure protection against retaliation, describe a confidential complaint process, and provide impartial investigation and corrective action.
- Take steps to prevent sexual harassment from occurring. For example, communicate to employees that the employer will not tolerate sexual harassment, and take immediate action when someone complains.
- Establish a management response system that includes an immediate reaction and investigation.
- Train supervisors and managers to increase their awareness of the issues, and discipline managers and employees involved in sexual harassment.

WHEN THE LAW ISN'T ENOUGH   Unfortunately, two practical considerations often trump the legal requirements. First, women react differently to possible harassment than do men. In one study, about 58% of employees reported experiencing at least some potentially harassment-type behaviors at work. Overall, about 25% found it fun and flattering and about half viewed it as benign. But on closer examination, about four times as many men as women found the behavior flattering or benign.[58] "Women perceive a broader range of socio-sexual behaviors (touching, for instance) as harassing."[59] Sexual harassment training and policies can reduce this problem.[60]

A second reason the usual precautions often aren't enough is that employees often won't use them. One study surveyed about 6,000 U.S. military employees. It turned out that reporting harassment often triggered retaliation, and could harm the victim "in terms of lower job satisfaction and greater psychological distress." Under such conditions, the most "reasonable" thing to do was to avoid reporting. The solution is to execute zealously the anti-harassment policies like those mentioned earlier.

WHAT THE EMPLOYEE CAN DO   First, remember that courts generally look to whether *the harassed employee used the employer's reporting procedures to file a complaint promptly.* To quote one EEO manual, "a victim has a duty to use reasonable means to avoid or minimize his or her damages. Generally, this is satisfied if the employer had an effectively communicated complaint procedure and the victim did not utilize it, or if the victim did make a complaint but then refused to cooperate in the investigation."[61] In that context, steps an employee can take include:

1. File a verbal contemporaneous complaint with the harasser and the harasser's boss, stating that the unwanted overtures should cease because the conduct is unwelcome.

2. If the unwelcome conduct does not cease, file verbal and written reports regarding the unwelcome conduct and unsuccessful efforts to get it to stop with the harasser's manager and/or the human resource director.

3. If the letters and appeals to the employer do not suffice, the accuser should turn to the local office of the EEOC to file the necessary claim. In very serious cases, the employee can also consult an attorney about suing the harasser for assault and battery, intentional infliction of emotional distress, injunctive relief, and to recover compensatory and punitive damages.

| 3 | Define *adverse impact* and explain how it is proved. |

DEFENSES AGAINST DISCRIMINATION ALLEGATIONS

To understand how employers defend themselves against employment discrimination claims, we should first briefly review some basic legal terminology.

Discrimination law distinguishes between disparate *treatment* and disparate *impact. Disparate treatment* means intentional discrimination. It "requires no more than a finding that women (or protected minority group members) were intentionally treated differently because of their gender" (or minority status). Disparate treatment "exists where an employer treats an individual differently because that individual is a member of a particular race, religion, gender, or ethnic group."[62] Having a rule that says "we do not hire bus drivers over 60 years of age" exemplifies this.

Disparate impact means that "an employer engages in an employment practice or policy that has a greater adverse impact (effect) on the members of a protected group under Title VII than on other employees, regardless of intent."[63] A rule that says "employees must have college degrees to do this particular job" exemplifies this (because more white males than some minorities earn college degrees).

Disparate impact claims do not require proof of discriminatory intent. Instead, the plaintiff must show that the

Source: Shutterstock.
Employees who believe they are victims of harassment should have a mechanism for filing a complaint.

apparently neutral employment practice (such as requiring a college degree) creates an **adverse impact**—a significant disparity—between the proportion of (say) minorities in the available labor pool and the proportion you hire. So, the key here is to show that the employment practice caused an adverse impact. If it has, then the employer will probably have to defend itself (for instance, by arguing that there is a business necessity for the practice).

The Central Role of Adverse Impact

Showing adverse impact therefore plays a central role in discriminatory practice allegations. Employers may not institute an employment practice that causes a disparate impact on a particular class of people unless they can show that the practice is job related and necessary.[64] Under Title VII and CRA 1991, a person who believes that (1) he or she was a victim of unintentional discrimination because of an employer's practices need only (2) establish a *prima facie* case of discrimination. This means showing, for instance, that the employer's selection procedures (like requiring a college degree for the job) did have an adverse impact on the protected minority group. Adverse impact "refers to the total employment process that results in a significantly higher percentage of a protected group in the candidate population being rejected for employment, placement, or promotion."[65] Then the burden of proof shifts to the employer.

So, for example, if a minority applicant feels he or she was a victim of discrimination, the person need only show that the employer's selection process resulted in an adverse impact on his or her group. (For example, if 80% of the white applicants passed the test, but only 20% of the black applicants passed, a black applicant has a *prima facie* case proving adverse impact.) Then the burden of proof shifts to the employer. It becomes the employer's task to prove that its test (or application blank or the like) is a valid predictor of performance on the job (and that it applied its selection process fairly and equitably to both minorities and nonminorities).

HOW CAN SOMEONE SHOW ADVERSE IMPACT?   An applicant or employee can use one of the following methods to show that one of an employer's procedures (such as a selection test) has an adverse impact on a protected group.

DISPARATE REJECTION RATES   **Disparate rejection rates** can be shown by comparing the rejection rates for a minority group and another group (usually the remaining nonminority applicants).[66]

Federal agencies use a **"4/5ths rule"** to assess disparate rejection rates: "A selection rate for any racial, ethnic, or sex group which is less than four-fifths or 80% of the rate for the group with the highest rate will generally be regarded as evidence of adverse impact, while a greater than four-fifths rate will generally not be regarded as evidence of adverse impact." For example, suppose the employer hires 60% of male applicants, but only 30% of female applicants. Four-fifths of the 60% male hiring rate would be 48%. Because the female hiring rate of 30% is less than 48%, adverse impact exists as far as these federal agencies are concerned.[67]

THE STANDARD DEVIATION RULE   Similarly, the courts have used the *standard deviation rule* to confirm adverse impact. (The standard deviation is a statistical measure of variability. Suppose we measure the heights of every person in your management class. In simplest terms, the standard deviation helps to describe, among other things, how wide a range there is between the shortest and tallest students.) In selection, the standard deviation rule holds that as a rule of thumb, the difference between the numbers of minority candidates we *would have expected* to hire and whom *we actually hired* should be less than two standard deviations.

Consider this example. Suppose 300 applicants apply for 20 openings; 80 of the applicants are women and the other 220 are men. We use our screening processes and hire 2 females and 18 males. Did our selection process have adverse impact? To answer this, we can compute the standard deviation:

$$SD = \sqrt{\frac{(Number\ of\ minority\ applicants)}{(Number\ of\ total\ applicants)} \times \frac{(Number\ of\ non\text{-}minority\ applicants)}{(Number\ of\ total\ applicants)} \times (Number\ of\ applicants\ selected)}$$

In our case:

$$SD = \sqrt{\left(\frac{80}{300} \times \frac{220}{300} \times 20\right)} = \sqrt{(0.2667 \times 0.7333 \times 20)}$$
$$= \sqrt{3.911} = SD = 1.977$$

In our example, women are 26% (80/300) of the applicant pool. We should therefore *expect* to hire 26% of 20 or about 5 women. We *actually* hired 2 women. The difference between the numbers of women we would expect to hire and whom we actually hired is $5 - 2 = 3$. We can use the standard deviation rule to gauge if there is adverse (disparate) impact. In our example, the standard deviation is 1.977. Again, the standard deviation rule holds that as a rule of thumb, the difference between the numbers of minority candidates we would have expected to hire and whom we actually hired should be less than two standard deviations. Two times 1.9777 is about 4. Since the difference between the number of women we would have expected to hire (5) and actually hired (2) is 3, the results suggest that our screening did not have adverse impact on women. (Put another way, in this case, hiring just 2 rather than 5 is not a highly improbable result.)[68]

RESTRICTED POLICY   The **restricted policy** approach means demonstrating that the employer's policy intentionally or unintentionally excluded members of a protected group. Here the problem is usually obvious—such as policies against hiring bartenders less than six feet tall. Evidence of restricted policies such as these is enough to prove adverse impact and to expose an employer to litigation.

POPULATION COMPARISONS   This approach compares (1) the percentage of minority/protected group and white workers in the organization with (2) the percentage of the corresponding group in the labor market. The EEOC usually defines labor market as the U.S. Census data for that Standard Metropolitan Statistical Area.

"Labor market," of course, varies with the job. For some jobs, such as laborer or secretary, it makes sense to compare the percentage of minority employees with the percentage of minorities in the surrounding community, since they will come from that community. But for jobs such as engineer, recruiting may be nationwide. Determining whether an employer has enough black engineers might thus involve determining the number available nationwide, not in the surrounding community.

Employers use *workforce analysis* to analyze the data regarding the firm's use of protected versus nonprotected employees in various job classifications.

---

adverse impact
The overall impact of employer practices that result in significantly higher percentages of members of minorities and other protected groups being rejected for employment, placement, or promotion.

disparate rejection rates
A test for adverse impact in which it can be demonstrated that there is a discrepancy between rates of rejection of members of a protected group and of others.

4/5ths rule
Federal agency rule that a minority selection rate less than 80% (4/5ths) of that for the group with the highest rate is evidence of adverse impact.

restricted policy
Another test for adverse impact, involving demonstration that an employer's hiring practices exclude a protected group, whether intentionally or not.

The process of comparing the percentage of minority employees in a job (or jobs) at the company with the number of similarly trained minority employees available in the relevant labor market is *utilization analysis.*

MCDONNELL-DOUGLAS TEST Lawyers in disparate impact cases use the previous approaches (such as population comparisons) to test whether an employer's policies or actions have the effect of unintentionally screening out disproportionate numbers of women or minorities. Lawyers use the McDonnell-Douglas test for showing (intentional) disparate treatment, rather than (unintentional) disparate impact.

This test grew out of a case at the former McDonnell-Douglas Corporation. The applicant was qualified but the employer rejected the person and continued seeking applicants. Did this show that the hiring company intentionally discriminated against the female or minority candidate? The U.S. Supreme Court set four rules for applying the McDonnell-Douglas test:

1. that the person belongs to a protected class;
2. that he or she applied and was qualified for a job for which the employer was seeking applicants;
3. that, despite this qualification, he or she was rejected; and
4. that, after his or her rejection, the position remained open and the employer continued seeking applications from persons with the complainant's qualifications.

If the plaintiff meets all these conditions, then a *prima facie* case of disparate treatment is established. At that point, the employer must articulate a legitimate nondiscriminatory reason for its action, and produce evidence but not prove that it acted based on such a reason. If it meets this relatively easy standard, the plaintiff then has the burden of proving that the employer's articulated reason is merely a pretext for engaging in unlawful discrimination.

ADVERSE IMPACT EXAMPLE Assume you turn down a member of a protected group for a job with your firm. You do this based on a test score (although it could have been interview questions or something else). Further, assume that this person feels he or she was discriminated against due to being in a protected class, and decides to sue your company.

Basically, all he or she must do is show that your human resources procedure (such as the selection test) had an adverse impact on members of his or her minority group. The plaintiff can apply three approaches here. These are disparate rejection rates, restricted policy, or population comparisons. Once the person proves adverse impact (to the court's satisfaction), the burden of proof shifts to the employer. The employer must defend against the discrimination charges.

Note that there is nothing in the law that says that because one of your procedures has an adverse impact on a protected group, you can't use the procedure. In fact, it may well happen that some tests screen out disproportionately higher numbers of, say, blacks than they do whites. What the law does say is that once your applicant has made his or her case (showing adverse impact), the burden of proof shifts to you. Now you (or your company) must defend use of the procedure.

There are then two basic defenses employers use to justify an employment practice that has an adverse impact on members of a minority group: the bona fide occupational qualification (BFOQ) defense and the business necessity defense.

Bona Fide Occupational Qualification

> **4** Explain and illustrate two defenses you can use in the event of discriminatory practice allegations.

An employer can claim that the employment practice is a **bona fide occupational qualification (BFOQ)** for performing the job. Title VII specifically permits this defense. Title VII provides that "it should not be an unlawful employment practice for an employer to hire an employee . . . on the basis of religion, sex, or national origin *in those certain instances where religion, sex, or national origin is a bona fide occupational qualification* reasonably necessary to the normal operation of that particular business or enterprise."

However, courts usually interpret the BFOQ exception narrowly. It is usually a defense to a disparate treatment case based upon direct evidence of *intentional* discrimination, rather than to disparate impact (unintentional) cases. As a practical matter, employers use it mostly as a defense against charges of intentional discrimination based on age.

AGE AS A BFOQ   The Age Discrimination in Employment Act (ADEA) permits disparate treatment in those instances when age is a BFOQ.[69] For example, age is a BFOQ when the Federal Aviation Agency sets a compulsory retirement age of 65 for commercial pilots.[70] Actors required for youthful or elderly roles suggest other instances when age may be a BFOQ. However, courts set the bar high: The reason for the age limit must go to the essence of the business. A court said a bus line's maximum-age hiring policy for bus drivers was a BFOQ. The court said the essence of the business was safe transportation of passengers, and given that, the employer could strive to employ the most qualified persons available.[71]

Employers who use the BFOQ defense admit they base their personnel decisions on age. However, they seek to justify them by showing that the decisions were reasonably necessary to normal business operations (for instance, the bus line arguing its age requirement is necessary for safety).[72]

RELIGION AS A BFOQ   Religion may be a BFOQ in religious organizations or societies that require employees to share their particular religion. For example, religion may be a BFOQ when hiring persons to teach in a religious school. However, remember courts construe the BFOQ defense very narrowly.

GENDER AS A BFOQ   Gender may be a BFOQ for positions like actor, model, and restroom attendant requiring physical characteristics possessed by one sex. However, for most jobs today, it's difficult to claim that gender is a BFOQ. For example, gender is not a BFOQ for parole and probation officers.[73] It is not a BFOQ for positions just because the positions require lifting heavy objects. A Texas man recently filed a complaint against Hooters of America alleging that one of its franchisees would not hire him as a waiter because it "merely wishes to exploit female sexuality as a marketing tool to attract customers and ensure profitability" and so was limiting hiring to females.[74] Hooters argued a BFOQ defense before reaching a confidential settlement.

NATIONAL ORIGIN AS A BFOQ   A person's country of national origin may be a BFOQ. For example, an employer who is running the Chinese pavilion at a fair might claim that Chinese heritage is a BFOQ for persons to deal with the public.

Business Necessity

"Business necessity" is a defense created by the courts. It requires showing that there is an overriding business purpose for the discriminatory practice and that the practice is therefore acceptable.

It's not easy to prove business necessity.[75] The Supreme Court made it clear that business necessity does not encompass such matters as avoiding an employer inconvenience, annoyance, or expense. For example, an employer can't generally discharge employees whose wages have been garnished merely because garnishment (requiring the employer to divert part of the person's wages to pay his or her debts) creates an inconvenience. The Second Circuit Court of Appeals held that business necessity

bona fide occupational qualification (BFOQ)
Requirement that an employee be of a certain religion, sex, or national origin where that is reasonably necessary to the organization's normal operation. Specified by the 1964 Civil Rights Act.

means an "irresistible demand." It said the practice "must not only directly foster safety and efficiency" but also be essential to these goals.[76] Furthermore, "the business purpose must be sufficiently compelling to override any racial impact. . . ."[77]

However, many employers have used the business necessity defense successfully. In an early case, *Spurlock v. United Airlines*, a minority candidate sued United Airlines. He said that its requirements that pilot candidates have 500 flight hours and college degrees were unfairly discriminatory. The court agreed that the requirements did have an adverse impact on members of the person's minority group. But it held that in light of the cost of the training program and the huge human and economic risks in hiring unqualified candidates, the selection standards were a business necessity and were job related.[78]

In general, when a job requires a small amount of skill and training, the courts closely scrutinize any preemployment standards or criteria that discriminate against minorities. There is a correspondingly lighter burden when the job requires a high degree of skill, and when the economic and human risks of hiring an unqualified applicant are great.[79]

Attempts by employers to show that their selection tests or other employment practices are *valid* are examples of the business necessity defense. Here the employer must show that the test or other practice is job related—in other words, that it is a valid predictor of performance on the job. Where the employer can establish such validity, the courts have generally supported using the test or other employment practice as a business necessity. In this context, *validity* means the degree to which the test or other employment practice is related to or predicts performance on the job; Chapter 6 explains validation.

Other Considerations in Discriminatory Practice Defenses

There are three other points to remember about discrimination charges:

1. First, *good intentions are no excuse.* As the Supreme Court held in the *Griggs* case,

   Good intent or absence of discriminatory intent does not redeem procedures or testing mechanisms that operate as built-in headwinds for minority groups and are unrelated to measuring job capability.

2. Second, one *cannot hide behind collective bargaining agreements* (for instance, by claiming that a union agreement necessitates some discriminatory practice). Equal employment opportunity laws take precedence.[80]

3. Third, a strong defense *is not your only recourse.* The employer can also respond by agreeing to eliminate the illegal practice and (when required) by compensating the people discriminated against.

ILLUSTRATIVE DISCRIMINATORY EMPLOYMENT PRACTICES

5 Cite specific discriminatory personnel management practices in recruitment, selection, promotion, transfer, layoffs, and benefits.

A Note on What You Can and Cannot Do

Before proceeding, we should review what federal fair employment laws allow (and do not allow) you to say and do.

Federal laws like Title VII usually don't expressly ban preemployment questions about an applicant's race, color, religion, sex, or national origin. In other words, "with the exception of personnel policies calling for outright discrimination against the members of some protected group," it's not the questions but their impact.[81] In other words, illustrative inquiries and practices such as those summarized on the next few pages are not illegal per se. For example, it isn't illegal to ask a job candidate about her marital status (although such a question might seem discriminatory). You can ask. However, be prepared to show either that you do not discriminate or that you can defend the practice as a BFOQ or business necessity.

But, in practice, there are two reasons to avoid such questions. First, although federal law may not bar such questions, many state and local laws do.

Second, the EEOC has said that it will disapprove of such practices, so just asking the questions may draw its attention. Such questions may identify and/or adversely affect an applicant as a member of a protected group. They become illegal if a complainant can show you use them to screen out a greater proportion of his or her protected group's applicants, and you can't prove the practice is required as a business necessity or BFOQ.

Let's look now at some of the potentially discriminatory practices to avoid.[82]

Recruitment

WORD OF MOUTH You cannot rely upon word-of-mouth dissemination of information about job opportunities when your workforce is all (or mostly all) white or all members of some other class such as all female, all Hispanic, and so on. Doing so reduces the likelihood that others will become aware of the jobs and thus apply for them.

MISLEADING INFORMATION It is unlawful to give false or misleading information to members of any group, or to fail or refuse to advise them of work opportunities and the procedures for obtaining them.

HELP WANTED ADS "Help wanted—male" and "help wanted—female" ads are violations unless gender is a bona fide occupational qualification for the job. The same applies to ads that suggest age discrimination. For example, you cannot advertise for a "young" man or woman.

Selection Standards

EDUCATIONAL REQUIREMENTS Courts have found educational qualifications to be illegal when (1) minority groups are less likely to possess the educational qualifications (such as a high school degree) and (2) such qualifications are also not job related. However, there may be jobs of course for which educational requirements (such as college degrees for pilot candidates) are a necessity.

TESTS Courts deem tests unlawful if they disproportionately screen out minorities or women *and* they are not job related. According to a former U.S. Supreme Court Chief Justice,

> Nothing in the [Title VII] act precludes the use of testing or measuring procedures; obviously they are useful. What Congress has forbidden is giving these devices and mechanisms controlling force unless they are demonstrating a reasonable measure of job performance.

The employer must be prepared to show that the test results are job related—for instance, that test scores relate to on-the-job performance.

PREFERENCE TO RELATIVES Do not give preference to relatives of current employees with respect to employment opportunities if your current employees are substantially nonminority.

HEIGHT, WEIGHT, AND PHYSICAL CHARACTERISTICS Physical requirements such as minimum height are unlawful unless the employer can show they're job related. For example, a U.S. Appeals Court upheld a $3.4 million jury verdict against Dial Corp. Dial rejected 52 women for entry-level jobs at a meat processing plant because they failed strength tests, although strength was not a job requirement.[83] *Maximum* weight rules generally don't trigger adverse legal rulings. To qualify for reasonable accommodation, obese applicants must be at least 100 pounds above their ideal weight or there must be a physiological cause for their disability. However, legalities aside, managers should be vigilant.[84] Studies leave little doubt that obese individuals are less likely to be hired, less likely to receive promotions, more likely to get less desirable sales assignments, and more likely to receive poor customer service as customers.[85]

RESEARCH INSIGHT   A study compared the wages of women whose weights ranged from very thin to average with the wages and salaries of men. The very thin women received the most severe "wage punishment" for adding their first few pounds. For example, for very thin American women, gaining 25 pounds produces an average predicted decrease in salary of approximately $15,572 per year. For women with above average weight, gaining that extra 25 pounds "costs" the women about $13,847. Conversely, "For men, gaining 25 pounds produced a predicted increase in wages of approximately $8,437 per year at below-average weights and a predicted increase of approximately $7,775 per year at above-average weights [to the point of obesity]."[86]

ARREST RECORDS   Unless the job requires security clearance, do not ask an applicant whether he or she has been arrested or spent time in jail, or use an arrest record to disqualify a person automatically. There are several reasons for this. Various racial minorities are more likely than whites to have arrest records.[87] There is always a presumption of innocence until proven guilty. And arrest records in general are not valid for predicting job performance. Thus, disqualifying applicants based on arrest records adversely impacts minorities. You can ask about conviction records. Then determine on a case-by-case basis whether the facts justify refusal to employ an applicant in a particular position.

APPLICATION FORMS   Employment applications generally shouldn't contain questions about applicants' disabilities, workers' compensation history, age, arrest record, or U.S. citizenship. In general it's best to collect personal information required for legitimate tax or benefit reasons (such as who to contact in case of emergency) after you hire the person.[88]

DISCHARGE DUE TO GARNISHMENT   A disproportionate number of minorities suffer garnishment procedures (in which creditors make a claim to some of the person's wages). Therefore, firing a minority member whose salary is garnished is illegal, unless you can show some overriding business necessity.

Sample Discriminatory Promotion, Transfer, and Layoff Practices

Fair employment laws protect not just job applicants but also current employees. For example, the Equal Pay Act requires that equal wages be paid for substantially similar work performed by men and women. Therefore, courts may hold that any employment practices regarding pay, promotion, termination, discipline, or benefits that

1. are applied differently to different classes of persons;
2. adversely impact members of a protected group; and
3. cannot be shown to be required as a BFOQ or business necessity are illegally discriminatory.

PERSONAL APPEARANCE REGULATIONS AND TITLE VII   Employees sometimes file suits against employers' dress and appearance codes under Title VII. They usually claim sex discrimination, but sometimes claim racial or even religious discrimination. A sampling of court rulings follows:[89]

- **Dress.** In general, employers do not violate the Title VII ban on sex bias by requiring all employees to dress conservatively. For example, a supervisor's suggestion that a female attorney tone down her attire was permissible when the firm consistently sought to maintain a conservative dress style and counseled men to dress conservatively. However, Alamo Rent-A-Car lost a case when they tried to prevent a Muslim woman employee from wearing a head scarf.

- **Hair.** Here, courts usually favor employers. For example, employer rules against facial hair do not constitute sex discrimination because they discriminate only between clean-shaven and bearded men, discrimination not qualified as sex bias under Title VII. Courts have also rejected arguments that prohibiting cornrow hair styles infringed on black employees' expression of cultural identification.

- **Uniforms.** When it comes to discriminatory uniforms and/or suggestive attire, however, courts frequently side with employees. For example, requiring female employees (such as waitresses) to wear sexually suggestive attire as a condition of employment has been ruled as violating Title VII in many cases.[90]
- **Tattoos and body piercings.** Tattoos and body piercings are an issue at work. For example, about 38% of millennials in one survey had tattoos as compared with 15% of baby boomers. About 23% of millennials had body piercings as compared with 1% of baby boomers. One case involved a waiter with religious tattoos on his wrists at a Red Robin Gourmet Burgers store. The company insisted he cover his tattoos at work; he refused. Red Robin subsequently settled a lawsuit after the waiter claimed that covering the tattoos would be a sin based on his religion.[91]

What the Supervisor Should Keep in Mind

The human resource manager plays a big role in helping the company avoid practices like these, but at the end of the day, the first-line supervisor usually triggers the problem. You make an ill-informed or foolish comment, and the employee is quick to sue. Even something apparently "nondiscriminatory"—like telling a female candidate you'd be concerned about her safety on the job after dark—might trigger a claim.

This is therefore a good point at which to emphasize three things. First, carefully learning this chapter's contents is important. For example, *understand the questions* you can and cannot ask when interviewing applicants, and know what *constitutes* sexual harassment. There is no substitute for that knowledge. Good intentions are no excuse.

Second, the courts may hold you (not just your employer) personally liable for your injudicious actions. *Management malpractice* is aberrant conduct on the part of the manager that has serious consequences for the employee's personal or physical well-being, or which, as one court put it, "exceeds all bounds usually tolerated by society."[92] In one outrageous example, the employer demoted a manager to janitor and took other steps to humiliate the person. The jury subsequently awarded the former manager $3.4 million. Supervisors who commit management malpractice may be personally liable for paying a portion of the judgment.

Third, know that *retaliation* is illegal under equal rights laws. To paraphrase the EEOC, "all of the laws we enforce make it illegal to fire, demote, harass, or otherwise 'retaliate' against people because they filed a charge, complained to their employer or other covered entity about discrimination, or because they participated in a discrimination investigation or lawsuit".[93] In one U.S. Supreme Court case, the employee complained to a government agency that her employer paid her less than male counterparts. Soon after the company heard about the complaint, it fired her fiancé, who also worked for the firm. Finding for the employee, the U.S. Supreme Court decision said, "a reasonable worker might be dissuaded from engaging in protected activity" if she knew that her fiancé would be fired.[94]

6 List the steps in the EEOC enforcement process.

THE EEOC ENFORCEMENT PROCESS

Even prudent employers eventually face employment discrimination claims and have to deal with EEOC officials. All managers (not just human resource managers) play roles in this process. Figure 2-3 provides an overview of the process.[95]

- **File Charge.** The process begins when someone files a claim with the EEOC. Either the aggrieved person or a member of the EEOC who has reasonable cause to believe that a violation occurred must file the claim in writing and under oath.[96] Under CRA 1991, the discrimination claim must be filed within 300 days (when there is a similar state law) or 180 days (where there is no similar state law)

FIGURE 2-3 The EEOC Charge-Filing Process
Note: Parties may settle at any time.

Source: Based on information at www.eeoc.gov.

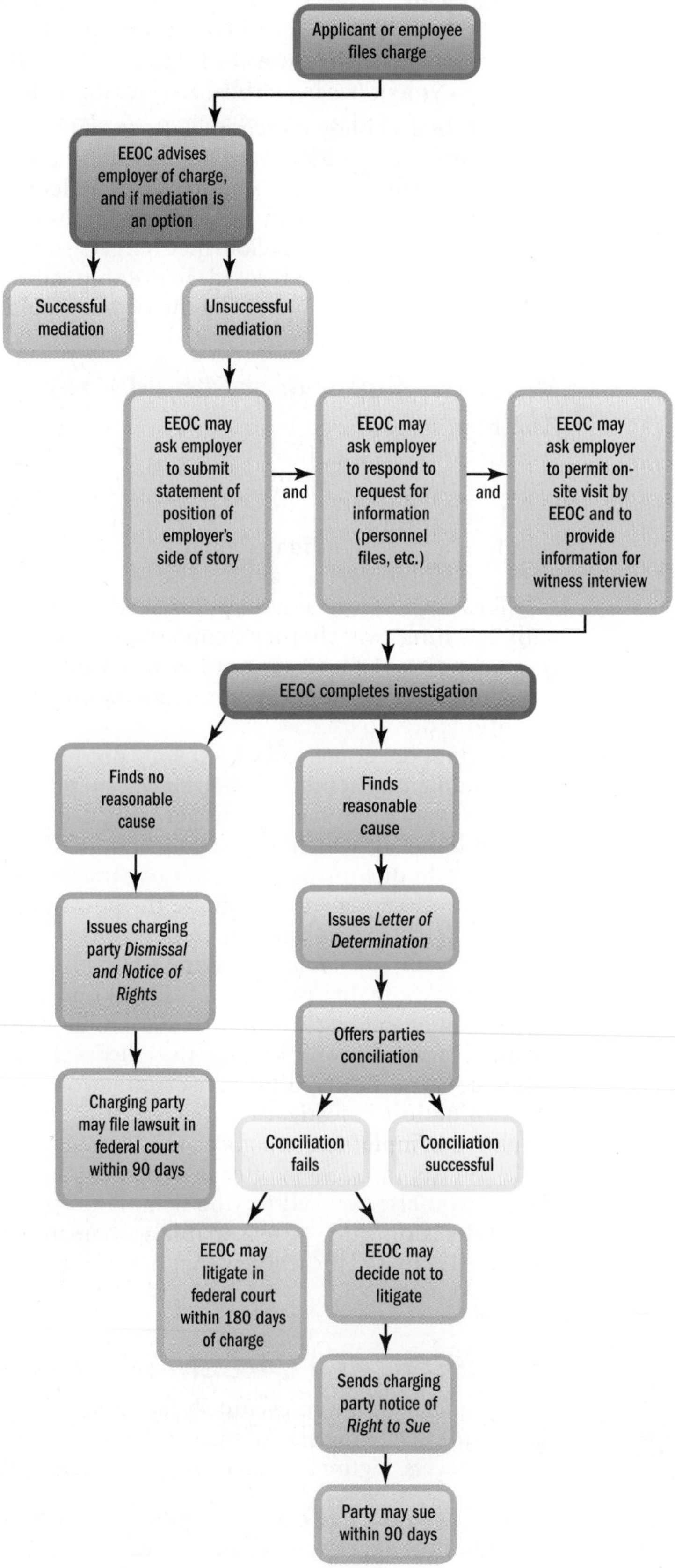

after the alleged incident took place (2 years for the Equal Pay Act).[97] The U.S. Supreme Court, in *Ledbetter v. Goodyear Tire & Rubber Company,* held that employees claiming Title VII pay discrimination must file their claims within 180 days of when they first receive the allegedly discriminatory pay. Congress then passed, and President Obama signed, the Lilly Ledbetter Fair Pay Act into law. Employees can now file such claims anytime, as long they're still receiving an "infected" paycheck. (In fiscal year 2010, individuals filed 99,922 charges with the EEOC; the two largest categories were for race discrimination [36% of total charges], and sex discrimination [29%].)[98]

- **Charge Acceptance.** The EEOC's common practice is to accept a charge and orally refer it to the state or local agency on behalf of the charging party. If the agency waives jurisdiction or cannot obtain a satisfactory solution, the EEOC processes it upon the expiration of the deferral period.[99]

- **Serve Notice.** After a charge is filed (or the state or local deferral period has ended), the EEOC has 10 days to serve notice on the employer. Figure 2-4 lists some questions to ask after receiving a bias complaint from the EEOC.

- **Investigation/Fact-Finding Conference.** The EEOC then investigates the charge to determine whether there is reasonable cause to believe it is true; it has 120 days to decide. Early in the investigation, the EEOC holds an initial *fact-finding conference.* However, the EEOC's focus here is often to find weak spots in each party's position. They use these to push for a settlement.

- **Cause/No Cause.** If it finds no reasonable cause, the EEOC must dismiss the charge, and must issue the charging party a Notice of Right to Sue. The person then has 90 days to file a suit on his or her own behalf.

- **Conciliation.** If the EEOC does find cause, it has 30 days to work out a conciliation agreement. The EEOC conciliator meets with the employee to determine what remedy would be satisfactory. It then tries to negotiate a settlement with the employer.

- **Notice to Sue.** If this conciliation is not satisfactory, the EEOC may bring a civil suit in a federal district court, or issue a Notice of Right to Sue to the person who filed the charge.

Voluntary Mediation

The EEOC refers about 10% of its charges to a voluntary mediation mechanism, "an informal process in which a neutral third party assists the opposing parties to reach a voluntary, negotiated resolution of a charge of discrimination."[100] If the parties don't reach agreement (or one of the parties rejects participation), the EEOC processes the charge through its usual mechanisms.[101]

FIGURE 2-4 Questions to Ask When an Employer Receives Notice That EEOC Has Filed a Bias Claim

Source: Fair Employment Practices Summary of Latest Developments, January 7, 1983, p. 3, Bureau of National Affairs, Inc. (800-372-1033); Kenneth Sovereign, *Personnel Law* (Upper Saddle River, NJ: Prentice Hall, 1999), pp. 36–37; "EEOC Investigations—What an Employer Should Know," Equal Employment Opportunity Commission (www.eoc.gov/employers/investigations.html), accessed May 6, 2007.

1. Exactly what is the charge and is your company covered by the relevant statutes? (For example, Title VII and the Americans with Disabilities Act generally apply only to employees with 15 or more employees.) Did the employee file his or her charge on time, and was it processed in a timely manner by the EEOC?
2. What protected group does the employee belong to?
3. Is the EEOC claiming disparate impact or disparate treatment?
4. Are there any obvious bases upon which you can challenge and/or rebut the claim? For example, would the employer have taken the action if the person did not belong to a protected group?
5. If it is a sexual harassment claim, are there offensive comments, calendars, posters, screensavers, and so on, on display in the company?
6. In terms of the practicality of defending your company against this claim, who are the supervisors who actually took the allegedly discriminatory actions and how effective will they be as potential witnesses? Have you received an opinion from legal counsel regarding the chances of prevailing?

Faced with an offer to mediate, the employer has three options: Agree to mediate the charge; make a settlement offer without mediation; or prepare a "position statement" for the EEOC. If the employer does not mediate or make an offer, the position statement is required. It should include a robust defense, including information relating to the company's business and the charging party's position; a description of any rules or policies and procedures that are applicable; and the chronology of the offense that led to the adverse action.[102]

Mandatory Arbitration of Discrimination Claims

Many employers, to avoid EEO litigation, require applicants and employees to agree to arbitrate such claims. The EEO does not favor mandatory arbitration, but the U.S. Supreme Court's decisions (in *Gilmer v. Interstate/Johnson Lane Corp.* and similar cases) make it clear that "employment discrimination plaintiffs [employees] may be compelled to arbitrate their claims under some circumstances."[103] Given this, employers "may wish to consider inserting a mandatory arbitration clause in their employment applications or employee handbooks."[104] To protect such a process against appeal, the employer should institute steps to protect against arbitrator bias, allow the arbitrator to offer a claimant broad relief (including reinstatement), and allow for a reasonable amount of prehearing fact finding.

After an expensive EEO lawsuit, Rockwell International implemented a grievance procedure that provides for binding arbitration as the last step. Called (as is traditional) an **alternative dispute resolution or ADR program**, Rockwell gradually extended the program to all nonunion employees at some locations. New hires at Rockwell must sign the agreement. Current employees must sign it prior to promotion or transfer. U.S. federal agencies must have ADR programs.[105] ADR plans are popular, although the EEOC generally prefers mediation for handling bias claims.[106] Figure 2-5 sums up guidelines employers should follow in addressing EEOC claims.

FIGURE 2-5 Management Guidelines for Addressing EEOC Claims

Sources: "Tips for Employers on Dealing with EEOC Investigations," *BNA Fair Employment Practices*, October 31, 1996, p. 130; "Conducting Effective Investigations of Employee Bias Complaints," *BNA Fair Employment Practices*, July 13, 1995, p. 81; Commerce Clearing House, *Ideas and Trends*, January 23, 1987, pp. 14–15; http://eeoc.gov/employers/investigations.html, accessed October 4, 2009.

During the EEOC Investigation:

Conduct your own investigation to get the facts.

Ensure that there is information in the EEOC's file *demonstrating lack of merit* of the charge.

Limit the information supplied to only those issues raised in the charge itself.

Get as much information as possible about the *charging party's claim.*

Meet with the employee who made the complaint to clarify all the relevant issues. For example, what happened? Who was involved?

Remember that *the EEOC can only ask (not compel) employers* to submit documents and ask for the testimony of witnesses under oath.

Give the EEOC a *position statement.* It should contain words to the effect that "the company has a policy against discrimination and would not discriminate in the manner charged in the complaint." Support the statement with documentation.

During the Fact-Finding Conference:

Because the only official record is the notes the EEOC investigator takes, *keep your own records.* Bring an *attorney.*

Make sure you are *fully informed* of the charges and facts of the case.

Before appearing, *witnesses (especially supervisors) need to be aware* of the legal significance of the facts they will present.

During the EEOC Determination and Attempted Conciliation:

If there is a finding of cause, *review it carefully*, and point out inaccuracies in writing to the EEOC.

Use this letter to try again to convince the parties that the charge is *without merit.*

Conciliate prudently. If you have properly investigated the case, there may be no real advantage in settling at this stage.

Remember: It is likely that *no suit will be filed* by the EEOC.

7 Discuss why diversity management is important and how to institutionalize a diversity management program.

DIVERSITY MANAGEMENT AND AFFIRMATIVE ACTION PROGRAMS

To some extent, demographic changes and globalization are rendering moot the goals of equitable and fair treatment driving equal employment legislation. White males no longer dominate the labor force, and women and minorities will represent the lion's share of labor force growth over the near future. Employers therefore often are striving for demographic balance not just because the law says they must, but due to self-interest.[107]

Furthermore, since many American workplaces are already diverse, the focus increasingly is on managing diversity at work.[108] **Diversity** means being diverse or varied, and at work means having a workforce comprised of two or more groups of employees with various racial, ethnic, gender, cultural, national origin, handicap, age, and religious backgrounds.[109]

Diversity's Potential Pros and Cons

The resulting workforce diversity produces both benefits and threats for employers.

SOME DIVERSITY DOWNSIDES   First, demographic differences can produce behavioral barriers that undermine work team collegiality and cooperation. Potential problems include:

- **Stereotyping** is a process in which someone ascribes specific behavioral traits to individuals based on their apparent membership in a group.[110] For example, "older people can't work hard." Prejudice means a bias toward prejudging someone based on that person's traits. For example, "we won't hire him because he's old."
- **Discrimination** is prejudice in action. **Discrimination** means taking specific actions toward or against the person based on the person's group.[111]

In the United States and many countries, it's generally illegal to discriminate at work based on a person' age, race, gender, disability, or country of national origin. But in practice, discrimination is often subtle. For example, many argue that a "glass ceiling," enforced by an "old boys' network" (friendships built in places like exclusive clubs), effectively prevents women from reaching top management. Insofar as it reflects national origin or religious discrimination, discrimination against Muslim employees is prohibited under Title VII. In the year 2001, the EEOC received 284 such charges from Muslim applicants or workers. The number rose to 803 charges by 2009.[112]

- **Tokenism** occurs when a company appoints a small group of women or minorities to high-profile positions, rather than more aggressively seeking full representation for that group.[113]
- **Ethnocentrism** is the tendency to view members of other social groups less favorably than one's own. For example, in one study, managers attributed the performance of some minorities less to their abilities and more to help they received from others. The same managers attributed the performance of *non*minorities to their own abilities.[114]
- Discrimination against women goes beyond glass ceilings. Working women also confront **gender-role stereotypes**, the tendency to associate women with certain (frequently nonmanagerial) jobs.

alternative dispute resolution or ADR program
Grievance procedure that provides for binding arbitration as the last step.

diversity
The variety or multiplicity of demographic features that characterize a company's workforce, particularly in terms of race, sex, culture, national origin, handicap, age, and religion.

discrimination
Taking specific actions toward or against the person based on the person's group

gender-role stereotypes
The tendency to associate women with certain (frequently nonmanagerial) jobs.

SOME DIVERSITY BENEFITS   The key is properly managing these potential threats. In one study, researchers examined the diversity climate in 654 stores of a large U.S. retail chain. They defined diversity climate as the extent to which employees in the stores reported believing that the firm promotes equal opportunity and inclusion. They found the greatest sales growth in stores with the highest pro-diversity climate, and the lowest in stores where subordinates and managers reported less hospitable diversity climates.[115] Another study found that racial discrimination was related negatively to employee commitment, but that organizational efforts to support diversity reduced such negative effects.[116] The following HR as a Profit Center feature provides another example.

HR AS A PROFIT CENTER

Workforce diversity makes strategic sense. With strong top-management support, IBM created several minority task forces focusing on groups such as women and Native Americans. One effect of these teams has been internal: In the 10 or so years since forming them, IBM has boosted the number of U.S.-born ethnic minority executives by almost 2 ½ times.[117]

However, the firm's diversity program also aided IBM's strategy of expanding its markets and business results. For example, one task force decided to focus on expanding IBM's market among multicultural and women-owned businesses. They did this in part by providing "much-needed sales and service support to small and midsize businesses, a niche well populated with minority and female buyers."[118] As a direct result, this IBM market grew from $10 million to more than $300 million in revenue in just 3 years.

Managing Diversity

Managing diversity means maximizing diversity's potential advantages while minimizing the potential barriers—such as prejudices and bias—that can undermine the functioning of a diverse workforce.

In practice, diversity management involves both compulsory and voluntary actions. However, compulsory actions (including EEO compliance) can't guarantee a close-knit and thriving community. Diversity management therefore also relies on taking steps to encourage employees to work together productively.[119]

TOP-DOWN PROGRAMS   Typically, this starts at the top. The employer institutes a diversity management program. One aim here is to make employees more sensitive to and better able to adapt to individual cultural differences. One diversity expert concluded that five sets of voluntary organizational activities are at the heart of the typical company-wide diversity management program. We can summarize these as follows:

Provide strong leadership. Companies with exemplary reputations in managing diversity typically have CEOs who champion the cause of diversity. Leadership means, for instance, becoming a role model for the behaviors required for the change.

Assess the situation. One study found that the most common tools for measuring a company's diversity include equal employment hiring and retention metrics, employee attitude surveys, management and employee evaluations, and focus groups.[120]

Provide diversity training and education. The most common starting point for a diversity management effort is usually some type of employee education program.

Diversity management can blend a diverse workforce into a close-knit and productive community.

Source: AGE Fotostock America Inc.

Change culture and management systems. Combine education programs with other concrete steps aimed at changing the organization's culture and management systems. For example, change the performance appraisal procedure to appraise supervisors based partly on their success in reducing inter-group conflicts.

Evaluate the diversity management program. For example, do employee attitude surveys now indicate any improvement in employees' attitudes toward diversity?

One writer advocates a four-step "AGEM" diversity training process: Approach, Goals, Executive commitment, and Mandatory attendance. First, determine if diversity training is the solution or if some other approach is more advisable. If training is the solution, then set measurable program goals, for instance, having training participants evaluate their units' diversity efforts. Next, make sure a high-visibility executive commits to the program. Finally, consider making participation in the training mandatory.[121]

EXAMPLE Baxter Healthcare Corporation began by adopting strong company policies advocating the benefits of a culturally, racially, and sexually diverse workforce: "Baxter International believes that a multicultural employee population is essential to the company's leadership in healthcare around the world." Baxter then publicizes this philosophy throughout the company.

Next, Baxter takes concrete steps to foster diversity at work. These steps include evaluating diversity program efforts, recruiting minority members to the board of directors, and interacting with representative minority groups and networks. Diversity training is another concrete activity. It aims at sensitizing all employees about the need to value cultural differences, build self-esteem, and generally create a more smoothly functioning and hospitable environment for the firm's diverse workforce.

Encouraging Inclusiveness

A big part of managing diversity involves overcoming barriers to inclusion—to bringing all employees "under the same tent," in a matter of speaking. Figure 2-6 illustrates strategies for overcoming barriers to inclusion, such as learning about other cultures and helping all employees to better understand the causes of prejudice.

managing diversity
Maximizing diversity's potential benefits while minimizing its potential barriers.

FIGURE 2-6 What the Manager Can Do to Overcome Barriers to Inclusion

Source: Norma Carr-Ruffino, *Making Diversity Work* (Upper Saddle River, NJ: Pearson Education, 2005), p. 104.

Inclusive Strategies	Barriers to Inclusion
Personal Level	
Become aware of prejudice and other barriers to valuing diversity	Stereotypes, prejudices
Learn about other cultures and groups	Past experiences and influences
Serve as an example, walk the talk	Stereotyped expectations and perceptions
Participate in managing diversity	Feelings that tend to separate, divide
Interpersonal Level	
Facilitate communication and interactions in ways that value diversity	Cultural differences
Encourage participation	Group differences
Share your perspective	Myths
Facilitate unique contributions	Relationship patterns based on exclusion
Resolve conflicts in ways that value diversity	
Accept responsibility for developing common ground	
Organizational Level	
All employees have access to networks and focus groups	Individuals who get away with discriminating and excluding
All employees take a proactive role in managing diversity and creating a more diverse workplace culture	A culture that values or allows exclusion
All employees are included in the inner circle that contributes to the bottom-line success of the company	Work structures, policies, and practices that discriminate and exclude
All employees give feedback to teams and management	
All employees are encouraged to contribute to change	

Developing a Multicultural Consciousness

In July 2009, after a heated exchange on his doorstep in Cambridge, Massachusetts, police arrested Professor Henry Louis Gates Jr., a nationally known African-American Harvard professor, for disorderly conduct. Professor Gates initially accused the police of racially profiling him. The arresting officer (who his department had appointed as a trainer to show fellow officers how to avoid racial profiling) denied any racial motives. President Obama, at a news conference, accused the Cambridge police of using less than good judgment. Whatever else one can say about the episode, it seems that three people who should know quite a bit about multicultural consciousness differed dramatically about how culturally sensitive the other person had been.

Being sensitive to and adapting to individual cultural differences is apparently easier said than done. Sometimes it's not easy for even the most well-meaning person to appreciate how people who are different from us may be feeling. This suggests that it's useful to take steps like these to develop a personal "diversity consciousness":[122]

1. **Take an active role in educating yourself.** For example, develop diverse relationships, and widen your circle of friends.

2. **Put yourself in a learning mode in any multicultural setting.** For example, suspend judgment and view the person you're dealing with just as an individual and in terms of the experiences you've actually had with him or her.

3. **Move beyond your personal comfort zone.** For example, put yourself in more situations where you are an "outsider."

4. **Don't be too hard on yourself if misunderstandings arise.** As one expert says, "The important thing is to acknowledge our mistakes and learn from them."[123]

5. **Realize that you are not alone.** Remember that there are other people including colleagues, friends, and mentors at work who you can turn to for advice as you deal with diversity issues.

Some employers encourage diversity through *affirmative action programs.* Affirmative action means making an extra effort to hire and promote those in protected groups, particularly when those groups are underrepresented. We turn to this next.

Equal Employment Opportunity Versus Affirmative Action

Equal employment opportunity aims to ensure that anyone, regardless of race, color, disability, sex, religion, national origin, or age, has an equal opportunity based on his or her qualifications. *Affirmative action* goes beyond this by having the employer take actions (in recruitment, hiring, promotions, and compensation) to eliminate the current effects of past discrimination.

Affirmative action is still a significant workplace issue today. The incidences of major court-mandated affirmative action programs are down, but courts still use them. Furthermore, many employers must still engage in voluntary programs. For example, Executive Order 11246 (issued in 1965) requires federal contractors to take affirmative action to improve employment opportunities for groups such as women and racial minorities. EO 11246 covers about 26 million workers—about 22% of the U.S. workforce.[124]

Implementing the Affirmative Action Program

Under guidelines such as EO 11246, the key aims of affirmative action programs are (1) to use numerical analysis to determine which (if any) target groups the firm is underutilizing relative to the relevant labor market, and (2) to eliminate the barriers to equal employment. Many employers pursue these aims with a **good faith effort strategy**; this emphasizes identifying and eliminating the obstacles to hiring and promoting women and minorities, and increasing the minority or female applicant flow. Reasonable steps to take include those shown in Figure 2-7.

RECRUITING MINORITIES ONLINE   One important step is to direct recruiting ads to one or more of the online minority-oriented job markets. For example, Recruiting-Online.com lists dozens of online diversity candidate resources (www.recruiting-online.com/course55.html). Diversity candidate Web sites with job banks include the National Urban League, Hispanic Online, Latino Web, Society of Hispanic Engineers, Gay.com, Association for Women in Science, and Minorities Job Bank.

EMPLOYEE RESISTANCE   Avoiding employee resistance to affirmative action programs is important. Studies suggest that current employees need to believe the program is fair. *Transparent selection procedures* (making it clear what selection tools and standards the company uses) help in this regard. *Communication* is also crucial. Make clear that the program doesn't involve preferential selection standards. Provide details on the qualifications of all new hires (both minority and nonminority). *Justifications* for the program should emphasize redressing past discrimination and the practical value of diversity, not underrepresentation.[125]

good faith effort strategy
An affirmative action strategy that emphasizes identifying and eliminating the obstacles to hiring and promoting women and minorities, and increasing the minority or female applicant flow.

FIGURE 2-7 Steps in an Affirmative Action Program

1. Issue a written equal employment policy indicating that the firm is an equal employment opportunity employer and the employer's commitment to affirmative action.
2. Demonstrate top-management support for the equal employment policy—for instance, appoint a high-ranking EEO administrator.
3. Publicize internally and externally the equal employment policy and affirmative action commitment.
4. Survey current minority and female employment by department and job classification to determine where affirmative action programs are especially desirable.
5. Carefully analyze employer human resources practices to identify and eliminate hidden barriers.
6. Review, develop, and implement specific HR programs to improve female and minority utilization.
7. Use focused recruitment to find qualified applicants from the target group(s).
8. Establish an internal audit and reporting system to monitor and evaluate progress.
9. Develop support for the affirmative action program, inside the company and in the community.

PROGRAM EVALUATION   How can one tell if the diversity initiatives are effective? Some commonsense questions can be asked:

- Are there women and minorities reporting directly to senior managers?
- Do women and minorities have a fair share of the jobs that are the traditional stepping-stones to successful careers in the company?
- Do women and minorities have equal access to international assignments?
- Is the employer taking steps that ensure that female and minority candidates will be in the company's career development pipeline?
- Are turnover rates for female and minority managers the same or lower than those for white males?
- Do employees report that they perceive positive behavior changes as a result of the diversity efforts?[126]

Reverse Discrimination

Courts have been grappling with the use of quotas (or de facto quotas) in hiring, particularly with claims of **reverse discrimination** (discriminating against *non*minority applicants and employees). Many cases addressed these issues, but until recently, few consistent answers emerged.

In one of the first such cases, *Bakke v. Regents of the University of California* (1978), the University of California at Davis Medical School denied admission to white student Allen Bakke, allegedly because of the school's affirmative action quota system, which required that a specific number of openings go to minority applicants. In a 5-to-4 vote, the U.S. Supreme Court struck down the policy that made race the only factor in considering applications for a certain number of class openings and thus allowed Bakke's admission.

Bakke was followed by many other cases. For example, in June 2001, the U.S. Supreme Court refused to hear Texas's challenge to a ruling that one of its law school affirmative action programs, which gives special consideration to black and Mexican American student applicants, discriminated against whites. In 2003, the U.S. Supreme Court decided against the University of Michigan's quota-based admissions programs. In June 2007, the Court ruled against race-based school assignment (busing) plans.[127]

In June 2009, the U.S. Supreme Court ruled in an important reverse discrimination suit brought by Connecticut firefighters. In *Ricci v. DeStefano*, 19 white firefighters and one Hispanic firefighter say the city of New Haven should have promoted them based on their successful test scores. The city argued that certifying the tests would have left them vulnerable to lawsuits from minorities for violating Title VII.[128] The Court ruled in favor of the (predominantly white) plaintiffs. In New Haven's desire to avoid making promotions that might appear to have an adverse impact on minorities, Justice Kennedy wrote that "The city rejected the test results solely because the higher scoring candidates were white." The consensus of observers was that the decision would make it much harder for employers to ignore the results obtained by valid tests, even if the results disproportionately impact minorities.[129]

The bottom line seems to be that employers should emphasize the external recruitment and internal development of better-qualified minority and female employees, "while basing employment decisions on legitimate criteria."[130]

REVIEW

MyManagementLab Now that you have finished this chapter, go back to **www.mymanagementlab.com** to continue practicing and applying the concepts you've learned.

CHAPTER SECTION SUMMARIES

1. Several of the most important **equal employment opportunity laws became law in the period from 1964 to 1991.**
   - Of these, Title VII of the 1964 Civil Rights Act was pivotal, and states that an employer cannot discriminate based on race, color, religion, sex, or national origin. This act established the Equal Employment Opportunity Commission, and covers most employees.
   - Under the Equal Pay Act of 1963 (amended in 1972), it is unlawful to discriminate in pay on the basis of sex when jobs involve equal work, skills, effort, and responsibility, and are performed under similar working conditions.
   - The Age Discrimination in Employment Act of 1967 made it unlawful to discriminate against employees or applicants who are between 40 and 65 years of age.
   - The Vocational Rehabilitation Act of 1973 requires most employers with federal contracts to take affirmative action when employing handicapped persons.
   - The Pregnancy Discrimination Act of 1978 prohibits using pregnancy, childbirth, or related medical conditions to discriminate in hiring, promotion, suspension, or discharge, or in any term or condition of employment.
   - The EEOC, Civil Service Commission, Department of Labor, and Department of Justice together issued uniform guidelines that set forth "highly recommended" procedures regarding HR activities like employee selection, record keeping, and preemployment inquiries.
   - One of the most important cases during this early period was *Griggs v. Duke Power Company.* Here, Chief Justice Burger held that in employment, discrimination does not have to be overt to be illegal, and an employment practice that discriminates must be job related.

2. Equal employment law continues to evolve, with important **new legislation being enacted since 1990–1991.**
   - The Civil Rights Act of 1991 reversed the effects of several Supreme Court rulings—for instance, underscoring that the burden of proof is the employer's once a plaintiff establishes possible illegal discrimination.
   - The Americans with Disabilities Act prohibits employment discrimination against qualified disabled individuals. It also says employers must make "reasonable accommodations" for physical or mental limitations unless doing so imposes an "undue hardship" on the business.
   - Although Title VII made sexual harassment at work illegal, the Federal Violence Against Women Act of 1994 provided women with another way to seek relief for (violent) sexual harassment. Basically, sexual harassment refers to unwelcome sexual advances, requests for sexual favors, and other verbal or physical conduct of a sexual nature that takes place, for

reverse discrimination
Claim that due to affirmative action quota systems, white males are discriminated against.

instance, when such conduct is made either explicitly or implicitly a term or condition of an individual's employment. Three main ways to prove sexual harassment include *quid pro quo*, hostile environment created by supervisors, and hostile environment created by coworkers who are not employees.

3. Employers use various **defenses against discrimination allegations**. In defending themselves against discrimination allegations, employers need to distinguish between disparate treatment (intentional discrimination) and disparate impact (a policy that has an adverse impact regardless of intent). Plaintiffs show adverse impact by the standard deviation rule or by showing disparate rejection rates, restricted policy, population comparisons, or by applying the McDonnell-Douglas test. Employers defend themselves by showing that the employment practice is a bona fide occupational qualification (for instance, gender is a BFOQ for a position such as model). Or they may defend themselves by using the business necessity defense, which requires showing that there is an overriding business purpose.

4. It's useful to have a working knowledge of **discriminatory employment practices**. For example, in recruitment, employers no longer use "help wanted—male" ads and endeavor to ensure that educational requirements are necessary to do the job. Similarly, in promotion and transfer, the Equal Pay Act requires that equal wages be paid for substantially similar work performed by men and women.

5. All managers play an important role in the **EEOC enforcement process**. The basic steps in this process include filing the charge, charge acceptance by the EEOC, serving notice on the employer, the investigation/fact-finding conference, a finding of cause/no cause, conciliation efforts, and (if necessary) a notice to sue. The EEOC refers about 10% of its charges to voluntary mediation mechanisms.

6. With an increasingly diverse workforce, **diversity management** is a key managerial skill. Managing diversity means maximizing diversity's potential benefits while minimizing the potential barriers. In one typical approach, the steps include providing strong leadership, assessing the situation, providing diversity training and education, changing the culture and management systems, and evaluating the diversity management program's results. Affirmative action generally means taking actions to eliminate the present effects of past discrimination. Many employers still pursue voluntary, good-faith effort strategies in identifying and eliminating the obstacles to hiring and promoting women and minorities, while some employers are under court-mandated requirement to do so.

DISCUSSION QUESTIONS

1. Explain the main features of Title VII, the Equal Pay Act, the Pregnancy Discrimination Act, the Americans with Disabilities Act, and the Civil Rights Act of 1991.
2. What important precedents were set by the *Griggs v. Duke Power Company* case? The *Albemarle v. Moody* case?
3. What is adverse impact? How can it be proved?
4. What is sexual harassment? How can an employee prove sexual harassment?
5. What are the two main defenses you can use in the event of a discriminatory practice allegation, and what exactly do they involve?
6. What is the difference between disparate treatment and disparate impact?

INDIVIDUAL AND GROUP ACTIVITIES

1. Working individually or in groups, respond to these three scenarios based on what you learned in this chapter. Under what conditions (if any) do you think the following constitute sexual harassment? (a) A female manager fires a male employee because he refuses her requests for sexual favors. (b) A male manager refers to female employees as "sweetie" or "baby." (c) A female employee overhears two male employees exchanging sexually oriented jokes.
2. Working individually or in groups, discuss how you would set up an affirmative action program.
3. Compare and contrast the issues presented in *Bakke* with more recent court rulings on affirmative action. Working individually or in groups, discuss the current direction of affirmative action.
4. Working individually or in groups, write a paper titled "What the Manager Should Know About How the EEOC Handles a Person's Discrimination Charge."
5. Explain the difference between affirmative action and equal employment opportunity.
6. Assume you are the manager in a small restaurant; you are responsible for hiring employees, supervising them, and recommending them for promotion. Working individually or in groups, compile a list of potentially discriminatory management practices you should avoid.
7. The HRCI Test Specifications appendix at the end of this book (pages 633–640) lists the knowledge someone studying for the HRCI certification exam needs to have in each area of human resource management (such as in Strategic Management, Workforce Planning, and Human Resource Development). In groups of four to five students, do four things: (1) review that appendix now; (2) identify the material in this chapter that relates to the required knowledge the appendix lists; (3) write four multiple-choice exam questions on this material that you believe would be suitable for inclusion in the HRCI exam; and (4) if time permits, have someone from your team post your team's questions in front of the class, so the students in other teams can take each others' exam questions.

EXPERIENTIAL EXERCISE

"Space Cadet" or Victim?

Discrimination lawsuits are rarely simple, because the employer will often argue that the person was fired due to poor performance, rather than discrimination. So, there's often a "mixed motive" element to such situations. The facts of a case illustrate this (*Burk v. California Association of Realtors*, California Court of Appeals, number 161513, unpublished, 12/12/03). The facts were as follows. The California Association of Realtors maintained a hotline service to provide legal advice to real estate agents. One of the 12 lawyers who answered this hotline on behalf of the Association was a 61-year-old California attorney who worked at the Association from 1989 to 2000. Until 1996 he received mostly good reviews and salary increases. At that time, Association members began filing complaints about his advice. His supervisor told him to be more courteous and more thorough in providing advice.

Two years later, Association members were still complaining about this individual. Among other things, Association members who called in to deal with him filed complaints referring to him as "a space cadet," "incompetent," and "a total jerk." Subsequently, his supervisor contacted six Association members whom the 61-year-old lawyer had recently counseled; five of the six said they had had bad experiences. The Association fired him for mistreating Association members and providing inadequate legal advice.

The 61-year-old lawyer sued the Association, claiming that the firing was age related. To support his claim, he noted, among other things, that one colleague had told him that he was "probably getting close to retirement" and that another colleague had told him that both he and another lawyer were "getting older." The appeals court had to decide whether the Association fired the 61-year-old lawyer because of his age or because of his performance.

Purpose: The purpose of this exercise is to provide practice in analyzing and applying knowledge of equal opportunity legislation to a real problem.

Required Understanding: Be thoroughly familiar with the material presented in this chapter. In addition, read the preceding "space cadet" case on which this experiential exercise is based.

How to Set Up the Exercise/Instructions:

1. Divide the class into groups of three to five students.
2. Each group should develop answers to the following questions:

   a. Based on what you read in this chapter, on what legal basis could the 61-year-old California attorney claim he was a victim of discrimination?

   b. On what laws and legal concepts did the employer apparently base its termination of this 61-year-old attorney?

   c. Based on what laws or legal concepts could you take the position that it is legal to fire someone for poor performance even though there may be a discriminatory aspect to the termination? (This is not to say that there necessarily was such a discriminatory aspect with this case.)

   d. If you were the judge called on to make a decision on this case, what would your decision be, and why?

   e. The court's decision follows, so please do not read this until you've completed the exercise.

In this case, the California State Appeals court held that "the only reasonable inference that can be drawn from the evidence is that [plaintiff] was terminated because he failed to competently perform his job of providing thorough, accurate, and courteous legal advice to hotline callers." ("On Appeal, Hotheaded Hotline Lawyer Loses Age, Disability Discrimination Claims," *BNA Human Resources Report*, January 12, 2004, p. 17.)

APPLICATION CASE

AN ACCUSATION OF SEXUAL HARASSMENT IN PRO SPORTS

The jury in a sexual harassment suit brought by a former high-ranking New York Knicks basketball team executive recently awarded her more than $11 million in punitive damages. They did so after hearing testimony during what the *New York Times* called a "sordid four-week trial." Officials of Madison Square Garden (which owns the Knicks) said they would appeal the verdict. However, even if they were to win on appeal (which one University of Richmond Law School professor said was unlikely), the case still exposed the organization and its managers to a great deal of unfavorable publicity.

The federal suit pitted Anucha Browne Sanders, the Knicks' senior vice president of marketing and business operations (and former Northwestern University basketball star), against the team's owner, Madison Square Garden, and its president, Isiah Thomas. The suit charged them with sex discrimination and retaliation. Ms. Browne Sanders accused Mr. Thomas of verbally abusing and sexually harassing her over a 2-year period. She said the Garden fired her about a month after she complained to top management about the harassment. "My pleas and complaints about Mr. Thomas' illegal and offensive actions fell on deaf ears," she said. At the trial, the Garden cited numerous explanations for the dismissal, saying she had "failed to fulfill professional responsibilities." At a news conference, Browne Sanders said that Thomas "refused to stop his demeaning and repulsive behavior and the Garden refused to intercede." For his part, Mr. Thomas vigorously insisted he was innocent, and said, "I will not allow her or anybody, man or woman, to use me as a pawn for their financial gain." According to one report of the trial, her claims of harassment and verbal abuse had little corroboration from witnesses, but neither did the Garden's claims that her performance had been subpar. After the jury decision came in, Browne Sanders' lawyers said, "This [decision] confirms what we've been saying all along, that [Browne Sanders] was sexually abused and fired for complaining about it." The Garden's statement said, in part, "We look forward to presenting our arguments to an appeals court and believe they will agree that no sexual harassment took place."

Questions

1. Do you think Ms. Browne Sanders had the basis for a sexual harassment suit? Why?
2. From what you know of this case, do you think the jury arrived at the correct decision? If not, why not? If so, why?

3. Based on the few facts that you have, what steps could Garden management have taken to protect itself from liability in this matter?
4. Aside from the appeal, what would you do now if you were the Garden's top management?
5. "The allegations against Madison Square Garden in this case raise ethical questions with regard to the employer's actions." Explain whether you agree or disagree with this statement, and why.

Sources: "Jury Awards $11.6 Million to Former Executive of Pro Basketball Team in Harassment Case," *BNA Bulletin to Management*, October 9, 2007, p. 323; Richard Sandomir, "Jury Finds Knicks and Coach Harassed a Former Executive," *The New York Times*, www.nytimes.com/2007/10/03/sports/basketball/03garden.html?em&ex=1191556800&en=41d47437f805290d&ei=5087%0A, accessed November 31, 2007; "Thomas Defiant in Face of Harassment Claims," espn.com, accessed November 31, 2007.

CONTINUING CASE

CARTER CLEANING COMPANY

A Question of Discrimination

One of the first problems Jennifer faced at her father's Carter Cleaning Centers concerned the inadequacies of the firm's current HR management practices and procedures.

One problem that particularly concerned her was the lack of attention to equal employment matters. Each store manager independently handled virtually all hiring; the managers had received no training regarding such fundamental matters as the types of questions they should not ask of job applicants. It was therefore not unusual—in fact, it was routine—for female applicants to be asked questions such as "Who's going to take care of your children while you are at work?" and for minority applicants to be asked questions about arrest records and credit histories. Non-minority applicants—three store managers were white males and three were white females—were not asked these questions, as Jennifer discerned from her interviews with the managers. Based on discussions with her father, Jennifer deduced two reasons for the laid-back attitude toward equal employment: (1) her father's lack of sophistication regarding the legal requirements and (2) the fact that, as Jack Carter put it, "Virtually all our workers are women or minority members anyway, so no one can really come in here and accuse us of being discriminatory, can they?"

Jennifer decided to mull that question over, but before she could, she was faced with two serious equal rights problems. Two women in one of her stores privately confided to her that their manager was making unwelcome sexual advances toward them, and one claimed he had threatened to fire her unless she "socialized" with him after hours. And during a fact-finding trip to another store, an older gentleman—he was 73 years old—complained of the fact that although he had almost 50 years of experience in the business, he was being paid less than people half his age who were doing the very same job. Jennifer's review of the stores resulted in the following questions.

Questions

1. Is it true, as Jack Carter claims, that "we can't be accused of being discriminatory because we hire mostly women and minorities anyway"?
2. How should Jennifer and her company address the sexual harassment charges and problems?
3. How should she and her company address the possible problems of age discrimination?
4. Given the fact that each of its stores has only a handful of employees, is her company covered by equal rights legislation?
5. And finally, aside from the specific problems, what other personnel management matters (application forms, training, and so on) have to be reviewed given the need to bring them into compliance with equal rights laws?

KEY TERMS

Title VII of the 1964 Civil Rights Act, 32

Equal Employment Opportunity Commission (EEOC), 32

affirmative action, 33

Office of Federal Contract Compliance Programs (OFCCP), 33

Equal Pay Act of 1963, 33

Age Discrimination in Employment Act of 1967 (ADEA), 33

Vocational Rehabilitation Act of 1973, 33

Pregnancy Discrimination Act, 34

uniform guidelines, 34

protected class, 34

Civil Rights Act of 1991 (CRA 1991), 35

"mixed motive" case, 36

Americans with Disabilities Act (ADA), 36

qualified individuals, 37

sexual harassment, 39

Federal Violence Against Women Act of 1994, 40

adverse impact, 44

disparate rejection rates, 44

4/5ths rule, 44

restricted policy, 45

bona fide occupational qualification (BFOQ), 46

alternative dispute resolution or ADR program, 54

diversity, 55

discrimination, 55

gender-role stereotypes, 55

managing diversity, 56

good faith effort strategy, 59

reverse discrimination, 60

ENDNOTES

1. Kevin McGowan, "Court Approves $175 Million Settlement of Novartis Sales Reps and Sex Bias Claims," *BNA Bulletin to Management*, November 30, 2010, p. 377.

2. Plaintiffs still bring equal employment claims under the Civil Rights Act of 1866. For example, in 2008 the U.S. Supreme Court held that the act prohibits retaliation against someone who complains of discrimination against others when contract rights (in this case, an employment agreement) are at stake. Charles Louderback, "U.S. Supreme Court Decisions Expand Employees' Ability to Bring Retaliation Claims," *Compensation & Benefits Review*, September/October 2008, p. 52.

3. Based on or quoted from *Principles of Employment Discrimination Law*, International Association of Official Human Rights Agencies, Washington, DC. See also Bruce Feldacker, *Labor Guide to Labor Law* (Upper Saddle River, NJ: Prentice Hall, 2000); "EEOC Attorneys Highlight How Employers Can Better Their Nondiscrimination Practices," *BNA Bulletin to Management*, July 20, 2008, p. 233; and www.eeoc.gov, accessed June 27, 2009. Employment discrimination law is a changing field, and the appropriateness of the rules, guidelines, and conclusions in this chapter and book may also be affected by factors unique to the employer's operation. They should be reviewed by the employer's attorney before implementation.

4. Individuals may file under the Equal Employment Act of 1972.

5. "The Employer Should Validate Hiring Tests to Withstand EEOC Scrutiny, Officials Advise," *BNA Bulletin to Management*, April 1, 2008, p. 107.

6. "Restructured, Beefed Up OFCCP May Shift Policy Emphasis, Attorney Says," *BNA Bulletin to Management*, August 18, 2009, p. 257.

7. "High Court: ADEA Does Not Protect Younger Workers Treated Worse Than Their Elders," *BNA Bulletin to Management* 55, no. 10 (March 4, 2004), pp. 73–80. See also D. Aaron Lacy, "You Are Not Quite as Old as You Think: Making the Case for Reverse Age Discrimination Under the ADEA," *Berkeley Journal of Employment and Labor Law* 26, no. 2 (2005), pp. 363–403; Nancy Ursel and Marjorie Armstrong-Stassen, "How Age Discrimination in Employment Affects Stockholders," *Journal of Labor Research* 17, no. 1 (Winter 2006), pp. 89–99; and, http://www.eeoc.gov/laws/statutes/adea.cfm, accessed October 3, 2011.

8. "Google Exec Can Pursue Claim," *BNA Bulletin to Management*, October 20, 2007, p. 342; "Fired Google Manager May Proceed with Age Bias Suit, California Justices Rule," *BNA Bulletin to Management*, August 10, 2010, p. 249.

9. http://www.eeoc.gov/laws/statutes/adea.cfm, accessed October 3, 2011.

10. The U.S. Supreme Court ruled in *California Federal Savings and Loan Association v. Guerra* that if an employer offers no disability leave to any of its employees, it can (but need not) grant pregnancy leave to a woman disabled for pregnancy, childbirth, or a related medical condition.

11. John Kohl, Milton Mayfield, and Jacqueline Mayfield, "Recent Trends in Pregnancy Discrimination Law," *Business Horizons* 48, no. 5 (September 2005), pp. 421–429, and http://www.eeoc.gov/eeoc/statistics/enforcement/pregnancy.cfm, accessed October 3, 2011.

12. Nancy Woodward, "Pregnancy Discrimination Grows," *HR Magazine*, July 2005, p. 79.

13. "Pregnancy Claims Rising; Consistent Procedures Paramount," *BNA Bulletin to Management*, November 23, 2010, p. 375.

14. www.uniformguidelines.com/uniformguidelines.html, accessed November 23, 2007.

15. *Griggs v. Duke Power Company*, 3FEP cases 175.

16. This is applicable only to Title VII and CRA 91; other statutes require intent.

17. James Ledvinka, *Federal Regulation of Personnel and Human Resources Management* (Boston: Kent, 1982), p. 41.

18. Bruce Feldacker, *Labor Guide to Labor Law* (Upper Saddle River, NJ: Prentice Hall, 2000), p. 513.

19. "The Eleventh Circuit Explains Disparate Impact, Disparate Treatment," *BNA Fair Employment Practices*, August 17, 2000, p. 102. See also Kenneth York, "Disparate Results in Adverse Impact Tests: The 4/5ths Rule and the Chi Square Test," *Public Personnel Management* 31, no. 2 (Summer 2002), pp. 253–262; and "Burden of Proof Under the Employment Non-Discrimination Act," http://www.civilrights.org/lgbt/enda/burden-of-proof.html, accessed August 8, 2011.

20. We'll see that the process of filing a discrimination charge goes something like this: The plaintiff (say, a rejected applicant) demonstrates that an employment practice (such as a test) has a disparate (or "adverse") impact on a particular group. *Disparate impact* means that an employer engages in an employment practice or policy that has a greater adverse impact [effect] on the members of a protected group under Title VII than on other employees, regardless of intent. (Requiring a college degree for a job would have an adverse impact on some minority groups, for instance.) Disparate impact claims do *not* require proof of discriminatory intent. Instead, the plaintiff's burden

is to show two things. First, he or she must show that a significant disparity exists between the proportion of (say) women in the available labor pool and the proportion hired. Second, he or she must show that an apparently neutral employment practice, such as word-of-mouth advertising or a requirement that the jobholder "be able to lift 100 pounds," is causing the disparity. Then, once the plaintiff fulfills his or her burden of showing such disparate impact, the *employer* has the heavier burden of proving that the challenged practice is job related. For example, the employer has to show that lifting 100 pounds is actually required for effectively performing the position in question, and that the business could not run efficiently without the requirement—that it is a business necessity.

21. Commerce Clearing House, "House and Senate Pass Civil Rights Compromise by Wide Margin," *Ideas and Trends in Personnel*, November 13, 1991, p. 179.

22. www.eeoc.gov/policy/cra91.html, accessed November 11, 2007. Note however that ". . . when an employer shows that it would have taken the same action even absent the discriminatory motive, the complaining employee will not be entitled to reinstatement, back pay, or damages," http://www.eeoc.gov/policy/docs/caregiving.html#mixed, accessed September 24, 2011.

23. Mark Kobata, "The Civil Rights Act of 1991," *Personnel Journal*, March 1992, p. 48.

24. Again, though, if the "employer shows that it would have taken the same action even absent the discriminatory motive, the complaining employee will not be entitled to reinstatement, back pay, or damages," http://www.eeoc.gov/policy/docs/caregiving.html#mixed, accessed September 24, 2011.

25. Elliot H. Shaller and Dean Rosen, "A Guide to the EEOC's Final Regulations on the Americans with Disabilities Act," *Employee Relations Law Journal* 17, no. 3 (Winter 1991–1992), pp. 405–430; and www.eeoc.gov/ada, accessed November 20, 2007.

26. "ADA: Simple Common Sense Principles," *BNA Fair Employment Practices*, June 4, 1992, p. 63; and http://www.eeoc.gov/facts/ada17.html, accessed September 24, 2011.

27. Shaller and Rosen, "A Guide to the EEOC's Final Regulations," p. 408. Other specific examples include "epilepsy, diabetes, cancer, HIV infection, and bipolar disorder," http://www1.eeoc.gov//laws/regulations/adaaa_fact_sheet, accessed October 3, 2011.

28. Shaller and Rosen, cit., p. 409.

29. James McDonald Jr., "The Americans with Difficult Personalities Act," *Employee Relations Law Journal* 25, no. 4 (Spring 2000), pp. 93–107; and Betsy Bates, "Mental Health Problems Predominate in ADA Claims," http://findarticles.com/p/articles/mi_hb4345, *Clinical Psychiatry News*,

http://findarticles.com/p/articles/mi_hb4 345/is_5_31, May 2003, at http://findarticles.com/p/articles/mi_hb4345/is_5_31/ai_n2 9006702, accessed September 24, 2011. For a detailed discussion of dealing with this issue, see http://www.eeoc.gov/facts/intellectual_disabilities.html, accessed September 2, 2011.

30. "EEOC Guidance on Dealing with Intellectual Disabilities," *Workforce Management*, March 2005, p. 16.

31. "Driver Fired After Seizure on Job Lacks ADA Claim," *BNA Bulletin to Management*, January 4, 2011, p. 6.

32. www.ada.gov/reg3a.html#Anchor-Appendix-52467, accessed January 23, 2009.

33. Martha Frase, "An Underestimated Talent Pool," *HR Magazine*, April 2009, pp. 55–58.

34. M. P. McQueen, "Workplace Disabilities Are on the Rise," *The Wall Street Journal*, May 1, 2007, p. A1.

35. "No Sitting for Store Greeter," *BNA Fair Employment Practices*, December 14, 1995, p. 150. For more recent illustrative cases, see Tillinghast Licht, "Reasonable Accommodation and the ADA-Courts Draw the Line," at http://library.findlaw.com/2004/Sep/19/133574.html, accessed September 6, 2011.

36. For example, a U.S. circuit court recently found that a depressed former kidney dialysis technician could not claim ADA discrimination after the employer fired him for attendance problems. The court said he could not meet the essential job function of predictably coming to work. "Depressed Worker Lacks ADA Claim, Court Decides," *BNA Bulletin to Management*, December 18, 2007, p. 406. See also www.eeoc.gov/press/5-10-01-b.html, accessed January 8, 2008.

37. *Toyota Motor Manufacturing of Kentucky, Inc. v. Williams.* - 534 U.S. 184 (2002).

38. "Supreme Court Says Manual Task Limitation Needs Both Daily Living, Workplace Impact," *BNA Fair Employment Practices*, January 17, 2002, p. 8.

39. Lawrence Postol, "ADAAA Will Result in Renewed Emphasis on Reasonable Accommodations," *Society for Human Resource Management Legal Report*, January 2009, pp. 1–3.

40. Mark Lengnick-Hall et al., "Overlooked and Underutilized: People with Disabilities Are an Untapped Human Resource," *Human Resource Management* 47, no. 2 (Summer 2008), pp. 255–273.

41. Susan Wells, "Counting on Workers with Disabilities," *HR Magazine*, April 2008, p. 45.

42. www.eeoc.gov/press/2-25-09.html, accessed April 3, 2009.

43. James Ledvinka and Robert Gatewood, "EEO Issues with Preemployment Inquiries," *Personnel Administrator* 22, no. 2 (February 1997), pp. 22–26.

44. "Expansion of Employment Laws Abroad Impacts U.S. Employers," *BNA Bulletin to Management*, April 11, 2006, p. 119; Richard Posthuma, Mark Roehling, and Michael Campion, "Applying U.S. Employment Discrimination Laws to International Employers: Advice for Scientists and Practitioners," *Personnel Psychology*, 2006, 59, pp. 705–739.

45. Guidelines based on Richard Posthuma et al., "Applying U.S. Employment Discrimination Laws to International Employees: Advice for Scientists and Practitioners," *Personnel Psychology* 59 (2006), p. 710. Reprinted by permission of Wiley Blackwell.

46. www.eeoc.gov/types/sexual_harassment.html, accessed April 24, 2009, and http://www.eeoc.gov/eeoc/statistics/enforcement/sexual_harassment.cfm, accessed October 3, 2011.

47. Larry Drake and Rachel Moskowitz, "Your Rights in the Workplace," *Occupational Outlook Quarterly* (Summer 1997), pp. 19–29.

48. Richard Wiener et al., "The Fit and Implementation of Sexual Harassment Law to Workplace Evaluations," *Journal of Applied Psychology* 87, no. 4 (2002), pp. 747–764. The Michigan Court of Appeals recently ruled that a male Ford Motor Company employee who claimed a male coworker sexually harassed him could proceed with his claim. "State Court Allows Same-Sex Harassment Case to Proceed," *BNA Bulletin to Management*, November 20, 2007, p. 382.

49. Jennifer Berdahl and Celia Moore, "Workplace Harassment: Double Jeopardy for Minority Women," *Journal of Applied Psychology* 91, no. 2 (2006), pp. 426–436.

50. Patricia Linenberger and Timothy Keaveny, "Sexual Harassment: The Employer's Legal Obligations," *Personnel* 58 (November/December 1981), p. 64; and "Court Examines Workplace Flirtation," http://hr.blr.com/HR-news/Discrimination/Sexual-Harassment/Court-Examines-Workplace-Flirtation, accessed October 2, 2011.

51. Edward Felsenthal, "Justice's Ruling Further Defines Sexual Harassment," *The Wall Street Journal*, March 5, 1998, p. B5.

52. Hilary Gettman and Michele Gelfand, "When the Customer Shouldn't Be King: Antecedents and Consequences of Sexual Harassment by Clients and Customers," *Journal of Applied Psychology* 92, no. 3 (2007), pp. 757–770.

53. See the discussion in "Examining Unwelcome Conduct in a Sexual Harassment Claim," *BNA Fair Employment Practices*, October 19, 1995, p. 124. See also Michael Zugelder et al., "An Affirmative Defense to Sexual Harassment by Managers and Supervisors: Analyzing Employer Liability and Protecting Employee Rights in the U.S.," *Employee Responsibilities and Rights* 18, no. 2 (2006), pp. 111–122.

54. Ibid., "Examining Unwelcome Conduct in a Sexual Harassment Claim," p. 124.

55. For example, a server/bartender filed a sexual harassment claim against Chili's Bar & Grill. She claimed that her former

boyfriend, also a restaurant employee, had harassed her. The court ruled that the restaurant's prompt response warranted ruling in favor of it. "Ex-Boyfriend Harassed, but Employer Acted Promptly," *BNA Bulletin to Management,* January 8, 2008, p. 14.

56. See Mindy D. Bergman et al., "The (Un)reasonableness of Reporting: Antecedents and Consequences of Reporting Sexual Harassment," *Journal of Applied Psychology* 87, no. 2 (2002), pp. 230–242. See also http://www.eeoc.gov/policy/docs/harassment-facts.html, accessed October 2, 2011.

57. Adapted from *Sexual Harassment Manual for Managers and Supervisors,* published in 1991, by CCH Incorporated, a Wolters-Kluwer Company; www.eeoc.gov/types/sexual_harrassment.html, accessed May 6, 2007; and http://www.eeoc.gov/policy/docs/harassment-facts.html, accessed October 2, 2011.

58. Jennifer Berdahl and Karl Aquino, "Sexual Behavior at Work: Fun or Folly?" *Journal of Applied Psychology* 94, no. 1, 2009, pp. 34–47.

59. Maria Rotundo et al., "A Meta-Analytic Review of Gender Differences in Perceptions of Sexual Harassment," *Journal of Applied Psychology* 86, no. 5 (2001): 914–922. See also Nathan Bowling and Terry Beehr, "Workplace Harassment from the Victim's Perspective: A Theoretical Model and Meta Analysis," *Journal of Applied Psychology* 91, no. 5 (2006): 998–1012.

60. Jathan Janov, "Sexual Harassment and the Three Big Surprises," *HR Magazine* 46, no. 11 (November 2001), p. 123ff. California mandates sexual harassment prevention training for supervisors. See "California Clarifies Training Law; Employers Take Note," *BNA Bulletin to Management,* November 20, 2007, p. 375.

61. Mary Rowe, "Dealing with Sexual Harassment," *Harvard Business Review,* May–June 1981, p. 43; the quoted material goes on to say that "The employer still bears the burden of proving that the employee's failure was unreasonable. If the employee had a justifiable fear of retaliation, his or her failure to utilize the complaint process may not be unreasonable," and is quoted from http://www.uiowa.edu/~eod/policies/sexual-harassment-guide/employer-liablity.htm, accessed October 3, 2011.

62. John Moran, *Employment Law* (Upper Saddle River, NJ: Prentice Hall, 1997), p. 166.

63. "The Eleventh Circuit Explains Disparate Impact, Disparate Treatment," p. 102.

64. Moran, *Employment Law,* p. 168.

65. John Klinefelter and James Thompkins, "Adverse Impact in Employment Selection," *Public Personnel Management,* May/June 1976, pp. 199–204; and http://www.eeoc.gov/policy/docs/factemployment_procedures.html, accessed October 2, 2011.

66. Employers use several types of statistics in addressing adverse impact. [For a discussion, see Robert Gatewood and Hubert Feild, *Human Resource Selection* (Fort Worth, TX: The Dryden Press, 1994), pp. 40–42, and Jean Phillips and Stanley Gulley, *Strategic Staffing* (Upper Saddle River, NJ: Pearson, 2012), pp. 68–69.] For example, *stock statistics* might compare *at a single point in time* (1) the percentage of female engineers the company has, as a percentage of its total number of engineers, with (2) the number of trained female engineers in the labor force as a percentage of the total number of trained engineers in the labor force. Here, the question of relevant labor market is important. For example, the relevant labor market if you're hiring unskilled assemblers might be the local labor market within, say, 20 miles from your plant, whereas the relevant labor market for highly skilled engineers might well be national and possibly international. *Flow statistics* measure proportions of employees, in particular, groups at two points in time: before selection and after selection takes place. For example, when comparing the percentage of minority applicants who applied with the percentage hired, the employer is using flow statistics. An employer's company-wide minority hiring statistics may be defensible company-wide but not departmentally. The employer therefore may employ *concentration statistics* to drill down and determine the concentration of minorities versus nonminorities in particular job categories.

67. One study found that using the 4/5ths rule often resulted in false-positive ratings of adverse impact, and that incorporating tests of statistical significance could improve the accuracy of applying the 4/5ths rule. See Philip Roth, Philip Bobko, and Fred Switzer, "Modeling the Behavior of the 4/5ths Rule for Determining Adverse Impact: Reasons for Caution," *Journal of Applied Psychology* 91, no. 3 (2006), pp. 507–522.

68. The results must be realistic. In this example, hiring 2 out of 5 women suggests there is no adverse impact. But suppose we had hired only one woman? Then the difference between those we would be expected to hire (5) and whom we actually hired (1) would rise to 4. Hiring just one less woman might then trigger adverse impact issues, because twice the standard deviation is also about 4. However, realistically, it probably would not trigger such concerns, because with such small numbers, one person makes such a difference. The point is that tools like the 4/5ths rule and the standard deviation rule are only rules of thumb. They do not themselves determine if the employer's screening process is discriminatory. This fact may work both for and against the employer. As the Uniform Guidelines (www.uniformguidelines.com/qandaprint.html) put it, "Regardless of the amount of difference in selection rates, unlawful discrimination may be present, and may be demonstrated through appropriate evidence . . ."

69. The ADEA does not just protect against intentional discrimination (disparate treatment). Under a Supreme Court decision (*Smith v. Jackson,* Miss., 2005), it also covers employer practices that seem neutral but that actually bear more heavily on older workers (disparate impact). "Employees Need Not Show Intentional Bias to Bring Claims Under ADEA, High Court Says," *BNA Bulletin to Management* 56, no. 14 (April 5, 2005), p. 105.

70. The Fair Treatment for Experienced Pilots Act raised commercial pilots' mandatory retirement age from 60 to 65 in 2008. Allen Smith, "Congress Gives Older Pilots a Reprieve," *HR Magazine,* February 2008, p. 24.

71. *Usery v. Tamiami Trail Tours,* 12FEP cases 1233.

72. Alternatively, an employer faced with an age discrimination claim may raise the FOA (factors other than age) defense. Here, it argues that its actions were "reasonable" based on some factor other than age, such as the terminated person's poor performance.

73. Ledvinka, *Federal Regulation.*

74. www.foxnews.com/story/0,2933,517334,00.html, accessed January 7, 2010.

75. Howard Anderson and Michael Levin-Epstein, *Primer of Equal Employment Opportunity* (Washington, DC: The Bureau of National Affairs, 1982), pp. 13–14.

76. *U.S. v. Bethlehem Steel Company,* 3FEP cases 589.

77. *Robinson v. Lorillard Corporation,* 3FEP cases 653.

78. *Spurlock v. United Airlines,* 5FEP cases 17.

79. Anderson and Levin-Epstein, *Primer of Equal Employment Opportunity,* p. 14.

80. This isn't ironclad, however. For example, the U.S. Supreme Court, in *Stotts,* held that a court cannot require retention of black employees hired under a court's consent decree in preference to higher-seniority white employees who were protected by a bona fide seniority system. It's unclear whether this decision also extends to personnel decisions not governed by seniority systems. *Firefighters Local 1784 v. Stotts* (BNA, April 14, 1985).

81. Ledvinka and Gatewood, "EEO Issues with Preemployment Inquiries," pp. 22–26.

82. Ibid.

83. "Eighth Circuit OKs $3.4 Million EEOC Verdict Relating to Pre-Hire Strength Testing Rules," *BNA Bulletin to Management,* November 28, 2006, p. 377.

84. Svetlana Shkolnikova, "Weight Discrimination Could Be as Common as Racial Bias," www.usatoday.com/news/ health/weightloss/2008-05-20-overweight-bias_N.htm, accessed January 21, 2009.

85. Jenessa Shapiro et al., "Expectations of Obese Trainees: How Stigmatized Trainee

Characteristics Influence Training Effectiveness," *Journal of Applied Psychology* 92, no. 1 (2007), pp. 239–249. See also Lisa Finkelstein et al., "Bias Against Overweight Job Applicants: Further Explanations of When and Why," *Human Resource Management* 46, no. 2 (Summer 2007), pp. 203–222.

86. T. A. Judge and D. M. Cable, "When It Comes to Pay, Do the Thin Win? The Effect of Weight on Pay for Men and Women," *Journal of Applied Psychology,* January 2011.

87. "EEOC Weighs Guidance on Use of Criminal Records in Hiring," *BNA Bulletin to Management,* November 20, 2008, p. 383.

88. See, for example, www.eeoc.gov/policy/docs/guidance-inquiries.html, accessed June 28, 2009.

89. This is based on *BNA Fair Employment Practices*, April 13, 1989, pp. 45–47; and "Crossed: When Religion and Dress Code Policies Intersect," http://www.mcguirewoods.com/news-resources/item.asp?item=3108, accessed October 2, 2011.

90. Eric Matusewitch, "Tailor Your Dress Codes," *Personnel Journal* 68, no. 2 (February 1989), pp. 86–91; Matthew Miklave, "Sorting Out a Claim of Bias," *Workforce* 80, no. 6 (June 2001), pp. 102–103, and "Laws and Cases Affecting Appearance," http://www.boardmanlawfirm.com/perspectives_articles/appearance.php, accessed September 8, 2011.

91. Rita Pyrillis, "Body of Work," *Workforce Management,* November 7, 2010, pp. 20–26.

92. Kenneth Sovereign, *Personnel Law,* 4th edition (Upper Saddle River, NJ: Prentice Hall, 1999), p. 220.

93. www.eeoc.gov/laws/types/retaliation.cfm, accessed August 19, 2011.

94. Adam Liptak, "Fiancés Firing Is Ruled an Illegal Reaction to a Discrimination Claim," *The New York Times,* January 25, 2011, p. A16.

95. Prudent employers often purchase employment practices liability insurance to insure against some or all of the expenses involved with defending against discrimination, sexual harassment, and wrongful termination–type claims. Antone Melton-Meaux, "Maximizing Employment Practices Liability Insurance Coverage," *Compensation & Benefits Review,* May/June 2008, pp. 55–59.

96. Litigants must watch the clock. In an equal pay decision, the U.S. Supreme Court held (in *Ledbetter v. Goodyear Tire & Rubber Company*) that the employee must file a complaint within 180 (or 300) days of the employer's decision to pay the allegedly unfair wage. The clock starts with that first pay decision, not with the subsequent paychecks that the employee receives. "Justices Rule 5–4 Claim-Filing Period Applies to Pay Decision, Not Subsequent Paycheck," *BNA Bulletin to Management* 58, no. 23 (June 5, 2007), pp. 177–184.

97. In 2007, the U.S. Supreme Court, in *Ledbetter v. Goodyear Tire & Rubber Company,* held that employees claiming Title VII pay discrimination must file their claims within 180 days of when they first receive the allegedly discriminatory pay. As of 2009, Congress was working to formulate new legislation enabling employees to file claims anytime, as long as the person was still receiving an "infected" paycheck.

98. http://eeoc.gov/eeoc/statistics/enforcement/charges.cfm, accessed May 20, 2010.

99. If the charge was filed initially with a state or local agency within 180 days after the alleged unlawful practice occurred, the charge may then be filed with the EEOC within 30 days after the practice occurred or within 30 days after the person received notice that the state or local agency has ended its proceedings.

100. www.eeoc.gov/mediate/facts.html, accessed June 29, 2009.

101. "EEOC's New Nationwide Mediation Plan Offers Option of Informal Settlements," *BNA Fair Employment Practices,* February 18, 1999, p. 21; and http://www.eeoc.gov/employees/mediation.cf, accessed October 2, 2011.

102. Timothy Bland, "Sealed Without a Kiss," *HR Magazine,* October 2000, pp. 85–92.

103. Stuart Bompey and Michael Pappas, "Is There a Better Way? Compulsory Arbitration of Employment Discrimination Claims After Gilmer," *Employee Relations Law Journal* 19, no. 3 (Winter 1993–1994), pp. 197–216, and http://www.eeoc.gov/policy/docs/mandarb.html, accessed September 5, 2011. The EEOC says here for instance that "the employer imposing mandatory arbitration is free to manipulate the arbitral mechanism to its benefit".

104. See Bompey and Pappas, pp. 210–211.

105. David Nye, "When the Fired Fight Back," *Across-the-Board,* June 1995, pp. 31–34, and http://www.eeoc.gov/federal/fed_employees/adr.cfm, accessed October 3, 2011.

106. "EEOC Opposes Mandatory Arbitration," *BNA Fair Employment Practices,* July 24, 1997, p. 85; and http://www.eeoc.gov/employees/mediation.cfm, accessed October 2, 2011.

107. See, for example, "Diversity Is Used as Business Advantage by Three Fourths of Companies, Survey Says," *BNA Bulletin to Management,* November 7, 2006, p. 355, and Claire Armstrong et al., "The Impact of Diversity and Equality Management on Firm Performance: Beyond High Performance Work Systems," *Human Resource Management* 49, no. 6 (November–December 2010), pp. 977–998.

108. Brian O'Leary and Bart Weathington, "Beyond the Business Case for Diversity in Organizations," *Employee Responsibilities and Rights* 18, no. 4 (December 2006), pp. 283–292.

109. See, for example, Michael Carrell and Everett Mann, "Defining Work-Force Diversity in Public Sector Organizations," *Public Personnel Management* 24, no. 1 (Spring 1995), pp. 99–111; Richard Koonce, "Redefining Diversity," *Training and Development Journal,* December 2001, pp. 22–33; Kathryn Canas and Harris Sondak, *Opportunities and Challenges of Workplace Diversity* (Upper Saddle River, NJ: Pearson, 2008), pp. 3–27. Others list race and ethnicity diversity, gender diversity, age diversity, disability diversity, sexual diversity, and cultural and national origin diversity as examples. Lynn Shore et al., "Diversity in Organizations: Where Are We Now and Where Are We Going?" *Human Resource Management Review,* 19 (2009), pp. 117–133.

110. Taylor Cox, Jr., *Cultural Diversity in Organizations* (San Francisco, CA: Berrett Kohler Publishers, Inc., 1993), p. 88; also see Stefanie Johnson, et al., "The strong, sensitive type: Effects of gender stereotypes and leadership prototypes on the evaluation of male and female leaders," *Organizational Behavior and Human Decision Processes* 106, no. 1 (May 2008), pp. 39–60.

111. Cox., p. 64.

112. "Workplace Bias Against Muslims Increasingly a Concern for Employers," *BNA Bulletin to Management,* October 26, 2010, p. 337.

113. Cox, *Cultural Diversity in Organizations,* pp. 179–80.

114. J. H. Greenhaus and S. Parasuraman, "Job Performance Attributions and Career Advancement Prospects: An Examination of Gender and Race Affects," *Organizational Behavior and Human Decision Processes* 55 (July 1993), pp. 273–298. Much research here focuses on how ethnocentrism prompts consumers to avoid certain products based on their country of origin. See for example, T.S. Chan, et al., "How Consumer Ethnocentrism and Animosity Impair the Economic Recovery of Emerging Markets." *Journal of Global Marketing* 23, no. 3 (July/August 2010), pp. 208–25.

115. Patrick McKay et al., "A Tale of Two Climates: Diversity Climate from Subordinates and Managers Perspectives and Their Role in Store Unit Sales Performance," *Personnel Psychology* 62 (2009), pp. 767–791.

116. Maria del Carmen Triana, Maria Fernandez Garcia, and Adrian Colella, "Managing Diversity: How Organizational Efforts to Support Diversity Moderate the Effects of Perceived Racial Discrimination on Affective Commitment," *Personnel Psychology* 63 (2010), pp. 817–843.

117. David Thomas, "Diversity as Strategy," *Harvard Business Review,* September 2004, pp. 98–104; see also J. T. Childs Jr., "Managing Global Diversity at IBM: A Global HR Topic that Has Arrived," *Human Resource Management* 44, no. 1 (Spring 2005), pp. 73–77.

118. Ibid., p. 99.

119. As another example, leaders who facilitated high levels of power sharing within their groups helped to reduce the frequently

observed positive relationship between increased diversity and increase turnover. But leaders who were inclusive of only a select few followers "may actually exacerbate the relationship between diversity and turnover" (p. 1422). Lisa Nishii and David Mayer, "Do Inclusive Leaders Help to Reduce Turnover in Diverse Groups? The Moderating Role of Leader—Member Exchange in the Diversity to Turn Over Relationship," *Journal of Applied Psychology* 94, no. 6 (2009), pp. 1412–1426.

120. Patricia Digh, "Creating a New Balance Sheet: The Need for Better Diversity Metrics," *Mosaics*, Society for Human Resource Management, September/October 1999, p. 1. For diversity management steps see Taylor Cox, Jr., *Cultural Diversity in Organizations: Theory, Research and Practice* (San Francisco: Berrett-Koehler, 1993), p. 236; see also Richard Bucher, *Diversity Consciousness* (Upper Saddle River, NJ: Pearson Prentice Hall, 2004), pp. 109–137.

121. Faye Cocchiara et al., "A Gem for Increasing the Effectiveness of Diversity Training," *Human Resource Management* 49, no. 6 (November–December 2010), pp. 1089–1106.

122. Richard Bucher, *Diversity Consciousness: Opening Our Minds to People, Cultures, and Opportunities* (Upper Saddle River, NJ: Pearson Prentice Hall, 2004), pp. 132–133.

123. Ibid., p. 133

124. David Harrison et al., "Understanding Attitudes Toward Affirmative Action Programs in Employment: Summary and Meta-Analysis of 35 Years of Research," *Journal of Applied Psychology* 91, no. 5 (2006), pp. 1013–1036; and Margaret Fiester et al., "Affirmative Action, Stock Options, I-9 Documents," *HR Magazine*, November 2007, p. 31.

125. David Harrison et al., "Understanding Attitudes Toward Affirmative Action Programs in Employment: Summary and Meta-Analysis of 35 Years of Research," *Journal of Applied Psychology* 91, no. 5 (2006), pp. 1013–1036.

126. Bill Leonard, "Ways to Tell if a Diversity Program Is Measuring Up," *HR Magazine*, July 2002, p. 21; and Ye Yang Zheng and Brenda White, "The Evaluation of a Diversity Program at an Academic Library," *Library Philosophy and Practice* 2007, http://unllib.unl.edu/LPP/yang.pdf, accessed October 2, 2011.

127. "Lawyers, Scholars Differ on Likely Impact of Affirmative Action Rulings on Workplace," *BNA Fair Employment Practices*, July 3, 2003, pp. 79–80.

128. http://newsfeedresearcher.com/data/articles_n17/tests-city-court.html, accessed April 24, 2009.

129. Adam Liptak, "Supreme Court Finds Bias Against White Firefighters," *The New York Times*, June 30, 2009, pp. A1, A13.

130. Ibid., p. 560.

3

Human Resource Management Strategy and Analysis

LEARNING OBJECTIVES

1. Explain why strategic planning is important to all managers.

2. Explain with examples each of the seven steps in the strategic planning process.

3. List with examples the main generic types of corporate strategies and competitive strategies.

4. Define strategic human resource management and give an example of strategic human resource management in practice.

5. Briefly describe three important strategic human resource management tools.

6. Explain with examples why metrics are important for managing human resources.

Several years ago, the Ritz-Carlton Company took over managing the Portman Hotel in Shanghai China. The new management reviewed the Portman's strengths and weaknesses, and its fast-improving local competitors. They decided that to be more competitive, they had to significantly improve the hotel's level of service. Achieving that aim in turn meant formulating secondary plans, particularly human resource management plans, for hiring, training, and rewarding hotel employees. It meant putting in place a new human resource strategy for the Portman Hotel, one aimed at improving customer service.

Access a host of interactive learning aids at **www.mymanagementlab.com** to help strengthen your understanding of the chapter concepts.

WHERE ARE WE NOW . . .

The next part of this book, Part 2, turns to the nuts and bolts of human resource management, topics such as analyzing jobs, and recruiting and selecting employees. But as at Shanghai's Portman Hotel, managers should know what they want to accomplish strategically before formulating and putting in place specific human resource management policies and practices. Therefore the main purpose of this chapter is to explain how managers formulate human resource strategies for their companies. The chapter addresses the strategic management process, strategic human resource management, human resource metrics and analysis, and building high-performance work systems.

1 Explain why strategic planning is important to all managers.

THE STRATEGIC MANAGEMENT PROCESS

As in the following Strategic Context feature, we can use the Shanghai Portman example to get a bird's eye view of the strategic human resource management process.

THE STRATEGIC CONTEXT

The Shanghai Portman Hotel

In Chapter 1, we said that *strategic human resource management* means formulating and executing human resource policies and practices that produce the employee competencies and behaviors the company needs to achieve its strategic aims. At the Shanghai Portman, the strategic human resource management process involved taking these steps:

- *Strategically*, they set the goal of making the Shanghai Portman outstanding by offering superior customer service.

- To achieve this, Shanghai Portman employees would have to exhibit new *skills and behaviors*, for instance, in terms of how they treated and responded to guests.

- To produce these employee skills and behaviors, management formulated new human resource management plans and policies. For example, they introduced the Ritz-Carlton Company's *human resource system* to the Portman. Thus, the hotel's new head and his managers personally interviewed each job candidate. They probed each candidate's values, selecting only employees who cared for and respected others: "Our selection focuses on talent and personal values because these are things that can't be taught . . . it's about caring for and respecting others."[1]

Management's efforts paid off. Their new human resource plans and practices produced the employee behaviors required to improve the Portman's level of service, thus attracting new guests. Travel publications were soon calling it the "best employer in Asia," "overall best business hotel in Asia," and "best business hotel in China." Profits soared, in no small part due to effective strategic human resource management.

In this chapter we look more closely at how managers formulate and implement plans, and how they analyze and evaluate their results. We will start with some basic planning-related definitions.

Goal-Setting and the Planning Process

Whether the manager is planning to boost a hotel's profitability or something more mundane, the basic *planning process* is the same. It involves setting objectives, making basic planning forecasts, reviewing alternative courses of action, evaluating which options are best, and then choosing and implementing your plan. A *plan* shows the course of action for getting from where you are to where you want to go—in other words, to the goal. *Planning* is always "goal-directed" (in this case, "to improve the hotel's level of service significantly").

THE HIERARCHY OF GOALS   In companies, it is traditional to view the goals from the top of the firm down to front-line employees as a chain or *hierarchy of goals*. Figure 3-1 illustrates this. At the top, the president sets long term or "strategic" goals (such as "Double sales revenue to $16 million in fiscal year 2011"). His or her vice presidents then set goals, such as "add one production line at plant," which flow from and make sense in terms of accomplishing the president's goal. (In other words, "What must I as production head do to help make sure that the company accomplishes its 'double sales' goal?") Then the vice presidents' subordinates set their own goals, and so on down the chain of command. The planning process thus traditionally starts with formulating top-level, long-term strategic plans and goals.

FIGURE 3-1 Sample Hierarchy of Goals Diagram for a Company

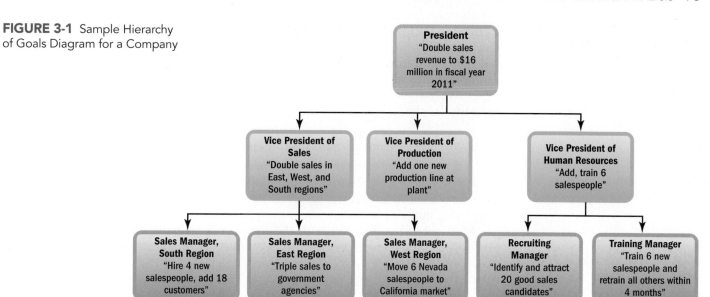

Strategic Planning

A **strategic plan** is the company's plan for how it will match its internal strengths and weaknesses with external opportunities and threats in order to maintain a competitive advantage. The essence of strategic planning is to ask, "Where are we now as a business, where do we want to be, and how should we get there?" The manager then formulates specific (human resources and other) plans to take the company from where it is now to where he or she wants it to be. When Yahoo! tries to figure out whether to sell its search business to Microsoft, it's engaged in strategic planning. A **strategy** is a course of action. If Yahoo! decides it must raise money and focus more on applications like Yahoo! Finance, one strategy might be to sell Yahoo! Search. **Strategic management** is the process of identifying and executing the organization's strategic plan, by matching the company's capabilities with the demands of its environment.

Figure 3-2 sums up the strategic management process. This process includes (1) defining the business and developing a mission, (2) evaluating the firm's internal and external strengths, weaknesses, opportunities, and threats, (3) formulating a new business direction, (4) translating the mission into strategic goals, and (5) formulating strategies or courses of action. Step (6) and step (7) entail implementing and then evaluating the strategic plan. Let's look at each step.

FIGURE 3-2 The Strategic Management Process

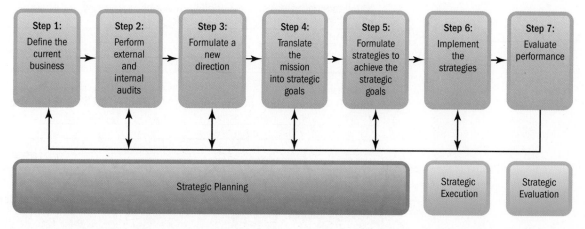

---

strategic plan
The company's plan for how it will match its internal strengths and weaknesses with external opportunities and threats in order to maintain a competitive advantage.

strategy
A course of action the company can pursue to achieve its strategic aims.

strategic management
The process of identifying and executing the organization's strategic plan, by matching the company's capabilities with the demands of its environment.

2 Explain with examples each of the seven steps in the strategic planning process.

STEP 1: DEFINE THE CURRENT BUSINESS   The logical place to start is by defining one's current business. Specifically, what products do we sell, where do we sell them, and how do our products or services differ from our competitor's. For example, Rolex and Casio both sell watches. However, Rolex sells a limited line of expensive watches. Casio sells a variety of relatively inexpensive but innovative specialty watches with features like compasses and altimeters.

STEP 2: PERFORM EXTERNAL AND INTERNAL AUDITS   The next step is to ask, "Are we heading in the right direction?" No one is immune to competitive pressures. Yahoo!'s search tool predominated until Google. Amazon's Kindle Reader forced even more bookstores to close. Prudent managers periodically assess what's happening in their environments.

Managers need to audit both the firm's environment, and the firm's strengths and weaknesses. The environmental scanning worksheet in Figure 3-3 is a simple

FIGURE 3-3 Worksheet for Environmental Scanning

Economic Trends
(such as recession, inflation, employment, monetary policies)

_____
_____
_____
_____

Competitive and Market Trends
(such as market/customer trends, entry/exit of competitors, new products from competitors)

_____
_____
_____
_____

Political Trends
(such as legislation and regulation/deregulation)

_____
_____
_____
_____

Technological Trends
(such as introduction of new production/distribution technologies, rate of product obsolescence, trends in availability of supplies and raw materials)

_____
_____
_____
_____

Social Trends
(such as demographic trends, mobility, education, evolving values)

_____
_____
_____
_____

Geographic Trends
(such as opening/closing of new markets, factors affecting current plant/office facilities location decisions)

_____
_____
_____
_____

FIGURE 3-4 SWOT Matrix, with Generic Examples

Potential Strengths
- Market leadership
- Strong research and development
- High-quality products
- Cost advantages
- Patents

Potential Opportunities
- New overseas markets
- Failing trade barriers
- Competitors failing
- Diversification
- Economy rebounding

Potential Weaknesses
- Large inventories
- Excess capacity for market
- Management turnover
- Weak market image
- Lack of management depth

Potential Threats
- Market saturation
- Threat of takeover
- Low-cost foreign competition
- Slower market growth
- Growing government regulation

guide for compiling relevant information about the company's environment. This includes the economic, competitive, and political trends that may affect the company. The SWOT chart in Figure 3-4 is the 800-pound gorilla of strategic planning; everyone uses it. Managers use it to compile and organize the company strengths, weaknesses, opportunities, and threats. The aim, of course, is to create a strategy that makes sense in terms of the company's strengths, weaknesses, opportunities, and threats.

STEP 3: FORMULATE A NEW DIRECTION   The question now is, based on the environmental scan and SWOT analysis, what should our new business be, in terms of what products we will sell, where we will sell them, and how our products or services will differ from competitors' products?

Managers sometimes formulate a vision statement to summarize how they see the essence of their business down the road. The **vision statement** is a general statement of the firm's intended direction; it shows, in broad terms, "what we want to become."[2] Rupert Murdoch, chairman of News Corporation (which owns the Fox network, and many newspapers and satellite TV businesses), built his company around a vision of an integrated, global satellite-based news-gathering, entertainment, and multimedia firm. PepsiCo's vision is "Performance with Purpose." PepsiCo CEO Indra Nooyi says the company's executives choose which businesses to be in based on Performance with Purposes' three pillars of human sustainability, environmental sustainability, and talent sustainability.[3]

Whereas vision statements usually describe in broad terms what the business should be, the company's **mission statement** summarizes what the company's main tasks are now. Several years ago, Ford adapted what was for several years a powerful mission for them—making "Quality Job One."

STEP 4: TRANSLATE THE MISSION INTO STRATEGIC GOALS   Next, translate the mission into strategic objectives. The company and its managers need strategic goals. At Ford, for example, what exactly did making "Quality Job One" mean for each department in terms of how they would boost quality? The answer is that its managers had to meet strict goals such as "no more than 1 initial defect per 10,000 cars."

vision statement
A general statement of the firm's intended direction that shows, in broad terms, "what we want to become."

mission statement
Summarizes the answer to the question, "What business are we in?"

STEP 5: FORMULATE STRATEGIES TO ACHIEVE THE STRATEGIC GOALS

Next, the manager chooses strategies—courses of action—that will enable the company to achieve its strategic goals. For example, what strategies could Ford pursue to hit its goal of no more than 1 initial defect per 10,000 cars? Perhaps open two new high-tech plants, reduce the number of car lines to better focus on just a few, and put in place new more rigorous employee selection, training, and performance appraisal procedures.

STEP 6: IMPLEMENT THE STRATEGIES   Strategy execution means translating the strategies into action. The company's managers do this by actually hiring (or firing) people, building (or closing) plants, and adding (or eliminating) products and product lines.

STEP 7: EVALUATE PERFORMANCE   Things don't always turn out as planned. For example, Ford bought Jaguar and Land Rover as a way to reduce reliance on lower-profit cars. With auto competition brutal, Ford announced in 2009 it was selling Jaguar and Land Rover (to Tata, a company in India). Ford wants to focus its scarce resources on modernizing and turning around its North American operations. Like all companies, Ford continually needs to assess its strategic decisions.

Improving Productivity Through HRIS

Using Computerized Business Planning Software

Business planning software packages are available to assist the manager in writing strategic plans. CheckMATE (www.chechmateplan.com) uses strategic planning tools such as SWOT analysis to enable even users with no prior planning experience to develop sophisticated strategic plans.4 Business Plan Pro from Palo Alto Software contains all the information and planning aids you need to create a business plan. It contains 30 sample plans, step-by-step instructions (with examples) for creating each part of a plan (executive summary, market analysis, and so on), financial planning spreadsheets, easy-to-use tables (for instance, for making sales forecasts), and programs for creating color 3-D charts for showing things like monthly sales and yearly profits.

Types of Strategies

In practice, managers formulate three strategies. There is *corporate-wide* strategic planning, business unit (or *competitive*) strategic planning, and *functional* (or departmental) strategic planning (see Figure 3-5). We'll look at each.

FIGURE 3-5 Type of Strategy at Each Company Level

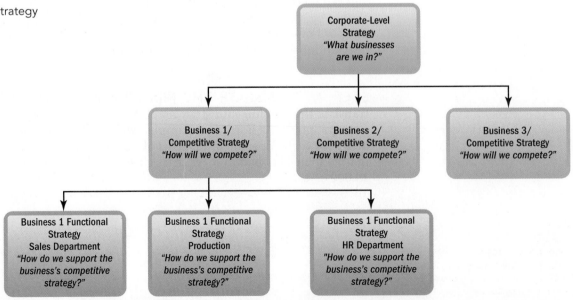

3 List with examples the main generic types of corporate strategies and competitive strategies.

CORPORATE STRATEGY The corporate strategy question is, "How many and what kind of businesses should we be in?" For example, PepsiCo doesn't just make Pepsi-Cola. Instead, PepsiCo is comprised of four main businesses: Frito-Lay North America, PepsiCo Beverages North America, PepsiCo International, and Quaker Oats North America.[5]

PepsiCo therefore needs a *corporate-level strategy*. A company's **corporate-level strategy** identifies the portfolio of businesses that, in total, comprise the company and how these businesses relate to each other.

- For example, with a *concentration* (single business) corporate strategy, the company offers one product or product line, usually in one market. WD-40 Company (which makes a spray hardware lubricant) is one example.

- A *diversification* corporate strategy implies that the firm will expand by adding new product lines. PepsiCo is diversified. Over the years, PepsiCo added chips and Quaker Oats. Such *related diversification* means diversifying so that a firm's lines of business still possess a logical fit. *Conglomerate diversification* means diversifying into products or markets not related to the firm's current businesses or to one another.

- A *vertical integration* strategy means the firm expands by, perhaps, producing its own raw materials, or selling its products direct. Thus, Apple opened its own Apple stores.

- With *consolidation* strategy, the company reduces its size.

- With *geographic expansion*, the company grows by entering new territorial markets, for instance, by taking the business abroad, as PepsiCo also did.

COMPETITIVE STRATEGY On what basis will each of our businesses compete? Each of these businesses (such as Frito-Lay) needs its own *business-level/competitive strategy*. A **competitive strategy** identifies how to build and strengthen the business's long-term competitive position in the marketplace.[6] It identifies, for instance, how Pizza Hut will compete with Papa John's or how Walmart competes with Target.

Managers endeavor to achieve competitive advantages for each of their businesses. We can define **competitive advantage** as any factors that allow a company to differentiate its product or service from those of its competitors to increase market share. Managers use several standard competitive strategies to achieve competitive advantage:

- *Cost leadership* means becoming the low-cost leader in an industry. Walmart is a classic example. It maintains its competitive advantage through its satellite-based distribution system, careful (usually suburban) site location, and expert control of purchasing and sales costs.

- *Differentiation* is a second possible competitive strategy. In a differentiation strategy, the firm seeks to be unique in its industry along dimensions that are widely valued by buyers.[7] Thus, Volvo stresses the safety of its cars, Papa John's stresses fresh ingredients, and Target stresses somewhat more upscale brands than Walmart. Like Mercedes-Benz, firms can usually charge a premium if they successfully stake a claim to being substantially different from competitors in some coveted way.

- *Focusers* carve out a market niche (like Ferrari). They compete by providing a product or service that their customers cannot get from their generalist competitors (such as Toyota).

HUMAN RESOURCES AS A COMPETITIVE ADVANTAGE A competitive advantage enables a company to differentiate its product or service from those of its competitors, but the competitive advantage needn't be tangible, such as

corporate-level strategy
Type of strategy that identifies the portfolio of businesses that, in total, comprise the company and the ways in which these businesses relate to each other.

competitive strategy
A strategy that identifies how to build and strengthen the business's long-term competitive position in the marketplace.

competitive advantage
Any factors that allow an organization to differentiate its product or service from those of its competitors to increase market share.

high-tech machines or satellite systems. *Bloomberg Businessweek* magazine recently described teams of empowered workers at a GE airfoils plant in Greenville, South Carolina. The teams run computer-controlled machine tools, interview prospective team members, and adjust assembly lines to maximize production.[8] For GE, the workers' skills and dedication are competitive advantages; they produce the quality and productivity that make GE an aerospace leader. Similarly, Apple's reputation for innovation reflects its competitive advantage in creative and brilliant engineers. Thus, the best competitive advantage is often "human capital"— knowledgeable, skilled, engaged employees working hard and with self-discipline.

FUNCTIONAL STRATEGY   Finally, what do our competitive choices (such as maintaining the lowest costs) mean for each of the departments that actually must do the work? Each individual business (like PepsiCo's Frito-Lay and Quaker Oats units) consists of departments such as manufacturing, sales, and human resource management. **Functional strategies** identify the broad guidelines that each department will follow in order to help the business accomplish its competitive goals. Each department's functional strategy should make sense in terms of the business/competitive strategy.

For example, the business's competitive strategy should mold the firm's human resource management policies and practices. As an example, the Portland hotel wants to differentiate itself with exceptional service, and so needs to select and train employees who are exceptionally customer oriented. Walmart's low cost competitive strategy translates into human resource management policies that many view as low-pay and antiunion.

STRATEGIC FIT   Strategic planning expert Michael Porter uses the term "strategic fit" to sum up the idea that each department's functional strategy should fit and support the company's competitive aims.

For example, Southwest Airlines is a low-cost leader. It aims to deliver low-cost, convenient service on its routes. To accomplish this, Southwest builds its departments' activities around supporting certain core aims. Southwest's core aims include limited passenger services (such as meals); short-haul, point-to-point service between mostly mid-size cities; high aircraft utilization; and lean highly productive ground crews. Achieving these aims means that each department's efforts needs to fit these aims. Southwest's ground crew department must get fast 15-minute turnarounds at the gate. That way, Southwest can keep its planes flying longer hours and have more departures with fewer aircraft. Its purchasing and marketing departments shun frills like meals and premium classes of service. To ensure highly productive ground crews, the HR department will provide high compensation, flexible union contracts, and employee stock ownership. Their aim is that:

$$\text{High Pay} \rightarrow \text{Highly Productive Ground Crews} \rightarrow \text{Frequent Departures} \rightarrow \text{Low Costs}$$

Top Managers' Roles in Strategic Planning

Devising a strategic plan is top management's responsibility. Top management must decide what businesses the company will be in and where, and on what basis it will compete. Southwest Airlines' top managers could never let lower-level managers make strategic decisions (such as unilaterally deciding that instead of emphasizing low cost, they were going to retrofit the planes with first-class cabins).

Departmental Managers' Strategic Planning Roles

However, the company's departmental managers (as for sales, manufacturing, and human resource management) also play roles in strategic planning. Specifically, they help the top managers *devise the strategic plan*; *formulate functional, departmental plans* that support the overall strategic plan; and then *execute the plans*. We'll look at each.

THEY HELP DEVISE THE STRATEGIC PLAN   It would be reckless for any top executive to formulate a strategic plan without the input of his or her lower-level managers. Few people know as much about the firm's competitive pressures, vendor capabilities, product and industry trends, and employee capabilities and concerns than do the company's department managers. So in practice, devising the strategic plan almost invariably involves frequent meetings and discussions among and between levels of managers. The top managers then lean heavily on the information from these interactions to hammer out their strategic plan.

For example, the human resource manager is in a good position to supply competitive intelligence. Details regarding competitors' incentive plans, employee opinion surveys that elicit information about customer complaints, and information about pending legislation such as labor laws are examples. And of course, human resource managers should be the masters of information about current employees' strengths and weaknesses. Input like this should all help win human resource managers a "seat at the (top management strategic planning) table." As other examples,

> From public information and legitimate recruiting and interview activities, you ought to be able to construct organization charts, staffing levels, and group missions for the various organizational components of each of your major competitors. Your knowledge of . . . who reports to whom can give important clues as to a competitor's strategic priorities. You may even know the track record and characteristic behavior of the executives.[9]

THEY FORMULATE SUPPORTING, FUNCTIONAL/DEPARTMENTAL STRATEGIES   Department managers also must translate the firm's strategic choices (such as becoming a low-cost leader) into functional strategies. For example, Walmart's cost leadership strategy means its purchasing department must pursue forcefully buying the lowest-cost goods it can find.

THEY EXECUTE THE PLANS   Whereas it would be reckless for top management to devise a plan without lower-level managers' advice, it is impossible for them to execute the plan without the company's other managers. Except in the tiniest of companies, no top manager could ever expect to do everything alone. With careful oversight, they therefore rely on their subordinate managers to do the planning, organizing, staffing, leading, and controlling that are required to execute the company's and each department's plans and goals.

Department Managers' Strategic Planning Roles in Action: Improving Mergers and Acquisitions

Mergers and acquisitions are among the most important strategic moves companies make. When mergers and acquisitions fail, it's often not due to financial or technical issues but to personnel-related ones. These may include, for example, employee resistance, mass exits by high-quality employees, and declining morale and productivity.[10] It's therefore ironic that, until relatively recently, human resource managers played limited roles in merger and acquisition (M&A) planning, according to a survey by

functional strategy
Strategy that identifies the broad activities that each department will pursue in order to help the business accomplish its competitive goals.

consultants Towers and Perrin. They tended to get involved only when management began integrating the two companies into one. By comparison, "close to two thirds of the [survey] participants are involved in M&A due diligence now."[11] How human resource managers assist top management with mergers illustrates how functional managers (and particularly human resource managers) can support the company's strategic aims.

DUE DILIGENCE STAGE   Before finalizing a deal, the merger partners usually perform "due diligence." These reviews assure they know what they're getting into. For the human resource team, due diligence includes reviewing things like employee compensation and benefits, labor relations, pending employee litigation, human resource policies and procedures, and key employees.[12] For example, do the target firm's health insurance contracts have termination clauses that could eliminate coverage for all employees if you lay off too many after the merger?[13]

INTEGRATION STAGE   Critical human resource issues during the first few months of a merger or acquisition include choosing the top management, communicating changes effectively to employees, and retaining key talent.[14] Several human resource consulting companies, such as Towers Perrin, assist firms with merger-related human resource management services. Their services help to illustrate human resource managers' roles in facilitating a merger.

- **Manage the deal costs.** Towers Perrin consultants identify and quantify people-related issues. These range from pension issues to redundancy costs and stock options.
- **Manage the messages.** "We support our clients in rapidly developing and deploying an employee communication strategy."
- **Secure the top team and key talent.** Towers Perrin helps clients to identify key talent, and then develop suitable retention strategies.
- **Define and implement an effective HR service delivery strategy.** Towers Perrin helps clients plan how to implement the delivery of HR services, such as in combining payroll systems.
- **Develop a workable change management plan.** "Especially in cross-border transactions, we assist companies in understanding and managing the cultural differences they face as part of the deal."
- **Design and implement the right staffing model.** Towers Perrin helps companies design the organization structure and determine which employee is best for which role.
- **Aligning total rewards.** "When integration [of pay plans] is desirable, we help companies' benchmarking and integration of compensation and benefit programs."[15]

4 Define strategic human resource management and give an example of strategic human resource management in practice.

STRATEGIC HUMAN RESOURCE MANAGEMENT

We've seen that once a company decides how it will compete, it turns to formulating functional departmental strategies to support its competitive aims. One of those departments is human resource management. Its functional strategies are *human resource management strategies.*

Defining Strategic Human Resource Management

Every company needs its human resource management policies and activities to make sense in terms of its broad strategic aims. **Strategic human resource management** means formulating and executing human resource policies and practices that

FIGURE 3-6 Linking Company-Wide and HR Strategies

Source: © Gary Dessler, Ph.D., 2010.

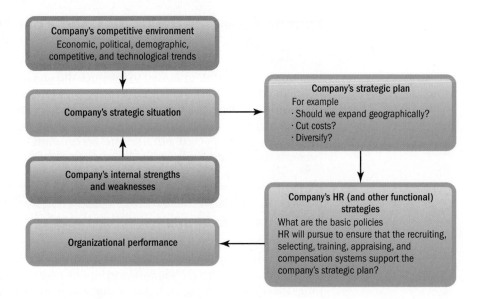

produce the employee competencies and behaviors the company needs to achieve its strategic aims. Figure 3-6 shows the link between human resource strategy and the company's strategic plans.

The basic idea behind strategic human resource management is this: In formulating human resource management policies and activities, the aim must be to produce the employee skills and behaviors that the company needs to achieve its strategic goals.

Figure 3-7 graphically outlines this idea. Management formulates a *strategic plan* and measurable strategic goals or aims. These plans and aims imply certain *workforce requirements,* in terms of the employee skills and behaviors required to achieve the firm's strategic aims. Given these workforce requirements, human resource management formulates *HR strategies (policies and practices)* to produce the desired workforce skills, competencies, and behaviors.

FIGURE 3-7 The Practices Behaviors Strategy Pyramid

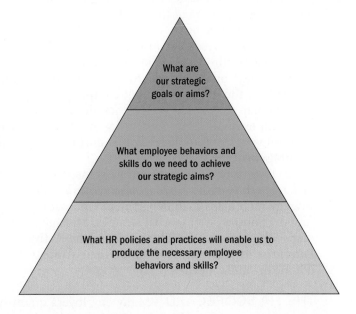

strategic human resource management
Formulating and executing human resource policies and practices that produce the employee competencies and behaviors the company needs to achieve its strategic aims.

Human Resource Strategies and Policies

Managers call the specific human resource management policies and practices they use to support their strategic aims *human resource strategies*.[16] The Shanghai Portman's human resource strategy aimed to produce the service-oriented employee behaviors the hotel needed to improve significantly the hotel's level of service. Its HR policies included installing the Ritz-Carlton Company's human resource system, having top management personally interview each candidate, and selecting only employees who cared for and respected others. The accompanying HR as a Profit Center feature presents another example.

HR AS A PROFIT CENTER

Albertsons Example

Several years ago, Albertsons Markets had to improve performance, and fast. With 2,500 stores and 230,000 workers, it faced competition not only from grocery chains, but also from Walmart and online sites. Albertsons' overall strategic aims included reducing costs, maximizing financial returns, becoming more customer-focused, and energizing employees. Albertsons turned to its human resource managers to help achieve these strategic aims. Its new human resource strategy entailed new screening, training, pay, and other human resources policies and practices, and using more technology to reduce its HR activities' costs.[17] The Albertsons human resource team's efforts helped Albertsons to cut costs, and to boost customer service by hiring and motivating customer-focused applicants.

| 5 | Briefly describe three important strategic human resource management tools. |

Strategic Human Resource Management Tools

Managers use several tools to translate the company's broad strategic goals into human resource management policies and activities. Three important tools include the strategy map, the HR Scorecard, and the digital dashboard.

STRATEGY MAP   The **strategy map** provides an overview of how each department's performance contributes to achieving the company's overall strategic goals. It helps the manager understand the role his or her department plays in helping to execute the company's strategic plan.

Figure 3-8 presents a strategy map example, in this case for Southwest Airlines. Recall that Southwest has a low-cost leader strategy. The strategy map for Southwest succinctly lays out the hierarchy of main activities required for Southwest Airlines to succeed. At the top is achieving company-wide, strategic financial goals. Then the strategy map shows the chain of activities that help Southwest Airlines achieve these goals. For example, as we saw earlier in this chapter, to boost revenues and profitability Southwest needs to fly fewer planes (to keep costs down), maintain low prices, and maintain on-time flights.

In turn (further down the strategy map), on-time flights and low prices require fast turnaround. And, fast turnaround requires motivated ground and flight crews. The strategy map helps each department (including HR) visualize what it needs to do to support Southwest's low-cost strategy. Managers can access their companies' strategy maps while on the go. They can use the ActiveStrategy Company's *ActiveStrategy Enterprise* to create and automate their strategy maps, and to access them through iPhone or similar devices.[18]

THE HR SCORECARD   Many employers quantify and computerize the strategy map's activities. The HR Scorecard helps them to do so. The **HR Scorecard** is not a scorecard. It refers to a process for *assigning financial and nonfinancial goals or metrics* to the human resource management–related chain of activities required for achieving the company's strategic aims.[19] (Metrics for Southwest might include airplane turnaround time, percent of on-time flights, and ground crew productivity.) Simply put, the idea is to take the strategy map and to quantify it.

FIGURE 3-8 Strategy Map for Southwest Airlines

Source: Based on TeamCHRYSALIS.com, accessed July 2006; http://mcknightkaney.com/Strategy_Maps_Primer.html, accessed August 3, 2011; http://www.strategymap.com.au/home/StrategyMapOverview.htm accessed August 3, 2011

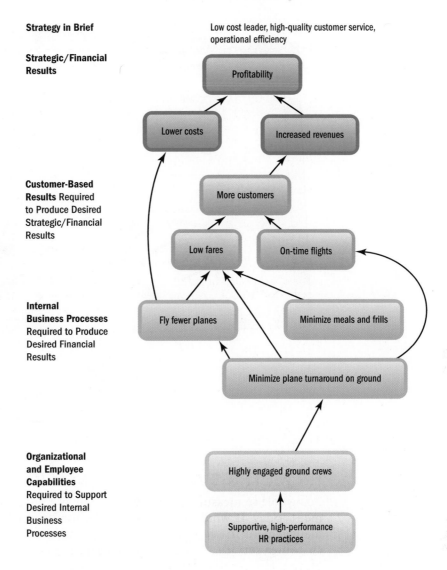

Strategy in Brief — Low cost leader, high-quality customer service, operational efficiency

Strategic/Financial Results — Profitability; Lower costs; Increased revenues

Customer-Based Results Required to Produce Desired Strategic/Financial Results — More customers; Low fares; On-time flights

Internal Business Processes Required to Produce Desired Financial Results — Fly fewer planes; Minimize meals and frills; Minimize plane turnaround on ground

Organizational and Employee Capabilities Required to Support Desired Internal Business Processes — Highly engaged ground crews; Supportive, high-performance HR practices

Managers use special scorecard software to facilitate this. The computerized scorecard process helps the manager quantify the relationships between (1) the HR activities (amount of testing, training, and so forth), (2) the resulting employee behaviors (customer service, for instance), and (3) the resulting firm-wide strategic outcomes and performance (such as customer satisfaction and profitability).[20]

DIGITAL DASHBOARDS   The saying "a picture is worth a thousand words" explains the purpose of the digital dashboard. A **digital dashboard** presents the manager with desktop graphs and charts, showing a computerized picture of how the company is doing on all the metrics from the HR Scorecard process. As in the illustration on the next page, a top Southwest Airlines manager's dashboard might display real-time trends for various strategy map activities. These might include fast turnaround, attracting and keeping customers, and on-time flights. This gives the manager time to take corrective action. For example, if ground crews are turning planes around slower today, financial results tomorrow may decline unless the manager takes action. Figure 3-9 summarizes the three strategic planning tools.

strategy map
A strategic planning tool that shows the "big picture" of how each department's performance contributes to achieving the company's overall strategic goals.

HR scorecard
A process for assigning financial and nonfinancial goals or metrics to the human resource management–related chain of activities required for achieving the company's strategic aims and for monitoring results.

digital dashboard
Presents the manager with desktop graphs and charts, and so a computerized picture of where the company stands on all those metrics from the HR Scorecard process.

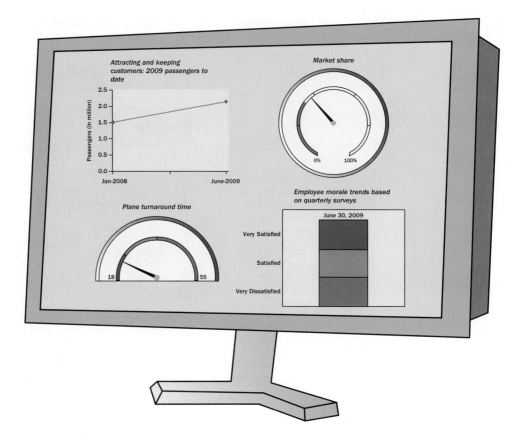

HR METRICS AND BENCHMARKING

Being able to measure what you are doing is a big part of human resource management today. It would have been futile, for instance, for the Portman Shanghai's management to set "better customer service" as a goal, if they couldn't measure customer service. Being able to measure what you are doing is an integral part of the HR strategy process. First, management translates its strategic plan into *workforce requirements*, in terms of measurable worker competencies and behaviors (such as outstanding service). Given these workforce requirements, the human resource manager then formulates supportive *HR strategies, policies, and practices (such as new training programs)*, intended to produce these workforce competencies.

Finally, the HR manager picks *measures* by which to gauge whether his or her new policies and practices are producing the required employee competencies and behaviors. At the Portman Shanghai, the measures might include, for instance, "hours of training per employee," "productivity per employee," and (via customer surveys) "customer satisfaction." The measures (or "metrics") you use may be broad organizational measures (such as return on investment, and profit margins). Or

FIGURE 3-9 Three Important Strategic HR Tools

Strategy Map	HR Scorecard	Digital Dashboard
Graphical tool that summarizes the chain of activities that contribute to a company's success, and so shows employees the "big picture" of how their performance contributes to achieving the company's overall strategic goals.	A process for managing employee performance and for aligning all employees with key objectives, by assigning financial and nonfinancial goals, monitoring and assessing performance, and quickly taking corrective action.	Presents the manager with desktop graphs and charts, so he or she gets a picture of where the company has been and where it's going, in terms of each activity in the strategy map.

they may focus narrowly on specific human resource management and activities (again, such as "hours of training per employee").[21] In any case, the bottom line is that measuring "how we're doing, and why" is important for managing one's human resources.

Types of Metrics

There are many measures that human resource managers use. For example, the HR-to-employee ratio averages about 1.12 HR employees per company employee for all employers. However, the ratio varies with employer size. For example, there is (on average) one human resource employee per 100 company employees for firms with 100–249 employees. The HR employee-to-employee ratio drops to about 0.79 for firms with 1,000–2,499 employees and to 0.72 for firms with more than 7,500 employees.[22]

Figure 3-10 illustrates more focused human resource management metrics. These include absence rate, cost per hire, and health care costs per employee.[23]

Improving Productivity Through HRIS

Tracking Applicant Metrics for Improved Talent Management

As an example of the benefits of using metrics, consider that most employers spend thousands of dollars (or more) each year recruiting employees, without measuring which hiring source produces the best candidates. The logical solution is to assess

---

Organizational Data
- Revenue
- Revenue per FTE
- Net Income Before Taxes
- Net Income Before Taxes per FTE
- Positions Included within the Organization's Succession Plan

HR Department Data
- Total HR Staff
- HR-to-Employee Ratio
- Percentage of HR Staff in Supervisory Roles
- Percentage of HR Staff in Professional/Technical Roles
- Percentage of HR Staff in Administrative Support Roles
- Reporting Structure for the Head of HR
- Types of HR Positions Organizations Expect to Hire in 2011

HR Expense Data
- HR Expenses
- HR Expense to Operating Expense Ratio
- HR Expense to FTE Ratio

Compensation Data
- Annual Salary Increase
- Salaries as a Percentage of Operating Expense
- Target Bonus for Non-Executives
- Target Bonus for Executives

Tuition/Education Data
- Maximum Reimbursement Allowed for Tuition/Education Expenses per Year
- Percentage of Employees Participating in Tuition/Education Reimbursement Programs

Employment Data
- Number of Positions Filled
- Time-to-Fill
- Cost-Per-Hire
- Employee Tenure
- Annual Overall Turnover Rate
- Annual Voluntary Turnover Rate
- Annual Involuntary Turnover Rate

Expectations for Revenue and Organizational Hiring
- Percentage of Organizations Expecting Changes in Revenue in 2011 compared to 2010
- Percentage of Organizations Expecting Changes in Hiring in 2011 compared to 2010

Metrics for More Profitable Organizations
- Total HR Staff
- HR-to-Employee Ratio
- HR Expenses
- HR Expense to Operating Expense Ratio
- HR Expense to FTE Ratio
- Annual Salary Increase
- Target Bonus for Non-Executives
- Target Bonus for Executives
- Maximum Reimbursement Allowed for Tuition/Education Expenses per Year
- Percentage of Employees Participating in Tuition/Education Reimbursement Programs
- Time-to-Fill
- Cost-Per-Hire
- Annual Overall Turnover Rate

FIGURE 3-10 Metrics for the SHRM® 2011–2012 Customized Human Capital Benchmarking Report

Source: Reprinted with permission from the Society for Human Resource Management. All rights reserved.

recruitment effectiveness, using measures or metrics. Metrics here might include "quality of new hires" and "which recruitment sources produce the most new hires."24

One way to track and analyze such data is by using an applicant tracking system (ATS). Many vendors provide ATSs. Vendors include specialized ATS vendors like Authoria, PeopleFilter, Wonderlic, eContinuum, and PeopleClick.

Regardless of the vendor, analyzing recruitment effectiveness using their software involves two basic steps.

- First, the employer (and vendor) decides how to measure the performance of new hires. For example, with Authoria's system, hiring managers input their evaluations of each new hire at the end of the employee's first 90 days, using a 1–5 scale.[25]

- Second, the applicant tracking system then enables the employer to track the recruitment sources that correlate with superior hires. It may show, for instance, that new employees hired through "employee referrals" stay longer and work better than those from newspaper ads do. Most applicant tracking systems enable hiring managers to track such hiring metrics on desktop dashboards.

Applicant tracking systems support an employer's talent management efforts in other ways. For example, installing an Authoria ATS enabled the Thomson Reuters Company to identify the sources, candidate traits, and best practices that work best in each geographic area where they do business.26 This in turn enabled them to reduce recruiting costs, for instance, by shifting recruitment dollars from less effective sources to ones that are more effective. Similarly, the ATS can also help hire better employees, for instance, by helping the employer see which applicant traits correlate with subsequent employee performance.

Benchmarking in Action

Measuring how one is doing (for instance in terms of employee turnover, or employee productivity) is rarely useful by itself. Instead, for a thorough analysis, you'll usually want to know "How are we doing?" in relation to something. That "something" may be historical company figures (for example, Are our accident rates going up or down?). Or, you will want to *benchmark* your results. *Benchmarking* means comparing the practices of high-performing companies to your own, in order to understand what they do that makes them better.[27]

SHRM provides a customized benchmarking service. This enables employers to compare their own HR-related metric results with those of other companies. SHRM's service provides benchmark figures for many industries. These include construction and mining, educational services, finance, manufacturing, and others. The employer can also request the comparable (benchmark) figures not just by industry, but broken down by employer size, company revenue, and geographic region. (See http://shrm.org/research/benchmarks/.)

Figure 3-11 illustrates one of the many sets of comparable benchmark measures you could obtain from SHRM's benchmark service. It shows how much employers are

FIGURE 3-11 SHRM Customized Human Capital Benchmarking Report

Tuition/Education Data					
	n	25th Percentile	Median	75th Percentile	Average
Maximum reimbursement allowed for tuition/ education expenses per year	32	$1,000	$5,000	$7,500	$6,000
Percentage of employees participating in tuition/ education reimbursement programs	32	1.0%	3.0%	5.0%	4.0%

Note: To ensure that the data are seen as credible, data for metrics with an "n" of less than 5 are not displayed.

spending on average for tuition reimbursement programs, and what percentage of employees typically participate in such programs.

Strategy and Strategy-Based Metrics

6 Explain with examples why metrics are important for managing human resources.

Benchmarking (comparing one firm's HR metrics with another's) only provides one way to look at how your company's human resource management system is performing.[28] It shows how your human resource management system's performance compares to the competition. It may *not* show the extent to which your firm's HR practices are helping your company to achieve its strategic goals. For example, if our strategy calls for doubling profits by improving customer service, to what extent are our new selection and training practices helping to improve customer service?

Managers use *strategy-based metrics* to answer that question. **Strategy-based metrics** are metrics that focus on measuring the activities that contribute to achieving a company's strategic aims.[29]

As an example:

- Let us say the owners of the "Paris International Hotel" decide to make their hotel one of the top 10 hotels in France.

- They believe doing so will translate into revenues and profits 50% higher than now.

- They decide that achieving those strategic aims requires improving customer service. They will measure customer service in terms of measures like *guest returns*, and *guest compliments* of employees.

- What can the hotel's human resource managers do to help achieve this improved customer service? They can take measurable steps to improve certain targeted HR practices, such as *increase training per year per employee* from 10 hours to 25, *boost incentive pay* (tied to guest service ratings) from zero now to 10% of total salaries, and move from no job candidates tested before hiring to *100% testing* prior to hiring.

- So, for the Paris Hotel, the strategic HR metrics would include (among others) 100% employee testing, 80% guest returns, incentive pay as a percent of total salaries, and sales up 50%. If changes in HR practices such as increased training and better incentives have their intended effects, then metrics like guest returns and guest compliments should also rise. And if so, the Paris Hotel should also achieve its strategic goal of being one of the top 10 hotels in France.

Workforce/Talent Analytics and Data Mining

Employers increasingly use workforce analytics (or "talent analytics") software applications to analyze their human resources data and to draw conclusions from it.[30] For example, a talent analytics team at Google analyzed data on employee backgrounds, capabilities, and performance. The team was able to identify the factors (such as an employee feeling underutilized) likely to lead to the employee leaving. In a similar project, Google analyzed data on things like employee survey feedback and performance management scores to identify the attributes of successful Google managers. Microsoft identified correlations among the schools and companies employees arrived from and the employee's subsequent performance. This enabled Microsoft to improve its recruitment and selection practices.[31] Software company SAS's employee retention program sifts through employee data on things like skills, tenure, performance, education, and friendships. The program can predict which high-value employees are more likely to quit in the near future.[32] Alliant Techsystems created a "flight risk model" to calculate the probability an employee would leave.

strategy-based metrics
Metrics that specifically focus on measuring the activities that contribute to achieving a company's strategic aims.

This enabled Alliant to predict unusually high turnover in one important group and to take corrective action.[33] IBM uses workforce analytics to identify employees who are "idea leaders" to whom other employees frequently turn for advice (for instance based on e-mail interactions and e-mail "mentions" by colleagues).

DATA MINING Such efforts usually employ data mining techniques. Data mining sifts through huge amounts of employee data to identify correlations that employers then use to improve their employee selection and other practices. *Data mining* is "the set of activities used to find new, hidden, or unexpected patterns in data."[34] Data mining systems use tools like statistical analysis to sift through data looking for relationships. Department stores often use data mining. For example, Macy's captures huge amounts of data on its customers—what they buy, when they buy it, how they pay for it, and what day of the week they tend to shop. Macy's can use data mining to make sense of it. For example, data mining reveals that some customers often come in to redeem "20% off" coupons they get in the mail. Other customers are more apt to buy new electronic gadgets with coupons than are others.

Thanks to data mining, the manager can discover patterns that he or she can then use to make predictions. He or she can answer questions such as "Which of our products would this customer be most likely to buy?" "Which of our customers are making too many returns?", and "What is the likelihood that this candidate will succeed here at Google?" The accompanying HR as a Profit Center presents other examples.

HR AS A PROFIT CENTER

Using Workforce/Talent Analytics

Talent analytics can produce striking profitability results. For example, Best Buy used talent analytics to determine that a 0.1% increase in employee engagement led to a more than $100,000 rise in a Best Buy store annual operating income.[35] Employers are using talent analytics to answer six types of talent management questions:[36]

Human capital facts. For example, "What are the key indicators of my organization's overall health?" JetBlue found that a key measure of employee engagement correlated with financial performance.

Analytical HR. For example, "Which units, departments, or individuals need attention?" Lockheed Martin collects performance data in order to identify areas needing improvement.

Human capital investment analysis. For example, "Which actions have the greatest impact on my business?" By monitoring employee satisfaction levels, Cisco was able to improve its employee retention rate from 65% to 85%, saving the company nearly $50 million in recruitment, selection, and training costs.

Workforce forecasts. For example, "How do I know when to staff up or cut back?" Dow Chemical uses a computerized model that predicts future required headcount for each business unit based on predictions for things like industry trends.

Talent value model. For example, "Why do employees choose to stay with—or leave—my company?" For example, Google was able to anticipate when an employee felt underutilized and was preparing to quit, thus reducing turnover costs.

Talent supply chain. For example, "How should my workforce needs adapt to changes in the business environment?" Thus, retail companies can use special analytical models to predict store volumes and release hourly employees early.

What Are HR Audits?

Human resource managers often collect data on matters such as employee turnover and safety with the help of *human resource audits*. One practitioner calls an **HR audit** "an analysis by which an organization measures where it currently stands and determines what it has to accomplish to improve its HR function."[37] Another calls it "a process of examining policies, procedures, documentation, systems, and practices with respect to an organization's HR functions."[38] In sum, the HR audit generally involves (1) reviewing the functioning of most aspects of the company's human resource function (recruiting, testing, training, and so on), usually using a checklist, as well as (2) ensuring that the employer is adhering to government regulations and company policies.

In conducting the HR audit, managers often benchmark—compare their results to those of comparable companies. Many private human resource management consulting firms (such as Mercer, www.mercer.com) offer such comparable data on a variety of HR activities. Sample activities include what other employers are paying and the ratio of HR professionals per company employee. We saw that the Society for Human Resource Management provides extensive benchmarking services. HR audits vary in scope and focus. As an example, typical broad areas to cover with the HR audit include:[39]

1. Roles and head count (including job descriptions, and employees by exempt/nonexempt and full/part-time status)
2. Legal issues (compliance with federal, state, local employment–related legislation)
3. Recruitment and selection (including selection tools, background checks, and so on)
4. Compensation (policies, incentives, survey procedures, and so on)
5. Employee relations (union agreements, performance management, disciplinary procedures, employee recognition)
6. Mandated benefits (social security, unemployment insurance, workers' compensation, and so on)
7. Group benefits (insurance, time off, flexible benefits, and so on)
8. Payroll (internal versus external payroll options, FLSA compliance)
9. Documentation and record keeping (HR information systems, personnel files, I-9 and other forms, and so on)
10. Training and development (new employee orientation, workforce development, technical and safety, career planning, and so on)
11. Employee communications (employee handbook, newsletter, recognition programs)
12. Internal communications (policies and procedures, and so on)
13. Termination and transition policies and practices

Drilling down to a finer level of analysis, here is what we might look for in several of these 13 items.

Item 9, Personnel Files Do our files contain information including résumés and applications, offer letters, job descriptions, performance evaluations, benefit enrollment forms, payroll change notices and/or documentation related to personnel actions, documents regarding performance issues, employee

---

HR audit
An analysis by which an organization measures where it currently stands and determines what it has to accomplish to improve its HR function.

handbook acknowledgments, I-9 forms, medical information (related to a medical leave of absence or FMLA leave), and workers' compensation information?[40]

Items 2 and 8, Wage and Hour Compliance Is our time record-keeping process in compliance with state and with federal law (for instance check-in/check-out no more than 3 minutes before starting/stopping work)? Do we conduct a random audit of timecards to ensure that practices are as they should be?[41]

Item 1, Headcount How many employees are currently on staff? How many employees of those on staff are currently

- Regular
- Probationary
- Temporary
- Full Time
- Part Time
- Exempt
- Non-Exempt[42]

Evidence-Based HR and the Scientific Way of Doing Things

In this chapter, we've seen that decision-making based on an objective review of the evidence is important for successful human resource management. Managers today strive to make decisions based on an analysis of the evidence. *Evidence-based human resource management* is the use of data, facts, analytics, scientific rigor, critical evaluation, and critically evaluated research/case studies to support human resource management proposals, decisions, practices, and conclusions.[43]

You may possibly sense that taking an evidence-based approach to making management decisions is similar to being scientific in how you do things, and if so, you are correct. A recent *Harvard Business Review* article even argues that managers must become more scientific and to "think like scientists" when making business decisions.[44]

HOW TO BE SCIENTIFIC   But how can managers do this? Two things are particularly important. First, in gathering evidence, scientists (or managers) need to be *objective*, or there's no way to trust their conclusions. For example, a medical school recently disciplined several of its professors. These doctors had failed to reveal that they were on the payroll of the drug company who supplied the drugs, the results of which the doctors were studying. Who could trust their objectivity—or their conclusions?

Being scientific also requires *experimentation*. An experiment is a test the manager sets up in such a way as to ensure (to the extent possible) that he or she understands the reasons for the results obtained. For example, in their *Harvard Business Review* article, "A Step-by-Step Guide to Smart Business Experiments," the authors argue that if you want to judge a new incentive plan's impact on corporate profits, don't start by implementing the plan with all employees. Instead, implement it with an "experimental" group (which gets the incentive plan), *and* with a "control" group (a group that does *not* get the incentive plan). Doing so will help you gauge if any performance improvement stemmed from the incentive or from some other cause (such as a new company-wide training program).[45]

If you've done a good job designing your business experiment, you should be able to use your results to explain and predict why, say, one plan succeeds and another fails. For example, you own a small business and a vendor suggests that you pay her $10,000 per year to use a personnel test to identify high-potential sales candidates. You conduct a study (we'll explain how in Chapter 5, Testing), using the test with some applicants but not with others. You conclude that by using that test you can *predict*, with high accuracy, which candidates will succeed. How many extra sales will that produce? You decide based on the evidence that the $10,000 would be well spent. Hopefully, your study will also help you *explain* your results, in other words to answer "Why." For example, "This test uncovers applicants who are highly self-confident, and that's a trait one needs to be a great salesperson in my business."

WHY SHOULD A MANAGER BE SCIENTIFIC?   For managers, the key point of being "scientific" is to make better decisions. The problem is that what's "intuitively obvious" can be misleading. "Does our expensive applicant testing program really produce better employees?" "Is this sales incentive plan really boosting sales?" "We've spent $40,000 in the past 5 years on our tuition-refund plan; what (if anything) did we get out of it?" What's the evidence?

EXAMPLES   Examples abound of human resource managers taking a scientific, evidence-based approach to making decisions. For example, an insurance firm was considering cutting costs by buying out senior underwriters, most of whom were earning very high salaries. But after analyzing the data, HR noticed that these underwriters also brought in a disproportionate share of the company's revenue. In fact, reviewing data on things such as employee salaries and productivity showed that it would be much more profitable to eliminate some low-pay call-center employees, replacing them with even less expensive employees. As another example, the chemical Company BASF Corp. analyzed data regarding the relationship among stress, health, and productivity in its 15,000 American headquarters staff. Based on that analysis, the company instituted health programs that it calculated would more than pay for themselves in increased productivity by reducing stress.[46]

Throughout this book we will show examples of how managers can use an evidence-based approach to making better human resource management decisions. For example, which recruitment source produces the best candidates for us? Does it pay to use this testing program? Should we raise salaries, or not? And, Does our safety program really result in fewer accidents?

WHAT ARE HIGH-PERFORMANCE WORK SYSTEMS?

One reason to measure, benchmark, and scientifically analyze human resource management practices is to identify and promote high-performance work practices. A **high-performance work system** is a set of human resource management policies and practices that together produce superior employee performance. As we saw in Chapter 1, one illustrative study looked at 17 manufacturing plants, some of which adopted high-performance work system practices. The high-performance plants paid more (median wages of $16 per hour compared with $13 per hour for all plants), trained more, used more sophisticated recruitment and hiring practices (tests and validated interviews, for instance), and used more self-managing work teams. These plants also had the best overall financial performance.[47] The bottom

high-performance work system
A set of human resource management policies and practices that promote organizational effectiveness.

TABLE 3-1 Comparison of HR Practices in High-Performance and Low-Performance Companies

Sample HR Practices	Low-Performance Company HR System Averages (Bottom 10%, 42 Firms)	High-Performance Company HR System Averages (Top 10%, 43 Firms)
Number of qualified applicants per position (*Recruiting*)	8.24	36.55
Percentage hired based on a validated *selection* test	4.26	29.67
Percentage of jobs *filled from within*	34.90	61.46
Number of hours of *training* for new employees (less than 1 year)	35.02	116.87
Number of hours of *training* for experienced employees	13.40	72.00
Percentage of employees receiving a regular *performance appraisal*	41.31	95.17
Percentage of workforce whose *merit increase* or *incentive pay* is tied to performance	23.36	87.27
Percentage of workforce who received *performance feedback* from multiple sources (360)	3.90	51.67
Target percentile for total compensation (market rate = 50%)	43.03	58.67
Percentage of the workforce eligible for *incentive pay*	27.83	83.56
Percentage of the workforce routinely working in a self-managed, *cross-functional,* or *project team*	10.64	42.28
Percentage of HR budget spent on *outsourced activities* (e.g., recruiting, benefits, payroll)	13.46	26.24
Number of employees per HR professional	253.88	139.51
Percentage of the eligible workforce covered by a union contract	30.00	8.98
Firm Performance		
Employee turnover	34.09	20.87
Sales per employee	$158,101	$617,576
Market value to book value	3.64	11.06

Source: Based on B. E. Becker, M. A. Huselid, and D. Ulrich, *The HR Scorecard: Linking People, Strategy and Performance* (Boston: Harvard Business School Press, 2001), pp. 16–17.

line is that, one way to improve performance is to design recruiting, selection, training, and other HR practices so that they produce superior employee performance—a high-performance work system.

High-Performance Human Resource Policies and Practices

What are these high-performance work practices? Studies show that high-performance work systems' human resource policies and practices do differ from less productive ones'. Table 3-1 illustrates this. For example, high-performing companies recruit more job candidates, use more selection tests, and spend many more hours training employees.

Table 3-1 illustrates four things.

First, it presents examples of human resource metrics. A **human resource metric** is a quantitative gauge of a human resource management activity such as employee turnover, hours of training per employee, or qualified applicants per position. (In Table 3-1, the metric for "Number of qualified applicants per position" is 36.55 in the high-performing companies.) Managers use such metrics to assess their companies' HR performance, and to compare one company's performance with another's.[48]

Second, Table 3-1 illustrates *the things employers must do* to have high-performance systems. For example, they hire based on validated selection tests. They fill more jobs from within. They organize work around self-managing teams. They extensively train employees.

Third, the table shows that high-performance work practices usually *aspire to help workers to manage themselves.* In other words, the point of such recruiting, screening, training, and other human resources practices is to foster an empowered, self-motivated, and flexible workforce.[49]

Fourth, Table 3-1 highlights *the measurable differences* between the human resource management systems in high-performance and low-performance companies. For example, high-performing companies have more than four times the number of qualified applicants per job than do low performers.

REVIEW

MyManagementLab   Now that you have finished this chapter, go back to **www.mymanagementlab.com** to continue practicing and applying the concepts you've learned.

CHAPTER SECTION SUMMARIES

1. **Strategic planning is important to all managers.** All managers' personnel and other decisions should be consistent with the goals that cascade down from the firm's overall strategic plan. Those goals form a hierarchy, starting with the president's overall strategic goals (such as double sales revenue to $16 million) and filtering down to what each individual manager needs to do in order to support that overall company goal.
2. Because each manager needs to make his or her decisions within the context of the company's plans, it's important for all managers to understand **management planning.** The management planning process includes setting an objective, making forecasts, determining what your alternatives are, evaluating your alternatives, and implementing and evaluating your plan.
3. Again, because all managers operate within the framework of their company's overall plans, it's important for all managers to be familiar with the **strategic management process.**
   • A strategic plan is the company's plan for how it will match its internal strengths and weaknesses with external opportunities and threats in order to maintain a competitive advantage. A strategy is a course of action.

• Strategic management is the process of identifying and executing the organization's strategic plan. Basic steps in the strategic management process include defining the current business, performing an external and internal audit, formulating a new direction, translating the mission into strategic goals, formulating strategies to achieve the strategic goals, implementing strategies, and evaluating performance.
• We distinguished among corporate-level, competitive-level, and functional strategies. Corporate strategies include, among others, diversification strategies, vertical integration, horizontal integration, geographic expansion, and consolidation. The main competitive strategies include cost leadership, differentiation, and focuser. Functional strategies reflect the specific departmental policies that are necessary for executing the business's competitive strategies.
• Department managers play an important role in strategic planning in terms of devising the strategic plan, formulating supporting functional/departmental strategies, and of course in executing the company's plans.

human resource metric
The quantitative gauge of a human resource management activity such as employee turnover, hours of training per employee, or qualified applicants per position.

4. Each function or department in the business needs its own functional strategy, and **strategic human resource management** means formulating and executing human resource policies and practices that produce the employee competencies and behaviors the company needs to achieve its strategic aims. Human resource strategies are the specific human resource management policies and practices managers use to support their strategic aims. The Shanghai Portman Hotel and Albertsons Markets are two examples of strategic human resource planning. Another is the use of HR consultants in improving mergers and acquisitions, for instance, with respect to managing the deal's costs, and aligning the total rewards necessary for the new entity. Important and popular strategic human resource management tools include the strategy map, the HR Scorecard, and digital dashboards.

5. The manager will want to **gather and analyze data** prior to making decisions. A high-performance work system is a set of human resource management policies and practices that promote organizational effectiveness. Human resource metrics (quantitative measures of some human resource management activities such as employee turnover) are critical in creating high-performance human resource policies and practices. This is because they enable managers to benchmark their own practices against those of successful organizations. A high-performance work system is a set of human resource management policies and practices that together produce superior employee performance.

DISCUSSION QUESTIONS

1. Give an example of hierarchical planning in an organization.
2. What is the difference between a strategy, a vision, and a mission? Give one example of each.
3. Define and give at least two examples of the cost leadership competitive strategy and the differentiation competitive strategy.
4. Explain how human resources management can be instrumental in helping a company create a competitive advantage.
5. What is a high-performance work system? Provide several specific examples of the typical components in a high-performance work system.

INDIVIDUAL AND GROUP ACTIVITIES

1. With three or four other students, form a strategic management group for your college or university. Your assignment is to develop the outline of a strategic plan for the college or university. This should include such things as mission and vision statements; strategic goals; and corporate, competitive, and functional strategies. In preparing your plan, make sure to show the main strengths, weaknesses, opportunities, and threats the college faces, and which prompted you to develop your particular strategic plans.
2. Using the Internet or library resources, analyze the annual reports of five companies. Bring to class examples of how those companies say they are using their HR processes to help the company achieve its strategic goals.
3. Interview an HR manager and write a short report on "The Strategic Roles of the HR Manager at XYZ Company."
4. Using the Internet or library resources, bring to class and discuss at least two examples of how companies are using an HR Scorecard to help create HR systems that support the company's strategic aims. Do all managers seem to mean the same thing when they refer to HR Scorecards? How do they differ?
5. In teams of 4–5 students, choose a company for which you will develop an outline of a strategic HR plan. What seem to be this company's main strategic aims? What is the firm's competitive strategy? What would the strategic map for this company look like? How would you summarize your recommended strategic HR policies for this company?
6. The HRCI "Test Specifications" appendix at the end of this book (pages 633–640) lists the things someone studying for the HRCI certification exam needs to know in each area of human resource management (such as in Strategic Management, Workforce Planning, and Human Resource Development). In groups of four to five students, do four things: (1) review that appendix now; (2) identify the material in this chapter that relates to the required knowledge the appendix lists; (3) write four multiple-choice exam questions on this material that you believe would be suitable for inclusion in the HRCI exam; and (4) if time permits, have someone from your team post your team's questions in front of the class, so the students in other teams can take each others' exam questions.

EXPERIENTIAL EXERCISE

Developing an HR Strategy for Starbucks

By 2010, Starbucks was facing serious challenges. Sales per store were stagnant or declining, and its growth rate and profitability were down. Many believed that its introduction of breakfast foods had diverted its "baristas" from their traditional jobs as coffee-preparation experts. McDonald's and Dunkin Donuts were introducing lower priced but still high-grade coffees. Starbucks' former CEO stepped back into the company's top job. You need to help him formulate a new direction for his company.

Purpose: The purpose of this exercise is to give you experience in developing an HR strategy, in this case, by developing one for Starbucks.

Required Understanding: You should be thoroughly familiar with the material in this chapter.

How to Set Up the Exercise/Instructions: Set up groups of three or four students for this exercise. You are probably already quite familiar with what it's like to have a cup of coffee or tea in a Starbucks coffee shop, but if not, spend some time in one prior to this exercise. Meet in groups and develop an outline for an HR strategy for Starbucks Corp. Your outline should include four basic elements: a basic business/competitive strategy for Starbucks, workforce requirements (in terms of employee competencies and behaviors) this strategy requires, specific HR policies and the activities necessary to produce these workforce requirements, and suggestions for metrics to measure the success of the HR strategy.

APPLICATION CASE

SIEMENS BUILDS A STRATEGY-ORIENTED HR SYSTEM

Siemens is a 150-year-old German company, but it's not the company it was even a few years ago. Until recently, Siemens focused on producing electrical products. Today the firm has diversified into software, engineering, and services. It is also global, with more than 400,000 employees working in 190 countries. In other words, Siemens became a world leader by pursuing a corporate strategy that emphasized diversifying into high-tech products and services, and doing so on a global basis.

With a corporate strategy like that, human resource management plays a big role at Siemens. Sophisticated engineering and services require more focus on employee selection, training, and compensation than in the average firm, and globalization requires delivering these services globally. Siemens sums up the basic themes of its HR strategy in several points. These include:

1. **A living company is a learning company.** The high-tech nature of Siemens' business means that employees must be able to learn on a continuing basis. Siemens uses its system of combined classroom and hands-on apprenticeship training around the world to help facilitate this. It also offers employees extensive continuing education and management development.

2. **Global teamwork is the key to developing and using all the potential of the firm's human resources.** Because it is so important for employees throughout Siemens to feel free to work together and interact, employees have to understand the whole process, not just bits and pieces. To support this, Siemens provides extensive training and development. It also ensures that all employees feel they're part of a strong, unifying corporate identity. For example, HR uses cross-border, cross-cultural experiences as prerequisites for career advances.

3. **A climate of mutual respect is the basis of all relationships—within the company and with society.** Siemens contends that the wealth of nationalities, cultures, languages, and outlooks represented by its employees is one of its most valuable assets. It therefore engages in numerous HR activities aimed at building openness, transparency, and fairness, and supporting diversity.

Questions

1. Based on the information in this case, provide examples for Siemens of at least four strategically required organizational outcomes, and four required workforce competencies and behaviors.

2. Identify at least four strategically relevant HR policies and activities that Siemens has instituted in order to help human resource management contribute to achieving Siemens' strategic goals.

3. Provide a brief illustrative outline of a strategy map for Siemens.

CONTINUING CASE

CARTER CLEANING COMPANY

The High-Performance Work System

As a recent graduate and as a person who keeps up with the business press, Jennifer is familiar with the benefits of programs such as total quality management and high-performance work systems.

Jack has actually installed a total quality program of sorts at Carter, and it has been in place for about 5 years. This program takes the form of employee meetings. Jack holds employee meetings periodically, but particularly when there is a serious problem in a store—such as poor-quality work or machine breakdowns. When problems like these arise, instead of trying to diagnose them himself or with Jennifer, he contacts all the employees in that store and meets with them as soon as the store closes. Hourly employees get extra pay for these meetings. The meetings have been useful in helping Jack to identify and rectify several problems. For example, in one store all the fine white blouses were coming out looking dingy. It turned out that the cleaner/spotter had been ignoring the company rule that required cleaning ("boiling down") the perchloroethylene

cleaning fluid before washing items like these. As a result, these fine white blouses were being washed in cleaning fluid that had residue from other, earlier washes.

Jennifer now wonders whether these employee meetings should be expanded to give the employees an even bigger role in managing the Carter stores' quality. "We can't be everywhere watching everything all the time," she said to her father. "Yes, but these people only earn about $8 to $15 per hour. Will they really want to act like mini-managers?" he replied.

Questions

1. Would you recommend that the Carters expand their quality program? If so, specifically what form should it take?
2. Assume the Carters want to institute a high-performance work system as a test program in one of their stores. Write a one-page outline summarizing important HR practices you think they should focus on.

TRANSLATING STRATEGY INTO HR POLICIES & PRACTICES CASE

THE HOTEL PARIS CASE

We present a "Translating Strategy into HR Policies and Practices Case: The Hotel Paris Case" in the end-of-chapter material of each chapter (starting with this chapter). This continuing case demonstrates how the Hotel Paris's HR director uses the concepts and techniques from each chapter to create a human resource management system that helps the Hotel Paris achieve its strategic goals.

As we explained in this chapter, the basic HR strategy process is as follows: Management formulates a *strategic plan*. This plan in turn implies certain required *organizational outcomes*, such as improved customer service. Those required outcomes in turn imply certain *workforce requirements*. Human resource management then formulates *HR strategies (policies and practices)* to produce the desired workforce skills, competencies, and behaviors. Finally, the human resource manager chooses measures to gauge the extent to which its new policies and practices are actually producing the required employee skills and behaviors. The Hotel Paris's human resource manager might for example use the following sequence of steps: [50]

Step 1: Define the Business Strategy. We saw first that translating strategy into human resource policies and activities starts by defining the company's strategic plans and goals.

Step 2: Outline a Strategy Map. As we also saw, a strategy map summarizes the chain of major interrelated

activities that contribute to a company's success in achieving its strategic goals.

Step 3: Identify the Strategically Required Organizational Outcomes. Every company must produce strategically relevant outcomes if it is to achieve its strategic goals. For the Portman Hotel in Shanghai, in this chapter's introduction, the main outcome management sought was excellent customer service, to help their hotel stand out from the rest.

Step 4: Identify the Required Workforce Competencies and Behaviors. Here, ask, "What competencies and behaviors must our employees exhibit if our company is to produce the strategically relevant organizational outcomes, and thereby achieve its strategic goals?"

Step 5: Identify the Required HR System Policies and Activities. Once the human resource manager knows the required employee competencies and behaviors, he or she can turn to formulating the HR activities and policies that will help to produce them.

Here it is important to be specific. It is not enough to say, "We need new training programs or disciplinary processes." Instead, the manager must now ask, "Exactly what sorts of new training programs do we need to produce the sorts of employee competencies and behaviors that we seek?"

Step 6: **Choose HR Scorecard Measures.** We saw that many managers quantify and computerize this chain of strategic goals, employee competencies, and required HR practices. The HR Scorecard process helps them to do so. Recall that the HR Scorecard is a process for assigning financial and nonfinancial goals or *metrics* to the HR-related chain of activities required for achieving the company's strategic aims and for monitoring results.

The task here is to choose the appropriate metrics. For example, if we decide to "improve the disciplinary system," how precisely will we measure improvement? Perhaps we would use the metric, "number of grievances."

The Hotel Paris International

Let us demonstrate how this process works by considering our fictitious company, the Hotel Paris International (Hotel Paris). Starting as a single hotel in a Paris suburb in 1990, the Hotel Paris now comprises a chain of nine hotels, with two in France, one each in London and Rome, and others in New York, Miami, Washington, Chicago, and Los Angeles. As a corporate strategy, the Hotel Paris's management and owners want to continue to expand geographically. They believe doing so will let them capitalize on their reputation for good service by providing multi-city alternatives for their satisfied guests. The problem is that their reputation for good service has been deteriorating. If they cannot improve service it would be unwise for them to expand, since their guests might actually prefer other hotels after trying the Hotel Paris.

The Strategy

Top management, with input from the human resource manager and other managers, and with the board of directors' approval, chooses a new competitive strategy and formulates new strategic goals. They decide: "The Hotel Paris International will use superior guest services to differentiate the Hotel Paris properties, and to thereby increase the length of stays and the return rate of guests, and thus boost revenues and profitability." All Hotel Paris managers—including the director of HR services—must now formulate strategies that support this competitive strategy.

The Strategy Map

Based on discussions with other managers, the HR director, Lisa Cruz, outlines a strategy map. This should help her visualize the HR activities that are crucial to helping the hotel achieve its strategic goals. For example, producing satisfied guests requires attending to all those activities where there is an opportunity to affect the guests' experiences. For the Hotel Paris, activities include getting the guest from the airport and checked in, cleaning the guest's room, and picking up baggage and getting the guest checked out.

The Strategically Required Organizational Outcomes

The Hotel Paris's basic strategy is to use superior guest services to expand geographically. Each step in the hotel's strategy map provides opportunities for improving guest service. For example, Lisa and her management colleagues must take steps that produce *fewer customer complaints* and more written compliments, more frequent *guest returns* and longer stays, and higher *guest expenditures* per visit.

The Strategically Relevant Workforce Competencies and Behaviors

Therefore, the question facing Lisa is this: What are the competencies and behaviors that our hotel's employees will have to exhibit if we are to produce the required organizational outcomes such as fewer customer complaints, more compliments, and more frequent guest returns? Thinking through the types of activities that occur at each step in the hotel's value chain helps Lisa answer that question. For example, the hotel's required employee competencies and behaviors would include "high-quality front-desk customer service," "taking calls for reservations in a friendly manner," "greeting guests at the front door," and "processing guests's room service meals efficiently." All require motivated, high-morale employees.

The Strategically Relevant HR System Policies and Activities

The HR manager's task now is to identify the human resource policies and activities that will enable the hotel to produce these crucial workforce competencies and behaviors. As one example, "high-quality front-desk customer service" is one such required behavior. From this, Lisa identifies human resource activities to produce such front-desk customer service efforts. For example, she decides to *institute practices to improve the disciplinary fairness and justice in the company*, with the aim of *improving employee morale*. Her assumption is that enhanced fairness will produce higher morale and that higher morale will produce improved front-desk service.

The HR Scorecard

Finally, Lisa may (or may not) decide to computerize all these cause-and-effect links among the HR activities, the workforce behaviors, and the organizational outcomes, using scorecard software to present results on digital dashboards. With a computerized scorecard software package, Lisa need not limit herself to assessing the effects of the handful of employee behaviors (such as percentage of calls answered on time). Instead, she could include metrics covering dozens of activities, from recruitment and selection through training, appraisal, compensation, and labor relations. Her HR Scorecard model could also include the effects of all these activities on a variety of workforce competencies and behaviors, and thus on organizational outcomes and on the company's performance. In this way, her HR Scorecard would become a comprehensive model representing the value-adding effects of the full range of Hotel Paris human resource activities.

How We Will Use the Hotel Paris Case in This Book

Table 3-2 presents some of the metrics that Lisa could use to measure human resource activities (by chapter). For example, she could endeavor to improve workforce competencies and behaviors by instituting (as per Chapter 5, Recruiting) improved recruitment processes, and measure the latter in terms of "number of qualified applicants per position."

TABLE 3-2 Examples of HR System Activities the Hotel Paris Can Measure as Related to Each Chapter in This Book

Chapter	Strategic Activities Metrics
2. EEOC	Number EEOC claims/year; cost of HR-related litigation; % minority/women promotions
3. Strategy	% employees who can quote company strategy/vision
4. Job Analysis	% employees with updated job descriptions
5. Recruiting	Number applicants per recruiting source; number qualified applicants/position
6. Testing	% employees hired based on validated employment test
7. Interview	% applicants receiving structured interview
8. Training	Number hours training/employee/year; number hours training new employee
9. Appraisal	Number employees getting feedback; % appraisals completed on time
10. Career Management	% employees with formal career/development plan
11. Compensation	Target percentile for total compensation (pay in top 25%)
12. Incentives	% workforce eligible for merit pay
13. Benefits	% employees 80% satisfied with benefits
14. Ethics	Number grievances/year; % employees able to quote ethics code
15. Labor Relations	% workforce in unions
16. Health and Safety	Number safety training programs/year; $ accident costs/year; hours lost time due to accidents
17. Global	% expatriates receiving predeparture screening, counseling
18. Entrepreneurship	Employee turnover
Overall HR Metrics	HR cost/employee; HR expense/total expenses; turnover costs

Similarly, she may recommend to management that they change the firm's pay policies (see Chapter 11, Pay Plans) so that the "target percentile for total compensation is in the top 25%." She could then show that doing so improves employee morale, employee service behavior, customer satisfaction, and the hotel chain's performance. In practice, all the HR activities we discuss in this book influence employee competencies and behaviors, and, thereby, organizational outcomes and performance.

Questions

1. Draw a simple strategy map for the Hotel Paris. Specifically, summarize in your own words an example of the hierarchy of links among the hotel's *HR practices*, necessary *workforce competencies* and behaviors, and required *organizational outcomes*.
2. Using Table 3-1 (page 92), list at least five metrics the Hotel Paris could use to measure its HR practices.

KEY TERMS

ENDNOTES

1. Arthur Yeung, "Setting Up for Success: How the Portman Ritz-Carlton Hotel Gets the Best from Its People," *Human Resource Management* 45, no. 2 (Summer 2006), pp. 67–75.

2. See, for example, Fred David, *Strategic Management* (Upper Saddle River, NJ: Prentice Hall, 2007), p. 11.

3. Tony Bingham and Pat Galagan, "Doing Good While Doing Well," *Training & Development*, June 2008, p. 33.

4. www.checkmateplan.com, accessed April 24, 2009.

5. www.pepsico.com/PEP_Company/ Overview, accessed December 7, 2007.

6. Paul Nutt, "Making Strategic Choices," *Journal of Management Studies*, January 2002, pp. 67–96.

7. Michael Porter, *Competitive Strategy* (New York: The Free Press, 1980), p. 14.

8. Peter Coy, "A Renaissance in U.S. Manufacturing," *Bloomberg Businessweek*, May 9–15, 2011, pp. 11–13.

9. Samuel Greengard, "You're Next! There's No Escaping Merger Mania!" *Workforce*, April 1997, pp. 52–62. The extent to which top executives rely on HR managers to support their strategic planning efforts is a matter of debate. Many employers still view HR managers mostly as strategy executors. On the other hand, a recent study found that 71% of the management teams do see HR as a "strategic player." See Patrick Kiger, "Survey: HR Still Battling for Leaders' Respect," *Workforce Management*, December 15, 2008, p. 8. See also E. E. Lawler et al., "What Makes HR a Strategic Partner?" *People & Strategy* 32, no. 1 (2009), p. 14.

10. Andy Cook, "Make Sure You Get a Prenup," *European Venture Capital Journal*, December/January 2007, p. 76. See www.accessmylibrary.com/coms2/summary_ 0286-29140938_ITM, accessed June 29, 2009.

11. www.towersPerrin.com, accessed December 4, 2007.

12. "Mergers & Acquisitions: Managing the HR Issues," *The M&A Spotlight*, January 1, 2007.

13. Leah Carlson, "Smooth Transition: HR Input Can Prevent Benefits Blunders During M&As," *Employee Benefit News*, June 1, 2005.

14. www.towersPerrin.com, accessed December 4, 2007. See also Ingmar Bjorkman, "The HR Function in Large-Scale Mergers and Acquisitions: The Case of Nordea," *Personnel Review* 35, no. 6 (2006), pp. 654–671; Elina Antila and Anne Kakkonen, "Factors Affecting the Role of HR Managers in International Mergers and Acquisitions: A Multiple Case Study," *Personnel Review* 37, no. 3 (2008), pp. 280–299; and Linda Tepedino and Muriel Watkins, "Be a Master of Mergers and Acquisitions," *HR Magazine*, June 2010, pp. 53–56.

15. This is paraphrased or quoted from "HR Services, Service Offerings: Mergers, Acquisitions and Restructuring," www.towersPerrin.com, accessed December 4, 2007.

16. See, for example, Evan Offstein, Devi Gnyawali, and Anthony Cobb, "A Strategic Human Resource Perspective of Firm Competitive Behavior," *Human Resource Management Review* 15 (2005), pp. 305–318.

17. "Automation Improves Retailer's Hiring Efficiency and Quality," *HR Focus* 82, no. 2 (February 2005), p. 3.

18. www.activestrategy.com/solutions/ strategy_mapping.aspx, accessed March 24, 2009.

19. When focusing on HR activities, managers call this an "HR Scorecard." When applying the same process broadly to all the company's activities, including, for example, sales, production, and finance, managers call it the "balanced scorecard process."

20. The idea for the HR Scorecard derives from a broader measurement tool managers call the "balanced scorecard." This does for the company as a whole what the HR Scorecard does for HR, summarizing instead the impact of various functions including HRM, sales, production, and distribution. The "balanced" in balanced scorecard refers to a balance of goals— financial and nonfinancial.

21. See, for example, "Using HR Performance Metrics to Optimize Operations and Profits," *PR Newswire*, February 27, 2008; and "How to 'Make Over' Your HR Metrics," *HR Focus* 84, no. 9 (September 2007), p. 3.

22. SHRM Human Capital Benchmarking Study: 2007 Executive Summary.

23. For additional information on HR metrics see, for example, Karen M. Kroll, "Repurposing Metrics for HR: HR Professionals Are Looking Through a People-Focused Lens at the CFO's Metrics on Revenue and Income per FTE," *HR Magazine* 51, no. 7 (July 2006), pp. 64–69; and http://shrm.org/ metrics/library_publishedover/measurementsystemsTOC.asp, accessed February 2, 2008.

24. Connie Winkler, "Quality Check: Better Metrics Improve HR's Ability to Measure— and Manage—the Quality of Hires," *HR Magazine* 52, no. 5 (May 2007), pp. 93–94, 96, 98.

25. Ibid.

26. Ibid.

27. See, for example, "Benchmarking for Functional HR Metrics," *HR Focus* 83, no. 11 (November 2006), p. 1; and John Sullivan, "The Last Word," *Workforce Management*, November 19, 2007, p. 42.

28. See Brian Becker and Mark Huselid, "Measuring HR? Benchmarking Is Not the Answer!" *HR Magazine* 8, no. 12 (December 2003), www.charmed.org, accessed February 2, 2008.

29. Ibid.

30. Ed Frauenheim, "Keeping Score with Analytics Software," *Workforce Management* 86, no. 10 (May 21, 2007), pp. 25–33.

31. Steven Baker, "Data Mining Moves to Human Resources," *Bloomberg Businessweek*, March 12, 2009, www.BusinessWeek.com/magazine/, accessed April 13, 2011.

32. Ibid.

33. Ed Frauenheim, "Numbers Game," *Workforce Management* 90, no. 3 (March 2011), p. 21.

34. George Marakas, *Decision Support Systems* (Upper Saddle River, NJ: Prentice-Hall), 2003, p. 326.

35. Thomas Davenport, Jeanne Harris, and Jeremy Shapiro, "Competing on Talent Analytics," *Harvard Business Review*, October 2010, pp. 52–58.

36. Ibid., p. 54.

37. Lin Grensing-Pophal, "HR Audits: Know the Market, Land Assignments," SHRM Consultants Forum, December 2004, www.shrm.org/hrdisciplines/consultants/ Articles/Pages/CMS_010705.aspx, accessed July 7, 2010.

38. Bill Coy, "Introduction to The Human Resources Audit," La Piana Associates, Inc., www.lapiana.org/consulting, accessed May 1, 2008.

39. Grensing-Pophal, "HR Audits: Know the Market, Land Assignments"; and Coy, "Introduction to The Humsan Resources Audit."

40. Dana R. Scott, "Conducting a Human Resources Audit," *New Hampshire Business Review*, August 2007.

41. Ibid.

42. Coy, "Introduction to The Human Resources Audit."

43. See for example, www.personneltoday.com/blogs/hcglobal-human-capital-management/2009/02/theres-no-such-thing-as-eviden.html, accessed April 18, 2009.

44. Eric Anderson and Duncan Simester, "A Step-by-Step Guide to Smart Business Experiments," *Harvard Business Review*, March 2011, pp. 98–105.

45. Ibid.

46. Bill Roberts, "How to Put Analytics on Your Side," *HR Magazine*, October 2009, pp. 43–46.

47. www.bls.gov/opub/ted/2006/may/wk2/art01.htm, accessed April 18, 2009; "Super Human Resources Practices Result in Better Overall Performance, Report Says," *BNA Bulletin to Management*, August 26, 2004, pp. 273–274. See also Wendy Boswell, "Aligning Employees with the Organization's Strategic Objectives: Out of Line of Sight, Out of Mind," *International Journal of Human Resource Management* 17, no. 9 (September 2006), pp. 1014–1041. A study found that some employers, which the researchers called cost minimizers, intentionally took a lower cost approach to human resource practices, with mixed results. See Soo Min Toh et al., "Human Resource Configurations: Investigating Fit with the Organizational Context," *Journal of Applied Psychology* 93, no. 4 (2008), pp. 864–882.

48. See, for example, www.personneltoday.com/blogs/hcglobal-human-capital-management/2009/02/theres-no-such-thing-as-eviden.html, accessed April 18, 2009.

49. Robert McNabb and Keith Whitfield, "Job Evaluation and High-Performance Work Practices: Compatible or Conflictual?" *Journal of Management Studies* 38, no. 2 (March 2001), p. 294.

50. This section is adapted in part from Brian Becker, Mark Huselid, and Dave Ulrich, *The HR Scorecard: Linking People, Strategy, and Performance* (Boston: Harvard Business School Press, 2001).

PART 1   VIDEO CASES APPENDIX

Video Title: Human Resource Management (Patagonia)

SYNOPSIS

The mission at Patagonia is to build the best product possible, cause no unnecessary environmental harm, and inspire solutions to the environmental crisis. The benefits to employees working for Patagonia are considerable. Although the pay is slightly below the industry average, employees are given time off work to try out the wetsuits the company produces, and employees are encouraged to put the needs of their families first. Employees can work flexible hours to accommodate this company value. Employees are also offered a period of 60 days in which they can work for a nonprofit environmental organization and still receive their full pay. Much thought is put into the hiring of new employees at Patagonia; ambitious, mission-driven people, with whom the core values of Patagonia resonate, are selected to fill open positions within this unique company.

Discussion Questions

1. How does the mission of Patagonia differ from most other companies?
2. Patagonia has often been selected as one of the country's best places to work. What Patagonia HR practices and employee benefits do you think help Patagonia earn this honor?
3. What characteristics would you use to describe a candidate likely to be hired by Patagonia? How do these characteristics reflect and support Patagonia's strategy?

Video Title: Equal Employment (UPS)

SYNOPSIS

A former HR director for UPS, now the president of "The Virtual HR Director," gives some perspective on what diversity means, and what its value can be to a company. Employees of a wide variety of backgrounds are intrinsically valuable to a company in the varied perspectives that they bring to the table, and can help a company find creative solutions to new problems that it has not encountered before.

In a diverse workplace, where employees come from a variety of backgrounds and ethnicities, there is always the possibility of harassment between employees. The video addresses the value of diversity sensitivity training in its capacity to help prevent incidence of employee harassment. Effective and constructive corrective measures for incidents of harassment are also discussed.

Discussion Questions

1. What kinds of things does Gary Wheeler think a diverse workforce can contribute to a company?
2. What typical avenues are open to an employee who feels he or she is being harassed, in order to make sure it is dealt with properly? Do you see any room for improvement based on our discussion in Chapter 3?
3. What does Gary Wheeler report is most often the basis of reported claims of harassment, and how are these cases dealt with?
4. What else would you do to deal with employees who are hostile to the idea of diversity?
5. To what extent do you believe that harassment, such as sexual harassment, is usually primarily a communications problem? Why?
6. In this video Mr. Wheeler focuses mostly on diversity and on sexual harassment. Discuss five other important aspects of equal employment opportunity at work that are also important.

Video Title: Strategic Management (Joie de Vivre Hospitality)

SYNOPSIS

Chip Conley is the founder of Joie de Vivre Hospitality (JDV), a collection of boutique hotels, restaurants, and spas in California. The kitschy atmosphere of the boutiques allows JDV to differentiate itself from both the luxury and the chain hotels. Customer loyalty is so great that JDV relies primarily on word-of-mouth advertising and spends little on traditional advertising methods.

Discussion Questions

1. How does Joie de Vivre Hospitality differentiate its boutique hotels from other hotel offerings in the area?
2. How did Chip Conley and Joie de Vivre Hospitality demonstrate great strategic flexibility during the dot-com crash and post-9/11 industry recession?
3. What is Joie de Vivre's philosophy on advertising for its hotels? How does this support the firm's strategic aims?
4. Similarly, list five specific human resource management practices that you would suggest JDV use in order to produce the employee behaviors required to achieve JDV's strategic aims.

4

Job Analysis and the Talent Management Process

LEARNING OBJECTIVES

1. Explain why talent management is important.

2. Discuss the nature of job analysis, including what it is and how it's used.

3. Use at least three methods of collecting job analysis information, including interviews, questionnaires, and observation.

4. Write job descriptions, including summaries and job functions, using the Internet and traditional methods.

5. Write a job specification.

6. Explain competency-based job analysis, including what it means and how it's done in practice.

W hen Daimler opened its Mercedes-Benz assembly plant in Alabama, its managers had a dilemma. They could not hire, train, or pay the plant employees unless the managers knew what each employee was expected to do—they needed, for each person, a "job description." But in this plant, self-managing teams of employees would assemble the vehicles, and their jobs and duties might change every day. How do you list job duties when the duties are a moving target?[1]

Access a host of interactive learning aids at **www.mymanagementlab.com** to help strengthen your understanding of the chapter concepts.

WHERE ARE WE NOW . . .

The human resource management process really begins with deciding what the job entails. The main purpose of this chapter is to show you how to analyze a job and write job descriptions. We'll see that analyzing jobs involves determining what the job entails and what kind of people the firm should hire for the job. We discuss several techniques for analyzing jobs, and explain how to draft job descriptions and job specifications. Then, in Chapter 5 (Personnel Planning and Recruiting), we'll turn to the methods managers use to actually find the employees they need. The main topics we'll cover in this chapter include the talent management process, the basics of job analysis, methods for collecting job analysis information, writing job descriptions, and writing job specifications.

THE TALENT MANAGEMENT PROCESS

This is the first chapter of the portion of the book (Parts Two, Three, and Four) which for many embodies the heart of human resource management, including recruitment and selection (staffing), training, appraisal, career development, and compensation. The traditional way to view staffing, training, appraisal, development, and compensation is as a series of steps:

1. Decide what positions to fill, through *job analysis, personnel planning, and forecasting.*
2. Build a pool of job candidates, by *recruiting* internal or external candidates.
3. Have candidates complete *application forms* and perhaps undergo initial screening interviews.
4. Use *selection tools* like tests, interviews, background checks, and physical exams to identify viable candidates.
5. Decide to whom to *make an offer.*
6. *Orient, train, and develop employees* to provide them with the competencies they need to do their jobs.
7. *Appraise employees* to assess how they're doing.
8. *Reward and compensate* employees to maintain their motivation.

This linear view makes sense. For example, the employer needs job candidates before selecting whom to hire. However, the step-by-step view also tends to mask the fact that the functions are more interrelated. For example, employers don't just train employees and appraise how they're doing; the appraisal results also loop back to shape the employee's subsequent training.

Therefore, employers today often view all these staff–train–reward activities as part of a single integrated *talent management* process. One survey of human resource executives found that "talent management" issues were among the most pressing ones they faced.[2] A survey of CEOs of big companies said they typically spent between 20% and 40% of their time on talent management.[3]

What Is Talent Management?

We can define **talent management** as the *goal-oriented* and *integrated* process of *planning, recruiting, developing, managing, and compensating* employees.[4] When a manager takes a talent management perspective, he or she:

1. **Understands that the talent management tasks** (such as recruiting, training, and paying employees) are parts of a single interrelated talent management process. For example, having employees with the right skills depends as much on recruiting, training, and compensation as it does on applicant testing.
2. **Makes sure talent management decisions such as staffing, training, and pay are goal-directed.** Managers should always be asking, "What recruiting, testing, or other actions should I take *to produce the employee competencies we need to achieve our strategic goals?*"
3. **Consistently uses the same "profile" of competencies, traits, knowledge, and experience for formulating recruitment plans for a job as for making selection, training, appraisal, and payment decisions for it.** For example, ask selection interview questions to determine if the candidate has the knowledge and skills to do the job, and then train and appraise the employee based on whether he or she shows mastery of that knowledge and skills.
4. **Actively segments and proactively manages employees.** Taking a talent management approach requires that employers *proactively manage* their employees' recruitment, selection, development, and rewards. As one example, IBM segmented its employees into three main groups (executive and technical employees, managers, and rank and file). This enables IBM to fine-tune its training, pay, and other practices

for employees in each segment. As another example, many employers pinpoint their "mission-critical" employees, and manage their development and rewards separately from the firms' other employees.

5. **Integrates/coordinates all the talent management functions.** Finally, an effective talent management process *integrates the underlying talent management activities* such as recruiting, developing, and compensating employees. For example, performance appraisals should trigger the required employee training. One simple way to achieve such integration is for HR managers to meet as a team to visualize and discuss how to coordinate activities like testing, appraising, and training. (For instance, they make sure the firm is using the same skills profile to recruit, as to select, train, and appraise for a particular job.) Another way to coordinate these activities is by using information technology.

- For example, Talent Management Solutions' (www.talentmanagement101.com) talent management suite includes e-recruiting software, employee performance management, a learning management system, and compensation management support. Among other things, this suite of programs "relieves the stress of writing employee performance reviews by automating the task," and ensures "that all levels of the organization are aligned—all working for the same goals."[5]

- SilkRoad Technology's talent management solution includes applicant tracking, onboarding, performance management, compensation, and an employee intranet support. Its talent management Life Suite "helps you recruit, manage, and retain your best employees."[6]

- Info HCM Talent Management "includes . . . tracking and monitoring performance metrics, interactive online training via WebEx, support for e-commerce integration to enable training. . . ."[7]

THE BASICS OF JOB ANALYSIS

> **2** Discuss the nature of job analysis, including what it is and how it's used.

Talent management begins with understanding what jobs need to be filled, and the human traits and competencies employees need to do those jobs effectively. **Job analysis** is the procedure through which you determine the duties of the positions and the characteristics of the people to hire for them.[8] Job analysis produces information for writing **job descriptions** (a list of what the job entails) and **job** (or "person") **specifications** (what kind of people to hire for the job). Virtually every personnel-related action you take—interviewing applicants, and training and appraising employees, for instance—depends on knowing what the job entails and what human traits one needs to do the job well.[9]

The supervisor or human resources specialist normally collects one or more of the following types of information via the job analysis:

- **Work activities.** First, he or she collects information about the job's actual work activities, such as cleaning, selling, teaching, or painting. This list may also include how, why, and when the worker performs each activity.

- **Human behaviors.** Information about human behaviors the job requires, like sensing, communicating, lifting weights, or walking long distances.

---

talent management
The goal-oriented and integrated process of planning, recruiting, developing, managing, and compensating employees.

job analysis
The procedure for determining the duties and skill requirements of a job and the kind of person who should be hired for it.

job descriptions
A list of a job's duties, responsibilities, reporting relationships, working conditions, and supervisory responsibilities—one product of a job analysis.

job specifications
A list of a job's "human requirements," that is, the requisite education, skills, personality, and so on—another product of a job analysis.

- **Machines, tools, equipment, and work aids.** Information regarding tools used, materials processed, knowledge dealt with or applied (such as finance or law), and services rendered (such as counseling or repairing).
- **Performance standards.** Information about the job's performance standards (in terms of quantity or quality levels for each job duty, for instance).
- **Job context.** Information about such matters as physical working conditions, work schedule, incentives, and, for instance, the number of people with whom the employee would normally interact.
- **Human requirements.** Information such as knowledge or skills (education, training, work experience) and required personal attributes (aptitudes, personality, interests).

Uses of Job Analysis Information

As Figure 4-1 summarizes, job analysis is important because managers use it to support just about all their human resource management activities.

RECRUITMENT AND SELECTION Information about what duties the job entails and what human characteristics are required to perform these activities helps managers decide what sort of people to recruit and hire.

EEO COMPLIANCE Job analysis is crucial for validating all major human resources practices. For example, to comply with the Americans with Disabilities Act, employers should know each job's essential job functions—which in turn requires a job analysis.

PERFORMANCE APPRAISAL A performance appraisal compares each employee's actual performance with his or her duties and performance standards. Managers use job analysis to learn what these duties and standards are.

COMPENSATION Compensation (such as salary and bonus) usually depends on the job's required skill and education level, safety hazards, degree of responsibility, and so on—all factors you assess through job analysis.

TRAINING The job description lists the job's specific duties and requisite skills— and therefore the training—that the job requires.

Job analysis is important in helping employers execute their overall strategic plans. The accompanying Strategic Context feature illustrates this.

FIGURE 4-1 Uses of Job Analysis Information

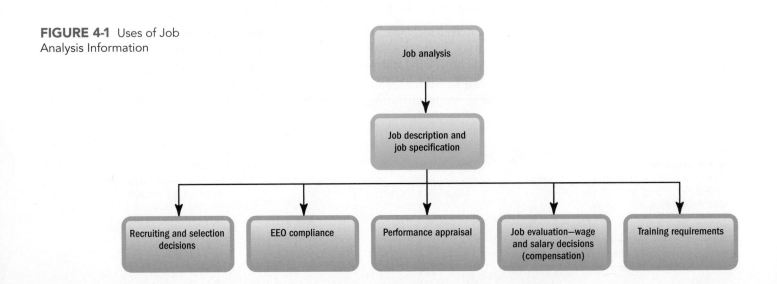

THE STRATEGIC CONTEXT

Daimler Alabama Example

In planning its Mercedes-Benz factory in Alabama, Daimler's strategy was to design a modern factory.[10] The plant emphasizes *just-in-time* inventory methods, so inventories stay negligible due to the arrival "just in time" of parts. It also organizes employees into *work teams*, and emphasizes that all employees must dedicate themselves to *continuous improvement.*

Production operations like those require certain employee competencies and behaviors. For example, they require multiskilled and flexible employees.

A modern approach to job analysis called *competencies-based job analysis* (which we'll discuss later in this chapter) therefore played an important role in staffing this factory. Written guidelines regarding who to hire and how to train them is based more on lists of worker competencies than on job descriptions that say, "these are your job duties." Without detailed job descriptions showing what "my job" is to constrain them, it's easier for employees to move from job to job within their teams. Not being pigeonholed also encourages workers to look beyond their own jobs to find ways to improve things. For instance, one team found a $0.23 plastic prong that worked better than the one for $2.50 the plant was using to keep car doors open during painting. Building its modern "continuous improvement" plant meant Daimler needed employees who thought for themselves; organizing its jobs around worker competencies and by using competency-based job analysis therefore helped Daimler achieve its strategic aims here.

Conducting a Job Analysis

There are six steps in doing a job analysis, as follows.

STEP 1: DECIDE HOW YOU'LL USE THE INFORMATION This will determine the data you collect. Some data collection techniques—like interviewing the employee—are good for writing job descriptions. Other techniques, like the position analysis questionnaire we describe later, provide numerical ratings for each job; these can be used to compare jobs for compensation purposes.

STEP 2: REVIEW RELEVANT BACKGROUND INFORMATION SUCH AS ORGANIZATION CHARTS, PROCESS CHARTS, AND JOB DESCRIPTIONS[11] **Organization charts** show the organization-wide division of work, and where the job fits in the overall organization. The chart should show the title of each position and, by means of interconnecting lines, who reports to whom and with whom the job incumbent communicates. A **process chart** provides a more detailed picture of the work flow. In its simplest form a process chart (like that in Figure 4-2) shows the flow of inputs to and outputs from the job you're analyzing. (In Figure 4-2, the quality control clerk is expected to review components from suppliers, check components going to the plant managers, and give information regarding component's quality to these managers.) Finally, the existing job description, if there is one, usually provides a starting point for building the revised job description.

WORKFLOW ANALYSIS AND JOB REDESIGN Job analysis enables the manager to list what a job's duties and demands are now. Job analysis does *not* answer questions such as "Does how this job relates to other jobs make sense?" or "Should this job even

---

organization chart
A chart that shows the organization-wide distribution of work, with titles of each position and interconnecting lines that show who reports to and communicates with whom.

process chart
A workflow chart that shows the flow of inputs to and outputs from a particular job.

FIGURE 4-2 Process Chart for Analyzing a Job's Workflow

Source: Compensation Management: Rewarding Performance by Richard J. Henderson. Reprinted by permission of Pearson Education, Upper Saddle River, NJ.

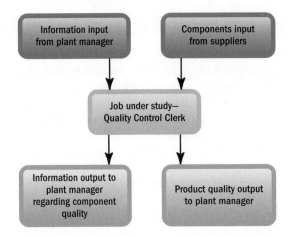

exist?" To answer such questions, it's necessary to conduct a *workflow analysis*. It may then be deemed necessary to redesign jobs. **Workflow analysis** is a detailed study of the flow of work from job to job in a work process. Usually, the analyst focuses on one identifiable work process, rather than on how the company gets all its work done. The accompanying HR as a Profit Center feature illustrates workflow analysis.

HR AS A PROFIT CENTER

Boosting Productivity through Work Redesign

The Atlantic American insurance company in Atlanta conducted a workflow analysis to identify inefficiencies in how it processes its insurance claims. The firm's HR Director described the workflow analysis as follows: "We followed the life of a claim to where it arrived in the mail and where it eventually ended up" in order to find ways to improve the process.[12]

American Atlantic's workflow analysis prompted several productivity-boosting changes. The firm reduced from four to one the number of people opening mail, replacing three people with a machine that does it automatically. A new date stamping machine lets staff stamp 20 pages at a time rather than 1. A new software program adds bar codes to each claim automatically, rather than manually. Thus, the firm used workflow analysis to view the process's "big picture" to automate work, redesign jobs, boost labor productivity, and redeploy claims processing employees.

In conducting a workflow analysis, the manager may use a *flow process chart*; this lists in order each step of the process. The manager may convert this step-by-step flow process chart into a diagrammatic process chart. This lays out, with arrows and circles, each step in the process from beginning to end.

BUSINESS PROCESS REENGINEERING   American Atlantic is an example of business process reengineering. **Business process reengineering** means redesigning business processes, usually by combining steps, so that small multifunction teams using information technology do the jobs formerly done by a sequence of departments. The basic approach is to

1. Identify a business process to be redesigned (such as approving a mortgage application)
2. Measure the performance of the existing processes
3. Identify opportunities to improve these processes
4. Redesign and implement a new way of doing the work
5. Assign ownership of sets of formerly separate tasks to an individual or a team that use new computerized systems to support the new arrangement

As another example, one bank reengineered its mortgage approval process by replacing the sequential operation with a multifunction mortgage approval team. Loan originators in the field now enter the mortgage application directly into wireless laptop computers, where software checks it for completeness. The information then goes electronically to regional production centers. Here, specialists (like credit analysts and loan underwriters) convene electronically, working as a team to review the mortgage together—at once. After they formally close the loan, another team of specialists takes on the task of servicing the loan.

As at Atlantic American and at this bank, reengineering usually requires redesigning individual jobs. For example, after creating the loan approval teams, the bank could eliminate the separate credit checking, loan approval, and home-inspecting departments from its organization chart. Reengineering also required delegating more authority to the loan approval teams, who now did their jobs with less supervisory oversight. Since loan team members may share duties, they tend to be more multiskilled than if they only had to do, say, loan analysis. Changes like these in turn prompt changes in individual jobs and job descriptions.

JOB REDESIGN Early economists wrote enthusiastically of how specialized jobs (doing the same small thing repeatedly) were more efficient (as in, "practice makes perfect"). But soon other writers were reacting to what they viewed as the "dehumanizing" aspects of pigeonholing workers into highly repetitive jobs. Many proposed job redesign solutions such as job enlargement, job rotation, and job enrichment to address such problems. **Job enlargement** means assigning workers additional same-level activities. Thus, the worker who previously only bolted the seat to the legs might attach the back as well. **Job rotation** means systematically moving workers from one job to another.

Psychologist Frederick Herzberg argued that the best way to motivate workers is through job enrichment. **Job enrichment** means redesigning jobs in a way that increases the opportunities for the worker to experience feelings of responsibility, achievement, growth, and recognition. It does this by *empowering* the worker—for instance, by giving the worker the skills and authority to inspect the work, instead of having supervisors do that. Herzberg said empowered employees would do their jobs well because they wanted to, and quality and productivity would rise. That philosophy, in one form or another, is the theoretical basis for the team-based self-managing jobs in many companies around the world today.

STEP 3: SELECT REPRESENTATIVE POSITIONS Whether or not the manager decides to redesign jobs via workforce analysis, process redesign, or job redesign, he or she must at some point select which positions to focus on for the job analysis. For example, it is usually unnecessary to analyze the jobs of 200 assembly workers when a sample of 10 jobs will do.

STEP 4: ACTUALLY ANALYZE THE JOB—BY COLLECTING DATA ON JOB ACTIVITIES, WORKING CONDITIONS, AND HUMAN TRAITS AND ABILITIES NEEDED TO PERFORM THE JOB In brief, analyzing the job involves greeting participants; briefly explaining the job analysis process and the participants' roles in this process; spending about 15 minutes interviewing the employees to get agreement on a basic summary of the job; identifying the job's broad areas of responsibility, such as "calling on potential clients"; and identifying duties/tasks within each area interactively with the employees.[13]

workflow analysis
A detailed study of the flow of work from job to job in a work process.

business process reengineering
Redesigning business processes, usually by combining steps, so that small multifunction process teams using information technology do the jobs formerly done by a sequence of departments.

job enlargement
Assigning workers additional same-level activities.

job rotation
Systematically moving workers from one job to another.

job enrichment
Redesigning jobs in a way that increases the opportunities for the worker to experience feelings of responsibility, achievement, growth, and recognition.

STEP 5: VERIFY THE JOB ANALYSIS INFORMATION WITH THE WORKER PERFORMING THE JOB AND WITH HIS OR HER IMMEDIATE SUPERVISOR This will help confirm that the information is factually correct and complete and help to gain their acceptance.

STEP 6: DEVELOP A JOB DESCRIPTION AND JOB SPECIFICATION The *job description* describes the activities and responsibilities of the job, as well as its important features, such as working conditions. The *job specification* summarizes the personal qualities, traits, skills, and background required for getting the job done.

Job Analysis Guidelines

Before actually analyzing the job, using one or more of the tools we turn to in the following section, keep several things in mind.

- Make the job analysis a *joint effort by a human resources manager, the worker, and the worker's supervisor.* The human resource manager might observe the worker doing the job, and have both the supervisor and worker fill out job questionnaires. Based on that, he or she lists the job's duties and required human traits. The supervisor and worker then review and verify the HR manager's list of job duties.

- *Make sure the questions and the process are both clear* to the employees. (For example, some might not know what you mean when you ask about the job's "mental demands.")

- *Use several different job analysis tools.* Do not rely just on a questionnaire, for instance, but supplement your survey with a short follow-up interview. (The problem is that each tool has potential drawbacks.) For example, the questionnaire might miss a task the worker performs just occasionally.

<table>
<tr><td>3</td><td>Use at least three methods of collecting job analysis information, including interviews, questionnaires, and observation.</td></tr>
</table>

METHODS FOR COLLECTING JOB ANALYSIS INFORMATION

There are various ways (interviews, or questionnaires, for instance) to collect information on a job's duties, responsibilities, and activities. We discuss the most important ones in this section.

The basic rule is to use those that best fit your purpose. Thus, an interview might be best for creating a list of job duties and a job description. The more quantitative position analysis questionnaire may be best for quantifying each job's relative worth for pay purposes.

The Interview

Job analysis interviews range from completely unstructured interviews ("Tell me about your job") to highly structured ones containing hundreds of specific items to check off.

Managers may conduct individual interviews with each employee, group interviews with groups of employees who have the same job, and/or supervisor interviews with one or more supervisors who know the job. They use group interviews when a large number of employees are performing similar or identical work, since this can be a quick and inexpensive way to gather information. As a rule, the workers' immediate supervisor attends the group session; if not, you can interview the supervisor separately.

Whichever kind of interview you use, be sure the interviewee fully understands the reason for the interview. There's a tendency for workers to view such interviews, rightly or wrongly, as "efficiency evaluations." If so, interviewees may hesitate to describe their jobs accurately.

Source: David Mager/Pearson Education.

It is helpful to spend several minutes prior to collecting job analysis information explaining the process that you will be following.

TYPICAL QUESTIONS Some typical interview questions include the following:

What is the job being performed?

What are the major duties of your position? What exactly do you do?

What physical locations do you work in?

What are the education, experience, skill, and [where applicable] certification and licensing requirements?

In what activities do you participate?

What are the job's responsibilities and duties?

What are the basic accountabilities or performance standards that typify your work?

What are your responsibilities? What are the environmental and working conditions involved?

What are the job's physical demands? The emotional and mental demands?

What are the health and safety conditions?

Are you exposed to any hazards or unusual working conditions?

STRUCTURED INTERVIEWS Many managers use a structured format to guide the interview. Figure 4-3 presents one example, a job analysis information sheet. It includes questions regarding matters like the general purpose of the job; supervisory responsibilities; job duties; and education, experience, and skills required.

Structured lists are not just for interviews. Job analysts who collect information by personally observing the work or by using questionnaires—two methods explained later—can also use structured lists.[14]

PROS AND CONS The interview's wide use reflects its advantages. It's a simple and quick way to collect information, including information that might not appear on a written form. For instance, a skilled interviewer can unearth important activities that occur only occasionally, or informal contacts that wouldn't be obvious from the organization chart. The employee can also vent frustrations that might otherwise go unnoticed.

Distortion of information is the main problem—whether due to outright falsification or honest misunderstanding.[15] Job analysis is often a prelude to changing a job's pay rate. As noted, employees therefore may legitimately view the interview as a sort of "efficiency evaluation" that may affect their pay. They may then tend to exaggerate certain responsibilities while minimizing others. In one study, researchers listed possible job duties either as simple task statements ("record phone messages and other routine information") or as ability statements ("ability to record phone messages and other routine information"). Respondents were more likely to include and report the ability-based versions of the statements. There may be a tendency for people to inflate their job's importance when abilities are involved, to impress the perceptions of others.[16] Employees will even puff up their job titles to make their jobs seem more important.[17] Obtaining valid information can thus be a slow process, and prudent analysts get multiple inputs.

INTERVIEWING GUIDELINES To get the best information possible, keep several things in mind when conducting job analysis interviews.

- Quickly establish rapport with the interviewee. Know the person's name, speak understandably, briefly review the interview's purpose, and explain how the person was chosen for the interview.

- Use a structured guide that lists questions and provides space for answers. This ensures you'll identify crucial questions ahead of time and that all interviewers (if more than one) cover all the required questions. (However, also make sure to ask, "Was there anything we didn't cover with our questions?")

FIGURE 4-3 Job Analysis Questionnaire for Developing Job Descriptions

Source: www.hr.blr.com. Reprinted with permission of the publisher Business and Legal Resources, Inc., Old Saybrook, CT. BLR® (Business & Legal Resources, Inc.).

Job Analysis Information Sheet

Job Title_____ Date _____

Job Code_____ Dept. _____

Superior's Title _____

Hours Worked _____ AM to _____ PM

Job Analyst's Name _____

1. **What is the job's overall purpose?**
   _____

2. **If the incumbent supervises others,** list them by job title; if there is more than one employee with the same title, put the number in parentheses following.
   _____

3. **Check those activities** that are part of the incumbent's supervisory duties.
   - ☐ Training
   - ☐ Performance appraisal
   - ☐ Inspecting work
   - ☐ Budgeting
   - ☐ Coaching and/or counseling
   - ☐ Others (please specify) _____

4. **Describe the type and extent of supervision** received by the incumbent.

5. **JOB DUTIES:** Describe briefly WHAT the incumbent does and, if possible, HOW he/she does it. Include duties in the following categories:

   a. daily duties (those performed on a regular basis every day or almost every day)
   _____

   b. periodic duties (those performed weekly, monthly, quarterly, or at other regular intervals)
   _____

   c. duties performed at irregular intervals
   _____

6. Is the incumbent performing duties he/she considers unnecessary? If so, describe.
   _____

7. Is the incumbent performing duties not presently included in the job description? If so, describe.
   _____

8. **EDUCATION:** Check the box that indicates the educational requirements for the job (not the educational background of the incumbent).

   - ☐ No formal education required
   - ☐ High school diploma (or equivalent)
   - ☐ 4-year college degree (or equivalent)
   - ☐ Eighth grade education
   - ☐ 2-year college degree (or equivalent)
   - ☐ Graduate work or advanced degree
     Specify: _____

   - ☐ Professional license
     Specify: _____

- When duties are not performed in a regular manner—for instance, when the worker doesn't perform the same duties repeatedly many times a day—ask the worker to list his or her duties in order of importance and frequency of occurrence. This will ensure that you don't overlook crucial but infrequently performed activities—like a nurse's occasional emergency room duties.

- After completing the interview, review the information with the worker's immediate supervisor and with the interviewee.

FIGURE 4-3 (Continued)

9. **EXPERIENCE:** Check the amount of experience needed to perform the job.

☐ None   ☐ Less than one month

☐ One to six months   ☐ Six months to one year

☐ One to three years   ☐ Three to five years

☐ Five to ten years   ☐ More than ten years

10. **LOCATION:** Check location of job and, if necessary or appropriate, describe briefly.

☐ Outdoor   ☐ Indoor

☐ Underground   ☐ Excavation

☐ Scaffold   ☐ Other (specify)

11. **ENVIRONMENTAL CONDITIONS:** Check any objectionable conditions found on the job and note afterward how frequently each is encountered (rarely, occasionally, constantly, etc.).

☐ Dirt   ☐ Dust

☐ Heat   ☐ Cold

☐ Noise   ☐ Fumes

☐ Odors   ☐ Wetness/humidity

☐ Vibration   ☐ Sudden temperature changes

☐ Darkness or poor lighting   ☐ Other (specify)

12. **HEALTH AND SAFETY:** Check any undesirable health and safety conditions under which the incumbent must perform and note how often they are encountered.

☐ Elevated workplace   ☐ Mechanical hazards

☐ Explosives   ☐ Electrical hazards

☐ Fire hazards   ☐ Radiation

☐ Other (specify)

13. **MACHINES, TOOLS, EQUIPMENT, AND WORK AIDS:** Describe briefly what machines, tools, equipment, or work aids the incumbent works with on a regular basis:

_____

14. Have concrete work standards been established (errors allowed, time taken for a particular task, etc.)? If so, what are they?

_____

15. Are there any personal attributes (special aptitudes, physical characteristics, personality traits, etc.) required by the job?

_____

16. Are there any exceptional problems the incumbent might be expected to encounter in performing the job under normal conditions? If so, describe.

_____

17. Describe the successful completion and/or end results of the job.

_____

18. What is the seriousness of error on this job? Who or what is affected by errors the incumbent makes?

_____

19. To what job would a successful incumbent expect to be promoted?

_____

[**Note:** This form is obviously slanted toward a manufacturing environment, but it can be adapted quite easily to fit a number of different types of jobs.]

Questionnaires

Having employees fill out questionnaires to describe their job-related duties and responsibilities is another popular way to obtain job analysis information.

Some questionnaires are very structured checklists. Here each employee gets an inventory of perhaps hundreds of specific duties or tasks (such as "change and splice wire"). He or she is asked to indicate whether he or she performs each task and, if so, how much time is normally spent on each. At the other extreme, the questionnaire may simply ask, "describe the major duties of your job."

In practice, the best questionnaire often falls between these two extremes. As illustrated in Figure 4-3, a typical job analysis questionnaire might include several open-ended questions (such as "What is the job's overall purpose?") as well as structured questions (concerning, for instance, education required).

All questionnaires have pros and cons. A questionnaire is a quick and efficient way to obtain information from a large number of employees; it's less costly than interviewing hundreds of workers, for instance. However, developing the questionnaire and testing it (perhaps by making sure the workers understand the questions) can be time-consuming. And as with interviews, employees may distort their answers.

Observation

Direct observation is especially useful when jobs consist mainly of observable physical activities—assembly-line worker and accounting clerk are examples. On the other hand, observation is usually not appropriate when the job entails a lot of mental activity (lawyer, design engineer). Nor is it useful if the employee only occasionally engages in important activities, such as a nurse who handles emergencies. And *reactivity*—the worker's changing what he or she normally does because you are watching—also can be a problem.

Managers often use direct observation and interviewing together. One approach is to observe the worker on the job during a complete work cycle. (The *cycle* is the time it takes to complete the job; it could be a minute for an assembly-line worker or an hour, a day, or longer for complex jobs.) Here you take notes of all the job activities. Then, ask the person to clarify points not understood and to explain what other activities he or she performs that you didn't observe.

Participant Diary/Logs

Another method is to ask workers to keep a **diary/log** of what they do during the day. For every activity engaged in, the employee records the activity (along with the time) in a log.

Some firms give employees pocket dictating machines and pagers. Then at random times during the day, they page the workers, who dictate what they are doing at that time. This approach can avoid relying on workers to remember what they did hours earlier when they complete their logs at the end of the day.

Quantitative Job Analysis Techniques

Qualitative methods like interviews and questionnaires are not always suitable. For example, if your aim is to compare jobs for pay purposes, a mere listing of duties may not suffice. You may need to say that, in effect, "Job A is twice as challenging as Job B, and so is worth twice the pay." To do this, it helps to have quantitative ratings for each job. The position analysis questionnaire and the Department of Labor approach are quantitative methods for doing this.

POSITION ANALYSIS QUESTIONNAIRE   The **position analysis questionnaire (PAQ)** is a very popular quantitative job analysis tool, consisting of a questionnaire containing 194 items (see Figure 4-4 for a sample).[18] The 194 items (such as "written materials") each represent a basic element that may play a role in the job. The items each belong to one of five PAQ basic activities: (1) having decision-making/communication/social responsibilities, (2) performing skilled activities, (3) being physically active, (4) operating vehicles/equipment, and (5) processing information (Figure 4-4 illustrates this last activity). The final PAQ "score" shows the job's rating on each of these five activities. The job analyst decides if each of the 194 items plays a role and, if so, to what extent. In Figure 4-4, for example, "written materials" received a rating of 4. Since the scale ranges from 1 to 5, a 4 suggests that written materials (such as books and reports) do play a significant role in this job. The analyst can use an online version of the PAQ (see www.paq.com) for each job he or she is analyzing.

The PAQ's strength is in assigning jobs to job classes for pay purposes. With ratings for each job's decision-making, skilled activity, physical activity, vehicle/equipment

FIGURE 4-4 Portion of a Completed Page from the Position Analysis Questionnaire. The 194 PAQ elements are grouped into six dimensions, and this figure illustrates the "information input" questions or elements. Other PAQ pages contain questions regarding mental processes, work output, relationships with others, job context, and other job characteristics.

Information Input

1 Information Input

	Extent of Use (U)
NA	Does not apply
1	Nominal/very infrequent
2	Occasional
3	Moderate
4	Considerable
5	Very substantial

1.1 Sources of Job Information
Rate each of the following items in terms of the extent to which it is used by the worker as a source of information in performing his job.

1.1.1 Visual Sources of Job Information

1 | 4 | Written materials (books, reports, office notes, articles, job instructions, signs, etc.)

2 | 2 | Quantitative materials (materials which deal with quantities or amounts, such as graphs, accounts, specifications, tables of numbers, etc.)

3 | 1 | Pictorial materials (pictures or picture-like materials used as *sources* of information, for example, drawings, blueprints, diagrams, maps, tracing, photographic films, x-ray films, TV pictures, etc.)

4 | 1 | Patterns/related devices (templates, stencils, patterns, etc., used as *sources* of information when *observed* during use; do not include here materials described in item 3 above)

5 | 2 | Visual displays (dials, gauges, signal lights, radarscopes, speedometers, clocks, etc.)

6 | 5 | Measuring devices (rulers, calipers, tire pressure gauges, scales, thickness gauges, pipettes, thermometers, protractors, etc., used to obtain visual information about physical measurements; do not include here devices describe in item 5 above)

7 | 4 | Mechanical devices (tools, equipment, machinery, and other mechanical devices which are *sources* of information when observed during use of operation)

8 | 3 | Materials in process (parts, material, objects, etc., which are sources of information when being modified, worked on, or otherwise processed, such as bread dough being mixed, workpiece being turned in a lathe, fabric being cut, shoe being resoled, etc.)

9 | 4 | Materials not in process (parts, materials, objects, etc., not in the process of being changed or modified, which are *sources* of information when being inspected, handled, packaged, distributed, or selected, etc., such as items or materials in inventory, storage, or distribution channels, items being inspected, etc.)

10 | 3 | Features of nature (landscapes, fields, geological samples, vegetation, cloud formations, and other features of nature which are observed or inspected to provide information)

11 | 2 | Man-made features of environment (structures, buildings, dams, highways, bridges, docks, railroads, and other "man-made" or altered aspects of the indoor environment which are observed or inspected to provide job information; do not consider equipment, machines, etc., that an individual uses in his work, as covered by item 7)

operation, and information-processing characteristics, you can quantitatively compare jobs relative to one another,[19] and then classify jobs for pay purposes.[20]

DEPARTMENT OF LABOR (DOL) PROCEDURE   Experts at the U.S. Department of Labor did much of the early work developing job analysis.[21] They used their results

diary/log
Daily listings made by workers of every activity in which they engage along with the time each activity takes.

position analysis questionnaire (PAQ)
A questionnaire used to collect quantifiable data concerning the duties and responsibilities of various jobs.

TABLE 4-1 Basic Department of Labor Worker Functions

	Data	People	Things
Basic Activities	0 Synthesizing	0 Mentoring	0 Setting up
	1 Coordinating	1 Negotiating	1 Precision working
	2 Analyzing	2 Instructing	2 Operating/controlling
	3 Compiling	3 Supervising	3 Driving/operating
	4 Computing	4 Diverting	4 Manipulating
	5 Copying	5 Persuading	5 Tending
	6 Comparing	6 Speaking/signaling	6 Feeding/offbearing
		7 Serving	7 Handling
		8 Taking instructions/helping	

Note: Determine employee's job "score" on data, people, and things by observing his or her job and determining, for each of the three categories, which of the basic functions illustrates the person's job. "0" is high; "6," "8," and "7" are lows in each column.[22]

to compile what was for many years the bible of job descriptions, the *Dictionary of Occupational Titles*. This mammoth book contained detailed information on virtually every job in America. We'll see in a moment that Internet-based tools have largely replaced the *Dictionary*. However, the U.S. Department of Labor job analysis procedure still offers a good example of how to quantitatively rate, classify, and compare different jobs, based on the DOL's "data, people, and things" ratings.

It works as follows. As Table 4-1 shows, the DOL method uses a set of standard basic activities called *worker functions* to describe what a worker must do with respect to data, people, and things. With respect to data, for instance, the possible functions include synthesizing, coordinating, and copying. With respect to people, they include mentoring, negotiating, and supervising. With respect to things, the basic functions include manipulating, tending, and handling.

Each worker function has an importance rating. Thus, "coordinating" is 1, whereas "copying" is 5. If you were analyzing the job of a receptionist/clerk, for example, you might label the job 5, 6, 7, to represent copying data, speaking/signaling people, and handling things. On the other hand, you might code a psychiatric aide in a hospital 1, 7, 5 in relation to data, people, and things. In practice, you would score each task that the worker performed as part of his or her job in terms of data, people, and things. Then you would use the highest combination (say 4, 6, 5) to rate the overall job, since this is the highest level that you would expect a successful job incumbent to attain. If you were selecting a worker for that 4, 6, 5 job, you'd expect him or her to be able to at least compute (4), speak/signal (6), and tend (5). If you were comparing jobs for pay purposes, then a 4, 6, 5 job should rank higher (see Table 4-1) than a 6, 8, 6 job. You can then present a summary of the job along with its 3-digit rating on a form such as in Figure 4-5.

Internet-Based Job Analysis

Methods such as questionnaires and interviews can be time-consuming. And collecting the information from geographically dispersed employees can be challenging.[23]

Conducting the job analysis via the Internet is an obvious solution.[24] Most simply, the human resource department can distribute standardized job analysis questionnaires to geographically disbursed employees via their company intranets, with instructions to complete the forms and return them by a particular date.

Of course, the instructions should be clear, and it's best to test the process first. Without a job analyst actually sitting there with the employee or supervisor, there's always a chance that the employees won't cover important points or that misunderstandings will cloud the results.

FIGURE 4-5 Sample Report Based on Department of Labor Job Analysis Technique

Job Analysis Schedule

1. Established Job Title ___DOUGH MIXER___

2. Ind. Assign ___(bake prod.)___

3. SIC Code(s) and Title(s) ___2051 Bread and other bakery products___

4. JOB SUMMARY:

Operates mixing machine to mix ingredients for straight and sponge (yeast) doughs according to established formulas, directs other workers in fermentation of dough, and curls dough into pieces with hand cutter.

5. WORK PERFORMED RATINGS:

Worker Functions	D Data	P People	(T) Things
	5	6	2

Work Field ___Cooking, Food Preparing___

6. WORKER TRAITS RATING (to be filled in by analyst):

Training time required
Aptitudes
Temperaments
Interests
Physical demands
Environment conditions

U.S. NAVY EXAMPLE The U.S. Navy used Web job analysis. The challenge was "to develop a system that would allow the collection of job-related information with minimal intervention and guidance, so that the system could be used in a distributed [long distance] manner."[25] To keep ambiguities to a minimum, they had the employees complete structured job analysis forms step-by-step, and duty by duty, as follows:

- First the online form *shows workers a set of work activities* (such as "getting information" and "monitor the process") from the Department of Labor online O*NET work activities list. (Figure 4-6 lists some of these activities, such as "Getting Information." You can access the site at www.onetcenter.org/content.html/4.A#cm_4.A.)

- Next the form directs them to *select those work activities* that are important to their job.

- Then the form asks them to *list actual duties* of their jobs that fit each of those selected work activities. For example, suppose an employee chose "Getting Information" as a work activity that was important to his or her job. In this final step, he or she would list next to "Getting Information" one or more specific job duties from the job, perhaps such as "watch for new orders from our vendors and bring them to the boss's attention."

Again, as here, the main issue with online job analysis is to strip the process of as many ambiguities as possible. The Navy's method proved to be an effective way to collect job-related information online.[26]

FIGURE 4-6 O*NET General Work Activities Categories

Note: The U.S. Navy employees were asked to indicate if their jobs required them to engage in work activities such as: Getting Information; Monitor Processes; Identifying Objects; Inspecting Equipment; and Estimating Quantifiable Characteristics.

Source: Reprinted by permission of O*NET OnLine.

Print-friendly Version
(Outline View | **Description View**)
▼▢ **Generalized Work Activities** — General types of job behaviors occurring on multiple jobs
  • Information Input — Where and how are the information and data gained that are needed to perform this job?
    • Looking for and Receiving Job-Related Information — How is information obtained to perform this job?
      Getting Information — Observing, receiving, and otherwise obtaining information from all relevant sources.
      Monitor Processes, Materials, or Surroundings — Monitoring and reviewing information from materials, events, or the environment, to detect or assess problems.
    • Identify and Evaluating Job-Relevant Information — How is information interpreted to perform this job?
      Identifying Objects, Actions, and Events — Identifying information by categorizing, estimating, recognizing differences or similarities, and detecting changes in circumstances or events.
      Inspecting Equipment, Structures, or Material — Inspecting equipment, structures, or materials to identify the cause of errors or other problems or defects.
      Estimating the Quantifiable Characteristics of Products, Events, or Information — Estimating sizes, distances, and quantities; or determining time, costs, resources, or materials needed to perform a work activity.

WRITING JOB DESCRIPTIONS

4 Write job descriptions, including summaries and job functions, using the Internet and traditional methods.

The most important product of job analysis is the job description. A job description is a written statement of what the worker actually does, how he or she does it, and what the job's working conditions are. You use this information to write a job specification; this lists the knowledge, abilities, and skills required to perform the job satisfactorily.

There is no standard format for writing a job description. However, most descriptions contain sections that cover:

1. Job identification
2. Job summary
3. Responsibilities and duties
4. Authority of incumbent
5. Standards of performance
6. Working conditions
7. Job specification

Figures 4-7 and 4-8 present two sample forms of job descriptions.

Job Identification

As in Figure 4-7, the job identification section (on top) contains several types of information.[27] The *job title* specifies the name of the job, such as supervisor of data processing operations, or inventory control clerk. The FLSA status section identifies the job as exempt or nonexempt. (Under the Fair Labor Standards Act, certain positions, primarily administrative and professional, are exempt from the act's overtime and minimum wage provisions.) *Date* is the date the job description was actually approved.

There may also be a space to indicate who approved the description and perhaps a space showing the location of the job in terms of its facility/division and department. This section might also include the immediate supervisor's title and information regarding salary and/or pay scale. There might also be space for the grade/level of the job, if there is such a category. For example, a firm may classify programmers as programmer II, programmer III, and so on.

JOB TITLE: Telesales Respresentative	JOB CODE: 100001
RECOMMENDED SALARY GRADE:	EXEMPT/NONEXEMPT STATUS: Nonexempt
JOB FAMILY: Sales	EEOC: Sales Workers
DIVISION: Higher Education	REPORTS TO: District Sales Manager
DEPARTMENT: In-House Sales	LOCATION: Boston
	DATE: April 2009

SUMMARY (Write a brief summary of job.)

The person in this position is responsible for selling college textbooks, software, and multimedia products to professors, via incoming and outgoing telephone calls, and to carry out selling strategies to meet sales goals in assigned territories of smaller colleges and universities. In addition, the individual in this position will be responsible for generating a designated amount of editorial leads and communicating to the publishing groups product feedback and market trends observed in the assigned territory.

SCOPE AND IMPACT OF JOB
Dollar responsibilities (budget and/or revenue)

The person in this position is responsible for generating approximately $2 million in revenue, for meeting operating expense budget of approximately $4000, and a sampling budget of approximately 10,000 units.

Supervisory responsibilities (direct and indirect)

None

Other

REQUIRED KNOWLEDGE AND EXPERIENCE (Knowledge and experience necessary to do job)
Related work experience

Prior sales or publishing experience preferred. One year of company experience in a customer service or marketing function with broad knowledge of company products and services is desirable.

Formal education or equivalent

Bachelor's degree with strong academic performance or work equivalent experience.

Skills

Must have strong organizational and persuasive skills. Must have excellent verbal and written communications skills and must be PC proficient.

Other

Limited travel required (approx 5%)

(Continued)

FIGURE 4-7 Sample Job Description, Pearson Education

Source: Courtesy of HR Department, Pearson Education.

Job Summary

The job summary should summarize the essence of the job, and include only its major functions or activities. Thus (in Figure 4-7), the telesales rep ". . . is responsible for selling college textbooks. . . ." For the job of mailroom supervisor, "the mailroom supervisor receives, sorts, and delivers all incoming mail properly, and he or she handles all outgoing mail including the accurate and timely posting of such mail."[28]

PRIMARY RESPONSIBILITIES (List in order of importance and list amount of time spent on task.)

Driving Sales (60%)

- Achieve quantitative sales goal for assigned territory of smaller colleges and universities.
- Determine sales priorities and strategies for territory and develop a plan for implementing those strategies.
- Conduct 15–20 professor interviews per day during the academic sales year that accomplishes those priorities.
- Conduct product presentations (including texts, software, and Web site); effectively articulate author's central vision of key titles; conduct sales interviews using the PSS model; conduct walk-through of books and technology.
- Employ telephone selling techniques and strategies.
- Sample products to appropriate faculty, making strategic use of assigned sampling budgets.
- Close class test adoptions for first edition products.
- Negotiate custom publishing and special packaging agreements within company guidelines.
- Initiate and conduct in-person faculty presentations and selling trips as appropriate to maximize sales with the strategic use of travel budget. Also use internal resources to support the territory sales goals.
- Plan and execute in-territory special selling events and book-fairs.
- Develop and implement in-territory promotional campaigns and targeted email campaigns.

Publishing (editorial/marketing) 25%

- Report, track, and sign editorial projects.
- Gather and communicate significant market feedback and information to publishing groups.

Territory Management 15%

- Track and report all pending and closed business in assigned database.
- Maintain records of customer sales interviews and adoption situations in assigned database.
- Manage operating budget strategically.
- Submit territory itineraries, sales plans, and sales forecasts as assigned.
- Provide superior customer service and maintain professional bookstore relations in assigned territory.

Decision-Making Responsibilities for This Position:

Determine the strategic use of assigned sampling budget to most effectively generate sales revenue to exceed sales goals.
Determine the priority of customer and account contacts to achieve maximum sales potential.
Determine where in-person presentations and special selling events would be most effective to generate the most sales.

Submitted By: Jim Smith, District Sales Manager	Date: April 10, 2007
Approval:	Date:
Human Resources:	Date:
Corporate Compensation:	Date:

FIGURE 4-7 (Continued)

While it's common to do so, include general statements like "performs other assignments as required" with care. Some experts state unequivocally that "one item frequently found that should never be included in a job description is a 'cop-out clause' like 'other duties, as assigned,'"[29] since this leaves open the nature of the job. Finally, make it clear in the summary that the employer expects the employee to carry out his or her duties efficiently, attentively, and conscientiously.

FIGURE 4-8 Marketing Manager Description from Standard Occupational Classification

Source: www.bls.gov/soc/soc_a2c1.htm, accessed May 10, 2007.

U.S. Department of Labor
Bureau of Labor Statistics
Standard Occupational Classification

www.bls.gov   **Advanced Search | A-Z Index**

BLS Home | Programs & Surveys | Get Detailed Statistics | Glossary | What's New | Find It! In DOL

11-2021 Marketing Managers

Determine the demand for products and services offered by a firm and its competitors and identify potential customers. Develop pricing strategies with the goal of maximizing the firm's profits or share of the market while ensuring the firm's customers are satisfied. Oversee product development or monitor trends that indicate the need for new products and services.

Relationships

There may be a "relationships" statement (not in Figure 4-7) that shows the jobholder's relationships with others inside and outside the organization. For a human resource manager, such a statement might look like this:[30]

Reports to: Vice president of employee relations.
Supervises: Human resource clerk, test administrator, labor relations director, and one secretary.
Works with: All department managers and executive management.
Outside the company: Employment agencies, executive recruiting firms, union representatives, state and federal employment offices, and various vendors.[31]

Responsibilities and Duties

This is the heart of the job description. It should present a list of the job's significant responsibilities and duties. As in Figure 4-7, list each of the job's major duties separately, and describe it in a few sentences. In the figure, for instance, the job's duties include "achieve quantitative sales goal . . ." and "determine sales priorities. . . ." Typical duties for other jobs might include making accurate postings to accounts payable, maintaining favorable purchase price variances, and repairing production-line tools and equipment.

This section may also define the limits of the jobholder's authority. For example, the jobholder might have authority to approve purchase requests up to $5,000, grant time off or leaves of absence, discipline department personnel, recommend salary increases, and interview and hire new employees.

Usually, the manager's basic question here is, "How do I determine what the job's duties are and should be?" The answer first is, from the *job analysis*; this should reveal what the employees on each job are doing now. Second, you can review various sources of standardized job description information. For example, the **Standard Occupational Classification (SOC)** (www.bls.gov/soc/socguide.htm) classifies all workers into one of 23 major groups of jobs, such as "Management Occupations" and "Healthcare Occupations." These in turn contain 96 minor groups of jobs, which in turn include 821 detailed occupations, such as the marketing manager description in Figure 4-8. The employer can use standard descriptions like these to identify a job's duties and responsibilities, such as "Determine the demand

Standard Occupational Classification (SOC)
Classifies all workers into one of 23 major groups of jobs that are subdivided into minor groups of jobs and detailed occupations.

for products." (The accompanying Managing the New Workforce feature expands on this.) The employer may also use other popular sources of job description information, such as www.jobdescription.com. O*NET online, as noted, is another option for finding job duties. We'll turn to this in a moment.

MANAGING THE NEW WORKFORCE

Writing Job Descriptions That Comply with the ADA

The list of job duties looms large in employers' efforts to comply with ADA regulations. Under the Americans with Disabilities Act (ADA), the individual must have the requisite skills, educational background, and experience to perform the job's essential functions. A job function is essential when it is the reason the position exists or when the function is so specialized that the firm hired the person doing the job for his or her expertise or ability to perform that particular function. If the disabled individual can't perform the job as currently structured, the employer is required to make a "reasonable accommodation," unless doing so would present an "undue hardship."

Is a function essential? Questions to ask include:

1. What activities/duties/tasks actually constitute the job? Is each really necessary?
2. Do the tasks necessitate sitting, standing, crawling, walking, climbing, running, stooping, kneeling, lifting, carrying, digging, writing, operating, pushing, pulling, fingering, talking, listening, interpreting, analyzing, seeing, coordinating, etc.?
3. Would removing a function fundamentally alter the job?
4. What happens if a task is not completed on time?
5. Does the position actually exist to perform that function?
6. Are employees in the position actually required to perform the function?[32]
7. What is the degree of expertise or skill required to perform the function?[33]

Standards of Performance and Working Conditions

A "standards of performance" section lists the standards the company expects the employee to achieve for each of the job description's main duties and responsibilities. Setting standards is never easy. However, most managers soon learn that just telling subordinates to "do their best" doesn't provide enough guidance. One straightforward way of setting standards is to finish the statement, "I will be completely satisfied with your work when. . . ." This sentence, if completed for each listed duty, should result in a usable set of performance standards. Here is an example:

Duty: Accurately Posting Accounts Payable

1. Post all invoices received within the same working day.
2. Route all invoices to proper department managers for approval no later than the day following receipt.
3. An average of no more than three posting errors per month.

The job description may also list the working conditions involved on the job. These might include things like noise level, hazardous conditions, or heat.

Using the Internet for Writing Job Descriptions

More employers are turning to the Internet for their job descriptions. One site, www.jobdescription.com, illustrates why. The process is simple. Search by alphabetical title, keyword, category, or industry to find the desired job title. This leads you to a generic job description for that title—say, "Computers & EDP Systems Sales Representative." You can then use the wizard to customize the generic description for this position. For example, you can add specific information about your organization, such as job title, job codes, department, and preparation date. And you can indicate whether the job has supervisory abilities, and choose from a number of possible desirable competencies and experience levels.

O*NET   The U.S. Department of Labor's occupational information network, called O*NET, is an increasingly popular Web tool (you'll find it at http://online. onetcenter.org). It allows users (not just managers, but workers and job seekers) to see the most important characteristics of various occupations, as well as the experience, education, and knowledge required to do each job well. Both the Standard Occupational Classification and O*NET include the specific tasks associated with many occupations. O*NET also lists skills, including *basic skills* such as reading and writing, *process skills* such as critical thinking, and *transferable skills* such as persuasion and negotiation.[34] You'll also see that an O*NET job listing includes information on worker requirements (required knowledge, for instance), occupation requirements (such as compiling, coding, and categorizing data, for instance), and experience requirements (including education and job training). You can also use O*NET to check the job's labor market characteristics, such as employment projections and earnings data.[35]

HOW TO USE O*NET   Many managers and small business owners face two hurdles when doing job analyses and job descriptions. First, they need a streamlined approach for developing a job description. Second, they fear that they will overlook duties that subordinates should be assigned.

You have three good options. The *Standard Occupational Classification*, mentioned earlier, provides detailed descriptions of thousands of jobs and their human requirements. Web sites like www.jobdescription.com provide customizable descriptions by title and industry. And the Department of Labor's O*NET is a third option. We'll focus here on how you can write a job description using O*NET (http://online.onetcenter.org).[36]

Step 1: **Decide on a Plan.** Ideally, the jobs you need should flow from your departmental or company plans. Therefore, you may want to review your plan. What do you expect your sales to be next year, and in the next few years? What areas or departments do you think will have to be expanded or reduced? What kinds of new positions do you think you'll need?

Step 2: **Develop an Organization Chart.** You may want to write an organization chart. Start with the organization as it is now. Then (depending upon how far you're planning), produce a chart showing how you'd like your chart to look in the future (say, in a year or two). Microsoft's MS Word includes an organization charting function. Software packages such as *OrgPublisher* from TimeVision of Irving, Texas, are another option.[37]

Step 3: **Use a Job Analysis Questionnaire.** Next, gather information about the job's duties. (You can use job analysis questionnaires, such as those shown in Figure 4-3 and Figure 4-9.)

Step 4: **Obtain Job Duties from O*NET.** The list of job duties you uncovered in the previous step may or may not be complete. We'll therefore use O*NET to compile a more complete list. (Refer to the A, B, and C examples pictured on page 125 as you read along.)

Start by going to http://online.onetcenter.org (A). Here, click on *Find Occupations*. Assume you want to create job descriptions for a retail salesperson. Key *Retail Sales* in the Keyword drop-down box. This brings you to the Occupations matching "retail sales" page (B).

Clicking on the *Retail Salespersons* summary produces the job summary and specific occupational duties for retail salespersons (C). For a small store, you might want to combine the duties of the "retail salesperson" with those of "first-line supervisors/managers of retail sales workers."

FIGURE 4-9 Simple Job Description Questionnaire

Source: Reprinted from www.hr.blr.com with the permission of the publisher. Business and Legal Resources, Inc., Old Saybrook, CT. BLR® (Business & Legal Resources, Inc.).

Instructions: Distribute copies of this questionnaire to supervisors, managers, personnel staff members, job analysts, and others who may be involved in writing job descriptions. Ask them to record their answers to these questions in writing.

1. What is the job title? _____

2. Summarize the job's more important, regularly performed/duties in a job summary. _____

3. In what department is the job located? _____

4. What is the title of the supervisor or manager to whom the job holder must report?

5. Does the job holder supervise other employees? If so, give their job titles and a brief description of their responsibilities.

Position Supervised	Responsibilities

6. What essential function duties does the job holder perform regularly? List them in order of importance.

Duty	Percentage of Time Devoted to This Duty
1.	
2.	
3.	
4.	
5.	
6.	

7. Does the job holder perform other duties periodically? Infrequently? If so, please list, indicating frequency.

8. What are the working conditions? List such items as noise, heat, outside work, and exposure to bad weather.

9. How much authority does the job holder have in such matters as training or guiding other people?

10. How much education, experience, and skill are required for satisfactory job performance?

11. At what stage is the job holder's work reviewed by the supervisor?

12. What machines or equipment is the job holder responsible for operating?

13. If the job holder makes a serious mistake or error in performing required duties, what would be the cost to management?

Step 5: List the Job's Human Requirements from O*NET. Next, return to the summary for *Retail Salesperson* (C). Here, click, for example, Knowledge, Skills, and Abilities. Use this information to help develop a job specification for your job. Use this information for recruiting, selecting, and training your employees.

Source: Reprinted by permission of O*NET OnLine.

A

B
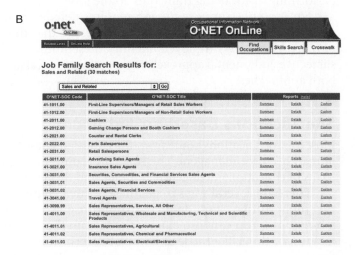

C

Step 6: Finalize the Job Description. Finally, perhaps using Figure 4-9 as a guide, write an appropriate job summary for the job. Then use the information obtained previously in steps 4 and 5 to create a complete listing of the tasks, duties, and human requirements of each of the jobs you will need to fill.

5 Write a job specification.

WRITING JOB SPECIFICATIONS

The job specification takes the job description and answers the question, "What human traits and experience are required to do this job effectively?" It shows what kind of person to recruit and for what qualities you should test that person. It may be a section of the job description, or a separate document. Often—as in Figure 4-7 on pages 119–120—the employer makes it part of the job description.[38]

Specifications for Trained Versus Untrained Personnel

Writing job specifications for trained employees is relatively straightforward. Here your job specifications might focus mostly on traits like length of previous service, quality of relevant training, and previous job performance.

The problems are more complex when you're filling jobs with untrained people (with the intention of training them on the job). Here you must specify qualities such as physical traits, personality, interests, or sensory skills that imply some potential for performing or for being trained to do the job.

For example, suppose the job requires detailed manipulation in a circuit board assembly line. Here you might want to ensure that the person scores high on a test of finger dexterity. Employers identify these human requirements either through a subjective, judgmental approach or through statistical analysis (or both). Let's examine both approaches.

Specifications Based on Judgment

Most job specifications come from the educated guesses of people like supervisors and human resource managers. The basic procedure here is to ask, "What does it take in terms of education, intelligence, training, and the like to do this job well?"

There are several ways to get these "educated guesses." You could simply review the job's duties, and deduce from those what human traits and skills the job requires. You can also choose them from the competencies listed in Web-based job descriptions like those at www.jobdescription.com. (For example, a typical job description there lists competencies like "Generates creative solutions" and "Manages difficult or emotional customer situations.") O*NET online is another option. Job listings there include complete lists of required education and other experience and skills.

Filling jobs with untrained employees requires identifying the personal traits that predict performance.

Source: Fotolia.

USE COMMON SENSE   In any case, use common sense when compiling your list. Don't ignore the behaviors that may apply to almost any job but that might not normally surface through a job analysis.

Industriousness is an example. Who wants an employee who doesn't work hard? One researcher collected supervisor ratings and other information from 18,000 employees in 42 different hourly entry-level jobs in predominantly retail settings.[39] Regardless of the job, here are the work behaviors (with examples) that he found to be important to all jobs:

Job-Related Behavior	Some Examples
Industriousness	Keeps working even when other employees are standing around talking; takes the initiative to find another task when finished with regular work.
Thoroughness	Cleans equipment thoroughly, creating a more attractive display; notices merchandise out of place and returns it to the proper area.
Schedule flexibility	Accepts schedule changes when necessary; offers to stay late when the store is extremely busy.
Attendance	Arrives at work on time; maintains good attendance.
Off-task behavior (reverse)	Uses store phones to make personal unauthorized calls; conducts personal business during work time; lets joking friends be a distraction and interruption to work.
Unruliness (reverse)	Threatens to bully another employee; refuses to take routine orders from supervisors; does not cooperate with other employees.
Theft (reverse)	(As a cashier) Under-rings the price of merchandise for a friend; cheats on reporting time worked; allows nonemployees in unauthorized areas.
Drug misuse (reverse)	Drinks alcohol or takes drugs on company property; comes to work under the influence of alcohol or drugs.

Job Specifications Based on Statistical Analysis

Basing job specifications on statistical analysis is the more defensible approach, but it's also more difficult. The aim here is to determine statistically the relationship between (1) some *predictor* (human trait, such as height, intelligence, or finger dexterity), and (2) some indicator or *criterion* of job effectiveness, such as performance as rated by the supervisor.

The procedure has five steps: (1) analyze the job and decide how to measure job performance; (2) select personal traits like finger dexterity that you believe should predict successful performance; (3) test candidates for these traits; (4) measure these candidates' subsequent job performance; and (5) statistically analyze the relationship between the human trait (finger dexterity) and job performance. Your objective is to determine whether the former predicts the latter.

This method is more defensible than the judgmental approach because equal rights legislation forbids using traits that you can't prove distinguish between high and low job performers. For example, hiring standards that discriminate based on sex, race, religion, national origin, or age may have to be shown to predict job performance. Ideally, you do this with a statistical validation study, as in the 5-step approach outlined earlier. In practice, most employers probably rely more on judgmental approaches.

Using Task Statements

Although employers traditionally use job descriptions and job specifications to summarize what their jobs entail, *task statements* are increasingly popular.[40] Each of a job's task statements shows *what* the worker does on one particular job task, *how* the worker does it, and for what *purpose*.[41] One task statement for a dry cleaning store counter person might be, "accepts an order of clothes from a customer and places it into a laundry bag and provides the customer with a receipt, in order to ensure that the customer's clothes items are together and identifiable and that the store and customer have an accurate record of the transaction." (In contrast, the traditional job duty might say, "accepts orders of clothes from customers and places them in laundry bags; gives customers receipts). Writing task statements such as that for each of the job's tasks is the first step in this process.

Next, for each task *identify the knowledge, skills, abilities*, and *other* characteristics (KSAOs) needed to do each task. For the sample task, the counter person would need to know how to operate the computerized cash register, would need the skill to identify fabrics so proper prices can be charged, and would need the ability or natural talent (for instance, cognitive ability or physical ability) to perform arithmetic computations and lift heavy laundry bags. Most jobs also require certain "other" human characteristics. For example, "conscientiousness" might be important for this and most other jobs.

Third, the job analyst takes the resulting 12 or 15 task statements for a job's tasks and groups them into four or five main job duties. Thus the four main counter person job duties might include accepts and returns customer's clothes, handles the cash register, fills in for the cleaner/spotter when he or she is absent, and supervises the tailor and assistant counter person.

Finally, the job analyst compiles all this information in a "Job Requirements Matrix" for this job. This matrix lists each of the four or five main job duties in column 1; the task statements associated with each job duty in column 2; the relative importance of each job duty and the time spent on each job duty in columns 3 and 4; and the knowledge, skills, ability, and other characteristics or competencies related to each job duty in column 5.[42] The task statement matrix provides a more comprehensive picture of what the worker does and how and why he or she does it than does a conventional job description. Such a list of required knowledge, skills, abilities, and other characteristics can provide powerful information for making staffing, training, and performance appraisal decisions, as can job profiling, to which we now turn.

PROFILES IN TALENT MANAGEMENT

6 Explain competency-based job analysis, including what it means and how it's done in practice.

A job is traditionally a set of closely related activities carried out for pay, but the concept of a job is changing. Employers such as Daimler are instituting high-performance work policies and practices. These include management practices (such as organizing around work teams) that depend on multiskilled employees who can tackle multiple jobs.

The problem is that in situations like these, relying on a list of conventional job duties can be counterproductive, because the person's job changes frequently.[43] Often, the better option is to create job profiles. *Job profiles* list the competencies, traits, knowledge, and experience that employees in these multi-skilled jobs *must be able to exhibit* to get the multiple jobs done. Then the manager can recruit, hire, train, appraise, and reward employees based on these profiles, rather than on a list of static job duties. Experts at the consulting firm DDI say that the aim of writing job profiles (also called "competency" or "success" profiles) is to create detailed descriptions of what is required for exceptional performance in a given role or job, in terms of required Competencies (necessary behaviors), Personal Attributes (traits, personality, etc.), Knowledge (technical and/or professional), and Experience (necessary educational and work achievements). Each job's profile then becomes the anchor for creating recruitment, selection, training, and evaluation and development plans for each job. (Many use the term *competency model* rather than *profile*.[44]) Figure 4-10 illustrates one type of profile, in the form of a competency model.

Competencies and Competency-Based Job Analysis

Employers often use competency-based job analysis to create such profiles. *Competencies* are observable and measurable behaviors of the person that make performance possible (we'll look at examples in a moment). To determine what a job's required competencies are, ask, "In order to perform this job competently, what should the employee be able to do?" Competencies are typically skills. Examples of

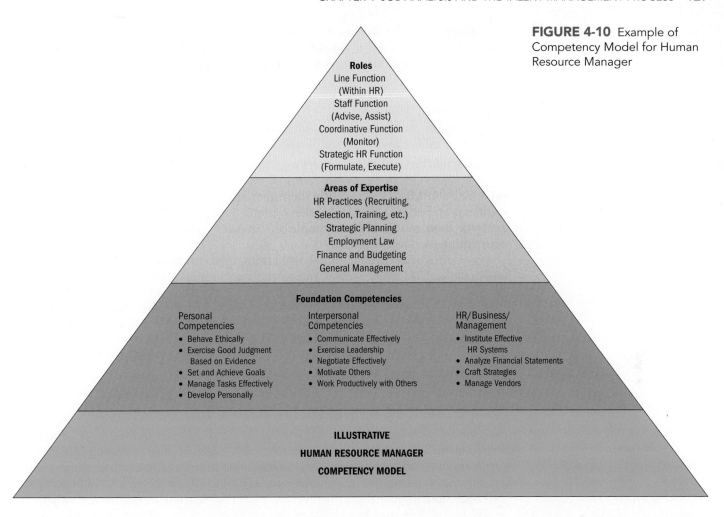

FIGURE 4-10 Example of Competency Model for Human Resource Manager

competencies include "program in HTML," "produce a lesson plan," and "engineer the struts for a bridge." **Competency-based job analysis** means describing the job in terms of measurable, observable, behavioral competencies (knowledge, skills, and/or behaviors) that an employee doing that job must exhibit.[45] Traditional job analysis is more job-focused (What are this job's duties?). Competency-based analysis is more worker-focused (What must employees be competent at to do this multiskilled job?).

Managers sometimes group competencies into various clusters, such as *general competencies* (reading and writing, for instance), *leadership competencies* (leadership, and strategic thinking, for instance), and *technical competencies*. Technical competencies for the job of systems engineer might include the following:

- Design complex software applications, establish protocols, and create prototypes.
- Establish the necessary platform requirements to efficiently and completely coordinate data transfer.[46]

Similarly, for a corporate treasurer, technical competencies might include:

- Formulate trade recommendations by studying several computer models for currency trends.
- Recommend specific trades and when to make them.[47]

Competency-based job analysis
Describing the job in terms of measurable, observable, behavioral competencies (knowledge, skills, and/or behaviors) that an employee doing that job must exhibit to do the job well.

In practice, competency-based analysis usually comes down to identifying the basic skills an employee needs to do the job. Thus, O*NET lists various skills within six skill groups (accessible at http://online.onetcenter.org/skills). A sampling includes:

"Mathematics—using mathematics to solve problems"

"Speaking—talking to others to convey information effectively"

"Complex problem-solving—identifying complex problems and reviewing related information to develop and evaluate options and implement solutions"

"Negotiation—bringing others together and trying to reconcile differences"

IBM EXAMPLE   IBM recently identified all of the possible roles (leader, analyst, engineer, and so on) that its workers, managers, and executives might fulfill. IBM analysts then studied what people do in each role and what skills effectively performing each role requires.

For doing what turned out to be 490 roles, IBM concluded there are 4,000 possible sets of skills. IBM now assesses and rates its employees' skills on a continuum from Zero—"You have not demonstrated a significant mastery of the skill set," to Three— "You have achieved a mastery level demonstrated by the fact that you're not only proficient, but that you're developing others around it." This enables IBM to tell each employee "where we see your skill sets, which skills you have that will become obsolete and what jobs we anticipate will become available down the road. . . . We'll direct you to training programs that will prepare you for the future."[48]

How to Write Competencies-Based Job Descriptions

Defining the job's competencies and writing them up is similar in most respects to traditional job analysis. In other words, you might interview job incumbents and their supervisors, ask open-ended questions regarding job responsibilities and activities, and perhaps identify critical incidents that pinpoint success on the job. However, instead of compiling lists of job duties, you will ask, *"In order to perform this job competently, the employee should be able to. . . ?"* Use your knowledge of the job to answer this, or use information from a source such as O*NET. There are also off-the-shelf competencies databanks. One is that of the Department of Labor's Office of Personnel Management (see www.opm.gov).

BP EXAMPLE   Several years ago, British Petroleum's (BP's) exploration division executives decided their unit needed a more efficient, faster-acting organization.[49] To help accomplish this, they felt they had to shift employees from a job duties–oriented "that's-not-my-job" attitude to one that motivated them to obtain the skills required to accomplish their broader responsibilities.

Their solution was a skills matrix like that in Figure 4-11. BP created skills matrices (such as in Figure 4-11) each job or job family (such as drilling managers).

FIGURE 4-11 The Skills Matrix for One Job at BP

Note: The light blue boxes indicate the minimum level of skill required for the job.

Technical expertise	Business awareness	Communication and interpersonal	Decision-making and initiative	Leadership and guidance	Planning and organizational ability	Problem-solving
H	H	H	H	H	H	H
G	G	G	G	G	G	G
F	F	F	F	F	F	F
E	E	E	E	E	E	E
D	D	D	D	D	D	D
C	C	C	C	C	C	C
B	B	B	B	B	B	B
A	A	A	A	A	A	A

As in Figure 4-11, each matrix listed (1) the types of skills required to do that job (such as technical expertise) and (2) the minimum level of each skill required for that job or job family. Talent management in this BP unit now involves recruiting, hiring, training, appraising, and rewarding employees based on the competencies they need to perform their ever-changing jobs, with the overall aim of creating a more flexible organization.

REVIEW

MyManagementLab Now that you have finished this chapter, go back to **www.mymanagementlab.com** to continue practicing and applying the concepts you've learned.

CHAPTER SECTION SUMMARIES

1. Employers today often view all the staff–train–reward activities as part of a single integrated *talent management* process. We defined talent management as the *goal-oriented* and *integrated* process of *planning, recruiting, developing, managing, and compensating* employees. When a manager takes a talent management perspective, he or she should keep in mind that the talent management tasks are parts of a single interrelated talent management process, make sure talent management decisions such as staffing and pay are goal-directed, consistently use the same "profile" for formulating recruitment plans for a job as you do for making selection, training, appraisal, and payment decisions for it, actively segment and manage employees, and integrate/coordinate all the talent management functions.

2. All managers need to be familiar with **the basics of job analysis.**
   - Job analysis is the procedure through which you determine the duties of the department's positions and the characteristics of the people to hire for them.
   - Job descriptions are a list of what the job entails, while job specifications identify what kind of people to hire for the job.
   - The job analysis itself involves collecting information on matters such as work activities; required human behaviors; and machines, tools, and equipment used.
   - Managers use job analysis information in recruitment and selection, compensation, training, and performance appraisal.
   - The basic steps in job analysis include deciding the use of the job analysis information, reviewing relevant background information including organization charts, analyzing the job, verifying the information, and developing job descriptions and job specifications.

3. There are various **methods for collecting job analysis information.** These include interviews, questionnaires, observation, participant diary/logs, and quantitative

techniques such as position analysis questionnaires. Employers increasingly collect information from employees via the Internet.

4. Managers should be familiar with the process for **writing job descriptions**. While there is no standard format, most descriptions contain sections that cover job identification, a job summary, a listing of responsibilities and duties, the job incumbent's authority, and performance standards. The job description may also contain information regarding the job's working conditions, and the job specifications. Many employers use Internet sources such as www.jobdescription.com to facilitate writing job descriptions.

5. In **writing job specifications**, it's important to distinguish between specifications for trained versus untrained personnel. For trained employees, the process is relatively straightforward, because you're looking primarily for traits like experience. For untrained personnel, it's necessary to identify traits that might predict success on the job. Most job specifications come from the educated guesses of people like supervisors, and are based mostly on judgment. Some employers use statistical analyses to identify predictors or human traits that are related to success on the job.

6. Employers are creating "profiles" for each of their jobs. The aim of creating profiles is to create detailed descriptions of what is required for exceptional performance in a given role or job, in terms of required competencies, personal attributes, knowledge, and experience. Each job's profile then becomes the anchor for creating recruitment, selection, training, and evaluation and development plans for each job. **Competency-based job analysis** means describing the job in terms of measurable, observable, behavioral competencies (such as specific skills) that an employee doing the job must exhibit to do the job well. With the job of, say, a team member possibly changing daily, one should identify the skills the employee may need to move among jobs.

DISCUSSION QUESTIONS

1. Why, in summary, should managers think of staffing, training, appraising, and paying employees as a talent management process?
2. Explain to the head of a company how he or she could use the talent management approach to improve his or her company's performance.
3. What items are typically included in the job description?
4. What is job analysis? How can you make use of the information it provides?
5. We discussed several methods for collecting job analysis data—questionnaires, the position analysis questionnaire, and so on. Compare and contrast these methods, explaining what each is useful for and listing the pros and cons of each.
6. Describe the types of information typically found in a job specification.
7. Explain how you would conduct a job analysis.
8. Do you think companies can really do without detailed job descriptions? Why or why not?
9. In a company with only 25 employees, is there less need for job descriptions? Why or why not?

INDIVIDUAL AND GROUP ACTIVITIES

1. Working individually or in groups, obtain copies of job descriptions for clerical positions at the college or university where you study, or the firm where you work. What types of information do they contain? Do they give you enough information to explain what the job involves and how to do it? How would you improve on the description?
2. Working individually or in groups, use O*NET to develop a job description for your professor in this class. Based on that, use your judgment to develop a job specification. Compare your conclusions with those of other students or groups. Were there any significant differences? What do you think accounted for the differences?
3. The HRCI "Test Specifications" appendix at the end of this book (pages 633–640) lists the knowledge someone studying for the HRCI certification exam needs to have in each area of human resource management (such as in Strategic Management, Workforce Planning, and Human Resource Development). In groups of four to five students, do four things: (1) review that appendix now; (2) identify the material in this chapter that relates to the required knowledge in the appendix lists; (3) write four multiple-choice exam questions on this material that you believe would be suitable for inclusion in the HRCI exam; and (4) if time permits, have someone from your team post your team's questions in front of the class, so the students in other teams can take each others' exam questions.

EXPERIENTIAL EXERCISE

The Instructor's Job Description

Purpose: The purpose of this exercise is to give you experience in developing a job description, by developing one for your instructor.

Required Understanding: You should understand the mechanics of job analysis and be thoroughly familiar with the job analysis questionnaires. (See Figures 4-3 and 4-9.)

How to Set Up the Exercise/Instructions: Set up groups of four to six students for this exercise. As in all exercises in this book, the groups should be separated and should not converse with each other. Half of the groups in the class will develop the job description using the job analysis questionnaire (Figure 4-3), and the other half of the groups will develop it using the job description questionnaire (Figure 4-9). Each student should review his or her questionnaire (as appropriate) before joining his or her group.

1. Each group should do a job analysis of the instructor's job: Half of the groups will use the Figure 4-3 job analysis questionnaire for this purpose, and half will use the Figure 4-9 job description questionnaire.
2. Based on this information, each group will develop its own job description and job specification for the instructor.
3. Next, each group should choose a partner group, one that developed the job description and job specification using the alternate method. (A group that used the job analysis questionnaire should be paired with a group that used the job description questionnaire.)
4. Finally, within each of these new combined groups, compare and critique each of the two sets of job descriptions and job specifications. Did each job analysis method provide different types of information? Which seems superior? Does one seem more advantageous for some types of jobs than others?

APPLICATION CASE

THE FLOOD

In May 2011, Mississippi River flooding hit Vicksburg, Mississippi, and the Optima Air Filter Company. Many employees' homes were devastated, and the firm found that it had to hire almost three completely new crews, one for each of its shifts. The problem was that the "old-timers" had known their jobs so well that no one had ever bothered to draw up job descriptions for them. When about 30 new employees began taking their places, there was general confusion about what they should do and how they should do it.

The flood quickly became old news to the firm's out-of-state customers, who wanted filters, not excuses. Phil Mann, the firm's president, was at his wits' end. He had about 30 new employees, 10 old-timers, and his original factory supervisor, Maybelline. He decided to meet with Linda Lowe, a consultant from the local university's business school. She immediately had the old-timers fill out a job questionnaire that listed all their duties. Arguments ensued almost at once: Both Phil and Maybelline thought the old-timers were exaggerating to make themselves look more important, and the old-timers insisted that the lists faithfully reflected their duties. Meanwhile, the customers clamored for their filters.

Questions

1. Should Phil and Linda ignore the old-timers' protests and write the job descriptions as they see fit? Why? Why not? How would you go about resolving the differences?
2. How would you have conducted the job analysis? What should Phil do now?

CONTINUING CASE

CARTER CLEANING COMPANY

The Job Description

Based on her review of the stores, Jennifer concluded that one of the first matters she had to attend to involved developing job descriptions for her store managers.

As Jennifer tells it, her lessons regarding job descriptions in her basic management and HR management courses were insufficient to fully convince her of the pivotal role job descriptions actually play in the smooth functioning of an enterprise. Many times during her first few weeks on the job, Jennifer found herself asking one of her store managers why he was violating what she knew to be recommended company policies and procedures. Repeatedly, the answers were either "Because I didn't know it was my job" or "Because I didn't know that was the way we were supposed to do it." Jennifer knew that a job description, along with a set of standards and procedures that specified what was to be done and how to do it, would go a long way toward alleviating this problem.

In general, the store manager is responsible for directing all store activities in such a way that quality work is produced, customer relations and sales are maximized, and profitability is maintained through effective control of labor, supply, and energy costs. In accomplishing that general aim, a specific store manager's duties and responsibilities include quality control, store appearance and cleanliness, customer relations, bookkeeping and cash management, cost control and productivity, damage control, pricing, inventory control, spotting and cleaning, machine maintenance, purchasing, employee safety, hazardous waste removal, human resource administration, and pest control.

The questions that Jennifer had to address follow.

Questions

1. What should be the format and final form of the store manager's job description?
2. Is it practical to specify standards and procedures in the body of the job description, or should these be kept separate?
3. How should Jennifer go about collecting the information required for the standards, procedures, and job description?
4. What, in your opinion, should the store manager's job description look like and contain?

TRANSLATING STRATEGY INTO HR POLICIES & PRACTICES CASE

THE HOTEL PARIS CASE

Job Descriptions

The Hotel Paris's competitive strategy is "To use superior guest service to differentiate the Hotel Paris properties, and to thereby increase the length of stay and return rate of guests, and thus boost revenues and profitability." HR manager Lisa Cruz must now formulate functional policies and activities that support this competitive strategy by eliciting the required employee behaviors and competencies.

As an experienced human resource director, the Hotel Paris's Lisa Cruz knew that recruitment and selection processes invariably influenced employee competencies and behavior and, through them, the company's bottom line. Everything about the workforce—its collective skills, morale, experience, and motivation—depended on attracting and then selecting the right employees.

In reviewing the Hotel Paris's employment systems, she was therefore concerned that virtually all the company's job descriptions were out of date, and that many jobs had no descriptions at all. She knew that without accurate job descriptions, all her improvement efforts would be in vain. After all, if you don't know a job's duties, responsibilities, and human requirements, how can you decide who to hire or how to train them? To create human resource policies and practices that would produce employee competencies and behaviors needed to achieve the hotel's strategic aims, Lisa's team first had to produce a set of usable job descriptions.

A brief analysis, conducted with her company's CFO, reinforced that observation. They chose departments across the hotel chain that did and did not have updated job descriptions. Although they understood that many other factors might be influencing the results, they believed that the relationships they observed did suggest that having job descriptions had a positive influence on various employee behaviors and competencies. Perhaps having the descriptions facilitated the employee selection process, or perhaps the departments with the descriptions just had better managers.

She knew the Hotel Paris's job descriptions would have to include traditional duties and responsibilities. However, most should also include several competencies unique to each job. For example, job descriptions for the front-desk clerks might include "able to check a guest in or out in 5 minutes or less." Most service employees' descriptions included the competency, "able to exhibit patience and guest supportiveness even when busy with other activities."

Questions

In teams or individually:

1. Based on the hotel's stated strategy, list at least four important employee behaviors for the Hotel Paris's staff.
2. If time permits, spend some time prior to class observing the front-desk clerk at a local hotel. In any case, create a job description for a Hotel Paris front-desk clerk.

KEY TERMS

ENDNOTES

1. Daimler is now expanding this plant; see www.autoblog.com/2009/03/23/rumormill-mercedes-benz-expected-to-expand-alabama-plant, accessed March 25, 2009, http://mbusi.com/ accessed August 20, 2011.
2. "Survey: Talent Management a Top Concern," *CIO Insight*, January 2, 2007.
3. Michael Laff, "Talent Management: From Hire to Retire," *Training and Development*, November 2006, pp. 42–48.
4. www.talentmanagement101.com, accessed December 10, 2007.
5. Ibid.
6. www.silkroadtech.com, accessed December 10, 2007.
7. "Software Facilitates Talent Management," *Product News Network,* May 18, 2007.
8. For a good discussion of job analysis, see James Clifford, "Job Analysis: Why Do It, and How Should It Be Done?" *Public Personnel Management* 23, no. 2 (Summer 1994), pp. 321–340; and "Job Analysis," www.paq.com/index.cfm?FuseAction=bulletins.job-analysis, accessed February 3, 2009.
9. One writer calls job analysis, "The hub of virtually all human resource management activities necessary for the successful functioning organizations." See Parbudyal Singh, "Job Analysis for a Changing Workplace," *Human Resource Management Review* 18 (2008), p. 87.
10. Lindsay Chappell, "Mercedes Factories Embrace a New Order," *Automotive News*, May 28, 2001. See also, www.autoblog.com/2009/03/23/rumormillmercedes-benz-expected-to-expandalabama-plant, accessed March 25, 2009,

http://mbusi.com, accessed August 20, 2011.

11. Richard Henderson, *Compensation Management: Rewarding Performance* (Upper Saddle River, NJ: Prentice Hall, 1994), pp. 139–150. See also T. A. Stetz et al., "New Tricks for an Old Dog: Visualizing Job Analysis Results," *Public Personnel Management* 38, no. 1 (Spring 2009), pp. 91–100.

12. Ron Miller, "Streamlining Claims Processing," *eWeek* 23, no. 25 (June 19, 2006), pp. 33, 35.

13. Darin Hartley, "Job Analysis at the Speed of Reality," *Training & Development*, September 2004, pp. 20–22.

14. See Henderson, *Compensation Management*, pp. 148–152.

15. Wayne Cascio, *Applied Psychology in Human Resource Management* (Upper Saddle River, NJ: Prentice Hall, 1998), p. 142. Distortion of information is a potential with all self-report methods of gathering information. See for example, http://apps.opm.gov/ADT/ContentFiles/AssessmentDecisionGuide071807.pdf, accessed October 1, 2011.

16. Frederick Morgeson et al., "Self Presentation Processes in Job Analysis: A Field Experiment Investigating Inflation in Abilities, Tasks, and Competencies," *Journal of Applied Psychology* 89, no. 4 (November 4, 2004), pp. 674–686; and Frederick Morgeson and Stephen Humphrey, "The Work Design Questionnaire (WDQ): Developing and Validating a Comprehensive Measure for Assessing Job Design and the Nature of Work," *Journal of Applied Psychology* 91, no. 6 (2006), pp. 1321–1339.

17. Arthur Martinez et al., "Job Title Inflation," *Human Resource Management Review* 18 (2008), pp. 19–27.

18. Note that the PAQ (and other quantitative techniques) can also be used for job evaluation, which is explained in Chapter 11.

19. We will see that job evaluation is the process through which jobs are compared to one another and their values determined. Although usually viewed as a job analysis technique, the PAQ, in practice, is actually as much or more of a job evaluation technique and could therefore be discussed in either this chapter or in Chapter 11.

20. Jack Smith and Milton Hakel, "Convergence Among Data Sources, Response Bias, and Reliability and Validity of a Structured Job Analysis Questionnaire," *Personnel Psychology* 32 (Winter 1979), pp. 677–692. See also Frederick Morgeson and Stephen Humphrey, "The Work Design Questionnaire (WDQ): Developing and Validating a Comprehensive Measure for Assessing Job Design and the Nature of Work," *Journal of Applied Psychology* 91, no. 6 (2006), pp. 1321–1339; www.paq.com/index.cfm?FuseAction=bulletins.job-analysis, accessed February 3, 2009.

21. www.paq.com/index.cfm?FuseAction=bulletins.job-analysis, accessed February 3, 2009.

22. Another technique, *functional job analysis*, is similar to the DOL method. However, it rates the job not just on data, people, and things, but also on the extent to which performing the task also requires four other things—specific instructions, reasoning and judgment, mathematical ability, and verbal and language facilities.

23. Roni Reiter-Palmon et al., "Development of an O*NET Web-Based Job Analysis and Its Implementation in the U.S. Navy: Lessons Learned," *Human Resource Management Review* 16 (2006), pp. 294–309.

24. Ibid., p. 294.

25. Ibid., p. 295.

26. Digitizing the information also enables the employer to quantify, tag, and electronically store and access it more readily. Lauren McEntire et al., "Innovations in Job Analysis: Development and Application of Metrics to Analyze Job Data," *Human Resource Management Review* 16 (2006), pp. 310–323.

27. Regarding this discussion, see Henderson, *Compensation Management*, pp. 175–184. See also Louisa Wah, "The Alphabet Soup of Job Titles," *Management Review* 87, no. 6 (June 1, 1998), pp. 40–43.

28. For discussions of writing job descriptions, see James Evered, "How to Write a Good Job Description," *Supervisory Management*, April 1981, pp. 14–19; Roger J. Plachy, "Writing Job Descriptions That Get Results," *Personnel*, October 1987, pp. 56–58; and Jean Phillips and Stanley Gulley, *Strategic Staffing* (Upper Saddle River, New Jersey: Pearson Education, 2012), pp. 89–95.

29. Evered, op cit., p. 16.

30. Ibid.

31. Ibid.

32. Deborah Kearney, *Reasonable Accommodations: Job Descriptions in the Age of ADA, OSHA, and Workers Comp* (New York: Van Nostrand Reinhold, 1994), p. 9. See also Paul Starkman, "The ADA's Essential Job Function Requirements: Just How Essential Does an Essential Job Function Have to Be?" *Employee Relations Law Journal* 26, no. 4 (Spring 2001), pp. 43–102; and Benjamin Wolkinson and Sarah Wolkinson, "The Pregnant Police Officer's Overtime Duties and Forced Leave Policies Under Title VII, the ADA, and FMLA," *Employee Relations Law Journal* 36, no. 1 (Summer 2010), pp. 3–20.

33. Kearney, op cit.

34. See, for example, Christelle Lapolice et al., "Linking O*NET Descriptors to Occupational Literacy Requirements Using Job Component Validation," *Personnel Psychology* 61 (2008), pp. 405–441.

35. Mariani, "Replace with a Database."

36. O*Net™ is a trademark of the U.S. Department of Labor, Employment, and Training Administration.

37. Jorgen Sandberg, "Understanding Competence at Work," *Harvard Business Review*, March 2001, p. 28. Other organization chart software vendors include Nakisa, Aquire, and HumanConcepts. See "Advanced Org Charting," *Workforce Management*, May 19, 2008, p. 34.

38. Based on Ernest J. McCormick and Joseph Tiffin, *Industrial Psychology* (Upper Saddle River, NJ: Prentice Hall, 1974), pp. 56–61.

39. Steven Hunt, "Generic Work Behavior: An Investigation into the Dimensions of Entry-Level, Hourly Job Performance," *Personnel Psychology* 49 (1996), pp. 51–83.

40. Jean Phillips and Stanley Gulley, *Strategic Staffing* (Upper Saddle River, NJ: Pearson Education, 2012), pp. 96–102.

41. Ibid., p. 96.

42. Ibid., p. 102.

43. Jeffrey Shippmann et al., "The Practice of Competency Modeling," *Personnel Psychology* 53, no. 3 (2000), p. 703.

44. Richard S. Wellins et al., "Nine Best Practices for Effective Talent Management," DDI Development Dimensions International, Inc. http://www.ddiworld.com/DDIWorld/media/white-papers/ninebestpracticetalentmanagement_wp_ddi.pdf?ext=pdf, accessed August 20, 2011. For a discussion of competency modeling, see Michael A. Campion, Alexis A. Fink, Brian J. Ruggeberg, Linda Carr, Geneva M. Phillips, and Ronald B. Odman, "Doing Competencies Well: Best Practices in Competency Modeling," *Personnel Psychology* 64, no. 1 (2011), pp. 225–262.

45. Wellins, et al., op cit.

46. Adapted from Richard Mirabile, "Everything You Wanted to Know About Competency Modeling," *Training & Development* 51, no. 8 (August 1997), pp. 73–78. See also Campion et al., op cit.

47. Mirabile, op cit.

48. Robert Grossman, "IBM'S HR Takes a Risk," *HR Magazine*, April 27, 2007, p. 57.

49. See, for example, Carol Spicer, "Building a Competency Model," *HR Magazine*, April 2009, pp. 34–36.

5
Personnel Planning and Recruiting

Source: Hannibal Hanschke/Reuters Pictures–Americas.

LEARNING OBJECTIVES

1. List the steps in the recruitment and selection process.
2. Explain the main techniques used in employment planning and forecasting.
3. Explain and give examples for the need for effective recruiting.
4. Name and describe the main internal sources of candidates.
5. List and discuss the main outside sources of candidates.
6. Develop a help wanted ad.
7. Explain how to recruit a more diverse workforce.

A s its board of directors began reviewing possible candidates to be IBM's next CEO, their thoughts turned to the sort of company IBM would be in the next few years. Some trends were clear. IBM had already sold off several "commodity" businesses such as personal computers and disk drives, replacing them with new software and service/consulting businesses. The new CEO would have to address new trends such as cloud computing. More sales would come from emerging markets in Asia and Africa. Strategic changes like these meant that IBM's employees would need new skills, and that the firm needed new personnel and succession plans for how to staff its new businesses.[1]

WHERE ARE WE NOW . . .

In Chapter 4, we discussed job analysis and the methods managers use to create job descriptions, job specifications, and competency profiles or models. The purpose of this chapter is to improve your effectiveness in recruiting candidates. The topics we discuss include personnel planning and forecasting, recruiting job candidates, and developing and using application forms. Then, in Chapter 6, we'll turn to the methods managers use to select the best employees from this applicant pool.

Access a host of interactive learning aids at **www.mymanagementlab.com** to help strengthen your understanding of the chapter concepts.

INTRODUCTION

Job analysis identifies the duties and human requirements for each of the company's jobs. The next step is to decide which of these jobs you need to fill, and to recruit and select employees for them. The traditional way to envision *recruitment and selection* is as a series of hurdles (Figure 5-1):

1. Decide what positions to fill, through *workforce/personnel planning and forecasting.*
2. Build a pool of candidates for these jobs, by *recruiting* internal or external candidates.
3. Have candidates complete *application forms* and perhaps undergo initial screening interviews.
4. Use *selection tools* like tests, background investigations, and physical exams to identify viable candidates.
5. Decide who to make an offer to, by having the supervisor and perhaps others *interview* the candidates.

This chapter focuses on personnel planning and on recruiting employees. Chapter 6 addresses tests, background checks, and physical exams. Chapter 7 focuses on interviewing—by far the most widely used selection technique.

WORKFORCE PLANNING AND FORECASTING

Recruitment and selection ideally starts with workforce planning. After all, if you don't know what your team's employment needs will be in the next few months, why should you be hiring?

Workforce (or employment or personnel) planning is the process of deciding what positions the firm will have to fill, and how to fill them. It embraces all future positions, from maintenance clerk to CEO. However, most firms call the process of deciding how to fill executive jobs *succession planning.*

Strategy and Workforce Planning

In either case, as at IBM (see page 137), employment planning should reflect the firm's strategic plans. Thus plans to enter new businesses or reduce costs all influence the types of positions you'll need to fill (or eliminate). Strategic issues are always crucial. In the short term, there's not much employers can do to overcome recessions, housing bubbles, or increases or decreases in consumer spending. However, the managers should control their strategy. So, knowing that the firm plans, say, to expand abroad, means making plans for ramping up hiring in the firm's international division. The accompanying Strategic Context feature illustrates this.

FIGURE 5-1 Steps in
Recruitment and Selection
Process

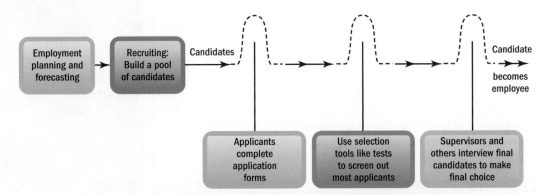

The recruitment and selection process is a series of hurdles aimed at selecting the best candidate for the job.

THE STRATEGIC CONTEXT

IBM

IBM has been transitioning from supplying mostly computers to supplying software and consulting services. Therefore, in terms of IBM's strategic workforce needs, "in three years, 22 percent of our workforce will have obsolete skills. Of the 22 percent, 85 percent have fundamental competencies that we can build on to get them ready for skills we'll need years from now." The remaining 15% will either self-select out of IBM or be let go.[2]

As at IBM, workforce and succession planning should entail thinking through the skills and competencies the firm needs to execute its overall strategy. At IBM, for instance, human resource executives review with finance and other executives the personnel ramifications of their company's strategic plans.[3] In other words, "What sorts of skills and competencies will we need to execute our strategic plans?"

Figure 5-2 summarizes the link between strategic and personnel planning. Like all plans, personnel plans require some forecasts or estimates, in this case, of three things: *personnel needs*, the *supply of inside* candidates, and the likely *supply of outside* candidates. The basic workforce planning process is to forecast the employer's demand for labor and supply of labor; then identify supply–demand gaps and develop action plans to fill the projected gaps.

We'll start with forecasting personnel needs.

Forecasting Personnel Needs (Labor Demand)

How many people will we need? Managers consider several factors.[4] For example, when Dan Hilbert took over staffing at Valero Energy, he reviewed Valero's demographics, growth plans, and turnover history. He discovered that projected employment shortfalls

FIGURE 5-2 Linking Employer's Strategy to Plans

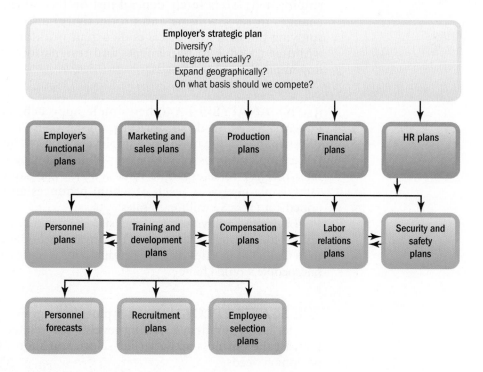

workforce (or employment or personnel) planning
The process of deciding what positions the firm will have to fill, and how to fill them.

were four times more than Valero could fill with its current recruitment procedures. He turned to formulating new personnel plans for boosting employee retention and recruiting and screening more candidates.[5]

A firm's staffing needs reflect demand for its products or services, adjusted for changes the firm plans to make in its strategic goals and for changes in its turnover rate and productivity. Forecasting workforce demand therefore starts with estimating what the demand will be for your products or services. Short term, management should be concerned with daily, weekly, and seasonal forecasts.[6] For example, retailers track daily sales trends because they know, for instance, that Mother's Day produces a jump in business and a need for additional store staff. Seasonal forecasts are critical for retailers contemplating end-of-year holiday sales, and for many firms such as landscaping and air-conditioning vendors.

Looking out a year or two isn't so easy. Managers will follow industry publications and economic forecasts closely, for instance from the *Conference Board*. Predicting a rise or fall in business activity a year of two in the future may not be precise. However, the planning process may help you to develop contingency staffing plans to address the potential changes in demand.

The basic process of forecasting personnel needs is to forecast revenues first. Then estimate the size of the staff required to support this sales volume. However, managers must also consider other, strategic factors. These include projected turnover, decisions to upgrade (or downgrade) products or services, productivity changes, and financial resources. There are several simple tools for projecting personnel needs, as follows.

TREND ANALYSIS   **Trend analysis** means studying variations in the firm's employment levels over the last few years. For example, you might compute the number of employees at the end of each of the last 5 years, or perhaps the number in each subgroup (like sales, production, secretarial, and administrative). The aim is to identify trends that might continue into the future.

Trend analysis can provide an initial estimate of future staffing needs, but employment levels rarely depend just on the passage of time. Other factors (like changes in sales volume and productivity) also affect staffing needs. Carefully studying the firm's historical and current workforce demographics and voluntary withdrawals (due to retirements and resignations, for instance) can help reveal impending labor force needs.

RATIO ANALYSIS   Another simple approach, **ratio analysis**, means making forecasts based on the historical ratio between (1) some causal factor (like sales volume) and (2) the number of employees required (such as number of salespeople). For example, suppose a salesperson traditionally generates $500,000 in sales. If the sales revenue to salespeople ratio remains the same, you would require six new salespeople next year (each of whom produces an extra $500,000) to produce a hoped-for extra $3 million in sales.

Like trend analysis, ratio analysis assumes that productivity remains about the same—for instance, that you can't motivate each salesperson to produce much more than $500,000 in sales. If sales productivity were to rise or fall, the ratio of sales to salespeople would change.

THE SCATTER PLOT   A **scatter plot** shows graphically how two variables—such as sales and your firm's staffing levels—are related. If they are, then if you can forecast the business activity (like sales), you should also be able to estimate your personnel needs.

For example, suppose a 500-bed hospital expects to expand to 1,200 beds over the next 5 years. The human resource director wants to forecast how many registered nurses they'll need. The human resource director realizes she must determine the relationship between size of hospital (in terms of number of beds) and number of nurses required. She calls eight hospitals of various sizes and gets the following figures:

Size of Hospital (Number of Beds)	Number of Registered Nurses
200	240
300	260
400	470
500	500
600	620
700	660
800	820
900	860

Figure 5-3 shows hospital size on the horizontal axis. It shows number of nurses on the vertical axis. If these two factors are related, then the points you plot (from the data above) will tend to fall along a straight line, as they do here. If you carefully draw in a line to minimize the distances between the line and each one of the plotted points, you will be able to estimate the number of nurses needed for each hospital size. Thus, for a 1,200-bed hospital, the human resource director would assume she needs about 1,210 nurses.

While simple, tools like scatter plots have drawbacks.[7]

1. They generally focus on historical sales/personnel relationships and assume that the firm's existing activities will continue as is.

2. They tend to support compensation plans that reward managers for managing ever-larger staffs, irrespective of the company's strategic needs.

3. They tend to institutionalize existing ways of doing things, even in the face of change.

MARKOV ANALYSIS Employers also use a mathematical process known as *Markov analysis* (or "transition analysis") to forecast availability of internal job candidates. Markov analysis involves creating a matrix that shows the probabilities that employees in the chain of feeder positions for a key job (such as from junior engineer, to engineer, to senior engineer, to engineering supervisor, to director

FIGURE 5-3 Determining the Relationship Between Hospital Size and Number of Nurses

Note: After fitting the line, you can project how many employees you'll need, given your projected volume.

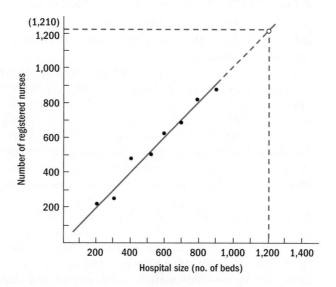

of engineering) will move from position to position and therefore be available to fill the key position.

Whichever forecasting tool you use, managerial judgment should play a big role. It's rare that any historical trend, ratio, or relationship will simply continue. You will therefore have to modify any forecast based on subjective factors—such as the feeling that more employees will be quitting—you believe will be important.

Improving Productivity Through HRIS

Computerized Personnel Forecasting

Computerized forecasts enable managers to build more variables into their personnel projections.[8] These systems rely on setting clear goals, such as reducing inventory on hand.[9] Other variables might include direct labor hours required to produce one unit of product (a measure of productivity), and minimum, maximum, and probable sales projections. Based on such input, a typical program generates average staff levels required to meet product demands, as well as separate forecasts for direct labor (such as assembly workers), indirect staff (such as secretaries), and exempt staff (such as executives).

With programs like these, employers can more accurately translate projected productivity and sales levels into personnel needs. Many firms particularly use computerized employee forecasting systems for estimating short-term needs. In retailing, for instance, labor scheduling systems help retailers estimate required staffing needs based on sales forecasts and estimated store traffic. As one vendor says, "[Our] Workforce Forecast Manager analyzes your business drivers to produce an accurate forecast down to 15 minute intervals. Seasonal variations, events, and current trends are consistently accounted for . . ."[10]

Perhaps because the demand for electric power is relatively predictable, utilities tend to do exemplary workforce planning. For example, at Chelan County Public Utility District, the development manager used spreadsheets to build a statistical model encompassing such things as age, tenure, turnover rate, and time to train new employees. This model helped them quickly identify five employment "hotspots" among 33 occupational groups at their company. This in turn prompted them to focus more closely on creating plans to retain and hire, for instance, more systems operators.[11]

Forecasting the Supply of Inside Candidates

Knowing your staffing needs satisfies only half the staffing equation. Next, you have to estimate the likely supply of both inside and outside candidates. Most firms start with the inside candidates.

The main task here is determining which current employees might be qualified for the projected openings. For this you need to know current employees' skills sets—their current qualifications. Sometimes it's obvious how you have to proceed. When Google's founders wanted a replacement for CEO Eric Schmidt, they chose one of their own.

Sometimes who to choose is not so obvious. Here, managers turn to **qualifications (or skills) inventories**. These contain data on employees' performance records, educational background, and promotability. Whether manual or computerized, these help managers determine which employees are available for promotion or transfer.

MANUAL SYSTEMS AND REPLACEMENT CHARTS   Department managers or owners of smaller firms often use manual devices to track employee qualifications. Thus a *personnel inventory and development record form* compiles qualifications information on each employee. The information includes education, company-sponsored courses taken, career and development interests, languages, desired assignments, and skills. **Personnel replacement charts** (Figure 5-4) are another option, particularly for the firm's top positions. They show the present performance and promotability for each position's potential replacement. As an alternative, you can develop a **position replacement card**. For this you create a card for each position, showing possible replacements as well as their present performance, promotion potential, and training.

FIGURE 5-4 Management Replacement Chart Showing Development Needs of Potential Future Divisional Vice Presidents

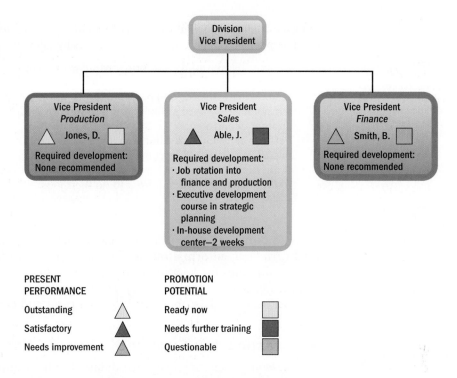

PRESENT PERFORMANCE

Outstanding

Satisfactory

Needs improvement

PROMOTION POTENTIAL

Ready now

Needs further training

Questionable

COMPUTERIZED SKILLS INVENTORIES   Larger firms obviously can't track the qualifications of hundreds or thousands of employees manually. Larger employers therefore computerize this information, using various packaged software systems such as SurveyAnalytics's Skills Inventory Software.

Such programs help management anticipate human resource shortages, and facilitate making employment recruitment and training plans.[12] Increasingly, they also link skills inventories with their other human resources systems. So, for instance, an employee's skills inventory might automatically update each time he or she is trained or appraised.

The usual process is for the employee, the supervisor, and human resource manager to enter information about the employee's background, experience, and skills via the system. Then, when a manager needs a person for a position, he or she uses key words to describe the position's specifications (for instance, in terms of education and skills). The computerized system then produces a list of qualified candidates. Computerized skills inventory data typically include items like *work experience codes, product knowledge*, the employee's *level of familiarity* with the employer's product lines or services, the person's *industry experience*, and *formal education*.

KEEPING THE INFORMATION PRIVATE   The employer should secure all its employee data.[13] Much of the data is personal (such as Social Security numbers and illnesses). Legislation gives employees legal rights regarding who has access to information about them. The legislation includes the Federal Privacy Act of 1974 (applies to federal workers), the New York Personal Privacy Act of 1985, HIPAA (regulates use of medical records), and the Americans with Disabilities Act. Employers should keep their manual records under lock and key.

Internet access makes it relatively easy for more people to access the firm's computerized files.[14] One solution is to incorporate an access matrix in the database management system. These define the rights of users to various kinds of access (such

qualifications (or skills) inventories
Manual or computerized records listing employees' education, career and development interests, languages, special skills, and so on, to be used in selecting inside candidates for promotion.

personnel replacement charts
Company records showing present performance and promotability of inside candidates for the most important positions.

position replacement card
A card prepared for each position in a company to show possible replacement candidates and their qualifications.

FIGURE 5-5 Keeping Data Safe

Source: HR Magazine by Caternicchia. Copyright 2005 by Society for Human Resource Management (SHRM). Reproduced with permission of Society for Human Resource Management (SHRM) in the format Textbook via Copyright Clearance Center.

Since intruders can strike from outside an organization or from within, HR departments can help screen out potential identity thieves by following four basic rules:

- Perform background checks on anyone who is going to have access to personal information.
- If someone with access to personal information is out sick or on leave, don't hire a temporary employee to replace him or her. Instead, bring in a trusted worker from another department.
- Perform random background checks such as random drug tests. Just because someone passed 5 years ago doesn't mean their current situation is the same.
- Limit access to information such as SSNs, health information, and other sensitive data to HR managers who require it to do their jobs.

as "read only" or "write only") to each database element. (So, those in accounting might *read only* information such as an employee's address.) Figure 5-5 summarizes some guidelines for keeping employee data safe. A growing problem is that peer-to-peer file-sharing applications jump firewalls and give outsiders quick access. Pfizer Inc. lost personal data on about 17,000 current and former employees this way.[15]

Forecasting the Supply of Outside Candidates

If there won't be enough inside candidates to fill the anticipated openings (or you want to go outside for another reason), you will turn to outside candidates.

Forecasting labor supply depends first on the manager's own sense of what's happening in his or her industry and locale. He or she will then supplement these observations with more formal labor market analyses, for instance, from the U.S. Bureau of Labor Statistics and from O*Net. For example, unemployment rates around 9% in the United States in 2011 signaled to HR managers that finding good candidates would be easier.[16]

Information like this is easy to find, both online and in print format. For example, look for economic projections online, for instance, from the U.S. Congressional Budget Office (www.cbo.gov/showdoc.cfm?index=1824&sequence=0) and the Bureau of Labor Statistics (www.bls.gov/news.release/ecopro.toc.htm). For hard-copy formats, *Bloomberg BusinessWeek* presents a weekly snapshot of the economy on its Outlook page, as well as a yearly forecast in December.

Your planning may also require forecasting specific occupations such as nurse, computer programmer, or teacher. Recently, for instance, there has been an under-supply of nurses. O*NET (discussed in Chapter 4) includes projections for most occupations. The U.S. Bureau of Labor Statistics publishes annual occupational projections both online and in the *Monthly Labor Review* and in *Occupational Outlook Quarterly*. Beyond specific occupations, the emphasis on technologically advanced jobs means many will lack basic skills such as communication, creativity, and teamwork.[17]

Talent Management and Predictive Workforce Monitoring

Traditionally, employers engage in formal workforce planning perhaps every year or so. However, this may not always provide enough time. For instance, having failed to do much such planning for years, Valero almost didn't have sufficient time to gear up its new employee development plan.

Applying a talent management philosophy to workforce planning requires being more proactive. Specifically, it requires *paying continuous attention* to workforce planning issues. Managers call this newer, continuous workforce planning approach *predictive workforce monitoring*. Some examples follow.

Intel Corporation example. Intel conducts semiannual "Organization Capability Assessments." The staffing department works with the firm's business heads twice a year to assess workforce needs—both immediate and up to 2 years in the future.[18]

Amerada Hess example. Amerada Hess uses its Organizational Capability (OC) group to monitor workforce attrition (such as retirement age, experience with Hess, education, etc.) and prospective talent requirements. It "then works with the lines of business to better prepare them for meeting changing global talent demands. The group considers how each line of business is evolving, examines what jobs at Hess will look like in the future, identifies sources for procuring the best talent, and assists in developing current and newly hired employees."[19]

Valero Energy example. Valero created a *labor supply chain* for monitoring steps in recruiting and hiring. It includes an analytic tool that predicts Valero's labor needs based on past experience. It also includes computer screen "dashboards" that show how components in the chain, such as ads placed on job boards, are performing according to cost, speed, and quality. In 2002, it took 41 pieces of paper to hire an employee and more than 120 days to fill a position. Each hire cost about $12,000. Soon, with the new labor supply chain in place, little paper was needed to bring an employee on board; the time-to-fill figure fell to below 40 days and cost per hire dropped to $2,300.[20]

ABB example. ABB's Talent Management process allows talent information to be stored on a global IT platform. For example, the system stores performance appraisals, career plans, and training and development information. It also shows a global overview of key management positions, including who holds them, and their potential successors. Potential successors get two kinds of assessments: by line managers, and against externally benchmarked leadership competency profiles.[21]

Developing an Action Plan to Match Projected Labor Supply and Labor Demand

Workforce planning should logically culminate in a workforce action plan. This lays out the employer's projected workforce demand–supply gaps, as well as staffing plans for filling the necessary positions. The staffing plan should identify the positions to be filled, potential internal and external sources for these positions, the required training, development, and promotional activities moving people into the positions will entail, and the resources that implementing the staffing plan will require. Resources might include, for instance, advertising costs, recruiter fees, relocation costs, and travel and interview expenses.[22]

The Recruiting Yield Pyramid

The manager should recognize that filling a relative handful of positions might require recruiting dozens or hundreds of candidates. Employers therefore use a staffing or **recruiting yield pyramid** as shown in Figure 5-6 to gauge the dimensions of the

FIGURE 5-6 Recruiting Yield Pyramid

50	New hires
100	Offers made (2:1)
150	Candidates interviewed (3:2)
200	Candidates invited (4:3)
1,200	Leads generated (6:1)

recruiting yield pyramid
The historical arithmetic relationships between recruitment leads and invitees, invitees and interviews, interviews and offers made, and offers made and offers accepted.

staffing issues it needs to address. In Figure 5-6, the company knows it needs 50 new entry-level accountants next year. From experience, the firm also knows the following:

- The ratio of offers made to actual new hires is 2 to 1.
- The ratio of candidates interviewed to offers made is 3 to 2.
- The ratio of candidates invited for interviews to candidates interviewed is about 4 to 3.
- Finally, the firm knows that of six leads that come in from all its recruiting sources, it typically invites only one applicant for an interview—a 6-to-1 ratio.

Given these ratios, the firm knows it must generate about 1,200 leads to be able to invite 200 viable candidates to its offices for interviews. The firm will then interview about 150 of those invited, and from these it will make 100 offers, and so on.

THE NEED FOR EFFECTIVE RECRUITING

> **3** Explain and give examples for the need for effective recruiting.

Assuming the company authorizes you to fill a position, the next step is to build up, through recruiting, an applicant pool. **Employee recruiting** means finding and/or attracting applicants for the employer's open positions.

Why Recruiting Is Important

It's hard to overemphasize the importance of effective recruiting. If only two candidates apply for two openings, you may have little choice but to hire them. But if 10 or 20 applicants appear, you can use techniques like interviews and tests to screen out all but the best.

Even high unemployment doesn't necessarily mean that it is easy to find good candidates. For example, a survey during an earlier slowdown (2003–2004) found that about half of respondents said they had "difficulty" finding qualified applicants. About 40% said it was "hard to find" good candidates.[23]

What Makes Recruiting a Challenge?

It's easy to assume that recruiting is easy—that all you need do is place a few ads on the Web. However, several things make it more complex.

- First, some recruiting methods are superior to others, depending on the type of job for which you are recruiting.
- Second, the success you have recruiting depends on nonrecruitment issues and policies. For example, paying 10% more than most firms in your locale should, other things being equal, help you build a bigger applicant pool faster.[24]
- Third, employment law prescribes what you can and cannot do when recruiting. For example, managers can't rely on word-of-mouth dissemination of information about job opportunities when the workforce is substantially all white or all members of some other class, such as Hispanic.[25]

Organizing How You Recruit

Should you centralize your firm's recruitment efforts, or let each plant or office do their own recruiting? For many firms, it's simply much easier to recruit centrally now that so much recruiting is on the Internet.[26] The accountants Deloitte & Touche Tohmatsu created a global recruitment site, thus eliminating the need to maintain 35 separate local recruiting Web sites.[27] Retailer 7-Eleven's site presents its worldwide job openings and lets prospective employees apply online.

THE SUPERVISOR'S ROLE   The human resource manager charged with filling an open position is seldom very familiar with the job itself. Someone has to tell this person what the position really entails, and what key things to look or watch out for. Only the position's supervisor can do this.

The supervisor should therefore know what sorts of questions to expect, and here your knowledge of job analysis should serve you well. For example, in addition to what the job entails now and its job specifications, the recruiter might want to know about the supervisor's leadership style and about the work group—is it a tough group to get along with, for instance?

INTERNAL SOURCES OF CANDIDATES

> **4** Name and describe the main internal sources of candidates.

Recruiting typically brings to mind LinkedIn, employment agencies, and classified ads, but internal sources—in other words, current employees or "hiring from within"—are often the best source of candidates.

Using Internal Sources: Pros and Cons

Filling open positions with inside candidates has several advantages. First, there is really no substitute for knowing a candidate's *strengths and weaknesses*, as you should after working with them for some time. Current employees may also be more *committed* to the company. *Morale* may rise if employees see promotions as rewards for loyalty and competence. And inside candidates should require *less orientation* and (perhaps) training than outsiders.

However, hiring from within can also backfire. Employees who apply for jobs and don't get them may become *discontented;* telling them why you rejected them and what remedial actions they might take is crucial. And too often internal recruiting is a *waste of time.* Many employers require managers to post job openings and interview all inside candidates. Yet the manager often knows whom he or she wants to hire. Requiring him or her to interview a stream of unsuspecting inside candidates can be a waste of time for everyone. *Inbreeding* is another potential drawback. When all managers come up through the ranks, they may have a tendency to maintain the status quo, when a new direction is required.

Finding Internal Candidates

Hiring from within ideally relies on job posting and the firm's skills inventories. **Job posting** means publicizing the open job to employees (usually by literally posting it on company intranets or bulletin boards). These postings list the job's attributes, like qualifications, supervisor, work schedule, and pay rate.

Qualifications skills banks also play a role. For example, the database may reveal persons who have potential for further training or who have the right background for the open job.

Rehiring

Should you rehire someone who left your employ? It depends. On the plus side, former employees are known quantities (more or less) and are already familiar with how you do things. On the other hand, employees who you let go may return with negative attitudes. A 2009 survey found that about 26 percent of employers who had laid people off recently planned to bring some back.[28]

In any event, you can reduce the chance of adverse reactions. After employees have been back on the job for awhile, credit them with the years of service they had accumulated before they left. In addition, inquire (before rehiring them) about what they did during the layoff and how they feel about returning: "You don't want someone coming back who feels they've been mistreated," said one manager.[29]

employee recruiting
Finding and/or attracting applicants for the employer's open positions.

job posting
Publicizing an open job to employees (often by literally posting it on bulletin boards) and listing its attributes, like qualifications, supervisor, working schedule, and pay rate.

Succession Planning

Hiring from within is particularly important when it involves filling the employer's top positions. Doing so requires **succession planning**—the ongoing process of systematically identifying, assessing, and developing organizational leadership to enhance performance.[30] About 36% of employers have formal succession planning programs.[31] As in IBM's search to eventually replace its CEO (outlined earlier in this chapter), succession planning should conform to basic talent management practices. In particular, the key is to profile the competencies that the firm's evolving strategy will require the new CEO to have; then use that profile to formulate an integrated development/appraisal/selection package for potential candidates.

Succession planning entails three steps: identify key needs, develop inside candidates, and assess and choose those who will fill the key positions.

IDENTIFY KEY NEEDS   First, based on the company's strategic and business plans, top management and the HR director identify what the company's future key position needs will be. Matters to address in this early stage include defining key positions, defining "high potentials", enlisting top management support, and reviewing the company's current talent. (Thus, plans to expand abroad may suggest bulking up the international division.[32])

DEVELOP INSIDE CANDIDATES   After identifying future key positions, management turns to creating candidates for these jobs. "Creating" means providing the inside or outside candidates you identify with the developmental experiences they require to be viable candidates. Employers develop high-potential employees through internal training and cross-functional experiences, job rotation, external training, and global/regional assignments.[33]

ASSESS AND CHOOSE   Finally, succession planning requires assessing these candidates and selecting those who will actually fill the key positions.[34]

Improving Productivity Through HRIS

Succession and Talent Planning Systems

More large employers use software to facilitate succession planning and talent management. These systems "Capture and search for information about employee competencies, skills, certifications, and experience . . . [and] Assess employees on key areas of leadership potential, job performance, and risk of leaving; Target employees for future roles."[35] As the user of one such system said, "The [SumTotal] platform allows us to track and assess the talent pool and promote people within the company. Our latest metrics show that 75% of key openings are fulfilled by internal candidates. The succession module helps us to identify who the next senior managers could be and build development plans to help them achieve their potential."[36]

Succession planning is an integral part of talent management. For example, when a new president took over at Dole Food Co., Inc., Dole was highly decentralized. The new president's strategy involved improving financial performance by reducing redundancies and centralizing certain activities, including succession planning.[37]

Web technology helped Dole do this. It contracted with application system providers (ASPs) to handle things like payroll management. For succession management, Dole chose software from Pilat NAI, which keeps all the data on its own servers for a monthly fee. Dole's managers access the program via the Web using a password. They fill out online résumés for themselves, including career interests, and note special considerations such as geographic restrictions.

The managers also assess themselves on four competencies. Once the manager provides his or her input, the program notifies that manager's boss. The latter then assesses his or her subordinate and indicates whether the person should be promoted. This assessment and the online résumés then go automatically to the division head and the divisional HR director. Dole's senior vice president for human resources then uses the information to create career development plans for each manager, including seminars and other programs.[38]

OUTSIDE SOURCES OF CANDIDATES

Firms can't always get all the employees they need from their current staff, and sometimes they just don't want to. We'll look at the sources firms use to find outside candidates next.

Recruiting via the Internet

For most employers and for most jobs, Internet-based recruiting is by far the recruiting source of choice.[39] For example, restaurant chain The Cheesecake Factory gets about a third of its management applicants via the Web. Most employers recruit through their own Web sites, or use job boards. Figure 5-7 highlights some top online

FIGURE 5-7 Some Top Online Recruiting Job Boards

Source: www.quintcareers.com/top_10_sites.html, accessed April 28, 2009. Used with permission of QuintCareers.com.

succession planning
The ongoing process of systematically identifying, assessing, and developing organizational leadership to enhance performance.

Source: www.careerbuilder.com/
MarketingWeb/iPhone/CBJobsAppli
cation.aspx?cbRecursionCnt=1&cbsi
d=7fd458dafd4a444fb192d9a24cee
d771-291142537-wx-6&ns_siteid=
ns_us_g_careerbuilder_ iphone,
accessed March 23, 2009.

recruiting job boards. Job boards account for about 12% of recent hires. Other major sources include company Web site, referrals, plus others such as temp to hire, rehires, and employment agencies.

The CareerBuilder.com iPhone application on the left offers a unique way to search nearly 2 million jobs on CareerBuilder.com, the largest U.S. job site.[40] Users may search for jobs by keyword, read job descriptions and salaries, save jobs to a list of favorites, and e-mail job links to anyone on their contact list. The application also takes advantage of the iPhone's geo-location capabilities. Users may direct it to search only for jobs in the region where they are located. Finally, the application integrates Google Maps by displaying a map of the city each job is located in.

Recruiting for professionals and managers is shifting from online job boards to social networking sites such as Facebook and LinkedIn. For example, Science Applications International Corp. cut the job boards it uses from 15 to 6 or so. Instead, its recruiters are searching for candidates on professional social networks instead. The problem is that many applications received via job boards didn't meet the job's qualifications. As one recruiter said, "recruiters had to put in all this extra time to read applications but we didn't get benefit from it." Instead, this company now hires recruiters who specialize in digging through social Web sites and competitors' publications to find applicants who may not even be looking for jobs.[41]

OTHER ONLINE RECRUITING PRACTICES   Again, in moving away from major job boards such as careerbuilder.com, recruiters are also seeking passive candidates (people not actively looking for jobs) by using social networking sites such as LinkedIn to find potential candidates.[42] One Massachusetts staffing firm uses its Facebook and LinkedIn pages to announce openings. Other firms use Twitter to announce job openings to jobseekers who subscribe to their Twitter feeds.[43] ResumePal, from the career site JobFox (www.jobfox.com/), is a recent recruiting innovation. ResumePal is an online standard universal job application. Jobseekers submit it to participating employers, who can then use the standardized application's keywords to identify viable candidates more easily.[44] McDonald's Corp. posted a series of employee testimonials on social networking sites like Second Life as a way to attract applicants.[45] Other employers simply screen through job boards' résumé listings.[46]

Sites such as Linkedin facilitate developing personal relationships for networking and employee referrals.[47] Accountants Deloitte & Touche asked employees to make short videos describing their experiences with Deloitte. It then took the 14 best (of 400 submitted) and posted them on YouTube.[48] Monster has a video product that helps employers integrate streaming video into their job postings.[49] Facebook makes it easy to start a company networking site, which many employers use for recruiting purposes.[50] McDonald's posted employee testimonials on networking sites like Second Life as a way to attract applicants.[51]

TEXTING   Some employers use text messaging to build an applicant pool. For example, at one diversity-oriented conference in New Orleans, consultants Hewitt Associates displayed posters asking attendees to text message *hewdiversity* to a specific five digit number. Each person texting then became part of Hewitt's "mobile recruiting network," periodically receiving text messages regarding Hewitt openings.[52]

THE DOT-JOBS DOMAIN   The *dot-jobs* domain gives job seekers a one-click conduit for finding jobs at the employers who register at www.goto.jobs. For example, applicants seeking a job at Disneyland can go to www.Disneyland.jobs. This takes them to Disney's Disneyland recruiting Web site.

VIRTUAL JOB FAIRS   Virtual (fully online) job fairs are another option. For example, the magazine *PR Week* organized such a fair for about a dozen public relations employers. At a virtual job fair, online visitors see a very similar setup to a regular job fair. They can listen to presentations, visit booths, leave résumés and business cards, participate in live chats, and get contact information from recruiters,

HR managers, and even hiring managers.[53] As one writer said, "virtual career fairs are appealing because they're a way to get your foot in the door without having to walk out the door."[54] The fairs last about 5 hours. Attendee might find 30 or more employers recruiting. Specialist virtual fair Web sites include Milicruit (for former military personnel) and Unicruit (for college students).

PROS AND CONS Web-based recruiting generates more responses quicker and for a longer time at less cost than just about any other method. But, it has two big potential problems.

First, fewer older people and some minorities use the Internet, so online application gathering may inadvertently exclude disproportionate numbers of older applicants (and certain minorities). To prove they've complied with EEO laws, employers should keep track of each applicant's race, sex, and ethnic group. The EEO says that, to be an "applicant," he or she must meet three conditions: he or she must express interest in employment; the employer must have taken steps to fill a specific job; and the individual must have followed the employer's standard application procedure.[55]

The second problem is Internet overload: Employers end up deluged with résumés. There are several ways to handle this. Realism helps. For example, The Cheesecake Factory posts detailed job duties listings, so those not interested need not apply. Another approach is to have job seekers complete a short online prescreening questionnaire. Then use these to identify those who may proceed in the hiring process.[56] Most employers also use applicant tracking systems, to which we now turn.

USING APPLICANT TRACKING Web-based ads tend to generate so many applicants that most firms use applicant tracking systems to support their on- and offline recruiting efforts. **Applicant tracking systems** (from firms such as Taleo Corporation and iTrack Solutions) are online systems that help employers attract, gather, screen, compile, and manage applicants.[57] They also provide other services, including requisitions management (for monitoring the firm's open jobs), applicant data collection (for scanning applicants' data into the system), and reporting (to create various recruiting-related reports such as cost per hire and hire by source).[58] Most are from *application service providers* (ASPs). The latter are companies that provide employers with online services by enabling the employer's applicants or employees to use the ASP's servers as if they're using the employer's own. Thus, applicants who log on to take a test at the employer are actually taking the test at the ASP's site.[59] Major suppliers of e-recruiting services include Automatic Data Processing (ADP.com), HRSmart (hrsmart.com), Silkroad Technology (silkroad.com), and Monster (monster.com).[60]

SUTTER HEALTH EXAMPLE For example, with 10,000 job openings per year, Sutter Health Corporation turned to online recruiting. But this actually complicated things.[61] Sutter Health had so many résumés coming in by e-mail and through its Web site (more than 300,000 per year) that the applications ended up in a pile, waiting for Sutter affiliates' HR departments to get to them.

Sutter Health's solution was to sign on with Taleo Corporation of San Francisco. Taleo is a recruiting applications service provider (ASP). It now does all the work of hosting Sutter Health's job site. Taleo doesn't just post Sutter Health job openings and collect its résumés; it also gives Sutter Health an automated way to evaluate, rank, and match IT and other job candidates with specific openings. For example, Taleo's system automatically screens incoming résumés, compares them with Sutter's job requirements, and flags high-priority applicants. This helped Sutter cut its recruiting process from weeks to days.

applicant tracking systems
Online systems that help employers attract, gather, screen, compile, and manage applicants.

FIGURE 5-8 Ineffective and Effective Web Ads

Ineffective Ad, Recycled from Magazine to the Web	Effective Web Ad (Space Not an Issue)
Process Engineer Pay: $65k–$85k/year	Do you want to help us make this a better world?
Immediate Need in Florida for a Wastewater Treatment Process Engineer. Must have a min. 4–7 years Industrial Wastewater exp. Reply KimGD@WatersCleanX.com	We are one of the top wastewater treatment companies in the world, with installations from Miami to London to Beijing. We are growing fast and looking for an experienced process engineer to join our team. If you have at least 4–7 years' experience designing processes for wastewater treatment facilities and a dedication to make this a better world, we would like to hear from you. Pay range depending on experience is $65,000–$85,000. Please reply in confidence to KimGD@WatersCleanX.com

IMPROVING ONLINE RECRUITING EFFECTIVENESS   Planning your online recruiting effort is crucial. Most Standard & Poor's 500 companies place employment information one click away from their home pages.[62] Applicants can submit their résumés online at almost all *Fortune* 500 firms' Web sites. Fewer companies give job seekers the option of completing online applications, although that's what most applicants prefer.[63]

One survey of 256 alumni from graduate business schools showed why many firms' Web-based recruiting turned them off. The objections included the following:

- Job openings lacked relevant information (such as job descriptions).
- It was often difficult to format résumés and post them in the form required.
- Many respondents expressed concerns about the privacy of the information.
- Poor graphics often made it difficult to use the Web site.
- Slow feedback from the employers (in terms of follow-up responses and receiving online applications) was annoying.[64]

Furthermore, the best Web ads don't just transpose newspaper ads to the Web. As one specialist put it, "getting recruiters out of the 'shrunken want ad mentality' is a big problem." Figure 5-8 is an example of recycling a print ad to the Web. The ineffective Web ad has needless abbreviations, and doesn't say much about why the job seeker should want that job.[65]

Now look at the effective Web ad in Figure 5-8. It uses compelling keywords such as "make this a better world." It provides good reasons to work for this company. It starts with an attention-grabbing heading and uses the extra space to provide more specific job information. Many employers often include the entire job description.[66] Ideally, an ad also should provide a way (such as a checklist of the job's human requirements) for potential applicants to gauge if the job is a good fit.[67]

Finally, online recruiting requires caution for applicants. Many job boards don't check the legitimacy of the "recruiters" who place ads. Many applicants submit personal details such as Social Security numbers, not realizing that ASPs are running the sites, rather than the firm to which they're applying.[68] U.S. laws generally do not prohibit job boards from sharing your data with other sources. One job board reportedly had personal information on more than 1 million subscribers stolen.[69]

Advertising

While Web-based recruiting is replacing help wanted ads, a glance at almost any paper or business or professional magazine will confirm that print ads are still popular. To use help wanted ads successfully, employers should address two issues: the advertising medium and the ad's construction.

THE MEDIA The best medium—the local paper, the *Wall Street Journal*, the Web (or some other)—depends on the positions for which you're recruiting. For example, the local newspaper is often a good source for local blue-collar help, clerical employees, and lower-level administrative employees. On the other hand, if recruiting for workers with special skills, such as furniture finishers, you'd probably want to advertise in places with many furniture manufacturers, such as the Carolinas, even if your plant is in Tennessee. The point is to target your ads where they'll reach your prospective employees.

For specialized employees, you can advertise in trade and professional journals like *American Psychologist, Sales Management, Chemical Engineering,* and *Women's Wear Daily*. Help wanted ads in papers like the *Wall Street Journal* and the *International Herald Tribune* can be good sources of middle- or senior-management personnel. Most of these print outlets now include online ads with the purchase of print help wanted ads.

Technology lets companies be more creative about the media they use.[70] For example, Electronic Arts (EA), a video-game publisher, uses its products to help solicit applicants. EA includes information about its internship program on the back of its video game manuals. Thanks to nontraditional techniques like these, EA has a database of more than 200,000 potential job candidates. It uses tracking software to identify potential applicants with specific skills, and to facilitate ongoing e-mail communications with everyone in its database.

> **6** Develop a help wanted ad.

CONSTRUCTING (WRITING) THE AD Experienced advertisers use the guide AIDA (attention, interest, desire, action) to construct ads. Of course, you must attract attention to the ad, or readers may just miss or ignore it. Figure 5-9 shows an ad from one classified section. Why does this ad attract attention? The phrase "next key player" certainly helps. Employers usually advertise key positions in display ads like this.

Next, develop interest in the job. You can create interest with lines such as "are you looking to make an impact?" or use other aspects of the job, such as its location.

Create desire by spotlighting words such as *travel* or *challenge*. As an example, having a graduate school nearby may appeal to engineers and professional people.

FIGURE 5-9 Help Wanted Ad That Draws Attention

Source: Giombetti Associates, Hampden, MA. Reprinted with permission.

Are You Our Next Key Player?

PLANT CONTROLLER   Northern New Jersey

Are you looking to make an impact? Can you be a strategic business partner and team player, versus a classic, "bean counter"? Our client, a growing **Northern New Jersey** manufacturer with two locations, needs a high-energy, self-initiating, technically competent Plant Controller. Your organizational skills and strong understanding of general, cost, and manufacturing accounting are a must. We are not looking for a delegator, this is a hands-on position. If you have a positive can-do attitude and have what it takes to drive our accounting function, read oh!

Responsibilities and Qualifications:
- Monthly closings, management reporting, product costing, and annual budget.
- Accurate inventory valuations, year-end physical inventory, and internal controls.
- 4-year Accounting degree, with 5–8 years experience in a manufacturing environment.
- Must be proficient in Microsoft Excel and have general computer skills and aptitude.
- Must be analytical and technically competent, with the leadership ability to influence people, situations, and circumstances.

If you have what it takes to be our next key player, tell us in your cover letter, *"Beyond the beans, what is the role of a Plant Controller?"* **Only cover letters addressing that question will be considered.** Please indicate your general salary requirements in your cover letter and email or fax your resume and cover letter to:

Ross Giombetti
Giombetti Associates
2 Allen Street, P.O. Box 720
Hampden, MA 01036
Email: Rossgiombetti@giombettiassoc.com
Fax: (413) 566-2009

Finally, the ad should prompt action with a statement like "call today." (Of course, the ad should also comply with equal employment laws, avoiding features like "man wanted.")

More information is usually better than less. Job applicants view ads with more specific job information as more attractive and more credible.[71] If the job has big drawbacks, then (depending on your risk preferences) consider a realistic ad. When the New York City Administration for Children's Services was having problems with employee retention, it began using these ads: "Wanted: men and women willing to walk into strange buildings in dangerous neighborhoods, [and] be screamed at by unhinged individuals. . . ." Realism reduces applicants, but improves employee retention.[72]

Employment Agencies

There are three main types of employment agencies: (1) public agencies operated by federal, state, or local governments; (2) agencies associated with nonprofit organizations; and (3) privately owned agencies.

PUBLIC AND NONPROFIT AGENCIES

Every state has a public, state-run employment service agency. The U.S. Department of Labor supports these agencies, through grants and through other assistance such as a nationwide computerized job bank. The National Job Bank enables agency counselors to advise applicants about available jobs in other states as well.

Some employers have mixed experiences with public agencies. For one thing, applicants for unemployment insurance are required to register and to make themselves available for job interviews. Some of these people are not interested in returning to work, so employers can end up with applicants who have little desire for immediate employment. And fairly or not, employers probably view some of these local agencies as lethargic in their efforts to fill area employers' jobs.

Yet these agencies are actually quite useful. Beyond just filling jobs, counselors will visit an employer's work site, review the employer's job requirements, and even assist the employer in writing job descriptions. Most states have turned their local state employment service agencies into "one-stop" shops—neighborhood training/employment/educational services centers.[73] One user said of the Queens New York Career Center in Jamaica: "I love it: I've made this place like a second home."[74] At Oregon State's centers, job seekers can use "iMatch" skills assessment software, while employers can get up-to-date local economic news and use the center's online recruitment tools.[75] More employers should be taking advantage of these centers (formerly the "unemployment offices" in many cities).

Most (nonprofit) professional and technical societies, such as the Institute for Electrical and Electronic Engineers (IEEE), have units that help members find jobs. Many special public agencies place people who are in special categories, such as those who are disabled.

PRIVATE AGENCIES

Private employment agencies are important sources of clerical, white-collar, and managerial personnel. They charge fees (set by state law and posted in their offices) for each applicant they place. Most are "fee-paid" jobs, in which the employer pays the fee.

Why use an agency? Reasons include:

1. Your firm doesn't have its own human resources department and feels it can't do a good job recruiting and screening.
2. You must fill an opening quickly.
3. There is a perceived need to attract more minority or female applicants.
4. You want to reach currently employed individuals, who might feel more comfortable dealing with agencies than with competing companies.
5. You want to reduce the time you're devoting to recruiting.[76]

Yet using employment agencies requires avoiding the potential pitfalls. For example, the employment agency's screening may let poor applicants go directly to the supervisors responsible for hiring, who may in turn naively hire them. Conversely, improper screening at the agency could block potentially successful applicants.

To help avoid problems:

1. Give the agency an accurate and complete job description.

2. Make sure tests, application blanks, and interviews are part of the agency's selection process.

3. Periodically review EEOC data on candidates accepted or rejected by your firm, and by the agency.

4. Screen the agency. Check with other managers to find out which agencies have been the most effective at filling the sorts of positions you need filled. Review the Internet and classified ads to discover the agencies that handle the positions you seek to fill.

5. Supplement the agency's reference checking by checking at least the final candidate's references yourself.

Temp Agencies and Alternative Staffing

Employers increasingly supplement their permanent workforces by hiring contingent or temporary workers, often through temporary help employment agencies. Also known as *part-time* or *just-in-time workers*, the contingent workforce is big and growing. In 2010, about 26% of all jobs private-sector employers added were temporary positions, two to three times the comparable figures for the last two recessions. Several things contribute to the trend toward using more temporary employees. One is continuing weak economic confidence among employers. Another is the trend towards organizing around short-term projects. For example, Makino, which manufactures machine tools, now outsources the installation of large machines to contract firms, who in turn hire temps to do the installations. Flexibility is another concern, with more employers wanting to quickly reduce employment levels if the economic turnaround proves short-lived.[77]

The contingent workforce isn't limited to clerical or maintenance staff. It includes thousands of engineering, science, or management support occupations, such as temporary chief financial officers, human resource managers, and chief executive officers.

Employers can hire temp workers either through direct hires or through temporary staff agencies. Direct hiring involves simply hiring workers and placing them on the job. The employer usually pays these people directly, as it does all its employees, but classifies them separately, as casual, seasonal, or temporary employees, and often pays few if any benefits.[78] The other approach is to have a temp agency supply the employees. Here the agency handles all the recruiting, screening, and payroll administration for the temps. Thus, Nike hired Kelly Services to manage Nike's temp needs.

PROS AND CONS Employers have long used "temps" to fill in for permanent employees who were out sick or on vacation. But today's desire for ever-higher productivity also contributes to temp workers' growing popularity. Productivity is measured in terms of output per hour paid for, and temps are generally paid only when they're working—not for days off, in other words. Many firms also use temporary hiring to give prospective employees a trial run before hiring them as regular employees.[79]

The benefits don't come without a price. Temps may be more productive, but generally cost employers 20% to 50% more than comparable permanent workers (per hour or per week), since the agency gets a fee. Furthermore, "people have a psychological reference point to their place of employment. Once you put them in the contingent category, you're saying they're expendable."[80]

When working with temporary agencies, ensure that basic policies and procedures are in place. For example, with temps, the time sheet is not just a verification of hours worked. Once the worker's supervisor signs it, it's usually an agreement to pay the

The numbers of temporary and freelance workers are increasing all over the world.

Source: Greg Balfour Evans/Alamy.

agency's fees. What is the policy if the client wants to hire one of the agency's temps as a permanent employee? How does the agency plan to recruit employees? Did you get a document from the agency stating that it is not discriminating when filling temp orders? Checking a temporary agency's references and its listing with the Better Business Bureau is advisable.[81]

WHAT SUPERVISORS SHOULD KNOW ABOUT TEMPORARY EMPLOYEES' CONCERNS   To make temporary relationships successful, managers supervising temps should understand these employees' main concerns. In one survey, six key concerns emerged. Temporary workers said they were:

1. Treated by employers in a dehumanizing and ultimately discouraging way.
2. Insecure about their employment and pessimistic about the future.
3. Worried about their lack of insurance and pension benefits.
4. Misled about their job assignments and in particular about whether temporary assignments were likely to become full-time.
5. "Underemployed" (particularly those trying to return to the full-time labor market).[82]

LEGAL GUIDELINES   Several years ago, federal agents rounded up about 250 illegal "contract" cleaning workers in 60 Walmart stores. The raid underscores the need to understand the status of the contract employees who work on your premises handling activities like security or after-hours store cleaning.[83] The fact that they actually work for another, temp-type company is no excuse. For purposes of most employment laws, with certain limited exceptions, employees of temporary staffing firms working in an employer's workplace will be considered to be employees both of the agency and of the employer.[84] The employer's liability basically comes down to the degree to which its supervisors control the temp employee's activities. For example, ask the staffing agency to handle training. Let it negotiate and set pay rates and vacation/time-off policies with the temp.

ALTERNATIVE STAFFING   Temporary employees are examples of **alternative staffing**—basically, the use of nontraditional recruitment sources. Other alternative staffing arrangements include "in-house temporary employees" (people employed directly by the company, but on an explicit short-term basis) and "contract technical employees" (highly skilled workers like engineers, who are supplied for long-term projects under contract from an outside technical services firm).

Offshoring and Outsourcing Jobs

Outsourcing and offshoring are perhaps the most extreme examples of alternative staffing. Rather than bringing people in to do the company's jobs, outsourcing and offshoring send the jobs out. *Outsourcing* means having outside vendors supply services (such as benefits management, market research, or manufacturing) that the company's own employees previously did in-house. *Offshoring* is a narrower term. It means having outside vendors or employees *abroad* supply services that the company's own employees previously did in-house.

Outsourcing and offshoring are both contentious. Particularly in challenging economic times, employees, unions, legislators, and even many business owners feel that "shipping jobs out" (particularly overseas) is ill-advised. That notwithstanding, employers are sending more jobs out, and not just blue-collar jobs. For example, GE's transportation division announced that it was shifting 17 mid-level drafting jobs from Pennsylvania to India.[85]

Sending out jobs, particularly overseas, presents employers with some special challenges. One is the potential for political tension in countries such as India. Others include the likelihood of cultural misunderstandings (such as between your home-based customers and the employees abroad); security and information privacy concerns; the need to deal with foreign contract, liability, and legal systems issues; and the fact that the offshore employees need special training (for instance, in using pseudonyms like "Jim" without discomfort). Rising overseas wages, higher oil prices, and quality issues are prompting more U.S. employers to bring their jobs back home.[86] The bottom line is that neither outsourcing nor offshoring always brings all the savings one would have hoped for, and both require careful consideration of human resource issues.

Executive Recruiters

Executive recruiters (also known as *headhunters*) are special employment agencies employers retain to seek out top-management talent for their clients. The percentage of your firm's positions filled by these services might be small. However, these jobs include key executive and technical positions. For executive positions, headhunters may be your only source of candidates. The employer always pays the fees.

There are two types of executive recruiters—contingent and retained. Members of the Association of Executive Search Consultants usually focus on executive positions paying $150,000 or more, and on "*retained* executive search." They are paid regardless of whether the employer hires the executive through the search firm's efforts. *Contingency-based recruiters* tend to handle junior- to middle-level management job searches in the $50,000 to $150,000 range. Whether retained or contingent, fees are beginning to drop from the usual 30% or more of the executive's first-year pay.[87] Top recruiters (all retained) include Heidrick and Struggles, Egon Zehnder International, Russell Reynolds, and Spencer Stuart.[88]

Executive recruiters are using more technology and becoming more specialized. The challenging part of recruiting has always been finding potential candidates—to find, say, "a sales manager with experience in chemical engineered products." Not surprisingly, Internet-based databases now dramatically speed up such searches. Executive recruiters are also becoming more specialized. The large ones are creating new businesses aimed at specialized functions (such as sales) or industries (such as oil products). So, it's advisable to look first for one that specializes in your field.

PROS AND CONS Recruiters bring a lot to the table. They have many contacts and are especially adept at finding qualified employed candidates who aren't actively looking to change jobs. They can keep your firm's name confidential until late into

alternative staffing
The use of nontraditional recruitment sources.

the search process. The recruiter can save top management's time by finding and screening an applicant pool. The recruiter's fee might actually turn out to be small when you compare it to the executive time saved.

The big issue is ensuring that the recruiter really understands your needs and then delivers properly vetted candidates who fill the bill. As an employer, it is essential to explain completely what sort of candidate is required—and why. Therefore, be prepared for some in-depth dissecting of your request. Some recruiters also may be more interested in persuading you to hire a candidate than in finding one who will really do the job. Understand that one or two of the "final candidates" may actually just be fillers to make the recruiter's one "real" candidate look better.

GUIDELINES   In choosing a recruiter, guidelines include:[89]

1. Make sure the firm is capable of conducting a thorough search. Under their ethics code, a recruiter can't approach the executive talent of a former client for a period of 2 years after completing a search for that client. Since former clients are off limits for 2 years, the recruiter must search from a constantly diminishing pool.[90]

2. Meet the individual who will actually handle your assignment.

3. Make sure to ask how much the search firm charges. Get the agreement in writing.[91]

4. Make sure the recruiter and you see eye to eye on what sort of person you need for the position.

5. *Never* rely solely on the executive recruiter (or other search professional, such as employment agency) to do all the reference checking. Certainly, let them check the candidates' references, but get notes of these references in writing from the recruiter (if possible). And, in any event, make sure to check at least the final candidate's references yourself.

On-Demand Recruiting Services

On-demand recruiting services (ODRS) provide short-term specialized recruiting assistance to support specific projects without the expense of retaining traditional search firms. They are recruiters who are paid by the hour or project, instead of a percentage fee. For example, when the human resource manager for a biotech firm had to hire several dozen people with scientific degrees and experience in pharmaceuticals, she used an ODRS firm. A traditional recruiting firm might charge 20% to 30% of each hire's salary, a prohibitive amount for a small company. The ODRS firm charged by time, rather than per hire. It handled recruiting and prescreening, and left the client with a short list of qualified candidates.[92]

College Recruiting

College recruiting—sending an employer's representatives to college campuses to prescreen applicants and create an applicant pool from the graduating class—is an important source of management trainees and professional and technical employees. One study several years ago concluded, for instance, that new college graduates filled about 38% of all externally filled jobs requiring a college degree.[93]

The problem is that on-campus recruiting is expensive and time-consuming. Schedules must be set well in advance, company brochures printed, interview records kept, and much time spent on campus. And recruiters themselves are sometimes ineffective. Some recruiters are unprepared, show little interest in the candidate, and act superior. Many don't screen candidates effectively. Employers need to train recruiters in how to interview candidates, how to explain what the company has to offer, and how to put candidates at ease. And even more than usual, the recruiter needs to be personable and preferably have a history of attracting good candidates.[94] GE hires 800 to 1,000 students each year from about 40 schools, and uses teams of employees and interns to build GE's brand at each school. Similarly, IBM has 10 recruiting staff who focus on improving the results of IBM's on-campus recruiting efforts.[95]

ON-CAMPUS RECRUITING GOALS   The campus recruiter has two main goals. One is to determine if a candidate is worthy of further consideration. Usual traits to assess include communication skills, education, experience, and interpersonal skills. The other aim is to attract good candidates. A sincere and informal attitude, respect for the applicant, and prompt follow-up letters can help sell the employer to the interviewee. Employers who send effective recruiters to campus and build relationships with opinion leaders such as career counselors and professors have better recruiting results.[96]

Building close ties with a college's career center can help employers achieve these goals. Doing so provides recruiters with useful feedback regarding things like labor market conditions and the effectiveness of one's on- and offline recruiting ads.[97] Shell Oil reduced the list of schools its recruiters visit, using factors such as quality of academic program, number of students enrolled, and diversity of the student body.[98]

THE ON-SITE VISIT   Employers generally invite good candidates to the office or plant for an on-site visit. There are several ways to make this visit fruitful. The invitation should be warm and friendly but businesslike, and should give the person a choice of dates to visit. Have someone meet the applicant, preferably at the airport or at his or her hotel, and act as host. A package containing the applicant's schedule as well as other information regarding the company—such as annual reports and employee benefits—should be waiting for the applicant at the hotel.

Plan the interviews and adhere to the schedule. Avoid interruptions; give the candidate the undivided attention of each person with whom he or she interviews. Have another recently hired graduate host the candidate's lunch. Make any offer as soon as possible, preferably at the time of the visit. If this is not possible, tell the candidate when to expect a decision. Frequent follow-ups to "find out how the decision process is going" may help to tilt the applicant in your favor.

A study of 96 graduating students from a major Northeastern university reveals some other things for which to watch out. For example, 53% said "on-site visit opportunities to meet with people in positions similar to those applied for, or with higher-ranking persons" had a positive effect. Fifty-one percent mentioned, "Impressive hotel/dinner arrangements and having well-organized site arrangements." "Disorganized, unprepared interviewer behavior, or uninformed, useless answers" turned off 41%. Forty percent mentioned "unimpressive cheap hotels, disorganized arrangements, or inappropriate behavior of hosts" as negatives.[99]

INTERNSHIPS   Many college students get their jobs through college internships. Internships can be win–win situations. For students, it may mean being able to hone business skills, learn more about potential employers, and discover their career likes (and dislikes). And employers can use the interns to make useful contributions while evaluating them as possible full-time employees. A recent study found that about 60% of internships turned into job offers.[100]

Referrals and Walk-Ins

Employee referral campaigns are an important recruiting option. Here the employer posts announcements of openings and requests for referrals on its Web site, bulletin, and/or wallboards. It often offers prizes or cash awards for referrals that lead

on-demand recruiting services (ODRS)
Services that provide short-term specialized recruiting to support specific projects without the expense of retaining traditional search firms.

college recruiting
Sending an employer's representatives to college campuses to prescreen applicants and create an applicant pool from the graduating class.

to hiring. For example, health care giant Kaiser Permanente says, "Our employee referral program encourages you to introduce your talented friends, family members, or former colleagues to career opportunities at Kaiser Permanente." Referring someone for one of its "award-eligible positions" can produces bonuses of $3,000 or more.[101] The Container Store uses a successful variant of the employee referral campaign. They train their employees to recruit new employees from among the firm's customers.

PROS AND CONS The big advantage here is that referrals tend to generate "more applicants, more hires, and a higher yield ratio (hires/applicants)."[102] Current employees will usually provide accurate information about the job applicants they are referring, since they're putting their own reputations on the line. The new employees may also come with a more realistic picture of what the firm is like. A survey by the Society for Human Resource Management (SHRM) found that of 586 employer respondents, 69% said employee referral programs are more cost-effective than other recruiting practices and 80% specifically said they are more cost-effective than employment agencies. On average, referral programs cost around $400–$900 per hire in incentives and rewards.[103]

There are a few things to avoid. If morale is low, you probably should address that prior to asking for referrals. And if you don't hire someone, explain to your employee/referrer why you did not hire his or her candidate. And we saw that relying on referrals might be discriminatory.

WALK-INS Particularly for hourly workers, walk-ins—direct applications made at your office—are a big source of applicants. From a practical point of view, simply posting a "Help Wanted" sign outside the door may be the most cost-effective way of attracting good local applicants. Treat walk-ins courteously and diplomatically, for both the employer's community reputation and the applicant's self-esteem. Many employers give every walk-in a brief interview, even if it is only to get information on the applicant "in case a position should be open in the future." Particularly in challenging times, you'll also receive many unsolicited application letters from professional and white-collar applicants. These can be good sources of leads. Good business practice requires answering all letters of inquiry from applicants promptly and courteously.

Telecommuters

Telecommuters are another option. For example, JetBlue Airways uses at-home agents to handle its reservation needs. These JetBlue employee "crewmembers" live in the Salt Lake City area and work out of their homes. They use JetBlue-supplied computers and technology, and receive JetBlue training.[104]

Military Personnel

Returning and discharged U.S. military personnel provide an excellent source of trained recruits. Several military branches have programs to facilitate soldiers finding jobs. For example, the U.S. Army's Partnership for Youth Success enables someone entering the Army to select a post-army corporate partner for an employment interview as a way to help soldiers find a job after leaving the Army.[105]

Recruiting Source Use and Effectiveness

Research reveals several guidelines employers can use to improve their recruiting efforts' effectiveness (see Table 5-1). For example, referrals from current employees yield applicants who are less likely to leave and more likely to perform better.[106]

TABLE 5-1 Recruitment: Practical Applications for Managers

Recruitment Research Finding[a]	Practical Applications for Managers
The recruitment source affects the characteristics of applicants you attract.	Use sources such as referrals from current employees that yield applicants more likely to be better performers.
Recruitment materials have a more positive impact if they contain more specific information.	Provide applicants with information on aspects of the job that are important to them, such as salary, location, and diversity.
Organizational image influences applicants' initial reactions.	Ensure all communications regarding an organization provide a positive message regarding the attractiveness of the organization as a place to work.
Applicants with a greater number of job opportunities are more attentive to early recruitment activities.	Ensure initial recruitment activities (e.g., Web site, brochure, on-campus recruiting) are attractive to candidates.
Realistic job previews that highlight both the advantages and the disadvantages of the job reduce subsequent turnover.	Provide applicants with a realistic picture of the job and organization, not just the positives.
Applicants will infer (perhaps erroneous) information about the job and company if the information is not clearly provided by the company.	Provide clear, specific, and complete information in recruitment materials so that applicants do not make erroneous inferences about the job or the employer.
Recruiter warmth has a large and positive effect on applicants' decisions to accept a job.	Choose individuals who have contact with applicants for their interpersonal skills.
Recruitment source also has a significant effect on reducing turnover.	Individuals recruited through personal recruitment sources such as employee referral programs are less likely to terminate their employment early.

[a]Selected research principles from M. S. Taylor and & C. J. Collins (2000), Strategic Recruitment. In C. L. Cooper & E. A. Locke. (Eds.) *I/O Psychology: Practice and Theory Book*. Oxford: Blackwell.

Sources: Adapted from Ann Marie Ryan and Nancy Tippins, "Attracting and Selecting: What Psychological Research Tells Us," *Human Resource Management* 43, no. 4 (Winter 2004), p. 311; and Ingo Weller et al., "Level and Time Effects of Recruitment Sources on Early Voluntary Turnover," *Journal of Applied Psychology* 94, no. 5 (2009), pp. 1146–1162 (1157). Reprinted by permission of Society for Human Resource Management via Copyright Clearance Center.

Evidenced-Based HR: Measuring Recruiting Effectiveness

Even small employers may spend tens of thousands of dollars per year recruiting applicants, yet few firms assess their recruitment efforts' effectiveness. Is it more cost-effective for us to advertise for applicants on the Web or in Sunday's paper? Should we use this employment agency or that one? One survey found that only about 44% of the 279 firms surveyed made formal attempts to evaluate their recruitment efforts.[107] Such inattention flies in the face of common sense.[108]

In terms of what to measure, one question is "How many applicants did we generate through each of our recruitment sources?"[109] Possible recruiting metrics include new hire job performance, new hire failure rate, new hire turnover, training success, and manager's satisfaction.[110]

The problem is that more applicants is not always better. The employer needs qualified, hirable applicants, not just applicants. An Internet ad may generate thousands of applicants, many from so far away that there's no chance they're viable. Even with computerized prescreening and tracking software, there are still more applicants to correspond with and screen.[111]

The applicant tracking system should help compare recruiting sources, but about 30% of them lack the necessary tools to effectively pinpoint source of hire.[112] And realistically, the manager looking to hire five engineers probably won't be twice as selective with 20,000 applicants as with 10,000. So, it is not just quantity but quality. It's therefore wise to compare your recruiting sources with measures of how employees from these sources did after about a year on the job. The accompanying HR as a Profit Center illustrates the role human resources can play.

HR AS A PROFIT CENTER

GE Medical Recruitment Process Outsourcing (RPO) Example

GE Medical hires about 500 technical workers a year to make sophisticated medical devices such as CT scanners. GE Medical must compete for talent with the likes of Microsoft. However, it has cut its hiring costs by 17%, reduced time to fill the positions by 20% to 30%, and cut in half the percentage of new hires who don't work out.[113]

GE Medical's HR team accomplished this in part by applying some of its purchasing techniques to its dealings with recruiters. For example, it called a meeting and told 20 recruiters that it would work with only the 10 best. To measure "best," the company created measurements inspired by manufacturing techniques, such as "percentage of résumés that result in interviews" and "percentage of interviews that lead to offers." Similarly, GE Medical discovered that current employees are very effective as references. For instance, GE Medical interviews just 1% of applicants whose résumés it receives, while 10% of employee referrals result in actual hires. So GE Medical took steps to double the number of employee referrals. It simplified the referral forms, eliminated bureaucratic submission procedures, and added a small reward like a Sears gift certificate for referring a qualified candidate. GE also upped the incentive—$2,000 if someone referred is hired, and $3,000 if he or she is a software engineer. GE is also moving to use recruitment process outsourcers. These "RPOs" handle tasks such as setting up interviews, making flight and hotel reservations and providing weekly reports on all open positions.[113].

Improving Productivity Through HRIS

An Integrated Approach to Recruiting

Ideally, an employer's computerized recruitment system should include several elements: a *requisition management system*, which facilitates requisition, routing, approval, and posting of job openings; a *recruiting solution*, including job advertisement, recruitment marketing, applicant tracking, and online recruitment vendor management, to increase and improve applicant pool quality; *screening services*, such as skills and behavioral assessment services; and *hiring management* software to capture and manage candidate information.[114]

RECRUITING A MORE DIVERSE WORKFORCE

| 7 | Explain how to recruit a more diverse workforce. |

As we explained in Chapter 2, recruiting a diverse workforce isn't just socially responsible. Given the rapid increase in minority, older worker, and women candidates, it is a necessity. The recruiting tools we have described to this point are certainly useful for minority and other applicants, too. However, in general, recruiting a more diverse workforce requires several special steps, to which we now turn.[115]

Single Parents

In 2010, there were almost 10 million single parent families with children under 18 maintained by the mother, about two-thirds of whom were employed. There were about 1.25 million single parent families with children under 18 maintained by the father, and three-fourths of those fathers were employed. Being a single parent isn't easy, and recruiting and keeping them requires understanding the problems they face in balancing work and family life.[116] In one survey,

> Many described falling into bed exhausted at midnight without even minimal time for themselves. . . . They often needed personal sick time or excused days off to care for sick children. As one mother noted, "I don't have enough sick days to get sick."[117]

Given such concerns, the first step in attracting (and keeping) single parents is to make the workplace as user friendly for them as practical.[118] Many firms have family friendly programs but these may not be extensive enough for single parents. For example, *flextime* programs provide employees some flexibility (such as 1-hour windows at the beginning or end of the day) around which to build their workdays. The problem is that for many single parents this limited flexibility may not be enough in the face of the conflicting work–home pressures that many face. CNN even offered a "Work/Life Balance Calculator" (www. cnn.com/2008/LIVING/worklife/06/ 04/balance.calculator/) to assess how far out of balance one's life may be.[119]

Flexible work schedules and child-care benefits are thus just two big single-parent magnets. In addition, surveys suggest that a supportive attitude on the supervisor's part can go far toward making the single parent's work–home balancing act more bearable.

Source: Mel Yates/Getty Images USA, Inc.

Not just single parents, but also their children may occasionally need some extra support.

Older Workers

When it comes to hiring older workers, employers don't have much choice.[120] Over the next few years, the fastest-growing labor force segment will be those from 45 to 64 years old. Those age 25 to 34 will decline by almost 3 million, reflecting fewer births in the late 1960s and early 1970s. On the positive side, a survey by AARP and SHRM concluded that older workers tend to have lower absenteeism rates, more reliability, and better work habits than younger workers.[121] Firms like Home Depot capitalize on this by hiring older employees, who "serve as a powerful draw to baby boomer shoppers by mirroring their knowledge and perspective."[122]

It therefore makes sense for employers to encourage older workers to stay (or to come to work at the company). Doing so involves several things. The big one is probably to provide opportunities for flexible (and often abbreviated) work schedules. One survey found that flexibility was the main concern for 71% of baby boomers, with those who continue working preferring to do so part time.[123] At one company, workers over 65 can progressively shorten their work schedules; another company uses "mini shifts" to accommodate those interested in working less than full time. Other suggestions include the following:

- Phased retirement that allows workers to ease out of the workforce.
- Portable jobs for "snowbirds" who wish to live in warmer climates in the winter.
- Part-time projects for retirees.
- Full benefits for part-timers.[124]

As always in recruiting, projecting the right image is essential. For example, one study found that writing the ad so that it sent the message "we're older-worker friendly" was important. The most effective ads emphasized schedule flexibility, and accentuated the firm's equal opportunity employment statement. This was much more effective than adding statements alluding to giving retirees opportunities to transfer their knowledge to the new work setting.[125]

Recruiting Minorities

The same prescriptions that apply to recruiting older workers apply to recruiting minorities. In practice, this requires a three-part effort: Understand the recruitment barriers, formulate the required recruitment plans, and institute the specific day-to-day programs.[126]

UNDERSTAND   First, understand the barriers that prevent minorities from applying. For example, many minority applicants don't meet the educational or experience standards for the job, so many companies offer remedial training in basic arithmetic and writing. For others, lack of role models is a problem. For example, in one retail chain, it was a lack of role models (plus what the one manager called a "rather macho culture") that stopped women from applying. Sometimes (as we saw) it's a lack of schedule flexibility, given the responsibility for caring and schooling of the children.

PLAN   After recognizing the potential impediments, you can turn to formulating plans for attracting and retaining minorities and women. This may include, for instance, developing flexible work options, redesigning jobs, and offering flexible benefits plans.

IMPLEMENT   Finally, translate these personnel plans into recruitment programs. Specifically, decide what the ads will say, and what recruiting sources you will use. Many job seekers check with friends or relatives as a strategy for looking for jobs, so encouraging your minority employees to assist in your recruitment efforts makes sense. Diversity recruitment specialists include www.diversity.com, www.2trabajo.com, and http://recruitersnetwork.com/resources/diversity.htm.

Other firms collaborate with specialist professional organizations. These include the National Black MBA Association (www.nbmbaa.org/home.aspx?PageID=637&), the National Society of Hispanic MBAs (www.nshmba.org/) and the Organization of Chinese Americans (http://ocanational.org/).

Welfare-to-Work

Some companies report difficulty in hiring and assimilating people previously on welfare. Applicants sometimes lack basic work skills, such as reporting for work on time, working in teams, and taking orders. The key to a welfare-to-work program's success seems to be the employer's pretraining program. Here, participants get counseling and basic skills training over several weeks.[127]

The Disabled

The EEOC estimates that nearly 70% of the disabled are jobless, but it certainly doesn't have to be that way.[128] The research is quite persuasive regarding the fact that in terms of virtually all work criteria, employees with disabilities are capable workers. Thousands of employers in the United States and elsewhere have found that disabled employees provide an excellent and largely untapped source of competent, efficient labor for jobs ranging from information technology to creative advertising to receptionist.

Employers can do several things to tap this huge potential workforce. The U.S. Department of Labor's Office of Disability Employment Policy offers several programs, including one that helps link disabled college undergraduates who are looking for summer internships with potential employers.[129] All states have local agencies (such as "Corporate Connections" in Tennessee) that provide placement services and other recruitment and training tools and information for employers seeking to hire the disabled. Employers also must use common sense. For example, employers who only post job openings online may miss potential employees who are visually impaired.[130]

DEVELOPING AND USING APPLICATION FORMS
Purpose of Application Forms

With a pool of applicants, the prescreening process can begin. The **application form** is usually the first step in this process (some firms first require a brief, prescreening interview or online test).

A filled-in application provides four types of information. First, you can make judgments on *substantive matters*, such as whether the applicant has the education

FIGURE 5-10 FBI Employment Application

Source: www.fbijobs.gov/employment/fd646c.pdf, accessed April 28, 2009.

FEDERAL BUREAU OF INVESTIGATION

Preliminary Application for
Honors Internship Program
(Please Type or Print in Ink)

Date: _____

I. PERSONAL HISTORY

Name in Full (Last, First, Middle, Maiden)	List College(s) attended, Major, Degree (if applicable), Grade Point Average

Birth Date (Month, Day, Year) Birth Place:	Social Security Number: (Optional)

Current Address

Street   Apt. No.

City   State   Zip Code

Home Phone

Work Phone

Area Code   Number

Area Code   Number

Are you: Licensed Driver ☐ Yes ☐ No   U. S. Citizen ☐ Yes ☐ No

Have you served on active duty in the Armed Forces of the United States? ☐ Yes ☐ No	Branch of military service and dates of active duty:	Type of Discharge

How did you learn or become interested in the FBI Honors Internship Program?

Do you have a foreign language background? ☐ Yes ☐ No List proficiency for each language on reverse side.

Have you ever been arrested or charged with any violation including traffic, but excluding parking tickets? ☐ Yes ☐ No If so, list all such matters even if found not guilty, not formally charged, no court appearance, or matter settled by payment of fine or forfeiture of collateral. Include date, place, charge, disposition, details, and police agency on reverse side.

II. EMPLOYMENT HISTORY

Identify your most recent three years FULL-TIME work experience, after high school (excluding summer, part-time and temporary employment).

From	To	Description of Work	Name/Location of Employer

III. PERSONAL DECLARATIONS

Persons with a disability who require an accommodation to complete the application process are required to notify the FBI of their need for the accommodation.

Have you used marijuana during the last three years or more than 15 times? ☐ Yes ☐ No

Have you used any illegal drug(s) or combination of illegal drugs, other than marijuana, more than 5 times or during the last 10 years? ☐ Yes ☐ No

All Information provided by applicants concerning their drug history will be subject to verification by a preemployment polygraph examination.

Do you understand all prospective FBI employees will be required to submit to an urinalysis for drug abuse prior to employment? ☐ Yes ☐ No

I am aware that willfully withholding information or making false statements on this application constitutes a violation of Section 1001, Title 18, U.S. Code and if appointed, will be the basis for dismissal from the Federal Bureau of Investigation. I agree to these conditions and I hereby certify that all statements made by me on this application are true and complete, to the best of my knowledge.

_____

Signature of Applicant as usually written. (**Do Not Use Nickname**)

The Federal Bureau of Investigation is an equal opportunity employer.

and experience to do the job. Second, you can draw conclusions about the applicant's *previous progress* and growth, especially important for management candidates. Third, you can draw tentative conclusions about the applicant's *stability* based on previous work record (although years of downsizing suggest the need for caution here). Fourth, you may be able to use the data in the application to *predict* which candidates will succeed on the job and which will not.

Most employers need several application forms. For technical and managerial personnel, the form may require detailed answers to questions about education and training. The form for hourly factory workers might focus on tools and equipment. Figure 5-10 presents one employer's approach to collecting application form information—the employment application for the FBI. In practice, most employers encourage online applications.

application form
The form that provides information on education, prior work record, and skills.

Application Guidelines

Managers should keep several practical guidelines in mind. In the "Employment History" section, request detailed information on each prior employer, including the name of the supervisor and his or her e-mail address and telephone number; this is essential for reference checking. Also, in signing the application, the applicant should certify his or her understanding that falsified statements may be cause for dismissal, that investigation of credit and employment and driving record is authorized, that a medical examination may be required, that drug screening tests may be required, and that employment is for no definite period.

APPLICANT EXAGGERATION Job applicants often exaggerate their qualifications. Estimates of how many applicants exaggerate range from 40% to 70%.[131] The most common exaggerations concern education and job experience. A majority of graduating seniors reportedly believe that employers expect a degree of exaggeration on resumes. Much of this exaggeration occurs on resumes, but may occur on application forms too. Therefore, always ensure applicants complete the form and sign a statement on it indicating that the information is true. The court will almost always support a discharge for falsifying information when applying for work.[132] Furthermore, doing a less-than-complete job of filling in the form may reflect poor work habits. Some applicants simply scribble "see résumé attached" on the application. This is not acceptable. You need the signed, completed form.

Application Forms and EEO Law

Carefully review application forms to ensure that they comply with equal employment laws. Questions to be aware of include:

Education. A question on the dates of attendance and graduation from various schools is one potential violation, insofar as it may reflect the applicant's age.

Arrest record. The courts have usually held that employers violate Title VII by disqualifying applicants from employment because of an arrest. This item has an adverse impact on minorities, and employers usually can't show it's required as a business necessity.

Notify in case of emergency. It is generally legal to require the name, address, and phone number of a person to notify in case of emergency. However, asking the relationship of this person could indicate the applicant's marital status or lineage.

Membership in organizations. Some forms ask the applicant to list memberships in clubs, organizations, or societies. Employers should include instructions not to include organizations that would reveal race, religion, physical handicaps, marital status, or ancestry.

Physical handicaps. It is usually illegal to require the listing of an applicant's physical handicaps or past illnesses unless the application blank specifically asks only for those that "may interfere with your job performance." Similarly, it is generally illegal to ask whether the applicant has ever received workers' compensation.

Marital status. In general, the application should not ask whether an applicant is single, married, divorced, separated, or living with anyone, or the names, occupations, and ages of the applicant's spouse or children.

Housing. Asking whether an applicant *owns, rents,* or *leases* a house may also be discriminatory. It can adversely affect minority groups and is difficult to justify on business necessity.

VIDEO RÉSUMÉS More candidates are submitting video résumés, a practice replete with benefits and threats. About half of responding employers in one survey thought video résumés might give employers a better feel for the candidate. The danger is that a video résumé makes it more likely that rejected candidates may claim discrimination.[133] To facilitate using video résumés, several Web sites compile for applicants, usually for a fee, multimedia résumés.[134]

Using Application Forms to Predict Job Performance

Finally, employers can use analyses of application information ("biodata") to *predict* employee tenure and performance. In one study, the researchers found that applicants who had longer tenure with previous employers were less likely to quit, and also had higher performance within 6 months after hire.[135] Examples of biodata items might include "quit a job without giving notice," "graduated from college," and "traveled considerably growing up."[136]

Choose biodata items with three things in mind. First, of course, equal employment law limits the items you'll want to use (don't use age, race, or gender, for instance). And, noninvasive items are best. In one study, subjects perceived items such as "dollar sales achieved" and "grade point average in math" as legitimate, and not invasive. Other items such as "birth order" and "frequent dates in high school" were more invasive, and unacceptable. Finally, consider that some applicants will fake biodata answers in an effort to impress the employer.[137]

Mandatory Arbitration

Many employers, aware of the high costs of employment litigation, require applicants to agree in writing to mandatory arbitration should a dispute arise. The practice is a matter of debate.

Different federal courts have taken different positions on the enforceability of these "mandatory alternative dispute resolution" clauses. The basic situation now is that they are generally enforceable, with two big caveats.

First, it must be a fair process.[138] For example, the agreement should be a signed and dated separate agreement. Use simple wording. Provide for reconsideration and judicial appeal if there is an error of law.[139] The employer must absorb most of the cost of the arbitration process. The arbitration process should be reasonably swift. The employee, if he or she prevails, should be eligible to receive the full remedies that he or she would have had if he or she had had access to the courts.

Second, mandatory arbitration clauses turn some candidates off. In one study, 389 MBA students read simulated employment brochures. Mandatory employment arbitration had a significantly negative impact on the attractiveness of the company as a place to work.[140]

REVIEW

MyManagementLab   Now that you have finished this chapter, go back to **www.mymanagementlab.com** to continue practicing and applying the concepts you've learned.

CHAPTER SECTION SUMMARIES

1. The **recruitment and selection process** entails five main steps: decide what positions to fill; build a pool of candidates for these jobs; have candidates complete application forms; use selection tools; and decide to whom to make an offer, in part by having the supervisor and others interview the candidates.

2. Recruitment and selection starts with **workforce planning and forecasting**. Workforce planning is the process of deciding what positions the firm will have to fill, and how to fill them. This often starts by forecasting personnel needs, perhaps using trend analysis, ratio analysis,

scatter plots, or computerized software packages. The other side of the equation is forecasting the supply of inside candidates. Here employers use manual systems and replacement charts, and computerized skills inventories. Forecasting the supply of outside candidates is important, particularly when entering periods of economic expansion where unemployment is low and good candidates are more difficult to come by.

3. All managers need to understand why **effective recruiting is important**. Without enough candidates, employers cannot effectively screen the candidates or hire the best.

Some employers use a recruiting yield pyramid to estimate how many applicants they need to generate in order to fill predicted job openings.

4. Filling open positions with **internal sources of candidates** has several advantages. For example, you're probably already more familiar with their strengths and weaknesses, and they require less orientation. Finding internal candidates often utilizes job posting. For filling the company's projected top-level positions, succession planning—the ongoing process of systematically identifying, assessing, and developing organizational leadership to enhance performance—is the process of choice.

5. Employers use a variety of **outside sources of candidates** when recruiting applicants.

   • Of these, recruiting via the Internet using job boards such as Monster.com represents the leading source. It is quick and cost-effective. One downside is too many applicants from too far away, but employers use applicant tracking software to screen online applicants.

   • Other sources include advertising and employment agencies (including public and nonprofit agencies, and private agencies).

   • Employers increasingly turn to temporary agencies and other alternative staffing methods to hire "alternative" types of employees, such as contract employees for special projects.

   • Executive recruiters, a special type of employment agency, are invaluable for finding and helping the employer hire top-level professionals and executives. However, the employer needs to ensure that the recruiter is conducting a thorough search and carefully checking references.

   • Other outside sources include college recruiting, referrals and walk-ins, and military personnel.

6. Understanding how to **recruit a more diverse workforce** is important. Whether the target is the single parent, older workers, or minorities, the basic rule is to understand their special needs and to create a set of policies and practices that create a more hospitable environment in which they can work.

7. The recruitment process inevitably includes **developing and using application forms** to collect essential background information about the applicant. The application should enable you to make judgments on substantial matters such as the person's education and to identify the person's job references and supervisors. Of course, it's important to make sure the application complies with equal employment laws, for instance with respect to questions regarding physical handicaps.

DISCUSSION QUESTIONS

1. What are the pros and cons of five sources of job candidates?

2. What are the four main types of information that application forms provide?

3. How, specifically, do equal employment laws apply to personnel recruiting activities?

4. What should employers keep in mind when using Internet sites to find job candidates?

5. What are the five main things you would do to recruit and retain a more diverse workforce?

INDIVIDUAL AND GROUP ACTIVITIES

1. Bring to class several classified and display ads from the Sunday help wanted ads. Analyze the effectiveness of these ads using the guidelines discussed in this chapter.

2. Working individually or in groups, develop a 5-year forecast of occupational market conditions for five occupations such as accountant, nurse, and engineer.

3. Working individually or in groups, visit the local office of your state employment agency (or check out their site online). Come back to class prepared to discuss the following questions: What types of jobs seem to be available through this agency, predominantly? To what extent do you think this particular agency would be a good source of professional, technical, and/or managerial applicants? What sorts of paperwork are applicants to the state agency required to complete before their applications are processed by the agency? What other services does the office provide? What other opinions did you form about the state agency?

4. Working individually or in groups, find at least five employment ads, either on the Internet or in a local newspaper, that suggest that the company is family friendly and should appeal to women, minorities, older workers, and single parents. Discuss what they're doing to be family friendly.

5. Working individually or in groups, interview a manager between the ages of 25 and 35 at a local business who manages employees age 40 or older. Ask the manager to describe three or four of his or her most challenging experiences managing older employees.

6. The HRCI "Test Specifications" appendix at the end of this book (pages 633–640) lists the knowledge someone studying for the HRCI certification exam needs to have in each area of human resource management (such as in Strategic Management, Workforce Planning, and Human Resource Development). In groups of four to five students, do four things: (1) review that appendix now; (2) identify the material in this chapter that relates to the required knowledge the appendix lists; (3) write four multiple-choice exam questions on this material that you believe would be suitable for inclusion in the HRCI exam; and (4) if time permits, have someone from your team post your team's questions in front of the class, so the students in other teams can take each others' exam questions.

EXPERIENTIAL EXERCISE

The Nursing Shortage

As of August 2011, U.S. unemployment was still disappointingly high, and employers were still holding back on their hiring. However, while many people were unemployed, that was not the case with nurse professionals. Virtually every hospital was aggressively recruiting nurses. Many were turning to foreign-trained nurses, for example, by recruiting nurses in the Philippines. Experts expected nurses to be in very short supply for years to come.

Purpose: The purpose of this exercise is to give you experience in creating a recruitment program.

Required Understanding: You should be thoroughly familiar with the contents of this chapter, and with the nurse recruitment program of a hospital such as Lenox Hill Hospital in New York (see http://lenoxhillhospital.org/careers_default.aspx).

How to Set Up the Exercise/Instructions: Set up groups of four to five students for this exercise. The groups should work separately and should not converse with each other. Each group should address the following tasks:

1. Based on information available on the hospital's Web site, create a hard-copy ad for the hospital to place in the Sunday edition of the *New York Times*. Which (geographic) editions of the *Times* would you use, and why?
2. Analyze the hospital's current online nurses' ad. How would you improve on it?
3. Prepare in outline form a complete nurses' recruiting program for this hospital, including all recruiting sources your group would use.

APPLICATION CASE

FINDING PEOPLE WHO ARE PASSIONATE ABOUT WHAT THEY DO

Trilogy Enterprises Inc. of Austin, Texas, is a fast-growing software company, and provides software solutions to giant global firms for improving sales and performance. It prides itself on its unique and unorthodox culture. Many of its approaches to business practice are unusual, but in Trilogy's fast-changing and highly competitive environment, they seem to work.

There is no dress code and employees make their own hours, often very long. They tend to socialize together (the average age is 26), both in the office's well-stocked kitchen and on company-sponsored events and trips to places like local dance clubs and retreats in Las Vegas and Hawaii. An in-house jargon has developed, and the shared history of the firm has taken on the status of legend. Responsibility is heavy and comes early, with a "just do it now" attitude that dispenses with long apprenticeships. New recruits are given a few weeks of intensive training, known as "Trilogy University" and described by participants as "more like boot camp than business school." Information is delivered as if with "a fire hose," and new employees are expected to commit their expertise and vitality to everything they do. Jeff Daniel, director of college recruiting, admits the intense and unconventional firm is not the employer for everybody. "But it's definitely an environment where people who are passionate about what they do can thrive."

The firm employs about 700 such passionate people. Trilogy's managers know the rapid growth they seek depends on having a staff of the best people they can find, quickly trained and given broad responsibility and freedom as soon as possible. CEO Joe Liemandt says, "At a software company, people are everything. You can't build the next great software company, which is what we're trying to do here, unless you're totally committed to that. Of course, the leaders at every company say, 'People are everything.' But they don't act on it."

Trilogy makes finding the right people (it calls them "great people") a company-wide mission. Recruiters actively pursue the freshest, if least experienced, people in the job market, scouring college career fairs and computer science departments for talented overachievers with ambition and entrepreneurial instincts. Top managers conduct the first rounds of interviews, letting prospects know they will be pushed to achieve but will be well rewarded. Employees take top recruits and their significant others out on the town when they fly into Austin for the standard, 3-day preliminary visit. A typical day might begin with grueling interviews but end with mountain biking, rollerblading, or laser tag. Executives have been known to fly out to meet and woo hot prospects who couldn't make the trip.

One year, Trilogy reviewed 15,000 résumés, conducted 4,000 on-campus interviews, flew 850 prospects in for interviews, and hired 262 college graduates, who account for over a third of its current employees. The cost per hire was $13,000; Jeff Daniel believes it was worth every penny.

Questions

1. Identify some of the established recruiting techniques that apparently underlie Trilogy's unconventional approach to attracting talent.
2. What particular elements of Trilogy's culture most likely appeal to the kind of employees it seeks? How does it convey those elements to job prospects?
3. Would Trilogy be an appealing employer for you? Why or why not? If not, what would it take for you to accept a job offer from Trilogy?
4. What suggestions would you make to Trilogy for improving its recruiting processes?

Sources: Chuck Salter, "Insanity, Inc.," *Fast Company*, January 1999, pp. 101–108; and www.trilogy.com/sections/careers/work, accessed August 24, 2007.

CONTINUING CASE

CARTER CLEANING COMPANY

Getting Better Applicants

If you were to ask Jennifer and her father what the main problem was in running their firm, their answer would be quick and short: hiring good people. Originally begun as a string of coin-operated laundromats requiring virtually no skilled help, the chain grew to six stores, each heavily dependent on skilled managers, cleaner/spotters, and pressers. Employees generally have no more than a high school education (often less), and the market for them is very competitive. Over a typical weekend, literally dozens of want ads for experienced pressers or cleaner/spotters can be found in area newspapers. All these people usually are paid around $15 per hour, and they change jobs frequently. Jennifer and her father thus face the continuing task of recruiting and hiring qualified workers out of a pool of individuals they feel are almost nomadic in their propensity to move from area to area and job to job. Turnover in their stores (as in the stores of many of their competitors) often approaches 400%. "Don't talk to me about human

resources planning and trend analysis," says Jennifer. "We're fighting an economic war and I'm happy just to be able to round up enough live applicants to be able to keep my trenches fully manned."

In light of this problem, Jennifer's father asked her to answer the following questions:

Questions

1. First, how would you recommend we go about reducing the turnover in our stores?
2. Provide a detailed list of recommendations concerning how we should go about increasing our pool of acceptable job applicants so we no longer face the need to hire almost anyone who walks in the door. (Your recommendations regarding the latter should include completely worded online and hard-copy advertisements and recommendations regarding any other recruiting strategies you would suggest we use.)

TRANSLATING STRATEGY INTO HR POLICIES & PRACTICES CASE

THE HOTEL PARIS CASE

The New Recruitment Process

The Hotel Paris's competitive strategy is "To use superior guest service to differentiate the Hotel Paris properties, and to thereby increase the length of stay and return rate of guests, and thus boost revenues and profitability." HR manager Lisa Cruz must now formulate functional policies and activities that support this competitive strategy by eliciting the required employee behaviors and competencies.

As a longtime HR professional, Lisa Cruz was well aware of the importance of effective employee recruitment. If the Hotel Paris didn't get enough applicants, it could not be selective about who to hire. And, if it could not be selective about who to hire, it wasn't likely that the hotels would enjoy the customer-oriented employee behaviors that the company's strategy relied on. She was therefore disappointed to discover that the Hotel Paris was paying virtually no attention to the job of recruiting prospective employees. Individual hotel managers slapped together help wanted ads when they had positions to fill, and no one in the chain had any measurable idea of how many recruits these ads were producing, or which recruiting approaches worked the best (or worked at all). Lisa knew that it was time to step back and get control of the Hotel Paris's recruitment function.

As they reviewed the details of the Hotel Paris's current recruitment practices, Lisa Cruz and the firm's CFO became increasingly concerned. What they found, basically, was that the recruitment function was unmanaged, totally. The previous HR director had simply allowed the responsibility for recruiting to remain with each separate hotel, and the hotel managers, not being human resources professionals, usually

took the path of least resistance when a job became available, such as by placing help wanted ads in their local papers. There was no sense of direction from the Hotel Paris's headquarters regarding what sorts of applicants the company preferred, what media and alternative sources of recruits its managers should use, no online recruiting, and no measurement at all of recruitment process effectiveness. The company ignored recruitment-source metrics that other firms used effectively, such as number of qualified applicants per position, percentage of jobs filled from within, the offer-to-acceptance ratio, acceptance by recruiting source, turnover by recruiting source, and selection test results by recruiting source.

It was safe to say that achieving the Hotel Paris's strategic aims depended on the quality of the people that it attracted to and then selected for employment at the firm. "What we want are employees who will put our guests first, who will use initiative to see that our guests are satisfied, and who will work tirelessly to provide our guests with services that exceed their expectations" said the CFO. Lisa and the CFO both knew this process had to start with better recruiting. The CFO gave her the green light to design a new recruitment process.

Questions

1. Given the hotel's stated employee preferences, what recruiting sources would you suggest they use, and why?
2. What would a Hotel Paris help wanted ad look like?
3. How would you suggest they measure the effectiveness of their recruiting efforts?

KEY TERMS

workforce (or employment or personnel) planning, *138*

trend analysis, *140*

ratio analysis, *140*

scatter plot, *140*

qualifications (or skills) inventories, *142*

personnel replacement charts, *142*

position replacement card, *142*

recruiting yield pyramid, *145*

employee recruiting, *146*

job posting, *147*

succession planning, *148*

applicant tracking systems, *151*

alternative staffing, *156*

on-demand recruiting services (ODRS), *158*

college recruiting, *158*

application form, *164*

ENDNOTES

1. Spencer Ante and Joann Lublin, "IBM Crafts Succession Plan," *The New York Times*, June 13, 2011, pp. B1, B12.
2. Robert Grossman, "IBM'S HR Takes a Risk," *HR Magazine*, April 27, 2007, p. 57.
3. "More Companies Turn to Workforce Planning to Boost Productivity and Efficiency," The Conference Board, press release/news, August 7, 2006; Carolyn Hirschman, "Putting Forecasting in Focus," *HR Magazine*, March 2007, pp. 44–49.
4. Jones Shannon, "Does HR Planning Improve Business Performance?" *Industrial Management*, January/February 2003, p. 20. See also Michelle Harrison et al., "Effective Succession Planning" *Training & Development*, October 2006, pp. 22–23.
5. Carolyn Hirschman, "Putting Forecasting in Focus," *HR Magazine*, March 2007, pp. 44–49.
6. Jean Phillips and Stanley Gully, *Strategic Staffing* (Upper Saddle River, NJ: Pearson Education, 2012), pp. 116–181.
7. Shannon, "Does HR Planning Improve Business Performance?" p. 16.
8. See, for example, Fay Hansen, "The Long View," *Workforce Management*, April 20, 2008, pp. 1, 14.
9. Chaman Jain and Mark Covas, "Thinking About Tomorrow: Seven Tips for Making Forecasting More Effective," *The Wall Street Journal*, July 7, 2008, p. 10.
10. For an example of a computerized personnel planning system, see Dan Kara, "Automating the Service Chain," *Software Magazine* 20 (June 2000), pp. 3, 42. http://www.kronos.com/scheduling-software/scheduling.aspx, accessed October 2, 2011.
11. Bill Roberts, "Can They Keep Our Lights On?" *HR Magazine*, June 2010, pp. 62–68.
12. www.surveyanalytics.com/skills-inventory-software.html, accessed June 1, 2011.
13. For a recent discussion see, for example, "Pitfalls Abound for Employers Lacking Electronic Information Retention Policies," *BNA Bulletin to Management*, January 1, 2008, pp. 1–2.
14. Ibid. See also Bill Roberts, "Risky Business," *HR Magazine*, October 2006, pp. 69–72.
15. "Traditional Security Insufficient to Halt File-Sharing Threat," *BNA Bulletin to Management*, January 20, 2008, p. 39.

16. See, for example, Society for Human Resource Management, "HR's Insight into the Economy," *Workplace Visions* 4 (2008), p. 5.
17. www.astd.org/NR/rdonlyres/CBAB6F0D-97FA-4B1F-920C-6EBAF98906D1/0/BridgingtheSkillsGap.pdf, accessed June 1, 2011.
18. "Next Generation Talent Management," www.hewittassociates.com/_MetaBasicCMAssetCache_/Assets/Articles/next_generation.pdf, accessed November 9, 2010.
19. Ibid.
20. Ed Frauenheim, "Valero Energy," *Workforce Management*, March 13, 2006.
21. Gunter Stahl et al., "Global Talent Management: How Leading Multinationals Build and Sustain their Talent Pipelines," Faculty & Research Working Paper, INSEAD, 2007.
22. Phillips and Gully, *Strategic Staffing*, pp. 116–181.
23. "Employers Still in Recruiting Bind Should Seek Government Help, Chamber Suggests," *BNA Bulletin to Management*, May 29, 2003, pp. 169–170. See also D. Mattioli, "Only the Employed Need Apply," *The Wall Street Journal* (Eastern Edition) (June 30, 2009), p. D1.
24. Tom Porter, "Effective Techniques to Attract, Hire, and Retain 'Top Notch' Employees for Your Company," *San Diego Business Journal* 21, no. 13 (March 27, 2000), p. b36.
25. Jonathan Segal, "Land Executives, Not Lawsuits," *HR Magazine*, October 2006, pp. 123–130.
26. Ibid.
27. Jessica Marquez, "A Global Recruiting Site Helps Far-Flung Managers at the Professional Services Company Acquire the Talent They Need—and Saves One Half-Million Dollars a Year," *Workforce Management*, March 13, 2006, p. 22.
28. "Hiring Works the Second Time Around," *BNA Bulletin to Management*, January 30, 1997, p. 40; and Issie Lapowsky, "How to Rehire Former Employees", *INC.*, May 18, 2010, available at http://www.inc.com/guides/2010/05/rehiring-former-employees.html, accessed October 3, 2011.
29. Ibid.
30. Where *succession planning* aims to identify and develop employees to fill specific slots,

talent management is a broader activity. *Talent management* involves identifying, recruiting, hiring, and developing high-potential employees. Soonhee Kim, "Linking Employee Assessments to Succession Planning," *Public Personnel Management* 32, no. 4 (Winter 2003), pp. 533–547. See also Michael Laff, "Talent Management: From Hire to Retire," *Training & Development*, November 2006, pp. 42–48.
31. "Succession Management: Identifying and Developing Leaders," *BNA Bulletin to Management* 21, no. 12 (December 2003); and David Day, Developing leadership talent, SHRM Foundation, http://www.shrm.org/about/foundation/research/Documents/Developing%20Lead%20Talent-%20FINAL.pdf, accessed October 4, 2011.
32. Quoted in Susan Wells, "Who's Next," *HR Magazine*, November 2003, p. 43. See also Christee Atwood, "Implementing Your Succession Plan," *Training & Development*, November 2007, pp. 54–57; and David Day, op cit.
33. See "Succession Management: Identifying and Developing Leaders," *BNA Bulletin to Management* 21, no. 12 (December 2003), p. 15; and David Day, op cit.
34. Soonhee Kim, "Linking Employee Assessments to Succession Planning," *Public Personnel Management*, Winter 2003.
35. www.sumtotalsystems.com/datasheets/sumt_succession_planning.pdf, accessed June 1, 2011.
36. Ibid.
37. Bill Roberts, "Matching Talent with Tasks," *HR Magazine*, November 2002, pp. 91–96.
38. Ibid., p. 34.
39. See, for example, J. De Avila, "Beyond Job Boards: Targeting the Source," *The Wall Street Journal* (Eastern Edition), July 2, 2009, pp. D1, D5; and C. Fernandez-Araoz et al., "The Definitive Guide to Recruiting in Good Times and Bad" [Financial crisis spotlight], *Harvard Business Review* 87, no. 5 (May 2009), pp. 74–84.
40. Reprinted from www.careerbuilder.com/MarketingWeb/iPhone/CBJobsApplication.aspx?cbRecursionCnt=1&cbsid=7fd458dafd4a444fb192d9a24ceed771-291142537-wx-6&ns_siteid=ns_us_g_careerbuilder_iphone, accessed March 23, 2009.

41. Joe Light, "Recruiters Rethink Online Playbook," online.wsj.com/article/SB100014240527487043074045760804926138 58846.html, accessed May 17, 2011.

42. Ed Frauenheim, "Logging Off of Job Boards," *Workforce Management*, June 22, 2009, pp. 25–27.

43. Jennifer Arnold, "Twittering at Face Booking While They Were," *HR Magazine*, December 2009, p. 54.

44. "ResumePal: Recruiter's Friend?" *Workforce Management*, June 22, 2009, p. 28.

45. "Innovative HR Programs Cultivate Successful Employees," *Nation's Restaurant News* 41, no. 50 (December 17, 2007), p. 74.

46. J. De Avila, "Beyond Job Boards: Targeting the Source," *The Wall Street Journal* (Eastern Edition), July 2, 2009, pp. D1, D5.

47. Jennifer Berkshire, "Social Network Recruiting," *HR Magazine*, April 2005, pp. 95–98. See also S. DeKay, "Are Business-Oriented Social Networking Web Sites Useful Resources for Locating Passive Jobseekers? Results of a Recent Study," *Business Communication Quarterly* 72, no. 1 (March 2009), pp. 101–105.

48. Josee Rose, "Recruiters Take Hip Path to Fill Accounting Jobs," *The Wall Street Journal*, September 18, 2007, p. 38.

49. Gina Ruiz, "Firms Tapping Web Videos to Lure Jobseekers," *Workforce Management*, October 8, 2007, p. 12.

50. Ed Frauenheim, "Social Revolution," *Workforce*, October 20, 2007, p. 30.

51. "Innovative HR Programs Cultivate Successful Employees," *Nation's Restaurant News* 41, no. 50 (December 17, 2007), p. 74.

52. Jennifer Taylor Arnold, "Recruiting on the Run," February 2010, *HR Magazine*, pp. 65–67.

53. Elizabeth Agnvall, "Job Fairs Go Virtual," *HR Magazine*, July 2007, p. 85.

54. Gary Stern, "Virtual Job Fairs Becoming More of a Reality," *Workforce Management*, February 2011, p. 11.

55. "EEOC Issues Much Delayed Definition of 'Applicant,'" *HR Magazine*, April 2004, p. 29; Valerie Hoffman and Greg Davis, "OFCCP's Internet Applicant Definition Requires Overhaul of Recruitment and Hiring Policies," *Society for Human Resources Management Legal Report*, January/February 2006, p. 2.

56. This carries legal risks, particularly if the device disproportionately screens out minority or female applicants. Lisa Harpe, "Designing an Effective Employment Prescreening Program," *Employment Relations Today* 32, no. 3 (Fall 2005), pp. 43–51.

57. William Dickmeyer, "Applicant Tracking Reports Make Data Meaningful," *Workforce*, February 2001, pp. 65–67; and, as an example, http://www.icims.com/prelude/1101/3009?_vsrefdom=google_ppc&gclid=CPHki_nx1KsCFcPt7QodmkjLDA, accessed October 4, 2011.

58. Paul Gilster, "Channel the Resume Flood with Applicant Tracking Systems," *Workforce*, January 2001, pp. 32–34;

William Dickmeyer, "Applicant Tracking Reports Make Data Meaningful," *Workforce*, February 2001, pp. 65–67; and, as an example, http://www.icims.com/prelude/1101/3009?_vsrefdom=google_ppc&gclid=CPHki_nx1KsCFcPt7QodmkjLDA, accessed October 4, 2011.

59. Note that the U.S. Department of Labor's office of federal contract compliance programs recently announced it would review federal contractors' online application tracking systems to ensure they're providing equal opportunity to qualify prospective applicants with disabilities. "Feds Want a Look at Online Job Sites," *HR Magazine*, November 2008, p. 12.

60. "E-Recruiting Software Providers," *Workforce Management*, June 22, 2009, p. 14.

61. Maria Seminerio, "E-Recruiting Takes Next Step," *eWeek*, April 23, 2001, pp. 49–51; http://www.sutterhealth.org/employment, accessed October 2, 2011.

62. "Does Your Company's Website Click with Job Seekers?" *Workforce*, August 2000, p. 260.

63. "Study Says Career Web Sites Could Snare More Job Seekers," *BNA Bulletin to Management*, February 1, 2001, p. 36.

64. Daniel Feldman and Brian Klaas, "Internet Job Hunting: A Field Study of Applicant Experiences with Online Recruiting," *Human Resource Management* 41, no. 2 (Summer 2002), pp. 175–192.

65. Sarah Gale, "Internet Recruiting: Better, Cheaper, Faster," *Workforce*, December 2001, p. 75.

66. "Help Wanted—and Found," *Fortune*, October 2, 2006, p. 40.

67. James Breaugh, "Employee Recruitment: Current Knowledge and Important Areas for Future Research," *Human Resource Management Review* 18 (2008), p. 114.

68. "Job Seekers' Privacy Has Been Eroded with Online Job Searchers, Report Says," *BNA Bulletin to Management*, November 20, 2003, p. 369.

69. James Breaugh, "Employee Recruitment."

70. Eric Krell, "Recruiting Outlook: Creative HR for 2003," *Workforce*, December 2002, pp. 40–44.

71. James Breaugh, "Employee Recruitment," p. 111.

72. James Breaugh, "Employee Recruitment," p. 113.

73. Find your nearest one-stop center at www.servicelocator.org.

74. Susan Saulney, "New Jobless Centers Offer More Than a Benefit Check," *The New York Times*, September 5, 2001, p. A1.

75. Lynn Doherty and E. Norman Sims, "Quick, Easy Recruitment Help: From a State?" *Workforce*, May 1998, p. 36.

76. Ibid.

77. "As Hiring Falters, More Workers Are Temporary," *The New York Times*, December 20, 2010, pp. A1, A4.

78. Robert Bohner Jr. and Elizabeth Salasko, "Beware the Legal Risks of Hiring Temps," *Workforce*, October 2002, pp. 50–57. See also Fay Hansen, "A Permanent Strategy for

Temporary Hires," *Workforce Management*, February 26, 2007, p. 27.

79. John Zappe, "Temp-to-Hire Is Becoming a Full-Time Practice at Firms," *Workforce Management*, June 2005, pp. 82–86.

80. Shari Cauldron, "Contingent Workforce Spurs HR Planning," *Personnel Journal*, July 1994, p. 60.

81. This is based on or quoted from Nancy Howe, "Match Temp Services to Your Needs," *Personnel Journal*, March 1989, pp. 45–51. See also Stephen Miller, "Collaboration Is Key to Effective Outsourcing," *HR Magazine* 58 (2008), pp. 60–61; and (as an example), http://www.bbb.org/shreveport/accredited-business-directory/employment-contractors-temporary-help/plain-dealing-la, accessed September 23, 2011.

82. Daniel Feldman, Helen Doerpinghaus, and William Turnley, "Managing Temporary Workers: A Permanent HRM Challenge," *Organizational Dynamics* 23, no. 2 (Fall 1994), p. 49. See also Kathryn Tyler, "Treat Contingent Workers with Care," *HR Magazine*, March 2008, p. 75; and http://www.employment.oregon.gov/EMPLOY/ES/BUS/index.shtml, accessed October 4, 2011.

83. Carolyn Hirschman, "Are Your Contractors Legal?" *HR Magazine*, March 2004, pp. 59–63.

84. Ibid.

85. This section is based on Robyn Meredith, "Giant Sucking Sound," *Forbes* 172, no. 6 (September 29, 2003), p. 158; Jim McKay, "Inevitable Outsourcing, Offshoring Stirred Passions at Pittsburgh Summit," *Knight Ridder/Tribune Business News*, March 11, 2004; Peter Panepento, "General Electric Transportation to Outsource Drafting Jobs to India," *Knight Ridder/Tribune Business News*, May 5, 2004; Julie Harbin, "Recent Survey Charts Execs' Willingness to Outsource Jobs," *San Diego Business Journal* 25, no. 14 (April 5, 2004), pp. 8–10; and Pamela Babcock, "America's Newest Export: White-Collar Jobs," *HR Magazine* 49, no. 4 (April 2004), pp. 50–57.

86. "Economics of Offshoring Shifting, as Some Reconsider Ventures," *BNA Bulletin to Management*, September 23, 2008, p. 311.

87. Susan Wells, "Slow Times for Executive Recruiting," *HR Magazine*, April 2003, pp. 61–67.

88. "Leading Executive Search Firms," *Workforce Management*, June 25, 2007, p. 24.

89. Michelle Martinez, "Working with an Outside Recruiter? Get It in Writing," *HR Magazine*, January 2001, pp. 98–105.

90. See, for example, Stephenie Overman, "Searching for the Top," *HR Magazine*, January 2008, p. 49.

91. Bill Leonard, "Recruiting from the Competition," *HR Magazine*, February 2001, pp. 78–86. See also G. Anders, "Secrets of the Talent Scouts," *New York Times* (Late New York Edition) (March 15, 2009), pp. 1, 7 (Sec 3).

92. Martha Frase-Blunt, "A Recruiting Spigot," *HR Magazine*, April 2003, pp. 71–79.

93. Sara Rynes, Marc Orlitzky, and Robert Bretz Jr., "Experienced Hiring Versus College Recruiting: Practices and Emerging Trends," *Personnel Psychology* 50 (1997), pp. 309–339. See also Lisa Munniksma, "Career Matchmakers: Partnering with Collegiate Career Centers Offers Recruiters Access to Rich Source of Applicants," *HR Magazine* 50, no. 2 (February 2005), p. 93.

94. See, for example, James Breaugh, "Employee Recruitment," p. 111.

95. "Recruiters look to be big man on campus," *Workforce Management*, September 2010, page 12

96. Greet Van Hoye and Filip Lievens, "Tapping the Grapevine: A Closer Look at Word-of-Mouth as a Recruitment Source," *Journal of Applied Psychology* 94, no. 2 (2009), pp. 341–352.

97. Lisa Munniksma, "Career Matchmakers," *HR Magazine*, February 2005, pp. 93–96.

98. Joe Mullich, "Finding the Schools That Yield the Best Job Applicant ROI," *Workforce Management*, March 2004, pp. 67–68.

99. Wendy Boswell et al., "Individual Job Choice Decisions and the Impact of Job Attributes and Recruitment Practices: A Longitudinal Field Study," *Human Resource Management* 42, no. 1 (Spring 2003), pp. 23–37. See also James Breaugh, "Employee Recruitment," p. 115.

100. Hao Zhao Oh and Robert Liden, "Internship: A Recruitment and Selected Perspective," *Journal of Applied Psychology* 96, no. 1 (2011), pp. 221–229.

101. www.kaiserpermanentejobs.org/employee-referral-program.aspx, accessed August 20, 2011.

102. James Breaugh, "Employee Recruitment," p. 109.

103. "Tell a Friend: Employee Referral Programs Earn High Marks for Low Recruiting Costs," *BNA Bulletin to Management*, June 28, 2001, p. 201.

104. Martha Frase-Blunt, "Call Centers Come Home," *HR Magazine*, January 2007, pp. 85–90.

105. Theresa Minton-Eversole, "Mission: Recruitment," *HR Magazine*, January 2009, pp. 43–45.

106. Ann Marie Ryan and Nancy Tippins, "Attracting and Selecting: What Psychological Research Tells Us," *Human Resource Management* 43, no. 4 (Winter 2004), p. 311.

107. Kevin Carlson et al., "Recruitment Evaluation: The Case for Assessing the Quality of Applicants Attracted," *Personnel Psychology* 55 (2002), pp. 461–490. For a recent survey of recruiting source effectiveness, see "The 2007 Recruiting Metrics and Performance Benchmark Report, 2nd ed.," Staffing.org, Inc., 2007.

108. Ibid., p. 461.

109. Ibid., p. 466.

110. Phillips and Gully, *Strategic Staffing*, p. 180.

111. Ibid., p. 466.

112. Gino Ruiz, "Special Report: Talent Acquisition," *Workforce Management*, July 23, 2007, p. 39.

113. Thomas Stewart, "In Search of Elusive Tech Workers," *Fortune*, February 16, 1998, pp. 171–172; and http://www.outsourcing-center.com/2006-10-ge-looks-to-recruitment-process-outsourcer-to-find-meat-and-potatoes-candidates-as-well-as-the-purple-squirrel-article-37479.html, accessed October 5, 2011.

114. Quoted or paraphrased from Robert Neveu, "Making the Leap to Strategic Recruiting," special advertising supplement to *Workforce Management*, 2005, p. 3.

115. "Internship Programs Help These Recruiters Toward Qualified Students with Disabilities," *BNA Bulletin to Management*, July 17, 2003, p. 225.

116. Judith Casey and Marcie Pitt-Catsouphes, "Employed Single Mothers: Balancing Job and Home Life," *Employee Assistance Quarterly* 9, no. 324 (1994), pp. 37–53; http://www.catalyst.org/publication/252/working-parents, accessed October 3, 2011.

117. Casey and Pitt-Catsouphes, op cit., p. 42.

118. "Barclaycard Helps Single Parents to Find Employment," *Personnel Today*, November 7, 2006.

119. Susan Glairon, "Single Parents Need More Flexibility at Work, Advocate in Denver Says," *Daily Camera*, February 8, 2002; http://www.cnn.com/2008/LIVING/worklife/06/04/balance.calculator, accessed October 5, 2011.

120. Sandra Block and Stephanie Armour, "Many Americans Retire Years Before They Want To," *USA Today*, July 26, 2006, http://usatoday.com, accessed December 23, 2007.

121. Phaedra Brotherton, "Tapping into an Older Workforce," *Mosaics* (Society for Human Resource Management, March/April 2000). See also Thomas Ng and Daniel Feldman, "The Relationship of Age to Ten Dimensions of Job Performance," *Journal of Applied Psychology* 90, no. 2 (2008), pp. 392–423.

122. Sue Shellenbarger, "Gray Is Good: Employers Make Efforts to Retain Older, Experienced Workers," *The Wall Street Journal*, December 1, 2005.

123. Alison Wellner, "Tapping a Silver Mine," *HR Magazine*, March 2002, p. 29.

124. Sue Shellenbarger, "Gray Is Good." See also Robert Grossman, "Keep Pace with Older Workers," *HR Magazine*, May 2008, pp. 39–46.

125. Gary Adams and Barbara Rau, "Attracting Retirees to Apply: Desired Organizational Characteristics of Bridge Employment," *Journal of Organizational Behavior* 26, no. 6 (September 2005), pp. 649–660.

126. Abby Ellin, "Supervising the Graybeards," *The New York Times*, January 16, 2000, p. B16; Derek Avery and Patrick McKay, "Target Practice: An Organizational Impression Management Approach to Attracting Minority and Female Job Applicants," *Personnel Psychology* 59 (2006), pp. 157–189.

127. Herbert Greenberg, "A Hidden Source of Talent," *HR Magazine*, March 1997, pp. 88–91.

128. Linda Moore, "Firms Need to Improve Recruitment, Hiring of Disabled Workers, EEO Chief Says," *Knight Ridder/Tribune Business News*, November 5, 2003. See also "Recruiting Disabled More Than Good Deed, Experts Say," *BNA Bulletin to Management*, February 27, 2007, p. 71.

129. "Students with Disabilities Available," *HR Briefing*, June 15, 2002, p. 5.

130. Moore, "Firms Need to Improve Recruitment."

131. This paragraph is based on Jennifer L. Wood, James M. Schmidtke, and Diane L. Decker, "Lying on Job Applications: The Effects of Job Relevance, Commission, and Human Resource Management Experience," *J Bus Psychology* 22 (2007), pp. 1–9.

132. Kenneth Sovereign, *Personnel Law* (Upper Saddle River, NJ: Pearson, 1999), p. 51.

133. Kathy Gurchiek, "Video Resumes Spark Curiosity, Questions," *HR Magazine*, May 2007, pp. 28–30; "Video Resumes Can Illuminate Applicants' Abilities, but Pose Discrimination Concerns," *BNA Bulletin to Management*, May 20, 2007, pp.169–170.

134. As of May 2010, these companies included resumebook.tv, optimalresume.com, interviewstudio.com, and brightab.com. Alina Dizik, "Wooing Job Recruiters with Video Resumes," *The Wall Street Journal*, May 20, 2010, p. D4.

135. Murray Barrick and Ryan Zimmerman, "Hiring for Retention and Performance," *Human Resource Management* 48, no. 2 (March/April 2009), pp. 183–206.

136. James Breaugh, "The Use of Biodata for Employee Selection: Test Research and Future Directions," *Human Resource Management Review* 19 (2009), pp. 219–231. Utilizing biodata items of course presumes that the employer can show that the items predict performance. Biodata items such as "graduated from college" may have an adverse impact on minorities but studies suggest that employers can avoid that problem through judicious choice of biodata items (p. 229).

137. Fred Mael, Mary Connerley, and Ray Morath, "None of Your Business: Parameters of Biodata Invasiveness," *Personnel Psychology* 49 (1996), pp. 613–650; and Kenneth Law et al., "Impression Management and Faking in Biodata Scores Among Chinese Job-Seekers," *Asia Pacific Journal of Management* 19, no. 4 (December 2002), p. 541–556.

138. "Supreme Court Denies Circuit City's Bid for Review of Mandatory Arbitration," *BNA Bulletin to Management*, June 6, 2002, p. 177.

139. "Supreme Court Gives the Employers Green Light to Hold Most Employees to Arbitration Pacts," *BNA Bulletin to Management*, March 29, 2001, pp. 97–98.

140. Douglas Mahony et al., "The Effects of Mandatory Employment Arbitration Systems on Applicants Attraction to Organizations," *Human Resource Management* 44, no. 4 (Winter 2005), pp. 449–470.

6

Employee Testing and Selection

LEARNING OBJECTIVES

1. Explain what is meant by reliability and validity.
2. Explain how you would go about validating a test.
3. Cite and illustrate our testing guidelines.
4. Give examples of some of the ethical and legal considerations in testing.
5. List eight tests you could use for employee selection, and how you would use them.
6. Give two examples of work sample/simulation tests.
7. Explain the key points to remember in conducting background investigations.

Google, famous for (among other things) its childcare and other employee benefits recently changed its employee screening process. Candidates used to have a dozen or more grueling interviews. But, with Google hiring thousands of people annually, this selection process proved too slow.[1] Now Google uses just four to five interviews, but lets all its employees express opinions on each candidate by e-mail, using a screening technique called "crowd sourcing." The changes bring the firm's hiring practices in line with its fast-growth strategy.[2]

Access a host of interactive learning aids at **www.mymanagementlab.com** to help strengthen your understanding of the chapter concepts.

Company's Strategic Goals

Employee Competencies and Behaviors Required for Company to Achieve These Strategic Goals

Recruitment and Placement

Strategic and Legal Environment

Training and Development

HR Policies and Practices Required to Produce Employee Competencies and Behaviors

Employee Relations

Compensation

WHERE ARE WE NOW . . .

Chapter 5 focused on the methods managers use to build an applicant pool. The purpose of Chapter 6 is to explain how to use various tools to select the best candidates for the job. The main topics we'll cover include the selection process, basic testing techniques, background and reference checks, ethical and legal questions in testing, types of tests, and work samples and simulations.

In Chapter 7, we will turn to the techniques you can use to improve your skills with what is probably the most widely used screening tool, the selection interview.

WHY CAREFUL SELECTION IS IMPORTANT

Once you review your applicants' résumés, the next step is selecting the best candidates for the job. This usually means whittling down the applicant pool by using the screening tools we cover in this chapter: tests, assessment centers, and background and reference checks. Then the supervisor can interview likely candidates and decide whom to hire. Nothing you do at work is more important than hiring the right employees. It is important for three main reasons: performance, costs, and legal obligations.

PERFORMANCE   First, your own performance always depends on your subordinates. Employees with the right skills will do a better job for you and the company. Employees without these skills or who are abrasive or obstructionist won't perform effectively, and your own performance and the firm's will suffer. The time to screen out undesirables is before they are in the door, not after.

COST   Second, it is important because it's costly to recruit and hire employees. Hiring and training even a clerk can cost $5,000 or more in fees and supervisory time. The total cost of hiring a manager could easily be 10 times as high once you add search fees, interviewing time, reference checking, and travel and moving expenses.

LEGAL OBLIGATIONS   Third, it's important because mismanaging hiring has legal consequences. For one thing (as we saw in Chapter 2), equal employment laws require nondiscriminatory selection procedures.[3] Furthermore, someone can sue an employer for *negligent hiring*. **Negligent hiring** means hiring employees with criminal records or other problems who then use access to customers' homes (or similar opportunities) to commit crimes.[4] In one case, *Ponticas v. K.M.S. Investments*, an apartment manager with a passkey entered a woman's apartment and assaulted her.[5] The court found the apartment complex's owner negligent for not checking the manager's background properly.[6]

Person and Job/Organization Fit

The main aim of employee selection is to achieve person-job fit. *Person-job fit* refers to matching (1) the knowledge, skills, abilities (KSAs), and competencies that are central to performing the job (as determined by job analysis) with (2) the prospective employee's knowledge, skills, abilities, and competencies. The aim is to achieve a match.

However, a candidate might be "right" for a job, but wrong for the organization.[7] For example, a highly experienced airline pilot might do well at American Airlines but perhaps not as well at Southwest, where the organizational values require that all employees help get the plane turned around fast, even if that means helping with baggage handling. Thus, while person-job fit is usually the main consideration in selection, employers should care about *person-organization fit* as well. The accompanying Strategic Context feature illustrates this.

THE STRATEGIC CONTEXT

Crowd Sourcing at Google

Google knows that to maintain its fast-growth strategy, it needs to keep new Google tools like Gmail and Google Maps coming. To support that strategy, Google needs its employees engaged and interacting with each other. Having employees thinking of themselves in isolated "silos" would inhibit the cross-pollination Google depends on. In formulating its employee selection practices, Google therefore found a way to foster the employee engagement and interaction its success depends on. Google uses "crowd sourcing" when it comes to making hiring decisions.[8]

Here's how it works.[9] When a prospective employee applies for a job, his or her information (such as school and previous employers) goes into Google's applicant-tracking system (ATS). The ATS then matches the applicant's information with that of current Google employees. When it finds a match, it asks those Google employees to comment on the applicant's suitability for the position. This helps give Google recruiters a valuable insight into how the Google employees actually doing the work think the applicant will do at Google. And it supports Google's strategy, by fostering a sense of community and interaction among Google employees, who see themselves working together to select new "Googlers."

BASIC TESTING CONCEPTS

1 Explain what is meant by reliability and validity.

A test is one popular selection tool. A test is basically a sample of a person's behavior. Using a test (or any selection tool) assumes the tool is both reliable and valid. Few things illustrate evidence-based HR—the deliberate use of the best-available evidence in making decisions about the human resource management practices you are focusing on—as do checking for reliability and validity.

Reliability

Reliability is a test's first requirement and refers to its consistency: "A reliable test is one that yields consistent scores when a person takes two alternate forms of the test or when he or she takes the same test on two or more different occasions."[10]

Reliability is very important. If a person scores 90 on an intelligence test on a Monday and 130 when retested on Tuesday, you probably wouldn't have much faith in the test.

You can measure reliability in several ways. One is to administer a test to a group of people one day, readminister the same test several days later to the same group, and then correlate the first set of scores with the second (*test-retest reliability estimates.*)[11] Or you could administer a test and then administer what experts believe to be an equivalent test later; this would be an *equivalent or alternate form estimate.* The Scholastic Assessment Test (SAT) is an example. Or, compare the test taker's answers to certain questions on the test with his or her answers to a separate set of questions on the same test aimed at measuring the same thing. For example, a psychologist includes 10 items on a test believing that they all measure interest in working outdoors. You administer the test and then statistically analyze the degree to which responses to these 10 items vary together. This is an *internal comparison estimate.* (Internal comparison is one reason that you find apparently repetitive questions on some test questionnaires.)

Many things cause a test to be unreliable. These include physical conditions (quiet tests conditions one day, noisy the next), differences in the test-taker (healthy one day, sick the next), and differences in the person administering the test (courteous one day, curt the next). Or the questions may do a poor job of sampling the material; for example, test one focuses more on Chapters 1, 3, and 7, while test two focuses more on Chapters 2, 4, and 8.

Because measuring reliability generally involves comparing two measures that assess the same thing, it is typical to judge a test's reliability in terms of a *reliability coefficient.* This basically shows the degree to which the two measures (say, test score one day and test score the next day) are correlated.

---

negligent hiring
Hiring workers with questionable backgrounds without proper safeguards.

reliability
The consistency of scores obtained by the same person when retested with the identical tests or with alternate forms of the same test.

FIGURE 6-1 Correlation
Examples

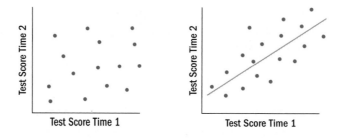

Figure 6-1 illustrates correlation. In both the left and the right scatter plots, the psychologist compared each applicant's time 1 test score (on the *x*-axis) with his or her subsequent test score (on the *y*-axis). On the left, the scatter plot points (each point showing one applicant's test score and subsequent test performance) are dispersed. There seems to be no correlation between test scores obtained at time 1 and at time 2. On the right, the psychologist tried a new test. Here the resulting points fall in a predictable pattern. This suggests that the applicants' test scores correlate closely with their previous scores.

Validity

Reliability, while indispensable, only tells you that the test is measuring something consistently. It does not prove that you are measuring what you intend to measure. A mismanufactured 33-inch yardstick will consistently tell you that 33-inch boards are 33 inches long. Unfortunately, if what you're looking for is a board that is 1 yard long, then your 33-inch yardstick, though reliable, is misleading you by 3 inches.

What you need is a valid yardstick. *Validity* tells you whether the test (or yardstick) is measuring what you think it's supposed to be measuring.[12]

A test, as we said, is a sample of a person's behavior, but some tests are more clearly representative of the behavior being sampled than others. A typing test, for example, clearly corresponds to an on-the-job behavior. At the other extreme, there may be no apparent relationship between the items on the test and the behavior. This is the case with projective personality tests. Thus, in the Rorschach Test sample in Figure 6-2, the psychologist asks the person to explain how he or she interprets an ambiguous picture. The psychologist uses that interpretation to draw conclusions about the person's personality and behavior. In such

FIGURE 6-2 A Slide from the Rorschach Test

Source: Fotolia LLC.

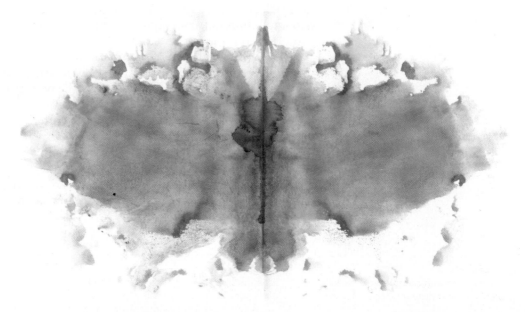

tests, it is more difficult to prove that the tests are measuring what they are said to measure, in this case, some trait of the person's personality—in other words, that they're valid.

TEST VALIDITY   **Test validity** answers the question "Does this test measure what it's supposed to measure?" Put another way, *validity* refers to the correctness of the inferences that we can make based on the test. For example, if Jane's scores on mechanical comprehension tests are higher than Jim's, can we be sure that Jane possesses more mechanical comprehension than Jim?[13] With employee selection tests, *validity* often refers to evidence that the test is job related—in other words, that performance on the test accurately predicts subsequent performance on the job. A selection test must be valid since, without proof of validity, there is no logical or legally permissible reason to continue using it to screen job applicants. You would not be too comfortable taking the GRE if you didn't think that your score on the GRE predicted, in some valid way, your likely performance in graduate school. Equal employment law (as we explained in Chapter 2) requires valid tests. In employment testing, there are two main ways to demonstrate a test's validity: criterion validity and content validity. A third option is construct validity.[14]

CRITERION VALIDITY   **Criterion validity** involves demonstrating statistically a relationship between scores on a selection procedure and job performance of a sample of workers. For example, it means demonstrating that those who do well on the test also do well on the job, and that those who do poorly on the test do poorly on the job. The test has validity to the extent that the people with higher test scores perform better on the job. In psychological measurement, a *predictor* is the measurement (in this case, the test score) that you are trying to relate to a *criterion*, such as performance on the job. The term *criterion validity* reflects that terminology.

CONTENT VALIDITY   **Content validity** is a demonstration that the content of a selection procedure is representative of important aspects of performance on the job. For example, employers may demonstrate the *content validity* of a test by showing that the test constitutes a fair sample of the job's content. The basic procedure here is to identify job tasks that are critical to performance, and then randomly select a sample of those tasks to test. In selecting students for dental school, many schools give applicants chunks of chalk, and ask them to carve something that looks like a tooth. If the content you choose for the test is a representative sample of what the person needs to know for the job, then the test is probably content valid. Clumsy dental students need not apply.

CONSTRUCT VALIDITY   **Construct validity** means demonstrating that (1) a selection procedure measures a construct (an abstract idea such as morale or honesty) and (2) that the construct is important for successful job performance.

---

test validity
The accuracy with which a test, interview, and so on measures what it purports to measure or fulfills the function it was designed to fill.

criterion validity
A type of validity based on showing that scores on the test (predictors) are related to job performance (criterion).

content validity
A test that is content valid is one that contains a fair sample of the tasks and skills actually needed for the job in question.

construct validity
A test that is construct valid is one that demonstrates that a selection procedure measures a construct and that construct is important for successful job performance.

2 Explain how you would go about validating a test.

Evidence-Based HR: How to Validate a Test

Employers often opt to demonstrate evidence of a test's validity using criterion validity. In order for a selection test to be useful, you need evidence that scores on the test relate in a predictable way to performance on the job. Thus, other things being equal, students who score high on the graduate admissions tests also do better in graduate school. Applicants who score high on mechanical comprehension tests perform better as engineers. In other words, you should validate the test before using it by ensuring that scores on the test are a good predictor of some *criterion* like job performance—thus demonstrating the test's *criterion validity*.[15]

At best, invalid tests are a waste of time. At worst, they may be discriminatory. Tests you buy "off the shelf" should include information on their validity. The Society for Industrial and Organizational Psychology says that "Experienced and knowledgeable test publishers have (and are happy to provide) information on the validity of their testing products."[16] But ideally, you should revalidate the tests for the job(s) at hand. In any case, tests rarely predict performance with 100% accuracy (or anywhere near it), so do not make tests your only selection tool; also use other tools like interviews and background checks.

An industrial psychologist usually conducts the validation study. The human resource department coordinates the effort. Strictly speaking, the supervisor's role is just to make sure that the job's human requirements and performance standards are clear to the psychologist. But in practice, anyone using tests (or test results) should know something about validation. Then you can better understand how to use tests and interpret their results. The validation process consists of five steps:

STEP 1: ANALYZE THE JOB The first step is to analyze the job and write job descriptions and job specifications. The point is to specify the human traits and skills you believe are required for job performance. For example, must an applicant be verbal, a good talker? Must the person assemble small, detailed components? These requirements become the *predictors*. These are the human traits and skills you believe predict success on the job.

In this first step, also define what you mean by "success on the job," since it's this success for which you want predictors. The standards of success are *criteria*. Here you could use production-related criteria (quantity, quality, and so on), personnel data (absenteeism, length of service, and so on), or judgments of worker performance (by persons like supervisors). For an assembler's job, *predictors* might include manual dexterity and patience. *Criteria* then might include number of rejects produced per hour.[17]

STEP 2: CHOOSE THE TESTS Once you know the predictors (such as manual dexterity) the next step is to decide how to test for them. Employers usually base this choice on experience, previous research, and "best guesses." They usually don't start with just one test. Instead, they choose several tests and combine them into a test battery. The test battery aims to measure an array of possible predictors, such as aggressiveness, extroversion, and numerical ability.

What tests are available and where do you get them? The best advice is probably to use a professional, such as a licensed industrial psychologist. However, many firms publish tests. Psychological Assessment Resources, Inc., in Odessa, Florida, is typical. Some tests are available to virtually any purchaser. Others are available only to qualified buyers (such as those with degrees in psychology). Wonderlic, Inc., publishes a well-known intellectual capacity test and other tests, including aptitude test batteries and interest inventories. G. Neil Company of Sunrise, Florida, offers employment testing materials including, for example, a clerical skills test, telemarketing ability test, service ability test, management ability test, team skills test, and sales abilities test.

Again, though, don't let the widespread availability of tests blind you to this fact: You should use tests in a manner consistent with equal employment laws, and in a

FIGURE 6-3 Examples of Web Sites Offering Information on Tests or Testing Programs

- www.hr-guide.com/data/G371.htm
Provides general information and sources for all types of employment tests.
- http://ericae.net
Provides technical information on all types of employment and nonemployment tests.
- www.ets.org/testcoll
Provides information on more than 20,000 tests.
- www.kaplan.com
Information from Kaplan test preparation on how various admissions tests work.
- www.assessments.biz
One of many firms offering employment tests.

manner that is ethical and protects the test taker's privacy. Figure 6-3 presents several Web sites that provide information about tests or testing programs.

STEP 3: ADMINISTER THE TEST

Next, administer the selected test(s). One option is to administer the tests to employees currently on the job. You then compare their test scores with their current performance; this is *concurrent (at the same time) validation*. Its main advantage is that data on performance are readily available. The disadvantage is that current employees may not be representative of new applicants (who, of course, are really the ones for whom you are interested in developing a screening test). Current employees have already had on-the-job training and screening by your existing selection techniques.

Predictive validation is the second and more dependable way to validate a test. Here you administer the test to applicants before you hire them. Then hire these applicants using only existing selection techniques, not the results of the new tests. After they have been on the job for some time, measure their performance and compare it to their earlier test scores. You can then determine whether you could have used their performance on the new test to predict their subsequent job performance.

STEP 4: RELATE YOUR TEST SCORES AND CRITERIA

The next step is to ascertain if there is a significant relationship between test scores (the predictor) and performance (the criterion). The usual way to do this is to determine the statistical relationship between (1) scores on the test and (2) job performance using correlation analysis, which shows the degree of statistical relationship.

If there is a correlation between test and job performance, you can develop an **expectancy chart**. This presents the relationship between test scores and job performance graphically. To do this, split the employees into, say, five groups according to test scores, with those scoring the highest fifth on the test, the second highest fifth, and so on. Then compute the percentage of high job performers in each of these five test score groups and present the data in an expectancy chart like that in Figure 6-4. In this case, someone scoring in the top fifth of the test has a 97% chance of being a high performer, while one scoring in the lowest fifth has only a 29% chance of being a high performer.[18]

STEP 5: CROSS-VALIDATE AND REVALIDATE

Before using the test, you may want to check it by "cross-validating"—in other words, by again performing steps 3 and 4 on a new sample of employees. At a minimum, have someone revalidate the test periodically.

expectancy chart
A graph showing the relationship between test scores and job performance for a group of people.

FIGURE 6-4 Expectancy Chart

Note: This expectancy chart shows the relation between scores made on the Minnesota Paper Form Board and rated success of junior draftspersons.

Example: Those who score between 37 and 44 have a 55% chance of being rated above average and those scoring between 57 and 64 have a 97% chance.

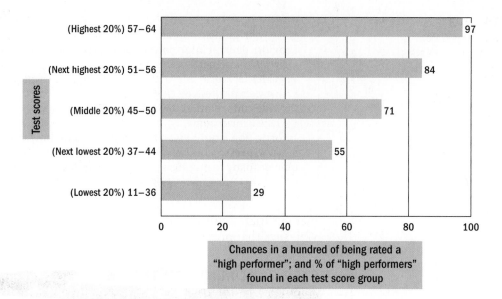

WHO SCORES THE TEST? Some tests (such as the 16PF® Personality Profile) are professionally scored and interpreted. Thus Wonderlic, Inc., lets an employer administer the 16PF. The employer then faxes (or scans) the answer sheet to Wonderlic, which scores the candidate's profile and faxes (or scans) back the interpretive report. Psychologists easily score many psychological tests online or using interpretive Windows-based software. However, managers can easily score many tests, like the Wonderlic Personnel Test, themselves.

> **3** Cite and illustrate our testing guidelines.

Bias

Most employers know they shouldn't use biased tests in the employee selection process.[19] In practice, two types of bias may arise. First, there may be bias in how the test *measures the trait* it purports to measure. For example, an IQ test may turn out to be a valid measure of cognitive ability for middle-class whites, but when used for minorities, it simply measures whether they are familiar with middle-class culture.[20] Second, *the predictions one makes* based on the test may be biased. For example, "If the test used in college admissions systematically over predicts the performance of males and under-predicts the performance of females, [then] that test functions as a biased predictor."[21] For many years, industrial psychologists believed they were adequately controlling test bias, but today that issue is under review.[22] For now, the bottom line is that employers should redouble their efforts to ensure that the tests they're using aren't producing biased decisions.

Utility Analysis

Knowing that a test is reliable and valid may not be of much practical use. For example, if it is going to cost the employer $1,000 per applicant for the test, and hundreds of applicants must be tested, the cost of the test may exceed the benefits the employer derives from hiring a few more capable employees.

Answering the question, "Does it pay to use the test?" requires *utility analysis*. Two selection experts say, "Using dollar and cents terms, [utility analysis] shows the degree to which use of a selection measure improves the quality of individuals selected over what would have happened if the measure had not been used."[23] The information required for utility analysis generally includes, for instance, the validity of the selection measure, a measure of job performance in dollars, applicants' average test scores, cost of testing an applicant, and the number of applicants tested and selected. The accompanying HR as a Profit Center feature provides an illustrative example.

HR AS A PROFIT CENTER

Reducing Turnover at KeyBank

Financial services firm KeyBank knew it needed a better way to screen and select tellers and call-center employees.[24] It calculated its cost about $10,000 to select and train an employee, but it was losing 13% of new tellers and call-center employees in the first 90 days. That turnover number dropped to 4% after KeyBank implemented a virtual job tryout candidate assessment screening tool. "We calculated a $1.7 million cost savings in teller turnover in one year, simply by making better hiring decisions, reducing training costs and increasing quality of hires," said the firm's human resources director.

Validity Generalization

Many employers, particularly smaller ones, won't find it cost-effective to conduct validity studies for the selection tools they use. These employers must find tests and other screening tools that have been shown to be valid in other settings (companies), and then bring them in-house in the hopes that they'll be valid there, too.[25]

If the test is valid in one company, to what extent can we generalize those validity findings to our own company? *Validity generalization* "refers to the degree to which evidence of a measure's validity obtained in one situation can be generalized to another situation without further study."[26] Being able to use it without your own validation study is of course the key. Factors to consider in arriving at a conclusion include existing validation evidence regarding using the test for various specific purposes, the similarity of the subjects on whom the test was validated with those in your organization, and the similarity of the jobs involved.[27]

Under the Uniform Guidelines, validation of selection procedures is desirable, but "the Uniform Guidelines require users to produce evidence of validity only when adverse impact is shown to exist." If there is no adverse impact, there is no validation requirement under the Guidelines."[28] Conversely, validating a test that suffers from adverse impact may not be enough. Under the Uniform Guidelines, the employer should also find an equally valid *but less adversely impacting* alternative.

Test Takers' Individual Rights and Test Security

> 4 Give examples of some of the ethical and legal considerations in testing.

Test takers have rights to privacy and feedback under the American Psychological Association's (APA) standard for educational and psychological tests; these guide psychologists but are *not* legally enforceable. Test takers have the following rights:

- The right to the confidentiality of test results.
- The right to informed consent regarding use of these results.
- The right to expect that only people qualified to interpret the scores will have access to them, or that sufficient information will accompany the scores to ensure their appropriate interpretation.
- The right to expect the test is fair to all. For example, no one taking it should have prior access to the questions or answers.

A complete discussion of the APA's "Ethical Principles of Psychologists and Code of Conduct" is beyond the scope of this book. But some of the points it addresses include competence, integrity, respect for people's dignity, nondiscrimination, and sexual harassment.[29]

PRIVACY ISSUES Common sense suggests that managers should keep their knowledge of employees' test results private. However, there are also privacy protections embedded in U.S. and common law. Certain U.S. Supreme Court decisions do protect individuals from intrusive governmental action in a variety of contexts.[30] Furthermore, the Federal Privacy Act gives federal employees the right to inspect their personnel files, and limits the disclosure of personnel information without the employee's consent, among other things.[31]

Common law provides some protection against disclosing information about employees to people outside the company. The main application here involves defamation (either libel or slander), but there are privacy issues, too.[32] The bottom line is this:

1. Make sure you understand the need to keep employees' information confidential.
2. Adopt a "need to know" policy. For example, if an employee has been rehabilitated after a period of drug use and that information is not relevant to his or her functioning in the workplace, then a new supervisor may not "need to know."

How Do Employers Use Tests at Work?

About 41% of companies that the American Management Association surveyed tested applicants for basic skills (defined as the ability to read instructions, write reports, and do arithmetic).[33] About 67% of the respondents required employees to take job skills tests, and 29% required some form of psychological measurement.[34] To see what such tests are like, try the short test in Figure 6-5. It shows how prone you might be to on-the-job accidents.

Tests are not just for lower-level workers. In general, as work demands increase (in terms of skill requirements, training, and pay), employers tend to rely more on testing in the selection process.[35] Employers don't use tests just to find good employees, but also to screen out bad ones. By one account, about 30% of all employees say they've stolen from their employers.[36] In retail, employers apprehended about one out of every 28 workers for stealing.[37] No wonder prudent employers test their applicants. We'll look at two examples.

OUTBACK STEAKHOUSE EXAMPLE Outback Steakhouse has used preemployment tests almost from when the company started. The testing seems successful. While annual turnover rates for hourly employees may reach 200% in the restaurant industry, Outback's turnover ranges from 40% to 60%. Outback wants employees

FIGURE 6-5 Sample Test

Source: Based on Sample Test Analysis according to John Kamp, an industrial psychologist.

CHECK YES OR NO	YES	NO
1. You like a lot of excitement in your life.		
2. An employee who takes it easy at work is cheating on the employer.		
3. You are a cautious person.		
4. In the past three years you have found yourself in a shouting match at school or work.		
5. You like to drive fast just for fun.		

Analysis: According to John Kamp, an industrial psychologist, applicants who answered no, yes, yes, no, no to questions 1, 2, 3, 4, and 5 are statistically likely to be absent less often, to have fewer on-the-job injuries, and, if the job involves driving, to have fewer on-the-job driving accidents. Actual scores on the test are based on answers to 130 questions.

Many employers administer online employment tests to job candidates.

Source: Fotolia LLC.

who are highly social, meticulous, sympathetic, and adaptable. They use a personality assessment test to screen out applicants who don't fit the Outback culture. This test is part of a three-step preemployment screening process. Applicants take the test, and managers then compare the candidates' results to the profile for Outback Steakhouse employees. Those who score low on certain traits (like compassion) don't move to the next step. Those who score high move on to be interviewed by two managers. The latter focus on behavioral questions such as "What would you do if a customer asked for a side dish we don't have on the menu?"[38]

CITY GARAGE EXAMPLE   City Garage, a 200-employee chain of 25 auto service and repair shops in Dallas–Fort Worth, implemented a computerized testing program to improve its operations. The original hiring process consisted of a paper-and-pencil application and one interview, immediately followed by a hire/don't hire decision. The result was high turnover. This inhibited the firm's growth strategy.

City Garage's solution was to purchase the Personality Profile Analysis online test from Thomas International USA. After a quick application and background check, likely candidates take the 10-minute, 24-question PPA. City Garage staff then enter the answers into the PPA Software system, and test results are available in less than 2 minutes. These show whether the applicant is high or low in four personality characteristics; it also produces follow-up questions about areas that might cause problems. For example, applicants might be asked how they handled possible weaknesses such as lack of patience in the past. If candidates answer those questions satisfactorily, they're asked back for extensive, all-day interviews, after which hiring decisions are made.

Computerized and Online Testing

As you can see, computerized and/or online testing is increasingly replacing conventional paper-and-pencil tests. Such tests are also becoming more sophisticated. For example, PreVisor (www.previsor.com/) offers online adaptive personality tests. As a candidate answers each question, these tests adapt the next question to the test taker's answers to the previous question. This improves test validity and may reduce cheating. For example, it makes it more unlikely that candidates can share test questions (since each candidate gets what amounts to a custom-made test).[39] Service firms like Unicru process and score online preemployment tests from employers' applicants. The applicant tracking systems we discussed in Chapter 5 often include an online prescreening test.[40] Most of the tests we describe on the following pages are available in computerized form. Vendors are making tests available for applicants to take via their iPhones. For example, www.iphonetypingtest.com offers an online typing test you can take on an iPhone.[41]

The Web site iphonetypingtest.com offers an online typing test you can take on an iPhone.

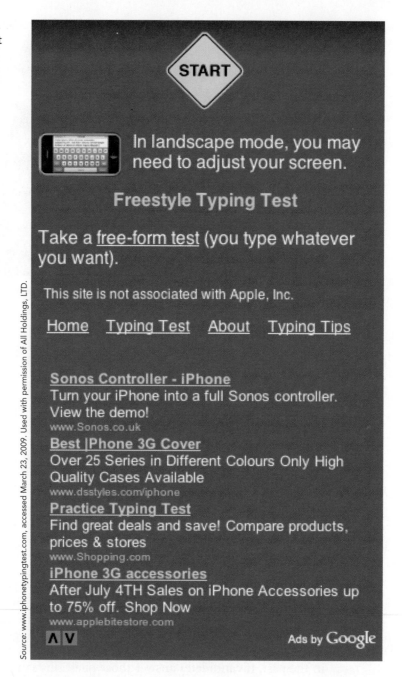

Source: www.iphonetypingtest.com, accessed March 23, 2009. Used with permission of All Holdings, LTD.

---

5 List eight tests you could use for employee selection, and how you would use them.

TYPES OF TESTS

We can conveniently classify tests according to whether they measure cognitive (mental) abilities, motor and physical abilities, personality and interests, or achievement.[42] We'll look at each.

Tests of Cognitive Abilities

Cognitive tests include tests of general reasoning ability (intelligence) and tests of specific mental abilities like memory and inductive reasoning.

INTELLIGENCE TESTS   Intelligence (IQ) tests are tests of general intellectual abilities. They measure not a single trait but rather a range of abilities, including memory, vocabulary, verbal fluency, and numerical ability. An adult's IQ score is a "derived" score. It reflects the extent to which the person is above or below the "average" adult's intelligence score.

FIGURE 6-6
Type of Question Applicant
Might Expect on a Test of
Mechanical Comprehension

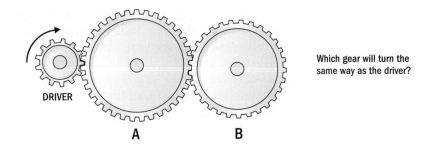

Which gear will turn the
same way as the driver?

Intelligence is often measured with individually administered tests like the Stanford-Binet Test or the Wechsler Test. Employers can administer other IQ tests such as the Wonderlic to groups of people. Other intelligence tests include the Kaufman Adolescent and Adult Intelligence Test, the Slosson Intelligence Test, and the Comprehensive Test of Nonverbal Intelligence. In a study of firefighter trainees' performance over 23 years, the researchers found that testing consisting of a measure of general intellectual ability and a physical ability assessment was highly predictive of firefighter trainee performance.[43]

SPECIFIC COGNITIVE ABILITIES There are also measures of specific mental abilities, such as deductive reasoning, verbal comprehension, memory, and numerical ability.

Psychologists often call such tests *aptitude tests*, since they purport to measure aptitude for the job in question. Consider the Test of Mechanical Comprehension in Figure 6-6, which tests applicants' understanding of basic mechanical principles. This may reflect a person's aptitude for jobs—like that of machinist or engineer—that require mechanical comprehension. Other tests of mechanical aptitude include the Mechanical Reasoning Test and the SRA Test of Mechanical Aptitude. The revised Minnesota Paper Form Board Test consists of 64 two-dimensional diagrams cut into separate pieces. It provides insights into an applicant's mechanical spatial ability; you'd use it for screening applicants for jobs such as designers, draftspeople, or engineers.

Tests of Motor and Physical Abilities

You might also want to measure motor abilities, such as finger dexterity, manual dexterity, and (if hiring pilots) reaction time. The Crawford Small Parts Dexterity Test is an example. It measures the speed and accuracy of simple judgment as well as the speed of finger, hand, and arm movements. Other tests include the Stromberg Dexterity Test, the Minnesota Rate of Manipulation Test, and the Purdue Peg Board.

Tests of physical abilities may also be required. These include static strength (such as lifting weights), dynamic strength (like pull-ups), body coordination (as in jumping rope), and stamina.[44] Thus applicants for the U.S. Marines must pass its Initial Strength Test (2 pull ups, 35 sit-ups, and a 1.5 mile run).

Measuring Personality and Interests

A person's cognitive and physical abilities alone seldom explain his or her job performance. Other factors, like motivation and interpersonal skills, are very important. As one consultant put it, most people are hired based on qualifications, but most are fired for nonperformance. And nonperformance "is usually the result of personal characteristics, such as attitude, motivation, and especially, temperament."[45] Even some online dating services, like eHarmony.com, have prospective members take online personality tests and reject those who its software judges as unmatchable.[46]

WHAT DO PERSONALITY TESTS MEASURE? Personality tests measure basic aspects of an applicant's personality, such as introversion, stability, and motivation.

Some of these tests are *projective*. The psychologist presents an ambiguous stimulus (like an inkblot or clouded picture) to the person. The person then reacts to it. Since the pictures are ambiguous, the person supposedly projects into the picture his or her attitudes. A security-oriented person might describe the ink blot in Figure 6-2 (page 178) as "A giant insect coming to get me." Other projective techniques include Make a Picture Story (MAPS), and the Forer Structured Sentence Completion Test.

Other personality tests are *self-reported*: applicants fill them out themselves. Figure 6-7 is an example. Thus, the Guilford-Zimmerman survey measures personality traits like emotional stability versus moodiness, and friendliness versus criticalness. The Minnesota Multiphasic Personality Inventory (MMPI) taps traits like hypochondria and paranoia. Available online, the Myers-Briggs test provides a personality type classification useful for decisions such as career selection and planning.[47]

FIGURE 6-7 Sample Online Personality Test Questions

Source: Elaine Pulakos, "Selection Assessment Methods," SHRM Foundation, 2005, p. 9.

HumanMetrics

Jung Typology Test™

After completing the questionnaire, you will obtain:

- Your type formula according to Carl Jung and Isabel Myers-Briggs typology along with the strengths of the preferences
- The description of your personality type
- The list of occupations and educational institutions where you can get relevant degree or training, most suitable for your personality type - Jung Career Indicator™

For Organizations and Professionals

Organizations and specialists interested in Jung personality assessments for team building, candidate assessment, leadership, career development, psychographics - visit **HRPersonality™** for practical and validated instruments and professional services.

1. You are almost never late for your appointments
   ○YES ○NO
2. You like to be engaged in an active and fast-paced job
   ○YES ○NO
3. You enjoy having a wide circle of acquaintances
   ○YES ○NO
4. You feel involved when watching TV soaps
   ○YES ○NO
5. You are usually the first to react to a sudden event: the telephone ringing or unexpected question
   ○YES ○NO
6. You are more interested in a general idea than in the details of its realization
   ○YES ○NO
7. You tend to be unbiased even if this might endanger your good relations with people
   ○YES ○NO
8. Strict observance of the established rules is likely to prevent a good outcome
   ○YES ○NO
9. It's difficult to get you excited
   ○YES ○NO
10. It is in your nature to assume responsibility
    ○YES ○NO
11. You often think about humankind and its destiny
    ○YES ○NO
12. You believe the best decision is one that can be easily changed
    ○YES ○NO
13. Objective criticism is always useful in any activity
    ○YES ○NO
14. You prefer to act immediately rather than speculate about various options
    ○YES ○NO
15. You trust reason rather than feelings
    ○YES ○NO
16. You are inclined to rely more on improvisation than on careful planning
    ○YES ○NO
17. You spend your leisure time actively socializing with a group of people, attending parties, shopping, etc.
    ○YES ○NO
18. You usually plan your actions in advance
    ○YES ○NO
19. Your actions are frequently influenced by emotions
    ○YES ○NO
20. You are a person somewhat reserved and distant in communication
    ○YES ○NO
21. You know how to put every minute of your time to good purpose
    ○YES ○NO
22. You readily help people while asking nothing in return
    ○YES ○NO
23. You often contemplate about the complexity of life
    ○YES ○NO
24. After prolonged socializing you feel you need to get away and be alone
    ○YES ○NO
25. You often do jobs in a hurry
    ○YES ○NO
26. You easily see the general principle behind specific occurrences
    ○YES ○NO
27. You frequently and easily express your feelings and emotions
    ○YES ○NO
28. You find it difficult to speak loudly
    ○YES ○NO

THE "BIG FIVE" What traits to measure? Industrial psychologists often focus on the "big five" personality dimensions: extraversion, emotional stability/neuroticism, agreeableness, conscientiousness, and openness to experience.[48]

Neuroticism represents a tendency to exhibit poor emotional adjustment and experience negative effects, such as anxiety, insecurity, and hostility. Extraversion represents a tendency to be sociable, assertive, active, and to experience positive effects, such as energy and zeal. Openness to experience is the disposition to be imaginative, nonconforming, unconventional, and autonomous. Agreeableness is the tendency to be trusting, compliant, caring, and gentle. Conscientiousness is comprised of two related facets: achievement and dependability.[49]

DO PERSONALITY TESTS PREDICT PERFORMANCE? It seems to make sense that personality tests would predict performance. After all, wouldn't an extroverted person do better in sales?

In fact, personality traits do often correlate with job performance. In one study, extraversion, conscientiousness, and openness to experience were strong predictors of leadership.[50] In another study, neuroticism was negatively related to motivation, while conscientiousness was positively related to it.[51] And, "in personality research, conscientiousness has been the most consistent and universal predictor of job performance."[52] So to paraphrase Woody Allen, it does seem that "90% of success is just showing up."

Other traits correlate with occupational success. For example, extraversion correlates with success in sales and management jobs.[53] The responsibility, socialization, and self-control scales of the California Psychological Inventory predicted dysfunctional job behaviors among law enforcement officers.[54] Emotional stability, extroversion, and agreeableness predicted whether expatriates would leave their overseas assignments early.[55]

CAVEATS However, there are three caveats. *First,* projective tests are hard to interpret. An expert must analyze the test taker's interpretations and infer from them his or her personality. The test's usefulness then assumes there's a measurable relationship between a personality trait (like introversion) and success on the job.

Second, personality tests can trigger legal challenges. For example, one court held that the MMPI is a medical test (because it can screen out applicants with psychological impairments), and so might violate the ADA.[56]

Third, some dispute that self-report personality tests predict performance at all. The journal *Personnel Psychology* convened a panel of distinguished industrial psychologists that said using self-report personality tests in selection "should be reconsidered [due to low validity]."[57] Other experts call such concerns "unfounded."[58] At a minimum, make sure that any personality tests you use predict performance.

INTEREST INVENTORIES **Interest inventories** compare one's interests with those of people in various occupations. Thus, a person who takes the Strong-Campbell Interests Inventory would receive a report comparing his or her interests to those of people already in occupations like accounting, engineering, or management. Someone taking the self-administered Self-Directed Search (SDS) (www.self-directed-search.com) receives an interests code to use in identifying likely high-potential occupations.

Interest inventories have many uses.[59] They're irreplaceable in career planning, since a person will likely do better in jobs that involve activities in which he or she is interested. They're also useful in selection. If you can select people whose interests are

interest inventory
A personal development and selection device that compares the person's current interests with those of others now in various occupations so as to determine the preferred occupation for the individual.

roughly the same as those of successful incumbents in the jobs for which you're recruiting, it's more likely that those applicants will be successful.

Achievement Tests

Achievement tests measure what someone has learned. Most of the tests you take in school are achievement tests. They measure your "job knowledge" in areas like economics, marketing, or human resources. Achievement tests are also popular at work. For example, the Purdue Test for Machinists and Machine Operators tests the job knowledge of experienced machinists with questions like "What is meant by 'tolerance'?" Some achievement tests measure the applicant's abilities; a typing test is one example.

WORK SAMPLES AND SIMULATIONS

With **work samples**, you present examinees with situations representative of the job for which they're applying, and evaluate their responses.[60] Experts consider these (and *simulations,* like the assessment centers we also discuss in this section) to be tests. However, they differ from most tests, because they measure job performance directly. For example, work samples for a cashier may include operating a cash register and counting money.[61]

Using Work Sampling for Employee Selection

6   Give two examples of work sample/simulation tests.

The **work sampling technique** tries to predict job performance by requiring job candidates to perform one or more samples of the job's tasks.

Work sampling has several advantages. It measures actual job tasks, so it's harder to fake answers. The work sample's content—the actual tasks the person must perform—is not as likely to be unfair to minorities (as might a personnel test that possibly emphasizes middle-class concepts and values).[62] Work sampling doesn't delve into the applicant's personality, so there's almost no chance of applicants viewing it as an invasion of privacy. Designed properly, work samples also exhibit better validity than do other tests designed to predict performance.

BASIC PROCEDURE   The basic procedure is to select a sample of several tasks crucial to performing the job, and then to test applicants on them.[63] An observer monitors performance on each task, and indicates on a checklist how well the applicant performs. Here is an example. In creating a work sampling test for maintenance mechanics, experts first listed all possible job tasks (like "install pulleys and belts" and "install and align a motor"). Four crucial tasks were installing pulleys and belts, disassembling and installing a gearbox, installing and aligning a motor, and pressing a bushing into a sprocket.

They then broke down these four tasks into the steps required to complete each step. Mechanics could perform each step in a slightly different way, of course. Since some approaches were better than others, the experts gave a different weight to different approaches.

Figure 6-8 shows one of the steps required for installing pulleys and belts—"checks key before installing." As the figure shows, possible approaches here include checking the key against (1) the shaft, (2) the pulley, or (3) neither. The right of the figure lists the weights (scores) reflecting the worth of each method. The applicant performs the task, and the observer checks off the approach used.

FIGURE 6-8 Example of a Work Sampling Question

Checks key before installing against:	
___shaft	score 3
___pulley	score 2
___neither	score 1
Note: This is one step in installing pulleys and belts.	

Situational Judgment Tests

Situational judgment tests are personnel tests "designed to assess an applicant's judgment regarding a situation encountered in the workplace." As an example, You are facing a project deadline and are concerned that you may not complete the project by the time it is due. It is very important to your supervisor that you complete a project by the deadline. It is not possible to get anyone to help you with the work. You would:[64]

  a. Ask for an extension of the deadline

  b. Let the supervisor know that you may not meet the deadline

  c. Work as many hours it as it takes to get the job done by the deadline

  d. Explore different ways to do the work so it can be completed by the deadline

  e. On the date it is due, hand in what you have done so far

  f. Do the most critical parts of the project by the deadline and complete the remaining parts after the deadline

  g. Tell your supervisor that the deadline is unreasonable

  h. Give your supervisor an update and express your concern about your ability to complete the project by the deadline

  i. Quit your job

Situational judgment tests are effective and widely used.[65]

Management Assessment Centers

A **management assessment center** is a 2- to 3-day simulation in which 10 to 12 candidates perform realistic management tasks (like making presentations) under the observation of experts who appraise each candidate's leadership potential. The center itself may be a simple conference room, but more likely a special room with a one-way mirror to facilitate observation. Many firms use assessment centers. For example, The Cheesecake Factory created its Professional Assessment and Development Center to help select promotable managers. Candidates spend 2 days of exercises, simulations, and classroom learning to see if they have the skills for key management positions.[66]

Typical simulated tasks include:

- **The in-basket.** This exercise confronts the candidate with an accumulation of reports, memos, notes of incoming phone calls, letters, and other materials collected in the actual or computerized in-basket of the simulated job he or she is about to start. The candidate must take appropriate action on each item. Trained evaluators then review the candidate's efforts.

- **Leaderless group discussion.** Trainers give a leaderless group a discussion question and tell members to arrive at a group decision. They then evaluate each group member's interpersonal skills, acceptance by the group, leadership ability, and individual influence.

- **Management games.** Participants solve realistic problems as members of simulated companies competing in a marketplace.

- **Individual presentations.** Here trainers evaluate each participant's communication skills and persuasiveness by having each make an assigned oral presentation.

---

work samples
Actual job tasks used in testing applicants' performance.

work sampling technique
A testing method based on measuring performance on actual basic job tasks.

management assessment center
A simulation in which management candidates are asked to perform realistic tasks in hypothetical situations and are scored on their performance. It usually also involves testing and the use of management games.

- **Objective tests.** An assessment center typically includes tests of personality, mental ability, interests, and achievements.
- **The interview.** Most also require an interview between at least one trainer and each participant, to assess the latter's interests, past performance, and motivation.

Supervisor recommendations usually play a big role in choosing center participants. Line managers usually act as assessors and typically arrive at their ratings through consensus.[67]

EFFECTIVENESS   Most experts view assessment centers as effective for selecting management candidates, but are they worth their cost? They are expensive to develop, take much longer than conventional tests, require managers acting as assessors, and often require psychologists. However, studies suggest they are worth it.[68] One study of 40 police candidates found that: "Assessment center performance shows a unique and substantial contribution to the prediction of future police work success, justifying the usage of such method." In this study, peers' evaluations of candidates during the center proved especially useful.[69]

Situational Testing and Video-Based Situational Testing

Situational tests require examinees to respond to situations representative of the job. Work sampling (discussed earlier) and some assessment center tasks (such as in-baskets) fall in this category. So do video-based tests and miniature job training (described next), and the situational interviews we address in Chapter 7.[70]

The **video-based simulation** presents the candidate with several online or PC-based video situations, each followed by one or more multiple-choice questions. For example, the scenario might depict an employee handling a situation on the job. At a critical moment, the scenario ends and the video asks the candidate to choose from several courses of action. For example:

(*A manager is upset about the condition of the department and takes it out on one of the department's employees.*)

> *Manager:* Well, I'm glad you're here.
> *Associate:* Oh? Why is that?
> *Manager:* Look at this place, that's why! I take a day off and come back to find the department in a mess. You should know better.
> *Associate:* But I didn't work late last night.
> *Manager:* Maybe not. But there have been plenty of times before when you've left this department in a mess.

(*The scenario stops here.*)
If you were this associate, what would you do?

a. Let the other associates responsible for the mess know that you had to take the heat.

b. Straighten up the department, and try to reason with the manager later.

c. Suggest to the manager that he talk to the other associates who made the mess.

d. Take it up with the manager's boss.[71]

Computerized Multimedia Candidate Assessment Tools

Employers increasingly use computerized multimedia candidate assessment tools. Development Dimensions International developed a multimedia skill test that Ford Motor Company uses for hiring assembly workers. "The company can test everything from how people tighten the ball, to whether they followed a certain procedure correctly, to using a weight-sensitive mat on the floor that, when stepped on at the wrong time, will mark a candidate down in a safety category."[72]

The Miniature Job Training and Evaluation Approach

Miniature job training and evaluation means training candidates to perform several of the job's tasks, and then evaluating the candidates' performance prior to hire. The approach assumes that a person who demonstrates that he or she can learn and perform the sample of tasks will be able to learn and perform the job itself. Like work sampling, *miniature job training and evaluation* tests applicants with actual samples of the job, so it's inherently content relevant and valid. The big problem is the expense involved in the instruction and training.

HONDA EXAMPLE When Honda built a new plant in Alabama, it had to hire thousands of new employees. Honda's recruiting ad sought applicants for a free training program Honda was offering as a precondition for applying for jobs at the new plant. Applicants needed at least a high school diploma or GED, employment for the past 2 years with no unexplainable gaps, and Alabama residency. Eighteen thousand people applied.

First Honda and the Alabama state employment agency screened the applicants by eliminating those who lacked the education or experience. They then gave preference to applicants near the plant. About 340 applicants per 6-week session received special training at a new facility, two evenings a week. This included classroom instruction, videos of Honda employees in action, and actually practicing particular jobs. (Thus, "miniature job training and evaluation.") Some candidates who watched the videos dropped out after seeing the work's pace.

Employers such as Honda first train and then have applicants perform several of the job tasks, and then evaluate the candidates before hiring them.

During training, Alabama state agency assessors scrutinized and rated the trainees. They then invited those who graduated to apply for plant jobs. Honda employees (from HR and departmental representatives) then interviewed the candidates, reviewed their training records, and decided who to hire. New employees take a one-time drug test, but no other paper-and-pencil tests or credentials are required. New hires receive a 3-day orientation. Then, assistant managers in each department coordinate their day-to-day training.[73]

Realistic Job Previews

Sometimes, a dose of realism makes the best screening tool. For example, Walmart found that many new associates quit within the first 90 days. When Walmart began explicitly explaining and asking about work schedules and work preferences, turnover improved.[74] In general, applicants who receive realistic job previews are more likely to turn down job offers, but firms are more likely to have lower turnover.[75]

HR in Practice: Testing Techniques for Managers

You may find that, even in large companies, when it comes to screening employees, you're on your own. The human resource department may work with you to design and administer screening tests. But more often HR may do little more than the recruiting and some prescreening (such as typing tests for clerical applicants), and run background checks and drug and physical exams.

Suppose you are, say, the marketing manager, and you want to screen your job applicants more formally. You could buy your own

Source: Issei Kato/Reuters Pictures–Americas.

---

situational test
A test that requires examinees to respond to situations representative of the job.

video-based simulation
A situational test in which examinees respond to video simulations of realistic job situations.

miniature job training and evaluation
Training candidates to perform several of the job's tasks, and then evaluating the candidates' performance prior to hire.

TABLE 6-1 Evaluation of Selected Assessment Methods

Assessment Method	Validity	Adverse Impact	Costs (Develop/ Administer)
Cognitive ability tests	High	High (against minorities)	Low/low
Job knowledge test	High	High (against minorities)	Low/low
Personality tests	Low to moderate	Low	Low/low
Integrity tests	Moderate to high	Low	Low/low
Structured interviews	High	Low	High/high
Situational judgment tests	Moderate	Moderate (against minorities)	High/low
Work samples	High	Low	High/high
Assessment centers	Moderate to high	Low to moderate, depending on exercise	High/high
Physical ability tests	Moderate to high	High (against females and older workers)	High/high

Source: Elaine Pulakos, *Selection Assessment Methods*, SHRM Foundation, 2005, p. 17. Reprinted by permission of Society for Human Resource Management via Copyright Clearance Center.

test battery. However, using packaged intelligence tests may violate company policy, raise validity questions, and even expose your employer to EEO liability.

A preferred approach is to devise and use screening tools, the validity of which is obvious ("face validity.") For example, create a work sampling test. Thus, it is reasonable for the marketing manager to ask an advertising applicant to spend an hour designing an ad, or to ask a marketing research applicant to spend a half hour outlining a marketing research program for a hypothetical product.

Summary

The employer needs to consider several things before deciding to use a particular selection tool. These include the tool's reliability and validity, its return on investment (in terms of utility analysis), applicant reactions, usability (in terms of your managers' and employees' willingness and ability to use it), adverse impact, and the tool's *selection ratio* (does it screen out, as it should, a high percentage of applicants or admit virtually all?).[76] Table 6-1 summarizes the validity, potential adverse impact, and cost of several popular assessment methods.

---

7 Explain the key points to remember in conducting background investigations.

BACKGROUND INVESTIGATIONS AND OTHER SELECTION METHODS

Testing is only part of an employer's selection process. Other tools may include background investigations and reference checks, preemployment information services, honesty testing, graphology, and substance abuse screening.

Why Perform Background Investigations and Reference Checks?

One of the easiest ways to avoid hiring mistakes is to check the candidate's background thoroughly. Doing so is cheap and (if done right) useful. There's usually no reason why even supervisors in large companies can't check the references of someone they're about to hire, as long as they know the rules.

Most employers therefore check and verify the job applicant's background information and references. In one survey of about 700 human resource managers,

87% said they conduct reference checks, 69% conduct background employment checks, 61% check employee criminal records, 56% check employees' driving records, and 35% sometimes or always check credit.[77] Commonly verified data include legal eligibility for employment (in compliance with immigration laws), dates of prior employment, military service (including discharge status), education, identification (including date of birth and address to confirm identity), county criminal records (current residence, last residence), motor vehicle record, credit, licensing verification, Social Security number, and reference checks.[78] Some employers are checking executive candidates' civil litigation records, with the candidate's prior approval.[79] As of 2010, Massachusetts and Hawaii prohibit private employers from asking about criminal records on initial written applications.[80]

WHY CHECK?   There are two main reasons to check backgrounds—to verify the applicant's information (name and so forth) and to uncover damaging information.[81] Lying on one's application isn't unusual. A survey found that 23% of 7,000 executive résumés contained exaggerated or false information.[82]

Even relatively sophisticated companies fall prey to criminal employees, in part because they haven't conducted proper background checks. In Chicago, a pharmaceutical firm discovered it had hired gang members in mail delivery and computer repair. The crooks were stealing close to a million dollars a year in computer parts, and then using the mail department to ship them to a nearby computer store they owned.[83]

How deeply you search depends on the position you seek to fill. For example, a credit and education check is more important for hiring an accountant than a groundskeeper. In any case, also periodically check the credit ratings of employees (like cashiers) who have easy access to company assets, and the driving records of employees who routinely use company cars.

EFFECTIVENESS   Most managers don't view references as very useful. This makes sense, given that few employers will talk freely about former employees. For example, in one 2010 poll, the Society for Human Resource Management (SHRM) found that 98% of 433 responding members said their organizations would verify dates of employment for current or former employees. However, 68% said they wouldn't discuss work performance; 82% said they wouldn't discuss character or personality; and 87% said they wouldn't disclose a disciplinary action.[84]

It's obvious why background checks have bad reputations. Many supervisors don't want to damage a former employee's chances for a job; others might prefer giving an incompetent employee good reviews if it will get rid of him or her.

The other reason is legal. Employers providing references generally can't be successfully sued for defamation unless the employee can show "malice"—that is, ill will, culpable recklessness, or disregard of the employee's rights.[85] But the managers and companies providing the references understandably still don't want the grief. Let's look at why.

The Legal Dangers and How to Avoid Them

In practice (as most people instinctively know), giving someone a bad reference can drag you into a legal mess. For example, if the courts believe you gave the bad reference to retaliate for the employee previously filing an EEOC claim, they might let him or her sue you.[86]

DEFAMATION   That is just the tip of the iceberg. Being sued for defamation is the real danger. First-line supervisors and managers, not just employers, are potentially at risk. Various federal laws[87] give individuals and students the right to know the nature and substance of information in their credit files and files with government agencies, and to review records pertaining to them from any private business that contracts with a federal agency. So, it's quite possible the person you're describing will see your comments and decide you defamed him or her. Common law (in particular, the tort of defamation) applies to any information you supply. A communication is *defamatory* if it is false and tends to harm the reputation of another by lowering the person in the estimation of the community or by deterring other persons from associating or dealing with him or her.

The person alleging defamation has various legal remedies, including suing the source of the reference for defamation.[88] In one case, a court awarded a man $56,000 after a company turned him down for a job because, among other things, the former employer called him a "character." As if that's not enough, there are companies that, for a small fee, will call former employers on behalf of employees who believe they're getting bad references. One supervisor thought his previous employer might bad-mouth him. He hired BadReferences.com to investigate. BadReferences.com (which uses trained court reporters for its investigations) found that a supervisor at the company suggested that the employee was "a little too obsessive . . . and not comfortable with taking risks, or making big decisions." The former employee sued his previous employer, demanding an end to defamation and $45,000 in compensation.[89]

PRIVACY   Furthermore, truth is not always a defense. Thus in some states, employees can sue employers for disclosing to a large number of people true but embarrassing private facts about the employee. Here truth is no defense.

One case involved a supervisor in a shouting match with an employee. The supervisor yelled out that the employee's wife had been having sexual relations with certain people. The employee and his wife sued the employer for invasion of privacy. The jury found the employer liable for invasion of the couple's privacy. It awarded damages to both of them, as well as damages for the couple's additional claim that the supervisor's conduct amounted to an intentional infliction of emotional distress.[90]

The net result is that most employers and managers are very restrictive about who can give references, and what they can say. As a rule, only authorized managers should provide information. Other suggestions include "Don't volunteer information," "Avoid vague statements," and "Do not answer trap questions such as, 'Would you rehire this person?'" In practice, many firms have a policy of not providing any information about former employees except for their dates of employment, last salary, and position titles.[91]

However, *not* disclosing relevant information can be dangerous, too. In one Florida case, a company fired an employee for allegedly bringing a handgun to work. After his next employer fired him (for absenteeism), he returned to that company and shot several employees before taking his own life. The injured parties and the relatives of the murdered employees sued the previous employer, who had provided the employee with a clean letter of recommendation allegedly because that first employer didn't want to anger the employee over his firing.

How to Check a Candidate's Background

Which brings us back to this point: In practice, the references you receive may not be useful. There are several things that managers and employers can do to get better information.

Most employers at least try to verify an applicant's current (or former) position and salary with his or her current (or former) employer by phone (assuming you cleared doing so with the candidate). Others call the applicant's current and previous supervisors to try to discover more about the person's motivation, technical competence, and ability to work with others (although again, many employers have policies against providing such information). Figure 6-9 shows one form you can use for phone references. Some employers get background reports from commercial credit rating companies for information about credit standing, indebtedness,

FIGURE 6-9 Reference Checking Form

Source: Society for Human Resource Management, © 2004. Reproduced with permission of Society for Human Resource Management.

(Verify that the applicant has provided permission before conducting reference checks.)

Candidate
Name _____

Reference
Name _____

Company
Name _____

Dates of Employment
From: _____ To: _____

Position(s)
Held _____

Salary
History _____

Reason for
Leaving _____

Explain the reason for your call and verify the above information with the supervisor (including the reason for leaving)
_____
_____
_____

1. Please describe the type of work for which the candidate was responsible.
_____
_____
_____

2. How would you describe the applicant's relationships with coworkers, subordinates (if applicable), and with superiors?
_____
_____
_____

3. Did the candidate have a positive or negative work attitude? Please elaborate.
_____
_____
_____

4. How would you describe the quantity and quality of output generated by the former employee?
_____
_____
_____

5. What were his/her strengths on the job?
_____
_____
_____

6. What were his/her weaknesses on the job?
_____
_____
_____

7. What is your overall assessment of the candidate?
_____
_____
_____

8. Would you recommend him/her for this position? Why or why not?
_____
_____
_____

9. Would this individual be eligible for rehire? Why or why not?
_____
_____

Other comments?
_____
_____
_____

reputation, character, and lifestyle. (Others check social network sites, as we will see in a moment.)

More employers are automating their reference checking process. Instead of the employer calling the references, the recruiter sends an e-mail link to each candidate.

The candidate then uses this link to contact five or more of his or her references, asking them to fill out a tailored online questionnaire. Special vendors then compile this information and create analytical reports for the employer.[92]

The Social Network: Checking Applicants' Social Postings

More employers are Googling applicants or checking social networking sites. After such online searches, recruiters found that 31% of applicants had lied about their qualifications and 19% had posted information about their drinking or drug use.[93] On Facebook.com, one employer found that a candidate had described his interests as smoking pot and shooting people. The student may have been kidding, but didn't get the job.[94] An article called "References You Can't Control" notes that you can use social networking sites to identify an applicant's former colleagues, and thus contact them.[95]

Googling is probably safe enough, but checking social networking sites raises legal issues. For example, while the Fair Credit Reporting Act refers more to getting official reports, it's probably best to get the candidate's prior approval for social networking searches.[96] And, of course, do not use a pretext or fabricate an identity.[97]

HR IN PRACTICE: MAKING THE BACKGROUND CHECK MORE VALUABLE
Is there any way to obtain better information? Yes.

- First, include on the application form a statement for applicants to sign explicitly authorizing a background check, such as:

    I hereby certify that the facts set forth in the above employment application are true and complete to the best of my knowledge. I understand that falsified statements or misrepresentation of information on this application or omission of any information sought may be cause for dismissal, if employed, or may lead to refusal to make an offer and/or to withdrawal of an offer. I also authorize investigation of credit, employment record, driving record, and, once a job offer is made or during employment, workers' compensation background if required.

- Second (since telephone references apparently produce assessments that are more candid), it's probably best to rely on telephone references. Use a form, such as the one in Figure 6-9. Remember that you can get relatively accurate information regarding dates of employment, eligibility for rehire, and job qualifications. It's more difficult to get other background information (such as reasons for leaving a previous job).[98]

- Third, persistence and attentiveness to potential red flags improves results. For example, if the former employer hesitates or seems to qualify his or her answer when you ask, "Would you rehire?" don't just go on to the next question. Try to unearth what the applicant did to make the former employer pause. If he says, "Joe requires some special care," say, "Special care?"

- Fourth, compare the application to the résumé; people tend to be more imaginative on their résumés than on their application forms, where they must certify the information.

- Fifth, try to ask open-ended questions (such as, "How much structure does the applicant need in his/her work?") in order to get the references to talk more about the candidate.[99] But in asking for information:

    Only ask for and obtain information that you're going to use.

    Remember that using arrest information is highly suspect.

    Use information that is specific and job related.

    Keep information confidential.

● Sixth, use the references offered by the applicant as a source for other references. You might ask each of the applicant's references, "Could you give me the name of another person who might be familiar with the applicant's performance?" In that way, you begin getting information from references that may be more objective, because they did not come directly from the applicant.

Using Preemployment Information Services

It is easy to have employment screening services check out applicants. Major employment screening providers include ADP (www.ADP.com), Employment Background Investigations (www.ebinc.com), First Advantage (www.FADV.com/employer), Hireright (www.hireright.com), and Talentwise (www.talentwise.com).[100] They use databases to access information about matters such as workers' compensation and credit histories, and conviction and driving records. For example, a South Florida firm advertises that for less than $50 it will do a criminal history report, motor vehicle/driver's record report, and (after the person is hired) a workers' compensation claims report history, plus confirm identity, name, and Social Security number. There are thousands of databases and sources for finding background information, including sex offender registries, and criminal and educational histories.

USE CAUTION   There are two reasons to use caution when delving into an applicant's criminal, credit, and workers' compensation histories.[101] First (as discussed in Chapter 2), it can be tricky complying with EEO laws. For example, the ADA prohibits employers from making preemployment inquiries into the existence, nature, or severity of a disability. Therefore, asking about a candidate's previous workers' compensation claims before offering the person a job is usually unlawful. Similarly, asking about arrest records may be discriminatory. Never authorize an unreasonable investigation.

Second, various federal and state laws govern how employers acquire and use applicants' and employees' background information. At the federal level, the Fair Credit Reporting Act is the main directive. In addition, at least 21 states impose their own requirements. Compliance with these laws essentially involves four steps, as follows:

STEP 1: DISCLOSURE AND AUTHORIZATION.   Before requesting reports, the employer must disclose to the applicant or employee that a report will be requested and that the employee/applicant may receive a copy. (Do this on the application.)

STEP 2: CERTIFICATION.   The employer must certify to the reporting agency that the employer will comply with the federal and state legal requirements—for example, that the employer obtained written consent from the employee or applicant.

STEP 3: PROVIDING COPIES OF REPORTS.   Under federal law, the employer must provide copies of the report to the applicant or employee if adverse action (such as withdrawing an offer of employment) is contemplated.[102]

STEP 4: NOTICE AFTER ADVERSE ACTION.   After the employer provides the employee or applicant with copies of the consumer and investigative reports and a "reasonable period" has elapsed, the employer may take an adverse action (such as withdrawing an offer). If the employer anticipates taking an adverse action, the employee or applicant must receive an adverse action notice. This notice contains information such as the name of the consumer reporting agency. The employee/applicant then has various remedies under the applicable laws.[103]

The Polygraph and Honesty Testing

Some firms still use the polygraph (or lie detector) for honesty testing, although the law severely restricts its use. The polygraph is a device that measures physiological changes like increased perspiration. The assumption is that such changes reflect changes in emotional state that accompany lying.

Complaints about offensiveness plus grave doubts about the polygraph's accuracy culminated in the Employee Polygraph Protection Act of 1988.[104] With a few exceptions, the law prohibits employers from conducting polygraph examinations of all job applicants and most employees. (Also prohibited are other mechanical or electrical devices that attempt to measure honesty or dishonesty, including psychological stress evaluators and voice stress analyzers.) Federal laws don't prohibit paper-and-pencil tests and chemical testing, as for drugs.

WHO CAN USE THE POLYGRAPH?

Local, state, and federal government employers (including the FBI) can use polygraphs, but state laws restrict many local and state governments. Private employers can use polygraph testing, but only under strictly limited circumstances. The latter include those with

- National defense or security contracts
- Nuclear power-related contracts with the Department of Energy
- Access to highly classified information
- Counterintelligence-related contracts with the FBI or Department of Justice
- Private businesses (1) hiring private security personnel, (2) hiring persons with access to drugs, or (3) doing ongoing investigations involving economic loss or injury to an employer's business, such as a theft

However, even if used for ongoing investigations of theft, the law restricts employers' rights. To administer a polygraph test for an ongoing investigation, an employer must meet four standards:

1. First, the employer must show that it suffered an economic loss or injury.
2. Second, it must show that the employee in question had access to the property.
3. Third, it must have a reasonable suspicion before asking the employee to take the polygraph.
4. Fourth, the employee must receive the details of the investigation before the test, as well as the questions to be asked on the polygraph test.

PAPER-AND-PENCIL HONESTY TESTS

The Polygraph Protection Act triggered a burgeoning market for paper-and-pencil (or online) honesty tests. These are psychological tests designed to predict job applicants' proneness to dishonesty and other forms of counterproductivity.[105] Most measure attitudes regarding things like tolerance of others who steal, acceptance of rationalizations for theft, and admission of theft-related activities. Tests include the Phase II profile. London House, Inc., and Stanton Corporation publish similar tests.[106]

Psychologists initially raised concerns about paper-and-pencil honesty tests, but studies support these tests' validity. One early study illustrates their potential usefulness. The study involved 111 employees hired by a convenience store chain to work at store or gas station counters.[107] The firm estimated that "shrinkage" equaled 3% of sales, and believed that internal theft accounted for much of this. Scores on an honesty test successfully predicted theft here, as measured by termination for theft. One large review of such tests concluded that the "pattern of findings" regarding the usefulness of such tests "continues to be consistently positive."[108]

CHECKING FOR HONESTY: WHAT YOU CAN DO

With or without testing, there's a lot a manager or employer can do to screen out dishonest applicants or employees. Specifically:

- **Ask blunt questions.**[109] Says one expert, there is nothing wrong with asking the applicant direct questions, such as, "Have you ever stolen anything from an employer?" "Have you recently held jobs other than those listed on your application?" and, "Is any information on your application misrepresented or falsified?"

- **Listen, rather than talk.** Allow the applicant to do the talking so you can learn as much about the person as possible.
- **Do a credit check.** Include a clause in your application giving you the right to conduct background checks, including credit checks and motor vehicle reports.
- **Check all employment and personal references.**
- **Use paper-and-pencil honesty tests and psychological tests.**
- **Test for drugs.** Devise a drug-testing program and give each applicant a copy of the policy.
- **Establish a search-and-seizure policy and conduct searches.** Give each applicant a copy of the policy and require each to return a signed copy. The policy should state, "All lockers, desks, and similar property remain the property of the company and may be inspected routinely."

Honesty testing still requires some caution. Having just taken and "failed" what is fairly obviously an "honesty test," the candidate may leave the premises feeling his or her treatment was less than proper. Some "honesty" questions also pose invasion-of-privacy issues. And there are state laws to consider. For instance, Massachusetts and Rhode Island limit paper-and-pencil honesty testing.

Graphology

Graphology is the use of handwriting analysis to determine the writer's basic personality traits. Graphology thus has some resemblance to projective personality tests, although graphology's validity is highly suspect.

In graphology, the handwriting analyst studies an applicant's handwriting and signature to discover the person's needs, desires, and psychological makeup. According to the graphologist, the writing in Figure 6-10 exemplifies traits such as "independence" and "isolation."

Graphology's place in screening sometimes seems schizophrenic. Studies suggest it is not valid, or that when graphologists do accurately size up candidates, it's because they are also privy to other background information. Yet some firms continue to swear by it. It tends to be popular in Europe, where "countries like France or Germany have one central graphology institute, which serves as the certifying body."[110] Fike Corporation in Blue Springs, Missouri, a 325-employee firm, uses profiles based on handwriting samples to design follow-up interviews. Exchange Bank in Santa Rosa, California, uses it as one element for screening officer candidates.[111] Most experts shun it.

"Human Lie Detectors"

While perhaps no more valid than graphology, some employers are using so-called "human lie detectors."[112] These are experts who may (or may not) be able to identify lying just by watching candidates. One Wall Street firm uses a psychologist and former FBI agent. He sits in on interviews and watches for signs of candidate deceptiveness. Signs include pupils changing size (which often corresponds to emotions, such as fear), irregular breathing (may flag nervousness), micro-expressions (quick transitory facial expressions that may portray emotions such as fear), crossing legs ("liars typically try to distance themselves from an untruth"), and quick verbal responses (possibly reflecting scripted statements).

Physical Exams

Once the employer extends the person a job offer, a medical exam is often the next step in the selection (although it may also occur after the new employee starts work).

There are several reasons for preemployment medical exams: to verify that the applicant meets the position's physical requirements, to discover any medical limitations you

FIGURE 6-10 The Uptight
Personality

Source: www.graphicinsight.co.za/
writingsamples.htm#The%20Uptight%
20Personality%2, accessed March 28,
2009. Used with permission of www.
graphicinsight.co.za.

The Uptight Personality

From The Graphology Review No 17

The following sample shows several uptight tendencies. We see independence, a critical, rather severe attitude and an economy of feeling. Notice too, how the words are separated by large spaces indicating that the writer has a feeling of personal isolation.

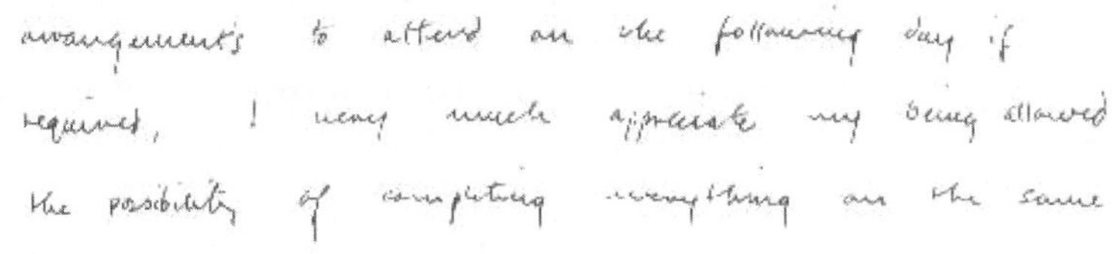

arrangements   to   attend   on   the   following   day   if
required,   I   very   much   appreciate   my   being   allowed
the   possibility   of   completing   everything   on   the   same

Here are some of the handwriting indicators for the uptight personality as discussed in The Graphology Review No 17;

- Small to middle size handwriting

- Upright slant

- Narrow letters

- Angular connections

- Economical use of space on the page

- Although the words here are not extremely cramped they are certainly not expansive. The spacing between the letters is very economical.

should consider in placing him or her, and to establish a baseline for future insurance or workers compensation claims. By identifying health problems, the examination can also reduce absenteeism and accidents and, of course, detect communicable diseases.

Under the Americans with Disabilities Act, an employer cannot reject someone with a disability if he or she is otherwise qualified and can perform the essential job functions with reasonable accommodation. Recall that the ADA permits a medical exam during the period between the job offer and commencement of work if such exams are standard practice for all applicants for that job category.[113]

Substance Abuse Screening

Many employers conduct drug screenings. The most common practice is to test candidates just before they're formally hired. Many also test current employees when there is reason to believe the person has been using drugs—after a work accident, or in the presence of obvious behavioral symptoms such as chronic lateness. Some firms routinely administer drug tests on a random or periodic basis, while others require drug tests when they transfer or promote employees to new positions.[114] Employers may use urine testing to test for illicit drugs, breath alcohol tests to determine amount of alcohol in the blood, blood tests to measure alcohol or drug in the blood at the time of the test, hair analyses to reveal drug history, saliva tests for substances such as marijuana and cocaine, and skin patches to determine drug use.[115]

SOME PRACTICAL CONSIDERATIONS   Drug testing, while ubiquitous, is neither as simple nor effective as it might first appear. First, no drug test is foolproof. Some urine sample tests can't distinguish between legal and illegal substances; for example, Advil can produce positive results for marijuana. Furthermore, "there is a swarm of products that promise to help employees (both male and female) beat drug tests."[116] (Employers should view the presence of adulterants in a sample as a positive test.) The alternative, hair follicle testing, requires a small sample of hair, which the lab analyzes.[117] But here, too, classified ads advertise chemicals to rub on the scalp to fool the test.

There's also the question of what is the point.[118] Unlike roadside breathalyzers for DUI drivers, tests for drugs only show whether drug residues are present, not impairment (or, for that matter, habituation or addiction).[119] Some therefore argue that testing is not justifiable on the grounds of boosting workplace safety.[120] Many feel the testing procedures themselves are degrading and intrusive. Many employers reasonably counter that they don't want drug-prone employees on their premises. Employers should choose the lab they engage to do the testing carefully.

LEGAL ISSUES Drug testing raises legal issues, too.[121] Several federal (and many state) laws affect workplace drug testing. As an example, under the ADA, a court would probably consider a former drug user (who no longer uses illegal drugs and has successfully completed or is participating in a rehabilitation program) a qualified applicant with a disability.[122] Under the Drug Free Workplace Act of 1988, federal contractors must maintain a workplace free from illegal drugs. Under the U.S. Department of Transportation workplace regulations, firms with more than 50 eligible employees in transportation industries (mass transit workers, school bus drivers, and so on) must conduct alcohol testing on workers with sensitive or safety-related jobs.[123]

WHAT TO DO IF AN EMPLOYEE TESTS POSITIVE What should one do when a job candidate tests positive? Most companies will not hire such candidates, and a few will immediately fire current employees who test positive. Current employees have more legal recourse. Employers must tell them the reason for dismissal if the reason is a positive drug test.[124]

Where sensitive jobs are concerned, courts tend to side with employers. In one case, the U.S. Court of Appeals for the First Circuit ruled that Exxon acted properly in firing a truck driver who failed a drug test. Exxon's drug-free workplace program included random testing of employees in safety-sensitive jobs. The employee drove a tractor-trailer carrying 12,000 gallons of flammable motor fuel and tested positive for cocaine. The union representing the employee challenged the firing, and an arbitrator reduced the penalty to a 2-month suspension. The appeals court reversed the arbitrator's decision. It ruled that the employer acted properly in firing the truck driver, given the circumstances.[125]

Complying with Immigration Law

Employees hired in the United States must prove they are eligible to work in the United States. A person does not have to be a U.S. citizen to be employable. However, employers should ask a person they're about to hire whether he or she is a U.S. citizen or an alien lawfully authorized to work in the United States. To comply with this law, employers should follow procedures outlined in the so-called I-9 Employment Eligibility Verification form.[126] More employers are using the federal government's voluntary electronic employment verification program, E-Verify.[127] Federal contractors must use it.[128]

PROOF OF ELIGIBILITY Applicants can prove their eligibility for employment in two ways. One is to show a document (such as a U.S. passport or alien registration card with photograph) that proves both the person's identity and employment eligibility. The other is to show a document that proves the person's identity, along with a second document showing the person's employment eligibility, such as a work permit.[129] In any case, it's always advisable to get two forms of proof of identity from everyone.

Some documents may be fakes. For example, a few years ago Immigration and Naturalization Service (INS) agents seized more than 2 million counterfeit documents ranging from green cards and Social Security cards to driver's licenses, from nine different states. The federal government is tightening restrictions on hiring undocumented workers. Realizing that many documents (such as Social Security cards) are fakes, the government is putting the onus on employers to make sure whom they're hiring. The Department of Homeland Security presses criminal charges against suspected employer violators.[130]

Employers can protect themselves in several ways. First, they can use E-Verify. Then, systematic background checks are important. Preemployment testing should include employment verification, criminal record checks, drug screens, and reference checks. You can verify Social Security numbers by calling the Social Security Administration. Employers can avoid accusations of discrimination by verifying the documents of all applicants, not just those they may think suspicious.[131]

AVOIDING DISCRIMINATION   In any case, employers should not use the I-9 form to discriminate based on race or country of national origin. The requirement to verify eligibility does not provide any basis to reject an applicant just because he or she is a foreigner, not a U.S. citizen, or an alien residing in the United States, as long as that person can prove his or her identity and employment eligibility. The latest I-9 forms contain a prominent "antidiscrimination notice."[132]

Improving Productivity Through HRIS
Using Automated Applicant Tracking and Screening Systems

The applicant tracking systems we introduced in Chapter 5 do more than compile incoming Web-based résumés and track applicants during the hiring process. They should also help with the testing and screening.

Thus, most employers also use their applicant tracking systems (ATS) to "knock out" applicants who don't meet minimum, nonnegotiable job requirements, like submitting to drug tests or holding driver's licenses.

Employers also use ATS to test and screen applicants online. This includes skills testing (in accounting, for instance), cognitive skills testing (such as for mechanical comprehension), and even psychological testing. For example, Recreation Equipment, Inc., wanted to identify applicants who were team-oriented. Its applicant tracking system helps it do that.[133]

Finally, the newer systems don't just screen out candidates, but discover "hidden talents." Thanks to the Internet, applicants often send their résumés out hoping a shotgun approach will help them hit a match. For most employers, this is a screening nuisance. But a good ATS can identify required talents in the applicant that even the applicant didn't know existed when he or she applied.[134]

REVIEW

MyManagementLab   Now that you have finished this chapter, go back to **www.mymanagementlab.com** to continue practicing and applying the concepts you've learned.

CHAPTER SECTION SUMMARIES

1. Careful **employee selection is important** for several reasons. Your own performance always depends on your subordinates; it is costly to recruit and hire employees; and mismanaging the hiring process has various legal implications including equal employment, negligent hiring, and defamation.

2. Whether you are administering tests or making decisions based on test results, managers need to understand several **basic testing concepts**. Reliability refers to a test's consistency, while validity tells you whether the test is measuring what you think it's supposed to be measuring. Criterion validity means demonstrating that those who do well on the test also do well on the job while content validity means showing that the test constitutes a fair sample of the job's content. Validating a test involves analyzing the job, choosing the tests, administering the test, relating your test scores and criteria, and cross-validating and revalidating. Test takers have rights to privacy and feedback as well as to confidentiality.

3. Whether administered via paper and pencil, by computer, or online, we discussed several main **types of tests**. Tests of cognitive abilities measure things like reasoning ability and include intelligence tests and tests of specific cognitive abilities such as mechanical comprehension. There are also tests of motor and physical abilities, and measures of personality and interests. With respect to personality, psychologists often focus on the "big five" personality dimensions: extroversion, emotional stability/neuroticism, agreeableness, conscientiousness, and openness to experience. Achievement tests measure what someone has learned.

4. With **work samples and simulations,** you present examinees with situations representative of the jobs for which they are applying. One example is the management assessment center, a 2- to 3-day simulation in which 10 to 12 candidates perform realistic management tasks under the observation of experts who appraise each candidate's leadership potential. Video-based situational testing and the miniature job training and evaluation approach are two other examples.

5. Testing is only part of an employer's selection process; you also want to conduct **background investigations and other selection procedures**.

- The main point of doing a background check is to verify the applicant's information and to uncover potentially damaging information. However, care must be taken, particularly when giving a reference, that the employee not be defamed and that his or her privacy rights are maintained.

- Given former employers' reluctance to provide a comprehensive report, those checking references need to do several things. Make sure the applicant explicitly authorizes a background check, use a checklist or form for obtaining telephone references, and be persistent and attentive to potential red flags.

- Given the growing popularity of computerized employment background databases, many or most employers use preemployment information services to obtain background information.

- For many types of jobs, honesty testing is essential and paper-and-pencil tests have proven useful.

- Most employers also require that new hires, before actually coming on board, take physical exams and substance abuse screening. It's essential to comply with immigration law, in particular by having the candidate complete an I-9 Employment Eligibility Verification Form and submit proof of eligibility.

DISCUSSION QUESTIONS

1. What is the difference between reliability and validity? In what respects are they similar?
2. Explain how you would go about validating a test. How can this information be useful to a manager?
3. Explain why you think a certified psychologist who is specifically trained in test construction should (or should not) be used by a small business that needs a test battery.
4. Give some examples of how to use interest inventories to improve employee selection. In doing so, suggest several examples of occupational interests that you believe might predict success in various occupations, including college professor, accountant, and computer programmer.
5. Why is it important to conduct preemployment background investigations? Outline how you would go about doing so.
6. Explain how you would get around the problem of former employers being unwilling to give bad references on their former employees.
7. How can employers protect themselves against negligent hiring claims?

INDIVIDUAL AND GROUP ACTIVITIES

1. Write a short essay discussing some of the ethical and legal considerations in testing.
2. Working individually or in groups, develop a list of specific selection techniques that you would suggest your dean use to hire the next HR professor at your school. Explain why you chose each selection technique.
3. Working individually or in groups, contact the publisher of a standardized test such as the Scholastic Assessment Test and obtain from it written information regarding the test's validity and reliability. Present a short report in class discussing what the test is supposed to measure and the degree to which you think the test does what it is supposed to do, based on the reported validity and reliability scores.
4. The HRCI "Test Specifications" appendix at the end of this book (pages 633–640) lists the knowledge someone studying for the HRCI certification exam needs to have in each area of human resource management (such as in Strategic Management, Workforce Planning, and Human Resource Development). In groups of four to five students, do four things: (1) review that appendix now; (2) identify the material in this chapter that relates to the required knowledge the appendix lists; (3) write four multiple-choice exam questions on this material that you believe would be suitable for inclusion in the HRCI exam; and (4) if time permits, have someone from your team post your team's questions in front of the class, so the students in other teams can take each others' exam questions.

EXPERIENTIAL EXERCISE

A Test for a Reservation Clerk

Purpose: The purpose of this exercise is to give you practice in developing a test to measure *one specific ability* for the job of airline reservation clerk for a major airline. If time permits, you'll be able to combine your tests into a test battery.

Required Understanding: Your airline has decided to outsource its reservation jobs to Asia. You should be fully acquainted with the procedure for developing a personnel test and should read the following description of an airline reservation clerk's duties:

Customers contact our airline reservation clerks to obtain flight schedules, prices, and itineraries. The reservation clerks look up the requested information on our airline's online flight schedule systems, which are updated continuously. The reservation clerk must speak clearly, deal courteously and expeditiously with the customer, and be able to find quickly alternative flight arrangements in order to provide the customer with the itinerary that fits his or her needs. Alternative flights and prices must be found quickly, so that the customer is not kept waiting, and so that our reservations operations group maintains its efficiency standards. It is often necessary to look under various routings, since there may be a dozen or more alternative routes between the customer's starting point and destination.

You may assume that we will hire about one-third of the applicants as airline reservation clerks. Therefore, your objective is to create a test that is useful in selecting a third of those available.

How to Set Up the Exercise/Instructions: Divide the class into teams of five or six students. The ideal candidate will need to have a number of skills and abilities to perform this job well. Your job is to select a single ability and to develop a test to measure that ability. Use only the materials available in the room, please. The test should permit quantitative scoring and may be an individual or a group test.

Please go to your assigned groups. As per our discussion of test development in this chapter, each group should make a list of the abilities relevant to success in the airline reservation clerk's job. Each group should then rate the importance of these abilities on a 5-point scale. Then, develop a test to measure what you believe to be the top-ranked ability. If time permits, the groups should combine the various tests from each group into a test battery. If possible, leave time for a group of students to take the test battery.

APPLICATION CASE

THE INSIDER

In 2011, a federal jury convicted a stock trader who worked for a well-known investment firm, along with two alleged accomplices, of insider trading. According to the indictment, the trader got inside information about pending mergers from lawyers. The lawyers allegedly browsed around their law firm picking up information about corporate deals others in the firm were working on. The lawyers would then allegedly pass their information on to a friend, who in turn passed it on to the trader. Such "inside" information reportedly helped the trader (and his investment firm) earn millions of dollars. The trader would then allegedly thank the lawyers, for instance, with envelopes filled with cash.

Of course, things like that are not supposed to happen. Federal and state laws prohibit it. And investment firms have their own compliance procedures to identify and head off, for instance, shady trades. The problem is that controlling such behavior once the firm has someone working for it who may be prone to engage in inside trading isn't easy. "Better to avoid hiring such people in the first place," said one pundit.

At lunch at the Four Seasons restaurant off Park Avenue in Manhattan, the heads of several investment firms were discussing the conviction, and what they could do to make sure something like that didn't occur in their firms. "It's not just compliance," said one, "we've got to keep the bad apples from ever getting in the door." They ask you for your advice.

Questions

1. We want you to design an employee selection program for hiring stock traders. We already know what to look for as far as technical skills are concerned—accounting courses, economics, and so on. What we want is a program for screening out potential bad apples. To that end, please let us know the following: What screening test(s) would you suggest, and why? What questions should we add to our application form? Specifically, how should we check candidates' backgrounds, and what questions should we ask previous employers and references?
2. What else (if anything) would you suggest?

CONTINUING CASE

HONESTY TESTING AT CARTER CLEANING COMPANY

Jennifer Carter, of the Carter Cleaning Centers, and her father have what the latter describes as an easy but hard job when it comes to screening job applicants. It is easy because for two important jobs—the people who actually do the pressing and those who do the cleaning/spotting—the applicants are easily screened with about 20 minutes of on-the-job testing. As with typists, Jennifer points out, "Applicants either know how to press clothes fast enough or how to use cleaning chemicals and machines, or they don't, and we find out very quickly by just trying them out on the job." On the other hand, applicant screening for the stores can also be frustratingly hard because of the nature of some of the other qualities that Jennifer would like to screen for. Two of the most critical problems facing her company are employee turnover and employee honesty. Jennifer and her father sorely need to implement practices that will reduce the rate of employee turnover. If there is a way to do this through employee testing and screening techniques, Jennifer would like to know about it because of the management time and money that are now being wasted by the never-ending need to recruit and hire new employees. Of even greater concern to Jennifer and her father is the need to institute new practices to screen out those employees who may be predisposed to steal from the company.

Employee theft is an enormous problem for the Carter Cleaning Centers, and one that is not limited to employees who handle the cash. For example, the cleaner/spotter and/or the presser often open the store themselves, without a manager present, to get the day's work started, and it is not unusual to have one or more of these people steal supplies or "run a route." Running a route means that an employee canvasses his or her neighborhood to pick up people's clothes for cleaning and then secretly cleans and presses them in the Carter store, using the company's supplies, gas, and power. It would also not be unusual for an unsupervised person (or his or her supervisor, for that matter) to accept a 1-hour rush order for cleaning or laundering, quickly clean and press the item, and return it to the customer for payment without making out a proper ticket for the item posting the sale. The money, of course, goes into the worker's pocket instead of into the cash register.

The more serious problem concerns the store manager and the counter workers who actually handle the cash.

According to Jack Carter, "You would not believe the creativity employees use to get around the management controls we set up to cut down on employee theft." As one extreme example of this felonious creativity, Jack tells the following story: "To cut down on the amount of money my employees were stealing, I had a small sign painted and placed in front of all our cash registers. The sign said: YOUR ENTIRE ORDER FREE IF WE DON'T GIVE YOU A CASH REGISTER RECEIPT WHEN YOU PAY. CALL 552–0235. It was my intention with this sign to force all our cash-handling employees to give receipts so the cash register would record them for my accountants. After all, if all the cash that comes in is recorded in the cash register, then we should have a much better handle on stealing in our stores. Well, one of our managers found a diabolical way around this. I came into the store one night and noticed that the cash register this particular manager was using just didn't look right, although the sign was placed in front of it. It turned out that every afternoon at about 5:00 P.M. when the other employees left, this character would pull his own cash register out of a box that he hid underneath our supplies. Customers coming in would notice the sign and, of course, the fact that he was meticulous in ringing up every sale. But unknown to them and us, for about 5 months the sales that came in for about an hour every day went into his cash register, not mine. It took us that long to figure out where our cash for that store was going."

Here is what Jennifer would like you to answer:

Questions

1. What would be the advantages and disadvantages to Jennifer's company of routinely administering honesty tests to all its employees?
2. Specifically, what other screening techniques could the company use to screen out theft-prone and turnover-prone employees, and how exactly could these be used?
3. How should her company terminate employees caught stealing, and what kind of procedure should be set up for handling reference calls about these employees when they go to other companies looking for jobs?

TRANSLATING STRATEGY INTO HR POLICIES & PRACTICES CASE

THE HOTEL PARIS CASE

Testing

The Hotel Paris's competitive strategy is "To use superior guest service to differentiate the Hotel Paris properties, and to thereby increase the length of stay and return rate of guests, and thus boost revenues and profitability." HR manager Lisa Cruz must now formulate functional policies and activities that support this competitive strategy by eliciting the required employee behaviors and competencies.

As she considered what she had to do next, Lisa Cruz, the Hotel Paris's HR director, knew that employee selection had to play a central role in her plans. The Hotel Paris currently had an informal screening process in which local hotel managers obtained application forms, interviewed applicants, and checked their references. However, a pilot project using an employment test for service people at the Chicago hotel had produced startling results. Lisa found consistent, significant relationships between test performance and a range of employee competencies and behaviors such as speed of check-in/out, employee turnover, and percentage of calls answered with the required greeting. Clearly, she was onto something. She knew that employee capabilities and behaviors like these translated into just the sorts of improved guest services the Hotel Paris needed to execute its strategy. She therefore had to decide what selection procedures would be best.

Lisa's team, working with an industrial psychologist, wants to design a test battery that they believe will produce the sorts of high-morale, patient, people-oriented employees they are

looking for. It should include, at a minimum, a work sample test for front-desk clerk candidates and a personality test aimed at weeding out applicants who lack emotional stability.

Questions

1. Provide a detailed example of the front-desk work sample test.
2. Provide a detailed example of two possible personality test questions.
3. What other tests would you suggest to Lisa, and why would you suggest them?

KEY TERMS

negligent hiring, *176*
reliability, *177*
test validity, *179*
criterion validity, *179*
content validity, *179*

construct validity, *179*
expectancy chart, *181*
interest inventory, *189*
work samples, *190*
work sampling technique, *190*

management assessment center, *191*
situational test, *192*
video-based simulation, *192*
miniature job training
  and evaluation, *193*

ENDNOTES

1. Kevin Delaney, "Google Adjusts Hiring Process as Needs Grow," *The Wall Street Journal*, October 23, 2006, pp. B1, B8; http://googleblog.blogspot.com/2009/01/changes-to-recruiting.html, accessed March 25, 2009.
2. Aliah D. Wright, "At Google, It Takes A Village to Hire an Employee," *HR Magazine* 56, no. 7 (2009 HR Trendbook supplement).
3. Even if they use a third party to prepare an employment test, contractors are "ultimately responsible" for ensuring the tests' job relatedness and EEO compliance. "DOL Officials Discuss Contractors' Duties on Validating Tests," *BNA Bulletin to Management*, September 4, 2007, p. 287. Furthermore, enforcement units are increasing their scrutiny of employers who rely on tests and screening. See "Litigation Increasing with Employer Reliance on Tests, Screening," *BNA Bulletin to Management*, April 8, 2008, p. 119. However, see also C. Tuna et al., "Job-Test Ruling Cheers Employers," *The Wall Street Journal*, July 1, 2009, p. B1–2.
4. See, for example, Ann Marie Ryan and Marja Lasek, "Negligent Hiring and Defamation: Areas of Liability Related to Pre-Employment Inquiries," *Personnel Psychology* 44, no. 2 (Summer 1991), pp. 293–319. See also Jay Stuller, "Fatal Attraction," *Across the Board* 42, no. 6 (November–December 2005), pp. 18–23.
5. Also see, for example, Ryan Zimmerman, "Wal-Mart to Toughen Job Screening," *The Wall Street Journal*, July 12, 2004, pp. B1–B8.

6. Negligent hiring highlights the need to think through what the job's human requirements really are. For example, "non-rapist" isn't likely to appear as a required knowledge, skill, or ability in a job analysis of an apartment manager, but in situations like this screening for such tendencies is obviously required. To avoid negligent hiring claims, "make a systematic effort to gain relevant information about the applicant, verify documentation, follow up on missing records or gaps in employment, and keep a detailed log of all attempts to obtain information, including the names and dates for phone calls or other requests." Fay Hansen, "Taking 'Reasonable' Action to Avoid Negligent Hiring Claims," *Workforce Management*, September 11, 2006, p. 31.
7. See for example, Jean Phillips and Stanley Gully, *Strategic Staffing* (Upper Saddle River, NJ: Pearson Education, 2012), pp. 234–235.
8. Wright, "At Google, It Takes a Village to Hire an Employee."
9. Ibid.
10. Kevin Murphy and Charles Davidshofer, *Psychological Testing: Principles and Applications* (Upper Saddle River, NJ: Prentice Hall, 2001), p. 73.
11. Ibid., pp. 116–119.
12. W. Bruce Walsh and Nancy Betz, *Tests and Assessment* (Upper Saddle River, NJ: Prentice Hall, 2001).
13. Murphy and Davidshofer, *Psychological Testing*, p. 74.
14. A third, less-used way to demonstrate a test's validity is *construct validity*.

A construct is an abstract trait such as happiness or intelligence. Construct validity generally addresses the question of "validity of measurement," in other words, of whether the test is really measuring, say, intelligence. To prove construct validity, an employer has to prove that the test measures the construct. Federal agency guidelines make it difficult to prove construct validity, however, and as a result few employers use this approach as part of their process for satisfying the federal guidelines. See James Ledvinka, *Federal Regulation of Personnel and Human Resource Management* (Boston: Kent, 1982), p. 113; and Murphy and Davidshofer, *Psychological Testing*, pp. 154–165.
15. The procedure you would use to demonstrate content validity differs from that used to demonstrate criterion validity (as described in steps 1 through 5). Content validity tends to emphasize judgment. Here, you first do a careful job analysis to identify the work behaviors required. Then combine several samples of those behaviors into a test. A typing and computer skills test for a clerk would be an example. The fact that the test is a comprehensive sample of actual, observable, on-the-job behaviors is what lends the test its content validity.
16. www.siop.org/workplace/employment%20testing/information_to_consider_when_cre.aspx, accessed March 22, 2009.
17. Murphy and Davidshofer, *Psychological Testing*, p. 73. See also Chad Van Iddekinge and Robert Ployhart, "Developments in the Criterion-Related Validation of Selection Procedures: A Critical Review

and Recommendations for Practice," *Personnel Psychology* 60, no. 1 (2008), pp. 871–925.

18. Experts sometimes have to develop separate expectancy charts and cutting points for minorities and nonminorities if the validation studies indicate that high performers from either group (minority or nonminority) score lower (or higher) on the test.

19. In employment testing, bias has a precise meaning. Specifically, "bias is said to exist when a test makes systematic errors in measurement or prediction." Murphy and Davidshofer, *Psychological Testing*, p. 303.

20. Ibid., p. 305.

21. Ibid., p. 308.

22. Herman Aguinis, Steven Culpepper, and Charles Pierce, "Revival of Test Bias Research in Preemployment Testing," *Journal of Applied Psychology* 95, no. 4 (2010), p. 648.

23. Robert Gatewood and Hubert Feild, *Human Resource Selection* (Mason, OH: South-Western, Cengage Learning, 2008, p. 243.

24. This is based on Dave Zielinski, "Effective Assessments," *HR Magazine*, January 2011, pp. 61–64

25. The Uniform Guidelines say, "Employers should ensure that tests and selection procedures are not adopted casually by managers who know little about these processes . . . . no test or selection procedure should be implemented without an understanding of its effectiveness and limitations for the organization, its appropriateness for a specific job, and whether it can be appropriately administered and scored."

26. Phillips and Gully, *Strategic Staffing*, p. 220.

27. Ibid., p. 220.

28. www.uniformguidelines.com/qandaprint. html, accessed August 20, 2011.

29. From "Ethical Principles of Psychologists and Code of Conduct," *American Psychologist* 47 (1992), pp. 1597–1611; and http://www.apa.org/ethics/code/index.aspx, accessed September 9, 2011.

30. Susan Mendelsohn and Kathryn Morrison, "The Right to Privacy at the Work Place, Part I: Employee Searches," *Personnel*, July 1988, p. 20. See also Talya Bauer et al., "Applicant Reactions to Selection: Development of the Selection Procedural Justice Scale," *Personnel Psychology* 54 (2001), pp. 387–419.

31. Mendelsohn and Morrison, "The Right to Privacy in the Work Place," p. 22.

32. Kenneth Sovereign, *Personnel Law* (Upper Saddle River, NJ: Prentice Hall, 1999), pp. 204–206.

33. "One-Third of Job Applicants Flunked Basic Literacy and Math Tests Last Year, American Management Association Survey Finds," *American Management Association*, www.amanet.org/press/amanews/bjp2001.htm, accessed January 11, 2008.

34. Ibid. See also Alison Wolf and Andrew Jenkins, "Explaining Greater Test Use for Selection: The Role of HR Professionals in a World of Expanding Regulation," *Human Resource Management Journal* 16, no. 2 (2006), pp. 193–213.

35. Steffanie Wilk and Peter Capelli, "Understanding the Determinants of Employer Use of Selection Methods," *Personnel Psychology* 56 (2003), p. 117.

36. Kevin Hart, "Not Wanted: Thieves," *HR Magazine*, April 2008, p. 119.

37. Sarah Needleman, "Businesses Say Theft by Their Workers Is Up," *The Wall Street Journal*, December 11, 2008, p. B8.

38. Sarah Gale, "Three Companies Cut Turnover with Tests," *Workforce*, Spring 2002, pp. 66–69.

39. Ed Frauenheim, "Personality Tests Adapt to the Times," *Workforce Management*, February 2010, p. 4.

40. Requiring job seekers to complete prescreening questionnaires and screening selected applicants out on this basis carries legal and business consequences. See, for example, Lisa Harpe, "Designing an Effective Employment Prescreening Program," *Employment Relations Today* 32, no. 3 (Fall 2005), pp. 41–43.

41. www.iphonetypingtest.com, accessed March 23, 2009.

42. Except as noted, this is based on Laurence Siegel and Irving Lane, *Personnel and Organizational Psychology* (Burr Ridge, IL: McGraw-Hill, 1982), pp. 170–185. See also Cabot Jaffee, "Measurement of Human Potential," *Employment Relations Today* 17, no. 2 (Summer 2000), pp. 15–27; Maureen Patterson, "Overcoming the Hiring Crunch; Tests Deliver Informed Choices," *Employment Relations Today* 27, no. 3 (Fall 2000), pp. 77–88; Kathryn Tyler, "Put Applicants' Skills to the Test," *HR Magazine*, January 2000, p. 74; Murphy and Davidshofer, *Psychological Testing*, pp. 215–403; Elizabeth Schoenfelt and Leslie Pedigo, "A Review of Court Decisions on Cognitive Ability Testing, 1992–2004," *Review of Public Personnel Administration* 25, no. 3 (2005), pp. 271–287.

43. Norman Henderson, "Predicting Long-Term Firefighter Performance from Cognitive and Physical Ability Measures," *Personnel Psychology* 60, no. 3 (2010), pp. 999–1039.

44. As an example, results of meta-analyses in one study indicated that isometric strength tests were valid predictors of both supervisory ratings of physical performance and performance on work simulations. See Barry R. Blakley, Miguel Quinones, Marnie Swerdlin Crawford, and I. Ann Jago, "The Validity of Isometric Strength Tests," *Personnel Psychology* 47 (1994), pp. 247–274; and http://www.military.com/military-fitness/marine-corps-fitness-requirements/marine-corps-fitness-test, accessed October 4, 2011.

45. William Wagner, "All Skill, No Finesse," *Workforce*, June 2000, pp. 108–116. See also, for example, James Diefendorff and Kajal Mehta, "The Relations of Motivational Traits with Workplace Deviance," *Journal of Applied Psychology* 92, no. 4 (2007), pp. 967–977.

46. James Spencer, "Sorry, You're Nobody's Type," *The Wall Street Journal*, July 30, 2003, p. D1.

47. www.myersbriggsreports.com/?gclid=CK71m6rEh6ACFVZS2godDEjgkw, accessed February 22, 2010.

48. See, for example, Joyce Hogan et al., "Personality Measurement, Faking, and Employee Selection," *Journal of Applied Psychology* 92, no. 5 (2007), pp. 1270–1285; and Colin Gill and Gerard Hodgkinson, "Development and Validation of the Five Factor Model Questionnaire (FFMQ): An Adjectival-Based Personality Inventory for Use in Occupational Settings," *Personnel Psychology* 60 (2007), pp. 731–766.

49. Timothy Judge et al., "Personality and Leadership: A Qualitative and Quantitative Review," *Journal of Applied Psychology* 87, no. 4 (2002), p. 765.

50. Ibid.

51. Timothy Judge and Remus Ilies, "Relationship of Personality to Performance Motivation: A Meta Analytic Review," *Journal of Applied Psychology* 87, no. 4 (2002), pp. 797–807.

52. L. A. Witt et al., "The Interactive Effects of Conscientiousness and Agreeableness on Job Performance," *Journal of Applied Psychology* 87, no. 1 (2002), pp. 164–169.

53. Murray Barrick et al., "Personality and Job Performance: Test of the Immediate Effects of Motivation Among Sales Representatives," *Journal of Applied Psychology* 87, no. 1 (2002), p. 43.

54. Charles Sarchione et al., "Prediction of Dysfunctional Job Behaviors Among Law-Enforcement Officers," *Journal of Applied Psychology* 83, no. 6 (1998), pp. 904–912. See also W. A. Scroggins et al., "Psychological Testing in Personnel Selection, Part III: The Resurgence of Personality Testing," *Public Personnel Management* 38, no. 1 (Spring 2009), pp. 67–77.

55. Paula Caligiuri, "The Big Five Personality Characteristics as Predictors of Expatriate Desire to Terminate the Assignment and Supervisor Rated Performance," *Personnel Psychology* 53 (2000), pp. 67–68. For some other examples, see Ryan Zimmerman, "Understanding the Impact of Personality Traits on Individuals' Turnover Decisions: A Meta-Analytic Path Model," *Personnel Psychology* 60, no. 1 (2008), pp. 309–348.

56. Diane Cadrain, "Reassess Personality Tests After Court Case," *HR Magazine* 50, no. 9 (September 2005), p. 30.

57. Frederick Morgeson et al., "Reconsidering the Use of Personality Tests in Personnel Selection Contexts," *Personnel*

Psychology 60 (2007), p. 683, and Frederick Morgeson et al., "Are We Getting Fooled Again? Coming to Terms with Limitations in the Use of Personality Tests for Personnel Selection," *Personnel Psychology* 60 (2007), p. 1046.

58. Robert Tett and Neil Christiansen, "Personality Tests at the Crossroads: A Response to Morgeson, Campion, Dipboye, Hollenbeck, Murphy, and Schmitt," *Personnel Psychology* 60 (2007), p. 967. See also Deniz Ones et al., "In Support of Personality Assessment in Organizational Settings," *Personnel Psychology* 60 (2007), pp. 995–1027.

59. See, for example, Chad Van Iddekinge, Dan Putka, and John Campbell, "Reconsidering Vocational Interest for Personnel Selection: The Validity of an Interest-Based Selection Testing Relation to Job Knowledge, Job Performance, and Continuance Intentions," *Journal of Applied Psychology* 96, no. 1 (2011) pp. 13–33.

60. Jeff Weekley and Casey Jones, "Video-Based Situational Testing," *Personnel Psychology* 50 (1997), p. 25.

61. Elaine Pulakos, *Selection Assessment Methods*, SHRM Foundation, 2005, p. 14.

62. However, studies suggest that blacks may be somewhat less likely to do well on work sample tests than are whites. See, for example, Philip Roth, Philip Bobko, and Lynn McFarland, "A Meta-Analysis of Work Sample Test Validity: Updating and Integrating Some Classic Literature," *Personnel Psychology* 58, no. 4 (Winter 2005), pp. 1009–1037; and Philip Roth et al., "Work Sample Tests in Personnel Selection: A Meta-Analysis of Black–White Differences in Overall and Exercise Scores," *Personnel Psychology* 60, no. 1 (2008), pp. 637–662.

63. Siegel and Lane, *Personnel and Organizational Psychology*, pp. 182–183.

64. Quoted from Deborah Whetzel and Michael McDaniel, "Situational Judgment Tests: An Overview of Current Research," *Human Resource Management Review* 19 (2009), pp. 188–202.

65. Ibid.

66. "Help Wanted—and Found," *Fortune*, October 2, 2006, p. 40.

67. Annette Spychalski, Miguel Quinones, Barbara Gaugler, and Katja Pohley, "A Survey of Assessment Center Practices in Organizations in the United States," *Personnel Psychology* 50, no. 1 (Spring 1997), pp. 71–90. See also Winfred Arthur Jr. et al., "A Meta Analysis of the Criterion Related Validity of Assessment Center Data Dimensions," *Personnel Psychology* 56 (2003), pp. 124–154.

68. See, for example, John Meriac et al., "Further Evidence for the Validity of Assessment Center Dimensions: A Meta-Analysis of the Incremental Criterion-Related Validity of Dimension Ratings," *Journal of Applied Psychology* 93, no. 5 (2008), pp. 1042–1052.

69. Kobi Dayan et al., "Entry-Level Police Candidate Assessment Center: An Efficient Tool or a Hammer to Kill a Fly?" *Personnel Psychology* 55 (2002), pp. 827–848.

70. Weekley and Jones, "Video-Based Situational Testing," p. 26.

71. Ibid., p. 30.

72. Except as noted, this is based on Dave Zielinski, "Effective Assessments," *HR Magazine*, January 2011, pp. 61–64.

73. Robert Grossman, "Made from Scratch," *HR Magazine*, April 2002, pp. 44–53.

74. Coleman Peterson, "Employee Retention, The Secrets Behind Wal-Mart's Successful Hiring Policies," *Human Resource Management* 44, no. 1 (Spring 2005), pp. 85–88. See also Murray Barrick and Ryan Zimmerman, "Reducing Voluntary, Avoidable Turnover Through Selection," *Journal of Applied Psychology* 90, no. 1 (2005), pp. 159–166.

75. James Breaugh, "Employee Recruitment: Current Knowledge and Important Areas for Future Research," *Human Resource Management Review* 18 (2008), pp. 106–107.

76. Phillips and Gully, *Strategic Staffing*, p. 223.

77. "Internet, E-Mail Monitoring Common at Most Workplaces," *BNA Bulletin to Management*, February 1, 2001, p. 34. See also "Are Your Background Checks Balanced? Experts Identify Concerns over Verifications," *BNA Bulletin to Management*, May 13, 2004, p. 153.

78. Merry Mayer, "Background Checks in Focus," *HR Magazine*, January 2002, pp. 59–62; and Carroll Lachnit, "Protecting People and Profits with Background Checks," *Workforce*, February 2002, p. 52.

79. Matthew Heller, "Special Report: Background Checking," *Workforce Management*, March 3, 2008, pp. 35–54.

80. Bill Roberts, "Close-up on Screening," *HR Magazine*, February 2011, pp. 23–29.

81. Seymour Adler, "Verifying a Job Candidate's Background: The State of Practice in a Vital Human Resources Activity," *Review of Business* 15, no. 2 (Winter 1993), p. 6.

82. Heller, "Special Report: Background Checking," p. 35.

83. This is based on Samuel Greengard, "Have Gangs Invaded Your Workplace?" *Personnel Journal*, February 1996, pp. 47–48.

84. Dori Meinert, "Seeing Behind the Mask," *HR Magazine* 56, no. 2 (February 2011), http://www.shrm.org/Publications/hrmagazine/EditorialContent/2011/0211/Pages/0211meinert.aspx, accessed August 20, 2011.

85. Ibid., p. 55.

86. For example, one U.S. Court of Appeals found that bad references might be grounds for a suit when they are retaliations for the employee having previously filed an EEOC claim. "Negative Reference Leads to Charge of Retaliation," *BNA Bulletin to Management*, October 21, 2004, p. 344.

87. Laws that affect references include the Privacy Act of 1974 (which applies only to federal workers), the Fair Credit Reporting Act of 1970, the Family Education Rights and Privacy Act of 1974 (and Buckley Amendment of 1974), and the Freedom of Information Act of 1966.

88. For additional information, see Lawrence E. Dube Jr., "Employment References and the Law," *Personnel Journal* 65, no. 2 (February 1986), pp. 87–91. See also Mickey Veich, "Uncover the Resume Ruse," *Security Management*, October 1994, pp. 75–76.

89. Eileen Zimmerman, "A Subtle Reference Trap for Unwary Employers," *Workforce*, April 2003, p. 22.

90. *Kehr v. Consolidated Freightways of Delaware*, Docket No. 86–2126, July 15, 1987, U.S. Seventh Circuit Court of Appeals. Discussed in *Commerce Clearing House, Ideas and Trends*, October 16, 1987, p. 165.

91. James Bell, James Castagnera, and Jane Patterson Young, "Employment References: Do You Know the Law?" *Personnel Journal* 63, no. 2 (February 1984), pp. 32–36. In order to demonstrate defamation, several elements must be present: (a) the defamatory statement must have been communicated to another party; (b) the statement must be a false statement of fact; (c) injury to reputation must have occurred; and (d) the employer must not be protected under qualified or absolute privilege. For a discussion, see Ryan and Lasek, "Negligent Hiring and Defamation," p. 307. See also James Burns Jr., "Employment References: Is There a Better Way?" *Employee Relations Law Journal* 23, no. 2 (Fall 1997), pp. 157–168.

92. Adrienne Fox, "Automated Reference Checking Puts Onus on Candidates," *HR Magazine* 66, no. 9 (2009, HR Trendbook supplement).

93. "Vetting via Internet Is Free, Generally Legal, but Not Necessarily Smart Hiring Strategy," *BNA Bulletin to Management*, February 20, 2007, pp. 57–58.

94. Alan Finder, "When a Risqué Online Persona Undermines a Chance for a Job," *The New York Times*, June 11, 2006, p. 1.

95. Anjali Athavaley, "Job References You Can't Control," *The Wall Street Journal*, September 27, 2007, p. B1.

96. Rita Zeidner, "How Deep Can You Probe?" *HR Magazine*, October 1, 2007, pp. 57–62.

97. "Web Searches on Applicants Are Potentially Perilous for Employers," *BNA Bulletin to Management*, October 14, 2008, p. 335.

98. See Paul Taylor et al., "Dimensionality and the Validity of a Structured Telephone Reference Check Procedure," *Personnel Psychology* 57 (2004), pp. 745–772, for a discussion of checking other work habits and traits.

99. "Getting Applicant Information Difficult but Still Necessary," *BNA Bulletin to Management*, February 5, 1999, p. 63.

See also Robert Howie and Laurence Shapiro, "Pre-Employment Criminal Background Checks: Why Employers Should Look Before They Leap," *Employee Relations Law Journal*, Summer 2002, pp. 63–77.

100. "Employment Related Screening Providers," *Workforce Management*, February 16, 2009, p. 14, and "Background and Screening Providers," *Workforce Management*, February 2011, at http://www.workforce.com/section/recruiting-staffing/feature/2011-background-screening-providers, accessed August 20, 2011.

101. Jeffrey M. Hahn, "Pre-Employment Information Services: Employers Beware?" *Employee Relations Law Journal* 17, no. 1 (Summer 1991), pp. 45–69. See also "Pre-Employment Background Screenings Have Evolved, But So Have Liability Risks," *BNA Bulletin to Management*, November 1, 2005, p. 345.

102. Under California law, applicants or employees must have the option of requesting a copy of the report regardless of action.

103. Teresa Butler Stivarius, "Background Checks: Steps to Basic Compliance in a Multistate Environment," *Society for Human Resource Management Legal Report*, March–April 2003, pp. 1–8.

104. Polygraphs are still widely used in law enforcement and reportedly are quite useful. See, for example, Laurie Cohen, "The Polygraph Paradox," *The Wall Street Journal*, March 22, 2008, p. A1.

105. John Jones and William Terris, "Post-Polygraph Selection Techniques," *Recruitment Today*, May–June 1989, pp. 25–31.

106. Norma Fritz, "In Focus: Honest Answers—Post Polygraph," *Personnel*, April 1989, p. 8. See also Richard White Jr., "Ask Me No Questions, Tell Me No Lies: Examining the Uses and Misuses of the Polygraph," *Public Personnel Management* 30, no. 4 (Winter 2001), pp. 483–493.

107. John Bernardin and Donna Cooke, "Validity of an Honesty Test in Predicting Theft Among Convenience Store Employees," *Academy of Management Journal* 36, no. 5 (1993), pp. 1097–1108.

108. Judith Collins and Frank Schmidt, "Personality, Integrity, and White Collar Crime: A Construct Validity Study," *Personnel Psychology* 46 (1993), pp. 295–311; Paul Sackett and James Wanek, "New Developments in the Use of Measures of Honesty, Integrity, Conscientiousness, Dependability, Trustworthiness, and Reliability for Personnel Selection," *Personnel Psychology* 49 (1996), p. 821. Some suggest that by possibly signaling mental illness, integrity tests may conflict with the Americans with Disabilities Act, but one review concludes these tests pose little such legal risk to employers. Christopher Berry et al., "A Review of Recent Developments in Integrity Test Research," *Personnel Psychology* 60, no. 2 (Summer 2007), pp. 271–301.

109. These are based on "Divining Integrity Through Interviews," *BNA Bulletin to Management*, June 4, 1987, p. 184; and *Commerce Clearing House, Ideas and Trends*, December 29, 1998, pp. 222–223. See also Bridget A. Styers and Kenneth S. Shultz, "Perceived Reasonableness of Employment Testing Accommodations for Persons with Disabilities," *Public Personnel Management* 38, no. 3 (Fall 2009), pp. 71–91.

110. Bill Leonard, "Reading Employees," *HR Magazine*, April 1999, pp. 67–73.

111. Ibid.

112. This is based on Kyle Stock, "Wary Investors Turn to Lie Pros," *The Wall Street Journal*, December 29, 2010, p. C3.

113. Mick Haus, "Pre-Employment Physicals and the ADA," *Safety and Health*, February 1992, pp. 64–65. See also Bridget A. Styers and Kenneth S. Shultz, "Perceived Reasonableness of Employment Testing Accommodations for Persons with Disabilities," *Public Personnel Management* 38, no. 3 (Fall 2009), pp. 71–91.

114. Scott MacDonald, Samantha Wells, and Richard Fry, "The Limitations of Drug Screening in the Workplace," *International Labor Review* 132, no. 1 (1993), p. 98. Not all agree that drug testing is worthwhile. See for example, Veronica I. Luzzi, et al., "Analytic Performance of Immunoassays for Drugs of Abuse Below Established Cutoff Values," *Clinical Chemistry* 2004; 50:717–722

115. Rita Zeidner, "Putting Drug Screening to the Test," *HR Magazine*, November 2010, p. 26.

116. Diane Cadrain, "Are Your Employees' Drug Tests Accurate?" *HR Magazine*, January 2003, pp. 40–45.

117. Chris Berka and Courtney Poignand, "Hair Follicle Testing—An Alternative to Urinalysis for Drug Abuse Screening," *Employee Relations Today*, Winter 1991–1992, pp. 405–409; for an example, see http://www.americanscreeningcorp.com/default.aspx, accessed October 8, 2011.

118. MacDonald et al., "The Limitations of Drug Screening," pp. 102–104.

119. R. J. McCunney, "Drug Testing: Technical Complications of a Complex Social Issue," *American Journal of Industrial Medicine* 15, no. 5 (1989), pp. 589–600; discussed in MacDonald et al., "The Limitations of Drug Screening," p. 102.

120. MacDonald et al., "The Limitations of Drug Screening," p. 103.

121. This is based on Ann M. O'Neill, "Legal Issues Presented by Hair Follicle Testing," *Employee Relations Today*, Winter 1991–1992, pp. 411–415.

122. Ibid., p. 413.

123. Richard Lisko, "A Manager's Guide to Drug Testing," *Security Management* 38, no. 8 (August 1994), p. 92. See also Randall Kesselring and Jeffrey Pittman, "Drug Testing Laws and Employment Injuries," *Journal of Labor Research*, Spring 2002, pp. 293–301.

124. Michael A. McDaniel, "Does Pre-Employment Drug Use Predict On-the-Job Suitability?" *Personnel Psychology* 41, no. 4 (Winter 1988), pp. 717–729.

125. *Exxon Corp. v. Esso Workers Union, Inc.*, CA1#96–2241, 7/8/97; discussed in *BNA Bulletin to Management*, August 7, 1997, p. 249.

126. For the form, see http://www.uscis.gov/files/form/i-9.pdf, accessed October 4, 2011.

127. "Conflicting State E-Verify Laws Troubling for Employers," *BNA Bulletin to Management*, November 4, 2008, p. 359.

128. "President Bush Signs Executive Order: Federal Contractors Must Use E-Verify," *BNA Bulletin to Management*, June 17, 2008, p. 193.

129. Note that the acceptable documents on page 3 of the current (as of 2009, but extended until 2012) I-9 form do not reflect the current list of acceptable documents. For this, refer to the Web site of the U.S. Department of Homeland Security. Margaret Fiester et al., "Affirmative Action, Stock Options, I-9 Documents," *HR Magazine*, November 2007, p. 32. See also, http://www.uscis.gov/USCIS/Office%20of%20Communications/Press%20Releases/FY%202009/August%202009/update_I-9_extension0827.pdf, accessed August 20, 2011.

130. Susan Ladika, "Trouble on the Hiring Front," *HR Magazine*, October 2006, pp. 56–62.

131. Russell Gerbman, "License to Work," *HR Magazine*, June 2000, pp. 151–160; the I-9 form clearly states that the employer may not discriminate. See http://www.uscis.gov/files/form/i-9.pdf, accessed October 4, 2011.

132. "As E-Verify, No Match Rules, I-9 Evolve, Employers Need to Stay on Top of Issues," *BNA Bulletin Management*, April 15, 2008, p. 121.

133. Note that unproctored Internet tests raise serious questions in employment settings. Nancy Tippins et al., "Unproctored Internet Testing in Employment Settings," *Personnel Psychology* 59 (2006), pp. 189–225.

134. From Bob Neveu, "Applicant Tracking's Top 10: Do You Know What to Look for in Applicant Tracking Systems?" *Workforce*, October 2002, p. 10.

7

Interviewing Candidates

LEARNING OBJECTIVES

1. List the main types of selection interviews.
2. List and explain the main errors that can undermine an interview's usefulness.
3. Define a structured situational interview.
4. Explain and illustrate each guideline for being a more effective interviewer.
5. Give several examples of situational questions, behavioral questions, and background questions that provide structure.

Can a company turn job candidates into customers? Whirlpool Corp. knows it can. Whirlpool makes and markets 17 major brands, including Whirlpool, KitchenAid, Maytag, Amana, and Jenn-Air.[1] With such a large product assortment and a global footprint, Whirlpool knows that every person it interviews for a job is either a current Whirlpool customer, or a potential one. That's why its strategy for building the Whirlpool brands' reputation and sales includes a special job applicant interviewing program. The program includes leaving all candidates—even those who don't get offers—with a positive impression of Whirlpool and its brands.

WHERE ARE WE NOW . . .

Chapter 6 focused on important tools managers use to select employees. Now we'll turn to one of these tools—interviewing candidates. The main topics we'll cover include types of interviews, things that undermine interviewing's usefulness, and designing and conducting effective selection interviews. In Chapter 8, we'll turn to training the new employee.

If the interview is just one of several selection tools, why devote a whole chapter to it? Because interviews are the most widely used selection procedure and most people aren't very good interviewers.[2]

Access a host of interactive learning aids at **www.mymanagementlab.com** to help strengthen your understanding of the chapter concepts.

1 List the main types of
selection interviews.

BASIC TYPES OF INTERVIEWS

An interview is more than a discussion. An *interview* is a procedure designed to obtain information from a person through oral responses to oral inquiries. Employers use several interviews at work, such as performance appraisal interviews and exit interviews. A *selection interview* (the focus of this chapter) is a selection procedure designed to predict future job performance based on applicants' oral responses to oral inquiries.[3] Many techniques in this chapter apply to appraisal and exit interviews. However, we'll postpone discussions of these two interviews until Chapters 9 and 10.

Interviewing should support the employer's strategic aims, as the accompanying Strategic Context feature illustrates.

THE STRATEGIC CONTEXT

Whirlpool Corp.

With its 17-brand assortment and global footprint, Whirlpool knows that every person it interviews is a current Whirlpool customer, or a potential one. The question is, how can Whirlpool use its applicant interview practices to ensure that every interview helps to build the Whirlpool brands' reputation and sales?

Whirlpool calls its candidate selection process the Exceptional Candidate Experience (ECE). The ECE doesn't just aim to select the best candidates. It also aims to make every candidate a loyal customer. ECE contains three elements: "initial candidate touch points," "candidate engagement," and "candidate closings."[4] *Initial candidate touch points* means that whether candidates first encounter Whirlpool via its careers Web site, at a job fair, or through some other means, Whirlpool carefully manages the process to make sure the candidate's impression of the company is consistent and positive.

Once a time is set for an interview, a Whirlpool guide contacts the candidate. His or her aim is to find out about the candidate's special situations. For example, does the candidate have special family responsibilities that the interviewing team should make scheduling adjustments for? Does he or she have special hobbies? The guide then helps to *engage* the candidate, for instance, by showing him or her how the geographic location in which he or she would be working can help support the candidate's preferences and needs, and by acting as a contact with the Whirlpool interviewing team. At the *candidate closings* the human resource team makes sure the candidate receives a thank-you note and a KitchenAid countertop appliance after the interviews.

Whirlpool believes that its interviewing and screening process directly supports the firm's strategy. In addition to ensuring that the firm's employees treat candidates with civility, the effect of the process is to leave the candidate with a positive impression of Whirlpool and its products and people.

We can classify selection interviews according to

1. How *structured* they are
2. Their "content"—the *types of questions* they contain
3. How the firm *administers* the interviews

Let's look at each.

Structured Versus Unstructured Interviews

First, most interviews vary in the degree to which the interviewer structures or standardizes the interview process.[5] You've almost certainly seen that some interviews are more structured or methodical than others. In **unstructured (or nondirective) interviews**, the manager follows no set format. A few questions might be specified in advance, but they're usually not, and there is seldom a formal guide for scoring "right" or "wrong" answers. This type of interview could even be described as little more than a general conversation.[6] Most selection interviews probably fall in this category.

At the other extreme, in **structured (or directive) interviews**, the employer lists the questions ahead of time, and may even list and score possible answers for appropriateness.[7] McMurray's Patterned Interview was one early example. The interviewer followed a printed form to ask a series of questions, such as "How was the person's present job obtained?" Comments printed beneath the questions (such as "Has he/she shown self-reliance in getting his/her jobs?") then guide the interviewer in evaluating the answers. Some experts still restrict the term "structured interview" to interviews like these, which are based on carefully selected job-oriented questions with predetermined answers.

But in practice, interview structure is a matter of degree. Sometimes the manager may just want to ensure he or she has a standard set of questions to ask so as to avoid skipping any questions. Here, he or she might just choose questions from a list like that in Figure 7-3 (page 228). The structured applicant interview guide in Figure 7-A1 (page 236) illustrates a more structured approach. As a third example, the Department of Homeland Security uses the structured guide in Figure 7-1 to help screen Coast Guard officer candidates. It contains a formal candidate rating procedure; it also enables geographically disbursed interviewers to complete the form via the Web.[8]

WHICH TO USE? Structured interviews are generally superior. In structured interviews, all interviewers generally ask all applicants the same questions. Partly because of this, these interviews tend to be more reliable and valid. Structured interviews can also help less talented interviewers conduct better interviews. Standardizing the interview also increases consistency across candidates, enhances job relatedness, reduces overall subjectivity and thus the potential for bias, and may "enhance the ability to withstand legal challenge."[9]

EEOC ASPECTS OF INTERVIEWS That last point is important. No one wants to have someone sue for discrimination, let alone lose the suit. A study of federal cases involving alleged employment interview discrimination is relevant. It's clear the courts will look at whether the interview process is structured and consistently applied. For example, did you (1) have objective/job-related questions, (2) standardize interview administration, and (3) preferably use multiple interviewers?[10]

However, blindly following a structured format isn't advisable either. Doing so may not provide enough opportunity to pursue points of interest as they develop. Therefore, the interviewer should always leave an opportunity to ask follow-up questions and pursue points of interest as they develop.

Interview Content (What Types of Questions to Ask)

We can also classify interviews based on the "content" or the types of questions you ask. Many (probably most) interviewers tend to ask relatively unfocused questions. These might include "What are your main strengths and weaknesses?" and "What do you want to be doing 5 years from now?" Generally, questions like these don't provide much insight into how the person will do on the job. At work, *situational, behavioral,* and *job-related* questions are most important.

SITUATIONAL QUESTIONS In a **situational interview**, you ask the candidate what his or her behavior *would be* in a given situation.[11] For example, you might ask a supervisory candidate how he or she would act in response to a subordinate coming to work late 3 days in a row.

unstructured (or nondirective) interview
An unstructured conversational-style interview in which the interviewer pursues points of interest as they come up in response to questions.

structured (or directive) interview
An interview following a set sequence of questions.

situational interview
A series of job-related questions that focus on how the candidate would behave in a given situation.

BEHAVIORAL QUESTIONS Whereas situational interviews ask applicants to describe how they would react to a hypothetical situation today or tomorrow, **behavioral interviews** ask applicants to describe *how they reacted* to actual situations in the past.[12] For example, when Citizen's Banking Corporation in Flint, Michigan, found that 31 of the 50 people in its call center quit in one year, Cynthia Wilson, the center's head, switched to behavioral interviews. Many of those who left did so because they didn't enjoy fielding questions from occasionally irate clients. So Wilson no longer tries to predict how candidates will act based on asking them if they want to work with angry clients. Instead, she asks behavioral questions like, "Tell me about a time you were speaking with an irate person, and how you turned the situation around." Wilson says this makes it much harder to fool the interviewer, and, indeed, only four people left her center in the following year.[13] In summary, *situational* questions start with phrases such as, "Suppose you were faced with the following situation . . . What would you do?" *Behavioral* questions start with phrases like, "Can you think of a time when . . . What did you do?"[14] More employers today are using (or planning to use) behavioral interviews.[15]

FIGURE 7-1 Officer Programs Applicant Interview Form

Source: www.uscg.mil/forms/cg/CG5527.pdf, accessed May 9, 2007.

U.S. Department of Homeland Security CG-5527 (06-04)	Officer Programs Applicant Interview Form	1. Date:

2. Name of Applicant (Last, First, MI)

3. Overall Impression: Compare this applicant to others you have interviewed or known. (Note: Scores of 4 through 7 constitute a recommendation for selection.)

NOT RECOMMENDED			RECOMMENDED			
Unsatisfactory 1☐	Limited Potential 2☐	Fair Performer 3☐	Good Performer 4☐	Excellent Performer 5☐	Exceptional Performer 6☐	Distinguished Performer 7☐

Comments:

4. Performance of Duties: Measures an applicant's ability to manage and to get things done.

Unsatisfactory 1☐ Limited Potential 2☐ Fair Performer 3☐ Good Performer 4☐ Excellent Performer 5☐ Exceptional Performer 6☐ Distinguished Performer 7☐

Comments:

5. Communication Skills: Measures an applicant's ability to communicate in a positive, clear, and convincing manner.

Unsatisfactory 1☐ Limited Potential 2☐ Fair Performer 3☐ Good Performer 4☐ Excellent Performer 5☐ Exceptional Performer 6☐ Distinguished Performer 7☐

Comments:

6. Names of Board Members	7. Rank	8. Command/Unit	9. Signature	10. Career Total of Interviews Conducted

PREVIOUS EDITIONS ARE OBSOLETE

CONTINUED ON REVERSE

Reset

FIGURE 7-1 (Continued)

Page 2 - CG-5527 (06-04)

11. **Leadership Skills:** Measures an applicant's ability to support, develop, direct, and influence others in performing work.

Unsatisfactory	Limited Potential	Fair Performer	Good Performer	Excellent Performer	Exceptional Performer	Distinguished Performer
1☐	2☐	3☐	4☐	5☐	6☐	7☐

Comments:

12. **Personal and Professional Qualities:** Measures qualities which illustrate the applicant's character.

Unsatisfactory	Limited Potential	Fair Performer	Good Performer	Excellent Performer	Exceptional Performer	Distinguished Performer
1☐	2☐	3☐	4☐	5☐	6☐	7☐

Comments:

Reset

INSTRUCTIONS

The Officer Programs Applicant Interview Form is designed to help Officer Programs selection panels select applicants to be Coast Guard officers. The form is heavily based on the Officer Evaluation Report (OER) and the scale for each category is based on OER performance standards. While it should be remembered that applicants are not yet Coast Guard officers, they should have had opportunities to exhibit qualities that show they possess the character and potential necessary to be successful officers. Provide written comments in support of numeric markings for each category. Base these comments on what you observe during the interview or see in the supporting documentation in the applicant's package. Much like an OER, both the numerical evaluation and written comments are used by selection panels. Officer interview boards should review Article 4.B.2 of the Recruiting Manual, COMDTINST M1100.2 (series) and Articles 1.B.8 and 1.B.9 of the Personnel Manual, COMDTINST M1000.6 (series), which provide guidance on officer interviews.

1.   Date of interview.
2.   Self-explanatory.
3.   Marks in the Overall Impression block should summarize the interview board's recommendation of the applicant's suitability for service as a Coast Guard Officer, and therefore should be completed last. Scores of 4 through 7 constitute a recommendation for selection.
4-5.   Self-explanatory.
6.   Last name, first name, and middle initial.
7-9.   Self-explanatory.
10.   Interviewer's career total of officer applicant interview boards.
11-12.   Self-explanatory.

PREVIOUS EDITIONS ARE OBSOLETE

OTHER TYPES OF QUESTIONS   In a **job-related interview**, the interviewer asks applicants questions about relevant past experiences. The questions here don't revolve around hypothetical or actual situations or scenarios. Instead, the interviewer asks job-related questions such as, "Which courses did you like best in business school?" The aim is to draw conclusions about, say, the candidate's ability to handle the financial aspects of the job the employer seeks to fill.

There are other, lesser-used types of questions. In a **stress interview**, the interviewer seeks to make the applicant uncomfortable with occasionally rude questions. The aim is supposedly to spot sensitive applicants and those with low (or high) stress tolerance. Thus, a candidate for a customer relations manager position

behavioral interview
A series of job-related questions that focus on how the candidate reacted to actual situations in the past.

job-related interview
A series of job-related questions that focus on relevant past job-related behaviors.

stress interview
An interview in which the applicant is made uncomfortable by a series of often rude questions. This technique helps identify hypersensitive applicants and those with low or high stress tolerance.

who obligingly mentions having had four jobs in the past 2 years might be told that frequent job changes reflect irresponsible and immature behavior. If the applicant then responds with a reasonable explanation of why the job changes were necessary, the interviewer might pursue another topic. On the other hand, if the formerly tranquil applicant reacts explosively with anger and disbelief, the interviewer might deduce that the person has a low tolerance for stress.

Stress interviews may help unearth hypersensitive applicants who might overreact to mild criticism with anger and abuse. However, the stress interview's invasive and ethically questionable nature demands that the interviewer be both skilled in its use and sure the job really calls for a thick skin and an ability to handle stress. This is definitely not an approach for amateur interrogators or for those without the skills to keep the interview under control.

Puzzle questions are popular. Recruiters like to use them to see how candidates think under pressure. For example, an interviewer at Microsoft asked a tech service applicant this: "Mike and Todd have $21 between them. Mike has $20 more than Todd does. How much money has Mike, and how much money has Todd?"[16] (You'll find the answer two paragraphs below.)

How Should We Administer the Interview?

Employers also administer interviews in various ways: *one-on-one or by a panel of interviewers, sequentially or all at once*, and *computerized or personally.*

Most selection interviews are *one-on-one* and *sequential.* In a one-on-one interview, two people meet alone, and one interviews the other by seeking oral responses to oral inquiries. Employers tend to schedule these interviews *sequentially.* In a *sequential (or serial) interview*, several persons interview the applicant, in sequence, one-on-one, and then make their hiring decision. In an **unstructured sequential interview**, each interviewer generally just asks questions as they come to mind. In a **structured sequential interview**, each interviewer rates the candidates on a standard evaluation form, using standardized questions. The hiring manager then reviews and compares the evaluations before deciding whom to hire.[17] (Answer: Mike had $20.50, Todd $.50.)

PANEL INTERVIEWS   A **panel interview**, also known as a board interview, is an interview conducted by a team of interviewers (usually two to three), who together interview each candidate and then combine their ratings into a final panel score. This contrasts with the *one-on-one interview* (in which one interviewer meets one candidate) and a *serial interview* (where several interviewers assess a single candidate one-on-one, sequentially).[18]

The panel format enables interviewers to ask follow-up questions, much as reporters do in press conferences. This may elicit more meaningful responses than are normally produced by a series of one-on-one interviews. On the other hand, some candidates find panel interviews more stressful, so they may actually inhibit responses. (An even more stressful variant is the **mass interview**. Here a panel interviews several candidates simultaneously. The panel poses a problem, and then watches to see which candidate takes the lead in formulating an answer.)

It's not clear whether as a rule panel interviews are more or less reliable and valid than sequential interviews, because how the employer actually does the panel interview determines this. For example, *structured* panel interviews in which members use scoring sheets with descriptive scoring examples for sample answers are more reliable and valid than those that don't. And, training the panel interviewers may boost the interview's reliability.[19]

PHONE INTERVIEWS   Employers do some interviews entirely by *telephone.* These can actually be more accurate than face-to-face interviews for judging an applicant's conscientiousness, intelligence, and interpersonal skills. Here, neither party need worry about things like appearance or handshakes, so each can focus on substantive answers. Or perhaps candidates—somewhat surprised by an unexpected call from the recruiter—just give answers that are more spontaneous (although more confident interviewees do better, of course".)[20] In a typical study, interviewers tended to evaluate applicants more favorably in telephone versus face-to-face interviews, particularly where the interviewees were less physically attractive. However, the interviewers came to about the same conclusions regarding the interviewees whether the interview was face-to-face or by *videoconference*. The applicants themselves preferred the face-to-face interviews.[21]

VIDEO/WEB-ASSISTED INTERVIEWS Firms have long used the Web to do selection interviews (particularly the initial, prescreening interviews). With iPad-type video functionalities and the widespread use of Skype™, their use is growing. For instance, Cisco Systems, Inc., recruiters conduct preliminary interviews online. Applicants use their own camera-supported PC or iPads (or go to a local FedEx Office or similar business). Then, at the appointed time, they link to Cisco via Web video for the prescreening interview. Naturally, such video interviews reduce travel and recruiting expenses. Job interviewing apps are available through Apple's App Store. One is from *Martin's iPhone Apps*. For people seeking technical jobs, this app includes hundreds of potential interview questions, such as Brain Teasers, Algorithms, C/C++, and Personal.[22]

Having a "Skype job interview" doesn't require special preparations for the employer, but Career FAQs (www.careerfaqs.com.au) says there are things that interviewees should keep in mind. Many of these may seem obvious. However, it's often the obvious things people overlook (for more on how to take interviews, see Appendix 2 to this chapter, pages 238–239):[23]

- **Make sure you look presentable.** You might feel silly sitting at home wearing a suit, but it could make all the difference.
- **Clean up the room.** Whether the interview is from your own home or a busy office environment, the interviewer does not want to see you sitting in front of a pile of junk.
- **Test first.** As Career FAQs says, "Five minutes before the video interview is not a good time to realize that your Internet is down, Skype isn't working, or your pet rabbit has chewed through the microphone cord."
- **Do a dry run.** Try recording yourself before the interview to try answering some imaginary questions.
- **Relax.** The golden rule with a Skype interview is to treat it like any other face-to-face meeting. There is a real person on the other end of the call, so treat them like one. Smile, look confident and enthusiastic, try to make eye contact, and don't shout, but do speak clearly.

COMPUTERIZED INTERVIEWS A *computerized selection interview* is one in which a job candidate's oral and/or computerized replies are obtained in response to computerized oral, visual, or written questions and/or situations. Most computerized interviews present the applicant with a series of questions regarding his or her background, experience, education, skills, knowledge, and work attitudes that relate to the job for which the person has applied. Some (video-based) computerized interviews also confront candidates with realistic scenarios (such as irate customers) to which they must respond. Such interviews are most often taken online.[24]

---

unstructured sequential interview
An interview in which each interviewer forms an independent opinion after asking different questions.

structured sequential interview
An interview in which the applicant is interviewed sequentially by several persons; each rates the applicant on a standard form.

panel interview
An interview in which a group of interviewers questions the applicant.

mass interview
A panel interviews several candidates simultaneously.

Typical computerized interviews present questions in a multiple-choice format, one at a time. The applicant has to respond to the questions on the screen by pressing a key. A sample interview question for a person applying for a job as a retail store clerk might be:

How would your supervisor rate your customer service skills?

   a. Outstanding

   b. Above average

   c. Average

   d. Below average

   e. Poor[25]

Questions on computerized interviews come in rapid sequence and require the applicant to concentrate.[26] The typical computerized interview program measures the response time to each question. A delay in answering certain questions such as "Can you be trusted?" flags a potential problem. The accompanying HR as a Profit Center feature illustrates the bottom line impact such systems can have.

HR AS A PROFIT CENTER

Great Western Bank

When Bonnie Dunn tried out for a teller's job at Great Western Bank, she faced a lineup of tough customers.[27] One young woman sputtered contradictory instructions about depositing a check and then blew her top when Bonnie didn't handle the transaction fast enough. Another customer said, "You people are unbelievably slow."

Both tough customers appeared on a computer screen, as part of a 20-minute computerized job interview. Ms. Dunn sat in front of the screen, responding via a touch screen and a microphone. She was tested on making change and on sales skills, as well as keeping her cool. When applicants sit down facing the computer, they hear it say, "Welcome to the interactive assessment aid." The computer doesn't understand what applicants say, although it records their comments for evaluation later. To begin the interview, applicants touch an icon on the screen, eliciting an ominous foreword: "We'll be keeping track of how long it takes you and how many mistakes you make. Accuracy is more important than speed."

Great Western reports success with its system. It dramatically reduced interviewing of unacceptable candidates, saving valuable HR time and resources. And, partly because the candidates see what the job is really like, those hired are reportedly 26% less likely to leave within 90 days of hiring, significantly reducing the bank's employee turnover costs.

SECOND LIFE Several employers such as Microsoft and Hewlett-Packard use the online virtual community Second Life to conduct job interviews. Job seekers create avatars to represent themselves in the interviews.[28]

SPEED DATING For better or worse, some employers are using a speed dating approach to interviewing applicants. One employer sent e-mails to all applicants for an advertised position. Four hundred (of 800 applicants) showed up. Over the next few hours, applicants first mingled with employees, and then (in a so-called "speed dating area") had one-on-one contacts with employees for a few minutes. Based on this, the recruiting team chose 68 candidates for follow-up interviews.[29]

BAIN & COMPANY CASE INTERVIEW Bain & Company uses case interviews as part of its candidate selection process. By having candidates explain how they would address the case "clients" problems, the case interview combines elements of behavioral and situational questioning to provide a more realistic assessment of the candidate's consulting skills. The accompanying screen grab shows Bain candidates how to prepare for the case-based interview.

Source: John Bain & Company, www.joinbain.com, accessed September 2011.

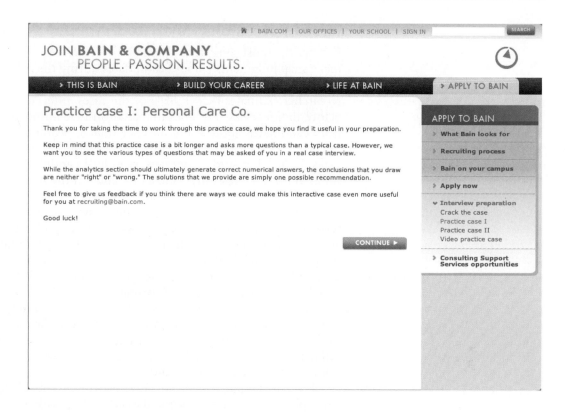

Three Ways to Make the Interview Useful

Interviews hold an ironic place in the hiring process: Everyone uses them, but they're generally not particularly valid. The knack is in doing them properly. If you do, then the interview is generally a good predictor of performance and is comparable with many other selection techniques.[30] There are three things to keep in mind.

USE STRUCTURED SITUATIONAL INTERVIEWS   First, *structure the interview.*[31] Structured interviews (particularly structured interviews using situational questions) are more valid than unstructured interviews for predicting job performance. They are more valid partly because they are more reliable—for example, the same interviewer administers the interview more consistently from candidate to candidate.[32] Situational interviews yield a higher mean validity than do job-related (or behavioral) interviews, which in turn yield a higher mean validity than do "psychological" interviews (which focus more on motives and interests).[33]

CAREFULLY SELECT TRAITS TO ASSESS   Interviews are better for revealing some traits than others. A typical study illustrates this. Interviewers were able to size up the interviewee's extraversion and agreeableness. What they could *not* assess accurately were the traits that often matter most on jobs—like conscientiousness and emotional stability.[34] The implication seems to be, don't focus (as many do) on hard-to-assess traits like conscientiousness.[35] Limit yourself mostly to situational and job knowledge questions that help you assess how the candidate will actually respond to typical situations on that job. We'll explain how to do this later in the chapter.

BEWARE OF COMMITTING INTERVIEWING ERRORS   Third, understand and avoid the *various errors that can undermine* any interview's usefulness. We turn to these next.

THE ERRORS THAT UNDERMINE AN INTERVIEW'S USEFULNESS

2 List and explain the main errors that can undermine an interview's usefulness.

One reason selection interviews are often less than useful is that managers make predictable, avoidable errors. We'll look at these next.

First Impressions (Snap Judgments)

Perhaps the most consistent finding is that interviewers tend to jump to conclusions—make snap judgments—about candidates during the first few minutes of the interview (or even before the interview starts, based on test scores or résumé data). One researcher estimates that in 85% of the cases, interviewers had made up their minds before the interview even began, based on first impressions the interviewers gleaned from candidates' applications and personal appearance.[36] In one typical study, giving interviewers the candidates' test scores biased the ultimate assessment of the candidates. In another study, interviewers judged candidates who they were told formerly suffered from depression or substance abuse more negatively.[37]

First impressions are especially damaging when the prior information about the candidate is negative. In one study, interviewers who previously received unfavorable reference letters about applicants gave those applicants less credit for past successes and held them more personally responsible for past failures after the interview. And the interviewers' final decisions (to accept or reject those applicants) always reflected what they expected of the applicants based on the references, quite aside from the applicants' actual interview performance.[38]

Add to this two more interviewing facts. First, interviewers are more influenced by unfavorable than favorable information about the candidate. Second, their impressions are much more likely to change from favorable to unfavorable than from unfavorable to favorable. Indeed, many interviewers really search more for negative information, often without realizing it.

The bottom line is that most interviews are probably loaded against the applicant. An applicant who starts well could easily end up with a low rating because unfavorable information tends to carry more weight in the interview. And pity the poor interviewee who starts out poorly. It's almost impossible to overcome that first bad impression.[39] Here's how one London-based psychologist who interviewed the chief executives of 80 top companies put it:

> "Really, to make a good impression, you don't even get time to open your mouth. . . . An interviewer's response to you will generally be preverbal—how you walk through the door, what your posture is like, whether you smile, whether you have a captivating aura, whether you have a firm, confident handshake. You've got about half a minute to make an impact and after that all you are doing is building on a good or bad first impression. . . . It's a very emotional response."[40]

Not Clarifying What the Job Requires

Interviewers who don't have an accurate picture of what the job entails and what sort of candidate is best suited for it usually make their decisions based on incorrect impressions or stereotypes of what a good applicant is. They then erroneously match interviewees with their incorrect stereotypes. You should clarify what sorts of traits you're looking for, and why, before starting the interview.

One classic study involved 30 professional interviewers.[41] Half got just a brief description of the jobs for which they were recruiting: It said, the "eight applicants here represented by their application blanks are applying for the position of secretary." The other 15 interviewers got much more explicit job information, in terms of typing speed and bilingual ability, for instance.

More job knowledge translated into better interviews. The 15 interviewers who had more job information generally all agreed among themselves about each candidate's potential; those without complete job information did not. The latter also didn't discriminate as well among applicants—they tended to give them all high ratings.

Candidate-Order (Contrast) Error and Pressure to Hire

Candidate-order (or contrast) error means that the order in which you see applicants affects how you rate them. In one study, managers had to evaluate a candidate who was "just average" after first evaluating several "unfavorable" candidates. They scored the average candidate more favorably than they might otherwise have done because, in contrast to the unfavorable candidates, the average one looked better than he actually was. This contrast effect can be huge: In some early studies, evaluators based only a small part of the applicant's rating on his or her actual potential.[42]

Pressure to hire accentuates this problem. Researchers told one group of managers to assume they were behind in their recruiting quota. They told a second group they were ahead of their quota. Those "behind" evaluated the same recruits much more highly than did those "ahead."[43]

Nonverbal Behavior and Impression Management

The applicant's nonverbal behavior (smiling, avoiding your gaze, and so on) can also have a surprisingly large impact on his or her rating. In one study, 52 human resource specialists watched videotaped job interviews in which *the applicants' verbal content was identical*, but their nonverbal behavior differed markedly. Researchers told applicants in one group to exhibit minimal eye contact, a low energy level, and low voice modulation. Those in a second group demonstrated the opposite behavior. Twenty-three of the 26 personnel specialists who saw the high-eye-contact, high-energy-level candidate would have invited him or her for a second interview. None who saw the low-eye-contact, low-energy-level candidate would have recommended a second interview.[44] It certainly seems to pay interviewees to "look alive."

Nonverbal behaviors are probably so important because interviewers infer your personality from the way you act in the interview. In one study, 99 graduating college seniors completed questionnaires; the questionnaires included measures of personality, among other things. The students then reported their success in generating follow-up interviews and job offers. The interviewee's personality, particularly his or her level of extraversion, had a pronounced influence on whether or not he or she received follow-up interviews and job offers.[45] Extraverted applicants seem particularly prone to self-promotion, and self-promotion is strongly related to the interviewer's perceptions of candidate–job fit.[46] Furthermore, "No matter how much an interview is structured, nonverbal cues cause interviewers to make [such] attributions about candidates."[47]

IMPRESSION MANAGEMENT   Clever candidates capitalize on that fact. One study found that some used ingratiation to persuade interviewers to like them. For instance, the candidates praised the interviewers or appeared to agree with their opinions. Ingratiation also involves, for example, agreeing with the recruiter's opinions and thus signaling that they share similar beliefs. Sensing that a perceived similarity in attitudes may influence how the interviewer rates them, some interviewees try to emphasize (or fabricate) such similarities.[48] Others make self-promoting comments about their own accomplishments.[49] Self-promotion means promoting one's own skills and abilities to create the impression of competence.[50] Psychologists call using techniques like ingratiation and self-promotion "impression management."

Effect of Personal Characteristics: Attractiveness, Gender, Race

Unfortunately, physical attributes such as applicants' attractiveness, gender, disability, or race may also distort their assessments.[51] For example, people usually ascribe more favorable traits and more successful life outcomes to attractive people.[52] Similarly, race can play a role, depending on how you conduct the interview. In one study, for example, the white members of a racially balanced interview panel rated white candidates higher, while the black interviewers rated black candidates higher. (In all cases, *structured* interviews produced less of a difference between minority and white interviewees than did unstructured interviews.)[53]

candidate-order (or contrast) error
An error of judgment on the part of the interviewer due to interviewing one or more very good or very bad candidates just before the interview in question.

Interviewers' reactions to stereotypical minority behavior are complex. In one study, the researchers dressed the "applicants" in either traditional Muslim attire (black scarf and full-length black robe) or simple two-piece black pantsuits. Both applicants got the same number of job offers. However, interactions were shorter and more interpersonally negative when applicants wore the Muslim attire.[54]

In general, candidates evidencing various attributes and disabilities (such as child-care demands, HIV-positive status, and being wheelchair-bound) had less chance of obtaining a positive decision, even when the person performed very well in the structured interview.[55]

MANAGING THE NEW WORKFORCE

Applicant Disability and the Employment Interview

Researchers surveyed 40 disabled people from various occupations. The basic finding was that the disabled people felt that interviewers tend to avoid directly addressing the disability, and therefore make their decisions without all the facts.[56]

What the disabled people prefer is a discussion that would allow the employer to clarify his or her concerns and reach a knowledgeable conclusion. Among the questions they said they would like interviewers to ask were these:

- Is there any kind of setting or special equipment that will facilitate the interview process for you?

- Is there any specific technology that you currently use or have used in previous jobs that assists the way you work?

- Other than technology, what other kind of support did you have in previous jobs? If none, is there anything that would benefit you?

- Discuss a barrier or obstacle, if any, that you have encountered in any of your previous jobs. How was that addressed?

- Do you anticipate any transportation or scheduling issues with the work schedule expected of this position?

Finally, remember that under the Americans with Disabilities Act, the interviewer must limit his or her questions to whether the applicant has any physical or mental impairment that may interfere with his or her ability to perform the job's essential tasks.[57]

EMPLOYMENT DISCRIMINATION "TESTERS"   Employment discrimination is abhorrent, but the use of employment discrimination "testers" makes nondiscriminatory interviewing even more important. As defined by the EEOC, testers are "individuals who apply for employment which they do not intend to accept, for the sole purpose of uncovering unlawful discriminatory hiring practices."[58] Although they're not really seeking employment, testers have legal standing with the courts and with the EEOC.[59]

For example, a civil rights group sent four university students—two white, two black—to an employment agency, supposedly in pursuit of a job. The civil rights group gave the four "testers" backgrounds and training to make them appear almost indistinguishable from each other in terms of qualifications. The white tester/applicants got interviews and job offers. The black tester/applicants got neither interviews nor offers.[60]

Interviewer Behavior

Finally, the *interviewer's* behavior also affects the interviewee's performance and rating.

Consider some examples. Some interviewers inadvertently telegraph the expected answers,[61] as in: "This job calls for handling a lot of stress. You can do that, can't you?" Even subtle cues (like a smile or nod) can telegraph the desired answer.[62] Some interviewers talk so much that applicants have no time to answer questions. At the other extreme, some interviewers let the applicant dominate the interview, and so don't ask all their questions.[63] When interviewers have favorable pre-interview impressions of the applicant, they tend to act more positively toward that person (smiling more, for instance).[64] Other interviewers play district attorney, forgetting that it is uncivil to play "gotcha" by gleefully pouncing on inconsistencies. Some interviewers play amateur psychologist, unprofessionally probing for hidden meanings in everything the applicant says. Others ask improper questions, forgetting, as one study found, that discriminatory questions "had a significant negative effect on participant's reactions to the interview and interviewer."[65] And, some interviewers are simply inept, unable to formulate decent questions.

In summary, interviewing errors to avoid include:

- First impressions (snap judgments)
- Not clarifying what the job involves and requires
- Candidate-order error and pressure to hire
- Nonverbal behavior and impression management
- The effects of interviewees' personal characteristics
- The interviewer's inadvertent behaviors

| 3 | Define a structured situational interview. |

HOW TO DESIGN AND CONDUCT AN EFFECTIVE INTERVIEW

There are two basic ways to avoid interview errors. One is obvious: Keep them in mind and avoid them (don't make snap judgments, for instance). The second is not so obvious: Use structured interviews. The single biggest rule for conducting effective selection interviews is to structure the interview around job-relevant situational and behavioral questions. We'll look next at how to do this.

Designing a Structured Situational Interview

There is little doubt that the **structured situational interview**—a series of job-relevant questions with predetermined answers that interviewers ask of all applicants for the job—produces superior results.[66] Ideally, the basic idea is to write situational (what would you do), behavioral (what did you do), or job knowledge questions, *and* have job experts (like those supervising the job) also write answers for these questions, rated from good to poor. The people who interview and rate the applicants then use rating sheets anchored with examples of good or bad answers to rate the interviewees' answers.[67] The procedure is as follows.[68]

STEP 1: ANALYZE THE JOB   Write a job description with a list of job duties; required knowledge, skills, and abilities; and other worker qualifications.

STEP 2: RATE THE JOB'S MAIN DUTIES   Rate each job duty, say from 1 to 5, based on its importance to job success.

STEP 3: CREATE INTERVIEW QUESTIONS   Create interview questions for each of the job duties, with more questions for the important duties. Recall that *situational questions* pose a hypothetical job situation, such as "What would you do if the machine suddenly began heating up?" *Job knowledge questions* assess knowledge essential to job performance (such as "What is HTML?"). *Willingness questions* gauge the applicant's willingness and motivation to meet the job's requirements—to do repetitive physical work or to travel, for instance. *Behavioral questions,* of course, ask candidates how they've handled similar situations.

structured situational interview
A series of job-relevant questions with predetermined answers that interviewers ask of all applicants for the job.

The people who create the questions usually write them in terms of critical incidents. For example, for a supervisory candidate, the interviewer might ask this situational question:

> Your spouse and two teenage children are sick in bed with colds. There are no relatives or friends available to look in on them. Your shift starts in 3 hours. What would you do in this situation?

STEP 4: CREATE BENCHMARK ANSWERS   Next, *for each question*, develop ideal (benchmark) answers for good (a 5 rating), marginal (a 3 rating), and poor (a 1 rating) answers. Three benchmark answers (from low to high) for the example question above might be, "I'd stay home—my spouse and family come first" (1); "I'd phone my supervisor and explain my situation" (3); and "Since they only have colds, I'd come to work" (5).

STEP 5: APPOINT THE INTERVIEW PANEL AND CONDUCT INTERVIEWS   Employers generally conduct structured situational interviews using a panel, rather than one-on-one. The panel usually consists of three to six members, preferably the same ones who wrote the questions and answers. It may also include the job's supervisor and/or incumbent, and a human resources representative. The same panel interviews all candidates for the job.[69]

The panel members generally review the job description, questions, and benchmark answers before the interview. One panel member introduces the applicant, and asks all questions of all applicants in this and succeeding candidates' interviews (to ensure consistency). However, all panel members record and rate the applicant's answers on the rating sheet. They do this by indicating where the candidate's answer to each question falls relative to the ideal poor, marginal, or good answers. At the end of the interview, someone answers any questions the applicant has.[70]

Web-based programs help interviewers design and organize behaviorally based selection interviews. For example, SelectPro (www.selectpro.net) enables interviewers to create behavior-based selection interviews, custom interview guides, and automated online interviews.

How to Conduct an Effective Interview

> **4** Explain and illustrate each guideline for being a more effective interviewer.

You may not have the time or inclination to create a structured situational interview. However, there is still much you can do to make your interviews more systematic and effective.

STEP 1: FIRST, MAKE SURE YOU KNOW THE JOB   Do not start the interview unless you understand the job and what human skills you're looking for. Study the job description.

STEP 2: STRUCTURE THE INTERVIEW   *Any* structuring is better than none. If pressed for time, you can do several things to ask more consistent and job-relevant questions, without developing a full-blown structured interview.[71] They include:[72]

- Base questions on *actual job duties.* This will minimize irrelevant questions.
- Use *job knowledge, situational, or behavioral questions*, and know enough about the job to be able to evaluate the interviewee's answers. Questions that simply ask for opinions and attitudes, goals and aspirations, and self-descriptions and self-evaluations allow candidates to present themselves in an overly favorable manner or avoid revealing weaknesses.[73] Figure 7-2 illustrates structured interview questions.
- *Use the same questions* with all candidates. When it comes to asking questions, the prescription is "the more standardized, the better." Using the same questions with all candidates improves reliability. It also reduces bias because of the obvious fairness of giving all the candidates the exact same opportunity.

FIGURE 7-2 Examples of Questions That Provide Interview Structure

Job Knowledge Questions
1. What steps would you follow in changing the fan belt on a Toyota Camry?
2. What factors would you consider in choosing a computer to use for work?

Experience Questions
3. What experience have you had actually repairing automobile engines?
4. What experience have you had creating marketing programs for consumer products?

Behavioral (Past Behavior) Questions
5. Tell me about a time when you had to deal with a particularly obnoxious person. What was the situation, and how did you handle it?
6. Tell me about a time when you were under a great deal of stress. What was the situation, and how did you handle it?

Situational (What Would You Do) Questions
7. Suppose your boss insisted that a presentation had to be finished by tonight, but your subordinate said she has to get home early to attend an online class, so she is unable to help you. What would you do?
8. The CEO just told you that he's planning on firing your boss, with whom you are very close, and replacing him with you. What would you do?

- Use *descriptive rating scales* (excellent, fair, poor) to rate answers. For each question, if possible, have several ideal answers and a score for each. Then rate each candidate's answers against this scale.

- If possible, use a *standardized interview form.* Interviews based on structured guides like the ones in Figures 7-1 (pages 216-217) or 7A-1 (pages 236–238) usually result in better interviews.[74] At the very least, list your questions before the interview.

STEP 3: GET ORGANIZED   Hold the interview in a private room where telephone calls are not accepted and you can minimize interruptions (including text messages). Prior to the interview, review the candidate's application and résumé, and note any areas that are vague or that may indicate strengths or weaknesses.

STEP 4: ESTABLISH RAPPORT   The main reason for the interview is to find out about the applicant. To do this, start by putting the person at ease. Greet the candidate and start the interview by asking a noncontroversial question, perhaps about the weather or the traffic conditions that day. As a rule, all applicants—even unsolicited drop-ins—should receive friendly, courteous treatment, not only on humanitarian grounds but also because your reputation is on the line.

> 5   Give several examples of situational questions, behavioral questions, and background questions that provide structure.

STEP 5: ASK QUESTIONS   Try to follow the situational, behavioral, and job knowledge questions you wrote out ahead of time. You'll find a sampling of other technical questions (such as "What did you most enjoy about your last job?") in Figure 7-3. As a rule,

Don't telegraph the desired answer.

Don't interrogate the applicant as if the person is on trial.

Don't monopolize the interview, nor let the applicant do so.

Do ask open-ended questions.

Do encourage the applicant to express thoughts fully.

Do draw out the applicant's opinions and feelings by repeating the person's last comment as a question (e.g., "You didn't like your last job?").

Do ask for examples.[75]

Do ask, "If I were to arrange for an interview with your boss, what's your best guess as to what he or she would say as your strengths, weaker points, and overall performance?, and "Tell me about a time when you had to deal with someone difficult–what did you do?"[76]

FIGURE 7-3 Suggested Supplementary Questions for Interviewing Applicants

Source: Reprinted from http://hr.blr.com with permission of the publisher Business and Legal Resources, Inc. 141 Mill Rock Road East, Old Saybrook, CT © 2004. BLR© (Business and Legal Resources, Inc.).

1. How did you choose this line of work?
2. What did you enjoy most about your last job?
3. What did you like least about your last job?
4. What has been your greatest frustration or disappointment on your present job? Why?
5. What are some of the pluses and minuses of your last job?
6. What were the circumstances surrounding your leaving your last job?
7. Did you give notice?
8. Why should we be hiring you?
9. What do you expect from this employer?
10. What are three things you will not do in your next job?
11. What would your last supervisor say your three weaknesses are?
12. What are your major strengths?
13. How can your supervisor best help you obtain your goals?
14. How did your supervisor rate your job performance?
15. In what ways would you change your last supervisor?
16. What are your career goals during the next 1–3 years? 5–10 years?
17. How will working for this company help you reach those goals?
18. What did you do the last time you received instructions with which you disagreed?
19. What are some of the things about which you and your supervisor disagreed? What did you do?
20. Which do you prefer, working alone or working with groups?
21. What motivated you to do better at your last job?
22. Do you consider your progress on that job representative of your ability? Why?
23. Do you have any questions about the duties of the job for which you have applied?
24. Can you perform the essential functions of the job for which you have applied?

STEP 6: TAKE BRIEF, UNOBTRUSIVE NOTES DURING THE INTERVIEW
Doing so may help avoid making a snap decision early in the interview, and may also help jog your memory once the interview is complete. Take notes, jotting down just the key points of what the interviewee says.[77]

STEP 7: CLOSE THE INTERVIEW Leave time to answer any questions the candidate may have and, if appropriate, to advocate your firm to the candidate.

Try to end the interview on a positive note. Tell the applicant whether there is any interest and, if so, what the next step will be. Make rejections diplomatically—for instance, "Although your background is impressive, there are other candidates whose experience is closer to our requirements." If the applicant is still under consideration but you can't reach a decision now, say so. Remember, as one recruiter says, "An interview experience should leave a lasting, positive impression of the company, whether the candidate receives and accepts an offer or not."[78]

In rejecting a candidate, one perennial question is, should you provide an explanation or not? In one study, rejected candidates who received an explanation detailing why the employer rejected them felt that the rejection process was fairer. Unfortunately, providing detailed explanations may not be practical. As the researchers put it,

> "We were unsuccessful in a number of attempts to secure a site for our applied study. Of three organizations that expressed interest in our research, all eventually declined to participate in the study because they were afraid that any additional information in the rejection letters might increase legal problems. They were reluctant to give rejected applicants information that can be used to dispute the decision."[79]

STEP 8: REVIEW THE INTERVIEW After the candidate leaves, review your interview notes, score the interview guide answers (if you used one), and make a decision.

Source: Dorling Kindersley Publishing, Inc. [US].

Go into the interview with an accurate picture of the traits of an ideal candidate, know what you're going to ask, and be prepared to keep an open mind about the candidate.

We'll address what *interviewees* can do to apply these findings and to excel in the interview in Appendix 2 to this chapter.

Talent Management: Profiles and Employee Interviews

Talent management is the goal-oriented and integrated process of planning for, recruiting, selecting, developing, and compensating employees. To ensure an integrated, goal-oriented effort, talent management therefore involves (among other things) using the same job profile (competencies, traits, knowledge, and experience) for recruiting as for selecting, training, appraising, and paying the employee.

Profiles can play an important role in employee selection. For example, we saw in Chapter 4 that IBM identified 490 possible roles that represented the building blocks of IBM's various jobs. IBM then identified a profile or set of required skills and competencies for each role (such as engineer).

Managers can use a job's profile to formulate job-related situational, behavioral, and knowledge interview questions when selecting someone for a job or set of roles. Consider a simple example. Table 7-1 summarizes illustrative competency, knowledge, trait, and experience elements for a chemical engineer, along with sample interview questions. Selecting engineers based on this profile helps to ensure that you focus your questions on the things that someone must be proficient at to do this job successfully. The same profile would similarly provide guidance for determining how to recruit candidates for this position, and on what basis to train, appraise, and pay him or her.

TABLE 7-1 Asking Profile-Oriented Interview Questions

Profile Component	Example	Sample Interview Question
Competency	Able to use computer drafting software	Tell me about a time you used CAD Pro computerized design software.
Knowledge	How extreme heat affects hydrochloric acid (HCL)	Suppose you have an application where HCL is heated to 400 degrees Fahrenheit at 2 atmospheres of pressure; what happens to the HCL?
Trait	Willing to travel abroad at least 4 months per year visiting facilities	Suppose you had a family meeting that you had to attend next week and our company informed you that you had to leave for a job abroad immediately, and stay 3 weeks. How would you handle that?
Experience	Designed pollution filter for acid-cleaning facility	Tell me about a time when you designed a pollution filter device for an acid-cleaning facility. How did it work? What particular problems did you encounter? How did you address them?

REVIEW

MyManagementLab   Now that you have finished this chapter, go back to **www.mymanagementlab.com** to continue practicing and applying the concepts you've learned.

CHAPTER SECTION SUMMARIES

1. A selection interview is a selection procedure designed to predict future job performance based on applicants' oral responses to oral inquiries; we discussed several **basic types of interviews**. There are structured versus unstructured interviews. We also distinguished between interviews based on the types of questions (such as situational versus behavioral) and on how you administer the interview, such as one-on-one, sequentially, or even via computer/ video/telephone. However you decide to conduct and structure the interview, be careful what sorts of traits

you try to assess, and beware of committing the sorts of interviewing errors we touch on next.

2. One reason selection interviews are often less useful than they should be is that managers make predictable **errors that undermine an interview's usefulness.** They jump to conclusions or make snap judgments based on preliminary information, they don't clarify what the job really requires, they succumb to candidate-order error and pressure to hire, and they let a variety of nonverbal behaviors and personal characteristics undermine the validity of the interview.

3. There are two basic ways to **avoid interview errors.** One is to keep them in mind, and the second is to use structured interviews.
   • The structured situational interview is a series of job-related questions with predetermined answers that interviewers ask of all applicants for the job.

Steps in creating a structured situational interview include analyzing the job, rating the job's main duties, creating interview questions, creating benchmark enters, and appointing the interview panel and conducting interviews.

4. Steps in **conducting an effective interview** include making sure you know the job, structuring the interview, getting organized, asking questions, taking brief unobtrusive notes during the interview, and reviewing the interview.

5. **Talent management profiles** can play an important role in employee selection. For example, we saw that IBM identified 490 possible roles employees might play, given IBM's strategic aims. IBM can then identify the skill sets each role requires. Managers can use a job's profile to formulate job-related situational, behavioral, and knowledge interview questions when selecting someone for a job or set of roles.

DISCUSSION QUESTIONS

1. Explain and illustrate the basic ways in which you can classify selection interviews.
2. Briefly describe each of the following types of interviews: unstructured panel interviews, structured sequential interviews, job-related structured interviews.
3. For what sorts of jobs do you think computerized interviews are most appropriate? Why?
4. Why do you think situational interviews yield a higher mean validity than do job-related or behavioral interviews, which in turn yield a higher mean validity than do psychological interviews?

5. Similarly, how would you explain the fact that structured interviews, regardless of content, are more valid than unstructured interviews for predicting job performance?
6. Briefly discuss and give examples of at least five common interviewing mistakes. What recommendations would you give for avoiding these interviewing mistakes?
7. Briefly discuss what an interviewer can do to improve his or her performance.

INDIVIDUAL AND GROUP ACTIVITIES

1. Prepare and give a short presentation titled "How to Be Effective as an Employment Interviewer."
2. Use the Internet to find employers who now do preliminary selection interviews via the Web. Print out and bring examples to class. Do you think these interviews are useful? Why or why not? How would you improve them?
3. In groups, discuss and compile examples of "the worst interview I ever had." What was it about these interviews that made them so bad? If time permits, discuss as a class.
4. In groups, prepare an interview (including a sequence of at least 20 questions) you'll use to interview candidates for the job of teaching a course in human resources management. Each group should present their interview questions in class.
5. Some firms swear by unorthodox interview methods. For example, Tech Planet, of Menlo Park, California, uses weekly lunches and "wacky follow-up sessions" as substitutes for first-round job interviews. During the informal meals, candidates are expected to mingle, and the Tech Planet employees they meet at the luncheons then review them. One Tech Planet employee asks candidates to ride a unicycle in her office to see if "they'll bond with the corporate culture or not." Toward the end of the screening process, the surviving group of interviewees has

to solve brainteasers, and then openly evaluate their fellow candidates' strengths and weaknesses. What do you think of a screening process like this? Specifically, what do you think are its pros and cons? Would you recommend a procedure like this? If so, what changes, if any, would you recommend?[80]

6. Several years ago, Lockheed Martin Corp. sued the Boeing Corp. in Orlando, Florida, accusing it of using Lockheed's trade secrets to help win a multibillion-dollar government contract. Among other things, Lockheed Martin claimed that Boeing had obtained those trade secrets from a former Lockheed Martin employee who switched to Boeing.[81] But in describing methods companies use to commit corporate espionage, one writer says that hiring away the competitor's employees or hiring people to go through its dumpster are just the most obvious methods companies use to commit corporate espionage. As he says, "one of the more unusual scams—sometimes referred to as 'help wanted'—uses a person posing as a corporate headhunter who approaches an employee of the target company with a potentially lucrative job offer. During the interview, the employee is quizzed about his responsibilities, accomplishments, and current projects. The goal is to extract important details without the employee realizing there is no job."[82]

Assume that you are the owner of a small high-tech company that is worried about the possibility that one or more of your employees may be approached by one of these sinister "headhunters." What would you do (in terms of employee training, or a letter from you, for instance) to try to minimize the chance that one of your employees will fall into that kind of a trap? Also, compile a list of 10 questions that you think such a corporate spy might ask one of your employees.

7. The HRCI "Test Specifications" appendix at the end of this book (pages 633–640) lists the knowledge someone studying for the HRCI certification exam needs to have in each area of human resource management (such as in Strategic Management, Workforce Planning, and Human Resource Development). In groups of four to five students, do four things: (1) review that appendix now; (2) identify the material in this chapter that relates to the required knowledge the appendix lists; (3) write four multiple-choice exam questions on this material that you believe would be suitable for inclusion in the HRCI exam; and (4) if time permits, have someone from your team post your team's questions in front of the class, so the students in other teams can take each others' exam questions.

EXPERIENTIAL EXERCISE

The Most Important Person You'll Ever Hire

Purpose: The purpose of this exercise is to give you practice using some of the interview techniques you learned from this chapter.

Required Understanding: You should be familiar with the information presented in this chapter, and read this: For parents, children are precious. It's therefore interesting that parents who hire "nannies" to take care of their children usually do little more than ask several interview questions and conduct what is often, at best, a perfunctory reference check. Given the often questionable validity of interviews, and the (often) relative inexperience of the father or mother doing the interviewing, it's not surprising that many of these arrangements end in disappointment. You know from this chapter that it is difficult to conduct a valid interview unless you know exactly what you're looking for and, preferably, structure the interview. Most parents simply aren't trained to do this.

How to Set Up the Exercise/Instructions:

1. Set up groups of five or six students. Two students will be the interviewees, while the other students in the group will serve as panel interviewers. The interviewees will develop an interviewer assessment form, and the panel interviewers will develop a structured situational interview for a "nanny."

2. Instructions for the interviewees: The interviewees should leave the room for about 20 minutes. While out of the room, the interviewees should develop an "interviewer assessment form" based on the information presented in this chapter regarding factors that can undermine the usefulness of an interview. During the panel interview, the interviewees should assess the interviewers using the interviewer assessment form. After the panel interviewers have conducted the interview, the interviewees should leave the room to discuss their notes. Did the interviewers exhibit any of the factors that can undermine the usefulness of an interview? If so, which ones? What suggestions would you (the interviewees) make to the interviewers on how to improve the usefulness of the interview?

3. Instructions for the interviewers: While the interviewees are out of the room, the panel interviewers will have 20 minutes to develop a short structured situational interview form for a "nanny." The panel interview team will interview two candidates for the position. During the panel interview, each interview should be taking notes on a copy of the structured situational interview form. After the panel interview, the panel interviewers should discuss their notes. What were your first impressions of each interviewee? Were your impressions similar? Which candidate would you all select for the position and why?

APPLICATION CASE

THE OUT-OF-CONTROL INTERVIEW

Maria Fernandez is a bright, popular, and well-informed mechanical engineer who graduated with an engineering degree from State University in June 2009. During the spring preceding her graduation, she went out on many job interviews, most of which she thought were conducted courteously and were reasonably useful in giving both her and the prospective employer a good impression of where each of them stood on matters of importance to both of them. It was, therefore, with great anticipation that she looked forward to an interview with the one firm in which she most wanted to work: Apex Environmental. She had always had a strong interest in cleaning up the environment and firmly believed that the best use of her training and skills lay in working for a

firm like Apex, where she thought she could have a successful career while making the world a better place.

The interview, however, was a disaster. Maria walked into a room where five men—the president of the company, two vice presidents, the marketing director, and another engineer—began throwing questions at her that she felt were aimed primarily at tripping her up rather than finding out what she could offer through her engineering skills. The questions ranged from being unnecessarily discourteous ("Why would you take a job as a waitress in college if you're such an intelligent person?") to being irrelevant and sexist ("Are you planning on settling down and starting a family anytime soon?"). Then, after the interview, she met with two of the gentlemen individually (including the president), and the discussions focused almost exclusively on her technical expertise. She thought that these later discussions went fairly well. However, given the apparent aimlessness and even mean-spiritedness of the panel interview, she was astonished when several days later the firm made her a job offer.

The offer forced her to consider several matters. From her point of view, the job itself was perfect. She liked what she would be doing, the industry, and the firm's location. And in fact, the president had been quite courteous in subsequent discussions, as had been the other members of the management team. She was left wondering whether the panel interview had been intentionally tense to see how she'd stand up under pressure, and, if so, why they would do such a thing.

Questions

1. How would you explain the nature of the panel interview Maria had to endure? Specifically, do you think it reflected a well-thought-out interviewing strategy on the part of the firm or carelessness on the part of the firm's management? If it were carelessness, what would you do to improve the interview process at Apex Environmental?

2. Would you take the job offer if you were Maria? If you're not sure, what additional information would help you make your decision?

3. The job of applications engineer for which Maria was applying requires (a) excellent technical skills with respect to mechanical engineering, (b) a commitment to working in the area of pollution control, (c) the ability to deal well and confidently with customers who have engineering problems, (d) a willingness to travel worldwide, and (e) a very intelligent and well-balanced personality. List 10 questions you would ask when interviewing applicants for the job.

CONTINUING CASE

CARTER CLEANING COMPANY

The Better Interview

Like virtually all the other HR-related activities at Carter Cleaning Centers, the company currently has no organized approach to interviewing job candidates. Store managers, who do almost all the hiring, have a few of their own favorite questions that they ask. But in the absence of any guidance from top management, they all admit their interview performance leaves something to be desired. Similarly, Jack Carter himself is admittedly most comfortable dealing with what he calls the "nuts and bolts" machinery aspect of his business and has never felt particularly comfortable having to interview management or other job applicants. Jennifer is sure that this lack of formal interviewing practices, procedures, and training account for some of the employee turnover and theft problems. Therefore, she wants to do something

to improve her company's batting average in this important area.

Questions

1. In general, what can Jennifer do to improve her employee interviewing practices? Should she develop interview forms that list questions for management and nonmanagement jobs? If so, how should these look and what questions should be included? Should she initiate a computer-based interview approach? If so, why and how?

2. Should she implement an interview training program for her managers, and if so, specifically what should be the content of such a training program? In other words, if she did decide to start training her management people to be better interviewers, what should she tell them and how should she tell it to them?

TRANSLATING STRATEGY INTO HR POLICIES & PRACTICES CASE

THE HOTEL PARIS CASE

The New Interviewing Program

The Hotel Paris's competitive strategy is "To use superior guest service to differentiate the Hotel Paris properties, and to thereby increase the length of stay and return rate of guests, and thus boost revenues and profitability." HR manager Lisa Cruz must now formulate functional policies and activities that support this competitive strategy by eliciting the required employee behaviors and competencies.

One thing that concerned Lisa Cruz was the fact that the Hotel Paris's hotel managers varied widely in their interviewing and hiring skills. Some were quite effective; most were not. Furthermore, the company did not have a formal

employment interview training program, nor, for that matter, did it have standardized interview packages that hotel managers around the world could use.

As an experienced HR professional, Lisa knew that the company's new testing program would go only so far. She knew that, at best, employment tests explained perhaps 30% of employee performance. It was essential that she and her team design a package of interviews that her hotel managers could use to assess—on an interactive and personal basis—candidates for various positions. It was only in that way that the hotel could hire the sorts of employees whose competencies and behaviors would translate into the kinds of outcomes—such as improved guest services—that the hotel required to achieve its strategic goals.

Lisa receives budgetary approval to design a new employee interview system. She and her team start by reviewing the job descriptions and job specifications for the positions of front-desk clerk, assistant manager, security guard, valet/door person, and housekeeper. Focusing on developing structured interviews for each position, the team sets about devising interview questions. For example, for the front-desk clerk and assistant manager, they formulate several *behavioral questions*, including, "Tell me about a time when you had to deal with an irate person, and what you did." And, "Tell me about a time when you had to deal with several conflicting demands at once, such as having to study for several final exams while at the same time

having to work. How did you handle the situation?" They also developed a number of *situational questions*, including, "Suppose you have a very pushy incoming guest who insists on being checked in at once, while at the same time you're trying to process the checkout for another guest who must be at the airport in 10 minutes. How would you handle the situation?"

Questions

1. For the job of security guard or valet, develop five situational, five behavioral, and five job knowledge questions, with descriptive good/average/poor answers.
2. Combine your questions into a complete interview that you would give to someone who must interview candidates for these jobs.

KEY TERMS

unstructured (or nondirective) interview, *214*

structured (or directive) interview, *215*

situational interview, *215*

behavioral interview, *216*

job-related interview, *217*

stress interview, *217*

unstructured sequential interview, *218*

structured sequential interview, *218*

panel interview, *218*

mass interview, *218*

candidate-order (or contrast) error, *222*

structured situational interview, *225*

ENDNOTES

1. This is based on Kristen Weirick, "The Perfect Interview," *HR Magazine* 53, no. 4 (April 2008), pp. 85–88.
2. Derek Chapman and David Zweig, "Developing a Nomological Network for Interview Structure: Antecedents and Consequences of the Structured Selection Interview," *Personnel Psychology* 58 (2005), pp. 673–702.
3. Michael McDaniel et al., "The Validity of Employment Interviews: A Comprehensive Review and Meta-Analysis," *Journal of Applied Psychology* 79, no. 4 (1994), p. 599. See also Laura Graves and Ronald Karren, "The Employee Selection Interview: A Fresh Look at an Old Problem," *Human Resource Management* 35, no. 2 (Summer 1996), pp. 163–180. For an argument against holding selection interviews, see D. Heath et al., "Hold the Interview," *Fast Company*, no. 136 (June 2009), pp. 51–52.
4. This is based on Weirick, "The Perfect Interview."
5. Therese Macan, "The Employment Interview: A Review of Current Studies and Directions for Future Research," *Human Resource Management Review* 19 (2009), pp. 203–218.
6. Duane Schultz and Sydney Schultz, *Psychology and Work Today* (Upper Saddle River, NJ: Prentice Hall, 1998), p. 830. A study found that interview structure "was best described by four dimensions: questioning consistency, evaluation standardization, question sophistication, and

rapport building." Chapman and Zweig, "Developing a Nomological Network."
7. McDaniel et al., "The Validity of Employment Interviews," p. 602.
8. We'll see later in this chapter that there are other ways to "structure" selection interviews. Many of them have nothing to do with using structured guides like these.
9. Laura Gollub Williamson et al., "Employment Interview on Trial: Linking Interview Structure with Litigation Outcomes," *Journal of Applied Psychology* 82, no. 6 (1996), p. 908. As an example, the findings of one recent study "Demonstrate the value of using highly structured interviews to minimize the potential influence of applicant demographic characteristics on selection decisions." Julie McCarthy, Chad Van iddekinge, and Michael Campion, "Are Highly Structured Job Interviews Resistant to Demographic Similarity Effects?" *Personnel Psychology* 60, no. 3 (2010), pp. 325–359.
10. Richard Posthuma, Frederick Morgeson, and Michael Campion, "Beyond Employment Interview Validity: A Comprehensive Narrative Review of Trends over Time," *Personnel Psychology*, 55 (2002), p. 47. See also Frederick P. Morgeson, Matthew H. Reider, and Michael A. Campion, "Review of Research on Age Discrimination in the Employment Interview," *Journal of Business & Psychology* 22, no. 3 (March 2008), pp. 223–232.
11. Williamson et al., "Employment Interview on Trial."

12. McDaniel et al., "The Validity of Employment Interviews," p. 602.
13. Bill Stoneman, "Matching Personalities with Jobs Made Easier with Behavioral Interviews," *American Banker*, November 30, 2000, p. 8a.
14. Paul Taylor and Bruce Small, "Asking Applicants What They Would Do Versus What They Did: A Meta-Analytic Comparison of Situational and Past Behavior Employment Interview Questions," *Journal of Occupational and Organizational Psychology* 75, no. 3 (September 2002), pp. 277–295.
15. Aparna Nancherla, "Anticipated Growth in Behavioral Interviewing," *Training & Development*, April 2008, p. 20.
16. Martha Frase-Blunt, "Games Interviewers Play," *HR Magazine*, January 2001, pp. 104–114.
17. Kevin Murphy and Charles Davidshofer, *Psychological Testing* (Upper Saddle River, NJ: Prentice Hall, 2001), pp. 430–431.
18. Marlene Dixon et al., "The Panel Interview: A Review of Empirical Research and Guidelines for Practice," *Public Personnel Management* 31, no. 3 (Fall 2002), pp. 397–429.
19. Ibid. See also M. Ronald Buckley, Katherine A. Jackson, and Mark C. Bolino, "The Influence of Relational Demography on Panel Interview Ratings: A Field Experiment," *Personnel Psychology* 60, no. 3 (Autumn 2007), pp. 627–646.
20. "Phone Interviews Might Be the Most Telling, Study Finds," *BNA Bulletin to Management*, September 1998, p. 273; and Lisa M. Moynihan, et al., "A Longitudinal

Study of the Relationships Among Job Search Self-Efficacy, Job Interviews, and Employment Outcomes," *Journal of Business and Psychology*, 18, no. 2 (Winter 2003), pp. 207–233. For phone interview job search suggestions, see for example, Janet Wagner, "Can You Succeed in a Phone Interview?" *Strategic Finance* 91, no. 10 (April 2010), p. 22, 61.

21. Susan Strauss et al., "The Effects of Video-conference, Telephone, and Face-to-Face Media on Interviewer and Applicant Judgments in Employment Interviews," *Journal of Management* 27, no. 3 (2001), pp. 363–381. If the employer records a video interview with the intention of sharing it with hiring managers who don't participate in the interview, it's advisable to first obtain the candidate's written permission. Matt Bolch, "Lights, Camera . . . Interview!" *HR Magazine*, March 2007, pp. 99–102.

22. www.martinreddy.net/iphone/interview, accessed July 5, 2009.

23. These are quoted or adapted from www.careerfaqs.com.au/getthatjob_video_interview.asp, accessed March 2, 2009.

24. Douglas Rodgers, "Computer-Aided Interviewing Overcomes First Impressions," *Personnel Journal*, April 1987, pp. 148–152; see also Linda Thornburg, "Computer-Assisted Interviewing Shortens Hiring Cycle," *HR Magazine*, February 1998, p. 73ff; and http://interviewstream.com/demorequest?gclid=COyxjOqd36sCFUbs7QodMziuOw, accessed October 2, 2011.

25. Rogers, "Computer-Aided Interviewing Overcomes First Impressions."

26. Gary Robins, "Dial-an-Interview," *Stores*, June 1994, pp. 34–35.

27. This is quoted from or paraphrased from William Bulkeley, "Replaced by Technology: Job Interviews," *The Wall Street Journal*, August 22, 1994, pp. B1, B7. For more on careers at Great Western see http://www.greatwesternbank.com/aboutus/careers, accessed October 6, 2011.

28. Anjali Athavaley, "A Job Interview You Don't Have to Show Up For," *The Wall Street Journal*, June 20, 2007, http://online.wsj.com/article/SB118229876637841321.html, accessed April 8, 2011.

29. Emily Maltby, "To Find the Best Hires, Firms Become Creative," *The Wall Street Journal*, November 17, 2009, p. B6.

30. For example, structured employment interviews using either situational questions or behavioral questions tend to yield high criterion-related validities (.63 versus .47). This is particularly so where the raters can use descriptively anchored rating scale answer sheets; these use short descriptors to illustrate good, average, or poor performance. Taylor and Small, "Asking Applicants What They Would Do Versus What They Did." See also, Julie McCarthy et al., "Are Highly Structured Job Interviews Resistant to Demographic Similarity Effects?" *Personnel Psychology* 63, no. 2 (Summer 2010), p. 325–359.

31. Williamson et al., "Employment Interview on Trial," p. 900.

32. Frank Schmidt and Ryan Zimmerman, "A Counterintuitive Hypothesis About Employment Interview Validity and Some Supporting Evidence," *Journal of Applied Psychology* 89, no. 3 (2004), pp. 553–561.

33. This validity discussion and these findings are based on McDaniel et al., "The Validity of Employment Interviews," pp. 607–610; the validities for situational, job-related, and psychological interviews were (.50), (.39), and (.29), respectively.

34. Murray Barrick et al., "Accuracy of Interviewer Judgments of Job Applicant Personality Traits," *Personnel Psychology* 53 (2000), pp. 925–951.

35. For example, with respect to the usefulness of selection interviews for assessing candidate intelligence or cognitive ability, see Christopher Berry et al., "Revisiting Interview–Cognitive Ability Relationships: Attending to Specific Range Restriction Mechanisms in Meta-Analysis," *Personnel Psychology* 60 (2007), pp. 837–874.

36. McDaniel et al., "The Validity of Employment Interviews," p. 608.

37. Anthony Dalessio and Todd Silverhart, "Combining Biodata Test and Interview Information: Predicting Decisions and Performance Criteria," *Personnel Psychology* 47 (1994), p. 313; and Nora Reilly, et al., "Benchmarks Affect Perceptions of Prior Disability in a Structured Interview," *Journal of Business & Psychology* 20, no. 4 (Summer 2006), pp. 489–500.

38. S. W. Constantin, "An Investigation of Information Favorability in the Employment Interview," *Journal of Applied Psychology* 61 (1976), pp. 743–749. It should be noted that a number of the studies discussed in this chapter involve having interviewers evaluate interviews based on written transcripts (rather than face to face) and that a study suggests that this procedure may not be equivalent to having interviewers interview applicants directly. See Charles Gorman, William Glover, and Michael Doherty, "Can We Learn Anything About Interviewing Real People from 'Interviews' of Paper People? A Study of the External Validity Paradigm," *Organizational Behavior and Human Performance* 22, no. 2 (October 1978), pp. 165–192; and Frederick P. Morgeson, Matthew H. Reider, Michael A. Campion, and Rebecca A. Bull, "Review of Research on Age Discrimination in the Employment Interview," *Journal of Business Psychology* 22 (2008), pp. 223–232.

39. David Tucker and Patricia Rowe, "Relationship Between Expectancy, Causal Attribution, and Final Hiring Decisions in the Employment Interview," *Journal of Applied Psychology* 64, no. 1 (February 1979), pp. 27–34. See also Robert Dipboye, Gail Fontenelle, and Kathleen Garner, "Effect of Previewing the Application on Interview Process and Outcomes," *Journal of Applied Psychology*

69, no. 1 (February 1984), pp. 118–128; and Nora Reilly, et al., "Benchmarks Affect Perceptions of Prior Disability in a Structured Interview," op cit.

40. Anita Chaudhuri, "Beat the Clock: Applying for Job? A New Study Shows That Interviewers Will Make Up Their Minds About You Within a Minute," *The Guardian*, June 14, 2000, pp. 2–6.

41. John Langdale and Joseph Weitz, "Estimating the Influence of Job Information on Interviewer Agreement," *Journal of Applied Psychology* 57 (1973), pp. 23–27.

42. R. E. Carlson, "Effect of Applicant Sample on Ratings of Valid Information in an Employment Setting," *Journal of Applied Psychology* 54 (1970), pp. 217–222.

43. R. E. Carlson, "Selection Interview Decisions: The Effect of Interviewer Experience, Relative Quota Situation, and Applicant Sample on Interview Decisions," *Personnel Psychology* 20 (1967), pp. 259–280.

44. See, for example, Scott T. Fleischmann, "The Messages of Body Language in Job Interviews," *Employee Relations* 18, no. 2 (Summer 1991), pp. 161–166; James Westphal and Ithai Stern, "Flattery Will Get You Everywhere (Especially if You're a Male Caucasian): How Ingratiation, Board Room Behavior, and a Demographic Minority Status Affect Additional Board Appointments at U.S. Companies," *Academy of Management Journal* 50, no. 2 (2007), pp. 267–288.

45. David Caldwell and Jerry Burger, "Personality Characteristics of Job Applicants and Success in Screening Interviews," *Personnel Psychology* 51 (1998), pp. 119–136.

46. Amy Kristof-Brown et al., "Applicant Impression Management: Dispositional Influences and Consequences for Recruiter Perceptions of Fit and Similarity," *Journal of Management* 28, no. 1 (2002), pp. 27–46. See also Lynn McFarland et al., "Impression Management Use and Effectiveness Across Assessment Methods," *Journal of Management* 29, no. 5 (2003), pp. 641–661.

47. Timothy DeGroot and Janaki Gooty, "Can Nonverbal Cues be Used to Make Meaningful Personality Attributions in Employment Interviews?" *Journal of Business Psychology* 24 (2009), p. 179.

48. Posthuma, Morgeson, and Campion, "Beyond Employment Interview Validity," 1–87.

49. C. K. Stevens and A. L. Kristof, "Making the Right Impression: A Field Study of Applicant Impression Management During Interviews," *Journal of Applied Psychology* 80, pp. 587–606; Schultz and Schultz, *Psychology and Work Today*, p. 82. See also Jay Stuller, "Fatal Attraction," *Across the Board* 42, no. 6 (November/December 2005), pp. 18–23.

50. Chad Higgins and Timothy Judge, "The Effect of Applicant Influence Tactics on Recruiter Perceptions of Fit and Hiring Recommendations: A Field Study," *Journal of Applied Psychology* 89, no. 4 (2004), pp. 622–632. Some researchers in this area

question results like these. The problem is that much of the interviewing research uses students as raters and hypothetical jobs, so it's not clear that we can apply the findings to the real world. For example, with respect to age bias in interviews, "Laboratory studies may create too much artificiality," in Frederick P. Morgeson, Matthew H. Reider, Michael A. Campion, and Rebecca A. Bull, "Review of Research on Age Discrimination in the Employment Interview," *Journal of Business Psychology* 22 (2008), 223–232.

51. See, for example, Madeline Heilmann and Lois Saruwatari, "When Beauty Is Beastly: The Effects of Appearance and Sex on Evaluations of Job Applicants for Managerial and Nonmanagerial Jobs," *Organizational Behavior and Human Performance* 23 (June 1979), pp. 360–372; and Cynthia Marlowe, Sandra Schneider, and Carnot Nelson, "Gender and Attractiveness Biases in Hiring Decisions: Are More Experienced Managers Less Biased?" *Journal of Applied Psychology* 81, no. 1 (1996), pp. 11–21.

52. Marlowe et al., "Gender and Attractiveness Biases," p. 11.

53. Allen Huffcutt and Philip Roth, "Racial Group Differences in Employment Interview Evaluations," *Journal of Applied Psychology* 83, no. 2 (1998), pp. 179–189.

54. Eden King and Afra Ahmad, "An Experimental Field Study of Interpersonal Discrimination Toward Muslim Job Applicants," *Personnel Psychology* 63, no. 4 (2010), pp. 881–906.

55. N. S. Miceli et al., "Potential Discrimination in Structured Employment Interviews," *Employee Responsibilities and Rights* 13, no. 1 (March 2001), pp. 15–38.

56. Andrea Rodriguez and Fran Prezant, "Better Interviews for People with Disabilities," *Workforce*, www.workforce.com, accessed November 14, 2003.

57. Pat Tammaro, "Laws to Prevent Discrimination Affect Job Interview Process," *The Houston Business Journal*, June 16, 2000, p. 48.

58. This is based on John F. Wymer III and Deborah A. Sudbury, "Employment Discrimination: 'Testers'—Will Your Hiring Practices 'Pass'?" *Employee Relations Law Journal* 17, no. 4 (Spring 1992), pp. 623–633.

59. Bureau of National Affairs, *Daily Labor Report*, December 5, 1990, p. D1.

60. Wymer and Sudbury, "Employment Discrimination," p. 629.

61. Arthur Pell, "Nine Interviewing Pitfalls," *Managers Magazine*, January 1994, p. 20.

62. Thomas Dougherty, Daniel Turban, and John Callender, "Confirming First Impressions in the Employment Interview: A Field Study of Interviewer Behavior," *Journal of Applied Psychology* 79, no. 5 (1994), p. 663.

63. See Pell, "Nine Interviewing Pitfalls," p. 29; Parth Sarathi, "Making Selection Interviews Effective," *Management and Labor Studies* 18, no. 1 (1993), pp. 5–7.

64. Posthuma, Morgeson, and Campion, "Beyond Employment Interview Validity," pp. 1–87.

65. Pell, "Nine Interviewing Pitfalls," p. 30; quote from, Alan M. Saks and Julie M. McCarthy, "Effects of Discriminatory Interview Questions and Gender on Applicant Reactions," *Journal of Business and Psychology* 21, No. 2 (Winter 2006), p. 175.

66. This section is based on Elliot Pursell et al., "Structured Interviewing," *Personnel Journal* 59 (November 1980), pp. 907–912; and G. Latham et al., "The Situational Interview," *Journal of Applied Psychology* 65 (1980), pp. 422–427. See also Michael Campion, Elliott Pursell, and Barbara Brown, "Structured Interviewing: Raising the Psychometric Properties of the Employment Interview," *Personnel Psychology* 41 (1988), pp. 25–42; and Paul R. Bernthal, "Recruitment and Selection," http://www.ddiworld.com/DDIWorld/media/trend-research/recruitment-and-selection_ere_es_ddi.pdf?ext=.pdf, accessed October 10, 2011. For a recent approach, see K. G. Melchers, et. al., "Is More Structure Really Better? A Comparison of Frame-of-Reference Training and Descriptively Anchored Rating Scales to Improve Interviewers' Rating Quality." *Personnel Psychology* 64, no. 1 (2011), pp. 53–87.

67. Taylor and Small, "Asking Applicants What They Would Do Versus What They Did." Structured employment interviews using either situational questions or behavioral questions tend to yield high validities. However, structured interviews with situational question formats yield the higher ratings. This may be because interviewers get more consistent (reliable) responses with situational questions (which force all applicants to apply the same scenario) than they do with behavioral questions (which require each applicant to find applicable experiences). However, there is some evidence that for higher-level positions, situational question–based interviews are inferior to behavioral question–based ones, possibly because the situations are "just too simple to allow any real differentiation among candidates for higher level positions." Allen Huffcutt et al., "Comparison of Situational and Behavioral Description Interview Questions for Higher Level Positions," *Personnel Psychology* 54, no. 3 (2001), p. 619.

68. See Phillip Lowry, "The Structured Interview: An Alternative to the Assessment Center?" *Public Personnel Management* 23, no. 2 (Summer 1994), pp. 201–215. See also Todd Maurer and Jerry Solomon, "The Science and Practice of a Structured Employment Interview Coaching Program," *Personnel Psychology* 59, no. 2 (Summer 2006), pp. 433–456.

69. Pursell et al., "Structured Interviewing," p. 910.

70. From a speech by industrial psychologist Paul Green and contained in *BNA Bulletin to Management*, June 20, 1985, pp. 2–3.

71. Williamson et al., "Employment Interview on Trial," p. 901; Michael Campion, David Palmer, and James Campion, "A Review of Structure in the Selection Interview," *Personnel Psychology* 50 (1997), pp. 655–702. See also Maurer and Solamon, "The Science and Practice of a Structured Employment Interview."

72. Unless otherwise specified, the following are based on Williamson et al., "Employment Interview on Trial," pp. 901–902.

73. Campion, Palmer, and Campion, "A Review of Structure," p. 668.

74. Carlson, "Selection Interview Decisions."

75. Pamela Kaul, "Interviewing Is Your Business," *Association Management*, November 1992, p. 29. See also Nancy Woodward, "Asking for Salary Histories," *HR Magazine*, February 2000, pp. 109–112. Gathering information about specific interview dimensions such as social ability, responsibility, and independence (as is often done with structured interviews) can improve interview accuracy, at least for more complicated jobs. See also Andrea Poe, "Graduate Work: Behavioral Interviewing Can Tell You If an Applicant Just Out of College Has Traits Needed for the Job," *HR Magazine* 48, no. 10 (October 2003): 95–96.

76. Edwin Walley, "Successful Interviewing Techniques," *The CPA Journal* 63 (September 1993), p. 70; and Randy Myers, "Interviewing Techniques: Tips From the Pros," *Journal of Accountancy* 202, no. 2 (August 2006), pp. 53–55.

77. Catherine Middendorf and Therese Macan, "Note Taking in the Employment Interview: Effects on Recall and Judgment," *Journal of Applied Psychology* 87, no. 2 (2002), pp. 293–303.

78. Weirick, "The Perfect Interview," p. 85.

79. Stephen Gilliland et al., "Improving Applicants' Reactions to Rejection Letters: An Application of Fairness Theory," *Personnel Psychology* 54 (2001), pp. 669–703.

80. Kris Maher, "New High-Tech Recruiting Tools: Unicycles, Yahtzee and Silly Putty," *The Wall Street Journal*, June 6, 2000, p. B14; see also Paul McNamara, "Extreme Interview," *Network World*, June 25, 2001, p. 65.

81. Tim Barker, "Corporate Espionage Takes Center Stage with Boeing Revelation," *Knight Ridder/Tribune Business News*, June 15, 2003.

82. Ibid.

83. See for example the classic excellent discussion of job-hunting and interviewing in Richard Payne, *How to Get a Better Job Quickly* (New York: New American Library, 1979).

APPENDIX 1 FOR CHAPTER 7

How to Create Applicant Interview Guide Process

STEP 1—Create a Structured Interview Guide

Instructions:
First, here in step 1, create a structured interview guide like this one (including a competency definition, a lead question, and benchmark examples and answers, for instance) for each of the job's required competencies:

Competency: Interpersonal Skills

Definition:
Shows understanding, courtesy, tact, empathy, concern; develops and maintains relationships; may deal with people who are difficult, hostile, distressed; relates well to people from varied backgrounds and situations; is sensitive to individual differences.

Lead Questions:
Describe a situation in which you had to deal with people who were upset about a problem. What specific actions did you take? What was the outcome or result?

Benchmark Level	Level Definition	Level Examples
5	Establishes and maintains ongoing working relationships with management, other employees, internal or external stakeholders, or customers. Remains courteous when discussing information or eliciting highly sensitive or controversial information from people who are reluctant to give it. Effectively handles situations involving a high degree of tension or discomfort involving people who are demonstrating a high degree of hostility or distress.	Presents controversial findings tactfully to irate organization senior management officials regarding shortcomings of a newly installed computer system, software programs, and associated equipment.
4		Mediates disputes concerning system design/ architecture, the nature and capacity of data management systems, system resources allocations, or other equally controversial/sensitive matters.
3	Cooperates and works well with management, other employees, or customers, on short-term assignments. Remains courteous when discussing information or eliciting moderately sensitive or controversial information from people who are hesitant to give it. Effectively handles situations involving a moderate degree of tension or discomfort involving people who are demonstrating a moderate degree of hostility or distress.	Courteously and tactfully delivers effective instruction to frustrated customers. Provides technical advice to customers and the public on various types of IT such as communication or security systems, data management procedures or analysis.
2		Familiarizes new employees with administrative procedures and office systems.
1	Cooperates and works well with management, other employees, or customers during brief interactions. Remains courteous when discussing information or eliciting non-sensitive or non-controversial information from people who are willing to give it. Effectively handles situations involving little or no tension, discomfort, hostility, or distress.	Responds courteously to customers' general inquiries. Greets and assists visitors attending a meeting within own organization.

FIGURE 7A-1 Three-Step Structured Interview Guide Process

Source: http://www.state.gov/documents/organization/107843.pdf, and United States Office of Personnel Management. Structured Interviews: Interview Guide and Evaluation Materials for Structured Interviews.

FIGURE 7A-1
(Continued)

STEP 2—INDIVIDUAL EVALUATION FORM

Instructions:
Next, in step 2, create a form for evaluating each job candidate on each of the job's competencies:

Candidate to be assessed: _____

Date of Interview:_____

Problem Solving

Definition:
Identifies problems; determines accuracy and relevance of information; uses sound judgment to generate and evaluate alternatives, and to make the recommendations.

Question:
Describe a situation in which you identified a problem and evaluated the alternatives to make a recommendation or decision. What was the problem and who was affected?

Probes:
How did you generate and evaluate your alternatives? What was the outcome?

Describe specific behaviors observed: (Use back of sheet, if necessary)

1–Low	2	3–Average	4	5–Outstanding
Uses logic to identify alternatives to solve routine problems. Reacts to and solves problems by gathering and applying information from standard materials or sources that provide a limited number of alternatives.		Uses logic to identify alternatives to solve moderately difficult problems. Identifies and solves problems by gathering and applying information from a variety of materials or sources that provide several alternatives.		Uses logic to identify alternatives to solve complex or sensitive problems. Anticipates problems and identifies and evaluates potential sources of information and generates alternatives to solve problems where standards do not exist.

Final Evaluation:	Printed Name:	Signature:

FIGURE 7A-1
(Continued)

STEP 3—PANEL CONSENSUS EVALUATION FORM

Instructions:
Finally, in step 3, create a panel consensus evaluation form like this one, which the members of the panel who interviewed the candidate will use to evaluate his or her interview performance.

Candidate: _____

Date:_____

<table>
<tr><th colspan="5">Panel Consensus Evaluation Form</th></tr>
<tr><td colspan="5">Instructions:
Translate each individual evaluation for each competency onto this form. If all of the individual competency evaluations are within one rating scale point, enter the average of the evaluations in the column labeled Group Evaluation. If more than one point separates any two raters, a consensus discussion must occur with each party justifying his/her evaluation. The lead interviewer or his/her designee should take notes on the consensus discussion in the space provided. Any changes in evaluation should be initialed and a final evaluation entered for each competency.</td></tr>
<tr><th rowspan="2">Competency</th><th colspan="3">Final Individual Evaluations</th><th rowspan="2">Group Evaluation</th></tr>
<tr><th>(1)</th><th>(2)</th><th>(3)</th></tr>
<tr><td>Interpersonal Skills</td><td></td><td></td><td></td><td></td></tr>
<tr><td>Self-Management</td><td></td><td></td><td></td><td></td></tr>
<tr><td>Reasoning</td><td></td><td></td><td></td><td></td></tr>
<tr><td>Decision Making</td><td></td><td></td><td></td><td></td></tr>
<tr><td>Problem Solving</td><td></td><td></td><td></td><td></td></tr>
<tr><td>Oral Communication</td><td></td><td></td><td></td><td></td></tr>
<tr><td>Total Score</td><td></td><td></td><td></td><td></td></tr>
<tr><td colspan="5">Consensus Discussion Notes:</td></tr>
</table>

Signature Panel Member 1: _____

Signature Panel Member 2: _____

Signature Panel Member 3: _____

APPENDIX 2 FOR CHAPTER 7

Interview Guide for Interviewees

Before managers move into positions where they have to interview others, they usually must navigate some interviews themselves. It's therefore useful to apply some of what we discussed in this chapter to navigating one's own interviews. Interviewers will tend to use the interview to try to determine what you are like as a person. In other words, how you get along with other people and your desire to work. They will look first at how you behave. Specifically, they will note whether you respond concisely, cooperate fully in answering questions, state personal opinions when relevant, and keep to the subject at hand; these are very important elements in influencing the interviewer's decision.

There are six things to do to get an extra edge in the interview.

1. **Preparation is essential.** Before the interview, learn all you can about the employer, the job, and the people doing the recruiting. On the Web or at the library, look through business periodicals to find out what is happening in the employer's field. Who is the competition? How are they doing? Try to unearth the employer's problems. Be ready to explain why you think you would be able to solve such problems, citing some of your *specific accomplishments* to make your case.

2. **Uncover the interviewer's real needs.** Spend as little time as possible answering your interviewer's first questions and as much time as possible getting him or her to describe his or her needs. Determine what the person is expecting to accomplish, and the type of person he or she feels is needed. Use open-ended questions here such as, "Could you tell me more about that?"

3. **Relate yourself to the interviewer's needs.** Once you know the type of person your interviewer is looking for and the sorts of problems he or she wants solved, you are in a good position to describe your own accomplishments *in terms of the interviewer's needs.* Start by saying something like, "One of the problem areas you've said is important to you is similar to a problem I once faced." Then state the problem, describe your solution, and reveal the results.[83]

4. **Think before answering.** Answering a question should be a three-step process: Pause—Think—Speak. *Pause* to make sure you understand what the interviewer is driving at, *think* about how to structure your answer, and then *speak.* In your answer, try to emphasize how hiring you will help the interviewer solve his or her problem.

5. **Remember that appearance and enthusiasm are important.** Appropriate clothing, good grooming, a firm handshake, and energy are important. Remember that your *nonverbal behavior* may broadcast more about you than does what you say. Maintain eye contact. In addition, speak with enthusiasm, nod agreement, and remember to take a moment to frame your answer (pause, think, speak) so that you sound articulate and fluent.

6. **Make a good first impression.** Remember that in most cases interviewers make up their minds about the applicant during the early minutes of the interview. A good first impression may turn to bad during the interview, but it is unlikely. Bad first impressions are almost impossible to overcome. Experts suggest paying attention to the following key interviewing considerations:

   - Appropriate clothing
   - Good grooming
   - A firm handshake
   - The appearance of controlled energy
   - Pertinent humor and readiness to smile
   - A genuine interest in the employer's operation and alert attention when the interviewer speaks
   - Pride in past performance
   - An understanding of the employer's needs and a desire to serve them

PART 2 VIDEO CASES APPENDIX

Video Title: Talent Management (The Weather Channel)

SYNOPSIS

This video discusses job analysis in some detail, including how employers use the job analysis, who contributes to a job analysis, and writing the job description and the job specification.

Discussion Questions

1. What job analysis tools would you suggest The Weather Channel use to supplement what it's doing now to analyze jobs?
2. What role do you think job analysis plays in talent management at The Weather Channel? What role should it play?
3. How is human resources at The Weather Channel involved in job analysis?
4. If Taylor asked you what strategic HR is, what would you tell her? Does The Weather Channel seem to be practicing strategic HR? Why or why not?
5. What indications, if any, are there that The Weather Channel takes a talent management approach?

Video Title: Recruiting (Hautelook)

SYNOPSIS

The online fashion retailer Hautelook is growing quickly and needs to recruit new employees at a rapid rate. The video discusses the company's methods for recruiting job applicants and for finding the best potential employees from among its applicants. Hautelook prefers to promote internal job candidates, but also to hire applicants who are most familiar with the company—ideally, previous customers.

Discussion Questions

1. Explain the importance of employee referrals to Hautelook's recruiting.
2. Based on the chapter, what other recruiting tools would you suggest a company like this use, and why?
3. How would you suggest Hautelook deal with the problem of receiving too many résumé applications?
4. Given that it loves to promote internally, what other steps would you suggest Hautelook take to facilitate this?
5. From what Hautelook says, is it really necessary for the company to use employment agencies? Why?

Video Title: Personnel Planning and Recruiting (Gawker Media)

SYNOPSIS

Gawker Media founder Nick Denton analyzes how his company responded to the 2007–2010 recession. A key was planning for staffing levels.

Discussion Questions

1. Based on what we discussed in Chapter 5, what advice would you give Gawker regarding how to improve its personnel planning?

2. How is it that some organizations succeed during a recession?
3. Evaluate Gawker Media's practice of recruiting new writers from the people who comment on its sites. How would you suggest the company improve its recruiting practices overall?

Video Title: Employee Testing and Selection (Patagonia)

SYNOPSIS

Patagonia strives to select employees whose values are in sync with the philosophies and values of the company. The interviewing process is a multi-faceted one, in which candidates take part in several group interviews. These interviews follow a very conversational style, in an attempt to reveal as much about a potential employee's interests, passions, and personality as possible. It is important that those hired by Patagonia not only have an interest in outdoor activities and the products the company produces, but also are passionate about preserving the environment, which is the mission of Patagonia.

Discussion Questions

1. If you had to create a talent management–type job profile for the average employee at Patagonia, what would the profile look like in terms of its specific contents?
2. What traits does Patagonia look for in its future employees during the interview process?
3. In what respects does Patagonia's employee selection process reflect a talent management approach to selection?
4. What is the employee turnover rate at Patagonia? Is this higher or lower than the industry average? What reason can you give for why Patagonia's turnover rate is as you described?
5. Describe the interview process used by Patagonia. How is this process similar to others in the industry? How does the process used by Patagonia differ?

Video Title: Interviewing Candidates (Zipcar)

SYNOPSIS

Zipcar is a company that allows customers to share a car for a fee as small as a short cab ride. Individuals who become Zipcar members are able to reserve a vehicle with as little advance notice as 1 hour through any wireless device, unlock a car with a card that members carry with them, and drive for the reserved period of time. The goal of Zipcar is to reduce the number of cars being driven and thereby reduce environmental pollution.

Zipcar is a fast-growing innovative company that supports the environment and is socially responsible. This makes it an attractive place to work for many who are looking for a company that is doing something new. When selecting new employees, Zipcar aims to find people who are passionate about the brand, professional, courteous, and presentable. It wants someone who understands the value of the organization and the culture within which the company operates.

Discussion Questions

1. What makes Zipcar an attractive employer for which to work?
2. What do those doing the actual hiring at Zipcar feel are important characteristics to find in potential employees?
3. List three behavioral and three situational questions that you would use to interview Zipcar employment applicants.
4. According to the video, what practices should you avoid during an interview? How do these compare with those we discussed in Chapter 7?

8

Training and Developing Employees

Source: Shutterstock.

LEARNING OBJECTIVES

1. Summarize the purpose and process of employee orientation.

2. List and briefly explain each of the four steps in the training process.

3. Describe and illustrate how you would identify training requirements.

4. Explain how to distinguish between problems you can fix with training and those you can't.

5. Discuss how you would motivate trainees.

6. Explain how to use five training techniques.

7. List and briefly discuss four management development programs.

8. List and briefly discuss the importance of the eight steps in leading organizational change.

9. Answer the question, "What is organizational development and how does it differ from traditional approaches to organizational change?"

For about 6 years after its merger with May Department Stores Co., Macy's Inc. was in a consolidation mode. First, it had to concentrate on integrating the regional department store chains under the single Macy's umbrella. Then the 2008 recession hit and the focus shifted to cutting costs. During these years, Macy's customer service suffered. Many Macy's sales associates just weren't providing the level of service that customers wanted. The question was, what should Macy's do about it now?

Access a host of interactive learning aids at **www.mymanagementlab.com** to help strengthen your understanding of the chapter concepts.

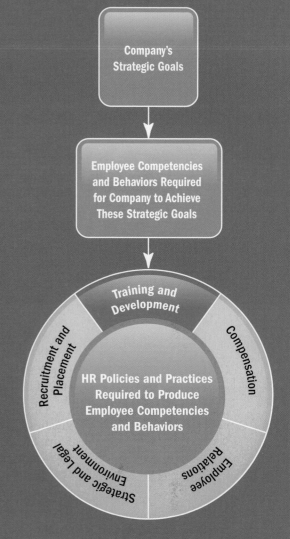

WHERE ARE WE NOW . . .

Chapters 6 and 7 focused on the methods managers use to interview and select employees. Once employees are on board, the employer must train them. The purpose of this chapter is to increase your effectiveness in training employees. The main topics we'll cover include orienting employees, the training process, analyzing training needs, implementing training and development programs, and evaluating the training effort. Then, in Chapter 9, we'll turn to appraising employees.

ORIENTING AND ONBOARDING NEW EMPLOYEES

Carefully selecting employees doesn't guarantee they'll perform effectively. Even high-potential employees can't do their jobs if they don't know what to do or how to do it. Making sure your employees do know what to do and how to do it is the purpose of orientation and training. The human resources department usually designs the company's orientation and training programs, but the rubber hits the road with the supervisor. He or she does most of the day-to-day orienting and training. Every manager therefore needs to know how to orient and train employees. We will start with orientation.

The Purposes of Employee Orientation/Onboarding

1 Summarize the purpose and process of employee orientation.

Employee orientation (or "onboarding") involves more than what most people realize.[1] **Employee orientation** still provides new employees with the information they need to function (such as computer passwords and company rules); ideally, though, it should also help new employees start getting emotionally attached to the firm. You want to accomplish four things by orienting new employees:

1. Make the new employee feel welcome and at home and part of the team.
2. Make sure the new employee has the basic information to function effectively, such as e-mail access, personnel policies and benefits, and what the employer expects in terms of work behavior.
3. Help the new employee understand the organization in a broad sense (its past, present, culture, and strategies and vision of the future).
4. Start the person on becoming socialized into the firm's culture, values, and ways of doing things.[2]

Getting the new employee to appreciate the company's culture and values distinguishes today's *onboarding* programs from traditional orientation.[3] For example, the Mayo Clinic's new "heritage and culture" program emphasizes core Mayo Clinic values such as teamwork, personal responsibility, innovation, integrity, diversity, customer service, and mutual respect.[4]

The Orientation Process

The length of the orientation program depends on what you cover. Traditional orientation programs take several hours. The human resource specialist (or, in smaller firms, the office manager) usually performs the first part of the orientation by explaining basic matters like working hours, benefits, and vacations. That person then introduces the new employee to his or her new supervisor. The supervisor continues the orientation by explaining (see Figure 8-1) the organization of the department and by introducing the person to his or her new colleagues, familiarizing the new employee with the workplace, and helping to reduce first-day jitters. Supervisors need to be vigilant. Follow up on and encourage new employees to engage in activities (such as taking breaks with current employees) that will enable each to "learn the ropes" and become productive. In firms like Toyota Motor USA, onboarding-type orientations take up to a week. These may include videos, lectures by company officers, and exercises covering matters like company history, vision, and values.

At a minimum, as in Figure 8-1, an orientation typically includes information on employee benefits, personnel policies, the daily routine, company organization and operations, safety measures and regulations, and a facilities tour.[5] New employees should receive (and sign for) print or Internet-based employee handbooks covering matters like these.

THE EMPLOYEE HANDBOOK Note that under certain conditions, courts may find that the employee handbook's contents represent legally binding employment commitments. Therefore, employers often include disclaimers. These make it clear that statements of company policies, benefits, and regulations do not constitute the terms and conditions of an employment contract, either expressed or implied. Also,

UNIVERSITY *of* CALIFORNIA, SAN DIEGO
MEDICAL CENTER

NEW EMPLOYEE DEPARTMENTAL ORIENTATION CHECKLIST
(Return to Human Resources within 10 days of Hire)

NAME:	HIRE DATE:	SSN:	JOB TITLE:
DEPARTMENT:	NEO DATE:	DEPARTMENTAL ORIENTATION COMPLETED BY:	

TOPIC	DATE REVIEWED	N/A
1. HUMAN RESOURCES INFORMATION a. Departmental Attendance Procedures and UCSD Medical Center Work Time & Attendance Policy b. Job Description Review c. Annual Performance Evaluation and Peer Feedback Process d. Probationary Period Information e. Appearance/Dress Code Requirements f. Annual TB Screening g. License and/or Certification Renewals	a. ____ b. ____ c. ____ d. ____ e. ____ f. ____ g. ____	☐☐☐☐☐☐☐
2. DEPARTMENT INFORMATION a. Organizational Structure-Department Core Values Orientation b. Department/Unit Area Specific Policies & Procedures c. Customer Service Practices d. CQI Effort and Projects e. Tour and Floor Plan f. Equipment/Supplies • Keys issued • Radio Pager issued • Other ____ g. Mail and Recharge Codes	a. ____ b. ____ c. ____ d. ____ e. ____ f. ____ ____ ____ ____ g. ____	☐☐☐☐☐☐☐☐☐☐
3. SAFETY INFORMATION a. Departmental Safety Plan b. Employee Safety/Injury Reporting Procedures c. Hazard Communication d. Infection Control/Sharps Disposal e. Attendance at annual Safety Fair (mandatory)	a. ____ b. ____ c. ____ d. ____ e. ____	☐☐☐☐☐
4. FACILITES INFORMATION a. Emergency Power b. Mechanical Systems c. Water d. Medical Gases e. Patient Room • Bed • Headwall • Bathroom • Nurse Call System	a. ____ b. ____ c. ____ d. ____ e. ____ ____ ____ ____ ____	☐☐☐☐☐☐☐☐
5. SECURITY INFORMATION a. Code Triage Assignment b. Code Blue Assignment c. Code Red – Evacuation Procedure d. Code 10 – Bomb Threat Procedure e. Departmental Security Measures f. UCSD Emergency Number 6111 or 911	a. ____ b. ____ c. ____ d. ____ e. ____ f. ____	☐☐☐☐☐☐

This generic checklist may not constitute a complete departmental orientation or assessment. Please attach any additional unit specific orientation material for placement in the employee's HR file

I have been oriented on the items listed above_____

D1999(R7-01)   **WHITE** – HR Records (8912)   **Yellow** – Department Retains

FIGURE 8-1 New Employee Departmental Orientation Checklist

Source: Used with permission of UC San Diego Medical Center.

employers generally should not insert statements such as "No employee will be fired without just cause" or statements that imply or state that employees have tenure. Indeed, it's best to emphasize that the employment relationship is strictly "at-will."

employee orientation
A procedure for providing new employees with basic background information about the firm.

ORIENTATION TECHNOLOGY   Employers use technology to support orientation. For example, some employers put all or some of their orientation media on the Web. At the University of Cincinnati, new employees spend about 45 minutes online learning about their new employer's mission, organization, and policies and procedures. IBM uses virtual environments like Second Life to support orientation, particularly for employees abroad. The new employees choose virtual avatars, which then interact with other company avatars, for instance to learn how to enroll for benefits.[6] ION Geophysical uses an online onboarding portal solution called RedCarpet. Ion's CEO uses RedCarpet to offer a streaming video welcome message. New hires can view things like photos and profiles of members of their work teams.[7] With Workday's iPhone app, employers can provide their employees easy mobile access to their employee directories. Users can search their company's worker directory for names, images, and contact information; call or e-mail coworkers directly; and view physical addresses on Google Maps.[8]

OVERVIEW OF THE TRAINING PROCESS

Directly after orientation, training should begin. **Training** means giving new or current employees the skills that they need to perform their jobs. This might mean showing new Web designers the intricacies of your site, new salespeople how to sell your firm's product, or new supervisors how to complete the firm's weekly payroll. It might involve simply having the current jobholder explain the job to the new hire, or a multi-week training process including classroom or Internet classes.

In any case, training is a task that managers ignore at their peril. Having high-potential employees doesn't guarantee they'll succeed. They must know what to do and how to do it. If they don't, they will improvise or do nothing useful at all.

Inadequate training can also trigger **negligent training** liability. As one expert puts it, "It's clear from the case law that where an employer fails to train adequately and an employee subsequently does harm to third parties, the court will find the employer liable."[9] Employers should confirm the applicant/employee's claims of skill and experience, provide adequate training (particularly where employees use dangerous equipment), and evaluate the training to ensure that it's actually reducing risks.

Aligning Strategy and Training

The employer's strategic plans should ultimately govern its training goals.[10] In essence, the task is to identify the employee behaviors the firm will require to execute its strategy, and from that deduce what competencies employees will need. Then, put in place training goals and programs to instill these competencies. As one trainer said, "We sit down with management and help them identify strategic goals and objectives and the skills and knowledge needed to achieve them."[11] For example, Caterpillar Inc. created Caterpillar University to oversee all its training and development programs. Company executives comprise the university's board of directors. They set the university's policies and oversee "the alignment of the corporation's learning needs with the enterprises' business strategy."[12] The accompanying Strategic Context feature illustrates strategy's role in training and development.

THE STRATEGIC CONTEXT

Having spent about 6 years consolidating and cutting costs to navigate its way through the recession, Macy's top management turned to a new strategy in 2011. As its CEO said, "We are [now] talking about a cultural shift . . . becoming more of a growth company."[13] However, Macy's top management knew that growth would not occur without a dramatic improvement in how its sales associates treated customers. (For example, studies by the consulting firm Bain & Co. showed that when customers had positive interactions with sales associates, customer purchases rose by as much as 50%.) To produce the improved customer service that Macy's new growth strategy depended on, Macy's installed a new training program. Rather than just watching a 90-minute interactive video as they previously did, sales associates now attended 3½-hour training sessions aimed at cultivating higher levels of customer service. Macy's management believes the training program and resulting improvement in customer service will be the biggest factor in achieving Macy's projected 3% growth in 2011 sales.[14]

Training and Performance

One survey found that "establishing a linkage between learning and organizational performance" was the number-one pressing issue facing training professionals.[15] Training experts often use the phrase "workplace learning and performance" in lieu of training to underscore training's dual aims of employee learning and organizational performance.[16] Training has an impressive record of influencing performance. It scores higher than appraisal and feedback and just below goal setting in its effect on productivity.[17] Companies recently spent on average $1,103 per employee for training per year and offered each about 28 hours of training.[18]

The ADDIE Five-Step Training Process

<table>
<tr><td>2</td><td>List and briefly explain each of the five steps in the training process.</td></tr>
</table>

Creating a training program involves more than contracting with an online training vendor and requiring your employees to take the course. The employer should use a rational training process. The gold standard here is still the basic analysis-design-develop-implement-evaluate (ADDIE) training process model that training experts have used for years.[19] As an example, one training vendor describes its training process as follows: [20]

- *Analyze* the training need.
- *Design* the overall training program.
- *Develop* the course (actually assembling/creating the training materials).
- *Implement* training, by actually training the targeted employee group using methods such as on-the-job or online training.
- *Evaluate* the course's effectiveness.

We'll look at each step next.

Conducting the Training Needs Analysis

The training needs analysis should address the employer's *strategic/longer term* training needs and/or its *current* training needs. If the program is to use technology, the manager should also include a review of the technology he or she plans to use for presenting the program, as part of the analysis. [21]

STRATEGIC TRAINING NEEDS ANALYSIS   Strategic goals (perhaps to enter new lines of business or to expand abroad) usually mean the firm will have to fill new jobs. *Strategic training needs analysis* focuses on identifying the training that employees will need to fill these new future jobs. For example, when Wisconsin-based Signicast Corp. decided to build a new, high-tech plant, the firm's top management knew the plant's employees would need new skills to run the computerized machines. They worked closely with their HR team to formulate hiring policies and training programs to ensure the firm would have the human resources required to populate the new plant.

Strategic training needs analysis is tied to succession planning. The latter, recall, means identifying the training and development that employees need to fill the firm's key positions, and then formulating plans to ensure that high-potential employees get the training and development to fill the firm's future positions.

---

training
The process of teaching new or current employees the basic skills they need to perform their jobs.

negligent training
A situation where an employer fails to train adequately, and the employee subsequently harms a third party.

CURRENT TRAINING NEEDS ANALYSIS   As important as strategic training is, most training efforts aim to improve current performance—specifically training new employees, and those whose performance is deficient.

How you analyze current training needs depends on whether you're training new or current employees. The main task in analyzing *new* employees' needs is to determine what the job entails and to break it down into subtasks, each of which you then teach to the new employee.

Analyzing *current* employees' training needs is more complex, because you must also decide whether training is the solution. For example, performance may be down because the standards aren't clear or because the person isn't motivated. Managers use *task analysis* to identify new employees' training needs, and *performance analysis* to identify current employees' training needs.

3 Describe and illustrate how you would identify training requirements.

TASK ANALYSIS: ANALYZING NEW EMPLOYEES' TRAINING NEEDS
Particularly with lower-level workers, it's common to hire inexperienced personnel and train them. Your aim here is to give these new employees the skills and knowledge they need to do the job. **Task analysis** is a detailed study of the job to determine what specific skills—like Java (in the case of a Web developer) or interviewing (in the case of a supervisor)—the job requires. For task analysis, job descriptions and job specifications are essential. These list the job's specific duties and skills, which are the basic reference points in determining the training required. Managers can also uncover training needs by reviewing performance standards, performing the job, and questioning current job holders and their supervisors.[22]

Some managers supplement the job description and specification with a *task analysis record form*. This consolidates information regarding required tasks and skills in a form that's especially helpful for determining training requirements. As Table 8-1 illustrates, the task analysis record form contains six types of information, such as "Skills or knowledge required."

TALENT MANAGEMENT: USING PROFILES AND COMPETENCY MODELS
Talent management is the goal-oriented and integrated process of planning for, recruiting, selecting, developing, and compensating employees. Among other things, talent management involves using the same competencies profile or model for recruiting the employee as for selecting, training, appraising, and paying him or her. For training, we can summarize this as follows:

Strategy → Employee Behaviors → Employee Competencies → Training and Development Needs → Training Implementation and Evaluation.

Many employers (including Sharp Electronics and IBM) therefore use competency models to help compile and summarize a job's training needs. The **competency model** consolidates, usually in one diagram, a precise overview of the competencies (the knowledge, skills, and behaviors) someone would need to do a job well. As noted, the employer can then formulate training goals and programs aimed at developing these competencies.

As an example, recall Figure 4-10 (page 129), the competency model for a human resource manager in Chapter 4. Recall that the top of the pyramid shows four main roles the human resource manager needs to fill. Beneath that are the areas of expertise such as selection and training, in which he or she must be expert in order to carry out these roles. Beneath are the HR manager's essential, "foundation" competencies, such as communicating effectively.[23]

The model's aim is to identify and compile in one place the competencies for executing the job. At Sharp, training managers interview senior executives to identify the firm's strategic objectives and to infer what competencies those objectives will require. Trainers also interview each job's top performers to identify the competencies (such as "able to focus on the customer") the latter believe comprise the job's core competencies. Subsequent training then aims to develop these competencies.[24]

As we've seen, the employer can use a competency model such as in Figure 4-10 to support all its talent management functions, such as selection and training.

TABLE 8-1 Sample Task Analysis Record Form

Task List		When and How Often Performed	Quantity and Quality of Performance	Conditions Under Which Performed	Skills or Knowledge Required	Where Best Learned
1.	Operate paper cutter	4 times per day		Noisy pressroom: distractions		
1.1	Start motor	4 times per day				On the job
1.2	Set cutting distance		± tolerance of 0.007 in.		Read gauge	On the job
1.3	Place paper on cutting table		Must be completely even to prevent uneven cut		Lift paper correctly	On the job
1.4	Push paper up to cutter				Must be even	On the job
1.5	Grasp safety release with left hand		100% of time, for safety		Essential for safety	On the job but practice first with no distractions
1.6	Grasp cutter release with right hand				Must keep both hands on releases	On the job but practice first with no distractions
1.7	Simultaneously pull safety release with left hand and cutter release with right hand				Must keep both hands on releases	On the job but practice first with no distractions
1.8	Wait for cutter to retract		100% of time, for safety		Must keep both hands on releases	On the job but practice first with no distractions
1.9	Retract paper				Wait until cutter retracts	On the job but practice first with no distractions
1.10	Shut off		100% of time, for safety			On the job but practice first with no distractions
2.	Operate printing press					
2.1	Start motor					

Note: Task analysis record form showing some of the tasks and subtasks performed by a printing press operator.

Thus *selecting* employees based on this model helps to ensure that you focus your questions on the things that someone must be proficient at to do this job successfully. The same model would help you to formulate training objectives. Thus a training objective for "testing skills" might be, "By completion of the ABC Company's HR manager training program, the trainee will be fully skilled at using the five testing tools that ABC uses to test its job applicants."

> **4** Explain how to distinguish between problems you can fix with training and those you can't.

PERFORMANCE ANALYSIS: ANALYZING CURRENT EMPLOYEES' TRAINING NEEDS For underperforming current employees, you can't assume that training is the problem. In other words, is it lack of training, or something else? **Performance analysis** is the process of verifying that there is a performance

---

task analysis
A detailed study of a job to identify the specific skills required.

competency model
A graphic model that consolidates, usually in one diagram, a precise overview of the competencies (the knowledge, skills, and behaviors) someone would need to do a job well.

performance analysis
Verifying that there is a performance deficiency and determining whether that deficiency should be corrected through training or through some other means (such as transferring the employee).

deficiency and determining whether the employer should correct such deficiencies through training or some other means (like transferring the employee).

The first step in performance analysis is usually to compare the person's actual performance to what it should be. Doing so helps to confirm that there is a performance deficiency, and (hopefully) helps the manager to identify its cause. Examples of performance deficiencies might be:

> *I expect each salesperson to make 10 new contracts per week, but John averages only six.*
>
> *Other plants our size average no more than two serious accidents per month; we're averaging five.*

There are several ways to identify how a current employee is doing. These include reviewing:

- Performance appraisals
- Job-related performance data (including productivity, absenteeism and tardiness, grievances, waste, late deliveries, product quality, downtime, repairs, equipment utilization, and customer complaints)
- Observations by supervisors or other specialists
- Interviews with the employee or his or her supervisor
- Tests of things like job knowledge, skills, and attendance
- Attitude surveys
- Individual employee daily diaries
- Assessment center results
- Special performance gap analytical software, such as from Saba Software, Inc.

CAN'T DO/WON'T DO   Ferreting out why performance is down is the heart of performance analysis. Why spend time training inefficient employees when the problem isn't training, but weak motivation?

The manager's aim is thus to distinguish between can't-do and won't-do problems. First, determine whether it is a *can't-do* problem and, if so, its specific causes. For example: The employees don't know what to do or what your standards are; there are obstacles in the system such as lack of tools or supplies; there are no job aids (such as color-coded wires that show assemblers which wire goes where); you've hired people who haven't the skills to do the job; or there is inadequate training.

On the other hand, it might be a *won't-do* problem. Here employees could do a good job if they wanted to. One expert says, "Perhaps the biggest trap that trainers fall into is [developing] training for problems that training just won't fix."[25] For instance, the solution may be to change the reward system.

Designing the Training Program

Armed with the needs analysis results, the manager next designs the overall training program. *Design* means planning the overall training program including training objectives, delivery methods, and program evaluation. Sub-steps include setting performance objectives, creating a detailed training outline (all training program steps from start to finish), choosing a program delivery method (such as lectures or Web), and verifying the overall program design with management. The design should include summaries of how you plan to set a training environment that motivates your trainees both to learn and to transfer what they learn to the job. It is also at the design stage that the manager reviews possible training program content (including workbooks, exercises, and activities), and estimates a budget for the training program.[26] We'll look more closely next at several specific program design issues. (Chapter 18 describes a streamlined training design process for a small business.)

SETTING LEARNING OBJECTIVES   Requests for training often start with line managers presenting concerns, such as "we're getting too many complaints from call

Most employers can build training programs like this one based on existing online and offline content offered by training content providers.

Source: Kim Kulish/Corbis Images.

center callers."[27] Training, development, or (more generally) *instructional objectives* should specify in measurable terms what the trainee should be able to accomplish after successfully completing the training program.[28] For example:

> The technical service representative will be able to adjust the color guidelines on this HP Officejet All-in-One printer copier within 10 minutes according to the device's specifications.

The learning objectives you choose should address rectifying the performance deficiencies that you identified with needs analysis. Thus, if the sales team's sales are 40% too low, the objectives should focus on ensuring they get the knowledge, skills, and attitudes they need to boost sales. But at the same time, the learning objectives must be practical, given the constraints. One constraint is financial. For all but the most trivial training programs, the employer will want to see and approve a *training budget* for the program. Typical costs include the development costs (of having, say, a human resource specialist working on the program for a week or two), the direct and indirect (overhead) costs of the trainers' time, participant compensation (for the time they're actually being trained), and the cost of evaluating the program. The question, of course, isn't just "Can we afford this program?" but "Does it pay to spend this much, given the benefits we'll devise from the program?" Therefore, be prepared to defend the training program on benefits-versus-costs grounds. There are also other constraints to consider. For example, time constraints may require reducing three or four desirable learning objectives down to one or two.

CREATING A MOTIVATIONAL LEARNING ENVIRONMENT Municipalities running driver's ed programs for traffic violators know there's often no better way to get a learner's attention than by presenting a terrifying filmed accident. In other words, they start the training not with a lecture but by making the material meaningful. They know that driver training is futile if the driver isn't motivated to benefit from the program.

The same is true in schools and at work. Learning requires both ability and motivation, and the training program's learning environment should take both into account. First, in terms of *ability*, the learner–trainee needs (among other things) the required reading, writing, and mathematics skills, and the educational level, intelligence, and knowledge base. It is rare that the prospective trainees will be homogeneous, for instance, in terms of intellectual capacity. Employees instinctively understand that if the material you want them to learn is beyond their ability to master, the training is a waste of time. In setting the learning environment, the manager therefore has to address several trainee-related ability issues. For example, how will our program accommodate differences in trainee abilities? Do we need to provide remedial training? And, do we need to use more personal, one-on-one trainers given our trainees' abilities?

Second, as every student (and driver's ed program) knows, the learner must also be motivated to learn the material. No manager should want to waste his or her time showing a disinterested employee how to do something (even if he or she has the requisite ability).

Many books have been written about how to motivate employees, but several specific observations are pertinent here.[29] It's likely that the training program's effects will be diminished if trainees return to their jobs to snide comments such as, "I hope you liked your little vacation" from peers or supervisors. Therefore, the low-hanging fruit in motivating trainees is to make sure the trainee's peers and supervisor support the training effort. Ideally, particularly for larger programs, top management should visibly support the program. Beyond that, various motivation theories provide useful guidance. From behavior modification, we know that the training should provide opportunities for positive reinforcement. Expectancy theory shows us that the trainees need to know they have the ability to succeed in the program, and that the value to them of completing the program is high. Self-efficacy is crucial—trainees must believe they have the capacity to succeed. We can summarize such motivational points as follows.

5   Discuss how you would motivate trainees.

MAKING THE LEARNING MEANINGFUL   Learners are always more motivated to learn something that has meaning for them. Therefore:

1. At the start of training, provide a bird's-eye view of the material that you are going to present. For example, show why it's important, and provide an overview.[30]
2. Use a variety of familiar examples.
3. Organize the information so you can present it logically, and in meaningful units.
4. Use terms and concepts that are already familiar to trainees.
5. Use as many visual aids as possible.
6. Again, create a perceived training need in trainees' minds.[31] In one study, pilots who experienced pretraining, accident-related events subsequently learned more from an accident-reduction training program than did those experiencing fewer such events.[32] Similarly, "before the training, managers need to sit down and talk with the trainee about why they are enrolled in the class, what they are expected to learn, and how they can use it on the job."[33]

MAKING SKILLS TRANSFER OBVIOUS AND EASY   Make it easy to *transfer* new skills and behaviors from the training site to the job site:

1. Maximize the similarity between the training situation and the work situation.
2. Provide adequate practice.
3. Label or identify each feature of the machine and/or step in the process.
4. Direct the trainees' attention to important aspects of the job. For example, if you're training a customer service rep to handle calls, explain the different types of calls he or she will encounter.[34]
5. Provide "heads-up" information. For example, supervisors often face stressful conditions. You can reduce the negative impact of such events by letting supervisory trainees know they might occur.[35]
6. Trainees learn best at their own pace. If possible, let them pace themselves.

REINFORCING THE LEARNING   Make sure the learner gets plenty of feedback. In particular:

1. Trainees learn best when the trainers immediately reinforce correct responses, perhaps with a quick "well done."
2. The schedule is important. The learning curve goes down late in the day, so that "full day training is not as effective as half the day or three-fourths of the day."
3. Provide follow-up assignments at the close of training, so trainees are reinforced by having to apply back on the job what they've learned.[36]

ENSURING TRANSFER OF LEARNING TO THE JOB   Unfortunately, less than 35% of trainees seem to be transferring what they learned in training to their jobs a year after training. Improving on that sad statistic requires taking special steps at each stage of training. *Prior to training*, get trainee and supervisor input in designing the program, institute a training attendance policy, and encourage employees to participate. *During training*, provide trainees with training experiences and conditions (surroundings, equipment) that resemble the actual work environment. *After training*, reinforce what trainees learned, for instance, by appraising and rewarding employees for using new skills, and by making sure that they have the tools and materials they need to use their new skills.[37]

OTHER TRAINING DESIGN ISSUES   Managers address several other issues during the training design stage. Most importantly, they review relevant alternative training methodologies (lectures, Web-based, and so on) and choose likely methods for their program. They also decide how they will organize the various training content components, choose how to evaluate the program, develop an overall summary plan for the program, and obtain management's approval to move ahead.

Developing the Program

Program development means actually assembling/creating the program's training content and materials. It means choosing the actual content the program will present, as well as designing/choosing the specific instructional methods (lectures, cases, Web-based, etc.) you will use. Training equipment and materials include (for example) iPads, workbooks, lectures, PowerPoint slides, Web- and computer-based activities, course activities, trainer resources (manuals, for instance), and support materials.

Some employers create their own training content, but there's also a vast selection of online and offline content from which to choose. You'll find turnkey, off-the-shelf programs on virtually any topic—from occupational safety to sexual harassment to Web design—from tens of thousands of online and offline providers. (See, for example, the American Society for Training and Development's Infoline at www.astd.org, www.trainerswarehouse.com, and www.gneil.com, among thousands of such suppliers.)[38] Turnkey training packages often include trainer's guide, self-study book, video, and other content.

Once you design, approve, and develop the program, management can implement and then evaluate it. *Implement* means to actually provide the training, using one or more of the instructional methods (such as lectures) that we discuss next. We address program *evaluation* at the end of this chapter.

IMPLEMENTING TRAINING PROGRAMS

> **6** Explain how to use five training techniques.

With objectives set and the program designed and budgeted, you can turn to implementing the training program. This means actually doing the training, using one or more of the training methods we turn to now. We'll start with simpler, low-tech methods and proceed to computer-based ones.

On-the-Job Training

On-the-job training (OJT) means having a person learn a job by actually doing it. Every employee, from mailroom clerk to CEO, gets on-the-job training when he or she joins a firm. In many firms, OJT is the only training available.[39] (Or worse: All too often the supervisor simply says, "Here's your desk; get started.")

on-the-job training
Training a person to learn a job while working on it.

TYPES OF ON-THE-JOB TRAINING   The most familiar on-the-job training is the *coaching or understudy method*. Here, an experienced worker or the trainee's supervisor trains the employee. This may involve simply acquiring skills by observing the supervisor, or (preferably) having the supervisor or job expert show the new employee the ropes, step-by-step. On-the-job training is part of multifaceted training at The Men's Wearhouse. It combines on-the-job training with comprehensive initiation programs and continuing-education seminars. Every Men's Wearhouse manager is accountable for the development of his or her direct subordinates.[40] *Job rotation*, in which an employee (usually a management trainee) moves from job to job at planned intervals, is another OJT technique. *Special assignments* similarly give lower-level executives firsthand experience in working on actual problems.

It is important that employers don't take the success of an on-the-job training effort for granted. Instead, the employer should formally plan out and structure the OJT process and experience. Train the trainers themselves (often the employees' supervisors), and provide the training materials. Trainers should know, for instance, the principles of motivating learners. Because low expectations may translate into poor trainee performance, supervisor/trainers should emphasize their high expectations. Many firms use "peer training" for OJT; for instance expert employees answer calls at selected times during the day or participate in in-house "radio programs" to answer their peers' call-in questions about technical aspects of doing their jobs.[41] Others use employee teams (instead of training professionals) to analyze the jobs and prepare training materials. The employees, already job experts, reportedly conduct task analyses more quickly and effectively than do training experts.[42]

THE OJT PROCES   Here are some steps to help ensure OJT success.

Step 1: Prepare the Learner

1. Put the learner at ease.
2. Explain why he or she is being taught.
3. Create interest and find out what the learner already knows about the job.
4. Explain the whole job and relate it to some job the worker already knows.
5. Place the learner as close to the normal working position as possible.
6. Familiarize the worker with equipment, materials, tools, and trade terms.

Step 2: Present the Operation

1. Explain quantity and quality requirements.
2. Go through the job at the normal work pace.
3. Go through the job at a slow pace several times, explaining each step. Between operations, explain the difficult parts, or those in which errors are likely to be made.
4. Again, go through the job at a slow pace several times; explain the key points.
5. Have the learner explain the steps as you go through the job at a slow pace.

Step 3: Do a Tryout

1. Have the learner go through the job several times, slowly, explaining each step to you. Correct mistakes and, if necessary, do some of the complicated steps the first few times.
2. Run the job at the normal pace.
3. Have the learner do the job, gradually building up skill and speed.
4. As soon as the learner demonstrates ability to do the job, let the work begin, but don't abandon him or her.

Step 4: Follow-Up

1. Designate to whom the learner should go for help.
2. Gradually decrease supervision, checking work from time to time.
3. Correct faulty work patterns before they become a habit. Show why the method you suggest is superior.
4. Compliment good work.

Apprenticeship Training

Apprenticeship training is a process by which people become skilled workers, usually through a combination of formal learning and long-term on-the-job training. It traditionally involves having the learner/apprentice study under the tutelage of a master craftsperson. When steelmaker Dofasco discovered that many of their employees would be retiring during the next 5 to 10 years, the company decided to revive its apprenticeship training. Applicants are prescreened. New recruits then spend about 32 months in an internal apprenticeship training program, learning various jobs under the tutelage of experienced employees.[43]

The U.S. Department of Labor's National Apprenticeship System promotes apprenticeship programs. More than 460,000 apprentices participate in 28,000 programs, and registered programs can receive federal and state contracts and other assistance.[44] Figure 8-2 lists popular recent apprenticeships.

Informal Learning

Surveys from the American Society for Training and Development estimate that as much as 80% of what employees learn on the job they learn through informal means, including performing their jobs on a daily basis with their colleagues.[45]

Although managers don't manage informal learning, there's still much they can do to ensure that it occurs. Most of the steps are simple. For example, Siemens Power Transmission and Distribution in Raleigh, North Carolina, places tools in cafeteria areas to take advantage of the work-related discussions taking place. Even installing whiteboards with markers can facilitate informal learning. Sun Microsystems implemented an informal online learning tool it called Sun Learning eXchange. This has evolved into a platform containing more than 5,000 informal learning items/suggestions addressing topics ranging from sales to technical support.[46]

Job Instruction Training

Many jobs (or parts of jobs) consist of a sequence of steps that one best learns step-by-step. Such step-by-step training is called **job instruction training (JIT)**. First, list the job's required steps (let's say for using a mechanical paper cutter) each in its proper sequence. Then (see the following page) list a corresponding "key point" (if any) beside each step. The steps in such a *job instruction training sheet* show trainees what to do, and the key points show how it's to be done—and why.

As an example, when training new UPS drivers to park and disembark, the company leaves nothing to chance. Among the steps it teaches new drivers are these: Shift into the

FIGURE 8-2 Some Popular Apprenticeships

Source: www.doleta.gov/oa, accessed July 3, 2009.

The U.S. Department of Labor's Registered Apprenticeship program offers access to 1,000 career areas, including the following top occupations:

- Able seaman
- Carpenter
- Chef
- Child care development specialist
- Construction craft laborer
- Dental assistant
- Electrician
- Elevator constructor
- Fire medic
- Law enforcement agent
- Over-the-road truck driver
- Pipefitter

apprenticeship training
A structured process by which people become skilled workers through a combination of classroom instruction and on-the-job training.

job instruction training (JIT)
Listing each job's basic tasks, along with key points, in order to provide step-by-step training for employees.

Steps	Key Points
1. Start motor	None
2. Set cutting distance	Carefully read scale—to prevent wrong-sized cut
3. Place paper on cutting table	Make sure paper is even—to prevent uneven cut
4. Push paper up to cutter	Make sure paper is tight—to prevent uneven cut
5. Grasp safety release with left hand	Do not release left hand—to prevent hand from being caught in cutter
6. Grasp cutter release with right hand	Do not release right hand—to prevent hand from being caught in cutter
7. Simultaneously pull cutter and safety releases	Keep both hands on corresponding releases—avoid hands being on cutting table
8. Wait for cutter to retract	Keep both hands on releases—to avoid having hands on cutting table
9. Retract paper	Make sure cutter is retracted; keep both hands away from releases
10. Shut off motor	None

lowest gear or into park; turn off the ignition; apply the parking brake; release the seatbelt with your left hand; open the door; and place the key on your ring finger.[47]

Lectures

Lecturing is a quick and simple way to present knowledge to large groups of trainees, as when the sales force needs to learn a new product's features.[48] Here are some guidelines for presenting a lecture:[49]

- Don't start out on the wrong foot. For instance, don't open with an irrelevant joke.
- Speak only about what you know well.
- Give your listeners signals. For instance, if you have a list of items, start by saying something like, "There are four reasons why the sales reports are necessary. . . . The first . . ."
- Use anecdotes and stories to show rather than tell.
- Be alert to your audience. Watch body language for negative signals like fidgeting. If they're not looking at you, they may be bored.
- Maintain eye contact with the audience.
- Make sure everyone in the room can hear. Repeat questions that you get from trainees.
- Control your hands. Leave them hanging naturally at your sides.
- Talk from notes rather than from a script. Write out notes on large index cards or on PowerPoint slides. Use these as an outline.
- Break a long talk into a series of short talks. Speakers often give a short overview introduction and then spend the rest of a 1-hour presentation going point by point through their material. Experts suggest instead breaking the long talk into a series of 10-minute talks, each with its own introduction. Write brief PowerPoint slides, and spend about a minute on each. Each introduction highlights what you'll discuss, why it's important to the audience, and your credibility—why they should listen to you.[50]
- Practice. If possible, rehearse under conditions similar to those under which you will actually give your presentation.

Programmed Learning

Whether the medium is a textbook, PC, or the Internet, **programmed learning** (or *programmed instruction*) is a step-by-step, self-learning method that consists of three parts:

1. Presenting questions, facts, or problems to the learner
2. Allowing the person to respond
3. Providing feedback on the accuracy of answers, with instructions on what to do next

Generally, programmed learning presents facts and follow-up questions frame by frame. When the learner responds, subsequent frames provide feedback on the answer's accuracy. What the next question is often depends on how the learner answers the previous question. The built-in feedback from the answers provides reinforcement.

Programmed learning reduces training time. It also facilitates learning by letting trainees learn at their own pace, get immediate feedback, and reduce their risk of error. Some argue that trainees do not learn much more from programmed learning than from a textbook. Yet studies generally support programmed learning's effectiveness. A typical study focused on 40 second year undergraduate students in an organic chemistry-I course. Some studied in a conventional lecture setting and others used programmed learning. The researchers concluded that "The findings suggest that programmed learning could be considered as a better alternative to conventional lecturing in teaching stereochemistry."[51]

Intelligent tutoring systems take programmed learning one step further. In addition to the usual programmed learning, computerized intelligent tutoring systems learn what questions and approaches worked and did not work for the learner, and then adjust the instructional sequence to the trainee's unique needs.

Audiovisual-Based Training

Although increasingly replaced by Web-based methods, audiovisual-based training techniques like DVDs, films, PowerPoint, and audiotapes are still popular.[52] The Ford Motor Company uses videos in its dealer training sessions to simulate problems and reactions to various customer complaints, for example. Consider using them in the following situations:

1. When there is a need to illustrate how to follow a certain sequence over time, such as when teaching machine repair. The stop-action, instant replay, and fast- or slow-motion capabilities of audiovisuals can be useful here.

2. When there is a need to show trainees events not easily demonstrable in live lectures, such as a visual tour of a factory.

Vestibule Training

With vestibule training, trainees learn on the actual or simulated equipment they will use on the job, but are trained off the job (perhaps in a separate room or *vestibule*). Vestibule training is necessary when it's too costly or dangerous to train employees on the job. Putting new assembly-line workers right to work could slow production, for instance, and when safety is a concern—as with pilots—simulated training may be the only practical alternative. As an example, UPS uses a life-size learning lab to provide a 40-hour, 5-day realistic training program for driver candidates.[53]

Electronic Performance Support Systems (EPSS)

Electronic performance support systems (EPSS) are computerized tools and displays that automate training, documentation, and phone support.[54] When you call a Dell service rep about a problem with your new computer, he or she is probably asking questions prompted by an EPSS; it takes you both, step-by-step, through an analytical sequence. Without the EPSS, Dell would have to train its service reps to memorize an unrealistically large number of solutions. Aetna Insurance cut its 13-week instructor-led training course for new call center employees by about 2 weeks by providing the employees with performance support tools.[55]

---

programmed learning
A systematic method for teaching job skills, involving presenting questions or facts, allowing the person to respond, and giving the learner immediate feedback on the accuracy of his or her answers.

electronic performance support systems (EPSS)
Sets of computerized tools and displays that automate training, documentation, and phone support; integrate this automation into applications; and provide support that's faster, cheaper, and more effective than traditional methods.

Performance support systems are modern job aids. **Job aids** are sets of instructions, diagrams, or similar methods available at the job site to guide the worker.[56] Job aids work particularly well on complex jobs that require multiple steps, or where it's dangerous to forget a step. Airline pilots use job aids (such as a checklist of things to do prior to takeoff). GM's former Electromotive Division gave workers job aids in the form of diagrams. These show, for example, where the locomotive wiring runs and which color wires go where.

Videoconferencing

Videoconferencing is popular for training geographically dispersed employees, and involves delivering programs via compressed audio and video signals over cable broadband lines, the Internet, or satellite. Vendors such as Cisco offer videoconference products such as Webex and TelePresence (www.cisco.com/en/US/products/ps10352/index.html). Employers typically use videoconferencing technology with other technology. For example, Cisco's Unified Video Conferencing (CUVC) product line combines Cisco group collaboration and decision-making software with videoconferencing, video telephony, and realistic "TelePresence" capabilities.[57] When Cisco organized a training program for its partners, it naturally used its videoconferencing capabilities. The course is "A hands-on course designed to assist System Engineers and IT managers to fully understand the features, benefits and overall operation of Cisco's videoconferencing network components."[58]

Computer-Based Training (CBT)

Computer-based training refers to training methods that use interactive computer-based systems to increase knowledge or skills. For example, employers use CBT to teach employees safe methods for avoiding falls; the system lets the trainees replay the lessons and answer questions, and are especially effective when paired with actual practice under a trainer's watchful eye.[59]

Computer-based training is increasingly interactive and realistic. For example, *interactive multimedia training* integrates the use of text, video, graphics, photos, animation, and sound to produce a complex training environment with which the trainee interacts.[60] In training a physician, for instance, such a system lets a medical student take a hypothetical patient's medical history, conduct an examination, and analyze lab tests. Then, by clicking the "examine chest" button, the student can choose a type of chest examination and even hear the sounds of the person's heart. The medical student can then interpret the sounds and draw conclusions upon which to base a diagnosis. *Virtual reality training* takes this realism a step further, by putting trainees into a simulated environment.

Simulated Learning

"Simulated learning" means different things to different people. A survey asked training professionals what experiences qualified as simulated learning experiences. The percentages of trainers choosing each experience were:

- Virtual reality-type games, 19%
- Step-by-step animated guide, 8%
- Scenarios with questions and decision trees overlaying animation, 19%
- Online role-play with photos and videos, 14%
- Software training including screenshots with interactive requests, 35%
- Other, 6%[61]

Virtual reality puts the trainee in an artificial three-dimensional environment that simulates events and situations that might be experienced on the job.[62] Sensory devices transmit how the trainee is responding to the computer, and the trainee "sees, feels and hears" what is going on, assisted by special goggles and auditory and sensory devices.[63]

U.S. ARMY EXAMPLE The U.S. Armed Forces use simulation-based training programs for soldiers and officers. For example, the army developed video game–type training programs called Full-Spectrum Command and Full-Spectrum Warrior for training troops in urban warfare. According to one description, the two games offer extremely realistic features, within a context that emphasizes real-time leadership and decision-making skills.[64]

OTHER EXAMPLES Employers use computerized simulations to inject more realism into their training. For example, Orlando-based Environmental Tectonics Corporation created an Advanced Disaster Management simulation for emergency medical response trainees. One of the simulated scenarios involves a passenger plane crashing into a runway. So realistic that it's "unsettling," trainees including firefighters and airport officials respond to the simulated crash's sights and sounds via pointing devices and radios.[65] When Cisco Systems decided it needed a better way to train the tens of thousands of Cisco trainees for Cisco certification exams it turned to gaming. Cisco embedded the learning within a video game–like atmosphere that included music, graphics, and sound effects.[66] Training simulations are expensive, but for larger companies the cost per employee is usually reasonable.[67]

One way to reduce the cost is to capitalize on virtual environments such as Second Life. For example, British Petroleum uses Second Life to train new gas station employees. The aim here is to show new gas station employees how to use the safety features of gasoline storage tanks. BP built three-dimensional renderings of the tank systems in Second Life. Trainees could use these to "see" underground and observe the effects of using the safety devices.[68]

ADVANTAGES In general, interactive and simulated technologies reduce learning time by an average of 50%.[69] Other advantages include instructional consistency (computers, unlike human trainers, don't have good days and bad days), mastery of learning (if the trainee doesn't learn it, he or she generally can't move on to the next step), increased retention, and increased trainee motivation (resulting from responsive feedback).

Specialist multimedia software houses such as Graphic Media of Portland, Oregon, produce much of the content for these programs. They produce both custom titles and generic programs such as a $999 package for teaching workplace safety.

Interactive Learning

Employers are also moving from textbook and classroom-based learning to interactive learning. For example, Cheesecake Factory employees use VideoCafé, a YouTube-type platform, to let employees "upload and share video snippets on job-related topics, including customer greetings and food preparation." The company is also emphasizing interactive games, including a simulation that shows employees how to build the "perfect hamburger." Amongst vendors, Learning Tree International "employs classroom, live online, and on-site training solutions that resonate with Gen Y learners because of their interactive features; hands-on exercises; and live, online experiences."[70]

Internet-Based Training

Trainers increasingly employ Internet-based learning to deliver programs. Until 2004, ADP's new sales associate training required two weeks of expensive classroom training at ADP's Atlanta, Georgia, training center. Today, ADP trains its new salespeople online, using a Blackboard learning management system similar to one used by many online college students.[71] The Italian eyewear company Luxottica (whose brands include LensCrafters, Pearl Vision, and Sunglass Hut) provides standardized training to its 38,000 employees worldwide via instant access online to information such as new products and regulations.[72]

There are two basic ways to offer online courses to employees. First, the employer can encourage and/or facilitate having its employees take relevant online courses from either

job aid
A set of instructions, diagrams, or similar methods available at the job site to guide the worker.

its own online (intranet) offerings or from the hundreds of online training vendors on the Web. For example, the employer might arrange with www.puresafety. com to let its employees take one or more occupational safety courses from those puresafety.com offers.

LEARNING PORTALS   The second approach is to arrange with an online training vendor to make its courses available via the employer's intranet-based learning portal. A *learning portal* is a section of an employer's Web site that offers employees online access to many or all of the training courses they need to succeed at their jobs. Most often, the employer contracts with applications service providers (ASPs). A Google search for e-learning companies reveals many vendors such as SkillSoft, Plateau Systems, and Employment Law Learning Technologies. When employees go to their firm's learning portal, they actually access the menu of training courses that the ASP offers for the employer.

Improving Productivity Through HRIS
Learning Management Systems

Learning management systems (LMS) are special software tools that support Internet training by helping employers identify training needs, and in scheduling, delivering, assessing, and managing the online training itself. For example, General Motors uses an LMS to help its dealers in Africa and the Middle East deliver training. The Internet-based LMS includes a course catalog, supervisor approved self-enrollment, and pre- and post-course tests. The system then automatically schedules the individual's training.73 Blackboard and WebCT are two familiar college-oriented learning management systems.

The movement today is toward integrating the e-learning system with the company's enterprisewide information systems. In that way, for instance, employers automatically update skills inventory and succession plans as employees complete their training.74

USING INTERNET-BASED LEARNING   Whether to use e-learning often comes down to efficiency. Web learning doesn't necessarily teach faster or better. In one review of the evidence, Web-based instruction was a bit more effective than classroom instruction for teaching memory of facts and principles, and Web-based instruction and classroom instruction were equally effective for teaching information about how to perform a task or action.[75] But of course, the need to teach large numbers of students remotely, or to enable students to study at their leisure, often makes e-learning so much more efficient that the small differences in Web-based versus classroom learning become somewhat meaningless.[76]

In practice, many employers opt for "blended learning." Here, the trainees make use of several delivery methods (such as manuals, in-class lectures, self-guided e-learning programs, and Web-based seminars or "webinars") to learn the material.[77] Intuit (which makes software such as TurboTax) uses instructor-led classroom training for bringing in new distributors and getting them up to speed. Then they use their virtual classroom systems to provide additional training, for monthly meetings with distributors, and for short classes on special software features.[78]

Mobile Learning

Mobile learning (or "on-demand learning") means delivering learning content on demand via mobile devices like cell phones, laptops, and iPads, wherever and whenever the learner has the time and desire to access it.[79] For example, using dominKnow's (www.dominknow.com) iPod touch and iPhone-optimized Touch Learning Center Portal, trainees can log in and take full online courses.[80]

Employers use mobile learning to deliver "corporate training and downloads on everything from how to close an important sales deal to optimizing organizational change to learning business Spanish . . . You can be . . . riding your bike" while listening to the training program.[81] Capital One purchased 3,000 iPods for trainees who had enrolled in one of 20 instructor-led courses at its Capital One University. The training department then had an Internet audio book provider create an audio learning site within Capital One's firewall. Employees used it to download the instructor-requested books and other materials to their iPods.[82] IBM uses mobile learning to deliver just-in-time information (for instance, about new product features) to its sales force. To increase such learning's accessibility, IBM's training department often breaks up, say, an hour program into 10-minute pieces. That way, employees needn't put away a full hour to listen. Some employers use blogs to communicate learning to trainees.[83] JP Morgan encourages employees to use instant messaging as a quick learning device, for instance, to quickly update colleagues about new products.

The Virtual Classroom

Conventional Web-based learning tends to be limited to the sorts of online learning with which many students are already familiar—reading PowerPoint presentations, participating in instant message type chat rooms, and taking online exams, for instance.

The virtual classroom takes online learning to a new level. A **virtual classroom** uses special collaboration software to enable multiple remote learners, using their PCs or laptops, to participate in live audio and visual discussions, communicate via written text, and learn via content such as PowerPoint slides.

The virtual classroom combines the best of Web-based learning offered by systems like Blackboard and WebCT with live video and audio. For example, Elluminate Live! enables learners to communicate with clear, two-way audio; build communities with user profiles and live video; collaborate with chat and shared whiteboards; and learn with shared applications such as PowerPoint slides.[84]

Lifelong and Literacy Training Techniques

Lifelong learning means providing employees with continuing learning experiences over their tenure with the firm, with the aims of ensuring they have the opportunity to learn the skills they need to do their jobs and to expand their horizons. For example, one senior waiter at the Rhapsody restaurant in Chicago received his undergraduate degree and began work toward a master of social work using the lifelong learning account (LiLA) program his employer offers. Lifelong learning may thus range from basic remedial skills (for instance, English as a second language) to college. Somewhat similar to 401(k) plans, employers and employees contribute to LiLA plans (without the tax advantages of 401(k) plans), and the employee can use these funds to better himself or herself.[85]

LITERACY TRAINING By one estimate, about 39 million people in the United States have learning disabilities. Another study called the American workforce ill-prepared.[86] Yet today's emphasis on teamwork and quality requires that employees read, write, and understand numbers.[87]

Employers often turn to private firms like Education Management Corporation to provide the requisite education.[88] Another simple literacy training approach is to have supervisors teach basic skills by giving employees writing and speaking exercises.[89] For example, if an employee needs to use a manual to find out how to change a part, teach that person how to use the index to locate the relevant section. Another approach is to bring in outside professionals (such as teachers from a local high school) to teach, say, remedial reading or writing. Having employees attend adult education or high school evening classes is another option.

virtual classroom
Teaching method that uses special collaboration software to enable multiple remote learners, using their PCs or laptops, to participate in live audio and visual discussions, communicate via written text, and learn via content such as PowerPoint slides.

lifelong learning
Provides employees with continuing learning experiences over their tenure with the firm, with the aims of ensuring they have the opportunity to learn the skills they need to do their jobs and to expand their occupational horizons.

MANAGING THE NEW WORKFORCE

Diversity Training

Diversity training aims to improve cross-cultural sensitivity, with the goal of fostering more harmonious working relationships among a firm's employees. Such training typically includes improving interpersonal skills, understanding and valuing cultural differences, improving technical skills, socializing employees into the corporate culture, indoctrinating new workers into the U.S. work ethic, improving English proficiency and basic math skills, and improving bilingual skills for English-speaking employees.[90] For example, IBM has online programs to educate managers regarding diversity, inclusive leadership, and sexual harassment. Training materials include interactive learning modules that enable trainees to practice what they've learned, testimonials from IBM executives, and self-assessment tools. [91]

Most employers opt for an off-the-shelf diversity training program such as *Just Be F.A.I.R.: A practical approach to diversity and the workplace*, from VisionPoint productions. The package includes streaming video, a facilitator and discussion guide, participant materials and workbook, a DVD with print materials, PowerPoint slides, and two videos (the purchase price for the entire program is about $1,000). It includes, for instance, vignettes illustrating such things as the importance of communicating, and the potential pitfalls of stereotyping people.[92]

Team Training

Teamwork is not something that always comes naturally. Companies therefore devote many hours to training new employees to listen to each other and to cooperate. Toyota's training process stresses dedication to teamwork. For example, the program uses short exercises to illustrate examples of good and bad teamwork, and to mold new employees' attitudes regarding good teamwork.

A team-building program at a Baltimore Coca-Cola plant illustrates what team training typically involves.[93] In this case, the plant suffered from high turnover and absenteeism. The new plant manager decided to reorganize around teams and to use team training to support the new organization.

Team training focused on technical, interpersonal, and team management issues. In terms of *technical training*, for instance, management encouraged team employees to learn each other's jobs, with the aim of encouraging flexible team assignments. **Cross training** means training employees to do different tasks or jobs than their own; doing so facilitates flexibility and job rotation, as when you expect team members to occasionally share jobs.

When teamwork fails, it is often due to interpersonal problems such as intra-team conflict, lack of agreement, guarded communications, and personal criticism. In this case, team training therefore included *interpersonal skills* training such as in listening, handling conflict, and negotiating.[94] In practice, effective teams also require certain team management skills. In this case, *team management skills* included training in problem solving, meetings management, consensus decision making, and team leadership (since each team member had to exercise team leadership at one time or another).

Employers also use team training to build stronger management teams. This often involves special training methods. For example, some use outdoor "adventure" or "extreme" training such as Outward Bound programs to build teamwork. Such training usually involves taking a firm's management team out into rugged, mountainous terrain. Activities might include, for instance, white water rafting, and maneuvering through obstacle courses.[95] The aim is to foster trust and cooperation among trainees. For example, the chief financial officer for a bank helped organize a retreat for 73 of his firm's financial officers and accountants. As he said, "They are very individualistic in their approach to their work. . . . What I have been trying to do is get them to see the power of acting more like a team."[96] Other team training methods include action learning and team building, both of which we'll address later in this chapter.

IMPLEMENTING MANAGEMENT DEVELOPMENT PROGRAMS

It's not always easy to tell where "training" leaves off and "management development" begins. The latter, however, tends to emphasize long-term development and a focus on developing current or future managers. **Management development** is any attempt to improve managerial performance by imparting knowledge, changing attitudes, or increasing skills.

Strategy and Development

The management development process consists of (1) assessing the company's strategic needs (for instance, to fill future executive openings or to boost competitiveness), (2) appraising managers' current performance, and then (3) developing the managers (and future managers).[97] As we explained in Chapter 5, development is usually part of the employer's *succession planning*. Succession planning refers to the process through which a company plans for and fills senior-level openings.[98]

Succession planning and management development both stem from the employer's strategy, vision, and personnel plans. For example, strategies to enter new businesses or expand overseas imply that the employer will need managers who have the skills to manage these new businesses.

Some management development programs are company-wide and involve all or most new (or potential) managers. Thus, new MBAs may join GE's management development program and rotate through various assignments and educational experiences. The aims include identifying their management potential and giving them the necessary developmental experience (in, say, production and finance). The firm may then slot superior candidates onto a "fast track," a development program that prepares them more quickly for senior-level commands.

Other development programs aim to fill specific top positions, such as CEO. For example, GE spent years developing, testing, and watching several potential replacements for CEO before finally choosing Jeffrey Immelt.

Assessment is usually part of development. At frozen foods manufacturer Schawn, senior executives first whittle 40 or more development candidates down to about 10. Then the program begins with a 1-day assessment by outside consultants of each manager's leadership strengths and weaknesses. The assessment involves managers addressing problems such as employee conflict. This assessment becomes the basis for each manager's individual development plan. Action-learning (practical) projects then supplement individual and group training activities.[99]

A survey listed the most popular management development activities. The most popular include classroom-based learning, executive coaching, action learning, 360° feedback, experiential learning, off-site retreats (where managers meet with colleagues for learning), mentoring, and job rotation.[100] We'll look at some of these.

Managerial On-the-Job Training

Managerial on-the-job training methods include job rotation, the coaching/understudy approach, and action learning. In the context of management development, **job rotation** means moving managers from department to department to broaden their understanding of the business and to test their abilities. The trainee may be a recent college graduate, and spend several months in each department, learning the department's business by actually doing it. Or he or she may be a senior manager being groomed for further promotion by being exposed to a range of domestic and foreign challenges.

---

cross training
Training employees to do different tasks or jobs than their own; doing so facilitates flexibility and job rotation.

management development
Any attempt to improve current or future management performance by imparting knowledge, changing attitudes, or increasing skills.

job rotation
A management training technique that involves moving a trainee from department to department to broaden his or her experience and identify strong and weak points.

COACHING/UNDERSTUDY APPROACH   Here the trainee works directly with a senior manager or with the person he or she is to replace; the latter is responsible for the trainee's coaching. Normally, the understudy relieves the executive of certain responsibilities, giving the trainee a chance to learn the job.

ACTION LEARNING   **Action learning** programs give managers and others released time to work analyzing and solving problems in departments other than their own. Its basics include carefully selected teams of 5 to 25 members, assigning the teams real-world business problems that extend beyond their usual areas of expertise, and structured learning through coaching and feedback. The employer's senior managers usually choose the projects and decide whether to accept the teams' recommendations.[101] For example, Pacific Gas & Electric Company's (PG&E) Action-Forum Process has three phases:

1. A "framework" phase of 6 to 8 weeks—basically, an intense planning period during which the team defines and collects data on an issue;

2. The action forum—2 to 3 days at PG&E's learning center discussing the issue and developing action-plan recommendations; and

3. Accountability sessions, when the teams meet with the leadership group at 30, 60, and 90 days to review their action plans.

Off-the-Job Management Training and Development Techniques

There are also many off-the-job techniques for training and developing managers.

THE CASE STUDY METHOD   As most everyone knows, the **case study method** presents a trainee with a written description of an organizational problem. The person then analyzes the case, diagnoses the problem, and presents his or her findings and solutions in a discussion with other trainees.

Integrated case scenarios expand the case analysis concept by creating long-term, comprehensive case situations. For example, the FBI Academy created an integrated case scenario. It starts with "a concerned citizen's telephone call and ends 14 weeks later with a simulated trial. In between is the stuff of a genuine investigation, including a healthy sampling of what can go wrong in an actual criminal inquiry." To create such scenarios, scriptwriters (often employees in the firm's training group) write the scripts. The scripts include themes, background stories, detailed personnel histories, and role-playing instructions. The scenarios aim to develop specific skills, such as interviewing witnesses.[102]

MANAGEMENT GAMES   Computerized **management games** enable trainees to learn by making realistic decisions in simulated situations. For example, *Interpret* is a team exercise that "explores team communication, the management of information and the planning and implementation of a strategy. It raises management trainees' communication skills, helps them to better manage the information flow between individuals and the team, and improves planning and problem solving skills".[103] With some games, trainees divide into teams, which compete in a simulated marketplace. Each team typically must decide, for example, (1) how much to spend on advertising, (2) how much to produce, (3) how much inventory to maintain, and (4) how many of which product to produce.

Management games are effective. People learn best by being involved, and games gain such involvement. They also help trainees develop their problem-solving skills, and to focus attention on planning rather than just putting out fires. The groups also usually elect their own officers and organize themselves. This can develop leadership skills and foster cooperation and teamwork.

OUTSIDE SEMINARS   Numerous companies and universities offer Web-based and traditional classroom management development seminars and conferences. The selection of 1- to 3-day training programs offered by the American Management Association illustrates what's available. Recently, for instance, their offerings ranged from "developing your emotional intelligence" to "assertiveness training," "assertiveness training for managers," "assertiveness training for women in business," "dynamic listening skills for successful communication," and "fundamentals of cost accounting."[104] Specialized associations, such as SHRM, provide specialized seminars for their profession's members.

UNIVERSITY-RELATED PROGRAMS   Many universities provide executive education and continuing education programs in leadership, supervision, and the like. These can range from 1- to 4-day programs to executive development programs lasting 1 to 4 months.

The Advanced Management Program of Harvard's Graduate School of Business Administration is one example.[105] Students are experienced managers from around the world. It uses cases and lectures to provide them with the latest management skills. When Hasbro wanted to improve its executives' creativity skills, it turned to Dartmouth University's Amos Tuck Business School. Tuck provided a "custom approach to designing a program that would be built from the ground up to suit Hasbro's specific needs."[106]

ROLE PLAYING   The aim of **role playing** is to create a realistic situation and then have the trainees assume the parts (or roles) of specific persons in that situation. Each trainee gets a role, such as:

> You are the head of a crew of telephone maintenance workers, each of whom drives a small service truck to and from the various jobs. Every so often you get a new truck to exchange for an old one, and you have the problem of deciding to which of your crew members you should give the new truck. Often there are hard feelings, since each seems to feel entitled to the new truck, so you have a tough time being fair.[107]

When combined with the general instructions and other roles, role playing can trigger spirited discussions among the role player/trainees. The aim is to develop trainees' skills in areas like leadership and delegating. For example, a supervisor could experiment with both a considerate and an autocratic leadership style, whereas in the real world the person might not have the luxury of experimenting. It may also train someone to be more aware of and sensitive to others' feelings.

BEHAVIOR MODELING   **Behavior modeling** involves (1) showing trainees the right (or "model") way of doing something, (2) letting trainees practice that way, and then (3) giving feedback on the trainees' performance. Behavior modeling training is one of the most widely used, well researched, and highly regarded psychologically based training interventions.[108] The basic procedure is as follows:

1. **Modeling.** First, trainees watch live or video examples showing models behaving effectively in a problem situation. Thus, the video might show a supervisor effectively disciplining a subordinate, if teaching "how to discipline" is the aim of the training program.

2. **Role playing.** Next, the trainees are given roles to play in a simulated situation; here they are to practice the effective behaviors demonstrated by the models.

3. **Social reinforcement.** The trainer provides reinforcement in the form of praise and constructive feedback.

4. **Transfer of training.** Finally, trainees are encouraged to apply their new skills when they are back on their jobs.

---

action learning
A training technique by which management trainees are allowed to work full-time analyzing and solving problems in other departments.

case study method
A development method in which the manager is presented with a written description of an organizational problem to diagnose and solve.

management game
A development technique in which teams of managers compete by making computerized decisions regarding realistic but simulated situations.

role playing
A training technique in which trainees act out parts in a realistic management situation.

behavior modeling
A training technique in which trainees are first shown good management techniques in a film, are asked to play roles in a simulated situation, and are then given feedback and praise by their supervisor.

CORPORATE UNIVERSITIES Many firms, particularly larger ones, establish **in-house development centers** (often called *corporate universities*). GE, Caterpillar, and IBM are examples. Such centers typically offer a catalogue of courses and programs aimed at supporting the employers' management development needs. Employers often collaborate with academic institutions, and with training and development program providers and Web-based educational portals, to create packages of programs and materials. Characteristics of effective corporate universities include (1) alignment with corporate strategic goals, (2) a focus on development of skills that support business needs, (3) evaluation of learning and performance, (4) using technology to support the learning, and (5) partnering with academia.[109]

Employers increasingly offer virtual—rather than bricks and morter—corporate university services. For example, Cerner, a health-care information technology company, offers its employees "Cerner KnowledgeWorks." This provides employees with three types of knowledge stores: Dynamic knowledge "is real-time content that flows back and forth, such as e-mails, instant messages, or conference calls;" Moderated content "includes best practices, such as case studies or wikis that capture information about situations where we did well and how we did it;" Codified content "is more formal documentation of official company practices, and includes installation guides, help files, and formal training or courses."[110] Bain & Company's virtual university provides a means for coordinating all the company's training efforts, and for delivering Web-based modules that cover topics from strategic management to mentoring.

EXECUTIVE COACHES Many firms retain executive coaches to develop their top managers' effectiveness. An **executive coach** is an outside consultant who questions the executive's boss, peers, subordinates, and (sometimes) family in order to identify the executive's strengths and weaknesses, and to counsel the executive so he or she can capitalize on those strengths and overcome the weaknesses.[111] Executive coaching can cost as much as $50,000 per executive. Experts recommend using formal assessments prior to coaching, to uncover strengths and weaknesses and to provide more focused coaching.[112]

Executive coaching can be effective. Participants in one study included about 1,400 senior managers who had received "360 degree" performance feedback from bosses, peers, and subordinates. About 400 worked with an executive coach to review the feedback. Then, about a year later, these 400 managers and about 400 who didn't receive coaching again received multisource feedback. The managers who received executive coaching were more likely to set more effective, specific goals for their subordinates, and to have received improved ratings from subordinates and supervisors.[113]

The coaching field is unregulated, so managers should do their due diligence. Check references carefully, and check with the International Coach Federation, a trade group.

THE SHRM LEARNING SYSTEM The Society for Human Resource Management, encourages HR professionals to qualify for certification by taking examinations. The society offers several preparatory training programs. The self-study option includes text and DVD. The college/university option provides classroom interaction with instructors and other students.

Leadership Development at GE

General Electric is known for its ability to develop executive talent. Their current mix of executive development programs illustrate what is available:[114]

Leadership programs: These multiyear training programs rotate about 3,000 employees per year through various functions with the aim of enabling people to run a large GE business.

Session C: This is GE's intense multi-level performance appraisal process. The CEO personally reviews GE's top 625 officers every year.

Crotonville: This is GE's corporate training campus in New York and offers a mix of conventional classroom learning and team-based training and cultural trips.

Boca Raton: At this annual meeting of GE's top 625 officers, they network, share their best ideas, and get to understand the company's strategy for the coming year.

The next big thing: Whether it's productivity and quality improvement through "Six Sigma" or "innovation," GE focuses its employees on central themes or initiatives.

Monthly dinners: Jeffrey Immelt, GE's CEO, meets periodically at dinners and breakfasts to learn more about his top executives and to "strengthen his connections with his top team."[115]

Perusing the development pages of GE's Website (http://www.ge.com/careers/students/entry-level.html) illustrates the breadth of training and development opportunities GE offers its employees. For example,

> The Edison Engineering Development Program (EEDP) develops technical problem-solving skills through advanced courses in engineering and technical projects and presentations to senior leadership that are aligned with business objectives.

> The Financial Management Program (FMP) develops leadership and analytical skills through classroom training and key assignments. Hands-on experience may include financial planning, accounting, operations analysis, auditing, forecasting, treasury/cash management, and commercial finance.

Talent Management and Mission-Critical Employees: Differential Development Assignments

Probably the most distinctive talent management best practice is to *actively manage employees*. In today's competitive environment, the traditional HR practice of allocating pay raises, development opportunities, and other scarce resources more-or-less across the board or based mostly on performance is no longer viable. Employers need to think through how to allocate those resources in a way that makes the most sense given their strategic aims. It therefore makes sense that talent management–oriented employers focus more of their development resources on their "mission-critical employees," those deemed critical to the companies' future growth.

We'll look closer at how employers do this in the following chapter. However, it is useful here to illustrate how employers implement this "differential" approach with several training-and-development examples.

- A telecommunications firm previously spread pay and development money evenly over its 8,000 employees. When the recent recession came, company leaders began segmenting their talent into four groups: business impact, high performers, high potentials, and critical skills. Then they shifted their dollars away from low performers and those not making an impact. "While the company lost some low performers, the high performers and high potentials felt like they finally received recognition."[116]

- One large manufacturer gives "rising stars" special access to online discussion boards, led by the CEO, that are dedicated to the company's biggest challenges. It encourages emerging leaders to visit the board daily to share ideas and opinions and to apply for assignments.[117]

- High potential participants in Johnson & Johnson's special "LeAD" leadership development program receive advice and regular assessments from coaches brought in from outside the company. As special projects, they also must develop a new product or service, or a new business model, intended to create value for their individual units.[118]

---

in-house development center
A company-based method for exposing prospective managers to realistic exercises to develop improved management skills.

executive coach
An outside consultant who questions the executive's associates in order to identify the executive's strengths and weaknesses, and then counsels the executive so he or she can capitalize on those strengths and overcome the weaknesses.

- Some companies share future strategies on a privileged basis with rising leaders. For example, these high-potentials receive e-mail updates detailing firm performance and strategic changes. Some invite them to quarterly meetings with high-level executives; some provide access to an online portal where the rising leaders can review the company's strategy and critical metrics.[119]

> 8 List and briefly discuss the importance of the eight steps in leading organizational change.

MANAGING ORGANIZATIONAL CHANGE PROGRAMS

Several years ago, Intel Corp. carried out a major reorganization that one writer says "may have badly damaged employee development, morale and the company's culture of innovation."[120] Managing change is important in today's challenging environment. Professor Edward Lawler says that as more employers face rapid competitive change, "focusing on strategy, organizational development, and organizational change is a high payoff activity for the HR organization."[121]

Major organizational changes like these are never easy, but perhaps the hardest part of leading a change is overcoming the resistance to it. Individuals, groups, and even entire organizations may resist the change, perhaps because they are accustomed to the usual way of doing things or because of perceived threats to their influence, or some other reason.[122]

What to Change

The first question is, "What should we change?" For example, a few years ago, Nokia was the worldwide leader in handsets and smartphones. Then, Apple introduced its first iPhone. Within a year, Nokia's smartphone market share plummeted, and its sales increasingly relied on low-priced handsets. By 2010, Nokia's board knew something had to be done. It appointed a new CEO with Silicon Valley experience, Stephen Elop (pictured).[123] He knew Nokia faced pressing problems. Its smartphone share was down, and it was losing low-cost handset business to Asian competitors. Nokia's R&D was behind the times. Its Symbian mobile operating system couldn't handle many of the leading applications that Apple's and Microsoft's systems could. Nokia was too slow in executing strategic changes. He had to jumpstart Nokia.

Faced with situations like these, managers like Stephen Elop can change one or more of five aspects of their companies—their *strategy, culture, structure, technologies,* or the *attitudes and skills* of the employees.

STRATEGIC CHANGE   Organizational turnarounds often start with a change in the firm's strategy, mission, and vision—with *strategic change.* For example, Elop embarked on a strategy to renew Nokia by streamlining Nokia's product development process and by entering into a partnership with Microsoft with the aim of introducing a new Microsoft-based smartphone within a year.

OTHER CHANGES   Nokia's new CEO instituted other organizational changes. In terms of *structure,* Nokia split responsibility for its smartphones and handsets into two new units. He replaced managers in Nokia's mobile phones unit and markets unit. In *technology,* Elop reduced the Symbian operating system's central role in its smartphones, replacing it with Microsoft's mobile operating system. With its *culture,* Elop had his new management team change the firm's culture, for instance, by impressing on Nokia's employees the need to eradicate bureaucratic decision making and to execute on Nokia's new strategy.

Of course, strategic, cultural, structural, and technological changes, no matter how logical, will fail without employees' active support. As one example, a nationwide beverage distributor encountered opposition from its sales force several years ago when it moved from its paper-based sales

Nokia CEO Stephen Elop.

management system to wireless laptops.[124] Organizational change therefore invariably involves bringing about *changes in the employees* themselves and in their attitudes, skills, and behaviors.[125]

Unfortunately, getting employees' active support is easier said than done. The change may require the cooperation of dozens or even hundreds of managers and supervisors, many of whom might well view the change as detrimental to their peace of mind. Resistance may therefore be formidable. Knowing how to deal with that resistance is the heart of implementing an organizational change.

Lewin's Change Process

Psychologist Kurt Lewin formulated a model to summarize what he believed was the basic process for implementing a change with minimal resistance. To Lewin, all behavior in organizations was a product of two kinds of forces: those striving to maintain the status quo and those pushing for change. Implementing change thus means reducing the forces for the status quo or building up the forces for change. Lewin's process consisted of three steps:

1. *Unfreezing* means reducing the forces that are striving to maintain the status quo, usually by presenting a provocative problem or event to get people to recognize the need for change and to search for new solutions.

2. *Moving* means developing new behaviors, values, and attitudes. The manager may accomplish this through organizational structure changes, through conventional training and development activities, and sometimes through the other organizational development techniques (such as the team building) we'll discuss later.

3. *Refreezing* means building in the reinforcement to make sure the organization doesn't slide back into its former ways of doing things.

Leading Organizational Change[126]

Of course, the challenge is in the details. A CEO such as Nokia's Stephen Elop needs a process for leading such a change. An 8-step process for leading organizational change follows.[127]

Unfreezing Stage

1. *Establish a sense of urgency.* Most managers start by creating a sense of urgency. This often requires creativity. For example, the CEO might present executives with a (fictitious) analyst's report describing the firm's imminent demise.

2. *Mobilize commitment* through joint diagnosis of problems. Having established a sense of urgency, the leader may then create one or more task forces to diagnose the problems facing the company. Such teams can produce a shared understanding of what they can and must improve, and thereby mobilize commitment.

Moving Stage

3. *Create a guiding coalition.* No one can really implement major organizational change alone. Most CEOs create a guiding coalition of influential people. They work together as a team to act as missionaries and implementers.

4. *Develop and communicate a shared vision.* Your organizational renewal may require communicating a new vision. For example, Stephen Elop's vision was of a streamlined Nokia moving fast to build advanced smartphones based on Microsoft's operating system. Guidelines here are *keep it simple* (for example, "We are going to become faster than anyone else in our industry at satisfying customer needs."), *use multiple forums* (meetings, e-mails, formal and informal interaction), and *lead by example.*[128]

5. *Help employees make the change.* Are there impediments to change? Does a lack of skills stand in the way? Do policies, procedures, or the firm's organization make it difficult to act? Do intransigent managers discourage employees from acting? If so, address the impediments. For example, Elop quickly replaced many of Nokia's top and mid-level managers.

6. *Consolidate gains* and produce more change. Aim for attainable short-term accomplishments. Use the credibility from these to change the remaining systems, structures, and policies that don't fit well with the company's new vision.[129]

Refreezing Stage

7. *Reinforce the new ways of doing things* with changes to the company's systems and procedures. For example, use new appraisal systems and incentives to reinforce the desired behaviors. Reinforce the new culture by ensuring that the firm's managers role-model the company's new values.

8. Finally, the leader must *monitor and assess progress.* In brief, this involves comparing where the company is today with where it should be, based on measurable milestones. At Nokia, for instance, "How many new products has the company introduced?" "What is our smartphone and handset market shares?"

Using Organizational Development

> 9 Answer the question, "What is organizational development and how does it differ from traditional approaches to organizational change?"

There are many ways to reduce resistance to change. Among the many suggestions are that managers impose rewards or sanctions that guide employee behaviors, explain why the change is needed, negotiate with employees, give inspirational speeches, or ask employees to help design the change.[130] Organizational development (OD) taps into the latter. **Organizational development** is a change process through which employees formulate the change that's required and implement it, often with the assistance of trained consultants. OD has several distinguishing characteristics:

1. It usually involves *action research*, which means collecting data about a group, department, or organization, and feeding the information back to the employees so they can analyze it and develop hypotheses about what the problems might be.

2. It applies behavioral science knowledge to improve the organization's effectiveness.

3. It changes the organization in a particular direction—toward empowerment, improved problem solving, responsiveness, quality of work, and effectiveness.

There are four basic categories of OD applications: human process, technostructural, human resource management, and strategic applications (see Table 8-2). Action research—getting the employees themselves to review the required data and to design and implement the solutions—is the basis of all four. We'll look at each.

TABLE 8-2 Examples of OD Interventions	
Human Process	**Human Resource Management**
T-groups	Goal setting
Process consultation	Performance appraisal
Third-party intervention	Reward systems
Team building	Career planning and development
Organizational confrontation meeting	Managing workforce diversity
Survey research	Employee wellness
Technostructural	**Strategic**
Formal structural change	Integrated strategic management
Differentiation and integration	Culture change
Cooperative union–management projects	Strategic change
Quality circles	Self-designing organizations
Total quality management	
Work design	

HUMAN PROCESS APPLICATIONS   The goal of human process OD techniques is to give employees the insight and skills required to analyze their own and others' behavior more effectively, so they can then solve interpersonal and intergroup problems. These problems might include, for instance, conflict among employees. Applications here include sensitivity training, team building, and survey research.

Sensitivity, laboratory, or *t-group* (the *t* is for "training") training's basic aim is to increase the participant's insight into his or her own behavior by encouraging an open expression of feelings in the trainer-guided t-group. Typically, 10 to 15 people meet, usually away from the job, with no specific agenda. Instead, the focus is on the feelings and emotions of the members in the group at the meeting. The facilitator encourages participants to portray themselves as they feel within the group rather than in terms of past behaviors. The t-group's success depends on the feedback each person gets from the others, and on the participants' willingness to be candid.[131]

T-group training is controversial. Its personal nature suggests that participation should be voluntary. Some view it as unethical because you can't consider participation "suggested" by one's superior as voluntary. Similarly, some practitioners have T-group trainees take personality tests, for instance assigning them letters, such as D for dominance and C for conscientiousness.[132] Others argue that it can be dangerous if led by an incompetent trainer.

Team building is another option. According to experts French and Bell, the typical team-building meeting begins with the consultant interviewing each of the group members and the leader before the meeting.[133] They are asked what their problems are, how they think the group functions, and what obstacles are keeping the group from performing better. The consultant then categorizes the interview data into themes (such as "inadequate communications") and presents the themes to the group at the start of the meeting. The group ranks the themes in terms of importance, and the most important ones become the agenda for the meeting. The group then explores and discusses the issues, examines the underlying causes of the problems, and begins devising solutions.

Survey research, another human process OD technique, requires that employees throughout the organization complete attitude surveys. The facilitator then uses those data as a basis for problem analysis and action planning. Surveys are a convenient way to unfreeze a company's management and employees. They provide a comparative, graphic illustration of the fact that the organization does have problems to solve.[134]

TECHNOSTRUCTURAL INTERVENTIONS   OD practitioners also get involved in changing firms' structures, methods, and job designs, using an assortment of technostructural interventions. For example, in a *formal structural change* program, the employees collect data on the company's existing organizational structure; they then jointly redesign and implement a new one.

HUMAN RESOURCE MANAGEMENT APPLICATIONS   OD practitioners use action research to enable employees to analyze and change their firm's human resources practices. Targets of change here might include the performance appraisal and reward systems, as well as installing diversity programs.

STRATEGIC OD APPLICATIONS   *Strategic interventions* aim to use action research to improve a company's strategic management. *Integrated strategic management* is one example. It consists of four steps: managers and employees (1) analyze current strategy and organizational structure, (2) choose a desired strategy and organizational structure, and (3) design a strategic change plan—"an action plan for moving the organization from its current strategy and organizational design to the desired future strategy and design."[135] Finally, (4) the team oversees implementing the strategic change and reviewing the results.[136]

organizational development
A special approach to organizational change in which employees themselves formulate and implement the change that's required.

EVALUATING THE TRAINING EFFORT

With today's emphasis on measuring results, it is crucial that the manager evaluate the training program. There are several things you can measure: participants' *reactions* to the program, what (if anything) the trainees *learned* from the program, and to what extent their on-the-job *behavior* or *results* changed as a result of the program. In one survey of about 500 U.S. organizations, 77% evaluated their training programs by eliciting reactions, 36% evaluated learning, and about 10% to 15% assessed the program's behavior and/or results.[137] Computerization facilitates evaluation. For example, Bovis Lend Lease uses learning management system software to monitor which employees are taking which courses, and the extent to which they're improving their skills.[138]

There are two basic issues to address when evaluating training programs. The first is the design of the evaluation study and, in particular, whether to use controlled experimentation. The second issue is, "What should we measure?"

Designing the Study

In evaluating the training program, the first question should be how to design the evaluation study. Your basic concern here is this: How can we be sure that the training caused the results? The *time series design* is one option. Here, as in Figure 8-3, you take a series of performance measures before and after the training program. This can provide at least an initial reading on the program's effectiveness.[139] However, you can't be sure from this analysis that the training (rather than, say, a new pay plan) caused any change.

Controlled experimentation is therefore the evaluation process of choice. A controlled experiment uses both a training group, and a control group that receives no training. Data (for instance, on quantity of sales or quality of service) are obtained both before and after the group is exposed to training and before and after a corresponding work period in the control group. This makes it possible to determine the extent to which any change in the training group's performance resulted from the training, rather than from some organization-wide change like a raise in pay. (The pay raise should have affected employees in both groups equally.)[140]

This controlled approach is feasible, but again, relatively few firms use it. Most simply measure trainees' reactions to the program; some also measure the trainees' job performance before and after training.[141]

FIGURE 8-3 Using a Time Series Graph to Assess a Training Program's Effects

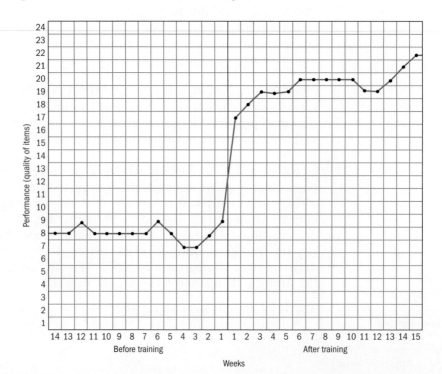

Training Effects to Measure

The manager can measure four basic categories of training outcomes:

1. **Reaction.** Evaluate trainees' reactions to the program. Did they like the program? Did they think it worthwhile?

2. **Learning.** Test the trainees to determine whether they learned the principles, skills, and facts they were supposed to learn.

3. **Behavior.** Ask whether the trainees' on-the-job behavior changed because of the training program. For example, are employees in the store's complaint department more courteous toward disgruntled customers?

4. **Results.** Probably most important, ask, "What results did we achieve, in terms of the training objectives previously set?" For example, did the number of customer complaints diminish? Reactions, learning, and behavior are important. But if the training program doesn't produce measurable results, then it probably hasn't achieved its goals.[142]

Evaluating any of these is straightforward. For example, Figure 8-4 presents one page from a sample evaluation questionnaire for assessing *reactions*. Or, you might assess trainees' *learning* by testing their new knowledge. The employer can also easily assess trainees' *behavioral change*. For example, assess the effectiveness of a supervisory performance appraisal training program by asking that person's subordinates, "Did your supervisor take the time to provide you with examples of good and bad performance when he or she appraised your performance most recently?" Finally, you can directly assess a training program's *results* by measuring, say, the percentage of phone calls that call center trainees subsequently answered correctly. The accompanying HR as a Profit Center feature illustrates measuring a program's impact.

FIGURE 8-4 A Training Evaluation Form

(Continued)

controlled experimentation
Formal methods for testing the effectiveness of a training program, preferably with before-and-after tests and a control group.

FIGURE 8-4
(Continued)

RATING OF INSTRUCTOR

1. Presentation, organization, delivery	○	○	○	○	○	○
2. Knowledge and command of the subject	○	○	○	○	○	○
3. Use of audio-visuals or other training aids	○	○	○	○	○	○
4. Stimulation of an open exchange of ideas, participation, & group interaction	○	○	○	○	○	○

STRONG POINTS OF THE COURSE

○

○

WEAK POINTS OF THE COURSE

○

○

ADDITIONAL DATA YOU WOULD LIKE TO HAVE COVERED IN COURSE

○

○

ADDITIONAL COMMENTS/OR RECOMMENDATIONS

HR AS A PROFIT CENTER

Judging Training's Impact

A careful comparison of the training program's costs and benefits can enable the human resource team to compute the program's return on investment. Online calculators such as the one shown below are available to facilitate such analyses.

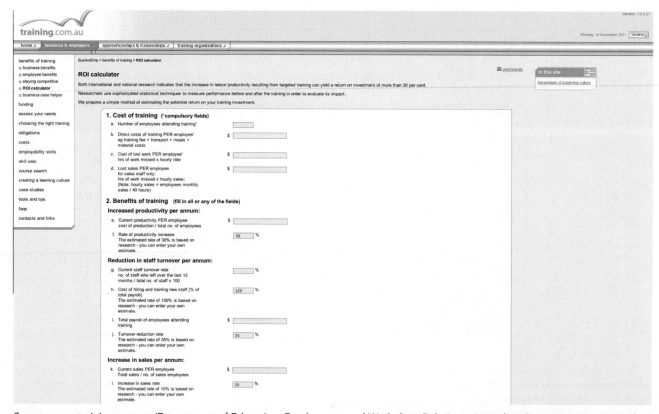

Source: www.training.com.au (Department of Education, Employment and Workplace Relations, Australian Government), accessed September 2011.

REVIEW

MyManagementLab   Now that you have finished this chapter, go back to **www.mymanagementlab.com** to continue practicing and applying the concepts you've learned.

CHAPTER SECTION SUMMARIES

1. Getting your new employee on board and up to speed begins with **orienting and training** him or her. Employee orientation means providing new employees with the information they need to function, and helping them start being emotionally attached to the firm. This may simply involve providing them with brief written orientation materials and an employee handbook, but sometimes involves a formal process aimed at instilling in the employee the company's cherished values. The four-step training process includes needs analysis, instructional design, implementation, and evaluation. Trainees need to be motivated to learn. Ensuring that they are motivated involves making the learning meaningful, making skills transfers easy, and reinforcing the learning.

2. We can use the acronym **ADDIE** to outline the training process: analyze, develop, design, implement, and evaluate. Before training employees, it's necessary to **analyze their training needs and design the training program**. In training new employees, employers use task analysis—basically, a detailed study of the job—to determine what skills the job requires. For current employees, performance analysis is required, specifically to verify that there is performance efficiency and to determine if training is the solution. Distinguishing between can't do and won't do problems is the main issue here. Once you understand the issues, you can design a training program, which means identifying specific training objectives, clarifying a training budget, and then actually designing the program in terms of the actual content.

3. With this in place, you can turn to **implementing the training program**. Specific training methods include on-the-job training, apprenticeship training, informal learning, job instruction training, lectures, programmed learning, audiovisual-based training, vestibule training, videoconferencing, electronic performance support systems, and computer-based training. Computerized training is increasingly popular, with many packaged programs available. Frequently, programs today are Internet-based, with employees accessing packaged online programs, backed up by learning management systems, through their company's learning portals. Employers also increasingly use mobile learning, for instance, delivering short courses and explanations to employees' iPods. With increasing demands for technologically literate employees, lifelong learning can help ensure employees have the basic educational backgrounds they need to succeed on their jobs. Diversity training aims to create better cross-cultural sensitivity with the goal of fostering more harmonious working relationships.

4. Most training methods are useful for all employees, but some are particularly appropriate for **management development programs**. Like all employees, new managers often get on-the-job training, for instance, via job rotation and coaching. In addition, it's usual to supply various off-the-job training and development opportunities—for instance, using the case study method, management games, outside seminars, university-related programs, corporate universities, executive coaches, and (for human resource managers) the SHRM learning system.

5. When facing economic, competitive, or other challenges, managers have to execute **organizational change programs**. These may aim at changing the company's strategy, culture, structure, technologies, or the attitudes and skills of the employees. Often, the trickiest part of organizational change is overcoming employees' resistance to it. With that in mind, steps in an effective organizational change program include establishing a sense of urgency, mobilizing commitment, creating a guiding coalition, developing and communicating a shared vision, helping employees make the change, consolidating gains, reinforcing new ways of doing things, and monitoring and assessing progress. Organizational development is a special approach to organizational change, one that involves action research, which means collecting data about a group and feeding the information back to the employees so they can analyze it and develop hypotheses about what the problems might be.

6. Whatever the training program, it's important to **evaluate the training effort**. You can measure reaction, learning, behavior, or results, ideally using a control group that is not exposed to training, in parallel with the group that you're training.

DISCUSSION QUESTIONS

1. "A well-thought-out orientation program is essential for all new employees, whether they have experience or not." Explain why you agree or disagree with this statement.

2. Explain how you would apply our "motivation points" (page 256) in developing a lecture, say, on orientation and training.

3. John Santos is an undergraduate business student majoring in accounting. He just failed the first accounting course, Accounting 101. He is understandably upset. How would you use performance analysis to identify what, if any, are John's training needs?

4. What are some typical on-the-job training techniques? What do you think are some of the main drawbacks of relying on informal on-the-job training for breaking new employees into their jobs?

5. One reason for implementing global training programs is the need to avoid business losses "due to cultural insensitivity." What sort of cultural insensitivity do you think is referred to, and how might that translate into lost business? What sort of training program would you recommend to avoid such cultural insensitivity?

6. Describe the pros and cons of five management development methods.

7. Do you think job rotation is a good method to use for developing management trainees? Why or why not?

INDIVIDUAL AND GROUP ACTIVITIES

1. You're the supervisor of a group of employees whose task is to assemble disk drives that go into computers. You find that quality is not what it should be and that many of your group's devices have to be brought back and reworked. Your boss says, "You'd better start doing a better job of training your workers."

    a. What are some of the staffing factors that could be contributing to this problem?

    b. Explain how you would go about assessing whether it is in fact a training problem.

2. Choose a task with which you are familiar—mowing the lawn, making a salad, or studying for a test—and develop a job instruction sheet for it.

3. Working individually or in groups, develop a short, programmed learning program on the subject "Guidelines for Giving a More Effective Lecture."

4. Find a provider of management development seminars. Obtain copies of its recent listings of seminar offerings. At what levels of managers are the offerings aimed? What seem to be the most popular types of development programs? Why do you think that's the case?

5. Working individually or in groups, develop several specific examples to illustrate how a professor teaching human resource management could use at least four of the techniques described in this chapter in teaching his or her HR course.

6. Working individually or in groups, develop an orientation program for high school graduates entering your university as freshmen.

7. The HRCI "Test Specifications" appendix at the end of this book (pages 633–640) lists the knowledge someone studying for the HRCI certification exam needs to have in each area of human resource management (such as in Strategic Management, Workforce Planning, and Human Resource Development). In groups of four to five students, do four things: (1) review that appendix now; (2) identify the material in this chapter that relates to the required knowledge the appendix lists; (3) write four multiple-choice exam questions on this material that you believe would be suitable for inclusion in the HRCI exam; and (4) if time permits, have someone from your team post your team's questions in front of the class, so the students in other teams can take each others' exam questions

8. Perhaps no training task in Iraq was more pressing than that involved in creating Iraq's country's new army, which is an ongoing task. These were the people who were to help the coalition bring security to Iraq. However, many new soldiers and even officers had no experience. There were language barriers between trainers and trainees. And some trainees found themselves quickly under fire from insurgents when they went as trainees out into the field. Based on what you learned about training from this chapter, list the five most important things you would tell the U.S. officer in charge of training to keep in mind as he designs the training program.

EXPERIENTIAL EXERCISE

Flying the Friendlier Skies

Purpose: The purpose of this exercise is to give you practice in developing a training program for the job of airline reservation clerk for a major airline.

Required Understanding: You should be fully acquainted with the material in this chapter and should read the following description of an airline reservation clerk's duties:

Customers contact our airline reservation clerks to obtain flight schedules, prices, and itineraries. The reservation clerks look up the requested information on our airline's online flight schedule systems, which are updated continuously. The reservation clerk must deal courteously and expeditiously with the customer, and be able to find quickly alternative flight arrangements in order to provide the customer with the itinerary that fits his or her needs. Alternative flights and prices must be found quickly, so that the customer is not kept waiting, and so that our reservations operations group maintains its efficiency standards. It is often necessary to look under various routings, *since there may be a dozen or more alternative routes between the customer's starting point and destination.*

You may assume that we just hired 30 new clerks, and that you must create a 3-day training program.

How to Set Up the Exercise/Instructions: Divide the class into teams of five or six students.

Airline reservation clerks obviously need numerous skills to perform their jobs. JetBlue Airlines has asked you to develop quickly the outline of a training program for its new reservation clerks. You may want to start by listing the job's main duties and by reviewing any work you may have done for the exercise at the end of Chapter 6. In any case, please produce the requested outline, making sure to be very specific about what you want to teach the new clerks, and what methods and aids you suggest using to train them.

APPLICATION CASE

REINVENTING THE WHEEL AT APEX DOOR COMPANY

Jim Delaney, president of Apex Door, has a problem. No matter how often he tells his employees how to do their jobs, they invariably "decide to do it their way," as he puts it, and arguments ensue between Jim, the employee, and the employee's supervisor. One example is the door-design department, where the designers are expected to work with the architects to design doors that meet the specifications. While it's not "rocket science," as Jim puts it, the designers invariably make mistakes—such as designing in too much steel, a problem that can cost Apex tens of thousands of wasted dollars, once you consider the number of doors in, say, a 30-story office tower.

The order processing department is another example. Jim has a very specific and detailed way he wants the order written up, but most of the order clerks don't understand how to use the multipage order form. They simply improvise when it comes to a detailed question such as whether to classify the customer as "industrial" or "commercial."

The current training process is as follows. None of the jobs has a training manual per se, although several have somewhat out-of-date job descriptions. The training for new people is all on the job. Usually, the person leaving the company trains the new person during the 1- or 2-week overlap period, but if there's no overlap, the new person is trained as well as possible by other employees who have filled in occasionally on the job in the past. The training is the same throughout the company—for machinists, secretaries, assemblers, engineers, and accounting clerks, for example.

Questions

1. What do you think of Apex's training process? Could it help to explain why employees "do things their way"? If so, how?
2. What role should job descriptions play in training at Apex?
3. Explain in detail what you would do to improve the training process at Apex. Make sure to provide specific suggestions, please.

Source: Copyright Dr. Gary Dessler.

CONTINUING CASE

CARTER CLEANING COMPANY

The New Training Program

The Carter Cleaning Centers currently have no formal orientation or training policies or procedures, and Jennifer believes this is one reason why the standards to which she and her father would like employees to adhere are generally not followed.

The Carters would prefer that certain practices and procedures be used in dealing with the customers at the front counters. For example, all customers should be greeted with what Jack refers to as a "big hello." Garments they drop off should immediately be inspected for any damage or unusual stains so these can be brought to the customer's attention, lest the customer later return to pick up the garment and erroneously blame the store. The garments are then supposed to be immediately placed together in a nylon sack to separate them from other customers' garments. The ticket also has to be carefully written up, with the customer's name and telephone number and the date precisely and clearly noted on all copies. The counter person is also supposed to take the opportunity to try to sell the customer additional services such as waterproofing, or simply notify the customer that "Now that people are doing their spring cleaning, we're having a special on drapery cleaning all this month." Finally, as the customer leaves, the counter person is supposed to make a courteous comment like "Have a nice day" or "Drive safely." Each of the other jobs in the stores—pressing, cleaning and spotting, and so forth—similarly contain certain steps, procedures, and most importantly, standards the Carters would prefer to see upheld.

The company has had problems, Jennifer feels, because of a lack of adequate employee training and orientation.

For example, two new employees became very upset last month when they discovered that they were not paid at the end of the week, on Friday, but instead were paid (as are all Carter employees) on the following Tuesday. The Carters use the extra two days in part to give them time to obtain everyone's hours and compute their pay. The other reason they do it, according to Jack, is that "frankly, when we stay a few days behind in paying employees it helps to ensure that they at least give us a few days' notice before quitting on us. While we are certainly obligated to pay them anything they earn, we find that psychologically they seem to be less likely to just walk out on us Friday evening and not show up Monday morning if they still haven't gotten their pay from the previous week. This way they at least give us a few days' notice so we can find a replacement."

There are other matters that could be covered during orientation and training, says Jennifer. These include company policy regarding paid holidays, lateness and absences, health benefits (there are none, other than workers' compensation), substance abuse, and eating or smoking on the job (both forbidden), and general matters like the maintenance of a clean and safe work area, personal appearance and cleanliness, time sheets, personal telephone calls, and personal e-mail.

Jennifer believes that implementing orientation and training programs would help to ensure that employees know how to do their jobs the right way. And she and her father further believe that it is only when employees understand the right way to do their jobs that there is any hope their jobs will be accomplished the way the Carters want them to be accomplished.

Questions

1. Specifically, what should the Carters cover in their new employee orientation program and how should they convey this information?

2. In the HR management course Jennifer took, the book suggested using a job instruction sheet to identify tasks performed by an employee. Should the Carter Cleaning Centers use a form like this for the counter person's job? If so, what should the form look like, say, for a counter person?

3. Which specific training techniques should Jennifer use to train her pressers, her cleaner/spotters, her managers, and her counter people? Why should these training techniques be used?

TRANSLATING STRATEGY INTO HR POLICIES & PRACTICES CASE

THE HOTEL PARIS CASE

The New Training Program

The Hotel Paris's competitive strategy is "To use superior guest service to differentiate the Hotel Paris properties, and to thereby increase the length of stay and return rate of guests, and thus boost revenues and profitability." HR manager Lisa Cruz must now formulate functional policies and activities that support this competitive strategy by eliciting the required employee behaviors and competencies.

As she reviewed her company's training processes, Lisa had reasons to be concerned. For one thing, the Hotel Paris relied almost exclusively on informal on-the-job training. New security guards attended a 1-week program offered by a law enforcement agency, but all other new hires, from assistant manager to housekeeping crew, learned the rudiments of their jobs from their colleagues and their supervisors, on the job. Lisa noted that the drawbacks of this informality were evident when she compared the Hotel Paris's performance on various training metrics with those of other hotels and service firms. For example, in terms of number of hours training per employee per year, number of hours training for new employees, cost per trainee hour, and percent of payroll spent on training, the Hotel Paris was far from the norm when benchmarked against similar firms.

Indeed, as Lisa and the CFO reviewed the measures of the Hotel Paris's current training efforts, it was clear that (when compared to similar companies) some changes were in order. Most other service companies provided at least 40 hours of training per employee per year, while the Hotel Paris offered, on average, no more than 5 or 6 hours. Similar firms offered at least 40 hours of training per new employee, while the Hotel Paris offered, at most, 10. Even the apparently "good" metrics comparisons simply masked poor results. For example, whereas most service firms spend about 8% of their payrolls on training, the Hotel Paris spent less than 1%. The problem, of course, was that the Hotel Paris's training was nonexistent. Given this and the common sense links between (1) employee training and (2) employee performance, the CFO gave his go-ahead for Lisa and her team to design a comprehensive package of training programs for all Hotel Paris employees.

Questions

1. Based on what you read in this chapter, what do you suggest Lisa and her team do first with respect to training? Why?

2. Have Lisa and the CFO sufficiently investigated whether training is really called for? Why? What would you suggest?

3. Based on what you read in this chapter and what you may access via the Web, develop a detailed training program for one of these hotel positions: security guard, housekeeper, or valet/door person.

KEY TERMS

employee orientation, *244*

training, *246*

negligent training, *246*

task analysis, *248*

competency model, *248*

performance analysis, *249*

on-the-job training (OJT), *253*

apprenticeship training, *255*

job instruction training (JIT), *255*

programmed learning, *256*

electronic performance support systems (EPSS), *257*

job aid, *258*

virtual classroom, *261*

lifelong learning, *261*

cross training, *262*

management development, *263*

job rotation, *263*

action learning, *264*

case study method, *264*

management game, *264*

role playing, *265*

behavior modeling, *265*

in-house development center, *266*

executive coach, *266*

organizational development, *270*

controlled experimentation, *272*

ENDNOTES

1. Marjorie Derven, "Management Onboarding," *Training & Development*, April 2008, pp. 49–52.

2. Sabrina Hicks, "Successful Orientation Programs," *Training & Development*, April 2000, p. 59. See also Howard Klein and Natasha Weaver, "The Effectiveness of an Organizational Level Orientation Program in the Socialization of New

Hires," *Personnel Psychology* 53 (2000), pp. 47–66; and Laurie Friedman, "Are You Losing Potential New Hires at Hello?" *Training & Development*, November 2006, pp. 25–27.

3. Charlotte Garvey, "The Whirlwind of a New Job," *HR Magazine*, June 2001, p. 111. See also Talya Bauer et al., "Newcomer Adjustment During Organizational Socialization: A Meta-Analytic Review of Antecedents, Outcomes, and Methods," *Journal of Applied Psychology* 92, no. 3 (2007), pp. 707–721.

4. Sheila Hicks et al., "Orientation Redesign," *Training & Development*, July 2006, pp. 43–46.

5. See, for example, John Kammeyer-Mueller and Connie Wanberg, "Unwrapping the Organizational Entry Process: Disentangling Multiple Antecedents and Their Pathways to Adjustments," *Journal of Applied Psychology* 88, no. 5 (2003), pp. 779–794.

6. Ed Frauenheim, "IBM Learning Programs Get a 'Second Life,'" *Workforce Management*, December 11, 2006, p. 6. See also J. T. Arnold, "Gaming Technology Used To Orient New Hires," *HRMagazine* (2009 HR Trendbook supp), pp. 36, 38.

7. Jennifer Taylor Arnold, "Ramping Up on Boarding," *HR Magazine*, May 2010, pp. 75–78.

8. www.workday.com/company/news/workdaymobility.php, accessed March 24, 2009.

9. Mindy Chapman, "The Return on Investment for Training," *Compensation &Benefits Review*, January/February 2003, pp. 32–33.

10. Rita Smith, "Aligning Learning with Business Strategy," *Training & Development*, November 2008, pp. 41–43.

11. Christine Ellis and Sarah Gale, "A Seat at the Table," *Training*, March 2001, pp. 90–96.

12. Christopher Glynn, "Building a Learning Infrastructure," *Training & Development*, January 2008, pp. 38–43. Training and development executives at Kelly Services Inc. meet periodically with the company's senior executives to "identify new priorities and reallocate training dollars as needed, based on the strategic needs of the business." Garry Kranz, "More to Learn," *Workforce Management*, January 2011, p. 27.

13. Rachel Dodes, "At Macy's, a Makeover on Service," *The Wall Street Journal*, April 11, 2011, p. B-10.

14. Ibid.

15. Nancy DeViney and Brenda Sugrue, "Learning Outsourcing: A Reality Check," *Training & Development*, December 2004, p. 41. See also "How Are Organizations Training Today?," *HR Focus* 86, no. 7 (July 2009), pp. 52–53.

16. Brenda Sugrue et al., "What in the World Is WLP?" *Training & Development*, January 2005, pp. 51–54.

17. "Companies Invested More in Training Despite Economic Setbacks, Survey Says," *BNA Bulletin to Management*, March 7, 2002, p. 73; "Employee Training Expenditures on the Rise," *American Salesman* 49, no. 1 (January 2004), pp. 26–28.

18. "Companies Invested More in Training"; Andrew Paradise, "The 2008 ASTD State of the Industry Report Shows Sustained Support for Corporate Learning," *Training & Development*, November 2008, pp. 45–51.

19. W. Clayton Allen, "Overview and Evolution of the ADDIE Training System," *Advances in Developing Human Resources* 8, no. 4 (November 2006), pp. 430–441.

20. www.intulogy.com/process//, accessed April 20, 2011.

21. P. Nick Blanchard and James Thacker, *Effective Training* (Upper Saddle River, NJ: Pearson, 2010), pp. 26–94, 153–199, 285–316; see also, Bruno Neal, "e-ADDIE!," *T+D* 65, no. 3 (March 2011), p. 76–77.

22. P. Nick Blanchard and James Thacker, *Effective Training: Systems, Strategies and Practices* (Upper Saddle River, NJ: Prentice Hall, 1999), pp. 138–139. See also Matthew Casey and Dennis Doverspike, "Training Needs Analysis and Evaluation for New Technologies Through the Use of Problem Based Inquiry," *Performance Improvement Quarterly* 18, no. 1 (2005), pp. 110–124.

23. See, for example, Jennifer Salopek, "The Power of the Pyramid," *Training and Development* (May 2009), pp. 70–73.

24. Richard Montier et al., "Competency Models Develop Top Performance," *Training and Development* (July 2006): 47–50. See also Jennifer Salopek, "The Power of the Pyramid," *Training and Development* (May 2009): 70–73.

25. Tom Barron, "When Things Go Haywire," *Training & Development*, February 1999, pp. 25–27.

26. Employers increasingly utilize learning content management systems (LCMS) to compile and author training content. See, for example, Bill Perry, "Customized Content at Your Fingertips," *Training and Development* (June 2009), pp. 29–30.

27. Jay Bahlis, "Blueprint for Planning Learning," *Training & Development*, March 2008, pp. 64–67.

28. P. Nick Blanchard and James Thacker, *Effective Training: Systems, Strategies, and Practices* (Upper Saddle River, NJ: Prentice Hall, 2007), p. 8; and G. Sadri, "Boosting Performance Through Self-Efficacy," *T+D* 65 no. 6 (June 2011), pp. 30–31.

29. Ibid.

30. Ibid., p. 90.

31. Kenneth Wexley and Gary Latham, *Developing and Training Human Resources in Organizations* (Upper Saddle River, NJ: Prentice Hall, 2002), p. 305.

32. Ibid.

33. Kathryn Tyler, "Focus on Training," *HR Magazine*, May 2000, pp. 94–102.

34. Janice A. Cannon-Bowers et al., "Framework for Understanding Pre-Practice Conditions and Their Impact on Learning," *Personnel Psychology* 51 (1998), pp. 291–320; see also, J. S. Goodman, et al., "Feedback Specificity, Information Processing, and Transfer of Training," *Organizational Behavior and Human Decision Processes* 115 no. 2 (July 2011), pp. 253–67.

35. Ibid., p. 305.

36. Ibid., and see Kendra Lee, "Reinforce Training," *Training* 48 no. 3(May/June 2011), p. 24.

37. Alan Saks and Monica Belcourt, "An Investigation of Training Activities and Transfer of Training in Organizations," *Human Resource Management* 45, no. 4 (Winter 2006), pp. 629–648. The percentage of managers transferring behaviors from training to the job may be as low as 10% to 20%. See George Vellios, "On the Level," *Training & Development*, December 2008, pp. 26–29. See also K. Lee, "Implement Training Successfully," *Training* 46, no. 5 (June 2009), p. 16.

38. Large training providers include Element K, Geo Learning, learn.com, Outsmart, Plateau, Saba People Systems, and Sum-Total Systems. "Training Providers," *Workforce Management*, January 2011, p. 8.

39. Wexley and Latham, *Developing and Training Human Resources*, pp. 78–79.

40. Donna Goldwasser, "Me a Trainer?" *Training*, April 2001, pp. 60–66; http://employment.menswearhouse.com/ats/advantageSelector.action;jsessionid=C6EA17158451F5A2902F7195B678CF6A?type=training, accessed June 1, 2011.

41. See for example, www.aps-online.net/consulting/structured_ojt.htm, accessed June 1, 2011; and Kathryn Tyler, "15 Ways to Train on the Job," *HR Magazine* 53 no. 9 (September 2008) pp. 105–108.

42. The following four steps in on-the-job training based on William Berliner and William McLarney, *Management Practice and Training* (Burr Ridge, IL: McGraw-Hill, 1974), pp. 442–443. For the discussion of employee task analysis, see "Eight Steps to Better On-the-Job Training," *HR Focus*, 80 no. 7 (July 2003), pp. 11, 13–14.

43. Cindy Waxer, "Steelmaker Revives Apprentice Program to Address Graying Workforce, Forge Next Leaders," *Workforce Management*, January 30, 2006, p. 40.

44. Kermit Kaleba, "New Changes to Apprenticeship Program Could Be Forthcoming," *Training & Development*, February 2008, p. 14.

45. Robert Weintraub and Jennifer Martineau, "The Just in Time Imperative," *Training & Development*, June 2002, p. 52; and Andrew Paradise, "Informal Learning: Overlooked or Overhyped?" *Training & Development*, July 2008, pp. 52–53.

46. Aparna Nancherla, "Knowledge Delivered in Any Other Form Is . . . Perhaps Sweeter," *Training & Development*, May 2009, pp. 54–60.

47. Nadira Hira, "The Making of a UPS Driver," *Fortune*, November 12, 2007, p. 120.

48. Arthur Winfred Jr. et al., "Effectiveness of Training in Organizations: A Meta Analysis of Design and Evaluation Features,"

Journal of Applied Psychology 88, no. 2 (2003), pp. 234–245.

49. Donald Michalak and Edwin G. Yager, *Making the Training Process Work* (New York: Harper & Row, 1979), pp. 108–111. See also Richard Wiegand, "Can All Your Trainees Hear You?" *Training & Development Journal* 41, no. 8 (August 1987), pp. 38–43; and "Dos and Don'ts at the Podium," *Journal of Accountancy* 200, no. 3 (September 2005).

50. Jacqueline Schmidt and Joseph Miller, "The Five-Minute Rule for Presentations," *Training & Development*, March 2000, pp. 16–17; and "Dos and Don'ts at the Podium," op cit.

51. G. N. Nash, J. P. Muczyk, and F. L. Vettori, "The Role and Practical Effectiveness of Programmed Instruction," *Personnel Psychology* 24 (1971), pp. 397–418; Duane Schultz and Sydney Ellen Schultz, *Psychology and Work Today* (Upper Saddle River, NJ: Prentice Hall, 1998), pp. 181–183; chemistry study based on N. Izzet Kurbanoglu, Yavuz Taskesenligil and Mustafa Sozbilir, "Programmed Instruction Revisited: A Study on Teaching Stereochemistry," *Chemistry Education Research and Practice* 7, no. 1 (2006), pp. 13–21.

52. Wexley and Latham, *Developing and Training*, pp. 131–133. See also Teri O. Grady and Mike Matthews, "Video . . . Through the Eyes of the Trainee," *Training* 24, no. 7 (July 1987), pp. 57–62; "New ARTBA PPE Video and Laborers' Night Work Suggestions Highlight Construction Safety Advances," *EHS Today* 2, no. 7 (July 2009), p. 51.

53. Paula Ketter, "What Can Training Do for Brown?" *Training & Development*, May 2008, pp. 30–36.

54. Craig Marion, "What Is the EPSS movement and What Does It Mean to Information Designers?" August 20, 1999.

55. Josh Bersin and Karen O'Leonard, "Performance Support Systems," *Training & Development*, April 2005, p. 68.

56. Blanchard and Thacker, *Effective Training*, p. 163.

57. www.radvision.com/Support/cisco.htm, accessed June 1, 2011.

58. Ibid.

59. Dina Berta, "Computer-Based Training Clicks with Both Franchisees and Their Employees," *Nation's Restaurant News*, July 9, 2001, pp. 1, 18; and, "Is Online Fall Protection Training Effective?" *EHS Today* 3, no. 7 (July 2010).

60. P. Nick Blanchard and James Thacker, *Effective Training: Systems, Strategies, and Practices* (Upper Saddle River, NJ: Pearson, 2003), p. 247; see also Michael Laff, "Simulations: Slowly Proving Their Worth," *Training & Development*, June 2007, pp. 30–34.

61. Laff, "Simulations."

62. Blanchard and Thacker, *Effective Training*, 2003, p. 248.

63. Ibid., p. 249. See also Kim Kleps, "Virtual Sales Training Scores a Hit," *Training & Development*, December 2006, pp. 63–64.

64. Paul Harris, "Simulation: The Game Is On," *Training & Development*, October 2003, p. 49. See also Jenni Jarventaus, "Virtual Threat, Real Sweat," *Training & Development*, May 2007, pp. 72–78.

65. Jarventaus, "Virtual Threat, Real Sweat."

66. Clark Aldrich, "Engaging Mini-Games Find Niche in Training," *Training & Development*, July 2007, pp. 22–24; and "Cisco's Global Training Machine," *Workforce Management*, November 17, 2008, p. 30.

67. "What Do Simulations Cost?" *Training & Development*, June 2007, p. 88; see also Paul Harris, "Immersive Learning Seeks a Foothold," *Training & Development*, January 2009, pp. 40–45; and R. S. Polimeni et al., "Using Computer Simulations to Recruit and Train Generation Y Accountants," *The CPA Journal* 79, no. 5 (May 2009), pp. 64–68.

68. Pat Galagan, "Second That," *Training & Development*, February 2008, pp. 34–37.

69. Garry Kranz, "More to Learn," *Workforce Management*, January 2011, p. 27; quote is from Ann Pace, "Spurring Innovation and Engaging the Learners of the 2011 Workplace," *T+D* 65, no. 8 (August 2011), pp. 64–69

70. See, for example, Rockley Miller, "New Training Looms," *Hotel and Motel Management*, April 4, 1994, pp. 26, 30; Albert Ingram, "Teaching with Technology," *Association Management* 48 (June 1996), pp. 31–34; Sandra Vera-Munoz et al., "Enhancing Knowledge Sharing in Public Accounting Firms," *Accounting Horizons* 20, no. 2 (June 2006), pp. 133–155.

71. Kevin Alansky, "Blackboard Pays Off for ADP," *T+D* 65, no. 6 (June 2011), pp. 68–69.

72. Greg Wright, "Retailers Buy into Relearning," *HR Magazine*, December 7, 2010, pp. 87–90.

73. John Zonneveld, "GM Dealer Training Goes Global," *Training & Development*, December 2006, pp. 47–51.

74. "The Next Generation of Corporate Learning," *Training & Development*, June 2003, p. 47.

75. Ibid.

76. For a list of guidelines for using e-learning, see, for example, Mark Simon, "E-Learning No How," *Training & Development*, January 2009, pp. 34–39.

77. "The Next Generation of Corporate Learning," *Training & Development*, June 2004, p. 47; Jennifer Hofmann and Nanatte Miner, "Real Blended Learning Stands Up," *Training & Development*, September 2008, pp. 28–31; J. Hofmann, "Top 10 Challenges of Blended Learning," *Training* (Minneapolis, Minn.) 48 no. 2 (March/April 2011), pp. 12–13; and Lee Salz, "Use Webinars for Training and Revenue," *Training* 48, no. 2 (March/April 2011), p. 14

78. Ruth Clark, "Harnessing the Virtual Classroom," *Training & Development*, November 2005, pp. 40–46.

79. Jennifer Taylor Arnold, "Learning On-the-Fly," *HR Magazine*, September 2007,

p. 137; see also, M. Donahue, "Mobile Learning is the Next Generation in Training." *Hotel Management* 226 no. 4 (April 4, 2011), p. 17.

80. www.dominknow.com, accessed March 23, 2009.

81. Elizabeth Agnvall, "Just-in-Time Training," *HR Magazine*, May 2006, pp. 67–78.

82. Ibid.

83. For a similar program at Accenture, see Don Vanthournout and Dana Koch, "Training at Your Fingertips," *Training & Development*, September 2008, pp. 52–57. For a discussion of blogs in training see Becky Livingston, "Harnessing Blogs for Learning," *T+D* 65, no. 5 (May 2011), pp. 76–77.

84. Traci Sitzmann et al., "The Comparative Effectiveness of Web-Based and Classroom Instruction: A Meta-Analysis," *Personnel Psychology* 59 (2006), pp. 623–664.

85. Susan Ladika, "When Learning Lasts a Lifetime," *HR Magazine*, May 2008, p. 57.

86. Jeremy Smerd, "New Workers Sorely Lacking Literacy Skills," *Workforce Management*, December 10, 2008, p. 6.

87. Paula Ketter, "The Hidden Disability," *Training & Development*, June 2006, pp. 34–40.

88. Jennifer Salopek, "The Growth of Succession Management," *Training & Development*, June 2007, pp. 22–24; and Kermit Kaleba, "Businesses Continue to Push for Lifelong Learning," *Training & Development*, June 2007, p. 14.

89. Rita Zeidner, "One Workforce—Many Languages," *HR Magazine*, January 2009, pp. 33–37.

90. Matthew Reis, "Do-It-Yourself Diversity," *Training & Development*, March 2004, pp. 80–81.

91. www.prismdiversity.com/resources/diversity_training.html, accessed June 1, 2011.

92. Jennifer Salopek, "Trends: Lost in Translation," *Training & Development*, December 2003, p. 15; www.visionpoint.com/training-solutions/title/just-be-fair-basic-diversity-training, accessed June 17, 2011.

93. Blanchard and Thacker, pp. 403–405.

94. Ibid., p. 404.

95. Holly Dolezalek, "Extreme Training," *Training* 47, no. 1 (January 2010), pp. 26–28.

96. Douglas Shuit, "Sound of the Retreat," *Workforce Management*, September 2003, p. 40.

97. For a discussion of leadership development tools, see John Beeson, "Building Bench Strength: A Tool Kit for Executive Development," *Business Horizons* 47, no. 6 (November 2004), pp. 3–9. See also Rita Smith and Beth Bledsoe, "Grooming Leaders for Growth," *Training & Development*, August 2006, pp. 47–50.

98. Paula Caligiuri, "Developing Global Leaders," *Human Resource Management Review* 16 (2006), pp. 219–228.

99. Ann Pomeroy, "Head of the Class," *HR Magazine*, January 2005, p. 57.

100. Mike Czarnowsky, "Executive Development," *Training & Development*, September 2008, pp. 44–45.

101. "Thrown into Deep End, Workers Surface as Leaders," *BNA Bulletin to Management*, July 11, 2002, p. 223. See also Ann Locke and Arlene Tarantino, "Strategic Leadership Development," *Training & Development*, December 2006, pp. 53–55.

102. Chris Whitcomb, "Scenario-Based Training at the FBI," *Training & Development*, June 1999, pp. 42–46. See also Michael Laff, "Serious Gaming: The Trainer's New Best Friend," *Training & Development*, January 2007, pp. 52–57.

103. http://teamcommunication.blogspot.com/, accessed June 17, 2011.

104. http://www.amanet.org/, accessed August 22, 2011.

105. For a list of Harvard programs, see, http://www.exed.hbs.edu/programs/Pages/default.aspx, accessed August 22, 2011.

106. Ann Pomeroy, "Head of the Class," *HR Magazine*, January 2005, p. 57. See also Michael Laff, "Centralized Training Leads to Nontraditional Universities," *Training & Development*, January 2007, pp. 27–29; and Chris Musselwhite, "University Executive Education Gets Real," *Training & Development*, May 2006, p. 57.

107. Norman Maier, Allen Solem, and Ayesha Maier, *The Role Play Technique* (San Diego, CA: University Associates, 1975), pp. 2–3. See also Karen Griggs, "A Role Play for Revising Style and Applying Management Theories," *Business Communication Quarterly* 68, no. 1 (March 2005), pp. 60–65.

108. Paul Taylor et al., "A Meta-Analytic Review of Behavior Modeling Training," *Journal of Applied Psychology* 90, no. 4 (2005), pp. 692–719.

109. Martha Peak, "Go Corporate U!" *Management Review* 86, no. 2 (February 1997), pp. 33–37; and Jessica Li and Amy Lui Abel, "Prioritizing and Maximizing the Impact of Corporate Universities," *T+D* 65, no. 5 (May 2011), pp. 54–57.

110. Russell Gerbman, "Corporate Universities 101," *HR Magazine*, February 2000, pp. 101–106; Holly Dolezalek, "University 2.0," *Training* 44, no. 8 (September 2007).

111. "Executive Coaching: Corporate Therapy," *The Economist*, November 15, 2003, p. 61. See also Steve Gladis, "Executive Coaching Builds Steam in Organizations," *Training & Development*, December 2007, pp. 59–61.

112. "As Corporate Coaching Goes Mainstream, Key Prerequisite Overlooked: Assessment," *BNA Bulletin to Management*, May 16, 2006, p. 153.

113. James Smither et al., "Can Working with an Executive Coach Improve Multisource Feedback Ratings over Time?" *Personnel Psychology* 56, no. 1 (Spring 2003), pp. 23–44.

114. This is based on Diane Brady, "Can GE Still Manage?" *Bloomberg Businessweek*, April 25, 2010, p. 29.

115. Ibid.

116. Quoted and abstracted from "Five Rules for Talent Management in the New Economy," May 2010, http://www.towerswatson.com/viewpoints/1988, accessed August 22, 2011.

117. Quoted and abstracted from Jean Martin and Conrad Schmidt, "How to Keep Your Top Talent," *Harvard Business Review* (May 2010): 53–61.

118. Ibid.

119. Ibid.

120. Ed Fraeuenheim, "Lost in the Shuffle," *Workforce Management*, January 14, 2008, p. 13.

121. Paul Harris, "A New Market Emerges," *Training & Development*, September 2003, pp. 30–38. For an example of a successful organizational change, see Jordan Mora et al., "Recipe for Change," *Training & Development*, March 2008, pp. 42–46.

122. See, for example, John Austin, "Mapping Out a Game Plan for Change," *HR Magazine*, April 2009, pp. 39–42.

123. Nokia examples based on www.engadget.com/2011/02/05/nokia-reportedly-planning-organizational-changes-mobile-phone/, and http://press.nokia.com/press-release/, accessed June 17, 2011.

124. Gina Gotsill and Meryl Natchez, "From Resistance to Acceptance: How to Implement Change Management," *Training & Development*, November 2007, pp. 24–26.

125. See for example, ibid.

126. The steps are based on Michael Beer, Russell Eisenstat, and Bert Spector, "Why Change Programs Don't Produce Change," *Harvard Business Review*, November–December 1990, pp. 158–166; Thomas Cummings and Christopher Worley, *Organization Development and Change* (Minneapolis, MN: West Publishing Company, 1993); John P. Kotter, "Leading Change: Why Transformation Efforts Fail," *Harvard Business Review*, March–April 1995, pp. 59–66; and John P. Kotter, *Leading Change* (Boston: Harvard Business School Press, 1996). Change doesn't necessarily have to be painful. See, for example, Eric Abrahamson, "Change Without Pain," *Harvard Business Review*, July–August 2000, pp. 75–79. See also David Herold et al., "Beyond Change Management: A Multilevel Investigation of Contextual and Personal Influences on Employees' Commitment to Change," *Journal of Applied Psychology* 92, no. 4 (2007), p. 949.

127. Ibid.

128. Kotter, "Leading Change," p. 85.

129. Beer, Eisenstat, and Spector, "Why Change Programs Don't Produce Change," p. 164.

130. Stacie Furst and Daniel Cable, "Employee Resistance to Organizational Change: Managerial Influence Tactics and Leader Member Exchange," *Journal of Applied Psychology* 3, no. 2 (2008), p. 453.

131. Beer, Eisenstat, and Spector, "Why Change Programs Don't Produce Change," p. 164.

132. Robert J. House, *Management Development* (Ann Arbor, MI: Bureau of Industrial Relations, University of Michigan, 1967), p. 71; Louis White and Kevin Wooten, "Ethical Dilemmas in Various Stages of Organizational Development," *Academy of Management Review* 8, no. 4 (1983), pp. 690–697.

133. Wendell French and Cecil Bell Jr., *Organization Development* (Upper Saddle River, NJ: Prentice Hall, 1995), pp. 171–193.

134. Benjamin Schneider, Steven Ashworth, A. Catherine Higgs, and Linda Carr, "Design Validity, and Use of Strategically Focused Employee Attitude Surveys," *Personnel Psychology* 49 (1996), pp. 695–705.

135. Cummings and Worley, *Organization Development and Change*, p. 501.

136. For a description of how to make OD a part of organizational strategy, see Aubrey Mendelow and S. Jay Liebowitz, "Difficulties in Making OD a Part of Organizational Strategy," *Human Resource Planning* 12, no. 4 (1995), pp. 317–329; and Valerie Garrow and Sharon Varney, "What Does OD Do?" *People Management* (June 4, 2009).

137. Wexley and Latham, *Developing and Training Human Resources in Organizations*, p. 128.

138. Todd Raphel, "What Learning Management Reports Do for You," *Workforce*, June 2001, pp. 56–58.

139. Wexley and Latham, *Developing and Training Human Resources in Organizations*, p. 153.

140. See, for example, Jack Phillips, and Patti Phillips, "Moving From Evidence to Proof," *T+D* 65, no. 8 (August 2011), pp. 34–39 for a discussion of a process for gathering training assessment data.

141. See, for example, Antonio Aragon-Sanchez et al., "Effects of Training on Business Results," *International Journal of Human Resource Management* 14, no. 6 (September 2003), pp. 956–980.

142. A recent review concluded that the relationship of training to human resource outcomes and organizational performance is positive, but that training "is only very weakly related to financial outcomes." Given this, managers may want to assess training results not just in terms of employee behavior and performance, but company financial performance as well. See Phyllis Tharenou et al., "A Review and Critique of Research on Training and Organizational Level Outcomes," *Human Resource Management Review* 17 (2007), pp. 251–273.

9

Performance Management and Appraisal

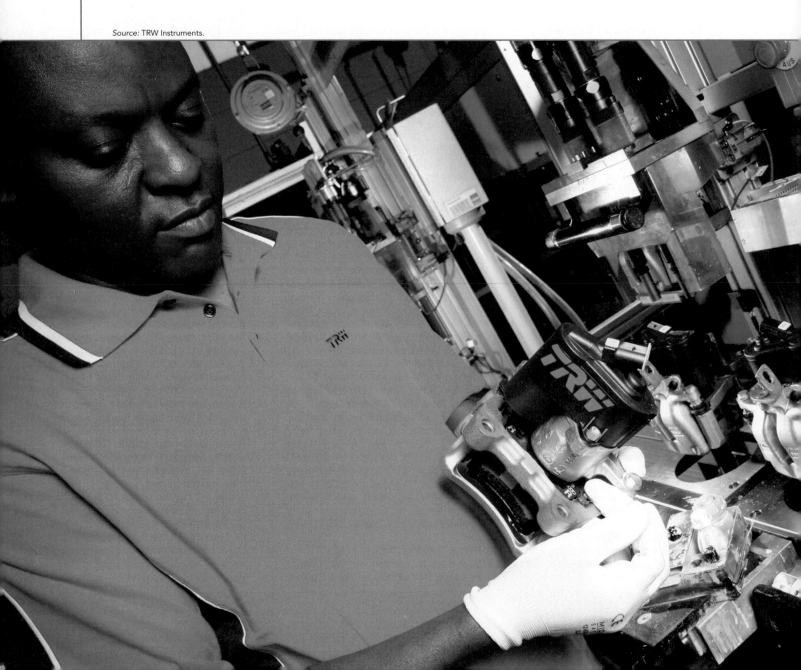

LEARNING OBJECTIVES

1. Define performance management and discuss how it differs from performance appraisal.

2. Describe the appraisal process.

3. Set effective performance appraisal standards.

4. Develop, evaluate, and administer at least four performance appraisal tools.

5. Explain and illustrate the problems to avoid in appraising performance.

6. Discuss the pros and cons of using different raters to appraise a person's performance.

7. Perform an effective appraisal interview.

TRW supplies automotive steering, braking, and safety and electronic equipment to customers worldwide.[1] Several years ago, TRW was deeply in debt.[2] With over 100,000 employees on five continents, TRW management knew it had to base its new strategy on improving competitiveness and performance. At the time, most of the firm's far-flung departments used their own paper-based performance appraisal systems. Top management decided it needed a new company-wide performance management system to help bring what TRW's employees were doing into synch with the firm's new strategic goals.

WHERE ARE WE NOW . . .

Chapters 6–8 explained selecting, training, and developing employees. After employees have been on the job for some time, you should appraise their performance. The purpose of this chapter is to show you how to do that. The main topics we cover include the performance appraisal process, appraisal methods, appraisal performance problems and solutions, performance management, and the appraisal interview. Career planning is a logical consequence of appraisal: We'll turn to career planning in Chapter 10.

Access a host of interactive learning aids at **www.mymanagementlab.com** to help strengthen your understanding of the chapter concepts.

1 Define performance management and discuss how it differs from performance appraisal.

BASIC CONCEPTS IN PERFORMANCE MANAGEMENT AND APPRAISAL

Few things supervisors do are fraught with more peril than appraising subordinates' performance. Employees tend to be overly optimistic about what their ratings will be. They also know that their raises, careers, and peace of mind may hinge on how you rate them. As if that's not enough, few appraisal processes are as fair as employers think they are. Hundreds of obvious and not-so-obvious problems (such as bias, and the tendency for supervisors to rate everyone "average") distort the process. However, the perils notwithstanding, performance appraisal plays a central role in human resource management.

2 Describe the appraisal process.

The Performance Appraisal Process

Performance appraisal means evaluating an employee's current and/or past performance relative to his or her performance standards. You may equate appraisal forms like Figure 9-1 with "performance appraisal," but appraisal involves more than forms.

FIGURE 9-1 Online Faculty Evaluation Form

Source: Used with permission of Central Oregon Community College.

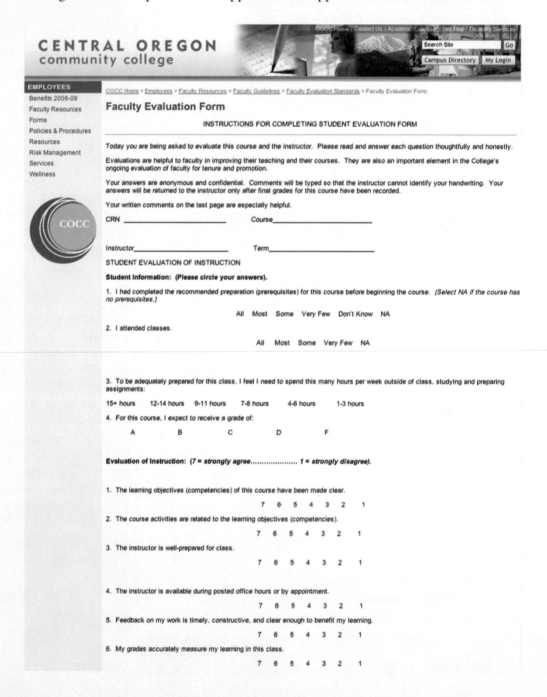

FIGURE 9-1 (Continued)

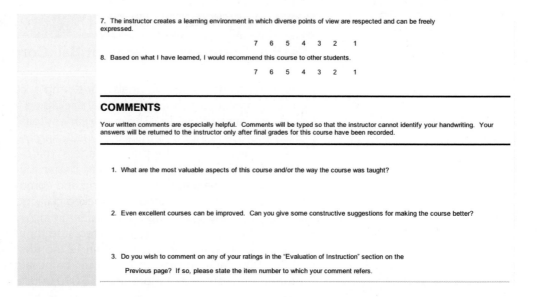

Effective appraisal also requires that the supervisor set performance standards. And it requires that the employee receives the training, feedback, and incentives required to eliminate performance deficiencies.

Effective appraisals begin before the actual appraisal, with the manager defining the employee's job and performance criteria. *Defining the job* means making sure that you and your subordinate agree on his or her duties and job standards and on the appraisal method you will use. Stripped to its essentials, performance appraisal always involves the 3-step **performance appraisal process**: (1) setting work standards; (2) assessing the employee's actual performance relative to those standards (this usually involves some rating form); and (3) providing feedback to the employee with the aim of helping him or her to eliminate performance deficiencies or to continue to perform above par.

Why Appraise Performance?

There are five reasons to appraise subordinates' performance.

- First, most employers still base pay, promotion, and retention decisions on the employee's appraisal.[3]

- Second, appraisals play a central role in the employer's *performance management* process. Performance management means continuously making sure that each employee's and team's performance makes sense in terms of the company's overall goals. The accompanying HR as a Profit Center feature illustrates this.

- Third, the appraisal lets you and the subordinate develop a plan for correcting any deficiencies, and to reinforce the things the subordinate does right.

- Fourth, appraisals should facilitate career planning. They provide an opportunity to review the employee's career plans in light of his or her exhibited strengths and weaknesses. We address career planning in Chapter 10.

- Finally, supervisors use appraisals to identify employees' training and development needs. The appraisal should enable the supervisor to identify if there is a "performance gap" between the employee's performance and his or her standards. And it should help identify the cause of any such gap, and the remedial steps required.

---

performance appraisal
Evaluating an employee's current and/or past performance relative to his or her performance standards.

performance appraisal process
A 3-step appraisal processing involving (1) setting work standards, (2) assessing the employee's actual performance relative to those standards, and (3) providing feedback to the employee with the aim of helping him or her to eliminate performance deficiencies or to continue to perform above par.

HR AS A PROFIT CENTER

Setting Performance Goals at Ball Corporation

Few HR practices have as pronounced an impact on a company's performance as does setting and measuring goals. For example, consider a report by management at Ball Corporation, which supplies metal packaging to customers such as food and paint manufacturers worldwide.[4] The management team at one Ball plant concluded that it could improve plant performance by instituting an improved process for setting goals and for ensuring that the plant's leaders' mind-sets and behaviors were in synch with these goals.[5] The new program began by training plant leaders on how to improve performance, and then setting and communicating daily performance goals. Management communicated and tracked daily goal attainment by distributing team scorecards to the plant's work teams. Plant employees received special coaching and training to ensure they had the skills required for achieving the goals.

According to management, within 12 months the plant increased production by 84,000,000 cans, improved customer complaints by 50 percent, and yielded a return-on-investment of more than $3,090,000.[6]

The Importance of Continuous Feedback

For accomplishing several of these aims, traditional annual or semiannual appraisal reviews make sense. For example, promotions and raises tend to be periodic decisions. Similarly, you probably wouldn't want to make career decisions without at least several months of data gathering and introspection.

However, it's usually a mistake to wait until the actual "appraisal" to let employees know what they're doing wrong and doing right. Aligning the employee's efforts with the job's standards should be a continuous process. When you see a performance problem, the time to take action is immediately—there is no substitute for nudging your employee's performance back into line continuously and incrementally. Similarly, when someone does something well, the best reinforcement comes immediately, not 6 months later.

Performance Management

Recognizing this, many employers today take a more continuous approach to the performance appraisal cycle. For example, at Toyota Motor's Lexington, Kentucky, Camry plant, the supervisors don't sit with individual employees to fill out forms and appraise them. Instead, teams of employees monitor their own results, even posting individual daily performance metrics. In frequent meetings, they continuously align those results with the work team's standards and with the plant's overall quality and productivity needs. They do this by continuously adjusting how they and their team members do things. Team members who need coaching and training receive it, and procedures that need changing are changed. This is *performance management* in action.

PERFORMANCE MANAGEMENT DEFINED   Performance management means different things to different people. Some use "performance management" as just a new way of saying "performance appraisal." Others say performance appraisal represents just the "appraisal" step of a three-step goal-setting/appraisal/feedback performance management process. In this book, we assume that **performance management** is a uniquely goal-oriented and continuous way to appraise and manage employees' performance. It is the "*continuous* process of identifying, measuring, and developing the performance of individuals and teams and *aligning* their performance with the organization's *goals*."[7]

The difference between performance management and performance appraisal is more than a matter of degree; it's a matter of substance. Many employers have what they call performance management processes, but in fact still use traditional performance appraisal. Continuous feedback and strategically related performance criteria are the two distinguishing characteristics of performance management. As one expert puts it, "a system that involves employee evaluations once a year without an ongoing effort to provide feedback and coaching so that performance can be improved is not a true performance management system."[8] Similarly, "performance management systems that do not make explicit the employee contribution to the organizational goals are not true performance management systems."[9] The accompanying Strategic Context feature illustrates this.

THE STRATEGIC CONTEXT

TRW

TRW management decided it needed a new company-wide performance management system to help bring its employees' actual performance into synch with the firm's new operating goals. Top management appointed a special team, and charged it with creating a "one company, one system" performance management system.

The team's aim was to quickly develop a performance management system that was *consistent* in that employees in all of TRW's far-flung organization could use the same system. It also had to be *comprehensive* in that it consolidated into a single integrated system the necessary goal setting, performance appraisal, professional development, and succession planning functions.

The new performance management system produced many benefits. Most notably, it focuses every employee's s attention on what each employee needs to do to contribute to achieving TRW's goals. It also identifies development needs that are relevant to both TRW and to the employee.

We'll discuss performance management more fully later in the chapter after we address some basics of performance appraisal.

Defining the Employee's Goals and Performance Standards

3 Set effective performance appraisal standards.

Most employees need and expect to know ahead of time on what basis their employer will appraise them.[10] Ideally, each employee's goals should derive from and contribute to the company's overall aims. The manager's goals flow from the vice president's, whose goals flow from the president's, for instance. However, setting useful goals is not as simple as it may appear. There is an art to setting effective goals.

First, the supervisor must decide what to measure. Many employers simply use packaged employee appraisal forms with generic scales, similar to that in Figure 9-1. That appraisal form shows what will be measured, for instance, "The instructor is well-prepared for class." Other firms use a management by objectives approach. Thus, the CEO may have a goal to double sales this year. Based on that, her vice president of sales has his or her own sales goals, and each salesperson has his or her sales goal, set in discussions with his or her supervisor.

It is typical to set measurable goals for each expectation you have for the employee. Suppose you expect your sales manager to "handle the company's three biggest accounts personally," and to "manage the sales force." You might measure the "personal selling" activity in terms of a money goal—how many dollars of sales the manager is to generate personally. You might measure "managing the sales force" in terms of a turnover goal (on the assumption that less than 10% of the sales force will quit in any given year if morale is high).

But is, say, a 10% turnover goal reasonable? One way to think of this is to remember that effective goals are "SMART." They are *specific*, and clearly state the desired results. They are *measurable*, and answer the question "How much?" They are

performance management
The *continuous* process of identifying, measuring, and developing the performance of individuals and teams and *aligning* their performance with the organization's *goals*.

attainable. They are *relevant,* and clearly derive from what the manager and company want to achieve. And they are *timely,* and reflect deadlines and milestones.[11]

HR IN PRACTICE: HOW TO SET EFFECTIVE GOALS   Behavioral science research studies suggest four guidelines for setting performance goals:

1. **Assign specific goals.** Employees who receive specific goals usually perform better than those who do not.
2. **Assign measurable goals.** Put goals in quantitative terms and include target dates or deadlines.
3. **Assign challenging but doable goals.** Goals should be challenging, but not so difficult that they appear impossible or unrealistic.
4. **Encourage participation.** The evidence suggests that participatively set goals do not consistently result in higher performance than assigned goals, nor do assigned goals consistently result in higher performance than participatively set ones. It is only when the participatively set goals are more difficult (are set higher) than the assigned ones that the participatively set goals produce higher performance. Because it tends to be easier to set higher standards when your employees participate in the process, participation tends to facilitate standards setting and performance.[12]

TALENT MANAGEMENT: BASING APPRAISAL STANDARDS ON REQUIRED COMPETENCIES   Other firms appraise employees based on the competencies and skills the job requires. For example, BP's exploration division appraises and rewards employees based on a skills matrix. This matrix shows (1) the basic skills required to do that job (such as "technical expertise") and (2) the minimum level of each skill that job requires.

THE ROLE OF JOB DESCRIPTIONS   Ideally, what to appraise and how to appraise it will be obvious from the job description. In terms of *what* criteria to appraise, the job description should list the job's duties or tasks, including how critical each is to the job, and how often it's performed. For example, a nurse's job description may include "safely administer patient medication" as a task. You might then appraise the nurse on "how well he or she safely administers patient medication," for instance using data from periodic hospital safety inspections.[13] The job description may also include strategically important behaviors such as "building patient trust and satisfaction." Their presence (either in the job description's list of duties or in a separate list of strategically relevant "core behaviors") enables the manager to identify competencies (such as "quality consciousness") to appraise that support the employers strategic aims.

Who Should Do the Appraising?

Appraisals by the immediate supervisor are still the heart of most appraisal processes. Getting a supervisor's appraisal is relatively straightforward and makes sense. The supervisor is usually in the best position to observe and evaluate his or her subordinate's performance. The supervisor is also responsible for that person's performance.

The human resources department serves a policy-making and advisory role. Generally, human resource managers provide the advice and the appraisal tool to use, but leave final decisions on procedures to operating division heads. The human resource team should also be responsible for training supervisors to improve their appraisal skills, for monitoring the appraisal system's effectiveness, and for ensuring that it complies with EEO laws.

Yet, although widely used, relying only on supervisors' appraisals isn't always advisable. For example, an employee's supervisor may not understand or appreciate how customers and colleagues see the employee's performance. Furthermore, there is always some danger of bias for or against the employee. If so, managers have several options.

PEER APPRAISALS   With more firms using self-managing teams, appraisal of an employee by his or her peers—peer appraisal—is popular. Typically, an employee due for an annual appraisal chooses an appraisal chairperson. The latter

Many employers use rating committees to appraise employees.

Source: Shutterstock.

then selects one supervisor and three peers to evaluate the employee's work.

Research indicates that peer appraisals can be effective. One study involved undergraduates placed into self-managing work groups. The researchers found that peer appraisals had "an immediate positive impact on [improving] perception of open communication, task motivation, social loafing, group viability, cohesion, and satisfaction."[14] Employees, in other words, seem to be motivated to meet their colleagues' expectations.

RATING COMMITTEES   A rating committee is usually composed of the employee's immediate supervisor and three or four other supervisors.[15]

Using multiple raters is advantageous. It can help cancel out problems such as bias on the part of individual raters.[16] It can also provide a way to include in the appraisal the different facets of an employee's performance observed by different appraisers. Multiple raters often see different facets of an employee's performance. Studies often find that the ratings obtained from different sources rarely match.[17] It's therefore advisable to obtain ratings from the supervisor, his or her boss, and at least one other manager who is familiar with the employee's work.[18] At a minimum, most employers require that the supervisor's boss sign off on any appraisals the supervisor does.

SELF-RATINGS   Some employers obtain employees' self-ratings, usually in conjunction with supervisors' ratings. The basic problem, of course, is that employees usually rate themselves higher than do their supervisors or peers.[19] One study found that, when asked to rate their own job performances, 40% of employees in jobs of all types placed themselves in the top 10%, and virtually all remaining employees rated themselves at least in the top 50%.[20] In another study, subjects' self-ratings correlated negatively with their subsequent performance in an assessment center—the higher they appraised themselves, the worse they did in the center. In contrast, an average of the person's supervisor, peer, and subordinate ratings predicted the subjects' assessment center performance.[21]

APPRAISAL BY SUBORDINATES   Many employers have subordinates rate their managers, usually for developmental rather than for pay purposes. Anonymity affects the feedback. Managers who receive feedback from subordinates who identify themselves view the upward feedback process more positively. However, subordinates prefer giving anonymous responses (not surprisingly), and those who must identify themselves tend to give inflated ratings.[22]

The evidence suggests that upward feedback can improve a manager's performance. One study focused on 252 managers during five annual administrations of an upward feedback program. Managers who were initially rated poor or moderate "showed significant improvements in [their] upward feedback ratings over the five-year period." In another study, cynicism toward management and inadequate time to interact with the boss reduced the upward appraisal's usefulness.[23] And, managers who met with their subordinates to discuss their upward feedback improved more than the managers who did not.[24]

360-DEGREE FEEDBACK   With 360-degree feedback, the employer collects performance information all around an employee—from his or her supervisors, subordinates, peers, and internal or external customers—generally for developmental rather than pay purposes.[25] The usual process is to have the raters complete online appraisal surveys on the ratee. Computerized systems then compile all this feedback into individualized reports to ratees (see the sample in Figure 9-2). The person may then meet with his or her supervisor to develop a self-improvement plan.

Results are mixed. Participants seem to prefer this approach, but one study concluded that multisource feedback led to "generally small" improvements in subsequent ratings by supervisors, peers, and subordinates. Improvement was most likely to occur when the feedback the person received indicated that change was necessary, and when the recipients believed that change was necessary and had a positive view of

FIGURE 9-2 Part of 360-Degree Feedback Survey

Source: www.hr-survey.com/sd3609q.htm, accessed April 28, 2009.

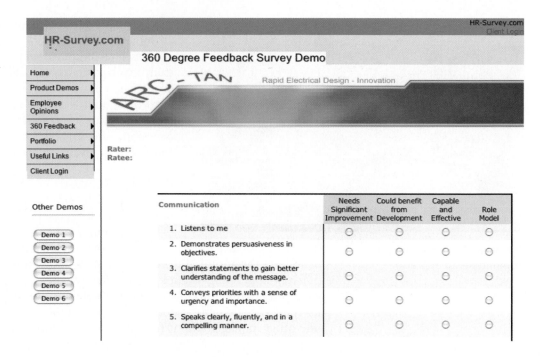

Supervisors must be familiar with appraisal techniques, understand and avoid problems that can cripple appraisals, and know how to conduct appraisals fairly.

the change process.[26] Also, 360-degree appraisals are more candid when subordinates know rewards or promotions are not involved.

There are several ways to improve 360-degree appraisals.

- Anchor the 360-degree rating dimensions (such as "conflict management") with specific behavioral examples (such as "effectively deals with conflicts").[27]
- Carefully train the people who are giving and receiving the feedback.[28]
- With so many appraisers involved, each potentially with his or her own ax to grind, make sure that the feedback the person receives is productive, unbiased, and development oriented.[29]
- Reduce the administrative costs associated with collecting multisource feedback by using a Web-based system such as the one in Figure 9-2. This lets the rater log in, open a screen with a rating scale, and rate the person along a series of competencies with ratings such as "capable and effective."[30]

TECHNIQUES FOR APPRAISING PERFORMANCE

The manager generally conducts the actual appraisal using a formal tool or method like one or more of those described next. The two basic questions in designing the actual appraisal tool are *what performance dimensions to measure,* and *how to measure* them. For example, in terms of *what dimensions to measure,* we might measure the employee's performance in terms of generic dimensions such as quality and timeliness, or with respect to achieving specific goals. In terms of *how to measure* it, you can use one or more of various tools or methods, such as graphic rating scales or forced distribution ("grading on a curve"). We'll start with the most popular, graphic rating scales.

Graphic Rating Scale Method

The **graphic rating scale** is the simplest and most popular method for appraising performance. Figure 9-3 shows one graphic rating scale. A graphic rating scale lists traits or performance dimensions (such as "communication" or "teamwork") and a range of performance values (from "below expectations" to "role model" or "unsatisfactory" to "outstanding,") for each trait. The supervisor rates each subordinate by

Sample Performance Rating Form

Employee's Name _____   Level: Entry-level employee

Manager's Name _____

Key Work Responsibilities   Results/Goals to Be Achieved
1. _____   1. _____
2. _____   2. _____
3. _____   3. _____
4. _____   4. _____

Communication

| 1 | 2 | 3 | 4 | 5 |

Below Expectations	Meets Expectations	Role Model
Even with guidance, fails to prepare straightforward communications, including forms, paperwork, and records, in a timely and accurate manner; products require minimal corrections.	With guidance, prepares straightforward communications, including forms, paperwork, and records, in a timely and accurate manner; products require minimal corrections.	Independently prepares communications, such as forms, paperwork, and records, in a timely, clear, and accurate manner; products require few, if any, corrections.
Even with guidance, fails to adapt style and materials to communicate straightforward information.	With guidance, adapts style and materials to communicate straightforward information.	Independently adapts style and materials to communicate information.

Organizational Know-How

| 1 | 2 | 3 | 4 | 5 |

Below Expectations	Meets Expectations	Role Model
<performance standards appear here>	<performance standards appear here>	<performance standards appear here>

Personal Effectiveness

| 1 | 2 | 3 | 4 | 5 |

Below Expectations	Meets Expectations	Role Model
<performance standards appear here>	<performance standards appear here>	<performance standards appear here>

Teamwork

| 1 | 2 | 3 | 4 | 5 |

Below Expectations	Meets Expectations	Role Model
<performance standards appear here>	<performance standards appear here>	<performance standards appear here>

Achieving Business Results

| 1 | 2 | 3 | 4 | 5 |

Below Expectations	Meets Expectations	Role Model
<performance standards appear here>	<performance standards appear here>	<performance standards appear here>

FIGURE 9-3 Sample Graphic Performance Rating Form

Source: Elaine Pulakos, "Performance Management," SHRM Foundation, 2004, pp. 16–17.

graphic rating scale
A scale that lists a number of traits and a range of performance for each. The employee is then rated by identifying the score that best describes his or her level of performance for each trait.

FIGURE 9-4 One Item from an Appraisal Form Assessing Employee Performance on Specific Job-Related Duties

Position: Pizza Chef			
Duty 1: Maintain adequate inventory of pizza dough		**Rating**	
Each round pizza dough must be between 12 and 14 ounces each, kneaded at least 2 minutes before being placed in the temperature and humidity-controlled cooler, and kept there for at least 5 hours prior to use. There should be enough, but no more for each day's demand.	Needs improvement	Satisfactory	Excellent

circling or checking the score that best describes the subordinate's performance for each trait. The manager then totals the assigned ratings for the traits.

4 Develop, evaluate, and administer at least four performance appraisal tools.

FIGURE 9-5 Appraisal Form for Assessing Both Competencies and Specific Objectives

Source: www.case.edu/finadmin/humres/policies/perfexempt.pdf, accessed May 17, 2007. Used with permission of Case Western Reserve University.

WHAT TO RATE?   We can use graphic ratings scales to illustrate the range of traits or performance dimensions one might evaluate. For example:

- As in Figure 9-3, some rating scales assess generic job dimensions such as communications, teamwork, know-how, and quantity.
- Another option is to rate the employee's performance on the job's actual duties. For example, Figure 9-4 shows part of an appraisal form for a pizza chef. This assesses the job's main specific duties, one of which is "Maintain adequate inventory of pizza dough." Here you would assess how well the employee did in exercising each of these duties.
- Or, you might rate (as in Section I of Figure 9-5) how well the employee did with respect to achieving specific performance expectations or objectives. Although not

SECTION I   Responsibilities/Objectives and Performance Standards in Support of Departmental Goals "Maximizing one's professional qualifications to make a difference"

SECTION II	Performance Competencies "Making a Difference by Working and Learning Together."	

	Mid-Year Progress Notes	End of Period Rating of Success and Effectiveness Comment and Place X on Scale to Rate Not Strong ———— Very Strong
Job Knowledge/Competency: Demonstrates the knowledge and skills necessary to perform the job effectively. Understands the expectations of the job and remains current regarding new developments in areas of responsibility. Performs responsibilities in accordance with job procedures and policies. Acts as a resource person upon whom others rely for assistance.		⊢—⊢—⊢—⊢—⊣
Quality/Quantity of Work: Completes assignments in a thorough, accurate, and timely manner that achieves expected outcomes. Exhibits concern for the goals and needs of the department and others that depend on services or work products. Handles multiple responsibilities in an effective manner. Uses work time productively.		⊢—⊢—⊢—⊢—⊣
Planning/Organization: Establishes clear objectives and organizes duties for self based on the goals of the department, division, or management center. Identifies resources required to meet goals and objectives. Seeks guidance when goals or priorities are unclear.		⊢—⊢—⊢—⊢—⊣
Initiative/Commitment: Demonstrates personal responsibility when performing duties. Offers assistance to support the goals and objectives of the department and division. Performs with minimal supervision. Meets work schedule/attendance expectations for the position.		⊢—⊢—⊢—⊢—⊣
Problem Solving/Creativity: Identifies and analyzes problems. Formulates alternative solutions. Takes or recommends appropriate actions. Follows up to ensure problems are resolved.		⊢—⊢—⊢—⊢—⊣
Teamwork and Cooperation: Maintains harmonious and effective work relationships with co-workers and constituents. Adapts to changing priorities and demands. Shares information and resources with others to promote positive and collaborative work relationships.		⊢—⊢—⊢—⊢—⊣
Interpersonal Skills: Deals positively and effectively with coworkers and constituents. Demonstrates respect for all individuals.		⊢—⊢—⊢—⊢—⊣
Communication (Oral and Written): Effectively conveys information and ideas both orally and in writing. Listens carefully and seeks clarification to ensure understanding.		⊢—⊢—⊢—⊢—⊣

Competencies Reviewed and Discussed:	Mid-Year Review	
Evaluator	Date	Employee Date

FIGURE 9-5 (Continued)

in the figure, "sell $600,000 worth of products per year" illustrates a performance expectation/objective.

- *Competency-based appraisal forms* are another option. Here you focus on the extent to which the employee exhibits the *competencies* (generally the skills and/or knowledge) needed to perform the job. Section II of Figure 9-5 illustrates this appraisal approach. To illustrate, one competency that a nurse supervisor should bring to the job might be "builds a culture that is open and receptive to improved clinical care." Why appraise such competencies? Suppose this hospital's strategic goals include improving quality of patient care. If so, then focusing the nurse supervisor's attention on improving his or her clinical care competencies better supports the hospital's strategy than would appraising how he or she rates on duties like "supervise one dozen nurses."[31]

Some graphic rating forms appraise several things. For example, Figure 9-5 (Sections I and II) assesses the employee's performance relating to both competencies and objectives. With respect to *competencies*, the employee is expected to develop and exhibit competencies (Section II) such as "identifies and analyzes problems" (Problem Solving), and "maintains harmonious and effective work relationships with co-workers and constituents" (Teamwork). The employee and supervisor would fill in the *objectives* section (Section I) at the start of the year, and then rate results and set new ones as part of the next appraisal.

FIGURE 9-6 Scale for
Alternate Ranking of Appraisee

ALTERNATION RANKING SCALE

Trait: _____

For the trait you are measuring, list all the employees you want to rank. Put the highest-ranking employee's name on line 1. Put the lowest-ranking employee's name on line 20. Then list the next highest ranking on line 2, the next lowest ranking on line 19, and so on. Continue until all names are on the scale.

Highest-ranking employee

1. _____   11. _____
2. _____   12. _____
3. _____   13. _____
4. _____   14. _____
5. _____   15. _____
6. _____   16. _____
7. _____   17. _____
8. _____   18. _____
9. _____   19. _____
10. _____   20. _____

Lowest-ranking employee

Alternation Ranking Method

Ranking employees from best to worst on a trait or traits is another option. Since it is usually easier to distinguish between the worst and best employees, an **alternation ranking method** is most popular. First, list all subordinates to be rated, and then cross out the names of any not known well enough to rank. Then, on a form like that in Figure 9-6, indicate the employee who is the highest on the performance dimension being measured and the one who is the lowest. Then choose the next highest and the next lowest, alternating between highest and lowest until all employees have been ranked.

Paired Comparison Method

The **paired comparison method** helps make the ranking method more precise. For every trait (quantity of work, quality of work, and so on), you pair and compare every subordinate with every other subordinate.

Suppose you have five employees to rate. In the paired comparison method, you make a chart, as in Figure 9-7, of all possible pairs of employees for each trait. Then, for each trait, indicate (with a + or −) who is the better employee of the pair. Next, add up the number of +'s for each employee. In Figure 9-7, Maria ranked highest (has the most + marks) for quality of work, whereas Art was ranked highest for creativity.

Forced Distribution Method

The **forced distribution method** is similar to grading on a curve. With this method, you place predetermined percentages of ratees into several performance categories. The proportions in each category need not be symmetrical; GE used top 20%, middle 70%, and bottom 10% for its managers. (GE now tells managers to use more discretion in assigning rankings, and no longer strictly adheres to its famous 20/70/10 split.)[32] Forced distribution makes some sense. It reflects the fact that top employees often outperform average or poor ones by as much as 100%.[33] About a fourth of *Fortune* 500 companies including Microsoft, Conoco, and Intel use versions of forced distribution.[34]

FIGURE 9-7 Ranking Employees by the Paired Comparison Method

Note: + means "better than." − means "worse than." For each chart, add up the number of +'s in each column to get the highest ranked employee.

FOR THE TRAIT "QUALITY OF WORK"

Employee rated:

As Compared to:	A Art	B Maria	C Chuck	D Diane	E José
A Art		+	+	−	−
B Maria	−		−	−	−
C Chuck	−	+		+	−
D Diane	+	+	−		+
E José	+	+	+	−	

Maria ranks highest here

FOR THE TRAIT "CREATIVITY"

Employee rated:

As Compared to:	A Art	B Maria	C Chuck	D Diane	E José
A Art		−	−	−	−
B Maria	+		−	+	+
C Chuck	+	+		−	+
D Diane	+	−	+		−
E José	+	−	−	+	

Art ranks highest here

As most students know, forced grading systems are unforgiving. With forced distribution, you're either in the top 5% or 10% (and thus get that "A"), or you're not. And, if you're in the bottom 5% or 10%, you get an "F," no questions asked. Your professor hasn't any wiggle room. Some students must fail. One survey found that 77% of responding employers using this approach were at least "somewhat satisfied" with forced ranking, while the remaining 23% were dissatisfied. The biggest complaints: 44% said it damages morale. Forty-seven percent said it creates interdepartmental inequities: "High performing teams must cut 10% of their workers while low performing teams are still allowed to retain 90% of theirs."[35] Some writers refer unkindly to forced rankings as "Rank and Yank."[36]

Given this, to protect against unfairness and bias claims, managers should take several steps.[37] Appoint a review committee to review any employee's low ranking. Train raters to be objective, and consider using multiple raters in conjunction with the forced distribution approach. And remember that distinguishing between top and bottom performers is usually not even the problem: "The challenge is to differentiate meaningfully between the other 80%."[38]

Critical Incident Method

With the **critical incident method**, the supervisor keeps a log of positive and negative examples (critical incidents) of a subordinate's work-related behavior. Every 6 months or so, supervisor and subordinate meet to discuss the latter's performance, using the incidents as examples.

Compiling incidents is useful. It provides examples of good and poor performance the supervisor can use to explain the person's rating. It makes the supervisor think about the subordinate's appraisal all during the year (so the rating does not just reflect the employee's most recent performance). And the list provides examples

alternation ranking method
Ranking employees from best to worst on a particular trait, choosing highest, then lowest, until all are ranked.

paired comparison method
Ranking employees by making a chart of all possible pairs of the employees for each trait and indicating which is the better employee of the pair.

forced distribution method
Similar to grading on a curve; predetermined percentages of ratees are placed in various performance categories.

critical incident method
Keeping a record of uncommonly good or undesirable examples of an employee's work-related behavior and reviewing it with the employee at predetermined times.

TABLE 9-1 Examples of Critical Incidents for Assistant Plant Manager		
Continuing Duties	**Targets**	**Critical Incidents**
Schedule production for plant	90% utilization of personnel and machinery in plant; orders delivered on time	Instituted new production scheduling system; decreased late orders by 10% last month; increased machine utilization in plant by 20% last month
Supervise procurement of raw materials and inventory control	Minimize inventory costs while keeping adequate supplies on hand	Let inventory storage costs rise 15% last month; overordered parts "A" and "B" by 20%; underordered part "C" by 30%
Supervise machinery maintenance	No shutdowns due to faulty machinery	Instituted new preventative maintenance system for plant; prevented a machine breakdown by discovering faulty part

of how the subordinate can eliminate deficiencies. The downside is that without some numerical rating, this method is not as useful for comparing employees or for salary decisions.

In any case, it is common to accumulate incidents to illustrate the reasons behind the employee's ratings. In Table 9-1, one of the assistant plant manager's continuing duties was to supervise procurement and to minimize inventory costs. The critical incident log shows that he or she let inventory storage costs rise 15%; this provides an example of what performance to improve.

Narrative Forms

All or part of the written appraisal may be in narrative form. Figure 9-8 presents an example. Here the person's supervisor assesses the employee's past performance and required areas of improvement. The supervisor's narrative assessment aids helps the employee understand where his or her performance was good or bad, and how to improve that performance.

Behaviorally Anchored Rating Scales

A **behaviorally anchored rating scale (BARS)** is an appraisal tool that anchors a numerical rating scale with specific illustrative examples of good or poor performance. Its proponents say it provides better, more equitable appraisals than do the other tools we discussed.[39]

Developing a BARS typically requires five steps:

1. **Write critical incidents.** Ask the job's jobholders and/or supervisors to write specific illustrations (critical incidents) of effective and ineffective performance on the job.

2. **Develop performance dimensions.** Have these people group the incidents into 5 or 10 performance dimensions, such as "salesmanship skills."

3. **Reallocate incidents.** To verify these groupings, have another team of people who also know the job reallocate the original critical incidents. They must reassign each incident to the cluster they think it fits best. Retain a critical incident if most of this second team assigns it to the same cluster as did the first group.

4. **Scale the incidents.** This second group then rates the behavior described by the incident as to how effectively or ineffectively it represents performance on the dimension (7- to 9-point scales are typical).

5. **Develop a final instrument.** Choose about six or seven of the incidents as the dimension's behavioral anchors.[40] We'll look at an example.

FIGURE 9-8 Appraisal-Coaching Worksheet

Source: Reprinted from www.HR.BLR.com with permission of the publisher *Business and Legal Resources, Inc.* 141 Mill Rock Road East, Old Saybrook, CT © 2004. BLR® (Business & Legal Resources, Inc.).

Appraisal-Coaching Worksheet

Instructions: This form is to be filled out by supervisor and employee prior to each performance review period.

Employee: _____   Position: _____

Supervisor: _____   Department: _____

Date: _____ Period of Work under Consideration: from _____ to _____

1. What areas of the employee's work performance are meeting job performance standards?

2. In what areas is improvement needed during the next six to twelve months?

3. What factors or events that are beyond the employee's control may affect (positively or negatively) his or her ability to accomplish planned results during the next six to twelve months?

4. What specific strengths has the employee demonstrated on this job that should be more fully used during the next six to twelve months?

5. List two or three areas (if applicable) in which the employee needs to improve his or her performance during the next six to twelve months (gaps in knowledge or experience, skill development needs, behavior modifications that affect job performance, etc.).

6. Based on your consideration of items 1–5 above, summarize your mutual objectives:

A. What supervisor will do:

B. What employee will do:

C. Date for next progress check or to re-evaluate objectives:

D. Data/evidence that will be used to observe and/or measure progress.

_____
Employee Signature   Supervisor Signature

_____
Date

RESEARCH INSIGHT   Three researchers developed a BARS for grocery checkout clerks.[41] They collected many critical incidents, and then grouped or clustered these into eight performance dimensions:

Knowledge and Judgment

Conscientiousness

Skill in Human Relations

Skill in Operation of Register

behaviorally anchored rating scale (BARS)
An appraisal method that aims at combining the benefits of narrative critical incidents and quantified ratings by anchoring a quantified scale with specific narrative examples of good and poor performance.

Skill in Bagging

Organizational Ability of Checkstand Work

Skill in Monetary Transactions

Observational Ability

They then developed behaviorally anchored rating scales for each of these dimensions. Each BARS contained a scale (ranging from 1 to 9) for rating performance from "extremely poor" to "extremely good." Then a specific critical incident (such as "by knowing the price of items, this checker would be expected to look for mismarked and unmarked items") helped anchor or specify what was meant by "extremely good" (9) performance. Similarly, they used several other critical incident anchors along the performance scale from (8) down to (1). To illustrate, Figure 9-9 shows a BARS for one performance dimension for a car sales person—the dimension "automobile salesmanship skills."

FIGURE 9-9 Example of a Behaviorally Anchored Rating Scale for the Dimension Salesmanship Skills

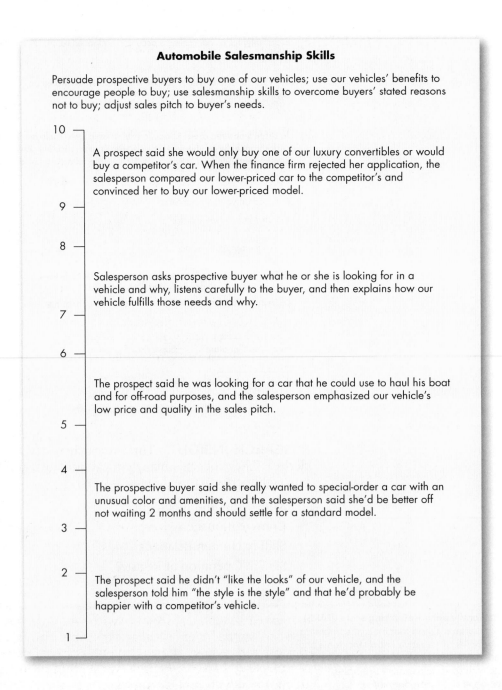

ADVANTAGES   It takes more time to develop a BARS, but the tool has advantages.

1. **A more accurate gauge.** People who know the job and its requirements better than anyone develop the BARS. This should produce a good gauge of job performance.

2. **Clearer standards.** The critical incidents along the scale illustrate what to look for in terms of superior performance, average performance, and so forth.

3. **Feedback.** The critical incidents make it easier to explain the ratings to appraisees.

4. **Independent dimensions.** Clustering the critical incidents into five or six performance dimensions (such as "salesmanship skills") helps to make the performance dimensions more independent of one another. For example, a rater should be less likely to rate an employee high on all dimensions simply because he or she was rated high in "salesmanship skills."

5. **Consistency.**[42] BARS evaluations seem to be relatively reliable, in that different raters' appraisals of the same person tend to be similar.

Mixed Standard Scales

Mixed standard scales are somewhat similar to behaviorally anchored scales. However, mixed scales generally list just a few (usually 3) behavioral examples (or "standards") for each of, say, 3 performance dimensions. The employer then "mixes" the resulting behavioral examples statements when listing them. The aim is to reduce rating errors by making it less obvious to the person doing the appraising (1) what performance dimensions he or she is rating; and (2) whether the behavioral example statements represent high, medium, or low performance. The supervisor rates the employee by indicating whether the latter's performance is better than, the same, or worse than the statement.

Suppose you want to appraise employees on the dimensions Quality of Work, Conscientiousness, and Gets Along with Others. You write three "high, medium, low" behavioral examples for each of these three dimensions, as follows.[43]

For *Quality of Work:*

Employee's work is striking in its accuracy, there is never any evidence of carelessness in it.

The accuracy of employee's work is satisfactory; it is not often that you find clear evidence of carelessness.

Frequent careless errors in this employee's work.

For *Conscientiousness:*

Is quick and efficient, able to keep work on schedule. Really gets going on a new task.

Is efficient enough, usually getting through assignments and work in reasonable time.

There is some lack of efficiency on employee's part. Employee may take too much time to complete assignments, and sometimes does not really finish them.

For *Gets Along with Others:*

Is on good terms with everyone. Can get along with people even when they disagree.

Only very occasionally has conflicts with others on the job, and these are likely to be minor.

Has a tendency to get into unnecessary conflicts with people.

Next, take the resulting nine high, medium, low statements, and list them randomly, in a mixed fashion, for instance with the "low" statement from Conscientiousness followed by the "high" Quality statement, and so on. Then the supervisor would appraise each employee by rating him or her "better," "the same" or "worse than" *for each of the 9 statements.* However, it is not clear that mixed standard appraisals are superior to others, such as graphic rating scales.

Management by Objectives

Some employers use management by objectives (MBO) as the primary appraisal method. Others use it to supplement a graphic rating or other appraisal method. You could engage in an informal MBO program with subordinates by jointly setting goals and periodically providing feedback. However, *MBO* generally refers to a comprehensive and formal organization-wide goal setting and appraisal program. Here goals cascade down by level and department, from company-wide strategic goals to tactical day-to-day goals.

Computerized and Web-Based Performance Appraisal

Employers increasingly use computerized or Web-based performance appraisal systems. These enable managers to compile computerized notes on subordinates during the year, and then to merge these with ratings for each employee on several performance traits. The software then generates written text to support each appraisal. Most such appraisals combine several appraisal methods, such as graphic ratings anchored by critical incidents.

EXAMPLES   There are many examples from which to choose. *Employee Appraiser* (developed by the Austin-Hayne Corporation, San Mateo, California) presents a menu of more than a dozen evaluation dimensions, including dependability, initiative, communication, decision making, leadership, judgment, and planning and productivity.[44] Within each dimension (such as "Communication") are separate performance factors for things like writing, verbal communication, and receptivity to criticism. When the user clicks on a performance factor, he or she is presented with a graphic rating scale. However, instead of numerical ratings, *Employee Appraiser* uses behaviorally anchored examples. For example, for *verbal communication* there are six choices, ranging from "presents ideas clearly" to "lacks structure." The manager chooses the phrase that most accurately describes the worker. Then "Employee Appraiser" generates an appraisal with sample text.

The eAppraisal system from Halogen Software is another example.[45] Employees using it can access the system year-round, track their progress against goals in real time, and enter significant accomplishments.[46] Seagate Technology uses "Enterprise Suite" for managing the performance of its 39,000 employees.[47] Early in Seagate's first fiscal quarter, employees enter the system and set goals and development plans for themselves that make sense in terms of Seagate's corporate objectives. Employees update their plans quarterly, and then do self-evaluations at the end of the year, with

Many employers today make use of online appraisals for evaluating employee performance.

Source: Corbis Images.

follow-up reviews by their supervisors. Figure 9-10 illustrates another good online appraisal tool, in this case from PerformancePro.

Electronic Performance Monitoring

Electronic performance monitoring (EPM) systems use computer network technology to allow managers to monitor their employees' computers. They thus allow managers to monitor the employees' rate, accuracy, and time spent working online.[48]

EPM can improve productivity. For example, for more routine, less complex jobs, highly skilled and monitored subjects keyed in more data entries than did highly skilled unmonitored participants. However, EPM can also backfire. In this same study, low-skilled but highly monitored participants did more poorly than did low-skilled, unmonitored participants. EPM also seems to raise employee stress. However, one researcher concludes that "Electronic Performance Monitoring (EPM) represents the future of performance feedback where supervisors can electronically monitor the amount and quality of work an employee is producing and have objective indicators of employee performance immediately available and visible."[49]

Appraisal in Practice

The best appraisal forms merge several approaches. Figure 9-3 (page 291) was an example. It supports a numerical graphic rating scale with illustrative behavioral incidents such as "Even with guidance, fails to. . . ."

FIGURE 9-10 Online Performance Appraisal Tool

Source: www.hrnonline.com/per_about.asp, accessed April 29, 2009.

(Continued)

electronic performance monitoring (EPM)
Having supervisors electronically monitor the amount of computerized data an employee is processing per day, and thereby his or her performance.

FIGURE 9-10 (Continued)

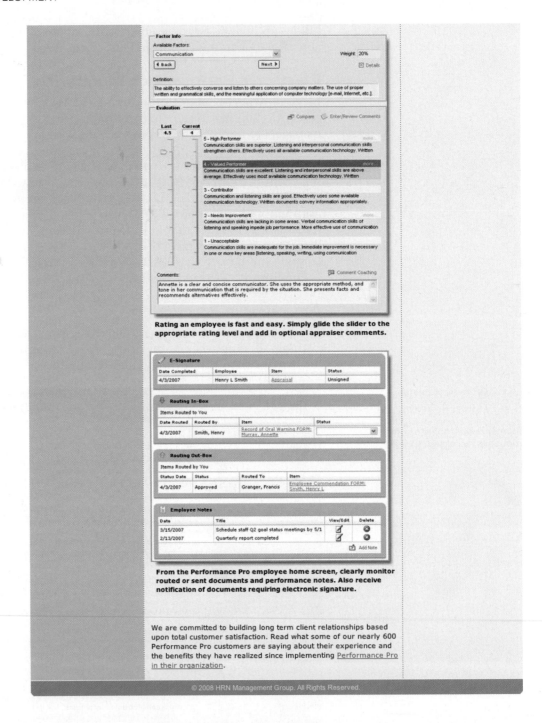

Rating an employee is fast and easy. Simply glide the slider to the appropriate rating level and add in optional appraiser comments.

From the Performance Pro employee home screen, clearly monitor routed or sent documents and performance notes. Also receive notification of documents requiring electronic signature.

We are committed to building long term client relationships based upon total customer satisfaction. Read what some of our nearly 600 Performance Pro customers are saying about their experience and the benefits they have realized since implementing Performance Pro in their organization.

Figure 9-3 illustrates an important point about appraisals. Even if the company uses a graphic rating scale with generic dimensions such as "Below Expectations," it can benefit from anchoring the scale, as here, with behavioral descriptions. Doing so improves the reliability and validity of the appraisal.

DEALING WITH APPRAISAL PROBLEMS AND INTERVIEWS

| 5 | Explain and illustrate the problems to avoid in appraising performance. |

As we said, few things managers do are fraught with more peril than appraising subordinates' performance.[50] We now turn to appraisal problems and how to solve them, and to several other appraisal issues.

TABLE 9-2 A Graphic Rating Scale with Unclear Standards				
	Excellent	Good	Fair	Poor
Quantity of work				
Quality of work				
Creativity				
Integrity				

Note: For example, what exactly is meant by "good," "quantity of work," and so forth?

Potential Appraisal Problems

Graphic-type rating scales in particular are susceptible to several problems: unclear standards, halo effect, central tendency, leniency or strictness, and bias.

UNCLEAR STANDARDS   Table 9-2 illustrates the **unclear standards** problem. This graphic rating scale seems objective. However, it would probably result in unfair appraisals, because the traits and degrees of merit are ambiguous. For example, different supervisors might define "good" performance, "fair" performance, and so on differently. The same is true of traits such as "quality of work" or "creativity."[51]

The best way to fix this problem is to include descriptive phrases that define or illustrate each trait, as in Figure 9-3. That form spells out what measures like "Role Model" or "Below Expectations" mean. This specificity results in more consistent and more easily explained appraisals.

HALO EFFECT   Experts define **halo effect** as "the influence of a rater's general impression on ratings of specific ratee qualities."[52] For example, supervisors often rate unfriendly employees lower on all traits, rather than just on "gets along well with others." Being aware of this problem is a step toward avoiding it. Supervisory training can also alleviate the problem, as can using a BARS (on which, recall, the performance dimensions are usually independent of each other).

CENTRAL TENDENCY   Some supervisors stick to the middle when filling in rating scales. For example, if the rating scale ranges from 1 to 7, they tend to avoid the highs (6 and 7) and lows (1 and 2) and rate most of their people between 3 and 5. **Central tendency** means rating all employees average. Doing so distorts the evaluations, making them less useful for promotion, salary, or counseling purposes. Ranking employees instead of using graphic rating scales can reduce this problem, since ranking means you can't rate them all average.

LENIENCY OR STRICTNESS   Other supervisors tend to rate all their subordinates consistently high or low, just as some instructors are notoriously high or low graders. This **strictness/leniency** problem is especially severe with graphic rating scales. On the other hand, ranking forces supervisors to distinguish between high and low performers.

There are other solutions. One is for the employer to recommend that supervisors avoid giving all their employees high (or low) ratings. A second is to basically enforce a

---

unclear standards
An appraisal that is too open to interpretation.

halo effect
In performance appraisal, the problem that occurs when a supervisor's rating of a subordinate on one trait biases the rating of that person on other traits.

central tendency
A tendency to rate all employees the same way, such as rating them all average.

strictness/leniency
The problem that occurs when a supervisor has a tendency to rate all subordinates either high or low.

distribution—that, say, about 10% of the people should be rated "excellent," 20% "good," and so forth. (But beware: Sometimes what appears to be an error—such as leniency—isn't an error at all, as when all subordinates really are superior performers.)[53]

RECENCY EFFECTS   The recency effect means letting what the employee has done recently blind you to what his or her performance has been over the year. The main solution is to accumulate critical incidents all year long.

BIAS   The number of things that can lead to **bias** during appraisals is limitless. One study focused on the rater's personality. Raters who scored higher on "conscientiousness" tended to give their peers lower ratings—they were stricter, in other words; those scoring higher on "agreeableness" gave higher ratings—they were more lenient.[54] In another study, "performance appraisal ratings obtained for administrative purposes [such as pay raises or promotions] were nearly one-third [higher] than those obtained for research or employee development purposes."[55] Another writer says, "performance ratings amplify the quality of the personal relationship between boss and employee. Good relationships tend to create good [appraisal] experiences, bad relationships bad ones."[56]

Unfortunately, personal characteristics (such as age, race, and sex) also affect ratings. A 36-year-old supervisor ranked a 62-year-old subordinate at the bottom of the department's rankings, and then fired him. The court held that the younger boss's discriminatory motives might have prejudiced the dismissal decision.[57] In one study, promoted women had to receive higher performance ratings than promoted men to be promoted, "suggesting that women were held to stricter standards for promotion."[58] Another study found that raters might actually penalize successful women for their success.[59] Other studies suggest that, "rater idiosyncratic biases account for the largest percentage of the observed variances in performance ratings."[60]

The bottom line is that the appraisal often says more about the appraiser than about the appraisee.[61] This is a powerful reason for using multiple raters, for having the supervisor's boss review the rating, and/or for having what some employers call "calibration" meetings; here supervisors discuss among themselves their reasons for the appraisals they gave each of their subordinates.[62]

Guidelines for Effective Appraisals

It's probably safe to say that problems like these can make an appraisal worse than no appraisal at all. Would an employee not be better off with no appraisal than with a seemingly objective but actually biased one? However, problems like these aren't inevitable, and you can minimize them. Do five things to have effective appraisals.

KNOW THE PERFORMANCE APPRAISAL PROBLEMS   First, learn and understand the potential appraisal problems (such as central tendency). Understanding and anticipating the problem can help you avoid it.

| 6 | Discuss the pros and cons of using different raters to appraise a person's performance. |

USE THE RIGHT APPRAISAL TOOL   Second, use the right appraisal tool—or combination of tools. Each has its own pros and cons. For example, the ranking method avoids central tendency but can cause bad feelings when employees' performances are in fact all "high."

In practice, employers choose an appraisal tool based on several criteria. Accessibility and ease-of-use is probably first. That is why graphic rating scales are still so popular, even within computerized appraisal packages. Table 9-3 summarizes each tool's pros and cons.

KEEP A DIARY   Third, keep a diary of employees' performances over the year.[63] One study involved 112 first-line supervisors. The conclusion of this and similar studies is that compiling critical incidents as they occur reduces appraisal problems.[64]

GET AGREEMENT ON A PLAN   Fourth, the aim of the appraisal should be to improve unsatisfactory performance (and/or to reinforce exemplary performance). The appraisal's end product should therefore always be a plan for what the employee must do to improve his or her efforts.

TABLE 9-3 Important Advantages and Disadvantages of Appraisal Tools

Tool	Advantages	Disadvantages
Graphic rating scale	Simple to use; provides a quantitative rating for each employee.	Standards may be unclear; halo effect, central tendency, leniency, bias can also be problems.
BARS	Provides behavioral "anchors." BARS is very accurate.	Difficult to develop.
Alternation ranking	Simple to use (but not as simple as graphic rating scales). Avoids central tendency and other problems of rating scales.	Can cause disagreements among employees and may be unfair if all employees are, in fact, excellent.
Forced distribution method	End up with a predetermined number or % of people in each group.	Employees' appraisal results depend on your choice of cutoff points.
Critical incident method	Helps specify what is "right" and "wrong" about the employee's performance; forces supervisor to evaluate subordinates on an ongoing basis.	Difficult to rate or rank employees relative to one another.
MBO	Tied to jointly agreed-upon performance objectives.	Time-consuming.

ENSURE FAIRNESS Fifth, make sure that every appraisal you give is fair. Studies confirm that, in practice, some managers ignore accuracy and honesty in performance appraisals. Instead, they use the process for political purposes (such as encouraging employees with whom they don't get along to leave the firm).[65] The employees' standards should be clear, employees should understand the basis on which you're going to appraise them, and the appraisals should be objective and fair.[66] One study found that a number of best practices, such as "have an appeal mechanism," distinguish fair appraisals. The checklist in Figure 9-11 summarizes these.

FIGURE 9-11 Checklist of Best Practices for Administering Fair Performance Appraisals

Source: Based on Richard Posthuma, "Twenty Best Practices for Just Employee Performance Reviews," *Compensation and Benefits Review,* January/February 2008, pp. 47–54.

☐ Base the performance review on duties and standards from a job analysis.
☐ Try to base the performance review on observable job behaviors or objective performance data.
☐ Make it clear ahead of time what your performance expectations are.
☐ Use a standardized performance review procedure for all employees.
☐ Make sure whoever conducts the reviews has frequent opportunities to observe the employee's job performance.
☐ Either use multiple raters or have the rater's supervisor evaluate the appraisal results.
☐ Include an appeals mechanism.
☐ Document the appraisal review process and results.
☐ Discuss the appraisal results with the employee.
☐ Let the employees know ahead of time how you're going to conduct the reviews.
☐ Let the employee provide input regarding your assessment of him or her.
☐ Indicate what the employee needs to do to improve.
☐ Train the supervisors who will be doing the appraisals. Make sure they understand the procedure to use, how problems (like leniency and strictness) arise, and how to deal with them.

bias
The tendency to allow individual differences such as age, race, and sex to affect the appraisal ratings employees receive.

FIGURE 9-12 Checklist for a Legally Defensible Appraisal

□ Preferably, conduct a job analysis to establish performance criteria and standards.
□ Communicate performance standards to employees and to those rating them, in writing.
□ When using graphic rating scales, avoid undefined abstract trait names
  (such as "loyalty" or "honesty").
□ Use subjective narratives as only one component of the appraisal.
□ Train supervisors to use the rating instrument properly.
□ Allow appraisers daily contact with the employees they're evaluating.
□ Don't use a single overall rating of performance.
□ Have more than one appraiser, and conduct all such appraisals independently.
□ One appraiser should never have absolute authority to determine a personnel action.
□ Give employees the opportunity to review and make comments.
□ Have a formal appeals process.
□ Document everything.
□ Provide corrective guidance to assist poor performers in improving.

Appraisals and the Law

One sure way to cause legal problems for an employer is to hold unfair appraisals. One court held that the firm had violated Title VII when it laid off several Hispanic-surnamed employees based on poor performance ratings.[67] The court concluded that the practice was illegal because:

1. The firm based the appraisals on subjective supervisory observations.
2. It didn't administer and score the appraisals in a standardized fashion.
3. Two of the three supervisory evaluators did not have daily contact with the employees.

If your case gets to court, what will judges look for? A review of about 300 U.S. court decisions is informative. Actions reflecting fairness and due process were most important. Figure 9-12 presents a checklist for developing a legally defensible appraisal process.[68]

Managing the Appraisal Interview

> 7 Perform an effective appraisal interview.

The appraisal typically culminates in an **appraisal interview**. Here you and the subordinate review the appraisal and make plans to remedy deficiencies and reinforce strengths. Interviews like these are often uncomfortable. Few people like to receive—or give—negative feedback. Adequate preparation and effective implementation are therefore essential.

TYPES OF APPRAISAL INTERVIEWS   Supervisors face four types of appraisal interviews, each with its unique objectives:

Satisfactory—Promotable is the easiest interview: The person's performance is satisfactory and there is a promotion ahead. Your objective is to discuss the person's career plans and to develop a specific professional development plan.

Satisfactory—Not promotable is for employees whose performance is satisfactory but for whom promotion is not possible. The objective here is to maintain satisfactory performance. The best option is usually to find incentives that are important to the person and sufficient to maintain performance. These might include extra time off, a small bonus, and reinforcement, perhaps in the form of an occasional "well done!"

When the person's performance is *unsatisfactory but correctable*, the interview objective is to lay out an action plan (see Figure 9-13) for correcting the unsatisfactory performance.

Finally, if the employee is *unsatisfactory* and the situation is *uncorrectable*, you can usually skip the interview. You either tolerate the person's poor performance for now, or (more likely) dismiss the person.

HOW TO CONDUCT THE APPRAISAL INTERVIEW   Beforehand, review the person's job description, compare performance to the standards, and review the previous appraisals. Give the employee at least a week's notice to review his or her work.

FIGURE 9-13 Sample Employee Development Plan

Source: www.career-change-mentor.com/support-files/sampleemployeedevelopmentplan.pdf, accessed April 28, 2009.

Sample Employee Development Plan

Employee Name: J. Citizen   Position Title: HR Analyst   Date Developed: _____   Date Last Revised: _____

A. Key objectives and core competencies

List top 3-5 business objectives for this year:	List core competencies for position:
1. Implement revised employee development system	1. Employee Development 4. Communication
2. Provide organization development support	2. Recruitment 5. Conflict Management
3. Reduce employee turnover by 5%	3. Organization Development 6. Grievance Management

B. Competency gaps and action plan

List top 2-3 core competencies that need development	List key gaps for each core competency	Briefly state how you will close each gap	Target completion date	Status R/Y/G
1. Employee Dev.	1. Succession Plng.	1. Participate in succession planning reviews in sister company to learn about process		G
2. Grievance Mgmt.	2. Elevation Process	2. Attend refresher training. Develop draft process. Pilot draft process and review.		Y
3.	3.	3.		

C. Comments/Notes – to be noted during Manager & Employee progress review of development plan

Succession Planning – good progress made on understanding process. Next step is to improve working knowledge of process by implementing it. Keep in close contact with mentor from sister company for advice and direction.
Elevation Process – refresher training attended but was inadequate. Plan in place to get assistance from HR Manager.

Status: Green – completed; Yellow – incomplete/plan in place to achieve objective; Red – not achieved/no plan in place

Manager's Name:_____   Signature:_____   Date Reviewed:_____

© www.career-change-mentor.com

Set a time for the interview and allow enough time. Interviews with lower-level personnel like clerical workers should take no more than an hour. Interviews with management employees often take 2 or 3 hours. Conduct the interview in a private place with no interruptions.

There are four things to keep in mind when conducting the interview:

1. **Talk in terms of objective work data.** Use examples such as absences, tardiness, quality records, orders processed, productivity records, and so on.

2. **Don't get personal.** Don't say, "You're too slow in producing those reports." Instead, try to compare the person's performance to a standard. ("These reports should normally be done within 10 days.") Similarly, don't compare the person's performance to that of other people. ("He's quicker than you are.")

3. **Encourage the person to talk.** Stop and listen to what the person is saying; ask open-ended questions such as, "What do you think we can do to improve the situation?" Use a command such as "Go on." Restate the person's last point as a question, such as, "You don't think you can get the job done?"

4. **Get agreement.** Make sure the person leaves knowing specifically what he or she is doing right and doing wrong and with agreement on how things will be improved, and by when. Write an action plan (Figure 9-13) with targets and dates.

Whether subordinates express satisfaction with their appraisal interview depends on several things. Subordinates will prefer:

1. not feeling threatened during the interview;

2. having an opportunity to present their ideas and feelings and to influence the course of the interview; and

3. having a helpful and constructive supervisor conduct the interview.

appraisal interview
An interview in which the supervisor and subordinate review the appraisal and make plans to remedy deficiencies and reinforce strengths.

FIGURE 9-14 Checklist During Appraisal Interview

Source: Reprinted from www.HR. BLR.com with permission of the publisher *Business and Legal Resources, Inc.* 141 Mill Rock Road East, Old Saybrook, CT © 2004. BLR® (Business & Legal Resources, Inc.).

CHECKLIST DURING THE APPRAISAL INTERVIEW

Yes No

- Did you discuss each goal or objective established for this employee?
- Are you and the employee clear on the areas of agreement? disagreement?
- Did you and the employee cover all positive skills, traits, accomplishments, areas of growth, etc.? Did you reinforce the employee's accomplishments?
- Did you give the employee a sense of what you thought of his or her potential or ability?
- Are you both clear on areas where improvement is required? expected? demanded? desired?
- What training or development recommendations did you agree on?
- Did you indicate consequences for noncompliance, if appropriate?
- Did you set good objectives for the next appraisal period?
  - Objective?
  - Specific?
  - Measurable?
- Did you set a standard to be used for evaluation?
- Time frame?
- Did you set a time for the next evaluation?
- Did you confirm what your part would be? Did the employee confirm his or her part?
- Did you thank the employee for his or her efforts?

Figure 9-14 provides an appraisal interview checklist.

HOW TO HANDLE A DEFENSIVE SUBORDINATE   Defenses are a familiar aspect of our lives. When a supervisor tells someone his or her performance is poor, the first reaction is often denial. Denial is a defense mechanism. By denying the fault, the person avoids having to question his or her own competence. Others react with anger and aggression. This helps them let off steam and postpones confronting the immediate problem.

In any event, understanding and dealing with defensiveness is an important appraisal skill. In his book *Effective Psychology for Managers*, psychologist Mortimer Feinberg suggests the following:

1. Recognize that defensive behavior is normal.
2. Never attack a person's defenses. Don't try to "explain someone to themselves" by saying things like, "You know the real reason you're using that excuse is that you can't bear to be blamed." Instead, concentrate on the fact ("sales are down").
3. Postpone action. Sometimes it is best to do nothing. Employees may react to sudden threats by instinctively hiding behind their defenses. But given sufficient time, a more rational reaction takes over.
4. Recognize your own limitations. The supervisor should not try to be a psychologist. Offering understanding is one thing; trying to deal with psychological problems is another.

HOW TO CRITICIZE A SUBORDINATE   When you must criticize, do so in a manner that lets the person maintain his or her dignity—in private, and constructively. Provide examples of critical incidents and specific suggestions of what to do and why. Avoid once-a-year "critical broadsides" by giving feedback periodically, so that the formal review contains no surprises. Never say the person is "always" wrong (since no one is ever "always" wrong or right). Criticism should be objective and free of personal bias.

HOW TO HANDLE A FORMAL WRITTEN WARNING An employee's performance may be so weak that it requires a formal written warning. Such warnings serve two purposes: (1) They may serve to shake your employee out of his or her bad habits, and (2) they can help you defend your rating, both to your own boss and (if needed) to the courts.

Written warnings should identify the employee's standards, make it clear that the employee was aware of the standard, specify any deficiencies relative to the standard, and show the employee had an opportunity to correct his or her performance.

REALISTIC APPRAISALS When the employee is not doing well, the manager will have to decide how candid to be. Not all managers are devotees of candor, but some firms, like GE, are famous for hard-hearted appraisals. GE's former CEO Jack Welch once said, for instance, that it is cruel to tell someone who's doing a mediocre job that their work is satisfactory.[69] Someone who might have had the chance to correct bad behavior or find a more appropriate vocation may instead spend years in a dead-end job, only to have to leave when a more demanding boss arrives.

There are many practical motivations for giving soft appraisals: the fear of having to hire and train someone new; the appraisee's unpleasant reactions; or a company appraisal process that's not conducive to candor, for instance. Ultimately, the person doing the appraising must decide if the drawbacks of less-than-candid appraisals outweigh the assumed benefits. They rarely do.

PERFORMANCE MANAGEMENT

Earlier in this chapter, we said that performance management is the continuous process of identifying, measuring, and developing the performance of individuals and teams and aligning their performance with the organization's goals.[70] We look at performance management more closely in this section.

Performance Management vs. Performance Appraisal

In comparing performance management and performance appraisal, "the distinction is the contrast between a year-end event—the completion of the appraisal form—and a process that starts the year with performance planning and is integral to the way people are managed throughout the year."[71] Three main things distinguish performance management from performance appraisal.

1. First, performance management never means just meeting with a subordinate once or twice a year to "review your performance." It means *continuous, daily, or weekly* interactions and feedback to ensure continuous improvement.[72]

2. Second, performance management is always *goal-directed*. The continuing performance reviews always involve comparing the employee's or team's performance against goals that specifically stem from and link to the company's strategic goals. *Strategic congruence* is central to performance management: each employee's goals must be aligned with departmental and company goals.

3. Third, performance management means continuously reevaluating and (if need be) *modifying how the employee and team get their work done*. Depending on the issue, this may mean additional training, changing work procedures, or instituting new incentive plans, for instance.

Furthermore, performance management systems increasingly use information technology to help managers automatically track employee performance and take immediate corrective action as required. By comparison, performance *appraisal* systems usually rely on paper forms, or perhaps online or computerized appraisal forms.

We can summarize performance management's six basic elements as follows:[73]

- *Direction sharing* means communicating the company's goals throughout the company and then translating these into doable departmental, team, and individual goals.
- *Goal alignment* means having a method that enables managers and employees to see the link between the employees' goals and those of their department and company.
- *Ongoing performance monitoring* usually includes using computerized systems that measure and then e-mail progress and exception reports based on the person's progress toward meeting his or her performance goals.
- *Ongoing feedback* includes both face-to-face and computerized feedback regarding progress toward goals.
- *Coaching and developmental support* should be an integral part of the feedback process.
- *Recognition and rewards* provide the consequences needed to keep the employee's goal-directed performance on track.

Using Information Technology to Support Performance Management

Performance management needn't be high-tech. For example, in many production facilities, work teams simply meet daily to review their performance and to get their efforts and those of their members aligned with their performance standards and goals.

On the other hand, information technology enables management to automate performance management and to monitor and correct deviations in real time. We can sum up this IT-supported performance management process as follows:

- *Assign financial and nonfinancial goals* to each team's activities along the strategy map chain of activities leading from the team's activities up to the company's overall strategic goals. (For example, an airline measures ground crew aircraft turnaround time in terms of "improve turnaround time from an average of 30 minutes per plane to 26 minutes per plane this year.")
- *Inform all employees* of their goals.
- *Use IT-supported tools* like scorecard software and digital dashboards to continuously display, monitor, and assess each team's and employee's performance. (We discussed this in Chapter 3, Strategy.)
- *Take corrective action* before things swing out of control. Figure 9-15 presents an example of an online performance management report for an employee.

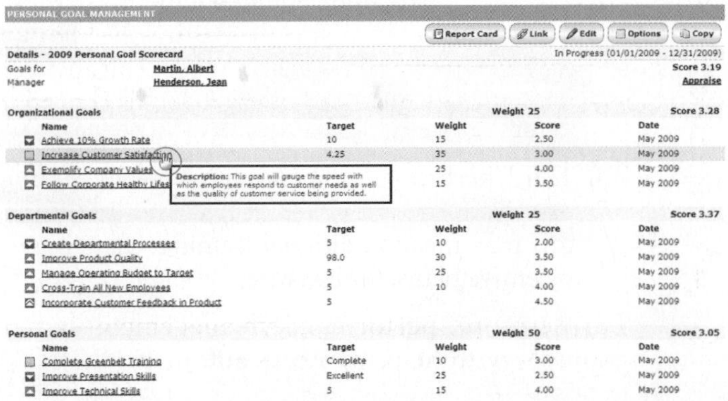

FIGURE 9-15 Summary of Performance Management Process Report

Source: Performance Management Report from www.activestrategy.com/images/7.2/PGM.jpg, accessed April 29, 2009. Used with permission of ActiveStrategy, Inc.

TALENT MANAGEMENT PRACTICES AND EMPLOYEE APPRAISAL

In Chapter 4, we defined talent management as the goal-oriented and integrated process of planning, recruiting, developing, appraising, and compensating employees. By way of review, we said five sets of practices distinguish talent management from merely recruiting, selecting, training, appraising, and paying employees. It requires:

1. Identifying the workforce profiles (competencies, knowledge, traits, and experiences) that the firm needs to achieve its strategic goals;

2. Consciously thinking through all the tasks (recruiting and so on) required for managing the company's talent;

3. Consistently using the same profile for formulating recruitment plans for the employee as you do for making the selection, training, appraisal, and payment decisions;

4. Actively managing different employees' recruitment, selection, development, and rewards; and

5. Integrating the underlying talent management activities (planning for, recruiting, developing, appraising, and compensating employees).

Appraising and Actively Managing Employees

Performance appraisal traditionally plays a predictable role when managers make pay raise and related decisions. Perhaps with the exception of selected "fast-track" employees, managers tend to allocate resources such as compensation and development opportunities either across-the-board or based on the employee's appraisal ratings (or both).

In contrast, talent management requires *actively managing* decisions like these. The point is that the traditional practice of allocating pay raises, development opportunities, and other scarce resources across the board or based just on performance makes less sense than it used to. Today, employers also need to focus their attention and resources on their company's mission-critical employees, those who are critical to the firm's strategic needs. Simply allocating awards across the board obviously does not fill that need. But allocating pay based solely on performance can also backfire. For example, is an employer really actively managing its employees if it gives the same percentage pay raise to every employee who rates "excellent," regardless of how important that employee is to the company's future success?

Increasingly, the answer from employers is "no." They continue to use performance appraisal to evaluate how their employees are performing. However, they also segment their employees based on how critical the employees are to the company's success. The point again is to focus your attention and resources on your company's mission-critical employees.

HOW TO SEGMENT EMPLOYEES Figure 9-16 illustrates one way to do this. Accenture uses a 4 × 4 Strategic Role Assessment matrix to plot employees by *Performance* (exceptional, high, medium, low) and *Value to the organization* (mission-critical, core, necessary, nonessential). As an example, consider a chemical engineering company that designs sophisticated pollution control equipment. The firm's experienced engineers may be mission-critical; engineer-trainees may be core; sales, accounting, and HR employees necessary; and peripheral, outsourceable employees such as those in maintenance non-essential. The company would then tie pay, development, dismissal, and other personnel decisions to each employee's position in the matrix.

Segmenting and Actively Managing Employees in Practice

Several examples can illustrate how employers implement this active-management segmented approach in practice.

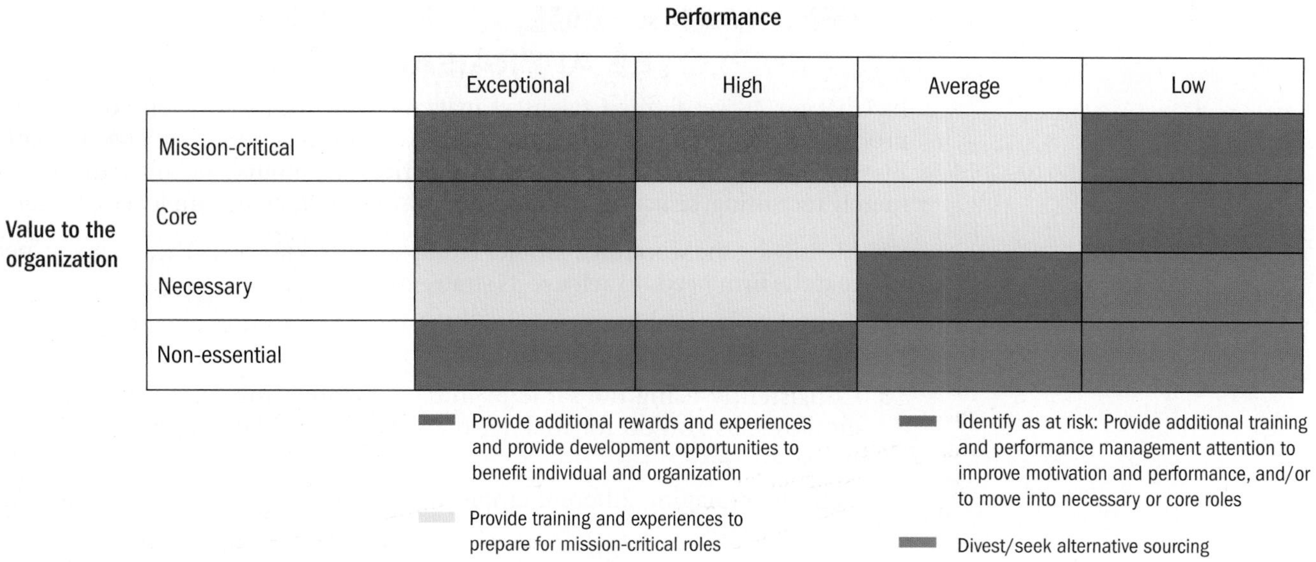

Performance

	Exceptional	High	Average	Low
Mission-critical				
Core				
Necessary				
Non-essential				

Value to the organization

▬▬ Provide additional rewards and experiences and provide development opportunities to benefit individual and organization

▬▬ Provide training and experiences to prepare for mission-critical roles

▬▬ Identify as at risk: Provide additional training and performance management attention to improve motivation and performance, and/or to move into necessary or core roles

▬▬ Divest/seek alternative sourcing

FIGURE 9-16 Accenture's Strategic Role Assessment Matrix

Source: "The New Talent Equation," *Outlook,* June 2009, an Accenture publication. © 2009 Accenture. All rights reserved. Chart reprinted by permission.

- Compass Group PLC identifies top performers. Then Compass assesses them for promotability, promotability time-frame, and leadership potential. Top employees then get special coaching and feedback, and development opportunities. Compass monitors their progress. GE prioritizes jobs and focuses on what it calls its employee "game changers."[74]

- Tesco PLC segments employees according to personal and professional goals to better communicate and motivate its employees.[75]

- McKinsey & Co. recommends limiting the "high potential group in whom the company invests heavily to no more than 10% to 20% of managerial and professional staff."[76]

- Unilever includes 15% of employees per management level in its high potential list each year, and expects these people to move to the next management level within 5 years.[77]

- Shell China appoints "career stewards" to meet regularly with "emerging leaders." They assess their level of engagement, help them set realistic career expectations, and make sure they're getting the right development opportunities.[78]

REVIEW

MyManagementLab   Now that you have finished this chapter, go back to **www.mymanagementlab.com** to continue practicing and applying the concepts you've learned.

CHAPTER SECTION SUMMARIES

1. Before appraising performance, managers should understand certain **basic concepts in performance management and appraisal**. Stripped to its essentials, performance appraisal involves setting work standards, assessing the employee's actual performance relative to those standards, and providing feedback to the employee. Managers should appraise employees based on the criteria previously assigned, and the actual

standards should be specific, measurable, attainable, relevant, and timely.

2. There are several basic **techniques managers use for appraising performance**.
   - Whichever tool you use, the appraisal should provide information on which to base pay and promotional decisions, clarify for the employee important company-relevant goals, develop a plan for correcting deficiencies, and support career planning.
   - In terms of specific techniques, the graphic rating scale lists a number of traits and a range of performance for each. Managers use generic job dimensions such as quantity, or focus on the job's actual duties or on competencies/skills.
   - With the alternation ranking method, you rank employees from best to worst on a particular trait.
   - The paired comparison method means ranking employees by making a chart of all possible pairs of the employees and indicating which is the better employee of the pair.
   - Many employers use the forced distribution method, which is similar to grading on a curve. Here you place predetermined percentages of appraisees in various performance categories.
   - Regardless of the specific methods used, the manager may want to maintain a record of critical incidents—uncommonly good or undesirable examples of employees' work behavior—to review with the employee.
   - A behaviorally anchored rating scale anchors a quantified scale with specific narrative examples of good and poor performance.
   - In practice, many employers use computerized and/or Web-based performance appraisal methods.

3. Many supervisors find appraisals difficult to administer, and it's important to understand **how to deal with performance appraisal problems**. Particularly with graphic rating scales, potential appraisal problems include unclear standards, halo effect, central tendency, leniency/strictness, recency effects, and bias. Guidelines for effective appraisals include knowing the problems (such as bias), using the right appraisal tool, keeping a diary of incidents, getting agreement on a plan, and being fair. Appraisals also need to be legally defensible, for instance, based on a job analysis and on defined rather than subjective standards. The appraisal may be administered by the immediate supervisor or by the employee's peers, a rating committee, via self-appraisal, by subordinates, or by 360-degree feedback. In any case, it's advisable to have at least the supervisor of the person completing the appraisal reviewing and approving it.

4. The supervisor needs to keep several points in mind during the **appraisal interview**. Preparation is essential, talk in terms of objective work, don't get personal, encourage the person to talk, and get agreement on how things will be improved. Minimize defensive reactions, for instance, by avoiding attacking the employee's defenses. Criticize objectively, in private, and constructively.

5. More employers are moving from traditional performance appraisals to **performance management**.
   - Performance management is the continuous process of identifying, measuring, and developing the performance of individuals and teams and aligning their performance with the organization's goals.
   - Its basic building blocks include direction (goals) sharing, goal alignment, ongoing performance monitoring, ongoing feedback, coaching, and rewards and recognition.
   - The performance management approach reflects a total quality philosophy toward performance. More importantly, it focuses on aligning and monitoring the link between the company's overall strategic goals and what each individual employee and team are supposed to accomplish.
   - In practice, employers use information technology to support performance management, for instance, using digital dashboards to monitor and correct each team's performance on a real-time basis.

DISCUSSION QUESTIONS

1. What is the purpose of a performance appraisal?
2. Discuss the pros and cons of four performance appraisal tools.
3. Explain how you would use the alternation ranking method, the paired comparison method, and the forced distribution method.
4. Explain in your own words how you would go about developing a behaviorally anchored rating scale.
5. Explain the problems to be avoided in appraising performance.
6. Discuss the pros and cons of using different potential raters to appraise a person's performance.
7. Compare and contrast performance management and performance appraisal.
8. Answer the question, "How would you avoid defensiveness during an appraisal interview?"

INDIVIDUAL AND GROUP ACTIVITIES

1. Working individually or in groups, develop a graphic rating scale for the following jobs: secretary, professor, directory assistance operator.
2. Working individually or in groups, describe the advantages and disadvantages of using the forced distribution appraisal method for college professors.

3. Working individually or in groups, develop, over the period of a week, a set of critical incidents covering the classroom performance of one of your instructors.
4. The "HRCI Test Specifications Appendix" at the end of this book (pages 633–640) lists the knowledge someone studying for the HRCI certification exam needs to have in each area of human resource management (such as in Strategic Management, Workforce Planning, and Human Resource Development). In groups of four to five students, do four things: (1) review that appendix now; (2) identify the material in this chapter that relates to the required knowledge the appendix lists; (3) write four multiple-choice exam questions on this material

that you believe would be suitable for inclusion in the HRCI exam; and (4) if time permits, have someone from your team post your team's questions in front of the class, so the students in other teams can take each others' exam questions
5. Every week, like clockwork, during the 2009 TV season, Donald Trump told another "apprentice," "You're fired!" Review recent (or archived) episodes of Donald Trump's *Apprentice* show and answer this: What performance appraisal system did Mr. Trump use, and do you think it resulted in valid appraisals? What techniques discussed in this chapter did he seem to apply? How would you suggest he change his appraisal system to make it more effective?

EXPERIENTIAL EXERCISE

Grading the Professor

Purpose: The purpose of this exercise is to give you practice in developing and using a performance appraisal form.

Required Understanding: You are going to develop a performance appraisal form for an instructor and should therefore be thoroughly familiar with the discussion of performance appraisals in this chapter.

How to Set Up the Exercise/Instructions: Divide the class into groups of four or five students.

1. First, based on what you now know about performance appraisal, do you think Figure 9-1 is an effective scale for appraising instructors? Why? Why not?

2. Next, your group should develop its own tool for appraising the performance of an instructor. Decide which of the appraisal tools (graphic rating scales, alternation ranking, and so on) you are going to use, and then design the instrument itself.
3. Next, have a spokesperson from each group post his or her group's appraisal tool on the board. How similar are the tools? Do they all measure the same factors? Which factor appears most often? Which do you think is the most effective tool on the board?
4. The class should select the top 10 factors from all of the appraisal tools presented to create what the class perceives to be the most effective tool for appraising the performance of the instructor.

APPLICATION CASE

APPRAISING THE SECRETARIES AT SWEETWATER U

Rob Winchester, newly appointed vice president for administrative affairs at Sweetwater State University, faced a tough problem shortly after his university career began. Three weeks after he came on board in September, Sweetwater's president, Rob's boss, told Rob that one of his first tasks was to improve the appraisal system used to evaluate secretarial and clerical performance at Sweetwater U. The main difficulty was that the performance appraisal was traditionally tied directly to salary increases given at the end of the year. Therefore, most administrators were less than accurate when they used the graphic rating forms that were the basis of the clerical staff evaluation. In fact, what usually happened was that each administrator simply rated his or her clerk or secretary as "excellent." This cleared the way for all support staff to receive a maximum pay increase every year.

But the current university budget simply did not include enough money to fund another "maximum" annual increase for every staffer. Furthermore, Sweetwater's president felt that the custom of providing invalid feedback to each secretary on his or her year's performance was not productive, so he had asked the new vice president to revise the system. In October, Rob sent a memo to all administrators, telling them that in the future no more than half the secretaries

reporting to any particular administrator could be appraised as "excellent." This move, in effect, forced each supervisor to begin ranking his or her secretaries for quality of performance. The vice president's memo met widespread resistance immediately—from administrators, who were afraid that many of their secretaries would begin leaving for more lucrative jobs, and from secretaries, who felt that the new system was unfair and reduced each secretary's chance of receiving a maximum salary increase. A handful of secretaries had begun picketing outside the president's home on the university campus. The picketing, caustic remarks by disgruntled administrators, and rumors of an impending slowdown by the secretaries (there were about 250 on campus) made Rob Winchester wonder whether he had made the right decision by setting up forced ranking. He knew, however, that there were a few performance appraisal experts in the School of Business, so he decided to set up an appointment with them to discuss the matter.

He met with them the next morning. He explained the situation as he had found it: The current appraisal system had been set up when the university first opened 10 years earlier. A committee of secretaries had developed it. Under that system, Sweetwater's administrators filled out forms similar to the one shown in Table 9-2. This once-a-year appraisal (in March) had run into problems almost immediately, since it was apparent from the start that administrators varied widely in their interpretations of job standards, as well as in how conscientiously they filled out the forms and supervised their secretaries. Moreover, at the end of the first year it became obvious to everyone that each secretary's salary increase was tied directly to the March appraisal. For example, those rated "excellent" received the maximum increases, those rated "good" received smaller increases, and those given neither rating received only the standard across-the-board cost-of-living increase. Since universities in general—and Sweetwater, in particular—have paid secretaries somewhat lower salaries than those prevailing in private industry, some secretaries left in a huff that first year. From that time on, most administrators simply rated all secretaries excellent in order to reduce staff turnover, thus ensuring each a maximum increase. In the process, they also avoided the hard feelings aroused by the significant performance differences otherwise highlighted by administrators.

Two Sweetwater experts agreed to consider the problem, and in 2 weeks they came back to the vice president with the following recommendations. First, the form used to rate the secretaries was grossly insufficient. It was unclear what "excellent" or "quality of work" meant, for example. They recommended instead a form like that in Figure 9-3. In addition, they recommended that the vice president rescind his earlier memo and no longer attempt to force university administrators to arbitrarily rate at least half their secretaries as something less than excellent. The two consultants pointed out that this was, in fact, an unfair procedure since it was quite possible that any particular administrator might have staffers who were all or virtually all excellent—or conceivably, although less likely, all below standard. The experts said that the way to get all the administrators to take

the appraisal process more seriously was to stop tying it to salary increases. In other words, they recommended that every administrator fill out a form like that in Figure 9-3 for each secretary at least once a year and then use this form as the basis of a counseling session. Salary increases would have to be made on some basis other than the performance appraisal, so that administrators would no longer hesitate to fill out the rating forms honestly.

Rob thanked the two experts and went back to his office to ponder their recommendations. Some of the recommendations (such as substituting the new rating form for the old) seemed to make sense. Nevertheless, he still had serious doubts as to the efficacy of any graphic rating form, particularly compared with his original, preferred forced ranking approach. The experts' second recommendation—to stop tying the appraisals to automatic salary increases—made sense but raised at least one very practical problem: If salary increases were not to be based on performance appraisals, on what were they to be based? He began wondering whether the experts' recommendations weren't simply based on ivory tower theorizing.

Questions

1. Do you think that the experts' recommendations will be sufficient to get most of the administrators to fill out the rating forms properly? Why? Why not? What additional actions (if any) do you think will be necessary?
2. Do you think that Vice President Winchester would be better off dropping graphic rating forms, substituting instead one of the other techniques we discussed in this chapter, such as a ranking method? Why?
3. What performance appraisal system would you develop for the secretaries if you were Rob Winchester? Defend your answer.

CONTINUING CASE

CARTER CLEANING COMPANY

The Performance Appraisal

After spending several weeks on the job, Jennifer was surprised to discover that her father had not formally evaluated any employee's performance for all the years that he had owned the business. Jack's position was that he had "a hundred higher-priority things to attend to," such as boosting sales and lowering costs, and, in any case, many employees didn't stick around long enough to be appraisable anyway. Furthermore, contended Jack, manual workers such as those doing the pressing and the cleaning did periodically get positive feedback in terms of praise from Jack for a job well done, or criticism, also from Jack, if things did not look right during one of his swings through the stores. Similarly, Jack was never shy about telling his managers about store problems so that they, too, got some feedback on where they stood.

This informal feedback notwithstanding, Jennifer believes that a more formal appraisal approach is required. She believes that there are criteria such as quality, quantity, attendance, and punctuality that should be evaluated periodically even if a worker is paid on piece rate. Furthermore, she feels quite strongly that the managers need to have a list of quality standards for matters such as store cleanliness, efficiency, safety, and adherence to budget on which they know they are to be formally evaluated.

Questions

1. Is Jennifer right about the need to evaluate the workers formally? The managers? Why or why not?
2. Develop a performance appraisal method for the workers and managers in each store.

TRANSLATING STRATEGY INTO HR POLICIES & PRACTICES CASE

THE HOTEL PARIS CASE

The New Performance Management System

The Hotel Paris's competitive strategy is "To use superior guest service to differentiate the Hotel Paris properties, and to thereby increase the length of stay and return rate of guests, and thus boost revenues and profitability." HR manager Lisa Cruz must now formulate functional policies and activities that support this competitive strategy by eliciting the required employee behaviors and competencies.

Lisa knew that the Hotel Paris's performance appraisal system was archaic. When the founders opened their first hotel, they went to an office-supply store and purchased a pad of performance appraisal forms. The hotel chain uses these to this day. Each form is a two-sided page. Supervisors indicate whether the employee's performance in terms of various standard traits including quantity of work, quality of work, and dependability was excellent, good, fair, or poor. Lisa knew that, among other flaws, this appraisal tool did not force either the employee or the supervisor to focus the appraisal on the extent to which the employee was helping the Hotel Paris to achieve its strategic goals. She wanted a system that focused the employee's attention on taking those actions that would contribute to helping the company achieve its goals, for instance, in terms of improved customer service.

Lisa and her team also wanted a performance management system that focused on both competencies and objectives. In designing the new system, their starting point was the job descriptions they had created for the hotel's employees. These descriptions each included required competencies. Consequently, using a form similar to Figure 9-5 (pages 292–293), the front-desk clerks' appraisals now focus on competencies such as "able to check a guest in or out in 5 minutes or less." Most service employees' appraisals include the competency, "able to exhibit patience and guest support even when busy with other activities." There were other required competencies. For example, the Hotel Paris wanted all service employees to show initiative in helping guests, to be customer-oriented, and to be team players (in terms of sharing information and best practices). Each of these competencies derives from the hotel's aim of becoming more service-oriented.

Questions

1. Choose one job, such as front-desk clerk. Based on any information you have (including job descriptions you may have created in other chapters), write a list of duties, competencies, and performance standards for that chosen job.
2. Based on that, create a performance appraisal form for appraising that job.

KEY TERMS

performance appraisal, *284*
performance appraisal process, *285*
performance management, *286*
graphic rating scale, *290*
alternation ranking method, *294*
paired comparison method, *294*

forced distribution method, *294*
critical incident method, *295*
behaviorally anchored rating scale (BARS), *296*
electronic performance monitoring (EPM), *301*

unclear standards, *303*
halo effect, *303*
central tendency, *303*
strictness/leniency, *303*
bias, *304*
appraisal interview, *306*

ENDNOTES

1. http://trw.com/, accessed June 1, 2011.
2. D. Bradford Neary, "Creating a Company-Wide, Online, Performance Management System: A Case at TRW, Inc.," *Human Resource Management* 41, no. 4 (Winter 2002), pp. 491–498.
3. Experts debate the pros and cons of tying appraisals to pay decisions. One side argues that doing so distorts the appraisals. A recent study concludes the opposite. Based on an analysis of surveys from over 24,000 employees in more than 6,000 workplaces in Canada, the researchers concluded: (1) linking the employees' pay to their performance appraisals contributed to improved pay satisfaction; (2) even when appraisals are *not* directly linked to pay, they apparently contributed to pay satisfaction, "probably through mechanisms related to perceived organizational justice"; and (3) whether or not the employees received performance pay, "individuals who do not receive performance appraisals are significantly less satisfied with their pay." Mary Jo Ducharme et al., "Exploring the Links Between Performance Appraisals and Pay Satisfaction," *Compensation and Benefits Review,* September/October 2005, pp. 46–52. See also Robert Morgan, "Making the Most of Performance Management Systems," *Compensation and Benefits Review,* September/October 2006, pp. 22–27.
4. www.ball.com/page.jsp?page=1, accessed June 1, 2011.
5. "Aligning People and Processes for Performance Improvement", *T+D* 65, no. 3 (March 2011), p. 80.
6. Ibid.
7. Peter Glendinning, "Performance Management: Pariah or Messiah," *Public Personnel Management* 31, no. 2 (Summer 2002), pp. 161–178. See also Herman Aguinis, *Performance Management* (Upper Saddle River, NJ: Prentice Hall 2007), p. 2.
8. Herman Aguinis, *Performance Management* (Upper Saddle River, NJ: Pearson, 2009), pp. 3–4
9. Ibid., p. 3.

10. Vesa Suutari and Marja Tahbanainen, "The Antecedents of Performance Management among Finnish Expatriates," *Journal of Human Resource Management* 13, no. 1 (February 2002), pp. 53–75.

11. "Get SMART about Setting Goals," *Asia Africa Intelligence Wire*, May 22, 2005.

12. See, for example, Robert Renn, "Further Examination of the Measurement of Properties of Leifer & McGannon's 1996 Goal Acceptance and Goal Commitment Scales," *Journal of Occupational and Organizational Psychology,* March 1999, pp. 107–114. One recent study found that, at least in China, a sense of cooperation improves the positive aspects of participative leadership. Yi Feng Chen and Dean Tjosvold, "Participative Leadership by American and Chinese Managers in China: The Role of Relationships," *Journal of Management Studies* (Oxford, England) 43 no. 8 (December 2006), pp. 1727–1752.

13. Aguinis, *Performance Management*, p. 35.

14. Vanessa Druskat and Steven Wolf, "Effects and Timing of Developmental Peer Appraisals in Self-Managing Work-Groups," *Journal of Applied Psychology* 84, no. 1 (1999), pp. 58–74. For a recent review, see Erich Dierdorff and Eric Surface, "Placing Peer Ratings in Context: Systematic Influences beyond Ratee Performance," *Personnel Psychology* 60, no. 1 (Spring 2007), pp. 93–126.

15. See, for example, Brian Hoffman and David Woehr, "Disentangling the Meaning of Multisource Performance Rating Source and Dimension Factors," *Personnel Psychology* 62 (2009), pp. 735–765.

16. As one study recently concluded, "Far from being a source of non-meaningful error variance, the discrepancies among ratings from multiple perspectives can in fact capture meaningful variance in multilevel managerial performance." In Sue Oh and Christopher Berry, "The Five Factor Model of Personality and Managerial Performance: Validity Gains through the Use of 360° Performance Ratings," *Journal of Applied Psychology* 94, no. 6 (2009), p. 1510.

17. Jeffrey Facteau and S. Bartholomew Craig, "Performance Appraisal Ratings from Different Rating Scores," *Journal of Applied Psychology* 86, no. 2 (2001), pp. 215–227.

18. See also Kevin Murphy et al., "Raters Who Pursue Different Goals Give Different Ratings," *Journal of Applied Psychology* 89, no. 1 (2004), pp. 158–164.

19. Such findings may be culturally related. One study compared self and supervisor ratings in "other-oriented" cultures (as in Asia, where values tend to emphasize teams). It found that self and supervisor ratings were related. M. Audrey Korsgaard et al., "The Effect of Other Orientation on Self: Supervisor Rating Agreement," *Journal of Organizational Behavior* 25, no. 7 (November 2004), pp. 873–891. See also Heike Heidemeier and Klaus Mosar, "Self Other Agreement in Job Performance Ratings: A Meta-Analytic Test of a Process Model," *Journal of Applied Psychology* 94, no. 2 (2009), pp. 353–370.

20. Forest Jourden and Chip Heath, "The Evaluation Gap in Performance Perceptions: Illusory Perceptions of Groups and Individuals," *Journal of Applied Psychology* 81, no. 4 (August 1996), pp. 369–379. See also Sheri Ostroff, "Understanding Self-Other Agreement: A Look at Rater and Ratee Characteristics, Context, and Outcomes," *Personnel Psychology* 57, no. 2 (Summer 2004), pp. 333–375.

21. Paul Atkins and Robert Wood, "Self versus Others Ratings as Predictors of Assessment Center Ratings: Validation Evidence for 360 Degree Feedback Programs," *Personnel Psychology* 55, no. 4 (Winter 2002), pp. 871–904.

22. David Antonioni, "The Effects of Feedback Accountability on Upward Appraisal Ratings," *Personnel Psychology* 47 (1994), pp. 349–355.

23. Alan Walker and James Smither, "A Five-Year Study of Upward Feedback: What Managers Do with Their Results Matters," *Personnel Psychology* 52 (1999), pp. 393–423, and Austin F. R. Smith and Vincent J. Fortunato, "Factors Influencing Employee Intentions to Provide Honest Upward Feedback Ratings," *Journal of Business Psychology* 22 (2008), pp. 191–207

24. The evidence from another study suggests also that "upward and peer 360-degree ratings may be biased by rater affect [whether the rater likes the ratee]; therefore, at this point, these ratings should be used for the sole purpose of providing ratees with developmental feedback." David Antonioni and Heejoon Park, "The Relationship Between Rater Affect and Three Sources of 360-Degree Feedback Ratings," *Journal of Management* 27, no. 4 (2001), pp. 479–495.

25. See, for example, "360-Degree Feedback on the Rise Survey Finds," *BNA Bulletin to Management,* January 23, 1997, p. 31; Leanne Atwater et al., "Multisource Feedback: Lessons Learned and Implications for Practice," *Human Resource Management* 46, no. 2 (Summer 2007), p. 285. However, a small number of employers are beginning to use 360-degree feedback for performance appraisals, rather than just development. See, for example, Tracy Maylett, "360° Feedback Revisited: The Transition from Development to Appraisal," *Compensation & Benefits Review,* September/October 2009, pp. 52–59.

26. James Smither et al., "Does Performance Improve Following Multi-Score Feedback? A Theoretical Model, Meta Analysis, and Review of Empirical Findings," *Personnel Psychology* 58 (2005), pp. 33–36.

27. Christine Hagan et al., "Predicting Assessment Center Performance with 360 Degree, Top-Down, and Customer-Based Competency Assessments," *Human Resource Management* 45, no. 3 (Fall 2006), pp. 357–390.

28. Bruce Pfau, "Does a 360-Degree Feedback Negatively Affect the Company Performance?" *HR Magazine,* June 2002, pp. 55–59.

29. Jim Meade, "Visual 360: A Performance Appraisal System That's 'Fun,'" *HR Magazine,* July 1999, pp. 118–119.

30. www.sumtotalsystems.com/performance/index.html?e=001&sitenbr=156896193&keys=visual+360&submit.x=11&submit.y=11&submit=submit, accessed April 20, 2008.

31. Howard Risher, "Getting Serious About Performance Management," *Compensation & Benefits Review,* November/December 2005, pp. 18–26.

32. Jena McGregor, "The Struggle to Measure Performance," *BusinessWeek,* January 9, 2006, p. 26.

33. Steve Bates, "Forced Ranking," *HR Magazine,* June 2003, pp. 63–68.

34. Steven Cullen et al., "Forced Distribution Rating Systems and the Improvement of Workforce Potential: A Baseline Simulation," *Personnel Psychology* 58 (2005), p. 1.

35. "Survey Says Problems with Forced Ranking Include Lower Morale and Costly Turnover," *BNA Bulletin to Management,* September 16, 2004, p. 297.

36. Steve Bates, "Forced Ranking: Why Grading Employees on a Scale Relative to Each Other Forces a Hard Look at Finding Keepers, Losers May Become Weepers," *HR Magazine* 48, no. 6 (June 2003), p. 62. See also D. J. Schleicher et al., "Rater Reactions to Forced Distribution Rating Systems," *Journal of Management* 35, no. 4 (August 2009), pp. 899–927.

37. "Straight Talk About Grading Employees on a Curve," *BNA Bulletin to Management,* November 1, 2001, p. 351.

38. Clinton Wingrove, "Developing an Effective Blend of Process and Technology in the New Era of Performance Management," *Compensation & Benefits Review,* January/February 2003, p. 26.

39. See, for example, Timothy Keaveny and Anthony McGann, "A Comparison of Behavioral Expectation Scales and Graphic Rating Scales," *Journal of Applied Psychology* 60 (1975), pp. 695–703. See also Neil Hauenstein et al., "BARS and Those Mysterious, Missing Middle Anchors," *Journal of Business & Psychology* 25, no. 4 (December 2010), pp. 663–672.

40. Based on Donald Schwab, Herbert Heneman III, and Thomas DeCotiis, "Behaviorally Anchored Scales: A Review of the Literature," *Personnel Psychology* 28 (1975), pp. 549–562. For a discussion, see also Uco Wiersma and Gary Latham, "The Practicality of Behavioral Observation Scales, Behavioral Expectation Scales, and Trait Scales," *Personnel Psychology* 30, no. 3 (Autumn 1986), pp. 619–689, and Neil Hauenstein et al., "BARS and Those Mysterious, Missing Middle Anchors," op cit.

41. Lawrence Fogli, Charles Hulin, and Milton Blood, "Development of First Level Behavioral Job Criteria," *Journal of Applied Psychology* 55 (1971), pp. 3–8. See also Joseph Maiorca, "How to Construct Behaviorally Anchored Rating Scales (BARS) for Employee Evaluations," *Supervision*, August 1997, pp. 15–19; and Neil Hauenstein et al., "BARS and Those Mysterious, Missing Middle Anchors," op cit.

42. Kevin R. Murphy and Joseph Constans, "Behavioral Anchors as a Source of Bias in Rating," *Journal of Applied Psychology* 72, no. 4 (November 1987), pp. 573–577; Aharon Tziner, "A Comparison of Three Methods of Performance Appraisal with Regard to Goal Properties, Goal Perception, and Ratee Satisfaction," *Group & Organization Management* 25, no. 2 (June 2000), pp. 175–191.

43. www.explorehr.org/articles/home/performance_appraisal_methods.html and http://jobsin.build-reciprocal-links.com/section-for-recruiters/performance-appraisal-management/2519110-performance-appraisal-method-mixed-standard-scales.html, accessed April 21, 2011.

44. www.employeeappraiser.com/index.php, accessed January 10, 2008.

45. www.halogensoftware.com/products/halogen-eappraisal, accessed January 10, 2008.

46. Drew Robb, "Appraising Appraisal Software," *HR Magazine*, October 2008, p. 68.

47. Drew Robb, "Building a Better Workforce," *HR Magazine*, October 2004, pp. 87–94.

48. See, for example, Stoney Alder and Maureen Ambrose, "Towards Understanding Fairness Judgments Associated with Computer Performance Monitoring: An Integration of the Feedback, Justice, and Monitoring Research," *Human Resource Management Review* 15, no. 1 (March 2005), pp. 43–67.

49. ibid., and David T. Goomas, "Electronic Performance Selfmonitoring and Engineered Labor Standards for "Man-Up" Drivers in a Distribution Center," *Journal of Business and Psychology* 21 no. 4 (Summer 2007), pp. 541–558.

50. See, for example, Jonathan Segal, "Performance Management Blunders," *HR Magazine*, November 2010, pp. 75–77.

51. See, for example, Adrienne Fox, "Curing What Ails Performance Reviews," *HR Magazine*, January 2009, pp. 52–55.

52. Andrew Solomonson and Charles Lance, "Examination of the Relationship Between True Halo and Halo Effect in Performance Ratings," *Journal of Applied Psychology* 82, no. 5 (1997), pp. 665–674.

53. Manuel London, Edward Mone, and John C. Scott, "Performance Management and Assessment: Methods for Improved Rater Accuracy and Employee Goal Setting," *Human Resource Management* 43, no. 4 (Winter 2004), pp. 319–336.

54. Ted Turnasella, "Dagwood Bumstead, Will You Ever Get That Raise?" *Compensation & Benefits Review*, September–October 1995, pp. 25–27. See also Solomonson and Lance, "Examination of the Relationship Between True Halo and Halo Effect," pp. 665–674.

55. I. M. Jawahar and Charles Williams, "Where All the Children Are Above Average: The Performance Appraisal Purpose Effect," *Personnel Psychology* 50 (1997), p. 921.

56. Annette Simmons, "When Performance Reviews Fail," *Training & Development* 57, no. 9 (September 2003), pp. 47–53.

57. "Flawed Ranking System Revives Workers' Bias Claim," *BNA Bulletin to Management*, June 28, 2005, p. 206.

58. Karen Lyness and Madeline Heilman, "When Fit Is Fundamental: Performance Evaluations and Promotions of Upper-Level Female and Male Managers," *Journal of Applied Psychology* 91, no. 4 (2006), pp. 767–775.

59. Madeleine Heilman et al., "Penalties for Success: Reactions to Women Who Succeed at Male Gender Type Tasks," *Journal of Applied Psychology* 89, no. 3 (2004), pp. 416–427. Managers may not rate successful female managers negatively (for instance, in terms of likability and boss desirability) when they see the woman as supportive, caring, and sensitive to their needs. Madeleine Heilmann and Tyler Okimoto, "Why Are Women Penalized for Success at Male Tasks? The Implied Communality Deficit," *Journal of Applied Psychology* 92, no. 1 (2007), pp. 81–92.

60. Gary Greguras et al., "A Field Study of the Effects of Rating Purpose on the Quality of Multisource Ratings," *Personnel Psychology* 56 (2003), pp. 1–21.

61. Wingrove, "Developing an Effective Blend of Process and Technology," pp. 25–30.

62. Joanne Sammer, "Calibrating Consistency," *HR Magazine*, January 2008, pp. 73–74. As one study recently concludes, "Far from being a source of non-meaningful error variance, the discrepancies among ratings from multiple perspectives can in fact capture meaningful variance in multi-level managerial performance." In-Sue Oh and Christopher Berry, "The Five Factor Model of Personality and Managerial Performance: Validity Gains through the Use of 360° Performance Ratings," *Journal of Applied Psychology* 94, no. 6 (2009), p. 1510.

63. Angelo DeNisi and Lawrence Peters, "Organization of Information in Memory and the Performance Appraisal Process: Evidence from the Field," *Journal of Applied Psychology* 81, no. 6 (1996), pp. 717–737. See also A. Fox, "Curing What Ails Performance Reviews," *HR Magazine* 54, no. 1 (January 2009), pp. 52–56.

64. Juan Sanchez and Phillip De La Torre, "A Second Look at the Relationship Between Rating and Behavioral Accuracy in Performance Appraisal," *Journal of Applied Psychology* 81, no. 1 (1996), p. 7. See also "How To . . . Improve Appraisals," *People Management* 15, no. 3 (January 29, 2009), p. 57.

65. M. Ronald Buckley et al., "Ethical Issues in Human Resources Systems," *Human Resource Management Review* 11 (2001), pp. 11, 29. See also Ann Pomeroy, "The Ethics Squeeze," *HR Magazine,* March 2006, pp. 48–55.

66. G. R Weaver and L. K.Treviño. "The role of human resources in ethics/compliance management: A fairness perspective," *Human Resource Management Review*, (2001), pp. 113–134. Researchers recently conducted studies of 490 police officers undergoing standardized promotional exams. Among their conclusions was that "Organizations should strive to ensure that candidates perceived justice both in the content of personnel assessments and in the way they are treated during the assessment process." Julie McCarthy et al., "Progression through the Ranks: Assessing Employee Reactions to High Stakes Employment Testing," *Personnel Psychology* 62 (2009), p. 826.

67. David Martin et al., "The Legal Ramifications of Performance Appraisal: The Growing Significance," *Public Personnel Management* 29, no. 3 (Fall 2000), pp. 381–383.

68. Wayne Cascio and H. John Bernardin, "Implications of Performance Appraisal Litigation for Personnel Decisions," *Personnel Psychology*, Summer 1981, pp. 211–212; Gerald Barrett and Mary Kernan, "Performance Appraisal and Terminations: A Review of Court Decisions Since *Brito v. Zia* with Implications

for Personnel Practices," *Personnel Psychology* 40, no. 3 (Autumn 1987), pp. 489–504; Elaine Pulakos, *Performance Management*, SHRM Foundation, 2004.

69. John (Jack) Welch, broadcast interview at Fairfield University, C-Span, May 5, 2001.

70. Peter Glendinning, "Performance Management: Pariah or Messiah," *Public Personnel Management* 31, no. 2 (Summer 2002), pp. 161–178. See also Aguinis, *Performance Management*, p. 2.

71. Howard Risher, "Getting Serious about Performance Management," *Compensation and Benefits Review,* November/December 2005, p. 19.

72. Clinton Wingrove, "Developing an Effective Blend of Process and Technology," p. 27.

73. These are quoted or paraphrased from Howard Risher, "Getting Serious about Performance Management," *Compensation and Benefits Review,* November/December 2005, p. 19.

74. Adapted or quoted from "Next Generation Talent Management," Hewitt.com, accessed June 2010.

75. Ibid.

76. Adapted or quoted from Gunter Stahl et al., "Global Talent Management: How Leading Multinationals Build and Sustain their Talent Pipelines," Faculty & Research Working Paper, INSEAD, 2007.

77. Ibid.

78. Ibid.

10
Employee Retention, Engagement, and Careers

LEARNING OBJECTIVES

1. Describe a comprehensive approach to retaining employees.

2. Explain why employee engagement is important, and how to foster such engagement.

3. Discuss what employers and supervisors can do to support employees' career development needs.

4. List and discuss the four steps in effectively coaching an employee.

5. List the main decisions employers should address in reaching promotion decisions.

IBM celebrated its centenary in 2011, marking 100 years since Charles Flint founded it to provide punch card tabulating machines for making business computations.[1] Staying in business that many years is a feat shared by few companies. Most credit IBM's ability to adapt to changing customer needs for its longevity. Today, IBM faces a new threat. Technology is changing so fast that IBM will soon need a workforce with dramatically different skills than its workforce has now. What should it do to build that new workforce, and to retain the employees it needs to move ahead?

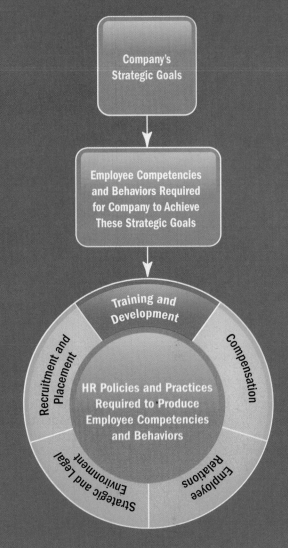

WHERE ARE WE NOW . . .

Having invested time and resources in selecting, training, and appraising employees, the employer naturally wants its employees to stay with the firm. Unfortunately, keeping good employees can be challenging. The main purpose of this chapter is to help you be more effective at improving employee retention, engagement, and careers. The main topics we'll address include employee retention, employee engagement, career development, coaching employees, and promotions.

Access a host of interactive learning aids at **www.mymanagementlab.com** to help strengthen your understanding of the chapter concepts.

MANAGING EMPLOYEE TURNOVER AND RETENTION

Turnover—the rate at which employees leave the firm—varies markedly among industries. For example, turnover in the accommodation and food services industry is chronically high, with over half the industry's employees voluntarily leaving each year. In contrast, voluntary turnover in educational services is about 12%.[2]

Furthermore, such figures only reflect employees who leave voluntarily, such as for better jobs or for retirement. They do not include involuntary separations, such as those due to poor performance, disability, or corporate downsizings.[3] Combining voluntary and involuntary turnover produces some astounding statistics. For example, the turnover in many food service organizations is around 100% per year. This means that (other things equal) many restaurants need to replace just about all their employees every year.

Costs of Turnover

The costs to employers of turnover are high.[4] The accompanying HR as a Profit Center feature illustrates this.

HR AS A PROFIT CENTER

A research team analyzed the tangible and intangible costs of turnover in a call center with 31 agents and 4 supervisors.[5] Tangible costs associated with an agent's leaving included, for instance, the costs of recruiting, screening, interviewing, and testing applicants, as well as the cost of wages while the new agent was oriented and trained. Intangible costs included the cost of lost productivity for the new agent (who is less productive at first than his or her predecessor), the cost of rework for errors the new agent makes, and the supervisory cost for coaching the new agent. For this call center, the researchers' mathematical model estimated the cost of an agent leaving at about $21,551. This call center averaged 18.6 vacancies per year (about a 60% turnover rate). Therefore, the researchers estimated the total annual cost of agent turnover at $400,853. Taking steps to cut this turnover rate in, say, half could save this firm about $200,000 per year.

Reducing turnover requires identifying and managing the reasons for both voluntary and involuntary turnover. We address managing voluntary turnover here, and managing involuntary turnover in Chapter 14 (ethics and fair treatment).

Managing Voluntary Turnover

Managing voluntary turnover requires identifying its causes and then addressing them. Unfortunately, identifying why employees voluntarily leave is easier said than done. People who are dissatisfied with their jobs are more likely to leave, but the sources of dissatisfaction are many and varied. Figure 10-1 provides an example.[6] The consultants collected survey data from 262 U.S. organizations having a minimum of 1,000 employees. In this survey, the five top reasons high commitment/top-performing employees gave for leaving (ranked from high to low) were pay, promotional opportunities, work–life balance, career development, and health care benefits. In contrast, employers ranked the top five reasons employees left as promotion, career development, pay, relationship with supervisor, and work–life balance. Other reasons employees voluntarily leave include unfairness, not having their voices heard, and a lack of recognition.[7] Sometimes simply asking, "All things considered, how satisfied are you with your job?" can be as effective as soliciting employees' attitudes toward various facets of the job (such as supervision and pay).[8] Practical considerations affect turnover. For example, high unemployment reduces voluntary turnover, and some locales have fewer job opportunities (and thus turnover) than do others.

FIGURE 10-1 Reasons Top-Performing Employees Leave an Organization

Source: www.worldatwork.org/waw/adimLink?id=17180, accessed April 3, 2011.

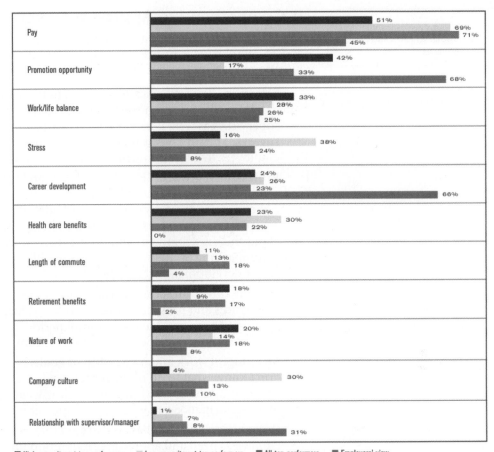

Pay	High-commitment top performers: 51%; Low-commitment top performers: 69%; All top performers: 71%; Employers' view: 45%
Promotion opportunity	High: 42%; Low: 17%; All: 33%; Employers' view: 68%
Work/life balance	High: 33%; Low: 28%; All: 26%; Employers' view: 25%
Stress	High: 16%; Low: 38%; All: 24%; Employers' view: 8%
Career development	High: 24%; Low: 26%; All: 23%; Employers' view: 66%
Health care benefits	High: 23%; Low: 30%; All: 22%; Employers' view: 0%
Length of commute	High: 11%; Low: 13%; All: 18%; Employers' view: 4%
Retirement benefits	High: 18%; Low: 9%; All: 17%; Employers' view: 2%
Nature of work	High: 20%; Low: 14%; All: 18%; Employers' view: 8%
Company culture	High: 4%; Low: 30%; All: 13%; Employers' view: 10%
Relationship with supervisor/manager	High: 1%; Low: 7%; All: 8%; Employers' view: 31%

■ High-commitment top performers   ▨ Low-commitment top performers   ▨ All top performers   ■ Employers' view
* Percentage reporting element as one of the top three reasons top-performing employees consider leaving an organization

Of course, turnover isn't necessarily bad. For example, losing low-performing employees isn't as problematical as losing high-performing ones. Some firms, such as the restaurant chain Applebee's, even incentivize their managers differentially, with higher incentives for reducing turnover among top-performing employees.[9]

Retention Strategies for Reducing Voluntary Turnover

In any case, given the variety of things prompting employees to leave voluntarily, what can one do to manage voluntary turnover? There is no silver bullet. The manager should understand that retaining employees is a talent management issue, and that the best retention strategies are therefore multifunctional. For example, employees who aren't interested in their jobs, sense that they're not suited for their jobs, or who feel undercompensated are more likely to leave. Employers can only address such issues by instituting effective and comprehensive talent management (recruitment, selection, training, appraisal, and compensation) practices. Put another way, turnovers (both voluntary and involuntary) often start with poor selection decisions, compounded by inadequate training, insensitive appraisals, and inequitable pay. Therefore trying to formulate a "retention strategy" without considering all of one's HR practices is generally futile.

Identifying the issues is an important first step in any retention strategy. As we'll explain in Chapter 14, effectively conducted exit interviews provide useful insights into potential turnover problem areas. Many employers routinely administer attitude surveys to monitor employees' feelings about matters such as supervision and pay. Open door policies and anonymous "hotlines" help management identify and remedy morale problems before they get out of hand. Sometimes, analyzing the situation leads to simple solutions. For example, Walmart discovered it could significantly reduce voluntary turnover by providing aggressively realistic previews about the job's demands and work hours. Then, having identified potential problems, the employer can take steps like the following to boost employee retention.

A Comprehensive Approach to Retaining Employees

Experts from the consulting company Development Dimensions International (DDI) and the employment firm Robert Half International suggest building comprehensive retention programs around the following steps.

Selection. "Retention starts up front, in the selection and hiring of the right employees."[10] Selection refers not just to the worker but to choosing the right supervisors as well. For example, FedEx conducts periodic employee attitude surveys. The supervisor then meets to review the results with his or her employees to address any problems the surveys raise.

Professional growth. Inadequate career and professional development prospects prompt many employees to leave. Conversely, a well-thought-out training and career development program can provide a strong incentive for staying with the company. As one expert says, "professionals who feel their company cares about their development and progress are much more likely to stay."[11] The accompanying Strategic Context feature illustrates this, and we also address career development later in the chapter.

Provide career direction. Periodically discuss with employees their career preferences and prospects at your firm, and help them lay out potential career plans. Furthermore, "don't wait until performance reviews to remind top employees how valuable they are to your company."[12]

Meaningful work and ownership of goals. People can't do their jobs if they don't know what to do or what their goals are. Therefore, an important part of retaining employees is making it clear what your expectations are regarding their performance and what their responsibilities are.

Recognition and rewards. We've seen that in addition to pay and benefits, employees need and appreciate recognition for a job well done.

Culture and environment. For example, companies that are very tense and "political" may prompt employees to leave, while companies that make them feel comfortable encourage them to stay.

Promote work–life balance. In one survey conducted by Robert Half and careerbuilder.com, workers identified "flexible work arrangements" and "telecommuting" as the two top benefits that would encourage them to choose one job or another.

Acknowledge achievements. When employees feel underappreciated, they're more likely to leave. Surveys suggest that frequent recognition of accomplishments is an effective nonmonetary reward.

THE STRATEGIC CONTEXT

IBM Aims for Flexibility

Technological change is occurring so fast that IBM will soon need a workforce with dramatically different skills than its workforce has now, one capable of reacting to customers' changing needs "on demand." IBM could, of course, merely size up its employees periodically and let go those who don't measure up. Instead, IBM chose to put in place an on-demand staffing strategy. This aims to ensure that its current employees get the training and coaching they need to play roles in IBM's future.[13] To do this, IBM budgeted $700 million per year to identify needed skills, spot gaps for skills that are in short supply, and to train and assess its executives, managers, and rank-and-file employees. IBM's on-demand staffing effort is having at least two big effects. It is supporting IBM's strategy, which depends on being able to offer the fast-evolving technological services its customers need, at once, on demand. The staffing program is also improving employee retention, by minimizing the layoffs and resignations that might occur if employees' skill sets were inconsistent with IBM's needs.

Managing Involuntary Turnover

We discuss involuntary turnover in Chapter 14, but several points are pertinent here. Involuntary turnovers are inevitable. Even under the best conditions, the employer will have to let some employers go when jobs are restructured, or when competitive pressures necessitate reductions in force. However, dismissals due to poor performance are sometimes avoidable. As with voluntary turnover, performance-based dismissals may stem from breakdowns in the employer's talent management system. Therefore, here, too, reviewing and improving one's recruitment, selection, training, appraisal, and compensation/incentive plans can reduce dismissals by addressing the reasons for poor performance. We discuss strategies for managing involuntary turnover in Chapter 14.

Talent Management and Employee Retention

All employees are important, but as we explained earlier in this book, talent management–oriented employers put special emphasis on developing and retaining their most critical employees. For example, we saw that Accenture uses a 4 × 4 strategic role assessment matrix. It plots employees by performance and by value to the organization. Accenture then ties pay, development, dismissal, and other personnel decisions to each employee's position in the matrix. Compass Group identifies top performers, and then assesses them for promotability and leadership potential. Shell China appoints career stewards to meet regularly with "emerging leaders." Novartis China uses a checklist to assess the attitudes of its most mission-critical employees. The point is that taking a talent management approach to retaining employees suggests focusing augmented retention efforts on the company's most important employees.

Job Withdrawal

Unfortunately, voluntary turnover is just one way that employees withdraw. Withdrawal in general means separating oneself from one's current situation—it's a means of escape for someone who is dissatisfied or fearful. At work, *job withdrawal* has been defined as "actions intended to place physical or psychological distance between employees and their work environments."[14]

Poor attendance and voluntary turnover are two job withdrawal examples. Other types of job withdrawal can be less obvious if no less corrosive. Some examples include "taking undeserved work breaks, spending time in idle conversation and neglecting aspects of the job one is obligated to perform."[15] Other employees stop "showing up" mentally ("psychological withdrawal"), perhaps daydreaming at their desks while productivity suffers.[16] The employee is there, but mentally absent. In fact, the *job withdrawal process* tends to be incremental, often evolving from daydreaming to absences to quitting: "[W]hen an employee perceives that temporary withdrawal will not resolve his/her problems, then the employee is apt to choose a more permanent form of withdrawal (i.e., turnover, assuming that alternative work opportunities are available)."[17]

DEALING WITH JOB WITHDRAWAL   Studies confirm the high costs of job withdrawal behavior, so understanding its causes is important.[18] Because many people have experienced the desire to withdraw—to "get away" from some situation—it's perhaps not difficult to empathize with those who feel they must escape. The simplest way to think about it is in terms of pain versus pleasure. People tend to move toward situations that make them feel good, and move away from those that make them feel bad. More technically, "negative emotional states make people aware that their current situation is problematic, and this awareness motivates them to take action."[19] People are repelled by situations that produce unpleasant, uncomfortable emotions, and are attracted to those that produce pleasant, comfortable ones.[20] The point is that the more negative and less positive the person's mood about a situation, the more likely he or she will try to avoid or withdraw from the situation.[21]

The manager can therefore think of withdrawal-reducing strategies in terms of reducing the job's negative effects, and/or of raising its positive effects. Because potential negatives and positives are virtually limitless, addressing withdrawal problems again requires a comprehensive human resource management approach. Illustrative potential negatives include, for instance, boring jobs, poor supervision, low pay, bullying, lack of career prospects, and poor working conditions. Potential positives include job enrichment, supportive supervision, equitable pay/family-friendly benefits, disciplinary/appeals processes, career development opportunities, safe and healthy working conditions, and having high-morale colleagues.[22] Interviews, surveys, and observation can help identify issues to address.

EMPLOYEE ENGAGEMENT

Poor attendance, voluntary turnover, and psychological withdrawal often also reflect diminished employee engagement. *Engagement* refers to being psychologically involved in, connected to, and committed to getting one's jobs done.

Why Engagement Is Important

> **2** Explain why employee engagement is important, and how to foster such engagement.

Employee engagement is an important topic, because many employee behaviors, including turnover, reflect the degree to which employees are "engaged." For example, based on surveys by the Gallup organization, business units with the highest levels of employee engagement have an 83% chance of performing above the company median, while those with the lowest employee engagement have only a 17% chance of performing better than the company median.[23] A survey by consultants Watson Wyatt Worldwide concluded that companies with highly engaged employees have 26% higher revenue per employee.[24] The director of recruiting at the nonprofit Fair Trade USA believes boosting engagement helps to explain the firm's subsequent 10% drop in turnover. A recent *Harvard Business Review* article notes that when it comes to customer service, satisfied employees aren't enough. Instead, "Employees should be engaged by providing them with reasons and methods to satisfy customers and then rewarded for appropriate behavior."[25] Yet studies, including one from the consulting firm TowersPerrin, concluded that only about 21% of the global workforce is engaged, while almost 40% is disengaged.[26]

Actions That Foster Engagement

The same TowersPerrin findings illustrate the sorts of managerial actions that can foster employee engagement. Figure 10-2 summarizes these findings.[27] Engagement-supporting actions include making sure employees (1) understand how their departments contribute to the company's success, (2) see how their own efforts contribute to achieving the company's goals, and (3) get a sense of accomplishment from working at the firm.

Monitoring Employee Engagement

Monitoring employee engagement needn't be complicated. With about 180,000 employees worldwide, the consulting firm Accenture uses a three-part "shorthand" method they call "say, stay, and strive" to identify which employees are engaged, and why. First, Accenture assesses the employee's pride in being with the organization in terms of how positively he or she speaks about the company and recommends it to others. Second, it looks at who stays with a company, and why. Finally, it looks at "strive." For instance, "do employees take an active role in the overall success of the organization by moving beyond just doing tasks to going above and beyond?"[28]

FIGURE 10-2 Employer Actions that Make Employees Feel More Engaged

Source: "Working Today: Understanding What Drives Employee Engagement," www.towersperrin. com/tp/getwebcachedoc?webc= hrs/usa/2003/200309/talent_2003.pdf, accessed April 3, 2011.

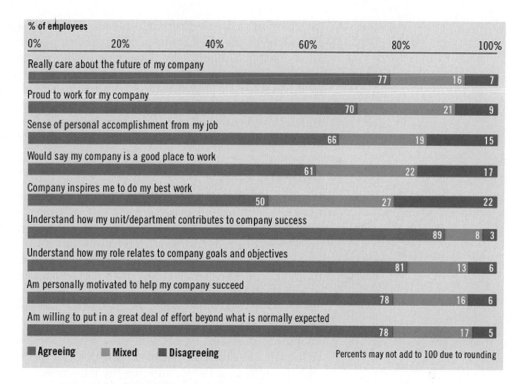

% of employees

	Agreeing	Mixed	Disagreeing
Really care about the future of my company	77	16	7
Proud to work for my company	70	21	9
Sense of personal accomplishment from my job	66	19	15
Would say my company is a good place to work	61	22	17
Company inspires me to do my best work	50	27	22
Understand how my unit/department contributes to company success	89	8	3
Understand how my role relates to company goals and objectives	81	13	6
Am personally motivated to help my company succeed	78	16	6
Am willing to put in a great deal of effort beyond what is normally expected	78	17	5

■ Agreeing   ■ Mixed   ■ Disagreeing   Percents may not add to 100 due to rounding

CAREER MANAGEMENT

Career development plays an important role in engaging and retaining employees. For example, a survey by the human resource management consulting firm Mercer found that as of 2010, employers planned to focus both on money and on career development to retain and engage the right talent.[29] One observer similarly says that "rather than focusing on incentives and perks to entice and retain employees, organizations . . . will hold onto the most talented workers . . . by offering them a range of professional experiences, broad functional and geographic exposure within the organization, and more targeted leadership opportunities."[30] These experiences become part of the employer's total rewards package.

Employers, not just employees, therefore benefit from offering employees career development support. The employees, armed with better insights about their occupational strengths, should be *better equipped* to serve the company.[31] Supporting your employees' career development may also *boost employee engagement* and support your *recruitment* and *retention* efforts. As one expert said, "The most attractive proposition an employer can make today is that in 5 years the employee will have more knowledge and be more employable than now. That should be the acid test for any career development program."[32]

Careers Terminology

We may define **career** as the occupational positions a person holds over the years. **Career management** is a process for enabling employees to better understand and develop their career skills and interests and to use these skills and interests most effectively both within the company and after they leave the firm. **Career development** is the lifelong series of activities (such as workshops) that contribute

career
The occupational positions a person has had over many years.

career management
The process for enabling employees to better understand and develop their career skills and interests, and to use these skills and interests more effectively.

career development
The lifelong series of activities that contribute to a person's career exploration, establishment, success, and fulfillment.

to a person's career exploration, establishment, success, and fulfillment. **Career planning** is the deliberate process through which someone becomes aware of personal skills, interests, knowledge, motivations, and other characteristics; acquires information about opportunities and choices; identifies career-related goals; and establishes action plans to attain specific goals.

We'll see that the employee's manager and employer should play roles in guiding and developing the employee's career. However, the employee must always accept full responsibility for his or her own career development and career success.

Careers Today

People once viewed careers as a sort of upward stairway from job to job, more often than not with one or at most a few firms. Today, recessions, mergers, outsourcing, consolidations, and more or less endless downsizings have changed the rules. Many people do still move up from job to job. But more often employees find themselves having to reinvent themselves. For example, the sales rep, laid off by a publishing firm that's just merged, may reinvent her career as an account executive at a media-oriented advertising firm.[33]

Careers today differ in other ways from a few years ago. With more women pursuing professional and managerial careers, families must balance the challenges associated with dual career pressures. At the same time, what people want from their careers seems to be changing. Baby boomers—those retiring in the next few years—tended to be job- and employer-focused. People entering the job market now often value work arrangements that provide more opportunities for balanced work–family lives.

Psychological Contract

One implication is that what employers and employees expect from each other is changing. What the employer and employee expect of each other is part of what psychologists call a *psychological contract*. This is "an unwritten agreement that exists between employers and employees."[34] The psychological contract identifies each party's mutual expectations. For example, the unstated agreement is that management will treat employees fairly and provide satisfactory work conditions, hopefully in a long-term relationship. Employees are expected to respond "by demonstrating a good attitude, following directions, and showing loyalty to the organization."[35]

But with today's tumultuous labor markets, neither the employer nor the employee can count on long term commitments from each other. That fact changes the terms of the psychological contract, and makes career management even more critical for the employee.

The Employee's Role in Career Management

The employer and manager have roles in guiding employees' careers, but particularly in today's environment, no employee should ever abandon this task to others. For the employee, career planning means matching individual strengths and weaknesses with occupational opportunities and threats. In other words, the person wants to pursue occupations, jobs, and a career that capitalize on his or her interests, aptitudes, values, and skills. He or she also wants to choose occupations, jobs, and a career that make sense in terms of projected future demand for various types of occupations. The consequences of a bad choice (or of no choice) are too severe to leave to others. There is a wealth of sources to turn to.

As one example, career-counseling expert John Holland says that personality (including values, motives, and needs) is one career choice determinant. For example, a person with a strong social orientation might be attracted to careers that entail interpersonal rather than intellectual or physical activities and to occupations such as social work. Holland found six basic personality types or orientations. Individuals can use his Self-Directed Search (SDS) test (available online at www.self-directed-search.com) to assess their occupational orientations and preferred occupations.

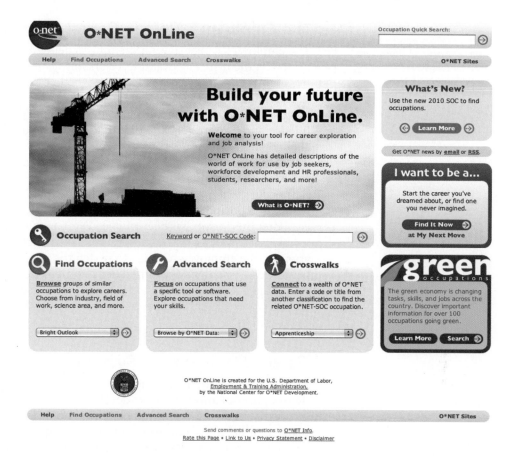

The SDS has an excellent reputation, but the career seeker needs to be wary of some of the other online career assessment sites. One study of 24 no-cost online career assessment Web sites concluded that they were easy to use, but suffered from insufficient validation and confidentiality. However, a number of online career assessment instruments such as Career Key (www.careerkey.org) do reportedly provide validated and useful information.[36] O*Net offers a free comprehensive online "My Next Move" occupations and career assessment system (http://www.onetcenter.org/mynextmove.html). You will find other examples at Workday.com, and in the following exercises.

EXERCISE 1   One useful exercise for identifying occupational skills is to head a page "The School or Occupational Tasks I Was Best At." Then write a short essay describing the tasks. Provide as much detail as you can about your duties and responsibilities, and what you found enjoyable about each task. (It's not necessarily the most enjoyable *job* you've had, but the most enjoyable *task* you've had to perform within your jobs.) Next, on other pages, do the same thing for two other tasks you've had. Now scrutinize the three essays. Underline the skills that you mentioned the most often. For example, did you especially enjoy the hours you spent in the library doing research for your boss when you worked one summer as an office clerk?[37]

EXERCISE 2   Another exercise can prove enlightening. On a page, answer the question: "If you could have any kind of job, what would it be?" Invent your own job if need be, and don't worry about what you can do—just what you want to do.[38]

career planning
The deliberate process through which someone becomes aware of personal skills, interests, knowledge, motivations, and other characteristics and establishes action plans to attain specific goals.

> **3** Discuss what employers and supervisors can do to support employees' career development needs.

The Employer's Role in Career Management

The employer's career development tasks depend partly on how long the employee has been with the firm. For example, *before hiring*, realistic job interviews can help prospective employees more accurately gauge whether the job is a good fit with the candidate's skills and interests.

Especially for recent college graduates, *the first job* can be crucial for building confidence and a more realistic picture of what he or she can and cannot do: Providing challenging first jobs (rather than relegating new employees to "jobs where they can't do any harm") and having an experienced mentor who can help the person learn the ropes are important. Some refer to this as preventing **reality shock**, a phenomenon that occurs when a new employee's high expectations and enthusiasm confront the reality of a boring, unchallenging job.

After the person has been *on the job* for a while, new employer career-management roles arise. Career-oriented appraisals—in which the manager is trained not just to appraise the employee but also to match the person's strengths and weaknesses with a feasible career path and required development work—is one important step. Similarly, providing periodic job rotation can help the person develop a more realistic picture of what he or she is (and is not) good at, and thus the sort of future career moves that might be best.

Career Management Systems

Most employers aren't inclined to provide a wide range of expensive career development options. However, career development systems needn't be complicated. Even just receiving performance feedback from supervisors, having individual development plans, and having access to training is enough for most employees. Beyond that, job postings, formal career-oriented performance appraisals, career development centers, formal counseling and mentoring with managers, and individual succession planning for high-potential employees are valuable career development tools.[39] Yet only about a fourth of the respondents in one survey even had individual development plans.[40]

Figure 10-3 illustrates a simple employee career planning form.[41]

CAREER CENTERS   Other systems are more comprehensive. Some employers create Web-based or offline libraries of career development materials, plus career workshops, workshops on related topics (such as time management), and individual career coaches for career guidance. First USA Bank has its "Opportunity Knocks" program. Its aim is to help employees crystallize their career goals and achieve them within the company. In addition to career development training and follow-up support, the program includes career development centers at work sites that employees use on company time. The latter contain materials such as career assessment and planning tools.[42]

CAREER PLANNING WORKSHOPS   A career planning workshop is "a planned learning event in which participants are expected to be actively involved, completing career planning exercises and inventories and participating in career skills practice sessions."[43] A typical workshop includes self-assessment exercises (skills, interests, values, and so on), an assessment of important occupational trends, and goal-setting and action-planning segments.

LIFELONG LEARNING BUDGETS   As we explained in Chapter 8 (Training), several employers provide 401(k)-type lifelong learning accounts for their employees. Both employers and employees contribute, and the employees can tap into these to get the career-related education and development they desire.[44]

PROVIDE CAREER COACHES   For example, Allmerica Financial Corp. hired 20 career development coaches to assist its 850-person information technology staff. The coaches helped individual employees identify their development needs and obtain the training, professional development, and networking opportunities that they require to satisfy those needs.[45]

FIGURE 10-3 Employee Career Development Plan

Source: Reprinted from www.HR.BLR.com with permission of the publisher *Business and Legal Resources, Inc.*, 141 Mill Rock Road East, Old Saybrook, CT © 2004. BLR® (Business and Legal Resources, Inc.).

Employee Career Development Plan

Employee: _____ Position: _____

Manager: _____ Department: _____

Date of Appraisal: _____

1. What is the next logical step up for this employee, and when do you think he or she will be ready for it?

Probable Next Job:	When Ready:			
	Now	6 Months	1 Year	2 Years
1.	☐	☐	☐	☐
2.	☐	☐	☐	☐
3.	☐	☐	☐	☐

2. What is the highest probable promotion within five years?

3. What does this employee need to prepare for promotion?

- Knowledge: _____
- Action Plan: _____
- Still Training: _____
- Action Plan: _____
- Management Training: _____
- Action Plan: _____

Career coaches generally help employees create 1- to 5-year plans showing where their careers with the firm may lead. Then, the employer and employee base the latter's development plans on what he or she will need to move up.[46]

OFFER ONLINE PROGRAMS   For example, WorkforceVision from Criterion, Inc., supplies online systems that help the employer analyze an employee's training needs. Clicking on the employee's name launches his or her work history, competencies, career path, and other information. For each competency (such as leadership and customer focus), a bar chart graphically shows a "gap analysis" highlighting the person's strengths and weaknesses. The firm can then organize developmental activities around the person's needs.[47]

CAREER-ORIENTED APPRAISALS   In brief, if you use the performance review only to tell the employee how he or she is doing, you'll miss an opportunity to support the employee's career development. Performance appraisals also provide an

reality shock
Results of a period that may occur at the initial career entry when the new employee's high job expectations confront the reality of a boring or otherwise unattractive work situation.

opportunity to discuss and link the employee's performance, career interests, and developmental needs into a coherent career plan.

Many employers have formal programs to do this. For example, JCPenney's managerial performance appraisal form contains a listing of all jobs by title, function, and level that employees could conceivably want to consider. The company trains its supervisors to link the employee's performance, career interests, and corporate needs, and develop a career plan including development activities for the employee.

However, even a simple form like the one shown in Figure 10-4 can suffice. The main thing is to help the manager and employee translate the latter's performance-based experiences for the year into tangible development plans and goals.

Gender Issues in Career Development

Women and men face different challenges as they advance through their careers. In one study, promoted women had to receive higher performance ratings than promoted men to get promoted, "suggesting that women were held to stricter standards for promotion."[48] Women report greater barriers (such as being excluded from informal

FIGURE 10-4 Sample Performance Review Development Plan

Source: Reprinted from www.HR.BLR.com with permission of the publisher *Business and Legal Resources, Inc.,* 141 Mill Rock Road East, Old Saybrook, CT © 2004. BLR® (Business and Legal Resources, Inc.).

HR Management Checklists

A. Employee's Major Strengths
   1. _____
   2. _____
   3. _____

B. Areas for Improvement/Development
   1. _____
   2. _____
   3. _____

C. Development Plans: Areas for Development
   1. _____
   2. _____
   3. _____
   4. _____
   Development Strategy:
   _____
   _____
   _____

D. Employee's Comments on This Review: _____
   _____
   _____
   _____

E. Reviewer's Comments: _____
   _____
   _____
   _____

   Growth potential in present position and future growth potential for increased responsibilities: _____
   _____
   _____

   Employer's Signature:_____   Date:_____
   Reviewer's Signature:_____   Date:_____
   Reviewer's Manager's Signature:_____   Date:_____

networks) than do men, and more difficulty getting developmental assignments and geographic mobility opportunities. Women have to be more proactive than men just to be considered for such assignments, and employers therefore need to focus on breaking down the barriers that impede women's career progress. One study concluded that three corporate career development activities—fast-track programs, individual career counseling, and career planning workshops—were less available to women than to men.[49] Many call this combination of subtle and not-so-subtle barriers to women's progress the *glass ceiling*. Because developmental experiences like these are so important, "organizations that are interested in helping female managers advance should focus on breaking down barriers that interfere with women's access to developmental experiences."[50]

The Manager's Role

It's hard to overstate the impact that a supervisor can have on his or her employee's career development. With little or no additional effort than realistic performance reviews and candid career advice, a competent supervisor can help the employee get on and stay on the right career track. At the other extreme, an uncaring or unsupportive supervisor may look back on years of having inhibited his or her employees' career development.

The manager can do several things to support his or her subordinates' career development needs. For example, when the subordinate first begins his or her job, make sure (through orientation and training) that he or she develops the skills required to get off to a good start. Schedule regular performance appraisals and, at these reviews, cover the extent to which the employee's current skills and performance are consistent with the person's career aspirations. Provide the employee with an informal career development plan like that in Figure 10-4. Keep subordinates informed about how they can utilize the firm's current career-related benefits, and encourage them to do so.[51] And, know how to coach employees and provide mentoring assistance. Let's look at this next.

IMPROVING COACHING SKILLS

4 List and discuss the four steps in effectively coaching an employee.

Coaching and the closely related *mentoring* are key managerial skills. **Coaching** means educating, instructing, and training subordinates. **Mentoring** means advising, counseling, and guiding. Coaching focuses on teaching shorter-term job-related skills. Mentoring focuses on helping employees navigate longer-term career hazards. Supervisors have coached and mentored employees from the dawn of management (in Greek mythology, Mentor advised Odysseus's son during Odysseus' absence). But with more managers leading highly trained employees and self-managing teams, supporting, coaching, and mentoring are fast replacing formal authority and giving orders for getting things done.

Employers understand that coaching and mentoring are important. One consulting firm surveyed about 2,500 senior human resource and training and development managers to see what their training programs offered.[52] The survey found that the top skills their firms' development programs taught were "coaching a performance problem" (72%), "communicating performance standards" (69%), "coaching a development opportunity" (69%), and "conducting a performance appraisal" (67%).

Building Your Coaching Skills

Coaching and mentoring require both analytical and interpersonal skills. They require *analysis* because it's futile to teach or advise someone if you don't know what the problem is. They require *interpersonal skills* because it's equally futile to know the problem if you can't get the person to listen or change.

coaching
Educating, instructing, and training subordinates.

mentoring
Advising, counseling, and guiding.

Some performance situations don't require coaching. For example, if your new employee learns the first time through how to do the job, or if your employee's performance review is flawless, you won't need to do much coaching. But things rarely go so smoothly. And when they don't, you're probably going to have to coach the employee.

Coaching does not mean just telling someone what to do. We can best think of coaching in terms of a four-step process: *preparation, planning, active coaching,* and *follow-up.*[53] *Preparation* means understanding the problem, the employee, and the employee's skills. Your aim is to formulate a hypothesis about what the problem is. You'll watch the employee to see what he or she is doing, and observe the workflow and how coworkers interact with the employee. In addition to observation, you may review (as we explained in Chapter 8, Training) objective data on things like productivity, absenteeism and tardiness, accidents, grievances, waste, product quality, downtime, repairs, customer complaints, and the employee's previous performance reviews and training.

Planning the solution is next. Perhaps the most powerful way to get someone to change is to obtain his or her enthusiastic agreement on what change is required. This requires reaching agreement on the problem and on what to change. In practice, you'll then lay out a change plan in the form of *steps to take, measures of success,* and *date to complete.*

With agreement on a plan, you can start the *actual coaching.* Here you are, in essence, the teacher. Your toolkit will include what you learned about on-the-job training in Chapter 8 ("Explain quantity and quality requirements," "Go through the job at the normal work pace," and so on). As one writer says, "[a]n effective coach offers ideas and advice in such a way that the subordinate can hear them, respond to them, and appreciate their value."[54]

Finally, bad habits sometimes reemerge. It's therefore necessary to *follow-up* and re-observe the person's progress periodically.

Figure 10-5 presents a self-evaluation checklist for assessing your coaching skills.

Building Your Mentoring Skills

Mentoring traditionally means having experienced senior people advising, counseling, and guiding employees' longer-term career development. An employee who agonizes over which career to pursue or how to navigate office politics might need mentoring.

Mentoring may be formal or informal. Informally, mid- and senior-level managers may voluntarily help less-experienced employees—for instance, by giving them career advice and helping them to navigate office politics. Many employers also have formal mentoring programs. For instance, the employer may pair protégés with potential mentors, and provide training to help mentor and protégé better understand their respective responsibilities. Either formal or informal, studies show that having a mentor give career-related guidance and act as a sounding board can significantly enhance one's career satisfaction and success.[55]

MENTORING CAVEATS For the supervisor, mentoring is both valuable and dangerous. It can be valuable insofar as it allows you to influence, in a positive way, the careers and lives of your less experienced subordinates and colleagues. The danger lies on the other side of that same coin. *Coaching* focuses on daily tasks that you can easily re-learn, so coaching's downside is usually limited. *Mentoring* focuses on relatively hard-to-reverse longer-term issues, and often touches on the person's psychology (motives, needs, aptitudes, and how one gets along with others, for instance). Because the supervisor is usually not a psychologist or trained career advisor, he or she must be extra cautious in the mentoring advice he or she gives.

THE EFFECTIVE MENTOR Research on what supervisors can do to be better mentors reveals few surprises. Effective mentors *set high standards,* are willing to *invest the time* and effort the mentoring relationship requires, and actively *steer protégés* into important projects, teams, and jobs.[56] Effective mentoring requires *trust,* and the level of trust reflects the mentor's *professional competence, consistency, ability to communicate,* and readiness to *share control.*[57]

FIGURE 10-5 Coach's Self-Evaluation Checklist

Source: Based on Richard Luecke, *Coaching and Mentoring* (Boston: Harvard Business School Press, 2004), pp. 8–9.

Coach's Self-Evaluation Checklist

The questions below relate to the skills and qualities needed to be an effective coach. Use this tool to evaluate your own effectiveness as a coach.

Question	Yes	No
1. Do you show interest in career development, not just short-term performance?		
2. Do you provide both support and autonomy?		
3. Do you set high yet attainable goals?		
4. Do you serve as a role model?		
5. Do you communicate business strategies and expected behaviors as a basis for establishing objectives?		
6. Do you work with the individual you are coaching to generate alternative approaches or solutions which you can consider together?		
7. Before giving feedback, do you observe carefully, and without bias, the individual you are coaching?		
8. Do you separate observations from judgments or assumptions?		
9. Do you test your theories about a person's behavior before acting on them?		
10. Are you careful to avoid using your own performance as a yardstick to measure others?		
11. Do you focus your attention and avoid distractions when someone is talking to you?		
12. Do you paraphrase or use some other method to clarify what is being said in a discussion?		
13. Do you use relaxed body language and verbal cues to encourage a speaker during conversations?		
14. Do you use open-ended questions to promote sharing of ideas and information?		
15. Do you give specific feedback?		
16. Do you give timely feedback?		
17. Do you give feedback that focuses on behavior and its consequences (rather than on vague judgments)?		
18. Do you give positive as well as negative feedback?		
19. Do you try to reach agreement on desired goals and outcomes rather than simply dictate them?		
20. Do you try to prepare for coaching discussions in advance?		
21. Do you always follow up on a coaching discussion to make sure progress is proceeding as planned?		
TOTALS		

When you have these characteristics and use these strategies, people trust you and turn to you for both professional and personal support.
*If you answered "**yes**" to most of these questions, you are probably an effective coach.*
*If you answered "**no**" to some or many of these questions, you may want to consider how you can further develop your coaching skills.*

Source: Harvard ManageMentor® Coaching.

However, studies suggest that traditional mentoring is less effective for women that it is for men. For example, in one survey of employees who had "active mentoring relationships" in one recent year, 72% of the men received one or more promotions in the ensuing 2 years, compared with 65% of the women. A CEO or other senior executive mentored 78% of the men, compared with 69% of women.[58]

Figures like these are prompting employers to assign women to "mentor/sponsors" who have more organizational clout. For example, when Deutsche Bank discovered that several female managing directors had left the firm for better jobs at competitors, it began pairing them with mentor/sponsors from the bank's executive committee. The latter were in a position to advocate the women for promotion.

THE PROTÉGÉ'S RESPONSIBILITIES   Effective mentoring is a two-way street. It's important to have effective mentors. But as the one with the most to gain, the protégé is still largely responsible for making the relationship work. Suggestions for protégés include:

- **Choose an appropriate potential mentor.** The mentor should be objective enough to offer good career advice. Many people seek out someone who is one or two levels above their current boss.
- **Don't be surprised if you're turned down.** Not everyone is willing to undertake this time-consuming commitment.
- **Make it easier for a potential mentor to agree to your request.** Do so by making it clear ahead of time what you expect in terms of time and advice.
- **Respect the mentor's time.** Be selective about the work-related issues that you bring to the table. The mentoring relationship generally should not involve personal problems or issues.[59]

Improving Productivity through HRIS: Integrating Talent Management and Career and Succession Planning

Talent management is the goal-oriented and integrated process of planning, recruiting, developing, managing, and compensating employees. Talent management–oriented employers therefore actively integrate related human resource functions. For example, the employee's career planning and development needs should reflect the employee strengths and weaknesses that the performance appraisal brings to light, while employees' career interests and appraisals should factor into the firm's succession planning.

Achieving such integration usually means using integrated talent management software. For example, the company that manages the trans-Alaska pipeline has a user-friendly portal that lets employees "see their full training history, development plans and upcoming deadlines, register for courses, or do career planning—usually without having to ask for help."[60] At the same time, "managers can get a quick picture of the training needs for a particular group, or see all the employees who have a specific qualification."[61]

Various talent management systems enable employers to achieve such appraisal, career development, training, and succession planning integration. For example, Kenexa CareerTracker "helps organizations optimize workforce productivity by providing an easily accessible platform for ongoing employee performance management, succession planning, and career development."[62] Halogen eSuccession™ enables the employer to "Identify the skills and competencies required to support your 3–5 year strategic plans and cultivate these in your high-potential employees with career and development planning . . . [and] establish and develop a large number of promotable employees for all key areas in your organization."[63] Cornerstone Succession manages succession management through automated talent profiles, career management, internal recruiting and comprehensive succession planning capabilities.[64] Sum-Total Succession Planning supports "a holistic, end-to-end talent management strategy" including:[65]

- **360 Feedback:** Competency reviews by peers can be used as inputs into succession gap analysis;
- **Career Development:** As employees map out their career progressions, plans can be established that address competency, skill, and behavior gaps;
- **Compensation Management:** Financial plans can be tied to future succession plans so that the financial impact can be modeled;
- **Career Progression:** Historical information regarding past positions and career progression can be used to guide future succession decisions;

- **Learning Management:** Learning paths and courses can be established for desired future positions;
- **Performance Management:** Performance reviews can identify consistent high performers and top talent in the organization; and
- **Recruiting & Hiring:** Job profiles can be shared with Succession Planning; External candidates can be tagged as successors.[66]

<table>
<tr><td>5</td><td>List the main decisions employers should address in reaching promotion decisions.</td></tr>
</table>

MAKING PROMOTION DECISIONS

Career planning and mentoring often precede promotion decisions. Most people crave promotions, which usually mean more pay, responsibility, and (often) job satisfaction. For employers, promotions can provide opportunities to reward exceptional performance, and to fill open positions with tested and loyal employees. Yet the promotion process isn't always a positive experience. Unfairness, arbitrariness, or secrecy can diminish the effectiveness of the process. Furthermore, with more employers downsizing, some "promotions" take the form of more challenging but not necessarily higher-ranked or better-paid jobs. Several decisions, therefore, loom large in any firm's promotion process.

Decision 1: Is Seniority or Competence the Rule?

Probably the most important decision is whether to base promotion on seniority or competence, or some combination of the two.

Today's focus on competitiveness favors competence. However, a company's ability to use competence as the criterion depends on several things. Union agreements sometimes contain clauses that emphasize seniority. Civil service regulations that stress seniority rather than competence often govern promotions in many public-sector organizations.

Decision 2: How Should We Measure Competence?

If the firm opts for competence, how should it define and measure competence? The question highlights an important managerial adage called the "Peter Principle," after its founder. In brief, the Peter Principle says that companies often promote competent employees up to their "level of incompetence," where they then sit, sometimes underperforming for years. The point is that defining and measuring *past* performance is relatively straightforward. But promotions should require something more. You also need a valid procedure for predicting the candidate's future performance.

For better or worse, most employers use prior performance as a guide, and assume that (based on exemplary prior performance) the person will do well on the new job. This is the simplest procedure. Many others use tests or assessment centers to evaluate promotable employees and to identify those with executive potential.

For example, given the public safety issues involved, police departments and the military tend to take a relatively systematic approach when evaluating candidates for promotion to command positions. For the police, traditional promotional reviews include a written knowledge test, an assessment center, credit for seniority, and a score based on recent performance appraisal ratings. Others include a personnel records review. This includes evaluation of job-related influences such as supervisory-related education and experience, ratings from multiple sources, and systematic evaluation of behavioral evidence.[67]

THE 9-BOX ASSESSMENT In assessing candidates for promotions, it's not just current performance but performance potential that's important. For example, some high-performing candidates may already be at their limit and have no potential for future growth. Some high potential candidates may be performing poorly but be salvageable. That idea is at the heart of the **9-box matrix** approach to assessing current employees' promotional prospects.[68] The 9-box matrix displays three levels of current job performance (exceptional, fully performing, not yet fully performing) across the top. It also shows three levels of likely potential (eligible for promotion, room for growth in current position, not likely to grow beyond current position) down the side. This 3×3 design results in 9 possible combinations of current job performance and likely potential. For example, an employee may be *eligible for promotion* and *exceptional in his or her current performance.* He or she is therefore ready for promotion. As another example, an employee may have *room to grow in his or her current position*, but *not fully performing yet.* Here you would want to identify the reasons for the underperformance and improve the employee's skills.

Decision 3: Is the Process Formal or Informal?

Many firms have informal promotion processes. They may or may not post open positions, and key managers may use their own "unpublished" criteria to make decisions. Here employees may (reasonably) conclude that factors like "who you know" are more important than performance, and that working hard to get ahead—at least in this firm—is futile.

Other employers set formal, published promotion policies and procedures. Employees receive a *formal promotion policy* describing the criteria by which the firm awards promotions. A *job posting policy* states the firm will post open positions and their requirements, and circulate these to all employees. As explained in Chapter 5 (Recruiting), many employers also maintain *employee qualification databanks* and use replacement charts and computerized employee information systems.

Decision 4: Vertical, Horizontal, or Other?

Promotions aren't necessarily upwards. For example, how do you motivate employees with the prospect of promotion when your firm is downsizing? And how do you provide promotional opportunities for those, like engineers, who may have little or no interest in managerial roles?

Several options are available. Some firms, such as the exploration division of British Petroleum (BP), create two parallel career paths, one for managers and another for "individual contributors" such as high-performing engineers. At BP, individual contributors can move up to nonsupervisory but senior positions, such as "senior engineer." These jobs have most of the financial rewards attached to management-track positions at that level.

Another option is to move the person horizontally. For instance, move a production employee to human resources, to develop his or her skills and to test and challenge his or her aptitudes. And, in a sense, "promotions" are possible even when leaving the person in the same job. For example, you can usually enrich the job and provide training to enhance the opportunity for assuming more responsibility.

Practical Considerations

In any case, there are practical steps to take in formulating promotion policies.[69] Establish eligibility requirements, for instance, in terms of minimum tenure and performance ratings. Require managers to review the job description, and revise if necessary. Vigorously review all candidates' performance and history, including those now in the firm. Preferably hire only those who meet the requirements.

Sources of Bias in Promotion Decisions

Women and people of color still experience relatively less career progress in organizations, and bias and more subtle barriers are often the cause. Yet this is not necessarily the result of decision makers' racist sentiments. Instead, secondary factors—such as having few people of color employed in the hiring department—may be the cause. In any case, the bottom line seems to be that whether it's bias or some other reason, barriers still exist. Employers and supervisors need to identify and abolish them.

Similarly, women still don't make it to the top of the career ladder in numbers proportionate to their numbers in U.S. industry. Women constitute more than

40% of the workforce, but hold less than 2% of top management positions. Blatant or subtle discrimination probably accounts for much of this. Some hiring managers erroneously believe that "women belong at home and are not committed to careers." The "old-boy network" of informal (mostly male) friendships forged over lunch, at social events, or at club meetings is still a problem. More women than men must also make the "career versus family" decision, since the responsibilities of raising children still fall disproportionately on women.

Similarly, a lack of female mentors makes it harder for women to find the role models and supporters they need to help guide their careers. Special networking and mentoring opportunities can reduce some of these problems, as can more flexible employment policies. For example, when the accounting firm Deloitte & Touche noticed it was losing good female auditors, it instituted a new flexible/reduced work schedule. This enabled many working mothers who might otherwise have left to stay with the firm.[70]

Promotions and the Law

In general, the employer's promotion processes must comply with all the same antidiscrimination laws as do procedures for recruiting and selecting employees or any other HR actions. But beyond that general caveat, there are several specific things to keep in mind regarding promotion decisions.

One concerns *retaliation*. Most federal and state employment laws contain anti-retaliation provisions. For example, one U.S. Appeals Court allowed a claim of retaliation to proceed when a female employee provided evidence that her employer turned her down for promotion because a supervisor she had previously accused of sexual harassment made comments that persuaded her current supervisor not to promote her.[71] The evidence confirmed that, in a meeting at which supervisors reviewed the person's performance, the former supervisor (and object of the sexual harassment accusation) made comments regarding the employee's "ability to work effectively with others."

A second concerns using inconsistent, unsystematic processes to decide who to promote. For example, one employer turned down a 61-year-old applicant for a promotion because of his interview performance; the person who interviewed him said he did not "get a real feeling of confidence" from the candidate.[72] In this case, "the court made it clear that while subjective reasons can justify adverse employment decisions, an employer must articulate any clear and reasonably specific factual bases upon which it based its decision." In other words, you should be able to provide objective evidence supporting your subjective assessment for promotion.

Managing Transfers

Source: Shutterstock.

Employers are transferring employees less often, partly because of family resistance.

A **transfer** is a move from one job to another, usually with no change in salary or grade. Employers may transfer a worker to vacate a position where he or she is no longer needed, to fill one where he or she is needed, or more generally to find a better fit for the employee within the firm. Many firms today boost productivity by consolidating positions. Transfers are a way to give displaced employees a chance for another assignment or, perhaps, some personal growth. Employees seek transfers for many reasons, including personal enrichment, more interesting jobs, greater convenience—better hours, location of work, and so on—or to jobs offering greater advancement possibilities.

9-box matrix
In workforce planning, this displays three levels of current job performance (exceptional, fully performing, not yet fully performing) across the top, and also shows three levels of likely potential (eligible for promotion, room for growth in current position, not likely to grow beyond current position) down the side.

transfer
Reassignments to similar positions in other parts of the firm.

Managing Retirements

For many employees, years of appraisals and career planning end with retirement.

Retirement planning is a significant long-term issue for employers. In the United States, the number of 25- to 34-year-olds is growing relatively slowly, and the number of 35- to 44-year olds is declining. So, with many employees in their 50s and 60s moving toward traditional retirement age, employers face a longer-term labor shortage: "companies have been so focused on downsizing to contain costs that they largely neglected a looming threat to their competitiveness . . . a severe shortage of talented workers."[73]

Many have wisely chosen to fill their staffing gaps in part with current or soon-to-be retirees. Fortuitously, 78% of employees in one survey said they expect to continue working in some capacity after normal retirement age (64% said they want to do so part-time). Only about a third said they plan to continue work for financial reasons; about 43% said they just wanted to remain active.[74]

The bottom line is that "retirement planning" is no longer just for helping current employees slip into retirement.[75] It can also enable the employer to retain, in some capacity, the skills and brain power of those who would normally retire and leave the firm.

WORKFORCE RETIREMENT PLANNING   A reasonable first step is to conduct numerical analyses of pending retirements. This should include a demographic analysis (including a census of the company's employees), a determination of the average retirement age for the company's employees, and a review of how retirement is going to affect the employer's health care and pension benefits. The employer can then determine the extent of the "retirement problem," and take fact-based steps to address it.[76]

METHODS   Employers seeking to attract and/or retain retirees need to take several steps. The general idea is to institute human resource policies that encourage and support older workers. Not surprisingly, studies show that employees who are more committed and loyal to the employer are more likely to stay beyond their normal retirement age.[77] This often starts by creating a culture that honors experience. For example, the CVS pharmacy chain knows that traditional recruiting media such as help-wanted signs might not attract older workers; CVS thus works through The National Council on Aging, city agencies, and community organizations to find new employees. They also made it clear to retirees that they welcome older workers: "I'm too young to retire. [CVS] is willing to hire older people. They don't look at your age but your experience," said one dedicated older worker.[78] Others modify selection procedures. For example, one British bank stopped using psychometric tests, replacing them with role-playing exercises to gauge how candidates deal with customers.

The techniques employers use to keep older workers include offering them part-time positions, hiring them as consultants or temporary workers, offering them flexible work arrangements, encouraging them to work past traditional retirement age, providing training to upgrade skills, and instituting a phased retirement program. The latter lets older workers ease into retirement with gradually reduced work schedules.[79]

REVIEW

MyManagementLab Now that you have finished this chapter, go back to **www.mymanagementlab.com** to continue practicing and applying the concepts you've learned.

CHAPTER SECTION SUMMARIES

1. Managing voluntary turnover requires identifying its causes and then addressing them. A comprehensive approach to **retaining employees should be multi-faceted**, and include improved selection, a well-thought-out training and career development program, assistance in helping employees lay out potential career plans, providing employees with meaningful work and recognition and rewards, promoting work–life balance, acknowledging employees' achievements, and providing all this within a supportive company culture.

2. **Employee engagement** is important. Numerous employee outcomes including turnover and performance reflect the degree to which employees are engaged. For example, business units with the highest levels of employee engagement have an 83% chance of performing above the company median, while those with the lowest employee engagement have only a 17% chance. Engagement-supporting actions include making sure employees (1) understand how their departments contribute to the company's success, (2) see how their own efforts contribute to achieving the company's goals, and (3) get a sense of accomplishment from working at the firm.

3. Employees ultimately need to take responsibility for their own careers, but employers and managers should also understand what **career management methods** are available. These include establishing company-based career centers, offering career planning workshops, providing employee development budgets, and offering online career development workshops and programs. Perhaps the simplest and most direct is to make the appraisal itself career-oriented, insofar as the appraisal feedback is a link to the employee's aspirations and plans. Supervisors can play a major role in their employee's career development. For example, make sure the employee gets the training he or she requires, and make sure appraisals are discussed in the context of the employee's career aspirations.

4. Getting employees to do better requires **improving your coaching skills**. Ideally, the coaching process involves preparation (in terms of analyzing the issues), developing an improvement plan, active coaching, and follow-up. Effective mentors set high standards, invest the time, steer protégés into important projects, and exhibit professional competence and consistency.

5. For employers, **promotions** can provide opportunities to reward exceptional performance, and to fill open positions with tested and loyal employees. Several decisions loom large in any firm's promotion process: Is seniority or competence the rule? How should we measure competence? Is the process formal or informal? and, Vertical, horizontal, or other? Women and people of color still experience relatively less career progress in organizations, and bias and more subtle barriers are often the cause. In general, the employer's promotion processes must comply with all the same antidiscrimination laws as do procedures for recruiting and selecting employees or any other HR actions.

DISCUSSION QUESTIONS

1. Why is it advisable for an employee retention effort to be comprehensive? To what extent does IBM's on-demand program fit that description, and why?

2. Explain why employee engagement is important, and how to foster such engagement. What exactly would you as a supervisor do to increase your employees' engagement?

3. What is the employee's role in the career development process? The manager's role? The employer's role?

4. List and discuss the four steps in effectively coaching an employee. How could (and would) a professional football coach apply these steps?

5. What are the main decisions employers should address in reaching promotion decisions?

INDIVIDUAL AND GROUP ACTIVITIES

1. Many rightfully offer IBM as an example of an employer that works hard to improve employee retention and engagement. Browse through the employment pages of IBM.com's Web site (such as www-03.ibm.com/employment/build_your_career.html). In this chapter, we discussed actions employers can take to improve employee retention and engagement. From the information on IBM's Web pages, what is IBM doing to support retention and engagement?

2. In groups of four or five students, meet with one or two administrators and faculty members in your college or university and, based on this, write a 2-page paper on the topic "the faculty promotion process at our college." What do you think of the process? Based on our discussion in this chapter, could you make any suggestions for improving it?

3. Working individually or in groups, choose two occupations (such as management consultant, HR manager, or salesperson) and use sources such as O*Net to size up the future demand for this occupation in the next 10 years or so. Does this seem like a good occupation to pursue? Why or why not?

4. In groups of four or five students, interview a small business owner or an HR manager with the aim of writing a 2-page paper addressing the topic "steps our company is taking to reduce voluntary employee turnover." What is this employer's turnover rate now? How would you suggest it improve its turnover rate?

5. The "HRCI Test Specifications Appendix" at the end of this book (pages 633–640) lists the knowledge someone studying for the HRCI certification exam needs to have in each area of human resource management (such as in Strategic Management, Workforce Planning, and Human Resource Development). In groups of four to five students, do four things: (1) review that appendix now; (2) identify the material in this chapter that relates to the required knowledge the appendix lists; (3) write four multiple-choice exam questions on this material that you believe would be suitable for inclusion in the HRCI exam; and (4) if time permits, have someone from your team post your team's questions in front of the class, so the students in other teams can take each others' exam questions

7. Several years ago, a survey of college graduates in the United Kingdom found that although many hadn't found their first jobs, most were already planning "career breaks" and to keep up their hobbies and interests outside work. As one report of the findings put it, "the next generation of workers is determined not to wind up on the hamster wheel of long hours with no play."[80] Part of the problem seems to be that many already see their friends "putting in more than 48 hours a week" at work. Career experts reviewing the results concluded that many of these recent college grads "are not looking for high-pay, high-profile jobs anymore."[81] Instead, they seem to be looking to "compartmentalize" their lives. They want to keep the number of hours they spend at work down, so they can maintain their hobbies and outside interests. If you were mentoring one of these people at work, what three bits of career advice would you give him or her? Why? What (if anything) would you suggest their employers do to accommodate these graduates' stated career wishes?

8. Sporting News (http://aol.sportingnews.com/ncaa-basketball/story/2009-07-29/sporting-news-50-greatest-coaches-all-time) ran a story listing what they called the 50 greatest basketball coaches. Look at this list, and pick out two of the names. Then research these people online to determine what behaviors they exhibited that seem to account for why they were great coaches. How do these behaviors compare with what this chapter had to say about effective coaching?

EXPERIENTIAL EXERCISE

Where Am I Going . . . and Why?

Purpose: The purpose of this exercise is to provide you with experience in analyzing your career preferences.

Required Understanding: Students should be thoroughly familiar with the "Employee's Role in Career Management" section in this chapter, as well as using O*Net (which we discussed in Chapter 4).

How to Set Up the Exercise/Instructions:

Using O*Net and the "Employee's Role in Career Management" section in this chapter, analyze your career-related inclinations (you can take the self-directed search for about $10 at www.self-directed-search.com). Based on this analysis, answer the following questions (if you wish, you may do this analysis in teams of three or four students).

1. What does your research suggest to you about what would be your preferable occupational options?

2. What are the prospects for these occupations?

3. Given these prospects and your own occupational inclinations, outline a brief, 1-page career plan for yourself, including current occupational inclinations, career goals, and an action plan listing four or five development steps you will need to take in order to get from where you are now career-wise to where you want to be, based on your career goals.

APPLICATION CASE

GOOGLE REACTS

On the face of it, Google would seem to be the last company that one would expect to have an employee retention problem. Google usually shows up in "Best Employers to Work for" lists; it's famous for full benefits, from dry-cleaning to free Web-enabled transportation from San Francisco to great pensions; it offers great stock options; and as a fast-growing company, it usually has many job applicants. So when its employee turnover began creeping up around 2010, Google's human resource team had to decide what to do. Part of the problem is that as attractive as Google is to work for, Silicon Valley is filled with attractive employers, from Apple to Facebook. One of Google's first steps was to boost compensation. It gave all 23,000 Google employees a 10% raise, plus a $1,000 tax-free holiday bonus.[82] But still,

Google management knew that pay was just part of the solution. It had to take other steps.

Questions

1. Without doing any further research than what you learned in this chapter, what other steps would you suggest Google take to improve employee retention?
2. Was there any information in previous chapters of this book that would help to illustrate other steps Google took to improve retention?
3. Use other Internet sources, including Google.com, to finalize an answer to the question, What other steps should Google take to improve employee retention?

CONTINUING CASE

CARTER CLEANING COMPANY

The Career Planning Program

Career planning has always been a pretty low-priority item for Carter Cleaning, since "just getting workers to come to work and then keeping them honest is enough of a problem," as Jack likes to say. Yet Jennifer thought it might not be a bad idea to give some thought to what a career planning program might involve for Carter. Many of their employees had been with them for years in dead-end jobs, and she frankly felt a little badly for them: "Perhaps we could help them gain a better perspective on what they want to do," she thought. And she definitely believed that career support would have an effect on improving Carter's employee retention.

Questions

1. What would be the advantages to Carter Cleaning of setting up a career planning program?
2. Who should participate in the program? All employees? Selected employees?
3. Outline and describe the career development program you would propose for the cleaners, pressers, counter people, and managers at the Carter Cleaning Centers.

TRANSLATING STRATEGY INTO HR POLICIES & PRACTICES CASE

THE HOTEL PARIS CASE

The New Career Management System

The Hotel Paris's competitive strategy is "To use superior guest service to differentiate the Hotel Paris properties, and to thereby increase the length of stay and return rate of guests, and thus boost revenues and profitability." HR manager Lisa Cruz must now formulate functional policies and activities that support this competitive strategy by eliciting the required employee behaviors and competencies.

Lisa Cruz knew that as a hospitality business, the Hotel Paris was uniquely dependent upon having committed, high-morale employees. In a factory or small retail shop, the employer might be able to rely on direct supervision to make

sure that the employees were doing their jobs. But in a hotel, just about every employee is "on the front line." There is usually no one there to supervise the limousine driver when he or she picks up a guest at the airport, or when the valet takes the guest's car, or the front-desk clerk signs the guest in, or the housekeeping clerk needs to handle a guest's special request. If the hotel wanted satisfied guests, they had to have committed employees who did their jobs as if they owned the company, even when the supervisor was nowhere in sight. But for the employees to be committed, Lisa knew the Hotel Paris had to make it clear that the company was also committed to its employees.

From her experience, she knew that one way to do this was to help her employees have successful and satisfying careers, and she was therefore concerned to find that the Hotel Paris had no career management process at all. Supervisors weren't trained to discuss employees' developmental needs or promotional options during the performance appraisal interviews. Promotional processes were informal. And the firm did not attempt to provide any career development services that might help its employees to develop a better understanding of what their career options were, or should be. Lisa was sure that committed employees were the key to improving the experiences of its guests, and that she couldn't boost employee commitment without doing a better job of attending to her employees' career needs.

For Lisa and the CFO, preliminary research left little doubt about the advisability of instituting a new career management system at the Hotel Paris. The CFO therefore gave the go-ahead to design and institute a new Hotel Paris career management program. Lisa and her team knew that they already had some of the building blocks in place, thanks to the new performance management system they had instituted just a few weeks earlier (as noted in the previous chapter). For example, the new performance management system required that the supervisor appraise the employee based on goals and competencies that were driven by the company's strategic needs, and the appraisal itself produced new goals for the coming year and specific development plans for the employee.

Questions

1. "Many hotel jobs are inherently 'dead end'; for example, maids, laundry workers, and valets either have no great aspirations to move up, or are just using these jobs temporarily, for instance, to help out with household expenses." First, do you agree with this statement—why, or why not? Second, list three specific career activities you would recommend Lisa implement for these employees.

2. Build on the company's current performance management system by recommending two other specific career development activities the hotel should implement.

3. What specific career development activities would you recommend in light of the fact that the Paris's hotels and employees are disbursed around the world?

KEY TERMS

career, *327*

career management, *327*

career development, *328*

career planning, *328*

reality shock, *330*

coaching, *333*

mentoring, *333*

9-box matrix, *339*

transfers, *339*

ENDNOTES

1. "IBM's Centenary: The Test of Time," *The Economist*, June 11, 2011, p. 20; "IBM is Founded," http://www.ibm.com/ibm100/us/en/icons/founded/, accessed August 28, 2011.

2. See, for example, www.nobscot.com/survey/index.cfm www.bls.gov/jlt/, accessed April 27, 2011.

3. Jean Phillips and Stanley Gulley, *Strategic Staffing* (Upper Saddle River, NJ: Pearson Education, 2012).

4. The following example is based on Barbara Hillmer, Steve Hillmer, and Gale McRoberts, "The Real Costs of Turnover: Lessons from a Call Center," *Human Resource Planning* 27, no. 3 (2004), pp. 34–41.

5. Ibid.

6. www.worldatwork.org/waw/adimLink?id=17180, accessed April 27, 2011.

7. Phillips and Gulley, *Strategic Staffing*, p. 329.

8. Stephen Robbins and Timothy Judge, *Organizational Behavior* (Upper Saddle River, NJ: Pearson Education, 2011), p. 81.

9. Phillips and Gulley, *Strategic Staffing*, p. 328.

10. Max Messmer, "Employee Retention: Why It Matters Now," *CPA Magazine*, June/July 2009, p. 28; and "The Employee Retention Challenge," Development Dimensions International, 2009.

11. Messmer, "Employee Retention."

12. Ibid.

13. Jessica Marquez, "IBM Cuts Costs and Reduces Layoffs as It Prepares Workers for an 'On Demand' World," *Workforce Management* 84, no. 5 (May 2005), pp. 84–85.

14. David Wilson, "Comparative Effects of Race/Ethnicity and Employee Engagement on Withdrawal Behavior," *Journal of Managerial Issues* 21, no. 2 (Summer 2009), pp. 165–166, 195–215.

15. Paul Eder and Robert Eisenberger, "Perceived Organizational Support: Reducing the Negative Influence of Coworker Withdrawal Behavior," *Journal of Management* 34, no. 1 (February 2008), pp. 55–68.

16. Wilson, "Comparative Effects of Race/Ethnicity and Employee Engagement."

17. Lisa Hope Pelled and Katherine R. Xin, "Down and Out: An Investigation of the Relationship between Mood and Employee Withdrawal Behavior," *Journal of Management* 25, no. 6 (1999), pp. 875–895.

18. Ibid.

19. Pelled and Xin, "Down and Out."

20. Ibid.

21. For an examination of this, see ibid.

22. See, for example, Margaret Shaffer and David Harrison, "Expatriates' Psychological Withdrawal from International Assignments: Work, Nonwork, and Family Influences," *Personnel Psychology* 51, no. 1 (Spring 1998), pp. 87–118; Karl Pajo, Alan Coetzer, and Nigel Guenole, "Formal Development Opportunities and Withdrawal Behaviors by Employees in Small and Medium-Sized Enterprises," *Journal of Small Business Management* 48, no. 3 (July 2010), pp. 281–301; and P. Eder, et. al., "Perceived Organizational Support: Reducing the Negative Influence of Coworker Withdrawal Behavior," *Journal of Management* 34 no. 1 (February 2008), pp. 55–68.

23. Adrienne Facts, "Raising Engagement," *HR Magazine*, May 2010, pp. 35–40.

24. Except as noted, this is based on Kathryn Tyler, "Prepare for Impact," *HR Magazine* 56, no. 3 (March 2011), pp. 53–56.

25. Rosa Chun and Gary Davies, "Employee Happiness Isn't Enough to Satisfy Customers," *Harvard Business Review* 87, no. 4 (April 2009), p. 19.

26. As another example, one recent study distinguished among physical engagement ("I work with intensity on my job, I exert my full effort to my job," and so on), emotional engagement ("I am enthusiastic in my job, I feel energetic at my job," and so on), and cognitive engagement ("at work, my mind is focused on my job," and "at work, I pay a lot of attention to my job"). Bruce Louis Rich et al., "Job Engagement: Antecedents and Effects on Job Performance," *Academy of Management Journal* 53, no. 3 (2010), pp. 617–635.

27. Rich, "Job Engagement."

28. Paula Ketter, "What's the Big Deal about Employee Engagement," *Training & Development*, January 2008, pp. 47–48.

29. "Organizations Focus on Employee Engagement to Attract and Retain Top Talent," www.Mercer.com, accessed July 24, 2010.

30. Robert Siegfried Jr., "Mapping a Career Path for Attracting & Retaining Talent," *Financial Executive*, November 2008, pp. 52–55.

31. Barbara Greene and Liana Knudsen, "Competitive Employers Make Career Development Programs a Priority," *San Antonio Business Journal* 15, no. 26 (July 20, 2001), p. 27.

32. Jim Bright, "Career Development: Empowering Your Staff to Excellence," *Journal of Banking and Financial Services* 17, no. 3 (July 2003), p. 12.

33. For example, see Phyllis Moen and Patricia Roehling, *The Career Mystique* (Boulder, CO: Rowman & Littlefield Publishers, 2005).

34. Robbins and Judge, *Organizational Behavior*, p. 285.

35. Ibid., p. 284.

36. Edward Levinson et al., "A Critical Evaluation of the Web-Based Version of the Career Key," *Career Development Quarterly* 50, no. 1 (September 1, 2002), pp. 26–36.

37. Richard Bolles, *What Color Is Your Parachute?* (Berkeley, CA: Ten Speed Press, 2003), pp. 5–6.

38. This example is based on Richard Bolles, *The Three Boxes of Life* (Berkeley, CA: Ten Speed Press, 1976). Richard Bolles updates his famous career book *What Color is Your Parachute* annually. It contains this and many other career exercises. The 2011 edition is published by Ten-Speed Press in Berkeley, California.

39. Yehuda Baruch, "Career Development in Organizations and Beyond: Balancing Traditional and Contemporary Viewpoints," *Human Resource Management Review* 16 (2006), p. 131.

40. Carla Joinson, "Employee, Sculpt Thyself with a Little Help," *HR Magazine*, May 2001, pp. 61–64.

41. Bright, "Career Development."

42. Patrick Kiger, "First USA Bank, Promotions and Job Satisfaction," *Workforce*, March 2001, pp. 54–56.

43. Fred Otte and Peggy Hutcheson, *Helping Employees Manage Careers* (Upper Saddle River, NJ: Prentice Hall, 1992), p. 143.

44. Greene and Knudsen, "Competitive Employers," p. 27.

45. Julekha Dash, "Coaching to Aid IT Careers, Retention," *Computerworld*, March 20, 2000, p. 52.

46. David Foote, "Wanna Keep Your Staff Happy? Think Career," *Computerworld*, October 9, 2000, p. 38.

47. Jim Meade, "Boost Careers and Succession Planning," *HR Magazine*, October 2000, pp. 175–178.

48. Karen Lyness and Madeline Heilman, "When Fit Is Fundamental: Performance Evaluations and Promotions of Upper-Level Female and Male Managers," *Journal of Applied Psychology* 91, no. 4 (2006), pp. 777–785.

49. Jan Selmer and Alicia Leung, "Are Corporate Career Development Activities Less Available to Female than to Male Expatriates?" *Journal of Business Ethics*, March 2003, pp. 125–137.

50. Karen Lyness and Donna Thompson, "Climbing the Corporate Ladder: Do Female and Male Executives Follow the Same Route?" *Journal of Applied Psychology* 85, no. 1 (2000), pp. 86–101.

51. Bill Hayes, "Helping Workers with Career Goals Boosts Retention Efforts," *Boston Business Journal* 21, no. 11 (April 20, 2001), p. 38.

52. Ann Pace, "Coaching Gains Ground," *Training & Development* 62, no. 7 (July 21, 2008), http://findarticles.com/p/articles/mi_m4467/is_200807/ai_n27996020/, accessed July 28, 2009.

53. This is based on Richard Luecke, *Coaching and Mentoring* (Boston: Harvard Business School Press, 2004), pp. 8–9.

54. Ibid., p. 9.

55. Michael Doody, "A Mentor Is a Key to Career Success," *Health-Care Financial Management* 57, no. 2 (February 2003), pp. 92–94.

56. Luecke, *Coaching and Mentoring*, pp. 100–101.

57. Ferda Erdem and Janset Özen Aytemur, "Mentoring—A Relationship Based on Trust: Qualitative Research," *Public Personnel Management* 37, no. 1 (Spring 2008), pp. 55–65.

58. Herminia Ibarra, Nancy Carter, and Christine Silva, "Why Men Still Get More Promotions than Women," *Harvard Business Review*, September 2010, pp. 80–85.

59. "Preparing Future Leaders in Health-Care," *Leaders*, c/o Witt/Kieffer, 2015 Spring Road, Suite 510, Oak Brook, IL 60523.

60. Tim Harvey, "Enterprise Training System Is Trans Alaska Pipeline's Latest Safety Innovation," *Pipeline and Gas Journal* 229, no. 12 (December 2002), pp. 28–32.

61. Ibid.

62. "Kenexa Announces a Latest Version of Kenexa Career Tracker," *Internet Wire*, March 22, 2004.

63. http://www.halogensoftware.com/products/halogen-esuccession/, accessed.

64. www.cornerstoneondemand.com/leadership-development-and-succession, accessed.

65. The following is quoted from http://www.sumtotalsystems.com/products/career-succession-planning.html, accessed August 28, 2011.

66. http://www.sumtotalsystems.com/products/career-succession-planning.html, accessed August 28, 2011.

67. George Thornton III and David Morris, "The Application of Assessment Center Technology to the Evaluation of Personnel Records," *Public Personnel Management* 30, no. 1 (Spring 2001), p. 55.

68. Phillips and Gulley, *Strategic Staffing*, pp. 282–283.

69. Pamela Babcock, quoting Terry Henley, SPHR, in "Promotions: Is There a 'New Normal'?" www.shrm.org/hrdisciplines/employeereltions/articles/Pages/PromotionsIsThereaNewNormal.aspx, accessed June 1, 2011.

70. Robin Shay, "Don't Get Caught in the Legal Wringer When Dealing with Difficult to Manage Employees," www.shrm.org http://moss07.shrm.org/Publications/hrmagazine/EditorialContent/Pages/0702toc.aspx, accessed July 28, 2009.

71. Maria Danaher, "Unclear Promotion Procedures Smack of Discrimination," www.shrm.org, accessed March 2, 2004.

72. In Susan Wells, "Smoothing the Way," *HR Magazine*, June 2001, pp. 52–58.

73. Ken Dychtwald et al., "It's Time to Retire Retirement," *Harvard Business Review*, March 2004, p. 49.

74. "Employees Plan to Work Past Retirement, but Not Necessarily for Financial Reasons," *BNA Bulletin to Management*, February 19, 2004, pp. 57–58. See also Mo Wang, "Profiling Retirees in the Retirement Transition and Adjustment Process: Examining the Longitudinal Change Patterns of Retirees' Psychological Well-Being," *Journal of Applied Psychology* 92, no. 2 (2007), pp. 455–474.

75. See, for example, Matt Bolch, "Bidding Adieu," *HR Magazine,* June 2006, pp. 123–127; and Claudia Deutsch, "A Longer Goodbye," *The New York Times*, April 20, 2008, pp. H1, H10.

76. Luis Fleites and Lou Valentino, "The Case for Phased Retirement," *Compensation & Benefits Review*, March/April 2007, pp. 42–46.

77. Andrew Luchak et al., "When Do Committed Employees Retire? The Effects of Organizational Commitment on Retirement Plans Under a Defined Benefit Pension Plan," *Human Resource Management* 47, no. 3 (Fall 2008), pp. 581–599.

78. Dychtwald et al., "It's Time to Retire Retirement," p. 52.

79. Eric Krell, "Ways to Phased Retirement," *HR Magazine*, October 2010, p. 90.

80. "New Trend in Career Hunt," *Europe Intelligence Wire*, February 10, 2004.

81. Ibid.

82. http://abclocal.go.com/kgo/story?section=news/business&id=7775524, accessed June 1, 2011.

PART 3 VIDEO CASES APPENDIX

Video Title: Training (Wilson Learning)

SYNOPSIS

Maxene Raices is a senior manager at Wilson Learning, a company that specializes in developing training programs. She describes the best practices that make training most effective. She explains how training sessions have to be planned carefully with an outcome in mind, and have to consist of more than just lecturing. Good training programs help employees do their jobs, and ideally produce measurable results. Managers can use technology to make training even more effective, giving opportunities for people spread over various locations to attend training sessions.

Discussion Questions

1. How does Wilson Learning's "know, show, do" approach fit with the training process that Chapter 8 described?
2. Explain what specific training tools and processes discussed in Chapter 8 you would use to implement a "know, show, do" training approach.
3. What you think of the experimental design Wilson used to assess the call-center training program? How would you suggest the company improve it?
4. Discuss four types of technology Wilson could use to deliver training, based on the Chapter 8.
5. What are two reasons that Maxene gives for thinking it is important for different learning styles to be recognized?
6. How does identifying the intended outcomes of a training shape the training itself?

Video Title: Training and Developing Employees (Witness.org)

SYNOPSIS

Witness.org trains human rights advocacy groups to capture on video the testimonies of survivors and witnesses to human rights abuses all over the world. The company's goal is to empower the people who are directly involved in the situations, by giving them the tools necessary to use the power of video to communicate their stories. Witness.org trains advocacy partners on how to use the video equipment, how to tell a story in such a way that it effects change in those who hear it, and how to get the video in front of the people who are able to make a positive change.

Witness.org is ran by a core of 28 people with experience in a variety of areas, including speaking multiple languages, managing a nonprofit organization, producing videos, and working with human rights issues. These employees train advocacy groups on the technical aspects of creating a video, as well as safety and security issues related to producing videos containing sensitive materials. The main goal of Witness.org is to achieve changes in policies, laws, or behaviors that are currently causing human suffering.

Discussion Questions

1. Explain how training and development play an important role in Witness.org.
2. Describe the challenges incurred in the training and development process at Witness.org.
3. Describe the group of experts who conduct the training for Witness.org.

Video Title: Performance Management (California Health Foundation)

SYNOPSIS

Kim Galvin, the human resources director of the California Health Foundation, explains the nature of the company's performance management system. The employee appraisal system is open-ended and includes just a few general categories, covering the employees' past performance with respect to their objectives set at the previous year's appraisal, and their future goals in the company.

Discussion Questions
1. Specifically what type of appraisal tool does the company seem to be using, based on what you read in Chapter 9? How would you modify it?
2. What you think of the idea of getting anonymous third-party feedback on the employee? Why?
3. Why does Kim Galvin think that, besides the human resources director, only an employee and his or her manager should review the employee's performance review? What (if any) is the drawback of not having the supervisor's own manager review the appraisal? Would you require some type of review, and why?
4. Suppose, as Kim Galvin says, you have an employee who is very well liked but not meeting the job expectations. What would you do?
5. How does the California Health Foundation handle employees who may be candidates for future promotion?

Video Title: Appraising (Hautelook)

SYNOPSIS

Performance appraisal can be performed both by employees and by their supervisors. The online clothing retail company Hautelook conducts evaluations by both a formal and an informal process. Informal evaluations can happen at any time during the year, whereas formal evaluations are in January, with an informal mid-year review in July. Hautelook has an informal culture, where managers have an open-door policy and employees are encouraged to have regular discussions with managers as to their performance, as well as to self-evaluate their own performance continually. Hautelook rewards employees in various ways, such as by recognition, raises, bonuses, and promotions. Filling positions by internal promotion is strongly emphasized, and employees are encouraged to think about how they might advance their position in the company in the future.

Discussion Questions
1. What appraisal tool or tools would you recommend using at Hautelook, and why?
2. What do you think of how Hautelook handled its attendance problem? Was this an appraisal or a discipline problem? What difference would it make in how you handle the problem?
3. Which appraisal problems from Chapter 9 would help to explain the "fairness and accuracy" issues that sometimes arise in the company's appraisals?
4. From what you've seen in this video, what exactly would you do to turn Hautelook's appraisal process into more of a performance management process?

Video Title: Appraising (The Weather Channel)

SYNOPSIS

Employee appraisals at The Weather Channel are recommended to be done on an ongoing, continual basis so that an employee always knows where he or she stands as far as what is expected and how well he or she is doing. This way, the employee can look forward to performance reviews instead of dreading them. The idea is that the appraisals will be a confirmation of the progress the employee has been making.

An employee is recognized not just for what he or she has achieved during the appraisal year, but for the ways in which his or her goals were accomplished. The employee can thereby have opportunities identified for building on his or her previous performance and better progress within the company.

Discussion Questions

1. From what Ms. Taylor says, does The Weather Channel really use a "performance management" process? Why do you conclude that?
2. How, specifically, does a firm's performance management process support its training process?
3. How would you reduce the anxiety and stress of an appraisal, based on what you read in Chapter 9?
4. How exactly would you appraise the employees' "competencies"? What tools would you use specifically, and why?

11

Establishing Strategic Pay Plans

Source: Tyler Olson/Shutterstock.

LEARNING OBJECTIVES

1. List the basic factors determining pay rates.
2. Define and give an example of how to conduct a job evaluation.
3. Explain in detail how to establish a market-competitive pay plan.
4. Explain how to price managerial and professional jobs.
5. Explain the difference between competency-based and traditional pay plans.
6. List and explain six important trends in compensation management.

The retail grocery business is highly competitive. Therefore, when Walmart moves into a grocery's area, the knee-jerk reaction is to cut costs, particularly wages and benefits. So as Wegman's Food Markets, Inc., adds more stores and increasingly competes with Walmart, its management needs to decide this: Should we cut pay to better compete based on cost, or pursue a different compensation policy?[1]

Access a host of interactive learning aids at **www.mymanagementlab.com** to help strengthen your understanding of the chapter concepts.

WHERE ARE WE NOW . . .

Once you've appraised and coached your employees, they'll expect to be paid. Of course, few firms just pay employees arbitrarily. Each employee's pay should make sense in terms of what other employees earn, and this requires a pay plan. The main purpose of this chapter is to show you how to establish a pay plan. We explain *job evaluation*—techniques for finding the relative worth of a job—and how to conduct online and offline salary surveys. We also explain how to price the jobs in your firm by developing pay grades and an overall pay plan. The next chapter focuses specifically on pay-for-performance and incentive plans.

1 List the basic factors determining pay rates.

BASIC FACTORS IN DETERMINING PAY RATES

Employee compensation includes all forms of pay going to employees and arising from their employment. It has two main components, **direct financial payments** (wages, salaries, incentives, commissions, and bonuses) and **indirect financial payments** (financial benefits like employer-paid insurance and vacations).

In turn, there are two basic ways to make direct financial payments to employees: based on increments of time or based on performance. Time-based pay is still the foundation of most employers' pay plans. Blue-collar and clerical workers receive hourly or daily wages, for instance. Others, like managers or Web designers, tend to be salaried and paid weekly, monthly, or yearly.

The second direct payment option is to pay for performance. For example, piecework ties compensation to the amount of production (or number of "pieces") the worker turns out. Sales commissions are another performance-based (in this case, sales-based) compensation. Other employers devise pay plans that combine time-based pay plus incentives.

In this chapter, we explain how to formulate plans for paying employees a time-based wage or salary. Subsequent chapters cover performance-based financial incentives and bonuses (Chapter 12) and employee benefits (Chapter 13).

Several factors determine the design of any pay plan: company strategy and policy, equity, legal, and union.

Aligning Total Rewards with Strategy

The compensation plan should first advance the firm's strategic aims—management should produce an *aligned reward strategy*. This means creating a compensation package including wages, incentives, and benefits that produces the employee behaviors the firm needs to support and achieve its competitive strategy.[2] We will see that many employers formulate a total rewards strategy. Total rewards encompass the traditional pay, incentives, and benefits, but also things such as more challenging jobs (job design), career development, and recognition programs.

Based on Chapter 3's strategy → behaviors → HR practices process (Figure 3-7, page 81), Table 11-1 lists illustrative questions to ask.

The accompanying Strategic Context feature illustrates strategic rewards.

THE STRATEGIC CONTEXT

Wegmans Foods

Strategic compensation management means asking, "What must the company do to achieve its strategic aims?"; then asking, "What are the employee behaviors or actions needed to support this strategic effort?"; and then putting in place compensation programs to reinforce those employee behaviors.

Wegmans exemplifies strategic compensation management. It competes in the retail food sector, where profit margins are notoriously thin and where online competitors and brick-and-mortar giants like Walmart excel at driving costs and prices down. The usual reaction, from competitors like Safeway, is to cut employee benefits and costs.[3] Wegmans takes a different approach. It views its workforce as an invaluable and integral part of achieving Wegmans' strategic aims of optimizing service while controlling costs by improving systems and productivity. For example, one dairy department employee designed a new way to organize the cooler, thus improving ordering decisions and inventory control.[4]

Wegmans' compensation policies aim to elicit just this sort of employee dedication. The firm offers above-market pay rates, affordable health insurance, a full range of employee benefits, and Wegmans hasn't laid off employees in 96 years.[5] In sum, Wegmans' pay policies aim to produce exactly the sorts of employee behaviors the company needs to achieve its strategic aims.

> **TABLE 11-1 Do Our Compensation Policies Support Our Strategic Aims?**
>
> - What are our strategic aims?
> - What employee behaviors and skills do we need to achieve our strategic aims?
> - What compensation policies and practices—salary, incentive plans, and benefits—will help to produce the employee behaviors we need to achieve our strategic aims?

Equity and Its Impact on Pay Rates

In studies at Emory University, researchers investigated how capuchin monkeys reacted to inequitable pay. They trained monkeys to trade pebbles for food. Some monkeys got grapes in return for pebbles; others got cucumber slices. Those receiving the sweeter grapes willingly traded in their pebbles. But if a monkey receiving a cucumber slice saw one of its neighbors get grapes, it slammed down the pebble or refused to eat the cucumber.[6] The moral seems to be that even lower primates are programmed to demand fair treatment when it comes to pay.

EQUITY THEORY OF MOTIVATION   Higher up the primate line, *the equity theory of motivation* postulates that people are strongly motivated to maintain a balance between what they perceive as their contributions and their rewards. Equity theory states that if a person perceives an inequity, a tension or drive will develop in the person's mind, and the person will be motivated to reduce or eliminate the tension and perceived inequity. Research tends to support equity theory, particularly as it applies to people who are underpaid.[7] For example, one study found that turnover of retail buyers is significantly lower when the buyers perceive fair treatment in the amount or rewards and in the methods by which employers allocate rewards.[8]

   With respect to compensation, managers should address four forms of equity: *external, internal, individual,* and *procedural.*[9]

- *External equity* refers to how a job's pay rate in one company compares to the job's pay rate in other companies.
- *Internal equity* refers to how fair the job's pay rate is when compared to other jobs within the same company (for instance, is the sales manager's pay fair, when compared to what the production manager is earning?).
- *Individual equity* refers to the fairness of an individual's pay as compared with what his or her coworkers are earning for the same or very similar jobs within the company, based on each individual's performance.
- *Procedural equity* refers to the "perceived fairness of the processes and procedures used to make decisions regarding the allocation of pay."[10]

ADDRESSING EQUITY ISSUES   Managers use various means to address such equity issues. For example, they use salary surveys (surveys of what other employers are paying) to monitor and maintain external equity. They use job analysis and comparisons of each job ("job evaluation") to maintain internal equity. They use performance appraisal and incentive pay to maintain individual equity. And they use communications, grievance mechanisms, and employees' participation to help ensure that employees view the pay process as procedurally fair. Some firms administer surveys to monitor employees' pay satisfaction. Questions typically include, "How satisfied are you with your pay?" and "What factors do you believe are used when your pay is determined?"[11]

---

employee compensation
All forms of pay or rewards going to employees and arising from their employment.

direct financial payments
Pay in the form of wages, salaries, incentives, commissions, and bonuses.

indirect financial payments
Pay in the form of financial benefits such as insurance.

When inequities do arise, conflicts ensue. To head off discussions that might prompt feelings of internal inequity, some firms maintain strict secrecy over pay rates, with mixed results.[12] But for external equity, online pay sites like Salary.com make it easy to see what one could earn elsewhere. Ironically, overpaying people relative to what they think they're worth can backfire too, perhaps "due to feelings of guilt or discomfort."[13]

Legal Considerations in Compensation

Employers do not have free reign in designing pay plans. Various laws specify things like minimum wages, overtime rates, and benefits.[14] Thus, the 1931 **Davis-Bacon Act** lets the secretary of labor set wage rates for laborers and mechanics employed by contractors working for the federal government. The 1936 **Walsh-Healey Public Contract Act** sets basic labor standards for employees working on any government contract that amounts to more than $10,000. It contains minimum wage, maximum hour, and safety and health provisions, and requires time-and-a-half pay for work over 40 hours a week. **Title VII of the 1964 Civil Rights Act** makes it unlawful for employers to discriminate against any individual with respect to hiring, compensation, terms, conditions, or privileges of employment because of race, color, religion, sex, or national origin.[15] We'll look next at other important compensation-related laws.

THE 1938 FAIR LABOR STANDARDS ACT The **Fair Labor Standards Act**, originally passed in 1938 and since amended many times, contains minimum wage, maximum hours, overtime pay, equal pay, record-keeping, and child labor provisions that are familiar to most working people.[16] It covers the majority of U.S. workers— virtually all those engaged in the production and/or sale of goods for interstate and foreign commerce. In addition, agricultural workers and those employed by certain larger retail and service companies are included. State fair labor standards laws cover most employers not covered by the Fair Labor Standards Act (FLSA).[17]

One familiar provision governs *overtime pay*. It says employers must pay overtime at a rate of at least one-and-a-half times normal pay for any hours worked over 40 in a workweek. Thus, if a worker covered by the act works 44 hours in one week, he or she must be paid for 4 of those hours at a rate equal to one-and-a-half times the hourly or weekly base rate the person would have earned for 40 hours. For example, if the person earns $12 an hour (or $480 for a 40-hour week), he or she would be paid at the rate of $18 per hour ($12 times 1.5) for each of the 4 overtime hours worked, or a total of $72 for the extra 4 hours. If the employee instead receives time off for the overtime hours, the employer must also compute the number of hours granted off at the one-and-a-half-times rate. So the person would get 6 hours off for the 4 hours of overtime, in lieu of overtime pay. Employers need to monitor when employees clock in and out, lest they become obligated for unexpected additional demands for overtime pay.[18]

Even giant firms make errors. Walmart agreed to pay up to $640 million to settle 63 wage and hour suits alleging infractions, such as failing to pay overtime and not providing required meal breaks.[19] The Chicago Police Department distributed Black-Berry smartphones to its officers in the field. One police officer subsequently sued, claiming that he wasn't paid overtime for the hours he spent using his smartphone off the clock. Vendors such as Pacific Timesheet (www.pacifictimesheet.com) provide mobile payroll time sheets. Employees who work outside the office can access and fill these in via their iPhones or similar devices. This improves attendance and payroll accuracy, and helps eliminate overpaying overtime.[20]

A great many employers today pay people as "independent contractors" rather than as employees. Strictly speaking, these people are like consultants, not covered by the FLSA. The accompanying Managing the New Workforce feature explains about paying this type of worker.

The FLSA also sets a *minimum wage*, which sets a floor for employees covered by the act (and usually bumps up wages for practically all workers when Congress raises

MANAGING THE NEW WORKFORCE

The Independent Contractor

Whether the person is an employee or an *independent contractor* is a continuing issue for employers.[21] For example, FedEx Ground is battling many lawsuits defending its right to maintain its roughly 15,000 delivery truck owner-operators as independent contractors. In December 2010, a federal district court in Indiana ruled that most of the FedEx ground package drivers were independent contractors, and that although FedEx encouraged the drivers to work fast, that didn't mean it controlled the means by which drivers achieved that result.[22]

For employers, there are advantages to claiming that someone is an independent contractor. For one thing, the FLSA's overtime and most other requirements do not apply. For another, the employer does not have to pay unemployment compensation payroll taxes, Social Security taxes, or city, state, and federal income taxes or compulsory workers' compensation for that worker. The problem is that many so-called independent contractor relationships aren't independent contractor relationships. There is no single rule or test for determining whether an individual is an independent contractor or a bona fide employee. Instead, the courts will look at the total activity or situation. The major consideration is this: The more the employer controls what the worker does and how he or she does it, the more likely it is that the courts will find the worker is actually an employee. Figure 11-1 lists some factors the courts will consider.

the minimum). The minimum wage for the majority of those covered by the act was $7.25 in 2011.[23] Many states have their own minimum wage laws. About 80 localities, including Boston and Chicago, require businesses that have contracts with the city to pay employees wages ranging from $8 to $12 an hour.[24] FLSA *child labor provisions* prohibit employing minors between 16 and 18 years old in hazardous occupations, and carefully restrict employment of those under 16.

EXEMPT/NONEXEMPT   Specific categories of employees are *exempt* from the FLSA or certain provisions of the act, and particularly from the act's overtime provisions—they are "exempt employees." A person's exemption depends on his or her responsibilities, duties, and salary. Bona fide executive, administrative (like office managers), and professional employees (like architects) are generally exempt from the minimum wage and overtime requirements of the act.[25] A white-collar worker earning more than $100,000 and performing any one exempt administrative, executive, or professional duty is automatically ineligible for overtime pay. Other employees can generally earn up to $23,660 per year and still automatically get overtime pay (so most employees earning less than $455 per week are nonexempt and earn overtime).[26] Figure 11-2 lists some examples of typically exempt and nonexempt jobs.

If an employee is exempt from the FLSA's minimum wage provisions, then he or she is also exempt from its overtime pay provisions. However, certain employees are *always* exempt from overtime pay provisions. They include, among others, agricultural employees, live-in household employees, taxi drivers, and motion picture theater employees.[27]

Davis-Bacon Act (1931)
A law that sets wage rates for laborers employed by contractors working for the federal government.

Walsh-Healey Public Contract Act (1936)
A law that requires minimum wage and working conditions for employees working on any government contract amounting to more than $10,000.

Title VII of the 1964 Civil Rights Act
This act makes it unlawful for employers to discriminate against any individual with respect to hiring, compensation, terms, conditions, or privileges of employment because of race, color, religion, sex, or national origin.

Fair Labor Standards Act (1938)
This act provides for minimum wages, maximum hours, overtime pay, and child labor protection. The law, amended many times, covers most employees.

FIGURE 11-1 Independent Contractor

Source: Reprinted from www.HR.BLR.com with permission of the publisher Business and Legal Resources Inc., 141 Mill Rock Road East, Old Saybrook, CT © 2004. BLR® (Business and Legal Resources, Inc.).

Independent Contractor

Managers are to use the following checklist to classify individuals as independent contractors. If more than three questions are answered "yes," the manager will confer with human resources regarding the classification. (EE = Employees, IC = Independent Contractors)

Factors which show control:

	Yes/EE	No/IC	N/A
1. Worker must comply with instructions.	☐	☐	☐
2. Worker is trained by person hired.	☐	☐	☐
3. Worker's services are integrated in business.	☐	☐	☐
4. Worker must personally render services.	☐	☐	☐
5. Worker cannot hire or fire assistants.	☐	☐	☐
6. Work relationship is continuous or indefinite.	☐	☐	☐
7. Work hours are present.	☐	☐	☐
8. Worker must devote full time to this business.	☐	☐	☐
9. Work is done on the employer's premises.	☐	☐	☐
10. Worker cannot control order or sequence.	☐	☐	☐
11. Worker submits oral or written reports.	☐	☐	☐
12. Worker is paid at specific intervals.	☐	☐	☐
13. Worker's business expenses are reimbursed.	☐	☐	☐
14. Worker is provided with tools or materials.	☐	☐	☐
15. Worker has no significant investment.	☐	☐	☐
16. Worker has no opportunity for profit/loss.	☐	☐	☐
17. Worker is not engaged by many different firms.	☐	☐	☐
18. Worker does not offer services to public.	☐	☐	☐
19. Worker may be discharged by employer.	☐	☐	☐
20. Worker can terminate without liability.	☐	☐	☐

Identifying exemptions is tricky. As noted, some jobs—for example, top managers and lawyers—are clearly exempt, while others—such as office workers earning less than $23,660 per year—are clearly nonexempt. Unfortunately, beyond the obvious categorizations, it's advisable to review the job before classifying it as exempt or nonexempt. Figure 11-3 presents a procedure for making this decision. In all but the clearest situations, carefully review the job description. Make sure, for instance, that the job currently does, in fact, require that the person perform, say, an exempt-type supervisory duty.[28]

FLSA exemption lawsuits are on the rise. For example, sales reps for a drug firm argue in one suit that the FLSA "outside salesperson" exemption doesn't cover them because they market and advise—not sell—drugs to doctors.[29] "Supervisors" are saying they don't really themselves supervise two or more employees.[30] So, again, it's not the title; it is what the employees actually do.[31]

FIGURE 11-2 Some Typical Exempt, Nonexempt Job Titles

Source: Based on www.flsa.com/coverage.html, accessed August 5, 2011.

EXEMPT	NONEXEMPT
Lawyers	Paralegals
Medical doctors	Accounting clerks
Dentists	Bookkeepers
Engineers (with degrees)	Licensed practical nurses
Teachers	Clerical employees
Scientists	Most secretaries (although some, such as the CEO's secretary, might be exempt)
Registered nurses	
General managers	Lab technicians
Pharmacists	
Administrative employees*	

* The administrative exemption is designed for relatively high-level employees whose main job is to "keep the business running." Examples of administrative functions, whose high level employees may typically be exempt, include labor relations and personnel (human resources employees), payroll and finance (including budgeting and benefits management), records maintenance, accounting and tax, marketing and advertising (as differentiated from direct sales), quality control, public relations (including shareholder or investment relations, and government relations), legal and regulatory compliance, and some computer-related jobs (such as network, internet and database administration).

1963 EQUAL PAY ACT   The **Equal Pay Act**, an amendment to the Fair Labor Standards Act, states that employees of one sex may not be paid wages at a rate lower than that paid to employees of the opposite sex for doing roughly equivalent work. Specifically, if the work requires equal skills, effort, and responsibility and involves similar working conditions, employees of both sexes must receive equal pay, unless the differences in pay stem from a seniority system, a merit system, the quantity or quality of production, or "any factor other than sex."

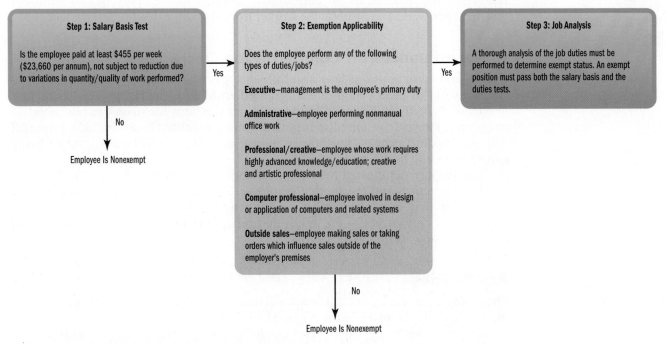

FIGURE 11-3 Who Is Exempt? Who Is Not Exempt?

Equal Pay Act (1963)
An amendment to the Fair Labor Standards Act designed to require equal pay for women doing the same work as men.

Source: Dreamstime LLC.

Two executives discuss a print layout; one happens to be in a wheelchair. Federal law mandates that the wheelchair-bound employee not suffer discrimination in compensation.

1974 EMPLOYEE RETIREMENT INCOME SECURITY ACT The **Employee Retirement Income Security Act (ERISA)** provided for the creation of government-run, employer-financed corporations to protect employees against the failure of their employers' pension plans. In addition, it sets regulations regarding vesting rights (*vesting* refers to the equity or ownership the employees build up in their pension plans should their employment terminate before retirement). ERISA also regulates *portability rights* (the transfer of an employee's vested rights from one organization to another). It also contains fiduciary standards to prevent dishonesty in pension plan funding.

OTHER LEGISLATION AFFECTING COMPENSATION Various other laws influence compensation decisions. For example, the *Age Discrimination in Employment Act* prohibits age discrimination against employees who are 40 years of age and older in all aspects of employment, including compensation.[32] The *Americans with Disabilities Act* prohibits discrimination against qualified persons with disabilities in all aspects of employment, including compensation. The *Family and Medical Leave Act* aims to entitle eligible employees, both men and women, to take up to 12 weeks of unpaid, job-protected leave for the birth of a child or for the care of a child, spouse, or parent. And various executive orders require employers that are federal government contractors or subcontractors to not discriminate, and to take affirmative action in certain employment areas, including compensation.

Each state has its own *workers' compensation laws.* Among other things, these aim to provide prompt, sure, and reasonable income to victims of work-related accidents. The *Social Security Act of 1935* (as amended) provides for unemployment compensation for workers unemployed through no fault of their own for up to 26 weeks (and recently extended), and for retirement benefits. (We'll discuss Social Security benefits in Chapter 13.) The federal wage garnishment law limits the amount of an employee's earnings that employers can withhold (garnish) per week, and protects the worker from discharge due to garnishment.

Union Influences on Compensation Decisions

Unions and labor relations laws also influence pay plan design. The National Labor Relations Act of 1935 (Wagner Act) granted employees the right to unionize, and to bargain collectively. Historically, the wage rate has been the main issue in collective bargaining. However, unions also negotiate other pay-related issues, including time off with pay, income security (for those in industries with periodic layoffs), cost-of-living adjustments, and health care benefits.

The Wagner Act created the National Labor Relations Board (NLRB) to oversee employer practices and ensure that employees receive their rights. For example, the NLRB says that employers must give the union a written explanation of the employer's "wage curves"—the graph that relates job to pay rate. The union is also entitled to know its members' salaries.[33]

Pay Policies

The employer's compensation strategy will manifest itself in *pay policies.* For example, a top hospital like Johns Hopkins might have a policy of paying nurses 20% above the prevailing market wage. Pay policies can influence the employer's performance and profitability, as the accompanying HR as a Profit Center illustrates.

Managers need to formulate pay policies covering a range of issues. One is whether to emphasize *seniority* or *performance.* For example, it takes 18 years for a U.S. federal employee to progress from step 1 to step 9 of the government's pay scale. Seniority-based pay may be advantageous to the extent that seniority is an objective standard. One disadvantage is that top performers may get the same raises as poor ones. Seniority-based pay might seem to be a relic reserved for some government agencies and unionized firms. However, one recent survey found that 60% of employees responding thought high-seniority employees got the most pay. Only about 35% said their companies paid high performers more.[34]

How to distinguish between *high and low performers* is a related policy issue. For example, for many years Payless ShoeSource was paternal in how it distributed raises—it paid everyone about the same. However, after seeing its market share drop over several years, management decided on a turnaround strategy. It necessitated revising the firm's compensation policies to differentiate more aggressively between top performers and others.[35] Other pay policies usually cover how to award salary increases and promotions, overtime pay, probationary pay, leaves for military service, jury duty, and holidays.

GEOGRAPHY   How to account for geographic differences in cost of living is another big pay policy issue. For example, the average base pay for an office supervisor ranges from $47,210 in Florida to $51,120 in Texas to $57,970 in New York.[36]

Employers handle cost-of-living differentials for transferees in several ways. One is to pay a differential for ongoing costs in addition to a one-time allocation. For example, one employer pays a differential of $6,000 per year to people earning $35,000 to $45,000 whom it transfers from Atlanta to Minneapolis. Others simply raise the employee's base salary. The problem is more complicated when you're sending employees overseas. Here, for instance, the person typically gets allowances including cost-of-living, relocation, housing, education, and hardship allowances (the latter for countries with a relatively hard quality of life, such as Zambia).[37]

HR AS A PROFIT CENTER

Wegmans Foods

As we saw, Wegmans' strategic pay policies aim to produce the employee behaviors the company needs to achieve its strategic aims. It is likely that those pay policies are one reason for the firm's exceptional profitability. For example, Wegmans employee turnover (from 38% for part-timers to 6%–7% for full timers) is well below the industry's average total of about 47%.[38] Its stores (which at about 120,000 square feet are much larger than competitors') average about $950,000 a week in sales (compared to a national average of $361,564), or about $46 million in sales annually, compared with a typical Walmart store's grocery sales of $23.5 million in sales.[39] Wegmans' human resource head was quoted as saying, "Our pay and benefits are at or above our competition's . . . It helps us attract a higher caliber of employee." As she also said, good employees assure higher productivity, and that translates into better bottom-line results.[40]

2 Define and give an example of how to conduct a job evaluation.

JOB EVALUATION METHODS

Employers use two basic approaches to setting pay rates: *market-based approaches* and *job evaluation methods*. Many firms, particularly smaller ones, simply use a *market-based* approach. Doing so involves conducting formal or informal salary surveys to determine what others in the relevant labor markets are paying for particular jobs. They then use these figures to price their own jobs. *Job evaluation methods* involve assigning values to each of the company's jobs. This helps to produce a pay plan in which each job's pay

Employee Retirement Income Security Act (ERISA)
The law that provides government protection of pensions for all employees with company pension plans. It also regulates vesting rights (employees who leave before retirement may claim compensation from the pension plan).

is equitable based on its value to the employer. However, we'll see that even with the job evaluation approach, managers must adjust pay rates to fit the market.[41]

Job evaluation is a formal and systematic comparison of jobs to determine the worth of one job relative to another. Job evaluation aims to determine a job's relative worth. Job evaluation eventually results in a *wage* or *salary structure* or hierarchy (this shows the pay rate for various jobs or groups of jobs). The basic principle of job evaluation is this: Jobs that require greater qualifications, more responsibilities, and more complex job duties should receive more pay than jobs with lesser requirements.[42] The basic job evaluation procedure is to compare jobs in relation to one another—for example, in terms of required effort, job complexity, and skills. Suppose you know (based on your job evaluation) the relative worth of the key jobs in your firm. You then conduct a salary survey to see what others are paying for similar jobs. You are then well on your way to being able to price all the jobs in your organization equitably.

Compensable Factors

You can use two basic approaches to compare the worth of several jobs. First, you can take an intuitive approach. You might decide that one job is more important than another is, and not dig any deeper. As an alternative, you could compare the jobs by focusing on certain basic factors the jobs have in common. Compensation management specialists call these **compensable factors**. They are the factors that establish how the jobs compare to one another, and that determine the pay for each job.

Some employers develop their own compensable factors. However, most use factors popularized by packaged job evaluation systems or by federal legislation. For example, the Equal Pay Act uses four compensable factors—skills, effort, responsibility, and working conditions. The method popularized by the Hay consulting firm emphasizes three factors: know-how, problem solving, and accountability. Walmart uses knowledge, problem-solving skills, and accountability requirements.

Identifying compensable factors plays a central role in job evaluation. You usually compare each job with all comparable jobs using the same compensable factors. However, the compensable factors you use depend on the job and the job evaluation method. For example, "decision making" might make sense for a manager's job, but not for a cleaner's job.[43]

Preparing for the Job Evaluation

Job evaluation is a judgmental process and demands close cooperation among supervisors, HR specialists, and employees and union representatives. The main steps include identifying the need for the program, getting cooperation, and then choosing an evaluation committee. The committee then performs the actual evaluation.

Identifying the need for job evaluation should not be difficult. For example, dissatisfaction reflected in high turnover, work stoppages, or arguments may result from paying employees different rates for similar jobs. Managers may express uneasiness with an informal way of assigning pay rates.

Employees may fear that a systematic evaluation of their jobs may reduce their pay rates, so *getting employees to cooperate* in the evaluation is important. For example, you can tell employees that because of the impending job evaluation program, pay rate decisions will no longer be made just by management whim, and that no current employee's rate will be adversely affected because of the job evaluation.

Third, *choose a job evaluation committee.* The committee usually consists of about five members, most of whom are employees. Management has the right to serve on such committees, but employees may view this with suspicion. However, a human resource specialist can usually be justified to provide expert assistance. Union representation is possible. In most cases, though, the union's position is that it is accepting the results of the job evaluation only as an initial decision and is reserving the right to appeal actual job pricing decisions through grievance or bargaining channels.[44] Once appointed, each committee member should receive a manual explaining the job evaluation process, and how to conduct the job evaluation.

The job evaluation committee typically includes at least several employees, and has the important task of evaluating the worth of each job using compensable factors.

The evaluation committee performs three main functions. First, it usually identifies 10 or 15 key **benchmark jobs**. These will be the first jobs they'll evaluate and will serve as the anchors or benchmarks against which the relative importance or value of all other jobs is compared. Next, the committee may select *compensable factors* (although the human resources department will usually choose these). Finally, the committee performs its most important function—actually *evaluating the worth of each job*. For this, the committee will probably use one of the following methods: ranking, job classification, or point method.

Job Evaluation Methods: Ranking

The simplest job evaluation method ranks each job relative to all other jobs, usually based on some overall factor like "job difficulty." There are several steps in the job **ranking method**.

1. **Obtain job information.** Job analysis is the first step. Here job descriptions for each job are prepared, and the information they contain about the job's duties is usually the basis for ranking jobs. (Sometimes job specifications are also prepared. However, the ranking method usually ranks jobs based on the whole job, rather than on several compensable factors. Therefore, job specifications, which tend to list job demands in terms of compensable factors such as problem solving, decision making, and skills, are not as important with this method as they are for other job evaluation methods.)

2. **Select and group jobs.** It is usually not practical to make a single ranking for all jobs in an organization. The usual procedure is to rank jobs by department or in clusters (such as factory workers or clerical workers). This eliminates the need for direct comparison of, say, factory jobs and clerical jobs.

3. **Select compensable factors.** In the ranking method, it is common to use just one factor (such as job difficulty) and to rank jobs based on the whole job. Regardless of the number of factors you choose, it's advisable to explain the definition of the factor(s) to the evaluators carefully so that they all evaluate the jobs consistently.

4. **Rank jobs.** For example, give each rater a set of index cards, each of which contains a brief description of a job. Then they rank these cards from lowest to highest. Some managers use an "alternation ranking method" for making the procedure more accurate. Here you take the cards, first choosing the highest and the lowest, then the next highest and next lowest, and so forth, until you've ranked all the cards. Table 11-2 illustrates a job ranking. Jobs in this small health facility rank from orderly up to office manager. The corresponding pay scales are on the right. After ranking, it is possible to slot additional jobs between those already ranked and to assign an appropriate wage rate. Online programs, as at www.hr-guide.com/data/G909.htm, can help you rank (and check the rankings of) your positions.

5. **Combine ratings.** Usually, several raters rank the jobs independently. Then the rating committee (or the employer) can simply average the raters' rankings.

This is the simplest job evaluation method, as well as the easiest to explain. And it usually takes less time than other methods.

---

job evaluation
A systematic comparison done in order to determine the worth of one job relative to another.

compensable factor
A fundamental, compensable element of a job, such as skills, effort, responsibility, and working conditions.

benchmark job
A job that is used to anchor the employer's pay scale and around which other jobs are arranged in order of relative worth.

ranking method
The simplest method of job evaluation that involves ranking each job relative to all other jobs, usually based on overall difficulty.

TABLE 11-2 Job Ranking at Jackson Hospital	
Ranking Order	**Annual Pay Scale**
1. Office manager	$43,000
2. Chief nurse	42,500
3. Bookkeeper	34,000
4. Nurse	32,500
5. Cook	31,000
6. Nurse's aide	28,500
7. Orderly	25,500

Note: After ranking, it becomes possible to slot additional jobs (based on overall job difficulty, for instance) between those already ranked and to assign each an appropriate wage rate.

Some of its drawbacks derive more from how it's used than from the method itself. For example, there's a tendency to rely too heavily on "guesstimates" (of things like overall difficulty), since ranking usually does not use compensable factors. Similarly, ranking provides no yardstick for quantifying the value of one job relative to another. For example, job number 4 may in fact be five times "more valuable" than job number 5, but with the ranking method all you know is that one job ranks higher than the other. Ranking is usually more appropriate for small employers that can't afford the time or expense of developing a more elaborate system.

The *factor comparison method*—a considerably more complicated method of ranking jobs according to various skill and difficulty factors, then adding up these rankings to arrive at an overall numerical rating for each job—is seldom used today.

Job Evaluation Methods: Job Classification

Job classification (or **job grading**) is a simple, widely used job evaluation method in which raters categorize jobs into groups; all the jobs in each group are of roughly the same value for pay purposes. We call the groups **classes** if they contain similar jobs or **grades** if they contain jobs that are similar in difficulty but otherwise different. Thus, in the federal government's pay grade system, a "press secretary" and a "fire chief" might both be graded "GS-10" (GS stands for "General Schedule"). On the other hand, in its job class system, the state of Florida might classify all "secretary IIs" in one class, all "maintenance engineers" in another, and so forth.

In practice, there are several ways to categorize jobs. One is to write class or grade descriptions (similar to job descriptions) and place jobs into classes or grades based on how well they fit these descriptions. A second is to write a set of compensable factor-based rules for each class (for instance, how much independent judgment, skill, and physical effort does the class of jobs require?). Then categorize the jobs according to these rules.

The latter is the most popular procedure—choose compensable factors, and then develop class or grade descriptions for each class or grade based on the amount or level of the compensable factor(s) in those jobs. For example, the U.S. government's classification system uses the following compensable factors: (1) difficulty and variety of work, (2) supervision received and exercised, (3) judgment exercised, (4) originality required, (5) nature and purpose of interpersonal work relationships, (6) responsibility, (7) experience, and (8) knowledge required. Based on these compensable factors, raters write a **grade definition** like that in Figure 11-4. This one shows one grade description (GS-7) for the federal government's pay grade system. Then the evaluation committee reviews all job descriptions and slots each job into its appropriate grade, by comparing each job description to the rules in each grade description. For instance, the federal government system classifies the positions automotive mechanic, welder, electrician, and machinist in grade GS-10.

FIGURE 11-4 Example of a Grade Level Definition

Source: www.opm.gov/fedclass/ gscler.pdf, accessed May 18, 2007.

Grade	Nature of Assignment	Level of Responsibility
GS-7	Performs specialized duties in a defined functional or program area involving a wide variety of problems or situations; develops information, identifies interrelationships, and takes actions consistent with objectives of the function or program served.	Work is assigned in terms of objectives, priorities, and deadlines; the employee works independently in resolving most conflicts; completed work is evaluated for conformance to policy; guidelines, such as regulations, precedent cases, and policy statements require considerable interpretation and adaptation.

The classification method has several advantages. The main one is that most employers usually end up grouping jobs into classes or grades anyway, regardless of the evaluation method they use. They do this to avoid having to price separately dozens or hundreds of jobs. Of course, the job classification automatically groups the employer's jobs into classes. The disadvantages are that it is difficult to write the class or grade descriptions, and considerable judgment is required to apply them. Yet many employers use this method with success.

Job Evaluation Methods: Point Method

The **point method**'s overall aim is to determine the degree to which the jobs you're evaluating contain selected compensable factors. It involves identifying several compensable factors for the jobs, as well as the degree to which each factor is present in each job. Assume there are five degrees of the compensable factor "responsibility" a job could contain. Further, assume you assign a different number of points to each degree of each compensable factor. Once the evaluation committee determines the degree to which each compensable factor (like "responsibility" and "effort") is present in a job, it can calculate a total point value for the job by adding up the corresponding degree points for each factor. The result is a quantitative point rating for each job. The point method of job evaluation is the most popular job evaluation method today.[45]

"PACKAGED" POINT PLANS A number of groups (such as the Hay Group, the National Electrical Manufacturer's Association, and the National Trade Association) have developed standardized point plans. Many thousands of employers use these systems. They contain ready-made factor and degree definitions and point assessments for a wide range of jobs. Employers can often use them with little or no modification.

Computerized Job Evaluations

Using quantitative job evaluation methods such as the point method can be time-consuming. Accumulating the information about "how much" of each compensable factor the job contains is a tedious process. The evaluation committees must debate the level of each compensable factor in each job. They then write down their consensus judgments and compute each job's point values or rankings.

job classification (or grading) method
A method for categorizing jobs into groups.

classes
Grouping jobs based on a set of rules for each group or class, such as amount of independent judgment, skill, physical effort, and so forth, required. Classes usually contain similar jobs.

grades
A job classification system like the class system, although grades often contain dissimilar jobs, such as secretaries, mechanics, and firefighters. Grade descriptions are written based on compensable factors listed in classification systems.

grade definition
Written descriptions of the level of, say, responsibility and knowledge required by jobs in each grade. Similar jobs can then be combined into grades or classes.

point method
The job evaluation method in which a number of compensable factors are identified and then the degree to which each of these factors is present on the job is determined.

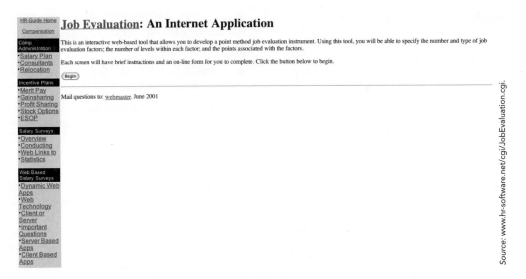

Source: www.hr-software.net/cgi/JobEvaluation.cgi.

Computer-aided job evaluation streamlines this process. The accompanying screen grab illustrates one. Most of these computerized systems have two main components. There is, first, a structured questionnaire. This contains items such as "enter total number of employees who report to this position." Second, all such systems use statistical models. These allow the computer program to price jobs more or less automatically, by assigning points.

> **3** Explain in detail how to establish a market-competitive pay plan.

HOW TO CREATE A MARKET-COMPETITIVE PAY PLAN

As we said, many firms simply price their jobs based on what other employers are paying—they use a market-based approach. However, most employers also base their pay plans on job evaluations. These evaluations assign values (such as point values) to each job. This helps to produce a pay plan in which each job's pay is internally equitable, based, as it is, on the job's value to the employer (as measured, for instance, by how many points it warrants). However, even with the job evaluation approach, managers must adjust pay rates to fit the market.[46] After all, you want employees' pay to be equitable internally—relative to what their colleagues in the firm earning—but also competitive to what other employers are paying. In a *market-competitive pay plan* a job's compensation reflects both the job's value in the company, as well as what other employers are paying for similar jobs in the marketplace. Because the point method (or "point-factor method") is so popular, we'll use it as the centerpiece of our step-by-step example for creating a market-competitive pay plan.[47] The 16 steps in creating a market-competitive pay plan begin with choosing benchmark jobs.

1. Choose Benchmark Jobs

Particularly when an employer has dozens or hundreds of different jobs, it's impractical and unnecessary to evaluate each of them separately. Therefore, the first step in the point method is to select benchmark jobs. Benchmark jobs are representative of the entire range of jobs the employer needs to evaluate. Like "accounting clerk" they should be common among employers (thus making it easier to survey what competitors are paying for similar jobs).[48]

2. Select Compensable Factors

The choice of compensable factors depends on tradition (as noted, the Equal Pay Act of 1963 uses four compensable factors: skill, effort, responsibility, and working conditions), and on strategic and practical considerations. For example, if your firm's competitive advantage is quality, you might substitute "responsibility for quality" for working conditions, or simply add it as a fifth factor.[49] Similarly, using "working conditions" makes little practical sense for evaluating executive jobs.

FIGURE 11-5 Illustrative Point Values and Degree Definitions for the Factor Job Complexity

Factor Definition: What Is Job Complexity? Job complexity generally refers to an amount of judgment, initiative, ingenuity, and complex data analysis that doing the job requires. To what extent does the person doing this job confront unfamiliar problems, deal with complex decisions, and have to exercise discretion?

Degree	Points	Job Complexity Degree Definitions: What to Look for in the Job
First	120	Here the job is routine and consists of repetitive operations requiring little or no choice of action and the automatic application of easily understood rules and procedures. For example, a filing clerk.
Second	240	Here the employee follows detailed instructions but may have to make limited decisions based on previously prescribed instructions which lay our prescribed alternatives. For example, a billing clerk or a receptionist.
Third	360	Here the employee again follows detailed instructions but because the number of matters to consider is more varied the employee needs to exhibit initiative and independent judgment, under direct supervision. For example, a nurse's aide.
Fourth	480	Here the employee can generally follow standard practices but the presence of nonroutine problems requires that the employee be able to use initiative and judgment to analyze and evaluate situations, possibly modifying the standard procedures to adjust to the new situations. For example, a nurse.
Fifth	600	On this job, the employee needs to use independent judgment and plan and perform complex work under only general supervision, often working independently toward achieving overall results. For example, medical intern.

The employer should carefully define each factor. This is to ensure that the evaluation committee members will each apply the factors with consistency. Figure 11-5 shows (on top) one such definition, in this case for the factor job complexity. The human resource specialist often draws up the definitions.

3. Assign Weights to Compensable Factors

Having selected compensable factors, the next step is to determine the relative importance (or weighting) of each factor (for instance, how much more important is "skill" then "effort"?). This is important because for each cluster of jobs some factors are bound to be more important than others are. Thus, for executive jobs the "mental requirements" factor would carry far more weight than would "physical requirements." To assign weights, we assume we have a total 100 percentage points to allocate for each job. Then (as an illustration), assign percentage weights of 60% for the factor job complexity, 30% for effort, and 10% for working conditions.[50]

4. Convert Percentages to Points for Each Factor

Next, we want to convert the percentage weights assigned to each compensable factor into point values for each factor (this is, after all, the point method). It is traditional to assume we are working with a total number of l,000 points (although one could use some other figure). To convert percentages to points for each compensable factor, *multiply the percentage weight for each compensable factor (from the previous step) by 1,000.*[51] This will tell you the *maximum number of points* for each compensable factor. The example above would translate into 1,000 × 0.60 = 600 possible points for job complexity, 1,000 × 0.30 = 300 points for effort, and 1,000 × 0.10 = 100 points for working conditions.

5. Define Each Factor's Degrees

Next, split each factor into degrees, and define each degree so that raters may judge the amount or degree of a factor existing in a job. Thus, for a factor such as "job complexity" you might choose to have five degrees, ranging from "here the job is routine" to "uses independent judgment." (Definitions for each degree are shown in Figure 11-5 under "Degree definitions: What to look for in each job"). The number of degrees usually does not exceed five or six, and the actual number depends mostly on judgment. Thus, if all employees work either in a quiet, air-conditioned office or in a noisy, hot factory, then two degrees would probably suffice for the factor "working conditions." You need not have the same number of degrees for each factor, and you should limit degrees to the number necessary to distinguish among jobs.

6. Determine for Each Factor Its Factor Degrees' Points

The evaluation committee must be able to determine the number of points each job is worth. To do this, the committee must be able to examine each job and (from each factor's degree definitions) determine what degree of each compensable factor that job has. For them to do this, we must first assign points to *each degree of each compensable factor*. For example, in our illustration, we have five possible degrees of job complexity, and the job complexity compensable factor is worth up to 600 points total. In our case, we decide that the first degree level of job complexity is worth 120 (or one-fifth of 600) points, the second degree level is worth 240 points, the third degree level is worth 360 points, the fourth degree level is worth 480 points, and the fifth degree is worth the full 600 points.[52] Do this for each factor (as in Table 11-3).

7. Review Job Descriptions and Job Specifications

The heart of job *evaluation* involves determining the amount or degree to which the job contains the selected compensable factors such as effort, job complexity, and working conditions. The team conducting the job evaluation will frequently do so by reviewing each job's job description and job specification. As we explained in Chapter 4 (Job Analysis), it is through the job analysis that the manager identifies the job's duties and responsibilities and writes the job description and job specification. Ideally, the job analysis should therefore include an explicit attempt to gather information about the compensable factors (such as job complexity) around which the employer plans to build its compensation plan.[53]

TABLE 11-3 Points Assigned to Factors and to Their Degrees (revised)

Factors	First-Degree Points	Second-Degree Points	Third-Degree Points	Fourth-Degree Points	Fifth-Degree Points
Job complexity (Total maximum points equal 600)	120	240	360	480	600
Effort (Total maximum points equal 300)	60	120	180	240	300
Working conditions (Total maximum points equal 100 points)	20	40	60	80	100

8. Evaluate the Jobs

The preceding steps provide us with the information on points and degrees we need to evaluate the jobs. Therefore, the committee now gathers job descriptions and job specifications for the benchmark jobs they want to focus on. Then for each of these jobs, the committee reviews the job description and job specification.

From this, the committee *determines the degree to which each compensable factor is present in each job*. Thus for, say, a job of master mechanic, the team might conclude (after studying the job description and job specification) that the master mechanic's job deserves the third degree level of job complexity points, the first degree level of effort, and the first-degree level of *working conditions*.

Knowing the job complexity, effort, and working conditions degrees for each job, *and knowing the number of points we previously assigned to each degree* of each compensable factor, we can now determine how many job complexity, effort, and working conditions points each benchmark job should contain. (We know the degree level for each factor for each job, so we merely check the corresponding points (see Table 11-3) that we previously assigned to each of these degrees.)

Finally, we add up these degree points for each job to determine each job's total number of points.[54] We thereby get a total point value for each benchmark job. This in turn enables us to list a hierarchy of jobs, based upon each job's points. We can then turn to assigning wage rates to each job (step nine). But first, we should define market-competitive pay plan, and **wage curve**.

WHAT IS A MARKET-COMPETITIVE PAY PLAN?   What should the pay rate be for each job? Of course, jobs with more points should command higher pay. The question is what pay rate to use. Our company's current, "internal" pay rates? Or pay rates based on what the "external" market is paying?[55]

With a **market-competitive pay system**, the employer's actual pay rates are competitive with those in the relevant labor, as well as equitable internally.[56] Put simply, the basic approach is to compare what the employer is *currently* paying for each job ("internal pay") with what the market is paying for the same or similar job ("external pay"), and then to combine this information to produce a market-competitive pay system.

WHAT ARE WAGE CURVES?   Wage curves play a central role in assigning wage rates to jobs. The wage curve typically shows the pay rates paid for jobs, relative to the points or rankings assigned to each job by the job evaluation. Figure 11-6 presents an example. Note that it shows pay rates for jobs on the vertical axis, and point values for these jobs along the horizontal axis. The purpose of the wage curve is to show the relationships between (1) the value of the job (expressed in points) as determined by one of the job evaluation methods and (2) the pay rates for the job. (We'll see that many employers may combine jobs into classes or grades. Here the wage curve shows the relationship between average pay rates for each grade, and each grade's average point value.) The pay rates on the wage curve are traditionally those now paid by the employer. However, if there is reason to believe the current pay rates are out of step with the market rates for these jobs, the employer will have to adjust them. One way to do this is to compare a wage curve that shows the jobs' *current* wage rates relative to the jobs' points, with a second curve that shows *market* wage rates relative to points. We do this as follows.

9. Draw the Current (Internal) Wage Curve

First, to study how each job's points relates to its current pay rate, we start by drawing an *internal wage curve*. Plotting each job's points and the wage rate the

---

wage curve
Shows the relationship between the value of the job and the average wage paid for this job.

market-competitive pay system
A pay system in which the employer's actual pay rates are competitive with those in the relevant labor market.

FIGURE 11-6 Plotting a Wage Curve

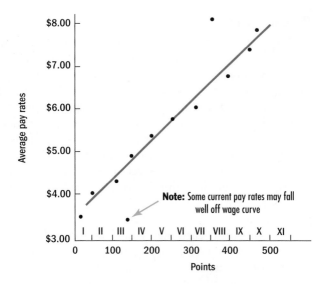

Note: Some current pay rates may fall well off wage curve

employer is now paying for each job (or wage rates, if there are several for each job) produces a scatter plot as in Figure 11-7 (left). We now draw a wage curve (on the right) through these plots that shows how point values relate to current wage rates. We can draw this wage line by just estimating a line that best fits the plotted points (by minimizing the distances between the plots and the curve). Or we can use regression, a statistical technique. Using the latter will produce a current/internal wage curve that best fits the plotted points. In any case, we show the results in Figure 11-7 (right).[57]

10. Conduct a Market Analysis: Salary Surveys

Next, we must compile the information needed to draw an *external wage curve* for our jobs, based on what other employers are paying for similar jobs. **Salary surveys—** surveys of what others are paying—play a big role in pricing jobs.[58] Employers use salary surveys in three ways. First, they use survey data to price benchmark jobs. Benchmark jobs are the anchor jobs around which they slot their other jobs, based on each job's relative worth to the firm. Second, employers typically price 20% or more of their positions directly in the marketplace (rather than relative to the firm's benchmark jobs), based on a survey of what comparable firms are paying for comparable jobs. (Google might do this for jobs like systems engineer, whose salaries fluctuate widely and often.) Third, surveys also collect data on benefits like insurance, sick leave, and vacations for decisions regarding employee benefits.

Salary surveys can be formal or informal. *Informal* phone or Internet surveys are good for checking specific issues, such as when a bank wants to confirm the salary at which to advertise a newly open teller's job, or whether some banks are really paying tellers an incentive. Some large employers can afford to send out their own *formal* surveys to collect compensation information from other employers. These ask about things like number of employees, overtime policies, starting salaries, and paid vacations.

FIGURE 11-7 The Current/Internal Wage Curve

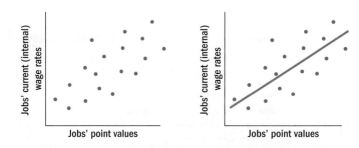

COMMERCIAL, PROFESSIONAL, AND GOVERNMENT SALARY SURVEYS

Many employers use surveys published by consulting firms, professional associations, or government agencies. For example, the U.S. Department of Labor's Bureau of Labor Statistics' (BLS) *National Compensation Survey (NCS)* provides comprehensive reports of occupational earnings, compensation cost trends, and benefits (www.bls.gov/bls/wages.htm).

Detailed occupational earnings are available from the national compensation survey for over 800 occupations in the United States, regions, states, and many metropolitan areas (http://stats.bls.gov/oes/current/oes_nat.htm). The Current Employment Statistics survey is a monthly survey of the payroll records of business establishments that provides data on earnings of production and nonsupervisory workers at the national level. This provides information about earnings as well as production bonuses, commissions, and cost-of-living increases. The National Compensation Survey—Benefits provides information on the share of workers who participate in specified benefits, such as health care, retirement plans, and paid vacations. These data also show the details of those benefits, such as amounts of paid leave. Internationally, the BLS reports comparative hourly compensation costs in local currencies and U.S. dollars for production workers and all employees in manufacturing in its international labor comparisons tables.

Private consulting and/or executive recruiting companies like Hay Associates, Heidrick and Struggles, Watson Wyatt Data Services, and Hewitt Associates publish data covering compensation for top and middle management and members of boards of directors. Professional organizations like the Society for Human Resource Management and the Financial Executives Institute publish surveys of compensation practices among members of their associations.[59]

USING THE INTERNET TO DO COMPENSATION SURVEYS
A rapidly expanding array of Internet-based options makes it easy for anyone to access published compensation survey information. Table 11-4 shows some popular salary survey Web sites.

TABLE 11-4 Some Pay Data Web Sites

Sponsor	Internet Address	What It Provides	Downside
Salary.com	Salary.com	Salary by job and zip code, plus job and description, for hundreds of jobs	Adapts national averages by applying local cost-of-living differences
U.S. Office of Personnel Management	www.opm.gov/oca/09Tables/index.asp	Salaries and wages for U.S. government jobs, by location	Limited to U.S. government jobs
Job Star	http://jobstar.org/tools/salary/sal-prof.php	Profession-specific salary surveys	Necessary to review numerous salary surveys for each profession
cnnmoney.com	cnnmoney.com	Input your current salary and city, and this gives you comparable salary in destination city	Based on national averages adapted to cost-of-living differences

salary survey
A survey aimed at determining prevailing wage rates. A good salary survey provides specific wage rates for specific jobs. Formal written questionnaire surveys are the most comprehensive, but telephone surveys and newspaper ads are also sources of information.

FIGURE 11-8 The Market/
External Wage Curve

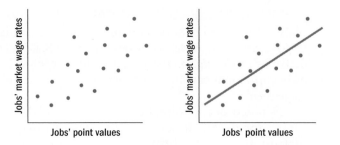

Many of these sites, such as Salary.com, provide national salary levels for jobs that the site then arithmetically adjusts to each locale based on cost-of-living formulas. To get a real-time picture of what employers in your area are actually paying for, say, accounting clerks, it's useful to access the online Internet sites of one or two of your local newspapers. For example, the *South Florida Sun-Sentinel* (and many papers) uses a site called careerbuilder.com. It lists career opportunities—in other words, just about all the jobs listed in the newspaper by category and, in many instances, their wage rates (www.sun-sentinel.com/classified/jobs).

11. Draw the Market (External) Wage Curve

The current/internal wage curve from step 9 is helpful. For example, showing, as it does, how a job's current pay rate compares with its points helps the employer identify jobs for which pay rates are currently too high or too low, relative to others in the company. (For example, if a job's current wage rate is well above the internal wage curve, it suggests that the present wage rate for that job is inequitably high, given the number of points we've assigned to that job.)

What the current (internal) wage curve does *not* reveal is whether our pay rates are too high, too low, or just right relative to what other firms are paying. For this, we need to draw a *market* or ex*ternal wage* curve.

To draw the market/external wage curve, we produce a scatter plot and wage curve as in Figure 11-8 (left and right). However, instead of using our firm's current wage rates, we use market wage rates (obtained from salary surveys). The market/external wage curve compares our jobs' points with market pay rates for our jobs.

12. Compare and Adjust Current and Market Wage Rates for Jobs

How different are the market rates others are paying for our jobs and the current rates we are now paying for our jobs? To determine this, we can draw both the current/internal and market/external wage curves on one graph, as in Figure 11-9. The market wage curve might be higher than our current wage curve (suggesting that our current pay rates may be too low), or below our current wage curve (suggesting that our current wage rates might be too high). Or perhaps market wage rates are higher for some of our jobs, and lower for others.[60]

Based on comparing the current/internal wage curve and market/external wage curve in Figure 11-9, we must decide whether to adjust the current pay rates for our jobs, and if so how. This calls for a policy decision by management. Strategic considerations influence this decision. Do our strategic aspirations suggest we should pay more, the same, or less than competitors? For example, we might decide to move our current internal wage curve up (and thereby give everyone a raise), or down (and thereby perhaps withhold pay increases for some time), or adjust the slope of the internal wage curve to increase what we pay for some jobs and decrease what we pay for others. In any case, the wage curve we end up (the green line in Figure 11-10, on page 372) should now be equitable internally (in terms of the point value of each job) and equitable externally (in terms of what other firms are paying).[61]

FIGURE 11-9 Plotting Both the Market and Internal Wage Curves

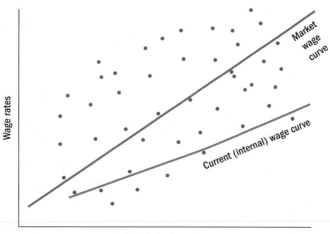

13. Develop Pay Grades

Employers typically group similar jobs (in terms of points) into grades for pay purposes. Then, instead of having to deal with hundreds of job rates, you might only have to focus on, say, pay rates for 10 or 12 pay grades. For example, Serco, a services firm which operates a London, England light railway system, set up pay grades after ranking jobs using a point system based on knowledge, management complexity, and the job's magnitude and impact on the organization.[62]

A **pay (or wage) grade** is comprised of jobs of approximately equal difficulty or importance as determined by job evaluation. If you used the point method of job evaluation, the pay grade consists of jobs falling within a range of points. If the ranking method was used, the grade consists of a specific number of ranks. If you use the classification system, then your jobs are already categorized into classes (or grades).

DETERMINING THE NUMBER OF PAY GRADES It is standard to establish grades of equal point spread. (In other words, each grade might include all those jobs falling between 50 and 100 points, 100 and 150 points, 150 and 200 points, etc.) Since each grade is the same width, the main issue involves determining how many grades to have. There doesn't seem to be any optimal number, although 10 to 16 grades for a given job cluster (shop jobs, clerical jobs, etc.) seems to be common. You need more pay grades if there are, say, 1,000 jobs to be graded than if there are only 100.

14. Establish Rate Ranges

Most employers do not pay just one rate for all jobs in a particular pay grade. For example, GE Medical won't want to pay all its accounting clerks, from beginners to long tenure, at the same rate, even though they may all be in the same pay grade. Instead, employers develop vertical pay (or "rate") ranges for each of the horizontal pay grades (or pay classes). These **pay (or rate) ranges** often appear as vertical boxes within each grade, showing minimum, maximum, and midpoint pay rates for that grade, as in Figure 11-10. (Specialists call this graph a *wage structure*. Figure 11-10 graphically depicts the range of pay rates—in this case, per hour—paid for each pay grade.) Alternatively, you may depict the pay range for each class or grade as steps in a table, such as Table 11-5, on page 373. Here you will have specific corresponding

---

pay (or wage) grade
A pay grade is comprised of jobs of approximately equal difficulty.

pay (or rate) ranges
A series of steps or levels within a pay grade, usually based upon years of service.

FIGURE 11-10
Wage Structure

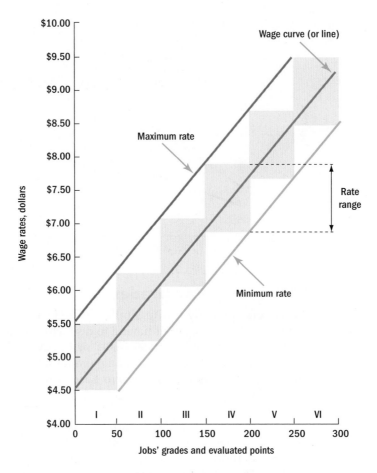

DEVELOPING RATE RANGES   The wage curve usually anchors the average pay rate for each vertical pay range. The firm might then arbitrarily decide on a maximum and minimum rate for each grade, such as 15% above and below the wage curve. As an alternative, some employers allow the pay range for each grade to become wider (they include more pay rates) for the higher pay ranges, reflecting the greater demands and performance variability inherent in more complex jobs. As in Figure 11-10, most employers structure their rate ranges to overlap a bit, so an employee in one grade who has more experience or seniority may earn more than would someone in an entry-level position in the next higher pay grade.[63]

There are several reasons to use pay ranges for each pay grade. First, it lets the employer take a more flexible stance in the labor market. For example, it makes it easier to attract experienced, higher-paid employees into a pay grade at the top of the range, since the starting salary for the pay grade's lowest step may be too low to attract them. Pay ranges also let companies provide for performance differences between employees within the same grade or between those with different seniorities.

Compensation experts sometimes use *compa ratios*. The **compa ratio** equals an employee's pay rate divided by the pay range midpoint for his or her pay grade. A compa ratio of 1 means the employee is being paid exactly at the pay range midpoint. If the compa ratio is above 1 then the person's pay rate exceeds the midpoint pay for the job. If it is below then the pay rate is less than the midpoint.

TABLE 11-5 Federal Government Salary Table[65]

SALARY TABLE 2009-GS

INCORPORATING THE 2.90% GENERAL SCHEDULE INCREASE EFFECTIVE JANUARY 2011

Annual Salary Rates by Grade and Step

Grade	Step 1	Step 2	Step 3	Step 4	Step 5	Step 6	Step 7	Step 8	Step 9	Step 10
1	17,803	18,398	18,990	19,579	20,171	20,519	21,104	21,694	21,717	22,269
2	20,017	20,493	21,155	21,717	21,961	22,607	23,253	23,899	24,545	25,191
3	21,840	22,568	23,296	24,024	24,752	25,480	26,208	26,936	27,664	28,392
4	24,518	25,335	26,152	26,969	27,786	28,603	29,420	30,237	31,054	31,871
5	27,431	28,345	29,259	30,173	31,087	32,001	32,915	33,829	34,743	35,657
6	30,577	31,596	32,615	33,634	34,653	35,672	36,691	37,710	38,729	39,748
7	33,979	35,112	36,245	37,378	38,511	39,644	40,777	41,910	43,043	44,176
8	37,631	38,885	40,139	41,393	42,647	43,901	45,155	46,409	47,663	48,917
9	41,563	42,948	44,333	45,718	47,103	48,488	49,873	51,258	52,643	54,028
10	45,771	47,297	48,823	50,349	51,875	53,401	54,927	56,453	57,979	59,505
11	50,287	51,963	53,639	55,315	56,991	58,667	60,343	62,019	63,695	65,371
12	60,274	62,283	64,292	66,301	68,310	70,319	72,328	74,337	76,346	78,355
13	71,674	74,063	76,452	78,841	81,230	83,619	86,008	88,397	90,786	93,175
14	84,697	87,520	90,343	93,166	95,989	98,812	101,635	104,458	107,281	110,104
15	99,628	102,949	106,270	109,591	112,912	116,233	119,554	122,875	126,196	129,517

The compa ratio can help reveal how many jobs in each pay grade are paid above and below competitive market pay rates.[64]

15. Address Remaining Jobs

To this point, we have focused our job evaluation on a limited number of benchmark jobs, as is traditional. We now want to add our remaining jobs to the wage structure. We can do this in two ways. We can evaluate each of the remaining jobs using the same process we just went through. Or we can simply slot the remaining jobs into the wage structure where we feel they belong, without formally evaluating and assigning points to these jobs. Jobs similar to our benchmark jobs we can easily slot into the wage structure. Jobs we're not sure about should undergo the same job evaluation process; we assign points to them and precisely slot them into the wage structure.[66]

16. Correct Out-of-Line Rates

Finally, the wage rate the firm is now paying for a particular job may fall well off the wage curve or well outside the rate range for its grade, as illustrated in Figure 11-6 (page 368). This means that the average pay for that job is currently too high or too low, relative to other jobs in the firm. For underpaid jobs, the solution is clear: Raise the wages of underpaid employees to the minimum of the rate range for their pay grade.

compa ratio
Equals an employee's pay rate divided by the pay range midpoint for his or her pay grade.

Current pay rates falling above the rate range are a different story. These are "red circle," "flagged," or "overrates." There are several ways to cope with this problem. One is to freeze the rate paid to these employees until general salary increases bring the other jobs into line. A second option is to transfer or promote the employees involved to jobs for which you can legitimately pay them their current pay rates. The third option is to freeze the rate for 6 months, during which time you try to transfer or promote the overpaid employees. If you cannot, then cut the rate you pay these employees to the maximum in the pay range for their pay grade.

PRICING MANAGERIAL AND PROFESSIONAL JOBS

4 Explain how to price managerial and professional jobs.

Developing compensation plans for managers or professionals is similar in many respects to developing plans for any employee. The basic aim is the same: to attract, motivate, and retain good employees. And job evaluation is about as applicable to managerial and professional jobs (below the top executive levels) as to production and clerical ones.

There are some big differences, though. Managerial jobs tend to stress harder-to-quantify factors like judgment and problem solving more than do production and clerical jobs. There is also more emphasis on paying managers and professionals based on their performance or on what they can do, rather than on static job demands like working conditions. And one must compete in the marketplace for executives who sometimes have the pay of rock stars. So, job evaluation, although still important, usually plays a secondary role to issues like bonuses, incentives, market rates, and benefits.

Compensating Executives and Managers

Compensation for a company's top executives usually consists of four main elements.[67] *Base pay* includes the person's fixed salary as well as, often, guaranteed bonuses such as "10% of pay at the end of the fourth fiscal quarter, regardless of whether or not the company makes a profit." *Short-term incentives* are usually cash or stock bonuses for achieving short-term goals, such as year-to-year increases in sales revenue. *Long-term incentives* aim to encourage the executive to take actions that drive up the value of the company's stock and include things like stock options; these generally give the executive the right to purchase stock at a specific price for a specific period. Finally, *executive benefits and perks* include things such as supplemental executive retirement pension plans, supplemental life insurance, and health insurance without a deductible or coinsurance. With so many complicated elements, employers must also be alert to the tax and securities law implications of their executive compensation decisions.[68]

What Determines Executive Pay?

For top executive jobs (especially the CEO), job evaluation typically has little relevance. The traditional wisdom is that company size and performance significantly affect top managers' salaries. Yet studies from the early 2000s showed that size and performance explained only about 30% of CEO pay: "In reality, CEO pay is set by the board taking into account a variety of factors such as the business strategy, corporate trends, and most importantly where they want to be in a short and long term."[69] One recent study concluded that three main factors, *job complexity* (span of control, the number of functional divisions over which the executive has direct responsibility, and management level), the employer's *ability to pay* (total profit and rate of return), and the executive's *human capital* (educational level, field of study, work experience) accounted for about two-thirds of executive compensation variance.[70] In practice, CEOs may have considerable influence over the boards of directors who theoretically set their pay. So, their pay sometimes doesn't reflect strictly arms-length negotiations.[71]

Shareholder activism and government oversight have tightened the restrictions on what companies pay top executives. For example, the banking giant HSBC recently shelved plans to raise its CEO's pay by over a third after shareholders rejected the proposals.[72]

ELEMENTS OF EXECUTIVE PAY   Salary is traditionally the cornerstone of executive compensation. On it, employers layer benefits, incentives, and perquisites—all normally conferred in proportion to base pay. Executive compensation emphasizes performance incentives more than do other employees' pay plans, since organizational results are likely to reflect executives' contributions more directly than those of lower-echelon employees.[73] Indeed, boards are boosting the emphasis on performance-based pay (in part due to shareholder activism). The big issue here is identifying the appropriate performance standards and then determining how to link these to pay. Typical short-term measures of shareholder value include revenue growth and operating profit margin. Long-term shareholder value measures include rate of return above some predetermined base, and what compensation experts call *economic value added.* We'll discuss such short and long-term incentives in Chapter 12.

Performance-based pay can focus a manager's attention. In 2010, Microsoft's board cut CEO Steve Ballmer's bonus in half, when (among other things) Microsoft failed to move fast enough to introduce a tablet to compete with the iPad.

MANAGERIAL JOB EVALUATION   Many employers use job evaluation for pricing managerial jobs (at least, below the top jobs) in most large firms. The basic approach is to classify all executive and management positions into a series of grades, each with a salary range.

As with nonmanagerial jobs, one alternative is to rank the executive and management positions in relation to each other, grouping those of equal value. However, firms also use the job classification and point evaluation methods, with compensable factors like position scope, complexity, and difficulty. Job analysis, salary surveys, and the fine-tuning of salary levels around wage curves also play roles.

Compensating Professional Employees

In compensating professionals, employers should first ensure that each employee is actually a "professional" under the law. The Fair Labor Standards Act "provides an exemption from both minimum wage and overtime pay for employees employed as bona fide executive, administrative, professional and outside sales employees."[74] However, calling someone a professional doesn't make him or her so. In addition to earning at least $455 per week, the person's main duty must "be the performance of work requiring advanced knowledge," and "the advanced knowledge must be customarily acquired by a prolonged course of specialized intellectual instruction."[75] One company hired a high school graduate as an exempt "Product design specialist II," earning $62,000 per year. The job required 12 years of relevant experience, but no particular education. The court ruled the job was non-exempt.[76]

Beyond that, compensating professional employees like engineers and scientists presents unique problems.[77] Analytical jobs emphasize compensable factors such as creativity and problem solving, compensable factors not easily compared or measured. Furthermore, how do you measure performance? For example, the success of an engineer's invention depends on how well the firm develops and markets it. Employers can use job evaluation for professional jobs. Compensable factors here tend to focus on problem solving, creativity, job scope, and technical knowledge and expertise. Firms use the point method and job classification.

Yet in practice, firms rarely rely on just job evaluation for pricing professional jobs. Factors like creativity are hard to measure, and other issues often influence professionals' job decisions. Competing for engineers in Silicon Valley illustrates the problem. Google recently raised its employees' salaries by 10% in the face of defections by even their highest paid professionals, such as the head of its Chrome OS team, to Facebook.[78] Many of these Google professionals, although well paid by national standards, still felt underpaid. Some undoubtedly moved to jobs they hoped would have more challenges. Many also probably felt that the best way to hit it big in terms of pay was to join a younger faster-growing firm and capitalize on new stock options.

Most employers therefore use a market-pricing approach. They price professional jobs in the marketplace as best they can, to establish the values for benchmark jobs. Then they slot these benchmark jobs and their other professional jobs into a salary structure. Each professional discipline usually ends up having four to six grade levels, each with a broad salary range. This helps employers remain competitive when bidding for professionals who literally have global employment possibilities.[79]

CONTEMPORARY TOPICS IN COMPENSATION

How employers pay employees has been evolving. In this final section, we'll look at six important contemporary compensation topics, competency-based pay, broadbanding, talent management, comparable worth, board oversight of executive pay, and total rewards. Chapter 12 then addresses performance-based pay.

Competency-Based Pay

> 5   Explain the difference between competency-based and traditional pay plans.

Employers traditionally base a job's pay rate on the relative worth of the job. The job evaluation committee compares jobs using compensable factors such as effort and responsibility. This allows them (1) to compare jobs to one another (as in, "based on its duties, this job seems to require about twice the effort of that one"), and (2) to assign internally equitable pay rates for each job. Therefore, the pay rate for the job principally depends on the job itself, not on who is doing it.

For reasons we'll explain shortly, some compensation experts and employers are moving away from assigning pay rates to jobs based on the jobs' numerically rated, intrinsic duties. Instead, they advocate basing the job's pay rate on the level of "competencies" the job demands of those who fill it.[80] "Title and tenure have been replaced with performance and competencies" is how one expert puts it.[81] Compensation specialists call this second approach *competency-based pay.*

WHAT IS COMPETENCY-BASED PAY?   In Chapter 4 (Job Analysis), we defined *competencies* as observable and measurable behaviors of the person that make performance possible. To determine what a job's required competencies are, ask, "In order to perform this job competently, the employee should be able to . . . ?" Competencies are most typically skills. Examples of competencies include "program in HTML," "produce a lesson plan," and "engineer the struts for a bridge."

In brief, **competency-based pay** means the company pays for the employee's skills and knowledge, rather than for the title he or she holds.[82] Experts variously call this competence-, knowledge-, or skill-based pay. With competency-based pay, an employee in a class I job who could (but may not have to at the moment) do class II work gets paid as a class II worker, not a class I.

In practice, competency-based pay usually comes down to *pay for knowledge* or *skill-based pay.*[83] Pay-for-knowledge pay plans reward employees for learning organizationally relevant knowledge—for instance, Microsoft pays new programmers more as they learn the intricacies of Windows. Skill-based pay tends to be used more for workers with manual jobs—thus, carpenters earn more as they become more proficient at finishing cabinets.

In sum, the biggest difference between traditional and competency-based pay is this:

- Traditional job evaluation ties the worker's pay to the worth of the job based on the job description and duties. Pay is *job oriented.*

- Competency-based pay ties the worker's pay to his or her competencies—pay is *person oriented.* Employees are paid based on what they know or can do—even if (at the moment), they don't have to do it.

WHY USE COMPETENCY-BASED PAY?   Why pay employees based on the skill, knowledge, or competency level they achieve, rather than based on the duties of the jobs to which they're assigned? For example, why pay an Accounting Clerk III who has achieved a exceptional mastery of accounting techniques the same (or more than) someone who is an Accounting Clerk IV?

There are three reasons. First, paying for competencies *enables the company to encourage employees* to develop the competencies the company requires to achieve its strategic aims. For example, Canon Corp. needs competencies in miniaturization and precision manufacturing to design and produce its cameras and copiers. It thus makes sense for Canon to pay employees based on the skills and knowledge they develop in these two strategically crucial areas.

Second, paying for measurable competencies provides a focus for the employer's *talent management process*. Thus at Canon, hiring, training, appraising, and rewards all focus on the competencies of miniaturization and precision manufacturing competencies.

Third, traditional pay plans can backfire if a *high-performance work system* is your goal. The whole thrust of these systems is to encourage employees to work in a self-motivated way. Employers do this by organizing the work around teams, by encouraging team members to rotate freely among jobs (each with its own skill set), and by pushing more responsibility for things like day-to-day supervision down to the workers. In such systems, the manager wants employees to be enthusiastic about learning and moving among jobs. Pigeonholing workers by classifying them too narrowly into jobs based on the job's points may actually discourage such enthusiasm and flexibility.

COMPETENCY-BASED PAY IN PRACTICE   In practice, a skill- (or competency- or knowledge-) based pay program generally has five main elements:

1. A system for defining required skills
2. A process for tying the person's pay to his or her skill level
3. A training system that lets employees acquire the skills
4. A formal skills competency testing system
5. A work design that lets employees move among jobs to permit work assignment flexibility[84]

GENERAL MILLS EXAMPLE   A General Mills manufacturing plant pays workers based on skill levels.[85] Plant management created four job clusters, corresponding to the plant's four production areas: mixing, filling, packaging, and materials. Within each cluster, workers could attain three levels of skill. Level 1 indicates limited ability, such as the ability to perform simple tasks.[86] Level 2 means the employee attained partial proficiency. Attaining Level 3 means the employee is fully competent. Each of the four job clusters had a different average wage rate. There were therefore 12 pay levels in the plant (four job clusters with three pay levels each).

General Mills set the wages for each job cluster's three levels by making the pay for the lowest of the three pay levels in each job cluster equal to the average entry-level pay rate for similar jobs in the community. A new employee could start in any job cluster, but always at Level 1. If after several weeks he or she was certified at the next higher skill level, General Mills raised his or her salary. Employees freely rotated from job cluster to cluster, as long as they could achieve Level 2 performance within their current cluster.

competency-based pay
Where the company pays for the employee's range, depth, and types of skills and knowledge, rather than for the job title he or she holds.

Many employers, such as General Mills, pay certain workers based on attained skill levels.

Source: Mark Richards/ PhotoEdit Inc.

THE BOTTOM LINE ON COMPETENCY-BASED PAY Some note that competency-based pay "ignores the cost implications of paying [employees] for knowledge, skills and behaviors even if they are not used."[87] There may also be simpler alternatives. For example, overlapping rate ranges allow workers to move from grade to grade, within limits. An article in *Compensation & Benefits Review* recently summed up the bottom line. It argued that, "after two decades of innovation in pay rate determination, it appears that old-fashioned job evaluation is back in vogue, if indeed it was ever gone."[88] In challenging times, perhaps the efficiencies of job evaluation sometimes outweigh the flexibility that comes with competency-based pay.

Broadbanding

6 List and explain six important trends in compensation management.

Most firms end up with pay plans that slot jobs into classes or grades, each with its own vertical pay rate range. For example, the U.S. government's pay plan consists of 18 main grades (GS-1 to GS-18), each with its own pay range. For an employee whose job falls in one of these grades, the pay range for that grade dictates his or her minimum and maximum salary.

The question is, "How wide should the salary grades be, in terms of the number of job evaluation points they include?" (For example, might the U.S. government want to collapse its 18 salary grades into 6 or 7 broader bands?) There is a downside to having (say, 18) narrow grades. For instance, if you want someone whose job is in grade 2 to fill in for a time in a job that happens to be in grade 1, it's difficult to reassign that person without lowering his or her salary. Similarly, if you want the person to learn about a job that happens to be in grade 3, the employee might object to the reassignment without a corresponding raise to grade 3 pay. Traditional grade pay plans thus may tend to encourage inflexibility.

That is why some firms are broadbanding their pay plans. **Broadbanding** means collapsing salary grades into just a few wide levels or bands, each of which contains a relatively wide range of jobs and pay levels. Figure 11-11 illustrates this. In this case, the company's previous six pay grades are consolidated into two broad grades or "broadbands."

A company may create broadbands for all its jobs, or for specific groups such as managers or professionals. The pay rate range of each broadband is relatively large, since it ranges from the minimum pay of the lowest grade the firm merged into the broadband up to the maximum pay of the highest merged grade. Thus, for example, instead of having 10 salary grades, each of which contains a salary range of $15,000, the firm might collapse the 10 grades into three broadbands, each with a set of jobs such that the difference between the lowest- and highest-paid jobs might be $40,000 or more. For the jobs that fall in this broadband, there is therefore a much wider range of pay rates. You can move an employee from job to job within the broadband more

FIGURE 11-11 Broadbanded
Structure and How It Relates
to Traditional Pay Grades
and Ranges

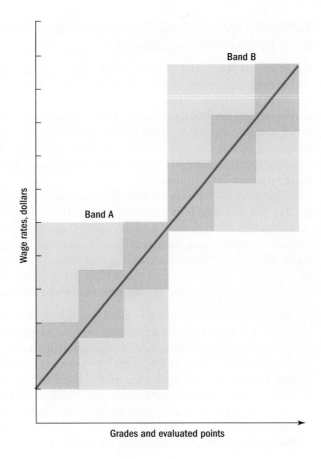

easily, without worrying about the employee's moving outside the relatively narrow
rate range associated with a traditional narrow pay grade. Broadbanding therefore
facilitates flexibility.

PROS AND CONS Companies create broadbands for several reasons. The basic
advantage is that it injects greater flexibility into employee assignments.[89] It is especially
sensible where firms organize into self-managing teams. The new, broad salary bands
can include both supervisors and subordinates and also facilitate moving employees
slightly up or down along the pay scale, without bumping the person into a new salary
range. For example, "the employee who needs to spend time in a lower-level job to
develop a certain skill set can receive higher-than-usual pay for the work, a circum-
stance considered impossible under traditional pay systems."[90] Similarly, one expert
argues that, say, point plans, may actually encourage inadaptability.[91] He says that jobs
narrowly defined by compensable factors such as "effort" are unlikely to encourage job
incumbents to be flexible. Instead, the tendency may be for workers to take a "that's not
my job" attitude and to concentrate on their usual assigned duties.

On the other hand, broadbanding can be unsettling, particularly for new employees.
For example, The Home Depot has used broadbanding for more than 10 years, and
"when employees want to learn something new, they play to the level [on that project]
that they're capable of," says the firm's head of information systems. Moving among jobs
is motivating once you get used to it. However, it can make a new employee feel adrift:
"There's a sense of permanence in the set of job responsibilities often attached to
job titles," he says. That sense of permanence isn't nearly as clear when employees move
frequently from project to project and job to job.[92]

broadbanding
Consolidating salary grades and ranges
into just a few wide levels or "bands," each
of which contains a relatively wide range
of jobs and salary levels.

Actively Managing Compensation Allocations, and Talent Management

As we saw in previous chapters, employers are increasingly segmenting their employees and actively assigning more resources to those they deem "mission-critical" in terms of the firm's strategy. Recall, for instance, that Accenture uses a 4×4 matrix to plot employees by Performance (exceptional, high, medium, low) and Value to the Organization (mission-critical, core, necessary, nonessential). It then allocates pay and other resources based on where the employee places in the matrix.[93] The decisions on whether to allocate pay on such a basis, and if so how to do so, are therefore important policy matters for employers.

Many employers are taking this more active, segmentation approach. For example, we saw that one telecommunications firm previously spread development money and compensation evenly over its 8,000 employees. When the recession came, it segmented its talent into business impact, high performers, high potentials, and critical skills. Then they shifted their dollars away from low performers and those not making an impact to high performers and high potentials.[94]

As another example, the human resources consulting company Hewitt says that,

"In the next generation of talent management, organizations will use consumer-marketing technologies to customize total rewards packages. Through personalized Web portals, organizations will offer rewards menus and associated dollar credits that are tailored to groups of workers and even individual workers. Dollar amounts will be tied to role and performance as opposed to age or seniority. Options offered will go beyond the traditional flexible benefits fare to include choice in work assignments and location, time and money for training, and working time flexibility. For example, AstraZeneca PLC offers workers customized rewards menus, allowing them to design the specifics of their rewards packages."[95]

Comparable Worth

Comparable worth refers to the requirement to pay men and women equal wages for jobs that are of *comparable* (rather than strictly *equal*) value to the employer. Thus, comparable worth may mean comparing quite dissimilar jobs, such as nurses to truck mechanics or secretaries to technicians. The question "comparable worth" seeks to address is this: Should you pay women who are performing jobs *equal* to men's or just *comparable* to men's the same as men? If it's only for equal jobs, then the tendency may be to limit women's pay to that of the other, lower-paid jobs in which women tend to predominate.

County of Washington v. Gunther (1981) was a pivotal case for comparable worth. It involved Washington County, Oregon, prison matrons who claimed sex discrimination. The county had evaluated roughly comparable but non-equal men's jobs as having 5% more "job content" (based on a point evaluation system) than the women's jobs, but paid the men 35% more.[96] Why should there be such a pay discrepancy for roughly comparable jobs? After seesawing through the courts to the U.S. Supreme Court, Washington County finally agreed to pay 35,000 employees in female-dominated jobs almost $500 million in pay raises over 7 years to settle the suit.

Comparable worth has implications for job evaluation. Virtually every comparable worth case that reached a court involved the use of the point method of job evaluation. By assigning points to dissimilar jobs, point plans facilitate comparability ratings among different jobs. Should employers still use point-type plans? Perhaps the wisest approach is for employers to price their jobs as they see fit (with or without point plans), but to ensure that women have equal access to all jobs. In other words, eliminate the wage discrimination issue by eliminating sex-segregated jobs.

THE PAY GAP All this notwithstanding, women in the United States earn only about 77% as much as men.[97] In general, education may reduce the wage gap somewhat. For example, studies suggest that schooling's impact on earnings is greater for females than for males, other things equal.[98] But gaps remain, even among the most highly trained. For example, new female medical doctors recently earned about

$17,000 per year less than their male counterparts did, and that gap has been widening for years.[99] Reasons put forward for the male-female gap range from the outdated notion that employers view women as having less leverage, to the fact that professional men change jobs more often (gaining more raises in the process) and that women tend to end up in departments that pay less.[100] In any case, it's a problem employers need recognize and to address.

Board Oversight of Executive Pay

Several years ago, the antivirus company McAfee apparently pushed out its president and saw its CEO leave after "a stock options investigation found accounting problems that will require financial restatements."[101]

There are various reasons why boards are clamping down on executive pay. As of 2005, the Financial Accounting Standards Board required that most public companies recognize as an expense the fair value of the stock options they grant.[102] The Sarbanes-Oxley Act makes executives personally liable, under certain conditions, for corporate financial oversight lapses. Writing in the *Harvard Business Review*, the chief justice of Delaware's Supreme Court said that governance issues, shareholder activism, and other changes have "created a new set of expectations for directors."[103] As of 2007, the Securities and Exchange Commission (SEC) required filing more compensation-related information, including a detailed listing of all individual "perks" or benefits if they total more than $100,000.[104] The economic downturn that began around 2008 exposed the enormous disconnect between what many executives were earning and their performance. The U.S. government's "pay czar" was soon overseeing certain pay awards in firms that had U.S. treasury loans. Yet none of these SEC or legislative actions seem (in retrospect) to have prevented some employers from dramatically overpaying their executives. The net result is that lawyers specializing in executive pay suggest that boards of directors (board compensation committees usually make executive pay decisions in large firms)[105] ask themselves these questions:

- Has our compensation committee thoroughly identified its duties and processes?
- Is our compensation committee using the appropriate compensation advisors? (Government regulators and commentators strongly encourage this.)
- Are there particular executive compensation issues that our committee should address?[106]
- Do our procedures demonstrate diligence and independence? (This demands careful deliberations and records.)
- Is our committee appropriately communicating its decisions? How will shareholders react?[107]

Total Rewards and Tomorrow's Pay Programs

Companies face severe economic and competitive challenges.[108] There will be what consultants McKinsey & Co. calls a "war for talent" as companies vie to hire and retain top employees. With reduced Social Security and company pensions, employees will have to build their own wealth for retirement. And younger "millennial" applicants will enter the workforce with greater expectations for recognition and feedback than did their predecessors.

Tomorrow's pay programs will therefore probably exhibit several features. Every company has jobs that are strategically crucial to their futures, and others, which while important, are supportive. Talent management–oriented employers will have to identify the strategically crucial jobs and pay them at premium levels. To engage the millennial

comparable worth
The concept by which women who are usually paid less than men can claim that men in comparable rather than in strictly equal jobs are paid more.

employees, it's essential that they know what's expected of them, and that they get continuing constructive feedback about their performance. Incentives will be a component of every compensation package. Employers will have to be creative about providing rewards like stock ownership options to provide young talent with the opportunity to create retirement wealth through their employment. And nonfinancial rewards including personal recognition will grow in importance as supplements to financial rewards.

That last point highlights the trend toward viewing rewards not just in terms of pay, incentives, and benefits, but as *total rewards*. As noted earlier, *total rewards* encompass the traditional compensation components, but also things such as recognition and redesigned more challenging jobs (as we discussed in this chapter), telecommuting programs, health and well being programs, and training and career development (discussed in Chapters 8 and 10). Some employers distribute annual total rewards statements to employees, to help them appreciate the full range of rewards that they are receiving.[109]

Improving Productivity through HRIS

Automating Strategic Compensation Administration

Traditionally, employers used spreadsheets to administer annual pay raise decisions, and many still do. The human resource department creates individual spreadsheets for each manager. The managers then record salary increase recommendations for their subordinates on these spreadsheets. The human resource team then compiles the spreadsheets by unit, department, division, and, finally, company-wide to add up who was spending what. This is a labor-intensive and costly process.

Today, companies more often use server-based intranet compensation planning programs to keep track of who is spending what.[110] This Web-based method has many advantages. The employer can quickly update its compensation programs (such as how much is available, and how much each manager can allocate) without having to modify the software on individual managers' computers. Automating the system reduces costs by eliminating manual processes. For example, one company estimated that it cost about $35 to complete a single manual compensation transaction (such as combining the raise budgets for two departments), but about $16 if it automated this process. Using a centralized application saves money in other ways. For example, employers often assign pay raise budgets to all their managers, only to find that (once the various department budgets all come together) the total accumulated raises are excessive. This generally doesn't happen with automated systems.

REVIEW

MyManagementLab   Now that you have finished this chapter, go back to **www.mymanagementlab.com** to continue practicing and applying the concepts you've learned.

CHAPTER SECTION SUMMARIES

1. In establishing strategic pay plans, managers first need to understand some **basic factors in determining pay rates**. Employee compensation includes both direct financial payments and indirect financial statements. The factors determining the design of any pay plan include legal, union, company strategy/policy, and equity. Legal considerations include, most importantly, the Fair Labor Standards Act, which governs matters such as minimum

wages and overtime pay. Specific categories of employees are exempt from the act or certain provisions of the act, particularly its overtime provisions. The Equal Pay Act of 1963 and the Employee Retirement Income Security Act are other important laws.

2. The process of **establishing pay rates** while ensuring external, internal, and procedural equity consists of five steps: conducting a salary survey, determining the worth of

each job, doing a job evaluation, grouping jobs comprised of approximately equal difficulty and pricing each pay grade with wage curves, and fine-tuning pay rates.

- Salary surveys may be informal phone or Internet surveys, or formal surveys conducted by the employer or utilizing commercial, professional, and/or government salary surveys.
- Job evaluation is a systematic comparison done in order to determine the worth of one job relative to another based on compensable factors.
- Compensable factors refer to compensable elements of a job such as skills and efforts.
- Popular job evaluation methods include ranking, job classification, the point method, and factor comparison. With ranking, for instance, you conduct a job analysis, group jobs by department, and have raters rank jobs.
- Once the committee uses job evaluation to determine the relative worth of each job, it can turn to the task of assigning pay rates to each job; it would usually first want to group jobs into pay grades to streamline the process.
- The team can then use wage curves to price each grade and then fine-tune pay rates.

3. **Pricing managerial and professional jobs** involves some special issues. Managerial pay typically consists of base pay, short-term incentives, long-term incentives, and executive benefits and, particularly at the top levels, doesn't lend itself to job evaluation but rather to understanding the job's complexity, the employer's ability to pay, and the need to be competitive in attracting top talent.

4. More employers are moving from paying jobs based on their intrinsic duties toward **paying jobs based on the competencies** the job requires. The main reason for doing so is to encourage employees to develop the competencies they need to move seamlessly from job to job. At General Mills, for instance, certain plant personnel are paid based on the skill levels they attain.

5. We addressed several important **special topics in compensation**. Broadbanding means consolidating several rates and ranges into a few wide levels or "bands," each of which contains a relatively wide range of jobs in salary levels. Broadbanding encourages employees to move freely from job to job and facilitates implementing team-based high-performance management systems. Comparable worth refers to the requirement to pay men and women equal pay for jobs that are of comparable rather than strictly equal value to the employee. With many stockholders concerned with excessive executive remuneration, board oversight of executive pay has become an important issue, and boards of directors should use qualified advisers and exercise diligence and independence in formulating executive pay plans. Total rewards encompass the traditional compensation components, but also things such as recognition and redesigned more challenging jobs.

DISCUSSION QUESTIONS

1. What is the difference between exempt and nonexempt jobs?
2. Should the job evaluation depend on an appraisal of the jobholder's performance? Why? Why not?
3. What is the relationship between compensable factors and job specifications?
4. Compare and contrast the following methods of job evaluation: ranking, classification, factor comparison, and point method.
5. What are the pros and cons of broadbanding, and would you recommend your current employer (or some other firm you're familiar with) use it? Why or why not?
6. It was recently reported in the news that the average pay for most university presidents was around $250,000 per year, but that a few earned much more. For example, the new president of Vanderbilt received $852,000 in one year. Discuss why you would (or would not) pay university presidents as much or more than many corporate CEOs.
7. Do small companies need to develop a pay plan? Why or why not?

INDIVIDUAL AND GROUP ACTIVITIES

1. Working individually or in groups, conduct salary surveys for the following positions: entry-level accountant and entry-level chemical engineer. What sources did you use, and what conclusions did you reach? If you were the HR manager for a local engineering firm, what would you recommend that you pay for each job?
2. Working individually or in groups, develop compensation policies for the teller position at a local bank. Assume that there are four tellers: two were hired in May and the other two were hired in December. The compensation policies should address the following: appraisals, raises, holidays, vacation pay, overtime pay, method of pay, garnishments, and time cards.
3. Working individually or in groups, access relevant Web sites to determine what equitable pay ranges are for these jobs: chemical engineer, marketing manager, and HR manager, all with a bachelor's degree and 5 years' experience. Do so for the following cities: New York, New York; San Francisco, California; Houston, Texas; Denver, Colorado; Miami, Florida; Atlanta, Georgia; Chicago, Illinois; Birmingham, Alabama; Detroit, Michigan; and Washington, D.C. For each position in each city, what are the pay ranges and the average pay? Does geographical location impact the salaries of the different positions? If so, how?
4. The "HRCI Test Specifications Appendix" (pages 633–640) lists the knowledge someone studying for the

HRCI certification exam needs to have in each area of human resource management (such as in Strategic Management, Workforce Planning, and Human Resource Development). In groups of four to five students, do four things: (1) review that appendix now; (2) identify the material in this chapter that relates to the required knowledge the appendix lists; (3) write four multiple-choice exam questions on this material that you believe would be suitable for inclusion in the HRCI exam; and (4) if time permits, have someone from your team post your team's questions in front of the class, so the students in other teams can take each others' exam questions.

5. Some of America's executives have come under fire recently because their pay seemed to some to be excessive, given their firms' performances. To choose just two of many: one Citigroup division head was due a $97 million bonus in 2009, and Merrill Lynch paid tens of millions in bonuses soon after Bank of America rescued it. However, big institutional investors are no longer sitting back and not complaining. For example, TV's *Nightly Business Line* says that pension manager TIAA-CREF is talking to 50 companies about executive pay. And the U.S. government's "pay czar" is looking to roll back some such payouts. Do you think they are right to make a fuss? Why?

EXPERIENTIAL EXERCISE

Ranking the College's Administrators

Purpose: The purpose of this exercise is to give you experience in performing a job evaluation using the ranking method.

Required Understanding: You should be thoroughly familiar with the ranking method of job evaluation and obtain job descriptions for your college's dean, department chairperson, director of admissions, library director, registrar, and your professor.

How to Set Up the Exercise/Instructions:

Divide the class into groups of four or five students. The groups will perform a job evaluation of the positions

of dean, department chairperson, and professor using the ranking method.

1. Perform a job evaluation by ranking the jobs. You may use one or more compensable factors.
2. If time permits, a spokesperson from each group can put his or her group's rankings on the board. Did the groups end up with about the same results? How did they differ? Why do you think they differed?

APPLICATION CASE

SALARY INEQUITIES AT ACME MANUFACTURING

Joe Black was trying to figure out what to do about a problem salary situation he had in his plant. Black recently took over as president of Acme Manufacturing. The founder and former president, Bill George, had been president for 35 years. The company was family owned and located in a small eastern Arkansas town. It had approximately 250 employees and was the largest employer in the community. Black was a member of the family that owned Acme, but he had never worked for the company prior to becoming president. He had an MBA and a law degree, plus 5 years of management experience with a large manufacturing organization, where he was senior vice president for human resources before making his move to Acme.

A short time after joining Acme, Black started to notice that there was considerable inequity in the pay structure for salaried employees. A discussion with the human resources director led him to believe that salaried employees' pay was very much a matter of individual bargaining with the past president. Hourly paid factory employees were not part of the problem because they were unionized and their wages were set by collective bargaining. An examination of the salaried payroll showed that there were 25 employees, ranging in pay from that of the president to that of the receptionist. A closer examination showed that 14 of the salaried employees were female. Three of these were front-line factory supervisors and

one was the human resources director. The other 10 were nonmanagement.

This examination also showed that the human resources director appeared underpaid, and that the three female supervisors earned somewhat less than any male supervisor did. However, there were no similar supervisory jobs with both male and female job incumbents. When asked, the HR director said she thought the female supervisors may have been paid at a lower rate mainly because they were women, and perhaps George, the former president, did not think that women needed as much money because they had working husbands. However, she added she personally thought that they were paid less because they supervised less-skilled employees than did the male supervisors. Black was not sure that this was true.

The company from which Black had moved had a good job evaluation system. Although he was thoroughly familiar with and capable in this compensation tool, Black did not have time to make a job evaluation study at Acme. Therefore, he decided to hire a compensation consultant from a nearby university to help him. Together, they decided that all 25 salaried jobs should be in the same job evaluation cluster; that a modified ranking method of job evaluation should be used; and that the job descriptions recently completed by the HR director were current, accurate, and usable in the study.

The job evaluation showed that the HR director and the three female supervisors were being underpaid relative to comparable male salaried employees.

Black was not sure what to do. He knew that if the underpaid female supervisors took the case to the local EEOC office, the company could be found guilty of sex discrimination and then have to pay considerable back wages. He was afraid that if he gave these women an immediate salary increase large enough to bring them up to where they should be, the male supervisors would be upset and the female supervisors might comprehend the total situation and want back pay. The HR director told Black that the female supervisors had never complained about pay differences.

The HR director agreed to take a sizable salary increase with no back pay, so this part of the problem was solved. Black believed he had four choices relative to the female supervisors:

1. To do nothing
2. To gradually increase the female supervisors' salaries
3. To increase their salaries immediately
4. To call the three supervisors into his office, discuss the situation with them, and jointly decide what to do

Questions

1. What would you do if you were Black?
2. How do you think the company got into a situation like this in the first place?
3. Why would you suggest Black pursue the alternative you suggested?

Source: This case was prepared by Professor James C. Hodgetts of the Fogelman College of Business and Economics of the University of Memphis. All names are disguised. Used by permission.

CONTINUING CASE

CARTER CLEANING COMPANY

The New Pay Plan

Carter Cleaning Centers does not have a formal wage structure nor does it have rate ranges or use compensable factors. Wage rates are based mostly on those prevailing in the surrounding community and are tempered with an attempt on the part of Jack Carter to maintain some semblance of equity between what workers with different responsibilities in the stores are paid.

Carter does not make any formal surveys when determining what his company should pay. He peruses the want ads almost every day and conducts informal surveys among his friends in the local chapter of the laundry and cleaners trade association. While Jack has taken a "seat-of-the-pants" approach to paying employees, his salary schedule has been guided by several basic pay policies. Although many of his colleagues adhere to a policy of paying minimum rates, Jack has always followed a policy of paying his employees about 10% above what he feels are the prevailing rates, a policy that he believes reduces

turnover while fostering employee loyalty. Of somewhat more concern to Jennifer is her father's informal policy of paying men about 20% more than women for the same job. Her father's explanation is, "They're stronger and can work harder for longer hours, and besides they all have families to support."

Questions

1. Is the company at the point where it should be setting up a formal salary structure based on a complete job evaluation? Why?
2. Is Jack Carter's policy of paying 10% more than the prevailing rates a sound one, and how could that be determined?
3. Similarly, is Carter's male–female differential wise? If not, why not?
4. Specifically, what would you suggest Jennifer do now with respect to her company's pay plan?

TRANSLATING STRATEGY INTO HR POLICIES & PRACTICES CASE

THE HOTEL PARIS CASE

The New Compensation Plan

The Hotel Paris's competitive strategy is "To use superior guest service to differentiate the Hotel Paris properties, and to thereby increase the length of stay and return rate of guests, and thus boost revenues and profitability." HR manager Lisa Cruz must now formulate functional policies and activities that support this competitive strategy by eliciting the required employee behaviors and competencies.

Like several other HR systems at the Hotel Paris, the compensation program was unplanned and unsophisticated. The company has a narrow target range for what it will pay employees in each job category (front-desk clerk, security guard, and so forth). Each hotel manager decides where to start a new employee within that narrow pay range. The company has given little thought to tying general pay levels or individual employees' pay to the company's strategic goals.

For example, the firm's policy is simply to pay its employees a "competitive salary," by which it means about average for what other hotels in the city are paying for similar jobs. Lisa knows that pay policies like these may actually run counter to what the company wants to achieve strategically, in terms of creating an extraordinarily service-oriented workforce. How can you hire and retain a top workforce, and channel their behaviors toward high-quality guest services, if you don't somehow link performance and pay? She and her team therefore turn to the task of assessing and redesigning the company's compensation plan.

Even a casual review by Lisa Cruz and the CFO made it clear that the company's compensation plan wasn't designed to support the firm's new strategic goals. For one thing, they knew that they should pay somewhat more, on average, than did their competitors if they expected employees to consistently exceed expectations when it came to serving guests. Yet their review of a variety of metrics (including the Hotel Paris's salary/competitive salary ratios, the total compensation expense per employee, and the target percentile for total compensation) suggested that in virtually all job categories the Hotel Paris paid no more than average, and, occasionally, paid somewhat less.

The current compensation policies had also bred what one hotel manager called an "I don't care" attitude on the part of most employees. What she meant was that most Hotel Paris employees quickly learned that regardless of what their performance was, they always ended up being paid about the same as employees who performed better and worse than they did. So, the firm's compensation plan actually was dysfunctional: It was not channeling employees' behaviors toward those required to achieve the company's goals. In some ways, it was doing the opposite.

Lisa and the CFO knew they had to institute a new, strategic compensation plan. They wanted a plan that improved employee morale, contributed to employee commitment, reduced employee turnover, and rewarded (and thus encouraged) the sorts of service-oriented behaviors that boosted guest satisfaction. After meeting with the company's CEO and the board, the CFO gave Lisa the go-ahead to redesign the company's compensation plan, with the overall aim of creating a new plan that would support the company's strategic aims.

Questions

1. Draw a diagram showing with arrows how compensation at Hotel Paris should influence employee performance, which should in turn influence Hotel Paris performance. Include at each level examples of relevant compensation policies, employee behavior, and Hotel Paris outcomes.

2. Would you suggest that Hotel Paris implement a competency-based pay plan for its nonmanagerial staff? Why or why not?

3. Devise a ranking job evaluation system for the Hotel Paris's nonmanagerial employees (housekeepers, valets, front-desk clerks, phone operators, waitstaff, groundskeepers, and security guards) and use it to show the worth of these jobs relative to one another.

KEY TERMS

employee compensation, *352*

direct financial payments, *352*

indirect financial payments, *352*

Davis-Bacon Act (1931), *354*

Walsh-Healey Public Contract Act (1936), *354*

Title VII of the 1964 Civil Rights Act, *354*

Fair Labor Standards Act (1938), *354*

Equal Pay Act (1963), *357*

Employee Retirement Income Security Act (ERISA), *358*

job evaluation, *360*

compensable factor, *360*

benchmark job, *361*

ranking method, *361*

job classification (or grading) method, *362*

classes, *362*

grades, *362*

grade definition, *362*

point method, *363*

wage curve, *367*

market-competitive pay system, *367*

salary survey, *368*

pay (or wage) grade, *371*

pay (or rate) ranges, *371*

compa ratio, *372*

competency-based pay, *376*

broadbanding, *378*

comparable worth, *380*

ENDNOTES

1. Elayne Robertson Demby, "Two Stores Refused to Join the Race to the Bottom for Benefits and Wages," *Workforce Management*, February 2004, pp. 57–59; www.wegmans.com/webapp/wcs/stores/servlet/CategoryDisplay?langId=1&storeId=10052&catalogId=10002&categoryId=256548, accessed March 25, 2009.

2. Richard Henderson, *Compensation Management* (Reston, VA: Reston Publishing, 1980), pp. 101–127; and Stacey L. Kaplan, "Total Rewards in Action: Developing a Total Rewards Strategy," *Benefits & Compensation Digest* 42 no. 8 (August 2005).

3. Demby, "Two Stores Refused to Join the Race."

4. Ibid.

5. www.wegmans.com, accessed June 1, 2011.

6. Nicholas Wade, "Play Fair: Your Life May Depend on It," *The New York Times*, September 12, 2003, p. 12.

7. Robert Bretz and Stephen Thomas, "Perceived Inequity, Motivation, and Final Offer

Arbitration in Major League Baseball," *Journal of Applied Psychology*, June 1992, pp. 280–282; Reginald ell, "Addressing Employees' Feelings of Inequity: Capitalizing on Equity Theory in Modern Management," *Supervision* 72 no. 5 (May 2011), pp. 3–6.

8. James DeConinck and Duane Bachmann, "An Analysis of Turnover Among Retail Buyers," *Journal of Business Research* 58, no. 7 (July 2005), pp. 874–882.

9. David Terpstra and Andre Honoree, "The Relative Importance of External, Internal, Individual, and Procedural Equity to Pay Satisfaction," *Compensation & Benefits Review*, November/December 2003, pp. 67–74.

10. Ibid., p. 68.

11. Millicent Nelson et al., "Pay Me More: What Companies Need to Know About Employee Pay Satisfaction," *Compensation & Benefits Review*, March/April 2008, pp. 35–42.

12. Pay inequities manifest in unexpected ways. In one study, the researchers studied the impact of keeping pay rates secret, rather than publicizing them on individual employees' test performance. They found that individuals with lower levels of tolerance for inequity reacted particularly harshly to pay secrecy in terms of weaker individual test performance. Peter Bamberger and Elena Belogolovsky, "The Impact of Pay Secrecy on Individual Test Performance," *Personnel Psychology* 60 no. 3 (2010), pp. 965–996.

13. Michael Harris et al., "Keeping Up with the Joneses: A Field Study of the Relationships Among Upward, Lateral, and Downward Comparisons and Pay Level Satisfaction," *Journal of Applied Psychology* 93, no. 3 (2008), pp. 665–673.

14. Henderson, *Compensation Management*; see also Barry Gerhart and Sara Rynes, *Compensation: Theory, Evidence, and Strategic Implications* (Thousand Oaks, CA: Sage Publications, 2003); and Joseph Martocchio, *Strategic Compensation* (Upper Saddle River, NJ: Prentice Hall, 2006), pp. 67–94.

15. In a recent case, *Ledbetter v. Goodyear Tire & Rubber Co.*, the U.S. Supreme Court notably restricted the amount of time (to 180 or 300 days) after each allegedly discriminatory pay decision under Title VII to file or forever lose the claim. Congress subsequently passed and President Obama assigned a new law significantly expanding the amount of time to file such claims. See, for example, "Following *Ledbetter* Ruling, Issue of Workers Sharing Pay Information Takes Center Stage," *BNA Bulletin to Management*, July 17, 2007, p. 225.

16. The recently approved Genetic Information Nondiscrimination Act amended the Fair Labor Standards Act to increase penalties for the death or serious injury of employees under age 18. Allen Smith,

"Penalties for Child Labor Violations Increase," *HR Magazine*, July 2008, p. 19.

17. Also note that 18 states have their own rules governing overtime. The states are Alaska, Arkansas, California, Colorado, Connecticut, Hawaii, Illinois, Kentucky, Maryland, Minnesota, Montana, New Jersey, North Dakota, Oregon, Pennsylvania, Washington, West Virginia, and Wisconsin. "DOL's Final Rule Is Not the Final Word on Overtime for Employers in 18 States," *BNA Bulletin to Management*, June 3, 2004, pp. 55, 177.

18. One company, Healthcare Management Group, estimates that "clock creep"—employees regularly clocking in a bit earlier late—costs as much as $250,000 per year in overtime. The company remedied the situation by installing an automated time and attendance system. These systems help provide real-time labor data to line managers, and automatically update timing systems for changes such as daylight savings time. Jennifer Arnold, "Reining in Overtime Costs," *HR Magazine*, April 2009, pp. 74–76.

19. "Wal-Mart to Settle 63 Wage and Hour Suits, Paying up to $640 Million to Resolve Claims," *BNA Bulletin to Management*, January 13, 2009, p. 11.

20. www.pacifictimesheet.com/timesheet_products/pacific_timesheet_handheld_pda_field_data_entry_software.htm, accessed March 23, 2009.

21. Recently, several state legislatures have moved to tighten regulations regarding misclassifying workers as independent contractors, some going so far as adding criminal penalties for violations. "Misclassification Cases Draw More Attention, Attorneys Say," *BNA Bulletin to Management*, December 15, 2009, p. 399.

22. "Federal Court Mostly Rules for FedEx Ground in Driver Lawsuits Alleging Misclassification," *BNA Bulletin to Management*, December 21, 2010, p. 403.

23. "Senate Passes Minimum Wage Increase That Includes Small-Business Tax Provisions," *BNA Bulletin to Management*, February 6, 2007, p. 41; www.dol.gov/esa/whd/flsa, accessed August 12, 2007.

24. Society for Human Resource Management, "The Evolution of Compensation," *Workplace Visions*, 2002, p. 2; www.dol.gov/esa/minwage/america.htm, accessed June 3, 2004.

25. For a description of exemption requirements, see Jeffrey Friedman, "The Fair Labor Standards Act Today: A Primer," *Compensation*, January/February 2002, pp. 51–54. See also www.shrm.org/issues/FLSA, accessed August 12, 2007; and www.dol.gov/esa/whd/flsa, accessed August 12, 2007.

26. "Employer Ordered to Pay $2 Million in Overtime," *BNA Bulletin to Management*, September 26, 1996, pp. 308–309. See also "Restaurant Managers Awarded $2.9 Million in Overtime Wages for Non-

management Work," *BNA Bulletin to Management*, August 30, 2001, p. 275.

27. Because the overtime and minimum wage rules only changed in 2004, exactly how to apply these rules is still in a state of flux. If there's doubt about exemption eligibility, it's probably best to check with the local Department of Labor Wage and Hour office. See, for example, "Attorneys Say FLSA Draws a Fine Line Between Exempt/Nonexempt Employees," *BNA Bulletin to Management*, July 5, 2005, p. 219; "DOL Releases Letters on Administrative Exemption, Overtime," *BNA Bulletin to Management*, October 18, 2005, p. 335. The U.S. Labor Department occasionally changes its positions. For example, in 2010 it concluded that mortgage loan officers are subject to the administrative exemption from federal overtime pay, although several years previously IT had ruled the opposite. Tim Watson and Barry Miller, "Tightening a White Collar Exemption," *HR Magazine*, December 2010, p. 95.

28. See, for example, Jeffrey Friedman, "The Fair Labor Standards Act Today: A Primer," *Compensation*, January/February 2002, p. 53; Andre Honoree, "The New Fair Labor Standards Act Regulations and the Sales Force: Who Is Entitled to Overtime Pay?" *Compensation & Benefits Review*, January/February 2006, p. 31; www.shrm.org/issues/FLSA, accessed August 12, 2007; www.dol.gov/esa/whd/flsa, accessed August 12, 2007.

29. "Drug Sales Reps Raise Questions About Outside Sales Exemption," *BNA Bulletin to Management*, April 1, 2008, p. 111.

30. Diane Cadrain, "Guard Against FLSA Claims," *HR Magazine*, April 2008, pp. 97–100.

31. For another example, this one involving technical writers working for Sun Microsystems, see "Court Certifies Class of Technical Writers Working for Sun Microsystems," *BNA Bulletin to Management*, May 20, 2008, p. 161.

32. Robert Nobile, "How Discrimination Laws Affect Compensation," *Compensation & Benefits Review*, July/August 1996, pp. 38–42.

33. See for example, http://www.bls.gov/opub/cwc/cm20030124ar01p1.htm, accessed October 9, 2011. See also Barry Hirsch and Edward Schumacher, "Unions, Wages, and Skills," *Journal of Human Resources* 33, no. 1 (Winter 1998), p. 115.

34. Peg Buchenroth, "Driving Performance: Making Pay Work for the Organization," *Compensation & Benefits Review*, May/June 2006, pp. 30–35.

35. Jessica Marquez, "Raising the Performance Bar," *Workforce Management*, April 24, 2006, pp. 31–32.

36. www.bls.gov/oes/current/oes431011.htm#st, accessed June 1, 2011.

37. Bobby Watson Jr. and Gangaram Singh, "Global Pay Systems: Compensation in

Support of Multinational Strategy," *Compensation & Benefits Review*, January/February 2005, pp. 33–36.

38. Demby, "Two Stores Refuse to Join the Race"; www.hoovers.com/company/Wegmans_Food_Markets_Inc/cfhtji-1.html, accessed June 1, 2011.

39. Ibid.

40. Demby, "Two Stores Refuse to Join the Race."

41. Joseph Martocchio, *Strategic Compensation* (Upper Saddle River, NJ: Pearson Education, 2011), p. 140.

42. Martocchio, *Strategic Compensation*, p. 138. See also Nona Tobin, "Can Technology Ease the Pain of Salary Surveys?" *Public Personnel Management* 31, no. 1 (Spring 2002), pp. 65–78.

43. You may have noticed that job analysis as discussed in Chapter 4 can be a useful source of information on compensable factors, as well as on job descriptions and job specifications. For example, a quantitative job analysis technique like the position analysis questionnaire generates quantitative information on the degree to which the following five basic factors are present in each job: having decision-making/communication/social responsibilities, performing skilled activities, being physically active, operating vehicles or equipment, and processing information. As a result, a job analysis technique like the PAQ is actually as (or some say, more) appropriate as a job evaluation technique (than for job analysis) in that jobs can be quantitatively compared to one another on those five dimensions and their relative worth thus ascertained. Another point worth noting is that you may find that a single set of compensable factors is not adequate for describing all your jobs. This is another reason why many managers therefore divide their jobs into job clusters. For example, you might have a separate job cluster for factory workers, for clerical workers, and for managerial personnel. You would then probably have a somewhat different set of compensable factors for each job cluster.

44. Michael Carrell and Christina Heavrin, *Labor Relations and Collective Bargaining* (Upper Saddle River, NJ: Prentice Hall, 2004), pp. 300–303.

45. John Kilgour, "Job Evaluation Revisited: The Point Factor Method," *Compensation & Benefits Review*, July/August 2008, p. 40.

46. Martocchio, *Strategic Compensation*, p. 140.

47. For a discussion, see, Roger Plachy, "The Point Factor Job Evaluation System: A Step-by-Step Guide, Part I," *Compensation & Benefits Review*, July/August 1987, pp. 12–27; Roger Plachy, "The Case for Effective Point-Factor Job Evaluation, Viewpoint I," *Compensation & Benefits Review*, March/April 1987, pp. 45–48; Roger Plachy, "The Point-Factor Job Evaluation System: A Step-by-Step Guide, Part II," *Compensation & Benefits Review*, September/October 1987, pp. 9–24; and particularly John Kilgour, "Job Evaluation Revisited: The Point Factor Method," *Compensation & Benefits Review*, July/August 2008, pp. 37–46.

48. Martocchio, *Strategic Compensation*, p. 141.

49. Kilgour, "Job Evaluation Revisited," pp. 37–46.

50. Ibid.

51. Ibid.

52. Ibid.

53. Ibid.

54. Ibid.

55. Ibid. Of course, the level of economic activity influences compensation expectations. For instance, salary increases were lower than expected in 2010 due to a lackluster economy, but were predicted to increase significantly for 2011. Fay Hansen, "Currents in Compensation and Benefits," *Compensation & Benefits Review* 42, no. 6 (2010), p. 435.

56. Martocchio, *Strategic Compensation*, p. 151.

57. Kilgour, "Job Evaluation Revisited," pp. 37–46.

58. Henderson, *Compensation Management*, pp. 260–269. See also "Web Access Transforms Compensation Surveys," *Workforce Management*, April 24, 2006, p. 34.

59. For more information on these surveys, see the company's brochure, "Domestic Survey References," Watson Wyatt Data Services, 218 Route 17 North, Rochelle Park, NJ 07662. See www.watsonwyatt.com/search/publications.asp?ArticleID=21432, accessed October 29, 2009.

60. Kilgour, "Job Evaluation Revisited," pp. 37–46.

61. Ibid.

62. David W. Belcher, *Compensation Administration* (Englewood Cliffs, NJ: Prentice Hall, 1974), pp. 257–276; and Nicola Sulliva, "Serco Introduces Pay Grade Structure for Senior Staff," *Employee Benefits*, July 2010, p. 5.

63. Martocchio, *Strategic Compensation*, p. 185.

64. Ibid., p 189.

65. www.opm.gov/oca/11tables/html/gs.asp accessed June 1, 2011.

66. Kilgour, "Job Evaluation Revisited," pp. 37–46.

67. Mark Meltzer and Howard Goldsmith, "Executive Compensation for Growth Companies," *Compensation & Benefits Review*, November/December 1997, pp. 41–50; Martocchio, *Strategic Compensation*, pp. 421–428. See also Martin J. Conyon, "Executive Compensation and Incentives," *The Academy of Management Perspectives* 20, no. 1 (February 2006), p. 25(20); and "Realities of Executive Compensation—2006/2007 Report on Executive Pay and Stock Options," www.watsonwyatt.com/research/resrender.asp?id=2006-US-0085&page=1, accessed May 20, 2007.

68. Douglas Tormey, "Executive Compensation: Creating a 'Legal' Checklist," *Compensation & Benefits Review*, July/August 1996, pp. 12–36. See also Bruce Ellig, "Executive Pay: A Primer," *Compensation & Benefits Review*, January/ February 2003, pp. 44–50.

69. James Reda, "Executive Pay Today and Tomorrow," *Corporate Board* 22, no. 126 (January 2001), p. 18.

70. Syed Tahir Hijazi, "Determinants of Executive Compensation and Its Impact on Organizational Performance," *Compensation & Benefits Review* 39, no. 2 (March–April 2007), p. 58(9).

71. For example, one book argues that executives of large companies use their power to have themselves compensated in ways that are not sufficiently related to performance. Lucian Bebchuk and Jesse Fried, *Pay Without Performance: The Unfulfilled Promise of Executive Compensation* (Boston: Harvard University Press, 2004).

72. http://uk.reuters.com/article/2010/02/23/uk-hsbc-idUKTRE61M6FT20100223, accessed June 23, 2011.

73. See, for example, Fay Hansen, "Current Trends in Compensation and Benefits," *Compensation & Benefits Review* 36, no. 2 (March/April 2004), pp. 7–8.

74. www.dol.gov/whd/regs/compliance/fairpay/fs17d_professional.pdf, accessed June 1, 2011.

75. Ibid.

76. Roger S. Achille, "FLSA Requires Education for Professional Exemption," www.shrm.org/LegalIssues/FederalResources/Pages/2ndFLSAProfessionalExemption.aspx, accessed August 28, 2011.

77. See, for example, Martocchio, *Strategic Compensation*; and Patricia Zingheim and Jay Schuster, "Designing Pay and Rewards in Professional Services Companies," *Compensation & Benefits Review*, January/February 2007, pp. 55–62.

78. Farhad Manjoo, "Engineers to the Valley: Pay Up," *Fast Company* 153, no. 38 (March 2011).

79. Dimitris Manolopoulos, "What Motivates Research and Development Professionals? Evidence from Decentralized Laboratories in Greece," *International Journal of Human Resource Management* 17, no. 4 (April 2006), pp. 616–647.

80. See, for example, Robert Heneman and Peter LeBlanc, "Development of and Approach for Valuing Knowledge Work," *Compensation & Benefits Review*, July/August 2002, p. 47.

81. Kevin Foote, "Competencies in the Real World: Performance Management for the Rationally Healthy Organization," *Compensation & Benefits Review*, July/August 2001, p. 25.

82. Gerald Ledford Jr., "Paying for the Skills, Knowledge, and Competencies of Knowledge Workers," *Compensation & Benefits Review*, July/August 1995, p. 56; see also P. K. Zingheim, et. al., "Competencies and Rewards: Substance or Just Style?" *Compensation and Benefits*

Review 35 no. 5 (September/October 2003), p. 40–44.

83. Joseph Martocchio, *Strategic Compensation*, p. 168.

84. Gerald Ledford Jr., "Three Case Studies on Skill-Based Pay," *Compensation & Benefits Review*, March/April 1981, p. 12. See also Kathryn Cofsky, "Critical Keys to Competency-Based Pay," *Compensation & Benefits Review*, November/December 1993, pp. 46–52; Murray and Gerhart, "Skill-Based Pay and Skills Seeking," *Human Resource Management* Review 10, no. 3 (2000), pp. 271–287.

85. Gerald Ledford Jr. and Gary Bergel, "Skill-Based Pay Case Number 1: General Mills," *Compensation & Benefits Review*, March/April 1991, pp. 24–38; as explained elsewhere in this section, competency based plans (including skill-based plans such as this one) require new selection, training, and appraisal practices to be successful. See for example, Frank L. Giancola, "A Framework for Understanding New Concepts in Compensation Management," *Benefits & Compensation Digest* 46 no. 9 (September 2009), pp. 7, 13–16.

86. This is based on Ledford and Bergel, "Skill-Based Pay Case Number 1," pp. 28–29.

87. Robert Heneman and Peter LeBlanc, "Work Evaluation Addresses the Shortcomings of Both Job Evaluation and Market Pricing," *Compensation & Benefits Review*, January/February 2003, p. 8.

88. Kilgour, "Job Evaluation Revisited," p. 37.

89. David Hofrichter, "Broadbanding: A 'Second Generation' Approach," *Compensation & Benefits Review*, September/October 1993, pp. 53–58. See also "The Future of Salary Management," *Compensation & Benefits Review*, July/August 2001, pp. 7–12.

90. Ibid., p. 55.

91. For example, see Sandra Emerson, "Job Evaluation: A Barrier to Excellence?" *Compensation & Benefits Review*, January/

February 1991, pp. 39–52; Nan Weiner, "Job Evaluation Systems: A Critique," *Human Resource Management Review* 1, no. 2 (Summer 1991), pp. 119–132; and Brian Klaas, "Compensation in the Jobless Organization," *Human Resource Management Review* 12, no. 1 (Spring 2002), pp. 43–62.

92. Dawne Shand, "Broadbanding the IT Worker," *Computerworld* 34, no. 41 (October 9, 2000).

93. "The New Talent Equation," www.accenture.com/NR/rdonlyres/7438E440-F7D5-4F81-B012-8D3271891D92/0/Accenture_Outlook_The_New_Talent_Equation.pdf, accessed November 9, 2010.

94. "Five Rules for Talent Management in the New Economy," www.towerswatson.com/viewpoints/2606, accessed November 9, 2010.

95. "Next Generation Talent Management," www.hewittassociates.com/_MetaBasicCMAssetCache_/Assets/Articles/next_generation.pdf, accessed November 9, 2010.

96. *County of Washington v. Gunther*, U.S. Supreme Court, no. 80–426, June 8, 1981.

97. Laura Fitzpatrick, "Why Do Women Still Earn Less Than Men?", www.time.com/time/nation/article/0,8599,1983185,00.html, accessed May 21, 2011.

98. Christopher Dougherty, "Why Are the Returns to Schooling Higher for Women Than for Men?" *Journal of Human Resources* 40, no. 4 (Fall 2005), pp. 969–988.

99. Rachel Silverman, "Women Doctors Face Pay Disparity," *The Wall Street Journal*, February 8, 2011, p. D4.

100. "Women Still Earned Less Than Men, BLS Data Show," *BNA Bulletin to Management*, June 8, 2000, p. 72. However, there is some indication that there is less gender-based pay gap among full-time workers ages 21 to 35 living alone. Kent Hoover, "Study Finds No Pay Gap for Young, Single Workers," *Tampa Bay Business Journal* 20, no. 19 (May 12,

2000), p. 10. See also, E. Frazier, "Raises for Women Executives Match Those for Men, but Pay Gap Persists," *The Chronicle of Philanthropy* 20 no. 24 (October 2, 2008), p. 33.

101. www.msnbc.msn.com/id/15219832/ns/business-corporate_scandals/t/mcafee-ousts-execs-after-stock-options-probe/, accessed June 1, 2011.

102. Mark Poerio and Eric Keller, "Executive Compensation 2005: Many Forces, One Direction," *Compensation & Benefits Review*, May/June 2005, pp. 34–40.

103. Ibid., p. 38.

104. Jennifer Dudley, "The New Executive Compensation Rule: The Tough Disclosures," *Compensation & Benefits Review*, July/August 2007, pp. 28–34.

105. Society for Human Resource Management, "Changing Leadership Strategies," *Workplace Visions*, no. 1 (2008), p. 3.

106. For a discussion of some of the issues that go into hammering out an executive employment agreement, see, for example, Jonathan Cohen and Laura Clark, "Is the Executive Employment Agreement Dead?" *Compensation & Benefits Review*, July/August 2007, pp. 50–55.

107. Ibid. See also Brent Longnecker and James Krueger, "The Next Wave of Compensation Disclosure," *Compensation & Benefits Review*, January/February 2007, pp. 50–54.

108. This is based on Howard Risher, "Planning and Managing Tomorrow's Pay Programs," *Compensation & Benefits Review*, July/August 2008, pp. 30–35.

109. Frank L. Giancola, "A Framework for Understanding New Concepts in Compensation Management," op cit.; and Georgina Fuller, "Total Reward Statements," *Employee Benefits*, January 2011, p. 47.

110. Al Wright, "Tools for Automating Complex Compensation Programs," *Compensation & Benefits Review*, November/December 2003, pp. 53–61.

12
Pay for Performance and Financial Incentives

LEARNING OBJECTIVES

1. Explain how you would apply five motivation theories in formulating an incentive plan.

2. Discuss the main incentives for individual employees.

3. Discuss the pros and cons of commissions versus straight pay incentives for salespeople.

4. Describe the main incentives for managers and executives.

5. Name and define the most popular organization-wide variable pay plans.

6. Outline the steps in designing effective incentive plans.

Ford Motor Company recently announced a new strategy for rejuvenating its Lincoln car brand. For several years, Ford simply built many Lincolns based on Ford chassis, and Lincoln sales suffered. The new strategy calls for spending $1 billion on new high-tech Lincoln car models, and requiring Lincoln dealers to build luxurious showrooms. Now the increased investments and prospects for car sales have some dealers wondering what employee sales incentives would best help them achieve their aims.

Access a host of interactive learning aids at **www.mymanagementlab.com** to help strengthen your understanding of the chapter concepts.

WHERE ARE WE NOW . . .

Chapter 11 focused on developing the overall pay plan and on salaries and wages. Incentives play an important role in any pay plan. The main purpose of this chapter is to explain how managers use performance-based incentives to motivate employees. After a brief overview of motivation theories, we'll discuss incentives for individual employees, for managers and executives, salespeople, and professionals, as well as organization-wide incentive plans. In Chapter 13 we'll turn to financial and nonfinancial benefits and services, which are the final part of the employee's compensation package.

MONEY AND MOTIVATION

Frederick Taylor popularized using **financial incentives**—financial rewards paid to workers whose production exceeds some predetermined standard—in the late 1800s. As a supervisor at the Midvale Steel Company, Taylor was concerned with what he called "systematic soldiering"—the tendency of employees to work at the slowest pace possible and to produce at the minimum acceptable level. What especially intrigued him was the fact that some of these workers had the energy to run home and work on their houses, even after a 12-hour day. Taylor knew that if he could harness this energy at work, Midvale could achieve huge productivity gains. **Productivity** "is the ratio of outputs (goods and services) divided by the inputs (resources such as labor and capital)."[1]

In pursuing that aim, Taylor turned to financial incentives. At the time, primitive incentive plans were in use, but were generally ineffective (because employers arbitrarily changed incentive rates). Taylor made three contributions. He saw the need for formulating what he called a **fair day's work**, namely standards of output for a job, which he devised for each job based on careful, scientific analysis. He spearheaded the **scientific management movement**, a management approach that emphasized improving work methods through observation and analysis. And he popularized the use of incentive pay as a way to reward employees who produced over standard. Graphically, we can summarize Taylor's aims as follows:

Financial Incentives → Boost Employee Performance → Productivity Gains.

Linking Strategy, Performance, and Incentive Pay

Today, incentive pay—tying workers' pay to their performance—is widely popular.[2] The problem is that doing so is easier said than done. Many such programs are ineffective, and some are disastrous. (One plan, at Levi Strauss, is widely assumed to have been the last nail in the coffin of Levi's U.S.-based production.) As logical as it seems to link pay to performance, about 83% of companies with such programs say their programs are at best somewhat successful. One study found that just 28% of the 2,600 U.S. workers it surveyed said their companies' incentive plans motivated them. "Employees don't see a strong connection between pay and performance, and their performance is not particularly influenced by the company's incentive plan," said one expert.[3,4] Equally problematical is the fact that some incentives incentivize the wrong behavior and performance. Thus, simply incentivizing "number of cars sold" in a dealership might produce high performance (in numbers of cars sold) but a low per-car profit. The accompanying Strategic Context feature illustrates this.

THE STRATEGIC CONTEXT

The Car Sales Commission

Strategic human resource management means "formulating and executing human resource policies and practices that produce the employee competencies and behaviors the company needs to achieve its strategic aims."

Few HR practices illustrate this better than designing car sales incentive plans. Car salespersons' compensation ranges from 100% commission to a small base salary with commission accounting for most of total compensation. Traditionally, the car salesperson's commission is based on a percentage of the difference between the dealer's invoice cost and the amount the car is sold for, minus an amount to cover the "pack" or dealer overhead (the pack being perhaps $300 for a new car to $800 for a used car, and rising for pricier cars).[5] This promotes precisely the sorts of behaviors the car dealer wants to encourage. For example, it encourages the salesperson to hold firm on the retail price, and to push "after-sale products" like floor mats and side moldings. There may also be extra incentives to sell packages such as rustproofing. For selling slow-moving vehicles, the salesperson may get a "spiff"—a car dealer term for an extra incentive bonus over commission. And there

> are bonuses, such as Salesperson of the Month (perhaps $300 for most cars sold), and a Monthly Car Count Bonus for selling, say, 10 or 12 cars.[6]
>
> Because maximizing car unit sales and profits still predominates as the strategy at many dealerships, commission plans like these still dominate, but they are not as popular as they once were. Many dealerships are substituting salary plus bonus plans for commissions. The transition to salary plus bonus reflects the growing emphasis on a dealer (and car company) strategy aimed at making the purchase process less tense, for instance, with "one price no hassle" pricing.[7] But in any case, the pay plan's aim is to produce the salesperson behaviors the dealership needs to support its strategic aims.

We'll see that there are many reasons for incentive plans' often-dismal results. Many employers, perhaps ignorant of Taylor and history, change their plans' standards arbitrarily. Others ignore the fact that incentive pay that may motivate some people won't motivate others.[8] Compensation experts therefore argue that managers should understand the motivational bases of incentive plans.[9] We'll review some motivation background next.

Motivation and Incentives

1 Explain how you would apply five motivation theories in formulating an incentive plan.

Several motivation theories have particular relevance to designing incentive plans. These include theories associated with the psychologists Abraham Maslow, Frederick Herzberg, Edward Deci, Victor Vroom, and B. F. Skinner.

THE HIERARCHY OF NEEDS AND ABRAHAM MASLOW Abraham Maslow propounded one widely quoted observation on what motivates people. Although lacking much scientific support, his theory is widely quoted.

He said that people have a hierarchy of five types of needs: *physiological* (food, water, warmth), *security* (a secure income, knowing one has a job), *social* (friendships and camaraderie), *self-esteem* (respect), and *self-actualization* (becoming the person you believe you can become). According to Maslow's *prepotency process principle*, people are motivated first to satisfy each lower-order need and then, in sequence, each of the higher-level needs. For example, if someone is out of work and insecure, getting a job may drive everything he or she does. (So, during periods of high unemployment, one may see even former executives taking low-level jobs to make ends meet.) A secure employee may then turn to being concerned with building friendships, getting respect, and going to school to get the degree required to be a top executive. On the other hand, don't try to motivate someone with more challenging work if he or she doesn't earn enough to pay the bills. We usually envision Maslow's hierarchy of five needs as a stepladder or pyramid.

MOTIVATORS AND FREDERICK HERZBERG Frederick Herzberg said the best way to motivate someone is to organize the job so that doing it provides the feedback and challenge that helps satisfy the person's "higher-level" needs for things like accomplishment and recognition. These needs are relatively insatiable, says Herzberg, so recognition and challenging work provide a sort of built-in motivation generator. Satisfying "lower level" needs for things like better pay and working conditions just keeps the person from becoming dissatisfied.

financial incentives
Financial rewards paid to workers whose production exceeds some predetermined standard.

productivity
The ratio of outputs (goods and services) divided by the inputs (resources such as labor and capital).

fair day's work
Output standards devised based on careful, scientific analysis.

scientific management
Management approach based on improving work methods through observation and analysis.

Herzberg says the factors ("hygienes") that satisfy lower-level needs are different from those ("motivators") that satisfy or partially satisfy higher-level needs. If *hygiene* factors (factors outside the job itself, such as working conditions, salary, and incentive pay) are inadequate, employees become dissatisfied. However, adding more of these hygienes (like incentives) to the job (supplying what Herzberg calls "extrinsic motivation") is an inferior way to try to motivate someone, because lower-level needs are quickly satisfied. Soon the person simply says, in effect, "What have you done for me lately? I want another raise."

Instead of relying on hygienes, says Herzberg, managers interested in creating a self-motivated workforce should emphasize "job content" or *motivator* factors. Managers do this by enriching workers' jobs so that the jobs are more challenging, and by providing feedback and recognition—they make doing the job intrinsically motivating, in other words. In organizational psychology, **intrinsic motivation** is motivation that derives from the pleasure someone gets from doing the job or task. It comes from "within" the person, rather than from some externally applied motivator, such as a boss's order or a financial incentive plan. When one is intrinsically motivated, just doing the job or task provides the motivation (as would a favorite hobby). Among other things, Herzberg's theory makes the point that relying exclusively on financial incentives is risky. The employer should also provide the recognition and challenging work that most people desire.

DEMOTIVATORS AND EDWARD DECI

Psychologist Edward Deci's work highlights another potential downside to relying too heavily on extrinsic rewards: They may backfire. Deci found that extrinsic rewards could at times actually detract from the person's intrinsic motivation.[10] For example, a Samaritan who risks danger by rushing to an accident victim's aid might be insulted if the victim said, "Thanks, here's some money for your trouble." The point may be stated thusly: Be cautious in devising incentive pay for highly motivated employees, lest you inadvertently demean and detract from the desire they have to do the job out of a sense of responsibility.

EXPECTANCY THEORY AND VICTOR VROOM

Another important motivational fact is that, in general, people won't pursue rewards they find unattractive, or where the odds of success are very low. Psychologist Victor Vroom's expectancy motivation theory echoes these commonsense observations. He says a person's motivation to exert some level of effort depends on three things: the person's **expectancy** (in terms of probability) that his or her effort will lead to performance;[11] **instrumentality**, or the perceived connection (if any) between successful performance and actually obtaining the rewards; and **valence**, which represents the perceived value the person attaches to the reward.[12] In Vroom's theory, motivation is thus a product of three things:

$$\text{Motivation} = (\text{E} \times \text{I} \times \text{V}),$$

where, of course, E represents expectancy, I instrumentality, and V valence. If E or I or V is zero or inconsequential, there will be no motivation.

Vroom's theory has three implications for how managers design incentive plans.

- First, if employees don't *expect* that effort will produce performance, no motivation will occur. So, managers must ensure that their employees have the skills to do the job, and believe they can do the job. Thus training, job descriptions, and confidence building and support are important in using incentives.

- Second, Vroom's theory suggests that employees must see the *instrumentality* of their efforts—they must believe that successful performance will in fact lead to getting the reward. Managers can accomplish this, for instance, by creating easy to understand incentive plans.

- Third, the reward itself must be of *value* to the employee. Ideally, the manager should take into account individual employee preferences.

BEHAVIOR MODIFICATION/REINFORCEMENT AND B. F. SKINNER

Using incentives also assumes you know something about how consequences affect behavior.[13] Psychologist B. F. Skinner's findings provide the foundation for much of what we know about this. Managers apply Skinner's principles by using *behavior modification*. **Behavior modification** means changing behavior through rewards or punishments that are contingent on performance. For managers, behavior modification boils down to two main principles. First, that behavior that appears to lead to a positive consequence (reward) tends to be repeated, whereas behavior that appears to lead to a negative consequence (punishment) tends not to be repeated; and second, that, therefore, managers can get someone to change his or her behavior by providing the properly scheduled rewards (or punishment).

Incentive Pay Terminology

Managers often use two terms synonymously with incentive plans.[14] Traditionally, all incentive plans are *pay-for-performance* plans. They all tie employees' pay to the employees' performance. **Variable pay** is more specific: It is usually an incentive plan that ties a group or team's pay to some measure of the firm's (or the facility's) overall profitability;[15] *profit-sharing plans* (discussed later) are one example. Variable pay is advantageous insofar as it reduces an employer's fixed pay, so that if sales or performance dips, pay declines too.[16] However, confusing as it may be, some experts have used the term "variable pay" to include incentive plans for individual employees.[17]

To arrange our discussion, we will organize the following sections around individual employee incentive and recognition programs, sales compensation programs, management and executive incentive compensation programs, and team and organization-wide incentive programs.

Employee Incentives and the Law

Under the Fair Labor Standards Act, if the incentive is in the form of a prize or cash award, the employer generally must *include the value of that award* when calculating the worker's overtime pay for that pay period.[18] Employers pay overtime rates to nonexempt employees based on the employees' previous week's earnings. So, unless you structure the incentive bonuses properly, the bonus itself becomes part of the week's wages. Suppose someone earning $10 per hour for a 40-hour week also earns performance incentive pay of $80 for the week, or $480 total. Further, assume she also works 2 hours overtime that week. The overtime rate for the 2 hours she works overtime that week equals 1.5 times $12 (which includes the $80/40 equals $2 per hour incentive pay) or $18; you must include the average $2 per hour ($80 divided by 40 hours) she earned in incentive pay.

Certain bonuses are excludable from overtime pay calculations. For example, Christmas and gift bonuses that are not based on hours worked, or are so substantial that employees don't consider them a part of their wages, do not have to be included in overtime pay calculations. Similarly, purely discretionary bonuses in which the employer retains discretion over how much if anything to pay are excludable.

Other types of incentive pay *must* be included. Under the Fair Labor Standards Act (FLSA), bonuses to include in overtime pay computations include those promised to newly hired employees; those provided for in union contracts or other agreements; and those announced to induce employees to work more productively, steadily, rapidly, or efficiently or to induce them to remain with the company. Such bonuses would include many of those we turn to next, such as individual and group production bonuses.

---

intrinsic motivation
Motivation that derives from the pleasure someone gets from doing the job or task.

expectancy
A person's expectation that his or her effort will lead to performance.

instrumentality
The perceived relationship between successful performance and obtaining the reward.

valence
The perceived value a person attaches to the reward.

behavior modification
Using contingent rewards or punishment to change behavior.

variable pay
Any plan that ties pay to productivity or profitability, usually as one-time lump payments.

2 Discuss the main incentives for individual employees.

INDIVIDUAL EMPLOYEE INCENTIVE AND RECOGNITION PROGRAMS

Several incentive plans are particularly suited for use with individual employees.

Piecework Plans

Piecework is the oldest and still most popular individual incentive plan. Here you pay the worker a sum (called a *piece rate*) for each unit he or she produces. Thus, if Tom the Web surfer receives $0.40 for each e-mail sales lead he finds for the firm, he would make $40 for bringing in 100 a day and $80 for 200.

In a perfect world, developing a workable piece rate plan requires industrial engineering. The crucial issue is the production standard, and industrial engineers often set this—for instance, in terms of a standard number of e-mail leads per hour or a standard number of minutes per e-mail lead. In Tom's case, a job evaluation indicated that his Web surfing job was worth $8 an hour. The industrial engineer determined that 20 good leads per hour was the standard production rate. Therefore, the piece rate (for each lead) was $8 divided by 20, or $0.40 per sales lead. (Of course, we need to ensure that Tom makes at least the minimum wage, so we'd probably pay him $7.25 per hour—the federal minimum wage as of 2011—whether or not he brought in 18 leads, and then pay him $0.40 per lead for each over 18.) But in practice, most employers set the piece rates more informally. Thus, at Safelite Glass Corp., workers earn an hourly wage plus a bonus based on how many windshields they install.

STRAIGHT PIECEWORK Piecework generally implies **straight piecework**, which entails a strict proportionality between results and rewards regardless of output. However, some piecework plans allow for sharing productivity gains between employer and worker; here the worker receives extra income for some above-normal production.[19] So, if Tom starts bringing in 30 leads per hour instead of the engineered "standard" 20, his piece rate for leads above 25 might bump to $.45 each.

STANDARD HOUR PLANS The **standard hour plan** is like the piece rate plan, with one difference. Instead of getting a rate per piece, the worker gets a premium equal to the percent by which his or her performance exceeds the standard. So if Tom's standard is 160 leads per day (and thus $64 per day), and he brings in 200 leads, he'd get an extra 25% (40/160), or $80 total for the day. Some firms find that expressing the incentive in percentages may reduce somewhat the workers' tendency to link their production standard to pay (thus making the standard easier to change). It also eliminates the need to recalculate piece rates whenever hourly wage rates are changed.

PROS AND CONS Piecework plans are understandable, appear equitable in principle, and can be powerful incentives, since rewards are proportionate to performance.

But from the time of Taylor, managers have seen piecework's disadvantages. Workers on piecework may resist even justified attempts to raise production standards. Because piecework plans usually tie incentive pay to quantity produced, employees may well downplay quality, or resist switching from job to job (since doing so could reduce productivity).[20] Attempts to introduce new technology or processes may trigger resistance, for much the same reason.

In some industries, the term *piecework* has a dreadful reputation. In one case, an electronics firm had a woman who assembled cables for the firm during the day take home parts to assemble at night. Working at home, she allegedly averaged only $2 to $2.50 an hour for the piecework.[21]

For these and other reasons, more employers are moving to other plans.[22] We'll look at these on the following pages.

Merit Pay as an Incentive

Merit pay or a **merit raise** is any salary increase the firm awards to an individual employee based on his or her individual performance. It is different from a bonus in that it usually becomes part of the employee's base salary, whereas a bonus is a one-time payment. Although the term *merit pay* can apply to the incentive raises given to any employee, the term is more often used for white-collar employees and particularly professional, office, and clerical employees.

Merit pay is the subject of much debate. Advocates argue that awarding pay raises across the board (without regard to individual merit) may actually detract from performance, by showing employees they'll be rewarded regardless of how they perform.

Detractors present good reasons why merit pay can backfire. One is the dubious nature of many appraisal processes. Since many appraisals are unfair, so too will be the merit pay you base them on.[23] Similarly, supervisors often give most employees about the same rating and raise, either because of a reluctance to alienate some employees or to give everyone a raise that will help them stay even with the cost of living. (Alienating employees is a problem. Almost every employee thinks he or she is above average, so getting a below-average merit increase can be demoralizing.) The evidence is mixed, but tends to support using merit pay. One study focused on 218 workers in a nuclear waste facility. The researchers found a "very modest relationship between merit pay increase and performance rating."[24] Research into tying merit pay increases to teachers' or faculty members' research and/or teaching performance suggest that merit pay is more clearly linked with research productivity than with teaching effectiveness.[25]

The solution is not to throw out merit raises, but to make them more effective. Among other things, this means establishing effective appraisal procedures and ensuring that managers tie merit pay awards to performance.

DIFFERENTIAL PAY INCREASES Merit plan effectiveness depends on truly differentiating among employees. For example, expected base pay increases by U.S. employers for their highest ranked employees recently were 5.6%, compared with only 0.6% for the lowest rated employees. Middle rated employees could expect about 3.3%. The same is true for incentive payouts. For example, the highest-paid office clerical employees could expect short-term incentive payouts of 13%, while lowest rated employees could expect 3%, and mid-rated employees 8%.[26]

MERIT PAY OPTIONS Two adaptations of merit pay plans are popular. One awards merit raises in a lump sum once a year and does *not* make the raise part of the employee's salary (making them, in effect, short-term bonuses for lower-level workers). Traditional merit increases are cumulative, but these *lump-sum merit raises* are not. This produces two potential benefits. First, the merit raise is not baked into the employee's salary, so you need not pay it year after year. Lump-sum merit increases can also be more dramatic motivators than a traditional merit raise. For example, a 5% lump-sum merit payment to a $30,000 employee is $1,500 cash, as opposed to a traditional weekly merit payout of $29 for 52 weeks.

The other adaptation ties merit awards to both individual and organizational performance. Table 12-1 presents a sample matrix for doing so. In this example, you might measure the company's performance by, say, sales divided by payroll costs. Company performance and the employee's performance (using his or her performance appraisal) receive equal weight in computing the merit pay. In Table 12-1 an

piecework
A system of pay based on the number of items processed by each individual worker in a unit of time, such as items per hour or items per day.

straight piecework
An incentive plan in which a person is paid a sum for each item he or she makes or sells, with a strict proportionality between results and rewards.

standard hour plan
A plan by which a worker is paid a basic hourly rate but is paid an extra percentage of his or her rate for production exceeding the standard per hour or per day. Similar to piecework payment but based on a percent premium.

merit pay (merit raise)
Any salary increase awarded to an employee based on his or her individual performance.

TABLE 12-1 Merit Award Determination Matrix (an Example)					
The Employee's Performance Rating (Weight = 0.50)	The Company's Performance (Weight = 0.50)				
	Outstanding	Excellent	Good	Marginal	Unacceptable
Outstanding	1.00	0.90	0.80	0.70	0.00
Excellent	0.90	0.80	0.70	0.60	0.00
Good	0.80	0.70	0.60	0.50	0.00
Marginal	—	—	—	—	—
Unacceptable	—	—	—	—	—

Note: To determine the dollar value of each employee's award: (1) multiply the employee's annual, straight-time wage or salary as of June 30 times his or her maximum incentive award (as determined by management or the board—such as, "10% of each employee's pay") and (2) multiply the resultant product by the appropriate percentage figure from this table. For example, if an employee had an annual salary of $20,000 on June 30 and a maximum incentive award of 7% and if her performance and the organization's performance were both "excellent," the employee's award would be $1,120: ($20,000 × 0.07 × 0.80 = $1,120).

outstanding performer would receive 70% of his or her maximum lump-sum award even if the organization's performance were marginal. However, employees with marginal or unacceptable performance would get no lump-sum awards even in years in which the firm's performance was outstanding. The bonus plan at Discovery Communications is an example. Executive assistants can receive bonuses of up to a maximum of 10% of their salaries. The boss's evaluation of the assistant's individual performance accounts for 80% of the potential bonus; 10% is based on how the division does, and 10% on how the company does.[27]

Incentives for Professional Employees

Professional employees are those whose work involves the application of learned knowledge to the solution of the employer's problems. They include lawyers, doctors, economists, and engineers.

Making incentive pay decisions for professional employees can be challenging. For one thing, firms usually pay professionals well anyway. For another, they're already driven by the desire to produce high-caliber work and receive recognition from colleagues.

However, it is unrealistic to assume that people like the engineers, systems analysts, and programmers at Microsoft and Google work only for professional gratification. Few firms therefore work harder to maintain competitive incentives for professionals. For example, Google reportedly pays higher incentives to engineers working on important projects. Those who choose the intrinsic motivation of working on more theoretical long-term projects are rewarded if their research pays off.[28] As at most Silicon Valley firms, Google's professionals also bask in the light of potentially millionaire-making stock option grants.

Dual-career ladders are another way to manage professionals' pay. At many employers, a bigger salary and bonus requires rerouting from, say, engineering into management. However, not all professionals want such paths. Therefore, many employers institute dual-career paths, in other words, one path for managers, and another for technical experts. The latter offer professionals such as engineers the prospect of using advanced technical skills and earning higher pay without switching to management.[29]

Nonfinancial and Recognition-Based Awards

Recognition programs are one of several types of nonfinancial rewards. The term *recognition program* usually refers to formal programs, such as employee-of-the-month programs. *Social recognition program* generally refers to informal manager–employee exchanges such as praise, approval, or expressions of appreciation for a job well done.

Performance feedback means providing quantitative or qualitative information on task performance to change or maintain performance; showing workers a graph of how their performance is trending is an example.[30]

Studies show that recognition has a positive impact on performance, either alone or in conjunction with financial rewards.[31] In one survey, 89% of surveyed companies reported having recognition programs in place, for things ranging from exceptional performance to attendance, safety, sales, and major life events.[32]

Many employers are bulking up their recognition programs. For example, Baudville, a workplace recognition vendor, recently unveiled an e-card service called ePraise. Employers use this to remind employees of how much they're appreciated. Intuit shifted its employee recognition, years of service, patent awards, and wellness awards programs from several vendors to Globoforce several years ago. The move "allowed us to build efficiencies and improved effectiveness" into the programs' management, says Intuit's vice president of performance, rewards, and workplace.[33]

At American Skandia, which provides insurance and financial planning products and services, customer service reps who exceed standards receive a plaque, a $500 check, their photo and story on the firm's internal Web site, and a dinner for themselves and their teams.[34] Most employers combine financial and nonfinancial awards. One survey of 235 managers found that the most-used rewards to motivate employees (top–down, from most used to least) were:[35]

- Employee recognition
- Gift certificates
- Special events
- Cash rewards
- Merchandise incentives
- E-mail/print communications
- Training programs
- Work/life benefits
- Variable pay
- Group travel
- Individual travel
- Sweepstakes

HR IN PRACTICE: INCENTIVES MANAGERS CAN USE   As you can see, the individual line manager should not rely just on the employer's incentive plans for motivating subordinates. Those plans may not be very complete, and there are simply too many opportunities to motivate employees every day to let those opportunities pass. There are three guides to follow.

First, the best option for motivating employees is also the simplest—*make sure the employee has a doable goal* and that he or she agrees with it. It makes little sense to try to motivate employees with financial incentives if they don't know their goals or don't agree with them. Psychologist Edwin Locke and his colleagues have consistently found that specific, challenging goals lead to higher task performance than specific, unchallenging goals, or vague goals or no goals.

Second, *recognizing an employee's contribution* is a powerful motivation tool. Studies (and theories like those of Maslow and Herzberg) show that recognition has a positive impact on performance, either alone or in combination with financial rewards. For example, in one study, combining financial rewards with recognition produced a 30% performance improvement in service firms, almost twice the effect of using each reward alone.

Third, the manager can use *social recognition* (such as compliments) as positive reinforcement on a day-to-day basis. Figure 12-1 presents a short list.[36]

• Challenging work assignments	• Being provided with ample encouragement
• Freedom to choose own work activity	• Being allowed to set own goals
• Having fun built into work	• Compliments
• More of preferred task	• Expression of appreciation in front of others
• Role as boss's stand-in when he or she is away	• Note of thanks
• Role in presentations to top management	• Employee-of-the-month award
• Job rotation	• Special commendation
• Encouragement of learning and continuous improvement	• Bigger desk
	• Bigger office or cubicle

FIGURE 12-1 Social Recognition and Related Positive Reinforcement Managers Can Use

Source: Bob Nelson, *1001 Ways to Reward Employees* (New York: Workman Pub, 1994), p. 19; Sunny C. L. Fong and Margaret A. Shaffer, "The Dimensionality and Determinants of Pay Satisfaction: A Cross-Cultural Investigation of a Group Incentive Plan," *International Journal of Human Resource Management* 14, no. 4 (June 2003), p. 559.

Online and IT-Supported Awards

Incentive programs can be expensive and complicated to administer.[37] For example, with more than 1,000 sales representatives, First Tennessee Bank was having problems managing its sales incentive programs.[38] Tracking the performance of dozens or hundreds of measures and then computing individual employees' incentives is time-consuming. Bank employees had to enter by hand sales information for each of the 1,000 sales reps onto Excel spreadsheets. The process, said one officer, "had begun to spiral out of control." As one solution, vendors provide *enterprise incentive management* (EIM) systems. These automate the planning, analysis, and management of incentive compensation plans.[39]

Administering recognition programs is similarly challenging. If a company has an Employee Anniversary Recognition Program, for instance, someone (probably in human resources) needs to compile a prizes catalog, distribute it, and keep track of who gets what. Many firms—including Levi Strauss & Co. and Walmart—now use online awards firms to expedite the process. Management consultant Hewitt Associates uses www.bravanta.com to help its managers more easily recognize exceptional employee service with special awards. Additional Internet incentive/recognition sites include www.premierechoiceaward.com/secure/home.asp, www.giveanything.com, www.incentivecity.com, and www.kudoz.com.

Job Design

Although not usually considered an "incentive," job design can have a significant impact on employee motivation and retention. A study by Harvard Business School researchers concluded that job design is a primary driver of employee engagement. A study by Sibson Consulting concluded that job responsibility and feedback from a job were the fifth and seventh most important drivers of employee engagement. A study by Towers Watson concluded that challenging work ranked as the seventh most important driver for attracting employees.[40] Job design is thus a useful part of an employer's total rewards program.

3 Discuss the pros and cons of commissions versus straight pay incentives for salespeople.

INCENTIVES FOR SALESPEOPLE

Sales compensation plans typically rely heavily on sales commissions, and should aim to achieve the company's strategic (and therefore sales) goals. As one survey said, "the performance metrics given to the sales team must drive behaviors that will help the company's go-to-market strategy to be successful."[41] Unfortunately, the same survey found that "30% of respondents believe their sales compensation program rewarded the right behaviors 'not well' or 'very poorly.'"[42] However, with the recent recession, employers are moving to align the metrics they use to reward their salespeople with the firms' strategies. For instance they're factoring in more growth-oriented metrics, and reviewing their sales pay plans more often.[43] In any case, some salespeople do get straight salaries; most receive a combination of salary and commissions.

Salary Plan

Some firms pay salespeople fixed salaries (perhaps with occasional incentives in the form of bonuses, sales contest prizes, and the like).[44] Why do this? Straight salaries particularly make sense when the main task involves prospecting (finding new clients) or account servicing (such as participating in trade shows). Turnover is another reason. Faced with the difficulty of attracting and keeping good salespeople, a Buick-GMC dealership in Lincolnton, North Carolina, offers straight salary as an option to salespeople who sell an average of at least eight vehicles a month (plus a small "retention bonus" per car sold).[45]

The straight salary approach also makes it easier to switch territories or to reassign salespeople, and it can foster sales staff loyalty. The main disadvantage, of course, is that straight salary can demotivate potentially high-performing salespeople.[46]

Commission Plan

Straight commission plans pay salespeople for results, and only for results. Commission plans tend to attract high-performing salespeople who see that effort clearly produces rewards. Sales costs are proportionate to sales rather than fixed, and the company's fixed sales costs are thus lower. It's a plan that's easy to understand and compute. Commission plan alternatives include quota bonuses (for meeting particular quotas), straight commissions, management by objectives programs (pay is based on specific metrics), and ranking programs (these reward high achievers but pay little or no bonuses to the lowest performing salespeople.)[47]

However, problems abound. In poorly designed plans, salespeople may focus on making the sale, and may neglect nonselling duties such as servicing small accounts, cultivating dedicated customers, and pushing hard-to-sell items. Wide variations in pay may occur; this can make some feel the plan is inequitable. Misjudging sales potential can lead to excessively high commissions and to the need to cut commission rates. In addition, salespersons' pay may be excessive in boom times and low in recessions. Furthermore, sales performance—like any performance—reflects not just motivation, but ability, too. If the person hasn't the sales skills, commissions won't produce sales.[48]

Combination Plan

Most companies pay salespeople a combination of salary and commissions, usually with a sizable salary component. An incentive mix of about 70% base salary/30% incentive seems typical; this cushions the salesperson's downside risk (of earning nothing), while limiting the risk that the commissions could get out of hand from the firm's point of view.[49]

Combination plans have pros and cons.[50] They give salespeople a floor to their earnings, let the company specify what services the salary component is for (such as servicing current accounts), and still provide an incentive for superior performance. However, the salary component isn't tied to performance, so the employer is obviously trading away some incentive value. Combination plans also tend to become complicated, and misunderstandings can result.

The latter might not be a problem with a simple salary-plus-commission plan, but most plans are not so simple. For example, in a "commission-plus-drawing-account" plan, the salesperson is paid based on commissions. However, he or she can draw on future earnings to get through low sales periods. Similarly, in the "commission-plus-bonus" plan, the firm pays its salespeople mostly based on commissions. However, they also get a small bonus for directed activities like selling slow-moving items.

Maximizing Sales Force Results

In setting sales quotas and commission rates, the employer wants to motivate sales activity but avoid excessive commissions. Unfortunately, the tendency is to set commission rates informally.[51]

Setting effective quotas is an art. Questions to ask include: Are quotas communicated to the sales force within 1 month of the start of the period? Does the sales force know how their quotas are set? Do you combine bottom–up information (like account forecasts) with top–down requirements (like the company business plan)? Are returns and de-bookings reasonably low? And, has your firm generally avoided compensation-related lawsuits?[52] One expert suggests the following rule as to whether the sales incentive plan is effective: 75% or more of the sales force achieving quota or better, 10% of the sales force achieving higher performance level (than previously), and 5% to 10% of the sales force achieving below-quota performance and receiving performance development coaching.[53]

A survey of sales effectiveness reveals that, among other things, salespeople at high-performing companies:

- Receive 38% of their total cash compensation in the form of *sales-related variable pay* (compared with 27% for salespeople at low-performing companies)
- Are twice as likely to receive stock, *stock options*, or other equity pay as their counterparts at low-performing companies (36% versus 18%)
- Spend 264 more hours per year on *high-value sales activities* (e.g., prospecting, making sales presentations, and closing) than salespeople at low-performing companies
- Spend 40% more time each year with their *best potential customers*—qualified leads and prospects they know—than salespeople at low-performing companies
- Compared with salespeople at low-performing companies, spend nearly 25% *less time on administration*, allowing them to allocate more time to core sales activities, such as prospecting leads and closing sales[54]

Evidence-Based HR: How Effective Are Your Incentives?

Somewhat astonishingly, given the amount of money employers pay out in commissions, about 60% of employers track sales performance and sales commissions much as they did decades ago, using spreadsheets.[55] But to maximize performance, the sales manager typically needs evidence, such as the following: Do the sales team members understand the compensation plans? Do they know how we measure and reward performance? Are quotas set fairly? Is there a positive correlation between performance and commission earnings? Are commissions more than covering total salespersons expenses? And, does our commission plan maximize sales of our most profitable products?[56] It is difficult or impossible to gather this evidence or answer these questions because the spreadsheets don't easily support these types of analyses.

Gathering this evidence and conducting these analyses require special enterprise incentive management software applications.[57] Several vendors supply these systems. One is VUE Software™, which supplies VUE Compensation Management®.[58] With the aid of VUE Compensation Management® the sales manager can analyze compensation and performance data, conduct "what-if" analyses and reports, and do trend analyses for performance data.[59]

Source: Used with permission of Computer Solutions & Software International, Inc.

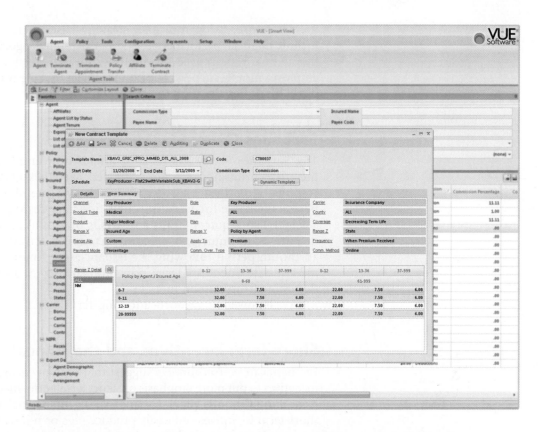

INCENTIVES FOR MANAGERS AND EXECUTIVES

Managers play a crucial role in divisional and company-wide profitability, and most firms therefore put considerable thought into how to reward them. Most managers get short-term and long-term incentives in addition to salary.[60] For firms offering short-term incentive plans, virtually all—96%—provide those incentives in cash. For those offering long-term incentives, about 48% offer them as stock options. The latter are to motivate and reward management for long-term corporate growth, prosperity, and shareholder value. A survey several years ago found that the average CEO pay mix was 16% salary, 22% bonus, and 62% long-term incentives.[61] Today, more employers are emphasizing short-term rather than long-term performance.

Strategy and the Executive's Long-Term and Total Rewards Package

Few human resource practices have as profound an impact on strategic success as the executive's long-term incentives. Whether building joint ventures abroad, consolidating operations, or pursuing growth, firms can't fully implement strategies in just 1 or 2 years. Therefore, the long-term signals you send managers and executives regarding what you will (or won't) reward can have a big effect on whether the firm's strategy succeeds.

In turn, the executives' total reward package—base salary, short- and long-term incentives, and perks—must align with each other and with the goal of achieving the company's strategic aims. Compensation experts suggest first defining the strategic context for the executive compensation plan. In other words, "What is our strategy and what are our strategic goals?" Then decide what long-term behaviors (boosting sales, cutting costs, and so on) the executives must exhibit to achieve the firm's strategic goals. Then shape each component of the executive total compensation package (base salary, short- and long-term incentives, and perks) and group them into a balanced plan that makes sense in terms of motivating the executive to achieve these aims. The rule is this: Each pay component should help focus the manager's attention on the behaviors required to achieve the company's strategic goals.[62]

Therefore, using multiple, strategy-based performance criteria is best. These include financial performance, number of strategic goals met, performance assessment by the board, employee productivity measures, customer satisfaction surveys, and employee morale surveys. The bottom line is that the top executive's pay package should direct his or her attention toward accomplishing the company's strategic goals.[63]

Sarbanes-Oxley

The Sarbanes-Oxley Act of 2002 affects how employers formulate their executive incentive programs. Congress passed Sarbanes-Oxley to inject a higher level of responsibility into executives' and board members' decisions. It makes them personally liable for violating their fiduciary responsibilities to their shareholders. The act also requires CEOs and CFOs of a public company to repay any bonuses, incentives, or equity-based compensation received from the company during the 12-month period following the issuance of a financial statement that the company must restate due to material noncompliance with a financial reporting requirement stemming from misconduct.[64]

We'll now look at short- and long-term management incentives.

Short-Term Incentives and the Annual Bonus

For better or worse, surveys suggest that employers are shifting away from long term incentives to put more emphasis on short term performance and incentives.[65] Most firms have **annual bonus** plans for motivating managers' short-term performance. Such short-term incentives can easily produce plus or minus adjustments of 25% or more to total pay. Four factors influence one's bonus: eligibility, fund size, individual performance, and formula.

ELIGIBILITY   Employers traditionally based annual bonus eligibility on job level/title, base salary, and/or officer status. Some simply based eligibility on job level or job title, or salary.[66] Recently, however, more employers are offering executives as well as employees below the executive level single annual incentive plans ". . . in which both executives and other employees participate."[67] The change reflects the fact that more employees—not just top managers—are now responsible for (and thus rewarded for) measurable contributions. The annual bonus is one such reward.

That trend to broader short-term bonus eligibility is evident from recent surveys of what factors determine bonus plan eligibility. Rather than job title or officer status, *salary grade or band* is now the most common eligibility determinant, reported by 42% of employers in a recent survey. This was followed by *title/reporting relationship* (24%), *officer status* (13%), *compensation committee approval* (11%), *discretionary* (6%), and *base salary* (2%).[68]

The percentage size of the bonus is typically greater for top-level executives. Thus, an executive earning $250,000 in salary may be able to earn another 80% of his or her salary as a bonus, while a manager in the same firm earning $100,000 can earn only another 30%. In 2010, Microsoft's CEO was eligible for an annual bonus of up to 100% of his salary (but he collected only half). A supervisor might be able to earn up to 15% of his or her base salary in bonuses. A typical breakdown might be executives, 45% of base salary; managers, 25%; and supervisory personnel, 12%.

FUND SIZE   How does one determine how big the annual bonus fund should be? Most employers (33% in a recent survey) traditionally use the Sum of Targets approach.[69] Specifically, they estimate the likely bonus for each eligible ("target") employee, and total these up to arrive at the bonus pool's size.

However, an increasing portion of employers (32%) are funding the short-term bonus fund based on financial results (32%). Here there are no fixed rules about the proportion of profits to pay out. One alternative is to reserve a minimal

Source: Shutterstock.

Even in retail stores, it's not unusual to compensate store managers partly based on short-term sales and profits.

amount of the profits, say, 10%, for safeguarding stockholders' investments, and then to establish a fund for bonuses equal to, say, 20% of the corporate operating profit before taxes in excess of this safeguard amount. Suppose the operating profits were $200,000 (after putting away 10% to safeguard stockholders). Then the management bonus fund might be 20% of $200,000 or $40,000. Most employers use more than one financial measure, with sales, earnings per share, and cash flow the most popular. [70] Other illustrative formulas might include:

- Twelve percent of net earnings after deducting 6% of net capital
- Ten percent of the amount by which net income exceeds 5% of stockholders' equity

Some firms don't use a formula at all, but make that decision on a discretionary basis.[71]

Other bases for determining fund size include simply summing up the actual awards and discretionary.

INDIVIDUAL PERFORMANCE   The third task is deciding the actual individual awards. Typically, the employer sets a target bonus (as well as maximum bonus, perhaps double the target bonus) for each eligible position. The actual award then reflects the manager's performance. For example, having previously decided which financial performance measures (return on assets, revenue growth, and so on) to use to measure each manager's performance, the employer computes preliminary total company bonus estimates, and compares the total amount of money required with the bonus fund available.[72] If necessary, it then adjusts the individual bonus estimates. In any case, outstanding managers should receive at least their target bonuses, and marginal ones should receive at best below-average awards. Use what you save on the marginal employees to supplement the outstanding employees.

One question is whether managers will receive bonuses based on individual performance, corporate performance, or both. Firms usually tie top-level executive bonuses mostly to overall corporate results (or divisional results if the executive heads a major division). This makes sense because the company's results are largely their own. But as one moves farther down the chain of command, corporate profits become a less accurate gauge of a manager's contribution. For, say, supervisors or the heads of functional departments, it often makes more sense to tie the bonus more closely to individual performance.

Many firms therefore end up tying short-term bonuses to both organizational and individual performance. Perhaps the simplest method is the *split-award plan*. This makes the manager eligible for two bonuses, one based on his or her individual effort and one based on the organization's overall performance. Thus, a manager might be eligible for an individual performance bonus of up to $10,000, but receive only $2,000 at the end of the year, based on his or her individual performance evaluation. But the person might also receive a second bonus of $3,000, based on the firm's profits for the year.

One drawback to this approach is that it may give marginal performers too much—for instance, someone could get a company-based bonus, even if his or her own performance is mediocre. One way to avoid this is to use the *multiplier method*. In other words, make the bonus a product of both individual and corporate performance. As Table 12-2 illustrates, multiply the target bonus by 1.00, .80, or zero (if the firm's performance is excellent, and the person's performance is excellent, good, fair, or poor). A manager whose own performance is poor does not even receive the company-based bonus.

FORMULA   The employer may also use a formula so as to base the bonus pool on those measures the employer wishes to emphasize. For example, Transocean Ltd., the firm that managed the Deepwater Horizon Gulf oil rig that sank in 2010, uses a

annual bonus
Plans that are designed to motivate short-term performance of managers and which are tied to company profitability.

TABLE 12-2 Multiplier Approach to Determining Annual Bonus

Individual Performance (Based on Appraisal, Weight = 0.50)	Company Performance (Based on Sales Targets, Weight = 0.50)			
	Excellent	Good	Fair	Poor
Excellent	1.00	0.90	0.80	0.70
Good	0.80	0.70	0.60	0.50
Fair	0.00	0.00	0.00	0.00
Poor	0.00	0.00	0.00	0.00

Note: To determine the dollar amount of a manager's award, multiply the maximum possible (target) bonus by the appropriate factor in the matrix.

formula that includes several financial factors such as new rig contracts. Safety accounts for 25% of the formula. After the Gulf explosion, senior Transocean executives donated their safety bonuses to the victims' families.[73]

Strategic Long-Term Incentives

Employers use long-term incentives to inject a long-term strategic perspective into their executives' decisions. With only short-term criteria to shoot for, a manager could conceivably boost profitability by reducing plant maintenance, for instance; this tactic might catch up with the company 2 or 3 years later. Long-term incentives such as stock options, if well-designed, should only pay off if the firm achieves its strategic goals, at which point the owners and investors should also benefit from the executives' efforts. Long-term incentives may also be "golden handcuffs," motivating executives to stay by letting them accumulate capital (usually options to buy company stock) that they can only cash in after a certain period. Popular long-term incentives include cash, stock, stock options, stock appreciation rights, and phantom stock. We'll look at each.

STOCK OPTIONS   A **stock option** is the right to purchase a specific number of shares of company stock at a specific price during a specific period. The executive thus hopes to profit by exercising his or her option to buy the shares in the future but at today's price. The assumption is that the price of the stock will go up. Unfortunately, this depends partly on considerations outside the manager's control, such as general economic conditions.[74] When stock markets dropped a few years ago, many employers including Intel and Google modified option plans to increase the likely payout.[75]

STOCK OPTION PROBLEMS   The chronic problem with stock options is that they often reward even managers who have lackluster performance, but there are also other issues. Many blame stock options for contributing to corporate scandals, in which executives allegedly manipulated the dates they received their options to maximize their returns. Options may also encourage executives to take perilous risks in pursuit of higher (at least short-term) profits.[76] The stock options provide an incentive to go for spectacular results, but since the managers haven't actually bought the stock yet, they don't risk their own money. One solution is to draft the option plan so that it forces recipients to convert their options to stock more quickly.[77]

OTHER STOCK PLANS   The trend is toward tying rewards more explicitly to performance goals. Instead of stock options, more firms are granting various types of performance shares such as *performance-contingent restricted stock*; the executive receives his or her shares only if he or she meets the preset performance targets.[78] With (time-based) *restricted stock plans*, the firm usually awards rights to the shares without cost to the executive but the employee is restricted from acquiring (and selling) the shares for, say, 5 years. The employer's aim is to retain the employee's services during that time.[79] With *indexed options*, the option's exercise price fluctuates with the performance of, say, a market index. Then, if the company's stock does no better than the index, the manager's options are worthless. With *premium priced options*, the exercise price is higher than the stock's closing price on the date of the grant, so the executive can't profit from the options until the stock makes significant gains.[80]

Stock appreciation rights (SARs) permit the recipient to exercise the stock option (by buying the stock) or to take any appreciation in the stock price in cash, stock, or some combination of these. Under *phantom stock plans*, executives receive not shares but "units" that are similar to shares of company stock. Then at some future time, they receive value (usually in cash) equal to the appreciation of the "phantom" stock they own. Both SARs and phantom stock essentially "are bonus plans that grant not stock but rather the right to receive an award based on the value of the company's stock." [81] A *performance achievement plan* awards shares of stock for the achievement of predetermined financial targets, such as profit or growth in earnings per share.

ETHICS AND INCENTIVES   "People put their efforts where they know they'll be rewarded" is a management truism with implications for long-term incentive plans. Simplistic, financial performance-oriented incentives, in the absence of strong ethical standards, may breed unethical behavior. As one article notes, "in today's cash focused culture, where new research suggests that money may have similar influences on individual actions as drugs or sex, the unexpected impact of plans that reward certain behaviors with cash is perhaps more than first thought."[82] For example, in describing one financial firm known for its high ethical standards, *Forbes* recently alleged that the firm's culture now "rewards hard-nosed aggressiveness and doesn't put the client's interests before those of the firm."[83] The solutions are to foster an ethical culture (see Chapter 14), and to include a sufficient array of bonus-able criteria in the incentive plan.

Other Executive Incentives

Companies also provide various incentives to persuade executives not to leave the firm. This is especially important when there is reason to believe another company is stalking the firm and wants to buy it. **Golden parachutes** are extraordinary payments companies make to executives in connection with a change in ownership or control of a company. For example, a company's golden parachute clause might state that, with a change in ownership of the firm, the executive would receive a one-time payment of $2 million.[84]

Other firms, perhaps more dubiously, guarantee large loans as incentives to directors and officers, for instance, to buy company stock. Thus, directors and officers of Conseco owed the company more than $500 million for such loans when shares of the company stock dropped precipitously.[85]

TEAM AND ORGANIZATIONWIDE INCENTIVE PLANS

> **5** Name and define the most popular organization-wide variable pay plans.

We've focused to this point on individual employee incentives such as piecework, commissions, and executive bonuses. Let's look now at incentives for teams, and for all employees company-wide.

How to Design Team Incentives

Firms increasingly rely on teams to manage their work. They therefore need incentive plans that encourage teamwork and focus team members' attention on performance. **Team (or group) incentive plans** pay incentives to the team based on the team's performance.

---

stock option
The right to purchase a stated number of shares of a company stock at today's price at some time in the future.

golden parachute
A payment companies make in connection with a change in ownership or control of a company.

team (or group) incentive plan
A plan in which a production standard is set for a specific work group, and its members are paid incentives if the group exceeds the production standard.

Source: Shutterstock.

Team incentives can foster a sense of cooperation and unanimity.

The main question here is how to reward the team's performance, and the wrong choice can prove lethal. Levi Strauss installed a team incentive plan that rewarded the team as a whole for its output, neglecting the fact that some employees worked harder than others did. The faster ones soon slowed down, production declined, and Levi's (as noted earlier) closed its U.S. factories.

So, the main thing is to make sure you have all your team pulling together. Yet the usual approach is still to tie rewards to some overall standard of group performance, such as "total labor hours per car." Doing so avoids the need for a precisely engineered piecework standard (in terms of wheels installed per hour, for instance).[86] One company established such an overall standard for its teams. If the firm reached 100% of its goal, the employees would share in about 5% of the improvement (in labor costs saved). The firm divided the 5% pool by the number of employees to compute the value of a "share." If the firm achieved less than 100% of its goal, the bonus pool was less. The results of this plan—in terms of changing employee attitudes and focusing teams on strategic goals—were reportedly "extraordinary."[87]

ENGINEERED STANDARDS   Some employers set an engineered production standard tied to the output of the group (again, such as in terms of wheels installed per hour). The employer typically uses either the piece rate or standard hour plan, but the latter is more prevalent. All team members then typically receive the same share of the team's incentive pay. Occasionally, the employer may want to pay all team members according to some other formula. For instance, instead of paying each team member based on how well the team as a whole does, pay everyone based on how well the *best* team member does. This counterintuitive option may make sense when an employer has reason to believe the new team incentive plan might demotivate high-performing team members. That's what happened at Levi's, for instance.

PROS AND CONS OF TEAM INCENTIVES   Team incentives often make sense. They reinforce team planning and problem solving, and can help ensure collaboration. In Asia in general, the tendency is to reward the group—to reduce jealousy, to make group members indebted to one another, and to encourage a sense of cooperation. Team incentives also facilitate training, since each member has an interest in getting new members trained as fast as possible. The main disadvantage is the demotivating effects of workers who share in the team-based pay but who don't put their hearts into it ("free riders").

Evidence-Based HR: Inequities That Undercut Team Incentives

Although about 85% of large employers reportedly use some type of group- or team-based incentives, studies suggest that team incentives are often counterproductive. What are the main things to beware of? A researcher studied business students enrolled in a graduate online MBA program.[88] She devised a method for systematically categorizing their qualitative observations about the team incentives they'd experienced.

The fundamental problem was inequity.[89] In many cases, each team member's financial compensation was the same, although one or two people "did the lion's share of the work." In other cases, the employer chose one or two team members for promotion, leaving others to feel they'd worked hard to support someone else's career. The bottom line seems to be that unless you actively minimize inequities, it's probably best to pay employees based on their individual contributions to the team, rather than on collective team performance.

Aside from avoiding inequities, the other thing to keep in mind is that successful teamwork reflects more than team incentives. Companies such as Honda screen, hire, train, and cultivate workers to be team members, so the incentives are just one component.

Many employers take the team incentive idea to the next logical level and institute incentive plans in which all or most employees participate. **Organization-wide incentive plans** are plans in which all or most employees can participate, and which generally tie the reward to some measure of company-wide performance. Also called *variable pay plans*, they include profit sharing, Scanlon/gainsharing plans, and employee stock ownership (ESOP) plans. We'll look at them next.

Profit-Sharing Plans

Profit-sharing plans are plans in which all or most employees receive a share of the firm's annual profits. Research on such plans' effectiveness is sketchy. One study concludes that there is ample evidence that profit-sharing plans boost productivity and morale, but that their effect on profits is insignificant, once you factor in the costs of the plans' payouts.[90] A recent study, conducted in Spain, concluded that profit-sharing plans enhance employees' commitment to the organization.[91]

There are several types of profit-sharing plans. With *current profit-sharing* or cash plans, employees share in a portion of the employer's profits quarterly or annually. In cash plans, the firm simply distributes a percentage of profits (usually 15% to 20%) as profit shares to employees at regular intervals. The Home Depot instituted such a cash program for all its store workers. It started paying store associates a bonus if their stores meet certain financial goals. In one recent year, The Home Depot distributed a total of $90 million under that company-wide incentive plan.[92]

With *deferred profit-sharing* plans, the employer puts cash awards into trust accounts for the employees' retirement.[93] These are essentially defined contribution pension plans "in which the employer has discretion to determine when and how much the company pays into the plan."[94] The employer generally distributes the awards based on a percentage of the employee's salary, or some measure of the employee's contribution to company profits.[95] Employees' income taxes on the distributions are deferred until the employee retires or withdraws funds from the plan.

Scanlon Plans

Few would argue with the idea that the most powerful way of ensuring employee commitment is to synchronize the company's goals with those of its employees—in other words, to ensure that by pursuing his or her goals, the worker pursues the employer's goals as well. Experts have proposed many techniques for attaining this ideal state. However, few plans are used as widely or successfully as the **Scanlon plan**, an incentive plan developed in 1937 by Joseph Scanlon, a United Steel Workers Union official.[96] It is still popular today.

The Scanlon plan is remarkably progressive, considering that it is now more than 70 years old. Scanlon plans have five basic features.[97] The first is Scanlon's *philosophy of cooperation*. This philosophy assumes that managers and workers must rid themselves of the "us" and "them" attitudes that normally inhibit employees from developing a sense of ownership in the company.

A second feature is what its practitioners call *identity*. This means that in order to focus employee involvement, the company must articulate its mission or purpose, and employees must understand how the business operates in terms of customers, prices, and costs. *Competence* is a third basic feature. The program, say three experts, "explicitly recognizes that a Scanlon plan demands a high level of competence from employees at all levels."[98] This suggests careful selection and training.

---

organization-wide incentive plan
Incentive plan in which all or most employees can participate.

profit-sharing plan
A plan whereby employees share in the company's profits.

Scanlon plan
An incentive plan developed in 1937 by Joseph Scanlon and designed to encourage cooperation, involvement, and sharing of benefits.

The fourth feature of the plan is the *involvement system*. Employees present improvement suggestions to the appropriate departmental-level committees, which transmit the valuable ones to the executive-level committee. The latter then decides whether to implement the suggestion.

The fifth element of the plan is the *sharing of benefits formula*. If a suggestion is implemented and successful, all employees usually share in 75% of the savings. For example, assume that the normal monthly ratio of payroll costs to sales is 50%. (Thus, if sales are $600,000, payroll costs should be $300,000.) Assume the firm implements suggestions that result in payroll costs of $250,000 in a month when sales were $550,000 and payroll costs therefore should have been $275,000 (50% of sales). The savings attributable to these suggestions is $25,000 ($275,000 minus $250,000). Workers would typically split 75% of this ($18,750), while $6,250 would go to the firm. In practice, the firm sets aside a portion, usually one-quarter of the $18,750, for the months in which payroll costs exceed the standard.

Other Gainsharing Plans

The Scanlon plan is one early version of today's **gainsharing plans**. Gainsharing is an incentive plan that engages many or all employees in a common effort to achieve a company's productivity objectives, with any resulting cost-savings gains shared among employees and the company.[99] In addition to the Scanlon plan, other popular gainsharing plans include the Lincoln, Rucker, and Improshare plans.

The basic difference among these plans is the formula employers use to determine employee bonuses. The Scanlon formula divides payroll expenses by total sales (or, sometimes, by total sales plus increases in inventory). In one version of the *Lincoln incentive system*, first instituted at the Lincoln Electric Company of Ohio, employees work on a guaranteed piecework basis. The company distributes total annual profits (less taxes, 6% dividends to stockholders, and a reserve) each year among employees based on their merit rating.

Most firms that use gainsharing implement customized versions. Recent results—from various efforts in hospitals, as well as manufacturing plants—suggest quite clearly that gainsharing plans can improve productivity and patient care, and reduce grievances, but often also entail considerable implementation costs.[100] Based on positive results, the U.S. Department of Health and Human Service's Office of Inspector General approved certain hospital gainsharing plans wherein the hospital pays physicians a share of any cost savings attributable in part to the physicians' efforts. In any case, there are eight basic steps in implementing a gainsharing plan:[101]

1. Establish general plan objectives, such as boosting productivity or lowering labor costs.
2. Choose specific performance measures, such as labor hours per unit produced.
3. Decide the portion of gains employees will receive. In the Scanlon example mentioned earlier, employees receive about 75% of the gains.
4. Decide on a method for dividing and distributing the employees' share of the gains. Popular methods include equal percentage of pay or equal shares.
5. Choose the form of payment, usually cash.
6. Decide how often to pay bonuses. Firms tend to pay based on financial performance measures annually and on labor productivity measures quarterly or monthly.
7. Develop the involvement system. The most commonly used systems include steering committees, update meetings, suggestion systems, and problem-solving teams.
8. Implement the plan.

At-Risk Pay Plans

In an **earnings-at-risk pay plan**, employees agree to put some portion of their normal pay (say, 6%) at risk (forego) if they don't meet their goals, in return for possibly obtaining a much larger bonus (say, 12%), if they exceed their goals. Suppose in one department the employees' base pay will be 94% of their counterparts' in a not-at-risk department. If the former department then achieves its goals, the employees get their full pay; if it exceeds its goals, they receive a 12% bonus.

Employee Stock Ownership Plans

Employee stock ownership plans (ESOPs) are company-wide plans in which the employer contributes shares of its own stock (or cash to be used to purchase such stock) to a trust established to purchase shares of the firm's stock for employees. The firm generally makes these contributions annually in proportion to total employee compensation, with a limit of 15% of compensation. The trust holds the stock in individual employee accounts and distributes it to employees upon retirement (or other separation from service), assuming the person has worked long enough to earn ownership of the stock. (*Stock options*, as discussed earlier in this chapter, go directly to the employees individually to use as they see fit, rather than into a retirement trust.)

ESOPs are popular. The company receives a tax deduction equal to the fair market value of the shares it transfers to the trustee, and can claim an income tax deduction for dividends paid on ESOP-owned stock. Employees, as noted, aren't taxed until they receive a distribution from the trust, usually at retirement. The Employee Retirement Income Security Act (ERISA) allows a firm to borrow against employee stock held in trust and then repay the loan in pretax rather than after-tax dollars, another tax incentive for using such plans.[102]

ESOPs can also help the shareholders of closely held corporations (in which, for instance, a family owns virtually all the shares) to diversify their assets. They do this by placing some of their own shares of the company's stock into the ESOP trust and purchasing other marketable securities for themselves in their place.[103]

Research suggests that ESOPs probably do encourage employees to develop a sense of ownership in and commitment to the firm, but their effects on motivation and performance are questionable. In any case, those responsible for the funds—usually, the firm's top executives—must be fastidious in executing their fiduciary responsibilities for the fund.[104]

BROAD-BASED STOCK OPTIONS
Companies have offered "broad-based stock option plans" in which all or most employees can participate. The basic thinking is that sharing ownership in the company with employees makes motivational and practical sense.[105]

Employers seem to be cutting back on these. For example, Time Warner, Microsoft, Aetna, and Charles Schwab announced they were discontinuing distributing stock options to most employees. Some of them, including Microsoft, are instead awarding stock. With current tax laws, companies must show the options as an expense when awarded, reducing their attractiveness as a "costless" reward. Microsoft and others apparently feel awarding stock instead of stock options is a more direct and immediate way to link pay to performance.[106]

| 6 | Outline the steps in designing effective incentive plans. |

DESIGNING EFFECTIVE INCENTIVE PROGRAMS

As we saw at the start of this chapter, roughly 70% of employees feel that their firms' incentive plans are ineffective. We now turn to why such plans fail, and to how to improve their effectiveness.[107] We'll start with an HR as a Profit Center example.[108]

---

gainsharing plan
An incentive plan that engages employees in a common effort to achieve productivity objectives and share the gains.

earnings-at-risk pay plan
Plan that puts some portion of employees' normal pay at risk if they don't meet their goals, in return for possibly obtaining a much larger bonus if they exceed their goals.

employee stock ownership plan (ESOP)
A corporation contributes shares of its own stock to a trust in which additional contributions are made annually. The trust distributes the stock to employees on retirement or separation from service.

HR AS A PROFIT CENTER

The Impact of Financial and Nonfinancial Incentives

Two researchers studied the impact of financial and nonfinancial incentives on business performance in 21 stores of a fast-food franchise in the Midwest.[109] The researchers carefully compared performance over time in stores that did and did not use financial and nonfinancial incentives. Each store had about 25 workers and two managers. The researchers trained the managers to identify observable, measurable employee behaviors that were currently deficient but that could influence store performance. Example behaviors included "keeping both hands moving at the drive-through window," "working during idle time," and "repeating the customer's order back to him or her."[110] Then they instituted the incentive plans. The researchers measured store performance in terms of gross profitability (revenue minus expenses), drive-through time, and employee turnover.

Financial Incentives

Some employees in some of the stores received financial incentives for exhibiting the desired behaviors. The financial incentives consisted of lump-sum bonuses in the workers' paychecks. For example, if the manager observed a work team exhibiting up to 50 behaviors during the observation period, he or she added $25 to the paychecks of all store employees that period; 50 to 100 behaviors added $50 per paycheck, and more than 100 behaviors added $75 per paycheck. Payouts rose over time as the employees learned more about the behaviors they were to exhibit.

Nonfinancial Incentives

The researchers also trained the managers in some stores to deliver nonfinancial incentives in the form of feedback and recognition. For example, for *performance feedback* managers maintained charts showing the drive-through times at the end of each day. They placed the charts by the time clocks, so all the store employees could keep track of their store's performance on things like drive-through times. The researchers also trained managers to administer *recognition* to employees, such as, "I noticed that today the drive-through times were really good. That is great since that is what we're really focusing on these days."[111]

Results

Both the financial and nonfinancial incentives improved employee and store performance.[112] For example, store profits rose 30% for those units where managers used financial rewards. Store profits rose 36% for those units where managers used nonfinancial rewards. During the same 9-month period, drive-through times decreased 19% for the financial incentives group, and 25% for the nonfinancial incentives groups. Turnover improved 13% for the financial incentives group, and 10% for the nonfinancial incentives group.

The Five Building Blocks of Effective Incentive Plans

The incentive plans in the accompanying feature exhibited the characteristics of effective incentive plans. We can summarize these as follows:

1. **Ask: Does it make sense to use incentives?**[113] It makes more sense to use an incentive plan when:
   - Motivation (and not ability) is the problem.
   - There is a clear relationship between employee effort and quantity or quality of output.
   - The employees can control the work you plan to incentivize.
   - Delays are few or consistent.

2. **Link the incentive with your strategy.** Link the incentive to behavior that is critical for achieving strategic goals.[114] For example, one incentive program at Sun Microsystems (now part of Oracle) supported Sun's customer satisfaction goals. Employees received incentives based on improvements in activities like on-time delivery and customer returns.[115]

3. **Make sure the program is motivational.** Victor Vroom would say there should be a clear link between *effort and performance*, and between *performance and reward*, and that the reward must be *attractive* to the employee. Employees must have the skills and training to do the job. Employers should support the incentive plan with performance feedback, as in the form of performance graphs.

4. **Set complete standards.** For example, don't just pay for quantity if quality is an issue, too.

5. **Be scientific.** Don't waste money on incentives that seem logical but that may not be contributing to performance. *Gather evidence* and analyze the effects of the incentive plan over time, to ascertain whether it is indeed influencing the measures (such as employee turnover, and so on) that you intended to improve through your plan.[116]

Incentive Plans in Practice: Nucor

Nucor Corp. is the largest steel producer in the United States. It also has the highest productivity and lowest labor cost per ton in the American steel industry.[117] Employees can earn bonuses of 100% or more of base salary, and all Nucor employees participate in one of four performance-based incentive plans. With the *production incentive plan*, operating and maintenance employees and supervisors get weekly bonuses based on their work groups' productivity. The *department manager incentive plan* pays department managers annual incentive bonuses based mostly on the ratio of net income to dollars of assets employed for their division. With the *professional and clerical bonus plan*, employees who are not in one of the two previous plans get bonuses based on their divisions' net income return on assets.[118] Finally, under the *senior officer incentive plan*, Nucor senior managers (whose base salaries are lower than those in comparable firms) get bonuses based on Nucor's annual overall percentage of net income to stockholders equity.[119] Nucor also divides 10% of its operating profits yearly among all employees (except senior officers). Depending on company performance, this may be from 1% to over 20% of an employee's pay.

REVIEW

MyManagementLab   Now that you have finished this chapter, go back to **www.mymanagementlab.com** to continue practicing and applying the concepts you've learned.

CHAPTER SECTION SUMMARIES

1. In designing an effective financial incentive plan, it's important to understand the relationship between **money and motivation**.
   - Abraham Maslow said that people have a hierarchy of five types of needs and that people are first motivated to satisfy each lower order need.
   - Frederick Hertzberg said the best way to motivate someone is to organize the job so that it provides the feedback and challenge that helps satisfy the person's higher-level needs.
   - Edward Deci found that extrinsic rewards may actually detract from a person's intrinsic motivation.
   - Victor Vroom's expectancy motivation theory says a person's motivation depends on expectancy, instrumentality, and valence.
   - Psychologist B. F. Skinner's behavior modification–based approach means changing behavior through rewards or punishments that are contingent on performance.

2. Several incentive plans are particularly suited for **individual employee incentives and recognition programs**. Piecework is an incentive plan in which a person is paid a sum for each item he or she makes. Merit pay refers to any salary increase awarded to an employee based on his or her individual performance. Nonfinancial and recognition-based awards are increasingly important and include awards in the form of employee recognition, gift certificates, and individual travel. Many employers use enterprise incentive management systems to automate the planning, analysis, and management of their incentive plans.

3. **Incentives for salespeople** are typically sales commissions. Although the percentage of pay in the form of sales commission may vary from zero to 100%, a survey found that salespeople at high-performing companies receive about 38% of their total cash compensation in the form of sales-related variable pay.

4. Managers take many things into consideration when formulating **incentives for managers and executives**. Most firms have annual bonus plans aimed at motivating managers' short-term performance. The actual award often depends on some combination of individual performance and organizational performance, so that, for instance, high-performing managers get a bonus even if the company itself underperforms. Long-term incentives include stock options, "golden parachutes," and stock appreciation rights.

5. With more employers organizing their efforts around teams, **team and organization-wide incentive plans are more important**. With team incentive plans, the main question is whether to reward members based on individual or team performance; both have pros and cons. Organization-wide incentive plans are plans in which all or most employees can participate. These include profit-sharing plans in which employees share in the company's profits; gainsharing plans, including the Scanlon plan, engage employees in a common effort to achieve productivity objectives and thereby share the gains. Employee stock ownership plans are company-wide plans in which the employer contributes shares of its own stock to a trust established to purchase shares of the firm's stock for employees.

6. Because so many incentive plans fail, **designing effective incentive programs** is crucial. Five important building blocks include determining whether using incentives makes sense, linking the incentive with your strategy, making sure the program is motivational, setting complete standards, and being scientific in terms of analyzing the effects of the incentive plan.

DISCUSSION QUESTIONS

1. Compare and contrast six types of incentive plans.
2. Explain five reasons why incentive plans fail.
3. Describe the nature of some important management incentives.
4. When and why would you pay a salesperson a combined salary and commission?
5. What is merit pay? Do you think it's a good idea to award employees merit raises? Why or why not?
6. In this chapter, we listed a number of guidelines for not instituting a pay-for-performance plan. Do you think these points make sense in terms of motivation theory? Why or why not?
7. What is a Scanlon plan? Based on what you've read in this chapter, what features of an effective incentive program does the Scanlon plan include?
8. Give four examples of when you would suggest using team or group incentive programs rather than individual incentive programs.

INDIVIDUAL AND GROUP ACTIVITIES

1. Working individually or in groups, create an incentive plan for the following positions: chemical engineer, plant manager, used-car salesperson. What factors did you have to consider in reaching your conclusions?
2. A state university system in the Southeast instituted a "Teacher Incentive Program" (TIP) for its faculty. Faculty committees within each university's colleges were told to award $5,000 raises (not bonuses) to about 40% of their faculty members based on how good a job they did teaching undergraduates, and how many courses they taught per year. What are the potential advantages and pitfalls of such an incentive program? How well do you think it was accepted by the faculty? Do you think it had the desired effect?
3. The "HRCI Test Specifications Appendix" (pages 633–640) lists the knowledge someone studying for the HRCI certification exam needs to have in each area of human resource management (such as in Strategic Management, Workforce Planning, and Human Resource Development). In groups of four to five students, do four things: (1) review that appendix now; (2) identify the material in this chapter that relates to the required knowledge the appendix lists; (3) write four multiple-choice exam questions on this material that you believe would be suitable for inclusion in the HRCI exam; and (4) if time permits, have someone from your team post your team's questions in front of the class, so the students in other teams can take each others' exam questions.
4. Several years ago, the pension plan of the Utility Workers Union of America proposed that shareholders change the corporate bylaws of Dominion Resources, Inc., so that in the future, management had to get shareholder approval of executive pay exceeding $1 million, as well as detailed information about the firm's executive incentive plans. Many unions—most of which have pension funds with huge investments in U.S. companies—are taking similar

steps. They point out that, usually, under Internal Revenue Service regulations, corporations can't deduct more than $1 million in pay for any of a company's top five paid executives. Under the new rules the unions are pushing, boards of directors will no longer be able to approve executive pay above $1 million; instead, shareholders would have to vote on it. In terms of effectively running a company, what do you think are the pros and cons of the unions' recommendations? Would you vote for or against the unions' recommendation? Why or why not?

EXPERIENTIAL EXERCISE

Motivating the Sales Force at Express Auto

Purpose: The purpose of this exercise is to give you practice developing an incentive plan.

Required Understanding: Be thoroughly familiar with this chapter, and read the following:

Express Auto, an automobile mega-dealership with more than 600 employees that represents 22 brands, has just received a very discouraging set of survey results. Customer satisfaction scores have fallen for the ninth straight quarter. Customer complaints include:

- It was hard to get prompt feedback from mechanics by phone.
- Salespeople often did not return phone calls.
- The finance people seemed "pushy."
- New cars were often not properly cleaned or had minor items that needed immediate repair or adjustment.

- Cars often had to be returned to have repair work redone.

Table 12-3 describes Express Auto's current compensation system.

How to Set Up the Exercise/Instructions:

Divide the class into groups of four to five students. One or more groups should analyze each of the five teams in column one. Each student group should analyze the compensation package for its Express Auto team. Each group should address these questions:

1. In what ways might your team's compensation plan contribute to the customer service problems?
2. What recommendations would you make to improve the compensation system in a way that would likely improve customer satisfaction?

TABLE 12-3 Express Auto Compensation System

Express Auto Team	Responsibility of Team	Current Compensation Method
1. Sales force	Persuade buyer to purchase a car.	Very small salary (minimum wage) with commissions. Commission rate increases with every 20 cars sold per month.
2. Finance office	Help close the sale; persuade customer to use company finance plan.	Salary, plus bonus for each $10,000 financed with the company.
3. Detailing	Inspect cars delivered from factory, clean, and make minor adjustments.	Piecework paid on the number of cars detailed per day.
4. Mechanics	Provide factory warranty service, maintenance, and repair.	Small hourly wage, plus bonus based on (1) number of cars completed per day and (2) finishing each car faster than the standard estimated time to repair.
5. Receptionists/phone service personnel	Primary liaison between customer and sales force, finance, and mechanics.	Minimum wage.

APPLICATION CASE

INSERTING THE TEAM CONCEPT INTO COMPENSATION—OR NOT

In his new position at Hathaway Manufacturing, one of the first things Sandy Caldwell wanted to do was improve productivity through teamwork at every level of the firm. As the new human resource manager for the suburban plant, Sandy set out to change the culture to accommodate the team-based approach he had become so enthusiastic about in his most recent position.

Sandy started by installing the concept of team management at the highest level, to oversee the operations of the entire plant. The new management team consisted of manufacturing, distribution, planning, technical, and human resource plant managers. Together they developed a new vision for the 500-employee facility, which they expressed in the simple phrase "Excellence Together." They drafted a new mission statement for the firm that focused on becoming customer driven and team based, and that called upon employees to raise their level of commitment and begin acting as "owners" of the firm.

The next step was to convey the team message to employees throughout the company. The communication process went surprisingly well, and Sandy was happy to see his idea of a "workforce of owners" begin to take shape. Teams trained together, developed production plans together, and embraced the technique of 360-degree feedback, in which an employee's performance evaluation is obtained from supervisors, subordinates, peers, and internal or external customers. Performance and morale improved, and productivity began to tick upward. The company even sponsored occasional celebrations to reward team achievements, and the team structure seemed firmly in place.

Sandy decided to change one more thing. Hathaway's long-standing policy had been to give all employees the same annual pay increase. But Sandy felt that in the new team environment, outstanding performance should be the criterion for pay raises. After consulting with CEO Regina Cioffi, Sandy sent a memo to all employees announcing the change to team-based pay for performance.

The reaction was immediate and 100% negative. None of the employees was happy with the change, and among their complaints, two stood out. First, because the 360-degree feedback system made everyone responsible in part for someone else's performance evaluation, no one was comfortable with the idea that pay raises might also be linked to peer input. Second, there was a widespread perception that the way the change was decided upon, and the way it was announced, put the firm's commitment to team effort in doubt. Simply put, employees felt left out of the decision process.

Sandy and Regina arranged a meeting for early the next morning. Sitting in her office, they began a painful debate. Should the new policy be rescinded as quickly as it was adopted, or should it be allowed to stand?

Questions

1. Does the pay-for-performance plan seem like a good idea? Why or why not?
2. What advice would you give Regina and Sandy as they consider their decision?
3. What mistakes did they make in adopting and communicating the new salary plan? How might Sandy have approached this major compensation change a little differently?
4. Assuming the new pay plan is eventually accepted, how would you address the fact that in the new performance evaluation system, employees' input affects their peers' pay levels?

Note: The incident in this case is based on an actual event at Frito-Lay's Kirkwood, New York, plant, as reported in C. James Novak, "Proceed with Caution When Paying Teams," *HR Magazine,* April 1997, p. 73.

CONTINUING CASE

CARTER CLEANING COMPANY

The Incentive Plan

The question of whether to pay Carter Cleaning Center employees an hourly wage or an incentive of some kind has always intrigued Jack Carter.

His basic policy has been to pay employees an hourly wage, except that his managers do receive an end-of-year bonus depending, as Jack puts it, "on whether their stores do well or not that year."

However, he is considering using an incentive plan in one store. Jack knows that a presser should press about 25 "tops" (jackets, dresses, blouses) per hour. Most of his pressers do not attain this ideal standard, though. In one instance, a presser named Walt was paid $8 per hour, and Jack noticed that regardless of the amount of work he had to do, Walt always ended up going home at about 3:00 P.M., so he earned about $300 at the end of the week. If it was a holiday week, for instance, and there were a lot of clothes to press, he might average 22 to 23 tops per hour (someone else did pants) and so he'd earn perhaps $300 and still finish each day in time to leave by 3:00 P.M. so he could pick up his children at school. But when things were very slow in the store, his productivity would drop to perhaps 12 to 15 pieces an hour, so that at the end of the week he'd end up earning perhaps $280, and in fact not go home much earlier than he did when it was busy.

Jack spoke with Walt several times, and while Walt always promised to try to do better, it gradually became apparent to Jack that Walt was simply going to earn his $300 per week no matter what. Though Walt never told him so directly, it dawned on Jack that Walt had a family to support and was

not about to earn less than his "target" wage, regardless of how busy or slow the store was. The problem was that the longer Walt kept pressing each day, the longer the steam boilers and compressors had to be kept on to power his machines, and the fuel charges alone ran close to $6 per hour. Jack clearly needed some way short of firing Walt to solve the problem, since the fuel bills were eating up his profits.

His solution was to tell Walt that, instead of an hourly $8 wage, he would henceforth pay him $0.33 per item pressed. That way, said Jack to himself, if Walt presses 25 items per hour at $0.33 he will in effect get a small raise. He'll get more items pressed per hour and will therefore be able to shut the machines down earlier.

On the whole, the experiment worked well. Walt generally presses 25 to 35 pieces per hour now. He gets to leave earlier and, with the small increase in pay, he generally earns his target wage. Two problems have arisen, though. The quality of Walt's work has dipped a bit, plus his manager has to spend a minute or two each hour counting the number of pieces Walt pressed that hour. Otherwise, Jack is fairly pleased with the results of his incentive plan, and he's wondering whether to extend it to other employees and other stores.

Questions

1. Should this plan be extended to pressers in the other stores?
2. Should other employees (cleaner/spotters, counter people) be put on a similar plan? Why? Why not? If so, how, exactly?

3. Is there another incentive plan you think would work better for the pressers? Describe it.

4. A store manager's job is to keep total wages to no more than 30% of sales and to maintain the fuel bill and the supply bill at about 9% of sales each. Managers can also directly affect sales by ensuring courteous customer service and by ensuring that the work is done properly. What suggestions would you make to Jennifer and her father for an incentive plan for store managers or front-desk clerks?

TRANSLATING STRATEGY INTO HR POLICIES & PRACTICES CASE

THE HOTEL PARIS CASE

The New Incentive Plan

The Hotel Paris's competitive strategy is "To use superior guest service to differentiate the Hotel Paris properties, and to thereby increase the length of stay and return rate of guests, and thus boost revenues and profitability." HR manager Lisa Cruz must now formulate functional policies and activities that support this competitive strategy by eliciting the required employee behaviors and competencies.

One of Lisa Cruz's biggest pay-related concerns is that the Hotel Paris compensation plan does not link pay to performance in any effective way. Because salaries were historically barely competitive, supervisors tended to award merit raises across the board. So, employees who performed well got only about the same raise as did those who performed poorly. Similarly, there was no bonus or incentive plan of any kind aimed at linking employee performance to strategically relevant employee capabilities and behaviors such as greeting guests in a friendly manner or providing expeditious check-ins and checkouts.

Based on their analysis, Lisa Cruz and the CFO concluded that by any metric, their company's incentive plan was inadequate. The percentage of the workforce whose merit increase or incentive pay is tied to performance is effectively zero, because managers awarded merit pay across the board. No more than 5% of the workforce (just the managers) was eligible for incentive pay. And, the percentage of difference in incentive pay between a low-performing and a high-performing employee was less than 2%. Lisa knew from industry studies that in top firms, more than 80% of the workforce had merit pay or incentive pay tied to performance. She also knew that in high-performing firms, there was at least a 5% or 6% difference in incentive pay between a low-performing and a high-performing employee. The CFO authorized Lisa to design a new strategy-oriented incentive plan for the Hotel Paris's employees. Their overall aim was to incentivize the pay plans of just about all the company's employees.

Lisa and the company's CFO laid out three measurable criteria that the new incentive plan had to meet. First, at least 90% (and preferably all) of the Hotel Paris's employees must be eligible for a merit increase or incentive pay that is tied to performance. Second, there must be at least a 10% difference in incentive pay between a low-performing and high-performing employee. Third, the new incentive plan had to include specific bonuses and evaluative mechanisms that linked employee behaviors in each job category with strategically relevant employee capabilities and behaviors. For example, front-desk clerks were to be rewarded in part based on the friendliness and speed of their check-ins and check-outs, and the housecleaning crew was to be evaluated and rewarded in part based on the percentage of room-cleaning infractions.

Questions

1. Discuss what you think of the measurable criteria that Lisa and the CFO set for their new incentive plan.
2. Given what you know about the Hotel Paris's strategic goals, list three or four specific behaviors you would incentivize for each of the following groups of employees: front-desk clerks, hotel managers, valets, housekeepers.
3. Lay out a complete incentive plan (including all long- and short-term incentives) for the Hotel Paris's hotel managers.

KEY TERMS

financial incentives, *392*	behavior modification, *395*	team (or group) incentive plan, *407*
productivity, *392*	variable pay, *395*	organization-wide incentive plan, *409*
fair day's work, *392*	piecework, *396*	
scientific management movement, *392*	straight piecework, *396*	profit-sharing plan, *409*
	standard hour plan, *396*	Scanlon plan, *409*
intrinsic motivation, *394*	merit pay (merit raise), *396*	gainsharing plan, *410*
expectancy, *394*	annual bonus, *404*	earnings-at-risk pay plan, *410*
instrumentality, *394*	stock option, *406*	employee stock ownership plan (ESOP), *411*
valence, *394*	golden parachute, *407*	

ENDNOTES

1. Jay Heizer and Barry Render, *Operations Management* (Upper Saddle River, NJ: Pearson, 2001), p. 15.

2. Even the traditional holiday bonus is being replaced by performance-based pay. A survey by consultants Hewitt Associates found that only about 5% of employers surveyed would distribute holiday cash bonuses. About 78% said they were offering performance-based awards, up from 51% about 15 years previously. "Cash Bonuses Are Ghosts of Holidays Past, Survey Says," *BNA Bulletin to Management*, December 13, 2005, p. 396. See also "Aligning Rewards with the Changing Employment Deal: 2006/2007 Strategic Rewards® Report," www.watsonwyatt.com/research/resrender.asp?id=2006-US-0038&page=1, accessed May 20, 2007.

3. "Few Employees See the Pay for Performance Connection," *Compensation & Benefits Review* 17, no. 2 (June 2003); "Most Workers Not Motivated by Cash," *Incentive Today*, July–August 2004, p. 19; and "Pay-for-Performance Plans' Impact Uncertain: Study," *Modern Healthcare*, May 24, 2004, p. 34.

4. Kathy Chu, "Employers See Lackluster Results Linking Salary to Performance," *The Wall Street Journal*, June 15, 2004, p. D2.

5. "Car Salesman Commission the Way It Works," http://carsalesprofessional.com/car-salesman-commission/, accessed June 26, 2011.

6. Ibid.

7. Peter Glendinning, "Kicking the Tires of Automotive Sales Compensation," *Compensation & Benefits Review*, September/October 2000, pp. 47–53; and Michele Marchetti, "Why Sales Contests Don't Work," *Sales and Marketing Management* 156 (January 2004), p. 19. See also "Salary and Bonus Gain Favor in Sales Pay (for Motor Vehicle Salespeople)," *Automotive News* 75, no. 5915 (February 5, 2001), p. 50.

8. Ted Turnasella, "Pay and Personality," *Compensation & Benefits Review*, March/April 2002, pp. 45–59.

9. Jason Shaw et al., "Reactions to Merit Pay Increases: A Longitudinal Test of a Signal Sensitivity Perspective," *Journal of Applied Psychology* 88, no. 3 (2003), pp. 538–544.

10. See, for example, Edward Deci, *Intrinsic Motivation* (New York: Plenum, 1975).

11. Ruth Kanfer, "Motivation Theory," in Harry C. Triandis, Marvin D. Dunnette, and Leaetta M. Hough, *Handbook of Industrial and Organizational Psychology* (Palo Alto, CA: Consulting Psychologists Press, 1994), p. 113. For a recent discussion about applying Vroom's principles, see B. Schaffer, "Leadership and Motivation." *Supervision* 69, no. 2 (February 2008), pp. 6–9.

12. For a discussion, see John P. Campbell and Robert Prichard, "Motivation Theory in Industrial and Organizational Psychology," in Marvin Dunnette (ed.), *Industrial and Organizational Psychology* (Chicago: Rand McNally, 1976), pp. 74–75; Kanfer, "Motivation Theory," pp. 115–116; and B. Schaffer, "Leadership and Motivation," op cit.

13. See, for example, Aubrey Daniels et al., "The Leader's Role in Pay Systems and Organizational Performance," *Compensation & Benefits Review*, May/June 2006, pp. 58–60; and Suzanne Peterson and Fred Luthans, "The Impact of Financial and Non-Financial Incentives on Business Unit Outcomes Over Time," *Journal of Applied Psychology* 91, no. 1 (2006), pp. 156–165.

14. See, for example, Mary Ducharme and Mark Podolsky, "Variable Pay: Its Impact on Motivation and Organisation Performance," *International Journal of Human Resources Development and Management* 6 (May 9, 2006), p. 68.

15. Ibid.

16. "Employers Use Pay to Lever Performance," *BNA Bulletin to Management*, August 21, 1997, p. 272; and "Variable Pay Is Superior to Bonus," *People Management*, February 24, 2011, p. 14.

17. See, for example, Kenan Abosch, "Variable Pay: Do We Have the Basics in Place?" *Compensation & Benefits Review*, July/August 1998, pp. 2–22.

18. See, for example, Diane Cadrain, "Cash Versus Non-Cash Rewards," *HR Magazine*, April 2003, pp. 81–87.

19. Richard Henderson, *Compensation Management* (Upper Saddle River, NJ: Prentice Hall, 2000), p. 463.

20. For a discussion of these, see Thomas Wilson, "Is It Time to Eliminate the Piece Rate Incentive System?" *Compensation & Benefits Review*, March/April 1992, pp. 43–49. For an example of piecework's use for workers working at home, see C. Tejada, "I Only Have 150 More to Go," *Wall Street Journal*, July 3, 2003, pp. B1, B2.

21. K. Oanh Ha, "California Workers Named in Articles Not Asked to Help in Piecework Probe," *Knight Ridder/Tribune News*, March 23, 2000, item 0008408e.

22. William Atkinson, "Incentive Pay Programs That Work in Textile," *Textile World* 151, no. 2 (February 2001), pp. 55–57.

23. See, for example, "Bias Creeps into Bonus Process, MIT Study Finds," *Workforce Management*, September 20, 2008, pp. 8–9.

24. The average uncorrected cross-sectional correlation was 17. Michael Harris et al., "A Longitudinal Examination of a Merit Pay System: Relationships Among Performance Ratings, Merit Increases, and Total Pay Increases," *Journal of Applied Psychology* 83, no. 5 (1998), pp. 825–831; see also, H. Risher, "Add Merit Pay for Performance," *Compensation and Benefits Review* 40 no. 6 (November/December 2008), pp. 22–29.

25. Eric R. Schulz and Denise Marie Tanguay, "Merit Pay in a Public Higher Education Institution: Questions of Impact and Attitudes," *Public Personnel Management* 35, no. 1 (Spring 2006), p. 71(18); Thomas S. Dee and Benjamin J. Keys, "Does Merit Pay Reward Good Teachers? Evidence from a Randomized Experiment," *Journal of Policy Analysis & Management* 23, no. 3 (Summer 2004), pp. 471–488. See also David N. Figlio and Lawrence W. Kenny, "Individual Teacher Incentives and Student Performance," *Journal of Public Economics* 91, no. 5–6 (June 2007), p. 901(14).

26. Fay Hansen, "Wage and Salary Trends," *Compensation & Benefits Review* 40, no. 5 (November/December 2008), p. 5.

27. Jonathan Glater, "Varying the Recipe Helps TV Operations Solve Morale Problem," *The New York Times*, March 7, 2001, p. C1.

28. Steve Yegge, quoted in http://glinden.blogspot.com/2006/09/management-and-incentives-at-google.html, accessed June 1, 2011.

29. Brian Skelton, "Dual-Career Tracks: Rewarding and Maintaining Technical Expertise," www.todaysengineer.org/2003/May/dual-ladder.asp, accessed June 1, 2011.

30. Peterson and Luthans, "The Impact of Financial and Nonfinancial Incentives."

31. See, for example, ibid., pp. 156–165.

32. "Employee Recognition," *WorldatWork*, April 2008, at www.worldatwork.org/waw/adimLink?id=25653, accessed November 3, 2009.

33. Michelle V. Rafter "Back in a Giving Mood," *Workforce Management* 88, no. 10 (September 14, 2009), pp. 25–29.

34. See, for example, Leslie Yerkes, *Fun Works: Creating Places Where People Love to Work* (San Francisco, CA: Berrett-Koehler Publishers, 2007).

35. Charlotte Huff, "Recognition That Resonates," *Workforce Management*, September 11, 2006, pp. 25–29. See also Scott Jeffrey and Victoria Schaffer, "The Motivational Properties of Tangible Incentives," *Compensation & Benefits Review*, May/June 2007, pp. 44–50.

36. Bob Nelson, *1001 Ways to Reward Employees* (New York: Workman Pub., 1994), p. 19. See also Sunny C. L. Fong and Margaret A. Shaffer, "The Dimensionality and Determinants of Pay Satisfaction: A Cross-Cultural Investigation of a Group Incentive Plan," *International Journal of Human Resource Management* 14, no. 4 (June 2003), p. 559(22).

37. William Bulkeley, "Incentives Systems Fine-Tune Pay/Bonus Plans," *The Wall Street Journal*, August 16, 2001, p. B4.

38. Jeremy Wuittner, "Plenty of Incentives to Use E.I.M. Software Systems," *American Banker* 168, no. 129 (July 8, 2003), p. 680.

39. Nina McIntyre, "Using EIM Technology to Successfully Motivate Employees," *Compensation & Benefits Review*, July/August 2001, pp. 57–60.

40. Frank Giancola, "Examining the Job Itself as a Source of Employee Motivation," *Compensation & Benefits Review* 43, no. 1 (2011), pp. 23–29.

41. www.deloitte.com/assets/Dcom-United-States/Local%20Assets/Documents/us_consulting_2010StrategicSalesCompensationSurvey_072910.pdf, accessed June 1, 2011.

42. Ibid.

43. Deloitte Varicent, 2010 Strategic Sales Compensation Survey, p. 6, at http://www.deloitte.com/assets/Dcom-United-States/Local%20Assets/Documents/us_consulting_2010StrategicSalesCompensationSurvey_072910.pdf, accessed August 29, 2011.

44. Straight salary by itself is not, of course, an incentive compensation plan as we use the term in this chapter.

45. Donna Harris, "Dealers Rethink How They Pay Salespeople," *Automotive News*, June 14, 2010, www.autonews.com/apps/pbcs.dll/article?AID=/20100614/RETAIL07/306149932m, accessed June 1, 2011.

46. Sonjun Luo, "Does Your Sales Incentive Plan Pay for Performance?" *Compensation & Benefits Review*, January/February 2003, pp. 18–24.

47. Scott Ladd, "May the Sales Force Be with You," *HR Magazine*, September 2010, p. 105.

48. Luo, "Does Your Sales Incentive Plan Pay for Performance," pp. 331–345. See also James M. Pappas and Karen E. Flaherty, "The Moderating Role of Individual-Difference Variables in Compensation Research," *Journal of Managerial Psychology* 21, no. 1 (January 2006), pp. 19–35; and T. B. Lopez, C. D. Hopkins, and M. A. Raymond, "Reward Preferences of Salespeople: How Do Commissions Rate?" *Journal of Personal Selling & Sales Management* 26, no. 4 (Fall 2006), p. 381(10).

49. Bill O'Connell, "Dead Solid Perfect: Achieving Sales Compensation Alignment," *Compensation & Benefits Review*, March/April 1996, pp. 46–47. See also C. Albrech, "Moving to a Global Sales Incentive Compensation Plan," *Compensation & Benefits Review* 41, no. 4 (July/August 2009), p. 52.

50. See, for example, Pankaj Madhani, "Realigning Fixed and Variable Pay in Sales Organizations: An Organizational Lifestyle Approach," *Compensation & Benefits Review* 42, no. 6, pp. 488–498.

51. Leslie Stretch, "From Strategy to Profitability: How Sales Compensation Management Drives Business Performance," *Compensation & Benefits Review*, May/June 2008, pp. 32–37.

52. S. Scott Sands, "Ineffective Quotas: The Hidden Threat to Sales Compensation Plans," *Compensation & Benefits Review* (March/April 2000), pp. 35–42. See also "Driving Profitable Sales Growth: 2006/2007 Report on Sales Effectiveness," www.watsonwyatt.com/research/resrender.asp?id=2006-US-0060&page=1, accessed May 20, 2007.

53. Peter Gundy, "Sales Compensation Programs: Built to Last," *Compensation & Benefits Review* (September/October 2002), pp. 21–28. See also T. B. Lopez, C. D. Hopkins, and M. A. Raymond, "Reward Preferences of Salespeople: How Do Commissions Rate?" *Journal of Personal Selling & Sales Management* 26, no. 4 (Fall 2006), p. 381(10).

54. "Driving Profitable Sales Growth: 2006/2007 Report on Sales Effectiveness," www.watsonwyatt.com/research/resrender.asp?id=2006-US-0060&page=1, accessed May 20, 2007.

55. Varicent, "2010 Strategic Sales."

56. Bob Conlin, "Best Practices for Designing New Sales Compensation Plans," *Compensation & Benefits Review*, March/April 2008, p. 51.

57. Ibid., p. 53.

58. www.vuesoftware.com/Product/Compensation_Management.aspx, accessed June 1, 2011.

59. Ibid.

60. Mark Meltzer and Howard Goldsmith, "Executive Compensation for Growth Companies," *Compensation & Benefits Review*, November/December 1997, pp. 41–50; and Barbara Kiviat, "Everyone into the Bonus Pool," *Time* 162, no. 24 (December 15, 2003), p. A5.

61. www.mercer.com/pressrelease/details.jhtml/dynamic/idContent/1263210, accessed January 2, 2007.

62. Meltzer and Goldsmith, "Executive Compensation for Growth Companies," pp. 41–50. See also Patricia Zingheim and Jay Schuster, "Designing Pay and Rewards in Professional Companies," *Compensation & Benefits Review*, January/February 2007, pp. 55–62; and Ronald Bottano and Russell Miller, "Making Executive Compensation Count: Tapping into the New Long-Term Incentive Portfolio," *Compensation & Benefits Review*, July/August 2007, pp. 43–47.

63. George Yancey, "Aligning the CEO's Incentive Plan with Criteria that Drive Organizational Performance," *Compensation & Benefits Review* 42, no. 3 (2010), pp. 190–196.

64. See "The Impact of Sarbanes-Oxley on Executive Compensation," www.thelenreid.com, accessed December 11, 2003. See also Brent Longnecker and James Krueger, "The Next Wave of Compensation Disclosure," *Compensation & Benefits Review*, January/February 2007, pp. 50–54.

65. James Reda, "Executive Compensation: Balancing Risk, Performance and Pay," *Financial Executive* 25, no. 9 (November 2009), pp. 46–50.

66. Meltzer and Goldsmith, "Executive Compensation for Growth Companies," pp. 44–45; Max Smith and Ben Stradley, "New Research Tracks the Evolution of Annual Incentive Plans," *Executive Compensation*, Towers Watson, 2010, Towerswatson.com, accessed August 28, 2011.

67. Max Smith and Ben Stradley, "New Research Tracks the Evolution of Annual Incentive Plans," *Executive Compensation*, Towers Watson, 2010, Towerswatson.com, accessed August 28, 2011.

68. Ibid.

69. Ibid.

70. Ibid.

71. Meltzer and Goldsmith, "Executive Compensation for Growth Companies," p. 44. Fay Hansen, "Salary and Wage Trends," *Compensation & Benefits Review*, March/April 2004, pp. 9–10.

72. Bruce Ellig, "Executive Pay Financial Measurements," *Compensation & Benefits Review*, September/October 2008, pp. 42–49.

73. Dionne Searcey, "Transocean Executives to Donate Bonuses," *The Wall Street Journal*, April 6, 2011, p. B1.

74. Benjamin Dunford et al., "Underwater Stock Options and Voluntary Executive Turnover: A Multidisciplinary Perspective Integrating Behavioral and Economic Theories," *Personnel Psychology* 61 (2008), pp. 687–726.

75. Phred Dvorak, "Slump Yields Employee Rewards," *The Wall Street Journal*, October 10, 2008, p. B2; Don Clark and Jerry DiColo, "Intel to Let Workers Exchange Options," *The Wall Street Journal*, March 24, 2009, p. B3.

76. Wm. Gerard Sanders and Donald Hambrick, "Swinging for the Fences: The Effects of CEO Stock Options on Company Risk-Taking and Performance," *Academy of Management Journal* 50, no. 5 (2007), pp. 1055–1078.

77. "Study Finds That Directly Owning Stock Shares Leads to Better Results," *Compensation & Benefits Review*, March/April 2001, p. 7. See also Ira Kay, "Whither the Stock Option? While Stock Options Lose More Luster as Executive Motivators, Compensation Committees Face Challenges, Including Selecting Other Forms of Stock Incentives," *Financial Executive* 20, no. 2 (March–April 2004), p. 46(3); and Lucian A. Bebchuk and Jesse M. Fried, "Pay Without Performance: Overview of the Issues," *Academy of Management Perspective* 20, no. 1 (February 2006), p. 5(20).

78. www.mercer.com/pressrelease/details.jhtml/dynamic/idContent/1263210, accessed January 2, 2007.

79. www.nceo.org/main/article.php/id/43/, accessed June 1, 2011.

80. Louis Lavelle, "How to Halt the Options Express," *BusinessWeek*, September 9, 2002.

81. www.nceo.org/main/article.php/id/43/, accessed June 1, 2011.

82. Christine Bevilacqua and Parbudyal Singh, "Pay for Performance—Panacea or Pandora's Box? Revisiting an Old Debate in the Current Economic Environment," *Compensation & Benefits Review*, September/October 2009, pp. 21–26.

83. www.forbes.com/2010/06/14/goldman-sachs-paulson-markets-lloyd-blankfein.html, accessed May 21, 2011.

84. Under IRS regulations, companies cannot deduct all golden parachute payments made to executives, and the executive must pay a 20% excise tax on the golden parachute payments. "Final Regs Issued for Golden Parachute Payments," *Executive Tax and Management Report* 66, no. 17 (September 2003), p. 1.

85. "Conseco Not Alone on Executive Perks," *Knight-Ridder/Tribune Business News*, August 28, 2003, item 03240015. See also "Realities of Executive Compensation—2006/2007 Report on Executive Pay and Stock Options," www.watsonwyatt.com/research/resrender.asp?id=2006-US-0085&page=1), accessed May 20, 2007.

86. Other suggestions are as follows: equal payments to all members on the team; differential payments to team members based on their contributions to the team's performance; and differential payments determined by a ratio of each group member's base pay to the total base pay of the group. See Kathryn Bartol and Laura Hagmann, "Team Based Pay Plans: A Key to Effective Team Work," *Compensation & Benefits Review*, November–December 1992, pp. 24–29. See also Charlotte Garvey, "Steer Teams with the Right Pay," *HR Magazine*, May 2002, pp. 70–71, and K. Merriman, "On the Folly of Rewarding Team Performance, While Hoping for Teamwork," *Compensation & Benefits Review* 41, no. 1 (January/February 2009), pp. 61–66.

87. Richard Seaman, "The Case Study: Rejuvenating an Organization with Team Pay," *Compensation & Benefits Review*, September/October 1997, pp. 25–30. See also Peter Wright, Mark Kroll, Jeffrey A. Krug, and Michael Pettus, "Influences of Top Management Team Incentives on Firm Risk Taking," *Strategic Management Journal* 28, no. 1 (January 2007), pp. 81–89.

88. K. Merriman, "On the Folly of Rewarding Team Performance, While Hoping for Teamwork," *Compensation & Benefits Review*, January/February 2009, pp. 61–66.

89. As another example, see, Bernd Irlenbusch and Gabriele K. Lünser, "Relative Rewards within Team-Based Compensation," November 2006. IZA Discussion Paper No. 2423. Available at SSRN: http://ssrn.com/abstract=947075, accessed May 21, 2011.

90. Seongsu Kim, "Does Profit Sharing Increase Firms' Profits?" *Journal of Labor Research*, Spring 1998, pp. 351–371. See also Jacqueline Coyle-Shapiro et al., "Using Profit-Sharing to Enhance Employee Attitudes: A Longitudinal Examination of the Effects on Trust and Commitment," *Human Resource Management* 41, no. 4 (Winter 2002), pp. 423–449.

91. Alberto Bayo-Moriones and Martin - Larraza-Kintana, "Profit Sharing Plans and Effective Commitment: Does the Context Matter?" *Human Resource Management* 48, no. 2 (March–April 2009), pp. 207–226.

92. Kaja Whitehouse, "More Companies Offer Packages Linking Pay Plans to Performance," *The Wall Street Journal*, December 13, 2005, p. B4.

93. Under the U.S. tax code, "any arrangement that provides for the deferral of compensation in a year later than the year in which the compensation was earned may be considered a deferred compensation arrangement." Steven Friedman, "2008 Compliance Strategies for Employers in Light of Final 409A Regulations," *Compensation & Benefits Review*, March/April 2008, p. 27.

94. www.axa-equitable.com/retirement/how-do-company-profit-sharing-plans-work.html, accessed June 1, 2011.

95. Joseph Martocchio, *Strategic Compensation* (Upper Saddle River, NJ: Prentice Hall, 2006), pp. 163–165.

96. Brian Graham-Moore and Timothy Ross, *The Scanlon Way to Improved Productivity: A Practical Guide* (New York: Wiley, 1978), p. 2. For a review of potential problems, see Denis Collins, "Death of a Gainsharing Plan: Power Politics and Participatory Management," *Organizational Dynamics* 24 (Summer 1995), pp. 23–37.

97. These are based in part on Steven Markham, K. Dow Scott, and Walter Cox Jr., "The Evolutionary Development of a Scanlon Plan," *Compensation & Benefits Review*, March/April 1992, pp. 50–56. See also Woodruff Imberman, "Are You Ready to Boost Productivity with a Gainsharing Plan? To Survive and Prosper in Our Hyper-competitive Environment, Board Converters Must Motivate Employees at All Levels," *Official Board Markets* 82, no. 47 (November 25, 2006), p. 5(2); and James Reynolds and Daniel Roble, "Combining Pay for Performance with Gainsharing," *Healthcare Financial Management* 60, no. 11 (November 2006), p. 50(6).

98. Markham et al., "The Evolutionary Development of a Scanlon Plan," p. 51.

99. Barry W. Thomas and Madeline Hess Olson, "Gainsharing: The Design Guarantees Success," *Personnel Journal*, May 1998, pp. 73–79; A. C. Gardner, "Goal Setting and Gainsharing: The Evidence on Effectiveness," *Compensation and Benefits Review* 43, no. 4 (July/August 2011), pp. 236–244.

100. Paraphrased from Woodruff Imbermann, "Boosting Plant Performance with Gainsharing," *Business Horizons*, November–December 1992, p. 77. See also Max Reynolds and Joane Goodroe, "The Return of Gainsharing: Gainsharing Appears to Be Enjoying a Renaissance," *Healthcare Financial Management* 59, no. 11 (November 2005), p. 114(6); and Dong-One Kim, "The Benefits and Costs of Employee Suggestions Under Gainsharing," *Industrial and Labor Relations Review* 58, no. 4 (July 2005), p. 631(22); hospital gainsharing discussion in Anjana Patel, "Gainsharing: Past, Present, and Future," *Healthcare Financial Management* 60, no. 9 (September 2006), pp. 124–128, 130.

101. Paul Rossler and C. Patrick Koelling, "The Effect of Gainsharing on Business Performance at a Paper Mill," *National Productivity Review*, Summer 1993, pp. 365–382; hospital gainsharing discussion in Anjana Patel, "Gainsharing: Past, Present, and Future," *Healthcare Financial Management* 60, no. 9 (September 2006), pp. 124–128, 130.

102. See for example, http://www.dol.gov/dol/topic/health-plans/erisa.htm, accessed October 2, 2011.

103. Steven Etkind, "ESOPs Create Liquidity for Share Holders and Help Diversify Their Assets," *Estate Planning* 24, no. 4 (May 1998), pp. 158–165. See also S. Coomes, "Employee Stock Plans Can Save Taxes, Attract Talent," *Nation's Restaurant News* 42, no. 36 (September 15, 2008), p. 12.

104. William Smith, Harold Lazarus, and Harold Murray Kalkstein, "Employee Stock Ownership Plans: Motivation and Moral Issues," *Compensation & Benefits Review*, September/October 1990, pp. 37–46. See also "ESOP Trustees Breached Their Fiduciary Duties Under ERISA by Failing to Make Prudent Investigation into Value of Stock Purchased by ESOP," *Tax Management Compensation Planning Journal* 30, no. 10 (October 4, 2002), p. 301(1); and J. D. Mamorsky, "Court Approves ERISA Action Against ENRON Executives, Trustee, and Plan Auditor for Retirement Plan Losses," *Journal of Compensation and Benefits* 20, no. 1 (January–February 2004), p. 46(7); G. Ledford, et al., "The Effects of Stock Ownership on Employee Attitudes and Behavior: Evidence from the Rewards of Work Studies," *Journal of Compensation & Benefits* 20, no. 2 (March/April 2004), pp. 24–30.

105. James Sesil et al., "Broad-Based Employee Stock Options in U.S. New Economy Firms," *British Journal of Industrial Relations* 40, no. 2 (June 2002), pp. 273–294.

106. Eric Dash, "Time Warner Stops Granting Stock Options to Most of Staff," *The New York Times*, February 19, 2005, item 128921996.

107. Peter Kurlander, "Building Incentive Compensation Management Systems: What Can Go Wrong?" *Compensation & Benefits Review*, July/August 2001, pp. 52–56. The average percentage of payroll employers spent on broad-based performance pay plans rose till 2005, and then has fallen for the past few years. "Companies Pull Back from Performance Pay," *Workforce Management*, October 23, 2006, p. 26. For one of many good discussions of why pay for performance tends to be ineffectual, see

Fay Hansen, "Where's the Merit-Pay Pay-off?" *Workforce Management*, November 3, 2008, pp. 33–39.

108. For a checklist for determining when pay for performance is advisable, see Myron Glassman et al., "Evaluating Pay for Performance Systems: Critical Issues for Implementation," *Compensation & Benefits Review* 42, no. 4 (2010), p. 236.

109. Suzanne Peterson and Fred Luthans, "The Impact of Financial and Nonfinancial Incentives on Business Unit Outcomes over Time," *Journal of Applied Psychology* 91, no. 1 (2006), pp. 156–165.

110. Ibid., p. 159.

111. Ibid., p. 159.

112. Ibid., p. 162. See also "Delivering Incentive Compensation Plans That Work," *Financial Executive* 25, no. 7 (September 2009), pp. 52–54.

113. Reed Taussig, "Managing Cash Based Incentives," *Compensation & Benefits Review*, March/April 2002, pp. 65–68. See also Nigel Nicholson, "How to Motivate Your Problem People," *Harvard Business Review*, January 2003, pp. 57–65; and "Incentives, Motivation and Workplace Performance," Incentive Research Foundation, www.incentivescentral.org/employees/whitepapers, accessed May 19, 2007.

114. "Two Frameworks for a More ROI-Minded Rewards Plan," *Pay for Performance Report,* February 2003, p. 1, www.ioma.com/issues/PFP/2003_02/518132-1.html, accessed November 3, 2009; and Alan Robinson and Dean Schroeder, "Rewards That Really Work," *Security Management*, July 2004, pp. 30–34. See also Patricia Zingheim and Jay Schuster, "What Are Key Pay Issues Right Now?" *Compensation & Benefits Review*, May/June 2007, pp. 51–55.

115. See, for example, Jessica Marquez, "Retooling Pay: Premium on Productivity," *Workforce Management* 84, no. 12 (November 7, 2005), pp. 1, 22–23, 25–26, 28, 30; www.scribd.com/doc/12824332/NUCOR-CORP-8K-Events-or-Changes-Between-Quarterly-Reports-20090224, accessed November 3, 2009; and www.nucor.com/careers, accessed November 3, 2009.

116. Theodore Weinberger, "Evaluating the Effectiveness of an Incentive Plan Design Within Company Constraints," *Compensation & Benefits Review*, November/December 2005, pp. 27–33; Howard Risher, "Adding Merit to Pay for Performance," *Compensation & Benefits Review*, November/December 2008, pp. 22–29.

117. Janet Wiscombe, "Can Pay for Performance Really Work?" *Workforce*, August 2001, p. 30.

118. Susan Marks, "Incentives That Really Reward and Motivate," *Workforce*, June 2001, pp. 108–114.

119. Although not an issue at Nucor, the employer needs to beware of instituting so many incentive plans (cash bonuses, stock options, recognition programs, and so on) tied to so many different behaviors that employees don't have a clear priority of the employer's priorities. See, for example, Stephen Rubenfeld and Jannifer David, "Multiple Employee Incentive Plans: Too Much of a Good Thing?" *Compensation & Benefits Review*, March/April 2006, pp. 35–43.

13

Benefits and Services

LEARNING OBJECTIVES

1. Name and define each of the main pay for time not worked benefits.

2. Describe each of the main insurance benefits.

3. Discuss the main retirement benefits.

4. Outline the main employees' services benefits.

5. Explain the main flexible benefit programs.

L ike many companies recently, NES Rentals Holdings Inc. wants to make cost control part of its strategy. NES (www.nesrentals.com) rents and sells construction equipment, such as the aerial lifts that roadside crews use to lift workers to repair traffic lights.[1] It's a competitive business, and the question was, where could they cut costs, without undermining their reputation for great products and service?

Access a host of interactive learning aids at **www.mymanagementlab.com** to help strengthen your understanding of the chapter concepts.

WHERE ARE WE NOW . . .

We've now covered two of the three pay plan components—salary (or wages) and incentives. The main purpose of this chapter is to discuss employee benefits. We discuss four main types of plans: supplemental pay benefits (such as sick leave and vacation pay), insurance benefits (such as workers' compensation), retirement benefits (such as pensions), and employee services (such as child-care facilities). Because legal considerations loom large in any benefits decision, we cover applicable federal laws and their implications for managers. This chapter completes our discussion of employee compensation. The next chapter, Chapter 14 (Ethics and Employee Rights), starts a new part of this book, and focuses on another important human resource task—managing employee relations.

THE BENEFITS PICTURE TODAY

"What are your benefits?" is the first thing many applicants ask. **Benefits**—indirect financial and nonfinancial payments employees receive for continuing their employment with the company—are an important part of just about everyone's compensation.[2] They include things like health and life insurance, pensions, time off with pay, and child care assistance.

Virtually all employers offer some health insurance coverage.[3] Employee benefits account for between 33%–40% of wages and salaries (or about 28% of total payrolls). Legally required benefits (like unemployment insurance) are the most expensive benefits costs, followed by health insurance. Figure 13-1 summarizes the breakdown of benefits as a percentage of employee compensation.

Health care benefit costs are rising. Health benefit costs rose 8% in 2011 and an estimated 8.5% in 2012, making total 2012 health benefit costs per employee well over $9,500.[4] Employers contend that the new Patient Protection and Affordable Care Act will raise this more, as we will see.

Employees understand the value of health benefits. In one survey, 78% of employees cited health care benefits as most crucial to retaining them; 75% cited compensation. But the same survey found that only 34% are satisfied with their health care benefits.[5]

Policy Issues

Employers therefore need to design benefits packages carefully. The list of policy issues includes what benefits to offer, who receives coverage, whether to include retirees in the plan, whether to deny benefits to employees during initial "probationary" periods, how to finance benefits, cost-containment procedures, and how to communicate benefits options to employees.[6]

Legal issues loom large. Federal laws mandate some benefits (such as Social Security) while other benefits are at the employer's discretion (see Table 13-1). However, federal law also impacts discretionary benefits such as vacation leave. And employers must adhere to the laws of the states in which they do business. For example, California requires most state contractors to provide domestic partner benefits for employees.[7]

There are many benefits and various ways to classify them. We will classify them as (1) pay for time not worked (such as vacations), (2) insurance benefits, (3) retirement benefits, and (4) services. We will start our discussion with pay for time not worked. But in any case, the benefits should make sense in terms of supporting the employer's strategy, as the accompanying Strategic Context feature illustrates.

FIGURE 13-1 Relative Importance of Employer Costs for Employee Compensation, March 2011

Sourc.e: www.bls.gov/news.release/ecec.nr0.htm, accessed June 1, 2011.

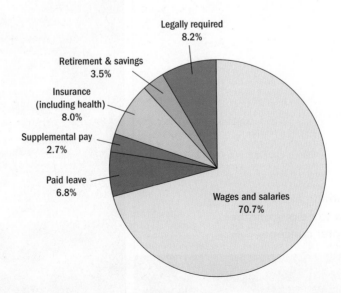

TABLE 13-1 Some Required and Discretionary Benefits

Benefits Required by Federal or Most State Law	Benefits Discretionary on Part of Employer[*]
Social Security	Disability, health, and life insurance
Unemployment insurance	Pensions
Workers' compensation	Paid time off for vacations, holidays, sick leave, personal leave, jury duty, etc.
Leaves under Family Medical Leave Act	Employee assistance and counseling programs, "family friendly" benefits for child care, elder care, flexible work schedules, etc., executive perquisites

[*]Although not required under federal law, all these benefits are regulated in some way by federal law, as explained in this chapter.

THE STRATEGIC CONTEXT

NES Rentals

As with a company's salary and incentive plans, its benefits plan must make sense in terms of, and support, the firm's strategy. As we saw in Chapters 11 and 12, managers must align each component of the employer's total rewards program so that each contributes in a meaningful way to fostering the employee behaviors that the company needs to achieve its strategic goals.

Seeking to cut costs while maintaining its reputation for great products and service, NES Rentals sent their employees home. Today, three-fourths of their customer support, collections, finance, and other back-office workers at their Chicago office work from home at least part of the week.[8] They therefore no longer have dedicated desks, but share space when in the office. The CEO says the results have been good. Productivity has increased 20%. Employee turnover dropped from 7% in 2009 to "virtually non-existent" in 2010. NES is leasing 40% less office space, and will save $100,000 in real estate expenses. And he estimates NES's total savings from instituting this new telecommuting benefit at about $350,000 annually. Introducing an employee benefit turned out to be a smart way to support NES's strategy.[9]

---

1 Name and define each of the main pay for time not worked benefits.

PAY FOR TIME NOT WORKED

Pay for time not worked—also called **supplemental pay benefits**—is the most costly benefit, because of the large amount of time off that most employees receive. Common time-off-with-pay include holidays, vacations, jury duty, funeral leave, military duty, personal days, sick leave, sabbatical leave, maternity leave, and unemployment insurance payments for laid-off or terminated employees.

Unemployment Insurance

All states have **unemployment insurance** (or **compensation**) laws. These provide benefits if a person is unable to work through no fault of his or her own. The benefits derive from a tax on employers that can range from 0.1% to 5% of taxable payroll in most states. An employer's unemployment tax rate reflects its rate of employee terminations. Although they all follow federal guidelines, states have their

---

benefits
Indirect financial and nonfinancial payments employees receive for continuing their employment with the company.

supplemental pay benefits
Benefits for time not worked such as unemployment insurance, vacation and holiday pay, and sick pay.

unemployment insurance (or compensation)
Provides benefits if a person is unable to work through some fault other than his or her own.

Unemployment insurance/compensation laws provide short-term benefits to people who lose their jobs through no fault of their own.

Source: Greta Pratt/Corbis Images.

own unemployment laws. Unemployment tax rates are rising in many states. For example, prior to the recent recession, Maryland's unemployment insurance tax rate was 0.3% or lower. The rate now averages 2.2% to 13.5% per employee, depending upon the employer's claim history.[10]

Firms aren't required to let everyone they dismiss receive unemployment benefits—only those released through no fault of their own. Thus, strictly speaking, a worker fired for chronic lateness can't legitimately claim benefits. But many managers take a lackadaisical attitude toward protecting their employers. Employers therefore spend thousands of dollars on unemployment taxes that would not be necessary if they protected themselves.

The main rule is to keep a list of written warnings. Beyond that, the checklist in Table 13-2 can help protect employers. Actions like these should enable you to demonstrate that the dismissal resulted from the person's inadequate performance. (Those you fire during their initial "90-day probation" *are* eligible for unemployment, so follow that checklist for them, too.)

TABLE 13-2 An Unemployment Insurance Cost-Control Checklist

Do You:

☐ Keep documented history of lateness, absence, and warning notices

☐ Warn chronically late employees before discharging them

☐ Have rule that 3 days' absence without calling in is reason for automatic discharge

☐ Request doctor's note on return to work after absence

☐ Make written approval for personal leave mandatory

☐ Stipulate date for return to work from leave

☐ Obtain a signed resignation statement

☐ Mail job abandonment letter if employee fails to return on time

☐ Document all instances of poor performance

☐ Require supervisors to document the steps taken to remedy the situation

☐ Document employee's refusal of advice and direction

☐ Require all employees to sign a statement acknowledging acceptance of firm's policies and rules

☐ File the protest against a former employee's unemployment claim on time (usually within 10 days)

☐ Use proper terminology on claim form and attach documented evidence regarding separation

☐ Attend hearings and appeal unwarranted claims

☐ Check every claim against the individual's personnel file

☐ Routinely conduct exit interviews to produce information for protesting unemployment claims

Vacations and Holidays

Most firms offer vacation leave benefits. About 90% of full time workers and 40% of part timers get paid holidays, an average of 8 paid holidays off.[11] The most common U.S. paid holidays include New Year's Day, Memorial Day, Independence Day, Labor Day, Thanksgiving Day, and Christmas Day. Other common holidays include Martin Luther King, Jr. Day, Good Friday, Presidents' Day, Veterans' Day, the Friday after Thanksgiving, and the days before Christmas Day and New Year's Day.[12] On average, American workers get about 9 days of vacation leave after 1 year's employment, about 14 days after 5 years, and 17 after 10 years.[13] Elsewhere, vacation allowances vary from 6 days in Mexico to 10 days in Japan to 25 days in Sweden and France.

Firms have to address several holiday- and vacation-related policy issues. They must decide, of course, how many days off employees will get, and which days (if any) will be the paid holidays. Other vacation policy decisions include:

- Will employees get their regular base pay while on vacation, or vacation pay based on average earnings (which may include overtime)?
- Will you pay employees for accrued vacation time if they leave before taking their vacations?
- Will you pay employees for a holiday if they don't come to work the day before and the day after the holiday?
- And, should we pay some premium—such as time and a half—when employees must work on holidays?

More firms are moving to a more flexible vacation leave approach. For example, IBM gives each of its 350,000 plus employees at least 3 weeks' vacation. However, IBM doesn't formally track how much vacation each person takes. Instead, employees simply make informal vacation arrangements with their direct supervisors.[14]

Wage surveys and Web sites like www.hrtools.com provide sample vacation policies for inclusion in the firm's employee manual.

SOME LEGAL ASPECTS OF VACATIONS AND HOLIDAYS Although federal law does not require vacation benefits, the employer must still formulate vacation policy with care. As an example, many employers' vacation policies say vacation pay accrues, say, on a biweekly basis. By doing so, these employers obligate themselves to pay employees pro rata vacation pay when they leave the firm. But if the employer's vacation policy requires that a new employee pass his or her first employment anniversary *before becoming entitled* to a vacation, the employee gets no vacation pay if he or she leaves during that first year.

One frequent question is whether the employer can cancel an employee's scheduled vacation, for instance, due to a rush of orders. Here it's important that the employer formulate its vacation policy so it's clear that the employer reserves the right to require vacation cancellation and rescheduling if production so demands.

Sick Leave

Sick leave provides pay to employees when they're out of work due to illness. Most sick leave policies grant full pay for a specified number of sick days—usually up to about 12 per year. The sick days usually accumulate at the rate of, say, 1 day per month of service.

Sick leave is problematical for employers. The problem is that while many employees use their sick days only when sick, others use it whether sick or not. In one survey, personal illnesses accounted for only about 45% of unscheduled sick leave absences. Family issues (27%), personal needs (13%), and a mentality of "entitlement" (9%) were other reasons cited.[15] Absenteeism costs U.S. employers perhaps $100 billion per year, with personal illness accounting for about a third of the absences.[16]

sick leave
Provides pay to an employee when he or she is out of work because of illness.

COST-REDUCTION TACTICS   Employers use several tactics to reduce excessive sick leave absence. Some repurchase unused sick leave at the end of the year by paying their employees a sum for each sick leave day not used. The problem is that legitimately sick employees may come to work. Others have held monthly lotteries in which only employees with perfect monthly attendance are eligible for a cash prize. At Marriott, employees can trade the value of some sick days for other benefits. Others aggressively investigate all absences, for instance, by calling the absent employees at their homes.[17]

Many employers use *pooled paid leave plans* (or *"banks"*).[18] These plans lump together sick leave, vacation, and personal days into a single leave pool. For example, one hospital previously granted new employees 25 days off per year (10 vacation days, 3 personal days, and 12 sick days). Employees used, on average, 5 of those 12 sick days (as well as all vacations and personal days).[19] The pooled paid leave plan allowed new employees to accrue 18 days to use as they saw fit. ("Catastrophic leaves"—short-term illnesses causing absences for more than 5 consecutive workdays, and special absences like bereavement leave—were handled separately.) The pooled plan reduced absences. Most firms don't include federal holidays in their paid time off "banks."[20]

Evidence-Based HR: Tracking Sick Leave

For many employers, sick leave is out of control simply because they don't measure it. In one survey, only 57% of employers formally tracked sick days for their exempt employees and only 46% tracked personal days.[21] Three-fourths of the employers could not even provide an estimate of what their sick pay was costing as a percentage of payrolls. Therefore, before taking other cost control steps the employer should have a system in place for monitoring sick leaves and for measuring their financial impact. The accompanying HR as a Profit Center feature expands on this.

The same applies to controlling health care costs. Some estimate that 5% to 15% of medical plans' enrollees may include ineligible dependents such as ex-spouses. Periodically auditing dependents can thus translate into significant health care cost savings.[22]

HR AS A PROFIT CENTER

Cutting Absences at the Driver and Vehicle Licensing Agency

Government agencies are as (if not more) susceptible to excessive sick leave claims as are private companies. So when she came in as a director of the United Kingdom's Driver and Vehicle Licensing Agency, part of the Department of Transport, Judith Whitaker saw that steps were needed to address the agency's sickness absence rate.[23] The rate had peaked at 14 days out per employee in 2005, at a cost of about $20 million per year (£10.3 million). The rate was down to 12.5 days by 2008, but was still too high.

The new director organized a multi-faceted human resource management initiative to address the sick leave absence problem.[24] The agency set a goal of reducing absences by 30% by 2010. Agency directors received absence-reduction goals, and their progress was tracked. The agency introduced new policies and procedures dealing with special leave, rehabilitation support, and keeping in touch with absentees. They introduced new policies to make it easier for employees to swap work shifts, and introduced a guaranteed leave day policy. They also introduced new smoking cessation classes and a weight management program.

These and similar actions were apparently very successful. The average annual sickness absence rate in 2010 was down to 7.5 days per employee. Improved attendance probably contributed to a 7% productivity increase in 2009–2010. This translates into a reduction in the agency's costs of about $48 million dollars (£24.4 million).

Parental Leave and the Family and Medical Leave Act

Parental leave is an important benefit. About half of workers are women, and about 80% will become pregnant during their work lives. Furthermore, many people head single-parent households. Under the Pregnancy Discrimination Act, employers must treat women applying for pregnancy leave as they would any other employee requesting a leave under the employer's policies. Beyond this, Congress passed, as noted, the Family and Medical Leave Act of 1993 (FMLA). Among other things (see Figure 13-2), the FMLA stipulates that:[25]

1. Private employers of 50 or more employees must provide eligible employees (women or men) up to 12 weeks of unpaid leave for their own serious illness, the birth or adoption of a child, or the care of a seriously ill child, spouse, or parent.

2. Employers may require employees to take any unused paid sick leave or annual leave as part of the 12-week leave provided in the law.

3. Employees taking leave are entitled to receive health benefits while they are on unpaid leave, under the same terms and conditions as when they were on the job.

4. Employers must guarantee most employees the right to return to their previous or equivalent position with no loss of benefits at the end of the leave.

FIGURE 13-2 Your Rights Under the Family and Medical Leave Act of 1993

Your Rights
under the
Family and Medical Leave Act of 1993

FMLA requires covered employers to provide up to 12 weeks of unpaid, job-protected leave to "eligible" employees for certain family and medical reasons. Employees are eligible if they have worked for their employer for at least one year, and for 1,250 hours over the previous 12 months, and if there are at least 50 employees within 75 miles. The FMLA permits employees to take leave on an intermittent basis or to work a reduced schedule under certain circumstances.

Reasons for Taking Leave:

Unpaid leave must be granted for *any* of the following reasons:

- to care for the employee's child after birth, or placement for adoption or foster care;
- to care for the employee's spouse, son or daughter, or parent who has a serious health condition; or
- for a serious health condition that makes the employee unable to perform the employee's job.

At the employee's or employer's option, certain kinds of *paid* leave may be substituted for unpaid leave.

Advance Notice and Medical Certification:

The employee may be required to provide advance leave notice and medical certification. Taking of leave may be denied if requirements are not met.

- The employee ordinarily must provide 30 days advance notice when the leave is "foreseeable."
- An employer may require medical certification to support a request for leave because of a serious health condition, and may require second or third opinions (at the employer's expense) and a fitness for duty report to return to work.

Job Benefits and Protection:

- For the duration of FMLA leave, the employer must maintain the employee's health coverage under any "group health plan."

- Upon return from FMLA leave, most employees must be restored to their original or equivalent positions with equivalent pay, benefits, and other employment terms.
- The use of FMLA leave cannot result in the loss of any employment benefit that accrued prior to the start of an employee's leave.

Unlawful Acts by Employers:

FMLA makes it unlawful for any employer to:
- interfere with, restrain, or deny the exercise of any right provided under FMLA.
- discharge or discriminate against any person for opposing any practice made unlawful by FMLA or for involvement in any proceeding under or relating to FMLA.

Enforcement:

- The U.S. Department of Labor is authorized to investigate and resolve complaints of violations.
- An eligible employee may bring a civil action against an employer for violations.

FMLA does not affect any Federal or State law prohibiting discrimination, or supersede any State or local law or collective bargaining agreement which provides greater family or medical leave rights.

For Additional Information:

If you have access to the Internet visit our FMLA website: **http://www.dol.gov.** To locate your nearest Wage-Hour Office, telephone our Wage-Hour toll-free information and help line at 1-866-4USWAGE (1-866-487-9243): a customer service representative is available to assist you with referral information from 8am to 5pm **in your time zone;** or log onto our Home Page at **http://www.wagehour.dol.gov.**

U.S. Department of Labor
Employment Standards Administration
Wage and Hour Division
Washington, D.C. 20210

WH Publication 1420
Revised August 2001

Employers have expressed some dissatisfaction with the FMLA. In a survey of 416 human resource professionals, about half said they approved leaves they believed were not legitimate, but felt they had to grant because of vague interpretations of the law.[26] Tracking leaves was another problem.[27]

FMLA leaves are usually unpaid, but they're not costless. The costs associated with hiring temporary replacements, training them, and compensating for their lower productivity can be considerable.

FMLA GUIDELINES Therefore, the manager who wants to avoid granting non-required FMLA leaves needs to understand the FMLA. For example, to be eligible for leave under the FMLA, the employee must have worked for the employer for at least a total of 12 months and have worked (not just been paid, as someone might be if on leave) for 1,250 or more hours in the past 12 consecutive months.[28] If these do not apply, no leave is required.

FIGURE 13-3 Online Request for Leave Form

Source: www.opm.gov/FORMS/PDF_FILL/opm71.pdf, accessed April 28, 2009.

Request for Leave or Approved Absence

1. Name *(Last, first, middle)*

2. Employee or Social Security Number

3. Organization

4. **Type of Leave/Absence**

Check appropriate box(es) and enter date and time below)	Date From	Date To	Time From	Time To	Total Hours
☐ Accrued annual leave					
☐ Restored annual leave					
☐ Advance annual leave					
☐ Accrued sick leave					
☐ Advance sick leave					

Purpose:
- ☐ Illness/injury/incapacitation of requesting employee
- ☐ Medical/dental/optical examination of requesting employee
- ☐ Care of family member, including medical/dental/optical examination of family member, or bereavement
- ☐ Care of family member with a serious health condition
- ☐ Other

☐ Compensatory time off					
☐ Other paid absence *(specify in remarks)*					
☐ Leave without pay					

5. **Family and Medical Leave**

If annual leave, sick leave, or leave without pay will be used under the Family and Medical Leave Act of 1993 (FMLA), please provide the following information:

☐ I hereby invoke my entitlement to family and medical leave for:
- ☐ Birth/Adoption/Foster care
- ☐ Serious health condition of spouse, son, daughter, or parent
- ☐ Serious health condition of self

Contact your supervisor and/or your personnel office to obtain additional information about your entitlements and responsibilities under the FMLA. Medical certification of a serious health condition may be required by your agency.

6. Remarks

7. **Certification:** I certify that the leave/absence requested above is for the purpose(s) indicated. I understand that I must comply with my employing agency's procedures for requesting leave/approved absence (and provide additional documentation, including medical certification, if required) and that falsification of information on this form may be grounds for disciplinary action, including removal.

7a. Employee signature

7b. Date signed

8a. Official action on request ☐ Approved ☐ Disapproved *(If disapproved, give reason. If annual leave, initiate action to reschedule.)*

8b. Reason for disapproval

8c. Signature

8d. Date signed

Privacy Act Statement

Section 6311 of title 5, United States Code, authorizes collection of this information. The primary use of this information is by management and your payroll office to approve and record your use of leave. Additional disclosures of the information may be: To the Department of Labor when processing a claim for compensation regarding a job connected injury or illness; to a State unemployment compensation office regarding a claim; to Federal Life Insurance or Health Benefits carriers regarding a claim; to a Federal, State, or local law enforcement agency when your agency becomes aware of a violation or possible violation of civil or criminal law; to a Federal agency when conducting an investigation for employment or security reasons; to the Office of Personnel Management or the General Accounting Office when the information is required for evaluation of leave administration; or the General Services Administration in connection with its responsibilities for records management.

Public Law 104-134 (April 26, 1996) requires that any person doing business with the Federal Government furnish a social security number or tax identification number. This is an amendment to title 31, Section 7701. Furnishing the social security number, as well as other data, is voluntary, but failure to do so may delay or prevent action on the application. If your agency uses the information furnished on this form for purposes other than those indicated above, it may provide you with an additional statement reflecting those purposes.

Office of Personnel Management
5 CFR 630

Local Reproduction Authorized

OPM Form 71
June 2001
Formerly Standard Form (SF) 71

Print Form Clear Form Save Form

Employers obviously need procedures for all leaves of absence (including those awarded under the Family and Medical Leave Act). These include:

- Give no employee a leave until the reason for the leave is clear.
- If the leave is for medical or family reasons, the employer should obtain medical certification from the medical practitioner.
- Use a standard form to record both the employee's expected return date and the fact that, without an authorized extension, the firm may terminate his or her employment (see Figure 13-3).
- One employment lawyer says employers should "kind of bend over backward" when deciding if an employee is eligible for leave based on an FMLA situation.[29] However, employers can require independent medical assessments before approving paid FMLA disability leaves.[30]

Some employers are enriching their parental leave plans to make it more attractive for mothers to return from maternity leave. Tactics include keeping in touch throughout the maternity leave, offering flexible jobs with reduced travel and hours, giving mothers fair access to bonuses and incentives, and facilitating longer leaves.[31]

Other laws apply to sick leaves. Under the Americans with Disabilities Act (ADA), a qualified employee with a disability may be eligible for a leave if such a leave is necessary to accommodate reasonably the employee. Under various state workers' compensation laws, employees may be eligible for leave in connection with work-related injuries. Many states also have their own, more restrictive versions of the FMLA.[32]

Severance Pay

Many employers provide **severance pay**, a one-time separation payment when terminating an employee. Severance pay makes sense. It is a humanitarian gesture, and good public relations. In addition, most managers expect employees to give them 1 or 2 weeks' notice if they plan to quit, so it seems appropriate to provide severance pay when dismissing an employee. Reducing the chances of litigation from disgruntled former employees is another reason. Severance pay plans also help reassure employees who stay on after a downsizing that they'll receive some financial help if they're let go, too. In one survey of 3,000 human resource managers, 82% of responding organizations reported having a severance policy.[33]

The reason for the dismissal affects whether the employee gets severance pay. About 95% of employees dismissed due to downsizings got severance pay, but only about a third of employers offer severance when terminating for poor performance. It is uncommon to pay when employees quit. The average maximum severance is 39 weeks for executives and about 30 weeks for other downsized employees.[34] About half of employers surveyed give white-collar and exempt employees 1 week of severance pay per year of service, and about one-third do the same for blue-collar workers.[35] If the employer obligates itself (for instance, in its employee handbook) to pay severance, then its "voluntary" plan will have to comply with additional rules under ERISA.[36]

GUIDELINES   In any event, there are several things to keep in mind when designing the severance plan. These include:

- List the situations for which the firm will pay severance, such as layoffs resulting from reorganizations. State that management will take other action as necessary.
- Require signing of a knowing and voluntary waiver/general release prior to remittance of any severance pay, absolving the employer from employment-related liability.
- Reserve the right to terminate or alter the severance policy.

severance pay
A one-time payment some employers provide when terminating an employee.

- Make it clear that any continuing severance payments continue until only the stated deadline or until the employee gets a new job, whichever occurs first.
- Remember that as with all personnel actions, employers must make severance payments, if any, equitably.[37]

Supplemental Unemployment Benefits

In some industries such as auto making, shutdowns to reduce inventories or change machinery are common, and laid-off or furloughed employees must depend on unemployment insurance. As the name implies, **supplemental unemployment benefits** are cash payments that supplement the employee's unemployment compensation, to help the person maintain his or her standard of living while out of work. They generally cover three contingencies: layoffs, reduced workweeks, and facility relocations.

INSURANCE BENEFITS

2 Describe each of the main insurance benefits.

Most employers also provide a number of required or voluntary insurance benefits, such as workers' compensation and health insurance.

Workers' Compensation

Workers' compensation laws aim to provide sure, prompt income and medical benefits to work-related accident victims or their dependents, regardless of fault. Every state has its own workers' compensation law and commission, and some run their own insurance programs. However, most require employers to carry workers' compensation insurance with private, state-approved insurance companies. Neither the state nor the federal government contributes any funds for workers' compensation.

HOW BENEFITS ARE DETERMINED   Workers' compensation can be monetary or medical. In the event of a worker's death or disablement, the person's dependents receive a cash benefit based on prior earnings—usually one-half to two-thirds the worker's average weekly wage, per week of employment. Most states have a time limit—such as 500 weeks—for which benefits can be paid. If the injury causes a specific loss (such as an arm), the employee may receive additional benefits based on a statutory list of losses, even though he or she may return to work. In addition to these cash benefits, employers must furnish medical, surgical, and hospital services as required for the employee.

For workers' compensation to cover an injury or work-related illness, one must only prove that it arose while the worker was on the job. It does not matter that he or she may have been at fault; if the person was on the job when the injury occurred, he or she is entitled to workers' compensation. For example, suppose you instruct all employees to wear safety goggles when at their machines. One worker does not and experiences an eye injury on the job. The company must still provide workers' compensation benefits.

Keep in mind that ADA provisions generally prohibit employers from inquiring about an applicant's workers' compensation history. Furthermore, failing to let an employee who is on injury-related workers' compensation return to work, or not accommodating him or her, could lead to lawsuits under ADA.

CONTROLLING WORKERS' COMPENSATION COSTS   It is important to control workers' compensation claims (and therefore costs). The employer's insurance company usually pays the claim, but the costs of the employer's premiums reflect the amount of claims.[38] Workers' comp claims also tend to correlate with injuries, so fewer claims is usually a good sign of fewer accidents.

There are several ways to reduce workers' compensation claims. Screen out accident-prone workers. Reduce accident-causing conditions in your facilities. And reduce the accidents and health problems that trigger these claims—for instance, by instituting effective safety and health programs and complying with government safety standards. Furthermore, although many workers' compensation claims are legitimate, some are not. Supervisors should therefore watch for typical fraudulent claim red flags. These include vague accident details, minor accidents resulting in major injuries, lack of witnesses, injuries occurring late Friday or very early Monday, and late reporting.[39]

Other workers' comp cost-control techniques include monitoring health care providers for compliance with their fee schedules and auditing medical bills.[40] *Case management* is a popular cost-control option. It is "the treatment of injured workers on a case-by-case basis by an assigned manager, usually a registered nurse, who coordinates with the physician and health plan to determine which care settings are the most effective for quality care and cost."[41]

Moving aggressively to support the injured employee and to get him or her back to work quickly is important. The involvement of an attorney and the duration of the claim both influence the workers claim cost.[42] Many firms have rehabilitation programs. These include physical therapy, and nursing assistance to help reintegrate claim recipients into the workforce.

Hospitalization, Health, and Disability Insurance

Health insurance looms large in many people's choice of employer, because it is so expensive. Hospitalization, health, and disability insurance helps protect employees against hospitalization costs and the loss of income arising from off-the-job accidents or illness. Many employers purchase insurance from life insurance companies, casualty insurance companies, or Blue Cross (for hospital expenses) and Blue Shield (for physician expenses) organizations. Others contract with health maintenance organizations or preferred provider organizations. The employer and employee usually both contribute to the plan. Table 13-3 illustrates the prevalence of health-related benefits.

COVERAGE   Most employer health plans provide at least basic hospitalization and surgical and medical insurance for all eligible employees at group rates. Insurance is

TABLE 13-3 Percentage of Employers Offering Some Popular Health Benefits—Change Over Time

	Yes (%) 2005	Yes (%) 2011
Prescription drug program coverage	97	96
Dental insurance	95	94
Mail order prescription program	90	91
PPO (preferred provider organization)	87	84
Chiropractic coverage	56	83
Mental health insurance	72	82
Vision insurance	80	76
Employee assistance program	73	75
Medical/Flexible spending account	80	73
HMO (health maintenance organization)	53	33

Source: Adapted from 2011 SHRM Employee Benefits Survey Report, p. 2. www.shrm.org/Research/SurveyFindings/Articles/Documents/Emp_Benefits_Tables.pdf, accessed, June 1, 2011. Reprinted with permission from the Society for Human Resource Management. All rights reserved.

supplemental unemployment benefits
Provide for a "guaranteed annual income" in certain industries where employers must shut down to change machinery or due to reduced work. These benefits are paid by the company and supplement unemployment benefits.

workers' compensation
Provides income and medical benefits to work-related accident victims or their dependents regardless of fault.

generally available to all employees—including new nonprobationary ones—regardless of health or physical condition. Most basic plans pay for hospital room and board, surgery charges, and medical expenses (such as doctors' visits to the hospital). Some also provide "major medical" coverage to meet the medical expenses resulting from serious illnesses.

Most employers' health plans also cover health-related expenses like doctors' visits, eye care, and dental services. Other plans pay for general and diagnostic visits to the doctor's office, vision care, hearing aids, and prescription drugs. *Disability insurance* provides income protection for salary loss due to illness or accident. Payments usually start when normal sick leave payments end, and may continue until age 65 or beyond. Disability benefits usually range from 50% to 75% of the employee's base pay if he or she is disabled.

HMOS Many employers offer membership in a **health maintenance organization (HMO)** as a hospital/medical insurance option. The HMO is a medical organization consisting of specialists (surgeons, psychiatrists, and so on), often operating out of a health care center. It provides routine medical services to employees who pay a nominal fee. Employees often have "gatekeeper" doctors who must approve appointments with specialist doctors. The HMO receives a fixed annual fee per employee from the employer (or employer and employee), regardless of whether it provides that person service.

PPOS **Preferred provider organizations (PPOs)** are a cross between HMOs and the traditional doctor–patient arrangement: They are "groups of health care providers that contract with employers, insurance companies, or third-party payers to provide medical care services at a reduced fee."[43] Unlike HMOs, PPOs let employees select providers (such as doctors) from a relatively wide list, and see them in their offices, often without gatekeeper doctor approval. The providers agree to provide discounts and submit to certain controls, for example, on testing. Employers are shifting from higher-cost HMOs to PPOs.[44]

MENTAL HEALTH BENEFITS The World Health Organization estimated that more than 34 million people in the United States between the ages of 18 and 64 suffer from mental illness.[45] Mental illnesses represent about 24% of all reported disabilities, more than disabling injuries, respiratory diseases, cardiovascular diseases, and cancer combined.

Mental health costs are rising. Reasons include widespread drug and alcohol problems, an increase in states that require employers to offer minimum mental health benefits, and the fact that mental health claims tend to trigger other health care claims. The Mental Health Parity Act of 1996 (as amended in 2008) sets minimum mental health care benefits; it also prohibits employer group health plans from adopting mental health benefits limitations without comparable limitations on medical and surgical benefits.[46]

The Legal Side of Health Benefits

With the U.S. introducing new health insurance laws, federal influence over health benefits will increase substantially in the next few years.

PROTECTION AND AFFORDABLE CARE ACT OF 2010 Signed into law by President Obama in 2010, employers will face a number of deadlines under the new Patient Protection and Affordable Care Act, unless Congress changes the law. For example, employers must begin reporting the value of health care benefits on employee's W-2 statements, contributions to health care flexible spending arrangements will be limited to $2,500 as of January 1, 2013, and in 2018 a 40% excise tax on high-cost health insurance plans goes into effect.[47] Individual and group health plans that already provide dependent coverage must expand eligibility up to age 26.[48] Among many other things, the act encourages employers with 50 or more employees to offer health insurance or pay a "shared responsibility payment" if the government has to subsidize an employee's health care.

Employers in one recent survey by the consulting firm Mercer expected this act to raise their health care expenses by from 2% to 5% in 2011.[49] As the act phases in over the next few years (assuming Congress makes no changes), the excise tax on high-cost plans was the employers' main cost concern. Other cost-raisers, the employers told Mercer, include the expanded coverage for older children, the ban on lifetime benefit dollar limits, the requirement that employers auto-enroll new hires into a health plan, and the rule that employers must offer coverage to employees including those working less than 30 hours per week (many of whom now have no health benefits).[50]

COBRA   COBRA—the Consolidated Omnibus Budget Reconciliation Act—requires most private employers to continue to make health benefits available to separated employees and their families for a time, generally 18 months after separation.[51] The former employee must pay for the coverage.

Employers ignore COBRA's regulations at their peril. Most importantly, you don't want separated employees to leave and be injured, and then claim you never told them they could have continued their insurance coverage. Therefore, when a new employee first becomes eligible for your company's insurance plan, the person *must* receive (and acknowledge receiving) an explanation of his or her COBRA rights. And, all employees separated from the company should sign a form acknowledging that they received and understand those rights. Figure 13-4 provides a COBRA checklist.

OTHER LAWS   Other federal laws are pertinent. For example, among other things, the *Employee Retirement Income Security Act* of 1974 (ERISA) sets minimum standards for most voluntarily established pension and health plans in private industry.[52] *The Newborn Mother's Protection Act of 1996* prohibits employers' health plans from using incentives to encourage employees to leave the hospital after childbirth after less than the legislatively determined minimum stay. Employers who provide health care services must follow the privacy rules of the *Health Insurance Portability and Accountability Act of 1996 (HIPAA)*.[53] Employers must provide the same health care benefits to employees over the age of 65 that they do to younger workers, even though the older workers are eligible for federal Medicare health insurance. Under the *Americans with Disabilities Act*, the plan generally shouldn't make distinctions based on disability. And, as explained earlier, the *Pregnancy Discrimination Act* requires employers to treat women affected by pregnancy, childbirth, or related medical conditions the same as any other employees not able to work, with respect to all benefits. Under the *Genetic Information Nondiscrimination Act* of 2008 (GINA), employers need to be vigilant about even apparently innocent situations. For example, if a health plan administrator learns that a member's mother passed away from breast cancer and makes a note to send a card, making the note and sending the card could conceivably be held as violations of the act.[54]

Trends in Employer Health Care Cost Control

Employers are endeavoring to rein in health care costs. Many retain *cost-containment specialists* to help reduce such costs. And most negotiate more aggressively with their health care insurance providers.[55] Most cost-control efforts necessarily start by instituting methods for measuring and tracking health care costs.[56]

---

health maintenance organization (HMO)
A prepaid health care system that generally provides routine round-the-clock medical services as well as preventive medicine in a clinic-type arrangement for employees, who pay a nominal fee in addition to the fixed annual fee the employer pays.

preferred provider organizations (PPOs)
Groups of health care providers that contract with employers, insurance companies, or third-party payers to provide medical care services at a reduced fee.

FIGURE 13-4 COBRA
Record-Keeping Compliance
Checklist

Source: Reprinted from
www.HR.BLR.com with permission
of the publisher Business and Legal
Resources, Inc., 141 Mill Rock Road
East, Old Saybrook, CT © 2004. BLR®
(Business and Legal Resources, Inc.).

Detailed record keeping is crucial for COBRA compliance. The following checklist is designed
to ensure that the proper records are maintained for problem-free COBRA compliance.

	Yes	No
• Do you maintain records so that it is easily determined who is covered by your group health care plan?	☐	☐
• Do you record terminations of covered employees as soon as terminations occur?	☐	☐
• Do you track reduction of hours of employees covered by group health care plans?	☐	☐
• Do you track deaths of employees covered by group health care plans?	☐	☐
• Do you track leaves of absence of employees covered by group health care plans?	☐	☐
• Do you track Medicare eligibility of employees covered by group health care plans?	☐	☐
• Do you track the disability status of employees covered by group health care plans?	☐	☐
• Do you track retirees covered by group health care plans?	☐	☐
• Do you maintain current addresses of employees?	☐	☐
• Do you maintain current addresses of individuals receiving COBRA benefits?	☐	☐
• Do you require employees to provide a written acknowledgment that they have received notice of their COBRA rights?	☐	☐
• Do you have a system to determine who has paid COBRA premiums on time?	☐	☐
• Do you have a system to determine who has obtained other group health coverage so that they are no longer eligible for COBRA under your plan?	☐	☐
• Do you maintain a telephone log of calls received about COBRA?	☐	☐
• Do you maintain a record of changes in your plan?	☐	☐
• Do you maintain a record of how premiums are calculated?	☐	☐
• Do you maintain a log of those employees who are denied COBRA coverage?	☐	☐
• Do you maintain a log of why employees are denied COBRA coverage?	☐	☐

For many employers, deductibles and co-pays are the low-hanging fruit in health care cost control. For example, 22% of employers imposed deductibles of at least $1,000 in 2011 for in-network services, up from 8% in 2008.[57] Even more—44%—imposed such deductibles for out-of-network services.[58] *Consumer-driven health plans (CDHPs)* are increasingly popular. These are high-deductible plans that give employees access to, for instance, a health savings account. (The Medicare Modernization Act of 2003 allows employers to establish tax-free health savings accounts (HSA).)[59] After the employer, employee, or both deposit pretax (and thus tax sheltered) pay in the employees' HSAs, employees or their families can use their HSA funds to pay for "low dollar" (not catastrophic) medical expenses.[60] The assumption is that this will motivate employees to utilize less expensive health care options, and thus avoid big deductibles.[61] Employers generally offer CDHPs as an option to traditional plans, such as PPOs.[62] We'll address other important cost-control trends.

COMMUNICATION AND EMPOWERMENT Most importantly, *make sure employees know the costs* of their medical benefits.[63] As one expert said, "the biggest criticism of managed care . . . is that the health care consumer has little financial stake in treatment decisions."[64] So, for example, periodically send a statement to each employee listing the employer's costs for each health benefit. *Online selection* lets employees choose the best of the employer's health care offerings, based on input from other employees concerning matters like doctor visits and specialists.

WELLNESS PROGRAMS   Many illnesses are preventable. In one study "employers who undertook prevention programs aimed at cardiovascular disease . . . reported an average 28% reduction in sick leave, [and] a 26% reduction in direct health-care costs."[65] Many employers therefore offer preventive services.[66] *Clinical prevention* programs include things like mammograms, immunizations, and routine checkups. Walgreens recently purchased two companies that provide *on-site health care services* such as mammograms for employers.[67] *Health promotion and disease prevention* programs include seminars and incentives aimed at improving unhealthy behaviors.[68] Top wellness program trends include obesity management, stress management, senior health improvement, and tobacco cessation programs.[69] Incentives, for instance, $50–$100, can boost wellness program participation, but may backfire.[70] Whirlpool gives nonsmoker discounts on health care premiums worth about $500. It suspended 39 workers it caught smoking outside the plant after claiming on their benefits enrollment forms that they were not tobacco users.

CLAIM AUDITS   It makes little sense to initiate cost cuts when employers are paying out thousands or millions of dollars in erroneous claims. Unfortunately, with health care plans increasingly complicated, it's easier for errors to occur. Human resource consultants Towers Perrin conducted a survey of claims payments. The industry standard for percentage of claims errors is 3%, but Towers Perrin found the *actual* percentage of claims with financial errors were about 6.3%. The industry standard for percentage of claims dollars actually paid in error was 1%; the *actual* percentage of claims dollars paid in error were 3.4%. So, setting standards for errors and then aggressively auditing all claims may be the most direct way to reduce employer health care expenses.[71]

LIMITED PLANS   Some employers are offering limited-benefit health care insurance plans. Unlike health care plans that may have lifetime coverage limits of $1 million or more, these "mini" medical plans have annual caps of about $2,000–$10,000 per year. The advantage, of course, is that the premiums are correspondingly lower.[72]

OUTSOURCING   Benefits management ranks high on the list of HR activities that employers outsource. For example, in one survey, 94% outsourced management of flexible spending accounts, 89% outsourced defined contribution plans, 72% outsourced defined benefit plans, and 68% outsourced the auditing of dependents.[73]

OTHER COST-CONTROL OPTIONS   Employers are taking other steps. One is using *defined contribution health care plans.* Here each employee gets a specific dollar amount allotment to use for co-payments or discretionary medical costs, rather than a specified health care benefits package with open-ended costs.[74] As noted, *outsourcing* health care plan administration and employee assistance and counseling to outside companies for a fee are other options.[75] Many employers reduce subsidized health benefits for their future *retirees.*[76] Small firms are joining *benefits purchasing alliances,* banding together to purchase health care benefits. Other employers are encouraging *medical tourism*, which means asking employees to have non-urgent medical procedures abroad, where costs are lower.[77] One simple method is just to ensure that any *dependents* enrolled are actually eligible for coverage.[78]

Long-Term Care

With baby-boomers in their 60s, long-term care insurance—for things like nursing assistance to former employees in their old age—is a key employee benefit. The Health Insurance Portability and Accountability Act of 1996 lets employers and employees deduct the cost of long-term care insurance premiums from their annual income taxes, making this benefit more attractive.[79] Employers can also provide insurance benefits for several types of long-term care, such as adult day care, assisted living, and custodial care.

Life Insurance

In addition to hospitalization and medical benefits, most employers provide **group life insurance** plans. Employees can usually obtain lower rates in a group plan. And group plans usually accept all employees—including new, nonprobationary ones—regardless of health or physical condition.

In general, there are three key personnel policies to address: the benefits-paid schedule (the amount of life insurance benefits is usually tied to the employee's annual earnings), supplemental benefits (continued life insurance coverage after retirement, for instance), and financing (the amount and percent the employee contributes).

Accidental death and dismemberment coverage provides a lump-sum benefit in addition to life insurance benefits when death is accidental. It also provides benefits in case of accidental loss of limbs or sight.

Benefits for Part-Time and Contingent Workers

About 19 million people work part-time (less than 35 hours a week). The recession, more phased retirements, a desire to better balance work and family life, and more women in the workforce help explain this phenomenon. In any case, most firms provide holiday, sick leave, and vacation benefits to part-timers, and more than 70% offer some form of health care benefits to them.[80] Again, employers should take care to not misclassify part-timers as "independent contractors."[81]

RETIREMENT BENEFITS

> **3** Discuss the main retirement benefits.

The first contingent of baby-boomers turned 65 in 2011, and many didn't wait until then to retire. This presents two challenges for employers. First (as we explained in Chapter 10, Employee Retention), employers are taking steps to entice older workers to keep working in some capacity.[82] Second, retirement funding is a big issue. We'll focus here on retirement benefits, including federal Social Security and employer pension/retirement plans like the 401(k).

Social Security

Most people assume that **Social Security** provides income only when they are older than 62, but it actually provides three types of benefits. The familiar *retirement benefits* provide an income if you retire at age 62 or thereafter and are insured under the Social Security Act. Second are *survivor's* or *death benefits*. These provide monthly payments to your dependents regardless of your age at death, again assuming you are insured under the Social Security Act. Finally, there are *disability payments*. These provide monthly payments to employees who become disabled totally (and to their dependents) if they meet certain requirements. The Social Security system also administers the Medicare program, which provides health services to people age 65 or older. "Full retirement age" for non-discounted social security benefits traditionally was 65— the usual age for retirement. It is now 67 for those born in 1960 or later.[83]

A tax on the employee's wages funds Social Security (technically, "Federal Old Age and Survivor's Insurance"). As of 2011, the maximum amount of earnings subject to Social Security tax was $106,800; the employer pays 6.2% and the employee pays 4.2%.[84]

Pension Plans

Pension plans provide income to individuals in their retirement, and just over half of full-time workers participate in some type of pension plan at work.

We can classify pension plans in three basic ways: contributory versus noncontributory plans, qualified versus nonqualified plans, and defined contribution versus defined benefit plans.[85] The employee contributes to the contributory pension plan, while the employer makes all contributions to the noncontributory pension plan. Employers derive certain tax benefits (such as tax deductions) for contributing to qualified pension plans (they are "qualified" for preferred tax treatment by the IRS); nonqualified pension plans get less favorable tax treatment. (As with all pay plan components, employers should ensure retirement benefits support their strategic needs. For example set guiding principles such as "assist in attracting employees" and "assist in retaining knowledgeable employees.")[86]

With **defined benefit plans**, the employee's pension is specified or "defined" ahead of time. Here the person knows ahead of time the pension benefits he or she will receive. How is this possible? There is usually a formula that ties the person's pension to (1) a percentage of (2) the person's pre-retirement pay (for example, to an average of his or her last 5 years of employment), multiplied by (3) the number of years he or she worked for the company. Due to tax law changes and other reasons, defined benefit plans now represent a minority of pension benefit plans.[87]

Defined contribution plans specify ("define") what contribution the employee and employer will make to the employee's retirement or savings fund. Here the contribution is defined, not the pension. With a *defined benefit* plan, the employee can compute what his or her retirement benefits will be upon retirement. With a *defined contribution* plan, the person only knows for sure what he or she is contributing to the pension plan; the actual pension will depend on the amounts contributed to the fund *and* on the success of the retirement fund's investment earnings. Defined contribution plans are popular among employers today due to their relative ease of administration, favorable tax treatment, and other factors. **Portability**—making it easier for employees who leave the firm prior to retirement to take their accumulated pension funds with them—is easier with defined contribution plans.

401(K) PLANS   The most popular defined contribution plans are based on section 401(k) of the Internal Revenue Code, and called **401(k) plans**. The employee authorizes the employer to deduct a sum from his or her paycheck before taxes, and to invest it in the bundle of investments in his or her 401(k). The deduction is pretax, so the employee pays no tax on those dollars until after he or she retires (or removes the money from the 401(k) plan). The person can decide to deduct any amount up to the legal maximum (the IRS sets an annual dollar limit—now about $15,000). The employer arranges, usually with an investment company such as Fidelity Investments, to administer the 401(k) plan and to make investment options available to the plan. The options typically include mutual stock funds and bond funds. As the recent downturn intensified, more employees made "hardship withdrawals" from their 401(k) plans (on which no taxes are due, for a time).[88]

Employers must choose their 401(k) providers with care. The employer has a fiduciary responsibility to its employees; it must monitor the fund and its administration.[89]

---

group life insurance
Provides lower rates for the employer or employee and includes all employees, including new employees, regardless of health or physical condition.

Social Security
Federal program that provides three types of benefits retirement income at the age of 62 and thereafter, survivor's or death benefits payable to the employee's dependents regardless of age at time of death, and disability benefits payable to disabled employees and their dependents. These benefits are payable only if the employee is insured under the Social Security Act.

pension plans
Plans that provide a fixed sum when employees reach a predetermined retirement age or when they can no longer work due to disability.

defined benefit plan
A plan that contains a formula for determining retirement benefits.

defined contribution plan
A plan in which the employer's contribution to employees' retirement savings funds is specified.

portability
Instituting policies that enable employees to easily take their accumulated pension funds when they leave employer.

401(k) plan
A defined contribution plan based on section 401(k) of the Internal Revenue Code.

Firms such as Vanguard, Fidelity, and others can establish online, fully Web-based 401(k) plans even for small firms with 10 to 50 employees.

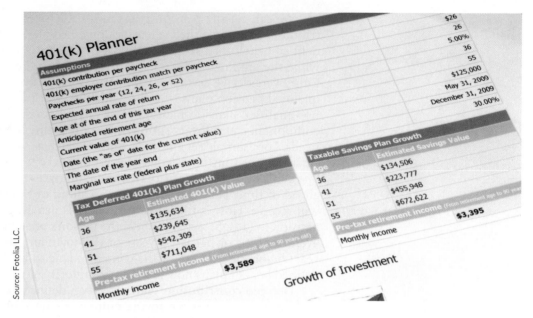

Source: Fotolia LLC.

Furthermore, changing 401(k) providers can be "grueling."[90] In addition to trustworthiness, the 401(k) plan provider should make it easy to enroll and participate in the plan.[91] Firms such as Vanguard, Fidelity, and others can establish Web-based 401(k) plans with online tools—such as an "asset allocation planner"—even for small firms. It's also crucial that employers monitor 401(k) housekeeping issues. For example, the IRS recently reported the top 10 most common violations that 401(k) plans encounter, including late deposits and incorrect employer matching contributions.[92]

Under the Pension Protection Act of 2006, employers who sponsor plans that facilitate both *automatic enrollment* and allocation to *default investments* (such as age-appropriate "lifestyle funds") reduce their compliance burdens.[93] Post-2008 stories, like that of "David," a 47-year-old engineer, suggest prudence. His adviser said that "if we saved very aggressively, I might be able to retire in my early 70s." Such experiences underscore the need for employee education, or perhaps directing funds into (relatively) prudent default investments.[94]

OTHER DEFINED CONTRIBUTION PLANS

The 401(k) plan is one example of a **savings and thrift plan**.[95] In any savings and thrift plan, employees contribute a portion of their earnings to a fund, and the employer usually matches this contribution completely or in part.

As discussed in Chapter 12 (Incentives), employers use a **deferred profit-sharing plan** to contribute a portion of their profits in cash to a pension fund, regardless of the level of employee contribution (income taxes on those contributions are deferred until the employee retires or leaves the employer). An **employee stock ownership plan (ESOP)** is a qualified, tax-deductible defined contribution plan in which employers contribute stock to a trust for eventual use by employees who retire.

CASH BALANCE PENSION PLANS

One problem with *defined benefits* plans is that to get your maximum pension, you generally must stay with your employer until you retire—the formula, recall, takes the number of years you work into consideration. With *defined contribution* plans, your pension is more portable—you can leave with it at any time, perhaps rolling it over into your next employer's pension plan. Without delving into all the details, **cash balance plans** are a hybrid; they have defined benefit plans' more predictable benefits, but the portability advantages of defined contribution plans.[96] The employer contributes a percentage of employees' current pay to the employees' pension plans every year, and employees earn interest on this amount.[97]

Pension Planning and the Law

No one wants to wake up and discover that his or her pension has vanished. Therefore, federal laws regulate pension planning and administration. As a rule, it is impossible to formulate a plan without expert help.

The **Employee Retirement Income Security Act of 1975 (ERISA)** is the basic law. It requires that employers have written pension plan documents and adhere to certain guidelines, such as regarding who is eligible for the employer's plan.[98] ERISA protects the employer's pension or health plans' assets by requiring that those who control the plans act responsibly. The Department of Labor says that the primary responsibility of *fiduciaries* is to run the plan solely in the interest of participants and beneficiaries.

Other laws are pertinent. Employers (and employees) want their pension contributions to be "qualified," or tax deductible, so they must adhere to the pertinent *income tax codes*. Under *labor relations laws*, the employer must let its unions participate in pension plan administration. The *Job Creation and Worker Assistance Act* provides guidelines regarding what rates of return employers should use in computing their pension plan values.

PBGC ERISA established the **Pension Benefits Guarantee Corporation (PBGC)** to oversee and insure a pension if a plan terminates without sufficient funds. The PBGC guarantees only defined benefit plans, not defined contribution plans. Furthermore, it will only pay an individual a pension of up to a maximum of about $54,000 per year for someone 65 years of age with a plan terminating in 2011.[99] So, high-income workers may still see most of their expected pensions evaporate if their employers go bankrupt.

MEMBERSHIP REQUIREMENTS When does the employee become eligible for a pension? Under the Tax Reform Act of 1986, an employer can require that an employee complete a period of no more than 2 years' service to the company before becoming eligible to participate in the plan. However, if it requires more than 1 year of service before eligibility, the plan must grant employees full and immediate vesting rights at the end of that period.

VESTING *Vested funds* are the money employer and employee have placed in the latter's pension fund that cannot be forfeited for any reason. The employees' contributions are always theirs, of course. However, until the passage of ERISA, the *employers'* contribution in many pension plans didn't vest until the employee retired. So, you could have worked for a company for 30 years and been left with no pension if the company went bust 1 year before you were to retire. That generally can't happen today, given the PBGC's guarantees.

Employers can choose one of two minimum vesting schedules (employers can allow funds to vest faster if they wish). With *cliff vesting*, the period for acquiring a nonforfeitable right to employer matching contributions (if any) is 3 years. So, the employee must have nonforfeitable rights to these funds by the end of 3 years. With the

savings and thrift plan
Plan in which employees contribute a portion of their earnings to a fund; the employer usually matches this contribution in whole or in part.

deferred profit-sharing plan
A plan in which a certain amount of profits is credited to each employee's account, payable at retirement, termination, or death.

employee stock ownership plan (ESOP)
A qualified, tax-deductible stock bonus plan in which employers contribute stock to a trust for eventual use by employees.

cash balance plans
Plans under which the employer contributes a percentage of employees' current pay to employees' pension plans every year, and employees earn interest on this amount.

Employee Retirement Income Security Act (ERISA)
Signed into law by President Ford in 1974 to require that pension rights be vested and protected by a government agency, the PBGC.

Pension Benefits Guarantee Corporation (PBGC)
Established under ERISA to ensure that pensions meet vesting obligations; also insures pensions should a plan terminate without sufficient funds to meet its vested obligations.

second (*graded vesting*) option, pension plan participants must receive nonforfeitable rights to the matching contributions as follows: 20% after 2 years, and then 20% for each succeeding year, with a 100% nonforfeitable right by the end of 6 years.

Pensions and Early Retirement

To trim their workforces or for other reasons, some employers are encouraging employees to retire early. Many of these plans take the form of **early retirement window** arrangements for specific employees (often age 50+). The "window" means that for a limited time, the employees can retire early. The financial incentive is generally a combination of improved or liberalized pension benefits plus a cash payment.

Early retirement programs can backfire for two reasons. Some are too successful. When Verizon Communications offered enhanced pension benefits to encourage what it hoped would be 12,000 employees to retire, more than 21,000 took the plan. Verizon had to replace 16,000 managers.[100]

Discrimination is the other potential problem. Unless structured properly, older employees can challenge early retirement programs as de facto ways for forcing them to retire against their will. Although it is generally legal to use incentives to encourage individuals to choose early retirement, the employee's decision must be voluntary. The Older Workers' Benefit Protection Act (OWBPA) imposes limitations. The employee's waiver must be knowing and voluntary, and give the employee ample time to think over the agreement and to seek legal advice, among other things.

Improving Productivity through HRIS

Online Benefits Management Systems

Left un-automated, benefits administration can require the employer to devote hundreds of human resource professionals' hours to answering employees' questions about comparative benefits and updating employees' benefits information.[101] Typical employee questions include, "In which option of the medical plan am I enrolled?" and "If I retire in 2 years, what will be my monthly retirement income?" Tasks like that cry out for online self-service benefits management applications.

BENELOGIC   For example, when the organization that assists Pennsylvania school districts with their insurance needs decided to help the school boards automate their benefits administration, they chose a company called Benelogic.[102] The solution, called the "Employee Benefit Electronic Service Tool," lets users manage all aspects of benefits administration, including enrollment, plan descriptions, eligibility, and premium reconciliation, via their browsers.[103]

Benelogic hosts and maintains the Web support application on its own servers, and creates customized, Web-based applications for each school district. The system facilitates Web-based employee benefit enrollment, and provides centralized call center support for benefit-related questions. It even handles benefits-related payroll, HRIS, and similar functions by collaborating with companies like ADP (for payroll) and Oracle PeopleSoft (which services many of the school boards' human resource information systems). Each school board employee accesses the Benelogic site via a link on his or her own board's Web site.

BENEFITS WEB SITES   Employers everywhere are adding new services to their own benefits Web sites. In addition to offering things like self-enrollment, the insurance company USAA's Web site (www.usaa.com) helps employees achieve better work life–balance. For example, click on the "today, I'm feeling . . . " menu. Here employees can respond to a list of words (such as "stressed"). From there, they see suggestions for dealing with (in this case) stress. Go to "my child is behaving badly," and the employee gets access to resources like "guide to addressing child behavior problems."[104] Boeing's Pay & Benefits Profile site gives employees real-time information about their salary and bonuses, benefits, pension, and even special services such as child care referrals.[105]

4 Outline the main employees' services benefits.

PERSONAL SERVICES AND FAMILY-FRIENDLY BENEFITS

Although time off, insurance, and retirement benefits account for the lion's share of benefits costs, most employers also provide various services benefits. These include personal services (such as legal and personal counseling), "family-friendly" services (such as child-care facilities), educational subsidies, and executive perquisites (such as company cars for its executives).

Personal Services

Many employers provide access to the sorts of personal services that employees sometimes need. These include credit unions, legal services, counseling, and social and recreational opportunities. (Some employers use the term *voluntary benefits* to cover personal services benefits that range from things like pet insurance to automobile insurance.[106]) We'll look at a few of these.

EMPLOYEE ASSISTANCE PROGRAMS   **Employee assistance programs (EAPs)** provide counseling and advisory services, such as personal legal and financial services, child and elder care referrals, adoption assistance, mental health counseling, and life event planning.[107] EAPs are increasingly popular, with more than 60% of larger firms offering such programs. One study found that personal mental health was the most common problem addressed by employee assistance programs, followed by family problems.[108]

For employers, EAPs produce advantages, not just costs. For example, sick family members and problems like depression account for many of the sick days employees take. Employee assistance programs can reduce such absences by providing expert advice on issues like elder care referrals.[109] Few but the largest employers establish their own EAPs. Most contract for the necessary services with vendors such as Magellan Health Services and CIGNA Behavioral Health.[110]

In either case, employers and managers need to keep several issues in mind. Everyone involved with the EAP, including supervisors, secretaries, and support staff, must understand the importance of *confidentiality*. Also, ensure files are locked, access is limited and monitored, and identifying information is minimized. *Be aware of legal issues.* For example, in most states counselors must disclose suspicions of child abuse to state agencies. *Define* the program's purpose, employee eligibility, the roles and responsibilities of EAP and employer personnel, and procedures for using the plan. And ensure the vendors you use fulfill *professional and state licensing requirements*.

Family-Friendly (Work–Life) Benefits

Several trends have changed the benefits landscape. There are more households where both adults work, more one-parent households, more women in the workforce, and more workers older than age 55. And, there's the "time bind"—people working more, without the time to do all they'd like to do. The issues involve working men, as well as women.[111]

These pressures have led many employers to bolster their **family-friendly (or work–life) benefits**. (The number of Americans who have never married is rising, and the newer "work–life benefits" terminology recognizes the need to improve all employees' work–life situations, not just those with families.)[112] These benefits include child care, elder care, fitness facilities, and flexible work schedules—benefits that help employees balance their family and work lives.[113] We'll look at some examples.

---

early retirement window
A type of offering by which employees are encouraged to retire early, the incentive being liberal pension benefits plus perhaps a cash payment.

employee assistance program (EAP)
A formal employer program for providing employees with counseling and/or treatment programs for problems such as alcoholism, gambling, or stress.

family-friendly (or work–life) benefits
Benefits such as child care and fitness facilities that make it easier for employees to balance their work and family responsibilities.

Software giant SAS Institute, Inc., offers generous employee benefits. The North Carolina firm keeps turnover at 4% in an industry where 20% is typical, partly by offering family-friendly benefits like paid maternity leave, day care on site, lunchtime piano concerts, massages, and yoga classes like this one.

Source: Fotolia LLC.

SUBSIDIZED CHILD CARE   Fulfilling work responsibilities while raising a family is a challenge, particularly for single parents. Most working people make private provisions to take care of their children. For example, relatives accounted for 48% of all child care providers in one study.[114] Organized day care centers accounted for another 30% of child care arrangements, and nonrelatives accounted for most of the remaining arrangements.

Employers who want to reduce the distractions associated with finding reliable child care can help in various ways. Some employers simply investigate the day care facilities in their communities and recommend certain ones to employees. Other employers set up company-sponsored and subsidized day care facilities, both to attract employees and to reduce absenteeism. For example, Abbott Laboratories built a $10 million child care center at its headquarters north of Chicago, daytime home to about 400 children of Abbott employees.[115]

By establishing subsidized day care, employers assumedly can benefit in several ways. These include improved recruiting results, lower absenteeism, improved morale, favorable publicity, and lower turnover. But, good planning is required. This often starts with a questionnaire to employees to answer questions like, "What would you be willing to pay for care for one child in a child care center near work?"

SICK CHILD BENEFITS   One study found that unexpected absences climbed to about 2.4% of payroll hours recently, with a cost per absence to employers of about $700 per episode (for temp employees and reduced productivity, for instance). More employers are thus offering emergency child care benefits, for example, when a young child's regular babysitter is a no-show. Texas Instruments built a Web database its employees use to find last-minute child care providers. Others, like Canadian financial services company CIBC, are expanding their on-site child care centers to handle last-minute emergencies.[116]

ELDER CARE   The responsibility for caring for an aging relative can affect the employee's performance.[117] One study found that, to care for an older relative, 64% of employees took sick days or vacation time, 33% decreased work hours, 22% took leaves of absence, 20% changed their job status from full- to part-time, 16% quit their jobs, and 13% retired early. One survey found that about 120 million Americans are now caring for—or in the past cared for—an adult relative or friend.[118]

So, more employers are providing elder care services. For example, the United Auto Workers and Ford Motor Company provide elder care referral services for Ford's salaried employees. The service provides a detailed assessment of the elderly relative's needs and recommendations on the care that would be best.[119] The National Council on Aging has a Web site to help elders and caregivers find benefit programs: www.benefitscheckup.org.

FAMILY-FRIENDLY BENEFITS AND THE BOTTOM LINE   It's not easy to evaluate the "profitability" of such programs. The costs are clear. For example, a few years ago Aetna found it saved $400,000 just by making employees at its Blue Bell, Pennsylvania, office buy their own coffee and tea.[120]

Measuring the program's positive consequences isn't so simple. "Family-friendly" firms such as SAS routinely turn up on "best companies to work for" lists. This almost undoubtedly makes it easier to recruit and retain good employees. Employees may even willingly forego somewhat higher pay for services like built-in day care. And some of the advantages to the employer are indirect. For example, employees who experience work–family conflict may experience anger that affects performance, a situation family-type benefits may improve.[121]

The bottom line is that employers are carefully reviewing these benefits. Even Google, long known for offering benefits that blow almost every other employer's away (free buses from the city, on-campus day care, and restaurants) has been cutting back of late.

Other Job-Related Benefits

Employers provide various other job-related benefits. Some provide subsidized *employee transportation*, such as increased mileage allowances or mass transit discounts.[122] Google's Web site lists benefits such as adoption assistance, the Google Child Care Center, free shuttle service from San Francisco, on-site dry cleaning, backup child care assistance, and on-site physician and dental care. Home Depot offers a "nose to tail coverage" pet health insurance program. Ben & Jerry's gives employees three pints of ice cream to take home every day.

EDUCATIONAL SUBSIDIES   Educational subsidies such as tuition refunds are popular benefits. Payments range from all tuition and expenses down to a flat limit of several hundred dollars per year. One survey found that about 72% of the 579 employers surveyed paid for college courses related to an employee's present job. Many employers also reimburse non–job-related courses (such as a Web designer taking an accounting class) that pertain to the company business.[123] Many employers provide college programs, taught on the employer's premises. We've seen that other educational programs include remedial work in basic literacy.

The problem is that you may be paying your best employees to leave. Researchers studied how employer-sponsored part-time college education reimbursements influenced job mobility. They focused on the U.S. Navy's tuition assistance program. Taking tuition assistance significantly decreased the probability the person stayed in the Navy.[124]

DOMESTIC PARTNER BENEFITS   When employers provide *domestic partner benefits* to employees, it generally means that employees' same-sex or opposite-sex domestic partners are eligible to receive the same benefits (health care, life insurance, and so forth) as do the husbands, wives, or legal dependents of the firm's other employees.[125] For example, Northrop Grumman Corp. extends domestic partner benefits to the 9,500 salaried workers at its Newport News shipyard.[126]

Executive Perquisites

When you reach the pinnacle of the organizational pyramid—or close to the top—you will find, waiting for you, the Executive Perk. Perquisites (perks, for short) usually only go to top executives. Perks can range from substantial (company planes) to relatively insignificant (private bathrooms).

Most perks fall between these extremes. These include *management loans* (which typically enable senior officers to exercise their stock options); *financial counseling* (to handle investments); and *relocation benefits*, often including subsidized mortgages, purchase of the executive's current house, and payment for the actual move. As we noted in Chapter 11 (Strategic Pay Plans), publicly traded companies must now itemize all executives' perks (if they total more than $100,000).

5   Explain the main flexible benefit programs.

FLEXIBLE BENEFITS PROGRAMS

Employees prefer choice in their benefits plans. In one survey of working couples, 83% took advantage of flexible hours (when available); 69% took advantage of the flexible-style benefits we'll discuss next; and 75% said that they prefer flexible benefits plans.[127] The online job listing service Jobtrak.com asked college students and recent graduates, "Which benefit do you desire most?" Thirty-five percent sought flexible hours; 19%, stock options; 13%, more vacation time; and 12%, a better health plan. Most of the preferred benefits had to do with lifestyle issues rather than financial ones.[128]

Given this, it is prudent to survey employees' benefits preferences, perhaps using a form like that in Figure 13-5. In any case, employers should provide for choice when designing benefits plans.

The Cafeteria Approach

One way to provide a choice is with an aptly named *cafeteria benefits plan.* (Pay specialists use **flexible benefits plan** and **cafeteria benefits plan** synonymously.) A *cafeteria plan* is one in which the employer gives each employee a benefits fund budget, and lets the person spend it on the benefits he or she prefers, subject to two constraints. First, the employer must of course limit the total cost for each employee's benefits package. Second, each employee's benefits plan must include certain required items—for example, Social Security, workers' compensation, and unemployment insurance. Employees can often make midyear changes to their plans if, for instance, their dependent care costs rise and they want to divert contributions.[129] IRS regulations require formal written plans describing the employer's cafeteria plan, including benefits and procedures for choosing them.[130]

TYPES OF PLANS   Cafeteria plans come in several varieties. To give employees more flexibility in what benefits they use, about 70% of employers offer *flexible spending accounts* for medical and other expenses. This option lets employees pay for certain

FIGURE 13-5 Online Survey of Employees' Benefits Preferences

Source: http://data.grapevinesurveys.com/survey.asp?sid=20062143964099, accessed April 29, 2009.

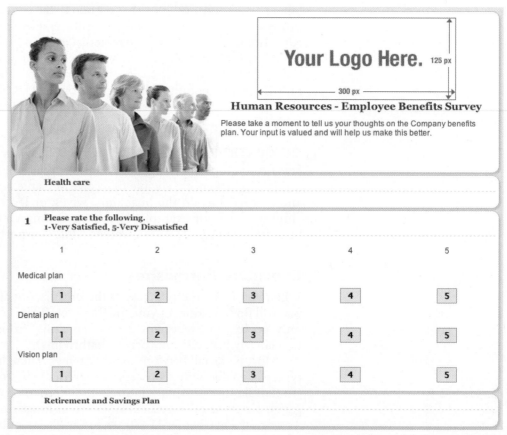

(Continued)

FIGURE 13-5 (Continued)

benefits expenses with pretax dollars (so the IRS, in effect, subsidizes some of the employee's expense). To encourage employees to use this option without laying out cash, some firms are offering *debit cards* that employees can use at their medical provider or pharmacy.[131] *Core plus option plans* establish a core set of benefits (such as medical insurance), which are usually mandatory for all employees. Beyond the core, employees can then choose from various benefits options.[132]

Benefits and Employee Leasing

As we'll explain in Chapter 18, many businesses—particularly smaller ones—don't have the resources or employee base to support the cost of many of the benefits we've discussed in this chapter. That's one big reason they turn to "employee leasing."

In brief, employee leasing firms (also called *professional employer organizations* or *staff leasing firms*) assume all or most of the employer's human resources chores. In doing so, they also become the employer of record for the employer's employees, by transferring them all to the employee leasing firm's payroll. The leasing firm thus becomes the employees' legal employer, and usually handles employee-related activities such as recruiting, hiring (with client firms' supervisors' approvals), and paying taxes (Social Security payments, unemployment insurance, and so on).

Insurance and benefits are usually the big attraction. Even group rates for life or health insurance can be quite high when only 20 or 30 employees are involved. That's where the leasing firm comes in. Remember that the leasing firm is the legal employer of your employees. The employees therefore are absorbed into a much larger insurable

flexible benefits plan/cafeteria benefits plan
Individualized plans allowed by employers to accommodate employee preferences for benefits.

group, along with other employers' former employees. As a result, a small business owner may be able to get insurance for its people that it couldn't otherwise afford.

Flexible Work Schedules

Flexible work schedules are increasingly popular.[133] Single parents often find them crucial for balancing work and family responsibilities. And for many millennial employees, flexible work schedules provide a way to pursue their careers without surrendering the quality of work life they desire. There are several flexible work schedule options.

FLEXTIME   **Flextime** is a plan whereby employees' workdays are built around a core of midday hours, such as 11:00 a.m. to 2:00 p.m. Workers determine their own starting and stopping hours. For example, they may opt to work from 7:00 a.m. to 3:00 p.m. or from 11:00 a.m. to 7:00 p.m. The number of employees in formal flextime programs—from 4% of operators to 17% of executive employees—doesn't tell the whole story. Many more employees, probably almost half, actually take advantage of informal flexible work schedules.[134] In practice, most employers hold fairly close to the traditional 9:00 a.m. to 5:00 p.m. workday. Therefore, the effect of flextime for most employees is to give them about 1 hour of leeway before 9:00 a.m. or after 5:00 p.m.

COMPRESSED WORKWEEKS   Many employees, like airline pilots, do not work conventional 5-day, 40-hour workweeks. Similarly, hospitals may want doctors and nurses to provide continuing care to a patient, or manufacturers may want to reduce the productivity lost whenever workers change shifts. Workers like these typically have **compressed workweek** schedules. This means they work fewer days each week, but each day they work longer hours. Nonconventional workweeks come in many flavors. Some firms have 4-day workweeks, with four 10-hour days. Some workers—in hospitals, for instance—work three 12-hour shifts, and then are off for the next 4 days.[135]

EFFECTIVENESS OF FLEXIBLE WORK SCHEDULE ARRANGEMENTS Studies show that flexible work schedules have positive effects on employee productivity, job satisfaction, and employee absenteeism; the positive effect on absenteeism was much greater than on productivity. Compressed workweeks positively affected job satisfaction; absenteeism did not increase, and productivity was not positively affected. Highly flexible programs were actually less effective than less flexible ones.[136]

Some experts argue that longer, 12-hour shifts may increase fatigue and accidents. However, one report suggests 12-hour shifts can actually be safer, in some respects. For example, 12-hour shifts reduce the "general workplace confusion" that often occurs during shift changes, since there are fewer shift changes per day. To reduce potential side effects, some employers install treadmills and exercise bikes, and special "light boxes" that mimic daylight.

WORKPLACE FLEXIBILITY   As anyone who has flown next to someone tapping away on a laptop knows, employees are increasingly conducting business from nontraditional settings, using technology like iPads and BlackBerry-type devices.[137] **Workplace flexibility** means arming employees with the information technology tools they need to get their jobs done wherever they are. For example, certain Capital One Bank employees received mobile technology tools such as wireless access laptops and BlackBerry-type cell phone devices. The program seems to have led to about a 41% increase in overall workplace satisfaction, a 31% reduction in time needed to get input from peers, and a 53% increase in those who say their workplace enhances group productivity.[138]

OTHER FLEXIBLE WORK ARRANGEMENTS   Employers are taking other steps to accommodate employees' scheduling needs. **Job sharing** allows two or more people to share a single full-time job. For example, two people may share a 40-hour-per-week job, with one working mornings and the other working afternoons. About 22% of the firms questioned in one survey indicated that they allow job sharing.[139] Job sharing can be particularly useful for retirement-aged employees. It allows them to reduce their hours while enabling the company to retain their expertise.[140] **Work sharing** refers to a temporary reduction in work hours by a group of employees during economic downturns as a way to prevent layoffs. Thus, 400 employees may all agree to work (and be paid for) only 35 hours per week, to avoid a layoff of 30 workers.

REVIEW

MyManagementLab Now that you have finished this chapter, go back to **www.mymanagementlab.com** to continue practicing and applying the concepts you've learned.

CHAPTER SECTION SUMMARIES

1. Because benefits are so important to employees, it's important that all managers understand **the benefits picture today**. In addition to the fact that benefits are very important to employees, the other big issue, of course, is that benefits in general and health care costs in particular are rising very fast. About 78% of employees cite health care benefits as most crucial to retaining them.

2. Employers provide numerous pay **for time not worked benefits**.
   - Unemployment insurance provides benefits if a person is unable to work due to some fault other than his or her own. To avoid unnecessary unemployment taxes, the main rule is to keep a list of written warnings.
   - American workers tend to get about 9 days of leave after 1 year of employment.
   - Sick pay provides pay to an employee when he or she is out of work because of illness. Minimizing sick leave pay is important, and here cost reduction tactics include repurchasing unused sick leave or simply using paid leave plans that lump sick leave, vacation, and holidays into one leave pool.
   - In formulating parental leave policies, the employer needs to keep in mind the Family and Medical Leave Act, which requires larger employers to provide up to 12 weeks of unpaid leave for family-related issues, and the Americans with Disabilities Act.

   - Severance pay is a one-time payment some employers provide when terminating an employee.

3. Most employers also provide a number of required or voluntary **insurance benefits**. Workers' compensation laws aim to provide sure, prompt medical benefits to work-related accident victims or their dependents, regardless of fault. Hospitalization, health, and disability insurance costs are rising fast, and most employer health plans provide at least basic hospitalization and surgical and medical insurance for eligible employees. Many employers provide these plans via preferred provider organizations or health management organizations. When an employee is terminated or terminates his or her employment, it is essential that the employer make the person aware of his or her COBRA rights. The basic overall trend in health care cost control is to take steps (for instance, in terms of communication and empowerment, health savings accounts, and claims audits) to try to keep the rising cost of health care insurance under control.

4. Particularly with stock markets volatile, **retirement benefits** are important to employees today. Social Security is a federal program that provides retirement income at the age of 62 and thereafter, as well as other benefits. Many employers make available pension plans; these provide an income when employees reach retirement age or when they can no longer work due to disability. Defined benefit plans contain a formula for determining retirement benefits, while defined contribution plans

flextime
A work schedule in which employees' workdays are built around a core of midday hours, and employees determine, within limits, what other hours they will work.

compressed workweek
Schedule in which employee works fewer but longer days each week.

workplace flexibility
Arming employees with the information technology tools they need to get their jobs done wherever they are.

job sharing
Allows two or more people to share a single full-time job.

work sharing
Refers to a temporary reduction in work hours by a group of employees during economic downturns as a way to prevent layoffs.

are plans in which the contribution to employees' retirement savings plans is specified. 401(k) plans are perhaps the most well-known of the latter, and are based on section 401(k) of the Internal Revenue Code. The Employee Retirement Income Security Act of 1975 requires that employers have written pension plan documents, and established the Pension Benefits Guarantee Corporation to oversee employers' pension plans. Key pension policy issues include membership requirements and testing.

5. Most employers also provide various **personal services and family-friendly benefits**. These include credit unions, employee assistance programs, and subsidized child care and elder care.

6. Employees prefer choice in their benefits plans, so **flexible benefits programs** are important. Flexible benefits or cafeteria benefits plans are individual plans that accommodate employee preferences for benefits. Some employers turn to employee leasing companies to capitalize on the advantage of the leasing firm's large employee base to get better employee benefits for their employees. Employers also are implementing various types of flexible work schedules, including flextime, compressed workweeks, and other flexible work arrangements such as job sharing.

DISCUSSION QUESTIONS

1. You are applying for a job as a manager and are at the point of negotiating salary and benefits. What questions would you ask your prospective employer concerning benefits? Describe the benefits package you would try to negotiate for yourself.

2. What is unemployment insurance? Is an organization required to pay unemployment benefits to all dismissed employees? Explain how you would go about minimizing your organization's unemployment insurance tax.

3. Explain how ERISA protects employees' pension rights.

4. What is "portability"? Why do you think it is (or isn't) important to a recent college graduate?

5. What are the main provisions of the FMLA?

INDIVIDUAL AND GROUP ACTIVITIES

1. Working individually or in groups, research the unemployment insurance rate and laws of your state. Write a summary detailing your state's unemployment laws. Assuming Company X has a 30% rate of annual personnel terminations, calculate Company X's unemployment tax rate in your state.

2. Assume you run a small business. Working individually or in groups, visit the Web site www.dol.gov/elaws. See the Small Business Retirement Savings Advisor. Write a 2-page summary explaining: (1) the various retirement savings programs available to small business employers, and (2) which retirement savings program you would choose for your small business and why.

3. You are the HR consultant to a small business with about 40 employees. Now the firm offers only 5 days of vacation, 5 paid holidays, and legally mandated benefits such as unemployment insurance payments. Develop a list of other benefits you believe it should offer, along with your reasons for suggesting them.

4. The "HRCI Test Specifications Appendix" (pages 633–640) lists the knowledge someone studying for the HRCI certification exam needs to have in each area of human resource management (such as in Strategic Management, Workforce Planning, and Human Resource Development). In groups of four to five students, do four things: (1) review that appendix now; (2) identify the material in this chapter that relates to the required knowledge the appendix lists; (3) write four-multiple choice exam questions on this material that you believe would be suitable for inclusion in the HRCI exam; and (4) if time permits, have someone from your team post your team's questions in front of the class, so the students in other teams can take each others' exam questions.

EXPERIENTIAL EXERCISE

Revising the Benefits Package

Purpose: The purpose of this exercise is to provide practice in developing a benefits package for a small business.

Required Understanding: Be very familiar with the material presented in this chapter. In addition, review Chapter 11 to reacquaint yourself with sources of compensation survey information, and come to class prepared to share with your group the benefits package for the small business in which you work or in which someone with whom you're familiar works.

How to Set Up the Exercise/Instructions:

Divide the class into groups of four or five students. Your assignment is as follows: Maria Cortes runs a small personnel recruiting office in Miami and has decided to start offering an expanded benefits package to her 25 employees. At the current time, the only benefits are 7 paid holidays per year and 5 sick days per year. In her company, there are 2 other managers, as well as 17 full-time recruiters and 5 secretarial staff members. In the time allotted, your group should create a benefits package in keeping with the size and requirements of this firm.

APPLICATION CASE

STRIKING FOR BENEFITS

By February 2004, the strike by Southern California grocery workers against the state's major supermarket chains was almost 5 months old. Because so many workers were striking (70,000), and because of the issues involved, unions and employers across the country were closely following the negotiations. Indeed, grocery union contracts were set to expire in several cities later in 2004, and many believed the California settlement—assuming one was reached—would set a pattern.

The main issue was employee benefits, and specifically how much (if any) of the employees' health care costs the employees should pay themselves. Based on their existing contract, Southern California grocery workers had unusually good health benefits. For example, they paid nothing toward their health insurance premiums, and paid only $10 co-payments for doctor visits. However, supporting these excellent health benefits cost the big Southern California grocery chains over $4 per hour per worker.

The big grocery chains were not proposing cutting health care insurance benefits for their existing employees. Instead, they proposed putting any new employees hired after the new contract went into effect into a separate insurance pool, and contributing $1.35 per hour for their health insurance coverage. That meant new employees' health insurance would cost each new employee perhaps $10 per week. And, if that $10 per week weren't enough to cover the cost of health care, then the employees would have to pay more, or do without some of their benefits.

It was a difficult situation for all the parties involved. For the grocery chain employers, skyrocketing health care costs were undermining their competitiveness; the current employees feared any step down the slippery slope that might eventually mean cutting their own health benefits. The unions didn't welcome a situation in which they'd end up representing two classes of employees, one (the existing employees) who had excellent health insurance benefits, and another (newly hired employees) whose benefits were relatively meager, and who might therefore be unhappy from the moment they took their jobs and joined the union.

Questions

1. Assume you are mediating this dispute. Discuss five creative solutions you would suggest for how the grocers could reduce the health insurance benefits and the cost of their total benefits package without making any employees pay more.
2. From the grocery chains' point of view, what is the downside of having two classes of employees, one of which has superior health insurance benefits? How would you suggest they handle the problem?
3. Similarly, from the point of view of the union, what are the downsides of having to represent two classes of employees, and how would you suggest handling the situation?

Source: Based on "Settlement Nears for Southern California Grocery Strike," *Knight-Ridder/Tribune Business News,* February 26, 2004, item 04057052.

CONTINUING CASE

CARTER CLEANING COMPANY

The New Benefit Plan

Carter Cleaning Centers has traditionally provided only legislatively required benefits for its employees. These include participation in the state's unemployment compensation program, Social Security, and workers' compensation (which is provided through the same insurance carrier that insures the stores for such hazards as theft and fire). The principals of the firm—Jack, Jennifer, and their families—have individual, family-supplied health and life insurance.

Jennifer can see several potential problems with the company's policies regarding benefits and services. One is turnover. She wants to do a study to determine whether similar companies' experiences with providing health and life insurance benefits suggest they enable these firms to reduce employee turnover and perhaps pay lower wages. Jennifer is also concerned with the fact that her company has no formal policy regarding vacations or paid days off or sick leave. Informally, at least, it is understood that employees get 1 week's vacation after 1 year's work, but in the past the policy regarding paid vacations for days such as New Year's Day and Thanksgiving Day has been very inconsistent. Sometimes employees who had been on the job only 2 or 3 weeks were paid fully for one

of these holidays, while at other times employees who had been with the firm for 6 months or more had been paid for only half a day. Jennifer knows that this policy must be made more consistent.

She also wonders whether it would be advisable to establish some type of day care center for the employees' children. She knows that many of the employees' children have either no place to go during the day (they are preschoolers) or have no place to go after school, and she wonders whether a benefit such as day care would be in the best interests of the company.

Questions

1. Draw up a policy statement regarding vacations, sick leave, and paid days off for Carter Cleaning Centers.
2. What would you tell Jennifer are the advantages and disadvantages to Carter Cleaning Centers of providing its employees with health, hospitalization, and life insurance programs?
3. Would you advise establishing some type of day care center for the Carter Cleaning employees? Why or why not?

TRANSLATING STRATEGY INTO HR POLICIES & PRACTICES CASE

THE HOTEL PARIS CASE

The New Benefits Plan

The Hotel Paris's competitive strategy is "To use superior guest service to differentiate the Hotel Paris properties, and to thereby increase the length of stay and return rate of guests, and thus boost revenues and profitability." HR manager Lisa Cruz must now formulate functional policies and activities that support this competitive strategy by eliciting the required employee behaviors and competencies.

Although the Hotel Paris's benefits (in terms of things like holidays and health care) were comparable to those of other hotels, Lisa Cruz knew they weren't good enough to support the high-quality service behaviors her company sought. Indeed, the fact that they were roughly comparable to those of similar firms didn't seem to impress the Hotel Paris's employees, at least 60% of whom consistently said they were deeply dissatisfied with the benefits they were getting. Lisa's concern (with which the CFO concurred) was that dissatisfaction with benefits contributed to morale and commitment being below what they should be, and thus to inhibiting the Hotel Paris from achieving its strategic aims. Lisa therefore turned to the task of assessing and redesigning the company's benefits plans.

As they reviewed the numbers relating to their benefits plan, Lisa Cruz and the CFO became increasingly concerned. They computed several benefits-related metrics for their firm, including *benefits costs as a percentage of payroll*, *sick days per full-time equivalent employee per year*, *benefits cost/competitor's benefits cost ratio*, and *workers' compensation experience ratings*. The results, as the CFO put it, offered a "good news–bad news" situation. On the good side, the ratios were generally similar to those of most competing hotels. The bad news was that the measures were strikingly below what they were when compared with the results for high-performing service-oriented businesses. The CFO authorized Lisa to design and propose a new benefits plan.

Lisa knew there were several things she wanted to accomplish with this plan. She wanted a plan that contributed to improved employee morale and commitment. She also wanted the plan to include elements that made it easier for her employees to do their jobs—so that, as she put it, "they could come to work and give their full attention to giving our guests great service, without worrying about child care and other major family-oriented distractions."

One of the metrics Lisa and her team specifically wanted to address was the relatively high absence rate at the Hotel Paris. Because so many of these jobs are front-line jobs—valets, limousine drivers, and front-desk clerks, for instance—it's impossible to do without someone in the position if there is absence. As a result, poor attendance had a particularly serious effect on metrics such as overtime pay and temporary help costs. At the urging of her compensation consultant, Lisa decided to look into a system similar to Marriott's "BENETRADE." With this benefit program, employees can trade the value of some sick days for other benefits. As Lisa put it, "I'd rather see our employees using their sick day pay for things like additional health care benefits, if it means they'll think twice before taking a sick day to run a personal errand."

Questions

1. Because employers typically make benefits available to all employees, they may not have the motivational effects of incentive plans. Given this, list five employee behaviors you believe Hotel Paris could try to improve through an enhanced benefits plan, and explain why you chose them.

2. Given your answer to question 1, explain specifically what benefits you would recommend the Hotel Paris implement to achieve these behavioral improvements.

KEY TERMS

ENDNOTES

1. John Pletz, "Workers, Go Home," *Crain's Chicago Business* 34, no. 8 (February 21, 2011), pp. 2, 14.

2. Based on Frederick Hills, Thomas Bergmann, and Vida Scarpello, *Compensation Decision Making* (Fort Worth, TX: The Dryden Press, 1994), p. 424. See also Fay Hansen, "The Cutting Edge of Benefit Cost Control," *Workforce*, March 2003, pp. 36–42; Crain's Benefits Outlook 2009, www.crainsbenefits.com/news/survey-finds-nearly-20-percent-of-employers-plan-to-drop-health-benefits.php, accessed July 28, 2009.

3. "Survey Finds 99 Percent of Employers Providing Health-Care Benefits," *Compensation & Benefits Review*, September/October 2002, p. 11. See also "National Compensation Survey: Employee Benefits in Private Industry in the United States, March 2006," U.S. Department of Labor, U.S. Bureau of Labor Statistics, August 2006.

4. "Costs This Year Increased at Highest Rate Since 2004, Survey Reveals," *HR Focus* 88, no. 1 (January 10, 2011); "Employee Medical Costs Expected to Increase by 8.5 Percent in 2012, According to PwC", http://www.pwc.com/us/en/pressreleases/2011/employer-medical-costs-expected-to-increase.jhtml accessed September 14, 2011.

5. "Trouble Ahead? Dissatisfaction with Benefits, Compensation," *HR Trendbook*, 2008, p. 16.

6. Joseph Martocchio, *Strategic Compensation* (Upper Saddle River, NJ: Prentice Hall, 2001), p. 262.

7. "California Domestic Partner Benefits Mandate Carries Likely Impact Beyond State's Borders," *BNA Bulletin to Management*, November 6, 2003, p. 353.

8. Pletz, "Workers, Go Home."

9. Ibid.

10. "HR Plays a Major Role in Curbing Company Unemployment Insurance Costs, Analysts Say," *BNA Bulletin to Management*, August 3, 2010, pp. 241–242.

11. www.bls.gov/opub/perspectives/issue2.pdf, accessed June 1, 2011.

12. Ibid.

13. www.bls.gov/opub/perspectives/issue2.pdf, accessed June 1, 2011.

14. Ken Belson, "At IBM, a Vacation Anytime, or Maybe No Vacation at All," *The New York Times*, August 31, 2007, pp. A1–A18.

15. "National Compensation Survey: Employee Benefits in Private Industry in the United States, March 2006," U.S. Bureau of Labor Statistics, August, 2006, p. 116. See also "Spurious Sick-Notes Spiral Upwards," *The Safety and Health Practitioner* 22, no. 6 (June 2004), p. 3.

16. "Unscheduled Employee Absences Cost Companies More Than Ever," *Compensation & Benefits Review*, March/April 2003, p. 19; Robert Grossman, "Gone but Not Forgotten," *HRMagazine* 56, no. 9 (September 2011), pp. 34–46.

17. "Making Up for Lost Time: How Employers Can Curb Excessive Unscheduled Absences," *BNA Human Resources Report*, October 20, 2003, p. 1097. See also W. H. J. Hassink et al., "Do Financial Bonuses Reduce Employee Absenteeism? Evidence from a Lottery," *Industrial and Labor Relations Review* 62, no. 3 (April 2009), pp. 327–342.

18. "SHRM Benefits Survey Finds Growth in Employer Use of Paid Leave Pools," *BNA Bulletin to Management*, March 21, 2002, p. 89.

19. See M. Michael Markowich and Steve Eckberg, "Get Control of the Absentee-Minded," *Personnel Journal*, March 1996, pp. 115–120; "Exploring the Pluses, Minuses, and Myths of Switching to Paid Time Off Banks," *BNA Bulletin to Management* 55, no. 25 (June 17, 2004), pp. 193–194.

20. Society for Human Resource Management 2009 employee benefits survey, quoted in Martha Frase, "Taking Time Off to the Bank," *HR Magazine*, March 2010, p. 42.

21. "Creating Holistic Time Off Programs Can Significantly Reduce Expenses," *Compensation & Benefits Review*, July/August 2007, pp. 18–19.

22. See, for example, Rita Zeidner, "Strategies for Saving in a Down Economy," *HR Magazine*, February 2009, p. 28.

23. Judith Whitaker, "How HR Made a Difference," *People Management* 27 (October 28, 2010).

24. Ibid.

25. The Department of Labor updated its revised regulations for administering the Family and Medical Leave Act in November 2008. See "DOL Issues Long-Awaited Rules; Address a Serious Health Condition, Many Other Issues," *BNA Bulletin to Management*, November 18, 2008, p. 369. In 2008, Congress amended the family and medical leave act to include, among other things, leave rights particularly for military families. See Sarah Martin, "FMLA Protection Recently Expanded to Military Families: Qualifying Exigency and Service Member Family Leave," *Compensation & Benefits Review*, September/October 2009, pp. 43–51.

26. "Ten Years After It Was Signed into Law, FMLA Needs Makeover, Advocates Contend," *BNA Bulletin to Management*, February 20, 2003, p. 58.

27. "HR Professionals Face Sundry Challenges Administering FMLA Leave, Survey Asserts," *BNA Bulletin to Management*, July 20, 2007, p. 233.

28. Based on Dennis Grant, "Managing Employee Leaves: A Legal Primer," *Compensation & Benefits Review* 35, no. 4 (2003), p. 41. There are several unresolved issues in what "12 months' employment" means. For example, several courts recently held that an employee *can* count previous periods of employment with the employer to satisfy the 12-month requirement. See Daniel Ritter et al., "Recent Developments Under the Family and Medical Leave Act," *Compensation & Benefits Review*, September/October 2007, p. 33.

29. Gillian Flynn, "Employers Need an FMLA Brush-Up," *Workforce*, April 1997, pp. 101–104. See also "Worker Who Was Employee for Less Than One Year Can Pursue FMLA Claim, Federal Court Determines," *BNA Fair Employment Practices*, April 26, 2001, p. 51.

30. "Workers Who Come and Go Under FMLA Complicate Attendance Policies, Lawyer Says," *BNA Bulletin to Management*, March 16, 2000, p. 81.

31. Sue Shellenbarger, "The Mommy Drain: Employers Beef Up Perks to Lure New Mothers Back to Work," *The Wall Street Journal*, September 28, 2006, p. D1.

32. Jill Fisher, "Reconciling the Family Medical Leave Act with Overlapping or Conflicting State Leave Laws," *Compensation & Benefits Review*, September/October 2007, pp. 39–44.

33. "Severance Practices," *BNA Bulletin to Management*, January 11, 1996, pp. 12–13; and Neil Grossman, "Shrinking the Workforce in an Economic Slowdown," *Compensation & Benefits Review*, Spring 2002, pp. 12–23.

34. "Severance Pay," July 2007, Culpepper Compensation & Benefits Surveys.

35. Terry Baglieri, "Severance Pay," www.SHRM.org, accessed December 23, 2006.

36. Ibid.

37. Ibid.

38. "Workers' Compensation Costs Are Rising Faster Than Wages," *BNA Bulletin to Management*, July 31, 2003, p. 244.

39. "Workers' Comp Claims Rise with Layoffs, But Employers Can Identify, Prevent Fraud," *BNA Bulletin to Management*, October 4, 2001, p. 313.

40. "Firms Cite Own Efforts as Key to Controlling Costs," *BNA Bulletin to Management*, March 21, 1996, p. 89. See also "Workers' Compensation Outlook: Cost Control Persists," *BNA Bulletin to Management*, January 30, 1997, pp. 33–44; and Annmarie Lipold, "The Soaring Costs of Workers' Comp," *Workforce*, February 2003, p. 42ff.

41. "Using Case Management in Workers' Compensation," *BNA Bulletin to Management*, June 6, 1996, p. 181; for other tactics, see for example, H. Jorgensen, "Overhauling Claims Management." *Risk Management* 54, no. 7 (July 2007), p. 50.

42. "Workers Comp Research Provides Insight into Curbing Health Care Costs," *EHS Today*, February 2010, p. 18.

43. Hills, Bergmann, and Scarpello, *Compensation Decision Making*, p. 137.

44. "Costs This Year Increased at Highest Rate Since 2004, Survey Reveals," *HR Focus* 88, no. 1 (January 10, 2011).

45. Society for Human Resource Management, "Mental Health Trends," *Workplace Visions*, no. 2, http://moss07.shrm.org/Research/FutureWorkplaceTrends/Pages/0303.aspx, accessed July 28, 2009.

46. "Mental-Health Parity Measure Enacted as Part of Financial Rescue Signed by Bush," *BNA Bulletin to Management*, October 7, 2008, p. 321.

47. "Deadlines Vary for Implementing Provisions of Health Care Law," *BNA Bulletin to Management*, May 4, 2010, p. 143.

48. "Regulation Will Allow Young Adults Up to Age 26 to Retain Dependent Coverage," *BNA Bulletin to Management*, May 18, 2010, p. 153.

49. www.mercer.com/press-releases/1380755, accessed July 25, 2011.

50. Ibid.

51. See, for example, Karli Dunkelberger, "Avoiding COBRA's Bite: Three Keys to Compliance," *Compensation & Benefits Review*, March/April 2005, pp. 44–48. As an example of the direction new federal health insurance may take post-2009, see A. Mathews, "Making Sense of the Debate on Health Care," *Wall Street Journal* (Eastern Edition), September 30, 2009, pp. D1, D5; and Patrick Muldowney, "Cobra and the Stimulus Act: A Sign of Things to Come?" *Compensation & Benefits Review* 42, no. 1 (January/February 2010), pp. 24–49.

52. www.DOL.gov, accessed December 23, 2006.

53. Larri Short and Eileen Kahanar, "Unlocking the Secrets of the New Privacy Rules," *Occupational Hazards*, September 2002, pp. 51–54.

54. Kevin Maroney, "Prognosis Negative? GINA's Interim Incentives Ruling a Concern for Wellness Programs," *Compensation & Benefits Review* 42, no. 2 (2010), pp. 94–101.

55. "Hewitt Says Employer Measures to Control Increases in Health Care Costs Are Working," *BNA Bulletin to Management*, October 7, 2008, p. 323.

56. James Curcio, "Creating Standardized Metrics and Benchmarking for Health, Absence and Productivity Management Programs: The EMPAQ Initiative," *Compensation & Benefits Review* 42, no. 2 (2010), pp. 109–126.

57. Jerry Geisel, "Employers Accelerate Health Care Cost-Shifting," *Business Insurance* 45, no. 21 (May 23, 2011), pp. 3, 21.

58. Ibid.

59. Christine Keller and Christopher Condeluci, "Tax Relief and Health Care Act Should Prompt Re-Examination of HSAs," *SHRM Legal Report*, July–August 2007, p. 1.

60. In contrast, with health reimbursement arrangements (HRA) only the employer makes contributions. See "Types of Tax Favored Health Accounts," *HR Magazine*, August 2008, p. 76.

61. Michael Bond et al., "Using Health Savings Accounts to Provide Low-Cost Health-Care," *Compensation & Benefits Review*, March/April 2005, pp. 29–32.

62. "Costs This Year Increased At Highest Rate Since 2004, Survey Reveals," *HR Focus* 88, no. 1 (January 10, 2011).

63. Alan Cohen, "Decision-Support in the Benefits Consumer Age," *Compensation & Benefits Review*, March/April 2006, pp. 46–51.

64. Ibid., p. 40. See also "Employers Explore Range of Tactics to Rein In Rising Health Costs for 2005 Plan Year," *BNA Bulletin to Management* 55, no. 27 (July 1, 2004), p. 219.

65. Ron Finch, "Preventive Services: Improving the Bottom Line for Employers and Employees," *Compensation & Benefits Review*, March/April 2005, p. 18. Note that prevention/wellness programs can run afoul of the Americans with Disabilities Act. So, for instance, employers should not make participation in such plans mandatory or use information obtained in such programs in such a way that violates ADA confidentiality requirements or discriminates against employees who are not physically fit. See "Despite Good Intentions, Wellness Plans Can Run Afoul of ADA, Attorney Cautions," *BNA Bulletin to Management* 56, no. 51 (December 20, 2005), p. 41.

66. "Employer Partners to Launch a Three-Year Wellness Initiative," *BNA Bulletin to Management*, August 7, 2007, p. 255.

67. "On-Site Clinics Aimed at Cutting Costs, Promoting Wellness," *BNA Bulletin to Management*, March 25, 2008, p. 103.

68. Ibid. See also Josh Cable, "The Road to Wellness," *Occupational Hazards*, April 2007, pp. 23–27.

69. George DeVries, "The Top 10 Wellness Trends for 2008 and Beyond," *Compensation & Benefits Review*, July/August 2008, pp. 60–63.

70. Susan Wells, "Getting Paid for Staying Well," *HR Magazine*, February 2010, p. 59.

71. Vanessa Fuhrmanns, "Oops! As Health Plans Become More Complicated, They're Also Subject to a Lot More Costly Mistakes," *The Wall Street Journal*, January 24, 2005, p. R4.

72. Martha Frase, "Minimalist Health Coverage," *HR Magazine*, June 2009, pp. 107–112.

73. Bill Roberts, "Outsourcing in Turbulent Times," *HR Magazine*, November 2009, p. 45.

74. "High Deductible Plans Might Catch On," *BNA Human Resources Report*, September 15, 2003, p. 967.

75. "HR Outsourcing: Managing Costs and Maximizing Provider Relations," *BNA, Inc.* 21, no. 11 (Washington, DC: November 2003), p. 10.

76. "One in Five Big Firms May Drop Coverage for Future Retirees, Health Survey Finds," *BNA Bulletin to Management*, December 12, 2002, p. 393. Reducing retiree benefits requires a preliminary legal review. See James McElligott Jr., "Retiree Medical Benefit Developments in the Courts, Congress, and EEOC," *Compensation & Benefits Review*, March/April 2005, pp. 23–28; and Natalie Norfus, "Retiree Benefits: Does an Employer's Obligation to Pay Ever End?" *Compensation & Benefits Review*, January/February 2008, pp. 42–45.

77. Robert Christadore, "Benefits Purchasing Alliances: Creating Stability in an Unstable World," *Compensation & Benefits Review*, September/October 2001, pp. 49–53. Betty Liddick, "Going the Distance for Health Savings," *HR Magazine*, March 2007, pp. 51–55. J. Wojcik, "Employers Consider Short-Haul Medical Tourism," *Business Insurance* 43, no. 29 (August 24, 2009), pp. 1, 20.

78. "Dependent Eligibility Audits Can Help Rein In Health Care Costs, Analysts Say," *BNA Bulletin to Management*, September 9, 2008, p. 289.

79. Carolyn Hirschman, "Will Employers Take the Lead in Long-Term Care?" *HR Magazine*, March 1997, pp. 59–66. For recent perspective, see A. D. Postal, "Industry Ramps Up Opposition To LTC Program In Senate Health Bill," *National Underwriter* (Life & Health/Financial Services Edition) 113, no. 14 (July 20, 2009), pp. 10, 32.

80. Bill Leonard, "Recipes for Part-Time Benefits," *HR Magazine*, April 2000, pp. 56–62.

81. As we explained earlier in this book, do not confuse independent contractors with part-time workers. As three attorneys put it, "Short-term, just-in-time workers provided by staffing agencies are not an issue. However, the employer's policy for workers who are still on the job after 1,000 to 1,500 hours should require that they be provided with benefits, either through the staffing agency or by outsourcing their administration to an administrative employer who can provide benefits." Bob Lanza et al., "Legal Status of Contingent Workers," *Compensation & Benefits Review*, July/August 2003, pp. 47–60.

82. Brenda Paik Sunoo, "Millions May Retire," *Workforce*, December 1997, p. 48. See also "Many Older Workers Choose to 'Un-Retire' or Not Retire at All," *Knight Ridder/Tribune Business News*, September 28, 2003, item 03271012; Patrick Purcell, "Older Workers: Recent Trends in Employment and Retirement," *Journal of Deferred Compensation* 8, no. 3 (Spring 2003), pp. 30–54; and "For Many Seniors, a Job Beats Retirement," *Knight Ridder/Tribune Business News*, February 9, 2003, item 3040001.

83. The U.S. Treasury has reportedly spent most of the trust fund on other government programs, so that changes (for

instance, in terms of reducing benefits, making people wait longer for benefits, or making some people pay more for benefits) will be necessary. John Kilgour, "Social Security in the 21st Century," *Compensation & Benefits Review* 42, no. 6 (2010), pp. 459–469.

84. In addition, tax rates under the Medicare program are 1.45 percent for employees and employers. http://ssa-custhelp.ssa.gov/app/answers/detail/a_id/240/~/2011-social-security-tax-rate-and-maximum-taxable-earnings, accessed June 1, 2011.

85. Martocchio, *Strategic Compensation*, pp. 245–248; and Lin Grensing-Pophal, "A Pension Formula that Pays Off," *HR Magazine* (February 2003), pp. 58–62.

86. For one recent example of how to do this, see Gail Nichols, "Reviewing and Redesigning Retirement Plans," *Compensation & Benefits Review*, May/June 2008, pp. 40–47.

87. Many employers are considering terminating their plans but most employers are considering instead either ceasing benefits accruals for all participants or just for future participants. Michael Cotter, "The Big Freeze: The Next Phase in the Decline of Defined Benefit Plans," *Compensation & Benefits Review*, March/April 2009, pp. 44–53.

88. Jessica Marquez, "More Workers Yanking Money Out of 401(k)s," *Workforce Management*, August 11, 2008, p. 4.

89. Nancy Pridgen, "The Duty to Monitor Appointed Fiduciaries Under ERISA," *Compensation & Benefits Review*, September/October 2007, pp. 46–51; "Individual 401(k) Plan Participant Can Sue Plan Fiduciary for Losses, Justices Rule," *BNA Bulletin to Management*, February 20, 2008, p. 65.

90. Lindsay Wyatt, "401(k) Conversion: It's as Easy as Riding a Bike," *Workforce*, April 1997, p. 66. See also Carolyn Hirschman, "Growing Pains. Employers and Employees Alike Have Lots to Learn About 401(k) Plans," *HR Magazine*, June 2002, pp. 30–38.

91. "Benefit Trends: Automatic Enrollment Takes Off," *Compensation & Benefits Review*, September/October 2008, p. 14.

92. For a discussion, see Jewel Esposito, "Avoiding 401(k) ERISA Disasters," *Compensation & Benefits Review* 42, no. 1 (January/February 2010), pp. 39–45.

93. Jack VanDerhei, "The Pension Protection Act and 401(k)s," *The Wall Street Journal*, April 20, 2008, p. 12.

94. Jessica Marquez, "Retirement Out of Reach," *Workforce Management*, November 3, 2008, pp. 1, 24.

95. Wyatt, "401(k) Conversion," p. 20.

96. "New Pension Law Plus a Recent Court Ruling Doom Age-Related Suits, Practitioners Say," *BNA Bulletin to Management* 57, no. 36 (September 5, 2006), pp. 281–282; and www.dol.gov/ebsa/FAQs/faq_consumer_cashbalanceplans.html, accessed January 9, 2010.

97. Harold Burlingame and Michael Gulotta, "Cash Balance Pension Plan Facilitates Restructuring the Workforce at AT&T," *Compensation & Benefits Review*, November/December 1998, pp. 25–31; Eric Lekus, "When Are Cash Balance Pension Plans the Right Choice?" *BNA Bulletin to Management*, January 28, 1999, p. 7; Jerry Geisel, "IRS releases long-awaited cash balance guidance," *Pensions & Investments* 38 no. 22 (November 1 2010), p. 22.

98. This is based on Eric Parmenter, "Employee Benefit Compliance Checklist," *Compensation & Benefits Review*, May/June 2002, pp. 29–38.

99. www.pbgc.gov/about/faq/pg/general-faqs-about-pbgc.html, accessed June 1, 2011.

100. Patrick Kiger, "Early-Retirement Plans Backfire, Driving Up Costs Instead of Cutting Them," *Workforce Management*, January 2004, pp. 66–68.

101. "Benefits Cost Control Solutions to Consider Now," *HR Focus* 80, no. 11 (November 2003), p. 1.

102. Johanna Rodgers, "Web Based Apps Simplify Employee Benefits," *Insurance and Technology* 28, no. 11 (November 2003), p. 21. See also www.benelogic.com/, accessed June 28, 2011.

103. Ibid.

104. Scott Harper, "Online Resources System Boosts Worker Awareness," *BNA Bulletin to Management*, April 10, 2007, p. 119.

105. Drew Robb, "A Total View of Employee Records," *HR Magazine*, August 2007, pp. 93–96.

106. Carolyn Hirschman, "Employees' Choice," *HR Magazine*, February 2006, pp. 95–99.

107. Joseph O'Connell, "Using Employee Assistance Programs to Avoid Crises," *Long Island Business News*, April 19, 2002, p. 10.

108. See Scott MacDonald et al., "Absenteeism and Other Workplace Indicators of Employee Assistance Program Clients and Matched Controls," *Employee Assistance Quarterly* 15, no. 3 (2000), pp. 51–58. See also Paul Courtis et al., "Performance Measures in the Employee Assistance Program," *Employee Assistance Quarterly* 19, no. 3 (2005), pp. 45–58.

109. See, for example, Donna Owens, "EAPs for a Diverse World," *HR Magazine*, October 2006, pp. 91–96.

110. "EAP Providers," *Workforce Management*, July 14, 2008, p. 16.

111. "Fathers Fighting to Keep Work–Life Balance Are Finding Employers Firmly in their Corner," *BNA Bulletin to Management* 56, no. 24 (June 14, 2005), p. 185.

112. Susan Wells, "Are You Too Family-Friendly?" *HR Magazine*, October 2007, pp. 35–39.

113. Maureen Hannay and Melissa Northam, "Low-Cost Strategies for Employee Retention," *Compensation & Benefits Review*, July/August 2000, pp. 65–72. See also Roseanne Geisel, "Responding to Changing Ideas of Family," *HR Magazine*, August 2004, pp. 89–98.

114. "Child Care Options," *BNA Bulletin to Management*, July 4, 1996, p. 212. See also "Child Care Report Boasts of Its Benefit to California Economy," *Knight Ridder/Tribune Business News*, January 9, 2003, item 03009011.

115. Patrick Kiger, "A Case for Childcare," *Workforce Management*, April 2004, pp. 34–40.

116. www.SHRM.org/rewards/library, accessed December 23, 2006. See also Kathy Gurchiek, "Give Us Your Sick," *HR Magazine*, January 2007, pp. 91–93.

117. Kelli Earhart, R. Dennis Middlemist, and Willie Hopkins, "Elder Care: An Emerging Assistance Issue," *Employee Assistance Quarterly* 8, no. 3 (1993), pp. 1–10. See also, "Finding a Balance Between Conflicting Responsibilities: Work and Caring for Aging Parents," *Monday Business Briefing*, July 7, 2004; and "Employers Feel Impact of Eldercare: Some Expanded Benefits for Workers," *Knight Ridder/Tribune Business News*, June 13, 2004, item 04165011.

118. "Employers Gain from Elder Care Programs by Boosting Workers' Morale, Productivity," *BNA Bulletin to Management* 57, no. 10 (March 7, 2006), pp. 73–74.

119. Rudy Yandrick, "Elder Care Grows Up," *HR Magazine*, November 2001, pp. 72–77.

120. Matthew Boyle, "How to Cut Perks Without Killing Morale," *Fortune*, February 19, 2001, pp. 241–244.

121. Susan Lambert, "Added Benefits: The Link Between Work Life Benefits and Organizational Citizenship Behavior," *Academy of Management Journal* 43, no. 5 (2000), pp. 801–815. Timothy Judge et al., "Work Family Conflict and Emotions: Effects at Work and Home," *Personnel Psychology* 59 (2006), pp. 779–814.

122. "Rising Gas Prices Prompting Employers to Consider Varied Computer Benefit Options," *BNA Bulletin to Management*, June 20, 2008, p. 201.

123. Mary Burke, Euren Esen, and Jessica Cullison, "2003 Benefits Survey," SHRM/SHRM Foundation, 1800 Duke Street, Alexandria VA, 2003, p. 30. See also Michael Laff, "U.S. Employers Tighten Reins on Tuition Reimbursement," *Training & Development*, July 2006, p. 18.

124. Richard Buddin and Kanika Kapur, "The Effect of Employer-Sponsored Education on Job Mobility: Evidence from the U.S. Navy," *Industrial Relations* 44, no. 2 (April 2005), pp. 341–363.

125. "What You Need to Know to Provide Domestic Partner Benefits," *HR Focus* 80, no. 3 (August 2003), p. 3.

126. Carolyn Shapiro, "More Companies Cover Benefits for Employee's Domestic Partners," *Knight-Ridder/Tribune Business News*, July 20, 2003.

127. "Couples Want Flexible Leave, Benefits," *BNA Bulletin to Management*, February 19, 1998, p. 53; SHRM, "2003 Benefits Survey," p. 14. See also Paul Harris, "Flexible Work

Policies Mean Business," *Training & Development*, April 2007, pp. 32–36.

128. "Money Isn't Everything," *Journal of Business Strategy* 21, no. 2 (March 2000), p. 4; see also "CEOs in the Dark on Employees' Benefits Preferences," *Employee Benefits News*, September 1, 2006, item 06244007.

129. Carolyn Hirshman, "Kinder, Simpler Cafeteria Rules," *HR Magazine*, January 2001, pp. 74–79.

130. "Employers Should Update Cafeteria Plans Now Based on Proposed Regs, Experts Say," *BNA Bulletin to Management*, September 4, 2007, pp. 281–282.

131. "Debit Cards for Health-Care Expenses Receive Increased Employer Attention," *BNA Bulletin to Management*, September 25, 2003, p. 305.

132. Martocchio, *Strategic Compensation*, p. 263.

133. Elka Maria Torpey, "Flexible Work: Adjusting the When and Where of Your Job," *Occupational Outlook Quarterly*, Summer 2007, pp. 14–27.

134. "Slightly More Workers Are Skirting 9–5 Tradition," *BNA Bulletin to Management*, June 20, 2002, p. 197.

135. See, for example, "Compressed Workweeks Gain Popularity, but Concerns Remain About Effectiveness," *BNA Bulletin to Management*, September 16, 2008, p. 297.

136. Boris Baltes et al., "Flexible and Compressed Workweek Schedules: A Meta-Analysis of Their Effects on Work-Related Criteria," *Journal of Applied Psychology* 84, no. 4 (1999), pp. 496–513. See also Charlotte

Hoff, "With Flextime, Less Can Be More," *Workforce Management*, May 2005, pp. 65–66.

137. Farrokh Mamaghani, "Impact of Information Technology on the Workforce of the Future: An Analysis," *International Journal of Management* 23, no. 4 (2006), pp. 845–850; Jessica Marquez, "Connecting a Virtual Workforce," *Workforce Management*, September 20, 2008, pp. 1–3.

138. Ann Pomeroy, "The Future Is Now," *HR Magazine*, September 2007, pp. 46–52.

139. SHRM, "2003 Benefits Survey," p. 2.

140. "With Job Sharing Arrangements, Companies Can Get Two Employees for the Price of One," *BNA Bulletin to Management* 56, no. 47 (November 22, 2005), pp. 369–370.

PART 4 VIDEO CASES APPENDIX

Video Title: Pay for Performance and Financial Incentives (Joie de Vivre Hospitality)

SYNOPSIS

Chip Conley is the founder of Joie de Vivre Hospitality (JDV), a collection of boutique hotels, restaurants, and spas in California. Conley aims to foster employee motivation using Maslow's Hierarchy of Needs and has written books and lectured on the subject. Joie de Vivre pays average wages, but experiences low turnover due to the nature of the relationships it has formed with each employee.

Discussion Questions

1. Chip Conley, founder of Joie de Vivre Hospitality, believes that most companies frame their financial incentives in the wrong way. Explain what he means. What does JDV do differently?
2. Why does Joie de Vivre offer free hotel stays to all employees as part of its incentive plan?
3. According to the video, what separates a world-class organization is its ability to care for its employees in good times and in bad? How did JDV accomplish this during the dot-com crash and post-9/11 industry recession?
4. Of the compensation, benefits, and incentives practices we discussed in Chapters 11, 12, and 13, which would you recommend JDV implement, and why?

Video Title: Compensation (Focus Pointe)

SYNOPSIS

In this video, two HR staff members, Cheryl and Gina, must determine if an employee, Angelo, is worthy of a pay raise. The company, Focus Pointe, provides market research services. One of these services involves recruiting consumer, medical, and other respondents for the market research industry. It's important to get good, qualified respondents. To distinguish itself from its competitors, Focus Pointe uses a special "triple screening" process to ensure that the respondents it recruits meet its clients' specifications. In this case, Angelo seems to be recruiting inadequate respondents. The two HR staff members are trying to determine if giving Angelo a raise would solve the problem.

As Angelo says in the video, he'd like to be better compensated. Cheryl and Gina point out to him that his pay is falling because his recruits often don't qualify. They ask him what he would like—an increase in salary or an increase in the amount per recruit that he is paid. He responds that he'd like both. They tell them they will go along with his request but that they must see higher levels of recruit qualifications within 3 months. As the panel's human resource managers (including Paul, from BMG) point out in assessing this video, they don't necessarily agree with giving someone who is underperforming a raise. As Paul says, "They should have just told him to improve first."

Discussion Questions

1. Do you think Angelo is underperforming as a result of motivation or something else, such as the need for improved training? How would you find out?
2. Is it a good idea to give someone who is underperforming a raise? Does it send the wrong signal, insofar as it seems to suggest that poor performance leads to rewards?
3. Do you think the idea of paying recruiters like Angelo per recruit might actually backfire, and if so how?

14

Ethics and Employee Rights and Discipline

LEARNING OBJECTIVES

1. Explain what is meant by ethical behavior at work.
2. Discuss important factors that shape ethical behavior at work.
3. Describe at least four specific ways in which HR management can influence ethical behavior at work.
4. Employ fair disciplinary practices.
5. List at least four important factors in managing dismissals effectively.

Not too long ago, Berkshire Hathaway spent $9 billion buying Lubrizol Corporation. Berkshire's CEO, Warren Buffett, at first declined to pursue Lubrizol, but a Berkshire top executive helped persuade him to do so. This executive did mention to Mr. Buffett that he (the executive) owned Lubrizol shares. However, Mr. Buffett apparently didn't pursue the matter, for instance by asking how many shares he owned. After it transpired that the executive bought about $10 million worth of shares just before bringing the potential acquisition to Mr. Buffett, Berkshire Hathaway said that the executive had now resigned. Questions remained, however. Why didn't Warren Buffett ask more questions about how many shares the executive owned and when he bought them? And, how could something like this even happen in a company still rightfully praised for its high ethical standards?

Access a host of interactive learning aids at **www.mymanagementlab.com** to help strengthen your understanding of the chapter concepts.

Company's Strategic Goals

Employee Competencies and Behaviors Required for Company to Achieve These Strategic Goals

Employee Relations

Strategic and Legal Environment

Compensation

HR Policies and Practices Required to Produce Employee Competencies and Behaviors

Training and Development

Recruitment and Placement

WHERE ARE WE NOW . . .

For many managers, recruitment and placement, training and development, and compensation are the heart of human resource management. But employees expect something more. They expect their employers to treat them fairly, and to have a safe work environment. Now, in Part 5, we turn to employee justice, safety, and union relations. The main purpose of this chapter is to explain ethics, employee rights, and fair treatment in human resource management, matters essential for positive employee relations. Topics include ethics and fair treatment at work, factors that shape ethical behavior at work, and managers' roles in fostering improved workplace ethics, employee discipline, and dismissals.

1 Explain what is meant by ethical behavior at work.

ETHICS AND FAIR TREATMENT AT WORK

THE STRATEGIC CONTEXT

Berkshire Hathaway

The situation with Berkshire Hathaway's purchase of Lubrizol illustrates the strategic nature of ethics at work. Berkshire Hathaway's strategy of investing in diverse businesses requires giving its division heads great latitude to run their divisions as they see fit. Berkshire's strategy therefore depends heavily on its managers sticking to the company's ethical rules. To help ensure such behavior, Berkshire's code of ethics is very clear. It says "A conflict of interest exists when a person's private interests interfere in any way with the interests of the company."[1]

So in this Lubrizol situation the strategic context was clear: Decentralized management was central to Berkshire's diversified strategy, which in turn made executives' ethical behavior critical to Berkshire maintaining control and achieving its goals. That such an alleged conflict of interest could arise at an exemplary firm like Berkshire underscores the challenge that employers face in managing ethical behavior.

FIGURE 14-1 The *Wall Street Journal* Workplace Ethics Quiz

Source: The *Wall Street Journal,* October 21, 1999, pp. B1–B4. Ethics Officer Association, Belmont, MA: Ethics Leadership Group.

People face ethical choices every day. Is it wrong to use a company credit card for personal purchases? Is a $50 gift to a client unacceptable? Compare your answers by answering the quiz in Figure 14-1.

Most everyone reading this book rightfully view themselves as ethical people, so why include ethics in a human resource management book? For two reasons: First, ethics is not theoretical. Instead, it greases the wheels that make businesses work.

The spread of technology into the workshop has raised a variety of new ethical questions and many old ones still linger. Compare your answers with those of other Americans surveyed, on page 490.

Office Technology

1. Is it wrong to use company e-mail for personal reasons?
   ☐ Yes   ☐ No

2. Is it wrong to use office equipment to help your children or spouse do schoolwork?
   ☐ Yes   ☐ No

3. Is it wrong to play computer games on office equipment during the workday?
   ☐ Yes   ☐ No

4. Is it wrong to use office equipment to do Internet shopping?
   ☐ Yes   ☐ No

5. Is it unethical to blame an error you made on a technological glitch?
   ☐ Yes   ☐ No

6. Is it unethical to visit pornographic Web sites using office equipment?
   ☐ Yes   ☐ No

Gifts and Entertainment

7. What's the value at which a gift from a supplier or client becomes troubling?
   ☐ $25   ☐ $50   ☐ $100

8. Is a $50 gift to a boss unacceptable?
   ☐ Yes   ☐ No

9. Is a $50 gift *from* the boss unacceptable?
   ☐ Yes   ☐ No

10. Of gifts from suppliers: Is it OK to take a $200 pair of football tickets?
    ☐ Yes   ☐ No

11. Is it OK to take a $120 pair of theater tickets?
    ☐ Yes   ☐ No

12. Is it OK to take a $100 holiday food basket?
    ☐ Yes   ☐ No

13. Is it OK to take a $25 gift certificate?
    ☐ Yes   ☐ No

14. Can you accept a $75 prize won at a raffle at a supplier's conference?
    ☐ Yes   ☐ No

Truth and Lies

15. Due to on-the-job pressure, have you ever abused or lied about sick days?
    ☐ Yes   ☐ No

16. Due to on-the-job pressure, have you ever taken credit for someone else's work or idea?
    ☐ Yes   ☐ No

Managers who promise raises but don't deliver, salespeople who say "The order's coming" when it's not, production managers who take kickbacks from suppliers—they all corrode the trust that day-to-day business transactions depend on. According to one lawsuit, marketers for Pfizer Inc. influenced Pfizer to suppress unfavorable studies about one of its drugs.[2] Plaintiffs sued for billions.

Second, ethical dilemmas are a familiar part of human resource management. For example, your team shouldn't start work on the new machine until all the safety measures are checked, but your boss is pressing you to get started: What should you do? You dismissed an employee in an angry moment, and now she has applied for unemployment insurance, saying you never warned her. Should you create and place in her file a note of warning, to protect your employer from paying higher unemployment taxes? One survey found that 6 of the 10 most serious ethical work issues—workplace safety, employee records security, employee theft, affirmative action, comparable work, and employee privacy rights—were HR-related.[3] Another found that 54% of human resource professionals surveyed had observed misconduct ranging from violations of Title VII to violations of the Occupational Safety and Health Act.[4] The bottom line is that all managers should understand the basics of ethics and the ethical dimensions of their people-related decisions. We'll start with what *ethics* means.

What Is Ethics?

Ethics refers to "the principles of conduct governing an individual or a group; specifically, the standards you use to decide what your conduct should be."[5]

Making ethical decisions always requires *normative judgments*.[6] A normative judgment means that something is good or bad, right or wrong, better or worse. "You are wearing a great outfit!" is a normative statement. Ethical decisions also always involve morality. *Morality* is society's highest accepted standards of behavior. Moral standards guide behaviors regarding serious matters such as murder, lying, and slander. Authoritative bodies like legislatures can't change what morality means. You can't make something that's immoral (such as murder) legal by passing a law that says it's legal. Violating moral standards often makes one feel ashamed or remorseful.[7] If the decision makes the person feel ashamed or remorseful, or requires doing something with serious consequence such as murder, then, chances are, it's unethical.

Ethics and the Law

Because legislative bodies can't change what morality means, asking, "Is what I'm doing legal?" won't necessarily reveal if it is ethical. Something may be legal but unethical or even illegal but ethical. Firing a 59-year-old employee with 40 years' tenure without cause may be legal, but some would view it as unethical. One executive put it this way: "Ethics means making decisions that represent what you stand for, not just what the laws are."[8]

Ethics, Justice, and Fair Treatment

Companies that employees view as "fair and just" also tend to score higher on ethics. One study concluded that, "to the extent that survey respondents believed that employees were treated fairly . . . [they] reported less unethical behavior in their organizations."[9] A company that is *just* is, among other things, equitable, fair, impartial, and unbiased. With respect to the workplace, experts generally define *organizational justice* in terms of distributive justice and procedural justice.

ethics
The principles of conduct governing an individual or a group; specifically, the standards you use to decide what your conduct should be.

FIGURE 14-2 Perceptions
of Fair Interpersonal
Treatment Scale

Source: Michelle A. Donovan
et al., "The Perceptions of Their
Interpersonal Treatment Scale:
Development and Validation
of a Measure of Interpersonal
Treatment in the Workplace,"
Journal of Applied Psychology 83,
no. 5 (1998), p. 692.

What is your organization like most of the time? Circle Yes if the item describes your organization, No if it does not describe your organization, and ? if you cannot decide.
 IN THIS ORGANIZATION:

1. Employees are praised for good work	Yes	?	No
2. Supervisors yell at employees (R)	Yes	?	No
3. Supervisors play favorites (R)	Yes	?	No
4. Employees are trusted	Yes	?	No
5. Employees' complaints are dealt with effectively	Yes	?	No
6. Employees are treated like children (R)	Yes	?	No
7. Employees are treated with respect	Yes	?	No
8. Employees' questions and problems are responded to quickly	Yes	?	No
9. Employees are lied to (R)	Yes	?	No
10. Employees' suggestions are ignored (R)	Yes	?	No
11. Supervisors swear at employees (R)	Yes	?	No
12. Employees' hard work is appreciated	Yes	?	No
13. Supervisors threaten to fire or lay off employees (R)	Yes	?	No
14. Employees are treated fairly	Yes	?	No
15. Coworkers help each other out	Yes	?	No
16. Coworkers argue with each other (R)	Yes	?	No
17. Coworkers put each other down (R)	Yes	?	No
18. Coworkers treat each other with respect	Yes	?	No

Note: R = the item is reverse scored.

- **Distributive justice** refers to the fairness and justice of the decision's *result* (for instance, did I get an equitable pay raise?).
- **Procedural justice** refers to the fairness of the *process* (for instance, is the process my company uses to allocate merit raises fair?).[10]

In practice, fair treatment reflects concrete actions such as "employees are treated with respect" (see Figure 14-2).[11] Most employees probably can't and won't unscramble what is ethical, fair, or just when it comes to how you treat them.[12]

Ethics, Public Policy, and Employee Rights

Recently, New York City's pension funds wanted Walmart to investigate allegations that its suppliers abroad were treating workers unfairly.[13] For instance, a Bangladeshi labor organizer alleged that one factory "does not enforce the law" on minimum wages.[14]

Societies don't rely on employers' ethics or sense of fairness or morality to ensure that they do what's right. Societies also institute various laws and procedures for enforcing these laws. These laws lay out what employers can and cannot do, for instance in terms of discriminating based on race. In so doing, these laws also carve out explicit rights for employees. For example, Title VII of The Civil Rights Act gives an employee the right to bring legal charges against an employer who he or she believes discriminated against him or her due to race.

UNALIENABLE RIGHTS However, not all rights derive from laws. Many rights flow from broader unwritten "human" or "unalienable" rights, rights that form the bedrock of American society.[15] For example, the 1776 U.S. Declaration of Independence famously states, "*We hold these truths to be self-evident, that all men are created equal, that they are endowed by their Creator with certain unalienable Rights, that among these are Life, Liberty and the pursuit of Happiness.*" Three years later, Congress passed the first 10 amendments to the U.S. Constitution, amendments now called the Bill of Rights. These rights govern Americans' rights vis-à-vis the government. For example, the first amendment gave Americans the right to practice their religions, to speak freely, and to assemble peacefully.

PUBLIC POLICY Although many laws, such as Title VII, aim to guarantee rights that people view as unalienable, reasonable people may differ over what the exact nature of those legal rights should be.

Most laws therefore also reflect public policy. In other words, governments enact laws so as to further their public policy aims. Thus, if New York decides that it's in its' citizens' best interests to lower fuel consumption by getting everyone to drive slower, its legislature may lower New York's speed limit. *Public policy* "consists of political decisions for implementing programs to achieve societal goals."[16] As with traffic laws, governments express their chosen public policies in the laws and regulations they set, and in the other decisions they make (such as how they spend their tax revenues). A government's public policy viewpoint propels the laws and the other decisions it makes, and the rights it decides to carve out, governing what its citizens can and cannot do.

EMPLOYMENT RIGHTS   *Protecting employee rights* is therefore part and parcel of all the employment laws we discuss in this book. As just a few examples, the National Labor Relations Act established the right of employees to engage in collective bargaining. The Landrum Griffin Act contained a "Bill of Rights" for union members, protecting them from mistreatment from their unions. The Fair Labor Standards Act gave employees the right to a minimum wage and overtime pay. The Occupational Safety and Health Act gave employees the right to refuse to work under unsafe conditions. The Consolidated Omnibus Budget Reconciliation Act (COBRA) gave employees rights to extended health insurance benefits. The bottom line is that although ethics, fairness, and morality help govern how employers treat their employees, the enforceable rights embedded in employment and other laws also govern employer behavior.

WHAT SHAPES ETHICAL BEHAVIOR AT WORK?

> **2** Discuss important factors that shape ethical behavior at work.

Whether a person acts ethically at work is usually not a consequence of any one thing. For example, could it be that everyone running the banks that triggered the sub-prime mess a few years ago was simply unethical? Not likely. There must have been more to it.

There's No One Smoking Gun

A recent review of over 30 years of ethics research concluded that three factors combine to determine the ethical choices a person makes.[17] The authors titled their paper "bad apples, bad cases, and bad barrels." They concluded that no single "smoking gun" determines ethical behavior. Instead, "bad apples" (people who make unethical choices), "bad cases" (ethical situations ripe for unethical choices), and "bad barrels" (environments which foster unethical choices) combine to determine what a person's ethical choices will be. The following summarizes their overall findings:

- *Individual characteristics: Who are the bad apples?* Some people are just more inclined to make unethical choices. The most principled people, with the highest level of "cognitive moral development," think through the implications of their decisions and apply ethical principles.

  However, most adults don't operate at this high level. Instead, most base their judgment about what is right on the expectations of their colleagues and other important people with whom they interact, or on company policies and what the law says.

  People at the lowest level make their ethical choices solely based on obeying what they're told and on avoiding punishment.

- *Which ethical situations make for bad (ethically dangerous) cases or situations?* Some ethical dilemmas are more likely to prompt unethical choices. Surprisingly, apparently "smaller" dilemmas prompt more bad choices. Why? Influential

---

distributive justice
The fairness and justice of a decision's result.

procedural justice
The fairness of the process.

factors in making such decisions include the total harm that can befall victims of an unethical choice, the likelihood that the action will result in harm, and the number of people potentially affected by the act. In less serious situations, it's more likely that someone might say, in effect, "It's okay to do this, even though I know it's wrong."

● *What are the "bad barrels"? What outside factors mold ethical choices?* These researchers also concluded that employers create bad and good cultures ("barrels") that shape ethical behavior, for good or for ill. Thus "a strong ethical culture that clearly communicates the range of acceptable and unacceptable behavior [such as through leader role models] is associated with fewer unethical decisions in the workplace."[18] For example, companies that promote an "everyone for himself" atmosphere are more likely to suffer unethical decisions. On the other hand, emphasizing that employees should focus on the well-being of everyone leads to more ethical choices.

We look more closely at "bad apples" and "bad barrels" next.

The Person (What Makes Bad Apples?)

Because people bring to their jobs their own ideas of what is morally right and wrong, each person must shoulder much of the credit (or blame) for his or her ethical choices. Some people are just more principled than others. For example, researchers surveyed CEOs to study the CEOs' intentions to engage in two questionable practices: soliciting a competitor's technological secrets, and making illegal payments to foreign officials. The researchers concluded that the CEOs' personal predispositions more strongly affected their decisions than did outside pressures or characteristics of their firms.[19]

TRAITS   The problem is it's hard to generalize about the characteristics of ethical or unethical people. Some studies suggest that age is a factor. One study surveyed 421 employees to measure the degree to which various traits influenced responses to ethical decisions. (Decisions included "doing personal business on company time" and "calling in sick to take a day off for personal use.") Older workers generally had stricter interpretations of ethical standards and made more ethical decisions than did younger ones.

Honesty testing (as we discussed in Chapter 5) can help pinpoint those people who are inclined to make bad ethical choices. How would you rate your own ethics? Figure 14-1 presented a short self-assessment survey for helping you answer that question.

Outside Forces That Shape Ethical Decisions (Bad Barrels)

COMPANY PRESSURES   We also saw that outside pressures weaken one's ethical compass. If people did unethical things at work solely for personal gain, it perhaps would be understandable (though inexcusable). The scary thing about unethical behavior at work is that it's often not driven by personal interests. As one former top executive said at his trial, "I took these actions, knowing they were wrong, in a misguided attempt to preserve the company to allow it to withstand what I believed were temporary financial difficulties."[20]

One study asked employees to list their reasons for taking unethical actions at work.[21] For most of these employees, "meeting schedule pressures," "meeting overly aggressive financial or business objectives," and "helping the company survive" were the three top causes. "Advancing my own career or financial interests" ranked about last. Thus (at least in this case) most ethical lapses seemed to occur because employees shifted their ethical compasses to "I must help my company." So the scary thing about unethical behavior at work is that it's often not just personal interests driving it. (A recent study suggests that people may not be so selfless. It found that people who took unethical actions out of loyalty were also more likely to expect reciprocity.)[22] In any case, guarding against pressures such as overly aggressive goals is one way to head off ethical lapses.

PRESSURE FROM THE BOSS   It's hard to resist even subtle pressure, let alone coercion, from your boss. According to one report, "the level of misconduct at work dropped dramatically when employees said their supervisors exhibited ethical behavior." Only 25% of employees who agreed that their supervisors "set a good example of ethical business behavior" said they had observed misconduct in the last year, compared with 72% of those who did not feel that their supervisors set good ethical examples.[23] Yet in another poll, only about 27% of employees strongly agreed that their organizations' leadership is ethical.[24]

Examples of how supervisors knowingly (or unknowingly) lead subordinates astray ethically include:

● Tell staffers to do whatever is necessary to achieve results.

● Overload top performers to ensure that work gets done.

● Look the other way when wrongdoing occurs.

● Take credit for others' work or shift blame.

● Be dishonest.[25]

ETHICS POLICIES AND CODES   An ethics policy and code is a good way to signal that the firm is serious about ethics. For example, IBM's code of ethics has this to say about tips, gifts, and entertainment:

> No IBM employee, or any member of his or her immediate family, can accept gratuities or gifts of money from a supplier, customer, or anyone in a business relationship. Nor can they accept a gift or consideration that could be perceived as having been offered because of the business relationship. "Perceived" simply means this: If you read about it in the local newspaper, would you wonder whether the gift just might have had something to do with a business relationship? No IBM employee can give money or a gift of significant value to a customer, supplier, or anyone if it could reasonably be viewed as being done to gain a business advantage.[26]

Sometimes ethics codes don't work. A number of years ago, Enron Corp. allegedly collapsed in part due to some executives' ethical misdeeds. Yet Enron's ethical principles were prominent on its Web site. It stated, that, "as a partner in the communities in which we operate, Enron believes it has a responsibility to conduct itself according to certain basic principles." Those include "respect, integrity, communication and excellence."[27]

Beyond the code, some firms urge employees to apply a quick "ethics test" to evaluate whether what they're about to do fits the company's code of conduct. For example, Raytheon Co. asks employees who face ethical dilemmas to ask:

Is the action legal?

Is it right?

Who will be affected?

Does it fit Raytheon's values?

How will it "feel" afterwards?

How will it look in the newspaper?

Will it reflect poorly on the company?[28]

However, codifying the rules without enforcing them is futile. As one study of ethics concludes, "strong statements by managers may reduce the risk of legal and ethical violations by their work forces, but enforcement of standards has the greatest impact."[29] More firms, such as Lockheed Martin Corp., therefore appoint chief ethics officers.[30] *Ethics audits* typically address topics like conflicts of interest, giving and receiving gifts, employee discrimination, and access to company information.[31]

THE ORGANIZATION'S CULTURE   These examples illustrate that employees take their signals about what's acceptable not just from what managers say, but from what they do. Those signals then mold the company's **organizational culture**, the "characteristic values, traditions, and behaviors a company's employees share." A *value* is a basic belief about what is right or wrong, or about what you should or shouldn't do. ("Honesty is the best policy" would be a value.) Values are important because they guide and channel behavior. Managing people and shaping their behavior therefore depends on shaping the values they use as behavioral guides. For example, if management really believes "honesty is the best policy," the written rules they follow and the things they do should reflect this value. Managers therefore have to think through how to send the right signals to their employees. Doing so includes:

- **Clarifying expectations.** First, managers should make clear their expectations with respect to the values they want subordinates to follow. For example, the Johnson & Johnson ethics code says, "We believe our first responsibility is to the doctors, nurses and patients, to mothers and fathers and all others who use our products and services."
- **Using signs and symbols.** *Symbolism*—what the manager actually does and thus the signals he or she sends—is crucial. Managers need to "walk the talk." They can't expect to say, "don't fudge the financials" and then do so themselves.
- **Providing physical support.** The physical manifestations of the manager's values—the firm's incentive plan, appraisal system, and disciplinary procedures, for instance—signal employees regarding what they should and should not do. For example, does the firm reward ethical behavior or penalize it? [32]

In Summary: Some Things to Keep in Mind About Ethical Behavior at Work

Several experts reviewed the research concerning things that influence ethical behavior in organizations. Here is what their findings suggest for managers:[33]

- Ethical behavior starts with *moral awareness*. In other words, does the person even recognize that a moral issue exists in the situation?
- *Managers* can do a lot to influence employee ethics by carefully cultivating the right norms, leadership, reward systems, and culture.
- Ethics slide when people undergo *"moral disengagement."* Doing so frees them from the guilt that would normally go with violating one's ethical standards. For example, you're more likely to harm others when you view the victims as "outsiders."
- The most powerful morality comes from *within*. In effect, when the moral person asks, "Why be moral?" the answer is, "Because that is who I am." Then, failure to act morally creates emotional discomfort.[34]
- Beware the seductive power of an *unmet goal*. Unmet goals pursued blindly can contribute to unethical behavior.[35]
- Offering *rewards* for ethical behavior can backfire. Doing so may actually undermine the intrinsic value of ethical behavior.
- Don't inadvertently reward someone for *bad behavior*. For example, don't promote someone who got a big sale through devious means.[36]
- Employers should *punish unethical behavior*. Employees who observe unethical behavior expect you to discipline the perpetrators.
- The degree to which employees *openly talk about ethics* is a good predictor of ethical conduct. Conversely, organizations characterized by "moral muteness" suffer more ethically problematic behavior.
- People tend to alter their *moral compasses* when they join organizations. They uncritically equate "What's best for this organization (or team, or department)?" with "What's the right thing to do?"

> **3** Describe at least four specific ways in which HR management can influence ethical behavior at work.

USING HUMAN RESOURCE MANAGEMENT METHODS TO PROMOTE ETHICS AND FAIR TREATMENT

Managers can use personnel activities to support the employer's ethics goals. We'll consider examples.

Selection

As one writer says, "The simplest way to tune up an organization, ethically speaking, is to hire more ethical people."[37] Employers can start by creating recruitment materials that emphasize ethics. (The Microsoft site in Figure 14-3 is an example.) Similarly, use honesty tests and background checks (discussed in Chapter 6) to screen out undesirables.[38] Ask behavioral questions such as, "Have you ever observed someone stretching the rules at work? What did you do about it?[39]

FAIRNESS   As two writers put it, "If prospective employees perceive that the hiring process does not treat people fairly, they may [also] assume that ethical behavior is not important."[40] Here, keep several things in mind:

- Applicants tend to view the *formal procedure* (such as the interview) as fair to the extent that it tests job-related criteria and provides an opportunity to demonstrate competence.
- Applicants expect respect. *Interpersonal treatment* reflects such things as the propriety of the questions, the politeness of interviewer, and the degree of two-way communication.
- Applicants see a selection system as fair to the extent that the employer provides *useful feedback* about the employee's or candidate's own performance.[41]

FIGURE 14-3 Using the Company Web Site to Emphasize Ethics

Source: www.microsoft.com/industry/government/GovGiftingCompliance.mspx, accessed April 28, 2009.

organizational culture
The characteristic values, traditions, and behaviors a company's employees share.

Ethics Training

Ethics training involves showing employees how to recognize ethical dilemmas, how to use codes of conduct to resolve problems, and how to use personnel activities like disciplinary practices in ethical ways.[42] In addition, the training should emphasize the moral underpinnings of the ethical choice and the company's deep commitment to integrity and ethics. Include participation by top managers to underscore that commitment.[43]

For all practical purposes, ethics training is mandatory. Federal sentencing guidelines reduced penalties for employers accused of misconduct who implemented codes of conduct and ethics training. An amendment to those guidelines now outlines stricter ethics training requirements.[44] Ethics training usually includes showing employees how to recognize ethical dilemmas, how to use ethical frameworks (such as codes of conduct) to resolve problems, and how to use human resource activities (such as interviews and disciplinary practices) in ethical ways.

Ethics training is often Internet-based. For example, Lockheed Martin's 160,000 employees take ethics and legal compliance training via the firm's intranet. Lockheed's online ethics program software also keeps track of how well the company and its employees are doing in terms of maintaining high ethical standards.[45] Online ethics training tools include *Business Ethics for Managers* from SkillSoft (skillsoftcom).[46] Some employers are switching from packaged ethics training to more company-relevant customized programs. For example, Yahoo! had a vendor produce an animated package containing ethical scenarios set in Yahoo! company offices around the world. The 45-minute program covers Yahoo!'s code of conduct as well as issues like the Foreign Corrupt Practices Act.[47]

Performance Appraisal

How you conduct appraisals is important. To send the signal that fairness is paramount, performance standards should be clear, employees should understand the basis upon which you're going to appraise them, and the appraisal itself should be objective.

Reward and Disciplinary Systems

To the extent that behavior is a function of its consequences, the manager needs to reward ethical behavior and penalize unethical behavior. "Employees expect the organization to dole out relatively harsh punishment for unethical conduct."[48] If not, it's often the ethical employees who feel punished.

Managing Ethics Compliance

Passage of the Sarbanes-Oxley Act of 2002 made ethics compliance obligatory.[49] Among other things, the act requires that the CEO and the CFO of publicly traded companies personally attest to the accuracy of their companies' financial statements, and to the fact that internal controls are adequate.[50] One study of *Fortune* 500 companies concluded than an HR officer was responsible for the program in 28% of responding firms. Another 28% gave the firm's legal officers responsibility, and 16% established separate ethics or compliance departments. The remaining firms spread the responsibility among auditing departments, or positions such as public affairs and corporate communications.[51]

| 4 | Employ fair disciplinary practices. |

MANAGING EMPLOYEE DISCIPLINE AND PRIVACY

The purpose of *discipline* is to encourage employees to behave sensibly at work (where *sensible* means adhering to rules and regulations). Discipline is necessary when an employee violates a rule.[52]

Proper disciplinary procedures are important for several reasons (beyond the fact that it's the ethical thing to do). One study surveyed 45 published arbitration awards in which tardiness had triggered discipline and/or discharge. When arbitrators overturned employers' decisions, it was usually because the employer had failed to clarify what it meant by "tardy." A lack of clarity regarding how often an employee may be late and an inappropriately severe penalty were other problems. Unfair disciplinary procedures can backfire in other ways. For example, an unfair disciplinary procedure can trigger retaliatory employee misbehavior. It is also hard to be seen as ethical when one's disciplinary practices are unfair. Discipline is not primarily a factory-bound problem. Managers increasingly discipline workers for misuse of social media and related devices in the workplace.[53]

Fairness in Disciplining

Disciplining employees is often unavoidable, but any such discipline must be rooted in the need to be fair. For most people the answer to "Why treat employees fairly?" is obvious, since most learn, early on, some version of the golden rule. But there are also concrete reasons to treat employees fairly. *Arbitrators and the courts* will consider the fairness of the disciplinary procedures when reviewing disciplinary decisions. Fairness also relates to a wide range of *positive employee outcomes.* These include enhanced employee commitment and enhanced satisfaction with the organization, and more "organizational citizenship behaviors" (the steps employees take to support their employers' interests).[54] *Job applicants* who felt treated unfairly expressed more desire to appeal the outcome. Those who view the firm's testing programs as fair view the company and the job as more attractive.[55] There are thus many practical reasons for treating employees fairly.

RESEARCH INSIGHT   A study illustrates this. College instructors completed surveys regarding the extent to which they saw their colleges as treating them with procedural and distributive justice. Procedural justice items included, "In general, the department/college's procedures allow for requests for clarification for additional information about a decision." Distributive justice items included, "I am fairly rewarded considering the responsibilities I have." The instructors also completed attitude surveys. These included items such as, "I am proud to tell others that I am part of this department/college." Their students also completed surveys. These contained items such as "The instructor was sympathetic to my needs," and "The instructor treated me fairly."

The results were impressive. Instructors who perceived high distributive and procedural justice reported being more committed to the college and to their jobs. Their students reported higher levels of instructor effort, pro-social behaviors, and fairness.[56]

Bullying and Victimization

Workplace unfairness is often subtle, but can be blatant. Some supervisors are workplace bullies, yelling at or even threatening subordinates. Employers should always prohibit such behavior. Many firms have anti-harassment policies. (For example, at one state agency, "It is the policy of the department that all employees, customers, contractors, and visitors to the work site are entitled to a positive, respectful, and productive work environment.")[57] Not surprisingly, employees of abusive supervisors are more likely to quit their jobs, and to report lower job and life satisfaction and higher stress.[58] Mistreatment makes it more likely the employee will also show higher levels of "work withdrawal" (show up for work, but not do his or her best).[59] They also exhibit more workplace deviance, for instance, in terms of theft and sabotage.[60]

Bullying—singling out someone to harass and mistreating them—is an increasingly serious problem. The U.S. government (www.stopbullying.gov/#) points out that while definitions of bullying vary, most would agree that bullying involves three things:

- **Imbalance of power:** People who bully use their power to control or harm and the people being bullied may have a hard time defending themselves.
- **Intent to cause harm:** Actions done by accident are not bullying; the person bullying has a goal to cause harm.
- **Repetition:** Incidents of bullying happen to the same person over and over by the same person or group.

Bullying can take many forms, such as:

- **Verbal:** name-calling, teasing
- **Social:** spreading rumors, leaving people out on purpose, breaking up friendships
- **Physical:** hitting, punching, shoving
- **Cyberbullying:** using the Internet, mobile phones, or other digital technologies to harm others

Lest there be any doubt, the person to blame for any bullying is the perpetrator. Employers must have systems in place, similar to those discussed elsewhere in this chapter, to ensure that the company can identify unfair treatment and deal with it expeditiously. This includes having policies in place to monitor employees' use of social media Web sites.[61]

However, numerous studies (usually conducted under the umbrella of "the victim precipitation model") show that certain people's traits and how they behave make them more vulnerable to bullying.[62] These include submissive victims (who seem more anxious, cautious, quiet, and sensitive), provocative victims (who show more aggressive behavior), and victims low in self-determination (who, in other words, seem to leave it to others to make decisions for them and determine the course of their careers).

RESEARCH INSIGHT   A recent study illustrates the interpersonal dynamics involved. Research suggests that people with higher intellectual capability often suffer bullying in school contexts, for instance, in the form of derogatory names such as geek and nerd. In this study, 217 employees of a health care organization completed a survey that measured cognitive ability, victimization, and how the person behaved at work.[63] The researchers found that it wasn't just whether the person was very smart that determined whether he or she became a victim, but how the person behaved. People with high cognitive ability who behaved more independently were more likely to be victimized by bullying. High-cognitive-ability people who were team players were less likely to be victimized.

What Causes Unfair Behavior

Some of the things that motivate managers to be fair may (or may not) be surprising. For one thing, the saying, "the squeaky wheel gets the grease" is true. One study investigated the extent to which assertiveness on the subordinate's part influenced the fairness with which the person's supervisor treated him or her.[64] Supervisors treated pushier employees more fairly: "Individuals who communicated assertively were more likely to be treated fairly by the decision maker." Furthermore, supervisors exposed to injustice exhibit abusive behavior against subordinates who they see as vulnerable or provocative.[65]

One study concluded that three supervisory actions influenced perceived fairness:[66]

- *Involving employees* in the decisions that affect them by asking for their input and allowing them to refute the others' ideas and assumptions;
- Ensuring that everyone involved and affected *understands why* final decisions are made and the thinking that underlies the decisions; and
- Making sure everyone knows up front by what *standards* you will judge him or her.

Many employers establish channels through which employees can air their concerns. For example, the FedEx Survey Feedback Action (SFA) program includes an anonymous survey that lets employees express their feelings about the company and their managers. Sample items include:

- I can tell my manager what I think.
- My manager tells me what is expected.
- My manager listens to my concerns.
- My manager keeps me informed.

Each manager then has an opportunity to discuss the department results with subordinates, and create an action plan for improving work group commitment.

Basics of a Fair and Just Disciplinary Process

The employer wants its discipline process to be both effective (in terms of discouraging unwanted behavior) and fair. Employers base such a process on three pillars: clear rules and regulations, a system of progressive penalties, and an appeals process.

RULES AND REGULATIONS   First, rules and regulations address issues such as theft, destruction of company property, drinking on the job, and insubordination. Examples include:

- **Poor performance is not acceptable.** Each employee is expected to perform his or her work properly and efficiently.
- **Alcohol and drugs have no place at work.** The use of either during working hours and reporting for work under the influence of either are both prohibited.

Rules inform employees ahead of time what is and is not acceptable behavior. Upon hiring, tell employees, preferably in writing, what is not permitted. The employee handbook usually contains the rules and regulations.

PROGRESSIVE PENALTIES   A system of progressive penalties is a second pillar of effective discipline. Penalties typically range from oral warnings to written warnings to suspension from the job to discharge.

The severity of the penalty usually reflects the type of offense and the number of times it has occurred. For example, most companies issue warnings for the first unexcused lateness (see the form in Figure 14-4). For a fourth offense, discharge is the usual disciplinary action.

FORMAL DISCIPLINARY APPEALS PROCESSES   In addition to rules and progressive penalties, the disciplinary process requires an appeals procedure (see Figure 14-5).

Virtually all union agreements contain disciplinary appeal procedures, but such procedures are not limited to unionized firms. For example, FedEx calls its 3-step appeals procedure *guaranteed fair treatment:*

- In *step 1, management review*, the complainant submits a written complaint to a member of management (manager, senior manager, or managing director) within 7 calendar days.
- If not satisfied with that decision, then in *step 2, officer complaint*, the complainant submits a written appeal to the vice president or senior vice president of the division.
- Finally, in *step 3, executive appeals review*, the complainant may submit a written complaint within 7 calendar days of the step 2 decision to the employee relations department. It then investigates and prepares a case file for the executive review appeals board. The appeals board—the CEO, the COO, the chief personnel officer, and three senior vice presidents—then reviews all relevant information and makes a decision to uphold, overturn, or initiate a board of review, or to take other appropriate action.

Some companies establish independent ombudsman, neutral counselors outside the normal chain of command to whom employees can turn for confidential advice.[67]

DISCIPLINE WITHOUT PUNISHMENT   Traditional discipline has two potential drawbacks. First, no one likes to be punished. Second, punishment tends to gain short-term compliance, but not the long-term cooperation employers often prefer.

FIGURE 14-4 Disciplinary
Action Form

Source: Reprinted from www.HR.BLR.
com with permission of the publisher
Business and Legal Resources, Inc.,
141 Mill Rock Road East, Old
Saybrook, CT © 2004. BLR®
(Business and Legal Resources, Inc.).

Disciplinary Action Form

Date: _____

Name: _____

Dept.: _____

Disciplinary Action:

❏ Verbal*   ❏ Written   ❏ Written & Suspension   ❏ Discharge

To the employee:

Your performance has been found unsatisfactory for the reasons set
forth below. Your failure to improve or avoid a recurrence will be
cause for further disciplinary action.

Details: _____

_____

_____

_____

_____

A copy of this warning was personally delivered to the above
employee by:

Supervisor: _____

Date: _____

I have received and read this warning notice. I have been informed
that a copy of this notice will be placed in my personnel file.

Employee: _____

Date: _____

*If action is *verbal*, completion of this form shall serve as documentation
only and should not be filed in the employee's personnel file.

Discipline without punishment (or **nonpunitive discipline**) aims to avoid these
drawbacks. It does this by gaining employees' acceptance of the rules while reducing
the punitive nature of the discipline itself. Here is how it works:[68]

1. **Issue an oral reminder.** The goal is to get the employee to agree to avoid future
   infractions.

2. **Should another incident arise within 6 weeks, issue a formal written reminder,
   a copy of which is placed in the employee's personnel file.** In addition, hold a
   second private discussion with the employee, again without any threats.

3. **Give a paid, 1-day "decision-making leave."** If another incident occurs in the next
   6 weeks or so, tell the employee to take a 1-day leave with pay, and to stay home and
   consider whether he or she wants to abide by the company's rules. When the
   employee returns to work, he or she meets with you and gives you his or her decision.

4. **If no further incidents occur in the next year or so, purge the 1-day paid suspension
   from the person's file.** If the behavior reoccurs, typically the next step is dismissal.

WAKE FOREST
U N I V E R S I T Y

Human Resources

STAFF GRIEVANCE FORM

This form is to be used by staff employees of Wake Forest University to initiate a **formal** grievance (Step II) that seeks resolution of a work-related problem or complaint. An employee who wishes to pursue a formal grievance must first have attempted to resolve the grievance informally through a discussion with his/her immediate supervisor (Step I) as outlined in *Staff Employee Grievance and Appeal Process*. Upon completion, this form is to be submitted to the Human Resources Department (Employee Relations), 116 Reynolda Hall.

Grievant: _____ Telephone #: _____

Job Title: _____

Employing Department/Office: _____

Name of Immediate Supervisor: _____

Date Grievance was informally discussed with immediate supervisor (Step I): _____

EMPLOYEE STATEMENT OF GRIEVANCE:
(Provide a concise statement of facts, including dates, to identify the work-related problem or complaint. Attach a continuation page, if necessary.)

REMEDY OR REDRESS SOUGHT BY THE GRIEVANT:
(Be specific as to what resolution you are seeking)

_____   _____
GRIEVANT'S SIGNATURE   DATE

_____   _____
DATE THE GRIEVANCE WAS RECEIVED BY HUMAN RESOURCES   INITIALS

PO Box 7424 | Winston-Salem, NC 27109 | p 336.758.4700 | f 336.758.6127 | askhr@wfu.edu   WFU-HR-0013
Issued: 5-17-00
Revised: 11-8-01

The process would not apply in exceptional circumstances. For example, criminal behavior or in-plant fighting might be grounds for immediate dismissal. And if several incidents occurred at very close intervals, you might skip step 2—the written warning.

IN SUMMARY: THE HOT STOVE RULE Supervisors traditionally apply the 4-point "hot stove rule" when applying discipline. When touching a hot stove that says, "Don't touch," the person has *warning*, and the pain is *consistent*, *impersonal*, and *immediate*. Figure 14-6 summarizes useful fair discipline guidelines.

nonpunitive discipline
Discipline without punishment, usually involving a system of oral warnings and paid "decision-making leaves" in lieu of more traditional punishment.

FIGURE 14-6 Summary of Fair
Discipline Guidelines

- Make sure the evidence supports the charge.
- Make sure the employee's due process rights are protected.
- Warn the employee of the disciplinary consequences.
- The rule that was allegedly violated should be "reasonably related" to the efficient and safe operation of the work environment.
- Fairly and adequately investigate the matter before administering discipline.
- The investigation should produce substantial evidence of misconduct.
- Apply all rules, orders, or penalties evenhandedly.
- The penalty should be reasonably related to the misconduct and to the employee's past work.
- Maintain the employee's right to counsel.
- Don't rob a subordinate of his or her dignity.
- Remember that the burden of proof is on you.
- Get the facts. Don't base a decision on hearsay or on your general impression.
- Don't act while angry.
- In general, do not attempt to deal with an employee's "bad attitude." Focus on improving the specific behaviors creating the workplace problem.

Employee Privacy

For most people, invasions of privacy are neither ethical nor fair.[69] The four main types of employee privacy violations upheld by courts are intrusion (locker room and bathroom surveillance), publication of private matters, disclosure of medical records, and appropriation of an employee's name or likeness for commercial purposes.[70] (Breaching security of personnel files is a related problem, as we discussed in Chapter 5 [Recruiting]). One survey of security professionals ranked human resources last among departments securing such confidential data.[71]) In practice, background checks, monitoring off-duty conduct and lifestyle, drug testing, workplace searches, and monitoring of workplace activities trigger most privacy violations.[72] Some employers, such as Eastman Kodak, are appointing chief privacy officers to ensure that the human resource management and other departments don't endanger the company by conducting inappropriate investigations of job applicants or employees.[73] We'll now look more closely at monitoring.

Employee Monitoring

Employee monitoring is pervasive. Biometrics—using physical traits such as fingerprints or iris scans for identification—is one example. Thus, New York's Bronx Lebanon Hospital uses biometric scanners to ensure that the employee who clocks-in in the

More employers are using iris scanning to verify employee identity.

Source: Tim Chapman/Getty Images USA, Inc.

morning is really who he or she says he is.[74] Iris scanning tends to be the most accurate authorization device. The Federal Aviation Authority uses it to control employees' access to its information systems.[75] More than half of employers say they monitor their employees' incoming and outgoing e-mail; 27% monitor internal e-mail as well.[76] One survey found that 41% of large employers have someone reading employee e-mails.[77] Ninety-six percent block access to adult Web sites; 61% block access to game sites.[78] Employers such as United Parcel Service use GPS units to monitor their truckers' and street sweepers' whereabouts. Indeed, iPhones, iPads, and Android devices track their owners more or less continuously.

Employers monitor employees' electronic activities mostly to improve productivity and to protect themselves from computer viruses, leaks of confidential information, and harassment suits.[79] In one case, a New Jersey court found an employer liable when one of its employees used his company computer at work to distribute child pornography. (Someone had previously alerted the employer to the suspicious activity and the employer had not taken action.)[80] When one employer noticed that employees were piling up overtime claims, it installed new software. It discovered many employees were spending hours on Facebook and shopping online. A recent U.S. Federal Trade Commission decision may make employers liable for deceptive endorsements that employees post on their own blogs or on social media sites such as Facebook, even if the employers didn't authorize the statements.[81] Security is a problem, too. One "4-gigabyte MP3 player, such as the first generation of iPod Mini . . . can take home a lot of corporate data," said one employer (a process some graphically describe as "pod slurping.")[82]

RESTRICTIONS There are two main restrictions on workplace monitoring: the **Electronic Communications Privacy Act (ECPA)** and *common-law protections* against invasion of privacy. The ECPA is a federal law intended to help restrict interception and monitoring of oral and wire communications. It contains two exceptions. The "business purpose exception" permits employers to monitor communications if they can show a legitimate business reason for doing so. The second, "consent exception," lets employers monitor communications if they have their employees' consent to do so.[83]

Electronic eavesdropping is thus legal—up to a point. Federal law and most state laws allow employers to monitor employees' phone calls in the ordinary course of business, but they must stop listening once it becomes clear that a conversation is personal rather than business related. Employers can also generally monitor their own e-mail systems (and possibly private accounts such as Hotmail, if used by employees on their company computer systems), which are, after all, their property. However, to be safe, employers should warn employees to use those systems for business purposes only.[84] Employers should have employees sign e-mail and telephone monitoring acknowledgment statements like that in Figure 14-7.

Videotaped workplace monitoring deserves more caution. In one case, a U.S. Court of Appeals ruled that an employer's continuous video surveillance of employees in an office setting was not an unconstitutional invasion of privacy.[85] But a Boston employer had to pay more than $200,000 to five workers it secretly videotaped in an employee locker room.[86]

Electronic Communications Privacy Act (ECPA)
Intended in part to restrict interception and monitoring of oral and wire communications, but with two exceptions: employers who can show a legitimate business reason for doing so, and employers who have employees' consent to do so.

FIGURE 14-7 Sample E-Mail
Monitoring Acknowledgment
Statement

I understand that XYZ Company periodically monitors any e-mail communications created, sent, or retrieved using this company's e-mail system. Therefore I understand that my e-mail communications may be read by individuals other than the intended recipient. I also understand that XYZ Company periodically monitors telephone communications, for example to improve customer service quality.

_____   _____
Signature   Date

_____   _____
Print Name   Department

| 5 | List at least four important factors in managing dismissals effectively. |

MANAGING DISMISSALS

Dismissal or termination is the most drastic disciplinary step the employer can take. Because of this, it requires special care. There should be sufficient cause for the dismissal, and (as a rule) you should only dismiss someone after taking reasonable steps to rehabilitate the employee. However, there will undoubtedly be times when dismissal is required, perhaps at once.

The best way to "handle" a dismissal is to avoid it in the first place. Many dismissals start with bad hiring decisions. Using effective selection practices including assessment tests, reference and background checks, drug testing, and clearly defined job descriptions can reduce the need for many dismissals.

Termination at Will and Wrongful Discharge

For more than 100 years, *termination at will* was the prevailing dismissal-related rule in the United States. **Termination at will** means that without a contract, either the employer or the employee could *terminate at will* the employment relationship. The employee can resign for any reason, at will, and the employer can dismiss an employee for any reason, at will.[87]

Today, however, dismissed employees are increasingly taking their cases to court, and many employers are discovering they no longer have a blanket right to fire. Instead, EEO and other laws and court rulings limit management's right to dismiss. For example, a statement in an employee handbook may imply a contractual agreement to keep an employee. Some employers—even when faced with employee theft—are reluctant to terminate disruptive employees for fear of lawsuits. In practice, plaintiffs only win a tiny fraction of such suits, but the cost of defending the suits is still huge.[88]

WRONGFUL DISCHARGE   **Wrongful discharge** refers to a dismissal that violates the law or that fails to comply with contractual arrangements stated or implied by the employer, for instance, in employee manuals.

Three main protections against wrongful discharge have eroded the termination-at-will doctrine—statutory exceptions, common law exceptions, and public policy exceptions.

First, in terms of *statutory exceptions*, federal and state equal employment and workplace laws prohibit specific types of dismissals. As just one example, occupational safety laws prohibit firing employees for reporting dangerous workplace conditions.[89]

Second, numerous *common law exceptions* exist. For example, some state courts recognize the concept of *implied contracts* in employment. Thus, a court may decide that an employee handbook promising termination only "for just cause" may create an exception to the at-will rule.

Finally, under the *public policy exception*, courts have held a discharge to be wrongful when it was against an explicit, well-established public policy (for instance, the employer fired the employee for refusing to break the law).

Grounds for Dismissal

There are four bases for dismissal: unsatisfactory performance, misconduct, lack of qualifications for the job, and changed requirements of (or elimination of) the job. We'll discuss each.

Unsatisfactory performance means persistent failure to perform assigned duties or to meet prescribed job standards.[90] Specific grounds include excessive absenteeism, tardiness, a persistent failure to meet normal job requirements, or an adverse attitude toward the company, supervisor, or fellow employees.

Misconduct is deliberate and willful violation of the employer's rules and may include stealing, rowdy behavior, and insubordination. Sometimes the misconduct is more serious, as when it causes someone else harm. For example, a coworker posted on YouTube a cook at a national pizza chain apparently putting vile foreign matter into the pizzas. Figure 14-8 shows how to identify such *gross misconduct*.

Lack of qualifications for the job is an employee's inability to do the assigned work although he or she is diligent. If the employee may be trying to do the job, it is reasonable to do what's possible to salvage him or her—perhaps by assigning the person to another job.

Changed requirements of the job refers to an employee's inability to do the job after the employer changed the nature of the job. Again, the employee may be industrious, so it is reasonable to retrain or transfer this person, if possible.

INSUBORDINATION   **Insubordination** is a form of misconduct. It basically refers to disobedience and/or rebelliousness. While things like stealing, chronic tardiness, and poor-quality work are easily understood grounds for dismissal, insubordination is

FIGURE 14-8 Was It Gross Misconduct?

- Was anyone physically harmed? How badly?
- Did the employee realize the seriousness of his or her actions?
- Were other employees significantly affected?
- Was the employer's reputation severely damaged?
- Will the employer lose significant business or otherwise suffer economic harm because of the misconduct?
- Could the *employer* lose its business license because of the employee's misconduct?
- Will the *employee* lose any license needed to work for the employer (e.g., driver's license)?
- Was criminal activity involved?
- Was fraud involved?
- Was any safety statute violated?
- Was any civil statute violated?
- Was the conduct purposeful?
- Did the conduct occur while on duty?
- Is the violated policy well-known to employees?
- Does the conduct justify immediate termination?
- Has the employer immediately fired other employees who did something similar?

dismissal
Involuntary termination of an employee's employment with the firm.

termination at will
In the absence of a contract, either the employer or the employee can terminate at will the employment relationship.

wrongful discharge
An employee dismissal that does not comply with the law or does not comply with the contractual arrangement stated or implied by the firm via its employment application forms, employee manuals, or other promises.

insubordination
Willful disregard or disobedience of the boss's authority or legitimate orders; criticizing the boss in public.

sometimes harder to translate into words. However, some acts are usually clearly insubordinate. These include, for instance:

1. Direct disregard of the boss's authority
2. Direct disobedience of, or refusal to obey, the boss's orders, particularly in front of others
3. Deliberate defiance of clearly stated company policies, rules, regulations, and procedures
4. Public criticism of the boss
5. Blatant disregard of reasonable instructions
6. Contemptuous display of disrespect
7. Disregard for the chain of command, shown by frequently going around the immediate supervisor with complaints, suggestions, or political maneuvers
8. Participation in (or leadership of) an effort to undermine or remove the boss[91]

FAIRNESS IN DISMISSALS   Dismissals are never pleasant. However, there are three things to do to make them fair.[92] First, "individuals who said that they were given *full explanations* of why and how termination decisions were made were more likely to perceive their layoff as fair . . . and indicate that they did not wish to take the past employer to court."

Second, institute a formal *multistep procedure* (including warning) and a neutral appeal process.

Third, *who actually does the dismissing* is important. Employees in one study whose managers informed them of an impending layoff viewed the dismissal procedure as much fairer than did those told by, say, a human resource manager. (One employer took a less diplomatic approach. The firm had an in-person meeting to announce the downsizing, but telecommuter employees got the news by e-mail. About 10% of respondents in one survey said they've used e-mail to fire employees.[93])

SECURITY MEASURES   Common sense requires using a checklist to ensure that dismissed employees return all keys and company property, and (often) accompanying them out of their offices and out of the building. The employer should disable Internet-related passwords and accounts of former employees, plug holes that could allow an ex-employee to gain illegal online access, and have rules for return of company laptops and handhelds. "Measures range from simply disabling access and changing passwords to reconfiguring the network and changing IP addresses, remote access procedures, and telephone numbers," says one chief technology officer.[94]

Avoiding Wrongful Discharge Suits

As noted earlier, wrongful discharge (or termination) occurs when an employee's dismissal does not comply with the law or with the contractual arrangement stated or implied by the employer. (In a *constructive discharge* claim, the plaintiff argues that he or she quit, but had no choice because the employer made the situation so intolerable at work.[95])

Avoiding wrongful discharge suits requires a three-pronged approach.[96] *First*, create employment policies including grievance procedures that help make employees feel you treated them fairly. Here employers can also use severance pay to blunt a dismissal's sting.[97] (Figure 14-9 summarizes typical severance policies in manufacturing and service industries.) There is no way to make termination pleasant, but the first line of defense is to handle it justly.[98]

Second, review and refine all employment-related policies, procedures, and documents to limit challenges. Have applicants sign the employment application. Make sure it contains a statement that employment is for no fixed term, and that the employer can terminate at any time. Pay particular attention to the employee

FIGURE 14-9 Length of Severance Period for Cash Payments (Number of weeks by year of service)

Source: Culpepper Pay Practices & Policies Surveys, March 2009, www.culpepper.com.

Job Level and Years of Service	Number of Weeks of Cash Severance Payments				
	10th Percentile	25th Percentile	(Median) 50th Percentile	75th Percentile	90th Percentile
Executives *					
1 Year of Service	1	2	4	12	26
2 Years of Service	2	2	6	16	26
3 Years of Service	3	4	9	18	26
5 Years of Service	5	5	13	24	29
10 Years of Service	9	10	20	33	52
15 Years of Service	10	15	26	38	52
20 Years of Service	10	20	26	43	52
Max # Weeks **	13	26	39	52	52
Directors & Managers					
1 Year of Service	1	2	2	4	11
2 Years of Service	2	2	4	7	12
3 Years of Service	3	3	6	8	13
5 Years of Service	5	5	8	10	19
10 Years of Service	5	10	12	20	26
15 Years of Service	7	13	17	26	30
20 Years of Service	8	13	20	29	40
Max # Weeks	9	13	20	29	52
Professional & Hourly					
1 Year of Service	1	1	2	4	6
2 Years of Service	2	2	4	4	8
3 Years of Service	3	3	4	6	12
5 Years of Service	5	5	7	10	13
10 Years of Service	8	10	10	18	20
15 Years of Service	8	13	15	24	30
20 Years of Service	8	13	20	26	40
Max # Weeks	8	13	20	26	52

*Nearly two-thirds of companies reported calculating executive severance cash payments by the number of years of service. Thirty percent calculate the amount of cash severance as a multiplier of one times base salary.

handbook. It should include an acknowledgment form as in Figure 14-10. Consider deleting statements such as "employees can be terminated only for just cause." Keep careful confidential records of all actions such as employee appraisals, warnings or notices, and memos outlining how improvement should be accomplished.

Third (but not least), make sure you clearly communicate job expectations to the employee; failing to do so triggers many wrongful termination claims.[99] The accompanying HR as a Profit Center feature illustrates what employers can gain from such actions.

HR AS A PROFIT CENTER

Wrongful Terminations

As we've seen, it is relatively easy for human resource managers to put in place procedures to minimize (and largely eliminate) wrongful discharge claims. As a result, this is one area where HR's profit center role is relatively clear, persuasive, and easy to implement. Steps like those in the accompanying text—such as instituting grievance procedures—are straightforward and essentially cost-less. On the other hand, the costs of wrongful terminations are real and material.

(Continued)

The costs don't just include obvious ones such as fighting the lawsuit in court. Wrongful termination can also trigger contractual clauses that require paying huge sums. Consider one recent case.[100] In this case, wrongfully terminating the employee caused two benefits that the employee might not otherwise be eligible for to vest: (1) five $14,000 annual deferred compensation payments and (2) a $275,000 benefit that otherwise would not have accumulated until the plaintiff completed 10 years of uninterrupted service (which the employee did not due to his wrongful termination).[101] In this case, the court did rule that the employer could pay those benefits out in monthly installments. But the fact remains that had the firm put in place procedures to minimize the possibility of a wrongful termination suit—had management terminated him for cause, for instance, or reached an agreement—they might have avoided the huge expense.

Personal Supervisory Liability

Courts sometimes hold managers personally liable for supervisory actions (including discipline and dismissal), particularly with respect to actions covered by the Fair Labor Standards Act and the Family and Medical Leave Act.[102]

There are several ways to avoid personal liability. Managers should be fully familiar with applicable federal, state, and local *statutes* (such as Title VII). *Follow company policies and procedures* (since an employee may allege you did not follow company policies and procedures). The essence of many charges is that the plaintiff was treated differently than others, so *consistent application* of the rule is important. Administer the discipline in a manner that does not add to the *emotional hardship* on the employee (as dismissing them publicly would). Most employees will try to present

FIGURE 14-10 Handbook Acknowledgment Form

Source: www.twc.state.tx.us, accessed April 28, 2009.

Table of Contents   Index   ⬅ ➡   Disclaimer

ACKNOWLEDGMENT OF RECEIPT OF EMPLOYEE HANDBOOK

The Employee Handbook contains important information about the Company, and I understand that I should consult the Administrator/Office Manager/General Manager/Branch Manager/Human Resources Manager [designate one] regarding any questions not answered in the handbook. I have entered into my employment relationship with the Company voluntarily, and understand that there is no specified length of employment. Accordingly, either the Company or I can terminate the relationship at will, at any time, with or without cause, and with or without advance notice.

I understand and agree that no person other than the Executive Director/President/Chief Executive Officer [designate one] may enter into an employment agreement for any specified period of time, or make any agreement contrary to the Company's stated employment-at-will policy.

Since the information, policies, and benefits described herein are subject to change at any time, I acknowledge that revisions to the handbook may occur, except to the Company's policy of employment-at-will. All such changes will generally be communicated through official notices, and I understand that revised information may supersede, modify, or eliminate existing policies. Only the President of the Company has the ability to adopt any revisions to the policies in this handbook.

Furthermore, I understand that this handbook is neither a contract of employment nor a legally-binding agreement. I have had an opportunity to read the handbook, and I understand that I may ask my supervisor or any employee of the Human Resources Department any questions I might have concerning the handbook. I accept the terms of the handbook. I also understand that it is my responsibility to comply with the policies contained in this handbook, and any revisions made to it. I further agree that if I remain with the Company following any modifications to the handbook, I thereby accept and agree to such changes.

I have received a copy of the Company's Employee Handbook on the date listed below. I understand that I am expected to read the entire handbook. Additionally, I will sign the two copies of this Acknowledgment of Receipt, retain one copy for myself, and return one copy to the Company's representative listed below on the date specified. I understand that this form will be retained in my personnel file.

_____ _____
Signature of Employee   Date

_____
Employee's Name - Printed

_____ _____
Company Representative   Date

Return to Businesses & Employers
Return to TWC Home

their side of the story, and allowing them to do so can provide the employee some measure of satisfaction. *Do not act in anger*, since doing so undermines any appearance of objectivity. Finally, *utilize the human resources department* for advice on how to handle difficult disciplinary matters.

The Termination Interview

Dismissing an employee is one of the most difficult tasks a manager faces at work. During one 5-year period, physicians interviewed 791 working people who had just undergone heart attacks to find out what might have triggered them. The researchers concluded that the stress associated with firing doubled the usual risk of a heart attack for the person doing the firing, during the week following the dismissal.[103] Furthermore, the dismissed employee, even if forewarned many times, may still react with disbelief or even violence.[104] Guidelines for the **termination interview** itself are as follows:

1. **Plan the interview carefully.** According to experts at Hay Associates, this includes the following:
   - Make sure the employee keeps the appointment time.
   - Allow 10 minutes as sufficient time for the interview.
   - Use a neutral site, not your own office.
   - Have employee agreements and release announcements prepared in advance.
   - Have phone numbers ready for medical or security emergencies.

2. **Get to the point.** Avoid small talk. *As soon as the employee enters*, give the person a moment to get comfortable and then inform him or her of your decision.

3. **Describe the situation.** Briefly explain why the person is being let go. For instance, "Production in your area is down 6%. We have talked about these problems several times in the past 3 months. We have to make a change." Stress the situation, rather than the employee and his or her shortcomings. Emphasize that the decision is final and irrevocable.

4. **Listen.** To the extent practical, continue the interview for several minutes until the person seems to be talking freely and reasonably calmly about the termination and the support package including severance pay.

5. **Review all elements of the severance package.** Briefly describe severance payments, benefits, access to office support people, and how references will be handled. (Human resources may address this with the employee.) However, make no promises beyond those already in the support package.

6. **Identify the next step.** The terminated employee may be disoriented and unsure what to do next. Explain where the employee should go upon leaving the interview. It's often best to have someone escort him or her until the person is out the door.

OUTPLACEMENT COUNSELING **Outplacement counseling** is a formal process by which a specialist trains and counsels a terminated person in the techniques of self-appraisal and securing a new position. Outplacement does not imply that the employer takes responsibility for placing the person in a new job. Instead, it is a counseling service whose purpose is to provide the person with advice, instructions, and a sounding board to help formulate career goals and successfully execute a job search for him or herself. Outplacement counseling is part of the terminated employee's support or severance package and is done by specialized outside firms.

Outplacement firms don't just counsel displaced employees; they also help the employer devise its dismissal plan. For example, prior to announcing a downsizing,

termination interview
The interview in which an employee is informed of the fact that he or she has been dismissed.

outplacement counseling
A formal process by which a terminated person is trained and counseled in the techniques of self-appraisal and securing a new position.

it might be sensible to work with an outplacement firm to decide things like how to break the news and deal with dismissed employees' emotional reactions.

EXIT INTERVIEW Many employers conduct **exit interviews** with employees who are leaving the firm for any reason. These are interviews, usually conducted by a human resource professional just prior to the employee leaving; they elicit information about the job or employer with the aim of giving employers insights into what is right—or wrong—about their companies. Exit interview questions include, "Why did you join the company?" "Was the job presented correctly and honestly?" "Were there any special problem areas?"[105] Women and minorities are more likely to quit early in their employment, so this might be one specific issue for which to watch.[106] Figure 14-11 presents an exit interview form.

The assumption of course is that because the employee is leaving, he or she will be candid. However, the information you get may be questionable.[107] Researchers found that at the time of separation, 38% of those leaving blamed

FIGURE 14-11 Employee Exit Interview Questionnaire

Source: www.fin.ucar.edu/forms/HR/exit_form/exit.pdf, accessed May 24, 2007. Used with permission.

University Corporation for Atmospheric Research

EXIT INTERVIEW

Employee Name ____________________ Supervisor ____________________

Division ____________________ Job Title ____________________

Hire Date ____________________ Termination Date ____________________

1. Why are you leaving UCAR?

____

____

____

2. What circumstances would have prevented your departure?

____

____

3. What did you like most about your job?

____

____

4. What did you like least about your job?

____

____

5. What did you think of your supervisor on the following points:

	Almost Always	Usually	Sometimes	Never
Was consistently fair	( )	( )	( )	( )
Provided recognition	( )	( )	( )	( )
Resolved complaints	( )	( )	( )	( )
Was sensitive to employees' needs	( )	( )	( )	( )
Provided feedback on performance	( )	( )	( )	( )
Was receptive to open communication	( )	( )	( )	( )
Followed UCAR's policies	( )	( )	( )	( )

salary and benefits, and only 4% blamed supervision. Followed up 18 months later, however, 24% blamed supervision and only 12% blamed salary and benefits. Getting to the real problem during the exit interview may thus require digging. Yet these interviews can be useful. When Blue Cross of Northeastern Pennsylvania dismissed employees, many said, in exit interviews, "This is not a stable place to work." The firm took steps to correct that misperception for those who stayed with Blue Cross.

Layoffs, Downsizing, and the Plant Closing Law

Nondisciplinary separations are a fact of corporate life.[108] For the employer, reduced sales or profits may require *layoffs* or *downsizing*. *Layoff* generally refers to having selected employees take time off, with the expectation that they will come back to work. **Downsizing** refers to permanently dismissing a relatively large proportion of employees in an attempt to improve productivity and competitiveness. Other employees may *resign* to *retire* or to look for better jobs.

THE PLANT CLOSING LAW
Until 1989, there were no federal laws requiring notification of employees when an employer decided to close a facility. However, in that year Congress passed the Worker Adjustment and Retraining Notification Act (popularly known as the WARN or *plant closing law*). It requires employers of 100 or more employees to give 60 days' notice before closing a facility or starting a layoff of 50 people or more. The law does not prevent the employer from closing down, nor does it require saving jobs. It simply gives employees time to seek other work or retraining by giving them advance notice. Although there are exceptions, the penalty for failing to give notice is 1 day's pay and benefits to each employee for each day's notice he or she should have received, up to 60 days. The act does not have any enforcement mechanism beyond suit in federal court. The law is not entirely clear about how to notify employees. However, a paragraph that might suit the purpose would be as follows:

> Please consider this letter to be your official notice, as required by the federal plant closing law, that your current position with the company will end 60 days from today because of a [layoff or closing] that is now projected to take place on [date]. After that day, your employment with the company will be terminated and you will no longer be carried on our payroll records. Any questions concerning the plant closing law or this notice will be answered in the HR office.[109]

THE LAYOFF PROCESS
A study illustrates one firm's downsizing process. In this company, senior management first met to make strategic decisions about the size and timing of the layoffs. These managers also debated the relative importance of the skill sets they thought the firm needed going forward. Front-line supervisors assessed their subordinates, rating their nonunion employees either A, B, or C (union employees were covered by a union agreement making layoffs dependant on seniority). The front-line supervisors then informed each of their subordinates about his or her A, B, or C rating, and told each that those employees with C grades were designated "surplus" and most likely to be laid off.[110]

Sensible layoff steps to take therefore include these:[111]

- **Identify objectives and constraints.** For example, decide how many positions to eliminate at which locations, and what criteria to use.

---

exit interviews
Interviews with employees who are leaving the firm, conducted for obtaining information about the job or related matters, to give the employer insight about the company.

downsizing
The process of reducing, usually dramatically, the number of people employed by a firm.

- **Form a downsizing team.** This team should prepare a communication strategy for explaining the downsizing, produce a downsizing schedule, and supervise the displaced employees' benefit programs.
- **Address legal issues.** Review factors such as age, race, and gender before finalizing and communicating any dismissals.
- **Plan post-implementation actions.** For those who remain, activities such as surveys and explanatory meetings can help maintain morale.
- **Address security concerns.** With large layoffs, it may be wise to have security personnel in place.
- **Try to remain informative.** When employees sue after mass layoffs, it's often because they're unhappy with how the employer handled the layoff. Providing advanced notice regarding the layoff and *interpersonal sensitivity* (in terms of the manager's demeanor during layoffs) can both help mitigate negative results.[112] The people who announce the downsizing and deal with the employee questions should explain what is happening truthfully.[113]

PREPARING FOR LAYOFFS　As the U.S. slipped into recession a few years ago, large layoffs climbed ominously, up by about 9.4%. How do managers prepare for the layoffs that almost invariably result from such challenging times?

Interestingly, the initial focus isn't on the layoffs, but on the employer's appraisal systems. One expert says that in preparing for large, scale layoffs, management needs to:[114]

- Make sure appraisals are up-to-date.
- Identify top performers and get them working on the company's future.
- Have leaders committed to the company's turnaround.

Another HR consultant says companies that "don't closely manage their performance appraisal systems suddenly learn during a reduction in force that everyone has been ranked a 'four' out of 'five'; that information is meaningless."[115]

So the essential point about layoffs is to prepare in advance by making sure to have an effective performance appraisal system in place. If you don't, then when the time comes to lay off significant numbers of employers, you may find yourself with no rational basis on which to decide who stays or leaves.

DISMISSAL'S EFFECTS　It's not surprising that layoffs often result in harmful psychological and physical health outcomes for employees who lose their jobs, as well as for the survivors who face uncertainty.[116]

Furthermore, not just the "victims" and "survivors" suffer. In one study, researchers "found that the more managers were personally responsible for handing out warning notices to employees, regardless of their age, gender, and marital status, the more likely they were to report physical health problems, to seek treatment for these problems, and to complain of disturbed sleep."[117]

BUMPING/LAYOFF PROCEDURES　As noted, *layoff* generally refers to having some employees take time off, with the expectation that they will come back to work. With layoffs, three conditions are usually present: (1) There is no work available for these employees, (2) management expects the no-work situation to be temporary and probably short term, and (3) management intends to recall the employees when work is again available. A layoff is therefore not a termination, which is a permanent severing of the employment relationship. Many employers, however, do use the term *layoff* as a euphemism for discharge or termination. (Others call them "productivity transformation programs.")[118]

Employers who encounter frequent business slowdowns may have bumping/ layoff procedures that let employees use their seniority to remain on the job. Here:

1. Seniority is usually the ultimate determinant of who will work.

2. Seniority can give way to merit or ability, but usually only when no senior employee is qualified for a particular job.

3. Seniority is usually based on the date the employee joined the organization, not the date he or she took a particular job.

4. Because seniority is usually company-wide, an employee in one job can usually bump or displace an employee in another job, provided the more senior person can do the job.

LAYOFF AND DOWNSIZING ALTERNATIVES Layoffs and downsizings are painful for all involved, and have the added disadvantage of stripping away trained personnel. Employers therefore often try to find alternatives.

There are alternatives. Suggestions include finding *volunteers* who are interested in reducing hours or part-time work, using *attrition*, and even networking with local employers concerning temporary or permanent *redeployments*. With the *voluntary reduction in pay plan*, all employees agree to reductions in pay to keep everyone working. Other employers arrange for all or most employees to *concentrate their vacations* during slow periods. They don't have to hire temporary help for vacationing employees during peak periods, and staffing automatically declines when business declines. Other employees agree to take *voluntary time off*, which again has the effect of reducing the employer's payroll and avoiding layoffs.

Many employers hire employees with the understanding their work is temporary. When layoffs are required, they are the first to leave. Some seek volunteers as an alternative to dismissing large numbers of employees. For example, many employers offer *early retirement* buyout packages to many of their employees.

Adjusting to Downsizings and Mergers

Firms usually downsize to improve their financial positions. Yet many firms discover profits don't improve after major personnel cuts. Low morale among those remaining is often part of the problem. Supportiveness in the face of downsizing is especially important in high performance work system–type firms that rely heavily on employee morale and expertise.[119] Options here include cut costs without reducing the workforce, perhaps through pay freezes or cuts; introduce a hiring freeze before reducing the workforce; provide candid communications about the need for the downsizing; give employees an opportunity to express their opinions about the downsizing; and be fair and compassionate in implementing the downsizing.[120]

MERGER GUIDELINES In terms of dismissal, *mergers and acquisitions* are usually one-sided. In such situations, the acquired firm's surviving employees may be hypersensitive to mistreatment of their soon-to-be former colleagues. It thus behooves the manager to treat those whom you let go fairly. As a rule, therefore:

● Avoid the appearance of power and domination.

● Avoid win–lose behavior.

● Remain businesslike and professional in all dealings.

● Maintain as positive a feeling about the acquired company as possible.

● Remember that the degree to which your organization treats the acquired group with care and dignity will affect the confidence, productivity, and commitment of those who remain.[121]

REVIEW

MyManagementLab　Now that you have finished this chapter, go back to **www.mymanagementlab.com** to continue practicing and applying the concepts you've learned.

CHAPTER SECTION SUMMARIES

1. **Ethics and fair treatment** play important roles in managing employees at work. Ethics refers to the principles of conduct governing an individual or a group. The concepts of ethics, justice, and fair treatment are intertwined. For example, fairness is inseparable from what most people think of as "justice" from the individual employee's point of view. Few societies rely solely on managers' ethics or sense of fairness, and therefore legislate employee rights, such as regarding employee pension rights, references rights, defamation rights, and union activity rights.

2. Many things influence **ethical behavior at work**. From research, we know that moral awareness, the managers themselves, moral engagement, morality, unmet goals, and rewards all influence ethical behavior. The person is important, in that people bring to their jobs their own ideas of what is morally right or wrong. The boss and how he or she molds the organizational culture have a prevailing effect on ethical behavior, because it's difficult to resist even subtle pressure from your boss. Employers themselves can take steps to support ethical behavior, for instance via training, whistle-blower programs, and ethics codes.

3. Managers can use **personnel methods to promote ethics and fair treatment**. For example, in selection, the manager can hire ethical people and emphasize the fairness of selection procedures. Similarly, ethics training, conducting fair and just performance appraisals, rewarding ethical behavior, and generally treating employees fairly all promote ethics and the perception of fair treatment. Communication plays an important role in fair treatment. For example, ask questions and listen carefully, set aside your defensive actions, and ask, "What would you like me to do?"

4. Managing **employee discipline and privacy** are important management skills. The basics of a fair and just disciplinary process include clear rules and regulations, a system of progressive penalties, and an appeals process. Some employers use nonpunitive discipline, which usually involves a system of oral warnings and paid "decision-making leaves." The "hot stove rule" means administering discipline in such a way that the person has warning, and the pain is consistent, impersonal, and immediate. With more employers using Internet monitoring and technologies such as biometrics, monitoring is widespread. The Electronic Communications Privacy Act and common law protections against invasion of privacy limit, somewhat, workplace monitoring. Employers should have employees sign e-mail and telephone monitoring acknowledgment statements.

5. Dismissals are usually traumatic for both the manager and the dismissed employee, and so managers need to take special care in **managing dismissals**.

   - Termination at will means that without a contract, either the employer or the employee could terminate, at will, the employment relationship.
   - Wrongful discharge refers to a dismissal that violates the law or that fails to comply with contractual arrangements stated or implied by the employer.
   - Grounds for dismissal include unsatisfactory performance, misconduct (including insubordination), lack of qualifications for the job, and changed requirements of the job.
   - Fairness in dismissals is enhanced when employees get explanations of why and how termination decisions were made; there is a formal multistep procedure, including warnings; and the supervisor rather than a third person does the dismissing.
   - Supervisors can be held personally liable for unjust dismissals, and so it is advisable that the supervisor not act in anger, follow company policies and procedures, and avoid adding to the emotional hardship on the employee.
   - The termination interview should be planned carefully, and the supervisor should then get to the point, describe the situation, listen, review all elements of the severance package, and then identify the next step. Some employers use outplacement counselors to facilitate the process.
   - The Worker Adjustment and Retraining Notification Act (plant closing law) requires larger employers to give 60 days' notice before closing a facility or starting to lay off 50 people or more.
   - To avoid wholesale dismissals during what may turn out to be short-term downturns, some employers are using attrition or voluntary reductions in pay plans to temporarily reduce headcount and compensation bills.

DISCUSSION QUESTIONS

1. Explain how you would ensure fairness in disciplining, discussing particularly the prerequisites to disciplining, disciplining guidelines, and the discipline without punishment approach.
2. Why is it important in our highly litigious society to manage dismissals properly?
3. What techniques would you use as alternatives to traditional discipline? What do such alternatives have to do with organizational justice? Why do you think alternatives like these are important, given industry's need today for highly committed employees?
4. Provide three examples of behaviors that would probably be unethical but legal, and three that would probably be illegal but ethical.
5. List 10 things your college or university does to encourage ethical behavior by students and/or faculty.
6. You need to select a nanny for your or a relative's child, and want someone ethical. Based on what you read in this chapter, what would you do to help ensure you ended up hiring someone ethical?
7. You believe your employee is being insubordinate. How would you verify this and what would you do about it if it is true?
8. Several years ago Walmart instituted a new employee scheduling system that makes it more difficult for its employees to know for sure what hours they would be working. Basically, the store supervisor calls them at the last minute if there's an opening that day. Based on what you read in this chapter, is the new system ethical? Why or why not? Is it fair? What would you do if you were a Walmart employee?

INDIVIDUAL AND GROUP ACTIVITIES

1. Working individually or in groups, interview managers or administrators at your employer or college in order to determine the extent to which the employer or college endeavors to build two-way communication, and the specific types of programs used. Do the managers think they are effective? What do the employees (or faculty members) think of the programs in use at the employer or college?
2. Working individually or in groups, obtain copies of the student handbook for your college and determine to what extent there is a formal process through which students can air grievances. Based on your contacts with other students, has it been an effective grievance process? Why or why not?
3. Working individually or in groups, determine the nature of the academic discipline process in your college. Do you think it is effective? Based on what you read in this chapter, would you recommend any modifications?
4. The "HRCI Test Specifications Appendix" (pages 633–640) lists the knowledge someone studying for the HRCI certification exam needs to have in each area of human resource management (such as in Strategic Management, Workforce Planning, and Human Resource Development). In groups of four to five students, do four things: (1) review that appendix now; (2) identify the material in this chapter that relates to the required knowledge the appendix lists; (3) write four multiple-choice exam questions on this material that you believe would be suitable for inclusion in the HRCI exam; and (4) if time permits, have someone from your team post your team's questions in front of the class, so the students in other teams can take each others' exam questions.
5. In a recent research study at Ohio State University, a professor found that even honest people, left to their own devices, would steal from their employers.[122] In this study, the researchers gave financial services workers the opportunity to steal a small amount of money after participating in an after-work project for which the pay was inadequate. Would the employees steal to make up for the underpayment? In most cases, yes. Employees who scored low on an honesty test stole whether or not their office had an ethics program that said stealing from the company was illegal. Employees who scored high on the honesty test also stole, but only if their office did not have such an employee ethics program—the "honest" people didn't steal if there was an ethics policy.

   In groups of four or five students, answer these questions: Do you think findings like these are generalizable? In other words, would they apply across the board to employees in other types of companies and situations? If your answer is yes, what do you think this implies about the need for and wisdom of having an ethics program?

EXPERIENTIAL EXERCISE

Discipline or Not?

Purpose: The purpose of this exercise is to provide you with some experience in analyzing and handling an actual disciplinary action.

Required Understanding: Students should be thoroughly familiar with the following case, titled "Botched Batch."

Do not read the "award" or "discussion" sections until after the groups have completed their deliberations.

How to Set Up the Exercise/Instructions:

Divide the class into groups of four or five students. Each group should take the arbitrator's point of view and assume that they are to analyze the case and make the arbitrator's decision. Review the case again at this point, but please do not read the award and discussion.

Each group should answer the following questions:

1. Based on what you read in this chapter, including all relevant guidelines, what would your decision be if you were the arbitrator? Why?

2. Do you think that after their experience in this arbitration the parties will be more or less inclined to settle grievances by themselves without resorting to arbitration?

Botched Batch

Facts: A computer department employee made an entry error that botched an entire run of computer reports. Efforts to rectify the situation produced a second set of improperly run reports. Because of the series of errors, the employer incurred extra costs of $2,400, plus a weekend of overtime work by other computer department staffers. Management suspended the employee for 3 days for negligence, and revoked a promotion for which the employee had previously been approved.

Protesting the discipline, the employee stressed that she had attempted to correct her error in the early stages of the run by notifying the manager of computer operations of her mistake. Maintaining that the resulting string of errors could have been avoided if the manager had followed up on her report and stopped the initial run, the employee argued that she had been treated unfairly because the manager had not been disciplined even though he compounded the problem, whereas she was severely punished. Moreover, citing her

"impeccable" work record and management's acknowledgment that she had always been a "model employee," the employee insisted that the denial of her previously approved promotion was "unconscionable."

(*Please do* **not** *read beyond this point until after you have answered the two questions.*)

Award: The arbitrator upholds the 3-day suspension, but decides that the promotion should be restored.

Discussion: "There is no question," the arbitrator notes, that the employee's negligent act "set in motion the train of events that resulted in running two complete sets of reports reflecting improper information." Stressing that the employer incurred substantial cost because of the error, the arbitrator cites "unchallenged" testimony that management had commonly issued 3-day suspensions for similar infractions in the past. Thus, the arbitrator decides, the employer acted with just cause in meting out an "evenhanded" punishment for the negligence.

Turning to the denial of the already approved promotion, the arbitrator says that this action should be viewed "in the same light as a demotion for disciplinary reasons." In such cases, the arbitrator notes, management's decision normally is based on a pattern of unsatisfactory behavior, an employee's inability to perform, or similar grounds. Observing that management had never before reversed a promotion as part of a disciplinary action, the arbitrator says that by tacking on the denial of the promotion in this case, the employer substantially varied its disciplinary policy from its past practice. Because this action on management's part was not "evenhanded," the arbitrator rules, the promotion should be restored.[123]

APPLICATION CASE

ENRON, ETHICS, AND ORGANIZATIONAL CULTURE

For many people, a company called Enron Corp. still ranks as one of history's classic examples of ethics run amok. During the 1990s and early 2000s, Enron was in the business of wholesaling natural gas and electricity. Rather than actually owning the gas or electric, Enron made its money as the intermediary (wholesaler) between suppliers and customers. Without getting into all the details, the nature of Enron's business—and the fact that Enron didn't actually own the assets—meant that its accounting procedures were unusual. For example, the profit statements and balance sheets listing the firm's assets and liabilities were unusually difficult to understand.

It turned out that the lack of accounting transparency enabled the company's managers to make Enron's financial performance look much better than it actually was. Outside experts began questioning Enron's financial statements in 2001. In fairly short order, Enron collapsed, and courts convicted several of its top executives of things like manipulating Enron's reported assets and profitability. Many investors (including former Enron employees) lost all or most of their investments in Enron.

It's probably always easier to understand ethical breakdowns like this in retrospect, rather than to predict they are going to happen. However, in Enron's case the breakdown is perhaps more perplexing than usual. As one writer said,

Enron had all the elements usually found in comprehensive ethics and compliance programs: a code of ethics, a reporting system, as well as a training video on vision and values led by [the company's top executives].[124]

Experts subsequently put forth many explanations for how a company that was apparently so ethical on its face could actually have been making so many bad ethical decisions without other managers (and the board of directors) noticing. The explanations ranged from a "deliberate concealment of information by officers" to more psychological explanations (such as employees not wanting to contradict their bosses) and the "surprising role of irrationality in decision-making."[125]

But perhaps the most persuasive explanation of how an apparently ethical company could go so wrong concerns organizational culture. The reasoning here is that it's not the rules but what employees feel they should do that determines ethical behavior. For example (speaking in general, not specifically about Enron), the executive director of the Ethics Officer Association put it this way:

[W]e're a legalistic society, and we've created a lot of laws. We assume that if you just knew what those laws meant that you would behave properly. Well, guess what? You can't write enough laws to tell us what to do at all times every day of the week in every part of the world. We've got to develop the critical thinking and critical reasoning skills of our people because most of the ethical issues that we deal with are in the ethical gray areas. Virtually every regulatory body in the last year has come out with language that has said in addition to law compliance, businesses are also going to be accountable to ethics standards and a corporate culture that embraces them.[126]

How can one tell or measure when a company has an "ethical culture"? Key attributes of a healthy ethical culture include:

- Employees feel a sense of responsibility and accountability for their actions and for the actions of others.[127]
- Employees freely raise issues and concerns without fear of retaliation.
- Managers model the behaviors they demand of others.
- Managers communicate the importance of integrity when making difficult decisions.

Questions

1. Based on what you read in this chapter, summarize in one page or less how you would explain Enron's ethical meltdown.
2. It is said that when one securities analyst tried to confront Enron's CEO about the firm's unusual accounting statements, the CEO publicly used vulgar language to describe the analyst, and that Enron employees subsequently thought doing so was humorous. If true, what does that say about Enron's ethical culture?
3. This case and chapter both had something to say about how organizational culture influences ethical behavior. What role do you think culture played at Enron? Give five specific examples of things Enron's CEO could have done to create a healthy ethical culture.

CONTINUING CASE

CARTER CLEANING COMPANY

Guaranteeing Fair Treatment

Being in the laundry and cleaning business, the Carters have always felt strongly about not allowing employees to smoke, eat, or drink in their stores. Jennifer was therefore surprised to walk into a store and find two employees eating lunch at the front counter. There was a large pizza in its box, and the two of them were sipping colas and eating slices of pizza and submarine sandwiches off paper plates. Not only did it look messy, but there were grease and soda spills on the counter and the store smelled from onions and pepperoni, even with the exhaust fan pulling air out through the roof. In addition to being a turnoff to customers, the mess on the counter increased the possibility that a customer's order might actually become soiled in the store.

Although this was a serious matter, neither Jennifer nor her father felt that what the counter people were doing was grounds for immediate dismissal, partly because the store manager had apparently condoned their actions. The problem was, they didn't know what to do. It seemed to them that the matter called for more than just a warning but less than dismissal.

Questions

1. What would you do if you were Jennifer, and why?
2. Should a disciplinary system be established at Carter Cleaning Centers?
3. If so, what should it cover? How would you suggest it deal with a situation such as the one with the errant counter people?
4. How would you deal with the store manager?

TRANSLATING STRATEGY INTO HR POLICIES & PRACTICES CASE

THE HOTEL PARIS CASE

The Hotel Paris's New Ethics, Justice, and Fair Treatment Process

The Hotel Paris's competitive strategy is "To use superior guest service to differentiate the Hotel Paris properties, and to thereby increase the length of stay and return rate of guests, and thus boost revenues and profitability." HR manager Lisa Cruz must now formulate functional policies and activities that support this competitive strategy by eliciting the required employee behaviors and competencies.

As the head of HR for the Hotel Paris, Lisa Cruz was especially concerned about her company maintaining the highest ethical standards. Her concerns were twofold. First, from a practical point of view, there are, in a hotel chain, literally thousands of opportunities on any given day for guests to have bad ethical experiences. For example, in any single hotel each day there are at least a dozen people (including housekeepers, front-desk clerks, security guards, and so on) with easy access to guests' rooms, and to their personal belongings. Guests—many younger, and many unwary—are continually walking the halls unprotected. So, in a service company like this, there is simply no margin for ethical errors.

But she was concerned about ethics for a second reason. She'd been around long enough to know that employees do not like being treated unfairly, and that unfairness in any form could manifest itself in low morale, commitment, and performance. Indeed, perhaps her employees' low morale and commitment—as measured by her firm's attitude surveys—stemmed in part from what they perceived as unjust treatment by the hotel's managers. Lisa therefore turned to the task of assessing and redesigning the Hotel Paris's ethics, justice, and fair treatment practices.

To do this, Lisa and her team wanted to proceed methodically through the company's entire HR process, starting with recruitment and selection. For example, working with the company's general counsel, they produced and presented to the CEO a new Hotel Paris code of ethics, as well as a more complete set of ethical guidelines. These now appear on the Hotel Paris's careers Web site link, and are part of each new employee's orientation packet. They contracted with a vendor to provide a customized, Web-based ethics training program, and made it clear that the first employees to participate in it were the company's top executives. However, she knew this was just the start.

Questions

1. List three specific steps Hotel Paris should take with respect to each individual human research function (selection, training, and so on) to improve the level of ethics in the company.
2. Based on what you read in this chapter, create in outline form a strategy map showing how the Hotel's HR functions can foster employee ethics.
3. Based on what you learned in this chapter, write a short (less than one page) explanation Lisa can use to sell to top management the need to improve the hotel chain's fairness and justice processes.

KEY TERMS

ethics, *461*

distributive justice, *462*

procedural justice, *462*

organizational culture, *466*

nonpunitive discipline, *472*

Electronic Communications Privacy Act (ECPA), *475*

dismissal, *476*

termination at will, *476*

wrongful discharge, *476*

insubordination, *477*

termination interview, *481*

outplacement counseling, *481*

exit interviews, *482*

downsizing, *483*

ETHICS QUIZ ANSWERS

Quiz is on page 460.

1. 34% said personal e-mail on company computers is wrong.
2. 37% said using office equipment for schoolwork is wrong.
3. 49% said playing computer games at work is wrong.
4. 54% said Internet shopping at work is wrong.
5. 61% said it's unethical to blame your error on technology.
6. 87% said it's unethical to visit pornographic sites at work.
7. 33% said $25 is the amount at which a gift from a supplier or client becomes troubling, while 33% said $50, and 33% said $100.
8. 35% said a $50 gift to the boss is unacceptable.
9. 12% said a $50 gift from the boss is unacceptable.
10. 70% said it's unacceptable to take the $200 football tickets.
11. 70% said it's unacceptable to take the $120 theater tickets.
12. 35% said it's unacceptable to take the $100 food basket.
13. 45% said it's unacceptable to take the $25 gift certificate.
14. 40% said it's unacceptable to take the $75 raffle prize.
15. 11% reported they lie about sick days.
16. 4% reported they take credit for the work or ideas of others.

ENDNOTES

1. James Stewart, "Is Buffett Whitewashing Soquel's Exit?" *The Wall Street Journal*, April 2–3, 2011, p. B7.
2. Keith Winstein, "Suit Alleges Pfizer Spun Unfavorable Drug Studies," *The Wall Street Journal*, October 8, 2008, p. B1.
3. Kevin Wooten, "Ethical Dilemmas in Human Resource Management: An Application of a Multidimensional Framework, A Unifying Taxonomy, and Applicable Codes," *Human Resource Management Review* 11 (2001), p. 161. See also Sean Valentine et al., "Employee Job Response as a Function of Ethical Context and Perceived Organization Support," *Journal of Business Research* 59, no. 5 (2006), pp. 582–588.
4. Paul Schumann, "A Moral Principles Framework for Human Resource Management Ethics," *Human Resource Management Review* 11 (2004), p. 94. A third survey found that roughly 10%–20% of employees observed specific personnel-related unethical behaviors at work, including abusive or intimidating behavior toward employees; lying to employees, customers, vendors, or to the public; violations of safety regulations; and misreporting of actual time worked. *2005 National Business Ethics Survey: How Employees Perceive Ethics at Work*, 2005, p. 25. Copyright © 2006, Ethics Resource Center (ERC). In O. C. Ferrell, John Fraedrich, and Linog Ferrell, *Business Ethics* (Boston: Houghton Mifflin, 2008), p. 61
5. Manuel Velasquez, *Business Ethics: Concepts and Cases* (Upper Saddle River, NJ: Prentice Hall, 1992), p. 9. See also O. C.

Ferrell, John Fraedrich, and Linda Ferrell, *Business Ethics* (Boston: Houghton Mifflin, 2008).

6. The following discussion, except as noted, is based on Manuel Velasquez, *Business Ethics*, pp. 9–12.

7. For further discussion of ethics and morality, see Tom Beauchamp and Norman Bowie, *Ethical Theory and Business* (Upper Saddle River, NJ: Prentice Hall, 2001), pp. 1–19.

8. Richard Osborne, "A Matter of Ethics," *Industry Week*, September 4, 2000, pp. 41–42.

9. Gary Weaver and Linda Trevino, "The Role of Human Resources in Ethics/Compliance Management: A Fairness Perspective," *Human Resource Management Review* 11 (2001): 115.

10. Daniel Skarlicki and Robert Folger, "Fairness and Human Resources Management," *Human Resource Management Review* 13, no. 1 (2003), p. 1.

11. Gary Weaver and Linda Trevino, "The Role of Human Resources in Ethics/Compliance Management: A Fairness Perspective," *Human Resource Management Review* 11 (2001), pp. 113–134.

12. Weaver and Trevino, "The Role of Human Resources in Ethics/Compliance Management," p. 115.

13. Stephanie Clifford, "Wal-Mart Is Being Pressed to Disclose How Global Suppliers Treat Workers," *The New York Times*, May 31, 2011, p. B3.

14. Ibid.

15. See http://archives.gov/exhibits/charters/bill_of_rights.html, accessed May 31, 2011.

16. http://focus.illinoisstate.edu/modules/policy/publicpolicy.shtml, accessed September 14, 2011.

17. Jennifer Kish-Gephart, David Harrison, and Linda Trevino, "Bad Apples, Bad Cases, and Bad Barrels: Meta-Analytic Evidence About Sources of Unethical Decisions That Work," *Journal of Applied Psychology* 95, no. 1, 2010, pp. 1–31.

18. This section based on Ibid., p. 21

19. Sara Morris et al., "A Test of Environmental, Situational, and Personal Influences on the Ethical Intentions of CEOs," *Business and Society* (August 1995), pp. 119–47. See also Dennis Moberg, "Ethics Blind Spots in Organizations: How Systematic Errors in Person's Perception Undermine Moral Agency," *Organization Studies* 27, no. 3 (2006), pp. 413–428; and Scott Reynolds et al., "Automatic Ethics: The Effects of Implicit Assumptions and Contextual Cues on Moral Behavior," *Journal of Applied Psychology* 95, no. 4 (2010), pp. 752–760.

20. "Former CEO Joins WorldCom's Indicted," *Miami Herald*, March 3, 2004, p. 4C.

21. O. C. Ferrell and John Fraedrich, *Business Ethics*, 3rd ed. (New York: Houghton Mifflin, 1997), p. 28; adapted from Rebecca Goodell, *Ethics in American Business: Policies, Programs, and Perceptions* (Washington, D.C.: Ethics Resource Center, 1994), p. 54; For other insights into unethical behavior's causes see, for example, F. Gino, et. al., "Nameless + Harmless = Blameless: When Seemingly Irrelevant Factors Influence Judgment of (Un)ethical Behavior," *Organizational Behavior and Human Decision Processes* 111, no. 2 (March 2010), p. 93–101, and J. Camps, et. al., "Learning Atmosphere and Ethical Behavior, Does It Make Sense?" *Journal of Business Ethics* 94, no. 1 (June 2010), pp. 129–147.

22. Elizabeth Umphress, John Bingham, and Marie Mitchell, "Unethical Behavior in the Name of the Company: The Moderating Effect of Organizational Identification and Positive Reciprocity Believes on Unethical Pro-Organizational Behavior," *Journal of Applied Psychology* 95, no. 4 (2010), pp. 769–770.

23. "Ethics Policies Are Big with Employers, but Workers See Small Impact on the Workplace," *BNA Bulletin to Management*, June 29, 2000, p. 201.

24. Jennifer Schramm, "Perceptions on Ethics," *HR Magazine*, November 2004, p. 176.

25. From Guy Brumback, "Managing Above the Bottom Line of Ethics," *Supervisory Management*, December 1993, p. 12. See also, E. Umphress et al., "The Influence of Distributive Justice on Lying for and Stealing from a Supervisor," *Journal of Business Ethics* 86, no. 4 (June 2009), pp. 507–518; and S. Chen, "The Role of Ethical Leadership Versus Institutional Constraints: A Simulation Study of Financial Misreporting by CEOs," *Journal of Business Ethics* 93 part supplement 1 (June 2010), p. 33–52.

26. Quoted in Tom Beauchamp and Norman Bowie, *Ethical Theory and Business* (Upper Saddle River, NJ: Prentice Hall, 2001), p. 109.

27. James Kunen, "Enron Division (and Values) Thing," *New York Times*, January 19, 2002, p. A19. For another example, see Heather Tesoriero and Avery Johnson, "Suit Details How J&J Pushed Sales of Procrit," *The Wall Street Journal (Eastern Edition)*, April 10, 2007, p. B1(1).

28. Dayton Fandray, "The Ethical Company," *Workforce* 79, no. 12 (December 2000): 74–77.

29. Richard Beatty et al., "HR's Role in Corporate Governance: Present and Prospective," *Human Resource Management* 42, no. 3 (Fall 2003), p. 268.

30. Dale Buss, "Corporate Compasses," *HR Magazine* (June 2004): 127–132.

31. Eric Krell, "How to Conduct an Ethics Audit," *HR Magazine*, April 2010, pp. 48–51.

32. Sometimes the most straightforward way of changing a company's culture is to move fast to change its top management. For example, some observers believe that the General Motors board fired CEO Fritz Henderson in part because he hadn't moved fast enough to telegraph the need for change in the company by changing the company's top management. Jeremy Smerd, "A Stalled Culture Change?" *Workforce Management*, December 14, 2009, pp. 1, 3.

33. This list based on Linda K. Trevino, Gary R. Weaver, and Scott J. Reynolds, "Behavioral Ethics in Organizations: A Review," *Journal of Management* 32, no. 6 (2006), pp. 951–990.

34. R. Bergman, "Identity as Motivation: Toward a Theory of the Moral Self." In D. K. Lapsley & D. Narvaez (Eds.), *Moral Development, Self and Identity* (Mahwah, NJ: Lawrence Erlbaum, 2004), pp. 21–46.

35. M. E. Schweitzer, L. Ordonez, and B. Douma, "Goal Setting as a Motivator of Unethical Behavior," *Academy of Management Journal* 47, no. 3 (2004), pp. 422–432.

36. N. M. Ashkanasy, C. A. Windsor, and L. K. Trevino, "Bad Apples in Bad Barrels Revisited: Cognitive Moral Development, Just World Beliefs, Rewards, and Ethical Decision Making." *Business Ethics Quarterly* 16 (2006), pp. 449–474.

37. J. Krohe Jr., "The Big Business of Business Ethics," *Across the Board* 34 (May 1997), pp. 23–29; Deborah Wells and Marshall Schminke, "Ethical Development and Human Resources Training: An Integrative Framework," *Human Resource Management Review* 11 (2001), pp. 135–158.

38. "Ethical Issues in the Management of Human Resources," *Human Resource Management Review* 11 (2001), p. 6; see also Joel Lefkowitz, "The Constancy of Ethics Amidst the Changing World of Work," *Human Resource Management Review* 16 (2006), pp. 245–268.

39. William Byham, "Can You Interview for Integrity?" *Across-the-Board* 41, no. 2 (March/April 2004), pp. 34–38. For a description of how the United States Military Academy uses its student admission and socialization processes to promote character development, see Evan Offstein and Ronald Dufresne, "Building Strong Ethics and Promoting Positive Character Development: The Influence of HRM at the United States Military Academy at West Point," *Human Resource Management* 46, no. 1 (Spring 2007), pp. 95–114.

40. Weaver and Trevino, "The Role of Human Resources," p. 123. See also Linda Andrews, "The Nexus of Ethics," *HR Magazine*, August 2005, pp. 53–58.

41. Russell Cropanzano and Thomas Wright, "Procedural Justice and Organizational Staffing: A Tale of Two Paradigms," *Human Resource Management Review* 13, no. 1 (2003), pp. 7–40.

42. "Ethical Issues in the Management of Human Resources," *Human Resource Management Review* 11 (2001), p. 6.

43. Weaver and Trevino, "The Role of Human Resources," p. 123.

44. Kathryn Tyler, "Do the Right Thing, Ethics Training Programs Help Employees Deal with Ethical Dilemmas," *HR Magazine*, February 2005, pp. 99–102.

45. M. Ronald Buckley et al., "Ethical Issues in Human Resources Systems," *Human Resource Management Review* 11, no. 1, 2 (2001), pp. 11, 29. See also Ann Pomeroy, "The Ethics Squeeze," *HR Magazine*, March 2006, pp. 48–55.

46. Tom Asacker, "Ethics in the Workplace," *Training & Development*, August 2004, p. 44; http://skillsoft.com/catalog/search.asp?title=Business+Ethics&type=Courses&submit.x=45&submit.y=15, accessed August 11, 2009.

47. Ed Finkel, "Yahoo Takes New Road on Ethics Training," *Workforce Management*, July 2010, p. 2.

48. Weaver and Trevino, "The Role of Human Resources," p. 114.

49. Ibid.

50. Michael Burr, "Corporate Governance: Embracing Sarbanes-Oxley," *Public Utilities Fortnightly*, October 15, 2003, pp. 20–22.

51. "Corporations' Drive to Embrace Ethics Gives HR Leaders Chance to Take Reins," *BNA Bulletin to Management*, November 7, 2002, p. 353.

52. Lester Bittel, *What Every Supervisor Should Know* (New York: McGraw-Hill, 1974), p. 308; and Thomas Salvo, "Practical Tips for Successful Progressive Discipline," SHRM White Paper July 2004, www.shrm.org/hrresources/whitepapers_published/CMS_009030.asp, accessed January 5, 2008.

53. David Campbell et al., "Discipline Without Punishment—At Last," *Harvard Business Review*, July/August 1995, pp. 162–178; J. F. Mason, "Myspace, Yourspace: What Employers Must Know About Social-Media Risks," *National Underwriter (P & C)* 115, no. 11 (March 28, 2011), pp. 18, 20.

54. Weaver and Trevino, "The Role of Human Resources," p. 117.

55. Russell Cropanzano and Thomas Wright, "Procedural Justice and Organizational Staffing: A Tale of Two Paradigms," *Human Resource Management Review* 13, no. 1 (2003), pp. 7–40.

56. Suzanne Masterson, "A Trickle-Down Model of Organizational Justice: Relating Employees' and Customers' Perceptions of and Reactions to Fairness," *Journal of Applied Psychology* 86, no. 4 (2001), pp. 594–601.

57. Rudy Yandrick, "Lurking in the Shadows," *HR Magazine*, October 1999, pp. 61–68. See also Helge Hoel and David Beale, "Workplace Bullying, Psychological Perspectives and Industrial Relations: Towards a Contextualized and Interdisciplinary Approach," *British Journal of Industrial Relations* 44, no. 2 (June 2006), pp. 239–262.

58. Bennett Tepper, "Consequences of Abusive Supervision," *Academy of Management Journal* 43, no. 2 (2000), pp. 178–190.

See also Samuel Aryee et al., "Antecedents and Outcomes of Abusive Supervision: Test of a Trickle-Down Model," *Journal of Applied Psychology*, no. 1 (2007), pp. 191–201.

59. Wendy Boswell and Julie Olson-Buchanan, "Experiencing Mistreatment at Work: The Role of Grievance Filing, Nature of Mistreatment, and Employee Withdrawal," *Academy of Management Journal* 47, no. 1 (2004), pp. 129–139. See also Samuel Aryee et al., "Antecedents and Outcomes of Abusive Supervision."

60. Bennett Tepper et al., "Abusive Supervision and Subordinates' Organization Deviance," *Journal of Applied Psychology* 93, no. 4 (2008), pp. 721–732.

61. "Facebook Harassment: Social Websites May Prompt Need for New Policies, Procedures," *BNA Bulletin to Management*, July 20, 2010, p. 225.

62. Eugene Kim and Teresa Glomb, "Get Smarty-Pants: Cognitive Ability, Personality, and Victimization," *Journal of Applied Psychology* 95, no. 3 (2010), pp. 889–901.

63. Ibid.

64. M. Audrey Korsgaard, Loriann Roberson, and R. Douglas Rymph, "What Motivates Fairness? The Role of Subordinate Assertive Behavior on Manager's Interactional Fairness," *Journal of Applied Psychology* 83, no. 5 (1998), pp. 731–744.

65. Bennett Tepper et al., "Procedural Injustice, Victim Precipitation, and Abusive Supervision," *Personnel Psychology* 59 (2006), pp. 11–23.

66. W. Chan Kim and Renee Mauborgne, "Fair Process: Managing in the Knowledge Economy," *Harvard Business Review*, July/August 1997, pp. 65–75.

67. For disciplinary best practices, see Lester Bittel, "What Every Supervisor Should Know," op. cit.; "Employers Turn to Corporate Ombuds to Defuse Internal Ticking Time Bombs," *BNA Bulletin to Management*, August 9, 2005, p. 249.

68. Dick Grote, "Discipline Without Punishment," *Across the Board* 38, no. 5 (September 2001), pp. 52–57.

69. Milton Zall, "Employee Privacy," *Journal of Property Management* 66, no. 3 (May 2001), p. 16.

70. Morris Attaway, "Privacy in the Workplace on the Web," *Internal Auditor* 58, no. 1 (February 2001), p. 30.

71. Rita Zeidner, "Out of the Breach," *HR Magazine*, August 2008, p. 38.

72. Declan Leonard and Angela France, "Workplace Monitoring: Balancing Business Interests with Employee Privacy Rights," *Society for Human Resource Management Legal Report*, May–June 2003, pp. 3–6; "Blogs, Networking Sites Drive Workplace Privacy Disputes," *BNA Bulletin to Management*, August 5, 2008, p. 255.

73. Rita Zeidner, "New Face in the C-suite," *HR Magazine*, January 2010, p. 39.

74. "Time Clocks Go High Touch, High Tech to Keep Workers from Gaming the System,"

BNA Bulletin to Management, March 25, 2004, p. 97.

75. Andrea Poe, "Make Foresight 20/20," *HR Magazine*, February 2000, pp. 74–80.

76. Rita Zeidner, "Keeping E-Mail in Check," *HR Magazine*, June 2007, pp. 70–74; P. Gralla, "Smartphone Privacy: IT Caught in the Crossfire," *Computerworld* 45, no. 9 (May 9, 2011), p. 16.

77. Frederic Leffler and Lauren Palais, "Filter Out Perilous Company E-Mails," *Society for Human Resource Management Legal Report*, August 2008, p. 3.

78. Bill Roberts, "Stay Ahead of the Technology Use Curve," *HR Magazine*, October 2008, pp. 57–61.

79. "Workers Sharing Music, Movies at Work Violates Copyrights, Employer Finds," *BNA Bulletin to Management*, June 19, 2003, p. 193.

80. "After Employer Found Liable for Worker's Child Porn, Policies May Need to be Revisited," *BNA Bulletin to Management*, March 21, 2006, p. 89.

81. "FTC Rules May Make Employers Liable for Worker Web Conduct," *BNA Bulletin to Management*, January 19, 2010, p. 23.

82. Kathy Gurchiek, "iPods Can Hit Sour Note in the Office," *HR Magazine*, April 2006.

83. *Vega-Rodriguez v. Puerto Rico Telephone Company*, CA1, #962061, 4/8/97, discussed in "Video Surveillance Withstands Privacy Challenge," *BNA Bulletin to Management*, April 17, 1997, p. 121. Also see, J. Greenwald, "Monitoring Communications? Know Legal Pitfalls," *Business Insurance* 45, no. 6 (February 7, 2011), pp. 1, 17.

84. *Quon v. Arch Wireless Operating Co.*, 529f.3d 892 (Ninth Circuit, 2008), "Employers Should Re-Examine Policies in Light of Ruling," *BNA Bulletin to Management*, August 12, 2008, p. 263.

85. "Secret Videotaping Leads to $200,000 Settlement," *BNA Bulletin to Management*, January 22, 1998, p. 17.

86. Bill Roberts, "Are You Ready for Biometrics?" *HR Magazine*, March 2003, pp. 95–96.

87. Charles Muhl, "The Employment at Will Doctrine: Three Major Exceptions," *Monthly Labor Review* 124, no. 1 (January 2001), pp. 3–11.

88. Michael Orey, "Fear of Firing," *BusinessWeek*, April 23, 2007, pp. 52–54.

89. Robert Lanza and Martin Warren, "United States: Employment at Will Prevails Despite Exceptions to the Rule," *Society for Human Resource Management Legal Report*, October–November 2005, pp. 1–8.

90. Joseph Famularo, *Handbook of Modern Personnel Administration* (New York: McGraw-Hill, 1982), pp. 65.3–65.5. See also Carolyn Hirschman, "Off Duty, Out of Work," *HR Magazine*, www.shrm.org/hrmagazine/articles/0203/0203hirschman.asp, accessed January 10, 2008.

91. Insubordinate and gross conduct acts based on Kenneth Sovereign, *Personnel Law*

(Upper Saddle River, NJ: Prentice Hall, 1999); Connie Wanberg et al., "Perceived Fairness of Layoffs Among Individuals Who Have Been Laid Off: A Longitudinal Study," *Personnel Psychology* 2 (1999), pp. 59–84.

92. Wanberg et al., "Perceived Fairness of Layoffs"; Brian Klass and Gregory Dell'omo, "Managerial Use of Dismissal: Organizational Level Determinants," *Personnel Psychology* 50 (1997), pp. 927–953; Nancy Hatch Woodward, "Smoother Separations," *HR Magazine*, June 2007, pp. 94–97.

93. "E-Mail Used for Layoffs, Humiliation," *BNA Bulletin to Management*, October 2, 2007, p. 315.

94. Jaikumar Vijayan, "Downsizings Leave Firms Vulnerable to Digital Attacks," *Computerworld* 25 (2001), pp. 6–7.

95. Paul Falcon, "Give Employees the (Gentle) Hook," *HR Magazine*, April 2001, pp. 121–128.

96. James Coil III and Charles Rice, "Three Steps to Creating Effective Employee Releases," *Employment Relations Today*, Spring 1994, pp. 91–94; Richard Bayer, "Termination with Dignity," *Business Horizons* 43, no. 5 (September 2000), pp. 4–10; Betty Sosnin, "Orderly Departures," *HR Magazine* 50, no. 11 (November 2005), pp. 74–78; "Severance Pay: Not Always the Norm," *HR Magazine*, May 2008, p. 28.

97. See, for example, Richard Hannah, "The Attraction of Severance," *Compensation & Benefits Review*, November/December 2008, pp. 37–44.

98. Jonathan Segal, "Severance Strategies," *HR Magazine*, July 2008, pp. 95–96.

99. "Lawyers Say Reasonable Employer Is Best Defense Against Wrongful Termination Claims," *BNA Bulletin to Management*, November 20, 2007, p. 379.

100. "Court Permits Wrongful Termination Benefit to Be Paid in Monthly Installments," *Benefits Magazine* 48, no. 3 (March 2011), pp. 59–60.

101. Ibid.

102. Based on Coil and Rice, "Three Steps to Creating Effective Employee Releases," pp. 91–94.

103. "One More Heart Risk: Firing Employees," *Miami Herald*, March 20, 1998, pp. C1, C7.

104. Kemba Dunham, "The Kinder Gentler Way to Lay Off Employees—More Human Approach Helps," *The Wall Street Journal*, March 13, 2001, p. B1.

105. Paul Barada, "Before You Go . . . ," *HR Magazine*, December 1998, pp. 89–102; Marlene Piturro, "Alternatives to Downsizing," *Management Review*, October 1999, pp. 37–42; "How Safe Is Your Job?" *Money*, December 1, 2001, p. 130.

106. Peter Hom et al., "Challenging Conventional Wisdom About Who Quits: Revelations from Corporate America," *Journal of Applied Psychology* 93, no. 1 (2008), pp. 1–34.

107. Joseph Zarandona and Michael Camuso, "A Study of Exit Interviews: Does the Last Word Count?" *Personnel* 62, no. 3 (March 1981), pp. 47–48. For another point of view, see "Firms Can Profit from Data Obtained from Exit Interviews," *Knight Ridder/Tribune Business News*, February 13, 2001, Item 0104 4446.

108. In the recession years of 2008 and 2009 combined, employers carried out a total of about 51,000 mass layoffs, idling over 5 million workers in total. "Mass Layoffs at Lowest Level Since July 2008, BLS Says," *BNA Bulletin to Management*, January 12, 2010, p. 13.

109. See Nancy Ryan, "Complying with the Worker Adjustment and Retraining Notification Act (WARN Act)," *Employee Relations Law Journal* 18, no. 1 (Summer 1993), pp. 169–176; and Emily Nelson, "The Job Cut Buyouts Favored by P&G Pose Problems," *The Wall Street Journal*, June 12, 2001, p. B1. See also Rodney Sorensen and Stephen Robinson, "What Employers Can Do to Stay Out of Legal Trouble When Forced to Implement Layoffs," *Compensation & Benefits Review*, January/February 2009, pp. 25–32.

110. Leon Grunberg, Sarah Moore, and Edward Greenberg, "Managers' Reactions to Implementing Layoffs: Relationship to Health Problems and Withdrawal Behaviors," *Human Resource Management* 45, no. 2 (Summer 2006), pp. 159–178.

111. These are suggested by attorney Ethan Lipsig and discussed in "The Lowdown on Downsizing," *BNA Bulletin to Management*, January 9, 1997, p. 16. See also Stephen Gilliland and Donald Schepers, "Why We Do the Things We Do: A Discussion and Analysis of Determinants of Just Treatment in Layoff Implementation Decisions," *Human Resource Management Review* 13, no. 1 (2003), pp. 59–84.

112. "Communication Can Reduce Problems, Litigation After Layoffs, Attorneys Say," *BNA Bulletin to Management*, April 24, 2003, p. 129.

113. John Kammeyer-Mueller and Hui Liao, "Workforce Reduction and Jobseeker Attraction: Examining Jobseekers' Reactions to Firm Workforce-Reduction Strategies," *Human Resource Management* 45, no. 4 (Winter 2006), pp. 585–603.

114. Adrienne Fox, "Prune Employees Carefully," *HR Magazine*, April 1, 2008.

115. Ibid.

116. Grunberg, Moore, and Greenberg, "Managers' Reactions to Implementing Layoffs."

117. In one recent year, U.S. employers implemented about 1,300 mass layoffs, involving a total of almost 133,000 workers. "Layoffs: 133,914 Workers Idled by Mass Layoffs in April, BLS Says," *BNA Bulletin to Management*, June 3, 2008, p. 181.

118. "Calling a Layoff a Layoff," *Workforce Management*, April 21, 2008, p. 41.

119. Roderick Iversen and Christopher Zatzick, "The Effects of Downsizing of Labor Productivity: The Value of Showing Consideration for Employees Morale and Welfare and High Performance Work Systems," *Human Resource Management* 50, no. 1 (January–February 2011), pp. 29–44.

120. Ibid., p. 40.

121. Steve Weinstein, "The People Side of Mergers," *Progressive Grocer* 80, no. 1 (January 2001), pp. 29–31.

122. Based on "Theft Is Unethical," *HR Solutions* 34 (October 2002), p. 66.

123. Bureau of National Affairs, *Bulletin to Management*, September 13, 1985, p. 3.

124. David Gebler, "Is Your Culture a Risk Factor?" *Business and Society Review* 111, no. 3 (Fall 2006), pp. 337–362.

125. John Cohan, "'I Didn't Know' and 'I Was Only Doing My Job': Has Corporate Governance Careened Out of Control? A Case Study of Enron's Information Myopia," *Journal of Business Ethics* 40, no. 3 (October 2002), pp. 275–299.

126. Gebler, "Is Your Culture a Risk Factor?"

127. Ibid.

15
Labor Relations and Collective Bargaining

Source: Elaine Thompson/AP Images.

LEARNING OBJECTIVES

1. Give a brief history of the American labor movement.
2. Discuss the main features of at least three major pieces of labor legislation.
3. Present examples of what to expect during the union drive and election.
4. Describe five ways to lose an NLRB election.
5. Illustrate with examples bargaining that is not in good faith.
6. Develop a grievance procedure.

Some people call Costco "The Anti-Walmart," because of how Costco treats its workers and unions.[1] For example, Walmart is famously anti-union. In comparison, when California grocery store workers picketed several chains a few years ago, "Costco Wholesale Corp. avoided the fray, quietly renegotiating a separate contract with its union employees there." The new contract boosted Costco workers' wages and the firm's contribution to their pension plans. Then in October 2011 Walmart announced it was cutting some employee health care benefits, and eliminating health insurance for future employees working less than 24 hours per week.[2]

WHERE ARE WE NOW . . .

Chapter 14 focused on employee ethics and justice—important issues in determining employees' tendencies to join unions. The main purpose of this chapter is to help you deal effectively with unions and grievances. After briefly discussing the history of the American labor movement, we describe the basic labor law, including unfair labor practices. We explain labor negotiations, including the union actions you can expect during the union campaign and election. And we explain what you can expect during the actual bargaining sessions, and how to handle grievances.

Access a host of interactive learning aids at **www.mymanagementlab.com** to help strengthen your understanding of the chapter concepts.

1 Give a brief history of the American labor movement.

THE LABOR MOVEMENT

Even with the pressures they've been under the past few years, about 14.7 million U.S. workers still belong to unions—about 11.9% of the total number of men and women working in this country.[3] Many are still blue-collar workers. But workers including doctors, psychologists, graduate teaching assistants, government office workers, and even fashion models are forming or joining unions.[4] In some industries— including transportation and public utilities, where more than 26% of employees are union members—it's still hard to get a job without joining a union.[5] Most union members are in the public sector, as opposed to the private sector.[6]

Furthermore, it's a mistake to assume that unions affect employers only negatively. For example, perhaps by professionalizing the staff and/or systematizing company practices, unionization may improve performance. Thus in one study, heart attack mortality among patients in hospitals with unionized registered nurses was 5% to 9% lower than in nonunion hospitals.[7] The accompanying Strategic Context feature provides another illustration of the potential positives of good union-management relations.

THE STRATEGIC CONTEXT

The "Anti-Walmart"

It's not easy competing with Walmart's always-low prices, but Costco may have found a way. Walmart Stores' Sam's Club is actually second in sales to Costco. How does Costco stay ahead? In part with "strong labor relations, low employee turnover and liberal benefits."[8] For example, Costco pays about 90% of the health insurance costs of its over 90,000 domestic employees, about $6,000 annually per employee.[9] And its relations with labor unions are comparatively benign. Costco's HR strategy is to fend off Walmart's low wages and labor costs by eliciting higher productivity and better service from its employees. The strategy seems to be working. Costco's sales per employee are about $500,000 a year versus $340,000 at Sam's Clubs.[10] Turnover among those employed with the company at least 1 year is about 6%, far below the retail industry average.[11] Aligning its labor relations strategy with its overall strategic aim to compete on the basis of better productivity and service seems to be working for Costco.

In any case, support for unions has always ebbed and flowed in America, and today pressures are building against unions. For example, critical budget problems following the 2008–2010 recession in states such as Wisconsin and New Jersey prompted those governments to reduce public employees' numbers, pensions, and pay. The number of U.S. workers belonging to unions actually declined by 612,000 from 2009 to 2010.

We'll look at unions and dealing with them in this chapter.

Why Do Workers Organize?

Experts have spent much time and money trying to discover why workers unionize, and they've proposed many theories. Yet there is no simple answer to the question, partly because each worker probably joins for his or her own reasons.

However, workers don't unionize just to get more pay or better working conditions, though these are important. For example, recent median weekly wages for union workers was $917, while that for nonunion workers was $717.[12] Union workers also generally receive significantly more holidays, sick leave, unpaid leave, insurance plan benefits, long-term disability benefits, and various other benefits than do nonunion workers. Unions also have been able to somewhat reduce the impact of (but obviously not eliminate) downsizings and wage cuts in most industries.[13]

Two other factors—employer unfairness and the union's power—are also important. In one Australia-based firm, researchers found that "individuals who believe that the company rules or policies were administered unfairly or to their detriment were more likely to turn to unions."[14] But, to vote pro-union, the employees also had to believe the union could improve their wages, benefits, and treatment.

Source: Library of Congress.

Making fenders at an early Ford factory in Ypsilanti, Michigan. In addition to heavy physical labor, workers faced health hazards—poor lighting, dust, and dangerous machinery.

THE BOTTOM LINE The bottom line is that the urge to unionize often boils down to the belief on the part of workers that it is only through unity that they can protect themselves from unilateral management whims. When Kaiser Permanente's San Francisco Medical Center cut back on vacation and sick leave for its pharmacists and other workers, the pharmacists' union, the Guild for Professional Pharmacists, won back the lost vacation days. As one staff pharmacist said, "Kaiser is a pretty benevolent employer, but there's always the pressure to squeeze a little."[15] One labor relations lawyer says, "The one major thing unions offer is making you a 'for cause' instead of an 'at will' employee, which guarantees a hearing and arbitration if you're fired."[16] So, in practice, low morale, fear of job loss, and arbitrary management actions help foster unionization. Employers ignore that at their peril.

In some respects, things have not changed in years. Here is how one writer describes the motivation behind the early (1900s) unionization of automobile workers:

In the years to come, economic issues would make the headlines when union and management met in negotiations. But in the early years, the rate of pay was not the major complaint of the autoworkers. . . . Specifically, the principal grievances of the autoworkers were the speed-up of production and the lack of any kind of job security. As production tapered off, the order in which workers were laid off was determined largely by the whim of foremen and other supervisors. . . . Generally, what the workers revolted against was the lack of human dignity and individuality, and a working relationship that was massively impersonal, cold, and nonhuman. They wanted to be treated like human beings—not like faceless clock card numbers.[17]

What Do Unions Want?

We can generalize by saying that unions have two sets of aims, one for *union security* and one for *improved wages, hours, working conditions*, and *benefits* for their members.

UNION SECURITY First and probably foremost, unions seek security for themselves. They fight hard for the right to represent a firm's workers, and to be the exclusive bargaining agent for all employees in the unit. (As such, they negotiate contracts for all employees, including those not members of the union.) Five types of union security are possible:

1. **Closed shop.**[18] The company can hire only current union members. Congress outlawed closed shops in interstate commerce in 1947, but they still exist in some states for particular industries (such as printing). They account for fewer than 5% of union contracts.

2. **Union shop.** The company can hire nonunion people, but they must join the union after a prescribed period and pay dues. (If not, they can be fired.) These account for about 73% of union contracts.

3. **Agency shop.** Employees who do not belong to the union still must pay the union an amount equal to union dues (on the assumption that the union's efforts benefit *all* the workers).

closed shop
A form of union security in which the company can hire only union members. This was outlawed in 1947 but still exists in some industries (such as printing).

union shop
A form of union security in which the company can hire nonunion people, but they must join the union after a prescribed period of time and pay dues. (If they do not, they can be fired.)

agency shop
A form of union security in which employees who do not belong to the union must still pay union dues on the assumption that union efforts benefit all workers.

4. **Preferential shop.** Union members get preference in hiring, but the employer can still hire nonunion members.

5. **Maintenance of membership arrangement.** Employees do not have to belong to the union. However, union members employed by the firm must maintain membership in the union for the contract period. These account for about 4% of union agreements.

Not all states give unions the right to require union membership as a condition of employment. **Right to work** is a term used to describe "state statutory or constitutional provisions banning the requirement of union membership as a condition of employment."[19] *Right-to-work laws* don't outlaw unions. They do outlaw (within those states) any form of union security. This understandably inhibits union formation in those states. There are 23 right-to-work states.[20] Several years ago, Oklahoma became the 22nd state to pass right-to-work legislation. Some believe that this—combined with a loss of manufacturing jobs—explains why Oklahoma's union membership dropped dramatically in the next 3 years.[21]

IMPROVED WAGES, HOURS, AND BENEFITS   Once the union ensures its security at the employer, it fights to improve its members' wages, hours, and working conditions. The typical labor agreement also gives the union a role in other human resource activities, including recruiting, selecting, compensating, promoting, training, and discharging employees.

The AFL-CIO and the SEIU

The American Federation of Labor and Congress of Industrial Organizations (AFL-CIO) is a voluntary federation of about 56 national and international labor unions in the United States. The separate AFL and CIO merged in 1955. For many people in the United States, the AFL-CIO is synonymous with the word *union.*

There are three layers in the structure of the AFL-CIO and most other U.S. unions. The worker joins the local union, to which he or she pays dues. The local is in turn a single chapter in the national union. For example, if you were a teacher in Detroit, you would belong to the local union there, which is one of hundreds of local chapters of the American Federation of Teachers, their national union (most unions actually call themselves international unions). The third layer in the structure is the national federation, in this case, the AFL-CIO.

The Service Employees International Union (SEIU) is a fast-growing federation of more than 2.2 million members. It includes the largest healthcare union, with more than 1.1 million members in the field, including nurses, LPNs, and doctors, and the second largest public employees union, with more than 1 million local and state government workers.[22]

Union federation membership is in flux. Several years ago, the SEIU, the International Brotherhood of Teamsters, and UNITE HERE left the AFL-CIO and established their own federation, called the Change to Win Coalition. Together, the departing unions represented over one-quarter of the AFL-CIO's membership and budget. Change to Win plans to be more aggressive about organizing workers than they say the AFL-CIO was.[23] Then the UNITE HERE union left Change to Win and rejoined the AFL-CIO, possibly slowing Change to Win's momentum.

Some people think of the federation (such as the AFL-CIO or SEIU) as the most important part of the labor movement, but it is not. Thus the president of the teachers' union wields more power in that capacity than in his capacity as a vice president of the AFL-CIO. Yet as a practical matter, the presidents of the AFL-CIO or SEIU do have political influence in excess of a figurehead president.

UNIONS AND THE LAW

As noted, the history of the American labor movement has been one of alternate expansion and contraction, in response to public policy changes. Until about 1930, there were no special labor laws. Employers were not required to engage in collective bargaining with employees and were virtually unrestrained in their behavior toward unions; the use of spies and firing of union agitators were widespread. "Yellow dog" contracts, whereby management could require nonunion membership as a condition for employment, were widely enforced. Most union weapons—even strikes—were illegal.

This one-sided situation lasted until the Great Depression (around 1930).[24] Since then, in response to changing public attitudes, values, and economic conditions, labor law has gone through three clear periods: from "strong encouragement" of unions, to "modified encouragement coupled with regulation," and finally to "detailed regulation of internal union affairs."[25]

<table>
<tr><td>2</td><td>Discuss the main features of at least three major pieces of labor legislation.</td></tr>
</table>

Period of Strong Encouragement: The Norris-LaGuardia (1932) and National Labor Relations (or Wagner) Acts (1935)

The **Norris-LaGuardia Act of 1932** set the stage for a new era in which union activity was encouraged. It guaranteed to each employee the right to bargain collectively "free from interference, restraint, or coercion." It declared yellow dog contracts unenforceable. And it limited the courts' abilities to issue injunctions (stop orders) for activities such as peaceful picketing and payment of strike benefits.

Yet this act did little to restrain employers from fighting labor organizations by whatever means they could find. So in 1935, Congress passed the **National Labor Relations (or Wagner) Act** to add teeth to Norris-LaGuardia. It did this by (1) banning certain unfair labor practices, (2) providing for secret-ballot elections and majority rule for determining whether a firm's employees would unionize, and (3) creating the **National Labor Relations Board (NLRB)** to enforce these two provisions.

UNFAIR EMPLOYER LABOR PRACTICES   The Wagner Act deemed "statutory wrongs" (but not crimes) five unfair labor practices used by employers:

1. It is unfair for employers to "interface with, restrain, or coerce employees" in exercising their legally sanctioned right of self-organization.

2. It is unfair for company representatives to dominate or interfere with either the formation or the administration of labor unions. Among other specific management actions found to be unfair under these first two practices are bribing employees, using company spy systems, moving a business to avoid unionization, and black-listing union sympathizers.

3. Employers are prohibited from discriminating in any way against employees for their legal union activities.

4. Employers are forbidden to discharge or discriminate against employees simply because the latter file unfair practice charges against the company.

5. Finally, it is an unfair labor practice for employers to refuse to bargain collectively with their employees' duly chosen representatives.

Unions file an unfair labor practice charge (see Figure 15-1) with the National Labor Relations Board. The board then investigates the charge and decides if it should take action. Possible actions include dismissal of the complaint, request for an injunction against the employer, or an order that the employer cease and desist.

---

preferential shop
Union members get preference in hiring, but the employer can still hire nonunion members.

right to work
A term used to describe state statutory or constitutional provisions banning the requirement of union membership as a condition of employment.

Norris-LaGuardia Act (1932)
This law marked the beginning of the era of strong encouragement of unions and guaranteed to each employee the right to bargain collectively "free from interference, restraint, or coercion."

National Labor Relations (or Wagner) Act
This law banned certain types of unfair practices and provided for secret-ballot elections and majority rule for determining whether a firm's employees want to unionize.

National Labor Relations Board (NLRB)
The agency created by the Wagner Act to investigate unfair labor practice charges and to provide for secret-ballot elections and majority rule in determining whether or not a firm's employees want a union.

FIGURE 15-1 NLRB Form 501: Filing an Unfair Labor Practice

FORM NLRB 501
(2 81)

FORM EXEMPT UNDER
44 U.S.C. 3512

UNITED STATES OF AMERICA
NATIONAL LABOR RELATIONS BOARD
CHARGE AGAINST EMPLOYER

INSTRUCTIONS: File an original and 4 copies of this charge with NLRB Regional Director for the region in which the alleged unfair labor practice occurred or is occurring.	DO NOT WRITE IN THIS SPACE	
	CASE NO.	DATE FILE

1. EMPLOYER AGAINST WHOM CHARGE IS BROUGHT

a. NAME OF EMPLOYER	b. NUMBER OF WORKERS EMPLOYED	
c. ADDRESS OF ESTABLISHMENT (*street and number, city, State, and ZIP code*)	d. EMPLOYER REPRESENTATIVE TO CONTACT	e. PHONE NO.
f. TYPE OF ESTABLISHMENT (*factory, mine, wholesaler, etc.*)	g. IDENTIFY PRINCIPAL PRODUCT OR SERVICE	

h. THE ABOVE-NAMED EMPLOYER HAS ENGAGED IN AND IS ENGAGING IN UNFAIR LABOR PRACTICES WITHIN THE MEANING OF SECTION 8(a), SUBSECTIONS (1) AND ______ (*list subsections*) OF THE NATIONAL LABOR RELATIONS ACT, AND THESE UNFAIR LABOR PRACTICES ARE UNFAIR LABOR PRACTICES AFFECTING COMMERCE WITHIN THE MEANING OF THE ACT.

2. BASIS OF THE CHARGE (*be specific as to facts, names, addresses, plants involved, dates, places, etc.*)

BY THE ABOVE AND OTHER ACTS, THE ABOVE-NAMED EMPLOYER HAS INTERFERED WITH, RESTRAINED, AND COERCED EMPLOYEES IN THE EXERCISE OF THE RIGHTS GUARANTEED IN SECTION 7 OF THE ACT.

3. FULL NAME OF PARTY FILING CHARGE (*if labor organization, give full name, including local name and number*)

4a. ADDRESS (*street and number, city, State, and ZIP code*)	4b. TELEPHONE NO.

5. FULL NAME OF NATIONAL OR INTERNATIONAL LABOR ORGANIZATION OF WHICH IT IS AN AFFILIATE OR CONSTITUENT UNIT (*to be filled in when charge is filed by a labor organization*)

6. DECLARATION

I declare that I have read the above charge and that the statements therein are true to the best of my knowledge and belief.

By ______
(signature of representative or person filing charge) (title, if any)

Address ______
(telephone number) (date)

WILLFULLY FALSE STATEMENTS ON THIS CHARGE CAN BE PUNISHED BY FINE AND IMPRISONMENT
(U.S. CODE, TITLE 18, SECTION 1001)

Such complaints are commonplace. For example, in 2011, the American Guild of Musical Artists said it would file an unfair labor charge against the New York City Opera if the latter carried through on its plan to cut staff and move to new quarters.

FROM 1935 TO 1947 Union membership increased quickly after passage of the Wagner Act in 1935. Other factors such as an improving economy and aggressive union leadership contributed to this rise. But by the mid-1940s, after the end of World War II, the tide had begun to turn. Largely because of a series of massive postwar strikes, public policy began to shift against what many viewed as union excesses. The stage was set for passage of the Taft-Hartley Act.

Period of Modified Encouragement Coupled with Regulation: The Taft-Hartley Act (1947)

The **Taft-Hartley** (*or Labor Management Relations*) **Act of 1947** reflected the public's less enthusiastic attitude toward unions. It amended the National Labor Relations (Wagner) Act by limiting unions in four ways: (1) prohibiting unfair union labor practices, (2) enumerating the rights of employees as union members, (3) enumerating the rights of employers, and (4) allowing the President of the United States to bar temporarily national emergency strikes.

Unfair Union Labor Practices

The Taft-Hartley Act enumerated several labor practices that unions were prohibited from engaging in:

1. First, it banned unions from *restraining or coercing employees* from exercising their guaranteed bargaining rights. (Some union actions courts have held illegal include stating to an anti-union employee that he or she will lose his or her job once the union gains recognition, and issuing patently false statements during union organizing campaigns.)

2. It is also an unfair labor practice for a union to *cause an employer to discriminate* in any way against an employee in order to encourage or discourage his or her membership in a union. For example, the union cannot try to force an employer to fire a worker because he or she doesn't attend union meetings or refuses to join a union. There is one exception: Where a closed or union shop prevails (and union membership is therefore a prerequisite to employment), the union may demand the discharge of someone who fails to pay his or her initiation fees and dues.

3. It is an unfair labor practice for a union to *refuse to bargain in good faith* with the employer about wages, hours, and other employment conditions. Certain strikes and boycotts are also unfair practices.

4. It is an unfair labor practice for a union to engage in *featherbedding* (requiring an employer to pay an employee for services not performed).

RIGHTS OF EMPLOYEES   The Taft-Hartley Act protected the rights of employees against their unions in other ways. For example, many people felt that compulsory unionism violated the basic right of freedom of association. Legitimized by Taft-Hartley, new right-to-work laws quickly sprung up in 19 (now 23) states (mainly in the South and Southwest). In New York, for example, in many printing firms you can't work as a press operator unless you belong to a printers' union. In Florida, such union shops—except those covered by the Railway Labor Act—are illegal, and printing shops typically employ both union and nonunion operators. Even today, union membership varies widely by state, from a high of 26.8% in New York to a low of 3.2% in North Carolina.[26] The Taft-Hartley act also required the employee's authorization before the union could have dues subtracted from his or her paycheck.

In general, the Labor Relations (Taft-Hartley) Act does not restrain unions from unfair labor practices to the extent that the law does employers. It says unions may not restrain or coerce employees. However, "violent or otherwise threatening behavior or clearly coercive or intimidating union activities are necessary before the NLRB will find an unfair labor practice."[27] Examples include physical assaults or threats of violence, economic reprisals, and mass picketing that restrains the lawful entry or leaving of a work site.

Taft-Hartley Act (1947)
Also known as the *Labor Management Relations Act,* this law prohibited unfair union labor practices and enumerated the rights of employees as union members. It also enumerated the rights of employers.

RIGHTS OF EMPLOYERS   The Taft-Hartley Act also explicitly gave *employers* certain rights. First, it gave them full freedom to express their views concerning union organization. For example, as a manager you can tell your employees that in your opinion unions are worthless, dangerous to the economy, and immoral. You can even (generally) hint that unionization and subsequent high-wage demands might result in the permanent closing of the plant (but not its relocation). Employers can set forth the union's record concerning violence and corruption, if appropriate. In fact, the only major restraint is that employers must avoid threats, promises, coercion, and direct interference with workers who are trying to reach a decision. There can be no threat of reprisal or force or promise of benefit.[28]

Furthermore, the employer (1) cannot meet with employees on company time within 24 hours of an election or (2) suggest to employees that they vote against the union while they are at home or in the employer's office (although he or she can do so while in their work area or where they normally gather).

NATIONAL EMERGENCY STRIKES   The Taft-Hartley Act also allows the U.S. President to intervene in **national emergency strikes**. These are strikes (for example, by railroad workers) that might "imperil the national health and safety." The President may appoint a board of inquiry and, based on its report, apply for an injunction restraining the strike for 60 days. If the parties don't reach a settlement during that time, the President can have the injunction extended for another 20 days. During this last period, employees take a secret ballot to ascertain their willingness to accept the employer's last offer.

PERIOD OF DETAILED REGULATION OF INTERNAL UNION AFFAIRS: THE LANDRUM-GRIFFIN ACT (1959)   In the 1950s, Senate investigations revealed unsavory practices on the part of some unions, and the result was the **Landrum-Griffin Act** (officially, the *Labor Management Reporting and Disclosure Act*) **of 1959**. An overriding aim of this act was to protect union members from possible wrongdoing on the part of their unions. Like Taft-Hartley, it also amended the National Labor Relations (Wagner) Act.

First, the law contains a bill of rights for union members. Among other things, it provides for certain rights in the nomination of candidates for union office. It also affirms a member's right to sue his or her union and ensures that the union cannot fine or suspend a member without due process.

This act also laid out rules regarding union elections. For example, national and international unions must elect officers at least once every 5 years, using a secret-ballot mechanism. And it regulates the kind of person who can serve as a union officer. For example, it bars persons convicted of felonies (bribery, murder, and so on) from holding union officer positions for a period of 5 years after conviction.

Senate investigators also discovered flagrant examples of employer wrongdoing. Employers and their "labor relations consultants" had bribed union agents and officers, for example. That had been a federal crime starting with the passage of the Taft-Hartley Act. But Landrum-Griffin greatly expanded the list of unlawful employer actions. For example, companies can no longer pay their own employees to entice them not to join the union, and must report use of labor consultants.

THE UNION DRIVE AND ELECTION

3 Present examples of what to expect during the union drive and election.

It is through the union drive and election that a union tries to be recognized to represent employees. Supervisors need to understand this process, which has five basic steps.[29]

Step 1. Initial Contact

During the initial contact stage, the union determines the employees' interest in organizing, and establishes an organizing committee.

The initiative for the first contact between the employees and the union may come from the employees, from a union already representing other employees of the firm, or from a union representing workers elsewhere. In any case, there is an initial contact.

Once an employer becomes a target, a union official usually assigns a representative to assess employee interest. The representative visits the firm to determine whether enough employees are interested to make a campaign worthwhile. He or she also identifies employees who would make good leaders in the organizing campaign and calls them together to create an organizing committee. The objective here is to educate the committee about the benefits of forming a union and the law and procedures involved in forming a local union.

The union must follow certain rules when it starts contacting employees. The law allows organizers to solicit employees for membership as long as the effort doesn't endanger the performance or safety of the employees. Therefore, much of the contact takes place off the job, perhaps at home or at eating places near work. Organizers can also safely contact employees on company grounds during off hours (such as lunch or break time). Yet, in practice, there will be much informal organizing going on at the workplace as employees debate organizing. Sometimes the first inkling management has of the campaign is the distribution or posting of handbills soliciting union membership.

Much soliciting today will be via e-mail, but prohibiting employees from sending pro-union e-mail messages on company e-mail is easier said than done. You can't discriminate against union activities, so prohibiting only union e-mail may violate NLRB decisions. And barring workers from using e-mail for all non–work-related topics may be futile if the company actually does little to stop it.

LABOR RELATIONS CONSULTANTS   Both management and unions typically use "labor relations consultants." The consultants may be law firms, researchers, psychologists, labor relations specialists, or public relations firms. Some are former union organizers who now represent the employers.[30]

In any case, their role is to provide advice and related services not just when a vote is expected (although this is when most of them are used), but at other times, too. For the employer, the consultant's services may range from ensuring that the firm properly fills out routine labor relations forms to managing the union campaign. Unions may use public relations firms to improve their image, or specialists to manage corporate campaigns. (These aim to pressure shareholders and creditors to get management to agree to the union's demands.)

The widespread use of such consultants—only some of whom are actually lawyers—raises the question of whether some have advised their clients to engage in questionable activities. One tactic, for instance, is to delay the union vote with lengthy hearings at the NLRB. The longer the delay in the vote, they argue, the more time the employer has to drill anti-union propaganda into the employees.

UNION SALTING   Unions are not without creative ways to win elections. The National Labor Relations Board defines **union salting** as "placing of union members on nonunion job sites for the purpose of organizing." Critics claim that "salts" also often interfere with business operations and harass employees.[31] The U.S. Supreme Court ruled that union salts are "employees" under the National Labor Relations Act; the NLRB will require that employers pay salts if they fire them for trying to organize.[32] For managers, the solution is to make sure you know whom you're hiring. However, not hiring someone simply because, as a member of the local union, he or she might be pro-union or a union salt would be discriminatory.[33]

---

national emergency strikes
Strikes that might "imperil the national health and safety."

Landrum-Griffin Act (1959)
Also known as the *Labor Management Reporting and Disclosure Act,* this law aimed at protecting union members from possible wrongdoing on the part of their unions.

union salting
A union organizing tactic by which workers who are in fact employed full-time by a union as undercover organizers are hired by unwitting employers.

Step 2. Obtaining Authorization Cards

For the union to petition the NLRB for the right to hold an election, it must show that a sizable number of employees may be interested in organizing. Therefore the next step for union organizers is to try to get the employees to sign **authorization cards** (see Figure 15-2). Among other things, these usually authorize the union to seek a representation election and state that the employee has applied to join the union. Thirty percent of the eligible employees in an appropriate bargaining unit must sign before the union can petition the NLRB for an election (although in Figure 15-2 this employer has agreed with SEIU to recognize the union without a follow-up vote if a majority of employees sign the authorization cards).

This is a dangerous time for supervisors. During this stage, both union and management use propaganda. The union claims it can improve working conditions, raise wages, increase benefits, and generally get the workers better deals. Management can attack the union on ethical and moral grounds and cite the cost of union membership. Management can also explain its accomplishments, express facts and opinions, and explain the law applicable to organizing campaigns. However, neither side can threaten, bribe, or coerce employees. And an employer (or supervisor) may not make promises of benefits to employees or make unilateral changes in terms and conditions of employment that were not planned to be implemented prior to the onset of union organizing activity.

STEPS TO TAKE Management can take several steps with respect to the authorization cards. For example, the NLRB ruled an employer might lawfully inform employees of their right to revoke their authorization cards, even when employees have not asked for such information. The employer can also distribute pamphlets that explain just how employees can revoke their cards. However, the law prohibits any material assistance to employees such as postage or stationery.

Similarly, it is an unfair labor practice to tell employees they can't sign a card. What you *can* do is prepare supervisors so they can explain what the card actually authorizes the union to do—including seeking a representation election, designating the union as bargaining representative, and subjecting the employee to union rules. The latter is especially important. The union, for instance, may force the employee to picket and fine any member who does not comply with union instructions. Explaining the serious legal and practical implications of signing the card can thus be an effective weapon.

One thing managers should *not* do is look through signed authorization cards if confronted with them by union representatives. The NLRB could construe that as an unfair labor practice, as spying on those who signed. Doing so could also later form the basis of a charge alleging discrimination due to union activity, if the firm subsequently disciplines someone who signed a card.

During this stage, unions can picket the company, subject to three constraints: (1) The union must file a petition for an election within 30 days after the start of picketing; (2) the firm cannot already be lawfully recognizing another union; and (3) there cannot have been a valid NLRB election during the past 12 months.

FIGURE 15-2
Authorization Card

Source: http://www.seiu503.org/admin/Assets/AssetContent/7c8327d7-9acf-4ebd-b068-c536cbe80e2a/546bfa9e-94e2-495f-9d30-54cc81f55e47/65ff6bf4-a58b-4cf8-b1cc-cd159b9c42b5/1/web%20ojdcard.pdf, accessed 1/15/10.

LOCAL 503 SEIU Stronger Together

Yes! I believe that by joining together with my co-workers to form a union, we can create a more democratic and fair workplace. I therefore authorize SEIU Local 503, OPEU to be my exclusive representative for the purposes of collective bargaining with my employer. I understand that my signature on this card may be used to obtain certification of SEIU Local 503, OPEU as our exclusive bargaining representative without an election.

Employer__________ Worksite__________

Signature__________ Date:__________

Printed Name:__________

Street Address:__________ City:__________ Zip:__________

Home Phone:__________ Cell Phone:__________ Home E-mail:__________

Department:__________ Job Title/Classification__________

Step 3. Hold a Hearing

Once the union collects the authorization cards, one of three things can occur. If the employer chooses not to contest *union recognition* at all, then the parties need no hearing, and a special "consent election" is held. If the employer chooses not to contest the union's *right to an election*, and/or the scope of the bargaining unit, and/or which employees are eligible to vote in the election, no hearing is needed and the parties can stipulate an election. If an employer *does* wish to contest the union's right, it can insist on a hearing to determine those issues. An employer's decision about whether to insist on a hearing is a strategic one. Management bases it on the facts of each case, and on whether it feels it needs more time to try to persuade employees not to elect a union.

Most companies do contest the union's right to represent their employees, claiming that a significant number of them don't really want the union. It is at this point that the National Labor Relations Board gets involved. The union usually contacts the NLRB, which requests a hearing. The regional director of the NLRB then sends a hearing officer to investigate. The examiner sends both management and union a notice of representation hearing (NLRB Form 852; see Figure 15-3) that states the time and place of the hearing.

The hearing addresses several issues. First, does the record indicate there is enough evidence to hold an election? (For example, did 30% or more of the employees in an appropriate bargaining unit sign the authorization cards?) Second, the examiner must decide what the bargaining unit will be. The **bargaining unit** is the group of employees that the union will be authorized to represent and bargain for collectively. If the entire organization is the bargaining unit, the union will represent all nonsupervisory, nonmanagerial, and nonconfidential employees, even though the union may be oriented mostly toward blue-collar workers. (Professional and nonprofessional employees can be included in the same bargaining unit only if the professionals agree.) If your firm disagrees with the examiner's bargaining unit decision, it can challenge the decision. This will require a separate NLRB ruling.

The NLRB hearing addresses other issues. These include, "Does the employer qualify for coverage by the NLRB?" and "Is the union a labor organization within the meaning of the National Labor Relations Act?"

If the results of the hearing are favorable for the union, the NLRB will order holding an election. It will issue a Notice of Election (NLRB Form 707) to that effect, for the employer to post.

Step 4. The Campaign

During the campaign that precedes the election, union and employer appeal to employees for their votes. The union will emphasize that it will prevent unfairness, set up grievance and seniority systems, and improve wages. Union strength, they'll say, will give employees a voice in determining wages and working conditions. Management will stress that improvements like those don't require unions and that wages are equal to or better than they would be with a union. Management will also emphasize the financial cost of union dues; the fact that the union is an "outsider"; and that if the union wins, a strike may follow. It can even attack the union on ethical and moral grounds, while insisting that employees will not be as well off and may lose freedom. But neither side can threaten, bribe, or coerce employees.

authorization cards
In order to petition for a union election, the union must show that at least 30% of employees may be interested in being unionized. Employees indicate this interest by signing authorization cards.

bargaining unit
The group of employees the union will be authorized to represent.

FIGURE 15-3 NLRB Form 852:
Notice of Representation
Hearing

FORM NLRB-852
(6-61)

UNITED STATES OF AMERICA
BEFORE THE NATIONAL LABOR RELATIONS BOARD

Case No.

NOTICE OF REPRESENTATION HEARING

The Petitioner, above named, having heretofore filed a Petition pursuant to Section 9 (c) of the National Labor Relations Act, as amended, 29 U.S.C. Sec 151 et seq., copy of which Petition is hereto attached, and it appearing that a question affecting commerce has arisen concerning the representation of employees described by such Petition.

YOU ARE HEREBY NOTIFIED that, pursuant to Section 3(b) and 9(c) of the Act, on the day of   , 20   , at

a hearing will be conducted before a hearing officer of the National Labor Relations Board upon the question of representation affecting commerce which has arisen, at which time and place the parties will have the right to appear in person or otherwise, and give testimony.

Signed at   on the   day of   , 20

Regional Director, Region
National Labor Relations Board

Step 5. The Election

The election occurs within 30 to 60 days after the NLRB issues its Decision and Direction of Election. The election is by secret ballot; the NLRB provides the ballots (see Figure 15-4), voting booth, and ballot box, and counts the votes and certifies the results.

The union becomes the employees' representative if it wins the election, and winning means getting a majority of the votes *cast*, not a majority of the total workers in the bargaining unit. (Also keep in mind that if an employer commits an unfair labor practice, the NLRB may reverse a "no union" election. As representatives of their employer, supervisors must therefore be careful not to commit unfair practices.)

Several things influence whether the union wins the certification election. Unions have a higher probability of success in geographic areas with a higher percentage of union workers. High unemployment seems to lead to poorer results for the union, perhaps because employees fear that unionization efforts might result in reduced job security or employer retaliation. Unions usually carefully pick the size of their bargaining unit (all clerical employees in the company, only those at one facility, and so on) because the larger the bargaining unit, the smaller the probability of union victory. The more workers vote, the less likely a union victory, probably because more workers who are not strong supporters vote. The union is important, too: The Teamsters union is less likely to win a representation election than other unions, for instance.[34]

FIGURE 15-4 Sample
NLRB Ballot

```
UNITED STATES OF AMERICA
National Labor Relations Board

OFFICIAL SECRET BALLOT
FOR CERTAIN EMPLOYEES OF
_____
Do you wish to be represented for purposes of collective bargaining by —



_____
MARK AN "S" IN THE SQUARE OF YOUR CHOICE

        YES                              NO
        [ ]                              [ ]

DO NOT SIGN THIS BALLOT. Fold and drop in ballot box.
If you spoil this ballot return it to the Board Agent for a new one.
```

4 Describe five ways to lose an NLRB election.

How to Lose an NLRB Election

Over the years, unions typically won about 55% of elections held each year.[35] According to expert Matthew Goodfellow, there is no sure way employers can win elections. However, there are several sure ways to lose one.[36]

REASON 1. ASLEEP AT THE SWITCH In one study, in 68% of the companies that lost to the union, executives were caught unaware. In these companies, turnover and absenteeism had increased, productivity was erratic, and safety was poor. Grievance procedures were rare. When the first reports of authorization cards began trickling back to top managers, they usually responded with a barrage of letters describing how the company was "one big family" and calling for a "team effort."[37]

REASON 2. APPOINTING A COMMITTEE Of the losing companies, 36% formed a committee to manage the campaign. According to the expert, there are three problems in doing so: (1) Promptness is essential in an election situation, and committees are notorious for moving slowly. (2) Most committee members are NLRB neophytes. Their views therefore are mostly reflections of hope rather than experience. (3) A committee's decision is usually a compromise decision. The result isn't necessarily the most knowledgeable or most effective one. This expert suggests giving full responsibility to a single, decisive executive. A human resource director and a consultant or adviser with broad experience in labor relations should in turn assist this person.

REASON 3. CONCENTRATING ON MONEY AND BENEFITS In 54% of the elections studied, the company lost because top management concentrated on the wrong issues: money and benefits. As this expert puts it:

> Employees may want more money, but quite often, if they feel the company treats them fairly, decently, and honestly, they are satisfied with reasonable, competitive rates and benefits. It is only when they feel ignored, uncared for, and disregarded that money becomes a major issue to express their dissatisfaction.[38]

REASON 4. DELEGATING TOO MUCH TO DIVISIONS For companies with plants scattered around the country, unionizing one or more plants tends to lead to unionizing others. The solution is, don't abdicate all personnel and industrial relations decisions to plant managers.[39] Dealing effectively with unions—monitoring employees' attitudes, reacting properly when the union appears, and so on—generally requires centralized guidance from the main office and its human resources staff.

The other side of the coin is this: What can unions do to boost their chances they'll win the election?

Evidence-Based HR: What to Expect the Union to Do to Win the Election

A researcher analyzed data from 261 NLRB elections. She found that the best way for unions to win is to pursue a "rank and file strategy." It includes union tactics such as the following:[40]

1. "Reliance on a slow, underground, person-to-person campaign using house calls, small group meetings, and pre-union associations to develop leadership and union commitment, and prepare workers for employer anti-union strategies before the employer becomes aware of the campaign."

2. The union will focus on building active rank-and-file participation, including an organizing committee reflecting the different interest groups in the bargaining unit.

3. The union will press for a first contract early in the organizing process.

4. The union will use "inside and outside pressure tactics to build worker commitment and compel the employer to run a fair campaign."

5. There will be an emphasis during the organizing campaign on issues such as respect, dignity, and fairness, not just traditional bread-and-butter issues like wages.

The Supervisor's Role

Supervisors are an employer's first line of defense in the unionizing effort. They are often in the best position to sense evolving employee attitude problems, for instance, and to discover the first signs of union activity. Unfortunately, there's another side to that coin: They can also inadvertently hurt their employer's union-related efforts.

Supervisors therefore need special training. Specifically, they must be knowledgeable about what they can and can't do legally to hamper organizing activities. Unfair labor practices could (1) cause the NLRB to hold a new election after your company has won a previous election, or (2) cause your company to forfeit the second election and go directly to contract negotiation.

In one case, a plant superintendent reacted to a union's initial organizing attempt by prohibiting distribution of union literature in the plant's lunchroom. Since solicitation of off-duty workers in nonwork areas is generally legal, the company subsequently allowed the union to post literature on the company's bulletin board and to distribute literature in nonworking areas inside the plant. However, the NLRB still ruled that the initial act of prohibiting distribution of the literature was an unfair labor practice, one not "made right" by the company's subsequent efforts. The NLRB used the superintendent's action as one reason for invalidating an election that the company had won.[41]

SOME TIPS   Supervisors can use the acronym TIPS to remember what *not* to do during the organizing or preelection campaigns.[42] *Do not* Threaten, Interrogate, make Promises to, or Spy on employees (for instance, do not threaten that you will close or move the business, cut wages, reduce overtime, or lay off employees). Use FORE for what you may do. *You may* give employees Facts (like what signing the authorization card means), express your Opinion about unions, explain factually correct Rules (such as that the law permits permanently replacing striking employees), and share your Experiences about unions.

Rules Regarding Literature and Solicitation

The employer can legally take steps to restrict union organizing activity.[43]

1. Employers can always bar nonemployees from soliciting employees during their work time—that is, when the employee is on duty and not on a break.

2. Employers can usually stop employees from soliciting other employees for any purpose if one or both employees are on paid-duty time and not on a break.

3. Most employers (generally not including retail stores, shopping centers, and certain other employers) can bar nonemployees from the building's interiors and work areas as a right of private property owners.[44]

4. Employers can deny on- or off-duty employees access to interior or exterior areas only if they can show the rule is required for reasons of production, safety, or discipline.

Again, such restrictions are valid only if the employer doesn't discriminate against the union. Thus, if the employer lets employees collect money for baby gifts, to sell Avon products or Tupperware, or to engage in other solicitation during their working time, it may not be able lawfully to prohibit them from union soliciting during work time. Here is one example of a specific rule aimed at limiting union organizing or activity:

> Solicitation of employees on company property during working time interferes with the efficient operation of our business. Nonemployees are not permitted to solicit employees on company property for any purpose. Except in break areas where both employees are on break or off the clock, no employee may solicit another employee during working time for any purpose.[45]

Decertification Elections: Ousting the Union

Winning an election and signing an agreement do not necessarily mean that the union is in the company to stay. The same law that grants employees the right to unionize also gives them a way to terminate legally their union's right to represent them. The process is **decertification**. There are around 450 to 500 decertification elections each year, of which unions usually win around 30%.[46] That's actually a more favorable win rate for management than the rate for the original, representation elections.

Decertification campaigns don't differ much from certification campaigns.[47] The union organizes membership meetings and house-to-house visits, mails literature into the homes, and uses phone calls, e-mails, NLRB appeals, and (sometimes) threats and harassment to win the election. Employers cannot legally start the decertification process, but once started management uses meetings—including one-on-one meetings, small-group meetings, and meetings with entire units—as well as legal or expert assistance, letters, improved working conditions, and subtle or not-so-subtle threats to try to influence the votes.[48]

THE COLLECTIVE BARGAINING PROCESS
What Is Collective Bargaining?

When and if the union becomes your employees' representative, a day is set for management and labor to meet and negotiate a labor agreement. This agreement will contain specific provisions covering wages, hours, and working conditions.

What exactly is **collective bargaining**? According to the National Labor Relations Act:

> For the purpose of [this act,] to bargain collectively is the performance of the mutual obligation of the employer and the representative of the employees to meet at reasonable times and confer in good faith with respect to wages, hours, and

decertification
Legal process for employees to terminate a union's right to represent them.

collective bargaining
The process through which representatives of management and the union meet to negotiate a labor agreement.

terms and conditions of employment, or the negotiation of an agreement, or any question arising thereunder, and the execution of a written contract incorporating any agreement reached if requested by either party, but such obligation does not compel either party to agree to a proposal or require the making of a concession.

In plain language, this means that both management and labor are required by law to negotiate wage, hours, and terms and conditions of employment "in good faith."

What Is Good Faith?

5 Illustrate with examples bargaining that is not in good faith.

Good faith bargaining is the cornerstone of effective labor–management relations. It means that both parties communicate and negotiate, that they match proposals with counterproposals, and that both make every reasonable effort to arrive at an agreement. It does not mean that one party compels another to agree to a proposal. Nor does it require that either party make any specific concessions (although as a practical matter, some may be necessary).[49]

How can you tell if bargaining is *not* in good faith? The following are some examples.

Surface bargaining. Going through the motions of bargaining without any real intention of completing an agreement.

Inadequate concessions. Unwillingness to compromise, even though no one is required to make a concession.

Inadequate proposals and demands. The NLRB considers the advancement of proposals to be a positive factor in determining overall good faith.

Dilatory tactics. The law requires that the parties meet and "confer at reasonable times and intervals." Obviously, refusal to meet with the union does not satisfy the positive duty imposed on the employer.

Imposing conditions. Attempts to impose conditions that are so onerous or unreasonable as to indicate bad faith.

Making unilateral changes in conditions. This is a strong indication that the employer is not bargaining with the required intent of reaching an agreement.

Bypassing the representative. The duty of management to bargain in good faith involves, at a minimum, recognition that the union representative is the one with whom the employer must deal in conducting negotiations.

Withholding information. An employer must supply the union with information, upon request, to enable it to discuss the collective bargaining issues intelligently.

Of course, requiring good faith bargaining doesn't mean that negotiations can't grind to a halt. For example, in 2011, the National Football League accused the NFL Players Association of not bargaining in good faith, using delays to "run out the clock" so that the players association could bring a suit against the NFL.[50]

The Negotiating Team

Both union and management send negotiating teams to the bargaining table, and both teams go into the bargaining sessions having "done their homework." Both sides today devote much time to preparations, because contracts today tend to be more detailed and complex. Union representatives will have sounded out union members on their desires and conferred with representatives of related unions.

Both sides will use several techniques to prepare for bargaining. First, they prepare the data on which to build their bargaining positions.[51] From compensation survey sources like those we discussed in Chapter 11, they compile data on pay and benefits that include comparisons with local pay rates and to rates paid for similar jobs within the industry. Data on the distribution of the workforce (in terms of age, sex, and seniority, for instance) are also important, because these factors determine what the company will actually pay out in benefits. Internal economic data regarding cost of benefits, overall-earnings levels, and the amount and cost of overtime are important as well.

Management will also "cost" the current labor contract and determine the increased cost—total, per employee, and per hour—of the union's demands. It will use information from grievances and feedback from supervisors to determine what the union's demands might be, and prepare counteroffers and arguments.[52] Other popular tactics include attitude surveys to test employee reactions to various sections of the contract that management may feel require change, and informal conferences with local union leaders to discuss the operational effectiveness of the contract and to send up trial balloons on management ideas for change.

HR AS A PROFIT CENTER

Costing the Contract

Collective bargaining experts emphasize the need to cost the union's demands carefully. One says,

> The mistake I see most often is [HR professionals who] enter the negotiations without understanding the financial impact of things they put on the table. For example, the union wants three extra vacation days. That doesn't sound like a lot, except that in some states, if an employee leaves, you have to pay them for unused vacation time. [So] now your employer has to carry that liability on their books at all times.[53]

Bargaining Items

Labor law sets out categories of specific items that are subject to bargaining: These are mandatory, voluntary, and illegal items.

Voluntary (or permissible) bargaining items are neither mandatory nor illegal; they become a part of negotiations only through the joint agreement of both management and union. Neither party can compel the other to negotiate over voluntary items. You cannot hold up signing a contract because the other party refuses to bargain on a voluntary item. Benefits for retirees might be an example.

Illegal bargaining items are forbidden by law. A clause agreeing to hire union members exclusively would be illegal in a right-to-work state, for example.

Table 15-1 presents some of the 70 or so **mandatory bargaining items** over which bargaining is mandatory under the law. They include wages, hours, rest periods, layoffs, transfers, benefits, and severance pay. Others, such as drug testing, are added as the law evolves.

Bargaining Hints

Expert Reed Richardson has the following advice for bargainers:

1. Be sure to set clear objectives for every bargaining item, and be sure you understand the reason for each.
2. Do not hurry.
3. When in doubt, caucus with your associates.
4. Be well prepared with firm data supporting your position.
5. Strive to keep some flexibility in your position.
6. Don't concern yourself just with what the other party says and does; find out why.

---

good faith bargaining
Both parties are making every reasonable effort to arrive at agreement; proposals are being matched with counterproposals.

voluntary (or permissible) bargaining items
Items in collective bargaining over which bargaining is neither illegal nor mandatory—neither party can be compelled against its wishes to negotiate over those items.

illegal bargaining items
Items in collective bargaining that are forbidden by law; for example, a clause agreeing to hire "union members exclusively" would be illegal in a right-to-work state.

mandatory bargaining items
Items in collective bargaining that a party must bargain over if they are introduced by the other party—for example, pay.

TABLE 15-1 Bargaining Items

Mandatory	Permissible	Illegal
Rates of pay	Indemnity bonds	Closed shop
Wages	Management rights as to union affairs	Separation of employees based on race
Hours of employment	Pension benefits of retired employees	Discriminatory treatment
Overtime pay	Scope of the bargaining unit	
Shift differentials	Including supervisors in the contract	
Holidays	Additional parties to the contract such as the international union	
Vacations	Use of union label	
Severance pay	Settlement of unfair labor charges	
Pensions	Prices in cafeteria	
Insurance benefits	Continuance of past contract	
Profit-sharing plans	Membership of bargaining team	
Christmas bonuses	Employment of strikebreaker	
Company housing, meals, and discounts		
Employee security		
Job performance		
Union security		
Management–union relationship		
Drug testing of employees		

Source: Carrell, Michael R.; Heavrin, Christina, *Labor Relations And Collective Bargaining: Cases, Practices, And Law*, 6th Edition, © 2001. Reprinted by permission of Pearson Education, Incl, Upper Saddle River, NJ.

7. Respect the importance of face saving for the other party.
8. Be alert to the real intentions of the other party—not only for goals, but also for priorities.
9. Be a good listener.
10. Build a reputation for being fair but firm.
11. Learn to control your emotions and use them as a tool.
12. As you make each bargaining move, be sure you know its relationship to all other moves.
13. Measure each move against your objectives.
14. Remember that collective bargaining is a compromise process. There is no such thing as having all the pie.
15. Try to understand the people and their personalities.[54]
16. Remember that excessive bargainer transparency and openness can backfire.[55]

Impasses, Mediation, and Strikes

In collective bargaining, an **impasse** occurs when the parties are not able to move further toward settlement. An impasse usually occurs because one party is demanding more than the other will offer. Sometimes an impasse can be resolved through a third party—a disinterested person such as a mediator or arbitrator. If the impasse is not resolved in this way, the union may call a work stoppage, or strike, to put pressure on management.[56]

THIRD-PARTY INVOLVEMENT Negotiators use three types of third-party interventions to overcome an impasse: mediation, fact finding, and arbitration. With **mediation**, a neutral third party tries to assist the principals in reaching agreement.

The mediator usually holds meetings with each party to determine where each stands regarding its position, and then uses this information to find common ground for further bargaining. The mediator is always a go-between, without authority to dictate terms or make concessions. He or she communicates assessments of the likelihood of a strike, the possible settlement packages available, and the like.

In certain situations, as in a national emergency dispute, a fact finder may be appointed. A **fact finder** is a neutral party who studies the issues in a dispute and makes a public recommendation for a reasonable settlement.[57] Presidential emergency fact-finding boards have successfully resolved impasses in certain critical transportation disputes.

Arbitration is the most definitive type of third-party intervention, because the arbitrator often has the power to determine and dictate the settlement terms. With *binding arbitration*, both parties are committed to accepting the arbitrator's award. With *nonbinding arbitration*, they are not. Arbitration may also be voluntary or compulsory (in other words, imposed by a government agency). In the United States, voluntary binding arbitration is the most prevalent.

There are two main topics of arbitration. **Interest arbitration** centers on working out a labor agreement; the parties use it when such agreements do not yet exist or when one or both parties are seeking to change the agreement. **Rights arbitration** really means "contract interpretation arbitration." It usually involves interpreting existing contract terms, for instance, when an employee questions the employer's right to have taken some disciplinary action.[58]

SOURCES OF THIRD-PARTY ASSISTANCE Various public and professional agencies make arbitrators and mediators available. For example, the American Arbitration Association (AAA) represents and provides the services of thousands of arbitrators and mediators to employers and unions. The U.S. government's Federal Mediation and Conciliation Service provides both arbitrators and mediators (see Figure 15-5).[59] In addition, most states provide arbitrator and mediation services.

STRIKES A **strike** is a withdrawal of labor. There are four main types of strikes. An **economic strike** results from a failure to agree on the terms of a contract. Unions call **unfair labor practice strikes** to protest illegal conduct by the employer. A **wildcat strike** is an unauthorized strike occurring during the term of a contract. A **sympathy strike** occurs when one union strikes in support of the strike of another union.[60] For example, in sympathy with South Korean Hyundai workers, the United Auto Workers organized a rally outside of Hyundai's technical center in Superior Township, Michigan and took steps to hold other rallies.[61]

The likelihood of and severity of a strike depends partly on the parties' willingness to "take a strike."[62] For instance, a number of years ago major-league baseball owners

---

impasse
Collective bargaining situation that occurs when the parties are not able to move further toward settlement, usually because one party is demanding more than the other will offer.

mediation
Intervention in which a neutral third party tries to assist the principals in reaching agreement.

fact finder
A neutral party who studies the issues in a dispute and makes a public recommendation for a reasonable settlement.

arbitration
The most definitive type of third-party intervention, in which the arbitrator usually has the power to determine and dictate the settlement terms.

interest arbitration
Arbitration enacted when labor agreements do not yet exist or when one or both parties are seeking to change the agreement.

rights arbitration
Arbitration that interprets existing contract terms, for instance, when an employee questions the employer's right to have taken some disciplinary action.

strike
A withdrawal of labor.

economic strike
A strike that results from a failure to agree on the terms of a contract that involve wages, benefits, and other conditions of employment.

unfair labor practice strike
A strike aimed at protesting illegal conduct by the employer.

wildcat strike
An unauthorized strike occurring during the term of a contract.

sympathy strike
A strike that takes place when one union strikes in support of the strike of another.

FIGURE 15-5 Online Request Form for Federal Mediation

FMCS Form F-53
Revised 5-92

Form Approved
OMB No. 3076-0005

FEDERAL SECTOR LABOR RELATIONS
NOTICE TO FEDERAL MEDIATION AND CONCILIATION SERVICE

Mail To:

Notice Processing Unit
FEDERAL MEDIATION AND CONCILIATION SERVICE
2100 K Street, N.W.
Washington, D.C. 20427

THIS NOTICE IS IN REGARD TO: (MARK "X")

① ☐ AN INITIAL CONTRACT   (INCLUDED FLRA CERTIFICATION NUMBER) # _____
☐ A CONTRACT REOPENER   REOPENER DATE _____
☐ THE EXPIRATION OF AN EXISTING AGREEMENT   EXPIRATION DATE: _____

② ☐ *OTHER REQUESTS FOR THE ASSISTANCE OF FMCS IN BARGAINING*   *(MARK "X")*
SPECIFY TYPE OF ISSUE(S)

③ ☐ *REQUEST FOR GRIEVANCE MEDIATION (SEE ITEM #10)*   *(MARK "X")*
ISSUE(S)

④ NAME OF FEDERAL AGENCY   NAME OF SUBDIVISION OR COMPONENT, IF ANY

STREET ADDRESS OF AGENCY   CITY   STATE   ZIP

AGENCY OFFICIAL TO BE CONTACTED   AREA CODE & PHONE NUMBER

⑤ NAME OF NATIONAL UNION OR PARENT BODY   NAME AND/OR LOCAL NUMBER

STREET ADDRESS   CITY   STATE   ZIP

UNION OFFICIAL TO BE CONTACTED   AREA CODE & PHONE NUMBER

LOCATION OF NEGOTIATIONS OR WHERE MEDIATION WILL BE HELD
⑥ STREET ADDRESS   CITY   STATE   ZIP

⑦ APPROX. # OF EMPLOYEES IN BARGAINING UNIT(S) >>   IN ESTABLISHMENT>>

⑧ THIS NOTICE OR REQUEST IS FILED ON BEHALF OF *(MARK "X")*   ☐ UNION   ☐ AGENCY

⑨ NAME AND TITLE OF OFFICIAL(S) SUBMITTING THIS NOTICE OR REQUEST   AREA CODE AND PHONE NUMBER

STREET ADDRESS   CITY   STATE   ZIP

FOR GRIEVANCE MEDIATION, THE SIGNATURES OF BOTH PARTIES ARE REQUIRED:*

⑩ SIGNATURE (AGENCY)   DATE   SIGNATURE (UNION)   DATE

*Receipt of this form does not commit FMCS to offer its services. Receipt of this form will not be acknowledged in writing by FMCS. While use of this form is voluntary, its use will facilitate FMCS service to respondents. Public reporting burden for this collection of information is estimated to average 10 minutes per response, including time for reviewing the collection of information. Send comments regarding this burden estimate or any other aspect of this collection of information, including suggestions for reducing this burden, to FMCS Division of Administrative Services, Washington, D.C. 20427, and to the Office of Management and Budget, Paperwork Reduction Project, Washington, D.C. 20603

For Instructions, See Back

were willing to let players strike and lose a whole season, because they had "consistently agreed that the players had been ruining the game by getting too much money and that only a hard line against such excesses" would stop that.[63]

The number of major work stoppages (strikes involving 1,000 workers or more) peaked at about 400 per year between 1965 and 1975, and today average around 20.

Picketing, or having employees carry signs announcing their concerns near the employer's place of business, is one of the first activities to occur during a strike. Its purpose is to inform the public about the existence of the labor dispute and often to encourage others to refrain from doing business with the struck employer.

Employers can make several responses when they become the object of a strike. One is to shut down the affected area and halt operations until the strike is over. A second is to contract out work in order to blunt the effects of the strike. A third response is to continue operations, perhaps using supervisors and other nonstriking workers to fill in for the striking workers. A fourth alternative is hiring replacements for the strikers.

Diminished union influence plus competitive pressures now prompt more employers to replace (or at least consider replacing) strikers with permanent replacement workers. One study of human resource managers found that of those responding, 18% "would

Picketing is one of the first activities to occur during a strike. The purpose is to inform the public about the labor dispute.

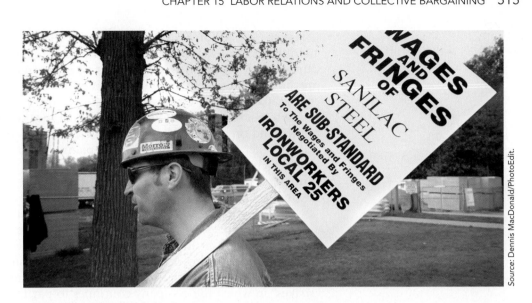

Source: Dennis MacDonald/PhotoEdit.

not consider striker replacements" in the event of a strike, while 31% called it "not very likely," 23% "somewhat likely," and 21% "very likely."[64] When the NFL locked out players in 2011, they also implied that they might use replacement players.[65]

Employers generally can replace strikers. In one very important labor relations case known as *Mackay*, the U.S. Supreme Court ruled that although the National Labor Relations Act does prohibit employers from interfering with employees' right to strike, employers still have the right to continue their operations and, therefore, to replace strikers. Subsequent decisions by the National Labor Relations Board put some limitations on *Mackay*. For example, employers cannot permanently replace strikers who are protesting unfair labor practices, and must rehire strikers who apply for reinstatement unconditionally.

STRIKE GUIDELINES FOR EMPLOYERS   When a strike is imminent, the employer should make plans to deal with it. For example, as negotiations between the Hibbing Taconite Steel Plant in Minnesota and the United Steelworkers of America headed toward a deadline, the firm brought in security workers and trailers to house them.

Two experts say that, with a strike imminent, following these guidelines can minimize confusion:

- Pay all striking employees what you owe them on the first day of the strike.
- Secure the facility. Management should control access to the property. Consider hiring guards to protect replacements coming to and from work, if necessary.
- Notify all customers, and prepare a standard official response to all queries.
- Contact all suppliers and other persons who will have to cross the picket line. Establish alternative methods of obtaining supplies.
- Arrange for overnight stays in the facility, and for delivered meals, if necessary.
- Notify the local unemployment office of your need for replacement workers.
- Photograph the facility before, during, and after picketing. If necessary, install videotape equipment to monitor picket line misconduct.
- Record all facts concerning strikers' demeanor and activities and such incidents as violence, threats, mass pickets, property damage, or problems.
- Gather the following evidence: number of pickets and their names; time, date, and location of picketing; wording on every sign carried by pickets; and descriptions of picket cars and license numbers.[66]

picketing
Having employees carry signs announcing their concerns near the employer's place of business.

OTHER "WEAPONS"   Management and labor each have other weapons to break an impasse and achieve their aims. The union, for example, may resort to a corporate campaign. A **corporate campaign** is an organized effort by the union that exerts pressure on the employer by pressuring the company's other unions, shareholders, corporate directors, customers, creditors, and government agencies.[67] Thus, the union might surprise individual members of the board of directors by picketing their homes, and organizing a **boycott** of the company's banks.[68] The head of the United Auto Workers recently said the union planned to begin a new campaign to organize hourly factory workers at foreign-owned car plants in the United States. As part of its campaign, the union began picketing the U.S. dealerships for Hyundai, Daimler, Toyota, and Nissan.[69]

Inside games are another union tactic. **Inside games** are union efforts to convince employees to impede or to disrupt production—for example, by slowing the work pace, refusing to work overtime, filing mass charges with government agencies, refusing to do work without receiving detailed instructions from supervisors, and engaging in other disruptive activities such as sick-outs.[70] Inside games are basically strikes—albeit "strikes" in which the company continues to pay the employees. In one inside game at Caterpillar's Aurora, Illinois, plant, United Auto Workers' grievances rose from 22 to 336. The effect was to tie up workers and management in unproductive endeavors on company time.[71]

Improving Productivity through HRIS

Unions Go High-Tech

E-mail and the Internet means unions can send mass e-mail announcements to collective-bargaining unit members and use e-mail to reach supporters and government officials for their corporate campaigns. For example, the group trying to organize Starbucks workers (the *Starbucks Workers' Union*) set up their own Web site (www. starbucksunion.org). It includes notes like "Starbucks managers monitored Internet chat rooms and eavesdropped on party conversations in a covert campaign to identify employees agitating for union representation at the coffee chain, internal emails reveal."[72]

For their part, employers can try to break an impasse with lockouts. A **lockout** is a refusal by the employer to provide opportunities to work. It (sometimes literally) locks out employees and prohibits them from doing their jobs (and being paid). In 2011, the National Football League (NFL) locked out football players when the two sides couldn't agree on a new contract.[73] The NLRB views lockouts as an unfair labor practice only when the employer acts for a prohibited purpose. It is not a prohibited purpose to try to bring about a settlement on terms favorable to the employer. Lockouts are not widely used today; employers are usually reluctant to cease operations when employees are willing to continue working.

Both employers and unions can seek a court injunction if they believe the other side is taking actions that could cause irreparable harm to the other party. An **injunction** is a court order compelling a party or parties either to resume or to desist from a certain action.[74]

The Contract Agreement

The actual contract agreement may be a 20- or 30-page document; it may be even longer. It may contain just general declarations of policy, or detailed rules and procedures. The tendency today is toward the longer, more detailed contract. This is largely a result of the increased number of items the agreements have been covering.

The main sections of a typical contract cover subjects such as these: (1) management rights; (2) union security and automatic payroll dues deduction; (3) grievance procedures; (4) arbitration of grievances; (5) disciplinary procedures; (6) compensation rates; (7) hours of work and overtime; (8) benefits: vacations, holidays, insurance, pensions; (9) health and safety provisions; (10) employee security seniority provisions; and (11) contract expiration date.

DEALING WITH DISPUTES AND GRIEVANCES

6 Develop a grievance procedure.

Hammering out a labor agreement is not the last step in collective bargaining. No labor contract can cover all contingencies and answer all questions. For example, suppose the contract says you can only discharge an employee for "just cause." You subsequently discharge someone for speaking back to you in harsh terms. Was speaking back to you harshly "just cause"?

The labor contract's grievance procedure usually handles problems like these. The **grievance procedure** provides an orderly system whereby both employer and union determine whether some action violated the contract.[75] It is the vehicle for administering the contract on a day-to-day basis. Remember, though, that this involves interpretation only: it usually doesn't involve negotiating new terms or altering existing ones.

Sources of Grievances

From a practical point of view, it is probably easier to list those items that *don't* precipitate grievances than to list the ones that do. Employees may use just about any factor involving wages, hours, or conditions of employment as the basis of a grievance.

However, certain grievances are more serious, since they're usually more difficult to settle. Discipline cases and seniority problems including promotions, transfers, and layoffs would top this list. Others would include grievances growing out of job evaluations and work assignments, overtime, vacations, incentive plans, and holidays.[76] Here are three examples of grievances:

- **Absenteeism.** An employer fired an employee for excessive absences. The employee filed a grievance stating that there had been no previous warnings related to excessive absences.

- **Insubordination.** An employee on two occasions refused to obey a supervisor's order to meet with him, unless a union representative was present at the meeting. As a result, the employee was discharged and subsequently filed a grievance protesting the discharge.

- **Plant rules.** The plant had a posted rule barring employees from eating or drinking during unscheduled breaks. The employees filed a grievance claiming the rule was arbitrary.[77]

A grievance is often a symptom of an underlying problem. Sometimes, bad relationships between supervisors and subordinates are to blame: This is often the cause of grievances over "fair treatment," for instance. Organizational factors such as ambiguous job descriptions that frustrate employees also cause grievances. Union activism is another cause; the union may solicit grievances from workers to underscore ineffective supervision. Problem employees are yet another underlying cause of grievances. These are individuals, who, by their nature, are negative, dissatisfied, and prone to complaints. Discipline and dismissal, discussed in Chapter 14 (Ethics), are also both major sources of grievances.

---

corporate campaign
An organized effort by the union that exerts pressure on the corporation by pressuring the company's other unions, shareholders, directors, customers, creditors, and government agencies, often directly.

boycott
The combined refusal by employees and other interested parties to buy or use the employer's products.

inside games
Union efforts to convince employees to impede or to disrupt production—for example, by slowing the work pace.

lockout
A refusal by the employer to provide opportunities to work.

injunction
A court order compelling a party or parties either to resume or to desist from a certain action.

grievance procedure
Formal process for addressing any factor involving wages, hours, or conditions of employment that is used as a complaint against the employer.

The Grievance Procedure

Most collective bargaining contracts contain a specific grievance procedure. It lists the steps in the procedure, time limits associated with each step, and specific rules such as "all charges of contract violation must be reduced to writing." Virtually every labor agreement signed today contains a grievance procedure clause. (Nonunionized employers need such procedures, too, as explained in Chapter 14, Ethics.)

Union grievance procedures differ from firm to firm. Some contain simple, two-step procedures. Here, the grievant, union representative, and company representative meet to discuss the grievance. If they don't find a satisfactory solution, the grievance goes before an independent, third-party arbitrator who hears the case, writes it up, and makes a decision. Figure 15-6 shows a grievance record form.

At the other extreme, the grievance procedure may contain six or more steps. The first step might be for the grievant and shop steward to meet informally with the supervisor of the grievant to try to find a solution. If they don't find one, the

FIGURE 15-6 Sample Online Grievance Form

Click to Fill in Text or Check a Box
Tab to Next Field

Date Received at Step B *(MM/DD/YYYY)*

UNITED STATES POSTAL SERVICE

USPS-NALC Joint Step A Grievance Form

INFORMAL STEP A — NALC Shop Steward Completes This Section

1. Grievant's Name *(Last, first, middle initial)* | 2. Home Telephone No.

3. Seniority Date *(MM/DD/YYYY)* | 4. Status *(Check one)* ☐ FT ☐ FTF ☐ PTR ☐ PTF ☐ TE | 5. Grievant's SSN

6. Installation/Work Unit | 7. Finance Number

8. NALC Branch No. | 9. NALC Grievance No. | 10. Incident Date *(MM/DD/YYYY)* | 11. Date Discussed with Supervisor *(Filing Date)*

12a. Companion MSPB Appeal? ☐ Yes ☐ No | 12b. Companion EEO Appeal? ☐ Yes ☐ No

13a. Supervisor's Printed Name and Initials *(Completed by Supervisor)* | 13b. Steward's Printed Name and Initials *(Completed by Steward)*

FORMAL STEP A — Formal Step A Parties Complete This Section

14. USPS Grievance No.

15. Issue Statement/Provide Contract Provision(s) and Frame the Issue(s)

16. Undisputed Facts *(List and Attach All Supporting Documents)* Attachments? ☐ No ☐ Yes Number____

17. UNION'S full, detailed statement of disputed facts and contentions *(List and Attach All Supporting Documents)* Attachments? ☐ No ☐ Yes Number____

18. MANAGEMENT'S full, detailed statement of disputed facts and contentions *(List and Attach All Supporting Documents)* Attachments? ☐ No ☐ Yes Number____

19. Remedy Requested/Offered

20. Disposition and Date *(Check one)* ☐ Resolved ☐ Withdrawn ☐ Not Resolved | Date of Formal Step A Meeting *(MM/DD/YYYY)*

21a. USPS Representative Name | 21b. Telephone No. *(Include Area Code)*

21c. USPS Representative Signature | 21d. Date *(MM/DD/YYYY)*

22a. NALC Representative Name | 22b. Telephone No. *(Include Area Code)*

22c. NALC Representative Signature | 22d. Date *(MM/DD/YYYY)*

PS Form 8190, August 2002 *(Page 1 of 2)*

employee files a formal grievance, and there's a meeting with the employee, shop steward, and the supervisor's boss. The next steps involve the grievant and union representatives meeting with higher-level managers. Finally, if top management and the union can't reach agreement, the grievance may go to arbitration.

Guidelines for Handling Grievances

The best way for a supervisor to handle a grievance is to develop a work environment in which grievances don't arise in the first place. Hone your ability to avoid, recognize, diagnose, and correct the causes of potential employee dissatisfaction (such as unfair appraisals or poor communications) before they become grievances.

Given that many factors including union pressures prompt grievances, it would be naïve to think that grievances arise only due to supervisor unfairness. However, there's little doubt that the quality of the interpersonal relations among you and your subordinates will influence your team's grievance rate. You should be thoroughly familiar with our discussions of supervisory fairness in Chapter 14, Ethics.

The supervisor is on the firing line and must steer a course between treating employees fairly and maintaining management's rights and prerogatives. One expert has developed a list of supervisor do's and don'ts as useful guides in handling grievances.[78] Some critical ones include:

Do:

1. Investigate and handle each case as though it may eventually result in arbitration.
2. Talk with the employee about his or her grievance; give the person a full hearing.
3. Require the union to identify specific contractual provisions allegedly violated.
4. Comply with the contractual time limits for handling the grievance.
5. Visit the work area of the grievance.
6. Determine whether there were any witnesses.
7. Examine the grievant's personnel record.
8. Fully examine prior grievance records.
9. Treat the union representative as your equal.
10. Hold your grievance discussions privately.
11. Fully inform your own supervisor of grievance matters.

Don't:

1. Discuss the case with the union steward alone—the grievant should be there.
2. Make arrangements with individual employees that are inconsistent with the labor agreement.
3. Hold back the remedy if the company is wrong.
4. Admit to the binding effect of a past practice.
5. Relinquish to the union your rights as a manager.
6. Settle grievances based on what is "fair." Instead, stick to the labor agreement.
7. Bargain over items not covered by the contract.
8. Treat as subject to arbitration claims demanding the discipline or discharge of managers.
9. Give long written grievance answers.
10. Trade a grievance settlement for a grievance withdrawal.
11. Deny grievances because "your hands have been tied by management."
12. Agree to informal amendments in the contract.

THE UNION MOVEMENT TODAY AND TOMORROW

About 35% of the non-farm U.S. workforce belonged to unions in the 1960s. Today, that figure is about 12%. Why has this drop occurred and what is the future for the union movement?

Why Union Membership Is Down

Several things contributed to union membership declines. *Laws* like OSHA and Title VII reduced the need for union protection. Increased global *competition* and *new technologies* like just-in-time production systems forced employers to reduce inefficiencies and cut costs—often by reducing payrolls by automating or by sending jobs abroad. New *foreign-owned* auto plants from Toyota and Daimler largely stayed union free. Only about 15% of U.S. workers now work in *manufacturing and construction*, so unions' traditional membership sources shrank. The 2008 recession triggered budget cuts in both the public and private sectors, prompting anti-union public policy attitudes, and the loss of about one million public sector union jobs.

All of this squeezes unions. For example, for years the head of Ford's United Auto Workers union fought for increased benefits for his members. More recently, he urged his colleagues to accept productivity-enhancing plans, such as outsourcing Ford's factory jobs to lower paid workers. "Ford is in a desperate situation," he says. "If this company goes down, I want to be able to look in the mirror and say I did everything I could."[79]

An Upswing for Unions?

However, the news is not all bleak. For one thing, we saw that it's not unusual for public policy attitudes to rotate from pro- to anti-union, and back. For another, the membership drop masks unions' real impact. Union membership varies widely by state, so unions are still quite influential in some states (such as Michigan and New York). Furthermore, about 35% of the nation's blue-collar workers—in particular those in manufacturing and construction jobs—belong to unions. Furthermore, a slight majority of all union members (about 51%) are now white-collar workers, which suggests unions are tapping this growing portion of the workforce. For example, an optical physicist at the National Aeronautics and Space Administration is also the president of his local union.[80] White-collar union members include about 40% of all college faculty members, 45,000 physicians, and 50,000 engineers. Almost 100,000 nurses belong to unions (as do most major league baseball, football, basketball, and hockey players). And, we'll see that unions themselves are becoming much more aggressive.

Unions are making inroads into traditionally hard-to-organize worker segments like professionals and white-collar workers.

Source: Stephen Chernin/iStockphoto.com.

Card Check and Other New Union Tactics

Unions are pushing Congress to pass the Employee Free Choice Act. This would make it more difficult for employers to inhibit workers from organizing. Instead of secret-ballot elections, the act would institute a "card check" system. Here, the union would win recognition when a majority of workers signed authorization cards saying they want the union. (Several large companies, including Cingular Wireless, have already agreed to the card check process.)[81] The act would also require binding arbitration to set a first contract's terms if the company and union can't negotiate an agreement within 120 days.[82]

Unions are also using class action lawsuits to support employees in nonunionized companies to pressure employers. For example, unions recently used class action lawsuits to support workers' claims under the Fair Labor Standards Act and the Equal Pay Act.[83] As another example, UNITE filed a $100 million class action suit against Cintas Corp. Then, Cintas workers in California filed a lawsuit claiming that the company was violating a nearby municipality's "living wage" law. UNITE then joined forces with the Teamsters union, which in turn began targeting Cintas' delivery people.[84]

UNIONS GO GLOBAL   Walmart, a company that traditionally works hard to prevent its stores from going union, recently had to agree to let the workers in its stores in China join unions. Walmart's China experience stems in part from efforts of global union campaigns by the Service Employees' International Union (SEIU). These campaigns reflect the belief that, as SEIU puts it, "huge global service sector companies routinely cross national borders and industry lines as they search for places where they can shift operations to exploit workers with the lowest possible pay and benefits."

SEIU is therefore strengthening its alliances with unions in other nations, with the goal of uniting workers in specific multinational companies and industries around the globe.[85] For example, SEIU recently worked with China's All China Federation of Trade Unions (ACFTU) to help the latter organize China's Walmart stores.[86] Recently, the United Steelworkers merged with the largest labor union in Britain to create "Workers Uniting" to better help the new union deal with multinational employers.[87] And the UAW is training activists about how to organize rallies and protests in support of union campaigns, and sending them abroad to help organize workers at car plants overseas.[88]

So, any company that thinks it can avoid unionization by sending jobs abroad may be in for a surprise. In fact, more U.S. companies are bringing jobs back "home," in part due to rising wages abroad.

High-Performance Work Systems, Employee Participation, and Unions

Many employers encourage employees to work together in teams. The aim is to help solve work-related problems and create high-performance work systems. In one such program, at UPS, hourly employees in self-directed teams establish priorities on how to do their jobs. Many unions believe that the result, if not the motive, of such programs is to usurp unions' traditional duties.

That presents a problem for employers. The National Recovery Act (1933) tried to give employees the right to organize and to bargain collectively. This triggered an increase in unions that were actually company-supported "sham unions" aimed at keeping legitimate unions out. Subsequent legislation outlawed such sham unions.

Employers can take steps to avoid having courts view their participation programs as sham unions. For example,[89]

- Involve employees in the formation of these programs.
- Continually emphasize to employees that the committees exist *only to address issues such as quality and productivity*, not to deal with mandatory bargaining-type items such as pay.

- Don't establish such committees when union organizing activities are beginning in your facility.
- Fill the committees with volunteers rather than elected employee representatives, and rotate membership.
- Minimize management's participation in the committees' day-to-day activities.

A recent review of union research and literature provides an additional insight. The author concludes that unions "that have a cooperative relationship with management can play an important role in overcoming barriers to the effective adoption of practices that have been linked to organizational competitiveness."[90] However, she also concludes that employers who want to capitalize on that potential need to change their way of thinking, avoiding adversarial industrial relations and emphasizing a cooperative partnership.

REVIEW

MyManagementLab   Now that you have finished this chapter, go back to **www.mymanagementlab.com** to continue practicing and applying the concepts you've learned.

CHAPTER SECTION SUMMARIES

1. The **labor movement** is important. About 14.7 million U.S. workers belong to unions—around 11.9% of the total. Workers unionize not just to get more pay or better working conditions; employer unfairness and the union's power are also important. Unions aim for union security, and then for improved wages, hours, and working conditions and benefits for their members. Union security options include the closed shop, union shop, agency shop, preferential shop, and maintenance of membership arrangement. The AFL-CIO plays an important role in the union movement as a voluntary federation of about 56 national and international labor unions in the United States.

2. To understand unions and their impact, it's necessary to understand the interplay between **unions and the law**. In brief, labor law has gone through periods of strong encouragement of unions, to modified encouragement coupled with regulation, and finally to detailed regulation of internal union affairs. Today, the legal environment seems to be moving toward increased encouragement of unions. Historically, the laws encouraging the union movement included the Norris-LaGuardia and National Labor Relations (Wagner) Acts of the 1930s. These outlawed certain unfair employer labor practices and made it easier for unions to organize. The Taft-Hartley or Labor Management Relations Act of 1947 addressed keeping unions from restraining or coercing employees, and listed certain unfair union labor practices. In the 1950s, the Landrum-Griffin Act (technically, the Labor Management Reporting and Disclosure Act) further protected union members from possible wrongdoing on the part of their unions.

3. When unions begin organizing, all managers and supervisors usually get involved, so it's essential to understand the mechanics of **the union drive and election**. The main steps include initial contact, obtaining authorization cards, holding a hearing, the campaign itself, and the election. Supervisors need to understand their role at each step in this process. Follow the acronym TIPS—do not threaten, interrogate, make promises, or spy. And follow FORE—provide facts, express your opinions, explain factually correct rules, and share your experiences. Managers need to understand rules regarding literature and solicitation. For example, employers can always bar nonemployees from soliciting employees during their work time, and can usually stop employees from soliciting other employees when both are on duty time and not on a break.

4. The employer and union hammer out an agreement via the **collective bargaining process**. The heart of collective bargaining is good faith bargaining, which means both parties must make reasonable efforts to arrive at agreement, and proposals are matched with counterproposals. Both negotiating teams will work hard to understand their respective clients' needs and to quantify their demands. In the actual bargaining sessions, there are mandatory bargaining items such as pay, illegal bargaining items, and voluntary bargaining items such as benefits for retirees. If things don't go smoothly during collective bargaining, the parties may utilize third-party intermediaries, including mediators, fact finders, and arbitrators. Strikes represent a withdrawal of labor. There are economic strikes resulting from a failure to agree on the terms of the contract, as well as unfair labor practice strikes, wildcat strikes, and sympathy strikes. During strikes, picketing may occur. Other tactics include a corporate campaign by the union, boycotting, inside games, or (for employers) lockouts.

5. Most managers become involved with **grievances** during their careers. Most collective bargaining agreements contain a specific grievance procedure listing the steps in the procedure. In general, the best way to handle a grievance is to create an environment in which grievances don't occur. However if a grievance does occur, things to do include investigate, handle each case as though it may eventually result in arbitration, talk with the employee about the grievance, and comply with the contractual time limits for handling the grievance. On the other hand, don't make arrangements with individual employees that are inconsistent with the labor agreement or hold back the remedy if the company is wrong.

6. Membership is down but in some ways unions are becoming more influential today, so it's important to understand the **union movement today and tomorrow**. For example, unions are becoming more aggressive in terms of pushing Congress to pass the Employee Free Choice Act, which, among other things, would enable employees to vote for the union by signing authorization cards, rather than going through a formal union election. New union federations, such as Change to Win, are being more aggressive about organizing workers, and unions are going global, for instance, by helping employees in China organize local Walmart stores.

DISCUSSION QUESTIONS

1. Why do employees join unions? What are the advantages and disadvantages of being a union member?
2. Discuss five sure ways to lose an NLRB election.
3. Describe important tactics you would expect the union to use during the union drive and election.
4. Briefly illustrate how labor law has gone through a cycle of repression and encouragement.
5. Explain in detail each step in a union drive and election.
6. What is meant by good faith bargaining? Using examples, explain when bargaining is not in good faith.
7. Define impasse, mediation, and strike, and explain the techniques that are used to overcome an impasse.

INDIVIDUAL AND GROUP ACTIVITIES

1. You are the manager of a small manufacturing plant. The union contract covering most of your employees is about to expire. Working individually or in groups, discuss how to prepare for union contract negotiations.
2. Working individually or in groups, use Internet resources to find situations where company management and the union reached an impasse at some point during their negotiation process, but eventually resolved the impasse. Describe the issues on both sides that led to the impasse. How did they move past the impasse? What were the final outcomes?
3. The "HRCI Test Specifications Appendix" (pages 633–640) lists the knowledge someone studying for the HRCI certification exam needs to have in each area of human resource management (such as in Strategic Management, Workforce Planning, and Human Resource Development). In groups of four to five students, do four things: (1) review that appendix now; (2) identify the material in this chapter that relates to the required knowledge the appendix lists;
(3) write four multiple-choice exam questions on this material that you believe would be suitable for inclusion in the HRCI exam; and (4) if time permits, have someone from your team post your team's questions in front of the class, so the students in other teams can take each others' exam questions.
4. Several years ago, 8,000 Amtrak workers agreed not to disrupt service by walking out, at least not until a court hearing was held. Amtrak had asked the courts for a temporary restraining order, and the Transport Workers Union of America was actually pleased to postpone its walkout. The workers were apparently not upset at Amtrak, but at Congress, for failing to provide enough funding for Amtrak. What, if anything, can an employer do when employees threaten to go on strike, not because of what the employer did, but what a third party—in this case, Congress—has done or not done? What laws would prevent the union from going on strike in this case?

EXPERIENTIAL EXERCISE

The Union-Organizing Campaign at Pierce U.

Purpose: The purpose of this exercise is to give you practice in dealing with some of the elements of a union-organizing campaign.[91]

Required Understanding: You should be familiar with the material covered in this chapter, as well as the following incident, "An Organizing Question on Campus."

INCIDENT: An Organizing Question on Campus: Art Tipton is human resource director of Pierce University, a private university located in a large urban city. Ruth Zimmer, a supervisor in the maintenance and housekeeping services division of the university, has just come into Art's office to discuss her situation. Zimmer's division is responsible for maintaining and cleaning physical facilities of the university. Zimmer is one of the department supervisors who supervise employees who maintain and clean on-campus dormitories.

In the next several minutes, Zimmer proceeds to express her concerns about a union-organizing campaign that has begun among her employees. According to Zimmer, a representative of the Service Workers Union has met with several of her employees, urging them to sign union authorization cards. She has observed several of her employees "cornering" other employees to talk to them about joining the union and to urge them to sign union authorization (or representation)

cards. Zimmer even observed this during working hours as employees were going about their normal duties in the dormitories. Zimmer reports that a number of her employees have come to her asking for her opinions about the union. They told her that several other supervisors in the department had told their employees not to sign any union authorization cards and not to talk about the union at any time while they were on campus. Zimmer also reports that one of her fellow supervisors told his employees that anyone who was caught talking about the union or signing a union authorization card would be disciplined and perhaps dismissed.

Zimmer says that her employees are very dissatisfied with their wages and with the conditions that they have endured from students, supervisors, and other staff people. She says that several employees told her that they had signed union cards because they believed that the only way university administration would pay attention to their concerns was if the employees had a union to represent them. Zimmer says that she made a list of employees who she felt had joined or were interested in the union, and she could share these with Tipton if he wanted to deal with them personally. Zimmer closed her presentation with the comment that she and other department supervisors need to know what they should do in order to stomp out the threat of unionization in their department.

How to Set Up the Exercise/Instructions:

Divide the class into groups of four or five students. Assume that you are labor relations consultants the university retained to identify the problems and issues involved and to advise Art Tipton on the university's rights and what to do next. Each group will spend the time allotted discussing the issues. Then, outline those issues, as well as an action plan for Tipton. What should he do next?

If time permits, a spokesperson from each group should list on the board the issues involved and the group's recommendations. What should Art do?

APPLICATION CASE

NEGOTIATING WITH THE WRITERS GUILD OF AMERICA

The talks between the Writers Guild of America (WGA) and the Alliance of Motion Picture & Television Producers (producers) began tense, and then got tenser. In their first meeting, the two sides got nothing done. As one producer said, "Everyone in the room is concerned about this."[92]

The two sides were far apart on just about all the issues. However, the biggest issue was how to split revenue from new media, such as when television shows move to DVDs or the Internet. The producers said they wanted a profit-splitting system rather than the current residual system. Under the residual system, writers continue to receive "residuals" or income from shows they write every time they're shown (such as when *Seinfeld* appears in reruns, years after the last original show was shot). Writers Guild executives did their homework. They argued, for instance, that the projections showed producers' revenues from advertising and subscription fees had recently jumped by about 40%.[93]

The situation grew tenser. After the first few meetings, one producers' representative said, "We can see after the dogfight whose position will win out. The open question there, of course, is whether each of us takes several lumps at the table, reaches an agreement, then licks their wounds later—none the worse for wear—or whether we inflict more lasting damage through work stoppages that benefit no one before we come to an agreement."[94] Even after meeting six times, it seemed that, "the parties' only apparent area of agreement is that no real bargaining has yet to occur."[95]

Soon, the Writers Guild asked its members for strike authorization, and the producers were claiming that the guild was just trying to delay negotiations until the current contract expired (at the end of October). As the president of the producers' group said, "We have had six across-the-table sessions and there was only silence and stonewalling from the WGA leadership. . . . We have attempted to engage on major issues, but no dialogue has been forthcoming from the WGA leadership. . . . The WGA leadership apparently has no intention to bargain in good faith."[96] As evidence, the producers claimed that the WGA negotiating committee left one meeting after less than an hour at the bargaining table.

Both sides knew timing in these negotiations was very important. During the fall and spring, television series production is in full swing. So, a strike now by the writers would have a bigger impact than waiting until, say, the summer to strike. Perhaps not surprisingly, some movement was soon discernible. In a separate set of negotiations, the Directors Guild of America reached an agreement with the producers that addressed many of the issues that the writers were focusing on, such as how to divide the new media income.[97] Then, the WGA and producers finally reached agreement. The new contract was "the direct result of renewed negotiations between the two sides, which culminated Friday with a marathon session including top WGA officials and the heads of the Walt Disney Co. and News Corp."[98]

Questions

1. The producers said the WGA was not bargaining in good faith. What did they mean by that, and do you think the evidence is sufficient to support the claim?
2. The WGA did eventually strike. What tactics could the producers have used to fight back once the strike began? What tactics do you think the WGA used?
3. This was a conflict between professional and creative people (the WGA) and TV and movie producers. Do you think the conflict was therefore different in any way than are the conflicts between, say, the Autoworkers or Teamsters unions against auto and trucking companies? Why?
4. What role (with examples) did negotiating skills seem to play in the WGA producers' negotiations?

CONTINUING CASE

CARTER CLEANING COMPANY

The Grievance

On visiting one of Carter Cleaning Company's stores, Jennifer was surprised to be taken aside by a long-term Carter employee, who met her as she was parking her car. "Murray (the store manager) told me I was suspended for 2 days without pay because I came in late last Thursday," said George. "I'm really upset, but around here the store manager's word seems to be law, and it sometimes seems like the only way anyone can file a grievance is by meeting you or your father like this in the parking lot." Jennifer was very disturbed by this revelation and promised the employee she would look into it and discuss the situation with her father. In the car heading back to headquarters, she began mulling over what Carter Cleaning Company's alternatives might be.

Questions

1. Do you think it is important for Carter Cleaning Company to have a formal grievance process? Why or why not?

2. Based on what you know about the Carter Cleaning Company, outline the steps in what you think would be the ideal grievance process for this company.

3. In addition to the grievance process, can you think of anything else that Carter Cleaning Company might do to make sure grievances and gripes like this one are expressed and are heard by top management?

TRANSLATING STRATEGY INTO HR POLICIES & PRACTICES CASE

THE HOTEL PARIS CASE

The Hotel Paris's New Labor Relations Practices

The Hotel Paris's competitive strategy is "To use superior guest service to differentiate the Hotel Paris properties, and to thereby increase the length of stay and return rate of guests, and thus boost revenues and profitability." HR manager Lisa Cruz must now formulate functional policies and activities that support this competitive strategy by eliciting the required employee behaviors and competencies.

Lisa Cruz's parents were both union members, and she had no strong philosophical objections to unions. However, as the head of human resources for the Hotel Paris, she did feel very strongly that her employer should do everything legally possible to remain union-free. She knew that this is what the hotel chain's owners and top executives wanted. Furthermore, the evidence seemed to support their position. At least one study that she'd seen concluded that firms with 30% or more of their eligible workers in unions were in the bottom 10% in terms of performance, while those with 8% to 9% of eligible workers in unions scored in the top 10%.[99] The problem was that the Hotel Paris really had no specific policies and procedures in place to help its managers and supervisors deal with union activities. With all the laws regarding what employers and their managers could and could not do to respond to a union's efforts, Lisa knew her company was "a problem waiting to happen." She turned her attention to deciding what steps she and her team should take with regard to labor relations and collective bargaining in the United States.

Lisa and the CFO knew that unionization was a reality for the Hotel Paris. About 5% of the hotel chain's U.S. employees were already unionized, and unions in this area were quite active. For example, as they were surfing the Internet to better gauge the situation, Lisa and the CFO came across an interesting Web site from the Boston Hotel Employees and Restaurant Employees Union, Local 26 (http://hotelworkersrising.org/Campaign/). It describes their success in negotiating contracts and their accomplishments at several hotels, including ones managed by the Westin and Sheraton chains. The CFO and Lisa agreed that it was important that she and her team develop and institute a new set of policies and practices that would enable the Hotel Paris to reduce the likelihood of further unionization and deal more effectively with their current unions. They set about that task with the aid of a labor–management attorney.

Questions

1. How should the details of the Hotel Paris's strategy influence the new union-related HR practices (perhaps such as grievance procedures) it establishes?

2. List and briefly describe what you believe are the three most important steps Hotel Paris management can take to reduce the likelihood unions will organize more of its employees.

3. Write a detailed 2-page outline for a "What You Need to Know When the Union Calls" manual. Lisa will distribute this manual to her company's supervisors and managers, telling them what they need to know about looking out for possible unionizing activity, and how to handle actual organizing process–related supervisory tasks.

KEY TERMS

closed shop, *497*

union shop, *497*

agency shop, *497*

preferential shop, *498*

right to work, *498*

Norris-LaGuardia Act (1932), *499*

National Labor Relations (or Wagner) Act, *499*

National Labor Relations Board (NLRB), *499*

Taft-Hartley Act (1947), *501*

national emergency strikes, *502*

Landrum-Griffin Act (1959), *502*

union salting, *503*

authorization cards, *504*

bargaining unit, *505*

decertification, *509*

collective bargaining, *509*

good faith bargaining, *510*

voluntary (or permissible) bargaining items, *511*

illegal bargaining items, *511*

mandatory bargaining items, *511*

impasse, *512*

ENDNOTES

1. For example, see http://articles.money central.msn.com/Investing/Extra/Costco TheAntiWalMart.aspx?page=1, accessed June 29, 2011.
2. Christine Frey, "Costco's Love of Labor: Employees' Well-Being Key to Its Success," www.seattlepi.com/default/article/ Costco-s-love-of-labor-Employees-well-being-key-1140722.php, accessed June 29, 2011; Steven Greenhouse and Reed Abelson, "Wal-Mart Cuts Some Health Care Benefits," *The New York Times*, (October 21, 2011), pp. B1,5
3. www.bls.gov/news.release/union2.nr0. htm, accessed June 5, 2011.
4. Ibid.; "Union Membership Rises," *Compensation & Benefits Review*, May/June 2008, p. 9.
5. Ibid.
6. Stephen Greenhouse, "Most US Union Members Are Working for the Government, New Data Shows," *The New York Times*, January 23, 2010, pages B1–B5.
7. Michael Ash and Jean Seago, "The Effect of Registered Nurses' Unions on Heart Attack Mortality," *Industrial and Labor Relations Review* 57, no. 3 (April 2004), pp. 422–442.
8. http://articles.moneycentral.msn.com/ Investing/Extra/CostcoTheAntiWalMart. aspx?page=1, accessed September 15, 2011.
9. Ibid.
10. Ibid.
11. Ibid.
12. www.bls.gov/news.release/union2.nr0. htm, accessed June 1, 2011.
13. Dale Belman and Paula Voos, "Changes in Union Wage Effects by Industry: A Fresh Look at the Evidence," *Industrial Relations* 43, no. 3 (July 2004), pp. 491–519.
14. Donna Buttigieg et al., "An Event History Analysis of Union Joining and Leaving," *Journal of Applied Psychology* 92, no. 3 (2007), pp. 829–839.
15. Kris Maher, "The New Union Worker," *The Wall Street Journal*, September 27, 2005, pp. B1, B11.
16. Robert Grossman, "Unions Follow Suit," *HR Magazine*, May 2005, p. 49.
17. Warner Pflug, *The UAW in Pictures* (Detroit: Wayne State University Press, 1971), pp. 11–12.
18. Arthur Sloane and Fred Witney, *Labor Relations* (Upper Saddle River, NJ: Prentice Hall, 2007), pp. 335–336.
19. Benjamin Taylor and Fred Witney, *Labor Relations Law* (Upper Saddle River, NJ: Prentice Hall, 1992), pp. 170–171; www. dol.gov/whd/state/righttowork.htm, accessed June 5, 2010.
20. www.dol.gov/whd/state/righttowork. htm, accessed June 5, 2010. (Indiana applicable only to school employees.)
21. Paul Monies, "Unions Hit Hard by Job Losses, Right to Work," *The Daily Oklahoman* (via *Knight Ridder/Tribune Business News*), February 1, 2005.
22. www.seiu.org/our-union/, accessed June 1, 2011.
23. Steven Greenhouse, "4th Union Quits AFL-CIO in a Dispute over Organizing," *The New York Times*, September 15, 2005, p. A14.
24. Some trace early U.S. labor relations legislation back to a fire at the Triangle Shirtwaist factory in 1911. Following that tragedy, in which 146 people died, New York State passed a number of legal reforms covering not only safety but also issues such as low wages, child labor, and long hours. New York City and New York State soon adopted 36 new laws, and many view these laws as the basis for and precursor to the U.S. labor legislation efforts that began in earnest in the 1930s. "The Birth of the New Deal," *The Economist*, March 19, 2011, p. 39.
25. The following material is based on Arthur Sloane and Fred Witney, *Labor Relations* (Upper Saddle River, NJ: Prentice Hall, 2001), pp. 46–124.
26. www.bls.gov/news.release/union2.nr0. htm, accessed June 1, 2011.
27. Michael Carrell and Christina Heavrin, *Labor Relations and Collective Bargaining* (Upper Saddle River, NJ: Prentice Hall, 2004), p. 180.
28. Sloane and Witney, *Labor Relations*, p. 121.
29. For examples from the unions' point of view, see www.twu.org/international/ steps, accessed June 29, 2011; www.opeiu. org/NeedAUnion/StepstoCreatinga UnionWorkplace/tabid/71/Default.aspx, accessed June 29, 2011; and http://ufcwone. org/steps-form-union, accessed June 29, 2011.
30. Kris Maher, "Unions' New Foe: Consultants," *The Wall Street Journal*, August 15, 2005, p. B1.
31. "Some Say Salting Leaves Bitter Taste for Employers," *BNA Bulletin to Management*, March 4, 2004, p. 79; and www.nlrb.gov/ global/search/index.aspx?mode=s&qt=sal ting&col=nlrb&gb=y, accessed January 14, 2008. For a management lawyer's perspective, see www.fklaborlaw.com/union_ salt-objectives.html, accessed May 25, 2007.
32. "Spurned Union Salts Entitled to Back Pay, D.C. Court Says, Affirming Labor Board," *BNA Bulletin to Management*, June 21, 2001, p. 193.
33. D. Diane Hatch and James Hall, "Salting Cases Clarified by NLRB," *Workforce*, August 2000, p. 92. See also www.fklaborlaw. com/union_salt-objectives.html, accessed May 25, 2007.
34. Edwin Arnold et al., "Determinants of Certification Election Outcomes in the Service Sector," *Labor Studies Journal* 25, no. 3 (Fall 2000), p. 51.
35. "Number of Elections, Union Wins Increased in 2002," *BNA Bulletin to Management*, June 19, 2003, p. 197.
36. This section is based on Matthew Goodfellow, "How to Lose an NLRB Election," *Personnel Administrator* 23 (September 1976), pp. 40–44. See also Matthew Goodfellow, "Avoid Unionizing: Chemical Company Union Election Results for 1993," *Chemical Marketing Reporter* 246 (July 18, 1994), p. SR14; Gillian Flynn, "When the Unions Come Calling," *Workforce*, November 2000, pp. 82–87.
37. Ibid.
38. Ibid.
39. Harry Katz, "The Decentralization of Collective Bargaining: A Literature Review and Comparative Analysis," *Industrial and Labor Relations Review* 47, no. 1 (October 1993), p. 11; and F. Traxler, "Bargaining (De)centralization, Macroeconomic Performance and Control over the Employment Relationship," *British Journal of Industrial Relations*, 41, no. 1 (March 2003), pp. 1–27.

40. The following are adapted and/or quoted from Kate Bronfenbrenner, "The Role of Union Strategies in NLRB Certification Elections," *Industrial and Labor Relations Review* 50 (January 1997), pp. 195–212; see also, J. Fiorito, et. al., "Understanding Organising Activity Among US National Unions," *Industrial Relations Journal*, 41, no. 1 (January 2010), pp. 74–92.

41. Frederick Sullivan, "Limiting Union Organizing Activity Through Supervisors," *Personnel* 55 (July/August 1978), pp. 55–65. See also Edward Young and William Levy, "Responding to a Union-Organizing Campaign: Do You and Your Supervisors Know the Legal Boundaries in a Union Campaign?" *Franchising World* 39, no. 3 (March 2007), pp. 45–49.

42. Ibid., pp. 167–168.

43. Jonathan Segal, "Unshackle Your Supervisors to Stay Union Free," *HR Magazine*, June 1998, pp. 62–65. See also www.nlrb.gov/workplace_rights/nlra_violations.aspx, accessed January 14, 2008.

44. Whether employers must give union representatives permission to organize on employer-owned property at shopping malls is a matter of legal debate. The U.S. Supreme Court ruled in *Lechmere, Inc. v. National Labor Relations Board* that employers may bar nonemployees from their property if the nonemployees have reasonable alternative means of communicating their message to the intended audience. However, if the employer lets other organizations like the Salvation Army set up at their workplaces, the NLRB may view discriminating against the union organizers as an unfair labor practice. See, for example, "Union Access to Employer's Customers Restricted," *BNA Bulletin to Management*, February 15, 1996, p. 49; "Workplace Access for Unions Hinges on Legal Issues," *BNA Bulletin to Management*, April 11, 1996, p. 113.

45. "Union Access to Employer's Customers Restricted," pp. 4–65. The appropriateness of these sample rules may be affected by factors unique to an employer's operation, and they should therefore be reviewed by the employer's attorney before implementation.

46. Clyde Scott and Edwin Arnold, "Deauthorization and Decertification Elections: An Analysis and Comparison of Results," *Working USA* 7, no. 3 (Winter 2003), pp. 6–20;www.nlrb.gov/nlrb/shared_files/brochures/rpt_september 2002.pdf, accessed January 14, 2008.

47. Carrell and Heavrin, *Labor Relations and Collective Bargaining*, pp. 120–121.

48. See, for example, David Meyer and Trevor Bain, "Union Decertification Election Outcomes: Bargaining Unit Characteristics and Union Resources," *Journal of Labor Research* 15, no. 2 (Spring 1994), pp. 117–136; Arthur Sloane and Fred Witney, *Labor Relations*, (Upper Saddle River, NJ: 2007), p. 96.

49. www.nlrb.gov/nlrb/shared_files/brochures/basicguide.pdf, accessed January 14, 2008.

50. For preceding examples of bad-faith bargaining see Carrell and Heavrin, *Labor Relations and Collective Bargaining*, pp. 176–177; see also www.bloomberg.com/news/2011-02-14/nfl-files-unfair-labor-practice-charge-against-union.html, accessed June 1, 2011.

51. John Fossum, *Labor Relations* (Dallas: BPI, 1982), pp. 246–250; Arthur Sloane and Fred Witney, *Labor Relations*, op cit., pp. 197–205.

52. *Boulwareism* is the name given to a strategy, now generally held in disfavor, by which the company, based on an exhaustive study of what it believed its employees wanted, made but one offer at the bargaining table and then refused to bargain any further unless convinced by the union on the basis of new facts that its original position was wrong. The NLRB subsequently found that the practice of offering the same settlement to all units, insisting that certain parts of the package could not differ among agreements, and communicating to the employees about how negotiations were going amounted to an illegal pattern. Fossum, *Labor Relations*, p. 267.

53. Kathryn Tyler, "Good-Faith Bargaining," *HR Magazine*, January 2005, p. 52.

54. Reed Richardson, *Collective Bargaining by Objectives* (Upper Saddle River, NJ: Prentice Hall, 1977), p. 150. Both sides will try to manipulate the media to jockey for better positions; for example see J. McCafferty, "Labor-Management Dispute Resolution & the Media," *Dispute Resolution Journal*, 56, no. 3 (August/October 2001), pp. 40–47.

55. Many negotiators pride themselves on being open, honest, and straightforward in their negotiations, but at least one study suggests that this can backfire. Specifically, people who are inclined to be straightforward may also develop a greater concern for their counterpart's interest, which in turn can lead to greater concession making during the negotiation. D. Scott DeRue et al., "When Is Straightforwardness a Liability in Negotiations? The Role of Integrative Potential and Structural Power," *Journal of Applied Psychology* 94, no. 4 (2009), pp. 1032–1047.

56. With or without reaching a solution, impasses and union–management conflict can leave union members demoralized. See, for example, Jessica Marquez, "Taking Flight," *Workforce*, June 9, 2008, pp. 1, 18.

57. Fossum, *Labor Relations*, p. 312.

58. Carrell and Heavrin, *Labor Relations and Collective Bargaining*, p. 501.

59. http://fmcs.gov/assets/files/annual%20reports/FY2006_Annual_Report.pdf, accessed January 14, 2008.

60. Fossum, *Labor Relations*, p. 317.

61. www.autoblog.com/2010/12/06/report-uaw-to-hold-sympathy-strike-for-hyundai-workers-in-korea/, accessed June 1, 2011.

62. This is based on Arthur Sloane and Fred Whitney, *Labor Relations* (Upper Saddle River, NJ: Prentice Hall, 2010), p. 213

63. Ibid.

64. "Striker Replacements," *BNA Bulletin to Management*, February 6, 2003, p. S7.

65. http://profootballtalk.nbcsports.com/2011/03/21/league-doesnt-rule-out-replacement-players-during-lockout/, accessed June 29, 2011.

66. Stephen Cabot and Gerald Cuerton, "Labor Disputes and Strikes: Be Prepared," *Personnel Journal* 60 (February 1981), pp. 121–126. See also Brenda Sunoo, "Managing Strikes, Minimizing Loss," *Personnel Journal* 74, no. 1 (January 1995), pp. 50ff.

67. Some labor lawyers report an increase in the use by unions of corporate campaigns. Janet Walthall, "Unions Increasingly Using Corporate Campaigns," *BNA Bulletin to Management*, February 16, 2010, p. 55.

68. For a discussion, see Herbert Northrup, "Union Corporate Campaigns and Inside Games as a Strike Form," *Employee Relations Law Journal* 19, no. 4 (Spring 1994), pp. 507–549.

69. Matthew Dolan, "UAW Targets Foreign Car Plants in US," *The Wall Street Journal*, December 23, 2010, p. B3.

70. Northrup, "Union Corporate Campaigns and Inside Games," p. 513.

71. Ibid., p. 518.

72. www.starbucksunion.org, accessed January 14, 2008.

73. "The Owners Take a Punt," *The Economist*, March 12, 2011, p. 40.

74. Clifford Koen Jr., Sondra Hartman, and Dinah Payne, "The NLRB Wields a Rejuvenated Weapon," *Personnel Journal*, December 1996, pp. 85–87; and D. Silverman, "The NLRA at 70: A New Approach to Processing 10(j)s [NLRA at Seventy conference in New York City, 2005]," *Labor Law Journal*, 56, no. 3 (Fall 2005), pp. 203-206.

75. Sloane and Witney, *Labor Relations*, 10th ed., pp. 221–227.

76. Carrell and Heavrin, *Labor Relations and Collective Bargaining*, pp. 417–418.

77. Richardson, *Collective Bargaining by Objectives*.

78. M. Gene Newport, *Supervisory Management* (St. Paul, MN: West Group, 1976), p. 273; see also Walter Baer, "Grievance Handling: 101 Guides for Supervisors," (New York: American Management Association, 1970); and Mark Lurie, "The Eight Essential Steps in Grievance Processing," *Dispute Resolution Journal*, 54 no. 4 (November 1999), pp. 61–65.

79. Jeffrey McCracken, "Desperate to Cut Costs, Ford Gets Union's Help," *The Wall Street Journal*, March 2, 2007, pp. A1, A9.

80. Kris Maher, "The New Union Worker," *The Wall Street Journal*, September 27, 2005, pp. B1, B11.

81. "The Limits of Solidarity," *The Economist*, September 23, 2006, p. 34.

82. Kris Maher, "Specter Won't Support Union-Backed Bill," *The Wall Street Journal*, March 20, 2009, p. A3.

83. "Unions Using Class Actions to Pressure Nonunion Companies," *BNA Bulletin to Management*, August 22, 2006, p. 271. Some believe that today, "long-term observers see more bark than bite in organized labor's efforts to revitalize." For example, Robert Grossman, "We Organized Labor and Code," *HR Magazine*, January 2008, pp. 37–40.

84. Andy Meisler, "Who Will Fold First?" *Workforce Management*, January 2004, pp. 28–38.

85. Ibid, p. 6.

86. Mei Fong and Kris Maher, "US Labor Chief Moves into China," *The Wall Street Journal* (Asia), June 22–24, 2007, p. 1.

87. Steven Greenhouse, "Steelworkers Merge with British Union," *The New York Times*, July 3, 2008, p. C4.

88. Matthew Dolan and Neil Boudette, "UAW to Send Activists Abroad," *The Wall Street Journal*, March 23, 2011, p. B2.

89. "Employer's System of Worker Empowerment Does Not Fall Prey to Labor Act, NLRB Rules," *BNA Bulletin to Management*, August 2, 2001, p. 241.

90. Carol Gill, "Union Impact on the Effective Adoption of High Performance Work Practices," *Human Resource Management Review* 19 (2009), pp. 39–50.

91. Raymond Hilgert and Cyril Ling, *Cases and Experiential Exercises in Management* (Upper Saddle River, NJ: Prentice Hall, 1996), pp. 201–203.

92. Chris Pursell, "Rhetoric Flying in WGA Talks," *TelevisionWeek*, July 23, 2007, pp. 3, 35; Peter Sanders, "In Hollywood, a Tale of Two Union Leaderships," *The Wall Street Journal*, January 7, 2008, p. B2.

93. Pursell, "Rhetoric Flying in WGA Talks."

94. Ibid.

95. James Hibberd, "Guild Talks Break with No Progress," *TVWeek* 26, no. 38 (October 8, 2007), pp. 1, 30.

96. Ibid.

97. "DGA Deal Sets the Stage for Writers," *TelevisionWeek*, January 21, 2008, pp. 3, 33.

98. "WGA, Studios Reach Tentative Agreement," *UPI NewsTrack*, February 3, 2008.

99. Brian Becker et al., *The HR Scorecard* (Boston: Harvard Business School Press, 2001), p. 16.

16

Employee Safety and Health

LEARNING OBJECTIVES

1. Explain the supervisor's role in safety.
2. Explain the basic facts about safety law and OSHA.
3. Answer the question, "What causes accidents?"
4. List and explain five ways to prevent accidents.
5. Minimize unsafe acts by employees.
6. List five workplace health hazards and how to deal with them.
7. Discuss the prerequisites for a security plan and how to set up a basic security program.

O n April 20, 2010, an explosion and fire on British Petroleum (BP)'s Deepwater Horizon rig in the Gulf of Mexico took the lives of 11 workers.[1] Reports from the scene said a malfunctioning blowout preventer failed to activate, causing the disaster. Past critics of BP's safety practices weren't so sure.

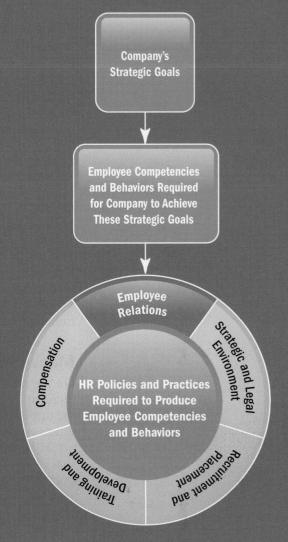

WHERE ARE WE NOW . . .

Safety, as are ethics and labor relations, is an important factor in the quality of employees' work lives. The main purpose of this chapter is to provide you with the basic knowledge to deal with workplace safety and health issues. We discuss the Occupational Safety and Health Act, and explain three causes of accidents: chance occurrences, unsafe conditions, and unsafe acts; as well as techniques for preventing accidents; and important employee health problems such as workplace violence.

Access a host of interactive learning aids at **www.mymanagementlab.com** to help strengthen your understanding of the chapter concepts.

SAFETY AND THE MANAGER

Why Safety Is Important

Safety and accident prevention concern managers for several reasons, one of which is the staggering number of workplace accidents. While accident rates are falling, in one recent year 4,551 U.S. workers died in workplace incidents.[2] Workplace accidents in the United States cause over 3.8 million occupational injuries and illnesses per year—roughly 3.6 cases per 100 equivalent full-time workers.[3] Such figures may actually underestimate the real number of injuries and illnesses by two or three times.[4] More than 80% of the workers in one survey ranked workplace safety as more important than minimum wages, sick days, and maternity leave.[5]

Injuries aren't just a problem in dangerous industries like construction. For example, new computers contribute to airtight "sick building" symptoms like headaches and sniffles. And office work is susceptible to things like repetitive trauma injuries related to computer use.

THE HIDDEN STORY   But even facts like these don't show the human suffering incurred by the injured workers and their families or the real economic costs incurred by employers.[6] For example, the direct injury costs of a forklift accident might be $4,500. However, the indirect costs for things like lost production time, maintenance time, and emergency supplies could raise that to $18,000 or more.[7]

Management's Role in Safety

On the next few pages, we'll see that reducing accidents often boils down to reducing accident-causing conditions and accident-causing acts. However, safety always starts at the top. Telling supervisors to "watch for spills" and employees to "work safely" is futile unless everyone knows management is serious about safety.[8]

Historically, for instance, DuPont's accident rate has been much lower than that of the chemical industry as a whole. This good safety record is partly due to an organizational commitment to safety, which is evident in the following description:

> One of the best examples I know of in setting the highest possible priority for safety takes place at a DuPont Plant in Germany. Each morning at the DuPont Polyester and Nylon Plant, the director and his assistants meet at 8:45 to review the past 24 hours. The first matter they discuss is not production, but safety. Only after they have examined reports of accidents and near misses and satisfied themselves that corrective action has been taken do they move on to look at output, quality, and cost matters.[9]

What Top Management Can Do

Policies like these start at the top.[10] The employer should institutionalize top management's commitment with a safety policy, and publicize it. It should give safety matters high priority in meetings: Louisiana-Pacific Corp., which makes building products, starts all meetings with a brief safety message.[11] Georgia-Pacific reduced its workers' compensation costs by requiring managers to halve accidents or forfeit 30% of their bonuses. The accompanying Strategic Context feature provides another example.

THE STRATEGIC CONTEXT

Deepwater Horizon

To many critics of BP's safety practices, the Deepwater Horizon disaster in the Gulf wasn't just due to a malfunctioning blowout preventer. To them, rightly or wrongly, the accident reflected the fact that BP's corporate strategy had long emphasized cost cutting and profitability at the expense of safety. For example, 5 years earlier, a report by the Chemical Safety Board blamed a huge blast at BP's Texas City, Texas, oil refinery on cost cutting, and on a safety strategy that aimed to reduce accidents but left in place "unsafe and antiquated equipment." To the Board and to some others who studied BP's safety practices, Deepwater was another example of how encouraging safe employee behavior must start at the top, and how top management's strategy can trump even earnest efforts to improve employee safety behaviors.[12]

Safety is not just a case of legality or humanitarianism. One study concluded that safety activities paid for themselves by a ratio of 10 to 1, just in direct savings of workers' compensation expenses over 4 years.[13]

The Supervisor's Role in Safety

1 Explain the supervisor's role in safety.

After inspecting a work site where workers were installing pipes in a 4-foot trench, an OSHA inspector cited an employer for violating the rule requiring employers to have a "stairway, ladder, ramp, or other safe means of egress" in deep trench excavations.[14] In the event the trench caved in, workers needed a quick way out. As in most such cases, the employer had the primary responsibility for safety, and the local supervisor was responsible for the day-to-day inspections. In this case the supervisor did not properly inspect for safety. The trench collapsed, injuring several employees.

The moral is that safety inspections should always be part of the supervisor's daily routine. For example, "a daily walk-through of your workplace—whether you are working in outdoor construction, indoor manufacturing, or any place that poses safety challenges—is an essential part of your work."[15] What to look for depends on the situation. However, in general you can use a checklist of unsafe conditions such as the one in Figure 16-5 (page 541) to spot problems.

OCCUPATIONAL SAFETY LAW

2 Explain the basic facts about safety law and OSHA.

Congress passed the **Occupational Safety and Health Act of 1970** "to assure so far as possible every working man and woman in the nation safe and healthful working conditions and to preserve our human resources."[16] The only employers it doesn't cover are self-employed persons, farms in which only immediate members of the employer's family work, and some workplaces already protected by other federal agencies or under other statutes. The act covers federal agencies, but usually not state and local governments.

The act created the **Occupational Safety and Health Administration (OSHA)** within the Department of Labor. OSHA's basic purpose is to administer the act and to set and enforce the safety and health standards that apply to almost all workers in the United States. The Department of Labor enforces the standards, and OSHA has inspectors working out of branch offices to ensure compliance.

OSHA Standards and Record Keeping

OSHA operates under the "general" standard clause that each employer:

... shall furnish to each of his [or her] employees employment and a place of employment which are free from recognized hazards that are causing or are likely to cause death or serious physical harm to his [or her] employees.

Occupational Safety and Health Act of 1970
The law passed by Congress in 1970 "to assure so far as possible every working man and woman in the nation safe and healthful working conditions and to preserve our human resources."

Occupational Safety and Health Administration (OSHA)
The agency created within the Department of Labor to set safety and health standards for almost all workers in the United States.

FIGURE 16-1 OSHA Standards Example

Source: www.osha.gov/pls/oshaweb/owadisp.show_document?p_id=9720&p_table=STANDARDS, accessed June 1, 2011.

Guardrails not less than 2" × 4" or the equivalent and not less than 36" or more than 42" high, with a midrail, when required, of a 1" × 4" lumber or equivalent, and toeboards, shall be installed at all open sides on all scaffolds more than 10 feet above the ground or floor. Toeboards shall be a minimum of 4" in height. Wire mesh shall be installed in accordance with paragraph [a] (17) of this section.

To carry out this basic mission, OSHA is responsible for promulgating legally enforceable standards. These are contained in five volumes covering general industry standards, maritime standards, construction standards, other regulations and procedures, and a field operations manual.

The standards are very complete, covering in detail just about every conceivable hazard. (Figure 16-1 presents a small part of the standard governing guardrails for scaffolds.) The regulations don't just list standards to which employers should adhere. They also lay out "how." For example, OSHA's respiratory protection standard also covers employee training.

Under OSHA, employers with 11 or more employees must maintain records of and report certain occupational injuries and occupational illnesses. An **occupational illness** is any abnormal condition or disorder caused by exposure to environmental factors associated with employment. This includes acute and chronic illnesses caused by inhalation, absorption, ingestion, or direct contact with toxic substances or harmful agents.

WHAT THE EMPLOYER MUST REPORT   As summarized in Figure 16-2, employers must report all occupational illnesses.[17] They must also report most occupational injuries, specifically those that result in medical treatment (other than first aid), loss

FIGURE 16-2 What Accidents Must Be Reported Under the Occupational Safety and Health Act?

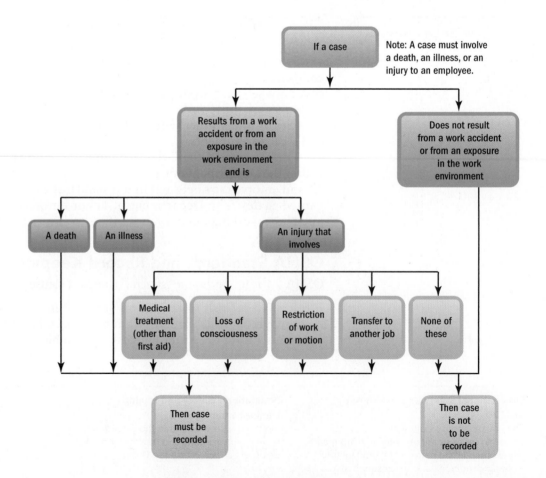

of consciousness, restriction of work (one or more lost workdays), restriction of motion, or transfer to another job.[18] If an on-the-job accident results in the death of an employee or in the hospitalization of five or more employees, all employers, regardless of size, must report the accident to the nearest OSHA office.

OSHA's current record-keeping rules allow the employer to conclude that an event needn't be reported if the facts so warrant—such as if a worker breaks an ankle after catching his foot on his car's seat belt when not at work and parked on the company lot.[19]

However, OSHA's record-keeping requirements are still broader than you might expect.[20] Examples of recordable conditions include food poisoning suffered by an employee after eating in the employer's cafeteria and ankle sprains that occur during voluntary participation in a company softball game at a picnic the employee was required to attend. Figure 16-3 shows the OSHA form for reporting occupational injuries or illness.

Inspections and Citations

OSHA enforces its standards through inspections and (if necessary) citations. The inspection is usually unannounced. OSHA may not conduct warrantless inspections without an employer's consent. However, it may inspect after acquiring an authorized search warrant or its equivalent.[21] With a limited number of inspectors, OSHA recently has focused on "fair and effective enforcement," combined with outreach, education and compliance assistance, and various OSHA–employer cooperative programs (such as its "Voluntary Protection Programs").[22]

INSPECTION PRIORITIES OSHA takes a "worst-first" approach in setting inspection priorities. Priorities include, from highest to lowest, imminent dangers, catastrophes and fatal accidents, employee complaints, high-hazard industries inspections, and follow-up inspections.[23] In one recent year, OSHA conducted just over 39,000 inspections. Referrals prompted about 8,000 of these.[24]

Under its priority system, OSHA conducts an inspection within 24 hours when a complaint indicates an immediate danger, and within 3 working days when a serious hazard exists. For a "nonserious" complaint filed in writing by a worker or a union, OSHA will respond within 20 working days. OSHA handles other nonserious complaints by writing to the employer and requesting corrective action.

THE INSPECTION The inspection begins when the OSHA officer arrives at the workplace.[25] He or she displays credentials and asks to meet an employer representative. (Always insist on seeing the credentials, which include photograph and serial number.) The officer explains the visit's purpose, the scope of the inspection, and the standards that apply. An authorized employee representative accompanies the officer during the inspection. The inspector can also stop and question workers (in private, if necessary). The act protects each employee from discrimination for exercising his or her disclosure rights.[26]

OSHA inspectors look for all types of violations, but some potential problem areas grab more attention. The five most frequent OSHA inspection violation areas are scaffolding, fall protection, hazard communication, lockout/tagout (electrical disengagement), and respiratory problems.

Finally, after checking the premises and employer's records, the inspector holds a closing conference with the employer's representative. Here the inspector discusses apparent violations for which OSHA may issue or recommend a **citation** and penalty. At this point, the employer can produce records to show compliance efforts. In one recent year, inadequate scaffolding/fall protection was one frequently cited hazard.

---

occupational illness
Any abnormal condition or disorder caused by exposure to environmental factors associated with employment.

citation
Summons informing employers and employees of the regulations and standards that have been violated in the workplace.

OSHA's FORM 301
Injury and Illness Incident Report

U.S. Department of Labor
Occupational Safety and Health Administration

Form approved OMB no. 1218-0176

Attention: This form contains information relating to employee health and must be used in a manner that protects the confidentiality of employees to the extent possible while the information is being used for occupational safety and health purposes.

This *Injury and Illness Incident Report* is one of the first forms you must fill out when a recordable work-related injury or illness has occurred. Together with the *Log of Work-Related Injuries and Illnesses* and the accompanying *Summary*, these forms help the employer and OSHA develop a picture of the extent and severity of work-related incidents.

Within 7 calendar days after you receive information that a recordable work-related injury or illness has occurred, you must fill out this form or an equivalent. Some state workers' compensation, insurance, or other reports may be acceptable substitutes. To be considered an equivalent form, any substitute must contain all the information asked for on this form.

According to Public Law 91-596 and 29 CFR 1904, OSHA's recordkeeping rule, you must keep this form on file for 5 years following the year to which it pertains.

If you need additional copies of this form, you may photocopy and use as many as you need.

Completed by _____

Title _____

Phone (_____) _____ - _____   Date ___/___/___

Information about the employee

1) Full name _____

2) Street _____
City _____ State _____ ZIP _____

3) Date of birth ___/___/___

4) Date hired ___/___/___

5) ☐ Male
☐ Female

Information about the physician or other health care professional

6) Name of physician or other health care professional _____

7) If treatment was given away from the worksite, where was it given?
Facility _____
Street _____
City _____ State _____ ZIP _____

8) Was employee treated in an emergency room?
☐ Yes
☐ No

9) Was employee hospitalized overnight as an in-patient?
☐ Yes
☐ No

Information about the case

10) Case number from the Log _____ *(Transfer the case number from the Log after you record the case.)*

11) Date of injury or illness ___/___/___

12) Time employee began work _____ AM/PM

13) Time of event _____ AM/PM
☐ Check if time cannot be determined

14) **What was the employee doing just before the incident occurred?** Describe the activity, as well as the tools, equipment, or material the employee was using. Be specific. *Examples:* "climbing a ladder while carrying roofing materials"; "spraying chlorine from hand sprayer"; "daily computer key-entry."

15) **What happened?** Tell us how the injury occurred. *Examples:* "When ladder slipped on wet floor, worker fell 20 feet"; "Worker was sprayed with chlorine when gasket broke during replacement"; "Worker developed soreness in wrist over time."

16) **What was the injury or illness?** Tell us the part of the body that was affected and how it was affected; be more specific than "hurt," "pain," or sore." *Examples:* "strained back"; "chemical burn, hand"; "carpal tunnel syndrome."

17) **What object or substance directly harmed the employee?** *Examples:* "concrete floor"; "chlorine"; "radial arm saw." If this question does not apply to the incident, leave it blank.

18) **If the employee died, when did death occur?**
Date of death ___/___/___

Public reporting burden for this collection of information is estimated to average 22 minutes per response, including time for reviewing instructions, searching existing data sources, gathering and maintaining the data needed, and completing and reviewing the collection of information. Persons are not required to respond to the collection of information unless it displays a current valid OMB control number. If you have any comments about this estimate or any other aspects of this data collection, including suggestions for reducing this burden, contact: US Department of Labor, OSHA Office of Statistical Analysis, Room N-3644, 200 Constitution Avenue, NW, Washington, DC 20210. Do not send the completed forms to this office.

FIGURE 16-3 Form Used to Record Occupational Injuries and Illnesses

Source: U.S. Department of Labor.

PENALTIES   OSHA can impose penalties. These generally range from $5,000 up to $150,000 for willful or repeat serious violations. However, penalties can be far higher—$1.5 million after a tragedy at Ford's Rouge Michigan plant, for instance.[27] The parties settle many OSHA cases before litigation, in "precitation settlements."[28] Non-serious violations may carry no penalties.

In general, OSHA calculates penalties based on the gravity of the violation and usually takes into consideration factors like the size of the business, the firm's compliance history, and the employer's good faith.[29] In practice, OSHA must have a final order from the independent Occupational Safety and Health Review Commission (OSHRC) to enforce a penalty.[30] An employer who files a notice of contest can drag out an appeal for years. Many employers do appeal, at least to the OSHA district office.[31]

To the chagrin of some employers, OSHA is publicizing its inspection results online. For example, OSHA's Web site (www.osha.gov) gives you easy access to your company's (or your competitors') OSHA enforcement history.[32]

MANAGERS' INSPECTION GUIDELINES   What should you do when OSHA inspectors unexpectedly show up? Guidelines include the following:

Initial Contact

- Restrict admittance until the manager in charge is on site.[33]
- Check the inspector's credentials.
- Ask the inspector why he or she is inspecting your workplace. Is it complaints? A scheduled visit?
- If the inspection stems from a complaint, you are entitled to know whether the person is a current employee, though not the person's name.
- Notify your counsel, who should review all documents and information.

Opening Conference

- Establish the focus and scope of the planned inspection.
- Discuss the procedures for protecting trade secret areas.
- Show the inspector you have safety programs in place. He or she may not even go to the work floor if your paperwork is complete and up to date.

Walk-Around Inspection

- Accompany the inspector and take detailed notes.
- If the inspector takes a photo or video, you should, too.
- Ask for duplicates of all physical samples and copies of all test results.
- Be helpful and cooperative, but don't volunteer information.
- To the extent possible, immediately correct any violation the inspector identifies.[34]

One survey asked 12 safety experts to identify the "10 best ways" to get into trouble with OSHA.[35] The top three were:

1. Ignore or retaliate against employees who raise safety issues.
2. Antagonize or lie to OSHA during an inspection.
3. Keep inaccurate OSHA logs and have disorganized safety files.

OSHA'S FREE ON-SITE INSPECTIONS   OSHA provides free on-site safety and health services for small businesses.[36] Employers can contact their nearest OSHA area office to speak to the compliance assistance specialist. According to OSHA, it issues no citations or penalties based on these inspections.

There is an opening conference with an OSHA safety expert, a walk-through, and a closing conference to discuss the expert's findings. The expert then sends a detailed report explaining the findings. The employer's only obligation is to commit to correcting serious job safety and health hazards in a timely manner.

Employees have rights and responsibilities under OSHA standards, such as to wear their hard hats, but OSHA can't cite them if they violate their responsibilities.

Responsibilities and Rights of Employers and Employees

Both employers and employees have responsibilities and rights under the Occupational Safety Health Act. *Employers* are responsible for providing "a workplace free from recognized hazards," for being familiar with mandatory OSHA standards, and for examining workplace conditions to make sure they conform to OSHA standards. Employers have the right to seek advice and off-site consultation from OSHA, request and receive proper identification of the OSHA compliance officer before inspection, and to be advised by the compliance officer of the reason for an inspection.

Employees also have rights and responsibilities, but OSHA can't cite them for violations of their responsibilities. Employees are responsible, for example, for complying with all applicable OSHA standards, for following all employer safety and health rules and regulations, and for reporting hazardous conditions to the supervisor. Employees have a right to demand safety and health on the job without fear of punishment. The act prohibits employers from punishing or discriminating against workers who complain to OSHA about job safety and health hazards. (See the accompanying OSHA safety poster in Figure 16-4.)

FIGURE 16-4 OSHA Safety Poster

You Have a Right to a Safe and Healthful Workplace.

IT'S THE LAW!

- You have the right to notify your employer or OSHA about workplace hazards. You may ask OSHA to keep your name confidential.
- You have the right to request an OSHA inspection if you believe that there are unsafe and unhealthful conditions in your workplace. You or your representative may participate in the inspection.
- You can file a complaint with OSHA within 30 days of discrimination by your employer for making safety and health complaints or for exercising your rights under the *OSH Act*.
- You have a right to see OSHA citations issued to your employer. Your employer must post the citations at or near the place of the alleged violation.
- Your employer must correct workplace hazards by the date indicated on the citation and must certify that these hazards have been reduced or eliminated.
- You have the right to copies of your medical records or records of your exposure to toxic and harmful substances or conditions.
- Your employer must post this notice in your workplace.

The *Occupational Safety and Health Act of 1970 (OSH Act)*, P.L. 91-596, assures safe and healthful working conditions for working men and women throughout the Nation. The Occupational Safety and Health Administration, in the U.S. Department of Labor, has the primary responsibility for administering the *OSH Act*. The rights listed here may vary depending on the particular circumstances. To file a complaint, report an emergency, or seek OSHA advice, assistance, or products, call 1-800-321-OSHA or your nearest OSHA office: • Atlanta (404) 562-2300 • Boston (617) 565-9860 • Chicago (312) 353-2220 • Dallas (214) 767-4731 • Denver (303) 844-1600 • Kansas City (816) 426-5861 • New York (212) 337-2378 • Philadelphia (215) 861-4900 • San Francisco (415) 975-4310 • Seattle (206) 553-5930. Teletypewriter (TTY) number is 1-877-889-5627. To file a complaint online or obtain more information on OSHA federal and state programs, visit OSHA's website at www.osha.gov. If your workplace is in a state operating under an OSHA-approved plan, your employer must post the required state equivalent of this poster.

1-800-321-OSHA
www.osha.gov

U.S. Department of Labor   •   Occupational Safety and Health Administration   •   OSHA 3165

DEALING WITH EMPLOYEE RESISTANCE Although employees have a responsibility to comply with OSHA standards, they often resist; the employer usually remains liable for any penalties. The refusal of some workers to wear hard hats typifies this problem.

Employers have attempted to defend themselves by citing worker intransigence. In most cases, courts still hold employers liable for workplace safety violations.

Yet employers can reduce their liability, since "courts have recognized that it is impossible to totally eliminate all hazardous conduct by employees."[37] In the event of a problem, the courts may consider whether the employer's safety procedures were adequate; whether the training gave employees the skills required to perform their duties safely; and whether the employer required employees to follow the procedures. The employer can bargain with its union for the right to discipline any employee who disobeys OSHA standards.[38] A formal employer–employee safety arbitration process and discussing with employees the reasons for their resistance are other options.

The independent three-member Occupational Safety and Health Review Commission that reviews OSHA decisions says employers must make "a diligent effort to discourage, by discipline if necessary, violations of safety rules by employees."[39] However, the only surefire way to eliminate liability is to make sure that no accidents occur.

WHAT CAUSES ACCIDENTS?

There are three basic causes of workplace accidents: chance occurrences, unsafe conditions, and employees' unsafe acts. Chance occurrences (such as walking past a window just as someone hits a ball through it) are more or less beyond management's control. We will therefore focus on unsafe conditions and unsafe acts.

What Causes Unsafe Conditions and Other Work-Related Safety Problems?

Unsafe conditions are a main cause of accidents. They include:

- Improperly guarded equipment
- Defective equipment
- Hazardous procedures in, on, or around machines or equipment
- Unsafe storage—congestion, overloading
- Improper illumination—glare, insufficient light
- Improper ventilation—insufficient air change, impure air source[40]

The solution here is to identify and eliminate the unsafe conditions. The main aim of the OSHA standards is to address these mechanical and physical accident-causing conditions. The employer's safety department (if any), and its human resource managers and top managers should take responsibility for identifying unsafe conditions.

3 Answer the question, "What causes accidents?"

DANGER ZONES While accidents can happen anywhere, there are some high-danger zones. About one-third of industrial accidents occur around forklift trucks, wheelbarrows, and other handling and lifting areas. The most serious accidents usually occur by metal and woodworking machines and saws, or around transmission machinery like gears, pulleys, and flywheels. Falls on stairs, ladders, walkways, and scaffolds are the third most common cause of industrial accidents. Hand tools (like chisels and screwdrivers) and electrical equipment (extension cords, electric droplights, and so on) are other major causes of accidents.[41]

Certain jobs are inherently more dangerous. For example, the job of crane operator results in about three times more hospital visits than does the job of supervisor.[42]

unsafe conditions
The mechanical and physical conditions that cause accidents.

Work schedules and fatigue also affect accident rates. Accident rates usually don't increase too noticeably during the first 5 or 6 hours of the workday. But after that, the accident rate increases faster. This is due partly to fatigue and partly to the fact that accidents occur more often during night shifts. In part due to reduced headcount and more people with second jobs, employee fatigue is a growing problem today.[43] Many employers are therefore taking steps to reduce employee fatigue, such as banning mandatory overtime.

Some of the most important working-condition–related causes of accidents involve workplace "climate" or psychology. One researcher reviewed the official hearings regarding the fatal accidents offshore oil workers suffered in the British North Sea.[44] A strong pressure to complete the work as quickly as possible, employees who are under stress, and a poor safety climate—for instance, supervisors who never mention safety—were some of the psychological conditions leading to accidents. Similarly, accidents occur more frequently in plants with high seasonal layoff rates, hostility among employees, many garnished wages, and blighted living conditions.

What Causes Unsafe Acts? (A Second Basic Cause of Accidents)

Unsafe employee acts can undo even the best attempts to reduce unsafe conditions. The problem is that there are no easy answers to the question of what causes people to act recklessly.

It may seem obvious that some people are simply accident prone, but the research isn't clear.[45] On closer inspection it turns out some "accident repeaters" were just unlucky, or may have been more meticulous about reporting their accidents.[46] However, there is growing evidence that people with specific traits may indeed be accident prone. For example, people who are impulsive, sensation seeking, extremely extroverted, and less conscientious (in terms of being less fastidious and dependable) are more likely to have accidents.[47]

Furthermore, the person who is accident prone on one job may not be so on another. Driving is one example. Personality traits that correlate with filing vehicular insurance claims include *entitlement* ("think there's no reason they should not speed"), *impatience* ("were 'always in a hurry'"), *aggressiveness* ("the first to move when the light turns green"), and *distractibility* ("frequently distracted by cell phones, eating, and so on").[48]

We'll turn to how employers can reduce unsafe acts and conditions next.

HOW TO PREVENT ACCIDENTS

4 List and explain five ways to prevent accidents.

In practice, accident prevention boils down to two basic activities: (1) reducing unsafe conditions and (2) reducing unsafe acts. In large firms, the chief safety officer (often called the "Environmental Health and Safety Officer") is responsible for this.[49] In smaller firms, managers, including those from human resources, plant management, and first-line managers, share these responsibilities.

Reducing Unsafe Conditions

Reducing unsafe conditions is always an employer's first line of defense in accident prevention. Safety engineers should design jobs to remove or reduce physical hazards. In addition, we saw that supervisors and managers play a role. Checklists like those in Figures 16-5 and 16-6, or the self-inspection checklist in Figure 16-8 (pages 566–569), can help identify and remove potential hazards.

Employers increasingly use computerized tools to design safer equipment. For example, Designsafe (from Designsafe Engineering, Ann Arbor, Michigan) helps automate the tasks of hazard analysis, risk assessment, and identifying safety options. Designsafe helps the safety designer choose the most appropriate safety control device for keeping the worker safe, such as adjustable enclosures, presence-sensing devices, and personal protective equipment.[50]

I. GENERAL HOUSEKEEPING

Adequate and wide aisles—no materials protruding into aisles
Parts and tools stored safely after use—not left in hazardous positions that could cause them to fall
Even and solid flooring—no defective floors or ramps that could cause falling or tripping accidents
Waste cans and sand pails—safely located and properly used

Material piled in safe manner—not too high or too close to sprinkler heads
Floors—clean and dry
Firefighting equipment—unobstructed
Work benches orderly
Stockcarts and skids safely located, not left in aisles or passageways
Aisles kept clear and properly marked; no air lines or electric cords across aisles

II. MATERIAL HANDLING EQUIPMENT AND CONVEYANCES

On all conveyances, electric or hand, check to see that the following items are all in sound working conditions:
Brakes—properly adjusted
Not too much play in steering wheel
Warning device—in place and working
Wheels—securely in place; properly inflated
Fuel and oil—enough and right kind

No loose parts
Cables, hooks, or chains—not worn or otherwise defective
Suspended chains or hooks conspicuous
Safely loaded
Properly stored

III. LADDERS, SCAFFOLD, BENCHES, STAIRWAYS, ETC.

The following items of major interest to be checked:
Safety feet on straight ladders
Guardrails or handrails
Treads, not slippery
Not cracked, or rickety

Properly stored
Extension ladder ropes in good condition
Toeboards

IV. POWER TOOLS (STATIONARY)

Point of operation guarded
Guards in proper adjustment
Gears, belts, shafting, counterweights guarded
Foot pedals guarded
Brushes provided for cleaning machines
Adequate lighting
Properly grounded

Tool or material rests properly adjusted
Adequate work space around machines
Control switch easily accessible
Safety glasses worn
Gloves worn by persons handling rough or sharp materials
No gloves or loose clothing worn by persons operating machines

V. HAND TOOLS AND MISCELLANEOUS

In good condition—not cracked, worn, or otherwise defective
Properly stored

Correct for job
Goggles, respirators, and other personal protective equipment worn where necessary

VI. WELDING

Arc shielded
Fire hazards controlled
Operator using suitable protective equipment

Adequate ventilation
Cylinder secured
Valves closed when not in use

VII. SPRAY PAINTING

Explosion-proof electrical equipment
Proper storage of paints and thinners in approved metal cabinets

Fire extinguishers adequate and suitable; readily accessible
Minimum storage in work area

VIII. FIRE EXTINGUISHERS

Properly serviced and tagged
Readily accessible

Adequate and suitable for operations involved

FIGURE 16-5 Checklist of Mechanical or Physical Accident-Causing Conditions

Source: Courtesy of the American Insurance Association. From "A Safety Committee Man's Guide," pp. 1–64.

Sometimes the solution for eliminating an unsafe condition is obvious, and sometimes it's more subtle. For example, slips and falls are often the result of debris or slippery floors.[51] Obvious remedies include floor mats and better lighting. Perhaps less obviously, personal safety gear, like slip-resistant footwear with grooved soles, can also reduce slips and falls. Cut-resistant gloves reduce the hazards of working with sharp objects.[52] (Hand injuries account for about 1 million emergency department visits annually by U.S. workers.[53])

FIGURE 16-6 Online Safety
Inspection Checklist

FORM **CD-574**
(9/02)

U.S. Department of Commerce
Office Safety Inspection Checklist for
Supervisors and Program Managers

Name:	Division:
Location:	Date:
Signature:	

This checklist is intended as a guide to assist supervisors and program managers in conducting safety and health inspections of their work areas. It includes questions relating to general office safety, ergonomics, fire prevention, and electrical safety. Questions which receive a "**NO**" answer require corrective action. If you have questions or need assistance with resolving any problems, please contact your safety office. More information on office safety is available through the Department of Commerce Safety Office website at http://ohrm.doc.gov/safetyprogram/safety.htm.

Work Environment

Yes	No	N/A	
O	O	⊙	Are all work areas clean, sanitary, and orderly?
O	O	⊙	Is there adequate lighting?
O	O	⊙	Do noise levels appear high?
O	O	⊙	Is ventilation adequate?

Walking / Working Surfaces

Yes	No	N/A	
O	O	⊙	Are aisles and passages free of stored material that may present trip hazards?
O	O	⊙	Are tile floors in places like kitchens and bathrooms free of water and slippery substances?
O	O	⊙	Are carpet and throw rugs free of tears or trip hazards?
O	O	⊙	Are hand rails provided on all fixed stairways?
O	O	⊙	Are treads provided with anti-slip surfaces?
O	O	⊙	Are step ladders provided for reaching overhead storage areas and are materials stored safely?
O	O	⊙	Are file drawers kept closed when not in use?
O	O	⊙	Are passenger and freight elevators inspected annually and are the inspection certificates available for review on-site?
O	O	⊙	Are pits and floor openings covered or otherwise guarded?
O	O	⊙	Are standard guardrails provided wherever aisle or walkway surfaces are elevated more than 48 inches above any adjacent floor or the ground?
O	O	⊙	Is any furniture unsafe or defective?
O	O	⊙	Are objects covering heating and air conditioning vents?

Ergonomics

Yes	No	N/A	
O	O	⊙	Are employees advised of proper lifting techniques?
O	O	⊙	Are workstations configured to prevent common ergonomic problems? (Chair height allows employees' feet to rest flat on the ground with thighs parallel to the floor, top of computer screen is at or slightly below eye level, keyboard is at elbow height. Additional information on proper configuration of workstations is available through the Commerce Safety website at http://ohrm.doc.gov/safetyprogram/safety.htm)
O	O	⊙	Are mechanical aids and equipment, such as; lifting devices, carts, dollies provided where needed?
O	O	⊙	Are employees surveyed annually on their ergonomic concerns?

FIGURE 16-6 (Continued)

FORM **CD-574**
(9/02)

Emergency Information (Postings)

Yes	No	N/A	
○	○	⊙	Are established emergency phone numbers posted where they can be readily found in case of an emergency?
○	○	⊙	Are employees trained on emergency procedures?
○	○	⊙	Are fire evacuation procedures/diagrams posted?
○	○	⊙	Is emergency information posted in every area where you store hazardous waste?
○	○	⊙	Is established facility emergency information posted near a telephone?
○	○	⊙	Are the OSHA poster, and other required posters displayed conspicuously?
○	○	⊙	Are adequate first aid supplies available and properly maintained?
○	○	⊙	Are an adequate number of first aid trained personnel available to respond to injuries and illnesses until medical assistance arrives?
○	○	⊙	Is a copy of the facility fire prevention and emergency action plan available on site?
○	○	⊙	Are safety hazard warning signs/caution signs provided to warn employees of pertinent hazards?

Fire Prevention

Yes	No	N/A	
○	○	⊙	Are flammable liquids, such as gasoline, kept in approved safety cans and stored in flammable cabinets?
○	○	⊙	Are portable fire extinguishers distributed properly (less than 75 feet travel distance for combustibles and 50 feet for flammables)?
○	○	⊙	Are employees trained on the use of portable fire extinguishers?
○	○	⊙	Are portable fire extinguishers visually inspected monthly and serviced annually?
○	○	⊙	Is the area around portable fire extinguishers free of obstructions and properly labeled?
○	○	⊙	Is heat-producing equipment used in a well ventilated area?
○	○	⊙	Are fire alarm pull stations clearly marked and unobstructed?
○	○	⊙	Is proper clearance maintained below sprinkler heads (i.e., 18" clear)?

Emergency Exits

Yes	No	N/A	
○	○	⊙	Are doors, passageways or stairways that are neither exits nor access to exits and which could be mistaken for exits, appropriately marked "NOT AN EXIT," "TO BASEMENT," "STOREROOM," etc.?
○	○	⊙	Are a sufficient number of exits provided?
○	○	⊙	Are exits kept free of obstructions or locking devices which could impede immediate escape?
○	○	⊙	Are exits properly marked and illuminated?
○	○	⊙	Are the directions to exits, when not immediately apparent, marked with visible signs?
○	○	⊙	Can emergency exit doors be opened from the direction of exit travel without the use of a key or any special knowledge or effort when the building is occupied?
○	○	⊙	Are exits arranged such that it is not possible to travel toward a fire hazard when exiting the facility?

(Continued)

JOB HAZARD ANALYSIS Recently, a Yale University science student, working late in a lab, was critically injured when her hair became caught in a spinning lathe. **Job hazard analysis** involves a systematic approach to identifying and eliminating

job hazard analysis
A systematic approach to identifying and eliminating workplace hazards before they occur.

FIGURE 16-6 (Continued)

FORM **CD-574**
(9/02)

Electrical Systems
(Please have your facility maintenance person or electrician accompany you during this part of the inspection)

Yes	No	N/A	
○	○	⊙	Are all cord and cable connections intact and secure?
○	○	⊙	Are electrical outlets free of overloads?
○	○	⊙	Is fixed wiring used instead of flexible/extension cords?
○	○	⊙	Is the area around electrical panels and breakers free of obstructions?
○	○	⊙	Are high-voltage electrical service rooms kept locked?
○	○	⊙	Are electrical cords routed such that they are free of sharp objects and clearly visible?
○	○	⊙	Are all electrical cords grounded?
○	○	⊙	Are electrical cords in good condition (free of splices, frays, etc.)?
○	○	⊙	Are electrical appliances approved (Underwriters Laboratory, Inc. (UL), etc)?
○	○	⊙	Are electric fans provided with guards of not over one-half inch, preventing finger exposures?
○	○	⊙	Are space heaters UL listed and equipped with shutoffs that activate if the heater tips over?
○	○	⊙	Are space heaters located away from combustibles and properly ventilated?
○	○	⊙	In your electrical rooms are all electrical raceways and enclosures securely fastened in place?
○	○	⊙	Are clamps or other securing means provided on flexible cords or cables at plugs, receptacles, tools, equipment, etc., and is the cord jacket securely held in place?
○	○	⊙	Is sufficient access and working space provided and maintained about all electrical equipment to permit ready and safe operations and maintenance? (This space is 3 feet for less than 600 volts, 4 feet for more than 600 volts)

FORM **CD-574**
(9/02)

Material Storage

Yes	No	N/A	
○	○	⊙	Are storage racks and shelves capable of supporting the intended load and materials stored safely?
○	○	⊙	Are storage racks secured from falling?
○	○	⊙	Are office equipment stored in a stable manner, not capable of falling?

such hazards before they cause accidents. According to OSHA, job hazard analysis "focuses on the relationship between the worker, the task, the tools, and the work environment," and ends by reducing the potential risks to acceptable levels.[54]

Consider a safety analyst looking at the Yale science lab, with the aim of identifying potential hazards. Performing a job hazard analysis here might involve looking at the situation and asking these questions:

- **What can go wrong?** A student's hair or clothing could come into contact with the lathe, a rotating object that "catches" it and pulls it into the machine.
- **What are the consequences?** The student could receive a severe injury as his or her body part or hair is caught and drawn into the spinning lathe.
- **How could it happen?** The accident could happen as a result of the student leaning too close to the lathe while working at the bench, or walking too close to the lathe, or bending to reach for an article that fell close to the lathe.
- **What are other contributing factors?** Speed is one contributing factor. The problem would occur so quickly that the student would be unable to take evasive action once the lathe ensnarled the hair.

The job hazard analysis should provide the basis for creating countermeasures. Given the speed with which any such accident would occur, it's unlikely that training by itself would suffice. Instead, the lathe area here should be ensconced in its own protective casing, and changes made to ensure that the lathe can't spin unless the student takes action via a foot pedal to keep the lathe power on.

OPERATIONAL SAFETY REVIEWS   After the Fukushima nuclear power plant in northern Japan exploded in 2011, many wondered if the International Atomic Energy Agency (IAEA) had conducted the necessary operational safety reviews. **Operational safety reviews** (or safety operations reviews) are conducted by agencies to ascertain whether units under their jurisdiction are complying with all the applicable safety laws, regulations, orders, and rules. For example, under IAEA's Operational Safety Review Program, "international teams of experts conduct in-depth reviews of operational safety performance at a nuclear power plant."[55]

PERSONAL PROTECTIVE EQUIPMENT   Getting employees to wear personal protective equipment (PPE) is a famously difficult chore.[56] Wearability is important. In addition to providing reliable protection, protective gear should fit properly; be easy to care for, maintain, and repair; be flexible and lightweight; provide comfort and reduce heat stress; have rugged construction; be relatively easy to put on and take off; and be easy to clean, dispose of, and recycle.[57] Many employers, such as Kimberly-Clark and MCR Safety, are tapping into the new fibers and fabrics used by runners, skiers, and NASCAR drivers to design easier wearing high-tech solutions.[58] Including employees in planning the safety program and addressing comfort issues contribute to employees' willingness to use the protective gear.[59]

Of course, it makes sense to require wearing the personal protective equipment before the accident, rather than after it. For example, a combustible dust explosion at a sugar refinery killed 14 employees and burned many others. The employer subsequently required that all employees wear fire resistant clothing, unfortunately too late for the victims.[60]

MANAGING THE NEW WORKFORCE

Protecting Vulnerable Workers

In designing safe and healthy environments, employers should pay special attention to vulnerable workers. Among others, these may include young, immigrant, aging, and women workers.[61] (The Fair Labor Standards Act strictly limits young people's exposure to dangerous jobs, but about 64 workers under age 18 died from work-related injuries in one recent year.[62]) For example, as the CEO of one safety engineering company said, "For decades, women essentially were ignored when it came to designing eye and face protection." Today, more products are available in smaller sizes.[63]

Similarly, with more workers postponing retirement, older workers are doing more manufacturing jobs.[64] They can do these jobs very effectively. However, there are numerous potential physical changes associated with aging, including loss of strength, loss of muscular flexibility, and reduced reaction time.[65] This means that employers should make special provisions such as designing jobs to reduce heavy lifting, and boosting lighting levels.[66] The fatality rate for older workers is about three times that of younger workers.[67]

But again, reducing unsafe conditions (such as enclosing noisy equipment) is always the first line of defense. Then use administrative controls (such as job rotation to reduce long-term exposure to the hazard). Only then should you turn to PPE.[68]

Reducing unsafe acts—by emphasizing safety and through screening, training, or incentive programs, for example—is the second basic way to reduce accidents. Let's look at how to do this.

Source: iStockphoto.com.

Emergency stop devices, such as buttons, override other machine controls to remove power from hazardous machine motion.

Reducing Unsafe Acts

Although reducing unsafe conditions is the first line of defense, human misbehavior can short-circuit even the best safety efforts. Sometimes the misbehavior is intentional, but often it's not.[69] In one accident, a maintenance worker obeyed the plant's lockout/tagout procedure, by calling the control room to have them shut off the roof exhaust fan he was about to work on. When he arrived on the roof, he noticed the fan was still turning, and assumed that the wind was turning the blades. After waiting several minutes, he wrapped a rag around his hand and tried to stop the blade with his hand, causing serious injury. He had obeyed the procedure by calling the control room. But the employer should have emphasized in its training that the point of the procedure was not to disconnect the power, but "to make sure that the fan is not turning before you touch it."[70]

For machinery, employees can use emergency stop devices like the one in the accompanying photo to cut power to hazardous machines.[71] But ironically, "making a job safer with machine guards or PPE lowers people's risk perceptions and thus can lead to an increase in at-risk behavior."[72]

As mentioned earlier, the manager plays a central role in reducing unsafe acts. For example, supervisors should:

- Praise employees when they choose safe behaviors;
- Listen when employees offer safety suggestions, concerns, or complaints; and
- Be a good example, for instance, by following every safety rule and procedure.[73]

Unfortunately, praising employees is usually not enough to banish unsafe acts. Instead, it requires a process. First, identify and try to eliminate potential risks, such as unguarded equipment. Next, reduce potential distractions, such as noise, heat, and stress. Then, carefully screen, train, and motivate employees, as we explain next.

5 Minimize unsafe acts by employees.

Reducing Unsafe Acts through Selection and Placement

Proper employee screening and placement reduces unsafe acts. Here, the employer's aim is to identify the traits that might predict accidents on the job in question, and then screen candidates for this trait. For example, the Employee Reliability Index (ERI) (see *http://www.ramsaycorp.com/catalog/view/?productid=208*) measures reliability dimensions such as emotional maturity, conscientiousness, and safe job performance.[74] Though not definitive, using the ERI in selection did seem to be associated with reductions in work-related accidents in one study. Others use *job simulation tests* (which attempt to measure the applicant by simulating physically demanding work activities) and *physical capabilities tests* (which measure muscle strength and motion) to predict who will have more accidents.[75]

Similarly, behavioral interview questions can be revealing. For example, ask, "What would you do if you saw another employee working in an unsafe way?" and "What would you do if your supervisor gave you a task, but didn't provide any training on how to perform it safely?"[76]

Under the Americans with Disabilities Act (ADA) it is unlawful to inquire (prior to hiring) about an applicant's workers' compensation injuries and claims. You also cannot ask applicants whether they have a disability, or about taking prescription drugs or require them to take tests that tend to screen out those with disabilities. However, you can usually ask, "Do you know of any reason why you would not be able to perform the various functions of the job you are seeking?"[77]

Reducing Unsafe Acts through Training

Safety training reduces unsafe acts, especially for new employees. You should instruct employees in safe practices and procedures, warn them of potential hazards, and work on developing a safety-conscious attitude. OSHA's standards require more than training. Employees must demonstrate that they actually learned what to do. (For example,

OSHA's respiratory standard requires that each employee demonstrate how to inspect, put on, and remove respirator seals.[78] OSHA has two booklets, "Training Requirements under OSHA" and "Teaching Safety and Health in the Workplace.")

However, note that the main aim of safety training is not to meet OSHA training standards. Rather, it is to impart the knowledge and skills required to reduce accidents. OSHA, the National Institute for Occupational Safety and Health (NIOSH), and numerous private vendors provide online safety training solutions.[79]

The nature of the safety training is important. Although lectures and online learning may be efficient, one study found that the most effective safety training demanded high employee engagement.[80] In this study, the "least engaging" programs included lectures, films, reading materials, and video-based training. Moderately engaging programs included computer interface instruction with feedback. The most engaging included behavioral modeling, simulation, and hands-on training.

MANAGING THE NEW WORKFORCE

Safety Training for Hispanic Workers

With increasing numbers of Spanish-speaking workers in the United States, experts are focusing more closely on their safety.[81] For example, many construction companies are offering specialized training programs for Hispanic workers. One example is a 40-hour training course at the Dallas–Fort Worth airport. Based on this program's apparent success, there are several useful conclusions one can draw about what a program like this should look like.

- First, the program should "*speak the workers' language.*"
- Second, the employer should also *recruit instructors who are from the ethnic groups they are training.*
- Third, provide for some *multilingual cross-training* for specific phrases. For example, the course teaches non-Hispanic trainees to say "peligro" (danger) or "cuidado" (be careful).[82]
- Fourth, *don't skimp on training.* Because of the added cultural and multilingual aspects, experts contend that a 24-hour course is the absolute minimum. The 40-hour course at the Dallas–Fort Worth airport cost about $500 tuition per student (not counting the workers' wages).

Employers also turn to the Web to support their safety training programs.[83] For example, PureSafety (www.puresafety.com) enables firms to create their own training Web sites, complete with a "message from the safety director." Once an employer installs the PureSafety Web site, it can populate the site with courses from companies that supply health and safety courses via that site. The courses themselves are available in various formats, including digital versions of videotape training, and PowerPoint presentations.[84]

CREATING A SUPPORTIVE ENVIRONMENT Although safety training is a key safety preventive method, a recent study suggests that creating a supportive supervisory environment is more important. "Organizations can develop a supportive environment by training supervisors to be better leaders, emphasizing the importance of teamwork and social support, and establishing the value of safety."[85]

Reducing Unsafe Acts through Motivation: Posters, Incentives, and Positive Reinforcement

Employers also use various tools to motivate workers to work safely. Safety posters are one. However, although safety posters can increase safe behavior, they are no substitute for a comprehensive safety program. Employers should combine them with other techniques (like screening and training) to reduce unsafe conditions and acts, and change the posters often.

One way to motivate and encourage safety in a factory is to tell employees how much management values it: This safety poster on an exterior factory wall tells employees how well they are doing.

Incentive programs are also useful.[86] Management at Tesoro Corporation's Golden Eagle refinery in California instituted one such plan. Employees earn "WINGS" (an acronym for Willing Involvement Nurtures Greater Safety) points for engaging in one or more specific safety activities, such as taking emergency response training. Employees can each earn up to $20 per month by accumulating points.[87]

Some contend that safety incentive programs are misguided. OSHA has argued, for instance, that such programs don't cut down on actual injuries or illnesses, but only on injury and illness *reporting*. One expert argues that by encouraging habitual behavior they can lull employees into letting their guard down.[88] One option is to emphasize nontraditional incentives, like recognition. For instance, recognize employees for identifying hazards.[89] In any case, the incentive program needs to be part of a comprehensive safety program.[90]

RESEARCH INSIGHT: POSITIVE REINFORCEMENT   Many employers successfully use *positive reinforcement programs* to improve safety. Such programs provide workers with continuing positive feedback, usually in the form of graphical performance reports and supervisory support, to shape the workers' safety-related behavior.

Researchers introduced one program in a wholesale bakery.[91] The new safety program included training and positive reinforcement. The researchers set and communicated a reasonable safety goal (in terms of observed incidents performed safely). Next, employees participated in a 30-minute training session by viewing pairs of slides depicting scenes that the researchers staged in the plant. One slide, for example, showed the supervisor climbing over a conveyor; the parallel slide showed the supervisor walking around the conveyor. After viewing an unsafe act, employees had to describe, "What's unsafe here?" Then the researchers demonstrated the same incident again but performed in a safe manner, and explicitly stated the safe-conduct rule ("go around, not over or under, conveyors").

At the conclusion of the training phase, supervisors showed employees a graph with their pretraining safety record (in terms of observed incidents performed safely) plotted. Supervisors then encouraged workers to consider increasing their performance to the new safety goal for their own protection, to decrease costs, and to help the plant get out of its last place safety ranking. Then the researchers posted the graph and a list of safety rules.

Whenever observers walked through the plant collecting safety data, they posted on the graph the percentage of incidents they had seen performed safely by the group as a whole, thus providing the workers with positive feedback. Workers could compare their current safety performance with both their previous performance and their assigned goal. In addition, supervisors praised workers when they performed selected incidents safely. Safety in the plant subsequently improved markedly.

Reducing Unsafe Acts through Behavior-Based Safety

Behavior-based safety means identifying the worker behaviors that contribute to accidents and then training workers to avoid these behaviors. Tenneco Corporation (which manufactures Monroe brand suspensions) implemented a behavior-based safety program. The firm selected internal consultants from among its quality managers, training managers, engineers, and production workers. After training, the internal consultants identified five critical behaviors for Tenneco's first safety program, such as, *Eyes on task: Does the employee watch his or her hands while performing a task?* The consultants made observations and collected data regarding the behaviors. Then they instituted training programs to get employees to perform these five behaviors properly.[92]

Reducing Unsafe Acts through Employee Participation

Employees are often your best source of ideas about what the safety problems are and how to solve them. For example, when the International Truck and Engine Corp.

FIGURE 16-7 Employee Safety Responsibilities Checklist

Source: Reprinted from www.HR.BLR.com with permission of the publisher *Business and Legal Resources, Inc.*, 141 Mill Rock Road East, Old Saybrook, CT © 2004. BLR® (Business and Legal Resources, Inc.).

Employee Safety Responsibilities Checklist

❑ Know what constitutes a safety hazard.
❑ Be constantly on the lookout for safety hazards.
❑ Correct or report safety hazards immediately.
❑ Know and use safe work procedures.
❑ Avoid unsafe acts.
❑ Keep the work area clean and uncluttered.
❑ Report accidents, injuries, illnesses, exposures to hazardous substances, and near misses immediately.
❑ Report acts and conditions that don't seem right even if you aren't sure if they're hazards.
❑ Cooperate with internal inspections and job hazard analyses.
❑ Follow company safety rules.
❑ Look for ways to make the job safer.
❑ Participate actively in safety training.
❑ Treat safety as one of your most important job responsibilities.

---

began designing its new robot-based plant in Springfield, Ohio, management chose to involve employees in designing the new facility.[93]

Management appointed joint labor–management safety teams for each department. These worked with project engineers to start designing safeguards for the robot equipment. The company even sent one safety team to Japan to watch the robot machines in action, and to identify items that the safety teams needed to address. Back in Ohio, this team worked with employees to identify possible hazards and to develop new devices (such as color-coded locks) to protect the employees.[94]

Once they are committed to the idea of safety, a checklist such as the one shown in Figure 16-7 can provide employees with a useful reminder.

Reducing Unsafe Acts by Conducting Safety and Health Audits and Inspections

Reducing unsafe acts is no substitute for eliminating hazards. Managers should therefore routinely inspect for problems using safety audit/checklists (as in Figures 16-6 and 16-7) as aids. Also, investigate all accidents and "near misses." Set up employee safety committees to evaluate safety adequacy, conduct and monitor safety audits, and suggest ways for improving safety.[95] Managers expedite safety audits by using personal digital assistants (PDAs).[96] For example, Process and Performance Measurement (PPM) is a Windows application for designing and completing safety audit questionnaires. To use this application, the manager gives the safety audit a name, enters the audit questions, and lists possible answers. Typical questions for a fire extinguisher audit might include, "Are fire extinguishers clearly identified and accessible?" and "Are only approved fire extinguishers used in the workplace?"[97] The supervisor or employee then uses his or her PDA to record the audit and transmit it to the firm's safety office.

With respect to safety and health, evidence-based management means identifying crucial metrics and then monitoring them. Metrics might include, for instance, the percent conformance to safety critical behaviors and processes, the level of exposure present in the workplace as measured through valid samples, and the rate of adverse outcomes such as injury rates.[98]

SAFETY AWARENESS PROGRAMS Employers also use safety awareness programs to improve employee safety behavior. A **safety awareness program** enables

---

behavior-based safety
Identifying the worker behaviors that contribute to accidents and then training workers to avoid these behaviors.

safety awareness program
Program that enables trained supervisors to orient new workers arriving at a job site regarding common safety hazards and simple prevention methods.

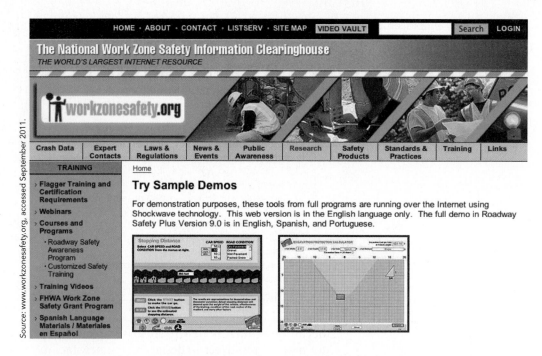

Source: www.workzonesafety.org, accessed September 2011.

trained supervisors to orient new workers arriving at a job site regarding common safety hazards and simple prevention methods. For example, the Roadway Safety Awareness Program covers trucker safety issues such as stopping distances required at various speeds (see the accompanying screen grab).

Table 16-1 summarizes suggestions for reducing unsafe conditions and acts.[99]

Controlling Workers' Compensation Costs

In the event an accident does occur, the employee may turn to the employer's workers' compensation insurance to cover his or her expenses and losses.[100] We addressed workers' compensation in Chapter 13 (Benefits), but address several safety-related points here.

BEFORE THE ACCIDENT   The time to start "controlling" workers' compensation claims is before the accident happens.[101] For example, LKL Associates, Inc., of Orem, Utah, cut its workers' compensation premiums in half by communicating written safety and substance abuse policies to workers and then strictly enforcing those policies.[102]

TABLE 16-1 Reducing Unsafe Conditions and Acts: A Summary
Reduce Unsafe Conditions
Identify and eliminate unsafe conditions.
Use administrative means, such as job rotation.
Use personal protective equipment.
Reduce Unsafe Acts
Emphasize top management commitment.
Emphasize safety.
Establish a safety policy.
Reduce unsafe acts through selection.
Provide safety training.
Use posters and other propaganda.
Use positive reinforcement.
Use behavior-based safety programs.
Encourage worker participation.
Conduct safety and health inspections regularly.

AFTER THE ACCIDENT The injury can be traumatic for the employee, and how the employer handles it is important. As noted in Chapter 13 (Benefits), moving aggressively to support the injured employee and to get him or her back to work quickly is important. The involvement of an attorney and the duration of the claim both influence the workers claim cost.[103]

It is important to be supportive and proactive. Provide first aid, and make sure the worker gets quick medical attention; make it clear that you are interested in the injured worker; document the accident; file required accident reports; and encourage a speedy return to work.[104] The HR as a Profit Center feature illustrates other steps HR can take.

HR AS A PROFIT CENTER

Reducing Workers Compensation Claims

Claims-tracking software helps employers understand and reduce their workers' compensation claims. For example, a health services agency in Bangor, Maine, purchased CompWatch, a workers' compensation claims management and tracking program. The agency entered all its previous claims, and used CompWatch to analyze trends. The agency discovered some of its auto accidents were apparently due to its drivers' need for training, so the agency introduced a driver safety program. In one department, this apparently led to a 42% reduction in auto accidents from one year to the next.[105]

> 6 List five workplace health hazards and how to deal with them.

WORKPLACE HEALTH HAZARDS: PROBLEMS AND REMEDIES

Most workplace hazards aren't as obvious as unguarded equipment or slippery floors. Many are unseen hazards (such as mold) that the company inadvertently produces as part of its production processes. Other problems, such as drug abuse, employees may create for themselves. Both such hazards can be as or more dangerous to workers' health and safety than are obvious hazards like slippery floors. Typical workplace exposure hazards include chemicals and other hazardous materials, temperature extremes, biohazards (including those that are naturally occurring, such as mold, and man-made, such as anthrax), and ergonomic hazards (such as uncomfortable equipment).[106]

Exposure to asbestos is a major potential source of occupational respiratory disease. This worker wears protective clothing and a respirator to remove asbestos from ceiling panels in a classroom.

Source: Stefan Hard/AP Images.

TABLE 16-2 OSHA Substance-Specific Health Standards

Substance	Permissible Exposure Limits*
Asbestos	.1001
Vinyl chloride	.1017
Inorganic arsenic	.1018
Lead	.1025
Cadmium	.1027
Benzene	.1028
Coke oven emissions	.1029
Cotton dust	.1043
1,2-Dibromo-3-chloropropane	.1044
Acrylonitrile	.1045
Ethylene oxide	.1047
Formaldehyde	.1048
4,4'-Methylenedianaline	.1050
Methylene chloride	.1051

*The actual measurement yardstick is substance-specific. For example, the yardstick for asbestos is Permissible Fiber per cubic centimeter, and for formaldehyde it is Parts formaldehyde per million parts of air

Source: John F. Rekus, "If You Thought Air Sampling Was Too Difficult to Handle, This Guide Can Help You Tackle Routine Sampling with Confidence, Part I," Occupational Hazards, May 2003, p. 43. See also www.osha.gov/SLTC/pel/, accessed June 30, 2011.

The Basic Industrial Hygiene Program

OSHA standards list exposure limits for about 600 chemicals. Table 16-2 lists some OSHA substance-specific health standards. Hazardous substances like these require air sampling and other preventive and precautionary measures.

Managing such exposure hazards comes under the area of *industrial hygiene* and involves recognition, evaluation, and control. First, the facility's health and safety officers (possibly working with teams of supervisors and employees) must *recognize* possible exposure hazards. This typically involves conducting plant/facility walk-around surveys, employee interviews, records reviews, and reviews of government (OSHA) and nongovernmental standards.

Having identified a possible hazard, *evaluation* involves determining how severe the hazard is. This requires measuring the exposure, comparing the measured exposure to some benchmark (as in Table 16-2), and determining whether the risk is within tolerances.[107]

Finally, hazard *control* involves eliminating or reducing the hazard. Note that personal protective gear is generally the *last* option for dealing with such problems. The employer must first install engineering controls (such as process enclosures or ventilation) and administrative controls (including training and improved housekeeping).

Asbestos Exposure at Work

There are four major sources of occupational respiratory diseases: asbestos, silica, lead, and carbon dioxide. Of these, asbestos is a major concern, in part because of publicity surrounding asbestos in buildings constructed before the mid-1970s. Major efforts are still underway to rid these buildings of the substance.

OSHA standards require several actions with respect to asbestos. Employers must monitor the air whenever they expect the level of asbestos to rise to one-half the allowable limit (which is 0.1 fibers per cubic centimeter). Engineering controls—walls, special filters, and so forth—are required to maintain an asbestos level that complies with OSHA standards. Only then can employers use respirators if additional efforts are required to achieve compliance.

Infectious Diseases

With many employees traveling to and from international destinations, monitoring and controlling infectious diseases has become an important safety issue.

Employers can take steps to prevent the entry or spread of infectious diseases into their workplaces. These steps include:[108]

1. Closely monitor Centers for Disease Control and Prevention (CDC) travel alerts about health concerns. Access this information at www.cdc.gov.
2. Provide daily medical screenings for employees returning from infected areas.
3. Deny access to your facility for 10 days to employees or visitors returning from affected areas.
4. Tell employees to stay home if they have a fever or respiratory system symptoms.
5. Clean work areas and surfaces regularly.
6. Stagger breaks. Offer several lunch periods to reduce overcrowding.
7. Emphasize the importance of frequent hand washing and make hand sanitizers easily available.

Air Quality

One of the downsides of opting for environmentally "green" office buildings is that sealed buildings can produce illnesses such as itchy eyes and trouble breathing, a phenomenon some call "sick building syndrome." The problem is that emissions from printers and photocopiers and other chemical pollutants, left unmonitored, can dramatically reduce air quality.[109] The solution is to institute continuous monitoring systems.

Alcoholism and Substance Abuse

Alcoholism and substance abuse are problems at work. About two-thirds of people with an alcohol disorder work full-time.[110] Some studies estimate that almost 13 million workers use drugs illicitly.[111] About 15% of the U.S. workforce (just over 19 million workers) "has either been hung over at work, been drinking shortly before showing up for work, or been drinking or impaired while on the job at least once during the previous year."[112] Employee alcoholism may cost U.S. employers about $226 billion per year, for instance, in higher absenteeism and accidents.[113] (Increasingly, it's not intoxicated drivers but "intexicated" employees causing the problem. Studies indicate that cell phone activity probably contributes to over 636,000 motor vehicle crashes per year. Many businesses are therefore banning cell phone use and texting activities among their drivers.)[114]

EFFECTS OF ALCOHOL ABUSE The effects of alcoholism on the worker and work are severe.[115] Both the quality and quantity of the work decline in the face of a sort of on-the-job absenteeism. The alcoholic's on-the-job accidents usually don't increase significantly, apparently, because he or she becomes much more cautious. However, the off-the-job accident rate is higher. Morale of other workers drops, as they have to shoulder the alcoholic's burdens.

Recognizing the alcoholic on the job is a problem. Early symptoms such as tardiness are similar to those of other problems and thus hard to classify. The supervisor is not a psychiatrist, and without specialized training, identifying—and dealing with—the alcoholic is difficult.

As you can see in Table 16-3, alcohol-related problems range from tardiness in the earliest stages of alcohol abuse to prolonged absences in its later stages.

SUPERVISOR TRAINING Training supervisors to identify alcoholics or drug abusers and the problems they create is advisable. However, supervisors are in a tricky position: They should be the company's first line of defense in combating workplace

TABLE 16-3   Observable Behavior Patterns Indicating Possible Alcohol-Related Problems

Alcoholism Stage	Some Possible Signs of Alcoholism Problems	Some Possible Alcoholism Performance Issues
Early	Arrives at work late	Reduced job efficiency
	Untrue statements	Misses deadlines
	Leaves work early	
Middle	Frequent absences, especially Mondays	Accidents
	Colleagues mentioning erratic behavior	Warnings from boss
	Mood swings	Noticeably reduced performance
	Anxiety	
	Late returning from lunch	
	Frequent multi-day absences	
Advanced	Personal neglect	Frequent falls, accidents
	Unsteady gait	Strong disciplinary actions
	Violent outbursts	Basically incompetent performance
	Blackouts and frequent forgetfulness	
	Possible drinking on job	

Sources: Gopal Patel and John Adkins Jr., "The Employer's Role in Alcoholism Assistance," *Personnel Journal* 62, no. 7 (July 1983), p. 570; Mary-Anne Enoch and David Goldman, "Problem Drinking and Alcoholism: Diagnosis and Treatment," *American Family Physician*, February 1, 2002, www.aafp.org/afp/20020201/441.html, accessed July 20, 2008; and Ken Pidd et al., "Alcohol and Work: Patterns of Use, Workplace Culture, and Safety," www.nisu.flinders.edu.au/pubs/reports/2006/injcat82.pdf, accessed July 20, 2008.

drug abuse, but should avoid becoming detectives or diagnosticians. Guidelines supervisors should follow include the following:

- If an employee appears to be under the influence of drugs or alcohol, ask how the employee feels and look for signs of impairment such as slurred speech. (See Table 16-3.) Send an employee judged unfit home.

- Make a written record of your observations and follow up each incident. In addition, inform workers of the number of warnings the company will tolerate before requiring termination.

- Refer troubled employees to the company's employee assistance program.

DEALING WITH SUBSTANCE ABUSE   For many employers, dealing with alcohol and substance abuse begins with substance abuse testing. As we saw in Chapter 6, it's unusual to find employers who don't at least test job candidates for substance abuse before hiring them. And many states are instituting mandatory random drug testing for high-hazard workers, such as electrical workers.[116] Several states also have laws making drug-test fraud a crime.[117]

Preemployment tests pick up only about half the workplace drug users, so ongoing random testing is advisable. One study concluded that preemployment drug testing had little effect on workplace accidents. However, a combination of preemployment and random ongoing testing was associated with a significant reduction in workplace accidents.[118] Preemployment drug testing also discourages those on drugs from applying for work or going to work for employers who test.[119]

Disciplining, discharge, in-house counseling, and referral to an outside agency are the four traditional prescriptions when a *current* employee tests positive. Most professionals seem to counsel treatment rather than outright dismissal, at least initially. Employers often make available employee assistance programs (EAPs) to provide the counseling necessary to support employees with alcohol or drug abuse problems.

SUBSTANCE ABUSE POLICIES The employers should establish and communicate a substance abuse policy. This policy should state management's position on alcohol and drug abuse and on the use and possession of illegal drugs on company premises. It should also list the methods (such as urinalysis) used to determine the causes of poor performance; state the company's views on rehabilitation, including workplace counseling; and specify penalties for policy violations. Additional steps employers take include conducting workplace inspections (searching employees for illegal substances) and using undercover agents.

Whether the alcohol abuse reflects a "disability" under the ADA depends on several things, including whether the person is alcohol dependent.[120] In general, employers can hold alcohol dependent employees to the same performance standards as they hold nonalcoholics. However, there are other legal risks. Employees have sued for invasion of privacy, wrongful discharge, defamation, and illegal searches. Therefore, before implementing a drug control program employers should use employee handbooks, bulletin board/intranet postings, and the like to publicize their substance abuse plans, and to explain the conditions under which testing might occur and what accommodations you make for employees who voluntarily seek treatment.

Stress, Burnout, and Depression

Problems such as alcoholism and drug abuse sometimes reflect underlying psychological causes such as stress and depression. In turn, a variety of workplace factors can lead to stress. These include work schedule, pace of work, job security, route to and from work, workplace noise, poor supervision, and the number and nature of customers or clients.[121]

Personal factors also influence stress. For example, Type A personalities—people who are workaholics and who feel driven to be on time and meet deadlines—normally place themselves under greater stress than do others. Add to job stress the stress caused by nonjob problems like divorce, and many workers are problems waiting to happen.

Job stress has serious consequences for both employer and employee. Human consequences include anxiety, depression, anger, cardiovascular disease, headaches, accidents, and even early onset Alzheimer's disease.[122] A Danish study recently found that nurses working under excessive pressure had double the risk for heart attacks.[123]

For the employer, consequences include diminished performance, and increased absenteeism and turnover. A study of 46,000 employees concluded that high-stress workers' health care costs were 46% higher than those of their less-stressed coworkers.[124] Yet only 5% of surveyed U.S. employers say they're addressing workplace stress.[125]

REDUCING JOB STRESS There are a number of ways to alleviate dysfunctional stress. These range from commonsense remedies (such as getting more sleep) to remedies like biofeedback and meditation. Finding a more suitable job, getting counseling, and planning and organizing each day's activities are other sensible responses.[126] In his book *Stress and the Manager*, Dr. Karl Albrecht suggests the following ways for a person to reduce job stress:[127]

- Build rewarding, pleasant, cooperative relationships with colleagues and employees.
- Don't bite off more than you can chew.
- Build an especially effective and supportive relationship with your boss.
- Negotiate with your boss for realistic deadlines on important projects.
- Learn as much as you can about upcoming events and get as much lead time as you can to prepare for them.
- Find time every day for detachment and relaxation.
- Take a walk around the office to keep your body refreshed and alert.
- Find ways to reduce unnecessary noise.
- Reduce the amount of trivia in your job; delegate routine work when possible.
- Limit interruptions.

- Don't put off dealing with distasteful problems.
- Make a constructive "worry list" that includes solutions for each problem.
- Get more and better quality sleep.[128]

Meditation is another option. Choose a quiet place with soft light and sit comfortably. Then meditate by focusing your thoughts (for example, count breaths or visualize a calming location such as a beach). When your mind wanders, bring it back to focusing your thoughts on your breathing or the beach.[129]

The employer and its human resource team and supervisors also play a role in reducing stress. Supportive supervisors and fair treatment are two obvious steps. Other steps include reducing personal conflicts on the job and encouraging open communication between management and employees. Huntington Hospital in Pasadena, California, introduced an on-site concierge service to help its employees reduce work-related stress. It takes care of tasks like making vacation plans for the employees.[130] Some employers use "resilience training" to help employees deal with stress. As one example, "participants consider previous stressful situations in their lives that they have overcome and identify factors that made the situations manageable."[131]

One British firm has a three-tiered employee stress-reduction program.[132] First is *primary prevention*. This focuses on ensuring that things like job designs and workflows are correct. Second is *intervention*. This includes individual employee assessment, attitude surveys to find sources of stress, and supervisory intervention. Third is *rehabilitation*, which includes employee assistance programs higher counseling.

BURNOUT   **Burnout** is a phenomenon closely associated with job stress. Experts define burnout as the total depletion of physical and mental resources caused by excessive striving to reach an unrealistic work-related goal. Burnout builds gradually, manifesting itself in symptoms such as irritability, discouragement, exhaustion, cynicism, entrapment, and resentment.[133]

Employers can head off burnout, for instance, by monitoring employees in potentially high-pressure jobs.[134] What can a burnout candidate do? In his book *How to Beat the High Cost of Success*, Dr. Herbert Freudenberger suggests:

- **Break your patterns.** First, are you doing a variety of things or the same one repeatedly? The more well-rounded your life is, the better protected you are against burnout.

- **Get away from it all periodically.** Schedule occasional periods of introspection during which you can get away from your usual routine.

- **Reassess your goals in terms of their intrinsic worth.** Are the goals you've set for yourself attainable? Are they really worth the sacrifices?

- **Think about your work.** Could you do as good a job without being so intense?

RESEARCH INSIGHTS   If you're thinking of taking a vacation to reduce your burnout, you might as well save your money, according to one classic study.[135] In this study, 76 clerks in the headquarters of an electronics firm in Israel completed questionnaires measuring job stress and burnout twice before a vacation, once during the vacation, and twice after the vacation.

The clerks' burnout did decline during the vacation. The problem was the burnout quickly returned. Burnout moved partway back toward its pre-vacation level by 3 days after the vacation, and all the way by 3 weeks after they returned to work.[136] One implication, as these researchers point out, is that mini vacations during the workday—"such as time off for physical exercise, meditation, power naps, and reflective thinking"—might help reduce stress and burnout. A later study concluded that the quality of a vacation—for instance, in terms of relaxation and nonwork hassles—affected the vacation's fade-out effects.[137]

One way to reduce burnout is to forget about your job once you go home. In one study, researchers measured psychological detachment from work during nonwork time with items such as "during after-work hours, I forget about work."[138] Lack of psychological detachment from work while off the job predicted higher emotional exhaustion one year later. The bottom line seems to be to leave your job behind once you go home (and to provide more time-off benefits for employees).

EMPLOYEE DEPRESSION   *Employee depression* is a serious problem at work. Experts estimate that depression results in more than 200 million lost workdays in the United States annually, and may cost U.S. businesses $24 billion or more per year just in absenteeism and lost productivity.[139] Depressed people also tend to have worse safety records.[140]

Employers need to work harder to ensure that depressed employees utilize available support services. One survey found that while about two-thirds of large firms offered employee assistance programs covering depression, only about 14% of employees with depression said they ever used one.[141]

Employers therefore need to train supervisors to identify depression's warning signs and to counsel those who may need such services to use the firm's employee assistance program.[142] Depression is a disease. It does no more good to tell a depressed person to "snap out of it" than it would to tell someone with a heart condition to stop acting tired. Typical depression warning signs (if they last for more than 2 weeks) include persistent sad, anxious, or "empty" moods; sleeping too little; reduced appetite; loss of interest in activities once enjoyed; restlessness or irritability; and difficulty concentrating.[143]

Solving Computer-Related Ergonomic Problems

Although many workers use computers at work, OSHA has no specific standards that apply to computer workstations. It does have general standards that might apply, regarding, for instance, radiation, noise, and electrical hazards.[144]

NIOSH provided general recommendations regarding computer screens. Most relate to *ergonomics* or design of the worker–equipment interface. These include:

- Employees should take a 3–5 minute break from working at the computer every 20–40 minutes, and use the time for other tasks, like making copies.
- Design maximum flexibility into the workstation so it can be adapted to the individual operator. For example, use adjustable chairs with midback supports. Don't stay in one position for long periods.
- Reduce glare with devices such as shades over windows and recessed or indirect lighting.
- Give workers a complete preplacement vision exam to ensure properly corrected vision for reduced visual strain.[145]
- Allow the user to position his or her wrists at the same level as the elbow.
- Put the screen at or just below eye level, at a distance of 18 to 30 inches from the eyes.
- Let the wrists rest lightly on a pad for support.
- Put the feet flat on the floor or on a footrest.[146]

Repetitive Motion Disorders

According to the U.S. National Institutes of Health, repetitive motion disorders include disorders such as carpal tunnel syndrome, bursitis, and tendonitis, and result from too many uninterrupted repetitions of an activity or motion, or from unnatural motions such as twisting the arm or wrist, or incorrect posture. It usually affects people who perform repetitive tasks such as assembly line or computer work. Employers can reduce the problem, for instance, with programs to help workers adjust their pace of work.[147]

burnout
The total depletion of physical and mental resources caused by excessive striving to reach an unrealistic work-related goal.

Workplace Smoking

Smoking is a serious health and cost problem for both employees and employers. For employers, these costs derive from higher health and fire insurance, increased absenteeism, and reduced productivity (as when a smoker takes a 10-minute break behind the store). The California Environmental Protection Agency estimated that each year in the United States, secondhand smoke causes 3,000 deaths due to lung cancer and 35,000 to 62,000 illnesses due to heart problems (not all work related).[148]

WHAT YOU CAN AND CANNOT DO   In general, you can probably deny a job to a smoker as long as you don't use smoking as a surrogate for some other kind of discrimination.[149] A "no-smokers-hired" policy does not, according to one expert, violate the Americans with Disabilities Act (since smoking is not considered a disability), and in general "employers' adoption of a no-smokers-hired policy is not illegal under federal law." Most employers these days ban indoor smoking, often designating small outdoor areas where smoking is permitted. Many states and municipalities now ban indoor smoking in public areas (see http://en.wikipedia.org/wiki/List_of_smoking_bans#United_States for a list).

Some firms take a hard-line approach. WEYCO Inc., a benefits services company in Michigan, first gave employees 15 months' warning and offered smoking secession assistance. Then they began firing or forcing out all its workers who smoke, including those who do so in the privacy of their homes.[150]

WELLNESS PROGRAMS   We discussed wellness programs in Chapter 13 (Benefits), but for many employers, wellness is part of their safety and health initiatives. Wegman's food markets Inc. has various health and fitness campaigns, and, for instance, encourages its employees to eat 5 cups of fruit and vegetables and walk 10,000 steps each day.[151] The accompanying HR as a Profit Center feature illustrates one program's advantages.

HR AS A PROFIT CENTER

Wellness Pays

The payback for wellness programs isn't theoretical. For example, over the past 20 or so years, the percentage of employees at Johnson & Johnson who smoke has dropped by more than two-thirds, in part thanks to J&J's comprehensive wellness effort. It's been reported that the company's leaders estimate that such wellness programs have saved the company about $250 million on health care costs from 2002 to 2008, a return of about $2.71 for every dollar spent on the wellness programs.[152]

Violence at Work

Violence against employees is an enormous problem at work. Homicide is the second biggest cause of fatal workplace injuries. Surveys by NIOSH found that nonfatal workplace assaults resulted in more than 1 million lost workdays in one recent year. While robbery was the main motive for homicide at work, a coworker or personal associate committed roughly one of seven workplace homicides.[153] In one survey, over half of human resource or security executives reported that disgruntled employees had threatened senior managers in the past 12 months.[154] Sadly, much of this violence involves acts by one intimate partner against another. For example, the U.S. Centers for Disease Control reported almost 5 million such attacks against women (and 3 million against men) recently (not all at work).[155] Women (and men) should have access to domestic crisis hotlines, such as www.ndvh.org, and to the employer's employee assistance programs.

WHO IS AT RISK?   Violence is associated with some jobs more than others. In one study, researchers constructed a "risk for violence scale." Jobs with a high likelihood for violence include those jobs that involve physical care of others or decisions that influence other people's lives, handling guns, security functions, physical control over others, interacting with frustrated individuals, and handling weapons other than guns.[156]

Although men have more fatal occupational injuries than do women, the proportion of women who are victims of assault is much higher. The Gender-Motivated Violence Act imposes significant liabilities on employers whose women employees become victims.[157] Most women (many working in retail establishments) murdered at work were victims of random criminal violence by an assailant unknown to the victim, as during a robbery. Coworkers, family members, or previous friends or acquaintances carried out the remaining homicides.

You can predict and avoid many workplace incidents. *Risk Management* magazine estimates that about 86% of past workplace violence incidents were apparent earlier to coworkers, who had brought them to management's attention. Yet, in most cases, management did little or nothing.[158] Employers can take several steps to reduce workplace violence. Let's look at them.

HEIGHTENED SECURITY MEASURES Heightened security measures are an employer's first line of defense. NIOSH suggests the following: Improve external lighting, use drop safes to minimize cash on hand and post signs noting that only a limited amount of cash is on hand, install silent alarms and surveillance cameras, increase the number of staff on duty, provide staff training in conflict resolution and nonviolent response, and close establishments during high-risk hours late at night.[159] Employers can also issue a weapons policy, for instance, barring firearms and other dangerous weapons.

Because about half of workplace homicides occur in the retail industry, OSHA issued voluntary recommendations aimed at reducing homicides and injuries in such establishments. The suggestions include the following: Install mirrors and improved lighting, provide silent and personal alarms, reduce store hours during high-risk periods, install drop safes and signs that indicate little cash is kept on hand, erect bullet-resistance enclosures, and increase staffing during high-risk hours.[160] Adopt a workplace violence policy that outlines unacceptable employee behavior and a zero-tolerance policy toward workplace violence.[161]

IMPROVED EMPLOYEE SCREENING That testing can screen out workplace aggressors is clear. In one study, researchers concluded that measurable individual differences like "attitude toward revenge" "account for more than 60% of the variance in our measure of the incidence of workplace aggression."[162] (We discussed bullying in Chapter 14, Ethics.)

At a minimum, carefully check references. Obtain a detailed employment application. Verify the applicant's employment history, educational background, and references. A personal interview, personnel testing, and a review and verification of all information should also be included. Sample interview questions might include, "What frustrates you?" and "Who was your worst supervisor and why?" Remember that certain questions, for instance concerning arrest records may violate one or more equal employment laws.[163]

Certain background facts suggest the need for a more in-depth background investigation (but note that the EEOC is preparing new guidelines for evidence-based violence background checks, to replace what are often checks made on "untested assumptions"):[164]

- An unexplained gap in employment
- Incomplete or false information on the résumé or application
- A negative, unfavorable, or false reference
- Prior insubordinate or violent behavior on the job
- A criminal history involving harassing or violent behavior
- A prior termination for cause with a suspicious (or no) explanation
- A history of significant psychiatric problems
- A history of drug or alcohol abuse
- Strong indications of instability in the individual's work or personal life, for example, frequent job changes or geographic moves
- Lapsed or lost licenses or accreditations[165]

Workplace Violence Supervisory Training

Employers should also train supervisors to identify the clues that typically precede violent incidents. These include:[166]

- **Typical profiles.** The typical perpetrator is male, between the ages of 25 and 40, and exhibits an inability to handle stress, manipulative behavior, and steady complaining. Of course, many nonviolent people exhibit such traits, too. However, perpetrators also tend to exhibit behaviors such as the following.
- **Verbal threats.** They harbor grudges and often talk about what they may do, such as, "That propane tank in the back could blow up easily."
- **Physical actions.** Troubled employees may try to intimidate others, gain access to places where they do not belong, or flash a concealed weapon.
- **Frustration.** Most cases involve an employee who has a frustrated sense of entitlement to a promotion, for example.
- **Obsession.** An employee may hold a grudge against a coworker or supervisor, and some cases stem from romantic interest.[167]

Vendors offer video violence training programs. These explain what workplace violence is, identify its causes and signs, and offer tips to supervisors on how to prevent it and what to do when it occurs.

Specific behaviors to watch out for include:

- An act of violence on or off the job
- Erratic behavior evidencing a loss of awareness of actions
- Overly defensive, obsessive, or paranoid tendencies
- Overly confrontational or antisocial behavior
- Sexually aggressive behavior
- Isolationist or loner tendencies
- Insubordinate behavior with a suggestion of violence
- Tendency to overreact to criticism
- Exaggerated interest in war, guns, violence, catastrophes
- The commission of a serious breach of security
- Possession of weapons, guns, knives at the workplace[168]
- Violation of privacy rights of others, such as searching desks or stalking
- Chronic complaining and frequent, unreasonable grievances
- A retribution-oriented or get-even attitude[169]

ORGANIZATIONAL JUSTICE   At work, violence often occurs in response to a perceived personal affront.[170] Consider one executive suspected of sabotaging his former employer's computer system, thus causing about $20 million in damage. He'd been earning $186,000 a year. A note he wrote anonymously to the president said this:

> I have been loyal to the Company in good and bad times for over thirty years. . . . What is most upsetting is the manner in which you chose to end our employment. I was expecting a member of top management to come down from his ivory tower to face us directly with a layoff announcement, rather than sending the kitchen supervisor with guards to escort us off the premises like criminals. . . . We will not wait for God to punish you—we will take measures into our own hands.[171]

DEALING WITH ANGRY EMPLOYEES   What do you do when confronted by an angry, potentially explosive employee? Here are some suggestions:[172]

- Make eye contact.
- Stop what you are doing and give your full attention.

- Speak in a calm voice and create a relaxed environment.
- Be open and honest.
- Let the person have his or her say.
- Ask for specific examples of what the person is upset about.
- Be careful to define the problem.
- Ask open-ended questions and explore all sides of the issue.
- Listen: As one expert says, "Often, angry people simply want to be listened to. They need a supportive, empathic ear from someone they can trust."[173]

DISMISSING VIOLENT EMPLOYEES   You should use caution when firing or disciplining potentially violent employees.

In dismissing potentially violent employees:

- Analyze and anticipate, based on the person's history, what kind of aggressive behavior to expect.
- Have a security guard nearby when the dismissal takes place.
- Clear away furniture and things the person might throw.
- Don't wear loose clothing that the person might grab.
- Don't make it sound as if you're accusing the employee; instead, say that according to company policy, you're required to take action.
- Maintain the person's dignity and try to emphasize something good about the employee.
- Provide job counseling for terminated employees, to help get the employee over the traumatic post-dismissal adjustment.[174]
- Consider obtaining restraining orders against those who have exhibited a tendency to act violently in the workplace.[175]

LEGAL ISSUES IN REDUCING WORKPLACE VIOLENCE   It is sensible to try to screen out potentially violent employees, but doing so incurs legal risks. For example, courts have interpreted Title VII of the Civil Rights Act of 1964 as restricting employers from making employment decisions based on arrest records, which may be discriminatory.

Aside from federal law, most states prohibit discrimination under any circumstances based on arrest records and on prior convictions unless a direct relationship exists between the prior conviction and the job, or the employment presents an unreasonable risk.[176] And developing a "violent employee" profile could end up merely describing a mental impairment and violate the Americans with Disabilities Act.[177]

7 Discuss the prerequisites for a security plan and how to set up a basic security program.

OCCUPATIONAL SECURITY AND SAFETY

A majority of employers have security arrangements.[178] A SHRM survey found that about 85% of responding organizations now have some type of formal disaster plan.[179] Many firms have also instituted special handling procedures for suspicious mail packages and hold regular emergency evacuation drills.

Many of these actions stemmed from employers' heightened focus on risk management in the past few years. Identifying security and other corporate risks falls within the domain of *enterprise risk management,* which means identifying risks, and planning to mitigate and actually mitigating these risks. Thus, as part of its risk management, Walmart asks questions such as, "What are the risks? And what are we going to do about these risks?"[180] Eliminating crime and enhancing facility security are two important issues here.

Basic Prerequisites for a Crime Prevention Plan

As one corporate security summary put it, "workplace security involves more than keeping track of who comes in a window, installing an alarm system, or employing guards for an after-hours watch. Organizations that are truly security conscious plan and implement policies and programs that involve employees in protecting against identified risks and threats."[181]

Ideally, a comprehensive corporate anticrime program should start with the following:

1. Company philosophy and policy on crime—In particular, make sure employees understand that no crime is acceptable and that the employer has a zero-tolerance policy with respect to workers who commit crimes.
2. Investigations of job applicants—Conduct full background checks as part of your selection process for every position.
3. Crime awareness training—Make it clear, during training and orientation, that the employer takes a tough approach to workplace crime.
4. Crisis management—Establish and communicate the procedures employees should follow in the event of a bomb threat, fire, or other emergency.

Setting Up a Basic Security Program

In simplest terms, instituting a basic facility security program requires four steps: analyzing the current *level* of risk, and then installing *mechanical, natural,* and *organizational* security systems.[182] Many organizations establish cross-functional threat assessment teams to monitor and address potential threats. At one university, for instance, "The team meets regularly to discuss issues relating to violence, security and potential threats directed at students, faculty and staff at the Metropolitan Campus."[183]

Security programs ideally start with an analysis of the facility's *current level of risk.* The employer, preferably with security experts, should assess the company's exposure. Here, start with the obvious. For example, what is the neighborhood like? Does your facility (such as the office building you're in) house other businesses or individuals (such as law enforcement agencies) that might bring unsafe activities to your doorstep? As part of this initial threat assessment, also review these six matters:

Many employers install video security cameras to monitor areas in and around their premises.

Source: Courtesy of Getty Images-Stockbyte, Royalty Free.

1. **Access to the reception area,** including number of access points, and need for a "panic button" for contacting emergency personnel;
2. **Interior security,** including possible need for key cards, secure restrooms, and better identification of exits;
3. **Authorities' involvement,** in particular emergency procedures developed with local law enforcement authorities;
4. **Mail handling,** including how employees screen and open mail and where it enters the building;
5. **Evacuation,** including a full review of evacuation procedures and training; and
6. **Backup systems,** such as those that let the company store data off site if disaster strikes.

Having assessed the potential current level of risk, the employer then turns its attention to assessing and improving natural, mechanical, and organizational security.[184]

NATURAL SECURITY *Natural security* means capitalizing on the facility's natural or architectural features in order to minimize security problems. For example, does having too many entrances mean it is difficult to control facility access?

MECHANICAL SECURITY   *Mechanical security* is the utilization of security systems such as locks, intrusion alarms, access control systems, and surveillance systems to reduce the need for continuous human surveillance.[185] Technological advances are making this easier. Many mail rooms now use scanners to check the safety of incoming mail. And for access security, biometric scanners that read thumb or palm prints or retina or vocal patterns make it easier to enforce plant security.[186]

ORGANIZATIONAL SECURITY   Finally, *organizational security* means using good management to improve security. For example, it means properly training and motivating security staff and lobby attendants. Also ensure that the security staff has written orders that define their duties, especially in situations such as fire, elevator entrapment, hazardous materials spills, medical emergencies, hostile intrusions, suspicious packages, civil disturbances, and workplace violence.[187] Other questions to ask include: Are you properly investigating the backgrounds of new hires? Are you requiring the same types of background checks for the contractors who supply security and other personnel to your facility? And, do you provide new employees with security orientations?

Evacuation Plans

The possibility of emergencies prompted by fires, explosions, and similar issues means that employers need facility notification and evacuation plans.[188] Such plans should cover *early detection of a problem, methods for communicating the emergency externally*, and *communications plans for initiating an evacuation and for providing information to those the employer wants to evacuate*. Ideally, an initial alarm should come first. The employer should then follow the initial alarm with an announcement providing specific information about the emergency and letting employees know what action they should take next. Most use social networks or text messaging.[189]

Company Security and Employee Privacy

Security programs have been accompanied by a significant rise in the monitoring of employee communications and workplace activities; this has prompted many to ask, are employee privacy rights being violated?

As noted in earlier in this book, employers must consider employee privacy when using monitoring to control or investigate possible employee security breaches. Ideally, employers should get employees' consent for monitoring. But the employer may also monitor if it's clear from the firm's existing policies and notices that employees should have known monitoring might take place.

The employer can take steps to make it easier to legally investigate employees for potential security breaches. These include:[190]

1. Distribute a policy that (a) says the company reserves the right to inspect and search employees as well as their personal property, electronic media, and files; and (b) emphasizes that company-provided conveniences such as lockers and desks remain the property of the company and are subject to its control and search.

2. Train investigators to focus on the facts and avoid making accusations.

3. Remember that employees can request that an employee representative be present during the investigative interview.

4. Make sure all investigations and searches are evenhanded and nondiscriminatory.

REVIEW

MyManagementLab Now that you have finished this chapter, go back to **www.mymanagementlab.com** to continue practicing and applying the concepts you've learned.

CHAPTER SECTION SUMMARIES

1. Safety and accident prevention concerns managers for several reasons, one of which is the staggering number of workplace accidents. Because of this, all managers need to be familiar with **occupational safety law**. The Occupational Safety and Health Act was passed by Congress in 1972 to ensure so far as possible every working man and woman in the nation safe and healthful working conditions and to preserve human resources. The act created the Occupational Safety and Health Administration (OSHA). OSHA, in turn, promulgates thousands of specific policies and standards with which employers must comply. It enforces these standards via a system of inspections and citations and, where necessary, penalties. Inspectors cannot make warrantless inspections, and managers need to make sure a designated OSHA coordinator is present if an inspector demands admittance.

2. There are three basic **causes of workplace accidents**: chance occurrences, unsafe conditions, and employees' unsafe acts. Unsafe conditions include things like improperly guarded equipment and hazardous procedures. Unsafe acts sometimes reflect personality traits such as impatience and distractibility.

3. In practice, **how to prevent accidents** boils down to reducing unsafe conditions and reducing unsafe acts. Reducing unsafe conditions is always the first line of defense and includes using checklists and following OSHA standards. Once all necessary steps are taken, employers need to encourage employees to use personal protective equipment. There are then several basic approaches to reducing unsafe acts, for instance, through proper selection and placement, training, motivation and positive reinforcement, behavior-based safety, employee participation, and conducting safety and health audits.

4. Most **workplace health hazards** aren't obvious, like unguarded equipment.

   - Typical exposure hazards include, for instance, chemicals, biohazards, and improperly designed equipment.
   - Managing exposure hazards like these comes under the area of industrial hygiene, and involves recognition, evaluation, and control. Obvious areas of concern include asbestos exposure and infectious diseases.
   - Managers need to be familiar with alcoholism, substance abuse, and their manifestations at work and particularly be familiar with signs of these problems and how to deal with them.
   - Stress, burnout, and depression are more serious at work than many people realize, and both the employee and employer can take steps to deal with them. Employers especially need to train supervisors to identify depression's warning signs and to counsel those who may need special services.
   - Violence against employees is an enormous problem. Women in particular are at risk. Heightened security measures are an employer's first line of defense and include, for instance, improving external lighting and using drop safes to minimize cash on hand.
   - Improved employee screening can reduce the risk of hiring potentially violent employees. However, employers also need to provide workplace violence training (for instance, including what to watch for such as verbal threats) and enhanced attention to employee retention and dismissal processes.

5. Most employers today have **occupational security and safety programs**. Instituting a basic facility security program involves analyzing the current level of risk, and then installing mechanical, natural, and organizational security systems.

DISCUSSION QUESTIONS

1. Explain how to reduce the occurrence of unsafe acts on the part of your employees.
2. Discuss the basic facts about OSHA—its purpose, standards, inspections, and rights and responsibilities.
3. Explain the supervisor's role in safety.
4. Explain what causes unsafe acts.
5. Describe at least five techniques for reducing accidents.
6. Explain how you would reduce stress at work.
7. Describe the steps employers can take to reduce workplace violence.

INDIVIDUAL AND GROUP ACTIVITIES

1. Working individually or in groups, answer the question, "Is there such a thing as an accident-prone person?" Develop your answer using examples of actual people you know who seemed to be accident prone on some endeavor.

2. Working individually or in groups, compile a list of the factors at work or in school that create dysfunctional stress for you. What methods do you use for dealing with the stress?

3. The "HRCI Test Specifications Appendix" (pages 633–640) lists the knowledge someone studying for the HRCI certification exam needs to have in each area of human resource management (such as in Strategic Management, Workforce Planning, and Human Resource Development). In groups of four to five students, do four things: (1) review that appendix now; (2) identify the material in this chapter that relates to the required knowledge the appendix lists; (3) write four multiple-choice exam questions on this material that you believe would be suitable for inclusion in the HRCI exam; and (4) if time permits, have someone from your team post your team's questions in front of the class, so the students in other teams can take each others' exam questions.

4. A safety journal presented some information about what happens when OSHA refers criminal complaints about willful violations of OSHA standards to the U.S. Department of Justice (DOJ). In one 20-year period, OSHA referred 119 fatal cases allegedly involving willful violations of OSHA to the DOJ for criminal prosecution. The DOJ declined to pursue 57% of them, and some were dropped for other reasons. Of the remaining 51 cases, the DOJ settled 63% with pretrial settlements involving no prison time. So, counting acquittals, of the 119 cases OSHA referred to the DOJ, only 9 resulted in prison time for at least one of the defendants. "The Department of Justice is a disgrace," charged the founder of an organization for family members of workers killed on the job. One possible explanation for this low conviction rate is that the crime in cases like these is generally a misdemeanor, not a felony, and the DOJ generally tries to focus its attention on felony cases. Given this information, what implications do you think this has for how employers and their managers should manage their safety programs, and why do you take that position?

5. A 315-foot-tall, 2-million-pound crane collapsed on a construction site in East Toledo, Ohio, killing four ironworkers. Do you think catastrophic failures like this are avoidable? If so, what steps would you suggest the general contractor take to avoid a disaster like this?

EXPERIENTIAL EXERCISE

How Safe Is My University?

Purpose: The purpose of this exercise is to give you practice in identifying unsafe conditions.

Required Understanding: You should be familiar with material covered in this chapter, particularly that on unsafe conditions and that in Figures 16-5 (page 541), 16-6 (pages 542–544), and 16-8 (pages 566–569).

How to Set Up the Exercise/Instructions:

Divide the class into groups of four. Assume that each group is a safety committee retained by your college's or university's safety engineer to identify and report on any possible unsafe conditions in and around the school building. Each group will spend about 45 minutes in and around the building you are now in for the purpose of identifying and listing possible unsafe conditions. (Make use of the checklists in Figures 16-5, 16-6, and 16-8.)

Return to the class in about 45 minutes. A spokesperson for each group should list on the board the unsafe conditions you have identified. How many were there? Do you think these also violate OSHA standards? How would you go about checking?

GENERAL

OK / ACTION NEEDED

1. Is the required OSHA workplace poster displayed in your place of business as required where all employees are likely to see it? ☐ ☐
2. Are you aware of the requirement to report all workplace fatalities and any serious accidents (where five or more are hospitalized) to a federal or state OSHA office within 48 hours? ☐ ☐
3. Are workplace injury and illness records being kept as required by OSHA? ☐ ☐
4. Are you aware that the OSHA annual summary of workplace injuries and illnesses must be posted by February 1 and must remain posted until March 1? ☐ ☐
5. Are you aware that employers with 10 or fewer employees are exempt from the OSHA record-keeping requirements, unless they are part of an official BLS or state survey and have received specific instructions to keep records? ☐ ☐
6. Have you demonstrated an active interest in safety and health matters by defining a policy for your business and communicating it to all employees? ☐ ☐
7. Do you have a safety committee or group that allows participation of employees in safety and health activities? ☐ ☐
8. Does the safety committee or group meet regularly and report, in writing, its activities? ☐ ☐
9. Do you provide safety and health training for all employees requiring such training, and is it documented? ☐ ☐
10. Is one person clearly in charge of safety and health activities? ☐ ☐
11. Do all employees know what to do in emergencies? ☐ ☐
12. Are emergency telephone numbers posted? ☐ ☐
13. Do you have a procedure for handling employee complaints regarding safety and health? ☐ ☐

WORKPLACE

ELECTRICAL WIRING, FIXTURES, AND CONTROLS

OK / ACTION NEEDED

Develop your own checklist.

These are only sample questions.

1. Are your workplace electricians familiar with the requirements of the National Electrical Code (NEC)? ☐ ☐
2. Do you specify compliance with the NEC for all contract electrical work? ☐ ☐
3. If you have electrical installations in hazardous dust or vapor areas, do they meet the NEC for hazardous locations? ☐ ☐
4. Are all electrical cords strung so they do not hang on pipes, nails, hooks, etc.? ☐ ☐
5. Is all conduit, BX cable, etc., properly attached to all supports and tightly connected to junction and outlet boxes? ☐ ☐
6. Is there no evidence of fraying on any electrical cords? ☐ ☐
7. Are rubber cords kept free of grease, oil, and chemicals? ☐ ☐
8. Are metallic cable and conduit systems properly grounded? ☐ ☐
9. Are portable electric tools and appliances grounded or double insulated? ☐ ☐
10. Are all ground connections clean and tight? ☐ ☐
11. Are fuses and circuit breakers the right type and size for the load on each circuit? ☐ ☐
12. Are all fuses free of "jumping" with pennies or metal strips? ☐ ☐
13. Do switches show evidence of overheating? ☐ ☐
14. Are switches mounted in clean, tightly closed metal boxes? ☐ ☐
15. Are all electrical switches marked to show their purpose? ☐ ☐
16. Are motors clean and kept free of excessive grease and oil? ☐ ☐
17. Are motors properly maintained and provided with adequate overcurrent protection? ☐ ☐
18. Are bearings in good condition? ☐ ☐
19. Are portable lights equipped with proper guards? ☐ ☐
20. Are all lamps kept free of combustible material? ☐ ☐
21. Is your electrical system checked periodically by someone competent in the NEC? ☐ ☐

FIGURE 16-8 Self-Inspection Safety and Health Checklist

EXITS AND ACCESS

OK | ACTION NEEDED | Develop your own checklist.

1. Are all exits visible and unobstructed? ☐ ☐
2. Are all exits marked with a readily visible sign that is properly illuminated? ☐ ☐
3. Are there sufficient exits to ensure prompt escape in case of emergency? ☐ ☐
4. Are areas with restricted occupancy posted and is access/egress controlled by persons specifically authorized to be in those areas? ☐ ☐
5. Do you take special precautions to protect employees during construction and repair operations? ☐ ☐

These are only sample questions.

FIRE PROTECTION

OK | ACTION NEEDED

1. Are portable fire extinguishers provided in adequate number and type? ☐ ☐
2. Are fire extinguishers inspected monthly for general condition and operability and noted on the inspection tag? ☐ ☐
3. Are fire extinguishers recharged regularly and properly noted on the inspection tag? ☐ ☐
4. Are fire extinguishers mounted in readily accessible locations? ☐ ☐
5. If you have interior standpipes and valves, are these inspected regularly? ☐ ☐
6. If you have a fire alarm system, is it tested at least annually? ☐ ☐
7. Are employees periodically instructed in the use of extinguishers and fire protection procedures? ☐ ☐
8. If you have outside private fire hydrants, were they flushed within the last year and placed on a regular maintenance schedule? ☐ ☐
9. Are fire doors and shutters in good operating condition? ☐ ☐
   Are they unobstructed and protected against obstruction? ☐ ☐
10. Are fusible links in place? ☐ ☐
11. Is your local fire department well acquainted with your plant, location, and specific hazards? ☐ ☐
12. Automatic sprinklers:
    Are water control valves, air, and water pressures checked weekly? ☐ ☐
    Are control valves locked open? ☐ ☐
    Is maintenance of the system assigned to responsible persons or a sprinkler contractor? ☐ ☐
    Are sprinkler heads protected by metal guards where exposed to mechanical damage? ☐ ☐
    Is proper minimum clearance maintained around sprinkler heads? ☐ ☐

HOUSEKEEPING AND GENERAL WORK ENVIRONMENT

OK | ACTION NEEDED

1. Is smoking permitted in designated "safe areas" only? ☐ ☐
2. Are NO SMOKING signs prominently posted in areas containing combustibles and flammables? ☐ ☐
3. Are covered metal waste cans used for oily and paint-soaked waste? ☐ ☐
   Are they emptied at least daily? ☐ ☐
4. Are paint spray booths, dip tanks, etc., and their exhaust ducts cleaned regularly? ☐ ☐
5. Are stand mats, platforms, or similar protection provided to protect employees from wet floors in wet processes? ☐ ☐
6. Are waste receptacles provided and are they emptied regularly? ☐ ☐
7. Do your toilet facilities meet the requirements of applicable sanitary codes? ☐ ☐
8. Are washing facilities provided? ☐ ☐
9. Are all areas of your business adequately illuminated? ☐ ☐
10. Are floor load capacities posted in second floors, lofts, storage areas, etc.? ☐ ☐
11. Are floor openings provided with toe boards and railings or a floor hole cover? ☐ ☐
12. Are stairways in good condition with standard railings provided for every flight having four or more risers? ☐ ☐
13. Are portable wood ladders and metal ladders adequate for their purpose, in good condition, and provided with secure footing? ☐ ☐
14. If you have fixed ladders, are they adequate, and are they in good condition and equipped with side rails or cages or special safety climbing devices, if required? ☐ ☐
15. For loading docks:
    Are dockplates kept in serviceable condition and secured to prevent slipping? ☐ ☐
    Do you have means to prevent car or truck movement when dockplates are in place? ☐ ☐

FIGURE 16-8 (Continued)

(Continued)

MACHINES AND EQUIPMENT

OK / ACTION NEEDED

1. Are all machines or operations that expose operators or other employees to rotating parts, pinch points, flying chips, particles, or sparks adequately guarded?
2. Are mechanical power transmission belts and pinch points guarded?
3. Is exposed power shafting less than 7 feet from the floor guarded?
4. Are hand tools and other equipment regularly inspected for safe condition?
5. Is compressed air used for cleaning reduced to less than 30 psi?
6. Are power saws and similar equipment provided with safety guards?
7. Are grinding wheel tool rests set to within $1/8$ inch or less of the wheel?
8. Is there any system for inspecting small hand tools for burred ends, cracked handles, etc.?
9. Are compressed gas cylinders examined regularly for obvious signs of defects, deep rusting, or leakage?
10. Is care used in handling and storing cylinders and valves to prevent damage?
11. Are all air receivers periodically examined, including the safety valves?
12. Are safety valves tested regularly and frequently?
13. Is there sufficient clearance from stoves, furnaces, etc., for stock, woodwork, or other combustible materials?
14. Is there clearance of at least 4 feet in front of heating equipment involving open flames, such as gas radiant heaters, and fronts of firing doors of stoves, furnaces, etc.?
15. Are all oil and gas fired devices equipped with flame failure controls that will prevent flow of fuel if pilots or main burners are not working?
16. Is there at least a 2-inch clearance between chimney brickwork and all woodwork or other combustible materials?
17. For welding or flame cutting operations:
    Are only authorized, trained personnel permitted to use such equipment?
    Have operators been given a copy of operating instructions and asked to follow them?
    Are welding gas cylinders stored so they are not subjected to damage?
    Are valve protection caps in place on all cylinders not connected for use?
    Are all combustible materials near the operator covered with protective shields or otherwise protected?
    Is a fire extinguisher provided at the welding site?
    Do operators have the proper protective clothing and equipment?

Develop your own checklist.

These are only sample questions.

MATERIALS

OK / ACTION NEEDED

1. Are approved safety cans or other acceptable containers used for handling and dispensing flammable liquids?
2. Are all flammable liquids that are kept inside buildings stored in proper storage containers or cabinets?
3. Do you meet OSHA standards for all spray painting or dip tank operations using combustible liquids?
4. Are oxidizing chemicals stored in areas separate from all organic material except shipping bags?
5. Do you have an enforced NO SMOKING rule in areas for storage and use of hazardous materials?
6. Are NO SMOKING signs posted where needed?
7. Is ventilation equipment provided for removal of air contaminants from operations such as production grinding, buffing, spray painting and/or vapor degreasing, and is it operating properly?
8. Are protective measures in effect for operations involved with x-rays or other radiation?
9. For lift truck operations:
    Are only trained personnel allowed to operate forklift trucks?
    Is overhead protection provided on high lift rider trucks?
10. For toxic materials:
    Are all materials used in your plant checked for toxic qualities?
    Have appropriate control procedures such as ventilation systems, enclosed operations, safe handling practices, proper personal protective equipment (such as respirators, glasses or goggles, gloves, etc.) been instituted for toxic materials?

FIGURE 16-8 (Continued)

Develop your own checklist.

These are only sample questions.

EMPLOYEE PROTECTION

	OK	ACTION NEEDED
1. Is there a hospital, clinic, or infirmary for medical care near your business?	☐	☐
2. If medical and first-aid facilities are not nearby, do you have one or more employees trained in first aid?	☐	☐
3. Are your first-aid supplies adequate for the type of potential injuries in your work-place?	☐	☐
4. Are there quick water flush facilities available where employees are exposed to corrosive materials?	☐	☐
5. Are hard hats provided and worn where any danger of falling objects exists?	☐	☐
6. Are protective goggles or glasses provided and worn where there is any danger of flying particles or splashing of corrosive materials?	☐	☐
7. Are protective gloves, aprons, shields, or other means provided for protection from sharp, hot, or corrosive materials?	☐	☐
8. Are approved respirators provided for regular or emergency use where needed?	☐	☐
9. Is all protective equipment maintained in a sanitary condition and readily available for use?	☐	☐
10. Where special equipment is needed for electrical workers, is it available?	☐	☐
11. When lunches are eaten on the premises, are they eaten in areas where there is no exposure to toxic materials, and not in toilet facility areas?	☐	☐
12. Is protection against the effect of occupational noise exposure provided when the sound levels exceed those shown in the OSHA noise standard?	☐	☐

FIGURE 16-8 (Continued)

APPLICATION CASE

THE NEW SAFETY AND HEALTH PROGRAM

At first glance, a dot-com company is one of the last places you'd expect to find potential safety and health hazards—or so the owners of LearnInMotion.com thought. There's no danger of moving machinery, no high-pressure lines, no cutting or heavy lifting, and certainly no forklift trucks. However, there are safety and health problems.

In terms of accident-causing conditions, for instance, the one thing dot-com companies have are cables and wires. There are cables connecting the computers to screens and to the servers, and in many cases separate cables running from some computers to separate printers. There are 10 telephones in this particular office, all on 15-foot phone lines that always seem to be snaking around chairs and tables. There is, in fact, an astonishing amount of cable considering this is an office with fewer so-called wireless connections and with fewer than 10 employees. When the installation specialists wired the office (for electricity, high-speed cable, phone lines, burglar alarms, and computers), they estimated they used well over 5 miles of cables of one sort or another. Most of these are hidden in the walls or ceilings, but many of them snake their way from desk to desk, and under and over doorways. Several employees have tried to reduce the nuisance of having to trip over wires whenever they get up by putting their plastic chair pads over the wires closest to them. However, that still leaves many wires unprotected. In other cases, they brought in their own packing tape and tried to tape down the wires in those spaces where they're particularly troublesome, such as across doorways.

The cables and wires are only one of the more obvious potential accident-causing conditions. The firm's programmer, before he left the firm, had tried to repair the main server while the unit was still electrically alive. To this day, they're not sure exactly where he stuck the screwdriver, but the result was that he was "blown across the room," as one manager put it. He was all right, but it was still a scare. And while they haven't received any claims yet, every employee spends hours at his or her computer, so carpal tunnel syndrome is a risk, as are a variety of other problems such as eyestrain and strained backs.

One recent accident particularly scared the owners. The firm uses independent contractors to deliver the firm's book- and DVD-based courses in New York and two other cities. A delivery person was riding his bike east at the intersection of Second Avenue and East 64th Street in New York when he was struck by a car going south on Second Avenue. Luckily, he was not hurt, but the bike's front wheel was wrecked, and the narrow escape got the firm's two owners, Mel and Jennifer, thinking about their lack of a safety program.

It's not just the physical conditions that concern the two owners. They also have some concerns about potential health problems such as job stress and burnout. Although the business may be (relatively) safe with respect to physical conditions, it is also relatively stressful in terms of the demands it makes in hours and deadlines. It is not at all unusual for employees to get to work by 7:30 or 8 o'clock in the morning and to work through until 11 or 12 o'clock at night, at least 5 and sometimes 6 or 7 days per week.

The bottom line is that both Jennifer and Mel feel quite strongly that they need to do something about implementing a health and safety plan. Now, they want you, their management consultants, to help them do it. Here's what they want you to do for them.

Questions

1. Based upon your knowledge of health and safety matters and your actual observations of operations that are similar to theirs, make a list of the potential hazardous conditions employees and others face at LearnInMotion.com.

What should they do to reduce the potential severity of the top five hazards?

2. Would it be advisable for them to set up a procedure for screening out stress-prone or accident-prone individuals? Why or why not? If so, how should they screen them?

3. Write a short position paper on the subject, "What should we do to get all our employees to behave more safely at work?"

4. Based on what you know and on what other dot-coms are doing, write a short position paper on the subject, "What can we do to reduce the potential problems of stress and burnout in our company?"

CONTINUING CASE

CARTER CLEANING COMPANY

The New Safety Program

Employees' safety and health are very important matters in the laundry and cleaning business. Each facility is a small production plant in which machines, powered by high-pressure steam and compressed air, work at high temperatures washing, cleaning, and pressing garments, often under very hot, slippery conditions. Chemical vapors are produced continually, and caustic chemicals are used in the cleaning process. High-temperature stills are almost continually "cooking down" cleaning solvents in order to remove impurities so that the solvents can be reused. If a mistake is made in this process—like injecting too much steam into the still—a boilover occurs, in which boiling chemical solvent erupts out of the still and over the floor, and on anyone who happens to be standing in its way.

As a result of these hazards and the fact that chemically hazardous waste is continually produced in these stores, several government agencies (including OSHA and the Environmental Protection Agency) have instituted strict guidelines regarding the management of these plants. For example, posters have to be placed in each store notifying employees of their right to be told what hazardous chemicals they are dealing with and what the proper method for handling each chemical is. Special waste-management firms must be used to pick up and properly dispose of the hazardous waste.

A chronic problem the Carters (and most other laundry owners) have is the unwillingness on the part of the cleaning/spotting workers to wear safety goggles. Not all the chemicals they use require safety goggles, but some—like the hydrofluoric acid used to remove rust stains from garments—are very dangerous. The latter is kept in special plastic containers, since it dissolves glass. The problem is that wearing safety goggles can be troublesome. They are somewhat uncomfortable, and they become smudged easily and thus cut down on visibility. As a result, Jack has always found it almost impossible to get these employees to wear their goggles.

Questions

1. How should the firm go about identifying hazardous conditions that should be rectified? Use checklists such as those in Figures 16-5 and 16-8 to list at least 10 possible dry-cleaning store hazardous conditions.

2. Would it be advisable for the firm to set up a procedure for screening out accident-prone individuals? How should they do so?

3. How would you suggest the Carters get all employees to behave more safely at work? Also, how would you advise them to get those who should be wearing goggles to do so?

TRANSLATING STRATEGY INTO HR POLICIES & PRACTICES CASE

THE HOTEL PARIS CASE

The New Safety and Health Program

The Hotel Paris's competitive strategy is "To use superior guest service to differentiate the Hotel Paris properties, and to thereby increase the length of stay and return rate of guests, and thus boost revenues and profitability." HR manager Lisa Cruz must now formulate functional policies and activities that support this competitive strategy by eliciting the required employee behaviors and competencies.

Although "hazardous conditions" might not be the first thing that comes to mind when you think of hotels, Lisa Cruz knew that hazards and safety were in fact serious issues for the Hotel Paris. Indeed, everywhere you look—from the valets leaving car doors open on the driveways to slippery areas around the pools, to tens of thousands of pounds of ammonia, chlorine, and other caustic chemicals that the hotels use each year for cleaning and laundry—hotels provide a fertile environment for accidents. Obviously, hazardous conditions are bad for the Hotel Paris. They are inhumane for the workers. High accident rates probably reduce employee morale and thus service. And accidents raise the company's costs and reduce its profitability, for instance in terms of workers' compensation claims and absences. Lisa knew that she had to clean up her firm's occupational safety and health systems.

Lisa and the CFO reviewed their company's safety records, and what they found disturbed them deeply. In terms of every safety-related metric they could find, including accident costs per year, lost time due to accidents, workers' compensation per employee, and number of safety training programs per year, the Hotel Paris compared unfavorably with most other hotel chains and service firms. "Why, just in terms of extra workers' compensation costs, the Hotel Paris must be spending $500,000 a year more than we should be," said the CFO. And that didn't include lost time due to accidents, or the likely negative effect accidents had on employee

morale, or the cost of litigation (as when, for instance, one guest accidentally burned himself with chlorine that a pool attendant had left unprotected). The CFO authorized Lisa to develop a new safety and health program.

Questions

1. Based on what you read in this chapter, what's the first step the Hotel Paris should take as part of its new safety and health program, and why?
2. List 10 specific high-risk areas in a typical hotel you believe Lisa and her team should look at first, including examples of the safety or health hazards that they should look for there.
3. Give three specific examples of how Hotel Paris can use HR practices to improve its safety efforts.
4. Write a 1-page summary addressing the topic, "How improving safety and health at the Hotel Paris will contribute to us achieving our strategic goals."

KEY TERMS

Occupational Safety and Health Act of 1970, *533*

Occupational Safety and Health Administration (OSHA), *533*

occupational illness, *534*

citation, *535*

unsafe conditions, *539*

job hazard analysis, *543*

operational safety reviews, *545*

behavior-based safety, *548*

safety awareness program, *549*

burnout, *556*

ENDNOTES

1. "BP Oil Spill Timeline," guardian.co.uk, July 22, 2010, www.guardian.co.uk/environment/2010/jun/29/bp-oil-spill-timeline-deepwater-horizon, accessed June 29, 2011.
2. Figures for 2009. www.bls.gov/iif/oshwc/cfoi/cfch0008.pdf, accessed June 1, 2011.
3. All data refer to 2009. www.bls.gov/news.release/archives/osh_10212010.pdf, accessed June 1, 2011.
4. "BLS Likely Underestimating Injury and Illness Estimates," *Occupational Hazards*, May 2006, p. 16; Tahira Probst et al., "Organizational Injury Rate Underreporting: The Moderating Effect of Organizational Safety Climate," *Journal of Applied Psychology* 93, no. 5 (2008), pp. 1147–1154.
5. "Workers Rate Safety Most Important Workplace Issue," *EHS Today*, October 2010, p. 17.
6. See, for example, "Workplace Fatalities: The Impact on Coworkers," *Occupational Hazards*, March 2008, p. 18.
7. David Ayers, "Mapping Support for an E. H. S. Management System," *Occupational Hazards*, June 2006, pp. 53–54.
8. One study recently concluded that, "employee perceptions of the extent to which managers and supervisors are committed to workplace safety likely influence employee safety behavior and, subsequently, injuries." Jeremy Beus et al., "Safety Climate and Juries: An Examination of Theoretical and Empirical Relationships," *Journal of Applied Psychology* 95, no. 4 (2010), pp. 713–727.
9. Willie Hammer, *Occupational Safety Management and Engineering* (Upper Saddle River, NJ: Prentice Hall, 1985), pp. 62–63. See also "DuPont's 'STOP' Helps Prevent Workplace Injuries and Incidents," *Asia Africa Intelligence Wire*, May 17, 2004.
10. F. David Pierce, "Safety in the Emerging Leadership Paradigm," *Occupational Hazards*, June 2000, pp. 63–66. See also, for example, Josh Williams, "Optimizing the Safety Culture," *Occupational Hazards*, May 2008, pp. 45–49.
11. Sandy Smith, "Louisiana-Pacific Corp. Builds Safety into Everything It Does," *Occupational Hazards*, November 2007, pp. 41–42.
12. See the BP case in the Appendix for further discussion.
13. Donald Hantula et al., "The Value of Workplace Safety: A Time Based Utility Analysis Model," *Journal of Organizational Behavior Management* 21, no. 2 (2001), pp. 79–98.
14. Ibid. In a similar case, in 2008 the owner of a Brooklyn, New York, construction site was arrested for manslaughter when a worker died in a collapsed trench. Michael Wilson, "Manslaughter Charge in Trench Collapse," *The New York Times*, June 12, 2008, p. B1.
15. "A Safety Committee Man's Guide," Aetna Life and Casualty Insurance Company, Catalog 87684, pp. 17–21.
16. Based on "All About OSHA" (Washington, DC: U.S. Department of Labor, 1980), www.OSHA.gov, accessed January 19, 2008.
17. "OSHA Hazard Communication Standard Enforcement," *BNA Bulletin to Management*, February 23, 1989, p. 13. See also William Kincaid, "OSHA vs. Excellence in Safety Management," *Occupational Hazards*, December 2002, pp. 34–36.
18. "What Every Employer Needs to Know About OSHA Record Keeping," U.S. Department of Labor, Bureau of Labor Statistics (Washington, DC), Report 412–3, p. 3.
19. Arthur Sapper and Robert Gombar, "Nagging Problems under OSHA's New

Record-Keeping Rule," *Occupational Hazards*, March 2002, p. 58.

20. Brian Jackson and Jeffrey Myers, "Just When You Thought You Were Safe: OSHA Record-Keeping Violations," *Management Review*, May 1994, pp. 62–63; http://www.osha.gov/recordkeeping/index.html, accessed October 26, 2011.

21. "Supreme Court Says OSHA Inspectors Need Warrants," *Engineering News Record*, June 1, 1978, pp. 9–10; W. Scott Railton, "OSHA Gets Tough on Business," *Management Review* 80, no. 12 (December 1991), pp. 28–29; Steve Hollingsworth, "How to Survive an OSHA Inspection," *Occupational Hazards*, March 2004, pp. 31–33.

22. http://osha.gov/as/opa/oshafacts.html, accessed January 19, 2008; Edwin Foulke Jr., "OSHA's Evolving Role in Promoting Occupational Safety and Health," *EHS Today*, November 2008, pp. 44–49. Some believe that under the new Democratic administration of President Obama, OSHA is moving from voluntary programs back to increased attention on inspections.

23. www.osha.gov/Publications/osha2098. pdf+OSHA+inspection+priorities&hl=en&ct=clnk&cd=1&gl=us, accessed January 19, 2008.

24. www.OSHA.gov, accessed May 28, 2005, and http://osha.gov/pls/oshaweb/owadisp.show_document?p_table=NEWS_RELEASES&p_id=14883, accessed January 19, 2008.

25. This section is based on "All About OSHA," pp. 23–25. See also "OSHA Final Rule Expands Employees' Role in Consultations, Protects Employer Records," *BNA Bulletin to Management*, November 2, 2000, p. 345.

26. D. Diane Hatch and James Hall, "A Flurry of New Federal Regulations," *Workforce*, February 2001, p. 98.

27. For example, OSHA settled with Murphy Oil USA, with Murphy paying just over $179,000 in OSHA fines for a variety of violations, and OSHA proposed a penalty of $195,200 against a masonry contractor with a total of 21 violations. See "Enforcement Briefs," *Occupational Hazards*, March 2008, p. 13.

28. www.osha.gov/Publications/osha2098. pdf+OSHA+inspection+priorities&hl=en&ct=clnk&cd=1&gl=us, accessed January 19, 2008.

29. "Enforcement Activity Increased in 1997," *BNA Bulletin to Management*, January 29, 1998, p. 28. See also www.osha.gov/as/opa/osha-faq.html, accessed May 26, 2007.

30. "Enforcement Activity Increased."

31. For a discussion of how to deal with citations and proposed penalties, see, for example, Michael Taylor, "OSHA Citations and Proposed Penalties: How to Beat the Rap," *EHS Today*, December 2008, pp. 34–36.

32. Employers with high injury rates may also be subject to additional monitoring. For example, OSHA recently sent about 15,000 letters to employers telling them that their injury and illness rates were much higher than the national average. ("OSHA Sends 15,000 Letters to Employers with High Injury Rates and Offers Assistance," *BNA Bulletin to Management*, March 16, 2010, p. 83.

33. Patricia Poole, "When OSHA Knocks," *Occupational Hazards*, February 2008, pp. 59–61.

34. Robert Grossman, "Handling Inspections: Tips from Insiders," *HR Magazine*, October 1999, pp. 41–50; and "OSHA Inspections," OSHA, www.osha.gov/Publications/osha2098.pdf, accessed May 26, 2007.

35. These are based on James Nash, "The Top Ten Ways to Get into Trouble with OSHA," *Occupational Hazards*, December 2003, pp. 27–30.

36. Sean Smith, "OSHA Resources Can Help Small Businesses with Hazards," *Westchester County Business Journal*, August 4, 2003, p. 4. See also www.osha.gov/as/opa/osha-faq.html, accessed May 26, 2007.

37. Charles Chadd, "Managing OSHA Compliance: The Human Resources Issues," *Employee Relations Law Journal* 20, no. 1 (Summer 1994), p. 106; as noted in the text, asking employees what is prompting their resistance may head off the problem. See J. Heitman, "Gaining Their Trust," *Occupational Health & Safety*, 71 no. 5 (May 2002), pp. 22–24.

38. These are based on Roger Jacobs, "Employee Resistance to OSHA Standards: Toward a More Reasonable Approach," *Labor Law Journal*, April 1979, pp. 227–230. See also "Half of All Working Americans Feel Immune to Workplace Injuries," www.mem-ins.com/newsroom/pr072803.htm, accessed August 11, 2009.

39. Arthur Sapper, "The Oft-Missed Step: Documentation of Safety Discipline," *Occupational Hazards*, January 2006, p. 59.

40. "A Safety Committee Man's Guide," Aetna Life and Casualty Insurance Company, Catalog 87684. See also Dan Petersen, "The Barriers to Safety Excellence," *Occupational Hazards*, December 2000, pp. 37–39.

41. "Did This Supervisor Do Enough to Protect Trench Workers?" *Safety Compliance Letter*, October 2003, p. 9.

42. Julian Barling et al., "High-Quality Work, Job Satisfaction, and Occupational Injuries," *Journal of Applied Psychology* 88, no. 2 (2003), pp. 276–283.

43. "The Dawning of a New Era," *Workforce Management*, December 2010, p. 3.

44. For a discussion of this, see David Hofmann and Adam Stetzer, "A Cross-Level Investigation of Factors Influencing Unsafe Behaviors and Accidents," *Personnel Psychology* 49 (1996), pp. 307–308. See also David Hofman and Barbara Mark, "An Investigation of the Relationship Between Safety Climate and Medication Errors as Well as Other Nurse and Patient Outcomes," *Personnel Psychology* 50, no. 9 (2006), pp. 847–869.

45. Duane Schultz and Sydney Schultz, *Psychology and Work Today* (Upper Saddle River, NJ: Prentice Hall, 2002), p. 332.

46. Robert Pater and Robert Russell, "Drop That 'Accident Prone' Tag: Look for Causes Beyond Personal Issues," *Industrial Safety and Hygiene News* 38, no. 1 (January 2004), p. 50, http://findarticles.com/p/articles/mi_hb5992/is_200401/ai_n24195869/, accessed August 11, 2009.

47. Discussed in Douglas Haaland, "Who's the Safest Bet for the Job? Find Out Why the Fun Guy in the Next Cubicle May Be the Next Accident Waiting to Happen," *Security Management* 49, no. 2 (February 2005), pp. 51–57.

48. "Thai Research Points to Role of Personality in Road Accidents," www.driveandstayalive.com/info%20section/news/individual%20news%20articles/x_050204_personality-in-crash-causation_thailand.htm, February 2, 2005, accessed August 11, 2009; Donald Bashline et al., "Bad Behavior: Personality Tests Can Help Underwriters Identify High-Risk Drivers," *Best's Review* 105, no. 12 (April 2005), pp. 63–64.

49. Todd Nighswonger, "Threat of Terror Impacts Workplace Safety," *Occupational Hazards*, July 2002, pp. 24–26.

50. Michael Blotzer, "Safety by Design," *Occupational Hazards*, May 1999, pp. 39–40; and www.designsafe.com/dsesoftware.php, accessed May 26, 2007.

51. Susannah Figura, "Don't Slip Up on Safety," *Occupational Hazards*, November 1996, pp. 29–31. See also Russ Wood, "Defining the Boundaries of Safety," *Occupational Hazards*, January 2001, pp. 41–43.

52. See, for example, Laura Walter, "What's in a Glove?" *Occupational Hazards*, May 2008, pp. 35–36.

53. Donald Groce, "Keep the Gloves On!" *Occupational Hazards*, June 2008, pp. 45–47.

54. www.osha.gov/Publications/osha3071.pdf, accessed, April 21, 2011.

55. www-ns.iaea.org/reviews/op-safety-reviews.asp, accessed April 21, 2011.

56. For example, when asked what accounted for injuries such as cuts and lacerations, contusions, and chemical exposure at their facilities, most employees concluded either that workers were not wearing the proper protective equipment or had been given the wrong protection for the task. Brian Perry, "Don't Invite an OSHA Citation with Lower Quality PPE," *EHS Today*, January 2011, p. 23.

57. James Zeigler, "Protective Clothing: Exploring the Wearability Issue," *Occupational Hazards*, September 2000, pp. 81–82.

58. Sandy Smith, "Protective Clothing and the Quest for Improved Performance," *Occupational Hazards*, February 2008, pp. 63–66.

59. Tim Andrews, "Getting Employees Comfortable with PPE," *Occupational Hazards*,

January 2000, pp. 35–38. Note that personal protective equipment can backfire. As one expert says, "making a job safer with machine guards or PPE lowers people's risk perceptions and thus can lead to an increase in at-risk behavior." Therefore, also train employees not to let their guard down. E. Scott Geller, "The Thinking and Seeing Components of People-Based Safety," *Occupational Hazards*, December 2006, pp. 38–40.

60. Laura Walter, "FR Clothing: Leaving Hazards in the Dust," *EHS Today*, January 2010, pp. 20–22.

61. Sandy Smith, "Protecting Vulnerable Workers," *Occupational Hazards*, April 2004, pp. 25–28.

62. Katherine Torres, "Challenges in Protecting a Young Workforce," *Occupational Hazards*, May 2006, pp. 24–27.

63. J. P. Sankpill, "A Clear Vision for Eye and Face Protection," *EHS Today*, November 2010, p. 29.

64. See, for instance, Laura Walter, "Training the Older Worker," *EHS Today*, February 2011, p. 39.

65. Robert Pater, "Boosting Safety with an Aging Workforce," *Occupational Hazards*, March 2006, p. 24.

66. Michael Silverstein, M.D., "Designing the Age Friendly Workplace," *Occupational Hazards*, December 2007, pp. 29–31.

67. Elizabeth Rogers and William Wiatrowski, "Injuries, Illnesses, and Fatalities Among Older Workers," *Monthly Labor Review* 128, no. 10 (October 2005), pp. 24–30.

68. "The Complete Guide to Personal Protective Equipment," *Occupational Hazards*, January 1999, pp. 49–60. See also Edwin Zalewski, "Noise Control: It's More Than Just Earplugs: OSHA Requires Employers to Evaluate Engineering and Administrative Controls Before Using Personal Protective Equipment," *Occupational Hazards* 68, no. 9 (September 2006), p. 48(3). You can find videos about personal protective products at "SafetyLive TV" at www.occupationalhazards.com, accessed March 14, 2009.

69. Robert Pater and Ron Bowles, "Directing Attention to Boost Safety Performance," *Occupational Hazards*, March 2007, pp. 46–48.

70. Jimi Michalscheck, "The Basics of Lock Out/Tag Out Compliance: Creating an Effective Program," *EHS Today*, January 2010, pp. 3–37.

71. Mike Carlson, "Machine Safety Solutions for Protecting Employees and Safeguarding Against Machine Hazards," *EHS Today*, July 2009, p. 24.

72. Geller, "The Thinking and Seeing Components of People-Based Safety."

73. William Kincaid, "10 Habits of Effective Safety Managers," *Occupational Hazards*, November 1996, pp. 41–43. See also Sandy Smith, "Breakthrough Safety Management," *Occupational Hazards*, June 2004, p. 43.

74. Gerald Borofsky, Michelle Bielema, and James Hoffman, "Accidents, Turnover, and the Use of a Preemployment Screening Inventory: Further Contributions to the Validation of the Employee Reliability Inventory," *Psychological Reports*, 1993, pp. 1067–1076; http://www.ramsaycorp.com/catalog/view/?productid=208, accessed October 26, 2011.

75. Ibid., p. 1072. See also Keith Rosenblum, "The Companion Solution to Ergonomics: Pretesting for the Job," *Risk Management* 50, no 11 (November 2003), p. 26(6).

76. Dan Hartshorn, "The Safety Interview," *Occupational Hazards*, October 1999, pp. 107–111.

77. Gaye Reese and Joy Waltemath, *Workers' Compensation Manual for Managers and Supervisors: A Guide to Effective Workers' Compensation Management* (Chicago, IL: CCH Incorporated, 1996), pp. 22–23; and J. Greenwald, "Safety Concern Doesn't Bar Claim for Hiring Bias," *Business Insurance*, 42 no. 28 (July 14 2008), pp. 3–6.

78. John Rekus, "Is Your Safety Training Program Effective?" *Occupational Hazards*, August 1999, pp. 37–39; see also, http://www.osha.gov/Publications/osha2254.pdf, accessed October 25, 2011.

79. Laura Walter, "Surfing for Safety," *Occupational Hazards*, July 2008, pp. 23–29.

80. Michael Burke et al., "The Dread Factor: How Hazards and Safety Training Influence Learning and Performance," *Journal of Applied Psychology* 96, no. 1 (2011), pp. 46–70.

81. James Nash, "Rewarding the Safety Process," *Occupational Hazards*, March 2000, pp. 29–34.

82. Quoted in Josh Cable, "Seven Suggestions for a Successful Safety Incentives Program," *Occupational Hazards* 67, no. 3 (March 2005), pp. 39–43. See also Jill Bishop, "Create a Safer Work Environment by Bridging the Language and Culture Gap," *EHS Today*, March 2009, pp. 42–44.

83. See, for example, Ron Bruce, "Online from Kazakhstan to California," *Occupational Hazards*, June 2008, pp. 61–65.

84. Michael Blotzer, "PDA Software Offers Auditing Advances," *Occupational Hazards*, December 2001, p. 11. See also Erik Andersen "Automating Health & Safety Processes Creates Value," *Occupational Hazards*, April 2008, pp. 53–63.

85. Jennifer Nahrgang et al., "Safety at Work: A Meta-Analytic Investigation of the Link Between Job Demands, Job Resources, Burnout, Engagement, and Safety Outcomes," *Journal of Applied Psychology* 96, no. 1 (2011), p. 86.

86. See, for example, Cable, "Seven Suggestions for a Successful Safety Incentive Program." See also J. M. Saidler, "Gift Cards Make Safety Motivation Simple," *Occupational Health & Safety* 78, no. 1 (January 2009), pp. 39–40.

87. Don Williamson and Jon Kauffman, "From Tragedy to Triumph: Safety Grows Wings at Golden Eagle," *Occupational Hazards*, February 2006, pp. 17–25; and www.tsocorp.com/TSOCorp/SocialResponsibility/HealthandSafety/HealthandSafety, accessed June 30, 2011.

88. See, for example, Josh Cable, "Safety Incentives Strategies," *Occupational Hazards* 67, no. 4 (April 2005), p. 37; Geller, "The Thinking and Seeing Components of People-Based Safety."

89. James Nash, "Construction Safety: Best Practices in Training Hispanic Workers," *Occupational Hazards*, February 2004, pp. 35–38.

90. Ibid., p. 37.

91. Judi Komaki, Kenneth Barwick, and Lawrence Scott, "A Behavioral Approach to Occupational Safety: Pinpointing and Reinforcing Safe Performance in a Food Manufacturing Plant," *Journal of Applied Psychology* 63 (August 1978), pp. 434–445. See also Anat Arkin, "Incentives to Work Safely," *Personnel Management* 26, no. 9 (September 1994), pp. 48–52; Peter Makin and Valerie Sutherland, "Reducing Accidents Using a Behavioral Approach," *Leadership and Organizational Development Journal* 15, no. 5 (1994), pp. 5–10; Sandy Smith, "Why Cash Isn't King," *Occupational Hazards*, March 2004, pp. 37–38.

92. Stan Hodson and Tim Gordon, "Tenneco's Drive to Become Injury Free," *Occupational Hazards*, May 2000, pp. 85–87. For another example, see Terry Mathis, "Lean Behavior-Based Safety," *Occupational Hazards*, May 2005, pp. 33–34.

93. Tim McDaniel, "Employee Participation: A Vehicle for Safety by Design," *Occupational Hazards*, May 2002, pp. 71–76.

94. For another good example, see Christopher Chapman, "Using Kaizen to Improve Safety and Ergonomics," *Occupational Hazards*, February 2006, pp. 27–29.

95. Lisa Cullen, "Safety Committees: A Smart Business Decision," *Occupational Hazards*, May 1999, pp. 99–104. See also www.osha.gov/Publications/osha2098.pdf, accessed May 26, 2007; and D. Kolman, "Effective Safety Committees," *Beverage Industry* 100, no. 3 (March 2009), pp. 63–65.

96. www.aihaaps.ca/palm/occhazards.html, accessed April 26, 2009.

97. Michael Blotzer, "PDA Software Offers Auditing Advances," *Occupational Hazards*, December 2001, p. 11.

98. Thomas Krause, "Steps in Safety Strategy: Executive Decision-Making & Metrics," *EHS Today*, September 2009, p. 24.

99. Note that the vast majority of workers' injury-related deaths occur not at work, but when the employees are off the job, often at home. More employers, including Johnson & Johnson, are therefore implementing safety campaigns encouraging employees to apply safe practices at home, as well as at work. Katherine Torres, "Safety Hits Home," *Occupational Hazards*, July 2006, pp. 19–23.

100. Michele Campolieti and Douglas Hyatt, "Further Evidence on the 'Monday Effect' in Workers' Compensation," *Industrial and Labor Relations Review* 59, no. 3 (April 2006), pp. 438–450.

101. See, for example, Rob Wilson, "Five Ways to Reduce Workers' Compensation Claims," *Occupational Hazards*, December 2005, pp. 43–46.

102. "Strict Policies Mean Big Cuts in Premiums," *Occupational Hazards*, May 2000, p. 51.

103. "Workers Comp Research Provides Insight into Curbing Health Care Costs," *EHS Today*, February 2010, p. 18.

104. See, for example, Reese and Waltemath *Workers' Compensation Manual for Managers and Supervisors*, pp. 36–39.

105. Donna Clendenning, "Taking a Bite Out of Workers' Comp Costs," *Occupational Hazards*, September 2000, pp. 85–86.

106. This is based on Paul Puncochar, "The Science and Art to Identifying Workplace Hazards," *Occupational Hazards*, September 2003, pp. 50–54.

107. Ibid., p. 52.

108. Sandy Smith, "SARS: What Employers Need to Know," *Occupational Hazards*, July 2003, pp. 33–35.

109. Gareth Evans, "Wireless Monitoring for a Safe Indoor Environment," *EHS Today*, December 2010, pp. 35–39.

110. Based on the report "Workplace Screening and Brief Intervention: What Employers Can and Should Do About Excessive Alcohol Use," www.ensuringsolutions.org/resources/resources_show.htm?doc_id=67 3239, accessed August 11, 2009.

111. "Employers Can Play Key Role in Preventing Painkiller Abuse, But Many Remain Reluctant," *BNA Bulletin to Management*, February 15, 2011, p. 49.

112. "15% of Workers Drinking, Drunk, or Hungover While at Work, According to New University Study," *BNA Bulletin to Management*, January 24, 2006, p. 27.

113. Samuel Bacharach et al.,"Alcohol Consumption and Workplace Absenteeism: The Moderating Effect of Social Support," *Journal of Applied Psychology* 95, no. 2 (2010), pp. 334–348.

114. Teresa Long, "Intexicated Drivers and Employer Liability," *EHS Today*, September 2009, pp. 22–23.

115. See, for example, Kathryn Tyler, "Happiness from a Bottle?" *HR Magazine*, May 2002, pp. 30–37.

116. "New Jersey Union Takes on Mandatory Random Drug Tests," *Record* (Hackensack, NJ), January 2, 2008.

117. Diane Cadrain,"Are Your Employees' Drug Tests Accurate?" *HR Magazine*, January 2003, pp. 41–45.

118. Frank Lockwood et al., "Drug Testing Programs and Their Impact on Workplace Accidents: A Time Series Analysis," *Journal of Individual Employment Rights* 8, no. 4 (2000), pp. 295–306; and Sally Roberts, "Random Drug Testing Can Help Reduce Accidents for Construction Companies; Drug Abuse Blamed for Heightened Risk in the Workplace," *Business Insurance* 40 (October 23, 2006), p. 6.

119. William Current, "Pre-Employment Drug Testing," *Occupational Hazards*, July 2002, p. 56. See also William Current, "Improving Your Drug Testing ROI," *Occupational Health & Safety* 73, no. 4 (April 2004), pp. 40, 42, 44.

120. Beth Andrus, "Accommodating the Alcoholic Executive," *Society for Human Resource Management Legal Report*, January 2008, pp. 1, 4.

121. Eric Sundstrom et al., "Office Noise, Satisfaction, and Performance," *Environment and Behavior*, no. 2 (March 1994), pp. 195–222; and "Stress: How to Cope with Life's Challenges," *American Family Physician* 74, no. 8 (October 15, 2006).

122. "Failing to Tackle Stress Could Cost You Dearly," *Personnel Today,* September 12, 2006; www.sciencedaily.com/releases/2007/06/070604170722.htm, accessed November 3, 2009.

123. Tara Parker-Pope, "Time to Review Workplace Reviews?" *The New York Times*, May 18, 2010, pp. D5.

124. "Drug-Free Workplace: New Federal Requirements," *BNA Bulletin to Management*, February 9, 1989, pp. 1–4. Note that the Drug-Free Workplace Act does not mandate or mention testing employees for illegal drug use. See also www.dol.gov/elaws/drugfree.htm and www.dot.gov/ost/dapc (this site contains detailed guidelines on urine sampling, who's covered, etc.), both accessed May 26, 2007.

125. "Few Employers Addressing Workplace Stress, Watson Wyatt Surveys Find," *Compensation & Benefits Review*, May/June 2008, p. 12.

126. See, for example, Elizabeth Bernstein, "When a Coworker Is Stressed Out," *The Wall Street Journal*, August 26, 2008, pp. B1, B2.

127. Karl Albrecht, *Stress and the Manager* (Englewood Cliffs, NJ: Spectrum, 1979). For a discussion of the related symptoms of depression, see James Krohe Jr., "An Epidemic of Depression?" *Across-the-Board*, September 1994, pp. 23–27; and Todd Nighswonger, "Stress Management," *Occupational Hazards*, September 1999, p. 100.

128. Sabine Sonnentag et al., "'Did You Have a Nice Evening?' A Day-Level Study on Recovery Experiences, Sleep, and Affect," *Journal of Applied Psychology* 93, no. 3 (2008), pp. 674–684.

129. "Meditation Gives Your Mind Permanent Working Holiday; Relaxation Can Improve Your Business Decisions and Your Overall Health," discussed in *Investors Business Daily*, March 24, 2004, p. 89. See also "Meditation Helps Employees Focus, Relieve Stress," *BNA Bulletin to Management*, February 20, 2007, p. 63.

130. Kathryn Tyler, "Stress Management," *HR Magazine*, September 2006, pp. 79–82.

131. William Atkinson, "Turning Stress into Strength," *HR Magazine*, January 2011, p. 51.

132. "Going Head to Head with Stress," *Personnel Today*, April 26, 2005, p. 1.

133. See, for example, Christina Maslach and Michael Leiter, "Early Predictors of Job Burnout and Engagement," *Journal of Applied Psychology* 93, no. 3 (2008), pp. 498–512.

134. Christina Maslach and Michael Leiter, "Early Predictors of Job Burnout and Engagement," *Journal of Applied Psychology* 93, no. 3 (2008), pp. 498–512.

135. Mina Westman and Dov Eden, "Effects of a Respite from Work on Burnout: Vacation Relief and Fade-Out," *Journal of Applied Psychology* 82, no. 4 (1997), pp. 516–527; these results notwithstanding, more employers are endeavoring to provide more time off benefits o head off burnout. See for example, S. Shellenbarger, "Companies Retool Time-Off Policies to Prevent Burnout, Reward Performance," *Wall Street Journal*, (January 5, 2006), p. D1.

136. Westman and Eden, op cit., p. 516.

137. Ibid., p. 526. See also Charlotte Fritz and Sabine Sonnentag, "Recovery, Well-Being, and Performance-Related Outcomes: The Role of Workload and Vacation Experiences," *Journal of Applied Psychology* 91, no. 4 (July 2006), p. 936(10).

138. Sabine Sonnentag et al., "Staying Well and Engaged When Demands Are High: The Role of Psychological Detachment," *Journal of Applied Psychology* 95, no. 5 (2010), pp. 965–976.

139. Todd Nighswonger, "Depression: The Unseen Safety Risk," *Occupational Hazards*, April 2002, pp. 38–42.

140. Ibid., p. 40.

141. "Employers Must Move from Awareness to Action in Dealing with Worker Depression," *BNA Bulletin to Management*, April 29, 2004, p. 137.

142. See, for example, Felix Chima, "Depression and the Workplace: Occupational Social Work Development and Intervention," *Employee Assistance Quarterly* 19, no. 4 (2004), pp. 1–20.

143. Ibid.

144. www.OSHA.gov, downloaded May 28, 2005.

145. Anne Chambers, "Computer Vision Syndrome: Relief Is In Sight," *Occupational Hazards*, October 1999, pp. 179–184; and www.OSHA.gov/ETOOLS/computerworkstations/index.html, downloaded May 28, 2005.

146. Sandra Lotz Fisher, "Are Your Employees Working Ergosmart?," *Personnel Journal*, December 1996, pp. 91–92. See also www.cdc.gov/od/ohs/Ergonomics/compergo.htm, accessed May 26, 2007.

147. www.ninds.nih.gov/disorders/repetitive_motion/repetitive_motion.htm, accessed February 28, 2010.

148. Ronald Davis, "Exposure to Environmental Tobacco Smoke: Identifying and Protecting Those at Risk," *Journal of the American Medical Association*, December 9, 1998, pp. 147–148; see also Al Karr, "Lighting Up," *Safety and Health* 162, no. 3 (September 2000), pp. 62–66.

149. However, note that some experts believe that in some circumstances the EEOC might see a smoking addiction as similar to use of illegal drugs, and thus possibly covered by the ADA. "Policies to Not Hire Smokers Raise Privacy, Bias Issues," *BNA Bulletin to Management*, December 14, 2010, p. 399.

150. Steve Bates, "Where There Is Smoke, There Are Terminations: Smokers Fired to Save Health Costs," *HR Magazine* 50, no. 3 (March 2005), pp. 28–29.

151. Susan Wells, "Does Work Make You Fat?" *HR Magazine*, October 2010, p. 28.

152. Leonard Berry et al., "What's the Hard Return on Employee Wellness Programs?" *Harvard Business Review*, December 2010, p. 105.

153. Guy Toscano and Janice Windau, "The Changing Character of Fatal Work Injuries," *Monthly Labor Review*, October 1994, p. 17. See also Robert Grossman, "Bulletproof Practices," *HR Magazine*, November 2002, pp. 34–42; and Chuck Manilla, "How to Avoid Becoming a Workplace Violence Statistic," *Training & Development*, July 2008, pp. 60–64.

154. Kelly Gurchiek, "Workplace Violence on the Upswing," *HR Magazine*, July 2005, p. 27.

155. www.cdc.gov/ncipc/dvp/ipv_factsheet. pdf, accessed February 28, 2010.

156. Manon Mireille LeBlanc and E. Kevin Kelloway, "Predictors and Outcomes of Workplace Violence and Aggression," *Journal of Applied Psychology* 87, no. 3 (2002), pp. 444–453.

157. Kenneth Diamond, "The Gender-Motivated Violence Act: What Employers Should Know," *Employee Relations Law Journal* 25, no. 4 (Spring 2000), pp. 29–41.

158. Paul Viollis and Doug Kane, "At Risk Terminations: Protecting Employees, Preventing Disaster," *Risk Management Magazine* 52, no. 5 (May 2005), pp. 28–33.

159. "Workplace Violence: Sources and Solutions," *BNA Bulletin to Management*, November 4, 1993, p. 345. See also "Creating a Safer Workplace: Simple Steps Bring Results," *Safety Now*, September 2002, pp. 1–2; and L. Claussen, "Disgruntled and Dangerous," *Safety & Health* 180, no. 1 (July 2009), pp. 44–47.

160. "OSHA Addresses Top Homicide Risk," *BNA Bulletin to Management*, May 14, 1998, p. 148. See also www.osha.gov/Publications/osha3148.pdf, accessed May 26, 2007.

161. Jean Thilmany, "In Case of Emergency," *HR Magazine*, November 2007, pp. 79–82; Chuck Mannila, "How to Avoid Becoming a Workplace Violence Statistic," *Training & Development*, July 2008, pp. 60–64.

162. Scott Douglas and Mark Martinko, "Exploring the Role of Individual Differences in the Prediction of Workplace Aggression," *Journal of Applied Psychology* 86, no. 4 (2001), p. 554.

163. Dawn Anfuso, "Deflecting Workplace Violence," *Personnel Journal*, October 1994, pp. 66–77; M. J. Camardella, "Interview Questions to Avoid; Accommodations for Prospective Employees; Preventing Workplace Violence," *Employment Relations Today* 29, no. 1 (Spring 2002), pp. 103–109.

164. Alfred Feliu, "Workplace Violence and the Duty of Care: The Scope of an Employer's Obligation to Protect Against the Violent Employee," *Employee Relations Law Journal*, 20, no. 3 (Winter 1994–5), p. 395; Fay Hansen, "Burden of Proof," *Workforce Management* 89, no. 2 (February 2010), pp. 27–28, 30, 32–33.

165. Ibid., p. 395.

166. "Preventing Workplace Violence," *BNA Bulletin to Management*, June 10, 1993, p. 177. See also Paul Viollis and Doug Kane, "At-Risk Terminations: Protecting Employees, Preventing Disaster," *Risk Management* 52, no. 5 (May 2005), p. 28(5).

167. Quoted or paraphrased from Beverly Younger, "Violence Against Women in the Workplace," *Employee Assistance Quarterly* 9, no. 3/4 (1994), p. 177, and based on recommendations from Chris Hatcher. See also Viollis and Kane, "At-Risk Terminations.

168. Florida has passed a law giving employees the right to carry guns in cars parked at work. See "Right to Carry Guns in Cars Parked at Work Becomes Loaded Issue in Florida, Elsewhere," *BNA Bulletin to Management*, May 13, 2008, p. 153.

169. Feliu, "Workplace Violence," pp. 401–402.

170. Karl Aquino et al., "How Employees Respond to Personal Offense: Effect of Blame Attribution, Victim Status, and Offender Status on Revenge and Reconciliation in the Workplace," *Journal of Applied Psychology* 86, no. 1 (2001), pp. 52–59. See also M. Sandy Hershcovis et al., "Predicting Workplace Aggression: A Meta-Analysis," *Journal of Applied Psychology* 92, no. 1 (2007), pp. 228–238.

171. Eve Tahmincioglu, "Employers Maintaining Vigilance in the Face of Layoff Rage," *The New York Times*, August 1, 2001, pp. C1, C6.

172. Donna Rosato, "New Industry Helps Managers Fight Violence," *USA Today*, August 8, 1995, p. 1.

173. Helen Frank Bensimon, "What to Do About Anger in the Workplace," *Training & Development* 51, no. 9 (September 1997), pp. 28–32. See also Viollis and Kane, "At-Risk Terminations."

174. Shari Caudron, "Target HR," *Workforce*, August 1998, pp. 44–52.

175. Diane Cadrain, "And Stay Out! Using Restraining Orders Can Be an Effective and Proactive Way of Preventing Workplace Violence," *HR Magazine*, August 2002, pp. 83–86.

176. Feliu, "Workplace Violence," p. 393.

177. Louis P. DiLorenzo and Darren J. Carroll, "The Growing Menace: Violence in the Workplace," *New York State Bar* Journal, January 1995, p. 27; and Fay Hansen, "Burden of Proof," op cit.

178. This is based on "New Challenges for Health and Safety in the Workplace," *Workplace Visions* (Society for Human Resource Management), no. 3 (2003), pp. 2–4. See also J. L. Nash, "Protecting Chemical Plants from Terrorists: Opposing Views," *Occupational Hazards*, February 2004, pp. 18–20.

179. "Survey Finds Reaction to September 11 Attacks Spurred Companies to Prepare for Disasters," *BNA Bulletin to Management*, November 29, 2005, p. 377.

180. Sources of *external* risk include legal/regulatory, political, and business environment (economy, e-business, etc.). *Internal* risks include financial, strategic, operational (including safety and security), and integrity (embezzlement, theft, fraud, etc.). William Atkinson, "Enterprise Risk Management at Wal-Mart," www.rmmag.com/MGTemplate.cfm?Section=RMMagazine&NavMenuID=128&template=/Magazine/DisplayMagazines.cfm&MGPreview=1&Volume=50&IssueID=205&AID=2209&ShowArticle=1, accessed April 1, 2009.

181. "Focus on Corporate Security," *BNA HR Executive Series*, Fall 2001, p. 4.

182. Unless otherwise noted, the following including the six matters to address is based on Richard Maurer, "Keeping Your Security Program Active," *Occupational Hazards*, March 2003, pp. 49–52.

183. http://view.fdu.edu/default.aspx?id=3705, accessed February 28, 2010.

184. Maurer, "Keeping Your Security Program Active," p. 50.

185. Ibid.

186. Bill Roberts, "Are You Ready for Biometrics?" *HR Magazine*, March 2003, pp. 95–99.

187. Maurer, "Keeping Your Security Program Active," p. 52.

188. Craig Schroll, "Evacuation Planning: A Matter of Life and Death," *Occupational Hazards*, June 2002, pp. 49–51.

189. Maurer, op cit., p. 52; and Li Yuan et al., "Texting When There's Trouble," *The Wall Street Journal*, April 18, 2007, p. B1.

190. Louis Obdyke, "Investigating Security Breaches, Workplace Theft, and Employee Fraud," *Society for Human Resource Management Legal Report*, January–February 2003, pp. 1–2.

17

Managing Global Human Resources

Source: Shutterstock.

LEARNING OBJECTIVES

1. List the HR challenges of international business.

2. Illustrate with examples how intercountry differences affect HRM.

3. List and briefly describe the main methods for staffing global organizations.

4. Discuss some important issues to keep in mind in training, appraising, and compensating international employees.

5. Explain with examples how to implement a global human resource management program.

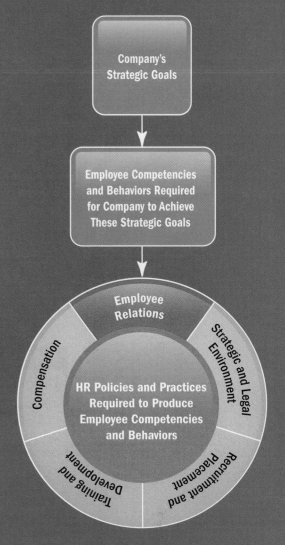

Walmart Stores, always resistant to unions, recently had a surprise. Opening stores in China at a fast clip, it tried to dissuade the local unions from organizing Walmart employees. However, the All China Federation of Trade Unions (ACFTU), with strong government backing, quickly established itself in several Walmart stores. At first, it seemed that the union would succeed in unionizing many Walmart Chinese workers. But Walmart's strategy has long included avoiding unions as one means of reducing costs, so the company was vigorously resisting.[1]

WHERE ARE WE NOW . . .

More managers and employers today find themselves managing people internationally. The purpose of this chapter is to improve your effectiveness at applying your human resource knowledge and skills when global issues are involved. The topics we'll discuss include the internationalization of business, intercountry differences affecting HR, improving international assignments through selection, and training and maintaining international employees.

Access a host of interactive learning aids at **www.mymanagementlab.com** to help strengthen your understanding of the chapter concepts.

1 List the HR challenges of international business.

The Manager's Global Challenge

With the globalization of the world economy, even small firms are discovering that success depends on marketing and managing abroad.[2] But expanding abroad requires putting in place management systems to control overseas activities. These systems include managerial controls, planning systems, and, of course, human resource management systems for recruiting, selecting, training, appraising, and compensating workers abroad.

Managing human resources internationally creates challenges. For one thing, differences in cultures and economic and legal systems influence employer HR practices from country to country. For example, "How should we appraise and pay our local employees?" "How should we deal with the unions in our offices abroad?" "How do we identify and get the right talent and skills to where we need them?" and "How do we spread state-of-the-art knowledge to our operations abroad?"[3]

Challenges like these don't just come from the vast distances involved (though this is important). The bigger issue is coping with the cultural, political, legal, and economic differences among countries. In China, for instance, government-backed unions are relatively powerful, and in Europe, firing an employee could take a year or more. The bottom line is that it's impossible to effectively manage human resource activities abroad without understanding how countries differ culturally, economically, and legally. The accompanying Strategic Context feature illustrates this.

THE STRATEGIC CONTEXT

Unionizing Walmart Stores in China

Walmart Stores' competitive strategy is to be retailing's low-cost leader, and avoiding unions has been one of its main tactics for keeping costs down. With more than 2.1 million employees,[4] Walmart wants to keep a tight reign on employee staffing, performance, wages, and benefits. Unions probably would drive up Walmart's labor costs, and impede its ability to make personnel changes.

With its powerful government-backed All-China Federation of Trade Unions, China's cultural, political, and labor relations and legal systems are a world away from what Walmart dealt with in America. Not surprisingly, therefore, several years ago the first trade union in Walmart China formed, followed by the firm's other stores.[5] Walmart China soon experienced the difference unions can make. The company offered three options—transfers to outlets in other cities, demotions, or leaving the company—to 54 local managers it wanted to transfer.[6] Not wanting to change, the China managers sprang into action. One led 11 colleagues to the local municipal federation of trade unions for assistance. Whatever they did, it worked. Walmart apparently halted its planned reshuffle. Walmart would definitely have to revise its HR strategy for China, and probably adjust its competitive strategy for China too.

2 Illustrate with examples how intercountry differences affect HRM.

ADAPTING HUMAN RESOURCE ACTIVITIES TO INTERCOUNTRY DIFFERENCES

Companies operating only within the United States generally have the luxury of dealing with a relatively limited set of economic, cultural, and legal variables. The United States is a capitalist, competitive society. And while the U.S. workforce reflects a multitude of cultural and ethnic backgrounds, shared values (such as an appreciation for democracy) help to blur cultural differences. Different states and municipalities certainly have their own employment laws. However, a basic federal framework helps produce a predictable set of legal guidelines regarding matters such as employment discrimination, labor relations, and safety and health.

A company operating multiple units abroad doesn't face such homogeneity. For example, minimum legally mandated holidays range from none in the United Kingdom to 5 weeks per year in Luxembourg. And while Italy has no formal

FIGURE 17-1 Critical Intercountry Differences That Influence International HR Practices

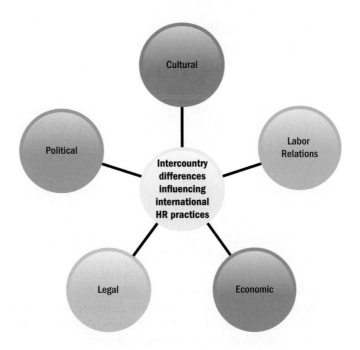

requirements for employee representatives on boards of directors, they're usually required in Denmark. The point is that managers have to be cognizant of and generally adapt their human resource policies and practices to the countries in which they're operating. Figure 17-1 sums up critical intercountry differences.

Cultural Factors

When Google founders Sergey Brin and Larry Page visited India a few years ago, they reportedly came across as "college backpackers."[7] They just seemed too informal, given their responsibilities for managing Google. Their experience illustrates the fact that countries differ widely in their *cultures*—in other words, in the basic values their citizens adhere to, and in how these values manifest themselves in the nation's arts, social programs, and ways of doing things.[8] Cultural differences manifest themselves in differences in how people from different countries think, act, and expect others to act. For example, in a study of about 330 managers from Hong Kong, Mainland China, and the United States, the U.S. managers tended to be most concerned with getting the job done. Chinese managers were most concerned with maintaining a harmonious environment. Hong Kong managers fell between these extremes.[9]

Employers need to adapt their HR practices to the cultures of the countries where they do business.

Source: Felipe Dupouy/Thinkstock.

THE HOFSTEDE STUDY A classic study by Professor Geert Hofstede illustrates other international cultural differences. For example, Hofstede says societies differ on five values, which he calls power distance, individualism, "masculinity," uncertainty avoidance, and long-term orientation. Thus, power distance represents the extent to which the less powerful members of institutions accept and expect an unequal distribution of power.[10] He concluded that acceptance of such inequality was higher in some countries (such as Mexico) than in others (such as Sweden).[11] In turn, such differences manifest themselves in different behaviors. To see how your country's culture compares with others, go to www.geert-hofstede.com/hofstede_dimensions.php.

Such cultural differences influence human resource policies and practices. For example, Americans' heavier emphasis on individuality may help to explain why European managers have more constraints, such as in dismissing workers.[12] As another example, in countries with a history of autocratic rule, employees often had to divulge information about their coworkers. Here, whistleblower rules, popular in America, are frowned upon.[13]

Economic Systems

Economists distinguish among market, planned, and mixed economies. In market economies (such as the United States), governments play a relatively restrained role in deciding things such as what will be produced and sold, at what prices. In planned economies (such as North Korea), the government decides and plans what to produce and sell, at what price. In mixed economies (such as China), many industries are still under direct government control, while others make pricing and production decisions based on market demand.

Differences in economic systems (and therefore in how "hands off" the government wants to be) tend to translate into differences in human resource management policies. For instance, eurozone countries tend to put more restrictions on things such as dismissing employees and allowable work hours per week. Portuguese workers average about 1,980 hours of work annually, while German workers average 1,648 hours. Labor costs also vary widely. For example, hourly compensation costs (in U.S. dollars) for production workers range from $2.92 in Mexico to $6.58 in Taiwan, $24.59 in the United States, $29.73 in the United Kingdom, and $37.66 in Germany.[14] The United Kingdom and Germany require substantial severance pay to departing employees, usually equal to at least 1 year's service in Germany.

Legal, Political, and Labor Relations Factors

Employers going abroad must be familiar with the labor law systems in the countries they're entering. For example, in India, companies with more than 100 workers must get government permission to fire anyone.[15] In Brazil, some labor laws stem from the labor code of pre–World War II Italy, and can be fantastically costly to employers.[16]

Legal differences blindside even sophisticated companies. After spending billions expanding into Germany, Walmart discovered that Germany's commercial laws discourage ads based on price comparisons. It soon left Germany.

As other examples, the U.S. practice of employment at will does not exist in Europe, where firing or laying off workers is usually expensive. And in many European countries, *work councils* replace the worker–management mediations typical in U.S. firms. *Work councils* are formal, employee-elected groups of worker representatives that meet monthly with managers to discuss topics ranging from no-smoking policies to layoffs.[17]

Codetermination is the rule in Germany and several other countries. **Codetermination** means employees have the legal right to a voice in setting company policies. Workers elect their own representatives to the supervisory board of the employer.[18] In the United States, by comparison, HR policies on most matters (such as wages and benefits) are set by the employer, or in negotiations with its labor unions.

Managing globally also requires monitoring political risks. *Political risks* "are any governmental actions or politically motivated events that could adversely affect the long run profitability or value of the firm."[19] For example, the president of Venezuela moved to nationalize his country's oil industries.

Ethics and Codes of Conduct

Employers also need to make sure their employees abroad are adhering to their firm's ethics codes. Doing so isn't easy. Exporting a firm's ethics rules requires more than having employees abroad use versions of its U.S. employee handbook. For example, few countries abroad adhere to "employment at will". Therefore even handbooks that say "we can fire employees at will" may not be enough to enable one to dismiss employees.[20] Instead of exporting the employee handbook, some recommend creating and distributing a global code of conduct.

Often, the employer's main concern is establishing global standards for adhering to U.S. laws that have cross-border impacts. For example, in 2011, IBM paid $10 million to settle accusations that it had bribed Chinese and South Korean officials to get $54 million in government contracts.[21] Such employers should set global policies on things like discrimination, harassment, bribery, and Sarbanes-Oxley.

HR Abroad Example: The European Union

Over the past four decades, the separate countries of the former European Community (EC) unified into a common market for goods, services, capital, and even labor called the *European Union (EU)*. Tariffs for goods moving across borders from one EU country to another generally disappeared, and employees (with some exceptions) now move freely between jobs in EU countries. The introduction of a single currency (the euro) further blurred differences.

Companies doing business in Europe must adjust their human resource policies and practices to EU directives, as well as to country-specific employment laws. The directives are basically EU-wide laws. The directives' objectives are binding on all member countries (although each country can implement the directives as they wish). For example, the EU directive on confirmation of employment requires employers to provide employees with written terms and conditions of their employment. However, these terms vary from country to country.[22] In England, a detailed written statement is required, including things like rate of pay, date employment began, and hours of work. Germany doesn't require a written contract, but it's still customary to have one specifying most particulars about the job.

This interplay of directives and country laws means that an employer's human resource practices must vary from country to country. For example:[23]

- **Minimum EU wages.** Most EU countries have minimum wage systems. Some set national limits. Others allow employers and unions to work out their own minimum wages.

- **Working hours.** The EU sets the workweek at 48 hours, but most EU countries set it at 40 hours a week.

- **Termination of employment.** Required notice periods when dismissing employees in Europe range from none in Spain to 2 months in Italy.

HR Abroad Example: China

For many years, employers inside and outside China relied on that country's huge workforce to provide products and services at very low cost. Part of the reason for the low labor cost was the relative lack of labor laws governing things like severance pay, minimum wages, and benefits.

Now that is changing. Several years ago, the People's Republic of China implemented its new labor contract law. This law adds numerous new employment protections for employees, and makes it correspondingly more expensive for employers in China to implement personnel actions such as layoffs. For example, multinational companies

codetermination
Employees have the legal right to a voice in setting company policies.

doing business in China argue that the new law will reduce employment flexibility, raise labor costs, and make it difficult to lay off employees by instituting new large severance package requirements.[24]

All employers in China deal with issues including problems retaining good employees and an increasingly active union movement. However, how they deal with these issues depends on the ownership of the firm. State-owned enterprises use fewer modern human resource management tools than do giant Chinese multi-nationals like Lenova, for instance. There are therefore wide variations in human resource management practices among companies in China, and between Chinese and Western firms.[25]

RECRUITING   Because of governmental constraints on migration and other legal constraints, it is relatively difficult to recruit, hire, and retain good employees. At least until recently, sporadic labor shortages were widespread and will likely return. China's Employment Contract Law requires, among many other things, that employers report the names, sexes, identification numbers, and contract terms for all employees they hire within 30 days of hiring to local labor bureaus.[26]

In China, recruiting effectiveness depends largely on non-recruitment human resource management issues. Employees are highly career oriented and gravitate toward employers that provide the best career advancement training and opportunities.[27] Firms like Siemens China, with impressive training and development programs, have the least difficulty attracting good candidates. Poaching employees is a serious matter in China. The employer must verify that the applicant is free to sign a new employment agreement.

SELECTION   The dominant employee selection method involves analyzing the applicant's résumé and then interviewing him or her. The ideal way to do this, as we saw in Chapter 6 (Interviewing), is to institute a structured interview process, as many of the foreign firms in China have done.

APPRAISING   Employee appraisal is particularly sensitive to the cultural realities in China. The appraisal therefore needs to follow the formalities of saving face and avoiding confrontational, tension-producing situations. In general, it's best to talk in terms of objective work data (as opposed to personal comments like "you're too slow").

COMPENSATION   Although many managers endorse performance-based pay in China, many employers, to preserve group harmony, make incentive pay a small part of the pay package. And, as in other parts of Asia, team incentives are advisable.[28]

STAFFING THE GLOBAL ORGANIZATION

3 List and briefly describe the main methods for staffing global organizations.

Employers' focus today is increasingly on managing human resource activities locally. In other words, their main concern is on selecting, training, appraising, and managing the in-country employees where they do business.

However, deciding whether to fill local positions with local versus expatriate ("imported") employees has been and continues to be a major concern. The process involves identifying and selecting the people who will fill the positions, and then placing them in those positions.

International Staffing: Home or Local?

Companies doing business internationally employ several types of international employees. *Locals* are citizens of the countries where they are working. **Expatriates ("expats")** are noncitizens of the countries in which they are working (an American working in France is an expat).[29] **Home-country nationals** are citizens of the country in which the multinational company has its headquarters (so an American working for GM's subsidiary in China is a home-country national, as well as an expat).

Third-country nationals are citizens of a country other than the parent or the host country—for example, a British executive working in the Tokyo branch of a U.S. multinational bank.[30] Expatriates still represent a minority of multinationals' managers. Locals fill most positions.[31]

USING LOCALS There are many reasons employers rely more on locals. For one thing, the cost of using expatriates is usually far greater than the cost of using local workers.[32] In one survey, employers reported a 21% attrition rate for expatriate employees, compared with an average of 10% for their general employee populations.[33] Local people may view the multinational as a "better citizen" if it uses local management talent; some governments even press for staffing with local management.[34] There may also be a fear that expatriates, knowing they're at the foreign subsidiary for only a few years, may overemphasize short-term results.[35] Some companies are surprised at what it costs to post someone abroad. Agilent Technologies routinely estimated that it cost about three times the expatriate's annual salary to keep the person abroad for 1 year. When Agilent outsourced its expatriate program, it discovered that the costs were much higher. The firm then dramatically reduced the number it sent abroad, from about 1,000 to 300 per year.[36]

It's also become more difficult to bring workers into the United States from abroad. Under rules now in effect, U.S. employers must try to recruit U.S. workers before filing foreign labor certification requests with the Department of Labor. In particular, employers must post open positions in the Department of Labor's job bank and (at least) run two Sunday newspaper advertisements before filing such requests.[37]

USING EXPATS Yet there are also reasons for using expatriates—either home-country or third-country nationals—for staffing subsidiaries. The main reason is usually that employers can't find local candidates with the required technical qualifications. Multinationals have also viewed a successful stint abroad as a required step in developing top managers. Control is another reason for using expatriates. The assumption is that home-country managers are already steeped in the firm's policies and culture, and thus more likely to apply headquarters' ways of doing things.

However, for the past 10 years or so the trend has definitely been toward using locals or other (non-expat) solutions. Posting expatriates abroad is expensive, security problems increasingly give potential expatriates' pause, returning expatriates often leave for other employers within a year or two of returning, educational facilities are turning out top-quality candidates abroad, and the recent global recession made the cost of posting employees abroad even more unattractive. As a result, new expatriate postings are not only down, but many employers are bringing them home early.[38] Another survey found that about 47% of U.S. multinationals were maintaining the size of their expat workforces; 18% were increasing it, and 35% were decreasing the number of expatriates.[39] The human resource team needs to control expat expenses, as the accompanying HR as a Profit Center explains.

HR AS A PROFIT CENTER

Reducing Expatriate Costs

Given the expense of sending employees (often, dozens or hundreds of employees) abroad for overseas assignments, the employer's human resource team plays a central role in controlling and reducing expatriate costs. A recent survey by Mercer (*Mercer's International Assignments Survey 2010*) shows some of the steps HR managers are taking to reduce these expenses. (Mercer provides consulting, outsourcing, and investment services to employers worldwide.)[40] First, companies

(continued)

---

expatriates (expats)
Noncitizens of the countries in which employees are working.

home-country nationals
Citizens of the country in which the multinational company has its headquarters.

third-country nationals
Citizens of a country other than the parent or the host country.

are upping the numbers of short-term assignments they make. This lets them use lower cost short-term assignments to replace some long-term assignments that require supporting expats (and their families) abroad for extended periods. Fifty percent of the companies Mercer surveyed are also replacing some expatriate postings with local hires. With an eye on cutting costs, many employers were reviewing their firms' policies regarding such things as housing, education and home leave, along with expatriate allowances and premiums (cost-of-living allowance and mobility/quality-of-living premiums).[41]

OTHER SOLUTIONS The choice is not just between expatriate versus local employees. For example, there are other "short-term" or "commuter" solutions. These involve frequent international travel but no formal relocation.[42]

One survey found that about 78% of surveyed employers had some form of "localization" policy. This is a policy of transferring a home-country national employee to a foreign subsidiary as a "permanent transferee." Here the employer doesn't treat the employee (who assumedly wants to move abroad) as an expatriate, but instead as a local hire.[43] For example, U.S. IBM employees originally from India eventually filled many of the 5,000 jobs that IBM recently shifted from the United States to India. These employees elected to move back to India, albeit at local India pay rates. Other firms use Internet-based video technologies and group decision-making software to enable global virtual teams to do business without either travel or relocation.[44]

USING TRANSNATIONAL VIRTUAL TEAMS Managing internationally may require the services of a "transnational" team, one composed of employees whose locations and activities span many countries.[45] For example, a European beverage manufacturer formed a 13-member "European Production Task Force" with members from its facilities in five countries. Its task was to analyze how many factories the firm should operate in Europe, what size they should be, and where to place them.[46]

Often, such teams don't meet face to face, but work in virtual environments. **Virtual teams** are groups of geographically dispersed coworkers who interact using a combination of telecommunications and information technologies to accomplish an organizational task.

Virtual teams are popular. Strategic partnerships and joint ventures often require employees of partner companies to act together as a team, although they work for different companies and in different locales.[47] To facilitate the merger of Marion Laboratories and Merrell Dow Pharmaceuticals the companies created a global virtual team comprised of members from production sites in Asia, Europe, and North America. The team helped overcome potential merger integration problems, and produced improved productivity and profits.[48]

Virtual teams depend on information technology. With desktop videoconferencing systems often the heart of such systems, communication among team members can embrace the body language and nuances of face-to-face communications.[49] Such teams also use collaborative software systems. Microsoft offers a NetMeeting conference system. When combined with products like Framework Technologies Corp.'s Active-Project 5.0, virtual team members can hold live project reviews and discussions and then store the sessions on the project's Web site.[50]

But the main challenges that virtual teams face are people related. These include building trust, cohesion, team identity, and overcoming the isolation among team members. Success therefore depends on various human resource management-related actions. In particular, train virtual team members in leadership, conflict management, and meetings management, and to respond swiftly to virtual teammates.[51] Give virtual team members a realistic preview of the potential for feeling detached. Select virtual team members using behavioral and situational interviews, where they describe how they'd respond to illustrative virtual team situations. And, use current virtual team members to help recruit and select new team members; and empower the virtual team to do its job.[52]

Offshoring

As explained in Chapter 4 (Recruiting), offshoring is an important international staffing issue. *Offshoring* means having local employees abroad do jobs that the firm's domestic employees previously did in-house. For example, IBM recently announced that it was shifting about 5,000 U.S. software and sales jobs to India.[53]

Offshoring is a uniquely human resource management–dependent activity. Firms once went abroad primarily to develop new markets or to open up new manufacturing facilities. Here marketing, sales, and production executives played the pivotal roles. Offshoring, on the other hand, depends on human resource management. Employers look to their HR managers to help identify high-quality, low-cost talent abroad, and to provide information on things like literacy, foreign wage rates, and working conditions. The human resource manager must also see that employees receive the screening, training, and compensation that they require. The firm may have to retain local legal counsel, both to navigate local laws and for advice on local hiring practices.[54]

Management Values and International Staffing Policy

Various factors like technical competence determine whether firms use locals or expatriates abroad. But (for better or worse) it's not just hard facts that influence such decisions. The top executives' personal inclinations and values also play a role. Some executives are just more "expat-oriented." For example, some experts classify top executives' values as *ethnocentric, polycentric,* or *geocentric.* We'll look at each.

ETHNOCENTRIC PRACTICES
In an ethnocentrically oriented corporation, "the prevailing attitude is that home-country attitudes, management style, knowledge, evaluation criteria, and managers are superior to anything the host country might have to offer."[55]

Such values translate into particular employment practices. With an **ethnocentric** staffing policy, the firm fills key management jobs with parent-country nationals.[56] Reasons given for ethnocentric staffing policies include lack of qualified host-country senior management talent, a desire to maintain a unified corporate culture and tighter control, and the desire to transfer the parent company's core competencies (for instance, a specialized manufacturing skill), to a foreign subsidiary more expeditiously.[57]

POLYCENTRIC PRACTICES
In the **polycentric** corporation, "there is a conscious belief that only host-country managers can ever really understand the culture and behavior of the host-country market; therefore, the foreign subsidiary should be managed by local people."[58]

A polycentric-oriented firm would staff its foreign subsidiaries with host-country nationals, and its home office with parent-country nationals. Such polices may reduce the local cultural misunderstandings that might occur if it used expatriate managers. It will also almost undoubtedly be less expensive.[59]

GEOCENTRIC PRACTICES
Geocentric executives believe that the best manager for a specific position anywhere may be in any of the countries in which the firm operates. Thus, Sony Corporation appointed as CEO someone from Wales who'd run the firm's U.S. operations.

---

virtual teams
Groups of geographically dispersed coworkers who interact using a combination of telecommunications and information technologies to accomplish an organizational task.

ethnocentric
The notion that home-country attitudes, management style, knowledge, evaluation criteria, and managers are superior to anything the host country has to offer.

polycentric
A conscious belief that only the host-country managers can ever really understand the culture and behavior of the host-country market.

A **geocentric** staffing policy "seeks the best people for key jobs throughout the organization, regardless of nationality."[60] This can let the global firm use its human resources more fully by transferring the best person to the open job, wherever he or she may be. Such cross-pollination can also help build a stronger and more consistent culture and set of values among the entire global management team.

Selecting Expatriate Managers

The processes that firms use to select managers for their domestic and foreign positions obviously have many similarities. For either assignment, candidates need the technical knowledge and skills to do the job, and the intelligence and people skills to be successful managers.[61] Testing, interviewing, and background checks are as applicable for selecting expatriates as for domestic assignments.

However, selection for foreign assignments is different. For example, there is the stress that being alone in a foreign land can put on the single manager. And if spouse and children will share the assignment, there are the pressures that the family will have to confront abroad. Furthermore, it's not just how different culturally the host country is from the person's home country. Rather, the person's adaptability is important. Some people adapt anywhere; others fail to adapt anywhere.[62]

How do firms select global managers? Recent analyses of expatriate practices across countries suggest several things. "Traditionally, most selection of expatriates appears to be done solely on the basis of successful records of job performance in the home country."[63] However, best practices in international assignee selection now include providing *realistic previews* to prospective international assignees, facilitating *self-selection* to enable expatriate candidates to decide for themselves if the assignments are right for them, and *traditional selection procedures* focusing on traits such as openness.[64] Over the past two decades there's also been an increase in the number of expatriate selection criteria that companies use. Selection criteria include technical/ professional skills, expatriates' willingness to go, experience in the country, personality factors (including flexibility), leadership skills, the ability to work with teams, and previous performance appraisals in the selection process. There has also been a big decline in U.S. companies' premature return rates, suggesting that employers are more successful at sending expatriates abroad.[65]

SELECTION TESTING   Selecting managers for assignments abroad therefore means testing them for traits that predict success in working abroad. Research here is evolving. An early study asked 338 international assignees from various countries to specify which traits were important for the success in a foreign assignment. They identified five factors: job knowledge and motivation, relational skills, flexibility/adaptability, extra-cultural openness, and family situation (spouse's positive opinion, willingness of spouse to live abroad, and so on). Figure 17-2 shows some of the specific items that comprise the five factors. Family situation was the most important.[66]

Subsequent research focused on one of these factors, adaptability. **Adaptability screening** aims to assess the assignees' (and spouses') probable success in handling the foreign transfer, and to alert them to issues (such as the impact on children) the move may involve.[67] Here, experience is often the best predictor of future success. Employers therefore look for overseas candidates whose work and nonwork experience, education, and language skills already demonstrate a commitment to and facility for living and working with different cultures. Even several summers traveling overseas or participating in foreign student programs might suggest that the potential transferee can adjust when he or she arrives overseas.

More recent research focuses on identifying what it takes to succeed in a global environment. In one study, researchers interviewed 200 senior international managers, and surveyed 5,000 managers worldwide.[68] They report that success

FIGURE 17-2 Five Factors Important in International Assignee Success and Their Components

Source: Based on Arthur Winfred Jr. and Winston Bennett Jr., "The International Assignee: The Relative Importance of Factors Perceived to Contribute to Success," *Personnel Psychology* 18 (1995), pp. 106–107.

I. Job Knowledge and Motivation
Managerial ability
Organizational ability
Imagination
Creativity
Administrative skills
Alertness
Responsibility
Industriousness
Initiative and energy
High motivation
Frankness
Belief in mission and job
Perseverance

II. Relational Skills
Respect
Courtesy
Display of respect
Kindness
Empathy
Nonjudgmental
Integrity
Confidence

III. Flexibility/Adaptability
Resourcefulness
Ability to deal with stress

Flexibility
Emotional stability
Willingness to change
Tolerance for ambiguity
Adaptability
Independence
Dependability
Political sensitivity
Positive self-image

IV. Extracultural Openness
Variety of outside
  interests
Interest in foreign cultures
Openness
Knowledge of local
  language(s)
Outgoingness and
  extroversion
Overseas experience

V. Family Situation
Adaptability of spouse
  and family
Spouse's positive opinion
Willingness of spouse
  to live abroad
Stable marriage

abroad hinges on having a "global mind-set," a mind-set that has intellectual, psychological, and social components:

intellectual capital, or knowledge of international business and the capacity to learn; *psychological capital*, or openness to different cultures and the capacity to change; and *social capital*, the ability to form connections, to bring people together, and to influence stakeholders—including colleagues, clients, suppliers, and regulatory agencies—who are unlike you in cultural heritage, professional background, or political outlook.[69]

Many firms use tests such as the Overseas Assignment Inventory (OAI). This identifies the characteristics and attitudes international assignment candidates should have. Its publisher establishes local norms and conducts ongoing validation studies.[70] Figure 17-3 illustrates the OAI. Realistic previews are also important. These should cover the problems to expect in the new job (such as extensive travel) as well as the cultural benefits, problems, and idiosyncrasies of the target country. The rule, say experts, should always be to "spell it all out" ahead of time.[71]

LEGAL ISSUES   In selecting employees for assignments abroad, managers need to consider the legal issues. As we explained in Chapter 2 (EEOC), American equal employment opportunity laws, including Title VII, the ADEA, and the ADA, affect qualified employees of U.S. employers doing business abroad, and foreign firms doing business in the United States or its territories.[72] If equal employment opportunity laws conflict with the laws of the country in which the U.S. employer is operating, the laws of the local country generally take precedence.[73]

geocentric
The belief that the firm's whole management staff must be scoured on a global basis, on the assumption that the best manager of a specific position anywhere may be in any of the countries in which the firm operates.

adaptability screening
A process that aims to assess the assignees' (and spouses') probable success in handling a foreign transfer.

Sample excerpt from the
OVERSEAS ASSIGNMENT INVENTORY

Welcome!

Enter the login information you were provided in the box on the left. This will direct you to a registration page before proceeding to your survey.

This site contains:

Overseas Assignment Inventory—A tool designed to assess cultural adaptability for employees and spouses going on international expatriate assignments.

Global Assessment Inventory—A development tool designed to assess factors related to success in multicultural interactions.

Demographics

Please complete the demographic information requested. Note, your answers will not impact the survey results. Upon completion, you will be directed to the survey.

Background Information

Employee or Spouse/Partner: ☐ Employee   ☐ Spouse/Partner

Gender: ☐ Male   ☐ Female

Nationality: _____

Age: _____

Number of Children: _____

Have Traveled Outside of Country of Citizenship: ☐ Yes   ☐ No

Have Lived Outside of Country of Citizenship: ☐ Yes   ☐ No

Employment

Destination Country: _____

Current Country Location: _____

[Submit]

Survey Questions *(page 1 of 6)*

Read each survey question carefully and select the bubble that corresponds to your choice. When answering the questions, keep in mind that there are no "right" or "wrong" answers. Choose the response that is reflective of what you think and do most of the time. Some of the questions appear similar; actually no two are exactly alike. Please answer each one without regard to the others.

Strongly Agree 1	Agree 2	Uncertain 3	Disagree 4	Strongly Disagree 5

1. I do not want to compromise my present standard of living.   ☐1 ☐2 ☐3 ☐4 ☐5

2. The environment I am comfortable with is similar to that in my destination country.   ☐1 ☐2 ☐3 ☐4 ☐5

3. Generally, my spouse/partner and I understand each other.   ☐1 ☐2 ☐3 ☐4 ☐5

4. I am generally one of the first to speak and take charge in a group.   ☐1 ☐2 ☐3 ☐4 ☐5

5. It is very clear to me how my work on this assignment will be evaluated.   ☐1 ☐2 ☐3 ☐4 ☐5

6. I am fluent in the language spoken in my destination country.   ☐1 ☐2 ☐3 ☐4 ☐5

FIGURE 17-3 Overseas Assignment Inventory

Avoiding Early Expatriate Returns

A major criterion of expatriate assignment failure is the early, unplanned return of the expatriate. Systematizing the entire expatriate management process is the first step in avoiding an early return. For example, employers should have an expatriate policy covering matters such as compensation and transfer costs. Have procedures, for instance, requiring that the managers responsible for the expat's budget obtain all chain of command approvals.[74] Similarly, before selecting someone to send abroad, understand where the main potential problems lie.

TRAITS OF SUCCESSFUL EXPATRIATES   As noted earlier, having the right traits improves the odds the expat will succeed. For example, in a study of 143 expatriate employees, extroverted, agreeable, and emotionally stable individuals were less likely to leave early.[75] Furthermore, *intentions* are important; people who want expatriate careers try harder to adjust to them.[76] Similarly, expatriates who are more satisfied with their jobs are more likely to adapt to the foreign assignment.[77] Some people are so culturally at ease that they adapt easily. [78]

FAMILY PRESSURES   Nonwork factors like *family pressures* loom large in expatriate failures. In one study, U.S. managers listed, in descending order of importance for leaving early: inability of spouse to adjust, managers' inability to adjust, other family problems, managers' personal or emotional immaturity, and inability to cope with larger overseas responsibility.[79]

Such findings underscore a truism about selecting international assignees: The problem is usually not incompetence, but family and personal problems. Yet, as noted, employers still often select expatriates mostly based on technical competence.[80]

Given the role of family problems in expatriate failures, the employer should understand just how unhappy and cut off the expatriate manager's spouse can feel in a foreign environment. Here is how the spouse of one expat put it:[81]

> It's difficult to make close friends. So many expats have their guard up, not wanting to become too close. Too many have been hurt, too many times already, becoming emotionally dependent on a friend only to have the inevitable happen—one or the other gets transferred. It's also difficult to watch your children get hurt when their best friend gets transferred. Although I have many acquaintances, I have nowhere near the close friends I had in the States. My spouse therefore has become my rock.[82]

One study identified three things that make it easier for spouses to adjust. First is *language fluency*, since spouses will feel even more cut off if they can't make themselves understood. Second, having *preschool-age children* (rather than school-age children or no children) seemed to make it easier for the spouse to adjust. "This suggests that younger children, perhaps because of their increased dependency, help spouses retain that part of their social identities: as parents, their responsibilities for these children remain the same."[83] Third, it helps that there be a *strong bond of closeness* between spouse and expat partner. This provides the continuing emotional and social support many spouses find lacking abroad.

WHAT EMPLOYERS CAN DO   So, employers can do several things to boost the odds that assignments abroad will go smoothly. Providing realistic previews of what to expect, carefully screening expat and spouse, improved orientation, and improved benefits packages are obvious solutions. Another is simply to shorten the length of the assignment. Person–job match is also important, insofar as expatriates who are more satisfied with their jobs are more likely to adapt to the foreign assignment.[84] Helping spouses get jobs abroad and providing more support to the expat and his or her family are also important.[85] Some employers set up "global buddy" programs. Here local managers mentor new expatriates.[86]

4 Discuss some important issues to keep in mind in training, appraising, and compensating international employees.

TRAINING AND MAINTAINING EMPLOYEES ABROAD
Orienting and Training Employees on International Assignment

When it comes to the orientation and training required for expatriate success overseas, the practices of most U.S. employers reflect more talk than substance. Executives tend to agree that international assignees do best when they receive the special training (in things like language and culture) that they require. Fewer actually provide it.

However, numerous training vendors do offer packaged cross-cultural pre-departure training programs. In general, the programs use lectures, simulations, videos, and readings to prepare trainees. Their offerings illustrate the aim and content of such programs. One program aims to provide the trainee with (1) the basics of the new country's history, politics, business norms, education system, and demographics; (2) an understanding of how cultural values affect perceptions, values, and communications; and (3) examples of why moving to a new country can be difficult, and how to manage these challenges.[87] Another aims to boost self-awareness and cross-cultural understanding, to provide opportunities for anxieties to be addressed, and to reduce stress and provide coping strategies.[88] A third prepares individuals and their families "to interact successfully in daily life and business situations abroad; understand the impact various factors have on cultural behaviors and attitudes to make the most of the living abroad experience; and to raise awareness of the challenges of moving abroad, culture shock and how to deal with exposure to new cultural experiences."[89]

Some employers use returning managers as resources to cultivate the global mind-sets of those departing. For example, Bosch holds regular seminars, where new arrived returnees pass on their experience to managers and their families going abroad.

ONGOING TRAINING   Beyond such pre-departure training, more firms are providing continuing, in-country cross-cultural training during the early stages of an overseas assignment.

For example, managers abroad (both expats and locals) continue to need traditional skills-oriented development. At many firms, including IBM, such development includes rotating assignments to help overseas managers grow professionally. IBM and other firms also have management development centers around the world where executives can hone their skills. And classroom programs (such as those at the London Business School or at INSEAD in France) provide overseas executives the educational opportunities (to acquire MBAs, for instance) that similar stateside programs do for their U.S.-based colleagues.

In addition to honing these managers' skills, international development activities hopefully have other, less tangible benefits. For example, rotating assignments can help managers form bonds with colleagues around the world. These can help the managers form the informal networks they need to make cross-border decisions more expeditiously.

Many global employers bring their international managers together periodically for training seminars.

Source: Shutterstock.

PepsiCo encourages expatriates to engage in local social activities, such as Latin dance lessons in Mexico City and table tennis tournaments in China, to help them become acclimated faster to local cultures.[90]

Appraising Managers Abroad

No single "best practice" global appraisal standard seems to exist, given the diversity of country environments and firm-specific differences involved.[91] However, several issues must be addressed.

The question of who actually appraises managers abroad is crucial.[92] Local management must have some input, but cultural differences may distort the appraisals. Thus, host-country bosses might evaluate a U.S. expatriate manager in India somewhat negatively if they find his or her use of participative decision making culturally inappropriate. On the other hand, home-office managers may be so out of touch that they can't provide valid appraisals. Similarly, the procedure may be to measure the expatriate by objective criteria such as profits and market share. However, local events (such as political instability) may affect the manager's performance while remaining "invisible" to home-office staff. Some suggestions for improving expatriate appraisals follow.

1. Stipulate the assignment's difficulty level, and adapt the performance criteria to the situation.

2. Weigh the evaluation more toward the on-site manager's appraisal than toward the home-site manager's appraisal.

3. If the home-office manager does the actual written appraisal, have him or her use a former expatriate from the same overseas location for advice.

Compensating Managers Abroad

The whole area of international compensation presents some tricky problems. On the one hand, there is logic in maintaining company-wide pay scales and policies so that, for instance, you pay divisional marketing directors throughout the world within the same range. This reduces the risk of perceived inequities, and simplifies the job of keeping track of country-by-country wage rates.

Yet not adapting pay scales to local markets will produce more problems than it solves. The fact is it can be enormously more expensive to live in some countries (like Japan) than others (like India); if these cost-of-living differences aren't considered, it will be almost impossible to get managers to take "high-cost" assignments. One way to handle this problem is to pay a similar base salary company-wide, and then add on various allowances according to individual market conditions.[93]

However, determining equitable wage rates in many countries is not simple. There is a wealth of "packaged" compensation survey data available in the United States, but such data are not so easy to come by overseas. As a result, one of the greatest difficulties in managing multinational compensation is obtaining consistent compensation measures between countries.

Some multinational companies conduct their own local annual compensation surveys. For example, Kraft conducts an annual study of total compensation in Belgium, Germany, Italy, Spain, and the United Kingdom. It focuses on all forms of compensation paid to each of 10 senior management positions held by local nationals in these firms.

THE BALANCE SHEET APPROACH   The most common approach to formulating expatriate pay is to equalize purchasing power across countries, a technique known as the *balance sheet approach*.[94] More than 85% of North American companies reportedly use this approach.

The basic idea is that each expatriate should enjoy the same standard of living he or she would have had at home. The balance sheet approach addresses four groups of expenses—income taxes, housing, goods and services, and discretionary expenses (child support, car payments, and the like). The employer estimates each of these four expenses in the expat's home country, and in the host country. The employer then pays any differences—such as additional income taxes or housing expenses.

The base salary will normally be in the same range as the manager's home-country salary. In addition, however, there might be an overseas or foreign service salary premium. The executive receives this as a percentage of his or her base salary, in part to compensate for the cultural and physical adjustments he or she will have to make.[95] There may also be several allowances, including a housing allowance and an education allowance for the expatriate's children. To help the expatriate manage his or her home and foreign financial obligations, most employers use a *split pay* approach; they pay, say, half a person's actual pay in home-country currency and half in the local currency.[96]

TABLE 17-1 The Balance Sheet Approach (Assumes U.S. Base Salary of $160,000)			
Annual Expense	Chicago, U.S.	Shanghai, China (US$ Equivalent)	Allowance
Housing & utilities	$35,000	$44,800	$9,800
Goods & services	6,000	7,680	1,680
Taxes	44,800	57,344	12,544
Discretionary income	10,000	12,800	2,800
Total	$95,800	$122,624	$26,824

Table 17-1 illustrates the balance sheet approach for someone transferring from Chicago to Shanghai, China. The U.S. Government State Departments estimates the cost of living in Shanghai at 128% of the U.S. cost of living.[97] In this case, the manager's base salary is $160,000, and she faces a U.S. income tax rate of 28%. Other costs are based on the index of living costs abroad published in the "U.S. Department of State Indexes of Living Costs Abroad, Quarters Allowances, and Hardship Differentials," available at http://aoprals.state.gov/content.asp?content_id= 186&menu_id=81.

Employers also pay their expatriates and local managers abroad performance incentives. Executive compensation systems around the world are becoming more similar.[98] U.S. firms that offer overseas managers long-term incentives often use overall corporate performance criteria (like worldwide profits) when awarding incentive pay.

EXPATRIATE PAY EXAMPLE   As a specific example, expats working for the company CEMEX:

> get foreign service premium equal to a 10% increase in salary. Some get a hardship premium, depending on the country; it ranges from zero in a relatively comfortable posting to, for example, 30% in Bangladesh. We pay for their housing. We pay for their children's schooling up to college. There's home leave—a ticket back to their home country for the entire family once a year. There are language lessons for the spouse. And we gross up the pay of all expats, to take out the potential effects of local tax law. Say you have an executive earning $150,000. This person would cost close to $300,000 as an ex-pat.[99]

INCENTIVES   Employers use various incentives in international compensation. First, as mentioned, employers pay various incentives to encourage the employee to take the job abroad. For example, **foreign service premiums** are financial payments over and above regular base pay. These typically range from 10% to 30% of base pay, and appear as weekly or monthly salary supplements. **Hardship allowances** compensate expatriates for hard living and working conditions at certain foreign locations. (U.S. diplomats posted to Iraq receive about a 70% boost in base salary, among other incentives.[100]) **Mobility premiums** are typically lump-sum payments to reward employees for moving from one assignment to another.

In terms of buying power, American managers don't rank near the top in terms of managerial pay. "Companies are operating in an increasingly open and competitive global economy, and emerging markets are offering managers higher disposable incomes than established countries." Average disposable income for managers ranges from about $72,000 in Indonesia to $98,000 in France; $105,000 in the United States; $124,000 in Brazil; $149,000 in the Ukraine; and $229,000 in Saudi Arabia.[101]

STEPS IN ESTABLISHING A GLOBAL PAY SYSTEM   Balancing global consistency in compensation with local considerations starts with establishing a rewards program that makes sense in terms of the employer's overall strategic needs.[102] Then the employer can turn to more micro issues, such as, is how we're paying our employees abroad competitive? And are we basing our overseas pay decisions on "credible and defendable market data"?[103] Steps to follow in creating a global pay system include these:[104]

Step 1: **Set strategy.** First, formulate strategic goals for the next five years, for instance, in terms of improving productivity or boosting market share.

Step 2: **Identify crucial executive behaviors.** Next, identify the actionable behaviors you expect your executives to exhibit in order to pursue these strategic goals.

Step 3: **Global philosophy framework.** Next, step back and ask how you want each pay component to contribute to prompting those executive actions and achieving the company's strategic goals.

Step 4: **Identify gaps.** Next, review your existing rewards programs around the world. The question is, "To what extent do our pay plans around the world support our strategic aims?"

Step 5: **Systematize pay systems.** Next, create more consistent performance assessment practices, and establish consistent job requirements and performance expectations for similar jobs worldwide.

Step 6: **Adapt pay policies.** Finally, review your global pay policies (for setting salary levels, incentives, and so forth). Conduct surveys and analyses to assess local pay practices. Then, fine-tune the firm's global pay policies so they make sense for each location.

Labor Relations Abroad

Firms opening subsidiaries abroad face substantial differences in labor relations practices among countries and regions. This is important, because while union membership is dropping in the United States, it is still relatively high abroad, and unions abroad thus tend to be more influential. Walmart, for instance, has successfully neutralized attempts to organize its U.S. employees, but had to accept unions in many of its stores in China.

As an example, unions in Europe are influential and labor–management bargaining and relations reflect this fact. In general, four issues characterize European labor relations:

- **Centralization.** Collective bargaining in Western Europe tends to be industry-wide, whereas in the United States it generally occurs at the enterprise or plant level.

- **Employer organization.** Due to the prevalence of industry-wide bargaining in Europe, employers tend to bargain via employer associations, rather than as individual employers.

- **Union recognition.** Union recognition is less formal than in the United States. For example, even if a union represents 80% of an employer's workers, another union can try to organize the other 20%.

- **Content and scope of bargaining.** U.S. labor–management agreements specify wages, hours, and working conditions. European agreements tend to be brief and to leave individual employers free to institute more generous terms.

Terrorism, Safety, and Global HR

TERRORISM Whether it's off the coast of Somalia or walking down the street in Brazil, businesspeople may be subject to "express kidnapping", wherein they're kidnapped, hopefully for just long enough to get a ransom payment from a bank or ATM.[105]

Even stationing employees in assumedly safe countries is no guarantee there won't be problems. A few years ago workers (certainly not terrorists) in French factories of Sony Corp., Caterpillar Inc., and 3M Co. took their managers hostage in order to

---

foreign service premiums
Financial payments over and above regular base pay, typically ranging between 10% and 30% of base pay.

hardship allowances
Payments that compensate expatriates for exceptionally hard living and working conditions at certain locations.

mobility premiums
Typically, lump-sum payments to reward employees for moving from one assignment to another.

negotiate better benefits for laid off employees.[106] Developments like these had already prompted employers to take steps to protect their expat and foreign employees better, for instance, evacuation plans to get employees to safety, if that becomes necessary.

TAKING PROTECTIVE MEASURES   Legally, employers have a duty of care for protecting international assignees and their dependents and international business travelers.[107] Employers are doing so in a variety of ways. Many employers purchase intelligence services for monitoring potential terrorist threats abroad. The head of one intelligence firm estimates such services as costing $6,000–$10,000 per year.[108] Many employers retain crisis management teams' services. They then call on these teams, for instance, when criminal elements kidnap one of their managers. As one insurance executive puts it, "When you have a specialist, there's a better chance to get the person back."[109]

Retaining risk management companies ahead of time can prove valuable in a volatile world. For example, when the protests erupted in Egypt in February 2011, Medex Global Solutions evacuated more than 500 client employees from Egypt, and had already been advising their employer clients about the possibilities for political unrest.[110]

KIDNAPPING AND RANSOM (K&R) INSURANCE   Hiring crisis teams and paying ransoms can be prohibitively expensive for all but the largest firms, so many employers buy kidnapping and ransom (K&R) insurance. Various events may trigger payments under such policies. The obvious ones are kidnapping (for instance, the employee is a hostage until the employer pays a ransom), extortion (threatening bodily harm), and detention (holding an employee without any ransom demand).

The insurance typically covers several costs associated with kidnappings, abductions, or extortion. These costs might include hiring a crisis team, the actual cost of the ransom payment to the kidnappers or extortionists, insuring the ransom money in transit, legal expenses, and employee death or dismemberment.[111]

Keeping business travelers out of crime's way is a specialty all its own, but suggestions here include the following.[112]

- Provide expatriates with general training about traveling, living abroad, and the destination, so they're more oriented when they arrive.
- Tell them not to draw attention to the fact that they're Americans—by wearing flag emblems, for instance.
- Have travelers arrive at airports as close to departure time as possible and wait in areas away from the main flow of traffic.
- Equip the expatriate's car and home with security systems.
- Tell employees to vary their departure and arrival times and take different routes to and from work.
- Keep employees current on crime and other problems by regularly checking the State Department's travel advisory service (click on Country Specific Information at http://travel.state.gov/).
- Advise employees to remain confident at all times: Body language can attract perpetrators, and those who look like victims often become victimized.[113]

Repatriation: Problems and Solutions

One of the most worrisome facts about sending employees abroad is that 40% to 60% of them will probably quit within 3 years of returning home.[114] Given the investment the employer makes in training and sending these high-potential people abroad, it makes sense to try to make sure they stay with the firm. For this, formal repatriation programs can be useful.[115] One study found that about 5% of returning employees resigned if their firms had formal repatriation programs, while about 22% of those left if their firms had no such programs.[116]

Probably the simplest thing the employer can do to improve repatriates' retention is to value their experience more highly. As one returnee put it: "My company was,

AT&T makes sure that the employee always feels that he or she is still "in the loop" with what's happening back at the home office.

in my view, somewhat indifferent to my experience in China as evidenced by a lack of monetary reward, positive increase, or leverage to my career in any way." Such feelings then prompt the person to look elsewhere for opportunities.[117]

Before repatriating the manager, it's essential that the expatriate and his or her family not feel that the firm left them adrift. To that end, AT&T has a 3-part repatriation program, one that starts before the employee goes abroad.[118] First, AT&T *matches the expat and his or her family with a psychologist* trained in repatriation issues. The psychologist meets with the family before they go abroad. The psychologist discusses the challenges they will face abroad, assesses with them how well he or she thinks they will adapt to their new culture, and stays in touch with them throughout their assignment. (Other firms provide written repatriation agreements. These guarantee in writing that the company won't keep the expat abroad for more than some period, such as 3 years, and that on return he or she will receive a mutually acceptable job.)

Second, AT&T makes sure that *the employee always feels that he or she is still "in the loop"* with what's happening back at the home office. For example, AT&T assigns the expatriate a mentor. It also periodically brings the expat back to the home office to meet with and to socialize with colleagues.

Third, once it's time for the expatriate employee and his or her family to return home, AT&T *provides formal repatriation services.* About 6 months before the overseas assignment ends, the psychologist and an HR representative meet with the expat and the family, to start preparing them for the return. For example, they help plan the employee's next career move, help the person update his or her résumé, and begin putting the person in contact with supervisors back home. They work with the person's family on the logistics of the move back. Then, about a month after returning home, the expat and family attend a "welcome home" seminar, to discuss matters like the stress of repatriation.[119]

Improving Productivity through HRIS

Taking the HRIS Global

For global firms, it makes particular sense to expand the firm's human resource information systems to the firm's operations abroad. For example, when Buildnet, Inc., decided to automate and integrate its separate systems for things like applicant tracking, training, and compensation, it chose a Web-based software package called MyHRIS from NuView, Inc. (www.nuviewinc.com). This Internet-based system includes human resource and benefits administration, applicant tracking and résumé scanning, training administration, and succession planning and development.[120] With MyHRIS, managers at any of the firm's locations around the world can access and update more than 200 built-in reports such as "termination summary" or "open positions."[121] The firm's home-office managers can access data on and monitor global human resource activities on a real-time basis.

Similarly, employers are taking their employee self-service HR portals international. For example, consider Time Warner's "Employee Connection" portal. It lets Time Warner's 80,000 worldwide employees self-manage much of their benefits, compensation planning, merit review, and personal information updating online.[122]

5	Explain with examples how to implement a global human resource management program.

MANAGING HR LOCALLY: HOW TO PUT INTO PRACTICE A GLOBAL HR SYSTEM

With employers increasingly relying on local rather than expatriate employees, transferring one's selection, training, appraisal, pay, and other human resource practices abroad is a top priority. But, given the cross-cultural and other differences, one could reasonably ask, "Is it realistic for a company to try to institute a standardized human resource management system in its facilities around the world?"

A study suggests that the answer is "yes." In brief, the study's results show that employers may have to defer to local managers on some specific human resource management policy issues. However, the findings also suggest that big intercountry

FIGURE 17-4 Best Practices
for Creating Global HR Systems

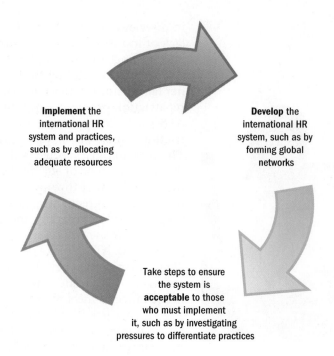

Implement the international HR system and practices, such as by allocating adequate resources

Develop the international HR system, such as by forming global networks

Take steps to ensure the system is **acceptable** to those who must implement it, such as by investigating pressures to differentiate practices

HR practice differences are often not necessary or even advisable. The important thing is how you implement the global human resource management system.

In this study, the researchers interviewed human resource personnel from six global companies—Agilent, Dow, IBM, Motorola, Procter & Gamble, and Shell Oil Co.—as well as international human resources consultants.[123] The study's overall conclusion was that employers who successfully implement global HR systems do so by applying several best practices. The basic idea is to *develop* systems that are *acceptable* to employees in units around the world, and ones that the employers can *implement* more effectively. Figure 17-4 summarizes this. We'll look at each of these three requirements' best practices.

Developing a More Effective Global HR System

First, these employers engage in two best practices in developing their worldwide human resource policies and practices.

Form global HR networks. To head off resistance, human resource managers around the world should feel that they're part of the firm's global human resource management team. The researchers found that in developing global HR systems, the most critical factor is "creating an infrastructure of partners around the world that you use for support, for buy-in, for organization of local activities, and to help you better understand their own systems and their own challenges."[124] Treat the local human resource managers as equal partners. For instance, they formed global teams to help develop the new human resources systems.

Remember that it's more important to standardize ends and competencies than specific methods. For example, IBM uses a more or less standardized recruitment and selection process worldwide. However, "details such as who conducts the interview (hiring manager vs. recruiter), or whether the prescreen is by phone or in person, differ by country."[125]

Making the Global HR System More Acceptable

Next, employers engage in three best practices so that the global human resource systems they develop will be *acceptable* to local managers around the world. These practices include:

Remember that truly global organizations find it easier to install global systems. For example, truly global companies require their managers to work on global teams, and to identify, recruit, and place the employees they hire globally. As one Shell manager put it, "If you're truly global, then you are hiring here [the United States] people who are going to immediately go and work in the Hague, and vice versa."[126] This global mind-set makes it easier for managers everywhere to accept the wisdom of having a standardized human resource management system.

Investigate pressures to differentiate and determine their legitimacy. Local managers will insist, "You can't do that here, because we are different culturally." These researchers found that these "differences" are usually not persuasive. For example, when Dow wanted to implement an online recruitment and selection tool abroad, the hiring managers there said that their managers would not use it. After investigating the supposed cultural roadblocks, Dow successfully implemented the new system.[127]

The operative word here is "investigate." Carefully assess whether the local culture or other differences might in fact undermine the new system. Be knowledgeable about local legal issues, and be willing to differentiate where necessary.

Try to work within the context of a strong corporate culture. Companies that create a strong corporate culture find it easier to obtain agreement among far-flung employees. For example, because of how P&G recruits, selects, trains, and rewards them, its managers have a strong sense of shared values. For instance, new recruits quickly learn to think in terms of "we" instead of "I." They learn to value thoroughness, consistency, self-discipline, and a methodical approach. Because all P&G managers worldwide tend to share these values, they are in a sense more similar to each other than they are geographically different. Having such global unanimity in values makes it easier to implement standardized human resource practices worldwide.

Implementing the Global HR System

Finally, two best practices helped ensure success in actually *implementing* the globally consistent human resource policies and practices.

"You can't communicate enough." "There's a need for constant contact with the decision makers in each country, as well as the people who will be implementing and using the system."[128]

Dedicate adequate resources. For example, don't require the local human resource management offices to implement new job analysis procedures unless the head office provides adequate resources for these additional activities.

REVIEW

MyManagementLab Now that you have finished this chapter, go back to **www.mymanagementlab.com** to continue practicing and applying the concepts you've learned.

CHAPTER SECTION SUMMARIES

1. **The internationalization of business influences employers' HR processes.** The big issue is coping with the cultural, political, legal, and economic differences among countries. For example, citizens of different countries adhere to different values, and countries have differing economic systems as well as different legal, political, and labor relations systems.

2. **Staffing the global organization** is a major challenge. Companies may use expatriates, home-country nationals, or third-country nationals. Offshoring means having local employees abroad do jobs that domestic employees previously did in-house. Employers seeking to gain cost advantages by offshoring rely on their HR managers to help identify high-quality, low-cost talent abroad.

Top management values will influence how they staff their operations abroad. Ethnocentric companies tend to emphasize home-country attitudes, polycentric companies focus more on host-country employees, and geocentric employers try to pick the best candidates from wherever they might be. Selecting employees to successfully work abroad depends on several things, most importantly on adaptability screening and on making sure that each employee's spouse and family get the realistic previews, counseling, and support necessary to make the transition abroad. Successful expatriates tend to be extroverted, agreeable, and emotionally stable individuals.

3. After selecting the employees to send abroad, attention turns to **training and maintaining your expatriate employees.**

   - In terms of pre-departure preparation, training efforts ideally first cover the impact of cultural differences; then, the focus moves to getting participants to understand how attitudes influence behavior, providing factual knowledge about the target country, and developing skills in areas like language and adjustment.
   - In compensating expatriates, most employers use the balance sheet approach; this focuses on four groups of expenses: income taxes, housing, goods and services, and discretionary expenses. The balance sheet approach aims to provide supplements in such a way that the employee's standard of living abroad is about what it would have been at home. It's usual to apply incentives such as foreign service premiums and hardship allowances to get employees to move abroad.
   - Distance complicates the issue of appraising expatriate managers, so it's prudent to let both the home-office supervisor and the manager's local superior contribute to the appraisal.

- Labor relations tend to be different abroad from what they are in the United States. For instance, there's a much greater emphasis on centralized bargaining in Europe.
- With terrorism a threat, most employers today take protective measures, including buying kidnapping and ransom insurance.
- To reduce the chronic problem of turnover among newly returned employees, it's important to have well-thought-out repatriation programs. These emphasize keeping employees in the loop as far as what's happening in their home offices, bringing them back to the office periodically, and providing formal repatriation services for the expatriate and his or her family to start preparing them for the return.

4. With employers increasingly relying on local rather than expatriate employees, it's important for managers to understand **how to implement a global HR system.** Studies suggest that it is realistic for a company to try to institute standardized human resource management practices at their facilities around the world, although it may be necessary to "fine-tune" them to the needs of the specific facility. The basic approach involves three steps. (1) Develop a more effective global HR system (by forming global HR networks and remembering that it's more important to standardize ends rather than specific methods). (2) Make the global HR system more acceptable (for instance, by taking a global approach to everything the company does, by investigating pressures to differentiate and determining their legitimacy, and by creating a strong company culture). (3) Implement the global system (by emphasizing continuing communications and by ensuring that adequate resources are available).

DISCUSSION QUESTIONS

1. You are the president of a small business. What are some of the ways you expect "going international" will affect HR activities in your business?
2. What are some of the specific, uniquely international activities an international HR manager typically engages in?
3. What intercountry differences affect HRM? Give several examples of how each may specifically affect HRM.
4. You are the HR manager of a firm that is about to send its first employees overseas to staff a new subsidiary. Your boss, the president, asks you why such assignments often fail, and what you plan to do to avoid such failures. How do you respond?

5. What special training do overseas candidates need? In what ways is such training similar to and different from traditional diversity training?
6. How does appraising an expatriate's performance differ from appraising that of a home-office manager? How would you avoid some of the unique problems of appraising the expatriate's performance?
7. As an HR manager, what program would you establish to reduce repatriation problems of returning expatriates and their families?

INDIVIDUAL AND GROUP ACTIVITIES

1. Working individually or in groups, outline an expatriation and repatriation plan for your professor, whom your school is sending to Bulgaria to teach HR for the next 3 years.

2. Give three specific examples of multinational corporations in your area. Check on the Internet or with each firm to determine in what countries these firms have operations. Explain the nature of some of their operations, and

summarize whatever you can find out about their international employee selection and training HR policies.

3. Choose three traits useful for selecting international assignees, and create a straightforward test to screen candidates for these traits.

4. Use a library or Internet source to determine the relative cost of living in five countries as of this year, and explain the implications of such differences for drafting a pay plan for managers being sent to each country.

5. The "HRCI Test Specifications Appendix" (pages 633–640) lists the knowledge someone studying for the HRCI certification exam needs to have in each area of human resource management (such as in Strategic Management, Workforce Planning, and Human Resource Development). In groups of four to five students, do four things: (1) review that appendix now; (2) identify the material in this chapter that relates to the required knowledge the appendix lists; (3) write four multiple-choice exam questions on this material that you believe

would be suitable for inclusion in the HRCI exam; and (4) if time permits, have someone from your team post your team's questions in front of the class, so the students in other teams can take each others' exam questions.

6. An issue of *HR Magazine* contained an article titled "Aftershocks of War," which said that soldiers returning to their jobs from Iraq would likely require HR's assistance in coping with "delayed emotional trauma." The term *delayed emotional trauma* refers to the personality changes such as anger, anxiety, or irritability and associated problems such as tardiness or absenteeism that exposure to the traumatic events of war sometimes triggers in returning veterans. Assume you are the HR manager for the employer of John Smith, who is returning to work next week after 1 year in Iraq. Based on what you read in this chapter, what steps would you take to help ensure that John's reintegration into your workforce goes as smoothly as possible?

EXPERIENTIAL EXERCISE

A Taxing Problem for Expatriate Employees

Purpose: The purpose of this exercise is to give you practice identifying and analyzing some of the factors that influence expatriates' pay.

Required Understanding: You should be thoroughly familiar with this chapter and with the Web site www.irs.gov.

How to Set Up the Exercise/Instructions:

Divide the class into teams of four or five students. Each team member should read the following: One of the trickiest aspects of calculating expatriates' pay relates to the question of the

expatriate's U.S. federal income tax liabilities. Go to the Internal Revenue Service's Web site, www.irs.gov. Scroll down to Individuals, and go to Overseas Taxpayers. Your team is the expatriate-employee compensation task force for your company, and your firm is about to send several managers and engineers to Japan, England, and Hong Kong. What information did you find on the site that will help your team formulate expat tax and compensation policies? Based on that, what are the three most important things your firm should keep in mind in formulating a compensation policy for the employees you're about to send to Japan, England, and Hong Kong?

APPLICATION CASE

"BOSS, I THINK WE HAVE A PROBLEM"

Central Steel Door Corporation has been in business for about 20 years, successfully selling a line of steel industrial-grade doors, as well as the hardware and fittings required for them.[129] Focusing mostly in the United States and Canada, the company had gradually increased its presence from the New York City area, first into New England and then down the Atlantic Coast, then through the Midwest and West, and finally into Canada. The company's basic expansion strategy was always the same: Choose an area, open a distribution center, hire a regional sales manager, and then let that regional sales manager help staff the distribution center and hire local sales reps.

Unfortunately, the company's traditional success in finding sales help has not extended to its overseas operations. With the introduction of the new "euro" European currency in 2002, Mel Fisher, president of Central Steel Door, decided to expand his company abroad, into Europe. However, the expansion has not gone smoothly at all.

He tried for 3 weeks to find a sales manager by advertising in the *International Herald Tribune*, which is read by businesspeople in Europe and by American expatriates living and working in Europe. Although the ads placed in the *Tribune* also ran for about a month on the *Tribune*'s Web site, Mr. Fisher so far has received only five applications. One came from a possibly viable candidate, whereas four came from candidates who Mr. Fisher refers to as "lost souls"— people who seem to have spent most of their time traveling aimlessly from country to country, sipping espresso in sidewalk cafés. When asked what he had done for the last 3 years, one told Mr. Fisher he'd been on a "walkabout."

Other aspects of his international HR activities have been equally problematic. Fisher alienated two of his U.S. sales managers by sending them to Europe to temporarily run the European operations, but neglecting to work out a compensation package that would cover their relatively high living expenses in Germany and Belgium. One ended up staying the better part of the year, and Mr. Fisher was rudely surprised to be informed by the Belgian government that his sales manager owed thousands of dollars in local taxes. The two managers had hired about 10 local people to staff each of the two distribution centers. However, the level of sales was disappointing, so Fisher decided to fire about half the distribution center employees. That's when he got an emergency phone call from his temporary sales manager in Germany: "I've just been told that all these employees should have had written employment agreements and that in any case we can't fire anyone without at least 1 year's

notice, and the local authorities here are really up in arms. Boss, I think we have a problem."

Questions

1. Based on this chapter and the case incident, compile a list of 10 international HR mistakes Mr. Fisher has made so far.
2. How would you have gone about hiring a European sales manager? Why?
3. What would you do now if you were Mr. Fisher?

CONTINUING CASE

CARTER CLEANING COMPANY

Going Abroad

With Jennifer gradually taking the reins of Carter Cleaning Company, Jack decided to take his first long vacation in years and go to Mexico for a month in January 2008. What he found surprised him: While he spent much of the time basking in the sun in Acapulco, he also spent considerable time in Mexico City and was surprised at the dearth of cleaning stores, particularly considering the amount of air pollution in the area. Traveling north, he passed through Juarez, Mexico, and was similarly surprised at the relatively few cleaning stores he found there. As he drove back into Texas, and back toward home, he began to think about whether it would be advisable to consider expanding his chain of stores into Mexico.

Aside from the possible economic benefits, he liked what he saw in the lifestyle in Mexico and was also attracted by the idea of possibly facing the sort of exciting challenge he had faced 20 years ago when he started Carter Cleaning in the United States: "I guess entrepreneurship is in my blood," is the way he put it.

As he drove home to have dinner with Jennifer, he began to formulate the questions he would have to ask before deciding whether to expand abroad.

Questions

1. Assuming they began by opening just one or two stores in Mexico, what do you see as the main HR-related challenges he and Jennifer would have to address?
2. How would you go about choosing a manager for a new Mexican store if you were Jack or Jennifer? For instance, would you hire someone locally or send someone from one of your existing stores? Why?
3. The cost of living in Mexico is substantially below that of where Carter is now located: How would you go about developing a pay plan for your new manager if you decided to send an expatriate to Mexico?
4. Present a detailed explanation of the factors you would look for in your candidate for expatriate manager to run the stores in Mexico.

TRANSLATING STRATEGY INTO HR POLICIES & PRACTICES CASE

THE HOTEL PARIS CASE

Managing Global Human Resources

The Hotel Paris's competitive strategy is, "To use superior guest service to differentiate the Hotel Paris properties, and to thereby increase the length of stay and return rate of guests, and thus boost revenues and profitability." HR manager Lisa Cruz must now formulate functional policies and activities that support this competitive strategy by eliciting the required employee behaviors and competencies.

With hotels in 11 cities in Europe and the United States, Lisa knew that the company had to do a better job of managing its global human resources. For example, there was no formal means of identifying or training management employees for duties abroad (either for those going to the United States or to Europe). As another example, recently, after spending upwards of $600,000 sending a U.S. manager and her family

abroad, they had to return her abruptly when the family complained bitterly of missing their friends back home. Lisa knew this was no way to run a multinational business. She turned her attention to developing the HR practices her company required to do business more effectively internationally.

On reviewing the data, it was apparent to Lisa and the CFO that the company's global human resource practices were probably inhibiting the Hotel Paris from being the world-class guest services company that it sought to be. For example, high-performing service and hotel firms had formal departure training programs for at least 90% of the employees they sent abroad; the Hotel Paris had no such programs. Similarly, with each city's hotel operating its own local hotel HR information system, there was no easy way for Lisa, the CFO, or the company's CEO to obtain reports on metrics like turnover, absences, or workers' compensation costs across all the different hotels. As the CFO summed it up, "If we can't measure how each hotel is doing in terms of human resource metrics like these, there's really no way to manage these activities, so there's no telling how much lost profits and wasted efforts are dragging down each hotel's performance." Lisa received approval to institute new global human resources programs and practices.

Questions

1. Provide a 1-page summary of what individual hotel managers should know in order to make it more likely incoming employees from abroad, like those in the Hotel Paris's management development program, will adapt to their new surroundings.

2. In previous chapters you recommended various human resource practices Hotel Paris should use. Choose one of these, and explain why you believe they could take this program abroad, and how you suggest they do so.

3. Choose one Hotel Paris human resources practice that you believe is essential to the company achieving its high-quality-service goal, and explain how you would implement that practice in the firm's various hotels worldwide.

KEY TERMS

codetermination, *580*	virtual teams, *584*	adaptability screening, *586*
expatriates (expats), *582*	ethnocentric, *585*	foreign service premiums, *592*
home-country nationals, *582*	polycentric, *585*	hardship allowances, *592*
third-country nationals, *583*	geocentric, *586*	mobility premiums, *592*

ENDNOTES

1. http://talkingunion.wordpress.com/2008/09/27/is-union-reform-possible-in-china, accessed March 25, 2009.
2. See, for example, Kimberly Manion, "Venturing Abroad," *HR Magazine*, June 2008, pp. 86–90.
3. See, for example, Chris Rowley and Malcolm Warner, "Introduction: Globalizing International Human Resource Management," *International Journal of Human Resource Management* 18, no. 5 (May 2007), p. 703(14).
4. www.hoovers.com/company/Wal-Mart_Stores_Inc/rrjiff-1.html, accessed June 1, 2011.
5. "First Wal-Mart Union Begins in China," www.huffingtonpost.com/2008/08/03/first-wal-mart-union-begi_n_116629.html, accessed June 30, 2011.
6. Based on "Wal-Mart's Reshuffle Plan in China Falters," www.chinadaily.com.cn/china/2009-04/21/content_7699105.htm, accessed June 30, 2011.
7. Claire Miller, "New Book on Google Shows Gaps in China," *The New York Times*, April 1, 2011, p. B3.
8. A. L. Lytle, J. M. Brett, Z. Barsness, C. H. Tinsley, and M. Janssens, "A Paradigm for Quantitative Cross-Cultural Research in Organizational Behavior," in B. M. Staw & L. L. Cummings (Eds), *Research in Organizational Behavior* 17 (1995), pp. 167–214.
9. David Ralston, David Gustafson, Priscilla Elsass, Fannie Cheung, and Robert Terpstra, "Eastern Values: A Comparison of Managers in the United States, Hong Kong, and the People's Republic of China," *Journal of Applied Psychology* 71, no. 5

(1992), pp. 664–671. See also P. Christopher Earley and Elaine Mosakowski, "Cultural Intelligence," *Harvard Business Review*, October 2004, pp. 139–146.
10. www.geert-hofstede.com/, accessed June 1, 2011.
11. See also Vas Taras, Bradley Kirkman, and Piers Steel, "Examining the Impact of Culture's Consequences: A Three Decade, Multilevel, Multi-Analytic Review of Hofstadter's Cultural Value Dimensions," *Journal of Applied Psychology* 95, no. 3 (2010), pp. 405–439.
12. Chris Brewster, "European Perspectives on Human Resource Management," *Human Resource Management Review* 14 (2004), pp. 365–382.
13. "SOX Compliance, Corporate Codes of Conduct Can Create Challenges for U.S. Multinationals," *BNA Bulletin to Management*, March 28, 2006, p. 97.
14. Annual 2007 figures, www.bls.gov/news.release/pdf/ichcc.pdf, accessed February 19, 2010.
15. "In India, 101 Employees Pose Big Problems," *Bloomberg Businessweek*, January 17–23, 2011, p. 13.
16. "Employer Beware," *The Economist*, March 12, 2011, p. 43.
17. See, for example, www.fedee.com/ewc1.html, accessed November 4, 2009.
18. This is discussed in E. Gaugler, "HR Management: An International Comparison," *Personnel*, 1988, p. 28. E. Poutsma et al., "The Diffusion of Calculative and Collaborative HRM Practices in European Firms," *Industrial Relations* 45, no. 4 (October 2006), pp. 513–546.

19. Helen Deresky, *International Management* (Upper Saddle River, NJ: Prentice Hall, 2008), p. 17.
20. Donald Dowling Jr., "Export Codes of Conduct, Not Employee Handbooks," *Society for Human Resource Management Legal Report*, January/February 2007, pp. 1–4.
21. www.nytimes.com/2011/03/19/business/global/19blue.html, accessed June 30, 2011.
22. Phillips Taft and Cliff Powell, "The European Pensions and Benefits Environment: A Complex Ecology," *Compensation & Benefits Review*, January/February 2005, pp. 37–50.
23. Ibid.
24. Lisbeth Clause, "What You Need to Know About the New Labor Contract Law of China," *SHRM Global Law Special Report*, October to November 2008.
25. See, for example, Syed Akhtar et al., "Strategic HRM Practices and Their Impact on Company Performance in Chinese Enterprises," *Human Resource Management* 47, no. 1 (Spring 2008), pp. 15–32.
26. Andreas Lauffs, "Chinese Law Spurs Reforms," *HR Magazine*, June 2008, pp. 92–98.
27. See, for example, Kathryn King-Metters and Richard Metters, "Misunderstanding the Chinese Worker," *The Wall Street Journal*, July 7, 2008, p. R11.
28. Gary Dessler, "Expanding into China? What Foreign Employers Entering China Should Know About Human Resource Management Today," *SAM Advanced Management Journal*, August 2006. See also Joseph Gamble, "Introducing Western-Style HRM Practices to China: Shop Floor

Perceptions in a British Multinational," *Journal of World Business* 41, no. 4 (December 2006), pp. 328–340; and Adrienne Fox, "China: Land of Opportunity and Challenge," *HR Magazine*, September 2007, pp. 38–44.

29. John Daniels and Lee Radebaugh, *International Business* (Upper Saddle River, NJ, Prentice Hall, 2001), p. 767.

30. Arvind Phatak, *International Dimensions of Management* (Boston: PWS Kent, 1989), p. 106. See also Charles Hill, *International Business: Competing in the Global Marketplace* (Burr Ridge, IL: Irwin McGraw-Hill, 2001), pp. 564–566.

31. Daniels and Radebaugh, *International Business*, p. 767.

32. Ibid., p. 769; Phatak, *International Dimensions of Management*, p. 106.

33. "Survey Says Expatriates Twice as Likely to Leave Employer as Home-Based Workers," *BNA Bulletin to Management*, May 9, 2006, p. 147.

34. Phatak, *International Dimensions of Management*, p. 108.

35. Daniels and Radebaugh, *International Business*, p. 769.

36. Leslie Klass, "Fed Up with High Costs, Companies Winnow the Ranks of Career Expats," *Workforce Management*, October 2004, pp. 84–88.

37. "DOL Releases Final Rule Amending Filing, Processing of Foreign Labor Certifications," *BNA Bulletin to Management*, January 11, 2005, p. 11.

38. Michelle Rafter, "Return Trip for Expats," *Workforce*, March 16, 2009, pp. 1, 3.

39. See "Workforce Trends: Companies Continue to Deploy Ex-Pats," *Compensation & Benefits Review* 42, no. 1 (January/February 2010), p. 6.

40. "Mercer's International Assignments Survey 2010," www.imercer.com/products/2010/intl-assignments-survey.aspx, accessed June 2, 2011; "Companies Juggle Cost Cutting with Maintaining Competitive Benefits for International Assignments," www.amanet.org/training/articles/Companies-Juggle-cost-cutting-with-Maintaining-Competitive-Benefits-for-International-Assignments.aspx, accessed June 2, 2011.

41. "Mercer's International Assignments Survey 2010," "Companies Juggle Cost Cutting with Maintaining Competitive Benefits for International Assignments."

42. Helene Mayerhofer et al., "Flexpatriate Assignments: A Neglected Issue in Global Staffing," *International Journal of Human Resource Management* 15, no. 8 (December 2004), pp. 1371–1389; and Martha Frase, "International Commuters," *HR Magazine*, March 2007, pp. 91–96.

43. Timothy Dwyer, "Localization's Hidden Costs," *HR Magazine*, June 2004, pp. 135–144.

44. Michael Harvey et al., "Global Virtual Teams: A Human Resource Capital Architecture," *International Journal of Human Resource Management* 16, no. 9 (September 2005), pp. 1583–1599.

45. Charles Snow, Scott Snell, Sue Canney Davison, and Donald Hambrick, "Use Transnational Teams to Globalize Your Company," *Organizational Dynamics*, Spring 1996, pp. 50–67.

46. Ibid.

47. Anthony Townsend, Samuel DiMarie, and Anthony Hendrickson, "Virtual Teams: Technology and the Workplace of the Future," *Academy of Management Executive* 12, no. 3 (1998), pp. 17–29. Christina Gibson and Susan Cohen, *Virtual Teams That Work: Creating Conditions for Virtual Team Effectiveness* (Jossey-Bass: San Francisco, 2004), provides practicing managers with valuable insights into organizing and managing virtual teams. Many companies use international virtual teams to coordinate research and development type projects. Bjorn Ambos and Bodo Schlemglmich, "The Use of International R&D Teams: An Empirical Investigation of Selected Contingency Factors," *Journal of World Business* 39, no. 1 (February 2004), pp. 37–48.

48. Michael Harvey et al., "Challenges to Staffing Global Virtual Teams," *Human Resource Management Review* 14 (2004), p. 281.

49. Ibid., p. 20.

50. Christa Degnan, "ActiveProject Aids Teamwork," *PC Week*, May 31, 1999, p. 35.

51. Except as noted, this is based on information in Bradley Kirkman et al., "Five Challenges to Virtual Team Success: Lessons from Sabre, Inc.," *Academy of Management Executive* 16, no. 3 (2002), p. 70.

52. This item based on Bradley Kirkman et al., "The Impact of Team Empowerment on Virtual Team Performance: The Moderating Role of Face-To-Face Interaction," *Academy of Management Journal* 47, no. 2 (2004), pp. 175–192.

53. William Bulkeley, "IBM to Cut US Jobs, Expand in India," *The Wall Street Journal*, March 26, 2009, p. B1.

54. Mary Medland, "Setting Up Overseas," *HR Magazine*, January 2004, p. 71.

55. Phatak, *International Dimensions of Management*, p. 129.

56. Charles Hill, *International Business: Competing in the Global Marketplace* (Burr Ridge, IL: Irwin, 1994), p. 507.

57. Ibid., pp. 507–510.

58. Ibid.

59. Ibid., p. 509.

60. Ibid. See also M. Harvey et al., "An Innovative Global Management Staffing System: A Competency-Based Perspective," *Human Resource Management* 39, no. 4 (Winter 2000), pp. 381–394.

61. Mason Carpenter et al., "International Assignment Experience at the Top Can Make a Bottom-Line Difference," *Human Resource Management* 30, no. 223 (Summer–Fall 2000), pp. 277–285. See also Gunter Stahl and Paula Caligiuri, "The Effectiveness of Expatriate Coping Strategies: The Moderating Role of Cultural Distance, Position Level, and Time on the International Assignment," *Journal of Applied Psychology* 90, no. 4 (2005), pp. 603–615.

62. Sunkyu Jun and James Gentry, "An Exploratory Investigation of the Relative Importance of Cultural Similarity and Personal Fit in the Selection and Performance of Expatriates," *Journal of World Business* 40, no. 1 (February 2005), pp. 1–8. See also Jan Selmer, "Cultural Novelty and Adjustment: Western Business Expatriates in China," *International Journal of Human Resource Management* 17, no. 7 (2006), pp. 1211–1222.

63. Mary G. Tye and Peter Y. Chen, "Selection of Expatriates: Decision-Making Models Used by HR Professionals," *Human Resource Planning* 28, no. 4 (December 2005), p. 15(6).

64. Paula Caligiuri et al., "Selection for International Assignments," *Human Resource Management Review* 19 (2009), pp. 251–262.

65. Zsuzsanna Tungli and Maury Peiperl, "Expatriate Practices in German, Japanese, UK and US Multinational Companies: A Comparative Survey of Changes," *Human Resource Management* 48, no. 1 (January–February 2009), pp. 153–171.

66. Winfred Arthur Jr. and Winston Bennett Jr., "The International Assignee: The Relative Importance of Factors Perceived to Contribute to Success," *Personnel Psychology* 48 (1995), p. 110; Gretchen Spreitzer, Morgan McCall Jr., and Joan Mahoney, "Early Identification of International Executive Potential," *Journal of Applied Psychology* 82, no. 1 (1997), pp. 62–69.

67. Phatak, *International Dimensions of Management*, p. 119. See also Arno Haslberger, "The Complexities of Expatriate Adaptation," *Human Resource Management Review* 15, no. 2 (June 2005), pp. 160–180.

68. Mansour Javidan, Mary Teagarden, and David Bowen, "Making It Overseas," *Harvard Business Review* 88, no. 4 (April 2010), pp. 109–113.

69. Ibid.

70. www.performanceprograms.com/Surveys/Overseas.shtm, accessed January 31, 2008.

71. Blocklyn, "Developing the International Executive," p. 45. See also Eric Krell, "Evaluating the Returns on Expatriates," *HR Magazine* 50, no. 3 (March 2005), pp. 61–65.

72. "The Equal Employment Opportunity Responsibilities of Multinational Employers," The U.S. Equal Employment Opportunity Commission, www.EEOC.gov/facts/multi-employers.html, accessed February 9, 2004.

73. See Donald Dowling Jr., "Choice of Law Contract Clauses May Not Fly Abroad," *Society for Human Resource Management Legal Report*, October–November 2008, pp. 1–2.

74. Chuck Csizmar, "Does Your Expatriate Program Follow the Rules of the Road?" *Compensation & Benefits Review*, January/February 2008, pp. 61–69.

75. P. Caligiuri, "The Big Five Personality Characteristics as Predictors of Expatriates' Desire to Terminate the Assignment and Supervisor-Rated Performance," *Personnel Psychology* 53, no. 1 (Spring 2000), pp. 67–88.

See also Margaret A. Shaffer, David A. Harrison, Hal Gregersen, J. Stewart Black, and Lori A. Ferzandi, "You Can Take It with You: Individual Differences and Expatriate Effectiveness," *Journal of Applied Psychology* 91, no. 1 (January 2006), p. 109(17).

76. Jan Selmer, "Expatriation: Corporate Policy, Personal Intentions and International Adjustment," *International Journal of Human Resource Management* 9, no. 6 (December 1998), pp. 997–1007.

77. Hung-Wen Lee and Ching-Hsing, "Determinants of the Adjustment of Expatriate Managers to Foreign Countries: An Empirical Study," *International Journal of Management* 23, no. 2 (2006), pp. 302–311.

78. Sunkyu Jun and James Gentry, "An Exploratory Investigation of the Relative Importance of Cultural Similarity and Personal Fit in the Selection and Performance of Expatriates," *Journal of World Business* 40, no. 1 (February 2005), pp. 1–8. See also Jan Selmer, "Cultural Novelty and Adjustment: Western Business Expatriates in China," *International Journal of Human Resource Management* 17, no. 7 (2006), pp. 1211–1222.

79. Discussed in Hill, *International Business*, pp. 511–515.

80. Barbara Anderson, "Expatriate Selection: Good Management or Good Luck?" *International Journal of Human Resource Management* 16, no. 4 (April 2005), pp. 567–583.

81. Margaret Shaffer and David Harrison, "Forgotten Partners of International Assignments: Development and Test of a Model of Spouse Adjustment," *Journal of Applied Psychology* 86, no. 2 (2001), pp. 238–254.

82. Ibid., p. 251.

83. Ibid., p. 250.

84. Hung-Wen Lee and Ching-Hsing, "Determinants of the Adjustment of Expatriate Managers to Foreign Countries: An Empirical Study," *International Journal of Management* 23, no. 2 (2006), pp. 302–311.

85. Gary Insch and John Daniels, "Causes and Consequences of Declining Early Departures from Foreign Assignments," *Business Horizons* 46, no. 6 (November–December 2002), pp. 39–48.

86. Eric Krell, "Budding Relationships," *HR Magazine* 50, no. 6 (June 2005), pp. 114–118.

87. Adapted from www.interchangeinstitute.org/html/cross_cultural.htm, accessed July 1, 2011.

88. Adapted from www.kwintessential.co.uk/cultural-services/articles/expat-cultural-training.html, accessed July 1, 2011.

89. www.global-lt.com/en/us/cultural-training/cultural-training-expatriate-training-courses.html#60Countries, accessed July 1, 2011.

90. Lynette Clemetson, "The Pepsi Challenge: Helping Ex-Pats Feel at Home," *Workforce Management*, December 2010, p. 36.

91. Jie Shen, "Effective International Performance Appraisals: Easily Said, Hard to Do," *Compensation and Benefits Review* 37, no. 4 (July/August 2005), pp. 70–79.

92. See, for example, Jie Shen, "Effective International Performance Appraisals: Easily Said, Hard to Do," *Compensation & Benefits Review*, July/August 2005, pp. 70–78.

93. See, for example, Victor Infante, "Three Ways to Design International Pay: Headquarters, Home Country, Host," *Workforce*, January 2001, pp. 22–24; and Gary Parker and Erwin Janush, "Developing Expatriate Remuneration Packages," *Employee Benefits Journal* 26, no. 2 (June 2001), pp. 3–51.

94. Stephenie Overman, "Focus on International HR," *HR Magazine*, March 2000, pp. 87–92; Sheila Burns, "Flexible International Assignee Compensation Plans," *Compensation & Benefits Review*, May/June 2003, pp. 35–44; Thomas Shelton, "Global Compensation Strategies: Managing and Administering Split Pay for an Expatriate Workforce," *Compensation & Benefits Review*, January/February 2008, pp. 56–59.

95. Phatak, *International Dimensions of Management*, p. 134. See also "China to Levy Income Tax on Expatriates," *Asia Africa Intelligence Wire*, August 3, 2004, Item A120140119.

96. Thomas Shelton, "Global Compensation Strategies: Managing and Administering Split Pay for an Expatriate Workforce," *Compensation & Benefits Review*, January/February 2008, pp. 56–59.

97. http://aoprals.state.gov/content.asp?content_id=186&menu_id=81, accessed July 1, 2011.

98. See, for example, "More Multinational Organizations Are Taking a Global Approach to Compensation," *Compensation & Benefits Review*, May/June 2008, p. 5.

99. Luis Hernandez, "On Why Ex-Pat Assignments Succeed—or Fail," *Harvard Business Review*, March 2011, p. 73.

100. Mark Schoeff Jr., "Danger and Duty," *Workforce*, November 19, 2007, pp. 1, 3.

101. "Managers Are Paid More in Emerging Economies," *Compensation & Benefits Review*, September/October 2007, p. 19.

102. Robin White, "A Strategic Approach to Building a Consistent Global Rewards Program," *Compensation & Benefits Review*, July/August 2005, p. 25.

103. "Recommendations for Managing Global Compensation Clause in a Changing Economy," Hewitt Associates, www.hewittassociates.com/_MetaBasicCMAssetCache_/Assets/Articles/2009/hewitt_pov_globalcomp_0109.pdf, accessed March 22, 2009.

104. White, "A Strategic Approach," pp. 23–40.

105. "For Employers Conducting Business Abroad, Kidnappings Remain an Ongoing Concern," *BNA Bulletin to Management*, November 23, 2010, p. 369.

106. Jessica Marquez, "Hostage-Taking in France has U.S. Observers on Their Guard," *Workforce Management*, April 20, 2009, p. 10.

107. Lisbeth Claus, "International Assignees at Risk," *HR Magazine*, February 2010, p. 73.

108. Fay Hansen, "Skirting Danger," *Workforce Magazine*, January 19, 2009, pp. 1, 3.

109. Frank Jossi, "Buying Protection from Terrorism," HR Magazine, June 2001, pp. 155-160.

110. "Unrest in Egypt Highlights Importance of Crisis Management Plans, Experts Say," *BNA Bulletin to Management*, February 8, 2011, pp. 41–42.

111. Frank Jossi, "Buying Protection from Terrorism," op cit.,

112. These are based on or quoted from Samuel Greengard, "Mission Possible: Protecting Employees Abroad," *Workforce*, August 1997, pp. 30–32. See also Z. Phillips, "Global Firms Consider Additional Cover for Overseas Execs," *Business Insurance* 43, no. 23 (June 15–22, 2009), pp. 4, 22.

113. Ibid., p. 32.

114. Carla Joinson, "Save Thousands Per Expatriate," *HR Magazine*, July 2002, p. 77. A survey by accountants KPMG found that only about 4% of the 430 human resource executives surveyed believed they were effectively managing the repatriation process. Tanya Mohn, "The Long Trip Home," *The New York Times*, March 10, 2009, p. 86.

115. Kathryn Tyler, "Retaining Repatriates," *HR Magazine*, March 2006, pp. 97–102.

116. Quoted in Leslie Klaff, "The Right Way to Bring Expats Home," *Workforce*, July 2002, p. 43.

117. Maria Kraimer et al., "The Influence of Expatriate and Repatriate Experiences on Career Advancement and Repatriate Retention," *Human Resource Management* 48, no. 1 (January–February 2009), pp. 27–47.

118. Ibid., p. 43.

119. Ibid.

120. Diane Turner, "NuView Brings Web-Based HRIS to Buildnet," *Workforce*, December 2000, p. 90.

121. Jim Meade, "Web-Based HRIS Meets Multiple Needs," *HR Magazine*, August 2000, pp. 129–133. See also "Dynamic HR: Global Applications from IBM," *Human Resource Management* 48, no. 4 (July/August 2009), pp. 641–648.

122. Drew Robb, "Unifying Your Enterprise with a Global HR Portal," *HR Magazine*, March 2006, pp. 119–120.

123. Ann Marie Ryan et al., "Designing and Implementing Global Staffing Systems: Part 2—Best Practices," *Human Resource Management* 42, no. 1 (Spring 2003), pp. 85–94.

124. Ibid., p. 89.

125. Ibid., p. 90.

126. Ibid., p. 86. See also M. Schoeff, "Adopting an HR Worldview," *Workforce Management* 87, no. 19 (November 17, 2008), p. 8.

127. Ryan, "Designing and Implementing Global Staffing Systems," p. 87.

128. Ibid., p. 92.

129. Written by and copyrighted by Gary Dessler, PhD.

18
Managing Human Resources in Small and Entrepreneurial Firms

Source: Bob Daemmrich/Alamy.

LEARNING OBJECTIVES

1. Explain why HRM is important to small businesses and how small business HRM is different from that in large businesses.

2. Give four examples of how entrepreneurs can use Internet and government tools to support the HR effort.

3. List five ways entrepreneurs can use their small size to improve their HR processes.

4. Discuss how you would choose and deal with a professional employee organization.

5. Describe how you would create a start-up human resource system for a new small business.

H is high school teacher told him he'd never make it in business. But today Carlos Ledezma owns two Chevrolet dealerships in Kansas City.[1] Those dealerships are more profitable than most, a fact that Mr. Ledezma attributes in no small part to his approach to human resource management. His business strategy was to boost profits by building repeat business from customers who like dealing with friendly, long-term employees, and that's what he's achieved.

WHERE ARE WE NOW . . .

Most people work for small businesses or create new small businesses of their own, and such businesses have special human resource management needs. The main purpose of this chapter is to help you apply what you know about human resource management to running a small business. The main topics we'll address include the small business challenge; using Internet and government tools to support the HR effort; leveraging small size with familiarity, flexibility, fairness, and informality; using professional employer organizations; and managing HR systems, procedures, and paperwork.

Access a host of interactive learning aids at **www.mymanagementlab.com** to help strengthen your understanding of the chapter concepts.

THE SMALL BUSINESS CHALLENGE

Why Small Business Is Important

In some respects there's nothing small about *small business*. More than half the people working in the United States—about 68 million out of 118 million—work for small firms.[2] Small businesses as a group also account for most of the 600,000 or so new businesses created every year, as well as for most of the business growth (small firms grow faster than big ones). And small firms create most of the new jobs in the United States.[3]

Statistically speaking, therefore, most people graduating from college in the next few years will work for small businesses—those with less than 200 or so employees. Anyone interested in human resource management thus needs to understand how managing human resources in small firms is different from doing so in huge multinationals.

1 Explain why HRM is important to small businesses and how small business HRM is different from that in large businesses.

How Small Business Human Resource Management Is Different

Managing human resources in small firms is different for four main reasons: *size*, *priorities*, *informality*, and the nature of the *entrepreneur*.

SIZE   For one thing, it would be very unusual to find a very small business—say, under 90 or so employees—with a dedicated human resource management professional.[4] The rule of thumb is that it's not until a company reaches the 100-employee milestone that it can afford an HR specialist. Yet even five- or six-person retail shops must recruit, select, train, and compensate employees. So in such situations, it's usually the owner and (sometimes) his or her assistant that does all the HR paperwork and tasks. SHRM's *Human Capital Benchmarking Study* found that even firms with under 100 employees often spend the equivalent of two-or-so people's time each year addressing human resource management issues.[5] But, that time is usually just coming out of the owner's very long workday.

PRIORITIES   It's not just size but the realities that drive many small business managers and entrepreneurs (the men and women who provide the vision and "spark" that starts a new business) to expend more time and resources on non-HR issues. After studying small e-commerce firms in the United Kingdom, one researcher concluded that, as important as human resource management is, it simply wasn't a high priority for these firms:

> Given their shortage of resources in terms of time, money, people and expertise, a typical SME [small- and medium-size enterprise] manager's organizational imperatives are perceived elsewhere, in finance, production and marketing, with HR of diminished relative importance.[6]

INFORMALITY   One effect of this is that human resource management tends to be more informal in smaller firms. For example, one study analyzed training practices in about 900 family and non-family small companies.[7] Training tended to be informal, with an emphasis on methods like coworker and supervisory on-the-job training.

Such informality isn't just due to a lack of expertise and resources (although that's part of it); it's also partly a "matter of survival." Entrepreneurs must be able to react quickly to changes in competitive conditions. Given that, there's logic in keeping things like compensation policies flexible. The need for small businesses to adapt quickly to competitive challenges often means handling matters like raises, appraisals, and time off "on an informal, reactive basis with a short time horizon."[8]

THE ENTREPRENEUR *Entrepreneurs* are people who create businesses under risky conditions, and starting new businesses from scratch is always risky. Researchers believe that small firms' relative informality partly stems from entrepreneurs' unique personalities. Entrepreneurs tend (among other things) to be controlling: "Owners tend to want to impose their stamp and personal management style on internal matters, including the primary goal and orientation of the firm, its working conditions and policies, and the style of internal and external communication and how this is communicated to the staff."[9]

IMPLICATIONS These four differences have several human resource management–related implications for small businesses.

- First, their more rudimentary human resource practices may put small business owners at a *competitive disadvantage*. A small business owner not using tools like Web-based recruiting is accumulating unnecessary costs, and probably deriving inferior results compared to larger competitors.

- Second, there is a *lack of specialized HR expertise*.[10] In most (larger) small businesses, there are at most one or two dedicated human resource management people. This makes it more likely that they'll miss problems in specific areas, such as equal employment law, or occupational safety. This may produce legal or other problems.

- Third, the smaller firm often hasn't the time or specialized expertise to understand the *legal implications*—for instance, of innocently (but inappropriately) asking a female job candidate if she's thinking of "starting a family."

- Fourth, the small business owner may not be fully complying with *compensation regulations and laws*. Examples include paying compensatory time for overtime hours worked, and distinguishing between employees and independent contractors.

- Fifth, paperwork duplication leads to *data entry errors*. Small businesses often don't use human resource information systems, so employee data (name, address, marital status, and so on) often appears on multiple human resource forms (medical enrollment forms, W-4 forms, and so on). Any personal data change requires manually changing all forms. This is time-consuming and inefficient, and can trigger errors.

Why HRM Is Important to Small Businesses

Entrepreneurs and all small business managers need to take these implications to heart. Small firms need all the advantages they can get, and effective human resource management is a competitive necessity. Small firms that have effective HR practices do better than those that do not.[11] For example, researchers studied 168 family-owned fast growth small- and medium-size enterprises (SMEs). They concluded that successful high-growth SMEs placed greater importance on training and development, performance appraisals, recruitment packages, maintaining morale, and setting competitive compensation levels than did low-performing firms: "These findings suggest that these human resource activities do in fact have a positive impact on performance [in smaller businesses]."[12]

For many small firms, effective human resource management is also mandatory for getting and keeping big customers. Most suppliers (and therefore *their* suppliers) must comply with international quality standards. Thus, to comply with ISO-9000 requirements, large customers "either directly checked for the presence of certain HR policies, or, satisfying their service demands indirectly necessitated changes in, for example, [the small vendor's] training and job design."[13] The accompanying Strategic Context feature provides an illustration.

THE STRATEGIC CONTEXT

The Dealership

Carlos Ledezma's strategy was to boost profits by building repeat business from customers who like dealing with friendly, long-term employees.[14] He knew his success therefore depended on building a dedicated and customer-oriented staff, and getting them to stay. To achieve that, he put in place an integrated, customer-oriented human resource management strategy. He tests each employment candidate to make sure the job is the right fit. There's a weeklong new-employee orientation that introduces them to their jobs and to the firm's mission and culture. Then he gives each new employee a senior employee to shadow for 90 days.[15] This person teaches by example. For the first 90 days, mentors receive $50 to $100 for each vehicle their trainee sells. In one recent year, Ledezma spent $150,000 on training.

Ledezma's HR strategy pays off in profits that are well above the industry average. Customers like dealing with dedicated, competent, long-term employees. His employee turnover is about 28%, and the average employee stays about 8 years, both much better than the industry average.

We turn in this chapter to methods entrepreneurs and small business managers can use to improve their human resource management practices, starting with Internet and government tools.

---

2 Give four examples of how entrepreneurs can use Internet and government tools to support the HR effort.

USING INTERNET AND GOVERNMENT TOOLS TO SUPPORT THE HR EFFORT

City Garage is an expanding service company in Texas. The firm's managers knew they would never implement their firm's growth strategy without changing how they tested and hired employees.[16] They needed mechanics who were comfortable interacting directly with customers in City Garage's "open service area" format. The old hiring process consisted of a paper-and-pencil application and one interview, followed by a hire/don't hire decision. The process ate up valuable management time, and was not effective. City Garage's solution was to purchase the Personality Profile Analysis (PPA) online test from Thomas International USA. Now, after a quick application and background check, likely candidates take the 10-minute, 24-question PPA. City Garage staff then enter the answers into the PPA Software system, and receive test results in less than 2 minutes. These show whether the applicant is high or low in four personality characteristics.

Like City Garage, no small business owner needs to cede the advantage to big competitors when it comes to human resource management. One can level the terrain by using Internet-based HR resources, including the free resources of the U.S. government. We'll next look at how small firms can do this.

Complying with Employment Laws

Complying with federal (and state and local) employment law is a thorny issue for entrepreneurs. For example, under the law, the entrepreneur needs to know, "What can I ask a job candidate?" "Must I pay this person overtime?" and, "Must I report this injury?"

Addressing such issues requires deciding which federal employment laws apply to the company. For example, Title VII of the Civil Rights Act of 1964 applies to employers with 15 or more employees, while the Age Discrimination in Employment Act of 1967 applies to those with 20 or more.[17] Small business owners will find the legal answers they need online at federal agencies' Web sites like the following.

City Garage's managers knew they would never implement their firm's growth strategy without changing how they tested and hired employees.

Source: PaulRapson/Alamy.

THE DOL   The U.S. Department of Labor's "*FirstStep* Employment Law Advisor" (see www.DOL.gov/elaws/firststep/) helps small businesses determine which laws apply to their business. First, the elaws wizard takes the owner through questions such as "What is the maximum number of employees your business or organization employs or will employ during the calendar year?" (See Figure 18-1.)

Proceeding through the wizard, the "results" page says, "Based on the information you provided in response to the questions in the Advisor, the following employment laws administered by the Department of Labor (DOL) may apply to your business or organization."[18] For a typical small firm, these laws might include the Consumer Credit Protection Act, Employee Polygraph Protection Act, Fair Labor Standards Act, Immigration and Nationality Act, Occupational Safety and Health Act, Uniformed Services Employment and Reemployment Rights Act, and Whistleblower Act.

A linked DOL site (www.dol.gov/whd/flsa/index.htm) provides information on the Fair Labor Standards Act (FLSA). It's "elaws Advisors" provide practical guidance on questions such as when to pay overtime. Figure 18-2 presents, from this Web site, a list of elaws Advisors.

FIGURE 18-1 *FirstStep* Employment Law Advisor

Source: www.dol.gov/elaws/firststep, accessed June 2008.

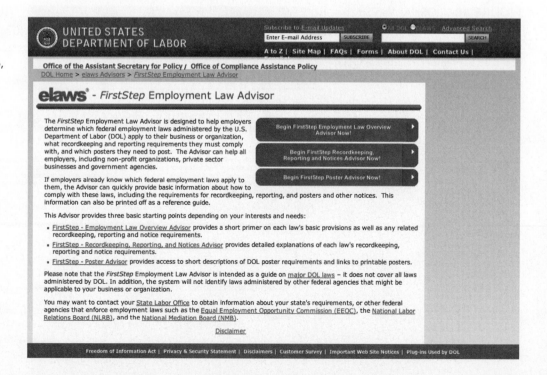

FIGURE 18-2 Sample DOL Elaws Advisors

Source: Adapted from www.dol.gov/whd/flsa/index.htm, accessed September 15, 2011.

- The *Coverage and Employment Status Advisor* helps identify which workers are employees covered by the FLSA.
- The *Hours Worked Advisor* provides information to help determine which hours spent in work-related activities are considered FLSA "hours worked" and, therefore, must be paid.
- The *Overtime Security Advisor* helps determine which employees are exempt from the FLSA minimum wage and overtime pay requirements under the Part 541 overtime regulations.
- The *Overtime Calculator Advisor* computes the amount of overtime pay due in a sample pay period based on information from the user.
- The *Child Labor Rules Advisor* answers questions about the FLSA's youth employment provisions, including at what age young people can work and the jobs they can perform.
- The *Section 14(c) Advisor* helps users understand the special minimum wage requirements for workers with disabilities.

THE EEOC The U.S. Equal Employment Opportunity Commission (EEOC) administers Title VII of the Civil Rights Act of 1964 (Title VII), the Age Discrimination in Employment Act of 1967 (ADEA), Title I of the Americans with Disabilities Act of 1990 (ADA), and the Equal Pay Act of 1963 (EPA). Its Web site (www.EEOC.gov/employers/) contains important information regarding matters such as:

- How do I determine if my business is covered by EEOC laws?
- Who may file a charge of discrimination with the EEOC?
- Can a small business resolve a charge without undergoing an investigation or facing a lawsuit?

As the EEOC says, "While the information in this section of our website applies to all employers, it has been specifically designed for small businesses which may not have a human resources department or a specialized EEO staff." (www.eeoc.gov/employers) The site provides small business owners with practical advice. For example, "What should I do when someone files a charge against my company?"

OSHA The DOL's Occupational Safety and Health Administration site (www.OSHA.gov/) similarly supplies small business guidance. (See Figure 18-3.) OSHA's

FIGURE 18-3 OSHA Web Site

Source: www.osha.gov/dcsp/smallbusiness/index.html, accessed September 15, 2011.

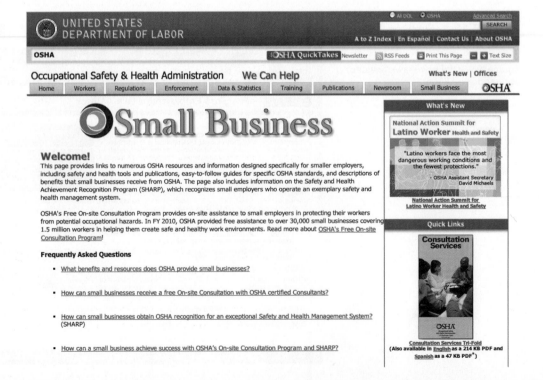

site provides, among other things, easy access to the *OSHA Small Business Handbook*. This contains practical information, including industry-specific safety and accident checklists.

Employment Planning and Recruiting

Internet resources can make small business owners as effective as their large competitors at writing job descriptions and building applicant pools. As we saw in Chapter 4 (Job Analysis), the Department of Labor's O*NET (http://online.onetcenter.org) illustrates this. Its online wizard enables business owners to create accurate and professional job descriptions and job specifications quickly.

WEB-BASED RECRUITING   Similarly, small business owners can use the online recruiting tools we discussed in Chapter 5. For example, it's easy to post positions on Internet job boards such as Careerbuilder.com, on the sites of professional associations, or on the sites of local newspapers.

Employment Selection

As with the earlier City Garage example, some tests are so easy to use they are particularly good for smaller firms. An example is the *Wonderlic Personnel Test*, which measures general mental ability. With questions somewhat similar to the SAT, it takes less than 15 minutes to administer the four-page booklet. The tester reads the instructions, and then keeps time as the candidate works through the 50 problems. The tester scores the test by totaling the number of correct answers. Comparing the person's score with the minimum scores recommended for various occupations shows whether the person achieved the minimally acceptable score for the job in question.

The *Predictive Index* is another example. It measures work-related personality traits, drives, and behaviors—in particular dominance, extroversion, patience, and blame avoidance. A template makes scoring simple. The Predictive Index program includes 15 standard benchmark personality patterns. For example, there is the "social interest" pattern, for a person who is generally unselfish, congenial, persuasive, patient, and unassuming. This person would be good with people and a good personnel interviewer, for instance.

Many vendors, including Wonderlic and the Predictive Index, offer online applicant compilation and screening services. Wonderlic's service (which costs about $8,500 per year for a small firm) first provides job analyses for the employer's jobs. Wonderlic then provides a Web site the small businesses' applicants can log into to take one or several selection tests (including the Wonderlic Personnel Test). Figure 18-4 shows a partial report for a sample applicant. The following are suggestions from *Inc.* magazine for supercharging a small business's recruiting and screening processes.

- **Keep It in the Industry.** Use online job boards that target a particular industry or city to minimize irrelevant applicants.[19] For example, Jobing.com maintains 41 city-specific job sites in 19 states. Beyond.com hosts more than 15,000 industry-specific communities.

- **Automate the Process.** Automated applicant processing systems are inexpensive enough for small employers. For example, systems from Taleo, NuView Systems, and Accolo accept résumés and help automate the screening process. NuView, which costs about $6 to $15 per month per user, can instantly ask applicants questions, and bump out those without, for instance, the required education.[20]

- **Test Online.** Use online tests, for instance, to test an applicant's typing speed, proficiency at QuickBooks, or even ability to sell over the phone. For example, PreVisor and Kenexa offer close to 1,000 online assessments, charging from several dollars to $50 a test.[21]

FIGURE 18-4 Wonderlic Personnel Test: Part of a Sample Report

Source: Wonderlic (www.wonderlic.com).

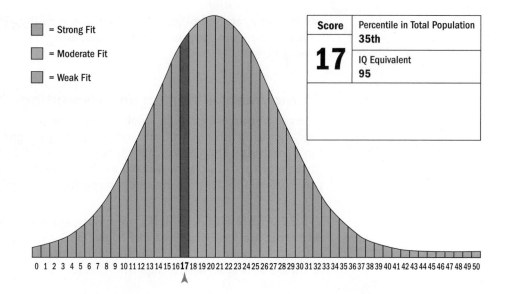

■ = Strong Fit
■ = Moderate Fit
■ = Weak Fit

Score	Percentile in Total Population
17	**35th**
	IQ Equivalent **95**

0 1 2 3 4 5 6 7 8 9 10 11 12 13 14 15 16 17 18 19 20 21 22 23 24 25 26 27 28 29 30 31 32 33 34 35 36 37 38 39 40 41 42 43 44 45 46 47 48 49 50

Score Interpretation

Job Fit: Test takers who score in this range do not meet the cognitive ability requirements identified for this job. The complexity present within this position may make it difficult for these individuals to meet minimum standards for job performance.

Training Potential: This test taker is likely to receive maximum benefit from training that follows a programmed or mastery approach to learning. Given enough time, this individual may have the ability to learn a limited number of lengthy, routine procedures. Allow for sufficient time with hands-on-training before requiring this individual to work independently.

- **Poll Your Inner Circle.** Tap friends and employees for recommendations and use social networking sites such as LinkedIn, Facebook, and MySpace. Many employers announce job openings through LinkedIn. One says, "I get people vouching for each applicant, so I don't have to spend hours sorting through résumés," he says.[22]

- **Send a Recording.** InterviewStream, in Bethlehem, Pennsylvania, records online video interviews for about $30 to $60. InterviewStream sends the candidate an e-mail invitation with a link. When he or she clicks the link, a video interviewer asks the company's prerecorded questions. A Webcam captures the candidate's answers. Employers can let candidates rerecord their answers. Hiring managers can review the videos at their leisure.[23]

COMPLYING WITH THE LAW Particularly when using tests at work, the employer must comply with equal employment laws. Unfortunately, given the time pressures facing most small business owners, confirming the validity of those tests one buys online or through office supply stores is probably the exception, not the rule. As Chapters 2 and 5 explained, there is no rational basis upon which to expose applicants to tests or devices, the validity of which are unknown. Many test providers will assist the employer in setting up a testing procedure. For example, as we noted, Wonderlic will review your job descriptions as part of its process.

Employment Training

Internet training can provide, at a relatively low cost, employee training that used to be beyond most small employers' reach.

PRIVATE VENDORS The small business owner can tap hundreds of suppliers of prepackaged training solutions. These range from self-study programs from the American Management Association (www.amanet.org) and SHRM (www.shrm.org), to specialized programs. For example, the employer might arrange with PureSafety to have its employees take occupational safety courses from www.puresafety.com.

FIGURE 18-5 Some Online Courses Offered by the Small Business Administration's Virtual Campus for Small Business Training

Source: http://www.sba.gov/category/navigation-structure/starting-managing-business/managing-business/running-business/human-resources, accessed September 18, 2011.

SkillSoft is another example (http://skillsoft.com/catalog/default.asp). Its courses include software development, business strategy and operations, professional effectiveness, and desktop computer skills. As an example, the course "interviewing effectively" targets managers, team leaders, and human resource professionals. About 2 1/2 hours long, it shows trainees how to use behavioral questioning to interview candidates.[24]

The buyer's guide from the American Society of Training and Development (www.astd.org/) is a good place to start to find a vendor (check under Resources).

THE SBA The federal government's Small Business Administration (www.SBA.gov/training/) provides a virtual campus that offers online courses, workshops, publications, and learning tools aimed toward supporting entrepreneurs.[25] For example, the small business owner can link under "Small Business Planner" to "Writing Effective Job Descriptions," "Employees versus Contractors: What's the Difference?" and "The Interview Process: How to Select the Right Person" (see Figure 18-5).

NAM The National Association of Manufacturers (NAM) is the largest industrial trade organization in the United States. It represents about 14,000 member manufacturers, including 10,000 small and mid-sized companies.

NAM's Virtual University (www.namvu.com) helps employees maintain and upgrade their work skills and continue their professional development. It offers almost 650 courses.[26] There are no long-term contracts to sign. Employers simply pay about $10–$30 per course taken by each employee. The catalog includes OSHA, quality, and technical training as well as courses in areas like business and finance, personal development, and customer service.

Employment Appraisal and Compensation

Small employers have easy access to computerized and online appraisal and compensation services. For example, Oracle Corporation's ePerformance (http://www.oracle.com/us/products/applications/peoplesoft-enterprise/hcm-resource-library/051027.pdf)

facilitates the performance management process by enabling managers to formalize the employee's goals and then assess progress toward meeting those goals.

The eAppraisal system from Halogen Software (http://www.halogensoftware.com/products/halogen-eappraisal/) is another example.[27]

Similarly, lack of easy access to salary surveys once made it difficult and time-consuming for smaller businesses to fine-tune their pay scales. Today, sites like onetonline.org facilitate the job analysis process and www.salary.com makes it easy to determine local pay rates.

Employment Safety and Health

Safety is an important issue for small employers. One European study found that the majority of all the workplace accidents and serious workplace accidents occur in firms with less than 50 employees.[28] OHSA provides several free services for small employers.

OSHA CONSULTATION[29]   OSHA provides free on-site safety and health services for small businesses. Employers can contact their nearest OSHA area office to speak to the compliance assistance specialist. (Employers can also check out the OSHA Training Institute training available in Chicago or in one of about 20 education centers located at U.S. colleges and universities.)

The employer triggers the process by requesting a voluntary consultation. There is an opening conference with a safety expert, a walk-through, and a closing conference at which the employer and safety expert discuss the latter's observations. The consultant then provides a detailed report explaining the findings. The employer's only obligation is to commit to correcting serious hazards in a timely manner.

OSHA SHARP   The OSHA Sharp program is a certification process. OSHA certifies that small employers have achieved commendable levels of safety awareness.[30] Employers request a consultation and visit, and undergo a complete hazard identification survey. The employer agrees to correct identified hazards, and to implement and maintain a safety and health management system. OSHA's on-site project manager may recommend that OSHA exempt the Sharp employer for 2 years from scheduled inspections.

3 List five ways entrepreneurs can use their small size to improve their HR processes.

LEVERAGING SMALL SIZE: FAMILIARITY, FLEXIBILITY, FAIRNESS, INFORMALITY, AND HRM

Because small businesses need to capitalize on their strengths, they should capitalize on their smallness when dealing with employees. Smallness should translate into personal *familiarity* with each employee's strengths, needs, and family situation. And it should translate into being *flexible* and *informal* in the human resource management policies and practices the company follows.[31]

Simple, Informal Employee Selection Procedures

Just as small business managers can use Internet-based recruitment and selection tools,[32] many low-tech tools are also available. We'll look at two, streamlined interviews, and work-sampling tests.

A Streamlined Interviewing Process

The small business owner, pressed for time, may use the following practical, streamlined employment interview process.[33]

PREPARING FOR THE INTERVIEW   Even a busy entrepreneur can quickly summarize the kind of person who would be best for the job. One way to do so is to focus

on four basic required factors—knowledge and experience, motivation, intellectual capacity, and personality. To proceed this way, ask the following questions:

- *Knowledge and experience:* What must the candidate know to perform the job? What experience is necessary to perform the job?
- *Motivation:* What should the person like doing to enjoy this job? Is there anything the person should not dislike? Are there any essential goals or aspirations the person should have?
- *Intellectual capacity:* Are there any specific intellectual aptitudes required (mathematical, mechanical, and so on)? How complex are the problems the person must solve? What must a person be able to demonstrate he or she can do intellectually?
- *Personality factor:* What are the critical personality qualities needed for success on the job (ability to withstand boredom, decisiveness, stability, and so on)? How must the job incumbent handle stress, pressure, and criticism? What kind of interpersonal behavior is required in the job?

SPECIFIC FACTORS TO PROBE IN THE INTERVIEW
Next, ask a combination of situational questions plus open-ended questions to probe the candidate's suitability for the job. For example:

- *Knowledge and experience factor:* Probe with situational questions such as "How would you organize such a sales effort?" or "How would you design that kind of Web site?"
- *Motivation factor:* Probe such areas as the person's likes and dislikes (for each thing done, what he or she liked or disliked about it), aspirations (including the validity of each goal in terms of the person's reasoning about why he or she chose it), and energy level, perhaps by asking what he or she does on, say, a "typical Tuesday."
- *Intellectual factor:* Ask questions that judge such things as complexity of tasks the person has performed, grades in school, test results (including scholastic aptitude tests, and so on), and how the person organizes his or her thoughts and communicates.
- *Personality factor:* Probe by looking for self-defeating behaviors (aggressiveness, compulsive fidgeting, and so on) and by exploring the person's past interpersonal relationships. Ask questions about the person's past interactions (working in a group at school, working with fraternity brothers or sorority sisters, leading the work team on the last job, and so on). Also, try to judge the person's behavior in the interview itself—Is the candidate personable? Shy? Outgoing?

CONDUCTING THE INTERVIEW
Devise and use a plan to guide the interview. According to interviewing expert John Drake, significant areas to touch on include the candidate's:

- College experiences
- Work experiences—summer, part-time
- Work experience—full-time (one by one)
- Goals and ambitions
- Reactions to the job you are interviewing for
- Self-assessments (by the candidate of his or her strengths and weaknesses)
- Military experiences
- Present outside activities[34]

FOLLOW YOUR PLAN
Perhaps start with an open-ended question for each topic, such as "Could you tell me about what you did when you were in high school?" Keep in mind that you are trying to elicit information about four main traits—knowledge and experience, motivation, intelligence, and personality. You can then accumulate the information in each of these four areas as the person answers. Follow up by asking questions like "Could you elaborate on that, please?"

MATCH THE CANDIDATE TO THE JOB   You should now be able to draw conclusions about the person's knowledge and experience, motivation, intellectual capacity, and personality, and to summarize the candidate's strengths and limits. Next, compare your conclusions to the job description and the list of requirements you developed when preparing for the interview. This should provide a rational basis for matching the candidate to the job—one based on an analysis of the traits and aptitudes the job actually requires.

Work-Sampling Tests

What should you do if you are trying to hire, say, a marketing manager, and want a simple way to screen your job applicants? Devising a *work-sampling test* is one solution. A work-sampling test means having the candidates perform actual samples of the job in question. Such tests have face validity (clearly measure actual job duties) and are easy to devise. Break down the job's main duties into component tasks. Then have the candidate complete a sample task. For example, for the marketing manager position, ask the candidate to spend an hour designing an ad for a hypothetical product.

Flexibility in Training

One study of 191 small and 201 large firms in Europe found that smaller firms were much more informal in their approaches to training and development.[35] Many of the small firms didn't systematically monitor their managers' skill needs, and fewer than 50% (as opposed to 70% of large firms) had career development programs. The smaller firms also tended to focus any management development training on learning specific firm-related competencies (such as how to sell the firm's products).[36] They did so due to resource constraints and a reluctance to invest too much in managers who may then leave.

FOUR-STEP TRAINING PROCESS   Limited resources or not, small businesses need training procedures. A simple but effective four-step training process follows.

Step 1:   **Write a Job Description.** A detailed job description is the heart of a training program. List the tasks of each job, along with a summary of the steps in each task.

Step 2:   **Develop a Task Analysis Record Form.** Rather than the full form we discussed in Chapter 8 (Training) the small business owner can use an abbreviated *Summary Task Analysis Record Form* (Table 18-1) containing four columns to guide the required coaching.

- In the first column, list *specific tasks*. Include what is to be performed in terms of each of the main tasks, and the steps involved in each task.
- In the second column, list *performance standards* (in terms of quantity, quality, accuracy, and so on).
- In the third column, list *trainable skills* required—things the employee must know or do to perform the task. Include skills (such as "Keep both hands on the wheel") that you want to emphasize in training.
- In the fourth column, list *aptitudes required*. These are the human aptitudes (such as mechanical comprehension) the employee must have to be trainable, and for which he or she should be screened.

Step 3:   **Develop a Job Instruction Sheet.** Next, develop a Job Instruction Sheet for the job. As in Table 18-2, a Job Instruction Sheet shows the steps in each task as well as key points for each.

Step 4:   **Prepare Training Program for the Job.** At a minimum, the job's training manual should include the job description, Task Analysis Record Form, and Job Instruction Sheet, all compiled in a training manual. Perhaps also include a brief overview/introduction to the job, and a graphical and/or written explanation of how the job fits with other jobs in the plant or office.

In terms of media, an on-the-job training program using current employees or supervisors as trainers often requires only the written materials we just listed. However, the job may require special training media. For many jobs, vendors like those we discussed in Chapter 8 provide packaged multi-media training programs.

TABLE 18-1 Sample Summary Task Analysis Record Form

Task List	Performance Standards	Trainable Skills Required	Aptitudes Required
1. Operate paper cutter			
1.1 Start motor	Start by push-button on first try	To start machine without accidentally attempting re-start while machine is running	Ability to understand written and spoken instructions
1.2 Set cutting distance	Maximum +/− tolerance of 0.007 inches	Read gauge	Able to read tolerances on numerical scale
1.3 Place paper on cutting table	Must be completely even to prevent uneven edges	Lift paper correctly	At least average manual dexterity
1.4 Push paper up to paper cutter blade	Must be even with blade	Check that paper is flat against blade	At least average manual dexterity
1.5 Grasp safety release with left hand	100% of the time, for safety	Must keep both hands on releases to prevent hand contact with cutting blade	Ability to understand written and spoken warnings

Note: This shows the first five steps in one of the tasks (operate paper cutter) for which a printing factory owner would train the person doing the cutting of the paper before placing the paper on the printing presses.

INFORMAL TRAINING METHODS Training expert Stephen Covey says small businesses can do many things to provide job-related training without actually establishing expensive formal training programs. His suggestions include:[37]

- Offer to cover the tuition for special classes
- Identify online training opportunities
- Provide a library of tapes and DVDs for systematic, disciplined learning during commute times
- Encourage the sharing of best practices among associates
- When possible, send people to special seminars and association meetings for learning and networking
- Create a learning ethic by having everyone teach each other what they are learning

Flexibility in Benefits and Rewards

The Family and Work Institute surveyed the benefits practices of about 1,000 small and large companies.[38] Not surprisingly, they found that large firms offer more *extensive* benefits packages than do smaller ones. However, many small firms overcame this by

TABLE 18-2 Sample Job Instruction Sheet

Steps in Task	Key Points to Keep in Mind
1. Start motor	None
2. Set cutting distance	Carefully read scale—to prevent wrong-sized cut
3. Place paper on cutting table	Make sure paper is even—to prevent uneven cut
4. Push paper up to cutter	Make sure paper is tight—to prevent uneven cut
5. Grasp safety release with left hand	Do not release left hand—to prevent hand from being caught in cutter
6. Grasp cutter release with right hand	Do not release right hand—to prevent hand from being caught in cutter
7. Simultaneously pull cutter and safety releases	Keep both hands on corresponding releases—avoid hands being on cutting table
8. Wait for cutter to retract	Keep both hands on releases—to avoid having hands on cutting table
9. Retract paper	Make sure cutter is retracted; keep both hands away from releases
10. Shut off motor	None

At Ward Furniture, workers can share job responsibilities and work part-time from home.

Source: Bill Aron/PhotoEdit.

offering more flexibility. "They've discovered how to turn tiny into tight-knit, earning employees' trust by keeping them in the loop on company news and financials, and their loyalty by providing frequent feedback on performance."[39] At ID Media, with 90 employees, CEO Lynn Fantom gives all new employees a welcome breakfast on their first day. Internet startup appssavvy Inc.'s CEO foregoes PowerPoint presentations in favor of humorous YouTube videos.[40]

A CULTURE OF FLEXIBILITY   Basically, the study found that small business owners, by personally interacting with all employees each day, did a better job of "understanding when work/life issues emerge."[41] Wards Furniture in Long Beach, California, exemplifies this. Many of its 17 employees have been with the firm for 10 to 20 years. Brad Ward, an owner, attributes this partly to his firm's willingness to adapt to its workers' needs. For example, workers can share job responsibilities, and work part-time from home.

WORK–LIFE BENEFITS   Here are some examples:[42]

- **Extra time off.** For example, Friday afternoons off in the summer.
- **Compressed workweeks.** For example, compressed summer workweeks.
- **Bonuses at critical times.** Small business owners are more likely to know what's happening with their employees. Use this knowledge to provide special bonuses, for instance, if an employee has a new baby.
- **Flexibility.** For example "if an employee is having a personal problem, help him or her create a work schedule that allows the person to solve problems without feeling like they're going to be in trouble."[43]
- **Sensitivity to employees' strengths and weaknesses.** The small business owner should be attuned to his or her employees' strengths, weaknesses, and aspirations. For example, ask them which jobs they feel most comfortable doing, and give them an opportunity to train for and move into the jobs they desire.
- **Help them better themselves.** For example, pay employees to take a class to help them develop their job skills.
- **Feed them.** Provide free meals every now and then, perhaps by taking your employees to lunch.
- **Make them feel like owners.** For example, endeavor to give your employees input into major decisions, let them work directly with clients, get them client feedback, share company performance data with them, and let them share in the company's financial success.

- **Make sure they have what they need to do their jobs.** Having motivated employees is only half the challenge. Also ensure they have the tools they need to do their jobs—for instance, the necessary training, procedures, computers, and so on.
- **Constantly recognize a job well done.** Capitalize on your day-to-day interactions with employees to "never miss an opportunity to give your employees the recognition they deserve."[44]

RECOGNITION Studies show that recognition can often be as powerful as financial rewards. The personal nature of small business interactions makes it easier to recognize employees. A short list includes:[45]

- Challenging work assignments
- Freedom to choose own work activity
- Having fun built into work
- More of preferred task
- Role as boss's stand-in when he or she is away
- Role in presentations to top management
- Job rotation
- Encouragement of learning and continuous improvement
- Being provided with ample encouragement
- Being allowed to set own goals
- Compliments
- Expression of appreciation in front of others
- Note of thanks
- Employee-of-the-month award
- Special commendation
- Bigger desk
- Bigger office or cubicle

SMALL BUSINESS BENEFITS FOR BAD TIMES The recession hit smaller businesses' benefits particularly hard.[46] Thus, when the monthly cost of a family policy for Brennan's Prime Meats, a meat wholesaler and retailer with six employees in Brooklyn, jumped almost 30%, to $1,780, its owner switched to a less expensive plan. Participating employees will have to absorb new co-payments and possibly pick up half of the premium cost.

With the recession, more firms were also focusing their retention efforts on "anything they can do to get high performers to feel appreciated."[47] For example, Intuit shifted its employee recognition awards programs from several vendors to Globoforce. The move "allowed us to build efficiencies and improved effectiveness" into the programs' management, says Intuit.[48]

SIMPLE RETIREMENT BENEFITS Access to retirement benefits is more prevalent in large firms than small ones. About 75% of large firms offer them, while only about 35% of small ones do.[49]

There are several ways for small firms to provide retirement plans. The Pension Protection Act of 2006 provides for a retirement benefit that combines traditional defined benefit and 401(k) (defined contribution) plans.[50] Only available to employers with less than 500 employees, it exempts employers from the complex pension rules to which large employers must adhere. The employees get a retirement plan that blends a defined pension, plus returns on the part of the investment that plan participants contributed.[51]

The easiest way for small businesses to provide retirement benefits is through a SIMPLE IRA plan. With the SIMPLE (for Savings Incentive Match Plan for Employees) IRA, employers must (and employees may) make contributions to traditional employee IRAs. These plans are for employers or small businesses with 100 or fewer employees and no other retirement plan.

SIMPLE IRAs are inexpensive and simple. The owner contacts an eligible financial institution and fills out several IRS forms. The IRS needs to have previously approved the financial institution. However, banks, mutual funds, and insurance companies that issue annuity contracts are generally eligible.[52] The plan has very low administrative costs. Employer contributions are tax-deductible.[53] A typical employer contribution might match employee contributions dollar for dollar up to 3% of pay. The financial institution usually handles the IRS paperwork and reporting.

Improved Communications

Effective communications are especially important in small businesses. With a thousand or more employees, one or two disgruntled employees may get lost in the shuffle. But with 5 or 10 employees, one or two disgruntled employees can destroy the business's service. That's why simple programs, like the one in the accompanying HR as a Profit Center feature, are important.

HR AS A PROFIT CENTER

IHOP

Half of all restaurant employees are less than 30 years old, and turnover of more than 100% per year is the norm.[54] So, when Joe Scripture, whose company runs 11 IHOP restaurants around Atlanta, looked at the industry's turnover statistics, he knew he and his partner needed to do something to get staffing costs down. But what?[55]

Seeking to shield their 11 IHOP restaurants from the industry's sky-high turnover rates, the owners hit on an HR solution. They dramatically reduced turnover with a new online system that lets new employees anonymously report their opinions about the hiring process.[56] Feedback from that simple communication tool enabled them to recalibrate their firm's hiring, training, and orientation methods, and to reduce turnover by about a third.

NEWSLETTER   Mel's Gourmet Diner in Bonita Springs, Florida, keeps employees informed with a quarterly newsletter. It distributes copies at the chain's 10 locations, but also posts it on the company Web site. "It sounds like a cliché, but our people are the keys to our success," says the owner. "We want to make sure we give them all the information and tools they need."[57]

ONLINE   Each time employees of Tampa, Florida–based Let's Eat! go to one of the firm's computers to input a guest's order, they can quickly review the chain's menu changes, special promotions, and mandatory employee meetings.[58]

THE HUDDLE   Sea Island Shrimp House in San Antonio, Texas, keeps employees in its seven restaurants communicating with its "cascading huddles." As in football parlance, the huddles are very quick meetings. At 9 A.M. top management meets in the first of the day's "huddles." The next huddle is a conference call with store managers. Then, store managers meet with hourly employees at each location before the restaurants open, to make sure the news of the day gets communicated. "It's all about alignment and good, timely communications," says the company.[59]

Fairness and the Family Business

Most small businesses are "family businesses," since the owner (and often one or more managers and employees) are family members.

Being a non-family employee here isn't easy. The tendency to treat family and non-family employees differently can undermine perceptions of fairness and morale.

If so, as one writer puts it, "It's a sure bet that their lower morale and simmering resentments are having a negative effect on your operations and sapping your profits."[60] Reducing such "fairness" problems involves several steps, including:[61]

- **Set the ground rules.** One family business consultant says,

  During the hiring process the [management] applicant should be informed as to whether he or she will be essentially a placeholder, or whether there will be potential for promotion. At a minimum, make the expectations clear, regarding matters such as the level of authority and decision-making the person can expect to attain.[62]

- **Treat people fairly.** Work hard to avoid "any appearance that family members are benefiting unfairly from the sacrifice of others."[63]
- **Confront family issues.** Discord and tension among family members distracts and demoralizes employees. Family members must confront and work out their differences.
- **Erase privilege.** Family members "should avoid any behavior that would lead people to the conclusion that they are demanding special treatment in terms of assignments or responsibilities."[64] Family employees should come in earlier, work harder, and stay later than other employees stay.

> **4** Discuss how you would choose and deal with a professional employee organization.

USING PROFESSIONAL EMPLOYER ORGANIZATIONS

As we explained in Chapter 13 (Benefits), many small business owners look at the issues involved with managing personnel, and decide to outsource most of their human resource functions to vendors.[65] These vendors go by the names *professional employer organizations* (PEOs), *human resource outsourcers* (HROs), or sometimes *employee* or *staff leasing firms*.

How Do PEOs Work?

These vendors range from specialized payroll companies to those that handle all an employer's human resource management requirements.[66] At a minimum, these firms take over the employer's payroll tasks.[67] Usually, however, PEOs assume most of the employer's human resources chores. By transferring the client firm's employees to the PEO's payroll, PEOs become co-employers of record for the employer's employees. The PEO can then fold the client's employees into the PEO's insurance and benefits program, usually at a lower cost. The PEO usually handles employee-related activities such as recruiting, hiring (with client firms' supervisors' approvals), and payroll and taxes. Most PEOs focus on employers with under 100 employees, and charge fees of 2% to 4% of a company's payroll. HROs usually handle these functions on an "administrative services only"—they're basically your "HR office," but your employees still work for you.[68]

Why Use a PEO?

Employers turn to PEOs for several reasons:

LACK OF SPECIALIZED HR SUPPORT   Small firms with fewer than about 100 employees typically have no dedicated HR managers. The owner has most of the human resource management burden on his or her shoulders.

PAPERWORK   The Small Business Administration estimates that small business owners spend up to 25% of their time on personnel-related paperwork, such as background checks and benefits sign-ups.[69] Because the PEO takes over most of this, many small businesses conclude that it's cheaper for them just to pay the employee leasing firm's fees.

FIGURE 18-6 Guidelines for Finding and Working with PEOs

Sources: Based on Robert Beck and J. Starkman, "How to Find a PEO that Will Get the Job Done," *National Underwriter* 110, no. 39 (October 16, 2006), pp. 39, 45; Lyle DeWitt, "Advantages of Human Resource Outsourcing," *The CPA Journal* 75, no. 6 (June 2005), p. 13; www.peo.com/dmn/, accessed April 28, 2008; Layne Davlin, "Human Resource Solutions for the Franchisee," *Franchising World* 39, no. 10 (October 2007), p. 27.

Employers should choose and manage the PEO relationship carefully. Guidelines for doing so include:

- *Conduct a needs analysis.* Know ahead of time exactly what human resource concerns your company wants to address.
- *Review the services* of all PEO firms you're considering. Determine which can meet all your requirements.
- *Determine if the PEO is accredited.* There is no rating system. However, the Employer Services Assurance Corporation of Little Rock, Arkansas (www.Escorp.org), imposes higher financial, auditing, and operating standards on its members. Also check the National Association of Professional Employer Organizations (www.NAPEO.org), and www.PEO.com.
- Check the provider's bank, credit, insurance, and professional references.
- Understand how the *employee benefits will be funded.* Is it fully insured or partially self-funded? Who is the carrier? Confirm that employers will receive first-day coverage.
- See if the contract assumes the *compliance liabilities in the applicable states.*
- *Review the service agreement carefully.* Are the respective parties' responsibilities and liabilities clear?
- Investigate how long the *PEO has been in business.*
- *Check out the prospective* PEO's staff. Do they seem to have the expertise to deliver on its promises?
- Ask, *how will firm deliver its services?* In person? By phone? Via the Web?
- Ask about upfront fees and how these are determined.
- *Periodically get proof that payroll that taxes and insurance premiums are being paid properly* and that any legal issues are handled correctly.

LIABILITY   Legally, PEOs generally "contractually share liability with clients and have a vested interest in preventing workplace injuries and employee lawsuits."[70] The PEO should thus help ensure the small business fulfills its Title VII, OSHA, COBRA, and Fair Labor Standards Act responsibilities.[71]

BENEFITS   As we saw in Chapter 13, insurance and benefits are often the big PEO attraction. Getting health and other insurance is a problem for smaller firms. That's where the leasing firm comes in. A small business owner may be able to get insurance [as well as benefits like a 401(k)] for its people that it couldn't otherwise.[72]

PERFORMANCE   Finally, the professionalism that the PEO brings to recruiting, screening, training, compensating, and maintaining employee safety and welfare will hopefully translate into improved employee and business results.

Caveats

There are several potential downsides to these firms. "If your PEO is poorly managed, or goes bankrupt, you could find yourself with an office full of uninsured workers."[73] Many employers view their human resource management processes (like training new engineers) as a strategic advantage, and aren't inclined to turn over tasks like these to outsiders. Another potential problem is determining who's responsible if things go wrong. For example, who is responsible if an employee gets hurt, the PEO or the employer? The contract should address this.[74]

WARNING SIGNS   Several things may signal problems with the prospective PEO. One is *lax due diligence.* For example, because they share liability with the employer, they should question you extensively about your firm's workplace safety and human resource policies and practices.[75] Figure 18-6 summarizes guidelines for finding and working with PEOs.

5 Describe how you would create a start-up human resource system for a new small business.

MANAGING HR SYSTEMS, PROCEDURES, AND PAPERWORK

Introduction

Consider the paperwork required to run a five-person retail shop. Just to start with, recruiting and hiring an employee might require a help wanted advertising listing, an employment application, an interviewing checklist, various verifications—of education and immigration status, for instance—and a telephone reference checklist. You then might need an employment agreement, confidentiality and noncompetition agreements, and an employer indemnity agreement. To process the new employee you might need a background verification, a new employee checklist, and forms for withholding tax and to obtain new employee data. And to keep track of the employee once on board, you'd need—just to start—a personnel data sheet, daily and weekly time records, an hourly employee's weekly time sheet, and an expense report. Then come all the performance appraisal forms, a disciplinary notice, an employee orientation record, separation notice, and employment reference response.

In fact, the preceding list barely scratches the surface of the policies, procedures, and paperwork you'll need to run the human resource management part of your business. Perhaps with just one or two employees you could keep track of everything in your head, or just write a separate memo for each HR action, and place it in a folder for each worker. But with more employees, you'll need to create a human resource system comprised of standardized forms. As the company grows, you'll then have to computerize various parts of the HR system—payroll, or appraising, for instance.

Basic Components of Manual HR Systems

Very small employers (say, with 10 employees or less) will probably start with a manual human resource management system. From a practical point of view, this generally means obtaining and organizing a set of standardized personnel forms covering each important aspect of the HR—recruitment, selection, training, appraisal, compensation, safety—process, as well as some means for organizing all this information for each of your employees.

BASIC FORMS   The number of forms you would conceivably need even for a small firm is quite large, as the illustrative list in Table 18-3 shows.[76] One simple way to obtain the basic component forms of a manual HR system is to start with one of the books or CDs that provide compilations of HR forms. The forms you

TABLE 18-3 Some Important Employment Forms

New Employee Forms	Current Employee Forms	Employee Separation Forms
Application	Employee Status	Retirement Checklist
New Employee Checklist	Change Request	Termination Checklist
Employment Interview	Employee Record	COBRA Acknowledgment
Reference Check	Performance Evaluation	Unemployment Claim
Telephone Reference Report	Warning Notice	Employee Exit Interview
Employee Manual	Vacation Request	
Acknowledgment	Probation Notice	
Employment Agreement	Job Description	
Employment Application	Probationary Evaluation	
Disclaimer	Direct Deposit Acknowledgment	
Employee Secrecy Agreement	Absence Report	
	Disciplinary Notice	
	Grievance Form	
	Expense Report	
	401(k) Choices	
	Acknowledgment	
	Injury Report	

want can then be adapted from these sources for your particular situation. Office supply stores (such as Office Depot and Staples) also sell packages of personnel forms. For example, Office Depot sells packages of individual personnel forms as well as a "Human Resource Kit" containing 10 copies of forms such as Application, Employment Interview, Reference Check, Employee Record, and Performance Evaluation.[77] Also available is a package of Employee Record Folders. Some employers still use such folders to maintain files on each employee; on the outside of the pocket is a place for recording information such as name, start date, company benefits, and so on.

OTHER SOURCES Several direct-mail catalog companies similarly offer HR materials. For example, HRdirect (www.hrdirect.com) offers packages of personnel forms. These include, for instance, Short- and Long-Form Employee Applications, Applicant Interviews, Employee Performance Reviews, and Absentee Calendars and Reports. Also available are various legal-compliance forms, including standardized Harassment Policy and FMLA Notice forms, as well as posters (for instance, covering legally required postings for matters such as the Americans with Disabilities Act).

G. Neil Company, of Sunrise, Florida (www.gneil.com), is another direct-mail personnel materials source. In addition to a complete line of personnel forms, documents, and posters, it also carries manual systems for matters like attendance history, job analyses, and for tracking vacation requests and safety records. It has a complete HR "start-up" kit containing 25 copies of each of the basic components of a manual HR system. These include, for instance, Long Form Application for Employment, Attendance History, Payroll/Status Change Notice, Absence Report, and Vacation Request & Approval, all organized in a file box.

Automating Individual HR Tasks

As the small business grows, it becomes unwieldy to rely on manual HR systems. It is therefore at this point that most small- to medium-sized firms begin computerizing individual human resource management tasks.

PACKAGED SYSTEMS Here again a variety of resources are available. For example, at the Web site for the International Association for Human Resource Information Management (www.ihrim.org) you'll find, within the Buyers Guide tab, a categorical list of HR software vendors.[78] These firms provide software solutions for virtually all personnel tasks, ranging from benefits management to compensation, compliance, employee relations, outsourcing, payroll, and time and attendance systems.

The G. Neil Company sells software packages for monitoring attendance, employee record keeping, writing employee handbooks, and conducting computerized employee appraisals. HRdirect offers software for tasks such as writing employee policy manuals, writing performance reviews, creating job descriptions, and tracking attendance and hours worked for each employee. For example, the Gradience® Records software they offer helps small businesses maintain employee records (including name, address, marital status, number of dependents, emergency contact and phone numbers, hire date, and job history).

As the company grows, the owner may decide to transition to an integrated human resource management system; we discuss this next.

Human Resource Information Systems (HRIS)

We can define an integrated human resource information system (*HRIS*) as interrelated components working together to collect, process, store, and disseminate information to support decision making, coordination, control, analysis, and visualization of an organization's human resource management activities.[79] There are several reasons for installing an HRIS. The first is improved transaction processing.

Improved Transaction Processing

The day-to-day minutiae of maintaining and updating employee records take an enormous amount of time. One study found that 71% of HR employees' time was devoted to transactional tasks like checking leave balances, maintaining address records, and monitoring employee benefits distributions.[80] HRIS packages substitute powerful computerized processing for a wide range of the firm's HR transactions.

Online Self-Processing

HR information systems also make it possible (or easier) to make the company's employees part of the HRIS. For example, at Provident Bank, an HR compensation system called Benelogic lets the bank's employees self-enroll in all their desired benefits programs over the Internet at a secure site. It also "support[s] employees' quest for 'what if' information relating to, for example, the impact on their take-home pay of various benefits options."[81] That's all work that HR employees would previously have had to do for Provident's employees.

Improved Reporting Capability

Because the HRIS integrates numerous individual HR tasks (training records, appraisals, employee personal data, and so on), installing an HRIS boosts HR's reporting capabilities. For example, reports might be available (company-wide and by department) for health care cost per employee, pay and benefits as a percent of operating expense, cost per hire, report on training, volunteer turnover rates, turnover costs, time to fill jobs, and return on human capital invested (in terms of training and education fees, for instance).

HR System Integration

Because the HRIS's software components (record keeping, payroll, appraisal, and so forth) are integrated, they enable the employer to reengineer its HR function. The system PeopleSoft (now part of Oracle Corporation) installed in its own offices provides an illustration. For example, its HRIS electronically routes salary increases, transfers, and other e-forms through the organization to the proper managers for approval. As one person signs off, it's routed to the next. If anyone forgets to process a document, a smart agent issues reminders until the task is completed. Installing the system in term enabled PeopleSoft to reorganize how the firm did these tasks.

HRIS Vendors

Many firms today offer HRIS packages. The Web site for the International Association for Human Resource Information Management (www.ihrim.org/), for instance, lists Automatic Data Processing, Inc., Business Information Technology, Inc., Human Resource Microsystems, Lawson Software, Oracle Corporation, SAP America, Inc., and about 25 other firms as HRIS vendors.

HR and Intranets

Employers increasingly use intranet-based HR information systems. For example, LG&E Energy Corporation uses its intranet for benefits communication. Employees can access the benefits homepage and (among other things) review the company's 401(k) plan investment options, get answers to frequently asked questions about the company's medical and dental plans, and report changes in family status. Other uses for human resource intranets include, for instance, automating job postings and applicant tracking, setting up training registration, providing electronic pay stubs, publishing an electronic employee handbook, and letting employees update their personal profiles and access their accounts, such as 401(k) accounts.

REVIEW

MyManagementLab Now that you have finished this chapter, go back to **www.mymanagementlab.com** to continue practicing and applying the concepts you've learned.

CHAPTER SECTION SUMMARIES

1. Many people reading this book will work for or own their own small businesses, so it's important to understand **the small business challenge**. In terms of managing human resources, small businesses are different in terms of size (not enough employees for a dedicated HR manager), priorities (sales come first), informality, and the nature of the entrepreneur. Without effective human resource management, small business owners run the risk that they'll be at a competitive disadvantage or that without the necessary HR expertise they may commit mistakes that lead to litigation.

2. Being small, small businesses can particularly capitalize on freely available **Internet and government tools to support their HR efforts**. For example, you can use Department of Labor elaws advisers to answer overtime questions, the EEOC's Web sites for answers on questions like "How can we resolve the charge?" and the Department of Labor's OSHA Web site to review, for instance, their small business handbook. To better compete, small business owners can also use online recruiting tools like those we discussed in Chapter 5 and training programs available online from companies such as puresafety.com, and from the SBA and National Association of Manufacturers.

3. Small businesses need to capitalize on their strengths, and in this case, it means capitalizing on **familiarity, flexibility, and informality**. For example, in many respects it's easier for small businesses to be flexible about extra time off, compressed workweeks, and job enrichment. They can also use relatively informal but still effective employee selection procedures such as the work-sampling test we discussed. Informal training methods include online training opportunities, encouraging the sharing of best practices among associates, and sending employees to seminars. Because small businesses are often family

businesses, it's important to make sure that nonfamily members are treated fairly, something that requires setting ground rules (for instance, regarding promotions), treating employees fairly, dealing with family discord and issues, and erasing privilege. Small businesses can also use simple methods for improving communications, for instance, online newsletters.

4. After reviewing all the challenges of managing human resources, many small business owners turn to **using professional employer organizations.** Also called *human resource outsourcers*, or *employee or staff leasing firms*, these firms generally transfer the client firm's employees to the PEO's own payroll and thus become the employer of record for the employer's employees. Reasons to turn to the PEOs include a lack of specialized HR support, a desire to reduce the paperwork burden, avoiding HR-related liability, obtaining better benefits for employees, and providing improved employee and business results.

5. Small business managers need to understand how their **HR systems, procedures, and paperwork** will evolve. At first, there may be a simple manual human resource management system, for instance, with employee records compiled on forms from office supply companies and maintained in manual files. The employer then may purchase one or more packaged systems for automating individual HR tasks, for instance, such as applicant tracking and performance appraisal. As companies grow, they will look to integrate the separate systems with a human resource information system, i.e., interrelated components working together to collect, process, store, and disseminate information to support decision making, coordination, control, analysis, and visualization of the company's human resource management activities.

DISCUSSION QUESTIONS

1. How and why is HR in small businesses different than that in large firms?
2. Explain why HRM is important to small businesses.
3. Explain and give at least four examples of how entrepreneurs can use Internet and government tools to support the HR effort.
4. Explain and give at least five examples of ways entrepreneurs can use small size—familiarity, flexibility, and informality—to improve their HR processes.

5. Discuss what you would do to find, retain, and deal with a professional employee organization on an ongoing basis.
6. Describe with examples how you would create a start-up, paper-based human resource system for a new small business.

INDIVIDUAL AND GROUP ACTIVITIES

1. Form teams of five or six persons, each with at least one person who owns or has worked for a small business. Based on their experiences, make a list of the "inadequate-HR risks" the business endured, in terms of competitive disadvantage, lack of specialized HR expertise, workplace litigation, compensation laws compliance, and paperwork/data-entry errors.

2. You own a small business, and you are confused about which of your employees is eligible for overtime pay. The employees in question include your secretary, two accounting clerks, one engineer, and two inside salespeople. Individually or in groups of four or five students, use the DOL's Overtime Security Advisor and DOL's Calculator to determine who gets overtime pay.

3. You have about 32 employees working in your factory. Working individually or in teams of four or five students, find and create a list of five online sources you could use to provide training to them, at no cost to you or to them.

4. The "HRCI Test Specifications Appendix" (pages 633–640) lists the knowledge someone studying for the HRCI certification exam needs to have in each area of human resource management (such as in Strategic Management, Workforce Planning, and Human Resource Development). In groups of four to five students, do four things: (1) review that appendix now; (2) identify the material in this chapter that relates to the required knowledge the appendix lists; (3) write four multiple-choice exam questions on this material that you believe would be suitable for inclusion in the HRCI exam; and (4) if time permits, have someone from your team post your team's questions in front of the class, so the students in other teams can take each others' exam questions.

EXPERIENTIAL EXERCISE

Building an HRIS

Purpose: The purpose of this exercise is to give you practice in creating a human resource management system (HRIS).

Required Understanding: You should be fully acquainted with the material in this chapter.

How to Set Up the Exercise/Instructions: Divide the class into teams of five or six students. Each team will need access to the Internet.

Assume that the owners of a small business come to you with the following problem. They have a company with less than 40 employees and have been taking care of all types of HR paperwork informally, mostly on little slips of paper and with memos. They want you to build them a human resource management information system—how computerized it is will be up to you, but they can only afford a budget of $5,000 upfront (not counting your consulting), and then about $500 per year for maintenance. You know from your HR training that there are various sources of paper-based and online systems. Write a 2-page proposal telling them exactly what your team would suggest, based on its accumulated existing knowledge, and from online research.

APPLICATION CASE

NETFLIX BREAKS THE RULES [82]

Why did Netflix survive as a startup when the dot-com bubble burst in the late 1990s? Probably because, from the day he started Netflix, founder Reed Hastings believed in breaking the rules. His direct-to-consumer mail and video streaming business model certainly helped Netflix to survive. But the firm's unorthodox human resource management practices helped the company to attract and keep the high producers who design the products that are the firm's lifeblood. Hastings knew that top Silicon Valley workers could choose where they worked, and high pay is pretty much standard throughout the Valley's industries. How to set oneself apart? Hastings and his start-up colleagues believed that a culture that balanced a flexible work environment with few constraints and high responsibility was the answer. They called the policy "Freedom and Responsibility."

Just how unorthodox are the Netflix HR practices? Consider this: As a Netflix professional you get unlimited vacations. One engineer takes 5-week vacations to Europe, because he likes (as he says) to take his time off in big chunks.

(An HR officer must approve time off in excess of 30 days annually.) As a Netflix employee, your pay isn't tied to performance appraisals, or even to a compensation plan. Frequent market salary surveys and pay hikes keeps everyone's pay aligned with Silicon Valley competitors'. Each employee decides whether to take his or her pay in cash or in Netflix stock. Options vest immediately. Netflix doesn't recruit much at college job fairs, instead hiring mostly highly experienced professionals. There's no training, professional development, or career planning at Netflix (except for legally required training, such as diversity training). You're in charge of your own career.

But with freedom like that comes responsibilities. The company expects its salaried employees to work hard—to "do the jobs of three or four people" as one report put it. And Netflix doesn't have the "frat party" free-wheeling atmosphere that many dot-coms do. It's an adult environment. Netflix does not coddle underperformers. Yearly 360-degree performance reviews provide "direct and honest feedback." Those that aren't cutting it are quickly let go, but (whenever possible) amicably. Rather than the sorts of litigiousness that often characterizes dismissals in other firms (having to prove the person was incompetent, for instance), Netflix writes a check. The company believes that a handsome severance payment helps maintain the person's dignity, makes it easier for supervisors to make tough calls with underperformers, and, of course, minimizes blowback from those it dismisses. It's more like a "no-fault divorce," as one observer put it.

Questions

In many respects, the Netflix HR strategy seems like a dream come true for small businesses. You don't need a pay plan; instead, you just update each person's pay every few months based on market surveys. You offer no training and development. And you don't track vacation time, more or less. If someone's not doing well, you just pay them to leave, with no hassles. Netflix seems to have hit upon its own version of "Netflix High-Performance Work Practices." Given that, answer the following questions (please be specific).

1. What (if anything) is it about Netflix that makes its HR practices work for Netflix?
2. Would you suggest using similar practices in other businesses, such as, say, a new restaurant? Why?
3. List the criteria you would use for deciding whether another company is right for Netflix-type HR practices.
4. What argument would you make in response to the following: "Netflix just lucked out; they'd have done even better with conventional HR practices."

CONTINUING CASE

CARTER CLEANING COMPANY

Cleaning in Challenging Times

As the economic downturn worsened, revenues at the Carter stores fell steeply. Many of their customers were simply out of work and didn't need (or couldn't afford) dry cleaning. Working customers were cutting back wherever they could. The Carters actually found themselves giving away some free cleaning services. They started a new program wherein existing customers could get one suit or dress cleaned free each month if they needed it for a job interview.

In the midst of this downturn, the Carters knew they had to do something to get their employment costs under control. The problem was that, realistically, there wasn't much room for cutting staffing in a store. Of course, if a store got very slow, they could double up by having a cleaner/spotter spend some of his or her time pressing, or having the manager displace the counter person. But if sales only fall 15% to 20% per store, there really wasn't much room for reducing employee head count because each store never really employed that many people in the first place.

The question therefore naturally arose as to whether the Carters could cut their employment expenses without dismissing too many people. Jennifer Carter has several questions for you.

Questions

1. Assume that we don't want to terminate any of our employees. What work-scheduling–related changes could we make that would reduce our payrolls by, say, 20% per week but still keep all our employees on board?
2. We are currently handling most of our personnel-related activities, such as sign-ons, benefits administration, and appraisals manually. What specific suggestions would you have for us in terms of using software systems to automate our HR processes?
3. Suggest at least five free Internet-based sources we could turn to for helping us to lower our total employment costs.

TRANSLATING STRATEGY INTO HR POLICIES & PRACTICES CASE

THE HOTEL PARIS CASE

The Hotel Paris's competitive strategy is "To use superior guest service to differentiate the Hotel Paris properties, and to thereby increase the length of stay and return rate of guests, and thus boost revenues and profitability." HR manager Lisa Cruz must now formulate functional policies and activities that support this competitive strategy by eliciting the required employee behaviors and competencies.

Challenging economic times brought the drawbacks of the Hotel Paris's relatively small size into sharp relief. Large chains like Marriott had vast online reservations capabilities

with huge centralized systems that easily and economically handled reservations requests from throughout the world. By comparison, the Hotel Paris still handled reservations much as hotels did 20 years ago, either with separate Web sites for each of their hotel locations, or by phone. Their human resource management information systems were similarly primitive. Lisa had managed to install several separate information systems, such as for performance appraisals. However, as she discussed one day over lunch with the CFO, these systems were not integrated. Therefore, if an employee changed his or her name, for instance, through marriage, people in Lisa's office had to execute all those name changes manually on all the various employee rosters and benefits plans.

This lack of integration was bad enough in boom times, but was increasingly unacceptable as the economy soured. In one of the most difficult discussions she ever had with the CFO, he pointed out to her that the amount of money they were spending on human resource management administration was about 30% higher than it was at larger chains such as Marriott. He understood that large size brings economies of scale. But on the other hand, he believed there had to be something they could do to bring down the cost of administering human resource management.

Questions

1. Using any benchmark data that you can find, including information from this textbook, what are some benchmark metrics that Lisa could be using to assess the efficiency of her human resource management operations? To what extent does the Hotel Paris's quality service orientation enter into how Lisa's metrics should compare?

2. Throughout this textbook, we've discussed various specific examples of how human resource management departments have been reducing the cost of delivering their services. Keeping in mind the Hotel Paris's service quality orientation, please list and explain with examples how Lisa Cruz could use at least five of these.

3. Focusing only on human resource information systems for a moment, what sorts of systems would you suggest Lisa consider recommending for the Hotel Paris?

4. Explain with detailed examples how Lisa can use free online and governmental sources to accomplish at least part of what you propose in your previous answers.

5. Give three examples of fee-based online tools you suggest Lisa use.

6. Do you suggest Lisa use a PEO? Why?

ENDNOTES

1. Based on Donna Harris, "Mentors Cut Turnover Costs, Boost Sales, Loyalty," *Automotive News* 64, no. 18 (June 28, 2010), p. 10.

2. "Statistics of U.S. Businesses and Non-Employer Status," www.sba.gov/advo/research/data.html, accessed November 5, 2009.

3. "Small Business Economic Indicators 2000," Office of Advocacy, U.S. Small Business Administration (Washington, D.C., 2001), p. 5. See also "Small Business Laid Foundation for Job Gains," www.sba.gov/advo, accessed March 9, 2006.

4. Studies show that the size of the business impacts human resource activities such as executive compensation, training, staffing, and HR outsourcing. Peter Hausdorf and Dale Duncan, "Firm Size and Internet Recruiting in Canada: A Preliminary Investigation," *Journal of Small-Business Management* 42, no. 3 (July 2004), pp. 325–334.

5. *SHRM Human Capital Benchmarking Study 2007*, Society for Human Resource Management, p. 12.

6. Graham Dietz et al., "HRM Inside UK E-commerce Firms," *International Small Business Journal* 24, no. 5 (October 2006), pp. 443–470.

7. Bernice Kotey and Cathleen Folker, "Employee Training in SMEs: Effect of Size and Firm Type—Family and Nonfamily," *Journal of Small-Business Management* 45, no. 2 (April 2007), pp. 14–39.

8. Dietz et al., "HRM Inside UK E-commerce Firms."

9. Ibid. See also N. Wasserman, "Planning a Start-Up? Seize the Day . . . Then Expect to Work All Night," *Harvard Business Review* 87, no. 1 (January 2009), pp. 27.

10. Points 2–5 based on Kathy Williams, "Top HR Compliance Issues or Small Businesses," *Strategic Finance* (February 2005), pp. 21–23.

11. However, one study concluded that the increased labor costs associated with high-performance work practices offset the productivity increases associated with high-performance work practices. Luc Sels et al., "Unraveling the HRM–Performance Link: Value Creating and Cost Increasing Effects of Small-Business HRM," *Journal of Management Studies* 43, no. 2 (March 2006), pp. 319–342. For supporting evidence of HR's positive effects on small companies, see also Andrea Rauch et al., "Effects of Human Capital and Long-Term Human Resources Development and Utilization on Employment Growth of Small-Scale Businesses: A Causal Analysis," *Entrepreneurship Theory and Practice* 29, no. 6 (November 2005), pp. 681–698; Andre Grip and Inge Sieben, "The Effects of Human Resource Management on Small Firms' Productivity and Employee's Wages," *Applied Economics* 37, no. 9 (May 20, 2005), pp. 1047–1054.

12. Dawn Carlson et al., "The Impact of Human Resource Practices and Compensation Design on Performance: An Analysis of Family-Owned SMEs," *Journal of Small-Business Management* 44, no. 4 (October 2006), pp. 531–543. See also Jake Messersmith and James Guthrie, "High Performance Work Systems in Emergent Organizations: Implications for Firm Performance," *Human Resource Management* 49, no. 2 (March–April 2010), pp. 241–264.

13. Dietz et al., "HRM Inside UK E-commerce Firms."

14. Based on Harris, "Mentors Cut Turnover Costs."

15. Ibid.

16. Gilbert Nicholson, "Automated Assessments for Better Hires," *Workforce* (December 2000): 102–107.

17. www.EEOC.gov/employers/overview.html, accessed February 10, 2008.

18. www.DOL.gov/elaws, accessed February 10, 2008.

19. Daren Dahl, "Recruiting: Tapping the Talent Pool . . . without Drowning in Resumes," *Inc.* 31, no. 3 (April 2009), PP. 121–122.

20. Ibid.

21. Ibid.

22. Ibid.

23. Ibid.

24. Paul Harris, "Small Businesses Bask in Training's Spotlight," *T+D* 59, no. 2 (Fall 2005), pp. 46–52.

25. Ibid.

26. Ibid.

27. www.halogensoftware.com/products/halogen-eappraisal, accessed January 10, 2008.

28. Jan de Kok, "Precautionary Actions within Small- and Medium-Sized Enterprises," *Journal of Small Business Management* 43, no. 4 (October 2005), pp. 498–516.

29. Sean Smith, "OSHA Resources Can Help Small Businesses Spot Hazards," *Westchester County Business Journal* (August 4, 2003), pp. 4. See also www.osha.gov/as/opa/osha-faq.html, accessed May 26, 2007.

30. www.osha.gov/dcsp/smallbusiness/sharp. html, accessed February 17, 2010.

31. Dietz et al., "HRM Inside UK E-commerce Firms."

32. Adrienne Fox, "McMurray Scouts Top Talent to Produce Winning Results," *HR Magazine* 51, no. 7 (July 2006), pp. 57.

33. This is based on John Drake, *Interviewing for Managers: A Complete Guide to Employment Interviewing* (New York, AMACOM, 1982).

34. Ibid.

35. Colin Gray and Christopher Mabey, "Management Development: Key Differences Between Small and Large Businesses in Europe," *International Small Business Journal* 23, no. 5 (October 2005), pp. 467–485.

36. Ibid. See also Essi Saru, "Organizational Learning and HRD: How Appropriate Are They for Small Firms?" *Journal of European Industrial Training* 31, no. 1 (January 2007), pp. 36–52.

37. From Stephen Covey, "Small Business, Big Opportunity," *Training* 43, no. 11 (November 2006), pp. 40.

38. Gina Ruiz, "Smaller Firms in Vanguard of Flex Practices," *Workforce Management* 84, no. 13 (November 21, 2005), pp. 10.

39. Kira Bindrum, "Little Firms Redefine Culture of Work," *Crain's New York Business* 25, no. 49 (December 7–13, 2009), p. 20.

40. Ibid., pp. 7–13.

41. Ruiz, "Smaller Firms in Vanguard of Flex Practices."

42. These are from Ty Freyvogel, "Operation Employee Loyalty," *Training Media Review,* September–October 2007.

43. Ibid.

44. Ibid.

45. Based on Bob Nelson, *1001 Ways to Reward Employees* (New York: Workmen Publishing, 1994), pp. 19. See also Sunny C. L. Fong and Margaret A. Shaffer, "The Dimensionality and Determinants of Pay Satisfaction: A Cross-Cultural Investigation of a Group Incentive Plan," *International Journal of Human Resource Management* 14, no. 4 (June 2003), p. 559(22).

46. Judith Medina, "No Help in Sight for Soaring Costs," *Crain's New York Business* 26, no. 2 (January 11–17, 2010), pp. 10, 13.

47. Michelle V. Rafter, "Back in a Giving Mood," *Workforce Management* 88, no. 10 (September 14, 2009), pp. 25–29.

48. Ibid.

49. Jeffrey Marshall and Ellen Heffes, "Benefits: Smaller Firm Workers Often Getting Less," *Financial Executive* 21, no. 9 (November 1, 2005), p. 10.

50. www.dol.gov/ebsa/pdf/ppa2006.pdf, accessed February 18, 2008.

51. Bill Leonard, "New Retirement Plans for Small Employers," *HR Magazine* 51, no. 12 (December 2006), pp. 30.

52. Kristen Falk, "The Easy Retirement Plan for Small Business Clients," *National Underwriter* 111, no. 45 (December 3, 2007), pp. 12–13.

53. Ibid.

54. Dina Berta, "Job Trekker's Odyssey Offers HR Insights," *Nation's Restaurant News* 42, no. 6 (February 11, 2008), pp. 1, 12.

55. Dina Berta, "IHOP Franchise Employs Post-Hiring Surveys to Get Off Turnover 'Treadmill,'" *Nation's Restaurant News* 41, no 39 (October 1, 2007), p. 6.

56. Dina Berta, "IHOP Franchisee Employs Post-Hiring Surveys to Get Off Turnover 'Treadmill,'" *Nation's Restaurant News* 41, no. 39 (October 1, 2007), p. 6.

57. Kate Leahy, "The 10 Minute Manager's Guide to . . . Communicating with Employees," *Restaurants & Institutions* 116, no. 11 (June 1, 2006), pp. 22–23.

58. Ibid.

59. Ibid.

60. Phillip Perry, "Welcome to the Family," *Restaurant Hospitality* 90, no. 5 (May 2006), pp. 73, 74, 76, 78.

61. Ibid.

62. Ibid.

63. Ibid.

64. Ibid.

65. Jane Applegate, "Employee Leasing Can Be a Savior for Small Firms," *Business Courier Serving Cincinnati–Northern Kentucky* (January 28, 2000), p. 23.

66. Robert Beck and Jay Starkman, "How to Find a PEO That Will Get the Job Done," *National Underwriter* 110, no. 39 (October 16, 2006), pp. 39, 45.

67. Layne Davlin, "Human Resource Solutions for the Franchisee," *Franchising World* 39, no. 10 (October 2007), pp. 27–28.

68. Beck and Starkman, "How to Find a PEO."

69. Lyle DeWitt, "Advantages of Human Resources Outsourcing," *The CPA Journal* 75, no. 6 (June 2005), pp. 13.

70. Max Chafkin, "Fed Up with HR?" *Inc.* 28, no. 5 (May 2006), pp. 50–52.

71. Ibid.

72. Ibid.

73. Ibid.

74. Diana Reitz, "Employee Leasing Breeds Liability Questions," *National Underwriter Property and Casualty Risk and Benefits Management* 104, no. 18 (May 2000), p. 12.

75. Max Chafkin, "Fed Up with HR?" *Inc.* 28, no. 5 (May 2006), pp. 50–52.

76. For a more complete list, see, for example, Sondra Servais, *Personnel Director* (Deerfield Beach, FL: Made E-Z Products, 1994); and www.hoovers.com/business-forms/—pageid_16436—/global-mktg-index.xhtml?cm_ven=PAID&cm_cat=GGL&cm_pla=FRM&cm_ite=employment_contract_forms, accessed July 20, 2008.

77. Office Depot, Winter 2003 Catalog (Delray Beach, FL: Office Depot, 2003).

78. www.ihrim.org, accessed April 28, 2008.

79. Adapted from Kenneth Laudon and Jane Laudon, *Management Information Systems: New Approaches to Organization and Technology* (Upper Saddle River, NJ: Prentice Hall, 1998), p. G7. See also Michael Barrett and Randolph Kahn, "The Governance of Records Management," *Directors and Boards* 26, no. 3 (Spring 2002), pp. 45–48; Anthony Hendrickson, "Human Resource Information Systems: Backbone Technology of Contemporary Human Resources," *Journal of Labor Research* 24, no. 3 (Summer 2003), pp. 381–395.

80. "HR Execs Trade Notes on Human Resource Information Systems," *BNA Bulletin to Management* (December 3, 1998), p. 1. See also Brian Walter, "But They Said Their Payroll Program Complied with the FLSA," *Public Personnel Management* 31, no. 1 (Spring 2002), pp. 79–94.

81. "HR Execs Trade Notes on Human Resource Information Systems," *BNA Bulletin to Management* (December 3, 1998), p. 2. See also Ali Velshi, "Human Resources Information," *The Americas Intelligence Wire* (February 11, 2004).

82. Copyright Gary Dessler, PhD, 2011; based on information in Michelle Conlin, "Netflix: Flex To The Max," September 24, 2007, www.businessweek.com/magazine/content/07_39/b4051059.htm, accessed July 3, 2011; Robert J. Grossman, "Tough Love at Netflix," April 1, 2010, www.shrm.org/Publications/hrmagazine/EditorialContent/2010/0410/Pages/0410grossman3.aspx, accessed July 3, 2011; and David F. Larcker, Allan McCall, and Brian Tayan, "Equity on Demand: The Netflix Approach to Compensation," January 15, 2010, http://hbr.org/product/equity-on-demand-the-netflix-approach-to-compensat/an/CG19-PDF-ENG, accessed July 3, 2011.

PART 5 VIDEO CASES APPENDIX

Video Title: Union-Management Relations (UPS)

SYNOPSIS

The former human resources head for UPS describes what it's like (for both an employer and an employee) to work with a labor union. The roles and functions of labor unions are discussed, and the advantages and disadvantages that can accrue to both employees and management are explained. The future of unions, and other arrangements that fulfill some of the same roles, are also discussed.

Discussion Questions

1. From what you know about UPS, what do you think would make the union believe that the company was ripe for being organized?
2. Do you agree that unions "stifle creativity"? Why or why not?
3. Do you agree that employees who excel in nonunion environments earn more than they would in unionized companies? Why?
4. What other "replacements" for unions have helped reduce union membership, according to the chapter?

Video Title: Safety (California Health Foundation)

SYNOPSIS

Company initiatives to promote safety and emergency preparedness are discussed. These include proactive measures to encourage employee health and to prevent injuries, especially ergonomic ones. Different methods of preventing injuries are discussed, including employee health programs that reimburse employees for gym memberships, smoking cessation, weight loss, and other programs. When the company helps foster better employee health, they are more likely to perform well and remain free of injuries.

Discussion Questions

1. What are some ways of lowering stress that the California Health Foundation emphasizes?
2. How are the employees at the California Health Foundation involved in ensuring an adequate response to an emergency?
3. Why are proactive measures the most appropriate for addressing ergonomic injuries?
4. Based on what you've seen to this point, how comprehensive would you say that the company's safety program is? What suggestions would you make for additional steps it should take?
5. What are the other economic side effects of accidents?
6. Do you agree that "safety in the office is a matter of attitude"? Why or why not?
7. What other steps would you suggest the company take to boost safety?; for instance, what would you have supervisors do to improve the company's safety and accident record?

Video Title: Safety (City of Los Angeles)

SYNOPSIS

In this video, Randall Macfarlane says, among other things, that they use four methods to ensure safety and health: training, providing personal protective equipment, providing a special 8-hour training course for their staff, and holding biweekly safety meetings.

He also says they train supervisors to recognize behaviors or other things that may be warning signs. Furthermore, an in-house review every year aims to make sure all information and videos, etc., are current. He also focuses on ergonomics in order to prevent problems like carpal tunnel syndrome. The company has periodic reviews from California's Occupational Safety and Health Administration.

Discussion Questions

1. What should the city do prior to issuing personal protective equipment, according to Chapter 16?
2. What do you think of the safety program? What else would you suggest, and why?
3. What are some of the issues and caveats the employer and its supervisors should follow when dealing with a visit from the Occupational Safety and Health Administration?
4. If you were asked to put together a list of items that supervisors should keep in mind with respect to supervising safety and health at work, what would you include on your list?

Video Title: Global HR Management (Joby)

SYNOPSIS

Joby is best known for its line of flexible camera tripods, called Gorillapods, and for its flexible flashlights, called Gorillatorches. Joby has only a few dozen employees, but has offices on three continents. It is often called "the smallest global company in the world."

Discussion Questions

1. Describe Joby's approach to managing globally. How does it coordinate design, manufacturing, and distribution in key world markets?
2. How does a small company like Joby hire employees to work in its facilities all over the world?
3. Based on what you read in Chapter 17, what suggestions would you make for improving this company's global HR practices?

PHR and SPHR knowledge Base

The PHR and SPHR exams are created using the following PHR and SPHR Knowledge Base, which outlines the responsibilities and knowledge needed to be a viable HR professional. The PHR and SPHR Knowledge Base is created by HR subject matter experts through a rigorous practice analysis study and then validated by HR professionals working in the field through an extensive survey instrument. The PHR and SPHR Knowledge Base periodically is updated to ensure it is consistent with current practices in the HR field. All questions appearing on the exams are linked to the responsibility and knowledge statements outlined below.

IF LAWS CHANGE

We realize that employment laws change constantly. Candidates are responsible for knowing the HR laws and regulations that are in effect as of the start of each exam period.

The percentages that follow each functional area heading are the PHR and SPHR percentages, respectively.

01 Strategic Business Management (12%, 29%)

Developing, contributing to and supporting the organization's mission, vision, values, strategic goals and objectives; formulating policies; guiding and leading the change process; and evaluating HR's contributions to organizational effectiveness.

RESPONSIBILITIES:

01 Interpret information related to the organization's operations from internal sources, including financial/accounting, business development, marketing, sales, operations, and information technology, in order to contribute to the development of the organization's strategic plan.

02 Interpret information from external sources related to the general business environment, industry practices and developments, technological developments, economic environment, labor pool, and legal and regulatory environment, in order to contribute to the development of the organization's strategic plan.

03 Participate as a contributing partner in the organization's strategic planning process.

04 Establish strategic relationships with key individuals in the organization to influence organizational decision-making.

05 Establish relationships/alliances with key individuals and organizations in the community to assist in achieving the organization's strategic goals and objectives.

06 Develop and utilize metrics to evaluate HR's contributions to the achievement of the organization's strategic goals and objectives.

07 Develop and execute strategies for managing organizational change that balance the expectations and needs of the organization, its employees, and all other stakeholders.

08 Develop and align the organization's human capital management plan with its strategic plan.

09 Facilitate the development and communication of the organization's core values and ethical behaviors.

10 Reinforce the organization's core values and behavioral expectations through modeling, communication, and coaching.

11 Develop and manage the HR budget in a manner consistent with the organization's strategic goals, objectives, and values.

12 Provide information for the development and monitoring of the organization's overall budget.

13 Monitor the legislative and regulatory environment for proposed changes and their potential impact to the organization, taking appropriate proactive steps to support, modify, or oppose the proposed changes.

14 Develop policies and procedures to support corporate governance initiatives (e.g., board of directors training, whistleblower protection, code of conduct).

15 Participate in enterprise risk management by examining HR policies to evaluate their potential risks to the organization.

16 Identify and evaluate alternatives and recommend strategies for vendor selection and/or outsourcing (e.g., human resource information systems [HRIS], benefits, payroll).

17 Participate in strategic decision-making and due diligence activities related to organizational structure and design (e.g., corporate restructuring, mergers and acquisitions [M&A], offshoring, divestitures). **SPHR ONLY**

18 Determine strategic application of integrated technical tools and systems (e.g., HRIS, performance management tools, applicant tracking, compensation tools, employee self-service technologies).

KNOWLEDGE OF:

01 The organization's mission, vision, values, business goals, objectives, plans, and processes.

02 Legislative and regulatory processes.

03 Strategic planning process and implementation.

04 Management functions, including planning, organizing, directing, and controlling.

05 Techniques to promote creativity and innovation.

06 Corporate governance procedures and compliance (e.g., Sarbanes-Oxley Act).

07 Transition techniques for corporate restructuring, M&A, offshoring, and divestitures. **SPHR ONLY**

02 Workforce Planning and Employment (26%, 17%)

Developing, implementing and evaluating sourcing, recruitment, hiring, orientation, succession planning, retention, and organizational exit programs necessary to ensure the workforce's ability to achieve the organization's goals and objectives.

RESPONSIBILITIES:

01 Ensure that workforce planning and employment activities are compliant with applicable federal, state, and local laws and regulations.

02 Identify workforce requirements to achieve the organization's short- and long-term goals and objectives (e.g., corporate restructuring, M&A activity, workforce expansion or reduction).

03 Conduct job analyses to create job descriptions and identify job competencies.

04 Identify and document essential job functions for positions.

05 Establish hiring criteria based on job descriptions and required competencies.

06 Analyze labor market for trends that impact the ability to meet workforce requirements (e.g., SWOT analysis, environmental scan, demographic scan). **SPHR ONLY**

07 Assess skill sets of internal workforce and external labor market to determine the availability of qualified candidates, utilizing third-party vendors or agencies as appropriate.

08   Identify internal and external recruitment sources (e.g., employee referrals, online job boards, resume banks) and implement selected recruitment methods.

09   Evaluate recruitment methods and sources for effectiveness (e.g., return on investment [ROI], cost-per-hire, time to fill).

10   Develop strategies to brand/market the organization to potential qualified applicants.

11   Develop and implement selection procedures, including applicant tracking, interviewing, testing, reference, and background checking, and drug screening.

12   Develop and extend employment offers and conduct negotiations as necessary.

13   Administer post-offer employment activities (e.g., execute employment agreements, complete I-9 verification forms, coordinate relocations, schedule physical exams).

14   Implement and/or administer the process for non-U.S. citizens to legally work in the United States.

15   Develop, implement and evaluate orientation processes for new hires, rehires, and transfers.

16   Develop, implement, and evaluate retention strategies and practices.

17   Develop, implement, and evaluate succession planning process.

18   Develop and implement the organizational exit process for both voluntary and involuntary terminations, including planning for reductions in force (RIF).

19   Develop, implement and evaluate an AAP, as required.

KNOWLEDGE OF:

08   Federal/state/local employment-related laws and regulations related to workforce planning and employment (e.g., Title VII, ADA, ADEA, USERRA, EEOC Uniform Guidelines on Employee Selection Procedures, Immigration Reform and Control Act, Internal Revenue Code).

09   Quantitative analyses required to assess past and future staffing effectiveness (e.g., cost-benefit analysis, costs-per-hire, selection ratios, adverse impact).

10   Recruitment sources (e.g., Internet, agencies, employee referral) for targeting passive, semi-active and active candidates.

11   Recruitment strategies.

12   Staffing alternatives (e.g., temporary and contract, outsourcing, job sharing, part-time).

13   Planning techniques (e.g., succession planning, forecasting).

14   Reliability and validity of selection tests/tools/methods.

15   Use and interpretation of selection tests (e.g., psychological/personality, cognitive, motor/physical assessments, performance, assessment center).

16   Interviewing techniques (e.g., behavioral, situational, panel).

17   Relocation practices.

18   Impact of total rewards on recruitment and retention.

19   International HR and implications of global workforce for workforce planning and employment. **SPHR ONLY**

20   Voluntary and involuntary terminations, downsizing, restructuring, and outplacement strategies and practices.

21   Internal workforce assessment techniques (e.g., skills testing, skills inventory, workforce demographic analysis) and employment policies, practices, and procedures (e.g., orientation and retention).

22   Employer marketing and branding techniques.

23   Negotiation skills and techniques.

03 Human Resource Development (17%, 17%)

Developing, implementing and evaluating activities and programs that address employee training and development, performance appraisal, talent and performance management, and the unique needs of employees to ensure that the knowledge, skills, abilities and performance of the workforce meet current and future organizational and individual needs.

RESPONSIBILITIES:

01   Ensure that human resource development programs are compliant with all applicable federal, state, and local laws and regulations.

02   Conduct a needs assessment to identify and establish priorities regarding human resource development activities. **SPHR ONLY**

03   Develop/select and implement employee training programs (e.g., leadership skills, harassment prevention, computer skills) to increase individual and organizational effectiveness. Note that this includes training design and methods for obtaining feedback from training (e.g., surveys, pre- and post-testing).

04   Evaluate effectiveness of employee training programs through the use of metrics (e.g., participant surveys, pre- and post-testing). **SPHR ONLY**

05   Develop, implement and evaluate talent management programs that include assessing talent, developing talent and placing high-potential employees. **SPHR ONLY**

06   Develop/select and evaluate performance appraisal process (e.g., instruments, ranking and rating scales, relationship to compensation, frequency).

07   Implement training programs for performance evaluators. **PHR ONLY**

08   Develop, implement and evaluate performance management programs and procedures (e.g., goal setting, job rotations, promotions).

09   Develop/select, implement and evaluate programs (e.g., flexible work arrangements, diversity initiatives, repatriation) to meet the unique needs of employees. **SPHR ONLY**

KNOWLEDGE OF:

24   Applicable federal, state, and local laws and regulations related to human resources development activities (e.g., Title VII, ADA, ADEA, USERRA, EEOC Uniform Guidelines on Employee Selection Procedures).

25   Career development and leadership development theories and applications.

26   Organizational development theories and applications.

27   Training program development techniques to create general and specialized training programs.

28   Training methods, facilitation techniques, instructional methods, and program delivery mechanisms.

29   Task/process analysis.

30   Performance appraisal methods (e.g., instruments, ranking and rating scales).

31   Performance management methods (e.g., goal setting, job rotations, promotions).

32   Applicable global issues (e.g., international law, culture, local management approaches/practices, societal norms). **SPHR ONLY**

33   Techniques to assess training program effectiveness, including use of applicable metrics (e.g., participant surveys, pre- and post-testing).

34   E-learning.

35   Mentoring and executive coaching.

04 Total Rewards (16%, 12%)

Developing/selecting, implementing/administering and evaluating compensation and benefits programs for all employee groups that support the organization's strategic goals, objectives, and values.

RESPONSIBILITIES:

01   Ensure that compensation and benefits programs are compliant with applicable federal, state, and local laws and regulations.

02   Develop, implement, and evaluate compensation policies/programs and pay structures based upon internal equity and external market conditions that support the organization's strategic goals, objectives, and values.

03   Administer payroll functions (e.g., new hires, deductions, adjustments, terminations).

04   Conduct benefits programs needs assessments (e.g., benchmarking, employee survey).

05   Develop/select, implement/administer, and evaluate benefits programs that support the organization's strategic goals, objectives, and values (e.g., health and welfare, retirement, stock purchase, wellness, employee assistance programs [EAP], time-off).

06   Communicate and train the workforce in the compensation and benefits programs and policies (e.g., self-service technologies).

07   Develop/select, implement/administer, and evaluate executive compensation programs (e.g., stock purchase, stock options, incentive, bonus, supplemental retirement plans). **SPHR ONLY**

08   Develop, implement/administer, and evaluate expatriate and foreign national compensation and benefits programs. **SPHR ONLY**

KNOWLEDGE OF:

36   Federal, state and local compensation, benefits, and tax laws (e.g., FLSA, ERISA, COBRA, HIPAA, FMLA, FICA).

37   Total rewards strategies (e.g., compensation, benefits, wellness, rewards, recognition, employee assistance).

38   Budgeting and accounting practices related to compensation and benefits.

39   Job evaluation methods.

40   Job pricing and pay structures.

41   External labor markets and/or economic factors.

42   Pay programs (e.g., incentive, variable, merit).

43   Executive compensation methods. **SPHR ONLY**

44   Non-cash compensation methods (e.g., stock options, ESOPs). **SPHR ONLY**

45   Benefits programs (e.g., health and welfare, retirement, wellness, EAP, time-off).

46   International compensation laws and practices (e.g., expatriate compensation, entitlements, choice of law codes). **SPHR ONLY**

47   Fiduciary responsibility related to total rewards management. **SPHR ONLY**

05 Employee and Labor Relations (22%, 18%)

Analyzing, developing, implementing/administering, and evaluating the workplace relationship between employer and employee, in order to maintain relationships and working conditions that balance employer and employee needs and rights in support of the organization's strategic goals, objectives, and values.

RESPONSIBILITIES:

01   Ensure that employee and labor relations activities are compliant with applicable federal, state, and local laws and regulations.

02   Assess organizational climate by obtaining employee input (e.g., focus groups, employee surveys, staff meetings).

03   Implement organizational change activities as appropriate in response to employee feedback.

04   Develop employee relations programs (e.g., awards, recognition, discounts, special events) that promote a positive organizational culture.

05   Implement employee relations programs that promote a positive organizational culture.

06   Evaluate effectiveness of employee relations programs through the use of metrics (e.g., exit interviews, employee surveys).

07   Establish workplace policies and procedures (e.g., dress code, attendance, computer use) and monitor their application and enforcement to ensure consistency.

08   Develop, administer and evaluate grievance/dispute resolution and performance improvement policies and procedures.

09   Resolve employee complaints filed with federal, state, and local agencies involving employment practices, utilizing professional resources as necessary (e.g., legal counsel, mediation/arbitration specialists and investigators).

10   Develop and direct proactive employee relations strategies for remaining union-free in non-organized locations.

11   Participate in collective bargaining activities, including contract negotiation and administration. **SPHR ONLY**

KNOWLEDGE OF:

48   Applicable federal, state, and local laws affecting employment in union and nonunion environments, such as antidiscrimination laws, sexual harassment, labor relations, and privacy (e.g., WARN Act, Title VII, NLRA).

49   Techniques for facilitating positive employee relations (e.g., employee surveys, focus groups, dispute resolution, labor/management cooperative strategies and programs).

50   Employee involvement strategies (e.g., employee management committees, self-directed work teams, staff meetings).

51   Individual employment rights issues and practices (e.g., employment at will, negligent hiring, defamation, employees' rights to bargain collectively).

52   Workplace behavior issues/practices (e.g., absenteeism and performance improvement).

53   Unfair labor practices (e.g., employee communication strategies and management training).

54   The collective bargaining process, strategies and concepts (e.g., contract negotiation and administration). **SPHR ONLY**

55   Positive employee relations strategies and non-monetary rewards.

06 Risk Management (7%, 7%)

Developing, implementing/administering, and evaluating programs, plans and policies that provide a safe and secure working environment and protect the organization from liability.

RESPONSIBILITIES:

01   Ensure that workplace health, safety, security, and privacy activities are compliant with applicable federal, state, and local laws and regulations.

02   Identify the organization's safety program needs.

03   Develop/select and implement/administer occupational injury and illness prevention, safety incentives and training programs. **PHR ONLY**

04   Develop/select, implement, and evaluate plans and policies to protect employees and other individuals and to minimize the organization's loss and liability (e.g., emergency response, evacuation, workplace violence, substance abuse, return-to-work policies).

05   Communicate and train the workforce on the plans and policies to protect employees and other individuals and to minimize the organization's loss and liability.

06   Develop and monitor business continuity and disaster recovery plans.

07   Communicate and train the workforce on the business continuity and disaster recovery plans.

08   Develop internal and external privacy policies (e.g., identity theft, data protection, HIPAA compliance, workplace monitoring).

09   Administer internal and external privacy policies.

KNOWLEDGE OF:

56   Federal, state and local workplace health, safety, security, and privacy laws and regulations (e.g., OSHA, Drug-Free Workplace Act, ADA, HIPAA, Sarbanes-Oxley).

57   Occupational injury and illness compensation and programs.

58   Occupational injury and illness prevention programs.

59   Investigation procedures of workplace safety, health, and security enforcement agencies (e.g., OSHA, National Institute for Occupational Safety and Health [NIOSH]).

60   Workplace safety risks.

61   Workplace security risks (e.g., theft, corporate espionage, asset and data protection, sabotage).

62   Potential violent behavior and workplace violence conditions.

63   General health and safety practices (e.g., evacuation, hazard communication, ergonomic evaluations).

64   Incident and emergency response plans.

65   Internal investigation, monitoring, and surveillance techniques.

66   Issues related to substance abuse and dependency (e.g., identification of symptoms, substance-abuse testing, discipline).

67   Business continuity and disaster recovery plans (e.g., data storage and backup, alternative work locations and procedures).

68   Data integrity techniques and technology (e.g., data sharing, firewalls).

Core Knowledge Required By HR Professionals

69   Needs assessment and analysis.

70   Third-party contract negotiation and management, including development of requests for proposals (RFPs).

71   Communication skills and strategies (e.g., presentation, collaboration, influencing, diplomacy, sensitivity).

72   Organizational documentation requirements to meet federal and state requirements.

73   Adult learning processes.

74   Motivation concepts and applications.

75   Training techniques (e.g., computer-based, classroom, on-the-job).

76   Leadership concepts and applications.

77   Project management concepts and applications.

78   Diversity concepts and applications.

79   Human relations concepts and applications (e.g., interpersonal and organizational behavior).

80   HR ethics and professional standards.

81   Technology to support HR activities (e.g., HRIS, employee self-service, e-learning, ATS).

82   Qualitative and quantitative methods and tools for analysis, interpretation, and decision-making purposes (e.g., metrics and measurements, cost/benefit analysis, financial statement analysis).

83   Change management methods.

84   Job analysis and job description methods.

85   Employee records management (e.g., electronic/paper, retention, disposal).

86   The interrelationships among HR activities and programs across functional areas.

87   Types of organizational structures (e.g., matrix, hierarchy).

88   Environmental scanning concepts and applications.

89   Methods for assessing employee attitudes, opinions, and satisfaction (e.g., opinion surveys, attitude surveys, focus groups/panels).

90   Basic budgeting and accounting concepts.

91   Risk management techniques.

Source: Used with permission of the HR Certificate Institute.

Comprehensive Cases

BANDAG AUTOMOTIVE*

Jim Bandag took over his family's auto supply business in 2005, after helping his father, who founded the business, run it for about 10 years. Based in Illinois, Bandag employs about 300 people, and distributes auto supplies (replacement mufflers, bulbs, engine parts, and so on) through two divisions, one that supplies service stations and repair shops, and a second that sells retail auto supplies through five "Bandag Automotive" auto supply stores.

Jim's father, and now Jim, have always endeavored to keep Bandag's organization chart as simple as possible. The company has a full-time controller, managers for each of the five stores, a manager that oversees the distribution division, and Jim Bandag's executive assistant. Jim (along with his father, working part-time) handles marketing and sales.

Jim's executive assistant administers the firm's day-to-day human resource management tasks, but the company outsources most HR activities to others, including an employment agency that does its recruiting and screening, a benefits firm that administers its 401(k) plan, and a payroll service that handles its paychecks. Bandag's human resource management systems consist almost entirely of standardized HR forms purchased from an HR supplies company. These include forms such as application and performance appraisal forms, as well as an "honesty" test Bandag uses to screen the staff that works in the five stores. The company performs informal salary surveys to see what other companies in the area are paying for similar positions, and use these results for awarding annual merit increases (which in fact are more accurately cost-of-living adjustments).

Jim's father took a fairly paternal approach to the business. He often walked around speaking with his employees, finding out what their problems were, and even helping them out with an occasional loan—for instance, when he discovered that one of their children was sick, or for part of a new home down payment. Jim, on the other hand, tends to be more abrupt, and does not enjoy the same warm relationship with the employees as did his father. Jim is not unfair or dictatorial. He's just very focused on improving Bandag's financial performance, and so all his decisions, including his HR-related decisions, generally come down to cutting costs. For example, his knee-jerk reaction is usually to offer fewer days off rather than more, fewer benefits rather than more, and to be less flexible when an employee needs, for instance, a few extra days off because a child is sick.

It's therefore perhaps not surprising that over the past few years Bandag's sales and profits have increased markedly, but that the firm has found itself increasingly enmeshed in HR/equal employment–type issues. Indeed, Jim now finds himself spending a day or two a week addressing HR problems. For example, Henry Jaques, an employee at one of the stores, came to Jim's executive assistant and told her he was "irate" about his recent firing and was probably going to sue. Henry's store manager stated on his last performance appraisal that Henry did the technical aspects of his job well, but that he had "serious problems interacting with his coworkers." He was continually arguing with them, and complaining to the store manager about working conditions. The store manager had told Jim that he had to fire Henry because he was making "the whole place poisonous," and that (although he felt sorry because he'd heard rumors that Henry suffered from some mental illness) he felt he had to go. Jim approved the dismissal.

*© Gary Dessler, Ph.D.

Gavin was another problem. Gavin had worked for Bandag for 10 years, the last two as manager of one of the company's five stores. Right after Jim Bandag took over, Gavin told him he had to take a Family and Medical Leave Act medical leave to have hip surgery, and Jim approved the leave. When Gavin returned from leave, Jim told him that his position had been eliminated. Bandag had decided to close his store and open a new, larger store across from a shopping center about a mile away, and had appointed a new manager in Gavin's absence. However, the company did give Gavin a (nonmanagerial) position in the new store as a counter salesperson, at the same salary and with the same benefits as he had before. Even so, "This job is not similar to my old one," Gavin insisted. "It doesn't have nearly as much prestige." His contention is that the FMLA requires that the company bring him back in the same or equivalent position, and that this means a supervisory position, similar to what he had before he went on leave. Jim said no, and they seem to be heading toward litigation.

In another sign of the times at Bandag, the company's controller, Miriam, who had been with the company for about 6 years, went on pregnancy leave for 12 weeks in 2005 (also under the FMLA), and then received an additional 3 weeks' leave under Bandag's extended illness days program. Four weeks after she came back, she asked Jim Bandag if she could arrange to work fewer hours per week, and spend about a day per week working out of her home. He refused, and about 2 months later fired her. Jim Bandag said, "I'm sorry, it's not anything to do with your pregnancy-related requests, but we've got ample reasons to discharge you—your monthly budgets have been several days late, and we've got proof you may have forged documents." She replied, "I don't care what you say your reasons are, you're really firing me because of my pregnancy, and that's illegal."

Jim felt he was on safe ground as far as defending the company for these actions, although he didn't look forward to spending the time and money that he knew it would take to fight each. However, what he learned over lunch from a colleague undermined his confidence about another case that Jim had been sure would be a "slam dunk" for his company. Jim was explaining to his friend that one of Bandag's truck maintenance service people had applied for a job driving one of Bandag's distribution department trucks, and that Jim had turned him down because the worker was deaf. Jim (whose wife has occasionally said of him, "No one has ever accused Jim of being politically correct") was mentioning to his friend the apparent absurdity of a deaf person asking to be a truck delivery person. His friend, who happens to work for UPS, pointed out that the U.S. Court of Appeals for the Ninth Circuit had recently decided that UPS had violated the Americans with Disabilities Act by refusing to consider deaf workers for jobs driving the company's smaller vehicles.

Although Jim's father is semi-retired, the sudden uptick in the frequency of such EEO-type issues troubled him, particularly after so many years of labor peace. However, he's not sure what to do about it. Having handed over the reins of the company to his son, he was loath to inject himself back into the company's operational decision making. On the other hand, he was afraid that in the short run these issues were going to drain a great deal of Jim's time and resources, and that in the long run they might be a sign of things to come, with problems like these eventually overwhelming Bandag Auto. He comes to you, who he knows consults in human resource management, and asks you the following questions.

Questions

1. Given Bandag Auto's size, and anything else you know about it, should we reorganize the human resource management function, and if so why and how?
2. What, if anything, would you do to change and/or improve upon the current HR systems, forms, and practices that we now use?
3. Do you think that the employee that Jim fired for creating what the manager called a poisonous relationship has a legitimate claim against us, and if so why and what should we do about it?
4. Is it true that we really had to put Gavin back into an equivalent position, or was it adequate to just bring him back into a job at the same salary, bonuses, and benefits as he had before his leave?

5. Miriam, the controller, is basically claiming that the company is retaliating against her for being pregnant, and that the fact that we raised performance issues was just a smokescreen. Do you think the EEOC and/or courts would agree with her, and, in any case, what should we do now?

6. An employee who is deaf has asked us to be one of our delivery people and we turned him down. He's now threatening to sue. What should we do, and why?

7. In the previous 10 years, we've had only one equal employment complaint, and now in the last few years we've had four or five. What should I do about it? Why?

Based generally on actual facts, but Bandag is a fictitious company. Bandag source notes: "The Problem Employee: Discipline or Accommodation?" *Monday Business Briefing*, March 8, 2005; "Employee Says Change in Duties After Leave Violates FMLA," *BNA Bulletin to Management*, January 16, 2007, p. 24; "Manager Fired Days After Announcing Pregnancy," *BNA Bulletin to Management*, January 2, 2007, p. 8; "Ninth Circuit Rules UPS Violated ADA by Barring Deaf Workers from Driving Jobs," *BNA Bulletin to Management*, October 17, 2006, p. 329.

ANGELO'S PIZZA*

Angelo Camero was brought up in the Bronx, New York, and basically always wanted to be in the pizza store business. As a youngster, he would sometimes spend hours at the local pizza store, watching the owner knead the pizza dough, flatten it into a large circular crust, fling it up, and then spread on tomato sauce in larger and larger loops. After graduating from college as a marketing major, he made a beeline back to the Bronx, where he opened his first Angelo's Pizza store, emphasizing its clean, bright interior; its crisp green, red, and white sign; and his all-natural, fresh ingredients. Within 5 years, Angelo's store was a success, and he had opened three other stores and was considering franchising his concept.

Eager as he was to expand, his 4 years in business school had taught him the difference between being an entrepreneur and being a manager. As an entrepreneur/small-business owner, he knew he had the distinct advantage of being able to personally run the whole operation himself. With just one store and a handful of employees, he could make every decision and watch the cash register, check in the new supplies, oversee the takeout, and personally supervise the service.

When he expanded to three stores, things started getting challenging. He hired managers for the two new stores (both of whom had worked for him at his first store for several years) and gave them only minimal "how to run a store"–type training, on the assumption that, having worked with him for several years, they already knew pretty much everything they needed to know about running a store. However, he was already experiencing human resource management problems, and he knew there was no way he could expand the number of stores he owned, or (certainly) contemplate franchising his idea, unless he had a system in place that he could clone in each new store to provide the manager (or the franchisee) with the necessary management knowledge and expertise to run their stores. Angelo had no training program in place for teaching his store managers how to run their stores. He simply (erroneously, as it turned out) assumed that by working with him they would learn how to do things on the job. Since Angelo really had no system in place, the new managers were, in a way, starting off below zero when it came to how to manage a store.

There were several issues that particularly concern Angelo. Finding and hiring good employees was number one. He'd read the new National Small Business Poll from the National Federation of Independent Business Education Foundation. It found that 71% of small-business owners believed that finding qualified employees was "hard." Furthermore, "the search for qualified employees will grow more difficult as demographic and education factors" continue to make it more difficult to find employees. Similarly, reading *The Kiplinger Letter* one day, he noticed that just about every type of business couldn't find enough good employees to hire. Small firms were particularly in jeopardy; the *Letter* said: Giant firms can outsource many (particularly entry-level) jobs abroad, and larger companies can also afford to pay better benefits and to train their employees. Small firms rarely have the resources or the economies of scale to allow

*© Gary Dessler, Ph.D.

outsourcing or to install the big training programs that would enable them to take untrained new employees and turned them into skilled ones.

Although finding enough employees was his biggest problem, finding enough honest ones scared him even more. Angelo recalled from one of his business school courses that companies in the United States are losing a total of well over $400 billion a year in employee theft. As a rough approximation, that works out to about $9 per employee per day and about $12,000 lost annually for a typical company. Furthermore, it was small companies like Angelo's that were particularly in the crosshairs, because companies with fewer than 100 employees are particularly prone to employee theft. Why are small firms particularly vulnerable? Perhaps they lack experience dealing with the problem. More importantly: Small firms are more likely to have a single person doing several jobs, such as ordering supplies and paying the delivery person. This undercuts the checks and balances managers often strive for to control theft. Furthermore, the risk of stealing goes up dramatically when the business is largely based on cash. In a pizza store, many people come in and buy just one or two slices and a cola for lunch, and almost all pay with cash, not credit cards.

And, Angelo was not just worried about someone stealing cash. They can steal your whole business idea, something he learned from painful experience. He had been planning to open a store in what he thought would be a particularly good location, and was thinking of having one of his current employees manage the store. Instead, it turned out that this employee was, in a manner of speaking, stealing Angelo's brain—what Angelo knew about customers, suppliers, where to buy pizza dough, where to buy tomato sauce, how much everything should cost, how to furnish the store, where to buy ovens, store layout—everything. This employee soon quit and opened up his own pizza store, not far from where Angelo had planned to open his new store.

That he was having trouble hiring good employees, there was no doubt. The restaurant business is particularly brutal when it comes to turnover. Many restaurants turn over their employees at a rate of 200% to 300% per year—so every year, each position might have a series of two to three employees filling it. As Angelo said, "I was losing two to three employees a month." As he said, "We're a high-volume store, and while we should have [to fill all the hours in a week] about six employees per store, we were down to only three or four, so my managers and I were really under the gun."

The problem was bad at the hourly employee level: "We were churning a lot at the hourly level," said Angelo. "Applicants would come in, my managers or I would hire them and not spend much time training them, and the good ones would leave in frustration after a few weeks, while often it was the bad ones who'd stay behind." But in the last 2 years, Angelo's three company-owned stores also went through a total of three store managers— "They were just blowing through the door," as Angelo put it, in part because, without good employees, their workday was brutal. As a rule, when a small-business owner or manager can't find enough employees (or an employee doesn't show up for work), about 80% of the time the owner or manager does the job himself or herself. So, these managers often ended up working 7 days a week, 10 to 12 hours a day, and many just burned out in the end. One night, working three jobs himself with customers leaving in anger, Angelo decided he'd never just hire someone because he was desperate again, but would start doing his hiring more rationally.

Angelo knew he should have a more formal screening process. As he said, "If there's been a lesson learned, it's much better to spend time up front screening out candidates that don't fit than to hire them and have to put up with their ineffectiveness." He also knew that he could identify many of the traits that his employees needed. For example, he knew that not everyone has the temperament to be a waiter (he has a small pizza/Italian restaurant in the back of his main store). As Angelo said, "I've seen personalities that were off the charts in assertiveness or overly introverted, traits that obviously don't make a good fit for a waiter a waitress."

As a local business, Angelo recruits by placing help wanted ads in two local newspapers, and he's been "shocked" at some of the responses and experiences he's had in response to the ads. Many of the applicants left voicemail messages (Angelo or the other workers in the store were too busy to answer), and some applicants Angelo "just axed" on the assumption that people without good telephone manners wouldn't have very good manners in the store, either. He also quickly learned that he had to throw out a very wide net, even if only hiring one or two people. Many people, as noted, he eliminated from consideration because of the messages they left, and about half the people he scheduled to come in for interviews didn't show up. He'd taken courses in human resource management, so (as he said) "I should know better," but he hired people based almost exclusively on a single interview (he occasionally made a feeble attempt to check references). In total, his HR approach was obviously not working. It wasn't producing enough good recruits, and the people he did hire were often problematical.

What was he looking for? Service-oriented courteous people, for one. For example, he'd hired one employee who used profanity several times, including once in front of a customer. On that employee's third day, Angelo had to tell her, "I think Angelo's isn't the right place for you," and he fired her. As Angelo said, "I felt bad, but also knew that everything I have is on the line for this business, so I wasn't going to let anyone run this business down." Angelo wants reliable people (who'll show up on time), honest people, and people who are flexible about switching jobs and hours as required.

Angelo's Pizza business has only the most rudimentary human resource management system. Angelo bought several application forms at a local Office Depot, and rarely uses other forms of any sort. He uses his personal accountant for reviewing the company's books, and Angelo himself computes each employee's paycheck at the end of the week and writes the checks. Training is entirely on-the-job. Angelo personally trained each of his employees. For those employees who go on to be store managers, he assumes that they are training their own employees the way that Angelo trained them (for better or worse, as it turns out). Angelo pays "a bit above" prevailing wage rates (judging by other help wanted ads), but probably not enough to make a significant difference in the quality of employees that he attracts. If you asked Angelo what his reputation is as an employer, Angelo, being a candid and forthright person, would probably tell you that he is a supportive but hard-nosed employer who treats people fairly, but whose business reputation may suffer from disorganization stemming from inadequate organization and training. He approaches you to ask you several questions.

Questions

1. My strategy is to (hopefully) expand the number of stores and eventually franchise, while focusing on serving only high-quality fresh ingredients. What are three specific human resource management implications of my strategy (including specific policies and practices)?
2. Identify and briefly discuss five specific human resource management errors that I'm currently making.
3. Develop a structured interview form that we can use for hiring (1) store managers, (2) wait staff, and (3) counter people/pizza makers.
4. Based on what you know about Angelo's, and what you know from having visited pizza restaurants, write a one-page outline showing specifically how you think Angelo's should go about selecting employees.

Based generally on actual facts, but Angelo's Pizza is a fictitious company. Angelo's Pizza source notes: Dino Berta, "People Problems: Keep Hiring from Becoming a Crying Game," *Nation's Business News* 36, no. 20 (May 20, 2002), pp. 72–74; Ellen Lyon, "Hiring, Personnel Problems Can Challenge Entrepreneurs," *Patriot-News*, October 12, 2004; Rose Robin Pedone, "Businesses' $400 Billion Theft Problem," *Long Island Business News*. 27 (July 6, 1998), pp. 1B–2B; "Survey Shows Small-Business Problems with Hiring, Internet," *Providence Business News* 16 (September 10, 2001), pp. 1B; "Finding Good Workers Is Posing a Big Problem as Hiring Picks Up," *The Kiplinger Letter* 81 (February 13, 2004).

GOOGLE*

Fortune magazine named Google the best of the 100 best companies to work for, and there is little doubt why. Among the benefits it offers are free shuttles equipped with Wi-Fi to pick up and drop off employees from San Francisco Bay area locations, unlimited sick days, annual all-expense-paid ski trips, free gourmet meals, five on-site free doctors, $2,000 bonuses for referring a new hire, free flu shots, a giant lap pool, on-site oil changes, on-site car washes, volleyball courts, TGIF parties, free on-site

*© Gary Dessler, Ph.D.

washers and dryers (with free detergent), Ping-Pong and foosball tables, and free famous people lectures. For many people, it's the gourmet meals and snacks that make Google stand out. For example, human resources director Stacey Sullivan loves the Irish oatmeal with fresh berries at the company's Plymouth Rock Cafe, near Google's "people operations" group. "I sometimes dream about it," she says. Engineer Jan Fitzpatrick loves the raw bar at Google's Tapis restaurant, down the road on the Google campus. Then, of course, there are the stock options—each new employee gets about 1,200 options to buy Google shares (recently worth about $480 per share). In fact, dozens of early Google employees ("Googlers") are already multimillionaires thanks to Google stock. The recession that began around 2008 did prompt Google and other firms to cut back on some of these benefits (cafeteria hours are shorter today, for instance), but Google still pretty much leads the benefits pack.

For their part, Googlers share certain traits. They tend to be brilliant, team oriented (teamwork is the norm, especially for big projects), and driven. *Fortune* describes them as people who "almost universally" see themselves as the most interesting people on the planet, and who are happy-go-lucky on the outside, but type A—highly intense and goal directed—on the inside. They're also super-hardworking (which makes sense, since it's not unusual for engineers to be in the hallways at 3 A.M. debating some new mathematical solution to a Google search problem). They're so team oriented that when working on projects, it's not unusual for a Google team to give up its larger, more spacious offices and to crowd into a small conference room, where they can "get things done." Historically, Googlers generally graduate with great grades from the best universities, including Stanford, Harvard, and MIT. For many years, Google wouldn't even consider hiring someone with less than a 3.7 average—while also probing deeply into the why behind any B grades. Google also doesn't hire lone wolves, but wants people who work together and people who also have diverse interests (narrow interests or skills are a turnoff at Google). Google also wants people with growth potential. The company is expanding so fast that it needs to hire people who are capable of being promoted five or six times—it's only, the company says, by hiring such overqualified people that it can be sure that the employees will be able to keep up as Google and their own departments expand.

The starting salaries are highly competitive. Experienced engineers start at about $130,000 a year (plus about 1,200 shares of stock options, as noted), and new MBAs can expect between $80,000 and $120,000 per year (with smaller option grants). Most recently, Google had about 10,000 staff members, up from its beginnings with just three employees in a rented garage.

Of course, in a company that's grown from three employees to 10,000 and from zero value to hundreds of billions of dollars, it may be quibbling to talk about "problems," but there's no doubt that such rapid growth does confront Google's management, and particularly its "people operations" group, with some big challenges. Let's look at these.

For one, Google, as noted earlier, is a 24-hour operation, and with engineers and others frequently pulling all-nighters to complete their projects, the company needs to provide a package of services and financial benefits that supports that kind of lifestyle, and that helps its employees maintain an acceptable work–life balance.

As another challenge, Google's enormous financial success is a two-edged sword. Although Google usually wins the recruitment race when it comes to competing for new employees against competitors like Microsoft or Yahoo!, Google does need some way to stem a rising tide of retirements. Most Googlers are still in their twenties and thirties, but many have become so wealthy from their Google stock options that they can afford to retire. One 27-year-old engineer received a million-dollar founder's award for her work on the program for searching desktop computers, and wouldn't think of leaving "except to start her own company." Similarly a former engineering vice president retired (with his Google stock profits) to pursue his love of astronomy. The engineer who dreamed up Gmail recently retired (at the age of 30).

Another challenge is that the work not only involves long hours but can also be very tense. Google is a very numbers-oriented environment. For example, consider a typical weekly Google user interface design meeting. Marisa Meyer, the company's vice president of search products and user experience, runs the meeting, where her employees work out the look and feel of Google's products. Seated around a conference table are about a dozen Googlers, tapping on laptops. During the 2-hour meeting, Meyer needs to evaluate various design proposals, ranging from minor tweaks to a new product's entire layout. She's previously given each presentation an allotted amount of time, and a large digital clock on the wall ticks off the seconds. The presenters must quickly present their ideas, but also handle questions such as "what do users do if the tab is moved from the side of the page to the top?" Furthermore, it's all about the numbers—no one at Google would ever say, for instance, "the tab looks better in red"—you need to prove your point. Presenters must come armed with usability experiment results, showing, for instance, that a certain percent preferred red or some other color. While the presenters are answering these questions as quickly as possible, the digital clock is ticking, and when it hits the allotted time, the presentation must end, and the next team steps up to present. It is a tough and tense environment, and Googlers must have done their homework.

Growth can also undermine the "outlaw band that's changing the world" culture that fostered the services that made Google famous. Even cofounder Sergi Brin agrees that Google risks becoming less "zany" as it grows. To paraphrase one of its top managers, the hard part of any business is keeping that original innovative, small-business feel even as the company grows.

Creating the right culture is especially challenging now that Google is truly global. For example, Google works hard to provide the same financial and service benefits every place it does business around the world, but it can't exactly match its benefits in every country because of international laws and international taxation issues. Offering the same benefits everywhere is more important than it might initially appear. All those benefits make life easier for Google staff, and help them achieve a work–life balance. Achieving the right work–life balance is the centerpiece of Google's culture, but this also becomes more challenging as the company grows. On the one hand, Google does expect all of its employees to work super hard; on the other hand, it realizes that it needs to help them maintain some sort of balance. As one manager says, Google acknowledges "that we work hard but that work is not everything."

Recruitment is another challenge. While Google certainly doesn't lack applicants, attracting the right applicants is crucial if Google is to continue to grow successfully. Working at Google requires a special set of traits, and screening employees is easier if it recruits the right people to begin with. For instance, Google needs to attract people who are super-bright, love to work, have fun, can handle the stress, and who also have outside interests and flexibility.

As the company grows internationally, it also faces the considerable challenge of recruiting and building staff overseas. For example, Google now is introducing a new vertical market–based structure across Europe, to attract more business advertisers to its search engine. (By vertical market–based structure, Google means focusing on key vertical industry sectors such as travel, retail, automotive, and technology.) To build these industry groupings abroad from scratch, Google promoted its former head of its U.S. financial services group to be the vertical markets director for Europe; he moved there recently. Google is thus looking for heads for each of its vertical industry groups for all of its key European territories. Each of these vertical market heads will have to educate their market sectors (retailing, travel, and so on) so Google can attract new advertisers. Google already has offices across Europe, and its London office had tripled in size to 100 staff in just 2 years.

However, probably the biggest challenge Google faces is gearing up its employee selection system, now that the company must hire thousands of people per year. When Google started in business, job candidates typically suffered through a dozen or more in-person interviews, and the standards were so high that even applicants with years of great work experience often got turned down if they had just average college grades. But recently, even Google's cofounders have acknowledged to security analysts that setting such an extraordinarily high bar for hiring was holding back Google's expansion. For Google's first few years, one of the company's cofounder's interviewed nearly every job candidate before he or she was hired, and even today one of them still reviews the qualifications of everyone before he or she gets a final offer.

The experience of one candidate illustrates what Google is up against. A 24-year-old was interviewed for a corporate communications job at Google. Google first made contact with the candidate in May, and then, after two phone interviews, invited him to headquarters. There he had separate interviews with about six people and was treated to lunch in a Google cafeteria. They also had him turn in several "homework" assignments, including a personal statement and a marketing plan. In August, Google invited the candidate back for a second round, which it said would involve another four or five interviews. In the meantime, he decided he'd rather work at a start-up, and accepted another job at a new Web-based instant messaging provider.

Google's new head of human resources, a former GE executive, says that Google is trying to strike the right balance between letting Google and the candidate get to know each other while also moving quickly. To that end, Google recently administered a survey to all Google's current employees in an effort to identify the traits that correlate with success at Google. In the survey, employees responded to questions relating to about 300 variables, including their performance on standardized tests, how old they were when they first used a computer, and how many foreign languages they speak. The Google survey team then went back and compared the answers against the 30 or 40 job performance factors they keep for each employee. They thereby identified clusters of traits that Google might better focus on during the hiring process. Google is also moving from the free-form interviews it used in the past to a more structured process.

Questions

1. What do you think of the idea of Google correlating personal traits from the employees' answers on the survey to their performance, and then using that as the basis for screening job candidates? In other words, is it or is it not a good idea? Please explain your answer.
2. The benefits that Google pays obviously represent an enormous expense. Based on what you know about Google and on what you read in this book, how would you defend all these benefits if you're making a presentation to the security analysts who were analyzing Google's performance?
3. If you wanted to hire the brightest people around, how would you go about recruiting and selecting them?
4. To support its growth and expansion strategy, Google wants (among other traits) people who are super-bright and who work hard, often round-the-clock, and who are flexible and maintain a decent work–life balance. List five specific HR policies or practices that you think Google has implemented or should implement to support its strategy, and explain your answer.
5. What sorts of factors do you think Google will have to take into consideration as it tries transferring its culture and reward systems and way of doing business to its operations abroad?
6. Given the sorts of values and culture Google cherishes, briefly describe four specific activities you suggest they pursue during new-employee orientation.

Source notes for Google: "Google Brings Vertical Structure to Europe," *New Media Age*, August 4, 2005, p. 2; Debbie Lovewell, "Employer Profile—Google: Searching for Talent," *Employee Benefits*, October 10, 2005, p. 66; "Google Looking for Gourmet Chefs," *Internet Week*, August 4, 2005; Douglas Merrill, "Google's 'Googley' Culture Kept Alive by Tech," *eWeek*, April 11, 2006; Robert Hof, "Google Gives Employees Another Option," *BusinessWeek Online*, December 13, 2005; Kevin Delaney, "Google Adjusts Hiring Process as Needs Grow," *The Wall Street Journal*, October 23, 2006, pp. B1, B8; Adam Lishinsky, "Search and Enjoy," *Fortune*, January 22, 2007, pp. 70–82; www.nypost.com/seven/10302008/business/frugal_google_cuts_perks_136011.htm, accessed July 12, 2009. Adam Bryant, "The Quest to Build a Better Boss," New York Times, March 13 2011, p. 1, 7.

MUFFLER MAGIC*

Muffler Magic is a fast-growing chain of 25 automobile service centers in Nevada. Originally started 20 years ago as a muffler repair shop by Ronald Brown, the chain expanded rapidly to new locations, and as it did so Muffler Magic also expanded the services it provided, from muffler replacement to oil changes, brake jobs, and engine repair. Today, one can bring an automobile to a Muffler Magic shop for basically any type of service, from tires to mufflers to engine repair.

---

*© Gary Dessler, Ph.D.

Auto service is a tough business. The shop owner is basically dependent upon the quality of the service people he or she hires and retains, and the most qualified mechanics find it easy to pick up and leave for a job paying a bit more at a competitor down the road. It's also a business in which productivity is very important. The single largest expense is usually the cost of labor. Auto service dealers generally don't just make up the prices that they charge customers for various repairs; instead, they charge based on standardized industry rates for jobs like changing spark plugs or repairing a leaky radiator. Therefore, if someone brings a car in for a new alternator and the standard number of hours for changing the alternator is an hour, but it takes the mechanic 2 hours, the service center's owner may end up making less profit on the transaction.

Quality is a persistent problem as well. For example, "rework" has recently been a problem at Muffler Magic. A customer recently brought her car to a Muffler Magic to have the car's brake pads replaced, which the service center did for her. Unfortunately, when she left she drove only about two blocks before she discovered that she had no brake power at all. It was simply fortuitous that she was going so slowly she was able to stop her car by slowly rolling up against a parking bumper. It subsequently turned out that the mechanic who replaced the brake pads had failed to properly tighten a fitting on the hydraulic brake tubes and the brake fluid had run out, leaving the car with no braking power. In a similar problem the month before that, a (different) mechanic replaced a fan belt, but forgot to refill the radiator with fluid; that customer's car overheated before he got four blocks away, and Muffler Magic had to replace the whole engine. Of course problems like these not only diminish the profitability of the company's profits, but, repeated many times over, have the potential for ruining Muffler Magic's word-of-mouth reputation.

Organizationally, Muffler Magic employs about 300 people, and Ron runs his company with eight managers, including himself as president, a controller, a purchasing director, a marketing director, and the human resource manager. He also has three regional managers to whom the eight or nine service center managers in each area of Nevada report. Over the past 2 years, as the company has opened new service centers, company-wide profits have diminished rather than increased. In part, these diminishing profits probably reflect the fact that Ron Brown has found it increasingly difficult to manage his growing operation ("Your reach is exceeding your grasp" is how Ron's wife puts it).

The company has only the most basic HR systems in place. It uses an application form that the human resource manager modified from one that he downloaded from the Web, and the standard employee status change request forms, sign-on forms, I-9 forms, and so on that it purchased from a human resource management supply house. Training is entirely on-the-job. Muffler Magic expects the experienced technicians that it hires to come to the job fully trained; to that end, the service center managers generally ask candidates for these jobs basic behavioral questions that hopefully provide a window into these applicants' skills. However, most of the other technicians hired to do jobs like rotating tires, fixing brake pads, and replacing mufflers are untrained and inexperienced. They are to be trained by either the service center manager or by more experienced technicians, on-the-job.

Ron Brown faces several HR-type problems. One, as he says, is that he faces the "tyranny of the immediate" when it comes to hiring employees. Although it's fine to say that he should be carefully screening each employee and checking their references and work ethic, from a practical point of view, with 25 centers to run, the centers' managers usually just hire anyone who seems to be breathing, as long as they can answer some basic interview questions about auto repair, such as, "What do you think the problem is if a 2001 Camry is overheating, and what would you do about it?"

Employee safety is also a problem. An automobile service center may not be the most dangerous type of workplace, but it is potentially dangerous. Employees are dealing with sharp tools, greasy floors, greasy tools, extremely hot temperatures (for instance, on mufflers and engines), and fast-moving engine parts including fan blades. There are some basic things that a service manager can do to ensure more safety, such as insisting that all oil spills be cleaned up immediately. However, from a practical point of view, there are a few ways to get around many of the problems—such as when the technician must check out an engine while it is running.

With Muffler Magic's profits going down instead of up, Brown's human resource manager has taken the position that the main problem is financial. As he says, "You get what you pay for" when it comes to employees, and if you compensate technicians better then your competitors do, then you get better technicians, ones who do their jobs better and stay longer with the company—and then profits will rise. So, the HR manager scheduled a meeting between himself, Ron Brown, and a professor of business who teaches compensation management at a local university. The HR manager has asked this professor to spend about a week looking at each of the service centers, analyzing the situation, and coming up with a compensation plan that will address Muffler Magic's quality and productivity problems. At this meeting, the professor makes three basic recommendations for changing the company's compensation policies.

Number one, she says that she has found that Muffler Magic suffers from what she calls "presenteeism"—in other words, employees drag themselves into work even when they're sick, because the company does not pay them if they are out; the company offers no sick days. In just a few days the professor couldn't properly quantify how much Muffler Magic is losing to presenteeism. However, from what she could see at each shop, there are typically one or two technicians working with various maladies like the cold or flu, and it seemed to her that each of these people was probably really only working about half of the time (although they were getting paid for the whole day). So, for 25 service centers per week, Muffler Magic could well be losing 125 or 130 personnel days per week of work. The professor suggests that Muffler Magic start allowing everyone to take 3 paid sick days per year, a reasonable suggestion. However, as Ron Brown points out, "Right now, we're only losing about half a day's pay for each employee who comes in and who works unproductively; with your suggestion, won't we lose the whole day?" The professor says she'll ponder that one.

Second, the professor recommends putting the technicians on a skill-for-pay plan. Basically, she suggests the following. Give each technician a letter grade (A through E) based upon that technician's particular skill level and abilities. An "A" technician is a team leader and needs to show that he or she has excellent diagnostic troubleshooting skills, and the ability to supervise and direct other technicians. At the other extreme, an "E" technician would typically be a new apprentice with little technical training. The other technicians fall in between those two levels, based on their individual skills and abilities.

In the professor's system, the "A" technician or team leader would assign and supervise all work done within his or her area but generally not do any mechanical repairs himself or herself. The team leader does the diagnostic troubleshooting, supervises and trains the other technicians, and test drives the car before it goes back to the customer. Under this plan, every technician receives a guaranteed hourly wage within a certain range, for instance:

A tech = $25–$30 an hour

B tech = $20–$25 an hour

C tech = $15–$20 an hour

D tech = $10–$15 an hour

E tech = $8–$10 an hour

Third, to directly address the productivity issue, the professor recommends that each service manager calculate each technician-team's productivity at the end of each day and at the end of each week. She suggests posting the running productivity total conspicuously for daily viewing. Then, the technicians as a group get weekly cash bonuses based upon their productivity. To calculate productivity, the professor recommends dividing the total labor hours billed by the total labor hours paid to technicians, in other words, total labor hours billed *divided by* total hours paid to technicians.

Having done some homework, the professor says that the national average for labor productivity is currently about 60%, and that only the best-run service centers achieve 85% or greater. By her rough calculations, Muffler Magic was attaining about industry average (about 60%—in other words, they were billing for only about 60 hours for each 100 hours that they actually had to pay technicians to do the jobs). (Of course, this was not entirely the technicians' fault. Technicians get time off for breaks and for lunch, and if a particular service center simply didn't have enough business on a particular day or during a particular week, then several technicians may well sit around idly waiting for the next car to come in.) The professor recommends setting a labor efficiency goal of 80% and posting each team's daily productivity results in the workplace to provide them with additional feedback. She recommends that if at the end of a week the team is able to boost its productivity ratio from the current 60% to 80%, then that team would get an additional 10% weekly pay bonus. After that, for every 5% boost of increased productivity above 80%, technicians would receive an additional 5% weekly bonus. So, if a technician's normal weekly pay is $400, that employee would receive an extra $40 at the end of the week when his team moves from 60% productivity to 80% productivity.

After the meeting, Ron Brown thanked the professor for her recommendations and told her he would think about it and get back to her. After the meeting, on the drive home, Ron was pondering what to do. He had to decide whether to institute the professor's sick leave policy, and whether to implement the professor's incentive and compensation plan. Before implementing anything, however, he wanted to make sure he understood the context in which he was making his decision. For example, did Muffler Magic really have an incentive pay problem, or were the problems more broad? Furthermore, how, if at all, would the professor's incentive plan impact the quality of the work that the teams were doing? And should the company really start paying for sick days? Ron Brown had a lot to think about.

Questions

1. Write a one-page summary outline listing three or four recommendations you would make with respect to each HR function (recruiting, selection, training, and so on) that you think Ron Brown should be addressing with his HR manager.
2. Develop a 10-question structured interview form Ron Brown's service center managers can use to interview experienced technicians.
3. If you were Ron Brown, would you implement the professor's recommendation addressing the presenteeism problem—in other words, start paying for sick days? Why or why not?
4. If you were advising Ron Brown, would you recommend that he implement the professor's skill-based pay and incentive pay plan as is? Why? Would you implement it with modifications? If you would modify it, please be specific about what you think those modifications should be, and why.

Based generally on actual facts, but Muffler Magic is a fictitious company. This case is based largely on information in Drew Paras, "The Pay Factor: Technicians' Salaries Can Be the Largest Expense in a Server Shop, as Well as the Biggest Headache. Here's How One Shop Owner Tackled the Problem," *Motor Age*, November 2003, pp. 76–79; see also Jennifer Pellet, "Health Care Crisis," *Chief Executive*, June 2004, pp. 56–61; "Firms Press to Quantify, Control Presenteeism," *Employee Benefits*, December 1, 2002.

BP TEXAS CITY*

When BP's Horizon oil rig exploded in the Gulf of Mexico in 2010, it triggered tragic reminders for experts in the safety community. In March 2005, an explosion and fire at British Petroleum's (BP) Texas City, Texas, refinery killed 15 people and injured 500 people in the worst U.S. industrial accident in more than 10 years. That disaster triggered three investigations: one internal investigation by BP, one by the U.S. Chemical Safety Board, and an independent investigation chaired by former U.S. Secretary of State James Baker and an 11-member panel that was organized at BP's request.

To put the results of these three investigations into context, it's useful to understand that under its current management, BP had pursued, for the past 10 or so years before the Texas City explosion, a strategy emphasizing cost-cutting and profitability. The basic conclusion of the investigations was that cost-cutting helped compromise safety at the Texas City refinery. It's useful to consider each investigation's findings.

The Chemical Safety Board's (CSB) investigation, according to Carol Merritt, the board's chairwoman, showed that "BP's global management was aware of problems

---

*© Gary Dessler, Ph.D.

with maintenance, spending, and infrastructure well before March 2005." Apparently, faced with numerous earlier accidents, BP did make some safety improvements. However, it focused primarily on emphasizing personal employee safety behaviors and procedural compliance, and on thereby reducing safety accident rates. The problem (according to the CSB) was that "catastrophic safety risks remained." For example, according to the CSB, "unsafe and antiquated equipment designs were left in place, and unacceptable deficiencies in preventive maintenance were tolerated." Basically, the CSB found that BP's budget cuts led to a progressive deterioration of safety at the Texas City refinery. Said Ms. Merritt, "In an aging facility like Texas City, it is not responsible to cut budgets related to safety and maintenance without thoroughly examining the impact on the risk of a catastrophic accident."

Looking at specifics, the CSB said that a 2004 internal audit of 35 BP business units, including Texas City (BP's largest refinery), found significant safety gaps they all had in common, including for instance, a lack of leadership competence, and "systemic underlying issues" such as a widespread tolerance of noncompliance with basic safety rules and poor monitoring of safety management systems and processes. Ironically, the CSB found that BP's accident prevention effort at Texas City had achieved a 70% reduction in worker injuries in the year before the explosion. Unfortunately, this simply meant that individual employees were having fewer accidents. The larger, more fundamental problem was that the potentially explosive situation inherent in the depreciating machinery remained.

The CSB found that the Texas City explosion followed a pattern of years of major accidents at the facility. In fact, there had apparently been an average of one employee death every 16 months at the plant for the last 30 years. The CSB found that the equipment directly involved in the most recent explosion was an obsolete design already phased out in most refineries and chemical plants, and that key pieces of its instrumentation were not working. There had also been previous instances where flammable vapors were released from the same unit in the 10 years prior to the explosion. In 2003, an external audit had referred to the Texas City refinery's infrastructure and assets as "poor" and found what it referred to as a "checkbook mentality," one in which budgets were not sufficient to manage all the risks. In particular, the CSB found that BP had implemented a 25% cut on fixed costs between 1998 and 2000 and that this adversely impacted maintenance expenditures and net expenditures, and refinery infrastructure. Going on, the CSB found that in 2004, there were three major accidents at the refinery that killed three workers.

BP's own internal report concluded that the problems at Texas City were not of recent origin, and instead were years in the making. It said BP was taking steps to address them. Its investigation found "no evidence of anyone consciously or intentionally taking actions or making decisions that put others at risk." Said BP's report, "The underlying reasons for the behaviors and actions displayed during the incident are complex, and the team has spent much time trying to understand them—it is evident that they were many years in the making and will require concerted and committed actions to address." BP's report concluded that there were five underlying causes for the massive explosion:

- A working environment had eroded to one characterized by resistance to change, and a lack of trust.
- Safety, performance, and risk reduction priorities had not been set and consistently reinforced by management.
- Changes in the "complex organization" led to a lack of clear accountabilities and poor communication.
- A poor level of hazard awareness and understanding of safety resulted in workers accepting levels of risk that were considerably higher than at comparable installations.
- Adequate early warning systems for problems were lacking, and there were no independent means of understanding the deteriorating standards at the plant.

The report from the BP-initiated but independent 11-person panel chaired by former U.S. Secretary of State James Baker contained specific conclusions and recommendations.

The Baker panel looked at BP's corporate safety oversight, the corporate safety culture, and the process safety management systems at BP at the Texas City plant as well at BP's other refineries.

Basically, the Baker panel concluded that BP had not provided effective safety process leadership and had not established safety as a core value at the five refineries it looked at (including Texas City).

Like the CSB, the Baker panel found that BP had emphasized personal safety in recent years and had in fact improved personal safety performance, but had not emphasized the overall safety process, thereby mistakenly interpreting "improving personal injury rates as an indication of acceptable process safety performance at its U.S. refineries." In fact, the Baker panel went on, by focusing on these somewhat misleading improving personal injury rates, BP created a false sense of confidence that it was properly addressing process safety risks. It also found that the safety culture at Texas City did not have the positive, trusting, open environment that a proper safety culture required. The Baker panel's other findings included the following.

- BP did not always ensure that adequate resources were effectively allocated to support or sustain a high level of process safety performance.
- BP's refinery personnel are "overloaded" by corporate initiatives.
- Operators and maintenance personnel work high rates of overtime.
- BP tended to have a short-term focus and its decentralized management system and entrepreneurial culture delegated substantial discretion to refinery plant managers "without clearly defining process safety expectations, responsibilities, or accountabilities."
- There was no common, unifying process safety culture among the five refineries.
- The company's corporate safety management system did not make sure there was timely compliance with internal process safety standards and programs.
- BP's executive management either did not receive refinery-specific information that showed that process safety deficiencies existed at some of the plants, or did not effectively respond to any information it did receive.[1]

The Baker panel made several safety recommendations for BP, including the following.

1. The company's corporate management must provide leadership on process safety.
2. The company should establish a process safety management system that identifies, reduces, and manages the process safety risks of the refineries.
3. The company should make sure its employees have an appropriate level of process safety knowledge and expertise.
4. The company should involve "relevant stakeholders" in developing a positive, trusting, and open process safety culture at each refinery.
5. BP should clearly define expectations and strengthen accountability for process safety performance.
6. BP should better coordinate its process safety support for the refining line organization.
7. BP should develop an integrated set of leading and lagging performance indicators for effectively monitoring process safety performance.
8. BP should establish and implement an effective system to audit process safety performance.
9. The company's board should monitor the implementation of the panel's recommendations and the ongoing process safety performance of the refineries.
10. BP should transform into a recognized industry leader in process safety management.

[1]These findings and the following suggestions based on "BP Safety Report Finds Company's Process Safety Culture Ineffective," *Global Refining & Fuels Report*, January 17, 2007.

In making its recommendations, the panel singled out the company's chief executive at the time, Lord Browne, by saying, "In hindsight, the panel believes if Browne had demonstrated comparable leadership on and commitment to process safety [as he did for responding to climate change] that would have resulted in a higher level of safety at refineries."

Overall, the Baker panel found that BP's top management had not provided "effective leadership" on safety. It found that the failings went to the very top of the organization, to the company's chief executive, and to several of his top lieutenants. The Baker panel emphasized the importance of top management commitment, saying, for instance, that "it is imperative that BP leadership set the process safety tone at the top of the organization and establish appropriate expectations regarding process safety performance." It also said BP "has not provided effective leadership in making certain its management and U.S. refining workforce understand what is expected of them regarding process safety performance."

Lord Browne, the chief executive, stepped down about a year after the explosion. About the same time, some BP shareholders were calling for the company's executives and board directors to have their bonuses more closely tied to the company's safety and environmental performance in the wake of Texas City. In October 2009, OSHA announced it was filing the largest fine in its history for this accident, for $87 million, against BP. One year later, BP's Horizon oil rig in the Gulf of Mexico exploded, taking 11 lives.

Questions

1. The textbook defines ethics as "the principles of conduct governing an individual or a group," and specifically as the standards one uses to decide what their conduct should be. To what extent do you believe that what happened at BP is as much a breakdown in the company's ethical systems as it is in its safety systems, and how would you defend your conclusion?

2. Are the Occupational Safety and Health Administration's standards, policies, and rules aimed at addressing problems like the ones that apparently existed at the Texas City plant? If so, how would you explain the fact that problems like these could have continued for so many years?

3. Since there were apparently at least three deaths in the year prior to the major explosion, and an average of about one employee death per 16 months for the previous 10 years, how would you account for the fact that mandatory OSHA inspections missed these glaring sources of potential catastrophic events?

4. The textbook lists numerous suggestions for "how to prevent accidents." Based on what you know about the Texas City explosion, what do you say Texas City tells you about the most important three steps an employer can take to prevent accidents?

5. Based on what you learned in Chapter 16(Safety), would you make any additional recommendations to BP over and above those recommendations made by the Baker panel and the CSB? If so, what would those recommendations be?

6. Explain specifically how strategic human resource management at BP seems to have supported the company's broader strategic aims. What does this say about the advisability of always linking human resource strategy to a company's strategic aims?

Source notes for BP Texas City: Sheila McNulty, "BP Knew of Safety Problems, Says Report," *The Financial Times*, October 31, 2006, p. 1; "CBS: Documents Show BP Was Aware of Texas City Safety Problems," *World Refining & Fuels Today*, October 30, 2006; "BP Safety Report Finds Company's Process Safety Culture Ineffective," *Global Refining & Fuels Report*, January 17, 2007; "BP Safety Record Under Attack," *Europe Intelligence Wire*, January 17, 2007; Mark Hofmann, "BP Slammed for Poor Leadership on Safety, Oil Firm Agrees to Act on Review Panel's Recommendations," *Business Intelligence*, January 22, 2007, p. 3; "Call for Bonuses to Include Link with Safety Performance," *The Guardian*, January 18, 2007, p. 24; www.bp.com/genericarticle.do?categoryId=9005029&contentId=7015905, accessed July 12, 2009; Steven Greenhouse, "BP Faces Record Fine For '05 Blast," *The New York Times*, October 30, 2009, pp. 1, 6. Kyle W Morrison,, "Blame to go around," Safety & Health v. 183 no. 3 (March 2011) p. 40.

GLOSSARY

action learning A training technique by which management trainees are allowed to work full-time analyzing and solving problems in other departments.

adaptability screening A process that aims to assess the assignee's (and spouse's) probable success in handling a foreign transfer.

ADDIE Process In training, Analyze the training need, Design the overall training program, Develop the course, Implement training, Evaluate the course's effectiveness.

adverse impact The overall impact of employer practices that result in significantly higher percentages of members of minorities and other protected groups being rejected for employment, placement, or promotion.

affirmative action Making an extra effort to hire and promote those in protected groups, particularly when those groups are underrepresented.

Age Discrimination in Employment Act of 1967 (ADEA) The act prohibiting arbitrary age discrimination and specifically protecting individuals over 40 years old.

agency shop A form of union security in which employees who do not belong to the union must still pay union dues on the assumption that union efforts benefit all workers.

alternation ranking method Ranking employees from best to worst on a particular trait, choosing highest, then lowest, until all are ranked.

alternative dispute resolution or ADR program Grievance procedure that provides for binding arbitration as the last step.

alternative staffing The use of nontraditional recruitment sources.

Americans with Disabilities Act (ADA) The act requiring employers to make reasonable accommodations for disabled employees; it prohibits discrimination against disabled persons.

annual bonus Plans that are designed to motivate short-term performance of managers and which are tied to company profitability.

applicant tracking systems Online systems that help employers attract, gather, screen, compile, and manage applicants.

application form The form that provides information on education, prior work record, and skills.

appraisal interview An interview in which the supervisor and subordinate review the appraisal and make plans to remedy deficiencies and reinforce strengths.

apprenticeship training A structured process by which people become skilled workers through a combination of classroom instruction and on-the-job training.

arbitration The most definitive type of third-party intervention, in which the arbitrator usually has the power to determine and dictate the settlement terms.

authority The right to make decisions, direct others' work, and give orders.

authorization cards In order to petition for a union election, the union must show that at least 30% of employees may be interested in being unionized. Employees indicate this interest by signing authorization cards.

bargaining unit The group of employees the union will be authorized to represent.

behavior modeling A training technique in which trainees are first shown good management techniques in a film, are asked to play roles in a simulated situation, and are then given feedback and praise by their supervisor.

behavior modification Using contingent rewards or punishment to change behavior.

behavioral interviews A series of job-related questions that focus on how the candidate reacted to actual situations in the past.

behaviorally anchored rating scale (BARS) An appraisal method that aims at combining the benefits of narrative critical incidents and quantified ratings by anchoring a quantified scale with specific narrative examples of good and poor performance.

behavior-based safety Identifying the worker behaviors that contribute to accidents and then training workers to avoid these behaviors.

benchmark job A job that is used to anchor the employer's pay scale and around which other jobs are arranged in order of relative worth.

benefits Indirect financial and nonfinancial payments employees receive for continuing their employment with the company.

bias The tendency to allow individual differences such as age, race, and sex to affect the appraisal ratings employees receive.

bona fide occupational qualification (BFOQ) Requirement that an employee be of a certain religion, sex, or national origin where that is reasonably necessary to the organization's normal operation. Specified by the 1964 Civil Rights Act.

boycott The combined refusal by employees and other interested parties to buy or use the employer's products.

broadbanding Consolidating salary grades and ranges into just a few wide levels or "bands," each of which contains a relatively wide range of jobs and salary levels.

bullying Singling out someone to harass and mistreat them.

bumping/layoff procedures Detailed procedures that determine who will be laid off if no work is available; generally allow employees to use their seniority to remain on the job.

burnout The total depletion of physical and mental resources caused by excessive striving to reach an unrealistic work-related goal.

business process reengineering Redesigning business processes, usually by combining steps so that small multi-function process teams using information technology do the jobs formerly done by a sequence of departments.

candidate-order (or contrast) error An error of judgment on the part of the interviewer due to interviewing one or more very good or very bad candidates just before the interview in question.

career The occupational positions a person has had over many years.

career development The lifelong series of activities that contribute to a person's career exploration, establishment, success, and fulfillment.

career management The process for enabling employees to better understand and develop their career skills and interests, and to use these skills and interests most effectively.

career planning The deliberate process through which someone becomes aware of personal skills, interests, knowledge, motivations, and other characteristics and establishes action plans to attain specific goals.

case study method A development method in which the manager is presented with a written description of an organizational problem to diagnose and solve.

cash balance plans Defined benefit plans under which the employer contributes a percentage of employees' current pay to employees' pension plans every year, and employees earn interest on this amount.

central tendency A tendency to rate all employees the same way, such as rating them all average.

citation Summons informing employers and employees of the regulations and standards that have been violated in the workplace.

Civil Rights Act of 1991 (CRA 1991) The act that places the burden of proof back on employers and permits compensatory and punitive damages.

classes Grouping jobs based on a set of rules for each group or class, such as amount of independent judgment, skill, physical effort, and so forth, required. Classes usually contain similar jobs.

closed shop A form of union security in which the company can hire only union members. This was outlawed in 1947 but still exists in some industries (such as printing).

coaching Educating, instructing, and training subordinates.

codetermination Employees have the legal right to a voice in setting company policies.

collective bargaining The process through which representatives of management and the union meet to negotiate a labor agreement.

college recruiting Sending an employer's representatives to college campuses to prescreen applicants and create an applicant pool from the graduating class.

compa ratio This equals an employee's pay rate divided by the pay range midpoint for his or her pay grade.

comparable worth The concept by which women who are usually paid less than men can claim that men in comparable rather than in strictly equal jobs are paid more.

compensable factor A fundamental, compensable element of a job, such as skills, effort, responsibility, and working conditions.

competency model Consolidates, usually in one diagram, a precise overview of the competencies (the knowledge, skills, and behaviors) someone would need to do a job well.

competency-based job analysis Describing a job in terms of the measurable, observable, and behavioral competencies an employee must exhibit to do a job well.

competency-based pay Where the company pays for the employee's range, depth, and types of skills and knowledge, rather than for the job title he or she holds.

competitive advantage Any factors that allow an organization to differentiate its product or service from those of its competitors to increase market share.

competitive strategy A strategy that identifies how to build and strengthen the business's long-term competitive position in the marketplace.

compressed workweek Schedule in which employee works fewer but longer days each week.

content validity A test that is construct valid is one that demonstrates that a selection procedure measures a construct and that construct is important for successful job performance.

controlled experimentation Formal methods for testing the effectiveness of a training program, preferably with before-and-after tests and a control group.

corporate campaign An organized effort by the union that exerts pressure on the corporation by pressuring the company's other unions, shareholders, directors, customers, creditors, and government agencies, often directly.

corporate-level strategy Type of strategy that identifies the portfolio of businesses that, in total, comprise the company and the ways in which these businesses relate to each other.

criterion validity A type of validity based on showing that scores on the test (predictors) are related to job performance (criterion).

critical incident method Keeping a record of uncommonly good or undesirable examples of an employee's work-related behavior and reviewing it with the employee at predetermined times.

cross training Training employees to do different tasks or jobs than their own; doing so facilitates flexibility and job rotation.

data mining The set of activities used to find new, hidden, or unexpected patterns in data.

Davis-Bacon Act (1931) A law that sets wage rates for laborers employed by contractors working for the federal government.

decertification Legal process for employees to terminate a union's right to represent them.

deferred profit-sharing plan A plan in which a certain amount of profits is credited to each employee's account, payable at retirement, termination, or death.

defined benefit pension plan A plan that contains a formula for determining retirement benefits.

defined contribution pension plan A plan in which the employer's contribution to employees' retirement savings funds is specified.

diary/log Daily listings made by workers of every activity in which they engage along with the time each activity takes.

digital dashboard Presents the manager with desktop graphs and charts, and thus a computerized picture of where the company stands on all the metrics from the HR Scorecard process.

direct financial payments Pay in the form of wages, salaries, incentives, commissions, and bonuses.

discrimination Taking specific actions toward or against the person based on the person's group.

dismissal Involuntary termination of an employee's employment with the firm.

disparate rejection rates A test for adverse impact in which it can be demonstrated that there is a discrepancy between rates of rejection of members of a protected group and of others.

distributive justice The fairness and justice of a decision's result.

diversity The variety or multiplicity of demographic features that characterize a company's workforce, particularly in terms of race, sex, culture, national origin, handicap, age, and religion.

downsizing The process of reducing, usually dramatically, the number of people employed by a firm.

early retirement window A type of offering by which employees are encouraged to retire early, the incentive being liberal pension benefits plus perhaps a cash payment.

earnings-at-risk variable pay plan Plan that puts some portion of employees' normal pay at risk if they don't meet their goals, in return for possibly obtaining a much larger bonus if they exceed their goals.

economic strike A strike that results from a failure to agree on the terms of a contract that involve wages, benefits, and other conditions of employment.

Electronic Communications Privacy Act (ECPA) Intended in part to restrict interception and monitoring of oral and wire communications, but with two exceptions: employers who can show a legitimate business reason for doing so, and employers who have employees' consent to do so.

electronic performance monitoring (EPM) Having supervisors electronically monitor the amount of computerized data an employee is processing per day, and thereby his or her performance.

electronic performance support systems (EPSS) Sets of computerized tools and displays that automate training, documentation, and phone support; integrate this automation into applications; and provide support that's faster, cheaper, and more effective than traditional methods.

employee assistance program (EAP) A formal employer program for providing employees with counseling and/or treatment programs for problems such as alcoholism, gambling, or stress.

employee compensation All forms of pay or rewards going to employees and arising from their employment.

employee orientation A procedure for providing new employees with basic background information about the firm.

employee recruiting Finding and/or attracting applicants for the employer's open positions.

Employee Retirement Income Security Act (ERISA) Signed into law by President Ford in 1974 to require that pension rights be vested and protected by a government agency, the PBGC.

employee stock ownership plan (ESOP) A qualified, tax-deductible stock bonus plan in which employers contribute stock to a trust for eventual use by employees.

Engagement The commitment and dedication of a firm's employees.

Equal Employment Opportunity Commission (EEOC) The commission, created by Title VII, is empowered to investigate job discrimination complaints and sue on behalf of complainants.

Equal Pay Act of 1963 The act requiring equal pay for equal work, regardless of sex.

ethics The principles of conduct governing an individual or a group; specifically, the standards you use to decide what your conduct should be.

ethnocentric The notion that home-country attitudes, management style, knowledge, evaluation criteria, and managers are superior to anything the host country has to offer.

executive coach An outside consultant who questions the executive's boss, peers, subordinates, and (sometimes) family in order to identify the executive's strengths and weaknesses, and to counsel the executive so he or she can capitalize on those strengths and overcome the weaknesses.

exit interviews Interviews with employees who are leaving the firm, conducted for the purpose of obtaining information about the job or related matters, to give the employer insight about the company.

expatriates (expats) Noncitizens of the countries in which employees are working.

expectancy A person's expectation that his or her effort will lead to performance.

expectancy chart A graph showing the relationship between test scores and job performance for a group of people.

fact finder A neutral party who studies the issues in a dispute and makes a public recommendation for a reasonable settlement.

fair day's work Standards of output which employers should devise for each job based on careful, scientific analysis.

Fair Labor Standards Act (1938) This act provides for minimum wages, maximum hours, overtime pay, and child labor protection. The law has been amended many times and covers most employees.

family-friendly (or work–life) benefits Benefits such as child care and fitness facilities that make it easier for employees to balance their work and family responsibilities.

Federal Violence Against Women Act of 1994 Provides that a person who commits a crime of violence motivated by gender shall be liable to the party injured.

financial incentives Financial rewards paid to workers whose production exceeds some predetermined standard.

flexible benefits plan/cafeteria benefits plan Individualized plans allowed by employers to accommodate employee preferences for benefits.

flextime A plan whereby employees' workdays are built around a core of mid-day hours, such as 11:00 A.M. to 2:00 P.M.

forced distribution method Similar to grading on a curve; predetermined percentages of ratees are placed in various performance categories.

foreign service premiums Financial payments over and above regular base pay, typically ranging between 10% and 30% of base pay.

4/5ths rule Federal agency rule that minority selection rate less than 80% (4/5ths) of that for the group with highest rate is evidence of adverse impact.

401(k) plan A defined contribution plan based on section 401(k) of the Internal Revenue Code.

functional authority (or functional control) The authority exerted by an HR manager as coordinator of personnel activities.

functional strategies Strategy that identifies the broad activities that each department will pursue in order to help the business accomplish its competitive goals.

gainsharing plan An incentive plan that engages employees in a common effort to achieve productivity objectives and share the gains.

gender-role stereotypes The tendency to associate women with certain (frequently nonmanagerial) jobs.

geocentric The belief that the firm's whole management staff must be scoured on a global basis, on the assumption that the best manager of a specific position anywhere may be in any of the countries in which the firm operates.

globalization The tendency of firms to extend their sales, ownership, and/or manufacturing to new markets abroad.

golden parachute A payment companies make in connection with a change in ownership or control of a company.

good faith bargaining Both parties are making every reasonable effort to arrive at agreement; proposals are being matched with counterproposals.

good faith effort strategy Employment strategy aimed at changing practices that have contributed in the past to excluding or underutilizing protected groups.

grade definition Written descriptions of the level of, say, responsibility and knowledge required by jobs in each grade. Similar jobs can then be combined into grades or classes.

grades A job classification system like the class system, although grades often contain dissimilar jobs, such as secretaries, mechanics, and firefighters. Grade descriptions are written based on compensable factors listed in classification systems.

graphic rating scale A scale that lists a number of traits and a range of performance for each. The employee is then rated by identifying the score that best describes his or her level of performance for each trait.

grievance procedure Formal process for addressing any factor involving wages, hours, or conditions of employment that is used as a complaint against the employer.

group life insurance Provides lower rates for the employer or employee and includes all employees, including new employees, regardless of health or physical condition.

halo effect In performance appraisal, the problem that occurs when a supervisor's rating of a subordinate on one trait biases the rating of that person on other traits.

hardship allowances Payments that compensate expatriates for exceptionally hard living and working conditions at certain locations.

health maintenance organization (HMO) A prepaid health care system that generally provides routine round-the-clock medical services as well as preventive medicine in a clinic-type arrangement for employees, who pay a nominal fee in addition to the fixed annual fee the employer pays.

high-performance work system An integrated set of human resources policies and practices that together produce superior employee performance.

home-country nationals Citizens of the country in which the multinational company has its headquarters.

HR audit An analysis by which an organization measures where it currently stands and determines what it has to accomplish to improve its HR function.

HR Scorecard Measures the HR function's effectiveness and efficiency in producing employee behaviors needed to achieve the company's strategic goals.

human capital The knowledge, education, training, skills, and expertise of a firm's workers.

human resource management (HRM) The policies and practices involved in carrying out the "people" or human resource aspects of a management position, including recruiting, screening, training, rewarding, and appraising.

human resource metric The fundamental financial and nonfinancial measures you will use to assess the HR unit's status and progress.

illegal bargaining items Items in collective bargaining that are forbidden by law; for example, a clause agreeing to hire "union members exclusively" would be illegal in a right-to-work state.

impasse Collective bargaining situation that occurs when the parties are not able to move further toward settlement, usually because one party is demanding more than the other will offer.

indirect financial payments Pay in the form of financial benefits such as insurance.

in-house development center A company-based method for exposing prospective managers to realistic exercises to develop improved management skills.

injunction A court order compelling a party or parties either to resume or to desist from a certain action.

inside games Union efforts to convince employees to impede or to disrupt production—for example, by slowing the work pace.

instrumentality The perceived relationships between successful performance and obtaining the reward.

insubordination Willful disregard or disobedience of the boss's authority or legitimate orders; criticizing the boss in public.

interest arbitration Arbitration enacted when labor agreements do not yet exist or when one or both parties are seeking to change the agreement.

interest inventory A personal development and selection device that compares the person's current interests with those of others now in various occupations so as to determine the preferred occupation for the individual.

internal wage curve Shows how each job's points relates to its current pay rate.

intrinsic motivation Motivation that derives from the pleasure someone gets from doing the job or task.

job aid A set of instructions, diagrams, or similar methods available at the job site to guide the worker.

job analysis The procedure for determining the duties and skill requirements of a job and the kind of person who should be hired for it.

job classification (or grading) method A method for categorizing jobs into groups.

job description A list of a job's duties, responsibilities, reporting relationships, working conditions, and supervisory responsibilities—one product of a job analysis.

job enlargement Assigning workers additional same-level activities, thus increasing the number of activities they perform.

job enrichment Redesigning jobs in a way that increases the opportunities for the worker to experience feelings of responsibility, achievement, growth, and recognition.

job evaluation A systematic comparison done in order to determine the worth of one job relative to another.

job hazard analysis A systematic approach to identifying and eliminating such hazards before they occur.

job instruction training (JIT) Listing each job's basic tasks, along with key points, in order to provide step-by-step training for employees.

job posting Publicizing an open job to employees (often by literally posting it on bulletin boards) and listing its attributes, like qualifications, supervisor, working schedule, and pay rate.

job-related interview A series of job-related questions that focus on relevant past job-related behaviors.

job rotation Systematically moving a worker from one job to another to enhance work team performance and/or to broaden his or her experience and identify strong and weak points to prepare the person for an enhanced role with the company.

job sharing Allows two or more people to share a single full-time job.

job specifications A list of a job's "human requirements," that is, the requisite education, skills, personality, and so on—another product of a job analysis.

job withdrawal Actions intended to place physical or psychological distance between employees and their work environments.

Landrum-Griffin Act (1959) The law aimed at protecting union members from possible wrongdoing on the part of their unions.

lifelong learning Providing employees with continuing learning experiences over their tenure with the firm, with the aims of ensuring they have the opportunity to learn the skills they need to do their jobs and to expand their horizons.

line authority The authority exerted by an HR manager by directing the activities of the people in his or her own department and in service areas (like the plant cafeteria).

line manager A manager who is authorized to direct the work of subordinates and is responsible for accomplishing the organization's tasks.

lockout A refusal by the employer to provide opportunities to work.

management assessment center A simulation in which management candidates are asked to perform realistic tasks in hypothetical situations and are scored on their performance.

It usually also involves testing and the use of management games.

management development Any attempt to improve current or future management performance by imparting knowledge, changing attitudes, or increasing skills.

management game A development technique in which teams of managers compete by making computerized decisions regarding realistic but simulated situations.

management process The five basic functions of planning, organizing, staffing, leading, and controlling.

manager The person responsible for accomplishing the organization's goals, and who does so by managing the efforts of the organization's people.

managing diversity Maximizing diversity's potential benefits while minimizing the potential barriers that can undermine the company's performance.

mandatory bargaining items Items in collective bargaining that a party must bargain over if they are introduced by the other party—for example, pay.

market competitive pay system A pay system where the employer's actual pay rates are competitive with those in the relevant labor markets.

market/external wage curve Compares job points with market pay rates for these jobs.

Markov analysis Mathematical tool that involves creating a matrix that shows the probabilities that employees in the chain of feeder positions for a key job will move from position to position and therefore be available to fill an end-point key position.

mass interview A panel interviews several candidates simultaneously.

mediation Intervention in which a neutral third party tries to assist the principals in reaching agreement.

mentoring Formal or informal programs in which mid- and senior-level managers help less experienced employees—for instance, by giving them career advice and helping them navigate political pitfalls.

merit pay (merit raise) Any salary increase awarded to an employee based on his or her individual performance.

miniature job training and evaluation Training candidates to perform several of the job's tasks, and then evaluating the candidates' performance prior to hire.

mission statement Summarizes the answer to the question, "What business are we in?"

"mixed motive" case A discrimination allegation case in which the employer argues that the employment action taken was motivated, not by discrimination, but by some nondiscriminatory reason such as ineffective performance.

mixed standard scales In performance appraisal, similar to behaviorally anchored scales, but mixed scales generally list just a few (usually three) behavioral examples (or "standards") for each of, say, three performance dimensions, and the employer then "mixes" the resulting behavioral statements in listing them.

mobility premiums Typically, lump-sum payments to reward employees for moving from one assignment to another.

national emergency strikes Strikes that might "imperil the national health and safety."

National Labor Relations (or Wagner) Act This law banned certain types of unfair practices and provided for secret-ballot elections and majority rule for determining whether or not a firm's employees want to unionize.

National Labor Relations Board (NLRB) The agency created by the Wagner Act to investigate unfair labor practice charges and to provide for secret-ballot elections and majority rule in determining whether or not a firm's employees want a union.

negligent hiring Hiring workers with questionable backgrounds without proper safeguards.

negligent training A situation where an employer fails to train adequately, and the employee subsequently harms a third party.

9-box matrix In workforce planning, this displays three levels of current job performance (exceptional, fully performing, not yet fully performing) across the top, and also shows three levels of likely potential (eligible for promotion, room for growth in current position, not likely to grow beyond current position) down the side.

nonpunitive discipline Discipline without punishment, usually involving a system of oral warnings and paid "decision-making leaves" in lieu of more traditional punishment.

Norris-LaGuardia Act (1932) This law marked the beginning of the era of strong encouragement of unions and guaranteed to each employee the right to bargain collectively "free from interference, restraint, or coercion."

occupational illness Any abnormal condition or disorder caused by exposure to environmental factors associated with employment.

Occupational Safety and Health Act The law passed by Congress in 1970 "to assure so far as possible every working man and woman in the nation safe and healthful working conditions and to preserve our human resources."

Occupational Safety and Health Administration (OSHA) The agency created within the Department of Labor to set safety and health standards for almost all workers in the United States.

Office of Federal Contract Compliance Programs (OFCCP) This office is responsible for implementing the executive orders and ensuring compliance of federal contractors.

on-demand recruiting services (ODRS) Services that provide short-term specialized recruiting to support specific projects without the expense of retaining traditional search firms.

on-the-job training Training a person to learn a job while working on it.

operational safety reviews (or safety operations reviews) Reviews conducted by agencies to ascertain whether units under their jurisdiction are complying with all the applicable safety laws, regulations, orders, and rules.

organization Consists of people with formally assigned roles who work together to achieve the organization's goals.

organization-person fit The goal of matching (1) the organization's values, culture, and ways of doing things with (2) the prospective employee's knowledge, skills, abilities and competencies.

organization chart A chart that shows the organization-wide distribution of work, with titles of each position and interconnecting lines that show who reports to and communicates to whom.

organizational culture The characteristic values, traditions, and behaviors a company's employees share.

organizational development A special approach to organizational change in which employees themselves formulate and implement the change that's required.

organization-wide incentive plans Plans in which all or most employees can participate, and that generally tie the reward to some measure of company-wide performance.

outplacement counseling A systematic process by which a terminated person is trained and counseled in the techniques of self-appraisal and securing a new position.

paired comparison method Ranking employees by making a chart of all possible pairs of the employees for each trait and indicating which is the better employee of the pair.

panel interview An interview in which a group of interviewers questions the applicant.

pay (or rate) ranges A series of steps or levels within a pay grade, usually based upon years of service.

pay (or wage) grade A pay grade is comprised of jobs of approximately equal difficulty.

Pension Benefits Guarantee Corporation (PBGC) Established under ERISA to ensure that pensions meet vesting obligations; also insures pensions should a plan terminate without sufficient funds to meet its vested obligations.

pension plans Plans that provide a fixed sum when employees reach a predetermined retirement age or when they can no longer work due to disability.

performance analysis Verifying that there is a performance deficiency and determining whether that deficiency should be corrected through training or through some other means (such as transferring the employee).

performance appraisal Evaluating an employee's current and/or past performance relative to his or her performance standards.

performance management Taking an integrated, goal-oriented approach to assigning, training, assessing, and rewarding employees' performance.

person-job fit The goal of matching (1) the knowledge, skills, abilities (KSAs), and competencies that are central to performing the job (as determined by job analysis) with (2) the prospective employee's knowledge, skills, abilities and competencies.

personnel appraisal process A 3-step appraisal process involving (1) setting work standards, (2) assessing the employee's actual performance relative to those standards, and (3) providing feedback to the employee with the aim of helping him or her to eliminate performance deficiencies or to continue to perform above par.

personnel replacement charts Company records showing present performance and promotability of inside candidates for the most important positions.

picketing Having employees carry signs announcing their concerns near the employer's place of business.

piecework A system of pay based on the number of items processed by each individual worker in a unit of time, such as items per hour or items per day.

point method The job evaluation method in which a number of compensable factors are identified and then the degree to which each of these factors is present on the job is determined.

polycentric A conscious belief that only the host-country managers can ever really understand the culture and behavior of the host-country market.

portability Making it easier for employees who leave the firm prior to retirement to take their accumulated pension funds with them.

position analysis questionnaire (PAQ) A questionnaire used to collect quantifiable data concerning the duties and responsibilities of various jobs.

position replacement card A card prepared for each position in a company to show possible replacement candidates and their qualifications.

predictive workforce monitoring Paying continuous attention to workforce planning issues.

preferential shop Union members get preference in hiring, but the employer can still hire nonunion members.

preferred provider organizations (PPOs) Groups of health care providers that contract with employers, insurance companies, or third-party payers to provide medical care services at a reduced fee.

Pregnancy Discrimination Act (PDA) An amendment to Title VII of the Civil Rights Act that prohibits sex discrimination based on "pregnancy, childbirth, or related medical conditions."

procedural justice The fairness of the process.

process chart A workflow chart that shows the flow of inputs to and outputs from a particular job.

productivity The ratio of outputs (goods and services) divided by the inputs (resources such as labor and capital).

profit-sharing plan A plan whereby employees share in the company's profits.

programmed learning A systematic method for teaching job skills involving presenting questions or facts, allowing the person to respond, and giving the learner immediate feedback on the accuracy of his or her answers.

protected class Persons such as minorities and women protected by equal opportunity laws, including Title VII.

psychological contract An unwritten agreement that exists between employers and employees governing each party's expectations regarding the other.

qualifications (or skills) inventories Manual or computerized records listing employees' education, career and development interests, languages, special skills, and so on, to be used in selecting inside candidates for promotion.

qualified individuals Under ADA, those who can carry out the essential functions of the job.

ranking method The simplest method of job evaluation that involves ranking each job relative to all other jobs, usually based on overall difficulty.

ratio analysis A forecasting technique for determining future staff needs by using ratios between, for example, sales volume and number of employees needed.

reality shock Results of a period that may occur at the initial career entry when the new employee's high job expectations confront the reality of a boring, unchallenging job.

recruiting yield pyramid The historical arithmetic relationships between recruitment leads and invitees, invitees and interviews, interviews and offers made, and offers made and offers accepted.

reliability The consistency of scores obtained by the same person when retested with the identical tests or with alternate forms of the same test.

restricted policy Another test for adverse impact, involving demonstration that an employer's hiring practices exclude a protected group, whether intentionally or not.

reverse discrimination Claim that due to affirmative action quota systems, white males are discriminated against.

right to work A term used to describe state statutory or constitutional provisions banning the requirement of union membership as a condition of employment.

rights arbitration Arbitration that interprets existing contract terms, for instance, when an employee questions the employer's right to have taken some disciplinary action.

role playing A training technique in which trainees act out parts in a realistic management situation.

safety awareness program This enables trained supervisors to orient new workers arriving at a jobsite regarding common safety hazards and simple prevention methods.

salary survey A survey aimed at determining prevailing wage rates. A good salary survey provides specific wage rates for specific jobs. Formal written questionnaire surveys are the most comprehensive, but telephone surveys and newspaper ads are also sources of information.

savings and thrift plan Plan in which employees contribute a portion of their earnings to a fund; the employer usually matches this contribution in whole or in part.

Scanlon plan An incentive plan developed in 1937 by Joseph Scanlon and designed to encourage cooperation, involvement, and sharing of benefits.

scatter plot A graphical method used to help identify the relationship between two variables.

scientific management Management approach based on improving work methods through observation and analysis.

severance pay A one-time payment some employers provide when terminating an employee.

sexual harassment Harassment on the basis of sex that has the purpose or effect of substantially interfering with a person's work performance or creating an intimidating, hostile, or offensive work environment.

sick leave Provides pay to an employee when he or she is out of work because of illness.

situational interview A series of job-related questions that focus on how the candidate would behave in a given situation.

situational test Examinees respond to situations representative of the job.

Social Security Federal program that provides three types of benefits: retirement income at the age of 62 and thereafter; survivor's or death benefits payable to the employee's dependents regardless of age at time of death; and disability benefits payable to disabled employees and their dependents. These benefits are payable only if the employee is insured under the Social Security Act.

staff authority Gives the manager the right (authority) to advise other managers or employees.

staff manager A manager who assists and advises line managers.

standard deviation rule In selection, the standard deviation rule holds that as a rule of thumb, the difference between the numbers of minority candidates we *would have expected* to hire and whom *we actually hired* should be less than two standard deviations.

standard hour plan A plan by which a worker is paid a basic hourly rate but is paid an extra percentage of his or her rate for production exceeding the standard per hour or per day. Similar to piecework payment but based on a percent premium.

Standard Occupational Classification (SOC) Classifies all workers into one of 23 major groups of jobs which are subdivided into minor groups of jobs and detailed occupations.

stock option The right to purchase a stated number of shares of a company stock at today's price at some time in the future.

straight piecework An incentive plan in which a person is paid a sum for each item he or she makes or sells, with a strict proportionality between results and rewards.

strategic human resource management Formulating and executing human resource policies and practices that produce the employee competencies and behaviors the company needs to achieve its strategic aims.

strategic management The process of identifying and executing the organization's mission by matching its capabilities with the demands of its environment.

strategic plan The company's plan for how it will match its internal strengths and weaknesses with external opportunities and threats in order to maintain a competitive advantage.

strategy The company's long-term plan for how it will balance its internal strengths and weaknesses with its external opportunities and threats to maintain a competitive advantage.

strategy-based metrics Metrics that specifically focus on measuring the activities that contribute to achieving a company's strategic aims.

strategy map Diagram that summarizes the chain of major activities that contribute to a company's success.

stress interview Interviewer seeks to make the applicant uncomfortable with occasionally rude questions.

strictness/leniency The problem that occurs when a supervisor has a tendency to rate all subordinates either high or low.

strike A withdrawal of labor.

structured (or directive) interview An interview following a set sequence of questions.

structured sequential interview An interview in which the applicant is interviewed sequentially by several persons; each rates the applicant on a standard form.

structured situational interview A series of job-oriented questions with predetermined answers that interviewers ask of all applicants for the job.

succession planning The ongoing process of systematically identifying, assessing, and developing organizational leadership to enhance performance.

supplemental pay benefits Benefits for time not worked such as unemployment insurance, vacation and holiday pay, and sick pay.

supplemental unemployment benefits Provide for a "guaranteed annual income" in certain industries where employers must shut down to change machinery or due to reduced work. These benefits are paid by the company and supplement unemployment benefits.

sympathy strike A strike that takes place when one union strikes in support of the strike of another.

Taft-Hartley Act (1947) Also known as the Labor Management Relations Act, this law prohibited unfair union labor practices and enumerated the rights of employees as union members. It also enumerated the rights of employers.

"Take" a strike Degree to which parties in a labor dispute are willing to tolerate employees going on strike.

talent management The goal-oriented and integrated process of planning, recruiting, developing, managing, and compensating employees throughout the organization.

task analysis A detailed study of a job to identify the specific skills required.

task statements Show what the worker does on a particular job task, how the worker does it, and for what purpose.

team (or group) incentive plan A plan in which a production standard is set for a specific work group, and its members are paid incentives if the group exceeds the production standard.

termination at will Without a contract, either the employer or the employee could terminate at will the employment relationship.

termination interview The interview in which an employee is informed of the fact that he or she has been dismissed.

test validity The accuracy with which a test, interview, and so on measures what it purports to measure or fulfills the function it was designed to fill.

third-country nationals Citizens of a country other than the parent or the host country.

Title VII of the 1964 Civil Rights Act The section of the act that says an employer cannot discriminate on the basis of race, color, religion, sex, or national origin with respect to employment.

training The process of teaching new employees the basic skills they need to perform their jobs.

transfers Reassignments to similar positions in other parts of the firm.

trend analysis Study of a firm's past employment needs over a period of years to predict future needs.

turnover The rate at which employees leave the firm.

unclear standards An appraisal that is too open to interpretation.

unemployment insurance (or compensation) Provides benefits if a person is unable to work through some fault other than his or her own.

unfair labor practice strike A strike aimed at protesting illegal conduct by the employer.

uniform guidelines Guidelines issued by federal agencies charged with ensuring compliance with equal employment federal legislation explaining recommended employer procedures in detail.

union salting A union organizing tactic by which workers who are in fact employed full-time by a union as undercover organizers are hired by unwitting employers.

union shop A form of union security in which the company can hire nonunion people, but they must join the union after a prescribed period of time and pay dues. (If they do not, they can be fired.)

unsafe conditions The mechanical and physical conditions that cause accidents.

unstructured (or nondirective) interview An unstructured conversational-style interview in which the interviewer pursues points of interest as they come up in response to questions.

unstructured sequential interview An interview in which each interviewer forms an independent opinion after asking different questions.

utility analysis The degree to which use of a selection measure improves the quality of individuals selected over what would have happened if the measure had not been used.

utilization analysis The process of comparing the percentage of minority employees in a job (or jobs) at the company with the number of similarly trained minority employees available in the relevant labor market.

valence The perceived value a person attaches to the reward.

validity generalization The degree to which evidence of a measure's validity obtained in one situation can be generalized to another situation without further study.

value chain Identifies the primary activities that create value for customers and the related support activities.

variable pay Any plan that ties pay to productivity or profitability, usually as one-time lump payments.

video-based simulation A situational test in which examinees respond to video simulations of realistic job situations.

virtual classroom Special collaboration software used to enable multiple remote learners, using their PCs or laptops, to participate in live audio and visual discussions, communicate via written text, and learn via content such as PowerPoint slides.

virtual teams Groups of geographically dispersed coworkers who are assembled and who interact using a combination of telecommunications and information technologies to accomplish an organizational task.

vision statement A general statement of the firm's intended direction that shows, in broad terms, "what we want to become."

Vocational Rehabilitation Act of 1973 The act requiring certain federal contractors to take affirmative action for disabled persons.

voluntary (or permissible) bargaining items Items in collective bargaining over which bargaining is neither illegal nor mandatory—neither party can be compelled against its wishes to negotiate over those items.

wage curve Shows the relationship between the value of the job and the average wage paid for this job.

Walsh-Healey Public Contract Act (1936) A law that requires minimum wage and working conditions for employees working on any government contract amounting to more than $10,000.

wildcat strike An unauthorized strike occurring during the term of a contract.

work samples Actual job tasks used in testing applicants' performance.

work sampling technique A testing method based on measuring performance on actual basic job tasks.

work sharing Refers to a temporary reduction in work hours by a group of employees during economic downturns as a way to prevent layoffs.

workers' compensation Provides income and medical benefits to work-related accident victims or their dependents regardless of fault.

workflow analysis A detailed study of the flow of work from job to job in a work process.

workforce analysis Employers use *workforce analysis* to obtain and to analyze the data regarding the firm's use of protected versus non protested employees in various job classifications.

workforce analytics Employers use workforce analytics (**or "talent analytics"**) software applications to analyze their human resources data and to draw conclusions from it.

workforce (or employment or personnel) planning The process of deciding what positions the firm will have to fill, and how to fill them.

workplace flexibility Arming employees with the information technology tools they need to get their jobs done wherever they are.

wrongful discharge An employee dismissal that does not comply with the law or does not comply with the contractual arrangement stated or implied by the firm via its employment application forms, employee manuals, or other promises.

NAME/ORGANIZATION INDEX

387*n*24, 389*n*105, 453*n*20, 454*n*45, 612, 629*n*5
Society for Human Resource Management Legal Report, 172*n*55
Society for Industrial and Organizational Psychology, 180
Society of Hispanic Engineers, 59
Software Magazine, 171*n*10
Solamon, Jerry, 235*n*68
Solem, Allen, 281*n*107
Solomonson, Andrew, 318*n*52
Sondak, Harris, 68*n*109
Sonnentag, Sabine, 574*n*128, 574*n*137–138
Sony Corporation, 585, 593
Southern California grocery workers, 451
South Florida Sun-Sentinel, 370
Southwest Airlines, 78, 82–84, 176
Sovereign, Kenneth, 68*n*92, 173*n*132, 209*n*32, 492*n*91
Sozbilir, Mustafa, 280*n*51
Spector, Bert, 281*n*126
Spencer, James, 209*n*46
Spicer, Carol, 135*n*49
Sporting News, 342
Spreitzer, Gretchen, 602*n*66
Spychalski, Annette, 210*n*67
Stahl, Gunter, 171*n*21, 319*n*76
Standard & Poor's, 12, 152
Stanton Corporation, 200
Staples, 624
Starbucks, 95, 516
Starkman, J., 622, 630*n*66
Starkman, Paul, 135*n*32
Staw, B. M., 601*n*8
Stern, Gary, 172*n*54
Stern, Ithai, 234*n*44
Stetz, T. A., 135*n*11
Stetzer, Adam, 572*n*44
Stevens, C. K., 234*n*49
Stewart, James, 490*n*1
Stewart, Thomas, 173*n*113
Stivarius, Teresa Butler, 211*n*103
Stock, Kyle, 211*n*112
Stoneman, Bill, 233*n*13
Strack, Rainer, 29*n*42
Stradley, Ben, 419*n*67
Strategic Management, 99*n*2
Strategic Staffing, 67*n*66, 135*n*40, 208*n*7, 209*n*26, 210*n*76
Strauss, Susan, 234*n*21
Stretch, Leslie, 419*n*51
Stuart, Spencer, 157
Stuller, Jay, 208*n*4, 234*n*49
Sudbury, Deborah A., 235*n*58
Sugrue, Brenda, 279*n*15–16
Sullivan, Frederick, 528*n*41
Sullivan, John, 99*n*27
Sundstrom, Eric, 574*n*121
Sun Microsystems, 255, 387*n*31, 413
Sunoo, Brenda Paik, 454*n*82

Supervisory Management, 135*n*28, 491*n*25
Sutter Health Corporation, 151
Suutari, Vesa, 317*n*10
Sweetwater State University, 314–315
Switzer, Fred, 67*n*67

T
Taft, Phillips, 601*n*22
Tahbanainen, Marja, 317*n*10
Tahmincioglu, Eve, 575*n*171
Talentwise, 199
Taleo Corporation, 151, 611
Tamiami Trail Tours, 67*n*71
Tammaro, Pat, 234*n*57
Tanguay, Denise Marie, 418*n*25
Target, 77
Taskesenligil, Yavuz, 280*n*51
Tata, 76
Taussig, Reed, 421*n*113
Tayan, Brian, 630*n*82
Taylor, Benjamin, 527*n*19
Taylor, Frederick, 392
Taylor, Michael, 572*n*31
Taylor, Paul, 210*n*98, 233*n*14, 281*n*108
T+D, 280*n*69, 280*n*71, 281*n*109, 281*n*140, 316*n*5
Teagarden, Mary, 602*n*68
Tech Planet, 230
TelevisionWeek, 528*n*92, 528*n*97
Tenneco Corporation, 548
Tepedino, Linda, 99*n*14
Tepper, Bennett, 492*n*58, 492*n*60, 492*n*65
Terpstra, David, 387*n*9
Terpstra, Robert, 601*n*9
Terris, William, 211*n*105
Tesco PLC, 312
Tesoro Corporation, 548
Tett, Robert, 210*n*58
Texas Instruments, 444
Textile World, 418*n*22
Thacker, James, 279*n*21–22, 279*n*28, 280*n*60
Thilmany, Jean, 575*n*161
Thomas, Barry W., 420*n*99
Thomas, David, 68*n*117
Thomas, Isiah, 63
Thomas, Stephen, 386*n*7
Thomas International USA, 185, 608
Thompkins, James, 67*n*65
Thompson, Donna, 345*n*50
Thomson Reuters Company, 86
Thornburg, Linda, 234*n*24
Thornton, George, III, 345*n*67
3M Co., 593
TIAA-CREF, 384
Tiffin, Joseph, 135*n*38
Time, 419*n*60
Time Warner, 411, 595
Tinsley, C. H., 601*n*8
Tippins, Nancy, 173*n*106, 211*n*133
Toh, Soo Min, 100*n*47

Tormey, Douglas, 388*n*68
Torpey, Elka Maria, 456*n*133
Torres, Katherine, 573*n*62, 573*n*99
Toscano, Guy, 575*n*153
Toulouse, Chad, 12, 13
Towers Perrin, 80, 326, 437
Towers Watson, 400
Townsend, Anthony, 602*n*47
Toyota, 11, 37, 77, 262, 520
Toyota Motor Manufacturing of Kentucky, Inc., 66*n*37
Toyota Motor USA, 244, 286
Training, 279*n*11, 279*n*37, 279*n*40, 280*n*52, 280*n*77, 280*n*95, 630*n*37
Training and Development, 28*n*36, 99*n*3, 134*n*3, 135*n*13, 135*n*46, 171*n*4, 171*n*30, 171*n*32, 233*n*15, 278–279*n*2, 278*n*1–2, 279*n*4, 279*n*10, 279*n*12, 279*n*15–16, 279*n*18, 279*n*23–27, 279*n*37, 279*n*44–46, 280*n*50, 280*n*53, 280*n*55, 280*n*60, 280*n*63–68, 280*n*73–74, 280*n*76–78, 280*n*83, 280*n*87–88, 280*n*90, 280*n*92, 280*n*97, 281*n*100, 281*n*102, 281*n*111, 281*n*121, 281*n*124, 318*n*56, 345*n*28, 345*n*52, 455*n*123, 492*n*46, 575*n*173
Training and Development Journal, 68*n*109, 280*n*49
Training Media Review, 630*n*42
Transocean Ltd., 405–406
Trevino, Linda, 318*n*66, 491*n*9, 491*n*11, 491*n*17, 491*n*33, 491*n*36
Triana, Maria del Carmen, 68*n*116
Triandis, Harry C., 418*n*11
Trilogy Enterprises Inc., 169
Trump, Donald, 26
TRW, 283, 287
Tucker, David, 234*n*39
Tulgan, Bruce, 28*n*38
Tuna, C., 208*n*3
Tungli, Zsuzsanna, 602*n*65
Turban, Daniel, 235*n*62
Turnasella, Ted, 318*n*54, 418*n*8
Turner, Diane, 603*n*120
Turnley, William, 172*n*82
TVWeek, 528*n*95
Tyco International, 26
Tye, Mary G., 602*n*63
Tyler, Kathryn, 29*n*40, 172*n*82, 209*n*42, 279*n*33, 279*n*41, 345*n*24, 492*n*44, 528*n*53, 574*n*115, 574*n*130, 603*n*115

U
UC San Diego Medical Center, 245
Ulrich, Dave, 20, 21, 28*n*9, 29*n*73, 100*n*50
Umphress, Elizabeth, 491*n*22
Unicru, 185

Wolkinson, Sarah, 135*n*32
Wolters-Kluwer Company, 67*n*57
Women's Wear Daily, 153
Wonderlic, Inc., 86, 180, 182, 611, 612
Wood, Jennifer L., 173*n*131
Wood, Robert, 317*n*21
Woodward, Nancy, 28*n*8, 65*n*12, 235*n*75
Wooten, Kevin, 29*n*60, 490*n*3
Workday.com, 246, 329
Workforce, 68*n*90, 99*n*9, 172*n*50,
    172*n*57–58, 172*n*65, 172*n*70,
    172*n*75, 172*n*78, 209*n*38, 209*n*45,
    210*n*89, 211*n*134, 234*n*56, 281*n*138,
    345*n*42, 421*n*117–118, 453*n*29,
    491*n*28, 527*n*33, 528*n*56, 572*n*26,
    575*n*174, 602*n*38, 603*n*100,
    603*n*108, 603*n*112, 603*n*116,
    603*n*120, 629*n*16
Workforce Management, 28*n*4, 28*n*9,
    28*n*14, 28*n*27, 29*n*56, 29*n*61, 29*n*80,
    68*n*91, 99*n*9, 99*n*27, 99*n*30, 99*n*33,
    135*n*37, 171*n*8, 171*n*20, 171*n*27,
    172*n*42, 172*n*44, 172*n*49, 172*n*54,
    172*n*60, 172*n*78–79, 172*n*88,
    173*n*95, 173*n*98, 173*n*112, 173*n*114,
    208*n*6, 210*n*79, 211*n*100, 279*n*6,
    279*n*12, 279*n*38, 279*n*43, 280*n*66,
    280*n*69, 280*n*86, 280*n*96, 281*n*120,
    344*n*13, 386*n*1, 387*n*35, 418*n*33,
    418*n*35, 420–421*n*107, 421*n*115,
    456*n*137, 528*n*84, 602*n*36, 630*n*38,
    630*n*47
WorkingUSA, 528*n*46
Workplace Visions, 28*n*15–16, 28*n*31,
    29*n*42, 171*n*16, 387*n*24,
    389*n*105, 454*n*45
World Health Organization, 434
Worley, Christopher, 281*n*126
Wright, Al, 389*n*110
Wright, Aliah D., 208*n*2
Wright, Benjamin, 28*n*17
Wright, Greg, 280*n*72
Wright, Thomas, 491*n*41, 492*n*55
Writers Guild of America (WGA), 525
Wuittner, Jeremy, 418*n*38
Wyatt, Lindsay, 455*n*90
Wymer, John F., III, 234*n*58

X

Xin, Katherine R., 344*n*17

Y

Yager, Edwin G., 280*n*49
Yahoo!, 73, 74, 468
Yale University, 543–544
Yancey, George, 419*n*63
Yandrick, Rudy, 455*n*119, 492*n*57
Yegge, Steve, 418*n*28

Yerkes, Leslie, 418*n*34
Yeung, Arthur, 99*n*1
York, Kenneth, 65*n*19
Young, Jane Patterson, 210*n*91
Younger, Beverly, 575*n*167
YouTube, 150, 477

Z

Zacharatos, Anthea, 28*n*33
Zalewski, Edwin, 573*n*68
Zall, Milton, 492*n*69
Zappe, John, 172*n*79
Zarandona, Joseph, 493*n*107
Zaslow, Jeffrey, 29*n*40
Zatzick, Christopher, 493*n*119
Zeidner, Rita, 29*n*44, 210*n*96, 211*n*115,
    280*n*89, 453*n*22, 492*n*71,
    492*n*73, 492*n*76
Zeigler, James, 572*n*57
Zheng, Ye Yang, 69*n*126
Zielinski, Dave, 209*n*24,
    210*n*72
Zimmerman, Eileen, 210*n*89
Zimmerman, Ryan, 173*n*135, 208*n*5,
    209*n*55, 234*n*32
Zipcar, 241
Zonneveld, John, 280*n*73
Zugelder, Michael, 66*n*53
Zweig, David, 233*n*2